TRAGIC
YEARS
1860-1865

TRAGIC YEARS 1860-1865

A DOCUMENTARY HISTORY
OF THE AMERICAN CIVIL WAR BY

Paul M. Angle AND Earl Schenck Miers

DA CAPO PRESS • NEW YORK

Library of Congress Cataloging in Publication Data

Tragic years, 1860-1865: a documentary history of the American Civil
War / [compiled by] Paul M. Angle and Earl Schenck Miers.—1st Da Capo
Press ed.
   p.   cm.
Originally published: New York: Simon and Schuster, 1960.
Includes index.
ISBN 0-306-80462-X (pbk.)
   1. United States—History—Civil War, 1861-1865—Sources. I. Angle, Paul M.
(Paul McClelland), 1900-1975. Miers, Earl Schenck, 1910-1972.
E464.T78 1992   91-34955
973.7—dc20   CIP

First Da Capo Press edition 1992

This Da Capo Press paperback edition of *Tragic Years 1860-1865* is an unabridged
republication of the edition published in two volumes in New York in 1960.

Published by Da Capo Press, Inc.
A Subsidiary of Plenum Publishing Corporation
233 Spring Street, New York, N.Y. 10013

Acknowledgement is gratefully made to the following for permission to quote from the books indicated:

American Heritage Publishing Company—*The Hanging of John Brown* by Boyd B. Stutler, copyright 1955.

Appleton-Century-Crofts, Inc.—*Lincoln in the Telegraph Office* by David Homer Bates, copyright 1907; *Under the Old Flag* by James Harrison Wilson, copyright 1912.

Brandt & Brandt—*John Brown's Body* by Stephen Vincent Benét, Rinehart & Company, Inc., copyright 1927, 1928 by Stephen Vincent Benét; renewed 1955, 1956 by Rosemary Carr Benét.

Thomas Y. Crowell Company—*South After Gettysburg: The Letters of Cornelia Hancock, 1863–1868*, copyright 1958 by Henrietta Stratton Jaquette.

Dodd, Mead & Company—*Lincoln and the Civil War*, edited by Tyler Dennett, copyright 1939.

Harvey S. Ford, Esquire—*The Memoirs of a Volunteer* by John Beatty, edited by Harvey S. Ford, copyright 1946.

Georgetown University Press—*John Dooley, Confederate Soldier*, edited by Joseph T. Durkin, copyright 1945.

Harcourt, Brace & Company—*Sherman, Fighting Prophet* by Lloyd Lewis, copyright 1932.

Houghton Mifflin Company—*An Autobiography* by Charles Francis Adams, copyright 1916; *The Education of Henry Adams* by Henry Adams, copyright 1906; *A Cycle of Adams Letters*, edited by Worthington C. Ford, copyright 1920; *Europe and the American Civil War* by Donaldson Jordan and Edwin J. Pratt, copyright 1931; *Diary of Gideon Welles*, copyright 1911; *The Life of Lyman Trumbull* by Horace White, copyright 1913.

Indiana University Press—*Grant and Lee* by J. F. C. Fuller, copyright 1957; *The Generalship of Ulysses S. Grant* by J. F. C. Fuller, copyright 1929; *With Sherman to the Sea* by Theodore F. Upson, edited by Oscar Osburn Winther, copyright 1943.

Little Brown & Company—*Meade's Headquarters, 1863–1865, Letters of Colonel Theodore Lyman from the Wilderness to Appomattox*, edited by George R. Agassiz, copyright 1922.

Longmans, Green & Company, Inc.—*Inside Lincoln's Cabinet: The Civil War Diaries of Salmon P. Chase*, edited by David Donald, copy-

right 1954; *Lincoln's Secretary: A Biography of John G. Nicolay* by Helen Nicolay, copyright 1949.

Louisiana State University Press—*Brokenburn: The Journal of Kate Stone*, edited by John Q. Anderson, copyright 1955; *Doctors in Gray: The Confederate Medical Service* by H. H. Cunningham, copyright 1958; *Behind the Lines in the Southern Confederacy* by Charles W. Ramsdell, copyright 1944; *The Plain People of the South* by Bell Irvin Wiley, copyright 1943.

McCowat-Mercer Press—*Cleburne and His Command* by Irving A. Buck, copyright 1908.

The Macmillan Company—*A History of the Southern Confederacy* by Clement Eaton, copyright 1954.

The Ohio Historical Society—*The Diary and Letters of Rutherford Birchard Hayes*, edited by Charles R. Williams, copyright 1922.

Oxford University Press—*Inside the Confederate Government: The Diary of Robert Garlick Hill Kean*, edited by Edward Younger, copyright 1957.

G. P. Putnam's Sons—*Letters of Ulysses S. Grant* by Jesse Grant Cramer, copyright 1912.

Charles Scribner's Sons—*War Years with Jeb Stuart* by W. W. Blackford, copyright 1945; *The Emergence of Lincoln* by Allan Nevins, copyright 1950.

University of Chicago Press—*The Civil War: A Soldier's View* by Col. G. F. R. Henderson, edited by Jay Luvaas, copyright 1958; *The Journal of Benjamin Moran, 1857–1865*, edited by Sarah Agnes Wallace and Frances Elma Gillespie, copyright 1948.

University of North Carolina Press—*Two Soldiers: The Campaign Diaries of Thomas J. Key, C. S. A. and Robert J. Campbell, U. S. A.*, edited by William A. Cate, copyright 1938; *I Rode with Stonewall* by Henry Kyd Douglas, copyright 1940.

University of South Carolina Press—*Mason Smith Family Letters, 1860–1868*, edited by Daniel E. H. Smith, Alice R. H. Smith and Arney R. Childs, copyright 1950.

University of Texas Press—*This Infernal War: The Confederate Letters of Sgt. Edwin H. Fay*, edited by Bell Irvin Wiley, copyright 1958.

CONTENTS

1863

1864

1865

*T*his *volume tells the story of a profound social revolution. The vehicle of its birth was the bloodiest civil war the world had known, yet that war resulted from the angry act of headstrong men unable to agree why they fought. A sense of duty to family and home, of loyalty to tradition, of honor for principle—these emotions soldiers of the North and South shared. Through four tragic years of bloodletting both parts of the warring nation were sustained by the same conviction of a just cause in the sight of God. So passionate was this belief that when at last an exhausted South could fight no longer, surrender was far more a physical necessity than a yielding of mind and heart.*

That ending, ragged and grudging, had cost a staggering price. The Federal dead were counted at 360,222 and the Federal wounded at 275,175. The Confederate dead were put at 258,000 and no one could say how many had been wounded. At the close of the conflict there were perhaps a million Union soldiers in the field, and during the years from 1861 to 1865 at least twice that number fought for Mr. Lincoln. How many served under arms for the Confederacy remains unknown. A reasonable estimate is between 600,000 and 700,000.

Looking back on the war in an effort to decide why it was fought— and for what purpose—Americans can find no grounds for complete agreement. The North's contention that the war was justified because the Union endured was only a partial truth. Emotionally, politically, the war remade the Union. Unexpectedly, nearing the halfway mark in what Mr. Lincoln called "a people's contest," the Emancipation Proclamation foreshadowed a change in the fundamental fabric of the American nation. When the guns were stilled, the dead were buried, and when succeeding springs had spread gentle cloaks over the scars of the battlefields, the indisputable decision—the Thirteenth Amendment—could not be ignored.

The angry act of Sumter plunged the nation on a heady wave of patriotism into a war that no sane person wanted; no one North or South could see how that contest must end. Still, in the First Inaugural, Mr. Lincoln said: "One section of our country believes slavery is right, and ought to be extended, while another believes it is wrong, and ought not to be extended. This is the only substantial dispute." And this dispute, if no other, the war settled.

As a story, the war contained many fascinations. It was a war fought with no holds barred, a war that posed problems of finance to strain the mind of an Alexander Hamilton and problems of military strategy and tactics to baffle the imagination of a Napoleon. Its politics were sometimes unbelievable, its corruption and cupidity often degrading, and its courage (on the field and at home) usually magnificent. Through each event, each mood ran a common thread that gives the pattern and dash of color to any mosaic depicting those four years of strife. In tidewater or upland Virginia, within sultry Mississippi bayous or along the raw frontier of the Southwest, this war was American in its style, in its villains and heroes, its practical and moral objectives.

The world watched this war. It had lessons for people everywhere. It was terrible and yet grand, fearful and yet inspiring, tragic and yet satisfying. In the end, it justified a time-honored faith—"that this nation, under God, shall have a new birth of freedom."

And with it, responsibilities still unmet.

1860

CHAPTER 1

PEACE
OR A SWORD?

S PRING CREPT OVER THE LAND. The year was 1860, the month April—the last April, for five years, that the nation would be at peace. No reasonable person, North or South, wanted war or expected war. America, caught in the pull of a booming industrial revolution, was shaking off the disagreeable effects of a depression. No one yet understood economic cycles in the deep sense of their social and political impact. In a country still dominated by frontier traditions, long hours of hard work filled the average day; dead tired by nightfall, most people were too exhausted by the physical struggle of survival to care much about the torments of the mind. A few made agitation their business—the abolitionists, professional secessionists like Robert Barnwell Rhett with his newspaper in Charleston—and transcendentalists like Emerson made a career of philosophy. Still others sought Utopia by reading bumps on their heads.

Men worked at jobs peculiar to the age. A son of the border states, Sam Clemens, piloted a steamboat between St. Louis and New Orleans. An ex–Army captain, Sam Grant, ran a leather business in Galena, Illinois. Along the Texas border, Colonel Robert E. Lee chased Indians. Homesteaders, with strings of kids tagging along, pushed into the wilderness; some were found later, their scalps gone, their bones bleached by the sun, their wagons burned. The sensitive mind of Walt Whitman recognized the epic they were living:

> *Through the battle, through defeat, moving yet and*
> *never stopping,*
> *Pioneers! O Pioneers!*

Cities throve—New York, Brooklyn still clinging to its separate identity, Philadelphia, Baltimore, Boston, Cincinnati, Louisville, Chicago. Canals, railroads, highways dusty from rolling stagecoach wheels crisscrossed the country. The nation's capital remained what it had always been—a mudhole with open sewers, mosquitoes and malaria breeding in Rock Creek, the little old juglike dome of the Capitol lost amid acres of roof. The Union, still intact, counted thirty-four states, and there would be more as soon as the settlers and the U. S. Cavalry drove the Indians to hell and gone. Gold in the Rockies, gold in the Sierra Nevadas—and gold in between, more than likely—these were discoveries and hunches that started human stampedes; but range land for cattle, soil that could grow wheat and a million miles of corn in sturdy rows were what peopled the territories that April, 1860.

In May in Chicago the Republican Party, now six years old, knocked together a platform that appealed to all shades of political dissent and opportunism, and nominated Abraham Lincoln for President. In Baltimore the Democratic Party fell apart over the question of slavery in the territories, the Northern wing supporting Stephen A. Douglas and the Southern wing nominating John C. Breckinridge. When that autumn Henry Adams returned from his schooling in Europe to the beloved Quincy of his ancestors, he saw the Wide-Awakes who campaigned for Lincoln marching up a hillside. Their torches lighted the night. In later years Adams realized that they had organized their clubs and parades "in a form military in all things except weapons."

I

Early in October, under blue skies and a golden sun, with the rice ripe, the cotton white, and the flowers almost as brilliant as in midsummer, the Governor of South Carolina dispatched by secret agent a letter to the several governors of the cotton states. William Henry Gist, wealthy planter, prohibitionist, former president of the Methodist State Sunday School Convention who once killed a man for a lady's honor, now threatened death to the Union:[1]

EXECUTIVE DEPARTMENT
UNIONVILLE, S. C., OCT. 5, 1860

DEAR SIR: The great probability, nay almost certainty, of Abraham Lincoln's election to the Presidency renders it important that there should be a full and free interchange of opinion between the

Executives of the Southern, and more especially of the Cotton, States, and while I unreservedly give you my views and the probable action of my State, I shall be much pleased to hear from you; that there may be concert of action, which is so essential to success. Although I will consider your communication confidential, and wish you so to consider mine so far as publishing in the newspapers is concerned, yet the information, of course, will be of no service to me unless I can submit it to reliable and leading men in consultation for the safety of our State and the South; and will only use it in this way. It is the desire of South Carolina that some other State should take the lead, or at least move simultaneously with her. She will unquestionably call a convention as soon as it is ascertained that a majority of the electors will support Lincoln. If a single State secedes, she will follow her. If no other State takes the lead, South Carolina will secede (in my opinion) alone, if she has any assurance that she will be soon followed by another or other States; otherwise it is doubtful. If you decide to call a convention upon the election of a majority of electors favorable to Lincoln, I desire to know the day you propose for the meeting, that we may call our convention to meet the same day, if possible. If your State will propose any other remedy, please inform me what it will probably be, and any other information you will be pleased to give me.

With great respect and consideration,

I am yours, etc.,

WM. H. GIST

II

A few days after Governor Gist's letter the voters of Pennsylvania, Ohio, and Indiana went to the polls to elect state officers. Decisive Republican majorities must have had their effect on the replies which Gist soon received. John W. Ellis of North Carolina, a secessionist whose personal convictions were tempered by the pro-Union views of thousands of his constituents, wrote on October 18:[2]

Our people are very far from being agreed as to what action the State should take in the event of Lincoln's election to the Presidency. . . . As a States-Rights man, believing in the sovereignty and reserved powers of the States, I will conform my actions to the action of North Carolina, whatever that may be. . . . I could not in any event assent to, or give my aid to, a political enforcement of the monstrous doctrine of coercion.

Governor A. B. Moore of Alabama wrote a week later:

It is my opinion that Alabama will not secede alone, but if two or more States will cooperate with her, she will secede with them; or if South Carolina or any other Southern State should go out alone and the Federal Government should attempt to use force against her, Alabama will immediately rally to her rescue.

Thomas O. Moore, the planter who had occupied the Governor's chair at Baton Rouge for the last ten months, cautiously restrained his fiery temper:

I shall not advise the secession of my State, and I will add that I do not think the people of Louisiana will ultimately decide in favor of that course. I shall recommend that Louisiana meet her sister slave-holding States in council to consult as to the proper course to be pursued, and to endeavor to effect a complete harmony of action. . . . I believe in the right of secession for just cause, of which the sovereignty must be the judge. If therefore the general Government shall attempt to coerce a State, and forcibly attempt the exercise of this right, I should certainly sustain the State in such a contest.

John J. Pettus of Mississippi made no reservations. He wrote on October 26:

I will call our Legislature in extra session as soon as it is known that the Black Republicans have carried the election. I expect Mississippi will ask a council of the Southern States, and if that council advise secession, Mississippi will go with them.

The ardently states'-rights and proslavery Governor of Georgia, Joseph E. Brown, predicted, on October 31, that his state would take the same action as Mississippi:

My opinion is that the people of Georgia will, in case of the election of Lincoln, decide to meet all the Southern States in convention and take common action for the protection of the rights of all. Events not yet foreseen may change their course and might lead to action on the part of Georgia without waiting for all the Southern States, if it should be found necessary to her safety.

The presidential election was three days old when M. S. Perry of Florida replied to Gist's letter:

I . . . am proud to say that Florida is ready to wheel into line with the gallant Palmetto State, or any other Cotton State or States, in any course which she or they may in their judgment think proper to adopt, looking to the vindication and maintenance of the rights, interest, honor, and safety of the South. . . . If there is sufficient manliness at the South to strike for our rights, honor, and safety, in God's name let it be done before the inauguration of Lincoln.

III

A troubled nation, the South defiant, the North worried but unable to believe that the disaffected section would carry out its threats, had gone to the polls on November 6. That night there was jubilation in the little city of Springfield, Illinois, the home of the Republican presidential candidate. The following morning an anonymous correspondent of the New York Tribune, *still under the excitement of the night before, rushed off a letter to his paper:*[3]

SPRINGFIELD, ILL., Nov. 7, 1860

About 9 o'clock last evening, when the returns began to tap in at the telegraph office, Mr. Lincoln, who had been notified beforehand, went over from the State House with a few friends, established himself comfortably near the instruments, and put himself into easy communication with the operators. The first fragments of intelligence were caught by the Superintendent as they ticked off at the tables, and, even before they could be recorded, were eagerly repeated and welcomed by all, for they came from the best counties in Illinois, and were full of good cheer. . . . Mr. Lincoln sat or reclined upon a sofa, while his companions mostly stood clustering around him. At length full sheets of returns were transcribed, and were taken apart, and were read aloud by Mr. Wilson—the listeners allowing no particle of good news to go by without their quick congratulations. . . .

As the evening advanced, other excitements were afforded by batches of private messages which came rushing in, mostly addressed to Mr. Lincoln, but in some cases to Senator Trumbull, who had joined the company a little after the time of assembling. For these messages an active watch soon began to be kept, and the moment that one was lifted from the table, it would be clutched by some of the ardent news-seekers, and sometimes, in the hurry and scramble, would be read by almost every person present before it reached him for whom it was intended. Whenever the information was of peculiarly gratifying character, as it often was, the documents would be taken out by some thoughtful friend of the populace outside, and read aloud in the State House, or elsewhere, to large crowds which had met and were enjoying celebrations on the strength of their own convictions that the expected news would be sure to justify them. Occasionally, a line or two would come in with so much force of encouragement as to set the little group beside itself with elation. A confident declaration from Gen. S. Cameron, promising abundance of good things from Pennsylvania, produced a sensation that quite took away the composure of the telegraph manipulators; and some superb items which came just after from Simeon Draper, setting aside all possibility of doubt as to New York, aroused demonstrations still more gleeful. There was just one person, however, who accepted everything with almost an immovable tranquility. Not that Mr. Lincoln undertook to conceal in the slightest degree the keen interest he felt in every new development; but, while he seemed to absorb it all with great satisfaction, the intelligence moved him to less energetic display of gratification than the others indulged in. He appeared, indeed, to be as fully alive to the smaller interests of some local districts, in which the fortunes of his friends were concerned, as to the wider and more universally important regions; and, in fact, his only departure from perfect quiet throughout the night was on hearing, just before he withdrew, of the complete success of the Republican ticket in his own precinct.

IV

On the morning after the election Abraham Lincoln arose early and proceeded, as he had for the last several weeks, to the Governor's office in the State House, where all day long he received the congratulations of his friends.

On the same day Mrs. James Chesnut, wife of one of South Carolina's United States Senators, was traveling from Charleston to Florida. As the train approached Fernandina one of the passengers, a woman, called out, "That settles the hash!" She had just learned that Lincoln had been elected.

In Columbia the South Carolina legislature, meeting in special session, debated measures for summoning a convention of delegates with the avowed purpose of taking the state out of the Union. In Charleston the foreman of the Federal grand jury announced to the presiding judge:[4]

The verdict of the Northern section of the Confederacy, solemnly announced to the country through the ballot-box on yesterday, has swept away the last hope for the permanence, for the stability, of the Federal Government of these sovereign States, and the public mind is constrained to lift itself above the consideration of details in the administration of law and justice up to the vast and solemn issues which have been forced upon us. These issues involve the existence of the Government of which this court is the organ and minister. In these extraordinary circumstances, the Grand Jury respectfully decline to proceed with their presentments.

The judge, Albert Gordon Magrath, replied:

In the political history of the United States an event has happened of ominous import to fifteen slaveholding States. The State of which we are citizens has been always understood to have deliberately fixed its purpose whenever that event should happen.

Feeling an assurance of what will be the action of the State, I consider it my duty, without delay, to prepare to obey its wishes. That preparation is made by the resignation of the office which I have held.

For the last time I have, as a Judge of the United States, administered the laws of the United States within the limits of the State of South Carolina. . . .

So far as I am concerned the Temple of Justice, raised under the Constitution of the United States, is now closed.

If it shall never again be opened, I thank God that its doors have been closed before its altar has been desecrated with sacrifices to tyranny.

Magrath had spoken with too much solemnity for the mood of the people, who immediately made him a hero. Mrs. Chesnut noted:[5]

This Judge Magrath . . . is a local celebrity of whom likenesses were suspended, in the frightfullest sign-post style of painting, across various thoroughfares in Charleston. The happy moment seized by the painter to depict him was while Magrath was in the act of dramatically tearing off his robes of office in rage and disgust at Lincoln's election.

The painting is in vivid colors, the canvas huge, and the rope hardly discernible. He is depicted with a countenance flaming with contending emotions—rage, disgust and disdain.

V

The people of Charleston were too excited to pay much attention to the arrival, on November 21, of a new commander of the Federal forces stationed there. Major Robert Anderson of the First Artillery, fifty-five-year-old career soldier, seemed to be an ideal selection for a post where a single hasty move could have the gravest consequences. A Virginian by ancestry, a Kentuckian by birth, proslavery in his sympathies, Anderson could be counted on to use the utmost restraint in dealing with the touchy local authorities. Secretary of War John B. Floyd, convinced that a collision at Charleston must be avoided at all costs, may have underestimated Anderson's devotion to duty—a devotion which a relative summed up in a sentence: "The Ten Commandments, the Constitution of the United States, and the Army Regulations were his guides in life."

Of the three forts in Charleston harbor only Moultrie, on Sullivan's Island north of the channel to the Atlantic, was garrisoned. Moultrie had been in bad repair and Sumter, in the center of the channel, unfinished, but Anderson found that workmen were rapidly putting both in defensible condition. His pressing concern was not the condition of the forts but their location. A few days after taking command he wrote a fateful report:[6]

FORT MOULTRIE, S. C., November 23, 1860

COL. S. COOPER,
ADJUTANT-GENERAL, U. S. ARMY:

COLONEL: In compliance with verbal instructions from the honorable Secretary of War, I have the honor to report that I have inspected the forts of the harbor. . . . At Fort Moultrie the Engineer, Captain Foster, is working very energetically on the outer defenses, which will, should nothing interfere to prevent, be finished and the guns mounted in two weeks. There are several sand hillocks within four hundred yards of our eastern wall, which offer admirable cover to approaching parties, and would be formidable points for sharp-shooters. Two of them command our work. These I shall be compelled to level, at least sufficiently to render our position less insecure than it now is. When the outworks are completed, this fort, with its appropriate war garrison, will be capable of making a very handsome defense. . . . The garrison now in it is so weak as to invite an attack, which is openly and publicly threatened. We are about sixty, and have a line of rampart of 1,500 feet in length to defend. If beleaguered, as every man of the command must be either engaged or held on the alert, they will be exhausted and worn down in a few days and nights of such service as they would then have to undergo.

At Fort Sumter the guns of the lower tier of casemates will be mounted, the Engineer estimates, in about seventeen days. That fort is now ready for the comfortable accommodation of one company, and, indeed, for the temporary reception of its proper garrison. . . . This work is the key to the entrance of this harbor; its guns command this work [Moultrie], and could drive out its occupants. It [Sumter] should be garrisoned at once.

Castle Pinckney, a small casemated work, perfectly commanding the city of Charleston, is in excellent condition, with the exception of a few repairs, which will require the expenditure of about $500. . . . It is, in my opinion, essentially important that this castle should be immediately occupied by a garrison, say, of two officers and thirty men. The safety of our little garrison would be rendered more certain, and our fort would be more secure from an attack by such a holding of Castle Pinckney than it would be from quadrupling our force. The Charlestonians would not venture to attack this place when they knew that their city was at the mercy of the commander of Castle Pinckney. So important do I consider the holding of Castle Pinckney by the Government that I recommend, if the troops asked for cannot be sent at once, then I be authorized to place an Engineer detachment, consisting, say, of one officer, two masons, two carpenters, and twenty-six laborers, to make the repairs needed there. . . . If my force was not so very small I would not hesitate to send a detachment at once to garrison that work. Fort Sumter and Castle Pinckney *must* be garrisoned immediately if the Government determines to keep command of this harbor.

I need not say how anxious I am—indeed, determined, so far as honor will permit—to avoid collision with the citizens of South Carolina. Nothing, however, will be better calculated to prevent bloodshed than our being found in such an attitude that it would be madness and folly to attack us. There is not so much of feverish excitement as there was last week, but that there is a settled determination to leave the Union, and to obtain possession of this work, is apparent to all.

Castle Pinckney, being so near the city, and having no one in it but an ordnance sergeant, they regard as already in their possession. The clouds are threatening, and the storm may break upon us at any moment. I do, then, most earnestly entreat that a re-enforcement be immediately sent to this garrison, and that at least two companies be sent at the same time to Fort Sumter and Castle Pinckney—half a company, under a judicious commander, sufficing, I think, for the latter work. I feel the full responsibility of making the above suggestions, because I firmly believe that as soon as the people of South Carolina learn that I have demanded re-enforcements, and that they have been ordered, they will occupy Castle Pinckney and attack this fort. It is therefore of vital importance that the troops embarked (say in war steamers) shall be designated for other duty. As we have no men who know anything about preparing ammunition, and our officers will be too much occupied to instruct them, I respectfully request that about half a dozen ordnance men, accustomed to the work of preparing fixed ammunition, be sent here, to be distributed at these forts. . . .

With these three works garrisoned as requested, and with a supply of ordnance stores, for which I shall send requisitions in a few days, I shall feel that, by the blessing of God, there may be a hope that no blood will be shed, and that South Carolina will not attempt to take these forts by force, but will resort to diplomacy to secure them. If we neglect, however, to strengthen ourselves, she will, unless these works are surrendered on their first demand, most assuredly immediately attack us. I will thank the Department to give me special instructions, as my position here is rather a politico-military than a military one.

Anderson received his answer in early December. "It is believed, from information thought to be reliable," Adjutant General Cooper wrote, "that an attack will not be made on your command, and the Secretary has only to refer to his conversation with you, and to caution you that, should his convictions unhappily prove untrue, your actions must be such as to be free from the charge of initiating a collision. If attacked, you are, of course, expected to defend the trust committed to you to the best of your ability. The increase of the force under your command, however much to be desired, would, the Secretary thinks, judging from the recent excitement produced on account of an anticipated increase, as mentioned in your letter, but add to that excitement, and might lead to serious results."

Anderson may well have wondered where Secretary Floyd obtained evidence that the Charlestonians would not attack the harbor forts. Those on the ground were impressed by preparations for war. Edward L. Wells, a young New Yorker of strong Southern sympathies, reported to his father on December 6, the day when the people of South Carolina elected delegates to the convention which would assuredly vote the state out of the Union:[7]

The all-absorbing question at present is secession. Men, women & children talk of nothing else. There is no difference of opinion as to whether Carolina shall secede or not; that is a fact settled beyond doubt by the unanimous consent of her people. The only questions are, *when* shall she secede, & *what* she shall then do. The delegates to the Convention, to meet on the 17, which will settle these points, were elected to-day. The enthusiasm with which people old & young, rich & poor, are rallying around their gallant little State, is truly admirable. The descendants of Marion, Sumter, & other revolutionary heroes are worthy of their ancestors. Every man able to bear a musket has joined a military company & is daily drilled. The merchants & their clerks, the lawyers, the mechanics & all classes of business men, after working all day for money to support their families, drill nearly half the night in order to be able to defend them. They must have the sympathy of every right-thinking, & honorable man.

Anderson reiterated his belief that the forts would be attacked and pressed for instructions. Secretary Floyd could no longer temporize, but instead of putting himself on record he sent Major Don Carlos Buell, Assistant Adjutant General, to Charleston with an oral message. Buell instructed Anderson:[8]

You are carefully to avoid every act which would needlessly tend to provoke aggression; and for that reason you are not, without evident and imminent necessity, to take up any position which could be construed into the assumption of a hostile attitude. But you are to hold possession of the forts in this harbor, and if attacked you are to defend yourself to the last extremity. The smallness of your force will not permit you, perhaps, to occupy more than one of the three forts, but an attack on or an attempt to take possession of any one of them will be regarded as an act of hostility, and you may then put your command into either of them which you may deem most proper to increase its power of resistance. You are also authorized to take similar steps whenever you have tangible evidence of a design to proceed to a hostile act.

VI

Anderson wondered what "tangible evidence of a design to proceed to a hostile act" might be. While he puzzled over the phrase the delegates to South Carolina's convention assembled at Columbia. Finding the capital in the grip of a smallpox epidemic, they decided to adjourn to Charleston, but they lingered long enough to give James L. Petigru, the only outspoken Unionist in the state, a chance to make a quip. Asked by a stranger the location of the insane asylum, Petigru pointed to the Baptist Church, where the convention was still in session. "It looks like a church," he said, "but it is now a lunatic asylum; go right there and you will find one hundred and sixty-four maniacs within."

On December 18 the convention reassembled at Charleston. Samuel Wylie Crawford, an Army surgeon in Anderson's command, looked on the scene with fascination. Twenty-five years later he wrote a vivid account of three crucial days in American history:[9]

. . . Crowds of excited people thronged the streets and open squares of the city, and filled the passage and stairways of the hall. Congratulations were exchanged on every side, while earnest dissatisfaction was freely expressed that the passage of the Secession Ordinance had been delayed.

Blue cockades and cockades of palmetto appeared in almost every hat; flags of all descriptions, except the National colors, were everywhere displayed. Upon the gavel that lay upon the Speaker's table, the word "Secession" had been cut in deep black characters. The enthusiasm spread to the more practical walks of trade, and the business streets were gay with bunting and flags, as the tradespeople, many of whom were Northern men, commended themselves to the popular clamor by a display of coarse representations on canvas of the public men, and of the incidents daily presenting themselves, and of the brilliant future in store for them.

The session of the Convention lasted but one hour; there was great unanimity. . . . On the 19th the Convention reassembled at St. Andrews Hall, when the President of the Convention submitted a communication from J. A. Elmore, the Commissioner from Alabama, enclosing a telegram received on the night of the 17th from Governor A. B. Moore, of Alabama.

"Tell the Convention," said he, "to listen to no propositions of compromise or delay"; and Mr. Elmore assures the President of the Convention that the Governor "offers it" in no spirit of dictation, but as the friendly counsel and united voice of the true men of Alabama. . . .

Early on the morning of the 20th knots of men were seen gathered here and there through the main streets and squares of Charleston. The Convention was not to meet until 12 o'clock, but it was understood that the Committee was ready to report the Ordinance of Secession, and that it would certainly pass the Convention that day. The report soon spread. Although this action had been fully anticipated, there was a feverish anxiety to know that the secession of the State was really accomplished, and as the hour of noon approached, crowds of people streamed along the avenues towards St. Andrews Hall and filled the approaches. A stranger passing from the excited throng outside into the hall of the Convention would be struck with the contrast. . . . Quietly the Convention had met, and had been opened with prayer to God. There was no excitement. There was no visible sign that the Commonwealth of South Carolina was about to take a step more momentous for weal or woe than had yet been known in her history.

Then followed the introduction of a resolution by Mr. R. B. Rhett, that a committee of thirteen be appointed to report an ordinance providing for a convention to form a Southern Confederacy, as important a step as the secession of the State itself. It was referred to the appropriate committee, when Chancellor Inglis of Chesterfield, the chairman of the committee to report an ordinance proper of secession, arose and called the attention of the President.

An immediate silence pervaded the whole assemblage as every eye turned upon the speaker. Addressing the chair, he said that the committee appointed to prepare a draft of an ordinance proper, to be adopted by the Convention in order to effect the secession of South Carolina from the Federal Union, respectfully report that they have had the matter under consideration, and believe that they would best meet the exigencies of the occasion by expressing in the fewest and simplest words all that was necessary to effect the end proposed, and so to exclude everything which was not a necessary part of the "solemn act of secession." They therefore submitted the following:

"AN ORDINANCE

to dissolve the Union between the State of South Carolina and other States united with her under the compact entitled 'The Constitution of the United States of America.'

"We, the People of the State of South Carolina, in Convention assembled, do declare and ordain, and it is hereby declared and ordained,

"That the Ordinance adopted by us in Convention, on the twenty-third day of May, in the year of our Lord one thousand seven hundred and eighty-eight, whereby the Constitution of the United States of America was ratified, and also, all Acts and parts of Acts of the General Assembly of this State, ratifying amendments to the said Constitution, are hereby repealed; and that the union now existing between South Carolina and other States, under the name of 'The United States of America,' is hereby dissolved."

A proposition that business be suspended for fifteen minutes was not agreed to, and the question was at once put, with the result of a unanimous vote, at 1:30 P.M., of 169 yeas, nays none. An immediate struggle for the floor ensued. Mr. W. Porcher Miles moved that an immediate telegram be sent to the Members of Congress, at Washington, announcing the result of the vote and the Ordinance of Secession. It was then resolved to invite the Governor and both branches of the Legislature to Institute Hall, at seven o'clock in the evening, and that the Convention should move in procession to that hall, and there, in the presence of the constituted authorities of the State and the people, sign the Ordinance of Secession. That a clergyman of the city should be invited to attend, and upon the completion of the signing of the Ordinance, he should "return thanks to Almighty God in behalf of the people of this State and to invoke His blessings upon our proceedings." The Ordinance was then turned over to the Attorney-General and solicitors to be engrossed.

The invitations to the Senate and House of Representatives having been accepted, the Convention moved in procession at the hour indicated to Institute Hall, amid the crowds of citizens that thronged the streets, cheering loudly as it passed. The galleries of the hall were crowded with ladies, who waved their handkerchiefs to the Convention as it entered, with marked demonstration. On either side of the President's chair were two large palmetto trees. The Hall was densely crowded. The Ordinance, having been returned engrossed and with the great seal of the State, attached by the Attorney-General, was presented and was signed by every member of the Convention, special favorites being received with loud applause. Two hours were thus occupied. The President then announced that "the Ordinance of Secession has been signed and ratified, and I proclaim the State of South Carolina an independent Commonwealth."

At once the whole audience broke out in a storm of cheers; the ladies again joined in the demonstration; a rush was made for the palmetto trees, which were torn to pieces in the effort to secure mementos of the occasion. . . .

The adjournment of the Convention was characterized by the same dignity that had marked its sessions. Outside, the whole city was wild with excitement as the news spread like wild-fire through its streets. Business was suspended everywhere; the peals of the church bells mingling with salvos of artillery from the citadel. Old men ran shouting down the street. Every one entitled to it, appeared at once in uniform. In less than fifteen minutes after its passage, the principal newspaper of Charleston had placed in the hands of the eager multitude a copy of the Ordinance of Secession. Private residences were illuminated, while military organizations marched in every direction, the music of their bands lost amid the shouts of the people. The whole heart of the people had spoken.

VII

The passage of the Ordinance of Secession and the belligerent attitude of the people of Charleston brought Anderson to a decision: on his own responsibility he would remove the garrison from Moultrie to Sumter, the only place from which he had a chance to hold the harbor forts. Keeping his decision to himself, he planned to make the transfer on Christmas Day, when the secessionists were not likely to be alert. Rain forced a postponement. On the afternoon of December 26, under a subterfuge, he sent the women and children with their household goods to Fort Johnson, a dilapidated work on the opposite side of the harbor. Shortly after dark he ordered officers and men to the boats, revealing their destination only at the last minute. Captain Abner Doubleday remembered:[10]

The chaplain, the Rev. Matthias Harris, being a non-combatant, and having his family in the village, was not notified. Neither was Surgeon Simons, of the army, who was living in a house adjoining the fort, and directly in line with our guns. When he saw the movement in progress, he hastened out with his family, to shelter them behind the sandhills as soon as possible.

Everything being in readiness, we passed out of the main gates, and silently made our way for about a quarter of a mile to a spot where the boats were hidden behind an irregular pile of rocks, which origi-

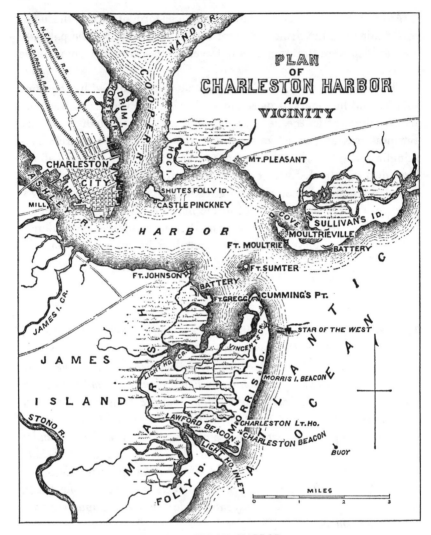

CHARLESTON HARBOR

From Benson J. Lossing, *Pictorial History of the Civil War*

nally formed part of the sea-wall. There was not a single human being in sight as we marched to the rendezvous, and we had the extraordinary good luck to be wholly unobserved. We found several boats awaiting us, under charge of two engineer officers, Lieutenants Snyder and Meade. They and their crews were crouched down behind the rocks, to escape observation. In a low tone they pointed out to me the boats intended for my company, and then pushed out rapidly to

return to the fort. Noticing that one of the guard-boats was approaching, they made a wide circuit to avoid it. I hoped there would be time
for my party to cross before the steamer could overhaul us; but as
among my men there were a number of unskillful oarsmen, we made
but slow progress, and it soon became evident that we would be overtaken in mid-channel. It was after sunset, and the twilight had deepened, so that there was a fair chance for us to escape. While the
steamer was yet afar off, I took off my cap, and threw open my coat
to conceal the buttons. I also made the men take off their coats, and use
them to cover up their muskets, which were lying alongside the row-
locks. I hoped in this way that we might pass for a party of laborers
returning to the fort. The paddle-wheels stopped within about a hundred yards of us; but, to our great relief, after a slight scrutiny, the
steamer kept on its way. In the mean time our men redoubled their
efforts, and we soon arrived at our destination. As we ascended the
steps of the wharf, crowds of workmen rushed out to meet us, most of
them wearing secession emblems. One or two Union men among them
cheered lustily, but the majority called out angrily, "What are these
soldiers doing here?" I at once formed my men, charged bayonets,
drove the tumultuous mass inside the fort, and seized the guard-room,
which commanded the main entrance. I then placed sentinels to prevent the crowd from encroaching on us. As soon as we had disembarked, the boats were sent back for Seymour's company. The major
landed soon after in one of the engineer boats, which had coasted
along to avoid the steamer. Seymour's men arrived in safety, followed
soon after by the remaining detachments, which had been left behind
as a rear-guard. The latter, however, ran a good deal of risk, for in
the dark it passed almost under the bow of the guard-boat *Niña*. The
whole movement was successful beyond our most sanguine expectations, and we were highly elated. The signal-gun was fired, and Hall
at once sailed over, and landed the soldiers' families and supplies. As
soon as the schooners were unloaded, the disloyal workmen were
placed on board and shipped off to the main-land. Only a few of the
best and most reliable were retained.

A small detachment remained at Moultrie with guns trained on the
route of the crossing. The secessionists suspected nothing. By 8 P.M.
Anderson stood on the parapet of Sumter and congratulated his officers
on the success of the movement. That night the men who had stayed
at Moultrie spiked all the guns and set fire to the gun carriages, giv-

ing the people of Charleston their first intimation that the fort had been abandoned.

Charleston raged. One of its newspapers, the News, *spoke for the city—and for much of the South:*[11]

Fort Moultrie in a mutilated state, with useless guns, and flames rising in different portions of it, will stand to show the cowardly conduct of the officers who had charge of it, and who in times of peace basely deserted their post and attempted to destroy a fortification which is surrounded with so many historical reminiscences that the arm of the base scoundrel who would have ruined it should have dropped from its socket.

The Boston Courier, *taking a different view, revealed the breadth of the gap which already separated the two sections:*

We must own that the news of the transaction in Charleston harbor was learned by us yesterday with a prouder beating of the heart. *We could not but feel once more that we had a country*—a fact which has been to a certain degree in suspense for some weeks past. What is given up for the moment is of no consequence, provided the one point stands out clear, that *the United States means to maintain its position, where its rights exist, and that its officers, civil and military, intend to discharge their duty.* The concentration of the disposable force in Charleston harbor in a defensible post, is thus a bond of Union. It is a decisive act, calculated to rally the national heart.

CHAPTER 2

THE BATTLEFIELD
OF POLITICS

T HE PASSAGE of the Ordinance of Secession and Anderson's occupation of Fort Sumter brought to a climax a chain of events that started in 1619, when a Dutch captain sold twenty-odd Negroes * to English colonists in Virginia.† Or in 1798, when Thomas Jefferson, author of the Virginia and Kentucky Resolutions, added the word *Nullification* to the American political vocabulary. Or on January 1, 1831, when the first issue of William Lloyd Garrison's militantly antislavery *Liberator* appeared. Or on November 7, 1837, when a proslavery mob killed the abolitionist editor Elijah P. Lovejoy at Alton, Illinois. But certainly by the spring of 1854, when Senator Stephen A. Douglas, with the full support of a Democratic administration, forced the Kansas–Nebraska Bill through a reluctant Congress, a nation's tormented conscience had become the battlefield of politics.

* In our text this word will be capitalized. In quoted material we will follow the prevailing usage, usually lower case.

† John Rolfe described the transaction in a letter written in 1620. "About the latter end of August, a Dutch man of Warr of the burden of a 160 tunes arrived at Point-Comfort, the Comandors name Capt Jobe, his Pilott for the West Indies one Mr. Marmaduke an Englishman. They mett with the *Trer* in the West Indyes, and determyned to hold consort shipp hetherward, but in their passage lost one the other. He brought not any thing but 20. and odd Negroes, which the Governor and Cape Marchant bought for victualles (Whereof he was in greate need as he pretended) at the best and easyest rates they could. He hadd a lardge and ample comyssion from his Excellency to range and to take purchase in the West Indyes."

The Kansas–Nebraska Bill destroyed the belief that a permanent solution of the slavery problem had been found—a belief that had prevailed since 1850. In that year, with new states formed from territory acquired in the Mexican War applying for admission to the Union, controversy over slavery threatened to bring on civil war. The break was averted when Henry Clay and Daniel Webster, revered above all other of the nation's statesmen, threw their influence behind the settlement that became known as the Compromise of 1850. One of the provisions reaffirmed the Missouri Compromise of 1820, which had stipulated that after the admission of Missouri, slavery would be prohibited in Federal territory north of the line of Missouri's southern boundary.

But Douglas' Kansas–Nebraska Bill, which provided for the organization of those territories, repealed the Missouri Compromise. In its place the author inserted "popular sovereignty." On this principle the people of Kansas and Nebraska, when they came to adopt constitutions preparatory to admission to the Union, could decide whether to admit slavery or rule it out. Thus the way was opened for the slave system to enter a vast area which its opponents had believed to be forever free.

Bitter resentment greeted the Kansas–Nebraska Bill. When Douglas returned to Illinois after the adjournment of Congress and attempted to address an open-air meeting in Chicago, where he had been a popular favorite, the crowd howled and booed until he finally shouted: "It is now Sunday morning—I'll go to church and you can go to hell!" In the Middle West, abolitionists formed a new party to which they gave the name Republican. Most of the dissidents, however, simply called themselves Anti-Nebraska Whigs or Anti-Nebraska Democrats, and sought to do no more than reverse the Kansas–Nebraska policy while retaining their old party affiliations.

I

Excitement over Kansas and Nebraska might have abated if extremists had not attempted a conquest of Kansas. But as soon as the territory was organized, proslavery groups, mostly from neighboring Missouri, moved in, determined that when the time came, Kansas should enter the Union as a slave state. Soon they faced emigrants from New England, equally determined that Kansas should be a free state. For the next four years the two factions stuffed ballot boxes, falsified election returns, set up rival governments, sacked each other's settlements, killed opponents in cold blood. "Popular sovereignty" might be

soundly democratic in principle; in practice it produced civil war.
In May, 1856, when Kansas seemed to be irrevocably bogged in
lawlessness, Charles Sumner of Massachusetts made a carefully pre-
pared speech in the United States Senate. Stanchly antislavery, Sum-
ner was able, pompous, without humor, contemptuous of anyone who
held opinions differing from his own, and unrestrained in speech. Tak-
ing "The Crime against Kansas" as his subject, he delivered a bitter
excoriation of the South and chose the elderly Senator from South
Carolina, Andrew P. Butler, as a target for personal insult:[1]

Before entering upon the argument, I must say something of a general character, particularly in response to what has fallen from Senators who have raised themselves to eminence on this floor in cham-
pionship of human wrongs. I mean the Senator from South Carolina
and the Senator from Illinois, who, though unlike as Don Quixote and
Sancho Panza, yet, like this couple, sally forth together in the same adventure. I regret much to miss the elder Senator from his seat, but
the cause, against which he has run atilt, with such activity of animosity, demands that the opportunity of exposing him should not be lost;
and it is for the cause that I speak. The Senator from South Carolina
has read many books of chivalry and believes himself a chivalrous
knight, with sentiments of honor and courage. Of course he has chosen
a mistress to whom he has made his vows, and who, though ugly to
others, is always lovely to him; though polluted in the sight of the
world, is chaste in his sight—I mean the harlot, Slavery. For her, his
tongue is always profuse in words. Let her be impeached in character,
or any proposition made to shut her out from the extension of her
wantonness, and no extravagance of manner or hardihood of assertion
is then too great for this Senator. The frenzy of Don Quixote in behalf
of his wench Dulcinea del Toboso, is all surpassed. The asserted rights
of Slavery, which shock equality of all kinds, are cloaked by a fantastic claim of equality. If the slave states cannot enjoy what, in mockery
of the great fathers of the Republic, he misnames equality under the
Constitution—in other words, the full power in the National Territories
to compel fellow men to unpaid toil, to separate husband and wife, and
to sell little children at the auction block—then, sir, the chivalric
Senator will conduct the State of South Carolina out of the Union!
Heroic knight! Exalted Senator! A second Moses come for a second
exodus!
. . . With regret I come again upon the Senator from South Caro-

lina, who, omnipresent in this debate, overflowed with rage at the simple suggestion that Kansas had applied for admission as a state; and,
with incoherent phrases, discharged the loose expectoration of his
speech, now upon her representative and then upon her people. There
was no extravagance of the ancient Parliamentary debate which he
did not repeat; nor was there any possible deviation from truth which
he did not make, with so much of passion, I am glad to add, as to save
him from the suspicion of intentional aberration. But the Senator
touches nothing which he does not disfigure—with error, sometimes of
principle, sometimes of fact. He shows an incapacity of accuracy,
whether in stating the Constitution or in stating the law, whether in the
details of statistics or the diversions of scholarship. He cannot open his
mouth, but out there flies a blunder. . . .

But it is against the people of Kansas that the sensibilities of the
Senator are particularly aroused. Coming, as he announces, from a
State—aye, sir, from South Carolina—he turns with lordly disgust
from this newly-formed community, which he will not recognize even
as "a body politic." Pray, sir, by what title does he indulge in this
egotism? Has he read the history of "the State" which he represents?
He cannot, surely, have forgotten its shameful imbecility from Slavery,
confessed throughout the Revolution, followed by its more shameful as-
sumptions for Slavery since. He cannot have forgotten its wretched
persistence in the slave trade as the very apple of its eye, and the condition of its participation in the Union. He cannot have forgotten its
Constitution, which is republican only in name, confirming power in
the hands of the few and founding the qualifications of its legislators
on "a settled freehold estate and ten negroes." And yet the Senator,
to whom that "State" has in part committed the guardianship of its
good name, instead of moving, with backward-treading steps, to cover
its nakedness, rushed forward, in the very ecstacy of madness, to expose it, by provoking a comparison with Kansas. South Carolina is
old; Kansas is young. . . . Were the whole history of South Carolina
blotted out of existence, from its very beginning down to the day of its
last election of the Senator to his present seat on this floor, civilization might lose—I do not say how little; but surely less than it has already gained by the example of Kansas, in its valiant struggle against
oppression, and in the development of a new science of emigration.
. . . Ah, sir, I tell the Senator that Kansas, welcomed as a Free State,
will be a "ministering angel" to the Republic, when South Carolina, in
the cloak of darkness which she hugs, "lies howling."

II

The day after Sumner finished his speech—he spoke on two days—he sat alone in the Senate Chamber. Preston Brooks, a member of the House of Representatives from South Carolina and Butler's nephew, approached the Senator from Massachusetts and without warning caned him over the head until he collapsed. By Brooks's code, the insults which Sumner had applied to the aged Butler and to the state of South Carolina justified the act. The North flamed with anger; the South showered Brooks with testimonial canes and hailed him as a hero.

Stirred by events in Kansas and aroused by the assault on Sumner, thousands of the Anti-Nebraskans of 1854 broke their old party allegiances and became avowed Republicans. The new party put its first national ticket, headed by John C. Frémont, into the field and polled 1,341,364 votes to 1,838,169 for the Democrat, James Buchanan, and 874,534 for Millard Fillmore, candidate of a remnant of Whigs and Know-Nothings. The Republican strength, essentially though not radically antislavery and drawn exclusively from the North, filled the South with foreboding.

Buchanan had been in office only two days when the Supreme Court aggravated sectional tensions. In the case of Dred Scott, a slave petitioning for his freedom, the Court held in effect that Congress had no power to prohibit slavery in the territories. The South cheered the decision. In the North the Republicans gained thousands of adherents.

The nation was fast approaching a crisis over slavery. In the summer of 1858 Abraham Lincoln shocked the complacent when he announced his candidacy for the United States Senate, in opposition to Douglas, with the assertion, " 'A house divided against itself cannot stand.' I believe this government cannot endure permanently half slave and half free. I do not expect the Union to be dissolved—I do not expect the house to fall—but I do expect it will cease to be divided." The campaign that followed drove home to all thoughtful persons the broad issues confronting the country. Douglas stated one position in his opening speech in the first debate, held at Ottawa, Illinois, on August 21:[2]

We are told by Lincoln that he is utterly opposed to the Dred Scott decision and will not submit to it, for the reason that he says it deprives the negro of the rights and privileges of citizenship. That is the first and main reason which he assigns for his warfare on the Supreme

Court of the United States and its decision. I ask you, are you in favor of conferring upon the negro the rights and privileges of citizenship? Do you desire to strike out of our state constitution that clause that keeps slaves and free negroes out of the state, and allow the free negroes to flow in and cover your prairies with black settlements? Do you desire to turn this beautiful state into a free negro colony, in order that when Missouri abolishes slavery she can send one hundred thousand emancipated slaves into Illinois, to become citizens and voters, on an equality with yourselves? If you desire negro citizenship, if you desire to allow them to come into the state and settle with the white man, if you desire them to vote on an equality with yourselves, and to make them eligible to office, to serve on juries, and to adjudge your rights, then support Mr. Lincoln and the Black Republican party, who are in favor of the citizenship of the negro. For one, I am opposed to negro citizenship in any and every form. I believe this government was made on the white basis. I believe it was made by white men, for the benefit of white men and their posterity for ever, and I am in favor of confining citizenship to white men, men of European birth and descent, instead of conferring it upon negroes, Indians and other inferior races. . . .

I do not hold that because the negro is our inferior that therefore he ought to be a slave. By no means can such a conclusion be drawn from what I have said. On the contrary, I hold that humanity and Christianity both require that the negro shall have and enjoy every right, every privilege, and every immunity consistent with the safety of the society in which he lives. On that point, I presume, there can be no diversity of opinion. You and I are bound to extend to our inferior and dependent every right, every privilege, every facility and immunity consistent with the public good. The question then arises, What rights and privileges are consistent with the public good? This is a question which each state and each territory must decide for itself—Illinois has decided it for herself. We have provided that the negro shall not be a slave, and we have also provided that he shall not be a citizen, but protect him in his civil rights, in his life, his person and his property, only depriving him of all political rights whatsoever, and refusing to put him on an equality with the white man. That policy of Illinois is satisfactory to the Democratic party and to me, and if it were to the Republicans, there would then be no question upon the subject; but the Republicans say that he ought to be made a citizen, and when he becomes a citizen he becomes your equal, with all your rights and privileges. They assert the Dred Scott decision to be monstrous because it denies that the negro is or can be a citizen under the Constitution. Now, I hold that Illinois had a right to abolish and prohibit slavery as she did, and I hold that Kentucky has the same right to continue and protect slavery that Illinois had to abolish it. I hold that New York had as much right to abolish slavery as Virginia has to continue it, and that each and every state of this Union is a sovereign power, with the right to do as it pleases upon this question of slavery, and upon all its domestic institutions. Slavery is not the only question which comes up in this controversy. There is a far more important one to you, and that is, What shall be done with the free negro? We have settled the slavery question as far as we are concerned; we have prohibited it in Illinois forever, and in doing so, I think we have done wisely, and there is no man in the state who would be more strenuous in his opposition to the introduction of slavery than I would; but when we settled it for ourselves, we exhausted all our power over that subject. We have done our whole duty and can do no more. We must leave each other and every other state to decide for itself the same question. . . .

Now, my friends, if we will only act conscientiously and rigidly upon this great principle of popular sovereignty which guarantees to each state and territory the right to do as it pleases on all things local and domestic instead of Congress interfering, we will continue at peace one with another.

As far as the Negro was concerned, Lincoln's position differed little from that of Douglas. In the debate at Charleston, Illinois, on September 18, Lincoln said:[3]

Judge Douglas has said to you that he has not been able to get from me an answer to the question whether I am in favor of negro citizenship. So far as I know, the Judge never asked me the question before. He shall have no occasion to ever ask it again, for I tell him very frankly that I am not in favor of negro citizenship. This furnishes me an occasion for saying a few words upon the subject. I mentioned in a certain speech of mine which has been printed, that the Supreme Court had decided that a negro could not possibly be made a citizen, and without saying what was my ground of complaint in regard to that, or whether I had any ground of complaint, Judge Douglas has from that thing manufactured nearly every thing that he ever says about my disposition to produce an equality between the negroes and the white people. If any one will read my speech, he will find I mentioned that as one of the points decided in the course of the Supreme Court opinions, but I did not state what objection I had to it. But Judge Douglas tells the people what my objection was when I did not tell them myself. Now my opinion is that the different states have the power to make a negro a citizen under the Constitution of the United States if they choose. The Dred Scott decision decides that they have not that power. If the state of Illinois had that power I should be opposed to the exercise of it. That is all I have to say about it.

But Lincoln put the controversy between the sections on a higher plane than expediency or even constitutionality. Summing up, in the next to the last debate, at Quincy, Illinois, on October 13, he defined the issue in terms that morally sensitive men could not ignore:[4]

We have in this nation this element of domestic slavery. It is a matter of absolute certainty that it is a disturbing element. It is the opinion of all the great men who have expressed an opinion upon it, that it is a dangerous element. We keep up a controversy in regard to it. That controversy necessarily springs from difference of opinion, and if we can learn exactly—can reduce to the lowest elements—what that difference of opinion is, we perhaps shall be better prepared for discussing the different systems of policy that we would propose in regard to that disturbing element. I suggest that the difference of opinion, reduced to its lowest terms, is no other than the difference between the men who think slavery a wrong and those who do not think it wrong. The Republican party think it wrong—we think it is a moral, a social and a political wrong. We think it is a wrong not confining itself merely to the persons or the states where it exists, but that it is a wrong in its tendency, to say the least, that extends itself to the existence of the whole nation. Because we think it wrong, we propose a course of policy that shall deal with it as a wrong. We deal with it as with any other wrong, in so far as we can prevent its growing any larger, and so deal with it that in the run of time there may be some promise of an end to it. We have a due regard to the actual presence of it amongst us and the difficulties of getting rid of it in any satisfactory way, and all the constitutional obligations thrown about it. I suppose that in reference both to its actual existence in the nation, and to our constitutional obligations, we have no right at all to disturb it in the states where it exists, and we profess that we have no more inclination to disturb it than we have the right to do it. We go further than that; we don't propose to disturb it where, in one instance, we think the Constitution would permit us. We think the Constitution would permit us to disturb it in the District of Columbia. Still we do not propose to do that, unless it should be in terms which I don't suppose the nation is very likely soon to agree to—the terms of making the emancipation gradual and compensating the unwilling owners. Where we suppose we have the constitutional right, we restrain ourselves in reference to the actual existence of the institution and the difficulties thrown about it. We also oppose it as an evil so far as it seeks to spread itself. We insist on the policy that shall restrict it to its present limits. We don't suppose that in doing this we violate anything due to the actual presence of the institution, or anything due to the constitutional guarantees thrown around it.

III

The Illinois election was close. In the vote for state officers the Republicans cast 125,430 votes against the Democratic total of 121,609, while the Buchanan Democrats could muster only 5,071. But the apportionment was such that votes in southern Illinois, where Douglas' strength lay, counted for more than votes in the northern part of the state, the Republican stronghold. As a result, Douglas won re-election by a vote of fifty-four to forty-six in the Illinois legislature.

But Lincoln lost only the immediate contest. He could not have realized at the time that through the debates with Douglas he had gained the national reputation without which he could not even have been considered for the Presidency two years later.

Now came the turn of old John Brown. For years this fanatical abolitionist had believed that only blood could wash out slavery. During the civil war in Kansas he and several of his sons had murdered proslavery settlers without provocation. Later, he had raided plantations in Missouri and carried slaves off to Canada. On October 16, 1859, with a band of blindly devoted followers, he attacked and captured the United States Arsenal at Harpers Ferry, Virginia, confident that the slaves would rise en masse and murder their white masters. The slaves made no move, but Virginia and the United States government acted quickly. Notified of the seizure of the arsenal, the War Department sent a detachment of Marines, the only troops then available, to the scene and then ordered Col. Robert E. Lee, who chanced to be at his home in Arlington, to take command. With Lee, as a volun-

*teer aide, went a young lieutenant of the First Cavalry home on leave,
J. E. B. Stuart. Lee's report to Adjutant General Samuel Cooper describes an action which could have been, except for its portent, merely
the quelling of a riot:*[5]

On arriving here on the night of the 17th [October], I learned that
a party of insurgents, about 11 P.M. on the 16th, had seized the
watchmen stationed at the armory, arsenal, rifle factory and bridge
across the Potomac, and taken possession of those points. They had
dispatched six men, under one of their party, to arrest the principal
citizens of the neighborhood and incite the negroes to join in the insurrection. The party took Colonel L. W. Washington from his bed about
1½ A.M. on the 17th, and brought him with four of his servants to this
place. Mr. J. H. Allstadt and six of his servants were in the same manner seized about 3 A.M. and arms placed in the hands of the negroes.
As day advanced and the citizens of Harper's Ferry commenced their
usual avocations, they were separately captured, to the number of
forty, and confined in one room of the fire-engine house of the armory,
which seems early to have been selected as a point of defense. . . .

I made preparations to attack the insurgents at daylight. But for the
fear of sacrificing the lives of some of the gentlemen held by them as
prisoners in a midnight assault, I should have ordered the attack at
once. Their safety was the subject of painful consideration, and to prevent if possible jeopardizing their lives, I determined to summon the
insurgents to surrender.

As soon after daylight as the arrangements were made, Lieutenant
J. E. B. Stuart, 1st Cavalry, who had accompanied me from Washington as a staff officer, was dispatched under a flag with a written summons, as follows: "Colonel Lee, United States Army, commanding the
troops sent by the President of the United States to suppress the insurrection at this place, demands the surrender of the persons in the armory buildings. If they will peaceably surrender themselves and restore
the pillaged property, they shall be kept in safety to await the orders of
the President. Colonel Lee represents to them, in all frankness, that it
is impossible for them to escape; that the armory is surrounded on all
sides by troops; and that if he is compelled to take them by force he
can not answer for their safety."

Knowing the character of the insurgents, I did not expect the summons would be accepted. I had therefore . . . prepared a storming
party of twelve Marines under their commander, Lieutenant Green,

and had placed them close to the engine-house and secure from its fire. Three marines were furnished with sledgehammers to break in the doors, and the men were instructed how to distinguish our citizens from the insurgents, to attack with the bayonet, and not to injure the blacks detained in custody unless they resisted. Lieutenant Stuart was also directed not to receive from the insurgents any counter proposi- tions. If they accepted the terms offered, they must immediately de- liver up their arms and release their prisoners. If they did not, he must, on leaving the engine-house, give me the signal. My object was, with a view of saving our citizens, to have as short an interval as possible between the summons and attack.

The summons, as I had anticipated, was rejected. At the concerted signal the storming party moved quickly to the door and commenced the attack. The fire-engines within the house had been placed by the besieged close to the doors. The doors were fastened by ropes, the spring of which prevented their being broken by the blows of the ham- mers. The men were therefore ordered to drop the hammers and to use as a battering-ram a heavy ladder, with which they dashed in a part of the door and gave admittance to the storming party. The fire of the insurgents up to this time had been harmless. At the threshold one Marine fell mortally wounded. The rest, led by Lieutenant Green and Major Russell, quickly ended the contest. The insurgents that resisted were bayoneted. Their leader, John Brown, was cut down by the sword of Lieutenant Green, and our citizens were protected by both officers and men. The whole was over in a few minutes. . . .

The survivors of the expedition I have delivered into the hands of the marshal of the western district of Virginia and the sheriff of Jeffer- son County. They were escorted to Charlestown by a detachment of Marines. . . .

IV

In the late morning of December 2, 1859, John Brown, convicted of murder, conspiracy, and treason against the State of Virginia, was brought to a field adjoining Charlestown for the purpose of hanging him by the neck until dead. Among those who watched was David Hunter Strother, a correspondent for Harper's Weekly:[6]

He [Brown] was seated in a furniture waggon on his coffin with his arms tied down above the elbows, leaving the forearms free. The drivers with two others occupied the front seat while the jailer sat in the after part of the waggon. I stood with a group of half a dozen gentlemen near the steps of the scaffold when the prisoner was driven up. He wore the same seedy and dilapidated dress that he had at Harper's Ferry and during his trial, but his rough boots had given place to a pair of particoloured slippers and he wore a low crowned broad brimmed hat (the first time I had ever seen him with a hat). He had entirely recovered from his wounds and looked decidedly better & stronger than when I last saw him. As he neared the gibbet his face wore a grim & grisly smirk which, but for the solemnity of the occasion, might have suggested ideas of the ludicrous. He stepped from the waggon with surprising agility and walked hastily toward the scaffold pausing a moment as he passed our group to wave his pinioned arm & bid us good morning. . . . He mounted the steps of the scaffold with the same alacrity and there as if by previous arrangement, he immediately took off his hat and offered his neck for the halter which was as promptly adjusted by Mr. Avis the jailer. A white muslin cap or hood was then drawn over his face and the Sheriff not remembering that his eyes were covered requested him to advance to the platform. The prisoner replied in his usual tone, "You will have to guide me there."

The breeze disturbing the arrangement of the hood the Sheriff asked his assistant for a pin. Brown raised his hand and directed him to the collar of his coat where several old pins were quilted in. The Sheriff took the pin and completed his work.

He was accordingly led forward to the drop, the halter hooked to the beam, and the officers supposing that the execution was to follow immediately took leave of him. In doing so, the Sheriff enquired if he did not want a handkerchief to throw as a signal to cut the drop. Brown replied, "No, I don't care; I don't want you to keep me waiting unnecessarily."

These were his last words, spoken with that sharp nasal twang peculiar to him, but spoken quietly & civilly, without impatience or the slightest apparent emotion. In this position he stood for five minutes or more, while the troops that composed the escort were wheeling into the positions assigned them. I stood within a few paces of him and watched narrowly during these trying moments to see if there was any indication of his giving way. I detected nothing of the sort. He had stiffened himself for the drop and waited motionless 'till it came.

During all these movements no sound was heard but the quick stern words of military command, & when these ceased a dead silence reigned. Col. Smith said to the Sheriff in a low voice, "We are ready." The civil officers descended from the scaffold. One who stood near me whispered earnestly, "He trembles, his knees are shaking." "You are mistaken," I replied, "it is the scaffold that shakes under the footsteps of the officers." The Sheriff struck the rope a sharp blow with a hatchet, the platform fell with a crash—a few convulsive struggles & a human soul had gone to judgment.

John Brown's raid and the execution of its leader stirred the country as nothing had stirred it since the passage of the Kansas–Nebraska Bill five years earlier. Allan Nevins in his superb study of the nation's agony, Ordeal of the Union, *portrays the effect on both sections:*[7]

While John Brown was being hanged; while the noonday sun shone down upon the far-sweeping Blue Ridge, the two winding rivers, the immobile lines of riflemen and horse, and the grim gallows; while the commanding officer proclaimed that the majesty of Virginia law had been satisfied, a mounting emotion swept the whole land from St. Croix to the Florida keys. Next day, the telegraph told how deep an imprint Brown's act and fate had laid upon the feeling of millions.

In many Northern communities, such as the Concord of Franklin Pierce and the Chicago of Douglas, bells were tolled at the hour of execution; in some, minute guns were fired; in still others, crowded public meetings were held. In Philadelphia, a gathering offered prayers for Brown, heard the Rev. W. H. Furness read letters from him, and applauded a speech by Lucretia Mott. In New York, Dr. George B. Cheever, author of *God Against Slavery*, addressed an audience at his Church of the Pilgrims. A crowd filling Tremont Temple in Boston heard a discourse by William Lloyd Garrison. In Albany, while a hundred guns were fired, meetings continued all afternoon and evening; in Syracuse, the city hall was packed with citizens who met for three hours of speechmaking; in Cleveland, buildings were hung with black, and a leading minister spoke to five thousand people. . . .

Emerson termed Brown a new saint in the calendar; Thoreau described him as an angel of light; Longfellow, on the day of execution, entered in his diary, "The date of a new revolution, quite as much needed as the old one." Dr. Cheever's sermon the following Sunday treated Brown as an incarnation of God's protest against slavery. But the significant fact was that men whose opinions fell far short of abolitionism spoke in similar terms. Wrote William Cullen Bryant: "History, forgetting the errors of his judgment in the contemplation of his unfaltering courage, of his dignified and manly deportment in the face of death, and of the nobleness of his aims, will record his name among those of its martyrs and heroes." Young William Dean Howells, writing his father from the capital of Ohio, predicted for the raider a great place in history: "Brown has become an idea, a thousand times purer and better and loftier than the Republican idea." Charles Eliot Norton, explaining to an English friend how the bitterness of the Virginia press, the hurry of the trial, the noble manliness of Brown under condemnation, his speech, his letters from prison, the visit from his wife, and, at last, his death, had wrought up popular emotion to the highest pitch, predicted that it would not die away. . . .

A great legend had been created in the North; a legend that was to place its mark on political thought, influence multitudes at the ballot box, and within two years send armies into battle singing "John Brown's Body." In the aura of that legend the real man was transfigured, and his crimes were palliated by his favorite text: "Without the shedding of blood there is no remission of sins." To be sure, conservative men in thousands denounced his raid. Washington Hunt termed it an infernal performance; Edward Everett confessed himself disgusted and alarmed; Richard Henry Dana, Jr., spoke of the man's insanity. Even Henry Wilson wrote that he knew of no Republican who did not condemn the John Brown blow, or at least regret it. Whittier, as a non-resistant Quaker, a believer in moral warfare alone, of course deplored such violence. Yet most Northerners believed that the man's character was noble, that his errors were those of a fanatic, and that if his act condemned himself, it also condemned slavery. It is the heaviest blow yet struck against the institution, said some; it brings the end of slavery ten years nearer, said others. . . .

It was just as inevitable that a very different legend of John Brown should spring up in the South. The bitter resentment aroused by his raid, felt by slaveholders and slaveless alike, embraced all Northerners suspected of being his helpers and abettors. . . .

At first, many Southerners were reluctant to believe that any but the more malignant abolitionists would express sympathy for treason, servile insurrection, and murder. Then, when they learned that Emerson, Longfellow, and Bryant had penned panegyrics of their assailant, that leading newspapers and hundreds of ministers were apotheosizing him, their tempers hardened. An observant young Tennesseean,

John W. Burgess, found that a revolution in sentiment occurred during the month after the raid. The tolling of Northern bells and half-staffing of Northern flags for Brown's execution were accepted as evidence of a wicked desire to destroy the South. Governor Wise's son noted the same change in Virginia. People of the Old Dominion began to look upon the Yankees as men who hated them, who were willing to see them assassinated at midnight by their own slaves and who were ready to support still more formidable invasions of Southern soil. . . .

It was natural that a great part of the Southern press should interpret John Brown's raid as evidence that the abolitionists would arm new bands of assailants, and that their section must now live under daily menace of attack. The scope of the conspiracy was vastly exaggerated. When maps of several Southern States were found in Brown's baggage, with marks indicating certain counties in which the colored people exceeded the whites, many jumped to the conclusion that abolition agents had been sent to these areas or would soon go thither. . . .

Unfortunately, the Republican Party was now widely misidentified with the abolitionists. Though most Republicans reprehended Brown's deed, the South was no longer in any mood to make the vital distinction between those who wished to contain slavery and those who wished its immediate extirpation. Howell Cobb, declining in a letter of October 31 to speak in New York, called the raid a practical result of Republican abuse of the South and talk of an irrepressible conflict. Much of the Democratic press in both sections took up the hue and cry. . . .

The unhappiest single result of the raid, in a practical sense, was this intensification of Southern hatred and suspicion of the Republican Party. It was universally called the Black Republican Party, its leaders were increasingly characterized as enemies of Southern institutions, and its doctrine of non-interference in the States but exclusion of slavery from the Territories was vituperatively distorted into a doctrine of warfare upon slavery everywhere.

1861

CHAPTER 3

CLAY WINGATE'S WAR

In the Governor's office of the Illinois State House, Abraham Lincoln, President-elect, watched in silence while the Union disintegrated. Stoically he saw state after state follow the lead of secessionist South Carolina—Mississippi on January 9, 1861; Florida on the 10th; Alabama on the 11th; Georgia on the 19th; Louisiana on the 26th; Texas on February 1. As Southern officers of the Army resigned their commissions and Southern Congressmen and Senators gave up their seats, Lincoln made no comment. He showed no concern as the armed forces of Southern states seized forts and arsenals within their boundaries. Engrossed in preparations for his own inauguration, he gave no sign that he even noticed the formation, in early February, of a Southern Confederacy and the election of Jefferson Davis and Alexander H. Stephens as provisional President and Vice President.

I

Lincoln left Springfield for Washington on February 11, 1861, stopping that night at Indianapolis. Only in this first of many speeches in the course of his long journey to the Capital did he give any public indication of the inflexible resolution he had formed at the beginning of the crisis.* From the balcony of his hotel he said:[1]

* The possible exception came on February 21, when he was wildly cheered by the New Jersey General Assembly for saying, "It may be necessary to put the foot down firmly."

The words "coercion" and "invasion" are in great use about these days. Suppose we were simply to try if we can, and ascertain what is the meaning of these words. Let us get, if we can, the exact definitions of these words—not from dictionaries, but from the men who constantly repeat them—what things they mean to express by the words. What, then, is "coercion"? What is "invasion"? Would the marching of an army into South Carolina, for instance, without the consent of her people, and in hostility against them, be coercion or invasion? I very frankly say, I think it would be invasion, and it would be coercion too, if the people of that country were forced to submit. But if the government, for instance, but simply insists upon holding its own forts, retaking those forts which belong to it—or even the withdrawal of the mails from those portions of the country where the mails themselves are habitually violated; would any or all of these things be coercion? Do the lovers of the Union contend that they will resist coercion or invasion of any State, understanding that any or all of these would be coercing or invading a State? If they do, then it occurs to me that the means for the preservation of the Union they so greatly love, in their own estimation, is of a very thin and airy character. If sick, they would consider the little pills of the homeopathist as already too large for them to swallow. In their view the Union, as a family relation, would not be anything like a regular marriage at all, but only as a sort of free-love arrangement—to be maintained on what that sect calls passionate attraction. But, my friends, enough of this.

What is the particular sacredness of a State? I speak not of that position which is given to a State in and by the Constitution of the United States, for that all of us agree to—we abide by; but that position assumed, that a State can carry with it out of the Union that which it holds in sacredness by virtue of its connection with the Union. I am speaking of that assumed right of a State, as a primary principle, that the Constitution should rule all that is less than itself, and ruin all that is bigger than itself. But, I ask, wherein does consist that right? If a State, in one instance, and a county in another, should be equal in extent of territory, and equal in the number of people, wherein is that State any better than the county? Can a change of name change the right? By what principle of original right is it that one-fiftieth or one-ninetieth of a great nation, by calling themselves a State, have the right to break up and ruin that nation as a matter of original principle? . . . I am deciding nothing, but simply giving something for

THE UNITED STATES IN 1861

FREE STATES

SLAVE STATES WHICH SECEDED

SLAVE STATES WHICH DID NOT SECEDE

TERRITORIES

you to reflect upon; and, with having said this much . . . I thank you again for this magnificent welcome, and bid you an affectionate farewell.

II

As Lincoln proceeded to Washington, Jefferson Davis made his way, reluctantly, from his estate in Mississippi to Montgomery, Alabama. A graduate of West Point and onetime lieutenant in the Regular Army, a volunteer colonel in the Mexican War, Secretary of War in Pierce's Administration, Davis looked forward to a military career in the armed conflict that he foresaw between North and South. After resigning from the United States Senate in January, he had accepted command of the state troops which Mississippi was raising, and preferred to continue in that capacity. Nevertheless, when notified of his election as provisional President and requested to proceed at once to the new seat of government, he neither demurred nor delayed. The Charleston Mercury reported his arrival:[2]

MONTGOMERY, February 16—President Davis' trip from Jackson, Mississippi, to Montgomery, was one continuous ovation. He made no less than twenty-five speeches upon the route, returning thanks for complimentary greetings from crowds of ladies and gentlemen. There were military demonstrations, salutes of cannon, &c., at the various depots.

The Committee of Reception, appointed by the Southern Congress, and also the Committee appointed by the Montgomery authorities, met President Davis about 80 miles from the city and formally welcomed him. Two fine companies from Columbus, Ga., formed an escort to Opelika. The *cortège* reached Montgomery Friday night at ten o'clock. Salvos of artillery greeted his approach, and a very large crowd assembled at the depot, hailing his appearance with tremendous cheering. President Davis, returning thanks, said that he was proud to receive the congratulations and hospitality of the people of Alabama. He briefly reviewed the present position of the South. The time for compromise, he said, had passed, and our only hope was in a determined maintenance of our position, and to make all who oppose us smell Southern powder and feel Southern steel. If coercion should be persisted in, he had no doubt as to the result. We would maintain our right to self-government at all hazards. We ask nothing, want nothing, and will have no complications. If other States should desire to join our Confederation, they can freely come on our terms. Our separation from the old Union is complete. NO COMPROMISE; NO RECONSTRUCTION CAN BE NOW ENTERTAINED.

Two days later, with bright sun and soft winds hinting of spring, Davis took the oath of office on the portico of the Alabama capitol. To cheering thousands he delivered his inaugural address. The tone was less belligerent than the impromptu remarks which he had made upon arriving at Montgomery, yet in several passages he left no doubt that the new Confederacy would go the limit to maintain its independence:[3]

The right solemnly claimed at the birth of the United States, and which has been solemnly affirmed and reaffirmed in the Bills of Rights of the States subsequently admitted into the Union of 1789, undeniably recognizes in the people the power to resume the authority delegated for the purposes of government. Thus the sovereign States here represented have proceeded to form this Confederacy; and it is by abuse of language that their act has been denominated a revolution. They formed a new alliance, but within each State its government has remained; so that the rights of person and property have not been disturbed. The agent through which they communicated with foreign nations is changed, but this does not necessarily interrupt their international relations. Sustained by the consciousness that the transition from the former Union to the present Confederacy has not proceeded from a disregard on our part of just obligations, or any failure to perform every constitutional duty, moved by no interest or passion to invade the rights of others, anxious to cultivate peace and commerce with all nations, if we may not hope to avoid war, we may at least expect that posterity will acquit us of having needlessly engaged in it. Doubly justified by the absence of wrong on our part and by wanton aggression on the part of others, there can be no cause to doubt that the courage and patriotism of the people of the Confederate States will be found equal to any measure of defense which their honor and security may require. . . .

We have entered upon the career of independence, and it must be inflexibly pursued. Through many years of controversy with our late associates of the Northern States, we have vainly endeavored to secure tranquillity and obtain respect for the rights to which we were entitled. As a necessity, not a choice, we have resorted to the remedy of separation, and henceforth our energies must be directed to the con-

duct of our own affairs and the perpetuity of the Confederacy which
we have formed. If a just perception of mutual interest shall permit
us peaceably to pursue our separate political career, my most earnest
desire will have been fulfilled. But if this be denied to us and the integrity of our territory and jurisdiction be assailed, it will but remain
for us with firm resolve to appeal to arms and invoke the blessing of
Providence on a just cause. . . .

As a consequence of our new condition and relations and with a
view to meet anticipated wants, it will be necessary to provide for
the speedy and efficient organization of branches of the Executive department having special charge of foreign intercourse, finance, military affairs, and the postal service. For purposes of defense, the Confederate States may, under ordinary circumstances, rely mainly upon
the militia; but it is deemed advisable, in the present condition of affairs, that there should be a well-instructed and disciplined army, more
numerous than would usually be required on a peace establishment.
I also suggest that, for the protection of our harbors and commerce on
the high seas, a navy adapted to those objects will be required. . . .

It is joyous in the midst of perilous times to look around upon a
people united in heart, where one purpose of high resolve animates
and actuates the whole; where the sacrifices to be made are not
weighed in the balance against honor and right and equality. Obstacles
may retard, but they cannot long prevent, the progress of a movement
sanctified by its justice and sustained by a virtuous people. Reverently let us invoke the God of our fathers to guide and protect us in
our efforts to perpetuate the principles which by His blessing they were
able to vindicate, establish, and transmit to their posterity. With the
continuance of His favor ever gratefully acknowledged, we may hopefully look forward to success, to peace, and to prosperity.

III

*On the fourth of March, 1861, Abraham Lincoln stood on the east
portico of the Capitol in Washington, placed his hand on the Bible, and
swore to "execute the office of President of the United States" and to
"preserve, protect, and defend the Constitution of the United States."
He faced a momentous fact. A new nation had come into existence.
Would there be war or a peaceable adjustment between the two countries—or could the wayward states be persuaded to return to their old
allegiance? To the hope that they could, he devoted much of his Inaugural Address.*[4]

That there are persons in one section or another who seek to destroy the Union at all events, and are glad of any pretext to do it, I will neither affirm nor deny; but if there be such, I need address no word to them. To those, however, who really love the Union, may I not speak?

Before entering upon so grave a matter as the destruction of our national fabric, with all its benefits, its memories, and its hopes, would it not be wise to ascertain precisely why we do it? Will you hazard so desperate a step, while there is any possibility that any portion of the ills you fly from, have no real existence? Will you, while the certain ills you fly to, are greater than all the real ones you fly from? Will you risk the commission of so fearful a mistake?

All profess to be content in the Union, if all constitutional rights can be maintained. Is it true, then, that any right, plainly written in the Constitution, has been denied? I think not. Happily the human mind is so constituted that no party can reach to the audacity of doing this. . . . All the vital rights of minorities, and of individuals, are so plainly assured to them, by affirmations and negations, guarantees and prohibitions in the Constitution, that controversies never arise concerning them. But no organic law can ever be framed with a provision specifically applicable to every question which may occur in practical administration. No foresight can anticipate, nor any document of reasonable length contain express provisions for all possible questions. Shall fugitives from labor be surrendered by national or by state authority? The Constitution does not expressly say. *May* Congress prohibit slavery in the territories? The Constitution does not expressly say. *Must* Congress protect slavery in the territories? The Constitution does not expressly say.

From questions of this class spring all our constitutional controversies, and we divide upon them into majorities and minorities. If the minority will not acquiesce, the majority must, or the government must cease. There is no other alternative; for continuing the government is acquiescence on one side or the other. If a minority, in such case, will secede rather than acquiesce, they make a precedent which, in turn, will divide and ruin them; for a minority of their own will secede from them, whenever a majority refuses to be controlled by such minority. For instance, why may not any portion of a new confederacy, a year or two hence, arbitrarily secede again, precisely as portions of the present Union now claim to secede from it? All who cherish disunion sentiments are now being educated to the exact temper of doing this. Is there such perfect identity of interests among the States to compose a new Union, as to produce harmony only, and prevent renewed secession?

Plainly, the central idea of secession is the essence of anarchy. A majority, held in restraint by constitutional checks and limitations, and always changing easily, with deliberate changes of popular opinions and sentiments, is the only true sovereign of a free people. Whoever rejects it does, of necessity, fly to anarchy or to despotism. Unanimity is impossible; the rule of a minority, as a permanent arrangement, is wholly inadmissible; so that, rejecting the majority principle, anarchy, or despotism in some form, is all that is left. . . .

Physically speaking, we cannot separate. We cannot remove our respective sections from each other, nor build an impassable wall between them. A husband and wife may be divorced, and go out of the presence, and beyond the reach of each other; but the different parts of our country cannot do this. They cannot but remain face to face; and intercourse, either amicable or hostile, must continue between them. Is it possible then to make that intercourse more advantageous, or more satisfactory, *after* separation than *before?* Can aliens make treaties easier than friends can make laws? Can treaties be more faithfully enforced between aliens, than laws can among friends? Suppose you go to war, you cannot fight always; and when, after much loss on both sides, and no gain on either, you cease fighting, the identical old questions, as to terms of intercourse, are again upon you. . . .

My countrymen, one and all, think calmly and *well,* upon this whole subject. Nothing valuable can be lost by taking time. If there be an object to *hurry* any of you, in hot haste, to a step which you would never take *deliberately,* that object will be frustrated by taking time; but no good object can be frustrated by it. Such of you as are now dissatisfied, still have the old Constitution unimpaired, and, on the sensitive point, the laws of your own framing under it; while the new administration will have no immediate power, if it would, to change either. If it were admitted that you who are dissatisfied, hold the right side in the dispute, there still is no single good reason for precipitate action. Intelligence, patriotism, Christianity, and a firm reliance on Him who has never yet forsaken this favored land, are still competent to adjust, in the best way, all our present difficulty.

In *your* hands, my dissatisfied fellow countrymen, and not in *mine,* is the momentous issue of civil war. The government will not assail *you.* You can have no conflict without being yourselves the aggressors.

You have no oath registered in Heaven to destroy the government, while *I* shall have the most solemn one to "preserve, protect and defend it."

I am loth to close. We are not enemies, but friends. We must not be enemies. Though passion may have strained, it must not break our bonds of affection. The mystic chords of memory, stretching from every battle-field, and patriot grave, to every living heart and hearth-stone, all over this broad land, will yet swell the chorus of the Union, when again touched, as surely they will be, by the better angels of our nature.

IV

Lincoln went to his office in the White House for the first time on the morning of March 5. There he found a letter from Joseph Holt, still acting as Secretary of War, informing him that information received from Charleston on the preceding day showed that Fort Sumter must either be reinforced or abandoned within a few weeks at most. John G. Nicolay and John Hay, embarking on their secretarial duties, described a crisis they had not expected:[5]

Here was a most portentous complication, not of Lincoln's own creating, but which he must nevertheless meet and overcome. He had counted on the soothing aid of time; time, on the contrary, was in this emergency working in the interest of rebellion. General Scott was at once called into council, but his sagacity and experience could afford neither suggestion nor encouragement. That same night he returned the papers to the President with a somewhat lengthy indorsement reciting the several events which led to, and his own personal efforts to avert, this contingency, but ending with the gloomy conclusion: "Evacuation seems almost inevitable, and in this view our distinguished Chief Engineer (Brigadier Totten) concurs—if indeed the worn-out garrison be not assaulted and carried in the present week."

This was a disheartening, almost a disastrous, beginning for the Administration. The Cabinet had only that day been appointed and confirmed. The Presidential advisers had not yet taken their posts—all had not even signified their acceptance. There was an impatient multitude clamoring for audience, and behind these swarmed an army of office-seekers. Everything was urgency and confusion, everywhere was ignorance of method and routine. Rancor and hatred filled the breasts of political opponents departing from power; suspicion and rivalry possessed partisan adherents seeking advantage and promotion. As yet, Lincoln virtually stood alone, face to face with the appalling problems of the present and the threatening responsibilities of the future. . . .

He referred the papers back to General Scott to make a more thorough investigation of all the questions involved. At the same time he gave him a verbal order touching his future policy, which a few days later was reduced to writing, and on the installation of the new Secretary of War transmitted by that functionary to the General-in-Chief through the regular official channels, as follows: "I am directed by the President to say he desires you to exercise all possible vigilance for the maintenance of all the places within the military department of the United States, and to promptly call upon all the departments of the Government for the means necessary to that end."

Four days later Lincoln called his first Cabinet meeting. Edward Bates, Attorney General, made this entry in his diary:[6]

March 9, 1861, Saturday night.—A Cabinet council upon the state of the country. I was astonished to be informed that Fort Sumter, in Charleston harbor, must be evacuated, and that General Scott, General Totten, and Major Anderson concur in opinion, that as the place has but twenty-eight days' provision, it must be relieved, if at all, in that time; and that it will take a force of twenty thousand men at least, and a bloody battle, to relieve it!

For several days after this, consultations were held as to the feasibility of relieving Fort Sumter, at which were present, explaining and aiding, General Scott, General Totten, Commodore Stringham, and Mr. Fox,* who seems to be *au fait* in both nautical and military matters. The army officers and navy officers differ widely about the degree of danger to rapid-moving vessels passing under the fire of land batteries. The army officers think destruction almost inevitable, where the navy officers think the danger but slight. The one believe that Sumter cannot be relieved—not even provisioned—without an army of twenty thousand men and a bloody battle. The other (the naval) believe that with light, rapid vessels they can cross the bar at high tide of a dark night, run the enemy's forts (Moultrie and Cummings

---

* Gustavus Vasa Fox had graduated from Annapolis in 1841 and had served in the Navy until 1856. He had no official standing at this time, but on May 9, 1861 was appointed chief clerk of the Navy Department, and on August 1, Assistant Secretary.

Point), and reach Sumter with little risk. They say that the greatest danger will be in landing at Sumter, upon which point there may be a concentrated fire. They do not doubt that the place can be and ought to be relieved.

Mr. Fox is anxious to risk his life in leading the relief, and Commodore Stringham seems equally confident of success.

The naval men have convinced me fully that the thing can be done, and yet as the doing of it would be almost certain to begin the war, and as Charleston is of little importance as compared with the chief points in the Gulf, I am willing to yield to the military counsel and evacuate Fort Sumter, at the same time strengthening the forts in the Gulf so as to look down opposition, and guarding the coast with all our naval power, if need be, so as to close any port at pleasure.

And to this effect I gave the President my written opinion on the 16th of March.

V

While Lincoln wrestled with the problem of Fort Sumter, Jefferson Davis's chief concern was that of making a new government function. Thomas C. De Leon, a South Carolinian who gave up his position in the office of Topographical Engineers as soon as Lincoln was inaugurated, described the Confederate President at work in Montgomery:[7]

"The President is at this house?" I queried of the ex-member of Congress next to me at dinner. "But he does not appear, I suppose?"

"Oh, yes; he's waiting here till his house is made ready. But he doesn't have a private table; takes his meals like an everyday mortal, at the ladies' ordinary."

He had scarcely spoken when Mr. Davis entered by a side door and took his seat, with only an occasional stare of earnest, but not disrespectful, curiosity from the more recent arrivals.

Even in the few weeks since I had seen him, there was a great change. He looked worn and thinner; and the set expression of the somewhat stern features gave a grim hardness not natural to their lines. With scarcely a glance around, he returned the general salutations, sat down absently and was soon absorbed in conversation with General Cooper, who had recently resigned the adjutant-generalship of the United States army and accepted a similar post and a brigadier's commission from Mr. Davis.

An after-dinner interview with the President of the Confederacy, to present the "very important" documents from one of the martyrs pining for hanging in Washington, proved them only a prolix report of the inauguration. Mr. Davis soon threw them aside to hear the verbal account from us.

At this time the southern chief was fifty-two years old—tall, erect and spare by natural habit, but worn thin to almost emaciation by mental and physical toil. Almost constant sickness and unremitting excitement of the last few months had left their imprint on face as well as figure. The features had sharpened and the lines had deepened and hardened; the thin lips had a firmer compression and the lower jaw—always firm and prominent—was closer pressed to its fellow. Mr. Davis had lost the sight of one eye many months previous, though that member scarcely showed its imperfection; but in the other burned a deep, steady glow, showing the presence within him of thought that never slept. And in conversation he had the habit of listening with eyes shaded by the lids, then suddenly shooting forth at the speaker a gleam from the stone-gray pupil which seemed to penetrate his innermost mind.

Little ceremony, or form, hedged the incubating government; and perfect simplicity marked every detail about Mr. Davis. His office, for the moment, was one of the parlors of the hotel. Members of the Cabinet and high officials came in and out without ceremony, to ask questions and receive very brief replies; or for whispered consultation with the President's private secretary, whose desk was in the same room. Casual visitors were simply announced by an usher, and were received whenever business did not prevent. Mr. Davis' manner was unvarying in its quiet and courtesy, drawing out all that one had to tell, and indicating by brief answer, or criticism, that he had extracted the pith from it. At that moment he was the very idol of the people; the grand embodiment to them of their grand cause; and they gave him their hands unquestioning, to applaud any move soever he might make.

In Washington, Lincoln came to a decision about Sumter: He would send a relief expedition, under Fox's command, but the ships would land provisions only and would make no attempt to put either men or munitions into the fort unless attacked. At a Cabinet meeting on March 29 a majority of the Secretaries agreed with the policy on which the President had already decided. In accordance with a previous *promise Lincoln, on April 6, sent a messenger to Governor Pickens ** *of South Carolina notifying him of the action the Federal government* *intended to take. Three days later the relief expedition sailed from* *New York.*

In Charleston the Confederate forces sprang into action. Brigadier *General Pierre Gustave Toutant Beauregard, the Louisiana Creole* *career soldier, recently resigned from the United States Army, whom* *Jefferson Davis had placed in command in South Carolina, sent a* *message to Anderson on April 11:*[8]

. . . I am ordered by the Government of the Confederate States to demand the evacuation of Fort Sumter. My aides, Colonel Chesnut and Captain Lee, are authorized to make such demand of you. All proper facilities will be afforded for the removal of yourself and command, together with company arms and property, and all private property, to any post in the United States which you may select. The flag which you have upheld so long and with so much fortitude, under the most trying circumstances, may be saluted by you on taking it down.

Anderson replied at once:

GENERAL: I have the honor to acknowledge the receipt of your communication demanding the evacuation of this fort, and to say, in reply thereto, that it is a demand with which I regret that my sense of honor, and of my obligations to my Government, prevent my compliance. Thanking you for the fair, manly, and courteous terms proposed, and for the high compliment paid me, I am, general, very respectfully, your obedient servant. . . .

The correspondence continued with all the punctiliousness of the code *duello. Beauregard rejoined:*

MAJOR: In consequence of the verbal observation made by you to my aides, Messrs. Chesnut and Lee, in relation to the condition of your supplies, and that you would in a few days be starved out if our guns did not batter you to pieces, or words to that effect, and desiring no useless effusion of blood, I communicated both the verbal observations and your written answer to my communication to my Government.

* Francis W. Pickens had succeeded William Henry Gist on December 17, 1860.

If you will state the time at which you will evacuate Fort Sumter, and agree that in the mean time you will not use your guns against us unless ours shall be employed against Fort Sumter, we will abstain from opening fire upon you. Colonel Chesnut and Captain Lee are authorized by me to enter into such an agreement with you. You are, therefore, requested to communicate to them an open answer. . . .

Anderson answered on the next day, April 12:

GENERAL: I have the honor to . . . state . . . that, cordially uniting with you in the desire to avoid the useless effusion of blood, I will, if provided with the proper and necessary means of transportation, evacuate Fort Sumter by noon on the 15th instant, and that I will not in the mean time open my fires upon your forces unless compelled to do so by some hostile act against this fort or the flag of my Government by the forces under your command, or by some portion of them, or by the perpetration of some act showing a hostile intention on your part against this fort or the flag it bears, should I not receive prior to that time controlling instructions from my Government or additional supplies. . . .

Beauregard's reply, dated April 12, 3:20 A.M., was transmitted by his two aides-de-camp:

SIR: By authority of Brigadier General Beauregard, commanding the Provisional Forces of the Confederate States, we have the honor to notify you that he will open the fire of his batteries on Fort Sumter in one hour after this time. . . .

VI

In his official report to the Confederate Secretary of War, Beauregard took up the story:[9]

On the refusal of Major Anderson to engage, in compliance with my demand, to designate the time when he would evacuate Fort Sumter, and to agree meanwhile not to use his guns against us, at 3:20 o'clock in the morning of the 12th instant I gave him formal notice that within one hour my batteries would open on his. In consequence of some circumstance of delay the bombardment was not begun precisely at the appointed moment, but at 4:30 the signal gun was fired, and within twenty minutes all our batteries were in full play. There was no response from Fort Sumter until about 7 o'clock, when the first shot from the enemy was discharged against our batteries on Cummings Point.

By 8 o'clock the action became general, and throughout the day was maintained with spirit on both sides. Our guns were served with skill and energy. The effect was visible in the impressions made on the walls of Fort Sumter. From our mortar batteries shells were thrown with such precision and rapidity that it soon became impossible for the enemy to employ his guns *en barbette*,* of which several were dismounted. The engagement was continued without any circumstance of special note until nightfall, before which time the fire from Sumter had evidently slackened. Operations on our side were sustained throughout the night, provoking, however, only a feeble response.

The damage to Sumter was less than the Confederate commander believed. Sergeant James Chester of Company E, First Artillery, described the way in which the garrison accepted the war's first challenge:[10]

Promptly at 4:30 A.M. a flash as of distant lightning in the direction of Mount Pleasant, followed by the dull roar of a mortar, told us that the bombardment had begun. The eyes of the watchers easily detected and followed the burning fuse which marked the course of the shell as it mounted among the stars, and then descended with ever-increasing velocity, until it landed inside the fort and burst. It was a capital shot. Then the batteries opened on all sides, and shot and shell went screaming over Sumter as if an army of devils were swooping around it. As a rule the guns were aimed too high, but all the mortar practice was good. In a few minutes the novelty disappeared in a realizing sense of danger, and the watchers retired to the bomb-proofs, where they discussed probabilities until reveille.

Habits of discipline are strong among old soldiers. If it had not been for orders to the contrary, the men would have formed for roll-call on the open parade, as it was their custom to do, although mortar-shells were bursting there at the lively rate of about one a minute. But they were formed under the bomb-proofs, and the roll was called as if nothing unusual was going on. They were then directed to get breakfast, and be ready to fall in when "assembly" was beaten. The break-

* Guns *en barbette* are so mounted as to fire over a fort's parapet.

fast part of the order was considered a grim joke, as the fare was reduced to the solitary item of fat pork, very rusty indeed. But most of
the men worried down a little of it, and were "ready" when the drum
called them to their work.

By this time it was daylight, and the effects of the bombardment
became visible. No serious damage was being done to the fort. The
enemy had concentrated their fire on the barbette batteries, but, like
most inexperienced gunners, they were firing too high. After daylight their shooting improved, until at 7:30 A.M., when "assembly"
was beaten in Sumter, it had become fairly good. At "assembly" the
men were again paraded, and the orders of the day announced. The
garrison was divided into two reliefs, and the tour of duty at the guns
was to be four hours. Captain Doubleday being the senior captain,
his battery took the first hour. . . .

At the end of the first four hours, Doubleday's men were relieved
from the guns and had an opportunity to look about them. Not a man
was visible near any of the batteries, but a large party, apparently of
non-combatants, had collected on the beach of Sullivan's Island, well
out of the line of fire, to witness the duel between Sumter and Moultrie.
Doubleday's men were not in the best of temper. They were irritated
at the thought that they had been unable to inflict any serious damage
on their adversary, and although they had suffered no damage in return they were dissatisfied. The crowd of unsympathetic spectators
was more than they could bear, and two veteran sergeants determined
to stir them up a little. For this purpose they directed two 42-pound-
ers on the crowd, and, when no officer was near, fired. The first shot
struck about fifty yards short, and, bounding over the heads of the
astonished spectators, went crashing through the Moultrie House. The
second followed an almost identical course, doing no damage except
to the Moultrie House, and the spectators scampered off in a rather
undignified manner. . . .

Major Anderson had given orders that only the casemate batteries
should be manned. While this was undoubtedly prompted by a desire
to save his men, it operated also, in some degree, to save the Confederates. Our most powerful batteries and all our shell guns were on
the barbette tier, and, being forbidden their use, we were compelled to
oppose a destructive shell fire with solid shot alone. This, especially as
we had no mortars, was a great disadvantage. Had we been permitted
to use our shell guns we could have set fire to the barracks and quarters in Moultrie; for, as it was, we wrecked them badly with solid

shot, although we could not see them. Then the cotton-bale shutters would have been destroyed, and we could have made it much livelier generally for our adversaries. This was so apparent to the men that one of them—a man named Carmody—stole up on the ramparts and deliberately fired every barbette gun in position on the Moultrie side of the work. The guns were already loaded and roughly aimed, and Carmody simply discharged them in succession; hence, the effect was less than it would have been if the aim had been carefully rectified. But Carmody's effort aroused the enemy to a sense of his danger. He supposed, no doubt, that Major Anderson had determined to open his barbette batteries, so he directed every gun to bear on the barbette tier of Fort Sumter, and probably believed that the vigor of his fire induced Major Anderson to change his mind. But the contest was merely Carmody against the Confederate States; and Carmody had to back down, not because he was beaten, but because he was unable, single-handed, to reload his guns.

VII

Meanwhile the relief expedition—or part of it—stood off the entrance to Charleston Harbor. Through a fantastic series of misunderstandings and conflicting orders, the frigate Powhatan, *the strongest ship in the expedition, was detached and sent to the relief of Fort Pickens in Pensacola Bay. Fox's report to the Secretary of War reveals understandable frustration and resentment:*[11]

STEAMER BALTIC,
NEW YORK, April 19, 1861

SIR: I sailed from New York in this vessel Tuesday morning, the 10th instant, having dispatched one steam-tug, the Uncle Ben, the evening previous to rendezvous off Charleston. The Yankee, another chartered tug, followed us to the Hook, and I left instructions to send on the Freeborn.

We arrived off Charleston the 12th instant, at 3 A.M., and found only the Harriet Lane. Weather during the whole time a gale. At 7 A.M. the Pawnee arrived, and, according to his orders, Captain Rowan anchored twelve miles east of the light, to await the arrival of the Powhatan. I stood in with the Baltic to execute my orders by offering, in the first place, to carry provisions to Fort Sumter. Nearing the bar it was observed that war had commenced, and, therefore, the peaceful offer of provisions was void.

The Pawnee and Lane immediately anchored close to the bar, notwithstanding the heavy sea, and though neither tugs or Powhatan or Pocahontas had arrived, it was believed a couple of boats of provisions might be got in. The attempt was to be made in the morning, because the heavy sea and absence of the Powhatan's gunboats crippled the night movement. All night and the morning of the 13th instant it blew strong, with a heavy sea. The Baltic stood off and on, looking for the Powhatan, and in running in during the thick weather struck on Rattlesnake Shoal, but soon got off. The heavy sea, and not having the sailors (three hundred) asked for, rendered any attempt from the Baltic absurd. I only felt anxious to get in a few days' provisions to last the fort until the Powhatan's arrival. The Pawnee and Lane were both short of men, and were only intended to afford a base of operations whilst the tugs and three hundred sailors fought their way in.

However, the Powhatan and tugs not coming, Captain Rowan seized an ice schooner and offered her to me, which I accepted, and Lieutenant Hudson of the Army, several Navy officers, and plenty of volunteers agreed to man the vessel, and go in with me the night of the 13th. The events of that day, so glorious to Major Anderson and his command, are known to you. As I anticipated, the guns from Sumter dispersed their naval preparations excepting small guard boats, so that with the Powhatan a re-enforcement would have been easy. . . .

I learned on the 13th instant that the Powhatan was withdrawn from duty off Charleston on the 7th instant, yet I was permitted to sail on the 9th, the Pawnee on the 9th, and the Pocahontas on the 10th, without intimation that the main portion—the fighting portion—of our expedition was taken away. In justice to itself as well as an acknowledgement of my earnest efforts, I trust the Government has sufficient reasons for putting me in the position they have placed me.

I have the honor to be, your obedient servant,.

G. V. Fox

In Charleston, Emma E. Holmes, a young woman confined to her home by a recent injury, caught the excitement of the day in her diary:[12]

I am writing about half-past four in the afternoon—just about twelve hours since the first shot was fired—and during the whole time shot and shell have been steadily pouring into Fort Sumter from Fort Stevens where our "Palmetto boys" have won the highest praise from Beauregard, from Fort Moultrie and the floating battery, placed at the cove. These are the principal batteries and just before dinner we received despatches saying *no one* has yet been hurt on either Morris or Sullivan's island and though the floating battery and Fort Stevens have both been hit several times, *no damage* has been done, while two or three breaches have been made in Fort Sumter. For more than two hours our batteries opened on Anderson, before he returned a single shot, as if husbanding his resources. At times the firing has been very rapid, then slow and irregular, and at times altogether upon Fort Moultrie. . . .

On the next day—April 13—Miss Holmes heard that Fort Sumter was on fire. She decided to see for herself:

I could not wait for the Dr.'s permission but drove hurriedly to cousin Sallie's, whence I had a splendid view of the harbor—with the naked eye. We could distinctly see the flames amidst the smoke. All the barracks were on fire. Beyond lay the fleet of four or five vessels off the bar, their masts easily counted. They did not make the slightest effort to go to Anderson's relief. . . .

The scene to the spectators in the city was intensely exciting. The Battery and every house, house top and spire was crowded. On White Point Garden were encamped about fifty cadets, having in charge five, six, & twelve pounders placed on the eastern promenade. It was thought the vessels might attempt to come in and bombard the city, and workmen were busy all day in mounting four twenty-fours directly in front of Cousin S.'s.

With the telescope I saw the shots as they struck the fort, and the masonry crumbling, while on Morris Island we saw the men moving about on the sand hills. All were anxious to see, and most had opera glasses which they coolly used till they heard a report from Sumter, when they dodged behind the sand hills.

VIII

As the Confederates found the range, their fire had a devastating effect. Surgeon Crawford, who had watched the South Carolina convention adopt the Ordinance of Secession, described the condition of the battered fortress at noon on the thirteenth:[13]

All of the woodwork was in flames. The officers, seizing the axes that were available, exerted themselves in cutting away whatever woodwork was accessible. It soon became evident that the magazine with its 300 barrels of powder was in danger of the flames, and every man that could be spared was placed upon the duty of removing the powder, toward which the fire was gradually progressing, now separated from the magazine by only one set of quarters. Not a third of the barrels could be removed; so thick was the cloud of smoke and burning cinders, that penetrated everywhere, that a cause of serious danger arose from the exposed condition of the powder taken from the magazine, and Major Anderson ordered that all but five barrels be thrown into the sea.

The men, almost suffocated as the south wind carried the cloud of hot smoke and cinders into the casemates, threw themselves upon the ground and covered their faces with wet cloths, or rushed to the embrasures, where the occasional draught made it possible to breathe. The enemy maintained his increased fire. The nine-inch shells which had been filled, and located in different parts of the work, to be used as grenades in repelling an assault, now exploded from time to time as the fire spread, adding greatly to the danger and destruction.

A large number had been placed in the towers on the spiral staircase of granite. They exploded, completely destroying these structures at the west gorge angle, as well as the interior of the other. It was at this moment that the writer, in obedience to Anderson's orders, had ascended to the parapet to report any movement of the fleet. It was with the greatest difficulty that he could make his way amid the destruction and reach the parapet at all. The fleet had made no movement.

The magazines were now closed, when a shot from the enemy's batteries "passed through the intervening shield, struck the door, and bent the lock in such a way that it could not be opened again."

. . . The scene was well nigh indescribable. . . . The enemy's fire from his mortars and gun batteries had been so increased that there was scarcely an appreciable moment that shot and shell were not searching the work. The flames of the burning quarters were still spreading, shooting upward amid the dense smoke as heavy masses of brick and masonry crumbled, and fell with loud noise. All of the woodwork had now been consumed. The heavy gates at the entrance of the work, as well as the planking of the windows on the gorge, were gone, leaving access to the fort easy and almost unobstructed.

Early in the afternoon Beauregard repeated the demand for surrender he had made on April 11. This time Anderson agreed, for reasons

stated in the terse official report he made to the Secretary of War on
April 18:[14]

Having defended Fort Sumter for thirty-four hours, until the quarters were entirely burned, the main gates destroyed by fire, the gorge walls seriously injured, the magazine surrounded by flames, and its door closed from the effects of heat, four barrels and three cartridges of powder only being available, and no provisions remaining but pork, I accepted terms of evacuation offered by General Beauregard, being the same offered by him on the 11th instant, prior to the commencement of hostilities. . . .

Word of Anderson's surrender spread instantly. Charleston moved at
once to repair the damage done by its own guns and to celebrate the
Confederacy's first victory. Emma Holmes described the city's exulta-
tion:[15]

What a change was wrought in a few moments in the appearance of the harbor. Steamers with fire engines were immediately despatched to the Fort. The garrison gathered on the wharf to breathe the fresh air and numbers of little sailing boats were seen darting like sea-gulls in every direction, conveying gentlemen to the islands to see their friends. . . .

As soon as the surrender was announced, the bells commenced to ring, and in the afternoon, salutes to the "magic seven" were fired from the cutter, "Lady Davis," school ship, and "Cadet's Battery" in honor of one of the most brilliant and bloodless victories in the records of the world. After thirty-three hours consecutive cannonading not one man hurt on either side *—no damages of any consequence done to any of our fortifications, though the officers quarters at Fort Moultrie and many of the houses on Sullivan's Island were riddled, and though the outer walls of Fort Sumter were much battered and many of the guns disabled. . . .

Sunday 14th. Major Anderson appointed 12 o'clock today to give up the fort. The Governor, his wife & suite, General Beauregard— suite—and many other military men besides Mrs. Isaac Hayne and Hattie Barnwell who went down with Lieut. Davis' sister, went down

---

* One Union soldier was killed and several were injured when a gun exploded while Anderson was saluting the flag after the surrender.

on board a steamer, whence they witnessed the ceremony of raising the Confederate and Palmetto flags. . . .

Sunday afternoon I went on the Battery, which was more crowded than ever. The cadets had a dress-parade at sunset and the harbor was gay with steamers with flags flying from every point. It did not seem at all like Sunday!

IX

John A. Campbell, associate justice of the United States Supreme Court, understood clearly why he had failed as a mediator between Seward and Confederate commissioners who had sought to negotiate a treaty between the dividing sections:[16]

The truth is that the grievances complained of by the cotton States are either not material or not remediable. What guarantee will prevent the denunciation of slavery and slaveholders in the pulpit, press and academy? What will prevent the pragmatical and conceited Yankee from making foreign newspapers and magazines the vehicle of his mendacity and spite? What will prevent their women and fanatics from making petitions to Congress and their politicians from irritating the Southern representatives? Who can give self-control to Southern members or prevent them from showing that slavery is ordained by Heaven?

The agitation is an agitation resulting from a fundamental difference between the sections on questions of active and living interest. This is the irrepressible conflict against which laws are powerless unless supported by an inquisition or an army.

Thus the tough-minded, realistic contemporary. A poet also understood that behind the legal arguments people followed different ways of life. Stephen Vincent Benét's Georgian, Clay Wingate, speaks:[17]

> *And yet—what happened to men in war*
> *Why were they all going out to war?*
>
> He brooded a moment. It wasn't slavery,
> That stale red-herring of Yankee knavery
> Nor even states-rights, at least not solely,
> But something so dim that it must be holy.
> A voice, a fragrance, a taste of wine,

A face half-seen in old candleshine,
A yellow river, a blowing dust,
Something beyond you that you must trust,
Something so shrouded it must be great,
The dead men building the living State
From 'simmon-seed on a sandy bottom,
The woman South in her rivers laving
That body whiter than new-blown cotton
And savage and sweet as wild-orange-blossom,
The dark hair streams on the barbarous bosom,
If there ever has been a land worth saving—
In Dixie land, I'll take my stand,
And live and die for Dixie!

CHAPTER 4

"THERE IS NO NORTH"

CENSORED REPORTS from Charleston gave work-bound Northerners on Saturday morning, April 13, fragments of the Sumter story. Shock and then anger rolled in waves across tideland, mountain and plain. People stopped work. Before newspaper offices in cities and towns, crowds awaiting dispatches jammed sidewalks and roads. Some stood in silence; some spoke, trying to disguise turbulent emotions by displaying rare gifts of prophecy; and a few, suspecting an acquaintance or a stranger of harboring secessionist sentiments, blustered that no time was better for fetching a rope and ridding the country of a treasonable dog. An overpowering patriotism welled up; and even those who offered scant comment and were without inspired speculations for the future agreed with the editorial writer for the Philadelphia *Press:*

"Henceforth each man, high and low, must take his position as a patriot or a traitor—as a foe or friend of his country—as a supporter of the flag of the stars and stripes or of the rebel banner."

I

To Lincoln's two young secretaries, John G. Nicolay and John Hay, the most composed man in America that Saturday morning occupied the White House:[1]

While the Sumter telegrams were on every tongue and revengeful indignation was in every heart, there was little variation in the business of the Executive Mansion. . . . The miscellaneous gathering was larger there, as it was larger at the Departments, the newspaper and telegraph offices, and the hotels. More leading men and officials called to learn or to impart news. The Cabinet, as by a common impulse, came together and deliberated. All talk, however, was brief, sententious, informal. The issue had not yet been reached. Sumter was still under fire. Nevertheless, the main question required no discussion, not even decision, scarcely an announcement. Jefferson Davis's order and Beauregard's guns had sufficiently defined the coming action of the Government. After this functionaries and people had but a single purpose, a single duty. Lincoln said but little beyond making inquiries about the current reports and criticizing the probability or accuracy of their details, and went on as usual receiving visitors, listening to suggestions, and signing routine papers throughout the day.

By next morning the news of Anderson's capitulation had reached Washington. Nicolay and Hay assisted the President in a swift and fateful decision:[2]

In the forenoon . . . Lincoln and his Cabinet, together with sundry military officers, were at the Executive Mansion, giving final shape to the details of the action the Government had decided to take. A proclamation, drafted by himself, copied on the spot by his secretary, was concurred in by his Cabinet, signed, and sent to the State Department to be sealed, filed, and copied for publication in the next morning's newspapers.

The document bears date April 15 (Monday), but was made and signed on Sunday. This proclamation, by authority of the Act of 1795, called into service seventy-five thousand militia for three months, and convened Congress in extra session on the coming 4th of July. It commanded treasonable combinations to disperse within twenty days, and announced that the first object of this military force was to repossess the forts and places seized from the Union. . . .

The action of the Government brought in its train countless new duties and details. Both at the departments and the executive Mansion the Sunday was one of labor, not of rest. . . . The President's room was filled all day as by a general reception. Already the patriotic echoes were coming in from an excited country. Senators and Representatives yet in Washington felt authorized to pledge the support of their States. Of all such words of cheer, it is safe to say none were personally so welcome and significant as the unreserved encouragement and adhesion of Senator Douglas of Illinois.

The brief report of the interview of these longtime political rivals, released by the Associated Press and published in the same newspapers that carried the text of Lincoln's proclamation, would be worth many thousands of muskets to the Union armies:[3]

WASHINGTON, April 14—Senator Douglas called on the President tonight. They had an interesting conversation on the present condition of the country. The substance of it was, on the part of Mr. Douglas, that while he was unalterably opposed to the Administration on all its political issues, he was prepared to sustain the President in the exercise of all his Constitutional functions. To preserve the Union, maintain the Government and defend the Federal Capital, firm policy and prompt action were necessary. The Capital of our country is in danger, and must be protected at all hazards, at any expense of men and money. He spoke of present and future, without reference to the past.

Mr. Lincoln was very much gratified with the interview.

II

The wires that carried the text of Lincoln's proclamation and the report of his interview with Douglas also carried telegrams from Simon Cameron, Secretary of War, to governors of states notifying them of the number of troops they would be expected to furnish. Some replies were dispatched the same day; others a day or two later.[4]

From Governor Oliver P. Morton, April 15:

On behalf of the State of Indiana I tender to you for the defense of the nation and to uphold the authority of the Government 10,000 men.

From Governor William Dennison, April 15:

Your dispatch calling on Ohio for thirteen regiments is just received and will be promptly responded to by this State.

From Zachariah Chandler, United States Senator from Michigan, April 17:

There is but one sentiment here. We will furnish you with the regiments in thirty days if you want them, and 50,000 men if you need them. General Cass subscribed $3,000 to equip the regiments. There are no sympathizers here worth hunting, and if there were, our population would diminish to the extent of their numbers forthwith.

From Governor John A. Andrew of Massachusetts, April 17:

Two of our regiments will start this afternoon—one for Washington, the other for Fort Monroe; a third will be dispatched tomorrow, and the fourth before the end of the week.

From Richard Yates, Governor of Illinois, and other state officers, April 17:

The Governor's call was published on yesterday and he has already received the tender of forty companies. . . . Our people burn with patriotism and all parties show the same alacrity to stand by the Government and the laws of the country.

From Governor Samuel J. Kirkwood of Iowa, April 18:

Present indications are that more than enough companies for one regiment will be offered. . . . Please assure the President that the people and the Executive of Iowa will stand by him unflinchingly. Ten days ago we had two parties in this State; today we have but one, and that one is for the Constitution and Union unconditionally.

Replies from the governors of the border states and of the Southern states which had not yet seceded were of different tenor.

Beriah Magoffin, Governor of Kentucky, wired on April 15:[5]

I say emphatically Kentucky will furnish no troops for the wicked purpose of subduing her sister Southern States.

John W. Ellis, Governor of North Carolina, on the same day:

I regard the levy of troops made by the Administration for the purpose of subjugating the States of the South as in violation of the

Constitution and a gross usurpation of power. I can be no party to this wicked violation of the laws of the country and to this war upon the liberties of a free people. You can get no troops from North Carolina.

From Governor John Letcher, April 16:

The militia of Virginia will not be furnished to the powers at Washington for any such use or purpose as they have in view. Your object is to subjugate the Southern States, and a requisition made upon me for such an object . . . will not be complied with. You have chosen to inaugurate civil war, and having done so, we will meet it in a spirit as determined as the Administration has exhibited toward the South.

From Governor Isham G. Harris, April 17:

Tennessee will not furnish a single man for purpose of coercion, but 50,000, if necessary, for the defense of our rights and those of our Southern brethren.

And from Claiborne Fox Jackson, Governor of Missouri, April 17:

Your requisition, in my judgment, is illegal, unconstitutional, and revolutionary in its object, inhuman and diabolical, and cannot be complied with. Not one man will the State of Missouri furnish to carry on any such unholy crusade.

To the Confederate Secretary of War, Leroy P. Walker, Southern governors and other officials responded to requisitions for troops with zeal and resolution.

On April 18 Governor Joseph E. Brown of Georgia wired Walker at Montgomery:[6]

I will have the 8,000 troops in readiness very soon. I have a division of volunteers nearly organized.

The same day Governor Francis W. Pickens promised:

Call for 5,000 more men will be responded to. South Carolina will always answer to the first tap of the drum.

M. S. Perry, of Florida, followed the next day:

I am engaged in raising the 1,500 troops called for, and will hurry them up.

On April 23 John J. Pettus, of Mississippi, acknowledged a requisition of two regiments with one curt sentence:

"Will be promptly responded to."

III

Although editors could print only a fraction of the dispatches that flowed over their desks, the greatest story in the country's history—the story of the gigantic response of the people to the cry of "To Arms!"—kept typesetters at their cases and flat-bed presses banging out newspapers day and night:[7]

DECATUR, ILL., April 16—The war news creates great excitement here. A large and enthusiastic meeting was held last night. Several speeches were made by prominent men of all parties in favor of upholding the Government in maintaining the Constitution and enforcing the laws. Today the Hon. Dick Oglesby is beating up recruits. Quite a number have already volunteered. . . .

BURLINGTON, IOWA, April 16— . . . Political distinctions are forgotten in the unanimous desire to support and sustain the Government. A muster roll is now open. The several companies of Iowa volunteers, who have tendered their services to the Government, are ordered to hand in the rolls of their companies, with the names of all the members who are willing to respond promptly to the orders of the Governor, to march as occasion may require. . . .

MILWAUKEE, WIS., April 16—An immense meeting was held at the Chamber of Commerce last night. Men of all parties participated and the excitement was very great. The feeling is unanimous for asserting the authority of the Government, and crowds of men are offering their services to the Adjutant General. Three Volunteer Rifle Companies were formed yesterday. . . .

DETROIT, MICH., April 16—At an informal meeting of citizens today, at which Gov. Blair was present, it was resolved, in order to expedite the equipment of the troops required from Michigan, to raise $100,000 by private subscription. A large portion of the amount was subscribed on the spot, and the balance will be raised immediately. . . .

CINCINNATI, OHIO, April 16— . . . The merchants have stopped shipping goods to the South. . . .

In New York City the New York East Methodist Conference opened with a prayer:[8]

Grant, O God, that all the efforts now being made to overthrow rebellion in our distracted country may be met with every success. Let the forces that have risen against our Government, and Thy law, be scattered to the winds, and may no enemies be allowed to prevail against us. Grant, O God, that those who have aimed at the very heart of the republic may be overthrown. We ask Thee to bring these men to destruction, and wipe them from the face of the country!

From the South came dispatches showing equally fervent loyalty to the Confederacy:[9]

PADUCAH, KY., April 16—A meeting irrespective of party, J. B. Husbands presiding, adopted resolutions recommending the Governor immediately to convene the Legislature; that we are with the South in interest and action; that the Governor be requested to issue a proclamation for a Convention at Frankfort at an early day as practicable to consider the position and future destiny of Kentucky; calling on the people of Kentucky to ignore party feelings and oppose to the last extremity the coercive and fratricidal policy of the Executive. . . .

MEMPHIS, TENN., April 16—Memphis is out of the Union. There are no Union men here. . . .

NEW ORLEANS, LA., April 16— . . . Lincoln's war proclamation was received with no astonishment. Everybody is highly pleased and the people are resolved to maintain their position at all hazards. Two more volunteer companies left today for Pensacola, and the rest will probably remain to defend the city. Volunteer regiments are forming throughout the state. . . .

MONTGOMERY, ALA., April 16—The people here are delighted that the uncertainty is at an end, and that we are now entirely justified in driving the invaders from our soil. No one feels a particle of doubt as to the result, and the only regret is that President Lincoln does not head the expedition.

The Cabinet were in council this forenoon. Mr. Lincoln's proclamation was read amid bursts of laughter. . . .

RICHMOND, VA., April 16—The Richmond *Whig* hauled down the
Stars and Stripes this afternoon, and ran up the flag of Virginia.

*Next day Virginia took the fateful step. In Richmond now was John
Beauchamp Jones, editor of the prosecessionist* Southern Monitor *of
Philadelphia, who had escaped from the City of Brotherly Love only
hours before an angry mob appeared with rope in hand and murder in
mind. For a quarter of a century Jones had championed the cause of
the South, living for this moment:*[10]

April 17th.—This was a memorable day. When we assembled at
Metropolitan Hall, it could be easily perceived that we were on the
threshold of momentous events. All other subjects, except that of a new
political organization of the State, seemed to be momentarily delayed,
as if awaiting action elsewhere. And this plan of political organization
filled me with alarm, for I apprehended it would result in a new conflict
between the old parties—Whig and Democrat. The ingenious discussion of this subject was probably a device of the Unionists, two or
three of them having obtained seats in the Revolutionary Convention. I
knew the ineradicable instincts of Virginia politicians, and their in-
veterate habit of public speaking, and knew there were well-grounded
fears that we should be launched and lost in an illimitable sea of argument, when the business was Revolution, and death to the coming invader. Besides, I saw no hope of unanimity if the old party distinctions
and designations were not submerged forever.

These fears, however, were groundless. The Union had received its
blessure mortelle, and no power this side of the Potomac could save
it. . . . Lieut.-Gov. Montague came in and announced the passage of
the ordinance. . . . This was succeeded by a moment too thrilling for
utterance, but was followed by tears of gladness and rapturous applause. Soon after, President Tyler and Gov. Wise were conducted
arm-in-arm, and bare-headed, down the center aisle amid a din of
cheers, while every member rose to his feet. They were led to the platform, and called upon to address the Convention. The venerable ex-
President of the United States first rose responsive to the call, but
remarked that the exhaustion incident to his recent incessant labors,
and the nature of his emotions at such a momentous crisis, superadded
to the feebleness of age, rendered him physically unable to utter what

he felt and thought on such an occasion. Nevertheless, he seemed to acquire supernatural strength as he proceeded, and . . . gave a brief history of all the struggles of our race for freedom, from *Magna Charta* to the present day; and he concluded with a solemn declaration that at no period of our history were we engaged in a more just and holy effort for the maintenance of liberty and independence than at the present moment. The career of the dominant party at the North was but a series of aggressions, which fully warranted the steps we were taking for resistance and eternal separation; and if we performed our whole duty as Christians and patriots, the same benign Providence which favored the cause of our forefathers in the Revolution of 1776, would again crown our efforts with similar success. He said he might not survive to witness the consummation of the work begun that day; but generations yet unborn would bless those who had the high privilege of being participators in it.

He was succeeded by Gov. Wise, who . . . electrified the assembly by a burst of eloquence, perhaps never surpassed by mortal orator. . . . At times the vast assembly rose involuntarily to their feet, and every emotion and expression of feature seemed responsive to his own. During his speech he alluded to the reports of the press that the oppressors of the North had probably seized one of his children sojourning in their midst. "But," said he, "if they suppose hostages of my own heart's blood will stay my hand in a contest for the maintenance of sacred rights, they are mistaken. Affection for kindred, property, and life itself sink into insignificance in comparison with the overwhelming importance of public duty in such a crisis as this. . . ."

Hon. J. M. Mason, and many other of Virginia's distinguished sons, were called upon, and delivered patriotic speeches, and finally, *Gov. Letcher* appeared upon the stage. He was loudly cheered by the very men who, two days before, would gladly have witnessed his execution. The governor spoke very briefly, merely declaring his concurrence in the important step that had been taken, and his honest purpose, under the circumstances, to discharge his whole duty as Executive of the State, in conformity to the will of the people and the provisions of the Constitution.

Before the *sine die* adjournment, it was suggested that inasmuch as the ordinance had been passed in secret session, and it was desirable that the enemy should not know it before certain preparations could be made to avert sudden injury on the border, etc., that the fact should not be divulged at present.

IV

Both North and South, men made personal decisions, sometimes with deliberation, sometimes on impulses stirred by patriotic oratory and martial music. The young Virginian Henry Kyd Douglas had no liking for secession, but he also had no doubt about his duty:[11]

. . . Having gone to college in the North and to law school in Lexington, Virginia, equally intimate with fellow students on both sides of Mason's and Dixon's line, I did not believe our people would ever take up arms against each other. In those days Virginia boys read *The Federalist* and all the debates of the framers of our government and Constitution. I had no more doubt of the right of a state to secede than I had of the truth of the catechism. Yet I could not make myself believe that there could be a dissolution of the Union; perhaps because I was so much opposed to it. In this hopefulness I went to St. Louis, after the election, to begin the practice of law. I had a winter of leisure for thought; and wisdom came in the spring.

When on the 17th of April 1861, Virginia passed the Ordinance of Secession, I had no doubt of my duty. In a week I was back on the Potomac. When I found my mother sewing on heavy shirts—with a heart doubtless heavier than I knew—I suspected for what and whom they were being made. In a few days I was at Harper's Ferry, a private in the Shepherdstown Company, Company "B," Second Virginia Infantry.

Another Virginian, Colonel Robert E. Lee, explained and justified his decision in a letter he wrote forty-eight hours after he had been offered a high command in the Union Army. His correspondent was his brother, Sydney Smith Lee, who would soon resign his commission as a captain in the United States Navy:[12]

ARLINGTON, VIRGINIA, April 20, 1861

MY DEAR BROTHER SMITH: The question which was the subject of my earnest consultation with you on the 18th inst. has in my own mind been decided. After the most anxious inquiry as to the correct course for me to pursue, I concluded to resign, and sent in my resignation this morning. I wished to wait till the Ordinance of Secession should be acted on by the people of Virginia; but war seems to have commenced, and I am liable at any time to be ordered on duty which I could not conscientiously perform. To save me from such a position, and to prevent the necessity of resigning under orders, I had to act at once, and before I could see you again on the subject, as I had wished, I am now a private citizen, and have no other ambition than to remain at home. Save in defense of my native State, I have no desire ever again to draw my sword. I send you my warmest love.

Your affectionate brother,
R. E. LEE

S. H. M. Byers had no intention of enlisting when he decided to attend a patriotic mass meeting in the village of Newton, Iowa, where he lived:[13]

It all came about through a confusion of names. . . . Everybody was there, and everybody was excited, for the war tocsin was sounding all over the country. A new regiment had been ordered by the governor, and no town was so quick in responding to the call as the village of Newton. We would be the very first. Drums were beating at the mass-meeting, fifes screaming, people shouting. There was a little pause in the patriotic noise, and then someone called out, "Myers to the platform!" "Myers! Myers! Myers!" echoed a hundred other voices. Mr. Myers never stirred, as he was no public speaker. I sat beside him near the aisle. Again the voices shouted "Myers! Myers!" Myers turned to me, laughed, and said, "They are calling you, Byers," and fairly pushed me out into the aisle. A handful of the audience seeing Myers would not respond, did then call my own name, and both names were cried together. Some of the audience becoming confused called loudly for me. "Go on," said Myers, half-rising and pushing me toward the platform.

I was young—just twenty-two—ambitious, had just been admitted to the bar, and now was all on fire with the newly awakened patriotism. I went up to the platform and stood by the big drum. The American flag, the flag that had been fired on by the South, was hanging over my head. In a few minutes I was full of the mental champagne that comes from a cheering multitude. I was burning with excitement, with patriotism, enthusiasm, pride, and my enthusiasm lent power to the words I uttered. I don't know why nor how, but I was moving my audience. The war was not begun to put down slavery, but what in the beginning had been an incident I felt in the end would become a cause.

The year before I had been for many months on a plantation in Mississippi, and there with my own eyes had seen the horrors of slavery. I had seen human beings flogged; men and women bleeding from an overseer's lash. Now in my excitement I pictured it all. I recalled everything. "And the war, they tell us," I cried, "is to perpetuate this curse!" In ten minutes after my stormy words one hundred youths and men, myself the first, had stepped up to the paper lying on the big drum and had put down our names for the war.

No one ever succeeded in stampeding Ulysses S. Grant; yet he knew very well what he would do when the time came. Although he would be thirty-nine within a week, he wanted to make sure that his father understood his position:[14]

GALENA, April 21st, 1861

DEAR FATHER: We are now in the midst of trying times when every one must be for or against his country, and show his colors too, by his every act. Having been educated for such an emergency, at the expense of the Government, I feel that it has upon me superior claims, such claims as no ordinary motives of self-interest can surmount. I do not wish to act hastily or unadvisedly in the matter, and as there are more than enough to respond to the first call of the President, I have not yet offered myself. I have promised, and am giving all the assistance I can in organizing the company whose services have been accepted from this place. I have promised further to go with them to the State capital, and if I can be of service to the Governor in organizing his state troops to do so. What I now ask is your approval of the course I am taking, or advice in the matter. A letter written this week will reach me in Springfield. I have not time to write to you but a hasty line, for, though Sunday as it is, we are all busy here. In a few minutes I shall be engaged in directing tailors in the style and trim of uniforms for our men.

Whatever may have been my political opinions before, I have but one sentiment now. That is, we have a Government, and laws and a flag, and they must all be sustained. There are but two parties now, traitors and patriots, and I want hereafter to be ranked with the latter, and I trust, the stronger party. I do not know but you may be placed in an awkward position, and a dangerous one pecuniarily, but costs cannot now be counted. My advice would be to leave where you are if you are not safe with the views you entertain. I would never stultify my opinion for the sake of a little security. . . .

Yours truly,
U. S. GRANT

William G. Stevenson, a young Kentucky-born New Yorker who had established a small business near Jeffersonville, Arkansas, early in 1861 enlisted to save his skin. As soon as the war broke out, Stevenson was taken before a local vigilance committee as a Northerner and suspected abolitionist. Escaping from his inquisitors, he immediately struck out for the North. At Memphis, Tennessee, he was apprehended:[15]

As the *St. Francis* touched the wharf on the morning of the 19th of April . . . I stepped upon the landing; meaning to look over the state of things in the city, and see if I could get out of it in the direction of Nashville, where I had friends who, I thought, would aid me homeward.

But I had not left the wharf when a "blue jacket," the sobriquet of the military policemen that then guarded the city, stepped up and said, "I see you are a stranger." "Yes, sir." "I have some business with you. You will please walk with me, sir." To my expression of astonishment, which was real, he replied, "You answer the description very well, sir. The Committee of Public Safety wish to see you, come along." As it was useless to parley, I walked with him, and was soon ushered into the presence of that body. . . .

They questioned me as to my home, political opinions, and destination, and received such answers as I thought it wise to give. Whereupon they confronted me, to my amazement, with a member of the Vigilance Committee which had tried me at Jeffersonville, one hundred and twenty miles distant, thirty hours before. I was amazed, because I did not imagine that any one of their number could have reached Memphis before me. He had ridden after me the night of my escape, and when I stopped for breakfast, he had passed on to Helena, and taking an earlier up-river boat, had reached Memphis some hours in advance of the *St. Francis;* long enough before me to post the Committee of Public Safety as to my person and story when before his committee. Even with this swift witness against me, they were unable to establish any crime, and after consultation, they told me I could retire. I was immediately followed by the policeman, who handed me a letter written by the chairman, suggesting that I would do well to go directly to a certain recruiting office, where young men were enlisting under the Provisional Government of Tennessee, and where I would find it to my interest to *volunteer*, adding, substantially, as follows: "Several members of the committee think if you do not see fit to follow this advice, you will probably stretch hemp instead of leaving Memphis; as they can not be responsible for the acts of an infuriated mob, who *may* hear that you came from the North." I was allowed no time for reflection, as the policeman stood waiting, he said, "to show me the way." I now saw at a glance, that the military power of the city had resolved to *compel* me to *volunteer*, and in my friendlessness I could think of no way to escape the cruel and dread necessity.

Still the hope remained that perhaps I might make a partial promise, and ask time, and yet elude the vigilance of the authorities. As the M. P. grew impatient, and at length imperious, showing that he well knew that he had me in his power, I walked on to avoid the crowd which was beginning to gather, and soon reached the recruiting station. I saw, the moment I was inside, that the only door was guarded by bayonets, crossed in the hands of determined men. The Blue Jacket, in a private conversation with the recruiting officer, soon gave him my *status;* when, turning to me, the officer said, with the air of a man who expects to carry his point, "Well, young man, I learn you have come to volunteer; glad to see you—good company," &c.

To which I replied, "I was advised to call and look at the matter, and will take some time to consider, if you please."

"No need of time, sir—no time to be lost; here is the roll—enter your name, put on the uniform, and then you can pass out," with a glance of his eye at the policeman and the crossed bayonets, which meant plainly enough, *"You do not go out before."*

To my suggestion that I had a horse on the boat which I must see about, he replied very promptly, *"That could all be done when this business was through."*

The meshes of their cursed net were around me, and there was no release; and with as good grace as I could assume, I wrote my name, and thus I *volunteered!*

The attack on Sumter found Major Thomas Jonathan Jackson, gradu-ate of West Point, veteran of the Mexican War, professor of artillery tactics and natural philosophy at the Virginia Military Institute since 1852, torn between two duties. It was his professional responsibility to prepare the cadet corps for service; but his Presbyterian conscience demanded that he participate in the meetings and services of the Pres-bytery of Lexington, then in session. Before the session ended, word came from the Governor of Virginia that the more advanced cadets would soon be wanted as drillmasters, but Jackson hoped that the call

*would not come until he could spend a quiet Sabbath in the church that
was so large a part of his life. The hope, as Mrs. Jackson related, would
not be realized:*[16]

About the dawn of that Sabbath morning, April 21st, our door-bell
rang, and the order came that Major Jackson should bring the cadets to
Richmond *immediately*. Without waiting for breakfast, he repaired at
once to the Institute, to make arrangements as speedily as possible for
marching, but finding that several hours of preparation would necessarily be required, he appointed the hour for starting at one o'clock
P.M. He sent a message to his pastor, Dr. White, requesting him to
come to the barracks and offer a prayer with the command before its
departure. All the morning he was engaged at the Institute, allowing
himself only a short time to return to his home about eleven o'clock,
when he took a hurried breakfast, and completed a few necessary
preparations for his journey. Then, in the privacy of our chamber, he
took his Bible and read that beautiful chapter in Corinthians beginning with the sublime hope of the resurrection—"For we know that
if our earthly house of this tabernacle be dissolved, we have a building
of God, a house not made with hands, eternal in the heavens"; and
then, kneeling down, he committed himself and her whom he loved to
the protecting care of his Father in heaven. . . .

When Dr. White went to the Institute to hold the short religious
service which Major Jackson requested, the latter told him the command
would march precisely at one o'clock, and the minister, knowing his
punctuality, made it a point to close the service at a quarter before
one. Everything was then in readiness, and after waiting a few moments an officer approached Major Jackson and said: "Major, everything is now ready. May we not set out?" The only reply he made was
to point to the dial-plate of the barracks clock, and not until the hand
pointed to the hour of one was his voice heard to ring out the order,
"Forward, march!"

*In St. Louis, William Tecumseh Sherman, a former Regular Army
officer who had recently headed the Louisiana State Military Academy,
decided that this was a war for others to fight. He described the thoughtless rebuff that threw him into a prolonged sulk:*[17]

I must have reached Washington about the 10th of March [1861]. I
found my brother there, just appointed Senator, in place of Mr. Chase,
who was in the cabinet, and I have no doubt my opinions, thoughts, and

feelings, wrought up by the events in Louisiana, seemed to him gloomy and extravagant. About Washington I saw but few signs of preparation, though the Southern Senators and Representatives were daily sounding their threats on the floors of Congress, and were publicly withdrawing to join the Confederate Congress at Montgomery.

One day, John Sherman took me with him to see Mr. Lincoln. . . . We found the room full of people, and Mr. Lincoln sat at the end of the table, talking with three or four gentlemen, who soon left. John walked up, shook hands, and took a chair near him, holding in his hand some papers referring to minor appointments in the State of Ohio, which formed the subject of conversation. Mr. Lincoln took the papers, said he would refer them to the proper heads of departments, and would be glad to make the appointments asked for, if not already promised. John then turned to me, and said, "Mr. President, this is my brother, Colonel Sherman, who is just up from Louisiana, he may give you some information you want." "Ah!" said Mr. Lincoln, "how are they getting along down there?" I said, "They think they are getting along swimmingly—they are preparing for war." "Oh, well!" said he, "I guess we'll manage to keep house." I was silenced, said no more to him, and we soon left. I was sadly disappointed, and remember that I broke out on John, damning the politicians generally, saying, "You have got things in a hell of a fix, and you may get them out as you best can," adding that the country was sleeping on a volcano that might burst forth at any minute, but that I was going to St. Louis to take care of my family, and would have no more to do with it. . . .

A Missourian, destined to become one of the most illustrious sons of the middle border, could tell his story with good humor. His occupation then was steamboat pilot; his name, Sam Clemens:[18]

I was visiting in a small town where my boyhood had been spent— Hannibal, Marion County. Several of us got together in a secret place by night and formed ourselves into a military company. One Tom Lyman, a young fellow of a good deal of spirit but of no military experience, was made captain; I was made second lieutenant. We had no first lieutenant; I do not know why; it was long ago. There were fifteen of us. By the advice of an innocent connected with the organization we called ourselves the Marion Rangers. I do not remember that any one found fault with the name. I did not; I thought it sounded quite well. The young fellow who proposed this title was perhaps a fair sample of the kind of stuff we were made of. He was young, ignorant, good-natured, well-meaning, trivial, full of romance, and given to reading chivalric novels and singing forlorn love-ditties. He had some pathetic little nickel-plated aristocratic instincts, and detested his name, which was Dunlap; detested it, partly because it was nearly as common in that region as Smith, but mainly because it had a plebeian sound to his ear. So he tried to ennoble it by writing it in this way: d'Unlap. . . .

That is one sample of us. Another was Ed Stevens, son of the town jeweler—trim-built, handsome, graceful, neat as a cat; bright, educated, but given over entirely to fun. There was nothing serious in life to him. As far as he was concerned, this military expedition of ours was simply a holiday. I should say that about half of us looked upon it in the same way; not consciously, perhaps, but unconsciously. We did not think; we were not capable of it. As for myself, I was full of unreasoning joy to be done with turning out of bed at midnight and four in the morning for a while; grateful to have a change, new scenes, new occupations, a new interest. In my thoughts that was as far as I went; I did not go into the details; as a rule, one doesn't at twenty-four.

Another sample was Smith, the blacksmith's apprentice. This vast donkey had some pluck, of a slow and sluggish nature, but a soft heart; at one time he would knock a horse down for some impropriety, and at another he would get homesick and cry. However, he had one ultimate credit to his account which some of us hadn't; he stuck to the war, and was killed in battle at last.

Jo Bowers, another sample, was a huge, good-natured, flax-headed lubber; lazy, sentimental, full of harmless brag, a grumbler by nature; an experienced, industrious, ambitious, and often quite picturesque liar, and yet not a successful one, for he had had no intelligent training, but was allowed to come up just any way. This life was serious enough to him, and seldom satisfactory. But he was a good fellow, anyway, and the boys all liked him. He was made orderly sergeant; Stevens was made corporal.

These samples will answer—and they are quite fair ones. Well, this herd of cattle started for the war. What could you expect of them? They did as well as they knew how; but, really, what was justly to be expected of them? Nothing, I should say. That is what they did.

V

While raw volunteers drew uniforms and stumbled through the manual of arms, military organizations already in existence were mobilized and started on their way to strategic points. One of the first to receive its orders was the Sixth Massachusetts, which entrained for Washington on the evening of April 17. On the morning of the nineteenth the long train carrying the troops pulled into the Philadelphia and Baltimore Railroad station in Baltimore. From that station their cars would have to be drawn by horses to the Baltimore and Ohio station, more than a mile distant.

Baltimore contained thousands of Southern sympathizers. On the afternoon of the eighteenth a pro-secession crowd threatened Regulars and Pennsylvania volunteers as they changed stations. The Sixth Massachusetts expected trouble—and found it. John W. Hanson, chaplain of the regiment and its historian, told the story:[19]

Orders were . . . given to the band, to confine their music to tunes that would not be likely to give offence, especially avoiding the popular air, "Dixie." Quartermaster Munroe distributed twenty rounds of ball cartridges; and Col. Jones went through the cars, issuing an order, that the regiment should march across Baltimore in column of sections. The regiment here loaded and capped their rifles. As soon as the cars reached the station, the engine was unshackled, horses were hitched to the cars, and they were drawn rapidly away. . . .

Some slight demonstrations were made on one or two of the cars containing the fifth and sixth companies; but nothing like an attack was made until the seventh car started. . . . It was attacked by clubs, paving-stones, and other missiles. The men were very anxious to fire on their assailants; but Maj. Watson forbade them, until they should be attacked by fire-arms. One or two soldiers were wounded by paving-stones and bricks; and at length one man's thumb was shot, when, holding the wounded hand up to the major, he asked leave to fire in return. Orders were then given to lie on the bottom of the car and load, and rising, to fire from the windows at will. These orders were promptly obeyed. . . . Moving with as much rapidity as possible, and receiving an occasional musket or pistol shot, or a shower of rocks and bricks, the car reached the main body of the regiment. . . .

The four companies that remained at the Philadelphia and Baltimore station soon discovered that they could not proceed by car; too many rails had been torn up, too many barricades erected. The troops formed to march to the Baltimore and Ohio station. Meanwhile, the mob had grown. Hanson sensed the impending danger:

Capt. Follansbee . . . took the command. There were but about two hundred and twenty in the column; and the mob soon reached ten thousand, at least. The air was filled with yells, oaths, taunts, all sorts of missiles, and soon pistol and musket shots; and Capt. Follansbee gave the order to fire at will. But few of the crowd were on the front of the column, but they pressed on the flank and rear more and more furiously. At one of the bridges in Pratt Street, a formidable barricade, with cannon to sweep the streets, not quite ready for service, had been arranged. Here the mob supposed that the column would be obliged to halt; but Capt. Follansbee ordered his command to scale the barricade. Before the ruffians could follow over the bridge, or run around to intercept them, the soldiers had succeeded in getting quite a distance up Pratt Street. . . . Cheers for "Jeff Davis," and for "South Carolina, and the South;" all sorts of insulting language,—such as "Dig your graves!"—"You can pray, but you cannot fight!" and the like,—were heard; but the little battalion went steadily ahead, with no thought of turning back.

As the gallant detachment passed along Pratt Street, pistols and guns were fired at them from the windows and doors of stores and houses; and our boys, getting a little accustomed to the strange circumstances in which they were placed, loaded their guns as they marched, dragging them between their feet, and, whenever they saw a hostile demonstration, they took as good aim as they could, and fired. There was no platoon firing whatever. At one place, at an upper window, a man was in the act of firing, when a rifle ball suggested to him the propriety of desisting, and he came headlong to the sidewalk. And thus the men, whose rare good fortune it was to contribute the first instalment of blood to pay the price of our redemption, hurried along their way. They were hampered by their orders to fire as little as possible; they were anxious to get to the capital, even then supposed to be in danger; they were separated from the larger part of the regiment, and knew not where their comrades were; and thus assaulted on each side, and by all sorts of weapons and missiles, they kept on their way, loading and firing at will, marching the entire distance,—a mile and a half,—bearing several of their wounded with them, and reached the station, and joined the rest of the regiment.

Yet their destination offered no safety. The mob engulfed the cars. Hanson continued:

Seeing the train about to start, the mob ran on ahead, and placed telegraph poles, anchors, etc., on the track. The train moved a short distance and stopped; a rail had been removed; it was replaced, and the cars went on; stopped again, the road was repaired, and the train went on again; stopped again, and the conductor reported to the colonel that it was impossible to proceed, that the regiment must *march* to Washington. Col. Jones replied, "We are ticketed through, and are going in these cars. If you or the engineer cannot run the train, we have plenty of men who can. If you need protection or assistance, you shall have it; but we go through."

The crowd went on for some miles out, as far as Jackson Bridge, near Chinkapin Hill, and the police followed, removing obstructions; and at several places shots were exchanged. At length, they reached the Relay House, where the double track ended, and where they waited two hours —and long hours they were—for a train from Washington that had the right of way; and at length started again, reaching Washington late in the afternoon.

VI

Thus the Sixth Massachusetts made its way through Baltimore, though barely. Other Northern regiments—the Eighth Massachusetts, the Seventh New York, the First Rhode Island—were routed around the secession-ridden city, traveling by water, foot, and finally rail to the Capital. In Washington, days dragged. Southern sympathizers became bold. John G. Nicolay watched the nerves of a harried President approach the breaking point:[20]

Washington took on the aspect of a city under siege. The supplies of flour and grain in the Georgetown mills were seized. Business was suspended, stores were closed and locked, the streets remained empty save for hurrying patrols. At the first news of burned railroad bridges and attacks on troops, all transient dwellers in Washington wanted to go home—and the desire was not lessened by a rumor that every able-bodied male might be impressed for the town's defense. On Monday the 22nd several hundred clerks in the government departments gave way to their southern sympathies and resigned their offices. Certain military and naval officers did likewise. One was Commodore Franklin Buchanan, who turned over the Washington Navy Yard with its ships and stores and priceless machinery to Commodore Dahlgren and departed, leaving him with scarcely enough marines to keep watch against possible incendiaries. Another was Captain John B. Magruder, who commanded a battery upon which General Scott had placed much reliance for the defense of the city. No case of desertion gave the President greater pain. "Only three days ago," he said, "Magruder came voluntarily to me in this room, and with his own lips, and in my presence, repeated over and over again, his asseverations and protestations of loyalty."

APPROACHES TO WASHINGTON

From Lossing, *Pictorial History of the Civil War*

The President had his emotions well under control. In the presence of others he gave little sign of the anxiety he was enduring, but on the 23rd, one of the days of darkest gloom, after the business of the day was over and he thought himself alone, one of the White House staff, passing the open door of the Executive Office, saw him pacing the floor, then pause and look wistfully out of the window in the direction from which help was expected, and heard him exclaim: "Why don't they come? Why don't they come!" Next day, when they still had not come, and he was talking to the wounded men of the Sixth Massachusetts, he spoke with an irony that only the intensest feeling could wring from him: "I begin to believe that there is no North. The Seventh Regiment is a myth. Rhode Island is another. You are the only real thing."

Two days later the Seventh New York reached Washington. To Nicolay and Hay, writing a quarter of a century later, the regiment's arrival remained an epochal event:[21]

Those who were in the Federal capital on that Thursday, April 25, will never, during their lives, forget the event. . . . As soon as the arrival was known, an immense crowd gathered at the depot to obtain ocular evidence that relief had at length reached the city. Promptly debarking and forming, the Seventh marched up Pennsylvania Avenue to the White House. As they passed up the magnificent street, with their well-formed ranks, their exact military step, their soldierly bearing, their gayly floating flags, and the inspiring music of their splendid regimental band, they seemed to sweep all thought of danger and all taint of treason out of that great national thoroughfare and out of every human heart in the Federal city. The presence of this single regiment seemed to turn the scales of fate. Cheer upon cheer greeted them, windows were thrown up, houses opened, the population came forth upon the streets as for a holiday. It was an epoch in American history. For the first time, the combined spirit and power of Liberty entered the nation's capital.

One of the regiments which poured into Washington once the dam broke was the Eleventh New York, the Fire Zouaves, commanded by Elmer Ellsworth, a twenty-four-year-old colonel who had brought a Chicago drill company to a spectacular state of proficiency and had then studied law in Lincoln's Springfield office. John Hay filled a page in his diary with a picture of Ellsworth and his men as they occupied an improvised bivouac in Washington:[22]

In the afternoon we went up to see Ellsworth's Zouave Firemen. They are the largest, sturdiest, and physically the most magnificent men I ever saw collected together. They played over the sward like kittens, lithe and agile in their strength.

Ellsworth has been intensely disgusted at the wild yarns afloat about them which are, for the most part, utterly untrue. A few graceless rascals have been caught in various lapses. These are in irons. One horrible story which has been terrifying all the maiden antiques of the city for several days, has the element of horror pretty well eliminated today, by the injured fair, who proves a most yielding seducee, offering to settle the matter for 25 dollars. Other yarns are due to the restless brains of the press-gang.

The youthful Colonel formed his men in a hollow square, and made a great speech at them. There was more commonsense, dramatic power, tact, energy, & that eloquence that naturally flowers into deeds in *le petit* Colonel's fifteen-minute harangue than in all the speeches that stripped the plumes from our unfortunate ensign in the spread-eagle days of the Congress that has flitted. He spoke to them as men. Made them proud in their good name; spoke bitterly & witheringly of the disgrace of the recreant; contrasted with cutting emphasis which his men delighted in, the enlistment of the dandy regiment for thirty days, with *theirs* for the war; spoke solemnly & impressively of the disgrace of expulsion; roused them to wild enthusiasm by announcing that he had heard of one officer who treated his men with less consideration than himself and that, if on inquiry the rumour proved true, he would strip him & send him home in irons. The men yelled with delight, clapped their hands, & shouted "Bully for you." He closed with wonderful tact and dramatic spirit by saying, "Now laddies, if anyone of you wants to go home, he had better sneak around the back alleys, crawl over fences, and get out of sight before we see him," which got them again. He must have run with this crowd sometime in his varied career. He knows them and handles them so perfectly.

VII

In Montgomery, Jefferson Davis likewise lived through hours of severe disappointment. Years afterward he still tried to indict Mr. Lincoln for acts that crippled the Confederate war effort:[23]

Already the Northern officer in charge had evacuated Harper's Ferry, after having attempted to destroy the public buildings there. His report says: "I gave the order to apply the torch. In three minutes or less, both of the arsenal buildings, containing nearly fifteen thousand stand of arms, together with the carpenter's shop, which was at the upper end of a long and connected series of workshops of the armory proper, were in a blaze. There is every reason for believing the destruction was complete." Mr. Simon Cameron, the Secretary of War, on

April 22d replied to his report in these words: "I am directed by the President of the United States to communicate to you, and through you to the officers and men under your command at Harper's Ferry Armory, the approbation of the Government of your and their judicious conduct there, and to tender you and them the thanks of the Government for the same." At the same time the ship-yard at Norfolk was abandoned after an attempt to destroy it. About midnight of April 20th, a fire was started in the yard, which continued to increase, and before daylight the work of destruction extended to two immense ship-houses, one of which contained the entire frame of a seventy-four-gun ship, and to the long ranges of stores and offices on each side of the entrance. The great ship Pennsylvania was burned, and the frigates Merrimac and Columbus, and the Delaware, Raritan, Plymouth, and Germantown were sunk. A vast amount of machinery, valuable engines, small-arms, and chronometers, was broken up and rendered entirely useless. The value of the property destroyed was estimated at several millions of dollars.

This property thus destroyed had been accumulated and constructed with laborious care and skillful ingenuity during a course of years to fulfill one of the objects of the Constitution, which was expressed in these words, "To provide for the common defense" (see Preamble of the Constitution). It had belonged to all the States in common, and to each one equally with the others. If the Confederate States were still members of the Union, as the President of the United States asserted, where can he find a justification of these acts?

In explanation of his policy to the Commissioners sent to him by the Virginia State Convention, he said, referring to his inaugural address, "As I then and therein said, I now repeat, the power confided in me will be used to hold, occupy, and possess property and places belonging to the Government." Yet he tendered the thanks of the Government to those who applied the torch to destroy this property belonging, as he regarded it, to the Government.

How unreasonable, how blind with rage must have been that administration of affairs which so quickly brought the Government to the necessity of destroying its own means of defense in order, as it publicly declared, "to maintain its life"! It would seem as if the passions that rule the savage had taken possession of the authorities at the United States capital! In the conflagrations of vast structures, the wanton destruction of public property, and still more in the issue of *lettres de cachet* by the Secretary of State, who boasted of the power of his little bell over the personal liberties of the citizen, the people saw, or might have seen, the rapid strides toward despotism made under the mask of preserving the Union. Yet these and similar measures were tolerated because the sectional hate dominated in the Northern States over the higher motives of constitutional and moral obligation.

CHAPTER 5

"IT WAS A PANIC, ALL AT ONCE"

B EFORE THE SPRING of 1861 many Americans had never seen a soldier in uniform; now armed men were everywhere. North and South, state militia, dazzled by the flashy troops of Napoleon III, dressed like the Zouaves of Algeria in baggy red trousers, white or yellow gaiters, short blue embroidered jackets and red fezzes with long blue tassels. The Thirty-ninth New York Infantry—the Garibaldi Guards—adopted the dress of Italian Bersaglieri, including the plumed hat; and the Seventy-ninth New York were Highlanders in Scottish sporrans and kilts. The Second Wisconsin were smartly uniformed in gray—to their sorrow, when Union troops fired on them in battle—and Confederate generals like Joe Johnston, Beauregard and Jackson often appeared in the old blue uniforms of their Regular Army days. On April 23, 1861, Secretary of War Cameron specified as the regulation Union uniform dark-blue flannel sack coat, light-blue kersey trousers, flannel shirt, forage cap, bootees and stockings, but Cameron issued an empty order until combat taught the ninety-day boys that peacock feathers were not the wisest garb where bullets whizzed. About the same time, the Confederate gray became official, but many Southern regiments clung to the smart blue uniforms in which they had already invested.

With bands playing, the boys gathered at county seats; here, usually, they were herded in pairs into a room where a doctor yelped "Strip!" looked them over like horses up for sale and told them to sign a paper; and so, within a few minutes, they lost their status as civilians. Mothers, wives and sweethearts wept and embraced. Fathers shook hands, and little brothers gazed in envy. Then by rail, steamer and on foot Reb and Yank journeyed to their state capitals.

In Richmond and Washington, the war departments struggled with the job of organizing the volunteers into armies. The regulation fire-arm of the U. S. infantry in 1861 was the muzzle-loading Springfield Model 1855, caliber .58, with a rear sight marked for ranges of 100, 200, 300 and 400 yards and an elevating leaf sight for ranges from 500 to 800 yards. When the arsenal at Harpers Ferry was destroyed, many of the Army's Model 1855 Springfields were lost. The only arse-nal equipped to make them, in Springfield, Massachusetts, had produc-tion schedules still geared to a country at peace. Outmoded firearms were substituted—the old Springfield Model 1842, caliber .69, a smoothbore that could hit only by luck at ranges over 200 yards; the Model 1841, caliber .54, renowned as the "Yager" or "Mississippi" rifle used in the Mexican War; and even flintlocks. Union and Con-federate agents scoured Europe for weapons. English caliber .577 Enfields—popularly called "Tower muskets" because English inspec-tors stamped them at the Tower of London—were much in demand. New York State in early 1861 bought 20,000 Enfields for its state troops; the Confederate government, with a chance to rush in Enfields before the blockade clamped down, was content to purchase 10,000!

I

North and South, each government moved first to protect its capital. Regiments raised in New England and the East were called to Wash-ington. The city was soon ringed with camps. With equal celerity the Confederate authorities sent troops to the vicinity of Manassas Junc-tion, thirty miles southwest of the Federal capital, where they threatened Washington at the same time they screened Richmond. Another Con-federate force seized Harpers Ferry, also a threat to Washington, while a third was assembled on the Peninsula between the York and James rivers to thwart a possible advance against Richmond from that di-rection.

With its forces in the East thus deployed, the South could afford to wait. The North could not. Only by military victory could the Union be restored. This was the logic of the situation; this was the demand of an aroused people.

Another problem plagued Washington. In the spring of 1861 the na-tional capital was without defenses except for old Fort Washington on the Potomac twelve miles below the city. A strip of land on the Virginia side of the river became a necessity to stave off rebel attack. Principally for this reason Winfield Scott, though apprehensive of "the impatience of our patriotic and loyal Union friends" who were urging "instant and vigorous action" regardless of consequences, ordered the first advance of the war—the occupation of Alexandria, Virginia.

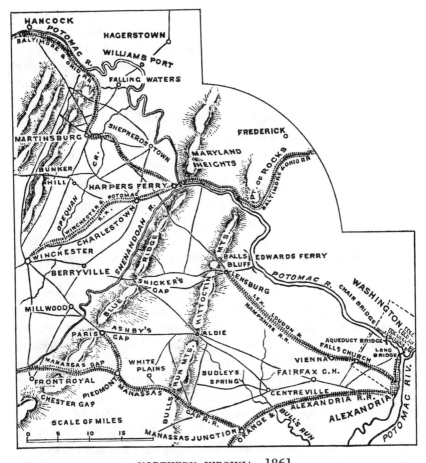

NORTHERN VIRGINIA, 1861

From Lossing, *Pictorial History of the Civil War*

At two o'clock on the moonlit morning of May 24, three regiments crossed over the Aqueduct Bridge at Georgetown; four moved across the Long Bridge at Washington. Elmer Ellsworth's Fire Zouaves—the Eleventh New York—came down river by steamer. The Confederate commander, warned of the approach of the enemy, hurried his infantry

onto a waiting train as the Union advance guard entered the town.
The occupation would have been bloodless except for an act of
boyish bravado. Judith Brockenbrough McGuire, wife of a school prin-
cipal, described the personal encounter which gave the war its first
martyr:[1]

FAIRFAX C. H., May 25.—The day of suspense is at an end. Alexandria and its environs, including, I greatly fear, our home, are in the
hands of the enemy. Yesterday morning, at an early hour, as I was in
my pantry, putting up refreshments for the barracks preparatory to a
ride to Alexandria, the door was suddenly thrown open by a servant,
looking wild with excitement, exclaiming, "Oh, madam, do you know?"
"Know what, Henry?" "Alexandria is filled with Yankees." "Are you
sure, Henry?" said I, trembling in every limb. "Sure, madam! I saw
them myself. Before I got up I heard soldiers rushing by the door; went
out, and saw our men going to the cars."

"Did they get off?" I asked, afraid to hear the answer. "Oh, yes, the
cars went off full of them, and some marched out, and then I went to
King Street, and saw such crowds of Yankees coming in! They came
down the turnpike, and some came down the river; and presently I
heard such noise and confusion, and they said they were fighting, so I
came home as fast as I could."

I lost no time in seeking Mr. ———, who hurried out to hear the
truth of the story. He soon met Dr. ———, who was bearing off one of
the editors in his buggy. He more than confirmed Henry's report, and
gave an account of the tragedy at the Marshall House. Poor Jackson
(the proprietor) had always said that the Confederate flag which
floated from the top of his house should never be taken down but over
his dead body. It was known that he was a devoted patriot, but his
friends had amused themselves at this rash speech. He was suddenly aroused by the noise of men rushing by his room-door, ran to the
window, and seeing at once what was going on, he seized his gun, his
wife trying in vain to stop him; as he reached the passage he saw
Colonel Ellsworth coming from the third story, waving the flag. As he
passed Jackson he said, "I have a trophy." Jackson immediately raised
his gun, and in an instant Ellsworth fell dead. One of the party immediately killed poor Jackson. The Federals then proceeded down the
street, taking possession of public houses, etc. I am mortified to write
that a party of our cavalry, thirty-five in number, was captured. It can
scarcely be accounted for. It is said that the Federals notified the au-

thorities in Alexandria that they would enter the city at eight, and the captain was so credulous as to believe them. Poor fellow, he is now a prisoner, but it will be a lesson to him and to our troops generally. Jackson leaves a wife and children. I know the country will take care of them. He is the first martyr. I shudder to think how many more there may be.

The North, too, had a martyr. In uncommon sorrow, Abraham Lincoln composed a letter:[2]

WASHINGTON, D. C.
May 25, 1861

To the Father and Mother of Col.
Elmer E. Ellsworth:

My dear Sir and Madam: In the untimely loss of your noble son, our affliction here, is scarcely less than your own. So much of promised usefulness to one's country, and of bright hopes for one's self and friends, have rarely been so suddenly dashed, as in his fall. In size, in years, and in youthful appearance, a boy only, his power to command men, was surpassingly great. This power, combined with a fine intellect, an indomitable energy, and a taste altogether military, constituted in him, as seemed to me, the best natural talent, in that department, I ever saw. But yet he was singularly modest and deferential in social intercourse. My acquaintance with him began less than two years ago; yet through the latter half of the intervening period, it was as intimate as the disparity of our ages, and my engrossing engagements, would permit. To me, he appeared to have no indulgences or pastimes; and I never heard him utter a profane, or an intemperate word. What was conclusive of his good heart, he never forgot his parents. The honors he labored for so laudably, and, in the sad end, so gallantly gave his life, he meant for them, no less than for himself.

In the hope that it may be no intrusion upon the sacredness of your sorrow, I have ventured to address you this tribute to the memory of my young friend, and your brave and early fallen child.

May God give you that consolation which is beyond all earthly power. Sincerely your friend in a common affliction—

A. LINCOLN

II

May 24 gave to the North its first hero; May 25 brought a new word into the language and a new direction to the war that had barely

started. The quick mind and tongue of Major General Benjamin F.
Butler, commanding at Fortress Monroe, guardian of the entrance to
Chesapeake Bay, were responsible:[3]

On the day after my arrival at the fort, May 23, three negroes were
reported coming in a boat from Sewall's Point, where the enemy was
building a battery. Thinking that some information as to that work
might be got from them, I had them before me. . . . The negroes said
they belonged to Colonel Mallory, who commanded the Virginia troops
around Hampton, and that he was now making preparation to take
all his negroes to Florida soon, and that not wanting to go away from
home they had escaped to the fort. I directed that they should be fed
and set at work.

On the next day I was notified by an officer in charge of the picket
line next Hampton that an officer bearing a flag of truce desired to be
admitted to the fort to see me. . . . Accompanied by two gentlemen of
my staff, Major Fay and Captain Haggerty, . . . I rode out to the
picket line and met the flag of truce there. It was under charge of
Major Carey, who introduced himself, at the same time pleasantly calling to mind that we last met at the Charleston convention. . . .

"I am informed," said Major Carey, "that three negroes belonging
to Colonel Mallory have escaped within your lines. I am Colonel Mallory's agent and have charge of his property. What do you mean to do
with those negroes?"

"I intend to hold them," said I.

"Do you mean, then, to set aside your constitutional obligation to return them?"

"I mean to take Virginia at her word, as declared in the ordinance of
secession passed yesterday. I am under no constitutional obligations to
a foreign country, which Virginia now claims to be."

"But you say we cannot secede," he answered, "and so you cannot
consistently detain the negroes."

"But you say you have seceded, so you cannot consistently claim
them. I shall hold these negroes as contraband of war, since they are
engaged in the construction of your battery and are claimed as your
property. The question is simply whether they shall be used for or
against the Government of the United States. Yet, though I greatly need
the labor which has providentially come to my hands, if Colonel Mallory will come into the fort and take the oath of allegiance to the United
States, he shall have his negroes, and I will endeavor to hire them from
him."

"Colonel Mallory is absent," was Major Carey's answer.

. . . I do not claim for the phrase "contraband of war," used in this connection, the highest legal sanction. . . . The effect upon the public mind, however, was most wonderful. Everybody seemed to feel a relief on this great slavery question. Everybody thought a way had been found through it. Everybody praised its author by extolling its great use, but whether right or wrong it paved the way for the President's proclamation of freedom to the slaves within eighteen months afterwards.

III

Two days before Butler coined a new word for slave, and one day before the death of Ellsworth, General Joseph E. Johnston, regarded as the ablest soldier in the Confederacy, took command at Harpers Ferry. He had been told by Lee and Davis that the position, at the junction of the Potomac and the Shenandoah, was a natural fortress. Johnston quickly concluded that artillery posted on the heights above the town could make it a deathtrap. He pressed for permission to transfer his command to Winchester, where he would be in better position to confront a strong Union force that was at Chambersburg, Pennsylvania, under General Robert Patterson. Permission was finally granted, and Johnston moved his troops to the northern end of the Shenandoah Valley where he would be in Patterson's way when that commander advanced.

But the North was paying little attention to Harpers Ferry and Winchester. All eyes were on Richmond. Greeley's Tribune spoke for millions when it carried at the head of its editorial column, day after day, the strident appeal:

"Forward to Richmond! Forward to Richmond! The Rebel Congress must not be allowed to meet there on the 20th of July! By that date the place must be held by the National Army!"

No administration could have resisted the popular demand without forfeiting popular confidence—an alternative worse than a lost battle. On June 29 Lincoln called the members of his Cabinet and several generals together to discuss a campaign against the Confederates at Manassas Junction. Scott demurred, preferring a massive advance down the Mississippi River in the fall. When overruled by the President and his advisors, the loyal old soldier presented a plan which General Irvin McDowell, who at forty-two had spent all his mature life in the Regular Army, had already prepared at Scott's request. If an advance were to be made, McDowell would command it. He had written:[4]

The Secession forces at Manassas Junction and its dependencies are supposed to amount at this time to—

Infantry	23,000
Cavalry	1,500
Artillery	500
	25,000

We cannot count on keeping secret our intention to overthrow this force. Even if the many parties intrusted with the knowledge of the plan should not disclose or discover it, the necessary preliminary measures for such an expedition would betray it, and they are alive and well informed as to every movement, however slight, we make. They have, moreover, been expecting us to attack their position, and have been preparing for it. When it becomes known positively we are about to march, and they learn in what strength, they will be obliged to call in their disposable forces from all quarters, for they will not be able, if closely pressed, to get away by railroad before we can reach them. If General J. E. Johnston's force is kept engaged by Major-General Patterson, and Major-General Butler occupies the force now in his vicinity, I think they will not be able to bring up more than ten thousand men. So we must calculate on having to do with about thirty-five thousand men. . . .

Leaving small garrisons in the defensive works, I propose to move against Manassas with a force of thirty-five thousand of all arms, organized into three columns, with a reserve of ten thousand. One column to move from Falls Church or Vienna (preferably the latter), to go between Fairfax Court-House and Centreville, and, in connection with another column moving by the Little River turnpike, cut off or drive in (the former, if possible) the enemy's advanced posts. The third column to move by the Orange and Alexandria Railroad, and leaving as large a force as may be necessary to aid in rebuilding it, to push on with the remainder to join the first and second columns.

The enemy is said to have batteries in position at several places in his front, and defensive works on Bull Run and Manassas Junction. I do not propose that these batteries be attacked, for I think they may all be turned. Bull Run, I am told, is fordable at most any place. After uniting the columns this side of it, I propose to attack the main position by turning it, if possible, so as to cut off communications by rail

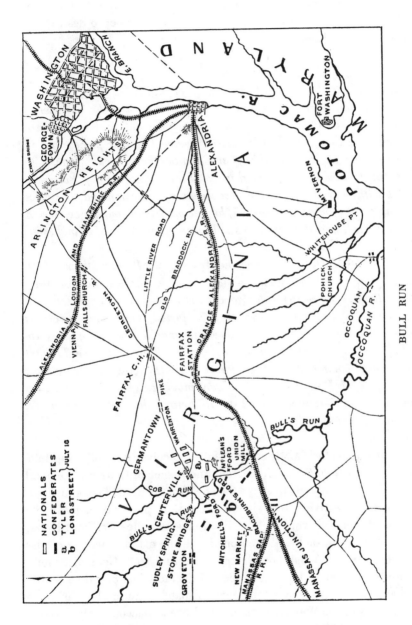

BULL RUN

From Lossing, *Pictorial History of the Civil War*

with the South, or threaten to do so sufficiently to force the enemy to leave his intrenchments to guard them; if necessary, and I find it can be done with safety, to move a force as far as Bristoe, to destroy the bridge at that place.

IV

"If General J. E. Johnston's force is kept engaged. . . ."

The question worried several of those who attended the President's council. Robert Patterson, now sixty-nine years old, had served with distinction in the Mexican War. Scott trusted him and placed him in charge of the troops assembling at Chambersburg, Pennsylvania, to drive the Confederates from Harpers Ferry. The elderly Patterson moved with energy during the first weeks of his command, but after crossing the Potomac on June 15, he became timid and indecisive. A month passed, and Patterson was still nine miles north of Winchester, where Johnston awaited him.

On July 16 McDowell ordered the Army of the Potomac forward. In Washington, in a house within a stone's throw of the Executive Mansion, a lady received a former government clerk who now acted as a Confederate spy. While the youth breakfasted, the woman wrote in cipher: "Order issued for McDowell to march upon Manassas tonight." The spy sped on to Manassas, and Pierre Gustave Toutant Beauregard, commanding there, knew of the Federal advance almost as soon as McDowell's troops began moving. The "Hero of Fort Sumter" immediately appealed to Richmond for Johnston's army. Johnston remembered:[5]

About one o'clock A.M., on the 18th, I received the following telegram from General Cooper, Adjutant and Inspector-General: "General Beauregard is attacked; to strike the enemy a decisive blow, a junction of all your effective force will be needed. If practicable, make the movement, sending your sick and baggage to Culpeper Court-House either by railroad or by Warrenton. In all the arrangements, exercise your discretion." A half-hour later, a telegram from General Beauregard informed me of his urgent need of the aid I had promised him in such an emergency. This intelligence, dispatched to me by him when he reported to the War Department, had been unaccountably delayed.

Being confident that the troops under my command could render no service in "the Valley," so important to the Confederacy as that of preventing a Federal victory at Manassas Junction, I decided, without hesitation, to hasten to that point with my whole force. The only question was, whether to attempt to defeat or to elude General Patterson.

Johnston need not have worried, for Patterson had already thrown away whatever chance he had of holding the wily Confederate in the Valley. General Sanford explained why to the Committee on the Conduct of the War, the inquisitorial body of three Senators and four Representatives who poked their noses into many phases of the war from December 1861 until the end:[6]

It was understood . . . that we were to march forward at daylight. I sent down Colonel Morell with 40 men to open a road down to the Opequan creek, within five miles of the camp at Winchester, on the side roads I was upon, which would enable me in the course of three hours to get between Johnston and the Shenandoah river, and effectually bar his way to Manassas. I had my ammunition all distributed, and ordered my men to have 24 hours' rations in their haversacks, independent of their breakfast. We were to march at four o'clock the next morning. I had this road to the Opequan completed that night. I had then with me, in addition to my eight regiments, amounting to about 8,000 men and a few cavalry, Doubleday's heavy United States battery of 20 and 30 pounders, and a very good Rhode Island battery. And I was willing to take the risk, whether General Patterson followed me up or not, of placing myself between Johnston and the Shenandoah river, rather than Johnston escape. And at four o'clock I should have moved over that road for that purpose, if I had had no further orders. But a little after 12 o'clock at night I received a long order of three pages from General Patterson, instructing me to move on to Charlestown, which is nearly at right angles to the road I was going to move on, and 22 miles from Winchester. This was after I had given my orders for the other movement.

[Mr. Chandler asked: What day was that?]

It was at 12 o'clock on the night of the 16th of July. I received that order—which was the first intimation I had of any kind or sort that we were not going to move on to Winchester—with a peremptory order to move at three o'clock in the morning to Charlestown. . . .

[The Chairman asked: And that left Johnston free?]

Yes, sir; left him free to make his escape, which he did.

When Johnston's cavalry reported that the Federal troops were too far away to interfere he lost no time in heading for Manassas:[7]

The troops left their camps about noon [July 18], Jackson's brigade leading. After the march was fairly begun, and the rear had left Winchester a mile or two, the different regiments were informed, at the same time, of the important object in view, of the necessity of a forced march, and exhorted to strive to reach the field in time to take part in the great battle then imminent.

The discouragement of that day's march to one accustomed, like myself, to the steady gait of regular soldiers, is indescribable. The views of military command and obedience, then taken by both officers and privates, confined those duties and obligations almost exclusively to the drill-ground and guards. In camps and marches they were scarcely known. Consequently, frequent and unreasonable delays caused so slow a rate of marching as to make me despair of joining General Beauregard in time to aid him. Major Whiting was therefore dispatched to the nearest station of the Manassas Gap Railroad, Piedmont, to ascertain if trains, capable of transporting the troops to their destination more quickly than they were likely to reach it on foot, could be provided there, and, if so, to make the necessary arrangements. That officer met me at Paris, after executing his instructions, with a report so favorable as to give me reason to expect that the transportation of the infantry over the thirty-four miles between Piedmont and Manassas Junction would be accomplished easily in twenty-four hours.

Jackson's brigade, his leading men, that is to say, reached Paris, seventeen miles from Winchester, about two hours after dark. The four others halted for the night on the Shenandoah, having marched thirteen miles; Jackson's brigade marched the six miles from Paris to Piedmont before eight o'clock, Friday morning; and, as trains enough for its transportation were found there, it moved in an hour or two. The other brigades came up separately in the afternoon—Bartow's first. Other trains, capable of transporting two regiments, being in readiness about three o'clock, the Seventh and Eighth Georgia regiments were dispatched in them. No other infantry had the means of moving that day. . . .

Enough of the cars, sent down in the morning to convey about two regiments, were brought back before midnight, but the conductors and engineers disappeared immediately, to pass the night probably in sleep, instead of on the road. And it was not until seven or eight o'clock Saturday morning that the trains could be put in motion, carrying the Fourth Alabama and Second Mississippi regiments, with two companies of the Eleventh. General Bee and myself accompanied these troops. Brigadier-General E. Kirby Smith was left at Piedmont to expedite the transportation of the remaining brigades—about three-fifths of the army.

But raw Union troops marched no better than Johnston's boys. Many ate or wasted their cooked rations before they reached the field of battle, and soon were almost starving as supply trains were delayed by "uninstructed and worthless teamsters and green teams." William T. Sherman, who had gone to war after all, recalled glumly:[8]

. . . Our division moved forward, leaving our camps standing; Keyes's brigade in the lead, then Schenck's, then mine, and Richardson's last. We marched via Vienna, Germantown, and Centreville, where all the army, composed of five divisions, seemed to converge. The march demonstrated little save the general laxity of discipline; for with all my personal efforts I could not prevent the men from straggling for water, blackberries, or anything on the way they fancied.

Sherman's experience was not unique. Lieutenant George W. Bicknell of the Fifth Maine Infantry described how a green regiment could decimate itself before it reached the firing line:[9]

Nine, ten o'clock, and yet we remained in the same position wondering what detained us. In the distance we could see the glistening bayonets moving across the plains, could hear peal after peal of artillery, and the sharp, quick reports of musketry. Soon an orderly dashes up, and the order, "Fifth Maine, fall in," was responded to with a will and readiness, indicative of our former impatience. We had moved but a short distance, when "double quick" came ringing on the air; and *such* a double quick, methinks, was never before or since experienced. Fortunately our course lay through a wooded country which served to shelter us, in a measure, from the intense heat of the sun. Our water was nearly gone, and, during that whole run of some six or seven miles, we were not once allowed a halt to replenish our canteens. Unaccustomed to such severe marches, suffering intensely from thirst and heat, pressed on at as rapid rate as possible, our thinning ranks began to show the effects of overexertion. Men seemed to fall in squads by the roadside, some sun-struck, some bleeding at nose, mouth, ears; others wind-broken, while others were exhausted to such a degree, that the threatening muzzle of the officer's pistol, failed to induce them a step further. While the boys were murmuring because they had no water, we suddenly came to a brook flowing across the road, through which thousands had undoubtedly passed before; and oh! ye people of the North, could you have witnessed the avidity with which our boys would drink of that water, in hundreds of cases using their shoes for dippers, horses and men side by side, the water thickened and yellow with dirt, your hearts would have bled for us. . . .

For miles the road was strewed with blankets, haversacks, coats, thrown aside by the almost exhausted soldiers. . . . On, on we ran, till suddenly a cannon ball, striking within a few feet of the head of the regiment, gave us to understand that we were "within range." Leaving the woods, we were hurried across an open plain. . . . Whiz! a man is struck immediately in our front, torn by a solid shot. Rapidly we pushed forward, soon passing into a ravine where we were temporarily shielded from the enemy's fire, though within a short distance of their position. Here we were met by wounded soldiers, disarmed and retreating federals, citizens, and negroes, all crying out, "go in boys," "the Johnnys are running," "the day is ours," etc., etc. It was not till half past one that we were formed into line of battle, though it was done as soon as we arrived on the field. Under the cover of a hill our regiment was halted, and the officers attempted to form our line. The regiment fronted, and oh! *what* a regiment! How sadly thinned from what it was in the morning! Nobly it had struggled through its fearful march; nor are those men who fell by the wayside to be remembered with other feelings than those of esteem, because they each and every one did all they could. . . . No one doubts that the greater portion of those men missing fell from sheer exhaustion. There was fearful blundering somewhere.

V

Johnston, who ranked Beauregard, took over the command of the Confederate army as soon as he reached Beauregard's headquarters. But the senior commander did not know the terrain or the troop dispositions; Beauregard would have to direct the impending battle. The Creole, trying hard to be the Napoleon in Gray, had devised one plan after another for smashing the Federal army before it could hit him. McDowell quashed them all simply by striking the Confederates at 6 A.M. on Sunday morning, July 21, two hours before Beauregard had planned to make his attack.

The Union commander opened the battle with a feint, waiting until later in the morning to deliver his real attack on the Confederate left flank. Beauregard, who had planned to strike the Union left and rear, had all he could do to prevent an immediate rout:[10]

The firing on the left began to increase so intensely as to indicate a severe attack, whereupon General Johnston said that he would go personally to that quarter.

After weighing attentively the firing, which seemed rapidly and heavily increasing, it appeared to me that the troops on the right would be unable to get into position before the Federal offensive should have made too much progress on our left, and that it would be better to abandon it altogether, maintaining only a strong demonstration so as to detain the enemy in front of our right and center, and hurry up all available reenforcements—including the reserves that were to have moved upon Centreville—to our left and fight the battle out in that quarter. Communicating this view to General Johnston, who approved it (giving his advice, as he said, for what it was worth, as he was not acquainted with the country), I ordered Ewell, Jones, and Longstreet to make a strong demonstration all along their front on the other side of the Run, and ordered the reserves below our position . . . to move swiftly to the left. General Johnston and I now set out at full speed for the point of conflict. We arrived there just as Bee's troops, after giving way, were fleeing in disorder behind the height in rear of the Stone Bridge. They had come around between the base of the hill and the Stone Bridge into a shallow ravine which ran up to a point on the crest where Jackson had already formed his brigade along the edge of the woods. We found the commanders resolutely stemming the further flight of the routed forces, but vainly endeavoring to restore order, and our own efforts were as futile. Every segment of the line we succeeded in forming was again dissolved while another was being formed; more than two thousand men were shouting each some suggestion to his neighbor, their voices mingling with the noise of the shells hurtling through the trees overhead, and all word of command drowned in the confusion and uproar. It was at this moment that General Bee used the famous expression, "Look at Jackson's brigade! It stands there like a stone wall"—a name that passed from the brigade to its immortal commander. The disorder seemed irretrievable, but happily the thought came to me that if their colors were planted out to the front the men might rally on them, and I gave the order to carry the standards forward some forty yards, which was promptly executed by the regimental officers, thus drawing the common eye of the troops. They now received easily the orders to advance and form on the line of their colors, which they obeyed with a general movement; and as General Johnston and myself rode forward shortly afterward with the colors of the 4th Alabama by our side, the line that had fought all morning, and had fled, routed and disordered, now advanced again into position as steadily as veterans.

Panic was averted, but the Union troops, though nearly as confused and disorganized as the Confederates, continued to advance. By midafternoon McDowell believed he had won his battle. So did Jefferson Davis, who had hurried up from Richmond as soon as he learned that a battle was being fought:[11]

On reaching the railroad junction, I found a large number of men, bearing the usual evidence of those who leave the field of battle under a panic. They crowded around the train with fearful stories of a defeat of our army. The railroad conductor announced his decision that the railroad train should proceed no farther. Looking among those who were about us for one whose demeanor gave reason to expect from him a collected answer, I selected one whose gray beard and calm face gave best assurance. He, however, could furnish no encouragement. Our line, he said, was broken, all was confusion, the army routed, and the battle lost. I asked for Generals Johnston and Beauregard; he said they were on the field when he left it. I returned to the conductor and told him that I must go on; that the railroad was the only means by which I could proceed, and that, until I reached the headquarters, I could not get a horse to ride to the field where the battle was raging. He finally consented to detach the locomotive from the train, and, for my accommodation, to run it as far as the army headquarters.

At the headquarters we found the Quartermaster-General, W. L. Cabell, and the Adjutant-General, Jordan, of General Beauregard's staff, who courteously agreed to furnish us horses, and also to show us the route. While the horses were being prepared, Colonel Jordan took occasion to advise my aide-de-camp, Colonel Davis, of the hazard of going to the field, and the impropriety of such exposure on my part. The horses were after a time reported ready, and we started to the field. The stragglers soon became numerous, and warnings as to the fate which awaited us if we advanced were not only frequent but evidently sincere.

There were, however, many who turned back, and the wounded generally cheered upon meeting us. I well remember one, a mere stripling, who, supported on the shoulders of a man, who was bearing him to the rear, took off his cap and waved it with a cheer, that showed within that slender form beat the heart of a hero—breathed a spirit that would dare the labors of Hercules.

As we advanced, the storm of the battle was rolling westward, and its fury became more faint. When I met General Johnston, who was upon a hill which commanded a general view of the field of the afternoon's operations, and inquired of him as to the state of affairs, he replied that we had won the battle.

Beauregard knew how the Federal drive had been broken—or thought he did:[12]

With superior numbers the Federals were pushing on new regiments in the attempt to flank my position, and several guns, in the effort to enfilade ours, were thrust forward so near the 33d Virginia that some of its men sprang forward and captured them, but were driven back by an overpowering force of Federal musketry. Although the enemy were held well at bay, their pressure became so strong that I resolved to take the offensive, and ordered a charge on my right for the purpose of recovering the plateau. The movement, made with alacrity and force by the commands of Bee, Bartow, Evans, and Hampton, thrilled the entire line, Jackson's brigade piercing the enemy's center, and the left of the line under Gartrell and Smith following up the charge, also, in that quarter, so that the whole of the open surface of the plateau was swept clear of the Federals.

Apart from its impressions on the enemy, the effect of this brilliant onset was to give a short breathing-spell to our troops from the immediate strain of conflict, and encourage them in withstanding the still more strenuous offensive that was soon to bear upon them. Reorganizing our line of battle under the unremitting fire of the Federal batteries opposite, I prepared to meet the new attack which the enemy were about to make, largely reenforced by the troops of Howard's brigade, newly arrived on the field. The Federals again pushed up the slope, the face of which partly afforded good cover by the numerous ravines that scored it and the clumps of young pines and oaks with which it was studded, while the sunken Sudley road formed a good ditch and parapet for their aggressive advance upon my left flank and rear. Gradually they pressed our lines back and regained possession of their lost ground and guns. With the Henry and Robinson houses once more in their possession, they resumed the offensive, urged forward by their commanders with conspicuous gallantry.

The conflict now became very severe for the final possession of this position, which was the key to victory. The Federal numbers enabled them so to extend their lines through the woods beyond the Sudley road as to outreach my left flank, which I was compelled partly to throw back, so as to meet the attack from that quarter; meanwhile their numbers equally enabled them to outflank my right in the direction of the Stone Bridge, imposing anxious watchfulness in that direction. I knew that I was safe if I could hold out till the arrival of reenforcements, which was but a matter of time; and, with the full sense of my own responsibility, I was determined to hold the line of the plateau, even if surrounded on all sides, until assistance should come, unless my forces were sooner overtaken by annihilation.

It was now between half-past 2 and 3 o'clock; a scorching sun increased the oppression of the troops, exhausted from incessant fighting, many of them having been engaged since the morning. Fearing lest the Federal offensive should secure too firm a grip, and knowing the fatal result that might spring from any grave infraction of my line, I determined to make another effort for the recovery of the plateau, and ordered a charge of the entire line of battle, including the reserves, which at this crisis I myself led into action. The movement was made with such keeping and dash that the whole plateau was swept clear of the enemy, who were driven down the slope and across the turnpike on our right and the valley of Young's Branch on our left, leaving in our final possession the Robinson and Henry houses, with most of Ricketts's and Griffin's batteries, the men of which were mostly shot down where they bravely stood by their guns.

Beauregard could ascribe his success to tactical shrewdness, but the fact was that both armies were made up of novices in the art of war; that no one, from commanding general to the rawest recruit, had more than a foggy notion of what he was doing; and that the side which panicked first would give victory to the other—all of which emerges in the story of Lieutenant Josiah M. Favill of the Fifty-seventh New York Infantry:[13]

Very soon we were relieved by the Sixty-ninth New York and a New Hampshire regiment, who followed up the enemy, while we fell back to the edge of the woods, stacked arms, and answered to roll call. We had lost seventeen men killed outright, and forty wounded; all the rest were accounted for; we then buried the dead and carried such of the wounded as had not already been cared for back to the field hospital, after which we compared notes and congratulated each other on the success of the fight. There served with us throughout the whole fight a tall, elderly gentleman, wearing plain clothes and a tall silk hat, in the front rank, who loaded and fired away in the most deliberate manner, apparently wholly indifferent to danger; he must have done a good deal of execution, as the excitement did not seem to affect him in the least. They say he is a noted abolitionist, and desired to do his share in the field, as well as in the forum; I am sorry I can not remember his name.* With a regiment of such men as he, what might we not have done?

Soon after we retired, General McDowell rode up, dressed in full uniform, including white gloves, and told us we had won a great victory, and that the enemy were in full retreat; we cheered him vociferously, and felt like veritable heroes.

The enemy having disappeared, some of us concluded to walk over the battle field, see how it looked, and pick up something as a souvenir of the fight. The Sixty-ninth and Seventy-ninth New York and the splendid line of the Marine corps, in their white cross belts, were moving without opposition, away off to the right, apparently intending to follow the enemy to Richmond. Butler and I strolled down the hill side, and were soon amongst the dead and dying rebels, who up to this time had been neglected. What a horrible sight it was! here a man, grasping his musket firmly in his hands, stone dead; several with distorted features, and all of them horribly dirty. Many were terribly wounded, some with legs shot off; others with arms gone, all of them, in fact, so badly wounded that they could not drag themselves away; many of the wretches were slowly bleeding to death, with no one to do anything for them. We stopped many times to give some a drink and soon saw enough to satisfy us with the horrors of war; and so picking up some swords, and bayonets, we turned about and retraced our steps. Suddenly a minnie ball whistled past us, making the dust fly just in front, where it lodged; we thought it must be from some of our men mistaking us for rebels, and so hurried along to join our regiment when, nearly at the summit of the hill, a whole volley of musket balls

* The copy of Favill's book in the Chicago Historical Society bears a marginal notation in pencil: "This 'tall elderly gentleman' was Wm. P. Thomasson, father of Nelson Thomasson, 117 No. Dearborn St., Chicago."

whizzed about us, one of them striking my companion, who dropped to the ground as though he had been killed, and I really thought he was; in looking him over, I found he was shot through the knee, and quite unable to stand, or walk; promising to bring him assistance, I started on the run, found the regiment, and with several good fellows quickly returned, picked up our comrade and carried him to the rear, and left him with the surgeons. This turn in affairs greatly puzzled everybody, and the only conclusion arrived at was, that some of our troops had mistaken us for the enemy. About half an hour after this, our attention was attracted to the distant hills and open ground by long lines of infantry extending across the whole face of the battle ground; the sound of distant musketry came floating along, followed by an occasional cannon shot. Presently the lines grew more distinct, finally developing into well defined lines of battle, marching in our direction; everybody was now alert, wondering what was going to happen; at last the glittering bayonets, reflecting the summer sun, were easily distinguished, and there was no longer a doubt but that the rebels had reformed, and with new forces were going to renew the fighting. The musketry increased and several batteries opened in our direction, but there were no indications on our part of making any resistance to the rapidly advancing foe; so far as we could see over the wide extended fields, not a single line of battle on our side was in position; the regiments about us had been gradually withdrawing, until few were left. All the guns had gone, except our two howitzers, and there was no general officer on the ground. As the long line came nearer and nearer, Colonel Martin ordered us to fall in, and with muskets in hand, we stood, simply watching the gradual approach of this overwhelming force, and the disappearance of our troops; wondering what had become of all the masses of men we not long ago thought numerous enough to thrash the world; now there was nobody left, and our colonel at length ordered us to counter march to the rear, and follow the crowd. We still supposed there was a new line forming in rear of us, and that in the confusion, our regiment had escaped attention, consequently, at first were not much alarmed, but as we continued going to the rear and saw no signs of fresh dispositions, we came to the conclusion we were running away, following the route we had marched over with so much confidence in the morning; presently we came up with the rear of the troops that had preceded us, but looked in vain for new defensive dispositions. Everywhere was hurry and confusion, the wagons and batteries filled the roads, while the men spread out on either side, gradually losing their formations and fast becoming reckless. There was no rear guard, nor any arrangements for holding the enemy in check, and if they really had appeared, they might have captured us all without difficulty. Now every one was anxious to be first, and so by degrees, the men of various regiments got mixed up together, and thus, finding themselves without officers, accelerated their steps until at last it became a precipitate flight to the rear.

McDowell knew that the basic causes of the Federal defeat were the inexperience of the army and the arrival on the field of the Confederate troops which Patterson should have held in the Shenandoah Valley. Yet even the Federal commander could not understand why a reverse should have turned so quickly into a rout:[14]

The enemy was evidently disheartened and broken. But we had then been fighting since 10:30 in the morning, and it was after 3 o'clock in the afternoon. The men had been up since 2 o'clock in the morning, and had made what to those unused to such things seemed a long march before coming into action, though the longest distance gone over was not more than 9½ miles; and though they had three days' provisions served out to them the day before, many, no doubt, either did not get them or threw them away on the march or during the battle, and were therefore without food. They had done much severe fighting. Some of the regiments which had been driven from the hill in the first two attempts of the enemy to keep possession of it had become shaken, were unsteady, and had many men out of the ranks.

It was at this time that the enemy's re-enforcements came to his aid from the railroad train (understood to have just arrived from the valley with the residue of Johnston's army). They threw themselves on the woods on our right, and opened a fire of musketry on our men, which caused them to break, and retire down the hill-side. This soon degenerated into disorder, for which there was no remedy. Every effort was made to rally them, even beyond the reach of the enemy's fire, but in vain. The battalion of regular infantry alone moved up the hill . . . and there maintained itself until our men could get down to and across the Warrenton turnpike on the way back to the position we occupied in the morning. The plain was covered with the retreating groups, and they seemed to infect those with whom they came in contact. The retreat soon became a rout, and this soon degenerated still further into a panic.

VI

Senator Lyman Trumbull of Illinois was one of many Congressmen who drove out from Washington on the day of Bull Run to watch the war end in one glorious Federal victory. In midafternoon he, Senator James A. McDougall of California, and Senator James W. Grimes of Iowa ate a pleasant picnic luncheon by the side of the road between Centreville and the battlefield. Then:[15]

Just as we were putting away the [luncheon] things we heard a great noise, and looking up towards the road saw it filled with wagons, horse-men and footmen in full run towards Centreville. We immediately mounted our horses and galloped to the road, by which time it was crowded, hundreds being in advance on the way to Centreville and two guns of the Sherman battery having already passed in full retreat. We kept on with the crowd, not knowing what else to do. On the way to Centreville many soldiers threw away their guns, knapsacks, etc. Gov. Grimes and I each picked up a gun. I soon came up to Senator Lane of Indiana, and the gun being heavy to carry and he better able to manage it, I gave it to him. Efforts were made to rally the men by civilians and others on their way to Centreville, but all to no purpose.

Literally, three could have chased ten thousand. All this stampede was occasioned, as I understand, by a charge of not exceeding two hundred cavalry upon Schenck's column down in the woods, which, in-stead of repulsing as they could easily have done, (having before be-come disordered and having lost some of their officers), broke and ran, communicating the panic to everybody they met. The rebel cavalry, or about one hundred of them, charged up past the hospital where we had been and took there some prisoners, as I am told, and released those we had. It was the most shameful rout you can conceive of. I suppose two thousand soldiers came rushing into Centreville in this disorgan-ized condition.

The cavalry which made the charge I did not see, but suppose they disappeared in double-quick time, not dreaming that they had put a whole division to flight. Several guns were left down in the woods, though I believe two were brought off. What became of Schenck I do not know. Tyler, I understand, was at Centreville when I got back there. Whether other portions of our army were shamefully routed just at the close of the day, after we had really won the battle, it seems im-possible for me to learn, though I was told that McDowell was at

Centreville when we were there and that his column had also been driven back. If this be so it is a terrible defeat.

At Centreville there was a reserve of 8000 or 10,000 men under Col. Miles who had not been in the action and they were formed in line of battle when we left there, but the enemy did not, I presume, advance to that point last night, as we heard no firing. We fed our horses at Centreville and left there at six o'clock last evening. Came on to Fairfax Court House, where we got supper, and leaving there at ten o'clock reached home at half-past two this morning, having had a sad day and witnessed scenes I hope never to see again. Not very many baggage wagons, perhaps not more than fifty, were advanced beyond Centreville. From them the horses were mostly unhitched and the wagons left standing in the road when the stampede took place. This side of Centreville there were a great many wagons, and the alarm if possible was greater than on the other. Thousands of shovels were thrown out upon the road, also axes, boxes of provisions, etc. In some instances wagons were upset to get them out of the road, and the road was full of four-horse wagons retreating as fast as possible, and also of flying soldiers who could not be made to stop at Centreville. The officers stopped the wagons and a good many of the retreating soldiers by putting a file of men across the road and not allowing them to pass. In this way all the teams were stopped, but a good many stragglers climbed the fences and got by. I fear that a great, and, of course, a terrible slaughter has overtaken the Union forces—God's ways are inscrutable. I am dreadfully disappointed and mortified.

VII

Trumbull, a devout man, could attribute the Bull Run disaster to the ways of an inscrutable but all-wise Providence. Colonel Louis Blenker of the Eighth New York, out of years of experience in the Bavarian Legion, needed no supernatural explanation:[16]

But still I do not think it is a blame for anybody to lose that battle. It was a panic, all at once. There was a panic which nobody can explain. The colonels there, a great many of them, never have a command. They look around and say: "What shall we do?" That is strange music— the bullet—and strange feeling to be killed. But what to do is the question. They are running. Some begin to retreat, and it is not possible to give orders to keep them together. If one regiment runs, the others go too. That has been the case in every army—French army, Austrian army, and every good army in the world. I would not blame any officer for that. . . . General McDowell, he was so much hurt that I feel the greatest sympathy for him today. I would not allow anybody to blame him today. . . . I do not speak good enough English to express myself.

THE MARTIAL
IMAGE

I F THE WAR had ended quickly, other heroes would have shaped its legends. With some sort of patched-up compromise the political and constitutional arguments would have been resolved, and Mr. Lincoln's contention that the war was "a people's contest" would have made him the simplest of Simple Susans. But the President was often haunted by a dream of being adrift toward a remote shore; he could not escape the mystery of the war. Nor could America. During those tragic years from 1861 to 1865 the people changed the nature and the purpose of their quarrel because the people themselves changed. They produced unexpected heroes, finding them among relatively obscure, neglected men. General George B. McClellan, with arms folded, striking the historic pose of Napoleon, would suffice as a Martial Image during the summer of 1861; but four years later the image was entirely a native product compounded of the stumpy, slouchy Grant, of Lee, the noble Virginian who shared the discomforts of camp life with his soldiers, of Sherman in the mussed-up uniform he must have slept in for weeks, and of Jackson who fastened his coat with safety pins.

What Americans had created in this new Martial Image was their own reflection, and the achievement was the more fascinating because by nature they never had been very long on introspection. A few had wrestled with tormented consciences over slavery; the many had not. Sometime during the conflict—perhaps after Bull Run, perhaps after Mr. Lincoln issued the Emancipation Proclamation—the truth became undeniable. The war was more than a mixed-up border raid, Indian scuffle, frontier brawl and Dixie knife-fight. A great many Americans had stumbled upon themselves in a new dimension. A posturing Napoleon no longer sufficed.

Americans, somewhat to their surprise, discovered that they always had been in dead earnest about their quarrel. The impact of their struggle shook Christian civilization. Morals had been wedded to politics and their offspring became a war that staggered imagination. A nation with the spottiest of military memories had raised, trained, equipped and transported stupendous armies. It had invented new tools of human destruction that revolutionized the nature of war on land and sea. Starting practically from scratch, it had evolved its own military tradition and breathed life into its own Martial Image, and had done so under civilian authority, in the name of freedom and democracy.

At home and abroad, in high office and low, men followed this war with growing intensity. All kinds of people found lessons in it—about themselves as people, about their responsibilities and their rights, about the strength of voluntary armies as opposed to professional military organizations, about man's humanity and inhumanity when put to the test of death.

I

The British, faced with the necessity of patrolling an empire and defending their island homeland, were confronted by a choice of Martial Images. The Franco-Prussian War supplied one, the American Civil War another. As time gave perspective, it became less unfashionable to impute intelligence to their cousins across the seas; the British picked at the American story, came back to it, and suddenly British military curiosity over the struggle between Billy Yank and Johnny Reb became an absorbing fascination. In a letter to Confederate Major Jed Hotchkiss, who planned to write a history of the war, Colonel G. F. R. Henderson, famous for his own searching studies of "Stonewall" Jackson and the Fredericksburg campaign, decided "to be impudent" and to suggest "what points we should like to hear about principally":[1]

1. The characters, demeanours, and appearance of your generals.

2. The character of the troops and of their fighting, and of their discipline.

3. The nature of entrenchments and breastworks constructed.

4. The way in which the fighting in the woods was carried out and the precautions taken to maintain order and direction.

5. The way intelligence of the enemy was obtained, and the country mapped. I would suggest that you give an example or two of the [maps].

6. The methods of the Confederacy [sic] marksmen—the efficiency of their fire and the manner in which it was controlled by their officers—or otherwise.

The more military your book is the better it will go down over here, as, owing to our number of volunteers and our constant little wars, the people generally understand and enjoy all details connected with the grand art of killing one's fellow men.

II

For Rebel or Yankee, the order was a tall one. It asked for preciseness of detail that was not characteristic of the war itself. In the beginning even the greatest soldier of the war would have seemed a sorry practitioner of Colonel Henderson's "grand art":[2]

My regiment was composed in large part of young men of as good social position as any in their section of the State. It embraced the sons of farmers, lawyers, physicians, politicians, merchants, bankers and ministers, and some men of maturer years who had filled such positions themselves. There were also men in it who could be led astray; and the colonel, elected by the votes of the regiment, had proved to be fully capable of developing all there was in his men of recklessness. It was said that he even went so far at times as to take the guard from their posts and go with them to the village near by and make a night of it. When there came a prospect of battle the regiment wanted to have some one else to lead them. I found it very hard work for a few days to bring all the men into anything like subordination; but the great majority favored discipline, and by the application of a little regular army punishment all were reduced to as good discipline as one could ask. . . .

I remained in Springfield with my regiment until the 3d of July, when I was ordered to Quincy, Illinois. By that time the regiment was in a good state of discipline and the officers and men were well up in the company drill. There was direct railroad communication between Springfield and Quincy, but I thought it would be good preparation for the troops to march there. We had no transportation for our camp and garrison equipage, so wagons were hired for the occasion and on the 3d of July we started. There was no hurry, but fair marches were made every day until the Illinois River was crossed. There I was overtaken by a dispatch saying that the destination of the regiment had been changed to Ironton, Missouri, and ordering me to halt where I was and await the arrival of a steamer which had been dispatched up the Illinois River to take the regiment to St. Louis. The boat, when it did come, grounded on a sand-bar a few miles below where we were in camp. We remained there several days waiting to have the boat get off the bar, but before this occurred news came that an Illinois regiment was surrounded by rebels at a point on the Hannibal and St. Joe Railroad some miles west of Palmyra, in Missouri, and I was ordered to proceed with all dispatch to their relief. . . .

My sensations as we approached what I supposed might be "a field of battle" were anything but agreeable. I had been in all the engagements in Mexico that it was possible for one person to be in; but not in command. If some one else had been colonel and I had been lieutenant-colonel I do not think I would have felt any trepidation. Before we were prepared to cross the Mississippi River at Quincy my anxiety was relieved; for the men of the besieged regiment came straggling into town. I am inclined to think both sides got frightened and ran away.

I took my regiment to Palmyra and remained there for a few days, until relieved by the 19th Illinois infantry. From Palmyra I proceeded to Salt River, the railroad bridge over which had been destroyed by the enemy. Colonel John M. Palmer at that time commanded the 13th Illinois, which was acting as a guard to workmen who were engaged in rebuilding this bridge. Palmer was my senior and commanded the two regiments as long as we remained together. The bridge was finished in about two weeks, and I received orders to move against Colonel Thomas Harris, who was said to be encamped at the little town of Florida, some twenty-five miles south of where we then were.

. . . We had no transportation and the country about Salt River was sparsely settled, so that it took some days to collect teams and drivers enough to move the camp and garrison equipage of a regiment nearly a thousand strong, together with a week's supply of provision and some ammunition. While preparations for the move were going on I felt quite comfortable; but when we got on the road and found every house deserted I was anything but easy. In the twenty-five miles we had to march we did not see a person, old or young, male or female, except two horsemen who were on a road that crossed ours. As soon as they saw us they decamped as fast as their horses could carry them. I kept my men in the ranks and forbade their entering any of the deserted houses or taking anything from them. We halted at night on the road and proceeded the next morning at an early hour.

Harris had been encamped in a creek bottom for the sake of being near water. The hills on either side of the creek extend to a considerable height, possibly more than a hundred feet. As we approached the brow of the hill from which it was expected we could see Harris' camp, and possibly find his men ready formed to meet us, my heart kept getting higher and higher until it felt to me as though it was in my throat. I would have given anything then to have been back in Illinois, but I had not the moral courage to halt and consider what to do; I kept right on.

When we reached a point from which the valley below was in full view I halted. The place where Harris had been encamped a few days before was still there and the marks of a recent encampment were plainly visible, but the troops were gone. My heart resumed its place. It occurred to me at once that Harris had been as much afraid of me as I had been of him. This was a view of the question I had never taken before; but it was one I never forgot afterwards. From that event to the close of the war, I never experienced trepidation upon confronting an enemy, though I always felt more or less anxiety. I never forgot that he had as much reason to fear my forces as I had his. The lesson was valuable. . . .

Actually Tom Harris had been willing to fight. Among those who frustrated the Confederate was young Samuel Langhorne Clemens, who told his side of the story:[3]

The last camp which we fell back upon was in a hollow near the village of Florida, where I was born—in Monroe County. Here we were warned one day that a Union colonel was sweeping down on us with a whole regiment at his heel. This looked decidedly serious. Our boys went apart and consulted; then we went back and told the other companies present that the war was a disappointment to us, and we were going to disband. They were getting ready themselves to fall back on some place or other, and we were only waiting for General Tom Harris, who was expected to arrive at any moment; so they tried to persuade us to wait a little while, but the majority of us said no, we were accustomed to falling back, and didn't need any of Tom Harris's help; we could get along perfectly well without him—and save time, too. So about half of our fifteen, including myself, mounted and left on the instant; the others yielded to persuasion and stayed—stayed through the war.

An hour later we met General Harris on the road, with two or three people in his company—his staff, probably, but we could not tell; none of them were in uniform; uniforms had not come into vogue among us yet. Harris ordered us back; but we told him there was a Union colonel coming with a whole regiment in his wake, and it looked as if there was going to be a disturbance; so we had concluded to go home. He raged a little, but it was of no use; our minds were made up. . . .

In time I came to know that Union colonel whose coming frightened me out of the war and crippled the Southern cause to that extent— General Grant. I came within a few hours of seeing him when he was as unknown as I was myself; at a time when anybody could have said, "Grant?—Ulysses S. Grant? I do not remember hearing the name before." It seems difficult to realize that there was once a time when such a remark could be rationally made; but there *was*, and I was within a few miles of the place and the occasion, too, though proceeding in the other direction.

"I could have become a soldier myself if I had waited," Sam Clemens said in later years. "I had got part of it learned; I knew more about retreating than the man that invented retreating."

Grant rummaged through his trunk for the manual of arms he had saved from West Point days. Next time he lined up his regiment he realized that he had wasted his time, for if he applied what he had studied, he would need to clear away houses and garden fences. But Grant always said little and thought much; he remembered his two commanders in the Mexican War, Winfield Scott and Zachary Taylor; Scott he admired and Taylor he copied:[4]

. . . The contrast between the two was very marked. General Taylor never wore uniform, but dressed himself entirely for comfort. He moved about the field in which he was operating to see through his own eyes the situation. Often he would be without staff officers, and when he was accompanied by them there was no prescribed order in which they followed. He was very much given to sit his horse side-ways—with both feet on one side—particularly on the battlefield. General Scott was the reverse in all these particulars. He always wore all the uniform prescribed or allowed by law when he inspected his lines; word would be sent to all divisions and brigade commanders in advance, notifying them of the hour when the commanding general might be expected. This was done so that all the army might be under arms to salute their chief as he passed. On these occasions he wore his dress uniform, cocked hat, aiguillettes, sabre and spurs. His staff proper, besides all officers constructively on his staff—engineers, inspectors, quartermasters, etc., that could be spared—followed, also in uniform and in prescribed order. Orders were prepared with great care and evidently with the view that they should be a history of what followed.

In their modes of expressing thought, these two generals contrasted quite as strongly as in their other characteristics. General Scott was precise in language, cultivated a style peculiarly his own; was proud of his rhetoric; not averse to speaking of himself, often in the third person, and he could bestow praise upon the person he was talking about without the least embarrassment. Taylor was not a conversationalist, but on paper he could put his meaning so plainly that there could be no mistaking it. He knew how to express what he wanted to say in the fewest well-chosen words, but would not sacrifice meaning to the construction of high-sounding sentences. But with their opposite characteristics both were great and successful soldiers; both were true, patriotic, and upright in all their dealings. Both were pleasant to serve under—Taylor was pleasant to serve with. Scott saw more through the eyes of his staff officers than through his own. His plans were deliberately prepared, and fully expressed in orders. Taylor saw for himself, and gave orders to meet the emergency without reference to how they would read in history.

III

The military heroes that America tried on for size during its first summer of discontent were of a different cut from Grant. The South was still entranced by the jaunty figure of Pierre Gustave Toutant Beauregard—the Grand Creole, the hero of Sumter, the little Napoleon in Gray—who would die insisting that the national government owed him the expenses incurred in returning from West Point to New Orleans to take part in the rebellion. The star that dazzled Yankee heavens belonged to George B. McClellan, a man of exceptional administrative abilities who, writing to his wife from western Virginia, saw himself as one general unafraid to keep a rendezvous with destiny:[5]

MARIETTA, June 21, 1861.—I must snatch a few moments to write you. We got off at 11.30 yesterday morning, and had a continual ovation all along the road. At every station where we stopped crowds had assembled to see the "young general": gray-headed old men and women, mothers holding up their children to take my hand, girls, boys, all sorts, cheering and crying, God bless you! I never went through such a scene in my life, and never expect to go through such another one. You would have been surprised at the excitement. At Chillicothe the ladies had prepared a dinner, and I had to be trotted through. They gave me about twenty beautiful bouquets and almost killed me with kindness. The trouble will be to fill their expectations, they seem to be so high. I could hear them say, "He is our own general"; "Look at him, how young he is"; "*He* will thrash them"; "He'll do," etc., etc. *ad infinitum*. . . .

We reached here about three in the morning, and at once went on board the boat, where I got about three hours' sleep until we reached Parkersburg. I have been hard at work all day, for I found everything in great confusion. Came up here in a boat about an hour ago, and shall go back to Parkersburg in two or three hours. . . . I shall have some eighteen regiments, two batteries, two companies of cavalry at my disposal—enough to thrash anything I find. I think the danger has been greatly exaggerated, and anticipate little or no chance of winning laurels. . . .

GRAFTON, Sunday, June 23, 1861.— . . . We did not reach here until about two in the morning, and I was tired out. . . . Everything here needs the hand of the master and is getting it fast. I shall hardly be able to move from here for a couple of days. . . .

GRAFTON, June 29.— . . . I am bothered half to death by delays in getting up supplies. Unless where I am in person, everything seems to go wrong. . . . I expect in the course of an hour or two to get to Clarksburg—will probably march twelve miles thence to-day—with Howe's battery, Mack's and the Chicago companies, and one company of cavalry. I shall have a telegraph line built to follow us up. Look on the maps and find Buckhannon and Beverly; that is the direction of my march. I hope to thrash the infamous scamps before a week is over. All I fear is that I won't catch them. . . .

BUCKHANNON, July 3.— . . . We had a pleasant march of sixteen miles yesterday through a beautiful mountain region: magnificent timber, lovely valleys running up from the main valley; the people all out, waving their handkerchiefs and giving me plenty of bouquets and kind words. . . .

We nearly froze to death last night. I retired, as I thought, at about

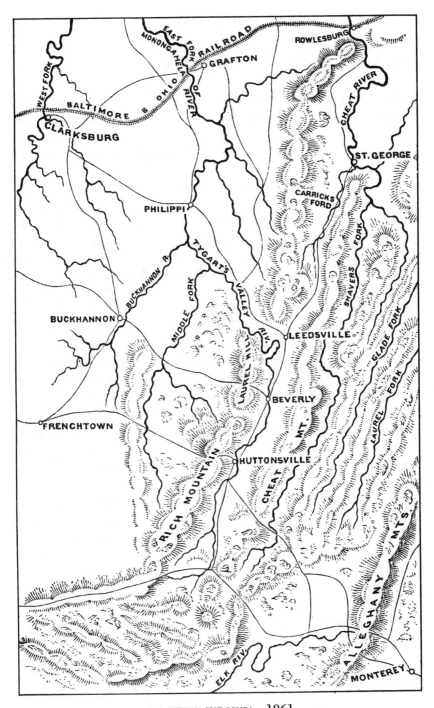

WESTERN VIRGINIA, 1861

From Lossing, *Pictorial History of the Civil War*

midnight, intending to have a good night's sleep. About half an hour after I shut up my tent a colonel in command of a detachment some fifteen miles distant came to report, so I received him in bed, and fell asleep about six times during the three hours I was talking with him. Finally, however, he left, and I alternately slept and froze until seven o'clock. This morning I sent Bates on an expedition and raked up a couple of horse-blankets, by the aid of which I hope hereafter to be reasonably comfortable. . . .

BUCKHANNON, July 7, 1861.—I have been obliged to inflict some severe punishments, and I presume the papers of the Western Reserve will be hard down on me for disgracing some of their friends guilty of the small crime of burglary. I believe the army is beginning to comprehend that they have a master over them who is stern in punishing and means what he says. I fear I shall have to have some of them shot or hung; that may convince some of the particular individuals concerned that they are not in the right track exactly. . . .

July 10, ROARING CREEK.—We have occupied the important position on this line without loss. The enemy are in sight, and I am about sending out a strong armed reconnoissance to feel him and see what he is. I have been looking at their camps with my glass; they are strongly entrenched, but I think I can come the Cerro Gordo over them.

Telegram—RICH MOUNTAIN, July 12, 1861.—Have met with complete success; captured the enemy's entire camp, guns, tents, wagons, etc. Many prisoners, among whom several officers. Enemy's loss severe, ours very small. No officers lost on our side. I turned the position. All well.

July 12, BEVERLY.—Have gained a decided victory at small cost, and move on to Huttonsville to-morrow in hope of seizing the mountain-pass near that point before it is occupied in force by the enemy. If that can be done I can soon clear up the rest of the business to be done out here, and return to see you for a time at least. . . .

I had an affecting interview to-day with a poor woman whom we liberated from prison, where she had been confined for three weeks by these scoundrels merely because she was a Union woman. I enclose a flower from a bouquet the poor thing gave me.

Telegram—July 12, 1861.—Success complete. Enemy routed. Lost everything he had—guns, tents, wagons, etc. Pegram was in command. We lost but 10 killed and 35 wounded. Garnett has abandoned his camp between this and Philippi, and is in full retreat into Eastern Virginia. I hope still to cut him off. All well.

IV

*True to his boast, McClellan had thrashed "the infamous scamps";
true to his own character, he hesitated to sweep into the Shenandoah
Valley and gain a complete victory. But within a week the North suffered defeat at Bull Run, and in desperate need of an authentic hero
accepted McClellan's small success in western Virginia with overflowing gratitude. Overnight McClellan's name became a household word
and the open facts of his life were familiar to anyone who read a newspaper. Soldier and student of war in Mexico and the Crimea, inventor
of the "McClellan saddle" used by the cavalry, railroad president—
clearly here was a "man of success," the pick of the West Point crop.*

*Among those who must have felt as green with envy as they were
green at war were the "political" generals, like the bustling Benjamin
Franklin Butler of Massachusetts and the incredible Daniel E. Sickles,
who had rushed out of his Tammany Wigwam with a war whoop no
Iroquois ever had surpassed. Only one in this crowd, however, had a
stature anywhere equal to McClellan's. Already renowned as the Path-
finder after three western explorations, son-in-law of Missouri's powerful Senator Thomas Hart Benton, presidential standard-bearer for the
Republicans in 1856, John Charles Frémont ruled over the western
military department in which Grant served so obscurely. Actually,
Robert Anderson, fresh from disaster at Sumter, and William Tecumseh
Sherman, fresh from disaster at Bull Run, managed an independent
command in Kentucky, but with Frémont in St. Louis the distinction
was entirely academic. Sherman sized up the situation:*[6]

McClellan and Fremont were the two men toward whom the country looked as the great Union leaders, and toward them were streaming the newly-raised regiments of infantry and cavalry, and batteries
of artillery; nobody seeming to think of the intervening link covered
by Kentucky. While I was to make this tour, Generals Anderson and
Thomas were to go to Louisville and initiate the department. None of
us had a staff, or any of the machinery for organizing an army, and,
indeed, we had no army to organize. Anderson was empowered to
raise regiments in Kentucky, and to commission a few brigadier-generals.

At Indianapolis I found Governor Morton and all the State officials
busy in equipping and providing for the new regiments, and my object
was to divert some of them toward Kentucky; but they were called for
as fast as they were mustered in, either for the army of McClellan or

Fremont. At Springfield also I found the same general activity and zeal, Governor Yates busy in providing for his men; but these men also had been promised to Fremont. I then went on to St. Louis, where all was seeming activity, bustle, and preparation. Meeting R. M. Renick at the Planters' House (where I stopped), I inquired where I could find General Fremont. Renick said, "What do you want with General Fremont?" I said I had come to see him on business; and he added, "You don't suppose that he will see such as you?" and went on to detail all the scandal of the day: that Fremont was a great potentate, surrounded by sentries and guards; that he had a more showy court than any real king; that he kept senators, governors, and the first citizens, dancing attendance for days and weeks before granting an audience, etc.; that if I expected to see him on business, I would have to make my application in writing, and submit to a close scrutiny by his chief of staff and by his civil surroundings. Of course I laughed at all this, and renewed my simple inquiry as to where was his office, and was informed that he resided and had his office at Major Brant's new house on Chouteau Avenue. It was then late in the afternoon, and I concluded to wait till the next morning; but that night I received a dispatch from General Anderson in Louisville to hurry back, as events were pressing, and he needed me.

Accordingly, I rose early next morning before daybreak, got breakfast with the early railroad-passengers, and about sunrise was at the gate of General Fremont's headquarters. A sentinel with drawn sabre paraded up and down in front of the house. I had on my undress uniform indicating my rank, and inquired of the sentinel, "Is General Fremont up?" He answered, "I don't know." Seeing that he was a soldier by his bearing, I spoke in a sharp, emphatic voice, "Then find out." He called for the corporal of the guard, and soon a fine-looking German sergeant came, to whom I addressed the same inquiry. He in turn did not know, and I bade him find out, as I had immediate and important business with the general. The sergeant entered the house by the front-basement door, and after ten or fifteen minutes the main front-door above was slowly opened from the inside, and who should appear but my old San Francisco acquaintance Isaiah C. Woods. . . . He ushered me in hastily, closed the door, and conducted me into the office on the right of the hall. We were glad to meet, after so long and eventful an interval, and mutually inquired after our respective families and special acquaintances. I found that he was a commissioned officer, a major on duty with Fremont, and Major Eaton, now of the Paymaster's Department, was in the same office with him. I explained to them that I had come from General Anderson, and wanted to confer with General Fremont in person. Woods left me, but soon returned, said the general would see me in a very few minutes, and within ten minutes I was shown across the hall into the large parlor, where General Fremont received me very politely. We had met before, as early as 1847, in California, and I had also seen him several times when he was senator. I then in a rapid manner ran over all the points of interest in General Anderson's new sphere of action, hoped he would spare us from the new levies what troops he could, and generally act in concert with us. He told me that his first business would be to drive the rebel General Price and his army out of Missouri, when he would turn his attention down the Mississippi. He asked my opinion about the various kinds of field-artillery which manufacturers were thrusting on him, especially the then newly-invented James gun, and afterward our conversation took a wide turn about the character of the principal citizens of St. Louis, with whom I was well acquainted. . . .

Returning to the Planters' House, I heard of Beard, another Californian, a Mormon, who had the contract for the line of redoubts which Fremont had ordered to be constructed around the city, before he would take his departure for the interior of the State; and while I stood near the office-counter, I saw old Baron Steinberger, a prince among our early California adventurers, come in and look over the register. I avoided him on purpose, but his presence in St. Louis recalled the maxim, "Where the vultures are, there is a carcass close by"; and I suspected that the profitable contracts of the quartermaster, McKinstry, had drawn to St. Louis some of the most enterprising men of California. I suspect they can account for the fact that, in a very short time, Fremont fell from his high estate in Missouri, by reason of frauds, or supposed frauds, in the administration of the affairs of his command.

v

In Kentucky, Sherman fell no less heavily than Frémont, though for another cause. Yet Sherman in time staged a comeback, achieving perhaps the greatest personal triumph of the war, whereas Frémont lacked any such recuperative genius. McClellan lasted considerably longer than his St. Louis rival. From western Virginia the Napoleon in Blue went to Washington, happy to accept a new role as savior of the Union. Again, a sampling of his "private letters" becomes painfully revealing:[7]

July 30, WASHINGTON.— . . . Had to work until nearly three this morning. . . . I am getting my ideas pretty well arranged in regard to the strength of my army; it will be a very large one. I have been employed in trying to get the right kind of general officers. . . . Have been working this morning at a bill allowing me to appoint as many aides as I please from civil life and from the army. . . .

I went to the Senate to get it through, and was quite overwhelmed by the congratulations I received and the respect with which I was treated. I suppose half a dozen of the oldest made the remark I am becoming so much used to: "Why, how young you look, and yet an old soldier!". . . When I was in the Senate chamber today and found those old men flocking around me; when I afterwards stood in the library, looking over the Capitol of our great nation, and saw the crowd gathering around to stare at me, I began to feel how great the task committed to me. Oh! how sincerely I pray to God that I may be endowed with the wisdom and courage necessary to accomplish the work. Who would have thought, when we were married, that I should so soon be called upon to save my country?

Aug. 8— . . . Rose early today (having retired at three A.M.), and was pestered to death with senators, etc., and a row with Gen. Scott until about four o'clock; then crossed the river and rode beyond and along the line of pickets for some distance. Came back and had a long interview with Seward about my "pronunciamento" against Gen. Scott's policy. . . . I have scarcely slept one moment for the last three nights, knowing well that the enemy intend some movement and fully recognizing our own weakness. If Beauregard does not attack to-night I shall look upon it as a dispensation of Providence. He ought to do it. Every day strengthens me. I am leaving nothing undone to increase our force; but the old general always comes in the way. He understands nothing, appreciates nothing. . . .

Aug. 9, 1861, 1 A.M.— . . . Gen. Scott is the great obstacle. He will not comprehend the danger. I have to fight my way against him. Tomorrow the question will probably be decided by giving me absolute control independently of him. I suppose it will result in enmity on his part against me; but I have no choice. The people call upon me to save the country. I must save it, and cannot respect anything that is in the way.

I receive letter after letter, have conversation after conversation, calling on me to save the nation, alluding to the presidency, dictatorship, etc. As I hope one day to be united with you for ever in heaven, I have no such aspiration. I would cheerfully take the dictatorship and agree to lay down my life when the country is saved. I am not spoiled by my unexpected new position. I feel sure that God will give me the strength and wisdom to preserve this great nation; but I tell you, who share all my thoughts, that I have no selfish feeling in this matter. I feel that God has placed a great work in my hands. I have not sought it. I know how weak I am, but I know that I mean to do right, and I believe that God will help me and give me the wisdom I do not possess. Pray for me, that I may be able to accomplish my task, the greatest, perhaps, that any poor, weak mortal ever had to do. . . . God grant that I may bring this war to an end and be permitted to spend the rest of my days quietly with you! . . .

WASHINGTON, 16th.— . . . I am here in a terrible place: the enemy have from three to four times my force; the President, the old general, cannot or will not see the true state of affairs. Most of my troops are demoralized by the defeat at Bull Run; some regiments even mutinous. I have probably stopped that; but you see my position is not pleasant. . . . I have, I believe, made the best possible disposition of the few men under my command; will quietly await events, and, if the enemy attacks, will try to make my movements as rapid and desperate as may be. If my men will only fight I think I can thrash him, notwithstanding the disparity of numbers. As it is, I trust to God to give success to our arms, though He is not wont to aid those who refuse to aid themselves. . . . I am weary of all this. I have no ambition in the present affairs; only wish to save my country, and find the incapables around me will not permit it. They sit on the verge of the precipice, and cannot realize what they see. Their reply to everything is, "Impossible! Impossible!" They think nothing possible which is against their wishes. . . .

I had another bouquet this morning, one from the "Lady President." Mr. Lincoln came this morning to ask me to pardon a man that I had ordered to be shot, suggesting that I could give as a reason in the order that it was by request of the "Lady President.". . .

Sept. 27.— . . . He (the President) sent a carriage for me to meet him and the cabinet at Gen. Scott's office. Before we got through the general "raised a row with me." I kept cool. In the course of the conversation he very strongly intimated that we were no longer friends. I said nothing, merely looked at him and bowed. He tried to avoid me when we left, but I walked square up to him, looked him fully in the eye, extended my hand, and said, "Good-morning, Gen. Scott." He had to take my hand, and so we parted. As he threw down the glove and I took it up, I presume war is declared. So be it. I have one strong point—that I do not care one iota for my present position. . . .

[No date; Sept. 30?]—A most unhappy thing occurred last night among some of W. F. Smith's raw regiments. They three times mistook each other for the enemy and fired into each other. At least six were killed and several wounded, besides two horses were killed. It is dangerous to make night-marches on that account; but Smith's march was delayed by causes I could not foresee, and it was necessary to advance at all hazards. The manoeuvring in advance by our flanks alarmed the enemy, whose centre at Munson's and Upton's was much advanced. As soon as our pickets informed me that he had fallen back I rushed forward and seized those very important points. We now hold them in strength and have at once proceeded to fortify them. The moral effect of this advance will be great, and it will have a bad influence on the troops of the enemy. They can no longer say that they are flaunting their dirty little flag in my face, and I hope they have taken their last look at Washington. . . .

VI

McClellan was now thirty-five; Scott was seventy-five, with a record of service to his country that went back to Lundy's Lane and Niagara. A good part of what McClellan had learned about the profession of war Scott had taught him in Mexico. Robert E. Lee, for whom the war had not yet found a dynamic role, likewise was indebted to Scott. When, in a holiday mood after the firing on Sumter, Virginia seceded from the Union, Lee had resigned from the U. S. Army, and within twenty-four hours had been en route to Richmond to assume command of all the forces of the Old Dominion. The politics of war under Jefferson Davis, the soldier President, forced Lee to step down in rank and authority once Virginia joined the Confederacy. Lee could be variously described as a "headquarters general" or "military advisor to the President"; the chief requirements were enormous tact, ceaseless energy and complete selflessness. The degree to which Lee possessed these qualities astonished young Lieutenant Walter Taylor, who served on Lee's staff:[8]

. . . I have never known a man more thorough and painstaking in all that he undertook. Early at his office, punctual in meeting all engagements, methodical to an extreme in his way of despatching business, giving close attention to details—but not, as is sometimes the concomitant if not the result of this trait, neglectful of the more important matters dependent upon his decision—he seemed to address himself to the accomplishment of every task that devolved upon him in a conscientious and deliberate way, as if he himself was directly accountable to some higher power for the manner in which he performed his duty. I then discovered, too, that characteristic of him that always marked his intercourse and relations with his fellowmen—scrupulous consideration for the feelings and interests of others; the more humble the station of one from whom he received appeal or request, the more he appeared to desire to meet the demand if possible or, if impracticable, to make denial in the most considerate way, as if done with reluctance and regret.

His correspondence, necessarily heavy, was constantly a source of worry and annoyance to him. He did not enjoy writing; indeed, he wrote with labor, and nothing seemed to tax his amiability so much as the necessity for writing a lengthy official communication; but he was not satisfied unless at the close of his office hours every matter requiring prompt attention had been disposed of.

After a day's work at his office he would enjoy above all things a ride on horseback. Accompanied by one or two of his military household, he would visit some point of interest around Richmond, making the ride one of duty as well as pleasure; and no sculptor can ever reproduce in marble or bronze the picture of manly grace and beauty that became in those days so familiar to the people in and around Richmond in the person of General Lee on his favorite horse. After his return from such excursions, in the closing hours of the day, he would take the greatest pleasure in having the little girls of the neighborhood gather around him, when he would talk and joke with them in the most loving and familiar way. . . .

Far removed from Lieutenant Taylor's mind was any thought of supplying a document of possible fascination to future psychologists; yet within Lee burned fires that other men called ambition and he identi-

*fied as Christian duty. He chafed bitterly at being left in Richmond
when the issue was joined at Manassas. After McClellan's small successes in western Virginia, Lee was sent to the pro-Union mountain
fastness to avert further Confederate disasters. By August he was in
camp at Valley Mountain, whence he wrote to his wife:*[9]

. . . We are on the dividing ridge looking north down Tygart's river
valley, whose waters flow into the Monongahela and South towards the
Elk River and Greenbrier, flowing into the Kanawha. In the valley
north of us lie Huttonsville and Beverly, occupied by our invaders,
and the Rich Mountains west, scene of our former disaster, and the
Cheat Mountains east, their present stronghold, are in full view.

The mountains are beautiful, fertile to the tops, covered with the
richest sward of bluegrass and white clover, the inclosed fields waving
with the natural growth of timothy. The habitations are few and population sparse. This is magnificent grazing country, and all it needs is
labour to clear the mountain-sides of its great growth of timber. There
surely is no lack of moisture at this time. It has rained, I believe, some
portion of every day since I left Staunton. . . . I find that our old
friend, J. J. Reynolds, of West Point memory, is in command of the
troops immediately in front of us. He is a brigadier-general. You may
recollect him as the Assistant Professor of Philosophy, and he lived
in the cottage beyond the west gate, with his little, pale-faced wife. He
resigned on being retired from West Point, and was made professor of
some college in the West. Fitzhugh * was the bearer of a flag the other
day, and he recognised him. He was very polite and made kind inquiries of us all. I am told they feel very safe and very confident of
success. Their numbers are said to be large, ranging from 12,000 to
13,000, but it is impossible for me to get correct information either as
to their strength or position. Our citizens beyond this are all on their
side. Our movements seem to be rapidly communicated to them, while
theirs come to us slowly and indistinctly. I have two regiments here,
with others coming up. I think we shall shut up this road to the Central
Railroad which they strongly threaten. . . .

*In a letter three weeks later to "My Precious Daughters" Lee remained
the self-effacing "headquarters general":*

. . . It rains here all the time, literally. There has not been sun-
shine enough since my arrival to dry my clothes. Perry [a servant] is

* Fitzhugh Lee, a nephew.

my washerman, and socks and towels suffer. But the worst of the rain is that the ground has become so saturated with water that the constant travel on the roads has made them impassable, so that I cannot get up sufficient supplies for the troops to move. It is raining now. Has been all day, last night, day before, day before that, etc., etc. But we must be patient.

The rain fell on both armies, as the diary of John Beatty of the Third Ohio Volunteers attested:[10]

. . . Tonight almost the entire valley is inundated. Many tents are waist high in water, and where others stood this morning the water is ten feet deep. Two men of the Sixth Ohio are reported drowned. The water got around them before they became aware of it, and in endeavoring to escape they were swept down the stream and lost. The river seems to stretch from the base of one mountain to the other, and the whole valley is one wild scene of excitement. Wherever a spot of dry ground can be found, huge log fires are burning, and men by the dozen are grouped around them, anxiously watching the water and discussing the situation. Tents have been hastily pitched on the hills, and campfires, each with its group of men, are blazing in many places along the side of the mountain. The rain has fallen steadily all day.

The South expected Robert E. Lee, as the son of "Light-Horse Harry" Lee of Revolutionary War fame, to step forward, a ready-made thunderbolt of war. Ignored were published reports that Lee had been sent to western Virginia merely to inspect and to consult on a plan of action. Generals already there were openly insubordinate, lax, incompetent, but Lee put up with their numerous faults—still the ever patient "advisor." Scouts brought him reports of a trail by which he could reach Cheat Mountain and surprise the Union's exposed flank. The hazards were many; Lee possessed no information of the Federal strength opposing him; yet he accepted the risks. Hindsight enabled Confederate General A. L. Long to discuss the impending disaster objectively:[11]

. . . The opposing forces were at this time about equal in numbers. Loring's force was now six thousand, General Jackson's about five thousand strong. General Reynolds' force * had been increased to about eleven thousand men; of these, two thousand were on Cheat Mountain, about five thousand in position on the Lewisburg Road in front of

* Reynolds' force was Federal; Loring's and Henry Jackson's were Confederate.

General Loring. The remainder of General Reynolds' force was held in reserve near the junction of the Parkersburg turnpike and the Lewisburg road.

General Lee determined to attack on the morning of the 28th [12th] of September. The plan was that Colonel Rust should gain the rear of the Federal position by early dawn, and begin the attack. General Anderson, with two Tennessee regiments from Loring's command, was to support him; while General Jackson was to make a diversion in front. Cheat Mountain Pass being carried, General Jackson, with his whole force, was to sweep down the mountain and fall upon the rear of the other Federal position; General Donaldson, with two regiments, was to gain a favorable position for attacking the enemy on the Lewisburg road, in flank or rear; and Loring was to advance, by the main road, on the Federal front. In case of failure, Anderson and Donaldson were to rejoin Loring, and Rust was to find his way back to Jackson. The troops gained their designated positions with remarkable promptness and accuracy in point of time, considering the distance and the difficulties to be overcome.

Colonel Rust's attack on Cheat Mountain was to be the signal for the general advance of all the troops. It was anxiously expected, from early dawn, throughout the day. On every side was continuously heard, "What has become of Rust?" "Why don't he attack?" "Rust must have lost his way." The Tennesseeans, under Anderson, became so impatient that they requested to be led to the attack without waiting for Rust; but General Anderson thought that he must be governed by the letter of his instructions, and declined granting the request of his men. Thus we see a plan that offered every prospect of success come to naught by the failure of a subordinate officer to come up to the expectations of his commander. Anderson and Donaldson, finding that their situation was becoming critical—being liable to discovery, and being between two superior forces—rejoined General Loring on the 29th [13th]. On the same day, Colonel Rust reported in person his operations, which amounted to this: he heard nothing of General Anderson; his heart failed him; he passed the day watching the Federals, and then retired. When Colonel Rust rendered his report, General Lee, perceiving the deep mortification he felt at the great blunder he had committed, permitted him to rejoin his regiment. . . .

General Long's account omitted the impatient Confederates who, firing their guns as they cleaned them, alerted a Federal cavalry detachment;

or of one assaulting column that, overrunning Federal pickets, believed
exaggerated stories of overwhelming Union strength and stopped the
assault; or of one Tennesseean who declared, "Never were men more
sick of Virginia and Virginians!" Lee poured out his distress in a letter
to his wife:[12]

. . . All the attacking parties with great labour had reached their
destination, over mountains considered impassable to bodies of troops,
notwithstanding a heavy storm that set in the day before and raged all
night, in which they had to stand up till daylight. Their arms were then
unserviceable, and they in poor condition for a fierce assault against
artillery and superior numbers. After waiting till 10 o'clock for the
assault on Cheat Mountain, which did not take place, and which was
to have been the signal for the rest, they were withdrawn, and, after
waiting three days in front of the enemy, hoping he would come out of
his trenches, we returned to our position [at Valley Mountain]. I can
not tell you my regret and mortification at the untoward events that
caused the failure of the plan. I had taken every precaution to ensure
success and counted on it. But the Ruler of the Universe ruled otherwise and sent a storm to disconcert a well-laid plan, and to destroy my
hopes. We are no worse off now than before, except the disclosure of
our plan, against which they will guard. . . .

"The righteous perisheth and no man layeth it to heart, and merciful
men are taken away, none considering that the righteous is taken away
from the evil to come." May God have mercy on us all! I suppose you
are at the Hot Springs and will direct to you there. Our poor sick, I
know, suffer much. They bring it on themselves by not doing what they
are told. They are worse than children, for the latter can be forced.

Robert E. Lee, failure—yet was he? More than any other general of
the war, Lee baffled the British. They had grown up believing it was
impossible to apply Christian principles to war. Lee contradicted
that dictum. Moreover, in the British estimate, Lee should have been
doomed by the sheer "want of authority" that he displayed in the
mountains of western Virginia. Instead, like Grant, he bided his time.
He became the war and the Cause for the South in the end. How?
Why? Major General J. F. C. Fuller, a perceptive British military au-
thority, tried to find the key to the Lee who would one day handle the
great Army of Northern Virginia as though it were a "divine instru-
ment" entrusted to his care by God:[13]

What this bootless, ragged, half-starved army accomplished is one of the miracles of history. It was led by a saint, it was endowed with the sanctity of its cause, and yet had its leader been more of a general and less of a saint, even if this had filched from it a little of its enthusiasm, its hardships would have been vastly reduced. Its spiritual morale was of the highest, its discipline of the lowest. It was full of young men full of life and quarrels, men who needed some show of severity to curb their discordant spirits. "Army of Northern Virginia, fabulous army," cried Stephen Vincent Benét:

"Strange army of ragged individualists,
The hunters, the riders, the walkers, the savage pastorals,
The unmachined, the men come out of the ground,
Still, for the most part, living close to the ground
As the roots of the cow-pea, the roots of the jessamine,
The lazy scorners, the rebels against the wheels,
The rebels against the steel combustion chamber
Of the half-born new age of engines and metal hands."

Physically such an army was beyond Lee's control. He could not be severe, he could not punish, he could only accept blame himself and shame it into some sort of discipline—set it an example. He sought discomfort, as once upon a time a Christian saint sought his hair shirt. Lord Wolseley informs us that his headquarters "consisted of about seven or eight pole-tents, pitched with their backs to a stake fence, upon a piece of ground so rocky that it was unpleasant to ride over it. . . . In front of the tents were some three four-wheeled wagons, drawn up without any regularity, and a number of horses roamed loose about the field. . . . No guard or sentries were to be seen in the vicinity; no crowd of aides-de-camp loitering about, making themselves agreeable to visitors. . . . A large farmhouse stands close by, which, in any other army, would have been the general's residence *pro tem.*; but, as no liberties are allowed to be taken with personal property, in Lee's army, he is particular in setting a good example himself. His staff are crowded together, two or three in a tent; none are allowed to carry more baggage than a small box each, and his own kit is but very little larger." The covering of the commander-in-chief was the same as that of the private soldier, his food generally inferior, as all dainties were sent to the sick and wounded; for as his nephew Edward Lee Childe tells us: "His guiding principle was that of setting his officers an example of not faring better than their soldiers."

That his example did influence his army is beyond doubt—it sanctified it and him; yet its discipline remained beneath contempt. Towards
it he acted like a soft-hearted father; he was its exalted leader, its high
priest, but not its general. "Colonel," he said to an officer who begged
for a visit, "a dirty camp gives me nausea. If you say your camps are
clean, I will go." A normal general would not have avoided dirty
camps, but would have sought them out, so that the officers in charge
might suffer for their uncleanliness. But Lee was not a normal general;
in place of the hot word he relied upon the half-disguised censure. He
was always tolerant, even when tolerance was little short of criminal.
"His one great aim and endeavor," writes Colonel Taylor, "was to
secure success for the cause in which he was enlisted; all else was
made subordinate to this." The cause was God's: who was he then to
judge the soldiers of the Almighty?

*Reading the black-and-white record of the war without intimate feeling
for its native connotations, the British often failed to realize how much
of the South was dominated by frontier manners and customs. In
large part Lee's troops, like the troops under Grant and Sherman, represented a democracy of individualists joined in a common enterprise
by their own consent and on their own terms. That fact may have been
the essence of their brotherhood; and the essence also of General
Fuller's puzzlement over Lee's warm relationship with Jackson, who
was individualism carried to infinity:*

Taylor says: "If Lee was the Jove of the war, Stonewall Jackson
was his thunderbolt." Jackson, though he believed in the omnipotence
of God as fervently as Lee did, could demand the impossible. "Did you
order me to advance over that field, sir?" said an officer to him. "Yes,"
answered Jackson. "Impossible, sir! My men will be annihilated!
Nothing can live there. They will be annihilated!" "General," replied
Jackson, "I always endeavour to take care of my wounded and to bury
my dead. You have heard my order—obey it."

Without Jackson, Lee was left a one-armed pugilist. Jackson possessed that brutality essential in war; Lee did not. He could clasp the
hand of a wounded enemy, whilst Jackson ground his teeth and mur-
mured: "No quarter to the violators of our homes and firesides," and
when someone deplored the necessity of destroying so many brave
men, he exclaimed: "No, shoot them all, I do not wish them to be
brave." With all his ability there was something repellent about Jack-

son; in spite of his many faults there was always something ennobling about Lee. Jackson was the Old Testament of War, Lee—the New.

VII

Lee, a failure in western Virginia; Grant, a kind of military wanderer in Missouri; McClellan, a headstrong idol in Washington; and Frémont, a virtual potentate in St. Louis—what did it all mean? Possibly these portraits signify nothing more than the fact that the generals all had much to learn, including how to use the new weapons soon to be placed in their hands; and they all had much to unlearn, including the still prevalent notion that it was cowardly to fight in trenches. They all had to adjust to new ideas about war as a social and political phenomenon— to telegraph operators linking Washington and Richmond to remote outposts, to newspaper reporters snooping out secrets and photographers lugging tons of equipment over roads clogged with marching men, to entertainers from the city roaming their camps and politicians like Governor Yates of Illinois arriving with a barrel of whisky to give the home town boys a treat, to female nurses and doctors snorting that death from the frying pan was the deadliest peril, to sutlers and cotton speculators and runaway slaves and hungry civilians. Growth became the mark of a man finally—growth in the qualities of survival: faith and zeal, courage and imagination, steadfastness of character and honesty of intellect. The one who seemed the poorest of the lot for a time—Sherman—came to know his trade so well that he emerged as one of the shrewdest military critics of his time:[14]

. . . I never saw the rear of an army engaged in battle but I feared that some calamity had happened at the front—the apparent confusion, broken wagons, crippled horses, men lying about dead and maimed, parties hastening to and fro in seeming disorder, and a general apprehension of something dreadful about to ensue; all these signs, however, lessened as I neared the front, and there the contrast was complete—perfect order, men and horses full of confidence, and it was not unusual for general hilarity, laughing, and cheering. Although cannon might be firing, the musketry clattering, and the enemy's shot hitting close, there reigned a general feeling of strength and security that bore a marked contrast to the bloody signs that had drifted rapidly to the rear; therefore, for comfort and safety, I surely would rather be at the front than the rear line of battle. So also on the march, the head of a column moves on steadily, while the rear is alternately halting and then rushing forward to close up the gap; and all sorts of rumors, especially the worst, float back to the rear. Old troops invariably deem it a special privilege to be in the front—to be at the "head of column"—because experience has taught them that it is the easiest and most comfortable place, and danger only adds zest and stimulus to this fact.

The hardest task in war is to lie in support of some position or battery, under fire without the privilege of returning it; or to guard some train left in the rear, within hearing but out of danger; or to provide for the wounded and dead of some corps which is too busy ahead to care for its own.

To be at the head of a strong column of troops, in the execution of some task that requires brain, is the highest pleasure of war—a grim one and terrible, but which leaves on the mind and memory the strongest mark; to detect the weak point of an enemy's line; to break through with vehemence and thus lead to victory; or to discover some keypoint and hold it with tenacity; or to do some other distinct act which is afterward recognized as the real cause of success. These all become matters that are never forgotten. Other great difficulties, experienced by every general, are to measure truly the thousand-and-one reports that come to him in the midst of conflict; to preserve a clear and well-defined purpose at every instant of time, and to cause all efforts to converge to that end.

To do these things he must know perfectly the strength and quality of each part of his own army, as well as that of his opponent, and must be where he can personally see and observe with his own eyes, and judge with his own mind. No man can properly command an army from the rear, he must be "at its front"; and when a detachment is made, the commander thereof should be informed of the object to be accomplished, and left as free as possible to execute it in his own way; and when an army is divided up into several parts, the superior should always attend that one which he regards as most important. Some men think that modern armies may be so regulated that a general can sit in an office and play on his several columns as on the keys of a piano; this is a fearful mistake. The directing mind must be at the very head of the army—must be seen there, and the effect of his mind and personal energy must be felt by every officer and man present with it, to secure the best results. Every attempt to make war easy and safe will result in humiliation and disaster. . . .

Generals sometimes dropped like flies beside their troops in this war; it became ultimately (and rather quickly) everybody's war, fought in over ten thousand places, and death had never been so democratic. The mystery it contained would one day be revealed when Grant stood before the nation as "the uncommon Common Man"; when the legend of the "Noble Lee" was supported by volumes of testimony; when Sherman as "Uncle Billy" became the idol of western armies; and when Jackson as the "Mighty Stonewall" seemed as vengeful as the predatory eagle, the national symbol. That the war had deeply religious undertones was vigorously disputed—but not by Lee, addressing his army after a crushing setback:[15]

Soldiers! we have sinned against Almighty God. We have forgotten His signal mercies, and have cultivated a revengeful, haughty, and boastful spirit. We have not remembered that the defenders of a just cause should be pure in His eyes; that "our times are in His hands"; and we have relied too much on our own arms for the achievement of our independence. God is our only refuge and our strength. Let us humble ourselves before Him. Let us confess our many sins, and beseech Him to give us a higher courage, a purer patriotism, and more determined will; that He will convert the hearts of our enemies; that He will hasten the time when war, with its sorrows and sufferings, shall cease, and that He will give us a name and place among the nations of the earth.

CHAPTER 7

GRASS FIRES

W ASHINGTON'S DISTRESS and Richmond's elation following the bloodletting at Bull Run began to dim before the sobering arguments over what, if anything, either side had won or lost. Insofar as Beauregard had been forced to share with Joseph E. Johnston such laurels as had been garnered on the field at Manassas, Beauregard became the first of the new Napoleons upon whom the shadows of history descended. Frémont's turn was coming soon, brought on by his own confusion over where military and civilian authority divided; and before the year closed even the jaunty McClellan would be disillusioned by the shifting breezes of popular sentiment.

Meanwhile for the average American this brothers' quarrel remained a half-truth, a vague reality. War letters home, garbled accounts in the newspapers supplied him with impressions rather than facts. If he lived near the borders of Missouri or Virginia, then he had some real sense of personal peril; and if he lived in Washington or Richmond his viewpoint was distorted by military personnel overrunning those seats of civilian government. If one had a son or husband in the army, wherever that son or husband was momentarily stationed became the apex of the war. Otherwise American attitudes generally were shaped by previous political prejudices, by local social pressures, or by the very personal experience of whether a pound of coffee was easy to come by.

A man of the prairies might have guessed wherein the true danger rested. Summer storms gathered quickly over the prairies; the vivid flashes of lightning, the wind moaning and roaring across the plain, the sudden interludes of intense, dark silence all bore an uncomfortable resemblance to a hurricane at sea. Then a dull copperish hue began to tinge the sky; to east, to west grass fires flamed and crackled; an hour later they were joined in a rolling wave of blood-colored destruction, and prairie wolves howled and prairie hens fluttered wildly.

During the hot, dry summer of 1861, the grass fires of the nation's storms in Missouri and Virginia were so widely separated that no one could guess their potential power. Other fires were so remote that even their presence was known to only a few. Less than a week after Bull Run a Confederate force under Colonel John R. Baylor swept down on Forts Fillmore and San Augustine in New Mexico and captured four hundred men belonging to the Seventh U. S. Infantry and Third U. S. Mounted Rifles. Already Rebel agents circulated among the Indian tribes, stirring up a witch's brew destined to spill over all the territories. When a regiment of Choctaw Indians joined the Confederate forces in western Virginia, Richmond papers announced gaily: SCALPERS ARRIVE.

Wilson's Creek and Belmont in Missouri—here clearly the nation's grass fires cast their blood color upon the sky.

I

Nowhere did the emotions of North and South meet more intimately than in Missouri. Neighborhoods, even households, split between secessionists and Unionists. Leader of the pro-Southerners was Governor Claiborne F. Jackson, who had supported the presidential aspirations of Stephen A. Douglas for the sound reason that "to have opposed him would have defeated his own election"—or so believed Colonel Thomas L. Snead, semiofficial historian of Missouri rebels. The dynamic force behind the Unionists in Missouri was Congressman Francis P. Blair, brother of Lincoln's Postmaster General, and even Colonel Snead admired "the courage, moderation and tact" with which Blair prevented a state convention, called in February by Jackson, from placing Missouri "unequivocally on the side of the South."

The Missouri story, filled with burning passions and bold intrigues, has frontier sinew. Nothing in Virginia yet equaled it. With storm clouds gathering over Sumter, Blair worried over the sixty-thousand stand of arms and the abundance of munitions in the United States Arsenal in St. Louis. It was no secret that secessionists drooled at the thought of them; and it was no secret that when Governor Jackson conferred with General Daniel M. Frost, then in command of a brigade of state militia, the conversation did not deal with saving the Union. After Lincoln's call for seventy-five thousand militia, Jackson played his hand. The President's act was "illegal, unconstitutional and revolutionary . . . inhuman and diabolical . . . an unholy crusade." From the Rebel side Colonel Snead, at various times an aide-de-camp to Jackson, spoke with authority:[1]

In the consultation with Frost it had been decided that the Governor, in pursuance of an existing law of the State, should order all its militia into encampment for the purpose of drill and discipline; and that, under cover of this order, Frost should camp his brigade upon the hills adjacent to and commanding the arsenal, so that when the opportunity occurred he might seize it and all its stores. A great difficulty in the way of the execution of this plan was the want of siege-guns and mortars. To remove this difficulty the Governor sent Captains Colton Greene and Basil W. Duke to Montgomery, Alabama, and Judge Cooke to Virginia to obtain these things. By Mr. Davis's order the arms were turned over to Duke and Greene at Baton Rouge, and were by them taken to St. Louis. Before they arrived there, however, the scheme to seize the arsenal had been completely frustrated by its commandant, Captain Nathaniel Lyon, who distributed a part of the coveted arms to Blair's Home Guards and removed the rest to Illinois, and then occupied with his own troops the hills around the arsenal. Frost consequently established Camp Jackson in a grove in the western part of the city, remote from the arsenal, and was drilling and disciplining his men there in conformity to the laws of the State and under the flag of the Union, when Jefferson Davis's gift to Missouri was taken into the camp.

Blair and Lyon, to whom every detail of the Governor's scheme had been made known, had been waiting for this opportunity. They had made up their minds to capture the camp and to hold the officers and men as prisoners of war. Frost went into camp on the 6th of May. The arms from the Confederacy were taken thither on the 8th. On Saturday, the 11th, the camp was to break up. Lyon had no time to lose. On Thursday he attired himself in a dress and shawl and other apparel of Blair's mother-in-law, Mrs. Alexander, and having completed his disguise by hiding his red beard and weather-beaten features under a thickly veiled sunbonnet, took on his arm a basket, filled, not with eggs, but with loaded revolvers, got into a barouche belonging to Blair's brother-in-law, Franklin A. Dick, and was driven out to Camp Jackson and through it. Returning to the city, he called the Union Safety Committee together, and informed them that he intended to capture the camp the next day. Some of the committee objected, but Blair and James O. Broadhead sustained him, and he ordered his men to be in readiness to move in the morning. Just as they were about to march, Colonel John S. Bowen came to Lyon with a protest from Frost. Lyon refused to receive it, and, marching out to the camp with about 7000 men, surrounded it and demanded its surrender. Frost, who had only 635 men, was obliged to comply.

While the surrender was taking place a great crowd of people, among whom were U. S. Grant and W. T. Sherman,* hurried to the scene. Most of the crowd sympathized with the prisoners, and some gave expression to their indignation. One of Lyon's German regiments thereupon opened fire upon them, and twenty-eight men, women, and children were killed. The prisoners were then marched to the arsenal, and paroled the next day.

The capture of Camp Jackson and the bloody scenes that followed —the shooting down then and the next day of unoffending men, women, and children—aroused the State. The General Assembly, which had reconvened in extra session, enacted instantly a law for organizing, arming, and equipping the Missouri State Guard, created a military fund, and conferred dictatorial power upon the Governor.

Hardly less important than these things—for it was what gave effect to them all—was the fact that the capture of the camp caused ex-Governor Sterling Price, President of the State Convention, and up to that time a Union man, to tender his services to the Governor. The General Assembly forthwith authorized the Governor to appoint a major-general to command all the forces which the State might put into the field, and Price was appointed to that position.

Colonel Snead stretched history—on both days Lyon fired only after mob attacks. Nor did Snead remark on the "Davis Avenue" and "Beauregard Street" that crisscrossed Frost's camp. Not that Lyon, a West Pointer, needed much urging—this fighting gamecock was devoted to the Union, Lincoln and Blair. He fought Rebels as he did Indians, believing that death purified their spirits. When General William S. Harney, in command in St. Louis, displayed a conciliatory attitude toward the Jackson element, Blair and Lyon greased the skids

* Grant, at this time mustering in regiments for the State of Illinois, had given himself a vacation in St. Louis. Sherman, sulking, still headed a St. Louis street railway.

for his departure. Now in exclusive command of a Federal force of about two thousand, Lyon marched on Jefferson City, found that Jackson had fled to Booneville and caught up with him there on June 17. Colonel Snead admitted that Lyon had outmaneuvered the rebels:[2]

From a military standpoint the affair at Booneville was a very insignificant thing, but it did in fact deal a stunning blow to the Southern-rights men of Missouri, and one which weakened the Confederacy during all of its brief existence. It was indeed the consummation of Blair's statesmanlike scheme to make it impossible for Missouri to secede, or out of her great resources to contribute liberally of men and material to the South, as she would have done could her people have had their own way. It was also the most brilliant achievement of Lyon's well-conceived campaign. The capture of Camp Jackson had disarmed the State, and completed the conquest of St. Louis and all the adjacent counties. The advance upon Jefferson City had put the State government to flight and taken away from the Governor the prestige which sustains established and acknowledged authority. The dispersion of the volunteers that were flocking to Booneville to fight under Price for Missouri and the South extended Lyon's conquest at once to the borders of Iowa, closed all the avenues by which the Southern men of North Missouri could get to Price and Jackson, made the Missouri River a Federal highway from its source to its mouth, and put an end to Price's hope of holding the rich and friendly counties in the vicinity of Lexington till the Confederacy could send an army to his support, and arms and supplies for the men whom he was concentrating there.

Price had, indeed, no alternative now but to retreat in all haste to the south-western part of the State, so as to organize his army within supporting distance of the force which McCulloch was assembling in western Arkansas for the protection of that State and the Indian Territory. He accordingly ordered Brigadier-General James S. Rains to take command of the militia at and near Lexington, and to move southward so as to effect a junction with the Governor in the vicinity of Lamar. . . . General Price himself, accompanied by his staff and a small escort, hastened rapidly toward Arkansas in order to bring McCulloch to the rescue of both the Governor and Rains. On the way he was joined, almost daily, by squads or companies, and by the time he reached Cowskin Prairie, in the extreme south-western corner of the State, he had collected about 1200 men.

War spread over southwestern Missouri. Federal forces under T. W. Sweeney and Franz Sigel were sent to intercept Jackson's retreat toward Arkansas. In a spirited battle at Carthage, although outnumbered four to one, that "damn Dutchman" Sigel, a pigheaded German who even refused to drink beer, retreated in perfect order. Jackson joined the bellicose Republican backslider Price at Cowskin Prairie, and another Rebel force under Ben McCulloch camped near Maysville,

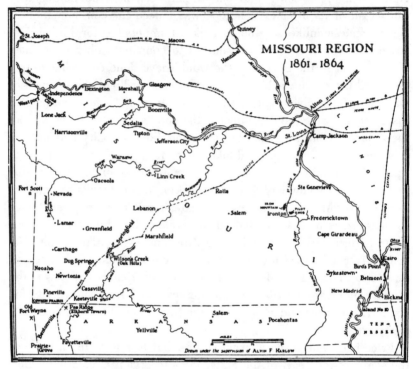

THE MISSOURI REGION, 1861–1864
From *Atlas of American History*

Arkansas. Lyon quit Booneville, called up regulars and Kansas volunteers under Major Samuel Sturgis, and reached Springfield on July 13. Colonel Snead drew a picture of a guerrilla camp where frontiersmen and backwoodsmen were whipped into soldiers:[3]

Lyon, on the one hand, and Price on the other now began to get their armies in readiness for active operations. For Lyon this was a simple undertaking; for Price it was one of great complexity and great difficulty. Of the 7000 or 8000 men that he had, only a few had been organized into regiments. Several thousand of them had no arms of any kind. The rest were for the most part armed with the shot-guns and rifles which they had brought from their homes. Of powder and lead they had an abundance, but no fixed ammunition for either their seven pieces of artillery or for their small-arms. Tents they had none, nor camp equipage of any kind. There were no quartermasters' supplies, nor subsistence; and neither the quartermaster-general nor the chief commissary had a dollar of funds. The men were not fighting for pay, they wanted none, nor did they get any; but they and their thousands of horses and mules had to be fed. For their animals there was nothing but the grass of the prairies, and for themselves nothing but a scant supply of lean beef and coarse corn-meal. There were enough good officers to organize and command the men; but it would have puzzled almost any one to drill a company of raw recruits, armed, some with shot-guns, some with rifles, a few with old-fashioned flint-lock muskets, and here and there a man with a percussion musket.

No better proof could be given of the dearth of material for the Staff, than the fact that I was myself assigned to duty by General Price as chief of ordnance of the army, though I told him at the time that I did not know the difference between a howitzer and a siege-gun, and had never seen a musket-cartridge in all my life; and a few days later I was assigned to the still more important position of acting Adjutant-General of the State Guard, though I had never then heard of a "morning report," and did not know the right of a company from its left. Had Hardee or any other West Pointer been in command, he would have kept us in camp six months, drilling and disciplining us, getting together wagons and teams, tents and cartridge-boxes, uniforms and haversacks, quartermasters and red tape, and all the other equipments and *impedimenta* of an army in the field, and then we would have gone into winter quarters; Lyon would have had his own way in Missouri, and the Federal armies that were sent thither to whip us would have been sent to fight in Virginia or in Tennessee instead, and the Confederacy might have been vanquished sooner than it was.

But Price had us all ready for the field in less than three weeks. We had no tents, it is true, but tents would only have been in our way; we had no uniforms, but a bit of flannel or calico fastened to the shoulder of an officer designated his rank sufficiently for all practical purposes; the ripening corn-fields were our depots of subsistence; the prairies furnished forage, and the people in defense of whose homes we were eager to fight gladly gave us of all their stores.

McCulloch, one of the bravest of men and best of scouts, looking at us through the eyes of the young army officers whom Mr. Davis had sent to teach him how to organize, equip, and fight an army scientifically, saw in the Missourians nothing but a half-armed mob, led by an ignorant old militia general, but he consented to go with Price in search of Lyon, who was at Springfield and not hard to find. General N. B. Pearce, commanding a brigade of Arkansas State troops, agreed to go along with them.

Hardee, who was at Pitman's Ferry, Arkansas, within a few hundred yards of the Missouri line, and almost as near to Springfield as were Price and McCulloch, and who had with him several thousand good soldiers, was begged by both Price and McCulloch to coöperate in the movement against Lyon, but he replied that he "did not wish to march to their assistance with less than 5000 men, well appointed, and a full complement of artillery"!

By order of General Polk, made at the earnest personal solicitation of Governor Jackson, who had gone to Memphis for that purpose, General Pillow moved into Missouri from Tennessee, with twelve thousand men, and occupied New Madrid on the 28th of July, with the intent to unite in the effort to repossess the State.

On the same day, Price, McCulloch, and Pearce, relying upon the coöperation of both Hardee and Pillow, concentrated their forces at Cassville, within about fifty miles of Springfield. There Price was reenforced by General McBride's command, consisting of two regiments of foot and three companies of mounted men, about 700 in all. They had come from the hill country lying to the south and south-east of Springfield, and were a unique body of soldiers. Very few of the officers had any knowledge whatever of military principles or practices, and only the most superficial experience in company tactics. The Staff was composed chiefly of country lawyers who took the ways of the court-room with them into the field. Colonels could not drill their regiments, nor captains their companies; a drum and a fife—the only ones in the entire command—sounded all the calls, and companies were paraded by the sergeant's calling out, "Oh, yes! Oh, yes! all you who belong to Captain Brown's company fall in here." Officers and men messed together, and all approached McBride without a salute, lounged around his quarters, listened to all that was said, and when they spoke to him called him "Jedge." Their only arms were the rifles with which they hunted the squirrels and other small game that abounded in their woods, but these they knew how to use. A powder-horn, a cap-pouch, "a string of patchin'," and a hunter's knife completed their equipment. I doubt whether among them all there was a man that had ever seen a piece of artillery.

But, for all this, they were brave and intelligent. Like all frontiersmen, they were shrewd, quick-witted, wary, cunning, and ready for all emergencies, and like all backwoodsmen, their courage was serene, steady, unconscious. While there was no attempt at military discipline, and no pretense of it, the most perfect order was maintained by McBride's mere force of character, by his great good sense, and by the kindness with which he exercised his patriarchal authority.

Leaving Cassville on the 31st of July, the combined Southern armies, nearly 11,000 strong, advanced toward Springfield. On the way they encountered Lyon, who had come out to meet them. McCulloch, who could not comprehend the Missourians or the able soldier who commanded them, refused to attack unless Price and Pearce would confer upon him the chief command. Price had been a brigadier-general in Mexico, when McCulloch was but a captain of scouts, and had won more battles there than McCulloch had ever witnessed; he was now a major-general with more than 5000 men, and McCulloch had barely 3000; and in intellect, in experience, and in generalship he was worth a dozen McCullochs; nevertheless, he cheerfully placed himself and his army under the Texan's command.

The order to advance was then given. Lyon had been encamped six miles in front with between 5000 and 6000 men. McCulloch moved at midnight, hoping to fall upon him unexpectedly, and to defeat him. To his amazement he learned on approaching the spot, that Lyon had left twenty hours before, and must now be almost in sight of Springfield. The Confederates kept on, and on the 6th of August went into camp on Wilson's Creek, within ten miles of Springfield. They were still lying there on the morning of the 10th of August, when they were surprised and suddenly attacked on the north by Lyon, and on the south by Sigel.

II

Even more surprised at the battle than the Confederates was Frémont in St. Louis:[4]

Before my arrival at St. Louis General Lyon had borne a decisive and important part in Missouri. Together with Francis P. Blair, the younger, he had saved Missouri from secession. For this reason I had left his movements to his own discretion, but had myself made every possible effort to reënforce him. The defeat at Bull Run had made a change in affairs from that which was existing when General Lyon left Booneville for Springfield on the 5th of July. To any other officer in his actual situation, I should have issued peremptory orders to fall back upon the railroad at Rolla.

On the 6th I had sent an officer by special engine to Rolla, with dispatches for Lyon, and for news of him. In his letter of August 9th, the day before the battle, Lyon states, in answer to mine of the 6th, that he was unable to determine whether he could maintain his ground or would have to retire. At a council of war a fortnight before the battle, the opinion of his officers was unanimous for retreating upon Rolla.

According to the New York Tribune, Colonel T. W. Sweeney had swayed Lyon's counselors against retreat, insisting that unless they stayed where they were, "the enemy would be flushed and boastful over such an easy conquest" and the Unionists in Missouri "crushed or estranged from us." Shoes, arriving from Rolla, were distributed to the troops; at one o'clock on the morning of August 10 Lyon marched his boys to battle and struck at about daylight. Surprise favored Lyon, then the Rebs rallied and superior numbers began to tell. It was a blazing battle straight through, and the New York Tribune captured its highest moment of drama:[5]

Up to this time Gen. Lyon had received two wounds, and had his fine dappled gray shot dead under him, which is sufficient evidence that he had sought no place of safety for himself while he placed his men in danger. Indeed, he had already unwisely exposed himself. Seeing blood upon his hat, I inquired, "General, are you badly hurt?" to which he replied, "I think not seriously." He had mounted another horse and was as busily engaged as ever. The Iowa First, under Lieutenant-Colonel Merritt, and part of the Kansas troops were now ordered forward to take the place of the Missouris. The former had all along the march been "gay and happy," passing the time with songs which were frequently joined in by the entire regiment, making together a chorus which could be heard for miles, and Gen. Lyon had often remarked that they had too much levity to do good fighting.

Mutual friends suggested that they ought at least to have an opportunity to show themselves in case of an engagement, and many argued that they would fight the better from keeping in good spirits. Gen. Lyon at one time replied, "Yes, I will give them an opportunity, but very much fear they will disgrace themselves." When they now came up to the front it was in splendid order and with a firm tread. The Missouri First had been almost overpowered, were almost exhausted from the severe fighting in which they had been engaged for over two hours, and had they not been relieved, must soon have fallen before the fourth body of fresh troops brought against them. The Iowas and Kansans now came upon the stage of action, and right well did they fight. The former fought like tigers, stood firm as trees, and saved us from utter and overwhelming defeat.

Gen. Lyon saw their indomitable perseverance and bravery, and with almost his last breath praised their behavior in glowing terms. Major Porter was all along the line, cheering his men forward, even when bullets fell like hail, and scores were dropping all around him. . . . Lying down close to the brow of the hill, they waited for another attempt of the enemy to retake their position. On they came, in overwhelming numbers. Not a breath was heard among the Iowas till their enemies came within thirty-five or forty feet, when they poured the contents of their Minié muskets into the enemy, and routed them, though suffering terribly themselves at the same time. Two Kansas companies afterward did the same thing on the eastern slope, and repulsed a vigorous attack of the enemy.

Lyon now desired the men to prepare to make a bayonet charge immediately after delivering their next fire, and the Iowas at once offered to go, and asked for a leader. On came the enemy. No time could be lost to select a leader. "I will lead you," exclaimed Lyon. "Come on, brave men," and with an unnatural glare in his eyes he had about placed himself in the van of the Iowas while Gen. Sweeney took a similar position to lead on a portion of the Kansas troops, when the enemy came only near enough to discharge their pieces, and retired before the destructive fire of our men.

Before the galling fire from the enemy fell the brave Gen. Lyon. An hour earlier, when the enemy had nearly regained the heights from which the Missouri, Iowa, and Kansas Volunteers had partially expelled them, when Lieut.-Col. Andrews had been wounded and his horse killed under him, when Col. Deitzler and Col. Mitchell of the two Kansas regiments had both been disabled from wounds, when the General had lost his own horse and received two wounds himself, he exclaimed wildly to his Adjutant, Major Schofield, that the day was lost, but the Major said "No, let us try once again." So the General gave orders to rally the men into line without reference to regiments, for the latter were so thoroughly cut to pieces as to make it an impossibility to get half of any one regiment together.

With Lyon's death—"He lies dead in a Springfield funeral parlor, dressed in his new uniform which he never wore in life," eulogized reporter Thomas Wallace Knox—the command fell on Sturgis, who wrote a spirited official report:[6]

. . . Our brave little army was scattered and broken; over 20,000 men were still in our front, and our men had had no water since 5 o'clock the evening before, and could hope for none short of Springfield, twelve miles distant; if we should go forward, our own success would prove our certain defeat in the end; if we retreated, disaster stared us in the face; our ammunition was well nigh exhausted, and should the enemy make this discovery through a slackening of our fire, total annihilation was all we could expect.

The great question in my mind was, "Where is Sigel?" If I could still hope for a vigorous attack by him on the enemy's right flank or rear, then we could go forward with some hope of success. If he had retreated, there was nothing left for us also. In this perplexing condition of affairs I summoned the principal officers for consultation. The great question with most of them was, "Is retreat possible?" The consultation was brought to a close by the advance of a heavy column of infantry from the hill, where Sigel's guns had been heard before.

Thinking they were Sigel's men, a line was formed for an advance, with the hope of forming a junction with him. These troops wore a dress much resembling that of Sigel's brigade, and carried the American flag. They were therefore permitted to move down the hill within easy range of Dubois' battery, until they had reached the covered position at the foot of the ridge on which we were posted, and from which we had been fiercely assailed before, when suddenly a battery was planted on the hill in our front, and began to pour upon us shrapnel and canister—a species of shot not before fired by the enemy. At this moment, the enemy showed his true colors, and at once commenced along our entire lines the fiercest and most bloody engagement of the day. . . .

The enemy could frequently be seen within twenty feet of Totten's guns, and the smoke of the opposing lines was often so confounded as to seem but one. Now, for the first time during the day, our entire line maintained its position with perfect firmness. Not the slightest disposition to give way was manifested at any point, and while Capt. Steele's battalion, which was some yards in front of the line, together with the troops on the right and left, were in imminent danger of being overwhelmed by superior numbers, the contending lines being almost muzzle to muzzle, Capt. Granger rushed to the rear and brought up the supports of Dubois' battery, consisting of two or three companies of the First Missouri, three companies of the First Kansas, and two companies of the First Iowa, in quick time, and fell upon the enemy's right flank, and poured into it a murderous volley, killing or wounding nearly every man within sixty or seventy yards. From this moment a perfect rout took place throughout the rebel front, while ours on the right flank continued to pour a galling fire into their disorganized masses. . . .

The order to retreat was given soon after the enemy gave way from our front and centre, Lieut. Dubois' battery having been previously sent to occupy with its supports the hill in our rear. Capt. Totten's battery, as soon as his disabled horses could be replaced, retired slowly with the main body of the infantry, while Capt. Steele was meeting the demonstrations upon our right flank. This having been repulsed, and no enemy being in sight, the whole column moved slowly to the high open prairie, about two miles from the battle-ground; meanwhile our ambulances passed to and fro, carrying off our wounded. After making a short halt on the prairie, we continued our march to Springfield.

It should be here remembered that, just after the order to retire was given, and while it was undecided whether the retreat should be continued, or whether we should occupy the more favorable position of our rear, and await tidings of Col. Sigel, one of his non-commissioned officers arrived, and reported that the Colonel's brigade had been totally routed, and all his artillery captured, Col. Sigel himself having been either killed or made prisoner. Most of our men had fired away all their ammunition, and all that could be obtained from the boxes of the killed and wounded. Nothing, therefore, was left to do but to return to Springfield, where two hundred and fifty Home Guards, with two pieces of artillery, had been left to take care of the train.

From Wilson's Creek Albert D. Richardson of the New York Tribune and the hard-drinking Franc Wilkie, in Missouri to report the war for the Dubuque Herald, clopped through seventy miles of Ozark foothills;

*by daylight they reached the log tavern at Lebanon, washed down
breakfast with a shot of whisky, then pushed on through bushwhacker
country to Rolla, whence they caught the cars to St. Louis. No war in
history had been so well reported! Jolting to St. Louis, Richardson gave
his Eastern readers the truth:*[7]

Gen. Sigel, upon hearing the battle opened by Gen. Lyon, at once
began the work on his side. He had already taken sixty prisoners, who,
with several wagons, were engaged on farms in the vicinity of the camp
digging potatoes, picking and roasting ears of corn, gathering to-
matoes and other vegetables for the rebel commissary department.
Sigel advanced upon the enemy without being seen, taking their pickets
prisoners except one, who was driven away from the camp, and drove
their force from their south-eastern camp, chasing them up as far as
the Fayetteville road. Here he was met by a regiment uniformed very
much like the Iowa First, coming over the summit from the northwest,
and supposing it was the latter men, allowed them to come within a few
paces of him, when they poured a murderous fire into his ranks and
scattered his men like sheep.

The enemy's cannon, also, now began against him, killing the horses
attached to his own six pieces, and he was forced to retire leaving
them behind. Capt. Flagg, seeing the position of affairs, took ropes,
fastened them to one cannon and placed them in the hands of his
prisoners, compelling them to draw the cannon off the field. One caisson also was saved, and another tipped into the creek. The others fell
into the hands of the enemy.

The cause of Sigel's repulse was owing very much to the behavior of
Col. Salomon's men, who were three months' men whose time had
expired, and who, at request, had agreed to serve ten days longer. At
the first severe fire, those, who in Carthage had fought like veterans,
began to lament that they had lengthened their time of service, and
wished they were with their families at home. Such men as these could
not be brought up to fight well against overwhelming numbers, and
their dissatisfaction communicated itself to many of Sigel's regiment.
Notwithstanding these very adverse circumstances, Sigel brought in
about one hundred prisoners and many horses.

*Union forces had been badly whipped, for all the cheerful tone Rich-
ardson gave his report. Of 5,400 Federals engaged, 223 were killed,
721 wounded, 291 missing; Confederate effectives numbered 11,600*

with 257 killed, 900 wounded and 27 missing. Southwestern Missouri had been cleared of "Northern scum," boasted the New Orleans Picayune, *losing its head completely:*

. . . The next word will be: On to St. Louis! That taken, the power of Lincolnism is broken in the whole West; and instead of shouting Ho! for Richmond! and Ho! for New Orleans! there will be hurryings to and fro among the frightened magnates at Washington, and anxious inquiries of what they shall do to save themselves from the vengeance to come. Good tidings reach us from the North and the West. Heaven smiles on the arms of the Confederate States; and through the brightly-beaming vistas of these battles we see golden promises of the speedy triumph of a righteous cause—in the firm establishment of Southern independence.

III

Athens and Potosi, Brunswick and Bird's Point—these were towns, hamlets, crossroads in Missouri where Confederate guerrillas struck. No single engagement amounted to much; together, these skirmishes stood for effective harassment. Frémont's answer to these hit-and-run raids came on August 30 in a proclamation that invoked martial law, confiscated the property of all Missourians in arms against the national government, and emancipated their slaves. Antislavery radicals rejoiced, but Lincoln instantly recognized the dangers. Frémont's edict would outrage border-state loyalists and convince a great many Northern Democrats that they had been tricked into supporting a war for the wrong purpose. Tactfully the President wrote Frémont:[8]

Private and confidential.

MAJOR GENERAL FRÉMONT:

WASHINGTON, D. C. Sept. 2, 1861

MY DEAR SIR: Two points in your proclamation of August 30th give me some anxiety. First, should you shoot a man, according to the proclamation, the Confederates would very certainly shoot our best man in their hands in retaliation; and so, man for man, indefinitely. It is therefore my order that you allow no man to be shot, under the proclamation, without first having my approbation or consent.

Secondly, I think there is great danger that the closing paragraph, in relation to the confiscation of property, and the liberating slaves of traitorous owners, will alarm our Southern Union friends, and turn them against us—perhaps ruin our rather fair prospect for Kentucky. Allow me therefore to ask, that you will as of your own motion, modify that paragraph so as to conform to the *first* and *fourth* sections of the act of Congress, entitled, "An act to confiscate property used for insurrectionary purposes," approved August, 6th, 1861, and a copy of which act I herewith send you. This letter is written in a spirit of caution and not of censure.

I send it by a special messenger, in order that it may certainly and speedily reach you. Yours very truly A. LINCOLN

Frémont replied that he would not change his proclamation "or shade it," insisting that "it was equal to a victory in the field." Mrs. Frémont brought this response to Washington, demanded an audience with the President, and hinted broadly that Mr. Lincoln should think twice before courting her husband's open opposition. Mr. Lincoln thought twice, then modified the order. The antislavery press erupted. Senator Grimes of Iowa called Frémont's edict "the only noble and true thing done during the war," and Senator Sumner of Massachusetts sneered how "vain" it became for Lincoln "to have the power of God and not use it godlike." When the President received a protest from his old friend, Senator Orville H. Browning, of Quincy, Illinois, his patience snapped. A tart letter instructed Browning in politics and the democratic process:[9]

Yours of the 17th is just received; and coming from you, I confess it astonishes me. That you should object to my adhering to a law, which you had assisted in making, and presenting to me, less than a month before, is odd enough. But this is a very small part. Genl. Fremont's proclamation, as to confiscation of property, and the liberation of slaves, is *purely political,* and not within the range of *military* law, or necessity. If a commanding General finds a necessity to seize the farm of a private owner, for a pasture, an encampment, or a fortification, he has the right to do so, and to so hold it, as long as the necessity lasts; and this is within military law, because within military necessity. But to say the farm shall no longer belong to the owner, or his heirs forever; and this as well when the farm is not needed for military purposes as when it is, is purely political, without the savor of military law about it. And the same is true of slaves. If the General needs them, he can seize them and use them; but when the need is past, it is not for him to fix their permanent future condition. That must be settled according to laws made by law-makers, and not by military proclamations. The proclamation in the point in question, is simply "dictatorship." It assumes that the general may do *anything* he pleases—confiscate the lands and free the slaves of *loyal* people, as well as of disloyal ones. And going the whole figure I have no doubt would be more popular with some thoughtless people, than that which has been done! But I cannot assume this reckless position; nor allow others to assume it on my responsibility. You speak of it as being the only means of *saving* the government. On the contrary it is itself the surrender of the government. Can it be pretended that it is any longer the government of the U. S.—any government of Constitution and laws,—wherein a General, or a President, may make permanent rules of property by proclamation?

I do not say Congress might not with propriety pass a law, on the point, just such as General Fremont proclaimed. I do not say I might not, as a member of Congress, vote for it. What I object to, is, that I as President, shall expressly or impliedly seize and exercise the permanent legislative functions of the government.

So much as to principle. Now as to policy. No doubt the thing was popular in some quarters, and would have been more so if it had been a general declaration of emancipation. The Kentucky Legislature would not budge till that proclamation was modified; and Gen. Anderson telegraphed me that on the news of Gen. Fremont having actually issued deeds of manumission, a whole company of our Volunteers threw down their arms and disbanded. I was so assured, as to think it probable, that the very arms we had furnished Kentucky would be turned against us. I think to lose Kentucky is nearly the same as to lose the whole game. Kentucky gone, we can not hold Missouri, nor, as I think, Maryland. These all against us, and the job on our hands is too large for us. We would as well consent to separation at once, including the surrender of this capitol. On the contrary, if you will give up your restlessness for new positions, and back me manfully on the grounds upon which you and other kind friends gave me the election, and have approved in my public documents, we shall go through triumphantly.

You must not understand I took my course on the proclamation *because* of Kentucky. I took the same ground in a private letter to General Fremont before I heard from Kentucky.

You think I am inconsistent because I did not also forbid Gen. Fremont to shoot men under the proclamation. I understand that part to be within military law; but I also think, and so privately wrote Gen.

Fremont, that it is impolitic in this, that our adversaries have the power, and will certainly exercise it, to shoot as many of our men as we shoot of theirs. I did not say this in the public letter, because it is a subject I prefer not to discuss in the hearing of our enemies.

IV

Mr. Lincoln had sound reason for concern over Kentucky. Early in September Confederate forces under Leonidas Polk, an Episcopal bishop turned general, occupied Columbus. Exactly what Polk was doing here, Richmond could not understand, but the bishop, who may have been obeying orders from a higher authority, insisted that he had acted upon "the necessity." Richmond allowed him to stay, and, tracing a line across the state of Kentucky from Columbus through Bowling Green to the Cumberland Gap, Confederate strategists exchanged the fiction of neutrality for the reality of a promising defensive line. Polk created another opportunity in an unexpected quarter. He gave Grant his chance.

This was more than Frémont had done. From the time Grant assumed his first command at Ironton, Missouri—where he functioned without a staff, without artillerymen to fire his cannon, and with horses that were mostly "barefoot"—his chief occupation seemed to be planning battles for other generals to fight. Successive commands at Jefferson City, Missouri, and Cairo, Illinois, found him "laboriously employed" in administrative detail, while his father ranted to neighbor and Congressman that 'Lyss's military talents were being wasted. Polk occupied Columbus almost simultaneously with the arrival of Grant's bright new stars as a brigadier general; as if to celebrate, Grant slipped under the nose of the bishop and seized Paducah, gateway to the Cumberland and Tennessee rivers. Frémont blustered that Grant had acted without specific orders. Angered by Lincoln's modification of his proclamation, tormented by another rash of guerrilla raids, and threatened by Price back in control of Lexington, Frémont never guessed that in Grant he held a bear by the tail. In early November, Frémont advanced against Price and ordered Grant to make a demonstration to hold Polk's forces in Columbus. Grant fought his first real battle:[10]

CAIRO,
November 8th, 1861

DEAR FATHER:

It is late at night and I want to get a letter into the mail for you before it closes. . . .

Day before yesterday, I left here with about 3000 men in five steamers, convoyed by two gun boats, and proceeded down the river to within twelve miles of Columbus. The next morning the boats were dropped down just out of range of the enemy's batteries and the troops debarked.

During this operation our gun boats exercised the rebels by throwing shells into their camps and batteries.

When all ready we proceeded about one mile towards Belmont opposite Columbus; then I formed the troops into line, and ordered two companies from each regiment to deploy as skirmishers, and push on through the woods and discover the position of the enemy. They had gone but a little way when they were fired upon, and the *ball* may be said to have fairly opened.

The whole command with the exception of a small reserve, was then deployed in like manner with the first, and ordered forward. The order was obeyed with great alacrity, the men all showing great courage. I can say with gratification that every Colonel without a single exception, set an example to his command that inspired a confidence that will always insure victory when there is the slightest possibility of gaining one. I feel truly proud to command such men. From here we fought our way from tree to tree through the woods to Belmont, about two and a half miles, the enemy contesting every foot of ground. Here the enemy had strengthened their position by felling the trees for two or three hundred yards and sharpening the limbs, making a sort of abatis. Our men charged through making the victory complete, giving us possession of their camp and garrison equipage, artillery and everything else.

We got a great many prisoners. The majority however succeeded in getting aboard their steamer and pushing across the river.

We burned everything possible and started back, having accomplished all that we went for and even more. Belmont is entirely covered by the batteries from Columbus and is worth nothing as a military position. It cannot be held without Columbus.

The object of the expedition was to prevent the enemy from sending a force into Missouri to cut off troops I had sent there for a special purpose, and to prevent reinforcing Price.

Besides being well fortified at Columbus their numbers far exceed ours, and it would have been folly to have attacked them. We found the Confederates well-armed and brave. On our return, stragglers that had been left in our rear, *now front*, fired into us, and more recrossed the river and gave us battle for fully a mile and afterwards at the boats when we were embarking. There was no hasty retreating or running away. Taking into account the object of the expedition the victory was most complete. It has given me a confidence in the officers and men of this command, that will enable me to lead them in any future engagement without fear of the result. General McClernand—who by the way acted with great coolness throughout, and proved that he is a soldier as well as statesman—and myself each had our horses shot under us. Most of the field-officers met with the same loss, besides nearly one third of them being killed or wounded themselves. As nearly as I can ascertain our loss was about 250 killed, wounded, and missing. . . .

U. S. GRANT

In his Memoirs—*secure in the distinguished military reputation which that day took its first toddling steps—Grant put another face on the affair at Belmont:*[11]

. . . The moment the camp was reached our men laid down their arms and commenced rummaging the tents to pick up trophies. Some of the higher officers were little better than the privates. They galloped about from one cluster of men to another and at every halt delivered a short eulogy upon the Union cause and the achievements of the command.

All this time the troops we had been engaged with for four hours, lay crouched under cover of the river bank, ready to come up and surrender if summoned to do so; but finding that they were not pursued, they worked their way up the river and came up on the bank between us and our transports. I saw at the same time two steamers coming from the Columbus side towards the west shore, above us, black—or gray— with soldiers from boiler-deck to roof. Some of my men were engaged in firing from captured guns at empty steamers down the river, out of range, cheering at every shot.

I tried to get them to turn their guns upon the loaded steamers above and not so far away. My efforts were in vain. At last I directed my staff officers to set fire to the camps. This drew the fire of the enemy's guns located on the heights of Columbus. They had abstained from firing before, probably because they were afraid of hitting their own men; or they may have supposed, until the camp was on fire, that it was still in the possession of their friends. About this time, too, the men we had driven over the bank were seen in line up the river between us and our transports. The alarm "surrounded" was given. The guns of the enemy and the report of being surrounded, brought officers and men completely under control.

At first some of the officers seemed to think that to be surrounded was to be placed in a hopeless position, where there was nothing to do but surrender. But when I announced that we had cut our way in and could cut our way out just as well, it seemed a new revelation to officers and soldiers. They formed line rapidly and we started back to our boats, with the men deployed as skirmishers as they had been on entering camp. The enemy was soon encountered, but his resistance this time was feeble. Again the Confederates sought shelter under the river banks. We could not stop, however, to pick them up, because the troops we had seen crossing the river had debarked by this time and were nearer our transports than we were. It would be prudent to get them behind us; but we were not again molested on our way to the boats. . . .

Confederate Lunsford P. Yandell gave his family another version of Belmont as "the battle swayed back and forth many times":[12]

. . . Once our men were driven clear under the river bank, having got out of cartridges. For several hours General Pillow held the enemy in check with two thousand men, the enemy having seven thousand infantry, four hundred and fifty cavalry, and I don't recollect their artillery. Pillow acted with great bravery. So did Polk and Cheatham, but they were not in the fight for several hours after Pillow. Pillow's escape is miraculous. Every one of his staff officers had his horse shot under him. One of them, Gus. Henry, had two shot under him. One of his aids was shot through the hip, and his horse was riddled with balls. Pillow wore a splendid uniform, very conspicuous, and rode the handsomest gray mare in the army. As we watched the fighting from the bluff, and saw our men advance and retreat, waver and fall back, and then saw the Arkansas troops' tents on fire, and the Stars and Stripes advancing toward the river, and some of our men crowding down to the very water's edge, I tell you my feelings were indescribable. The scene was grand, but it was terrible, and when I closed my eyes about four o'clock next morning, I could see regiments charging and retreating— men falling and yelling—horses and men torn and mangled—and myriads of horrid spectacles. It was a bloody enjoyment, but we do not know the loss on either side yet.

It is roughly estimated that we lost two hundred and fifty in killed, wounded, and missing, and the enemy five hundred in killed and wounded. An immense number of horses were killed. I rode over the battle-field yesterday. For several miles the trees are torn and barked by balls, and many horses lie upon the ground, some torn open by shells and others riddled by balls. You can see innumerable stains of blood upon the ground. Where poor, gallant Armstrong was killed, there were eleven dead bodies. At the time of his death, he had a cap upon his sword waving it, rallying his men. My friend Captain Billy Jackson was shot in the hip while leading a portion of Russell's brigade. I think he will recover. I am afraid Jimmy Walker (James' son) will not recover. I think he is shot through the rectum.

. . . I have given you but a poor account of what I saw, but I have not time to go more into details now, and I am out of kelter besides. You will see a full account in the papers of the fight. I wish the war would close. Such scenes as that of Thursday are sickening; and this destruction of life is so useless. . . .

v

Belmont in 1861 consisted of three shanties stuck in the Missouri mud; it is remembered today because Grant fought there. But what of West Liberty, Kentucky? It, too, knew a stark day of war:[13]

Col. Len. Harris, with his regiment, Second Ohio, two guns of Capt. Konkles' Ohio battery, and Capt. Laughlin's Cavalry, set out at three o'clock Tuesday afternoon of last week, from a point thirty-six miles this side of West Liberty, for a march upon that town, intending to surprise it at daylight the following morning [stated the Cincinnati *Commercial*]. It was reported that the rebels, several hundred strong, were advantageously posted in the neighborhood of West Liberty, which is situated on the head waters of the Licking River, is the county seat of Morgan County, and thirty-five miles from Prestonburg, the headquarters of the rebels in Eastern Kentucky.

The gallant boys of the Ohio Second pressed forward with great spirit and vigor, but a heavy rain came up and fell for six hours without intermission, making the roads so bad as to cause detention. The men toiled forward steadily all night, wading the Licking River—the water up to their belts—three times. At eight o'clock Wednesday morning they had marched thirty-six miles, and the bushwhackers of the enemy, posted on a rocky hillside and in a corn-field, opened fire upon the advance, doing no injury, as they were in manifest trepidation.

Col. Harris saw that the fight was to be a mere skirmish, and that the first thing to be done was to clean the enemy out of the bushes. Giving directions to the artillery (one gun had been left behind, owing to the wretched condition of the roads, and there was but one on the spot) to send a few shells into the town, and a suspicious neck of the woods, the colonel gave his horse in charge of a servant, and went into the bushes with his flank companies, which were armed with Enfield rifles. They had a very exciting hunt after the rebels, who were popped over in all directions and driven like a flock of frightened animals through the bushes and fields.

The captain says Col. Harris and his men returned from this rebel hunt covered all over with burrs and Spanish needles. Not one of the boys was so much as scratched by an enemy's ball, though they had killed seventeen rebels, most of whom were men living in that vicinity. There was no mistake about the killing, for coffins have been the articles most in demand since that time in the little town of West Liberty. Three well-known citizens of the town were killed, and another, the leading secesh of the place, was seen running away, his right arm dangling as if it had been shattered by a rifle ball. . . . The rebels were terrified at the bombshells sent screeching through the woods, and fled as if they had discovered the devil suddenly on a dark night. There was a party of cavalry—a motley array—drawn up near the Court House. A shell howled up the street and exploded near them. The captain shouted, "Disperse!" and there was a wild scamper.

One fellow, well mounted and armed with a good rifle, lingered behind, and fired with deliberate aim at Col. Harris, as the latter rode into the town. He, luckily, missed his aim. The moment he fired he put his horse to the top of his speed to make his escape, but a volley was fired after him, and he fell headlong. On coming up with him, he was found stretched in the road insensible. A close examination of his person disclosed the fact that, though his clothes had been cut in several places by balls, the only wound was a bullet hole through his right hand. The fellow was secured.

The town was deserted by its inhabitants, only a few negroes remaining behind. The people had been taught that the Union soldiers would be guilty of most awful atrocities. Several women made their appearance on Thursday; trembling with cold and fear, and said that they had remained in the woods all night after the fight. They were afraid they would be ill-used if they were in the power of the Union soldiers, and were greatly surprised and gratified to learn that they had been mistaken. The poor creatures had been told by the secesh that the Abolition troops rejoiced to kill Southern babies and were in the habit of carrying little children about on their bayonets in the towns which they took; and this was actually believed. . . .

CHAPTER 8

THE MANY FACES
OF WAR

Offices of newspapers antagonistic to the Lincoln Administration were sacked by angry mobs in New Haven, Connecticut, and in Concord, New Hampshire. Runaway slaves were jailed in Washington. In Charleston the *Mercury* launched a series of attacks upon the policies of Jefferson Davis. Among items disappearing from Southern households were candles and oil. Rumors of slave insurrection persisted over a wide area. A clergyman in Boston told his congregation to think of the Stars and Stripes as nailed to the Cross, for Christ and the Union were inseparable. In Webster, Massachusetts, troops en route to camps along the Potomac kissed all the girls in town. Pritchard's Mills in Maryland, Hanging Rock in West Virginia, Santa Rosa in Florida, Wet Glaze, Shawnee Mound and Salem in Missouri, Fort Hatteras and Port Royal in the Carolinas, Galveston Harbor in Texas, Ball's Bluff, Pohick Church and Drainesville in Virginia—these were new place names in the war news.

Clearly, a war wore many faces. Where next its grim visage would appear no one could say with assurance. Mr. Lincoln's blockade had given the British government some legal excuse for recognizing the Confederacy as a belligerent; the British policy of neutrality was largely a diplomatic dodge, insisted many who should have been well informed; and alone of the great European powers Britain neglected to send to the Washington government a friendly note hoping for the speedy restoration of national harmony. Against this tense background Charles Francis Adams arrived at the Court of St. James's to carry on the quarrels with the British ministers which, in the phrase of son Henry, had been "the only public occupation of all the Adamses for a hundred and fifty years at least." Before the end of November America added to the complexities of civil strife the unwanted peril of a war with Great Britain.

I

A big, loose country was fighting a big, loose war. To give the struggle reason and pattern became Lincoln's chief concern. During the early fall he wrote down his meditations:[1]

Memorandum for a PLAN of Campaign
[c. October 1, 1861]

On, or about the 5th. of October, (the exact day to be determined hereafter) I wish a movement made to seize and hold a point on the Railroad connecting Virginia and Tennessee, near the Mountain pass called Cumberland Gap.

That point is now guarded against us by Zolicoffer, with 6000 or 8000, rebels at Barboursville, Kentucky, say twentyfive miles from the Gap towards Lexington.

We have a force of 5000 or 6000, under General Thomas, at Camp Dick Robinson, about twentyfive miles from Lexington, and seventyfive from Zollicoffer's camp on the road between the two, which is not a Railroad, anywhere between Lexington and the point to be seized— and along the whole length of which the Union sentiment among the people largely predominates.

We have military possession of the Railroads from Cincinnati to Lexington, and from Louisville to Lexington, and some Home Guards under General Crittenden are on the latter line.

We have possession of the Railroad from Louisville to Nashville, Tenn, so far as Muldraugh's Hill, about forty miles, and the rebels have possession of that road all South of there. At the Hill we have a force of 8000 under Gen. Sherman; and about an equal force of rebels is a very short distance South, under Gen. Buckner.

We have a large force at Paducah, and a smaller at Fort-Holt, both on the Kentucky side, with some at Bird's Point, Cairo, Mound City, Evansville, & New-Albany, all on the other side; and all which, with the Gun-Boats on the River, are, perhaps, sufficient to guard the Ohio from Louisville to it's mouth.

About supplies of troops, my general idea is that all from Wisconsin,

Minesota, Iowa, Illinois, Missouri, and Kansas, not now elsewhere, be left to *Fremont*.

All from Indiana and Michigan, not now elsewhere, be sent to Anderson at Louisville.

All from Ohio, needed in Western Virginia be sent there; and any remainder, be sent to Mitchell at Cincinnati, for Anderson.

All East of the Mountains be appropriated to McClellan, and to the coast.

As to movements, my idea is that the one for the coast, and that on Cumberland Gap be simultaneous; and that, in the mean time, preparation, vigilant watching, and the defensive only be acted upon—(this however, not to apply to Fremonts operations in Northern and middle Missouri)—that before these movements, Thomas and Sherman shall respectively watch, but not attack Zollicoffer, and Buckner.

That when the coast and Gap movements shall be ready, Sherman is merely to stand fast; while all at Cincinnati, and all at Louisville with all on the lines, concentrate rapidly at Lexington, and thence to Thomas' camp joining him, and the whole thence upon the Gap.

It is for the Military men to decide whether they can find a pass through the mountains at or near the Gap, which can not be defended by the enemy, with a greatly inferior force, and what is to be done in regard to this.

The Coast and Gap movements made, Generals McClellan and Fremont, in their respective Departments, will avail themselves of any advantages the diversions may present.

II

Mr. Lincoln had suggested a movement against the coast. On October 19, 1861, the steam frigate Wabash, *Flag Officer Samuel F. Du Pont commanding, left New York harbor. A number of sloops of war and four ninety-day gunboats—so called since by contract they must be built within that time—followed the* Wabash. *Transports carrying troops under General Thomas W. Sherman joined the fleet at Hampton Roads off Old Point Comfort, Virginia. Approaching the Atlantic graveyard off Cape Hatteras, one hundred miles to the south, Daniel Ammen, executive officer of the North Atlantic blockading squadron, expected the worst:*[2]

. . . There are few nights in the year when lightning cannot be seen from the top of the lighthouse, usually to seaward over the Gulf

Stream, which here approaches nearer to the coast than at any other point. An ocean depth of 2,000 fathoms or more stretches almost in a direct line from the low sand islands east of Nassau to within a distance of 12 miles of the cape; from the shore the water deepens very rapidly to 100 fathoms, and then falls abruptly to a depth of 2,500 fathoms. This great depth, so near the land, and the Gulf Stream sweeping even nearer, are the probable causes of the sudden and violent changes of the weather there prevailing. . . .

On rounding the cape, the wind rose, the sea became heavy, a dull

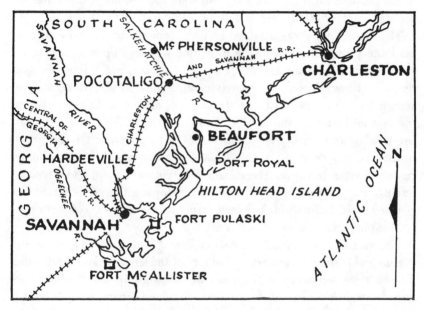

PORT ROYAL AND VICINITY

leaden sky shut out the light, and not long after midday there were assurances of a south-east gale. About 2:30 P.M. the weather was so rough that signal was made from the flag-ship to commanders of vessels to disregard the order of sailing and take care of their individual commands.

In order to make the best of our way, and the better to avoid collisions with other vessels of the fleet, the *Seneca* was kept on the port tack, and "hove to," barely turning the engines, the vessel being under close-reefed fore and main sails. Had she been square-rigged, the other tack would have been necessary to her safety. In the drifting mists and rain, it soon grew dark. The greater part of that night I stood under the

lee of the weather bulwark, near the wheel, casting glances to windward, to be in readiness to bear away should a vessel be seen coming
down upon us. It was a long, weary, and anxious night. On peering to
windward, the rain-drops pelted the face like sleet, and the phosphorescent spray broke over us in superlative grandeur. At 3 o'clock I
observed what had been an object of watchfulness—an arch rising in
the west, precursor of a sudden change of wind. The mainsail was
lowered, and when the squall struck us the foresheet was shifted over.
At 9 or 10 A.M. the gale had abated greatly, and the flag-ship was well
under our lee; we then wore ship and were soon in her wake. Later in
the day several other vessels fell into line. . . .

The *Isaac Smith* was disabled and her commander forced to throw
his battery overboard, with the exception of one 30-pounder rifle, to
enable him to go to the assistance of the *Governor*, which foundered at
sea. The *Young Rover*, fortunately coming up, was able to signal the
sailing frigate *Sabine* in the distance, and, after strenuous exertions,
the marine battalion and crew of the *Governor*, with the exception of
seven who were lost, were transferred to the *Sabine*. Of the army
transports, the *Peerless*, laden with stores, went down, the crew being
rescued by the *Mohican*. The steamers *Belvidere*, *Union*, and *Osceola*,
having army stores on board, but no troops, either sank or never
reached their destination. The large army transport *Winfield Scott* was
so disabled that she never left Port Royal harbor after entering.

The morning of November 3d was a bright Sunday, with a moderate
breeze and a smooth sea. Several others of the small steamers with the
Seneca were following in the wake of the flag-ship. In obedience to
signal, I went on board that vessel, and received orders to be delivered
to Captain Lardner of the *Susquehanna*, the senior officer blockading
Charleston, distant about thirty miles. These directed certain vessels
to rendezvous off Port Royal entrance, but not to leave the line of
blockade until after nightfall. No sooner was the *Seneca* fairly in sight
of Sumter than the signal guns were fired, to announce the arrival of
the *avant-courier* of the fleet that they knew was intended for the attack
of Port Royal. After passing Bull's Bay, I had the belief that we were
bound for Port Royal, but no actual knowledge of the fact until going
on board of the *Wabash*, as my orders were marked "Confidential—
not to be opened unless separated from the flag-ship." At the very instant we were weathering the gale, the following telegram was sent:

"RICHMOND, Nov. 1, '61. GOV. PICKENS, S. C. I have just received
information, which I consider entirely reliable, that the enemy's ex-

pedition is intended for Port Royal. J. P. BENJAMIN, *Acting Secretary of War.*"

Robert E. Lee now was back in Richmond after his unhappy adventure in western Virginia. Except for Jefferson Davis the general seemed not to have a devoted supporter in the Confederate capital; even the chatty Mrs. Chesnut joined in the gossip about Lee: "So far his bonnie face has only brought us ill luck." Lee, homesick, was looking up the schedules of river steamers when a summons came to report to the War Office. The President handed him a new assignment: He commanded now the Department of South Carolina, Georgia and Florida. The railroad station nearest Port Royal was Coosawhatchie, South Carolina. From there, amid wild rumors that Forts Walker and Beauregard were taking the worst of a vicious duel with Du Pont's fleet, Lee galloped off on horseback. He saw the disaster; Ammen, aboard the Wabash, with the hatches battened down, beheld the "grand view":[3]

. . . A faint light only came from the ports, as did the flashes from the discharged guns, which recoiled violently with a heavy thud. As far as the smoke would permit, hundreds of men were visible in rapid motion, loading and running out the guns with the greatest energy. Such a view, accompanied by the noise of battle, is weird and impressive to the highest degree.

The vessels in the main line slowly passed toward the sea, throwing their shells into the earth-work with the utmost precision, and this destruction was supplemented by the fire of ten of the vessels from an enfilading position. . . .

At 1:15 the *Ottawa* signaled that the enemy was leaving the fort [Walker], and fifteen minutes later the same signal was made by the *Pembina.* . . . Two pivot guns fired from the flag-ship received no response, and signal was made to cease firing. Captain John Rodgers, who was serving as aide to the flag-officer, was sent on shore with a flag of truce. On landing he found no garrison, and at 2:20 P.M. hoisted the Union flag over the fort. When that honored emblem appeared, the rigging was manned in an instant on board the flag-ship and on all the vessels of war at anchor; three cheers were wafted over the waters, so loud that they startled the defenders of Fort Beauregard. . . .

III

Port Royal fell on November 7 and Lee was confronted, in his own words, with "another forlorn hope expedition." The vital seaports of

Charleston and Savannah were now dangerously exposed and Lee, somehow, was expected to defend the Confederacy's entire Atlantic coastline with four wooden steamers, each mounting two guns, and fewer than seven thousand troops. On this same day Grant fought at Belmont, starting up the long, steep road to military renown. And perhaps that day Mrs. McClellan read a letter from her husband, raised now to supreme command in the East, who recently had parted company with an old antagonist:[4]

Nov. 3.—I have already been up once this morning—that was at four o'clock to escort Gen. Scott to the depot. It was pitch-dark and a pouring rain; but with most of my staff and a squadron of cavalry I saw the old man off. He was very polite to me; sent various kind messages to you and the baby; so we parted. The old man said that his sensations were very peculiar in leaving Washington and active life. I can easily understand them; and it may be that at some distant day I, too, shall totter away from Washington, a worn-out soldier, with naught to do but make my peace with God. The sight of this morning was a lesson to me which I hope not soon to forget. I saw there the end of a long, active, and ambitious life, the end of the career of the first soldier of his nation; and it was a feeble old man scarce able to walk; hardly any one there to see him off but his successor. Should I ever become vainglorious and ambitious, remind me of that spectacle. I pray every night and every morning that I may become neither vain nor ambitious, that I may be neither depressed by disaster nor elated by success, and that I may keep one single object in view—the good of my country. At last I am the "major-general commanding the army." I do not feel in the least elated, for I do feel the responsibility of the position. And I feel the need of some support. I trust that God will aid me.

In Kentucky that same November personal disaster stalked William Tecumseh Sherman. He had begged Lincoln not to trust him with the responsibility of a command, and his lack of faith in himself was quickly shared by a growing circle of Kentuckians. Sherman despised newspaper men; he hated female nurses; he "mothered" his troops; and in his hallucinations over nonexistent Rebel forces that were about to overwhelm him he talked like a wild man. On December 11, the Cincinnati Commercial *declared:*[5]

GENERAL WILLIAM T. SHERMAN INSANE

The painful intelligence reaches us, in such form that we are not at liberty to disclose it, that Gen. William T. Sherman, late commander of the Department of the Cumberland, is insane. It appears that he was at the time while commanding in Kentucky, stark mad. We learn that he at one time telegraphed to the War Department three times in one day for permission to evacuate Kentucky and retreat into Indiana. He also, on several occasions, frightened leading Union men of Louisville almost out of their wits by the most astounding representation of the overwhelming force of Buckner and the assertion that Louisville could not be defended. The retreat from Cumberland Gap was one of his mad freaks. When relieved of the command in Kentucky he was sent to Missouri and placed at the head of a brigade at Sedalia, when the shocking fact that he was a madman was developed by orders that his subordinates knew to be preposterous and refused to obey. He has of course been relieved altogether from command. The harsh criticisms that have been lavished on this gentleman, provoked by his strange conduct, will now give way to feelings of deepest sympathy for him in his great calamity. It seems providential that the country has not to mourn the loss of an army through the loss of mind of a general into whose hands was committed the vast responsibility of the command of Kentucky.

IV

The tempo of the war quickened. Suddenly it threatened to become a world conflict. The critical figure now was Charles Francis Adams, son of one President and grandson of another, who had arrived in London with official British policy formulated and unofficial British practice operating in anything but a straight-from-the-shoulder fashion. In Liverpool the banking firm of Fraser, Trenholm & Company, a branch of the old house of John Fraser and Company of Charleston, chartered vessels under the British flag for purposes that fooled no one; and since the outbreak of hostilities three Confederate agents—Pierre A. Rost, William L. Yancey and Ambrose D. Mann—had enjoyed a hospitable reception in England and on the Continent. Adams functioned under diplomatic difficulties such as only British eccentricity could invent. Son Henry witnessed the peculiar situation firsthand:[6]

. . . Familiar as the whole tribe of Adamses had been for three generations with the impenetrable stupidity of the British mind, and weary of the long struggle to teach it its own interests, the fourth generation could still not quite persuade itself that this new British prejudice was natural. The private secretary suspected that Americans in New York and Boston had something to do with it. The Copperhead was at home in Pall Mall. Naturally the Englishman was a coarse animal and liked coarseness. Had Lincoln and Seward been the ruffians supposed, the average Englishman would have liked them the better. The exceedingly quiet manner and the unassailable social position of Minister Adams in no way conciliated them. They chose to ignore him, since they could not ridicule him. Lord John Russell set the example. Personally the Minister was to be kindly treated; politically he was negligible; he was there to be put aside. London and Paris imitated Lord John. Every one waited to see Lincoln and his hirelings disappear in one vast *débâcle*. All conceived that the Washington Government would soon crumble, and that Minister Adams would vanish with the rest.

This situation made Minister Adams an exception among diplomats. European rulers for the most part fought and treated as members of one family, and rarely had in view the possibility of total extinction; but the Governments and society of Europe, for a year at least, regarded the Washington Government as dead, and its Ministers as nullities. Minister Adams was better received than most nullities because he made no noise. Little by little, in private, society took the habit of accepting him, not so much as a diplomat, but rather as a member of opposition, or an eminent counsel retained for a foreign Government. He was to be received and considered; to be cordially treated as, by birth and manners, one of themselves. This curiously English way of getting behind a stupidity gave the Minister every possible advantage over a European diplomat. Barriers of race, language, birth, habit, ceased to exist. Diplomacy held diplomats apart in order to save Governments, but Earl Russell could not hold Mr. Adams apart. He was undistinguishable from a Londoner. In society few Londoners were so widely at home. None had such double personality and corresponding double weight.

Charles Francis Adams quickly required every advantage of personal charm and social position that he could exert. On the day after Port Royal two additional Confederate agents—James M. Mason, bound for England, and John Slidell, en route to France—sailed from Havana aboard the Trent, *a British contract mailpacket. A Federal warship under Captain Charles Wilkes, who acted without orders, intercepted the* Trent, *removed Mason and Slidell, and carried them to an American port. The North rejoiced at Wilkes's audacity, adding insult to national affront in the British view. Benjamin Moran, a secretary of the American legation in London, revealed how close to breaking the gathering storm came:*[7]

Wed. 27 Nov. '61. . . . At about ½ past 12 this morning we received a telegram from Capt. Britton at Southampton announcing that the West India steamer at that port brought news in there this morning that Capt. Wilkes, of the U. S. Ship of War San Jacinto, had stopped the British mail steamer Trent in the Bahama Channel, not far from St. Thomas, on the 9th Inst, & had forcibly taken Mason, Slidell, Eustis, & Macfarlane [McFarland] out of her: and at 1 o'clk a telegram from Reuter confirmed the statement. That the capture of these arch-rebels gave us great satisfaction at the first blush, was natural: & we gave free vent to our exultation. But on reflection I am satisfied that the act will do more for the Southerners than ten victories, for it touches John Bull's honor, and the honor of his flag. At present the people have hardly recovered from the paralysing effect of the news; but they are beginning to see that their flag has been insulted, and if that devil *The Times*, feeds their ire to-morrow, as it assuredly will, nothing but a miracle can prevent their sympathies running to the South, and Palmerston getting up a war. We have no particulars, but from what we hear, it would seem that Capt. Wilkes acted on his own responsibility, and not on that of the Govt.

I telegraphed the news at once to Mr. Adams, and fear it has not added to his enjoyment of rural retirement. . . .

Friday, 29 Nov. 61. Mr. Adams returned to town last night. It appears he got my telegram promptly. He regards the Trent affair as serious, and is very grave about it. To-day he has been writing home concerning it, and I have had a vast deal of hard work. Earl Russell fixed quarter to two for an interview, but beyond asking a few questions about the orders of the Capt. of the James Adger, his Lordship said nothing. It is quite evident that Ministers consider the question as serious, and many of them feel very sore and hostile about it. As I was detained late, I remained to dinner. Mr. Adams expressed apprehensions that we would not be here a month and from this I suspect he has reason to believe that the people at the head of the Gov't are not altogether capable of dealing wisely with so delicate a question. We shall certainly be in an unpleasant state of mind concerning this affair for a month, or until we hear from Washington. . . .

There has been a great crowd of anxious visitors to-day, mostly Americans, to know if war will result, but we can't tell. . . .

Monday, 2 Dec. '61. There is no time for rest now. I was here nearly all day yesterday recording, and putting our accumulated documents to rights. During the morning Mr. Adams called our attention to a curious statement in the *Observer* about American *espionage* in England, in which there are some facts strangely mingled up with a great deal of speculation. From this it is quite clear to me that some person either in the Foreign Office, or Lord Palmerston's confidence, communicates facts to this *Observer,* and does the work very clumsily. . . .

Tuesday 3 Dec. '61. . . . At present the excitement in England is truly terrific. The Europa was detained at Cork or Queenstown, until last night, or this morning, to carry out an Ultimatum, and the purport of that is indicated by the London papers of yesterday and to-day. It is alleged that the Law Officers of the Crown have decided that Wilkes did not insult England enough, and the result is a demand for an apology, and the restoration of the men. By harping on this, and asserting that Capt. Wilkes' act was an authorized and deliberate insult of our Gov't, the journals have lashed the nation into a most indecent rage, and the consequence is that mob rule reigns supreme, and the natural English hatred of the American people, which is ordinarily concealed, has been allowed to gush up in its full bitterness from all hearts, high and low. This polite and calm nation is in the throes of a vulgar and coarse excitement such as one might naturally look for among a crowd of the London Fancy, but the like of which no one, not even their worst enemy, would ever expect to seize upon the inoffensive and harmless upper classes of the realm. That pink of modesty and refinement, *The Times,* is filled with such slatternly abuse of us and ours, that it is fair to conclude that all the Fishwifes of Billingsgate have been transferred to Printing House Square to fill the ears of the writers there with their choicest phraseology. There is something positively infernal in the way these assassins are goading the nation on to a war. They daily feed the public mind with the most palpable lies, & stick at nothing. If a war should follow this wicked conduct, reflecting Englishmen will blush in after years at the bigotry and blindness which hurried them into the struggle. . . .

Moran's subsequent complaint that "the mob and The Times *have the mastery," and "will drive the nation to war" is supported by two modern scholars, Donaldson Jordan and Edwin J. Pratt:*[8]

. . . The excitement was tremendous—greater, men said, than at any time in their generation. Spontaneous public meetings were held in various towns to urge the Government to take strong measures; on the streets men talked of almost nothing else; and everywhere it was assumed that this meant war. Hardly any one stopped to ask whether the American commander had by any chance been within his legal rights; hardly any one doubted that the act of Captain Wilkes had been ordered by his Government and that it was the consequence of a direct purpose to insult and defy England. The public feeling was very righteous. England had done nothing to provoke a war, but on the contrary it was being deliberately forced on her. She was assailed at two of her dearest points: freedom of the seas and the right of asylum. Both were infringed by the same deed, and reparation, ample and prompt, was required.

"Of course," said Henry Sidgwick, who in the main favored the cause of the Union, "if Seward wants a war with England, he must have it." Matthew Arnold thought the time had come when it was necessary to give the Americans a lesson. Sir George Cornewall Lewis, a member of the Cabinet and the coolest of all public men, could hardly believe that Seward really wanted war; Sir John Acton took the same point of view; and scarcely a well-known man is to be found on record who did not think that Seward desired a conflict.

If this conviction was all but universal at first, there were some who welcomed the Trent incident more heartily than others. "The Times," comparatively calm for a day or two, grew more and more belligerent as it grasped the popular trend. Its editorials called Seward a reckless adventurer who could evoke at will all the wild passions of a sovereign mob, and remarked that it was very seldom possible in a polite and decorous age to "accumulate so much evidence of a deliberate and long-cherished intention to do us an injury as we are able to bring against Mr. Seward, the present Prime Minister of the Northern States of America." The "Bucks Herald," a Tory journal in Disraeli's region, rejoiced in the unanimity of English opinion, which it felt was only the proper consequence of a hostility to the North which had been of long and steady growth. "The cause is simple. . . . With the North is to be associated insolence and defiance of almost every diplomatic conventuality. . . . For years the Cabinet of Washington has left not a stone unturned to lower us in the opinion of Europe. Our forebearance has been called cowardice. . . . Now the most plausible defence cannot screen the American ministers from the charge of aiming at a rupture between our country and their own. The curtain has been drawn aside, the machinery is exposed, and we, without hesitation, pronounce that President Lincoln and his colleagues are doing their utmost to compel us to relinquish our neutrality, and by that means to bring on a European war."

Other editors were more violent still. The "Wakefield Journal and Examiner," in its only leading article of the week, said that "whatever the law of nations may be, we are certain that the law of English feeling will be that Lord Palmerston will ill sustain his ancient reputation for courage if he allow us to submit tamely to such indignity. . . . Ever since the Union of the States we have allowed the Americans to provoke, insult, and bully us. They have with impunity robbed us of our trade, our territory, and our good name. There is, however, a limit even to an Englishman's patience, and our own opinion is, that had we shown a little more determination in years gone by the present indignity would not have been offered to us. The feeling of the people of England before this happened was decidedly in favor of the Southern States, in spite of the fact that those States are mainly supported by slavery, which we have spent millions of money and oceans of blood to put down. We hope that that feeling will now be allowed to have vent, and that we shall show those Northerners that we are no longer disposed to cripple our commerce and ruin our cotton manufacture for the sake of keeping up what they are pleased to call a blockade. If France and England break the blockade, and protect our merchant ships, there will very soon be an end of the American war, for the Southerners will be able to carry it on as they have hitherto done, vigorously and effectively, and in spite of all their boast and bluster the Northerners must submit. We shall then be fully avenged for the insults they have heaped upon us."

Reports from Buckingham Palace gave Moran reason for concern— and hope:[9]

Sat. 14 Dec. '61. This morning's papers announce the serious illness of Prince Albert. This is so unexpected as to create much alarm. In fact The Times of this morning evidently regards his life in danger, and has a notice almost amounting to an obituary. He has been ill for several days, but no intimation of anything like the possibility of his death has been whispered until now. From his appearance, I shall not be astonished at his death, in case his disease should prove to be a violent fever. . . .

We are told that the Queen is opposed to a war with the United States, and that she and Prince Albert greatly modified the demands, and the tone of the despatch to our Gov't. on the Trent affair. . . .

By late December cool heads had prevailed in the United States. On the 26th Seward announced that Mason and Slidell had been "cheerfully liberated." In a letter to Cassius M. Clay, minister to Russia, Charles Francis Adams contended that the right principle had prevailed:[10]

. . . My situation has not, very certainly, been a particularly pleasant one during the continuance of the difficulty about the *Trent* even if it were tolerable at any other time. That affair has been settled, and, as I think, correctly. For whatever opinion I may have of the consistency of Great Britain, or of the temper in which she has prosecuted her latest convictions, that does not in my judgment weigh a feather in the balance against the settled policy of the United States which has uniformly condemned every and any act like that of Captain Wilkes when authorised by other nations. The extension of the rights of neutrals on the ocean and the protection of them against the arbitrary exercise of mere power have been cardinal principles in the system of American statesmen ever since the foundation of the Government. It is not for us to abandon them under the transient impulse given by the capture of a couple of unworthy traitors. What are they that a country like ours should swerve one hair from the line of its ancient policy, merely for the satisfaction of punishing them? In such a struggle they could lose nothing, for they have nothing to lose; whereas the Government of the United States might appear seriously to derogate from its dignity if on their account it were to involve itself in the necessity of disavowing the sound doctrines to which it has been heretofore pledged in order to embrace such as have become odious in the civilized world, even among the very people who were formerly the most strenuous assertors of them. . . .

V

Domestic diplomacy also occupied Mr. Lincoln. The President could not escape the slave question. The Conscription Act of August 6, 1861, freed slaves used to assist the rebellion, but what of Negroes who ran away or were abandoned by their owners? Butler's device of calling them "contraband" did not help the President. Faithful to his pledge not to attack slavery in the states, he enforced the Fugitive Slave Law. But the President knew deep in his heart that there had to be some better solution; and sometime during November his thoughts turned to the slave state of Delaware. Two plans for "compensated emancipation" for Delaware were drafted. The second, here quoted, was preferred by the President, who added his reasons:[11]

Be it enacted by the State of Delaware that on condition the United States of America will, at the present session of Congress, engage by law to pay, and thereafter faithfully pay to the said State of Delaware, in the six per cent bonds of said United States, the sum of seven hundred and nineteen thousand, and two hundred dollars, in thirty one equal annual instalments, there shall be neither slavery nor involuntary servitude, at any time after the first day of January in the year of our Lord one thousand eight hundred and ninety three, within the said State of Delaware, except in the punishment of crime, whereof the party shall have been duly convicted; nor, except in the punishment of crime as aforesaid, shall any person who shall be born after the passage of this act, nor any person above the age of thirty five years, be held in slavery, or to involuntary servitude, within said State of Delaware, at any time after the passage of this act.

And be it further enacted that said State shall, in good faith prevent, so far as possible, the carrying of any person out of said state, into involuntary servitude, beyond the limits of said State, at any time after the passage of this act.

And be it further enacted that said State may make provision of apprenticeship, not to extend beyond the age of twentyone years for males, nor eighteen for females, for all minors whose mothers were not free at the respective births of such minors.

On reflection, I like No. 2 the better. By it the Nation would pay the State $23,200 per annum for thirtyone years—and

All born after the passage of the act would be born free—and

All slaves above the age of 35 years would become free on the passage of the act—and

All others would become free on arriving at the age of 35 years, until January 1893—when

All remaining of all ages would become free, subject to apprenticeship for minors born of slave mothers, up to the respective ages of 21 and 18.

If the State would desire to have the money sooner, let the bill be altered only in fixing the time of final emancipation earlier, and making the annual instalments correspondingly fewer in number, by which they would also be correspondingly larger in amount. For instance, strike out "1893," and insert "1872"; and strike out "thirtyone" annual instalments, and insert "ten" annual instalments. The instalments would then be $71,920 instead of $23,200 as now. In all other particulars let the bill stand precisely as it is.

VI

In myriad shapes and guises America's big, fast-growing war appeared almost everywhere. Miles of tiny newspaper type were set by hand to chronicle the significant battles, the crossroads brushes, the humor of camp life, the malicious rumors. By the year's end, the war was the principal American reality for anyone who could read; it was an unfailing topic of conversation, and, like the weather, there wasn't much the average American could do about it. By flickering lamplight his eyes followed the newspaper dispatches; here are items he pasted into scrapbooks:[12]

. . . When the Tiger Rifles, who played such havoc with Lincoln's "Pet Lambs" at Manassas, on the memorable 21st July, passed through this city, we thought that we had seen a specimen of the roughest and most ferocious set of men on earth; but when we speak of the Tenth Louisiana regiment, of New Orleans, which passed through this city on Sunday, language is inadequate to give a description, composed as it was of English, French, Germans, Dutch, Italians, Sicilians, Spaniards, Portuguese, Swiss, Mexicans, Indians, and Creoles, who, in their jabbering, seemed to represent a second Babel. The commander, together with many other officers, are veterans who served throughout the Crimean war. The commands are given in French, Dutch, Spanish, or something else which we could not exactly understand, but seemed to be executed with promptness and a remarkable degree of precision. The Mexicans, particularly, were objects of much curiosity with our citizens, most of whom had never seen one before.—*Lynchburg Virginian.*

May 31.—A strange spectacle was witnessed on the Illinois River a few days ago. In tow of the Resolute, going North, was a barge on which reposed a two-story frame house. This house is the property of a man who lived in it in St. Louis. Becoming alarmed at the late commotion, he had his house moved as stated, and taken to a free State. His family went along with him. While going up the river, the man's dog sat in the door, the cat reclined lazily at a window, and the good wife carried on the household work as usual.—*N. Y. Commercial*, June 3.

ABE LINCOLN ASSASSINATED!—ARREST OF THE ASSASSIN!— GREAT EXCITEMENT

WASHINGTON, August 7, 10 A.M.—Abe Lincoln was shot through the heart last night, just as he was entering his carriage, after leaving his cabinet in consultation. The assassin, a Southerner, is now in the hands of the authorities. There is great excitement, and "On to Richmond!" is the cry.

Later—11 A.M.—Abe is still alive, but there is no chance for him to survive. The excitement here is great.

Still Later—12 M.—Abe was wounded in the abdomen and not in the heart. His physician thinks he will recover. The excitement is abating.

Later Still—1 P.M.—It is now currently reported that Abe was only slightly wounded in the leg. No excitement.

The Latest—2 P.M.—An investigation now proves that the bullet intended for Abe's heart missed its mark, and only killed one of his footmen. The people are returning to their business.

Later Still—3 P.M.—Abe's footman was not killed, as reported, but badly wounded. He will recover.

The Very Latest—4 P.M.—It has been officially announced from the capital, that Old Abe's footman was very slightly wounded in the hand by the accidental discharge of a gun which he was cleaning.

The President was not in consultation with his cabinet last night as first stated. "Nobody hurt."—*Memphis Appeal*, August 15.

Female Rebels—How to Manage Them—The Louisville *Courier* is very pathetic in speaking of a little paragraph of ours, wherein we stated that crinoline contains many a contraband article, and advised the detectives to be on the look-out. Sturdy patriotism, however, is getting to be proof against sickly pathos. It is notorious that hundreds, if not thousands of pistols, have been smuggled under the cover of crinoline into the Southern Confederacy, for the killing of citizens of the United States, and the thing should be stopped. Our neighbor appears to think that the only way to prevent contrabands from being smuggled under ladies' dresses, is to employ the great "he creatures" to search the blushing innocents. He is a greenhorn. Doesn't he know with what delicacy, and yet how effectively, these things are managed in foreign ports? If a woman, carrying under her dress deadly weapons to be used by rebels against our people, blushes at being examined in a private room by another woman, let her blush. Better that her blood should mount to her face, than that the blood of our countrymen should be shed through her crime. Smuggling pistols under female hoops is not a legitimate mode of hooping barrels.—*Louisville Journal.*

Secession of the Indian Nations—The Galveston *News,* of the 25th of June, has the following intelligence from the Indian nations:—

Mr. J. A. Echols, Secretary of the Commissioners sent by the Texas Convention to the Indian nations, returned recently. He informs us that the Chickasaw Legislature passed an act of secession by a unanimous vote about the 1st inst. A convention was to be held by the Choctaws about the 14th inst. for the same purpose, and there is no doubt that that nation has also seceded. The Creek nation had a convention about the 12th of May, but they sat with closed doors, and their action is not therefore certainly known, but as delegates to the Southern Confederacy were immediately sent, no doubt is entertained that an act of secession was passed.

Mr. Echols has brought to Austin the treaties that have been executed by commissioners on the part of Texas and the Chickasaw nation, with five wild tribes west of the civilized Indians, including the Texas Reserves. The Kickapoos, the Delawares, the Keechies, &c., bind themselves to co-operate with the Southern Confederacy in the present war with the Lincoln Government.

The slaves who run away from their masters in Virginia, are set to work at once by Gen. Butler, and made to keep at it, much to their annoyance. One of them having been put to it rather strong, said, "Golly, Massa Butler, dis nigger never had to work so hard before; guess dis chile will secede once moah."—*Ohio Statesman,* Aug. 2.

The battle-field of Bull Run is owned by George Leary, of New York, son of the famous hatter. As soon as the war is over, certain parties, with the consent of Mr. Leary, intend building an immense hotel there, to accommodate the curious, who will flock there to inspect the battlefield.—*Woonsocket Patriot,* Oct. 4.

Camp Phrases—An enterprising publisher might make money by getting up a camp dictionary for the benefit of those who visit the army, and are mystified by the extraordinary words and phrases used. The word "arms" has been distorted into "uum," brought forcibly forth like the last groan of a dying cat, and in place of "march" we hear "utch." A tent is jocularly termed "the canvas," a sword is a "toad-sticker," and any of the altered patterns of muskets are known as "howitzers." Mess beef is "salt horse," coffee is "boiled rye," vegetables are "cow feed," and butter "strong grease." "Bully" is the highest term of commendation, while dissent is expressed in the remark "I don't see it." Almost every regiment has its nickname, and few officers or privates receive their legal appellations or titles when spoken of in their absence.—*Cincinnati Commercial,* Nov. 20.

Blasted B's—The B's have swarmed upon us for some time, and are more provocative of nightmare than mince pie at ten o'clock. We had Buchanan, Breckinridge, Black, Bright, Bigler, Bayard, Benjamin, and Brown to curse the nation in the civil ranks, and now we are haunted by Bull Run, Ball's Bluff, Big Bethel, and Bull's Bay, boldly entered by our fleet, notwithstanding the ominous prestige against B's. Blast the B's. We hope they will cease to swarm on the boughs of the Tree of Liberty. We hope our fleet will make no Bull in Bull's Bay, and regret that Beaufort begins with B.—*Cleveland Plain Dealer.*

There seems to be another "blasted B" down at Belmont, Mo.

ST. LOUIS, Sept. 11—Mrs. Willow and a free colored woman named Hannah Courtena, were arrested yesterday for selling poisoned pies to the soldiers at Camp Benton.—*N. Y. World,* Sept. 12.

1862

CHAPTER 9

"ALL QUIET ON THE POTOMAC"

URING THE EARLY WINTER the weather in Virginia continued clear and mild. The roads remained hard and dry. "What is such weather *for*, if not for fighting?" an artillery officer asked Horace Greeley. The editor of the New York *Tribune* described the uneasiness and dissatisfaction that the New Year brought to the North:

"The loyal masses—awed by the obloquy heaped on those falsely accused of having caused the disaster at Bull Run by their ignorant impatience and precipitancy—stood in silent expectation. They still kept raising regiment after regiment, battery after battery, and hurrying them forward to the all-ingulfing Army of the Potomac, to be in time for the decided movement that must be just at hand—but the torrent was there drowned in a lake of Lethean stagnation. First, we were waiting for reenforcements—which was most reasonable; then, for the requisite drilling and fitting for service—which was just as helpful to the Rebels as to us; then for the leaves to fall—so as to facilitate military movements in a country so wooded and broken as Virginia; then, for cannon—whereof we had already more than 200 first-rate field-pieces in Virginia, ready for instant service; and so the long, bright Autumn, and the colder but still favorable December, wore heavily away, and saw nothing of moment attempted. Even the Rebel batteries obstructing the lower Potomac were not so much as menaced—the Navy laying the blame on the Army; the Army throwing it back on the Navy—probably both right, or, rather, both wrong; but the net result was nothing done; until the daily repetition of the stereotyped telegraphic bulletin, 'All quiet on the Potomac'—which had at first been received with satisfaction; afterward with complacency; at length evoked a broad and general roar of disdainful merriment."

I

McClellan, stricken with typhoid, ran a high fever. Many feared for his life. With drill and discipline the Army of the Potomac began to resemble an efficient military organization, yet those who visited its camps across the river from the capital often departed, as one witness said, with the impression that the army "lived its own life as if it were hundreds of miles away from Washington." The growing "nervousness of the administration and Congress, caused by the delay and the alarming sickness of General McClellan," General William B. Franklin believed, explained why he was summoned to a special meeting in the White House:[1]

On Friday evening, January 10th, 1862, I received a dispatch from the Assistant Secretary of War, informing me that the President wished to see me at eight o'clock that evening, if I could safely leave my command. I went to Washington, and arrived at the White House at eight o'clock. I was received in a small room in the northeast corner of the house, and found the President, Secretaries Seward and Chase, the Assistant Secretary of War, and General McDowell. The President was in great distress over the condition of the country. He complained that he was abused in Congress for the military inaction; that, notwithstanding the enormous amount of money which had been spent, nothing was doing East or West; that there was a general feeling of depression on account of the inaction; and that, as he expressed it, the bottom appeared to be falling out of everything. He was exceedingly sorry for the sickness of General McClellan. He was not allowed to see him to talk over military matters, and he wanted to produce some concerted action between Generals Halleck and Buell,* who did not appear to pull together. He could, of course, do nothing with the Western armies; they were out of his reach; but he thought that he could, in a very short time, do something with the Army of the Potomac, if he were allowed to have his own way, and had sent for General McDowell and me so that

* Henry W. Halleck commanded the Department of the Missouri, including the states of Missouri, Arkansas and that part of Kentucky that lay west of the Cumberland River. Don Carlos Buell commanded the Department of Ohio, including the state of Tennessee and the remaining portion of Kentucky.

he might have somebody to talk to on the subject. In fact, he wanted, he said to *borrow* the Army of the Potomac from General McClellan for a few weeks, and wanted us to help him as to how to do it. He complained of the rise of gold, of the unreasonableness of Congress, of the virulence of the press, and, in general, told us all that depressed him, in a plain, blunt way that was touching to a degree. Mr. Seward told us that an Englishman whom he had sent into the enemy's lines had returned, giving him information of the number of rebel troops at Centreville, Richmond, Norfolk, etc.; and I inferred that Johnston, who commanded at Centreville, could have raised about 75,000 men to meet any attack which we might make within a moderate time.

Mr. Chase said very little, but what he did say left it plainly to be inferred that he thought that the army ought to be moved at once. General McDowell said that, in his opinion, the army ought to be formed into army corps, and that a vigorous movement in the direction of Centreville would enable us, he thought, to get into position by which we could cut the enemy's lines of communication, and that by the use of the railroad from Alexandria, and the connection of the Baltimore and Ohio Road with those south of the river by a railroad over the Long Bridge, large wagon trains would be avoided. He, however, did not know how long a time would be required to get ready to make the movement which he advocated. I said that I was ignorant of the things necessary to enable me to form a judgment on the subject, only knowing my own division, which was ready for the field. That I thought that the proper disposition to make of the Army of the Potomac was to transport it by the easiest and quickest route to York river, to operate against Richmond, leaving force enough to prevent any danger to Washington.

The Assistant Secretary of War thought that the transportation of this force in a reasonable time would be a very difficult work. As General McDowell and I both felt too ignorant of the proper state of the supply departments to justify us in speaking any more definitely, it was determined by the President that the same party should meet on the next evening at the same time, and that General McDowell and I should in the meantime get all the information from the chiefs of the various staff departments of the Army of the Potomac, as to their status with regard to a movement of the army within a short time.

So on Saturday we met in the morning, and went to all of the chiefs of the staff departments, and obtained from them such information as to their departments as they could give us. We learned from Mr. Chase the destination of Burnside's expedition [Roanoke Island, N. C.], which, until then, had been unknown to us, and he relieved our minds as to the apparent impropriety of our obtaining information from the chiefs of the staff departments without the authority of the commanding general, by reminding us that as we were acting by the direct orders of the President, we ought to execute those orders. He also told us what was McClellan's plan of operations for the Army of the Potomac.

In the evening we again met at the White House. The party of the evening before were there with the addition of Judge Blair, the Postmaster General. General McDowell read a paper embodying our joint views, which were in substance, that if the Army of the Potomac was to be moved *at once*, it would be better to march it into Virginia than to transport it by vessels. General McDowell was, however, in favor of the immediate movement into Virginia. I was not. Just here the presence of Judge Blair was felt. He strongly opposed any movement toward Centreville at that time, denounced it as bad strategy, said that a second Bull Run would occur, and strenuously and ably advocated the movement to the Peninsula by transports. Mr. Seward and Judge Chase were of opinion that victory over the enemy was what was required, whether gained in front of Washington or further South, and that our difficulties would probably be as great on the Peninsula as they would be at Centreville. I thought that the President, who said little, was much impressed by what Judge Blair said, and he adjourned the meeting until three o'clock the next day, directing General McDowell and myself to see the Quartermaster General in the meantime as to water transportation for the army.

Quartermaster General Montgomery Meigs told McDowell and Franklin that a month or six weeks would be required to collect the necessary water transportation for a movement of the army. At three o'clock on Sunday afternoon they returned to the White House. Hard on their heels came the Secretary of State to explode a verbal bombshell:

. . . Suddenly Mr. Seward hurried in, threw down his hat in great excitement, and exclaimed, "Gentlemen, I have seen General McClellan, and *he is a well man.* I think that this meeting would better adjourn." A general discussion was entered upon as to what was the best course to pursue with regard to the army, and it was understood that we would meet again on Monday, at one o'clock, when General McClellan would be present. On Monday, January 13th, at one o'clock, the same party was gathered at the President's. General McClellan shortly afterward appeared, looking exceedingly pale and weak. The President explained, in an apologetic way, why he had called General McDowell and me to these conferences, and asked General McDowell to explain the proposed plan of operations. General McDowell did so, he and I differing slightly as to the time of commencement of the movement from our front. In answer to some statement from General McDowell as to the delicate position in which we were placed, General McClellan stated that we were, of course, entitled to our opinions. I stated that in giving my opinion as to the Peninsula movement, I knew that my judgment coincided with General McClellan's. General McDowell stated that he was in ignorance of any plan of General McClellan's.

The President went over the subject of discussion in a general way, and then there was a silence. It was broken by Governor Chase, who asked General McClellan if he had any objection to telling the persons there assembled what his plan for the movement of the Army of the Potomac was. After a long silence the General made a few general remarks, and ended by saying to the President that he knew when his plans had hitherto been told to the Cabinet that they had leaked out, and he would therefore decline to divulge them now, unless the President would order him so to do. Then there was another long silence, and the President broke it by asking the General if he had matured a plan for the movement of the Army of the Potomac. The General answered that he had. After another silence the President said, "Then, General, I shall not order you to give it."

During this time Governor Chase, General McDowell and I were standing in one of the window embrasures. When General McClellan declined to give his plans to the meeting, Governor Chase said to us, "Well, if that is Mac's decision, he is a ruined man."

II

McClellan's fundamental weakness, then and later, was his inability to recognize the fact that a commanding general must be an instrument of government. He was never capable of rolling with the political punches. For Lincoln, mocked by antislavery radicals who opposed the President's moderate approach to emancipation, the dangers of the moment included a bold intrigue within his Cabinet. Secretary of War Cameron, a darling of the radical Republicans, had not consulted Lincoln before inserting in his annual report paragraphs calling for emancipation and the arming of slaves. Lincoln ordered the report recalled from the post offices and the offending passage was deleted. He had never wanted Cameron in his official family. Now he acted quietly to mend this political fence:[2]

EXECUTIVE MANSION
WASHINGTON, Jan. 11, 1862

PRIVATE

DEAR SIR:

Though I have said nothing hitherto in response to your wish, expressed long since, to resign your seat in the cabinet, I have not been unmindful of it. I have been only unwilling to consent to a change at a time, and under circumstances which might give occasion to misconstruction, and unable, till now to see how such misconstruction could be avoided.

But the desire of Mr. Clay to return home and to offer his services to his country in the field enables me now to gratify your wish, and at the same time evince my personal regard for you, and my confidence in your ability, patriotism, and fidelity to public trust.

I therefore tender to your acceptance, if you still desire to resign your present position, the post of Minister to Russia. Should you accept it, you will bear with you the assurance of my undiminished confidence, of my affectionate esteem, and of my sure expectation that, near the great sovereign whose personal and hereditary friendship for the United States, so much endears him to Americans, you will be able to render services to your country, not less important than those you could render at home.

Very sincerely
Your friend
A. LINCOLN

III

The war remained a giant that was still awakening. On the day that Lincoln wrote Cameron, Kansas delegations representing the Weas, Peorias, Miamis and Piankashaws gathered in Leavenworth for a meeting with William P. Dole, the Commissioner of Indian Affairs. Chief Y-O-To-Wah spoke for the tribesmen:[3]

I came to visit your city, and most of the way on foot. I came to get arms and a force to guard our frontier. I told General Hunter we would gladly fight if our homes and firesides could be protected—that we would fight with white soldiers, and go wherever wanted. Our chiefs say they will go out if the women and children can be protected. They said the Government had not called for them to fight; there was no fence down and no chance to jump over. We are willing to put in our mite and share the same fate with the pale faces. We are on the border; we have been insulted, but the tomahawk is buried under our orchards, and we want to go as men. We don't want to pull the tomahawk —we would rather prune our trees. If I am driven from my little farm, I want to die like a man. Peace is my motto. I will make a child's bargain with the Missouri rebels—if they'll let me alone, I'll let them alone.

I came up here partly for the white men around me. They solicited my aid. They told me to ask Gen. Hunter and the great men around here, to station a guard on the border for their protection. And I wish to thank Gen. Hunter and your citizens, for the aid they extended to me.

Last June my life was assailed by Missourians. I was driven from home, and went to Lawrence and Wyandotte with my family.

I want to harmonize with my chiefs, and do nothing against white man or red man.

Loyal men are accustomed to come to me; they leave their arms and money with my wife to be secreted.

If I have had some troubles, I have had more pleasure from being a Union man.

Our Agent, Major Colton, has encouraged us in agricultural pursuits. He takes pride in interesting me in the ways of the white man. Other agents have never had the care of us that he has.

I give my most cordial feeling to the people of Kansas and to the First and Second Kansas regiments who have fought so bravely for us.

This is my story. You can put in the pinks, and roses, and flowers.

IV

From the time McClellan became commander in chief his basic strategy was to strike by sea at Richmond. Since any operation against Knoxville and Chattanooga would draw Confederate forces from Richmond, McClellan supported Lincoln's somewhat sentimental proposal for a campaign in east Tennessee, where Unionist sympathy predominated. One grave weakness of this plan was the fact that as long as strong Confederate forces operated in Missouri and western Tennessee they

*could fall on the rear of a Federal army advancing to their south and
east. And with McClellan dividing the West between Halleck's Department of the Missouri and Buell's Department of the Ohio there was
one commander too many for the combined movement that would be
needed. Halleck was a rigid, stiff-necked military pedant and Buell a
man of imagination. Nature had made them poor partners in any uni-
fied operation.*

*November and December had been lost in a series of argumentative
exchanges between McClellan in Washington and Buell and Halleck in
the West. Buell's position—a sound one—was that a movement into
east Tennessee was foolhardy without a co-ordinated operation in western Kentucky and western Tennessee; thus he wished to send flotilla
columns up the Tennessee and the Cumberland and move against
Nashville at the same time he advanced into east Tennessee. Halleck's
position—a customary one—was to do nothing and yell for reinforcements. In early January, while McClellan was ill, Lincoln instructed
Buell and Halleck to work out their own plan. Nothing in Halleck's
textbooks led him to approve the movements up the rivers that Buell
was urging; then McClellan recovered, and apparently consulting the
same textbooks, ordered Buell to move into east Tennessee without
waiting for Halleck. Reluctantly Buell sent a force under Brigadier
General George H. Thomas to attack the Confederate army of Felix
Zollicoffer, then near Somerset on the Cumberland. On January 19 a
brisk battle was fought at Mill Springs. Lincoln's new Secretary of War
issued his first congratulatory order:*[4]

WAR DEPARTMENT, Jan. 22, 1862.

The President, Commander-in-chief of the army and navy, has received information of a brilliant victory achieved by the United States
forces over a large body of armed traitors and rebels at Mill Springs,
in the State of Kentucky.

He returns thanks to the gallant officers and soldiers who won that
victory; and when the official reports shall be received, the military
skill and personal valor displayed in battle will be acknowledged and
rewarded in a fitting manner.

The courage that encountered and vanquished the greatly superior
numbers of the rebel force, pursued and attacked them in their intrenchments, and paused not until the enemy was completely routed,
merits and receives commendation.

The purpose of this war is to attack, pursue, and destroy a rebellious enemy, and to deliver the country from danger menaced by traitors. Alacrity, daring, courageous spirit, and patriotic zeal, on all occasions and under every circumstance, are expected from the army of the United States.

In the prompt and spirited movements and daring battle of Mill Springs, the nation will realize its hopes, and the people of the United States will rejoice to honor every soldier and officer who proves his courage by charging with the bayonet and storming intrenchments, or in the blaze of the enemy's fire.

By order of the President.

EDWIN M. STANTON,
Secretary of War

The reporter for the Cincinnati Commercial *offered a somewhat startling opinion of what constituted civilized war:*[5]

. . . I shall not attempt to describe the battle-field, the dead or the dying. Of course, in all battles, somebody must be killed, and somebody must be wounded; this was no exception to the general rule. I shall mention only one of the dead—that one Zollicoffer. He lay by the side of the road along which we all passed, and all had a fair view of what was once Zollicoffer. I saw the lifeless body as it lay in a fence-corner by the side of the road, but Zollicoffer himself is now in hell. Hell is a fitting abode for all such arch-traitors. May all the other chief conspirators in this rebellion soon share Zollicoffer's fate—shot dead through the instrumentality of an avenging God—their spirits sent straightway to hell, and their lifeless bodies lie in a fence-corner, their faces spattered with mud, and their garments divided up, and even the hair of their head cut off and pulled out by an unsympathizing soldiery of a conquering army, battling for the right.

The correspondent for the Nashville paper supplied an account of rebel vengeance:[6]

At eight o'clock in the morning of Sunday last, the nineteenth instant, the battle commenced, the enemy opening fire. The Mississippi regiment was ordered to the right, and Battle's to the left, and immediately afterward, riding up in front, Gen. Zollicoffer advanced to within a short distance of an Ohio regiment, which had taken a position at a point unknown to him, and which he supposed to be one of his own regiments.

The first intimation he had of his dangerous position was received when it was too late. "There's old Zollicoffer," cried out several of the regiment in front of him. "Kill him!" and in an instant their pieces were levelled at his person. At that moment Henry M. Fogg, aid to Gen. Zollicoffer, drew his revolver and fired, killing the person who first recognized Gen. Zollicoffer. With the most perfect coolness, Gen. Zollicoffer approached to the head of the enemy, and drawing his sabre, cut the head of the Lincoln colonel from his shoulder. As soon as this was done, twenty bullets pierced the body of our gallant leader, and Gen. Zollicoffer fell from his horse a mangled corpse.

V

For weeks Grant had urged Halleck to break the rebel line on the Tennessee, arguing that the South would suffer a disaster from which it might never recover. After repeated requests Halleck finally consented to see Grant in St. Louis on January 23. "I was cut short as if my plan was preposterous," Grant commented, recalling that unhappy interview. The truth was that three days earlier, unsettled by the success at Mill Springs that could make Buell the coming man in the West, Halleck had thought well enough of Grant's proposal to adopt it as his own and to present it to McClellan. Halleck then consulted the commander of the gunboat fleet, Andrew Foote, and was assured that the plan for a combined land and naval operation was feasible. On the twenty-ninth Grant received the order to move against Fort Henry on the Tennessee. Slender, spry Charlie Coffin, night editor turned war correspondent, gave the readers of the Boston Journal *a clear view of the risks involved:*[7]

When the rebels took possession of Columbus, and made a stand at Bowling Green, they saw the necessity of also shutting the two gates midway the two places, the Cumberland and Tennessee Rivers, which open into the heart of the seceded States. Taking now the map, you will observe that the two rivers are very near together at the dividing line between Kentucky and Tennessee. Two important points were selected on those rivers, near the State line, strong natural positions, which military science and engineering had made, it was thought, impregnable to any attack by land or water. The points selected are below the railroad which connects Memphis with Bowling Green, thus guarding against any interruption of communication, a matter very important to the rebels, not only in subsisting their armies, but in enabling

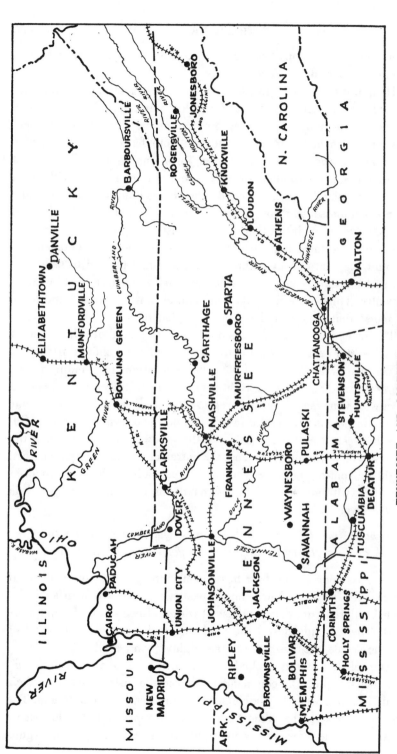

TENNESSEE AND SOUTHERN KENTUCKY

them to transfer troops from either division, as might be necessary to counteract our movements.

The point selected for fortification on the Tennessee, is about ninety miles from the Ohio River, at Pine Bluff Landing, on the east side, where, in addition to the strong battery commanding the river, there was an entrenched camp, protected on both flanks by creeks and a pond, and on the river by felled trees, for a long distance. The river at this point runs nearly due north. A mile and a quarter below the Fort is Panther Island, heavily wooded. The channel on the east side of the island is impassable at low water, the main channel being on the west side. The rebel engineer, therefore, in constructing the work, arranged the angles and faces to command the main channel, but had taken into account the contingency of high water, and had planted torpedoes in the east passage, which were fished up by Commodore Foote without difficulty. Three were first taken up, and all but one were found to be so moist that they would not have exploded.

The front face of the Fort is about twenty feet above the water. It contains four or five acres, and the intrenched camp about thirty acres.

You can obtain an idea of the relative positions by standing facing the north, and raising your right arm, half bent, till your hand is on a level with your face. Your arm represents the river; the Fort is at your elbow, in position to send a raking fire down toward your wrist. Midway between the wrist, and above the elbow, you are to locate the creeks, which will almost enclose the entrenched camp behind the Fort. Right in front of your face, you are to locate a high bluff, one hundred feet high, with a redan, which commands the Fort on the opposite side of the river.

Bad roads slowed down Grant's troops so that Foote's gunboats led the attack on Fort Henry unsupported. Coffin witnessed that action:[8]

. . . As soon as the four boats came into position, the Cincinnati opened fire at thirty-four minutes past twelve o'clock, with an eight-inch Dahlgren gun, throwing a shell with a fifteen-second fuse into the Fort. The Carondelet and the St. Louis each gave the same kind of missile, while the Essex threw an eighty-pound shell.

The rebels instantly replied, and the firing became general, though not at first rapid. The commanders obeyed the instructions, kept their boats in a line with the Cincinnati, and fired with deliberate aim. The consequence was, that almost every shell dropped in the right place.

As only the bow-guns were used, there were only twelve guns

brought to bear upon the Fort, and in return about the same number of guns were brought to bear by the rebels upon the boats. As soon as the four boats were sufficiently advanced, the Lexington, Tyler, and Conestoga reached the head of the island, elevated their guns and joined in the fight, taking deliberate aim and dropping their shells into the Fort and camp.

Steadily onward moved the boats, so nearly equal that at times they were almost in even line, throwing their shells as if practising at a target.

And now there was a visible commotion in the rebel camp. The first shell from the Cincinnati threw the troops into disorder, and at the fourth round, unable to stand the terrible hail which was bringing sure destruction, they broke and fled, leaving arms, ammunition, provisions, blankets, tents—everything, and poured out of the intrenchment a motley, panic-stricken rabble, taking the road toward Dover. A portion jumped on board a small steamboat which was lying in the creek above the Fort, and escaped up the river. A few shells from the boats would have stopped them, and doubtless would have caused terrible slaughter, but Com. Foote had a definite purpose in view—the taking of the Fort, and he was not to be swerved from that.

When the cannonade opened, the troops which were marching to gain the rear of the enemy, impeded by the swollen creeks, were not more than half-way to their designed positions, but with the first gun from the Cincinnati they gave a loud hurrah, and of their own accord broke into the double-quick, fearing they would be too late to have a hand in it. Their fears were well grounded. . . .

Straight onward moved the boats, swerving neither to the right nor the left. As they neared the Fort their fire became more and more destructive. The sand-bags and gabions were knocked about, covering the guns and smothering those who served them. At an early moment in the fight the rifled gun of the rebels burst, but they did not slacken fire or seem discouraged. They fired with great accuracy. . . . The gunboats were repeatedly hit, and those portions which were not plated with iron were badly riddled.

After fifty minutes of fighting the rebels landed a shot in the starboard boiler of the Essex, *disabling her and drawing from tough little Joe McCullagh of the Cincinnati* Commercial *the best unpublished reporting of the day: "Jeeesus!" Coffin, in his report, jumped quickly to the climactic moments:*

. . . At forty-six minutes past one, or one hour and twelve minutes from the commencement of the fight, when the gunboats were within three or four hundred yards of the Fort, the rebel flag came down by the run. In an instant all firing ceased. The rebels had raised a white flag, signifying a desire for a truce, but the smoke hid it from view, and no one on board the fleet observed it, and the shells were pouring in at such a rate which would not admit of delay, after the thought had once taken possession of the rebels' minds that it was time to give in. Conditions were of minor consideration.

The St. Louis being nearest, immediately sent a boat on shore, and the Stars and Stripes went up with a wild huzzah from the crews. Gen. Tilghman, who commanded the rebels, asked for Commodore Foote. Word was sent from the Cincinnati that Commodore Foote would be happy to receive him on board that gunboat, and the Cincinnati's gig was sent to the shore. The rebel General entered it and soon stood before the Commodore.

Gen. Tilghman asked for terms. "No, sir," said the Commodore, "your surrender must be unconditional."

"Well, sir, if I must surrender, it gives me pleasure to surrender to so brave an officer as you."

"You do perfectly right to surrender, sir; but I should not have surrendered on any condition."

"Why so? I do not understand you."

"Because I was fully determined to capture the Fort or go to the bottom."

The rebel General opened his eyes at this remark, replied: "I thought I had you, Commodore, but you were too much for me."

"But how could you fight against the old flag?"

"Well, it did come hard at first; but if the North had only let us alone, there would have been no trouble. But they would not abide by the Constitution."

Commodore Foote assured him that he and all the South were mistaken.

VI

Grant never denied that Foote handed him the victory at Henry. Grant slept little that first night inside the rebel works. Plans to take Fort Donelson, ten miles east of Henry, possessed him.[9]

On the 7th [of February], the day after the fall of Fort Henry, I took my staff and the cavalry—a part of one regiment—and made a reconnaissance to within about a mile of the outer line of works at Donelson. I had known General Pillow in Mexico, and judged that with any force, no matter how small, I could march up to within gunshot of any intrenchments he was given to hold. I said this to the officers of my staff at the time. I knew that Floyd was in command, but he was no soldier, and I judged that he would yield to Pillow's pretensions. I met, as I expected, no opposition in making the reconnaissance and, besides learning the topography of the country on the way and around Fort Donelson, found that there were two roads available for marching; one leading to the village of Dover, the other to Donelson.

Fort Donelson is two miles north, or down the river, from Dover. The fort, as it stood in 1861, embraced about one hundred acres of land. On the east it fronted the Cumberland; to the north it faced Hickman's creek, a small stream which at that time was deep and wide because of the back-water from the river; on the south was another small stream [Indian Creek], or rather a ravine, opening into the Cumberland. This also was filled with back-water from the river. The fort stood on high ground, some of it as much as a hundred feet above the Cumberland. Strong protection to the heavy guns in the water batteries had been obtained by cutting away places for them in the bluff. To the west there was a line of rifle-pits some two miles back from the river at the farthest point. This line ran generally along the crest of high ground, but in one place crossed a ravine which opens into the river between the village and the fort. The ground inside and outside of this intrenched line was very broken and generally wooded. The trees outside of the rifle-pits had been cut down for a considerable way out, and had been felled so that their tops lay outwards from the intrenchments. The limbs had been trimmed and pointed, and thus formed an abatis in front of the greater part of the line. Outside of this intrenched line, and extending about half the entire length of it, is a ravine running north and south and opening into Hickman creek at a point north of the fort. The entire side of this ravine next to the works was one long abatis.

General Halleck commenced his efforts in all quarters to get reinforcements forward to me immediately on my departure from Cairo. General Hunter sent men freely from Kansas, and a large division under General Nelson, from Buell's army, was also dispatched. Orders went out from the War Department to consolidate fragments of companies that were being recruited in the Western States so as to make full companies, and to consolidate companies into regiments. General Halleck did not approve or disapprove of my going to Fort Donelson.

He said nothing whatever to me on the subject. He informed Buell on the 7th that I would march against Fort Donelson the next day; but on the 10th he directed me to fortify Fort Henry strongly, particularly to the land side, saying that he forwarded me intrenching tools for that purpose. I received this dispatch in front of Fort Donelson.

I was very impatient to get to Fort Donelson because I knew the importance of the place to the enemy and supposed he would reinforce it rapidly. I felt that 15,000 men on the 8th would be more effective than 50,000 a month later. I asked Flag-officer Foote, therefore, to order his gunboats still about Cairo to proceed up the Cumberland River and not to wait for those gone to Eastport and Florence; but the others got back in time and we started on the 12th. . . .

I started from Fort Henry with 15,000 men, including eight batteries and part of a regiment of cavalry, and, meeting with no obstruction to detain us, the advance arrived in front of the enemy by noon. That afternoon and the next day were spent in taking up ground to make the investment as complete as possible. General Smith had been directed to leave a portion of his division behind to guard forts Henry and Heiman. He left General Lew. Wallace with 2,500 men. With the remainder of his division he occupied our left, extending to Hickman creek. McClernand was on the right and covered the roads running south and south-west from Dover. His right extended to the back-water up the ravine opening into the Cumberland south of the village. The troops were not intrenched, but the nature of the ground was such that they were just as well protected from the fire of the enemy as if rifle-pits had been thrown up.

Our line was generally along the crest of ridges. The artillery was protected by being sunk in the ground. The men who were not serving the guns were perfectly covered from fire on taking position a little back from the crest. The greatest suffering was from want of shelter. It was midwinter and during the siege we had rain and snow, thawing and freezing alternately. It would not do to allow camp-fires except far down the hill out of sight of the enemy, and it would not do to allow many of the troops to remain there at the same time. In the march over from Fort Henry numbers of the men had thrown away their blankets and overcoats. There was therefore much discomfort and absolute suffering.

Grant understood the case. Franc B. Wilkie, now filing the story for the New York Times, filled in the grim details:[10]

Friday night was one of the severest description. The men being without tents, and in many cases without fire, suffered intensely. Hundreds were frost-bitten, and from facts related to me since the surrender by some of the rebels, I have no doubt but that many of our wounded men, who fell in the fight of Friday, and were unable to walk in, were actually frozen to death. This circumstance is a terrible one, and inexpressibly shocking, but there was no help for it. During the various conflicts of Friday, the scene was constantly changed from point to point, and not again visited by our troops. Men would fall at these places, and being unable to get away, were obliged to stay where they fell. In some cases, a few of our wounded were cared for by the rebels, although they were without fire, and could give them but little valuable assistance.

Wilkie saw the battle start:

Early on the morning of Friday—almost before it was fairly light— the enemy poured forth in a mass of not less than three thousand men, and hurled themselves with tremendous force against the Forty-fifth and Twelfth Illinois regiments, that were nearly on the extreme right. Accompanying them were twelve batteries of artillery. The Forty-fifth and Twelfth sustained the shock manfully for a short time, and then withdrew. The Eighteenth and Ninth Illinois soon after came to their support, and for a short time held the enemy in check. Soon after, the Thirtieth, Thirty-first, and Eleventh Illinois regiments, the Eighth Missouri, Fifty-eighth Ohio, and Twenty-fifth Kentucky, and Willard's battery were added to the National force, and the fight became of terrific proportions. McAllister's battery took position on an eminence, and for four hours their heavy twenty-four-pounders were not silent for a single instant. During all this time they were exposed to a heavy fire from the rebels, who had erected batteries so as to command McAllister's position from three points—two directly in front, and one on his right. Taylor's battery stood a little to the rear of the other, and somewhat to the left—the other National batteries were distributed at various points along the line, as the nature of the ground would permit—all kept the air incessantly filled with their music, and with showers of grape and shell.

This is but an outline of the position of the National forces, for there can be strictly no correct sketch given, as at no time during the fight were the regiments stationary. Now they pushed forward, again fell

back, withdrew, and were replaced by others. The fight itself was prolonged and desperate. Now it rolled over a hill, anon poured along
a ravine, always in the woods, and always marking its track in characters of blood. The conflict was not conducted according to any particular military plan—men stationed themselves behind trees, logs,
rocks, anything that would afford shelter, and blazed away whenever
a hostile head appeared.

The Twenty-fifth Kentucky regiment was on the extreme right, and
was attacked by a swarm of the enemy with such vigor that they broke
and fled in disorder. At another part of the National line the attack
was conducted by such overwhelming numbers that the line was broken
through, and the battle seemed well-nigh likely to become a total rout
on the part of the National forces. It was at this last gap broken through
the National line that McAllister's battery was stationed, and where
for a time it fell in the hands of the rebels. The battery had only one
hundred and fifty rounds of ammunition, and at about ten o'clock these
were all fired away—not a single shot was left. Capt. McAllister in
vain endeavored to obtain a supply from the rear; a shot from the enemy passed through three of his horses; another tore off the trail from
one of the guns; a third smashed the wheel of a second gun. Just at
this time, a heavy force of the enemy obtained a cover near him, and
opened fire at about two hundred yards with musketry. Hitching six
horses to the only undamaged gun, he endeavored to haul it off, but the
weight was so great, and the road in such a muddy condition, that it
was found impossible to get along with it, and after dragging it a half-
mile, it became mired, and he was reluctantly obliged to leave it. The
horses were driven off, dragging the limbers and empty caissons, and
the guns were left to their fate. In the course of the day a tremendous
charge on the part of our troops reöccupied the lost ground, closed up
the gap and recovered the pieces. They were found where they were
left, their great weight—being twenty-four-pound siege-guns—probably preventing the enemy from taking them away. . . .

The whole of the fight was of the most terrific character. Without a
single moment's cessation the rebels poured into our forces perfect
torrents of canister, shell, and round-shot, while their thousands of
riflemen hurled in a destructive fire from every bush, tree, log, or obstruction of any kind that afforded shelter. The roar of the battle was
like that of a heavy tornado, as it sweeps through some forest on its
mission of destruction. Small arms kept up an incessant cracking,
mingling with which came up occasionally the roar of company or di-

vision firing, while over all came every moment or two the resonant thunders of the batteries.

Gloomily, the Richmond Dispatch *prepared the South for a disaster on the Cumberland:*[11]

Saturday was the rubicon of Fort Donelson. The enemy had received strong reënforcements during the week, and now they numbered, according to their own estimates, fifty thousand men.* Snow lay on the ground to the depth of three inches, and a cold, blinding sleet poured incessantly in the faces of our soldiers. Still, with all these odds, they faltered not. Early in the day the order came from headquarters to make a vigorous attack on the right flank of the Union army, which, thirty-five thousand strong, was posted on the opposite hills, under command of Gen. Grant. Not more than ten thousand of our men engaged in this movement, but such was the impetuosity of their advance that the enemy fled in confusion from their intrenchments.

Charge after charge was made by our regiments, and the ground was covered with the slain. Three hundred prisoners, including several officers belonging to an Illinois regiment, four batteries, and three thousand five hundred stand of arms, were captured. The former are now in a Confederate prison. The two latter may have been retaken, but this is not yet known. Everywhere in the earlier part of the day, our flag was victorious.

The Union commander, finding that his right had been turned, and that the day would be lost but for some decisive effort, concentrated his troops in the afternoon on our right, and making a sudden plunge, after a long and desperate struggle, redeemed the morning's loss by capturing a portion of our intrenchments. The dead lay piled up in heaps, their gore trickling in red lines along the snow in every direction. Still our troops fought on, contesting inch by inch the ground they were compelled to vacate. At nightfall the firing ceased, and at twelve o'clock Pillow telegraphed to Nashville: "The day is ours; we have repulsed the enemy with great loss to them, and with considerable loss to ourselves. We want reënforcements." Reënforcements were not forthcoming, however, and Sunday morning found the Union army strengthened by thirty thousand fresh men, encompassing the place

* The figure is ridiculous. Of 27,000 Federals engaged, 500 were killed, 2,108 wounded, and 224 missing. Of 21,000 Confederates engaged, 2,000 were killed and wounded and 14,623 missing and captured.

and completely surrounding our forces. The fight was renewed at five o'clock A.M.; but it being useless to contend against such odds, the Fort and army capitulated to the enemy on their own terms. . . .

Had reënforcements been sent forward, so that eight or ten thousand fresh men could have stood the brunt of the battle on Saturday afternoon instead of our jaded soldiers, Fort Donelson would not have fallen; but the lack of this effective strength enabled the enemy to completely hem our little army in, and extend their lines in crescent shape from river-bank to river-bank around us.

VII

Confederate General Buckner, grimly accepting Grant's terms of "unconditional surrender," gave new meaning to the "U. S." before the victorious general's name. Pillow's exaggerated reports of success left Nashville quite unprepared for Yankee visitors—among them Franc Wilkie of the New York Times:[12]

Up to Sunday morning, the sixteenth inst., the day upon which Fort Donelson surrendered, the impression was prevalent in Nashville that the "Yankees" were being "cleaned out" in the usual wholesale slaughter, buncombe style, customary in the cases of the gallant sons of chivalry. Saturday a despatch was published as follows: "ENEMY RETREATING!—GLORIOUS RESULT!!—OUR BOYS FOLLOWING AND PEPPERING THEIR REAR!!—A COMPLETE VICTORY."

Gen. Pillow also sent up a despatch: "ON THE HONOR OF A SOLDIER THE DAY IS OURS!!"

. . . Of course the virtuous and Christianly traitors of Nashville were highly delighted Sunday morning, to receive these encouraging assurances of the thrifty progress of rebellion. They were mingling this glad intelligence with their devotions—indulging in cheerful anticipations of the future of Dixie, while they gave vent to Old Hundred and other *Te Deums*, when suddenly the delicious union of religion and rebellion was strangled as mercilessly as one throttles a litter of blind puppies, by the advent of the gallant Floyd, who commanded the vanguard of the retreat from Donelson.

Old Hundred was dropped instanter—devotion was silenced—and if the name of Him they had met to worship was again mentioned in the course of that memorable Sunday, it was generally with the addition of an emphatic "d--n."

[Governor Isham G.] Harris instantly convened his Legislature, but, finding no parliamentary remedy against the approach of Yankees with rifles and armored gunboats, they adjourned without calling for the nays, and took a special train for Memphis.

Before night, Johnston, with his retreating hordes from Bowling Green, entered the city and struck straight south for Dixie. This added to the general panic, and when a rumor became current that the dreaded gunboats had taken Clarksville and were advancing up the river, the excitement grew to be tremendous. . . . *

The Federal forces occupying Nashville, as Wilkie recorded for the titillation of his Northern readers, were not likely ever to forget that experience:[13]

The ladies of Nashville—that is, the few of them who have not struck for the warmer and less Yankee-haunted portions of Dixie—are, of course as full of treason as they are, in occasional cases, of loveliness. I have seen only two cases of women who are loyal, and both of these are among what might be called the "lower walks" of social life. One of these was a bare-armed, bare-headed female that issued from a shanty on the bluffs as we passed along the front of the city, and commenced waving her hands wildly up and down, at the same time *teetering* violently on her toes, like some devotee before the altar of an Aztec idol. She continued this demonstrative but original welcome, till a couple of other females issued from the same shanty and forcibly carried her in-doors. It may be suspected that her loyal recognition sprang rather from whisky than patriotism—a suspicion that my own mind is not altogether free from, as I have carefully reflected upon this singular and almost isolated case of Union feeling.

The other case was also that of an Irish lady, and seemed more the result of genuine loyalty than of stimulants. As Gen. Grant and staff were riding through the city, a woman rushed out from a house, and throwing up her hands in the style adopted by cruel parents when they say, "Bless you, my children," in fifteen-cent novels, exclaimed: "God bless ye, gintlemen! Success go wid ye! Arrah, git in there, ye thafe, and don't be boderin' the life out o'me!" The last remark, I may say, was accompanied by a resounding slap, and was addressed to a dirty-faced gossoon that thrust his unkempt head beyond the

* Johnston left Nashville on February 18 and Federal forces under Buell occupied the city on February 24. Grant determined that he would go to Nashville on the twenty-eighth "if I received no orders to the contrary." Go he did.

doorway—and not, as may be surmised, to the Illinoisian hero. The youth set up one of those vigorous howls so peculiar to offended juvenility, and amid a chorus of slaps, blessings, and the roars of the suffering infant, the General turned a corner and disappeared.

A little further, and the party passed slowly by a costly carriage, out of one of whose windows was thrust the head of an elegantly-dressed lady. She was giving some directions to the liveried darkey that held the reins; but looking up as the party passed, she caught sight of the Federal uniforms. With a "baugh!" as if she had swallowed a toad, she spat toward the ground, and with a contemptuous and expressive grimace of disgust upon her features, drew in her head, and threw herself back in her carriage. Quite possibly such movements are the very height of Southern breeding—further North, in the land of Yankees and wooden clocks, a woman who would perpetrate an act of the kind, under similar circumstances, would be regarded—well, to use a convenient everyday expression, as "no better than she should be"—a somebody closely akin to, if not the identical scarlet feminine spoken of in Revelation.

Occasionally I met other specimens of Nashville ladies, who, in many cases, supposing me to be a soldier, from the possession of a blue overcoat, described upon meeting a wide semicircle of avoidance, swinging, as they did so, their rotundant skirts with a contemptuous flirt far out, as if the very touch of a blue coat would be contamination. And then the angle at which the noses of the naughty darlings went up, and the extent to which their lips and eyes went down, were not the least interesting portion of these little by-plays, and assisted materially in showing the exquisite breeding of these amiable demoiselles.

VIII

The lively times that Grant had stirred up along the Tennessee and the Cumberland brought scant cheer to McClellan, still sitting quietly on the Potomac. He had been ordered by Lincoln to make some movement on or before February 22; that date now had passed. Meanwhile the Northern press lavished extravagant attention on "Unconditional Surrender" Grant as the first real hero of the war—a circumstance that nettled McClellan and infuriated Halleck, who had jumped from Buell's fire into Grant's frying pan. Suddenly the wires between St. Louis and Washington began to thrum with angry dispatches. McClellan told the story of this battle of the clicking keys:[14]

On the morning of Sunday, March 2, 1862, desiring to give orders for the further movements of Buell's and Halleck's commands, I went to the military telegraph-office—then in the headquarters of the Army of the Potomac at the corner of Pennsylvania avenue and Jackson square—and caused communication to be cut off from all wires except those leading to Halleck's headquarters at St. Louis and Buell's at Nashville. I then called Buell and Halleck to their respective offices, and asked for a full report of the condition of affairs, number, position, and condition of their troops, that of the enemy, etc. Buell promptly gave me the information needed. Halleck replied the same day:

". . . I have had no communication with Gen. Grant for more than a week. He left his command without my authority and went to Nashville. His army seems to be as much demoralized by the victory of Fort Donelson as was that of the Potomac by the defeat of Bull Run. It is hard to censure a successful general immediately after a victory, but I think he richly deserves it. I can get no returns, no reports, no information of any kind from him. Satisfied with his victory, he sits down and enjoys it without any regard to the future. I am worn out and tired with this neglect and inefficiency. C. F. Smith is almost the only officer equal to the emergency." To this I replied:

"Your despatch of last evening received. The success of our cause demands that proceedings such as Grant's should be at once checked. Generals must observe discipline as well as private soldiers. Do not hesitate to arrest him at once, if the good of the service requires it, and place C. F. Smith in command. You are at liberty to regard this as a positive order, if it will smooth your way. I appreciate the difficulties you have to encounter, and will be glad to relieve you from trouble as far as possible."

On the 4th Halleck telegraphed me:

"A rumor has just reached me that since the taking of Fort Donelson Grant has resumed his former bad habits. If so, it will account for his repeated neglect of my often-repeated orders. I do not deem it advisable to arrest him at present, but have placed Gen. Smith in command of the expedition up the Tennessee. I think Smith will restore order and discipline. . . ."

On the 6th Halleck telegraphed to Grant:

"Gen. McClellan directs that you report to me daily the number and position of the forces under your command. Your neglect of repeated orders to report the strength of your command has created great dissatisfaction and seriously interfered with military plans. Your going to Nashville without authority, and when your presence with your troops was of the greatest importance, was a matter of serious complaint at Washington, so much so that I was advised to arrest you on your return."

On the 31st of March Halleck informed Grant:

"Gen. McClellan directed me to place Gen. Smith in command of the expedition until you were ordered to join it."

On the 10th of March the adjutant-general of the army, by direction of the President, required from Halleck a report as to Grant's unauthorized visit to Nashville and as to his general conduct. On the 15th Halleck replied that Grant had gone to Nashville to communicate with Buell, that his motives were proper, and advised that no further proceedings be had in the case.*

Now to the story which prompts me to insert these despatches. More than a year after the events in question Franklin wrote to me that on meeting Grant at Memphis, or some such point on the Mississippi, Grant asked what had made me hostile to him. Franklin replied that he knew that I was not hostile but very friendly to him. Grant then said that that could not be so, for, without any reason, I had ordered Halleck to relieve him from command and arrest him soon after Fort Donelson, and that Halleck had interfered to save him. I took no steps to undeceive Grant, trusting to time to elucidate the question.

Not only was McClellan involved in a testy controversy over Grant, but in Washington, by his own account, he also was spending an uncomfortable morning at the White House:[15]

. . . On the 8th of March, the President sent for me at an early hour in the morning, about half-past seven, and I found him in his office. He appeared much concerned about something, and soon said that he

---

* The letter giving his command to General C. F. Smith, Grant declared, "was the first intimation I had received that General Halleck had called for information as to the strength of my command." On March 11 Halleck was given command of all forces in the West and two days later restored Grant for the possible reason that he no longer saw him as a rival. Grant was willing to concede that Smith was "a much fitter officer for the command," adding: "But this did not justify the dispatches which General Halleck sent to Washington, or his subsequent concealment of them from me when pretending to explain the actions of my superiors."

wished to talk with me about "a very ugly matter." I asked what it was; and, as he still hesitated, I said that the sooner and more directly such things were approached the better. . . .

He then adverted to the more serious—or ugly—matter, and now the effects of the intrigues by which he had been surrounded became apparent. He said that it had been represented to him (and he certainly conveyed to me the distinct impression that he regarded these representations as well founded) that my plan of campaign (which was to leave Washington under the protection of a sufficient garrison, its numerous well-built and well-armed fortifications, and the command of Banks, then in the Shenandoah Valley, and to throw the whole active army suddenly by water from Annapolis and Alexandria to the forts on James river, and thence by the shortest route upon Richmond) was conceived with the traitorous intent of removing its defenders from Washington, and thus giving over to the enemy the capital and the government, thus left defenceless.

It is difficult to understand that a man of Mr. Lincoln's intelligence could give ear to such abominable nonsense. I was seated when he said this, concluding with the remark that it did look to him much like treason. Upon this I arose, and, in a manner perhaps not altogether decorous towards the chief magistrate, desired that he should retract the expression, telling him that I could permit no one to couple the word treason with my name. He was much agitated, and at once disclaimed any idea of considering me a traitor, and said that he merely repeated what others had said, and that he did not believe a word of it. I suggested caution in the use of language, and again said that I would permit no doubt to be thrown upon my intentions; whereupon he again apologized and disclaimed any purpose of impugning my motives.

IX

Frayed nerves were not a Washington monopoly. In Richmond, where Robert Garlick Hill Kean labored as Head of the Bureau of War, the bitter taste of each dawn had a cause other than the preceding evening's whisky and branch water. Following the Confederate defeat at Mill Springs, Kean used his diary to release his pent-up frustration:[16]

There seems to me to be a more general feeling of despondency prevailing at this time than ever before since the war began. Nor is it the fruit of the late disaster; it existed before that. I suppose the vast preparation of the enemy, the obstinacy with which they persist in the purpose of subjugating, their success in raising enormous sums of money for the war, and the seeming willingness to go to any length of taxation, has produced a general disappointment of the hopes founded on the late bankrupt condition of their treasury. Many too are disappointed at the stiffness with which McClellan has withstood all outside pressure, and gone on with his plans and preparations developing the vast system of attacks by which he proposes to outflank the entire Confederacy. Some are disappointed that the Mason–Slidell affair was so disastrously managed by Seward and that England seems no nearer our ally than last summer. But the most just cause of alarm of all is the apathy of the people, their anxious desire to avoid military service, and the apparent cowardice of the legislature, which seems afraid to do anything worthy of the occasion. There seems a probability that the men from the Southern states will go home when their term is out, and not return. The naval expeditions are probably designed to have, and will have, this effect.

Virginia must fight her own battles, defend as best she may her own soil and in so doing defend the whole eastern part of the Confederacy. If the rulers will only bring out her sons and the general government give them back the army she has furnished, they will do it. Noble, grand old State! I love her dearer in her days of tribulation than in her prosperity, and while life is spared me I will fight in her behalf so long as a foe is on her soil, or raises a hand against her; nor if, like Poland it is written in the Book of Fate that she shall "close her bright eyes, and curb her high career," will I cease to strive for her deliverance while Life lasts. Never! Never! Never! will I be a subject to the power which rules in Washington, unless as a captive bound in chains.

No less depressed was Robert E. Lee, toiling night and day to strengthen coastal defenses along the Atlantic. After the disasters at Henry and Donelson, Lee wrote home that the Southern people must be "humbled and taught to be less boastful, less selfish, and more devoted to right and justice to all the world"; then in early February a Federal force captured Roanoke Island. Lee grumbled in another letter that "our soldiers have not realized the necessity for the endurance and labor they are called upon to undergo, and that it is better to sacrifice themselves than our cause." Fresh disaster smote the Confederacy when a Federal force, descending from Roanoke Island, captured New Bern,

North Carolina on March 14, but Lee by then was no longer responsible for coastal defense:

RICHMOND, VA., March 2, 1862

GENERAL R. E. LEE,
    SAVANNAH:
If circumstances will, in your judgment, warrant your leaving, I wish to see you here with the least delay.

JEFFERSON DAVIS

X

Many were the visitors to the Union tent-fields across the all-quiet Potomac. One who saw the "hundred circling camps" was Julia Ward Howe, who in the late fall of 1861 visited Washington accompanied by her husband, Governor Andrew of Massachusetts, and James Freeman Clarke, her pastor. She was deeply affected by the experience:[17]

We returned from the review of troops near the city very slowly . . . to beguile the rather tedious drive, we sang from time to time snatches of the army songs so popular at that time, concluding, I think, with "John Brown's body." The soldiers . . . answered back, "Good for you!" Mr. Clarke said, "Mrs. Howe, why do you not write some good words for that stirring tune?" I replied that I had often wished to do this, but had not as yet found in my mind any leading toward it.

I went to bed that night as usual, and slept, according to my wont, quite soundly. I awoke in the gray of the morning twilight; and as I lay waiting for the dawn, the long lines of the desired poem began to twine themselves in my mind. Having thought out all the stanzas, I said to myself, "I must get up and write those verses down, lest I fall asleep and forget them." So, with a sudden effort, I sprang out of bed, and found in the dimness an old stump of a pen which I remembered to have used the day before. I scrawled the verses almost without looking at the paper. I had learned to do this when, on previous occasions, attacks of versification had visited me in the night, and I feared to have recourse to a light lest I should wake the baby, who slept near me. I was always obliged to decipher my scrawl before another night should intervene, as it was only legible while the matter was fresh in my mind. At this time, having completed my writing, I returned to bed and fell asleep, saying to myself, "I like this better than most things that I have written."

In February, 1862, The Atlantic Monthly *published Mrs. Howe's poem. The war for the North acquired new purpose and dignity:*[18]

BATTLE-HYMN OF THE REPUBLIC

Mine eyes have seen the glory of the coming of the Lord:
He is trampling out the vintage where the grapes of wrath are stored;
He hath loosed the fateful lightning of his terrible swift sword:
  His truth is marching on.

I have seen Him in the watch-fires of a hundred circling camps;
They have builded Him an altar in the evening dews and damps;
I can read His righteous sentence by the dim and flaring lamps.
  His day is marching on.

I have read a fiery gospel, writ in burnished rows of steel;
"As ye deal with my contemners, so with you my grace shall deal;
Let the Hero, born of woman, crush the serpent with his heel,
  Since God is marching on."

He has sounded forth the trumpet that shall never call retreat;
He is sifting out the hearts of men before his judgment-seat:
Oh! be swift, my soul, to answer Him! be jubilant, my feet!
  Our God is marching on.

In the beauty of the lilies Christ was born across the sea,
With a glory in his bosom that transfigures you and me:
As He died to make men holy, let us die to make men free,
  While God is marching on.

                     —JULIA WARD HOWE

CHAPTER 10

SURPRISES, THICK AND FAST

O N AN AUGUST DAY in 1861 a dour man, writing in a neat long-hand, addressed a letter "To His Excellency Abraham Lincoln, President of the United States":

"The writer, having introduced the present system of naval propulsion and constructed the first screw ship of war, now offers to construct a vessel for the destruction of the rebel fleet at Norfolk and for scouring the Southern rivers and inlets of all craft protected by rebel batteries. Having thus briefly noticed the object of my addressing you, it will be proper for me most respectfully to state that in making this offer I seek no private advantage or emolument of any kind. Fortunately I have already upward of one thousand of my caloric engines in successful operation, with affluence in prospect. Attachment to the Union alone impels me to offer my services at this fearful crisis—my life if need be—in the great cause which Providence has called upon you to defend."

Perhaps Lincoln did not see this letter; in any event, John Ericsson never received a reply. In September the Swedish inventor, who was now a naturalized American citizen, addressed another letter to Washington, this time assuring the Committee on Ironclads that he could build a vessel with a revolving gun turret that would "split the rebel fleet at Norfolk into matches in half an hour." Again he received no answer. In succeeding weeks in his studio-office at 95 Franklin Street, New York City, Ericsson glowered at the long table that held his books and sketches. In naval circles rumors were rife of how at Norfolk the

Rebels were converting the captured *Merrimack* * into an ironclad of revolutionary design. Ericsson could guess what this development portended. If, thinking of the Committee on Ironclads, Ericsson muttered "Fools! Fools! Fools!" who could blame him?

Then in late September a knock sounded on the door at 95 Franklin Street. Ericsson's caller was Cornelius Scranton Bushnell, Connecticut industrialist and warm friend of Secretary of the Navy Welles. The inventor and his caller discussed ironclads generally before Ericsson, warming to Bushnell, produced the dust-covered box in which he had stored the model of his proposed *Monitor*. "I was perfectly overjoyed," Bushnell remembered, "when, at the close of the interview, Captain Ericsson entrusted the box with its precious contents to my care."

Bushnell saw Lincoln at the White House. The President was instantly impressed. Next day Mr. Lincoln and the industrialist, model under his arm, appeared before the Committee on Ironclads. A few thought Ericsson's model possessed possibilities; others pronounced it ridiculous. Suddenly all eyes turned toward Mr. Lincoln. What did he think?

"All I can say," the President remarked, "is what the girl said when she put her foot in the stocking: 'It strikes me there's something in it.' "

I

Secretary of the Navy Welles recalled how he learned the Merrimack *soon would menace the Union fleet at Hampton Roads:*[1]

Late in February, a negro woman, who resided in Norfolk, came to the Navy Department and desired a private interview with me. She and others had closely watched the work upon the "Merrimac," and she, by their request, had come to report that the ship was nearly finished, had come out of the dock, and was about receiving her armament. The woman had passed through the lines, at great risk to herself, to bring me the information, and, in confirmation of her statement, she took from the bosom of her dress a letter from a Union man, a mechanic in the Navy Yard, giving briefly the facts as stated by her. This news, of course, put an end to the test, which had been originally designed, of destroying the "Merrimac" in the dry-dock. . . .

Doubtless Welles's heart was chilled by the information the Negro woman brought him. Commissioned at the Boston Navy Yard in De-

* The vessel was christened the *Merrimack*, and so appears in the official *Navy Register*. Most writers, however, refer to the ship as the *Merrimac*.

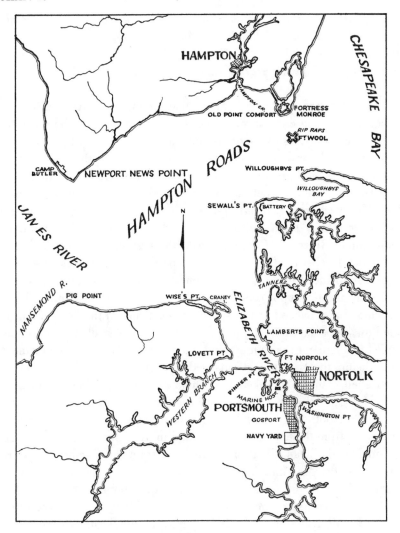

HAMPTON ROADS

cember, 1855, the Merrimack *had been sent through the West Indies and around the Horn to the Pacific as an example to the world of America's prowess at shipbuilding. The Confederates, however, had completely remodeled the proud ship, cutting her down to the waterline and raising a new 160-foot-long superstructure of oak and pine on her berth deck. Armor plate, three inches thick, now covered the slanting sides of this gun deck. She carried a fighting crew of 350 and her ten guns handled 150-pound shot.*

Low and ugly, the Merrimack, *black smoke pouring from her stack, appeared off Hampton Roads on March 8, 1862. A Federal officer shouted: "That* Thing *is coming down!" Readers of the* Baltimore American *were given a grim account of what followed:*[2]

The Merrimac made her appearance, coming out from Elizabeth River about noon on Saturday. She stood directly across the roads toward Newport News. As soon as she was made out and her direction ascertained, the crews were beat to quarters on both the Cumberland and Congress, and preparations made for what was felt to be an almost hopeless fight, but the determination to make it as desperate as possible. The Merrimac kept straight on, making, according to the best estimates, about eight miles an hour. As she passed the mouth of Nansemond River, the Congress threw the first shot at her, which was immediately answered. The Merrimac passed the Congress, discharging a broadside at her, (one shell from which killed and disabled every man except one at gun No. Ten,) and kept on toward the Cumberland, which she approached at full speed, striking her on the port side near the bow, her stem knocking port No. One and the bridle-port into one, whilst her ram cut the Cumberland under water. Almost at the moment of collision, the Merrimac discharged from her forward gun an eleven-inch shell. This shell raked the whole gun-deck, killing ten men at gun No. One, among whom was master mate John Harrington, and cutting off both arms and legs of quarter-gunner Wood. The water rushed in from the hole made below, and in five minutes the ship began to sink by the head. Shell and solid shot from the Cumberland were rained on the Merrimac as she passed ahead, but the most glanced harmlessly from the incline of her iron-plated bombproof.

As the Merrimac rounded to and came up she again raked the Cumberland with heavy fire. At this fire sixteen men at gun No. Ten were killed or wounded, and were all subsequently carried down in the sinking ship.

Advancing with increased momentum, the Merrimac struck the Cumberland on the starboard side, smashing her upper works and cutting another hole below the water-line.

The ship now began to rapidly settle, and the scene became most horrible. The cockpit was filled with the wounded, whom it was impossible to bring up. The forward magazine was under water, but powder was still supplied from the after-magazine, and the firing kept steadily up by men who knew that the ship was sinking under them. They worked desperately and unremittingly, and amid the din and horror of the conflict gave cheers for their flag and the Union, which were joined in by the wounded. The decks were slippery with blood, and arms and legs and chunks of flesh were strewed about. The Merrimac laid off at easy point-blank range, discharging her broadsides alternately at the Cumberland and the Congress. The water by this time had reached the after-magazine of the Cumberland. The men, however, kept at work, and several cases of powder were passed up and the guns kept in play. Several men in the after shell-room lingered there too long in their eagerness to pass up shell, and were drowned.

The water had at this time reached the berth or main gun-deck, and it was felt hopeless and useless to continue the fight longer. The word was given for each man to save himself, but after this order gun No. Seven was fired, when the adjoining gun, No. Six, was actually under water. This last shot was fired by an active little fellow named Matthew Tenney, whose courage had been conspicuous throughout the action. As his port was left open by the recoil of the gun, he jumped to scramble out, but the water rushed in with so much force that he was washed back and drowned. When the order was given to cease firing, and to look out for their safety in the best way possible, numbers scampered through the port-holes, whilst others reached the spar-deck by the companionways. Some were incapable to get out by either of these means, and were carried by the rapidly sinking ship. Of those who reached the upper deck, some swam off to the tugs that came out from Newport News.

The Cumberland sank in water nearly to her cross-trees. She went down with her *flag still flying,* and it still flies from the mast above the water that overwhelmed her, a memento of the bravest, most daring, and yet most hopeless defence that has ever been made by any vessel belonging to any navy in the world. The men fought with a courage that could not be excelled. There was no flinching, no thought of surrender.

The whole number lost of the Cumberland's crew was one hundred and twenty.

In salty idiom, Seaman Willard afterward recalled for a New York audience his experiences aboard the Congress:[3]

Gentlemen and ladies, I am not acquainted with this kind of speaking. I am not used to it; I have been too long in a man-of-war. I enlisted in a man-of-war when I was thirteen years of age; I am now forty. I have been in one ever since. We had been a long time in the Congress, waiting for the Merrimac, with the Cumberland. I claim a timber-head in both ships. I belonged to the Cumberland in the destroying of the navy-yard and the ships at Norfolk. On the eighth of March, when the Merrimac came out, we were as tickled as a boy would be with his father coming home with a new kite for him. [Loud laughter and applause.] She fired a gun at us. It went clean through the ship, and killed nobody. The next one was a shell. It came in at a port-hole, killed six men, and exploded and killed nine more. The next one killed ten. Then she went down to the Cumberland. She had an old grudge against her, and she took her hog-fashion, as I should say. [Great laughter.] The Cumberland fought her as long as she could. She fired her spar-deck guns at her after the gun-deck was under water, but the shot had no more effect than peas. She sunk the Cumberland in about seven fathoms of water. You know what a fathom is—six feet. We lay in nine fathoms, and it would not do to sink in that. We slipped our cable and ran into shallower water, to get our broadside on the Merrimac, but we got her bows on; that gave them a chance to rake us, as they did. The commander opened a little port-hole, and said: "Smith, will you surrender the ship?" Says he: "No, not as long as I have got a gun or a man to man it." They fired a broadside. The men moved the dead bodies away, and manned the guns again. They fired another broadside, and dismounted both the guns and killed the crews. When they first went by us, they sot us a-fire by a shell exploding near the magazine. I know where the magazine is; you folks don't. Last broadside she killed our commander, Mr. Smith, our sailing-master, and the pilot. We had no chance at all. We were on the spar-deck, most of us; the other steamers firing at us, and we dodging the shot; no chance to dodge down below, because you could not see the shot till they were inside of the ship. We had no chance, and we surrendered. The rebel officers—we knowed 'em all—all old playmates, shipmates—came home in the Germantown with them—all old playmates, but rascals now. She left us, and she went toward Norfolk to get out of the way. . . . I have no more to say, people, but there is the flag that the fathers of our country left us, and by the powers of God above us, we'll—[Tremendous cheering.]

In a single afternoon the Merrimack *was rendering obsolete the wooden navies of nations around the world. The Baltimore* American *continued its narrative of fast-changing naval history:*[4]

After sinking the Cumberland and firing the Congress, the Merrimac, with the Yorktown and Jamestown, stood off in the direction of the steam-frigate Minnesota, which had been for some hours aground, about three miles below Newport News. This was about five o'clock on Saturday evening. The rebel commander of the Merrimac, either fearing the greater strength of the Minnesota, or wishing, as it afterward appeared, to capture this splendid ship without doing serious damage to her, did not attempt to run the Minnesota down, as he had run down the Cumberland. He stood off about a mile distant, and with the Yorktown and Jamestown threw shell and shot at the frigate. The Minnesota, though from being aground unable to manoeuvre or bring all her guns to bear, was fought splendidly. She threw a shell at the Yorktown which set her on fire, and she was towed off by her consort the Jamestown. From the reäppearance of the Yorktown next day, the fire must have been suppressed without serious damage. The after-cabins of the Minnesota were torn away in order to bring two of her large guns to bear from her stern-ports, the position in which she was lying enabling the rebels to attack her there with impunity. She received two serious shots: one, an eleven-inch shell, entered near the waist, passed through the chief engineer's room, knocking both rooms into ruins, and wounding several men. Another shot went clear through the chain-plate, and another passed through the main-mast. Six of the crew were killed outright, on board the Minnesota, and nineteen wounded. The men, though fighting at great disadvantage, stuck manfully to their guns, and exhibited a spirit that would have enabled them to compete successfully with any ordinary vessel.

About nightfall, the Merrimac, satisfied with her afternoon's work of death and destruction, steamed in under Sewall's Point. The day thus closed most dismally for our side, and with the most gloomy apprehensions of what would occur the next day. The Minnesota was at the mercy of the Merrimac, and there appeared no reason why the iron monster might not clear the Roads of our fleet, destroy all the stores and warehouses on the beach, drive our troops into the Fortress, and command Hampton Roads, against any number of wooden vessels the Government might send there. Saturday was a terribly dismal night at Fortress Monroe.

II

From Fortress Monroe, General Wool telegraphed the Secretaries of War and Navy news of the disaster that had struck at Hampton Roads.

Stanton scurried to the White House, telegram in hand. A worried President sent for Welles. Seward and Chase also had been summoned, and when Welles reached the Executive Mansion one question burst at him from Lincoln, Stanton, Seward, Chase: What could be done to meet and check this formidable monster? Looking around the room, Welles judged his audience:[5]

Mr. Stanton, impulsive, and always a sensationalist, was terribly excited, walked the room in great agitation, and gave brusque utterances, and deprecatory answers to all that was said, and censured everything that had been done or was omitted to be done. Mr. Seward, usually buoyant and self-reliant, overwhelmed with the intelligence, listened in responsive sympathy to Stanton, and was greatly depressed, as, indeed, were all the members, who, in the meantime, had arrived, with the exception of Mr. Blair, as well as one or two others—naval and military officers—among them, Commander Dahlgren and Colonel Meigs.

"The 'Merrimac,' " said Stanton, who was vehement, and did most of the talking, "will change the whole character of the war; she will destroy, seriatim, every naval vessel; she will lay all the cities on the seaboard under contribution. I shall immediately recall Burnside; Port Royal must be abandoned. I will notify the Governors and municipal authorities in the North to take instant measures to protect their harbors." It is difficult to repeat his language, which was broken and denunciatory, or to characterize his manner, or the panic under which he labored, and which added to the apprehension of others. He had no doubt, he said, that the monster was at this moment on her way to Washington, and, looking out of the window, which commanded a view of the Potomac for many miles, "not unlikely we shall have a shell or cannon-ball from one of her guns in the White House before we leave this room." Most of Stanton's complaints were directed to me, and to me the others turned—not complainingly, but naturally for information or suggestion that might give relief.

I had little to impart, except my faith in the untried "Monitor" experiment, which we had prepared for the emergency; an assurance that the "Merrimac," with her draught, and loaded with iron, could not pass Kettle Bottom Shoals, in the Potomac, and ascend the river and surprise us with a cannon-ball; and advised that, instead of adding to the general panic, it would better become us to calmly consider the situation, and inspire confidence by acting, so far as we could, intelligently, and with discretion and judgment. Mr. Chase approved the suggestion, but thought it might be well to telegraph Governor Morgan and Mayor Opdyke, at New York, that they might be on their guard. Stanton said he should warn the authorities in all the chief cities. I questioned the propriety of sending abroad panic missives, or adding to the alarm that would naturally be felt, and said it was doubtful whether the vessel, so cut down and loaded with armor, would venture outside of the Capes; certainly, she could not, with her draught of water, get into the sounds of North Carolina to disturb Burnside and our forces there; nor was she omnipresent, to make general destruction at New York, Boston, Port Royal, etc., at the same time; that there would be general alarm created; and repeated that my dependence was on the "Monitor," and my confidence in her great.

"What," asked Stanton, "is the size and strength of this 'Monitor?' How many guns does she carry?" When I replied two, but of large calibre, he turned away with a look of mingled amazement, contempt, and distress, that was painfully ludicrous. Mr. Seward said that my remark concerning the draught of water which the "Merrimac" drew, and the assurance that it was impossible for her to get at our forces under Burnside, afforded him the first moment of relief and real comfort he had received. It was his sensitive nature to be easily depressed, but yet to promptly rally and catch at hope. Turning to Stanton, he said we had, perhaps, given away too much to our apprehensions. He saw no alternative but to wait and hear what our new battery might accomplish.

Stanton left abruptly after Seward's remark. The President ordered his carriage, and went to the Navy Yard to see what might be the views of the naval officers.

Ericsson's preposterous "cheesebox on a raft," built in scarcely a hundred days, reached Hampton Roads Saturday night. Her crew of forty-eight, battered by rough seas on their voyage to Virginia, stood wearily at their battle stations. Two guns against ten on the Merrimack—*what match was this pygmy for the Confederate giant? Gulls circling over Hampton Roads next morning looked down on a "little black mass" as Ericsson's* Monitor *steamed gamely to its test. The reporter for the* Baltimore American *admitted: "Never was a greater hope placed upon more insignificant means." At a mile's distance, he thought,*

"she might be taken for a raft, with an army ambulance amidship."
Captain G. J. Van Brunt, commanding the frigate Minnesota, reported to Gideon Welles the story of an immortal battle:[6]

At six A.M. the enemy again appeared, coming down from Craney
Island, and I beat to quarters; but they ran past my ship, and were
heading for Fortress Monroe, and the retreat was beaten, to allow my
men to get something to eat. The Merrimac ran down near the Rip
Raps, and then turned into the channel through which I had come.
Again all hands were called to quarters, and I opened upon her with my
stern-guns, and made signal to the Monitor to attack the enemy. She immediately ran down in my wake, right within the range of the Merrimac, completely covering my ship, as far as was possible with her
diminutive dimensions, and, much to my astonishment, laid herself
right alongside of the Merrimac, and the contrast was that of a pigmy
to a giant.

Gun after gun was fired by the Monitor, which was returned with
whole broadsides from the rebels, with no more effect, apparently,
than so many pebble-stones thrown by a child. After a while they commenced manoeuvring, and we could see the little battery point her bow
for the rebel's, with the intention, as I thought, of sending a shot
through her bow-porthole; then she would shoot by her, and rake her
through her stern. In the mean time the rebels were pouring broadside
after broadside, but almost all her shot flew over the little submerged
propeller; and when they struck the bomb-proof tower, the shot glanced
off without producing any effect, clearly establishing the fact that
wooden vessels cannot contend successfully with iron-clad ones, for
never before was anything like it dreamed of by the greatest enthusiast
in maritime warfare.

The Merrimac, finding that she could make nothing of the Monitor,
turned her attention once more to me in the morning. She had put one
eleven-inch shot under my counter, near the water-line, and now, on her
second approach, I opened upon her with all my broadside-guns and
ten-inch pivot—a broadside which would have blown out of water any
timber-built ship in the world. She returned my fire with her rifled bow-
gun, with a shell which passed through the chief engineer's state-room,
through the engineer's mess-room amidships, and burst in the boat-
swain's room, tearing four rooms all into one, in its passage exploding
two charges of powder, which set the ship on fire, but it was promptly

extinguished by a party headed by my first lieutenant. Her second went through the boiler of the tugboat Dragon, exploding it, and causing some consternation on board my ship for the moment, until the matter was explained.

This time I had concentrated upon her an incessant fire from my gun-deck, spar-deck and forecastle pivot-guns, and was informed by my marine officer, who was stationed on the poop, that at least fifty solid shot struck her on her slanting side, without producing any apparent effect. By the time she had fired her third shell, the little Monitor had come down upon her, placing herself between us, and compelled her to change her position, in doing which she grounded, and again I poured into her all the guns which could be brought to bear upon her. As soon as she got off, she stood down the bay, the little battery chasing her with all speed, when suddenly the Merrimac turned around, and ran full speed into her antagonist. For a moment I was anxious, but instantly I saw a shot plunge into the iron roof of the Merrimac, which surely must have damaged her, for some time after the rebels concentrated their whole battery upon the tower and pilot-house of the Monitor, and soon after the latter stood down for Fortress Monroe, and we thought it probable she had exhausted her supply of ammunition, or sustained some injury.

Soon after the Merrimac and the two other steamers headed for my ship, and I then felt to the fullest extent my condition. I was hard and immovable aground, and they could take position under my stern and rake me. I had expended most of my solid shot, and my ship was badly crippled, and my officers and men were worn out with fatigue; but even in this extreme dilemma I determined never to give up the ship to the rebels, and after consulting my officers, I ordered every preparation to be made to destroy the ship, after all hope was gone to save her. On ascending the poop-deck, I observed that the enemy's vessels had changed their course, and were heading for Craney Island; then I determined to lighten the ship by throwing overboard my eight-inch guns, hoisting out provisions, starting water, etc. At two P.M. I proceeded to make another attempt to save the ship, by the use of a number of powerful tugs and the steamer S. R. Spaulding—kindly sent to my assistance by Captain Talmadge, Quartermaster at Fortress Monroe— and succeeded in dragging her half a mile distant, and then she was again immovable, the tide having fallen. At two A.M. this morning I succeeded in getting the ship once more afloat, and am now at anchor opposite Fortress Monroe.

But the Merrimack *knew she had lost the game; after firing volley upon volley, one of her officers grumbled: "I can do about as much damage to the* Monitor *by snapping my fingers at her." The* Merrimack *limped back to Norfolk, "sagging" at the stern as though "badly aleak."*

The North, wild with joy at the news of the victory, soon was smoking cigars called "El Monitor" and dancing "Ericsson's Gallope." It is doubtful, however, whether any tribute pleased Ericsson more than the letter he received from Alban G. Stimers, engineer aboard the Monitor:[7]

IRON-CLAD MONITOR

HAMPTON ROADS, March 9, 1862

MY DEAR SIR: After a stormy passage, which proved us to be the finest sea-boat I was ever in, we fought the Merrimac for more than three hours this forenoon, and sent her back to Norfolk in a sinking condition. Iron-clad against iron-clad. We manoeuvred about the bay here, and went at each other with mutual fierceness. I consider that both ships were well fought; we were struck twenty-two times: pilot-house twice, turret nine times, side-armor eight times, deck three times. The only vulnerable point was the pilot-house. One of your great logs (nine by twelve inches thick) is broken in two. The shot struck just outside of where the captain had his eye, and it has disabled him by destroying his left eye and temporarily blinding the other. The log is not quite in two, but is broken and pressed inward one and a half inches. [The "log" alluded to is made of wrought iron of the best material.] She tried to run us down and sink us as she did the Cumberland yesterday, but she got the worst of it. Her bow passed over our deck, and our sharp upper-edged side cut through the light iron shoe upon her stem and well into her oak. She will not try that again. She gave us a tremendous thump, but did not injure us in the least. We are just able to find the point of contact.

The turret is a splendid structure. I don't think much of the shield, but the pendulums are fine things, though I cannot tell you how they would stand the shot, as they were not hit.

You were very correct in your estimate of the effect of shot upon the man inside the turret when it was struck near him. Three men were knocked down, of whom I was one; the other two had to be carried below, but I was not disabled at all, and the others recovered before the battle was over. Captain Worden stationed himself at the pilot-house, Greene fired the guns, and I turned the turret until the Captain was

disabled and was relieved by Greene, when I managed the turret myself, Master Stodden having been one of the two stunned men.

Captain Ericsson, I congratulate you upon your great success. Thousands have this day blessed you. I have heard whole crews cheer you.
Every man feels that you have saved this place to the nation by furnish-
ing us with the means to whip an iron-clad frigate that was, until our
arrival, having it all her own way with our most powerful vessels.

I am, with much esteem, very truly yours,

ALBAN C. STIMERS

CAPTAIN J. ERICSSON,

NO. 95 FRANKLIN STREET, NEW-YORK.

*In the American legation in London that indefatigable diarist, Ben-
jamin Moran, noted joyfully:*[8]

. . . This startling battle has dumfounded and dismayed all England.
After loud-mouthed exultations over their iron-armoured Warrior, and
savage boasts of her power to destroy us & ours, the nation has awaked
this morning to the agreeable fact that their navy is worthless. Instead
of being the ruler of the seas, they now stand like other maritime powers, literally without a Navy. It remains to be seen what nation will
build up iron fleets quickest.

The battle between the Monitor and Merrimac is the absorbing topic
of conversation in the Clubs, in Parliament, & in Society. And but few
Englishmen care to conceal their chagrin that the Americans have been
the first to demonstrate the power of iron ships, and the comparative
uselessness of stone forts.

III

*Dispatches reaching the war offices in Washington and Richmond told a
story of fighting or of preparations for battle wherever the sun warmed
the earth. Even McClellan was on the point of venturing from the
banks of the Potomac. In northern Arkansas, from March 6 to 8, eleven
thousand Union troops under General Samuel Curtis collided with
fourteen thousand Confederates at Pea Ridge or Elkhorn Tavern;
Curtis claimed his one victory of the war, but he owed it principally to
those solid German saloonkeepers, shoemakers, merchants and farmers who "fought mit Sigel." On March 14 at New Madrid, Missouri, a
victory by Union troops under Brigadier General John Pope secured*

the upper reaches of the Mississippi for the North. In the far southwest, where Confederates under H. H. Sibley were fighting an almost ignored war, the capture of Santa Fe, New Mexico on March 4 was followed by a defeat on the twenty-eighth in Apache Canyon at Pigeon's Ranch (Glorieta). Obviously Mr. Lincoln and his government were doing much better at the trade of war than most informed observers had expected three short months before; nerves in Richmond were at least jangled to the point where Jefferson Davis reshuffled the portfolios of State, War and Attorney General in his official family.

April brought the scent of peach blossoms along the Tennessee. With the evacuation of Nashville, Albert Sidney Johnston began concentrating his Confederate forces at Corinth. Grant had been restored to command, and in early March had argued that he should strike at Corinth before Johnston effected his concentration there. Halleck said No—Grant should wait until later in the month when Buell could join forces with him; and for once both Grant and Halleck were right, depending on the style of war one favored. Curtis' victory at Pea Ridge, falling within Halleck's department, had brought him the supreme command in the West—proof at least that Mr. Lincoln still had something to learn about separating his military sheep and goats. Yet it was not really Halleck's fault that the Rebels destroyed the bridges over the Duck River, delaying by ten days Buell's scheduled juncture with Grant.

At Pittsburg Landing on the Tennessee, where the camping ground around Shiloh Meetinghouse could have accommodated the tents of one hundred thousand troops, Grant waited impatiently for Buell. On April 4 Grant's horse stumbled, so severely injuring the general's ankle that his boot had to be cut off. Grant could neither walk nor sleep. His position at Pittsburg Landing, and also the assurances he received from Sherman, gave him a false sense of security—or so, in retrospect, Colonel Wills De Hass believed:[9]

The country is undulating table-land, the bluffs rising to the height of one hundred and fifty feet above the alluvial. Three principal streams and numerous tributaries cut the ground occupied by the army, while many deep ravines intersect, rendering it the worst possible battle-ground. The principal streams are Lick creek, which empties into the Tennessee above the landing; Owl creek, which rises near the source of Lick creek, flows south-east, encircling the battle-field, and falls into Snake creek, which empties into the Tennessee below the

landing, or about three miles below Lick creek. The country . . . was
a primeval forest, except where occasional settlers had opened out into
small farms. The Army of the Tennessee lay within the area indicated,
extending three and a half miles from the river and nearly the same
distance north and south. . . .

When the writer reached Shiloh (April 2d) he found the impression
general that a great battle was imminent. Experienced officers believed

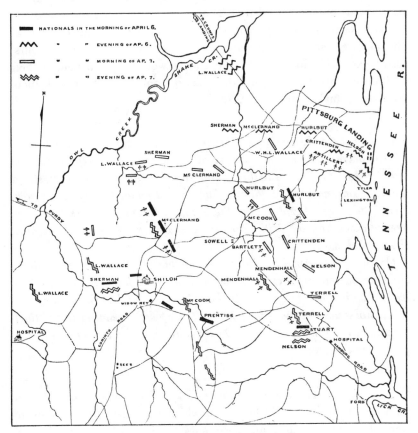

SHILOH, APRIL 6 AND 7, 1862

From Lossing, *Pictorial History of the Civil War*

that Beauregard and Johnston would strike Grant or the Army of the
Tennessee before Buell could unite the Army of the Ohio. We found
the army at Shiloh listless of danger, and in the worst possible condition of defense. The divisions were scattered over an extended space,

with great intervals, and at one point a most dangerous gap. Not the semblance of a fortification could be seen. The entire front was in the most exposed condition. One or two sections of batteries at remote points, no scouts, no cavalry pickets, a very light infantry picket within one mile of camp, were all that stood between us and the dark forest then filling with the very flower of the Southern army. To my inexperienced judgment, all this appeared very strange, and I communicated these views to our brigade commander, who expressed himself in the same spirit, but remarked that he was powerless. One day's work in felling trees would have placed the camp in a tolerable state of defense. The men were actually sick from inaction and over-eating. A few hours' active exercise with the axe and shovel would have benefited their health, and might have saved their camp from destruction, with thousands of valuable lives. . . .

Shiloh, in the end, would be a battle of ten thousand different stories, all true according to what the individual narrators had experienced on those yellow bluffs at Pittsburg Landing. In later years Grant stated that his "only military engineer" had argued against digging intrenchments, adding: "Besides this, the troops with me, officers and men, needed discipline and drill more than they did experience with the pick, shovel and axe."

On Saturday, April 5, Grant learned that Buell would arrive down river at Savannah next day. Sherman assured him again that there was no immediate danger at Pittsburg Landing, and so Grant, hobbling to his horse on that painful ankle, left the field, intending to see Buell in person on Sunday. Colonel De Hass did not share Sherman's easygoing confidence:[10]

. . . Colonel Hildebrand and myself occupied the same tent; it stood adjacent the primitive little church which was destined to fill so important a page in our country's annals. Colonel Hildebrand, not feeling well, retired early, but I remained up late writing letters, and preparing for the morrow. The men were ordered to stack arms in front of their tents, prepared to advance or repel attack, and that if firing were heard during the night to remain quiet—await the long-roll or bugle-call. . . . How unconscious of danger lay the army of the Union that night! Outside of the immediate brigades named, few dreamed of danger; but their visions were of home and the loved ones who looked so fondly for their return; but, alas! how hopeless to thousands, who, that night, slept their last sleep on earth.

On our front—in the depth of the dark forest—how different the scene! At midnight, stepping from my tent, beneath the shadow of that quiet church, I listened for a premonition of the coming storm. But all was still save the measured tread of the sentinel, and the gentle whispers of the genial night breeze. No sound came from the distant wood; no camp-fires shed their lurid light against the walls of living green; no drum-beats or bugle-blasts were heard, for quietness reigned by imperious command throughout the rebel camps. Those who slept dreamed of booty and glory, for Beauregard had assured them that they should sleep in the enemy's camp to-morrow night, eat well-baked bread and meat, and drink real coffee. It is also alleged, of the same commander, that he declared he would water his horse on Sunday evening in the Tennessee, or another place where water is supposed not to be very abundant. He did not redeem either of the latter promises, but he did the first. Long before early dawn on the calm, Sabbath morn, the rebel army had breakfasted, and stripped for the bloody work before them. Their blankets, knapsacks, etc., were laid aside, their only incumbrance being their arms, haversacks, and canteens. The latter, it has been asserted, were filled with "powder and whisky," which, of course, is a popular delusion. Certain it is, however, they fought with the desperation of men inflamed with something more stirring than Yankee hatred and Southern patriotism. By three o'clock they were on the move. At daybreak General A. Sidney Johnston said to General Beauregard: "Can it be possible they are not aware of our presence?" "It can scarcely be possible," replied the latter; "they must be laying some plan to entrap us."

Beauregard explained the Confederate plan:[11]

By a rapid and vigorous attack on Gen. Grant, it was expected he would be beaten back into his transports and the river, or captured, in time to enable us to profit by the victory, and remove to the rear all the stores and munitions that would fall into our hands in such an event, before the arrival of Gen. Buell's army on the scene. It was never contemplated, however, to retain the position thus gained, and abandon Corinth, the strategic point of the campaign.

Want of proper officers, needful for the proper organization of divisions and brigades of an army brought thus suddenly together, and other difficulties in the way of effective organization, delayed the movement until the night of the second inst., when it was heard from a reliable quarter that the junction of the enemy's armies was near at hand. It was then, at a late hour, determined that the attack should be attempted at once, incomplete and imperfect as were our preparations for such a grave and momentous adventure. Accordingly, that night, at one o'clock A.M., the preliminary orders to the commanders of corps were issued for the movement.

On the following morning the detailed orders of movement . . . were issued, and the movement, after some delay, commenced—the troops being in admirable spirits. It was expected we should be able to reach the enemy's lines in time to attack them early on the fifth instant. The men, however, for the most part, were unused to marching—the roads narrow, and traversing a densely wooded country, became almost impassable after a severe rain-storm on the night of the fourth, which drenched the troops in bivouac; hence our forces did not reach the intersection of the roads from Pittsburg and Hamburg, in the immediate vicinity of the enemy, until late Saturday afternoon.

It was then decided that the attack should be made on the next morning, at the earliest hour practicable, in accordance with the orders of movement—that is, in three lines of battle: the first and second extending from Owl Creek on the left to Lick Creek on the right—a distance of about three miles—supported by the third and the reserve. . . .

At eight A.M., on the sixth, a reconnoitring party of the enemy having become engaged with our advanced pickets, the commander of the forces gave the orders to begin the movement and attack as determined upon. . . .

IV

For the first time since those unhappy days in Kentucky when Sherman had been publicly called insane, the red-bearded general was back in command. His combat experience amounted to the fiasco at Bull Run; and when with the breaking dawn that Sabbath morning scared rabbits began overrunning his camp, he appeared singularly uninterested in what was causing this invasion.

Young Whitelaw Reid of the Cincinnati Gazette *wrote his story "fresh from the field of the great battle, with its pounding and roaring of artillery, and its keener-voiced rattle of musketry sounding in my ears; with all its visions of horror still seeming seared upon my eyeballs, while scenes of panic-stricken rout and brilliant charges, and obstinate defences, and succor, and intoxicating success are burned alike confusedly and indelibly upon my brain . . ." At seven o'clock on Sunday morning Reid watched the Rebels under Johnston and Beauregard burst upon Sherman's camps:*[12]

. . . Some, particularly among our officers, were not yet out of bed. Others were dressing, others washing, others cooking, a few eating their breakfasts. Many guns were unloaded, accoutrements lying pell-mell, ammunition was ill-supplied—in short, the camps were virtually surprised—disgracefully, it might be added, unless some one can hereafter give some yet undiscovered reason to the contrary—and were taken at almost every possible disadvantage.

The first wild cries from the pickets rushing in, and the few scattering shots that preceded their arrival, aroused the regiments to a sense of their peril; an instant afterward, shells were hurtling through the tents, while, before there was time for thought of preparation, there came rushing through the woods, with lines of battle sweeping the whole fronts of the division-camps and bending down on either flank, the fine, dashing, compact columns of the enemy.

Into the just-aroused camps thronged the rebel regiments, firing sharp volleys as they came, and springing toward our laggards with the bayonet. Some were shot down as they were running, without weapons, hatless, coatless, toward the river. The searching bullets found other poor unfortunates in their tents, and there, all unheeding now, they still slumbered, while the unseen foe rushed on. Others fell, as they were disentangling themselves from the flaps that formed the doors to their tents; others as they were buckling on their accoutrements; a few, it was even said, as they were vainly trying to impress on the cruelly-exultant enemy their readiness to surrender.

Officers were wounded in their beds, and left for dead, who, through the whole two days' fearful struggle, lay there gasping in their agony, and on Monday evening were found in their gore, inside their tents, and still able to tell the tale.

The confusion mounted. Brutal, bruising Shiloh grew into a patchwork of personal horrors. Wild stories were related:[13]

Frank W. Reilly, writing in the Cincinnati *Times:* "I hope my eyes never look upon such sights. Men with their entrails protruding, others with bullets in their breasts or shoulders, and one poor wretch I found whose eyes had been shot entirely away."

Lieutenant William George Stevenson,* of Beauregard's staff, explaining why his horse balked at the edge of a little ravine: "He hesitated and I glanced down to detect the cause. The rain had washed the leaves out of the narrow channel down the gully some six inches wide, leaving the hard clay exposed. Down this pathway ran a band of blood nearly an inch thick, filling the channel. Striking my rowels into the horse to escape the horrible sight, he plunged his foot into the stream of blood and threw the already thickening mass in ropy folds up on the dead leaves on the bank."

L. M. Blakely, Iowa Sixth, fighting with Sherman: "Our regiment . . . lost everything, among which was the subscriber's establishment containing $5,000 worth of merchandise; my tents Gen. Beauregard made his headquarters (a mighty good place). . . ."

"One of Many," Iowa Eleventh, fighting with McClernand: ". . . as a specimen of the moral status of the rebels, I may say that the Surgeon of the 13th Iowa, in the same Brigade with us, who left a barrel of medical whiskey standing in his tent, had it all sucked dry—they not even leaving enough for bitters for the hospital corps the next morning."

A clergyman, exhorting Union boys to "rally for God and country," hears from Colonel Jacob Ammen, in civilian life a pious Episcopalian: "Shut-up, you God-damned old fool! Get out of the way!"

A Kentuckian, calling to his brother: "Hold on Bill, don't shoot there any more! That's father!"

Sergeant H. M. White, Iowa Eleventh, fighting with McClernand: ". . . They came running back in the wildest disorder. One frightened fugitive in particular I noticed, who, as he came along and ran through our ranks, exclaimed, 'Give them h-ll, boys. I gave them h-ll as long as I could.' Whether he had really given them any of the *sulphurous* or not, I can not say, but assuredly he had given them everything else he possessed, including his gun, cartridge-box, coat and hat, and was in a fair way to leave his unmentionables and undergarments, to be accounted for perhaps by the return so commonly made—'lost in action.' "

Leonard B. Houston, Iowa Second, fighting with Wallace: ". . .

---

* The same Stevenson who had been told (page 74) to join the Rebel army or climb a rope.

While the battle was raging most terrifically, and when it seemed like a mighty hurricane sweeping everything before it; when the great storm of cannon balls made the forest in places fall before its sweep; when men and horses were dying, and a blaze of unearthly fire lit up the scene; at this moment of horror when our Regiment was lying close to the ground to avoid the storm of balls, the *little birds* were singing in the green trees over our heads!—They were as happy as if all were perfect calmness beneath them and around them!"

Union Lieutenant Elijah C. Lawrence, boasting: ". . . The fact that our line was so short, our resistance so determined and that we made no show of artillery deceived them. The stampede and rally, followed by 'column by file,' and the hollow square in the woods, as we were told by officers captured the next day, were looked upon as Yankee tricks to draw them on masked batteries, and repeatedly, the commanding officer, when urged to allow a charge upon us, replied, 'No, you will get into a trap; no such little body of men could ever stand up and fight like that without something back of them.' They never thought that 'something' was pure pluck."

William Tecumseh Sherman: "Several times during the battle, cartridges gave out; but General Grant had thoughtfully kept a supply coming from the rear. When I appealed to the regiments to stand fast, although out of cartridges, I did so because to retire a regiment for any cause has a bad effect on others."

Prentiss, Sherman, McClernand—each had been driven back before Grant limped onto the field toward midmorning. By then Albert Sidney Johnston had been carried off, mortally wounded. Ed Russell, shot through the stomach, had shaken hands with every man in his battery before dropping dead. Four horses had been shot from under Sherman and powder smoke had changed the color of his beard. Whitelaw Reid, standing near Grant, described the final scenes of that savage afternoon:[14]

We have reached the last act in the tragedy of Sunday. It is half-past four o'clock. Our front line of divisions has been lost since half-past ten. Our reserve line is now gone, too. The rebels occupy the camps of every division save that of W. H. L. Wallace. Our whole army is crowded in the region of Wallace's camps, and to a circuit of one half to two thirds of a mile around the Landing. We have been falling back all day. We can do it no more. The next repulse puts us into the river, and there are not transports enough to cross a single division till the enemy would be upon us.

Lew. Wallace's division might turn the tide for us—it is made of fighting men—but where is it? Why has it not been thundering on the right for three hours past? We do not know yet that it was not ordered up till noon. Buell is coming, but he has been doing it all day, and all last week. His advance-guard is across the river now, waiting ferriage; but what is an advance-guard, with sixty thousand victorious foes in front of us?

We have lost nearly all our camps and camp equipage. We have lost nearly half our field artillery. We have lost a division general and two or three regiments of our soldiers as prisoners. We have lost—how dreadfully we are afraid to think—in killed and wounded. The hospitals are full to overflowing. A long ridge bluff is set apart for surgical uses. It is covered with the maimed, the dead and dying. And our men are discouraged by prolonged defeat. Nothing but the most energetic exertion, on the part of the officers, prevents them from becoming demoralized. Regiments have lost their favorite field-officers; companies the captains whom they have always looked to, with that implicit faith the soldier learns, to lead them to battle.

Meanwhile there is a lull in the firing. For the first time since sunrise you fail to catch the angry rattle of musketry or the heavy booming of the field-guns. Either the enemy must be preparing for the grand, final rush that is to crown the day's success and save the Southern Confederacy, or they are puzzled by our last retreat, and are moving cautiously lest we spring some trap upon them. Let us embrace the opportunity, and look about the Landing. We pass the old-log house, lately post-office, now full of wounded and surgeons, which constitutes the "Pittsburg" part of the Landing. General Grant and staff are in a group beside it. The General is confident. "We can hold them off till to-morrow; then they'll be exhausted, and we'll go at them with fresh troops." A great crowd is collected around the building—all in uniforms, most of them with guns. And yet we are needing troops in the front so sorely!

On the bluffs above the river is a sight that may well make our cheeks tingle. There are not less than five thousand skulkers lining the banks! Ask them why they don't go to their places in the line: "Oh! our regiment is all cut to pieces." "Why don't you go to where it is forming again?" "I can't find it," and the hulk looks as if that would be the very last thing he would want to do.

Officers are around among them, trying to hunt up their men, storming, coaxing, commanding—cursing I am afraid. One strange fellow—a Major, if I remember aright—is making a sort of elevated, superfine Fourth of July speech to everybody that will listen to him. He means well, certainly: "Men of Kentucky, of Illinois, of Ohio, of Iowa, of Indiana, I implore you, I beg of you, come up now. Help us through two hours more. By all that you hold dear, by the homes you hope to defend, by the flag you love, by the States you honor, by all your love of country, by all your hatred of treason, I conjure you, come up and do your duty now!" And so on for quantity. "That feller's a good speaker," was the only response I heard, and the fellow who gave it nestled more snugly behind his tree as he spoke.

With darkness close at hand, with his men exhausted after twelve hours of combat without food, Beauregard called a halt:[15]

I accordingly established my headquarters at the church at Shiloh, in the enemy's encampment, with Maj.-Gen. Bragg, and directed our troops to sleep on our arms, in such positions, in advance and rear, as corps commanders should determine, hoping, from news received by a special despatch, that delay had been encountered by Gen. Buell in his march from Columbia, and that his main force could not reach the field of battle in time to save Gen. Grant's shattered fugitive forces from capture or destruction on the following day.

During the night the rain fell in torrents, adding to the discomfort and harassed condition of the men; the enemy, moreover, had broken their rest by a discharge, at measured intervals, of heavy shells, thrown from the gunboats; therefore on the following morning, the troops under my command were not in condition to cope with an equal force of fresh troops. . . .

"Grant's worst battle," say many historians of Shiloh; the reporter for the New York World *wondered if Grant's middle name might not be "Surprise." A brilliant military scholar, Major General J. F. C. Fuller, examines Grant's conduct once he reached Shiloh and draws another conclusion:*[16]

John Codman Ropes is an author whose opinions rightly carry weight. He possessed a legal mind, and was one of the first of the Civil War historians to base the history of the war on the Official Records. What he cannot find substantiated in the Records he frequently doubts.

This is the weak link in many of his arguments, for, when a chaotic situation arises, there is no time, certainly during battle, to record anything beyond the main orders. I have been fortunate enough to witness two such events, namely the German counter-attack of November 30, 1917, and the British defeat in March the following year, and all I can say is that should any writer attempt to base the history of these operations on official records his work will be fantastic and unreal.

What were the conditions which confronted Grant on the morning of the 6th? The country was thickly wooded and broken; the front of his army had been pulverized and driven back two miles; some 10,000 panic-stricken non-combatants were crowding towards the river bank; 5,000 stragglers were spreading confusion broadcast: and as is always the case when such situations arise, every form of rumour was in the air, the enemy's numbers being exaggerated to 100,000. Such was the situation which faced Grant when on crutches he hobbled off his ship to be assisted onto his horse. What did he then do?

I will answer this question categorically:

(1) Remembering his lesson at Fort Donelson, he at once organized ammunition trains.

(2) The 23rd Missouri regiment he hurried forward to reinforce Prentiss.

(3) The 15th and 16th Iowa regiments he directed to form line, arrest the stragglers, and reorganize them as a reserve.

(4) He then rode to the front after sending word to Lewis Wallace and Nelson to advance forthwith.

(5) He visited Hurlbut's, W. H. L. Wallace's and Prentiss's divisions.

(6) At 10 A.M., he visited Sherman and McClernand, and finding them short of ammunition sent an aide back to send more forward.

(7) He next formed up a large number of stragglers, and, constantly under fire, visited every part of the field.

(8) Then he sent back to urge on Lewis Wallace and Nelson. The first had taken the wrong road, and the second in place of marching at 7 A.M. did not start until 1.30 P.M.!

(9) To make up for their delay he sent an order to General Wood of Buell's army to march his division with all speed to Savannah, and arranged for transports to meet him there.

(10) He wrote a message to Buell to urge him on.

(11) He ordered two Iowa regiments to reinforce McClernand.

(12) Between 1 and 2 P.M., he returned to the Landing, and met General Buell on the steamer *Tigress*.

(13) Then he once again rode to the front to Snake Creek, and sent an aide to find General Wallace and guide him to the battlefield.

(14) At 3 P.M., he ordered forward the 81st Ohio regiment, and placed it in position.

(15) Then he once again visited Sherman, who, in his *Memoirs*, says: "He ordered me to be ready to assume the offensive in the morning, saying that, as he observed at Fort Donelson at the crisis of the battle, both sides seemed defeated and whoever assumed the offensive was sure to win."

(16) After this he rode back to the Landing and was present on the left when the final attack was made.

(17) Then he placed in position the two leading regiments of Nelson's division.

(18) Finally, at nightfall, he sent an order to all his divisional commanders to be ready early on the 7th to push out a heavy line of skirmishers followed by entire divisions at supporting distance, and to engage the enemy as soon as found.

Here we have eighteen important movements and actions carried out in the space of about nine hours. Many of these are not such as might be expected of a general commanding a highly trained army. But Grant's army was far from being highly trained, he had no staff worthy of the name, and very few trained subordinate officers. That, in the circumstances, "he left the division-commanders entirely to themselves" shows his wisdom; and to me it seems, that had not this half-crippled man, who on the night of the 6th/7th slept among his men in torrents of rain, and could get no rest because his ankle was much swollen, acted as he did, the battle would have been lost. Before he was engaged, his oversights were many; but, during the turmoil, his activity and generalship appear to me, in the circumstances which surrounded him, to have been quite wonderful. To say: "He seems to have given few orders, and in fact to have done little during the day except to show himself" is, in my opinion, a gross calumny, a calumny which Ropes would never have perpetrated had he himself experienced the chaos of war. This eminent writer may certainly have been misled by the scantiness of the recorded reports—this was inevitable—and also by Grant himself, who was no lawyer, for he says nothing about himself in his Shiloh Report,* in place—all the good he can of others. Ropes, throughout his highly documented studies, seldom gauges the modesty of Grant's nature.

Next day, throwing in 20,000 reinforcements under Buell and another 6,000 under Wallace, Grant drove the Confederates from Pittsburg Landing. The cost of the two-day battle staggered North and South:

	EFFECTIVES	KILLED	WOUNDED	MISSING
Union	62,682	1,754	8,408	2,885
Confederate	40,335	1,723	8,012	959

The unburied dead on the field sickened the civilian nurses and surgeons who arrived to care for the wounded. In abusive language the Lieutenant Governor of Ohio lashed out at Grant as a bloody blunderer. Some circulated the untrue story that during the battle Grant had been too drunk to mount a horse. Sherman remembered how these criticisms almost lost for the North its greatest general:[17]

A short time before leaving Corinth I rode from my camp to General Halleck's headquarters, then in tents just outside of the town, where we sat and gossiped for some time, when he mentioned to me casually that General Grant was going away the next morning. I inquired the cause, and he said that he did not know, but that Grant had applied for a thirty days' leave, which had been given him. Of course we all knew that he was chafing under the slights of his anomalous position, and I determined to see him on my way back. His camp was a short distance off the Monterey road, in the woods, and consisted of four or five tents, with a sapling railing around the front. As I rode up, Majors Rawlins, Lagow, and Hilyer, were in front of the camp, and piled up near them were the usual office and camp chests, all ready for a start in the morning. I inquired for the general, and was shown to his tent, where I found him seated on a camp-stool, with papers on a rude camp-table; he seemed to be employed in assorting letters, and tying them up with

* Actually Grant never wrote a full report on Shiloh. A few days after the battle Halleck moved his headquarters to Pittsburg Landing, and Grant observed: "I was ignored as much as if I had been at the most distant point of territory within my jurisdiction." Grant, under the circumstances, let Halleck seek his information on the battle from those to whom the commander of the western department was still talking.

red tape into convenient bundles. After passing the usual compliments, I inquired if it were true that he was going away. He said, "Yes." I then inquired the reason, and he said: "Sherman, you know. You know that I am in the way here. I have stood it as long as I can, and can endure it no longer." I inquired where he was going to, and he said, "St. Louis." I then asked if he had any business there, and he said, "Not a bit." I then begged him to stay, illustrating his case by my own.

Before the battle of Shiloh, I had been cast down by a mere newspaper assertion of "crazy"; but that single battle had given me new life, and now I was in high feather; and I argued with him that, if he went away, events would go right along, and he would be left out; whereas, if he remained, some happy accident might restore him to favor and his true place. He certainly appreciated my friendly advice, and promised to wait awhile; at all events, not to go without seeing me again, or communicating with me. Very soon after this, I was ordered to Chewalla, where, on the 6th of June, I received a note from him, saying that he had reconsidered his intention, and would remain. I cannot find the note, but my answer I have kept.

Grant admitted that he was now a changed man:[18]

Up to the battle of Shiloh I, as well as thousands of other citizens, believed that the rebellion against the Government would collapse suddenly and soon, if a decisive victory could be gained over any of its armies. Donelson and Henry were such victories. An army of more than 21,000 men was captured or destroyed. Bowling Green, Columbus and Hickman, Kentucky, fell in consequence, and Clarksville and Nashville, Tennessee, the last two with an immense amount of stores, also fell into our hands. The Tennessee and Cumberland rivers, from their mouths to the head of navigation, were secured. But when Confederate armies were collected which not only attempted to hold a line farther south, from Memphis to Chattanooga, Knoxville and on to the Atlantic, but assumed the offensive and made such a gallant effort to regain what had been lost, then, indeed, I gave up all idea of saving the Union except by complete conquest. Up to that time it had been the policy of our army, certainly of that portion commanded by me, to protect the property of the citizens whose territory was invaded, without regard to their sentiments, whether Union or Secession. After this, however, I regarded it as humane to both sides to protect the persons of those found at their homes, but to consume everything that could be used to support or supply armies. Protection was still continued over such supplies as were within lines held by us and which we expected to continue to hold; but such supplies within the reach of Confederate armies I regarded as much contraband as arms or ordnance stores. Their destruction was accomplished without bloodshed and tended to the same result as the destruction of armies.

CHAPTER 11

ANYTHING GOES!

I N EARLY APRIL, 1862, the country recoiled from the tragedy at Pittsburg Landing. Yet with the cyclonic proportions that the conflict was now attaining, even the horror of Shiloh was an incident of headlines today, editorializing tomorrow, and memory a day afterward. Shock and sorrow, victory and elation, derring-do and astonishment— from day to day the changing story of the war tantalized the nation's imagination, haunted its dreams, jangled its nerves and stirred its emotions. Take the highlights of a week's dispatches: On April 6 the Confederates caught the Federals breakfasting or sleeping at Shiloh; on April 7, on the Mississippi, the strongly fortified Confederate post at Island Number 10 surrendered; on April 11 Union forces occupied Huntsville, Alabama. Triumph and disaster competed for the nation's attention.

What next? No one could guess. An America learning how to fight total war improvised as it went. Anything was worth a try, and so for eight hours along the tracks of a Georgia railroad on a wet Saturday the antagonists in this brothers' contest staged a race without parallel in history. To award the participants of this adventure Congress created the Medal of Honor.

I

Twenty * *Union soldiers, attired in civilian clothes, had worked their way deep into the hill country of Georgia that Saturday. Under the com-*

* One raider never joined the group in Georgia. Two others, captured en route (though their identity was not discovered), were forced into the Southern Army. Another pair of raiders who reached Marietta failed to report at the rendezvous.

mand of Captain John J. Andrews, a valuable spy on Buell's staff,
these raiders proposed to steal a locomotive somewhere in the vicinity
of Atlanta. With luck, they expected to run north to Chattanooga,
burning bridges along the way and turning Southern communications
into a shambles.

At Marietta they boarded a train and waited quietly for the eight-
mile run around the base of Kenesaw Mountain. At Big Shanty, the
depot beyond, they gazed apprehensively at the white tents of a Con-
federate encampment. The locomotive hissed to its scheduled stop.
The raw, gloomy morning suddenly exploded. The Reverend William
Pittenger, Second Ohio Volunteers, one of the train thieves, told why:[1]

When we stopped, the conductor, engineer, and many of the passengers hurried to breakfast, leaving the train unguarded. Now was the
moment of action! Ascertaining that there was nothing to prevent a
rapid start, Andrews, our two engineers, Brown and Knight, and the
fireman hurried forward, uncoupling a section of the train consisting
of three empty baggage or box cars, the locomotive and tender. The
engineers and fireman sprang into the cab of the engine, while Andrews, with hand on the rail and foot on the step, waited to see that the
remainder of the band had gained entrance into the rear box car. This
seemed difficult and slow, though it really consumed but a few seconds,
for the car stood on a considerable bank, and the first who came were
pitched in by their comrades, while these, in turn, dragged in the others,
and the door was instantly closed. A sentinel, with musket in hand,
stood not a dozen feet from the engine watching the whole proceeding,
but before he or any of the soldiers and guards around could make up
their minds to interfere, all was done, and Andrews, with a nod to his
engineer, stepped on board. The valve was pulled wide open, and for a
moment the wheels of the "General" slipped around ineffectively; then,
with a bound that jerked the soldiers in the box car from their feet, the
little train darted away, leaving the camp and station in the wildest uproar and confusion. The first step of the enterprise was triumphantly
accomplished.

According to the time-table, of which Andrews had secured a copy,
there were two trains to be met. These presented no serious hindrance
to our attaining high speed, for we could tell just where to expect them.
There was also a local freight not down on the time-table, but which
could not be far distant. Any danger of collision with it could be avoided
by running according to the schedule of the captured train until it was

passed; then, at the highest possible speed, we would run to the Oostanaula and Chickamauga bridges, lay them in ashes, and pass on through Chattanooga to Mitchel,* at Huntsville, or wherever eastward of that point he might be found, arriving long before the close of the day. It was a brilliant prospect, and, so far as human estimates can determine, it would have been realized had the day been Friday instead of Saturday. On Friday every train had been on time, the day dry, and the road in perfect order. Now the road was in disorder, every train far behind time, and two "extras" were approaching us. But of these unfavorable conditions we knew nothing, and pressed confidently forward.

We stopped frequently, at one point tore up the track, cut telegraph wires, and loaded on crossties to be used in bridge burning. Wood and water were taken without difficulty, Andrews telling, very coolly, the story to which he adhered throughout the run, namely, that he was an agent of General Beauregard's running an impressed powder train through to that officer at Corinth. We had no good instruments for track-raising, as we had intended rather to depend upon fire; but the amount of time spent in taking up a rail was not material at this stage of our journey, as we easily kept on the time of our captured train. There was a wonderful exhilaration in passing swiftly by towns and stations through the heart of an enemy's country in this manner. It possessed just enough of the spice of danger—in this part of the run—to render it thoroughly enjoyable. The slightest accident to our engine, however, or a miscarriage in any part of our programme, would have completely changed the conditions.

At Etowah Station we found the "Yonah," an old locomotive owned by an iron company, standing with steam up; but not wishing to alarm the enemy till the local freight had been safely met, we left it unharmed. . . .

Back at Big Shanty, the conductor of the "General," W. A. Fuller, his engineer, J. Cain, and a road superintendent, Anthony Murphy, stood with jaws gaping as the train began to move north without them. A writer in the Southern Confederacy *reconstructed that astonishing scene:*[2]

These three determined men, without a moment's delay, put out after the flying train *on foot,* amidst shouts of laughter by the crowd, who,

* Major General Ormsby M. Mitchel.

though lost in amazement at the unexpected and daring act, could not repress their risibility at seeing three men start after a train on foot, which they had just witnessed depart at lightning speed. They put on all their speed and ran along the track for three miles, when they came across some track-raisers who had a small truck-car, which is shoved along by men so employed on railroads, on which to carry their tools. This truck and men were at once "impressed." They took it by turns of two at a time to run behind this truck and push it along all up-grades and level portions of the road, and let it drive at will on all the down-grades.

A little way further up the fugitive adventurers had stopped, cut the telegraph-wires, and torn up the track. Here the pursuers were thrown at pell-mell, truck and men, upon the side of the road. Fortunately "nobody was hurt on our side." The truck was soon placed on the road again, enough hands were left to repair the track, and with all the power of determined will and muscle they pushed on to Etowah station, some twenty miles above. Here, most fortunately, Major Cooper's old coal-engine, the "Yonah," one of the first engines on the State road, was standing out fired up. This venerable locomotive was immediately turned upon her old track, and, like an old racer at the tap of the drum, pricked up her ears, and made fine time to Kingston. . . .

Arriving there, and learning the adventurers were but twenty min-utes ahead, they left the "Yonah" to blow off while they mounted the engine of the Rome Branch road, which was ready fired up, and waiting for the arrival of the passenger-train nearly due, when it would have proceeded to Rome. A large party of gentlemen volunteered for the chase, some at Acworth, Allatoona, Kingston, and other points, taking such arms as they could lay their hands on at the moment, and with this fresh engine they set out with all speed, but with "great care and caution," as they had scarcely time to make Adairsville before the down freight-train would leave that point. Sure enough they discovered this side of Adairsville three rails torn up, and other impediments in the way. They "took up" in time to prevent an accident, but could proceed with the train no further. This was most vexatious, and it may have been in some degree disheartening, but it did not cause the slightest relaxation of efforts, and, as the result proved, was but little in the way of the *dead game*, pluck and resolution of Fuller and Murphy, who left the engine and again *put out on foot alone*. After running two miles they met the down freight-train one mile out from Adairsville. They immediately reversed the train and ran backwards to Adairsville, put the cars on the siding and pressed forward, making fine time to Calhoun, where they met the regular down passenger-train. Here they halted a moment, took on board a telegraph operator and a number of men, who again volunteered, taking their guns along, and continued the chase. Mr. Fuller also took in here a company of track-hands to repair the track as they went along. A short distance above Calhoun they *flushed their game* on a curve, where they doubtless supposed themselves out of danger, and were quietly oiling the engine, taking up the track, etc. . . .

The Reverend Mr. Pittenger never forgot that moment:[3]

. . . Not far behind we heard the scream of a locomotive bearing down upon us at lightning speed! The men on board were in plain sight and well armed! Two minutes—perhaps one—would have removed the rail at which we were toiling; then the game would have been in our own hands, for there was no other locomotive beyond that could be turned back after us. But the most desperate efforts were in vain. The rail was simply bent, and we hurried to our engine and darted away, while remorselessly after us thundered the enemy.

Now the contestants were in clear view, and a most exciting race followed. Wishing to gain a little time for the burning of the Oostanaula bridge we dropped one car, and shortly after, another; but they were "picked up" and pushed ahead to Resaca station. We were obliged to run over the high trestles and covered bridge at that point without a pause. This was the first failure in the work assigned us.

The Confederates could not overtake and stop us on the road, but their aim was to keep close behind so that we might not be able to damage the road or take in wood or water. In the former they succeeded, but not the latter. Both engines were put at the highest rate of speed. We were obliged to cut the wire after every station passed, in order that an alarm might not be sent ahead, and we constantly strove to throw our pursuer off the track or to obstruct the road permanently in some way so that we might be able to burn the Chickamauga bridges, still ahead. The chances seemed good that Fuller and Murphy would be wrecked. We broke out the end of our last box car and dropped cross-ties on the track as we ran, thus checking their progress and getting far enough ahead to take in wood and water at two separate stations. Several times we almost lifted a rail, but each time the coming of the Confederates, within rifle range, compelled us to desist and speed on.

Our worst hindrance was the rain. The previous day (Friday) had been clear, with a high wind, and on such a day fire would have been easily and tremendously effective. But to-day a bridge could be burned only with abundance of fuel and careful nursing.

Thus we sped on, mile after mile, in this fearful chase, around curves and past stations in seemingly endless perspective. Whenever we lost sight of the enemy beyond a curve we hoped that some of our obstructions had been effective in throwing him from the track and that we would see him no more; but at each long reach backward the smoke was again seen, and the shrill whistle was like the scream of a bird of prey. The time could not have been so very long, for the terrible speed was rapidly devouring the distance, but with our nerves strained to the highest tension each minute seemed an hour. On several occasions the escape of the enemy from wreck seemed little less than miraculous. At one point a rail was placed across the track so skillfully on a curve that it was not seen till the train ran upon it at full speed. . . .

Well might the Southern Confederacy *report with pride that nothing could daunt the redoubtable Mr. Fuller:*[4]

. . . Coming to where the rails were torn up, they stopped, tore up the rails behind them and laid them down before till they had passed over that obstacle. When the cross-ties were reached they hauled to and threw them off, and then proceeded, and under these difficulties gained on the frightened fugitives. At Dalton they halted a moment. Fuller put off the telegraph operator, with instructions to telegraph to Chattanooga to have them stopped in case he should fail to overhaul them. Fuller pressed on in hot chase, sometimes in sight, as much to prevent their cutting the wires before the message could be sent, as to catch them. The daring adventurers stopped just opposite, and very near to, where Colonel Glenn's regiment is encamped, and cut the wires; but the operator at Dalton *had put the message through about two minutes before.* They also again tore up the track, cut down a telegraph-pole, and placed the two ends of it under the cross-ties, and the middle over the rail on the track. The pursuers stopped again, and got over this impediment in the same manner they did before—taking up rails behind and laying them down before. Once over this, they shot on and passed through the great tunnel at Tunnel Hill, being only five minutes behind. The fugitives, finding themselves closely pursued, uncoupled two of the box-cars from the engine, to impede the progress of the pursuers. Fuller hastily coupled them to the front of his engine, and pushed them ahead of him to the first turn-out or siding, where they were left, thus preventing the collision the adventurers intended. Thus the engine-thieves passed Ringgold, where they began to fag. They were out of wood, water, and oil. Their rapid running and inattention to the engine had melted all the brass from the journals. They had no time to repair and refit, for an iron horse of more bottom was close behind. Fuller and Murphy and their men soon came within four hundred yards of them, when the fugitives jumped from the engine and left it—three on the north side, and five on the south—all fleeing precipitately, and scattering through the thicket. Fuller and his party also took to the woods after them. Some gentlemen, also well armed, took the engine and some cars of the down passenger-train at Calhoun, and followed up Fuller and Murphy and their party in the chase but a short distance behind, and reached the place of the stampede but a very few minutes after the first pursuers did.

A large number of men were soon mounted, armed, and scouring the entire country in search of them. Fortunately there was a militia muster at Ringgold. A great many countrymen were in town. Hearing of the case, they put out on foot and on horseback in every direction in search of the daring but now thoroughly frightened and fugitive men.

In a report to Secretary of War Stanton, Judge Advocate General Joseph Holt chronicled the sad climax of the story:[5]

The twenty-two captives, when secured, were thrust into the negro-jail of Chattanooga. They occupied a single room, half under ground, and but thirteen feet square, so that there was not space enough for them all to lie down together, and a part of them were, in consequence, obliged to sleep sitting and leaning against the walls. The only entrance was through a trap-door in the ceiling, that was raised twice a day to let down their scanty meals, which were lowered in a bucket. They had no other light or ventilation than that which came through two small, triple-grated windows. They were covered with swarming vermin, and the heat was so oppressive that they were often obliged to strip themselves entirely of their clothes to bear it. Add to this, they were all handcuffed, and, with trace-chains secured by padlocks around their necks, were fastened to each other in companies of twos and threes. Their food, which was doled out to them twice a day, consisted of a little flour wet with water and baked in the form of bread, and spoiled pickled beef. They had no opportunity of procuring any supplies from the outside, nor had they any means of doing so—their pockets having been rifled of their last cent by the confederate authorities, prominent among whom was an officer wearing the rebel uniform of a major. No part of the money thus basely taken was ever returned.

During this imprisonment at Chattanooga their leader, Mr. Andrews, was tried and condemned as a spy, and was subsequently executed at Atlanta, the seventh of June. They were strong and in perfect health when they entered this negro-jail, but at the end of something more than three weeks, when they were required to leave it, they were so exhausted from the treatment to which they had been subjected, as scarcely to be able to walk, and several staggered from weakness as they passed through the streets to the cars.

Finally, twelve of the number, including the five who have deposed, and Mr. Mason, of Co. K, Twenty-first regiment Ohio volunteers—who was prevented by illness from giving his evidence—were transferred to the prison of Knoxville, Tenn. On arriving there, seven of them were arraigned before a court-martial, charged with being spies. Their trial of course was summary. They were permitted to be present, but not to hear either the argument of their own counsel or that of the judge advocate. . . .

. . . Soon thereafter all the prisoners were removed to Atlanta, Ga., and they left Knoxville under a belief that their comrades, who had been tried, either had been or would be acquitted. In the mean time, however, the views entertained and expressed to them by the members of the court were overcome, it may be safely assumed, under the prompting of the remorseless despotism at Richmond. On the eighteenth of June, after their arrival at Atlanta, where they rejoined the comrades from whom they had been separated at Chattanooga, their prison-door was opened, and the death sentences of the seven who had been tried at Knoxville were read to them. No time for preparation was allowed them. They were told to bid their friends farewell, "and to be quick about it." They were at once tied and carried out to execution. Among the seven was private Samuel Robinson, Co. G, Thirty-third Ohio volunteers, who was too ill to walk. He was, however, pinioned like the rest, and in this condition was dragged from the floor on which he was lying to the scaffold. In an hour or more the cavalry escort, which had accompanied them, was seen returning with the cart, but the cart was empty—the tragedy had been consummated! On that evening and following morning the prisoners learned from the provost-marshal and guard that their comrades had died, as all true soldiers of the republic should die in the presence of its enemies. Among the revolting incidents which they mentioned in connection with this cowardly butchery, was the fall of two of the victims from the breaking of the ropes after they had been for some time suspended. On their being restored to consciousness, they begged for an hour in which to pray and to prepare for death, but this was refused them. The ropes were readjusted and the execution at once proceeded. . . .

Fourteen prisoners now remained jailed in Atlanta. In October a conversation between the jailer and an officer left no doubt that they also would hang. They struck boldly:

. . . On the evening of the next day, [they seized] the jailer when he opened the door to carry away the bucket in which their supper had been brought. This was followed by the seizure also of the seven guards on duty, and before the alarm was given eight of the fugitives were beyond the reach of pursuit. It has been since ascertained that six of these, after long and painful wanderings, succeeded in reaching our lines. Of the fate of the other two, nothing is known.* The remaining six of the fourteen, consisting of the five witnesses who have deposed, and Mr. Mason, were recaptured and confined in the barracks, until December, when they were removed to Richmond. There they were shut up in a room in Castle Thunder, where they shivered through the winter, without fire, thinly clad, and with but two small blankets, which they had saved with their clothes, to cover the whole party. So they remained until a few days since, when they were exchanged; and thus, at the end of eleven months, terminated their pitiless persecutions in the prisons of the South—persecutions begun and continued amid indignities and sufferings on their part, and atrocities on the part of their traitorous foes, which illustrate far more faithfully than any human language could express it, the demoniac spirit of a revolt, every throb of whose life is a crime against the very race to which we belong.

* Martin Hawkins and Daniel Allen Dorsey, who, wandering through Rebel country, did not reach the safety of the Union lines in Kentucky until November 18, 1862.

II

By the second spring of the war, life in America had changed completely. In the vast area east of the Mississippi no city, town or country crossroads could any longer take peace for granted. Spies stealing a train, raiders bursting from the cover of a woods, large invading forces appearing from the mists of the sea—anything was possible now, at any moment. In the "Paris of America"—New Orleans —young George W. Cable was learning that new ways quickly tend to become old habits:[6]

In the spring of 1862, we boys of Race, Orange, Magazine, Camp, Constance, Annunciation, Prytania, and other streets had no game. Nothing was "in"; none of the old playground sports that commonly fill the school-boy's calendar. We were even tired of drilling. Not one of us between seven and seventeen but could beat the drum, knew every bugle-call, and could go through the manual of arms and the facings like a drill-sergeant. We were *blasé* old soldiers—military critics.

Who could tell us anything? I recall but one trivial admission of ignorance on the part of any lad. On a certain day of grand review, when the city's entire defensive force was marching through Canal street, there came along, among the endless variety of good and bad uniforms, a stately body of tall, stalwart Germans, clad from head to foot in velveteen of a peculiarly vociferous fragrance, and a boy, spelling out the name upon their banner, said:

"H-u-s-s-a-r-s: what's them?"

"Aw, you fool!" cried a dozen urchins at once, "them's the Hoosiers. Don't you smell 'em?"

But that was earlier. The day of grand reviews was past. Hussars, Zouaves, and numberless other bodies of outlandish name had gone to the front in Tennessee and Virginia. Our cultivated eyes were satisfied now with one uniform that we saw daily. Every afternoon found us around in Coliseum Place, standing or lying on the grass watching the dress parade of the "Confederate Guards." Most of us had fathers or uncles in the long, spotless, gray, white-gloved ranks that stretched in such faultless alignment down the hard, harsh turf of our old ballground.

This was the flower of the home guard. The merchants, bankers, underwriters, judges, real-estate owners, and capitalists of the Anglo-American part of the city were "all present or accounted for" in that long line. Gray heads, hoar heads, high heads, bald heads. Hands

flashed to breast and waist with a martinet's precision at the command
of "Present arms,"—hands that had ruled by the pen—the pen and
the dollar—since long before any of us young spectators was born, and
had done no harder muscular work than carve roasts and turkeys these
twenty, thirty, forty years. Here and there among them were individuals who, unaided, had clothed and armed companies, squadrons, battalions, and sent them to the Cumberland and the Potomac. A good
three-fourths of them had sons on distant battle-fields, some living,
some dead. . . .

In those beautiful spring afternoons there was scarcely a man to
be found, anywhere, out of uniform. Down on the steamboat landing,
our famous Levee, a superb body of Creoles drilled and paraded in
dark-blue uniform. The orders were given in French; the manual was
French; the movements were quick, short, nervy. Their "about march"
was four sharp stamps of their neatly shod feet—*un, deux, trois,
quatre*—that brought them face about and sent them back, tramp,
tramp, tramp, over the smooth white pavement of powdered oyster-
shells. Ah, the nakedness of that once crowded and roaring mart!

And there was a "Foreign Legion." Of course, the city had always
been full of foreigners; but now it was a subject of amazement, not un-
mixed with satire, to see how many whom every one had supposed to
be Americans or "citizens of Louisiana" bloomed out as British, or
French, or Spanish subjects. But, even so, the tremendous pressure of
popular sentiment crowded them into the ranks and forced them to
make every show of readiness to "hurl back the foe," as we used to
call it. And they really served for much. Merely as a gendarmerie they
relieved just so many Confederate soldiers of police duty in a city under martial law, and enabled them to man forts and breastworks at
short notice whenever that call should come.

*Scoff though Southern newspapers did at the effectiveness of Mr. Lin-
coln's "paper blockade," New Orleans lived with its reality:*[7]

There had come a great silence upon trade. Long ago the custom-
warehouses had begun to show first a growing roominess, then empti-
ness, and then had remained shut, and the iron bolts and cross-bars
of their doors were gray with cobwebs. One of them, in which I had
earned my first wages as a self-supporting lad, had been turned into
a sword-bayonet factory, and I had been turned out. For some time
later the Levee had kept busy; but its stir and noise had gradually de-

clined, faltered, turned into the commerce of war and the clatter of calkers and ship-carpenters, and faded out. Both receipts and orders from the interior country had shrunk and shrunk, and the brave, steady fellows, who at entry and shipping and cash and account desks could no longer keep a show of occupation, had laid down the pen, taken up the sword and musket, and followed after the earlier and more eager volunteers. There had been one new, tremendous sport for moneyed men for a while, with spoils to make it interesting. The sea-going tow-boats, of New Orleans were long, slender side-wheelers, all naked power and speed, without either freight or passenger room, each with a single tall, slim chimney and hurrying walking-beam, their low, taper hulls trailing behind scarcely above the water, and perpetually drenched with the yeast of the wheels. Some merchants of the more audacious sort, restless under the strange new quiet of Tchoupitoulas street, had got letters of mark and reprisal, and let slip these sharp-nosed deerhounds upon the tardy, unsuspecting ships that came sailing up the Passes unaware of the declaration of war. But that game too was up. The blockade had closed in like a prison-gate: the lighter tow-boats, draped with tarpaulins, were huddled together under Slaughterhouse Point, with their cold boilers and motionless machinery yielding to rust; the more powerful ones had been moored at the long wharf vacated by Morgan's Texas steamships; there had been a great hammering, and making of chips, and clatter of railroad iron, turning these tow-boats into iron-clad cotton gun-boats, and these had crawled away, some up and some down the river, to be seen in that harbor no more. At length only the foundries, the dry-docks across the river, and the ship-yard in suburb Jefferson, where the great ram *Mississippi* was being too slowly built, were active, and the queen of Southern commerce, the city that had once believed it was to be the greatest in the world, was absolutely out of employment.

There was, true, some movement of the sugar and rice crops into the hands of merchants who had advanced the money to grow them; and the cotton-presses and cotton-yards were full of cotton, but there it all stuck; and when one counts in a feeble exchange of city for country supplies, there was nothing more. Except—yes—that the merchants had turned upon each other, and were now engaged in a mere passing back and forth among themselves in speculation the daily diminishing supply of goods and food. Some were too noble to take part in this, and dealt only with consumers. I remember one odd little old man, an extensive wholesale grocer, who used to get tipsy all by himself every day, and go home so, but who would not speculate on the food of a distressed city. He had not got down to that.

What had happened at Pittsburg Landing on the Tennessee wrenched hearts in New Orleans:[8]

. . . The times were grim. Opposite the rear of the store where I was now employed,—for it fronted in Common street and stretched

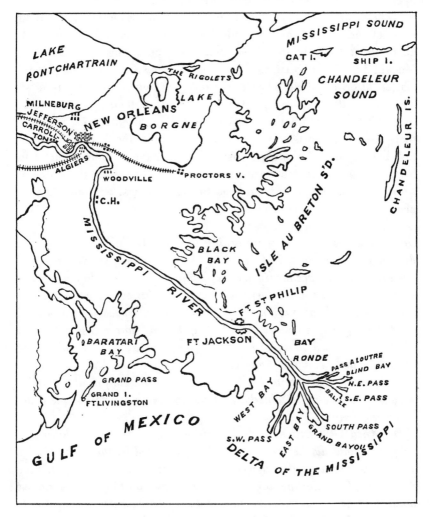

NEW ORLEANS AND VICINITY

From Lossing, *Pictorial History of the Civil War*

through to Canal,—the huge, unfinished custom-house reared its lofty granite walls, and I used to go up to its top now and then to cast my eye over the broad city and harbor below. When I did so, I looked down upon a town that had never been really glad again after the awful day of Shiloh. She had sent so many gallant fellows to help Beauregard, and some of them so young,—her last gleaning,—that when, on the day of their departure, they marched with solid column and firm-set, unsmiling mouths down the long gray lane made by the open ranks of those old Confederate Guards, and their escort broke into cheers and tears and waved their gray shakoes on the tops of their bayonets and seized the dear lads' hands as they passed in mute self-devotion and steady tread, while the trumpets sang "Listen to the Mockingbird," that was the last time; the town never cheered with elation afterward; and when the people next uncovered it was in silence, to let the body of Albert Sidney Johnston, their great chevalier, pass slowly up St. Charles street behind the muffled drums, while on their quivering hearts was written as with a knife the death-roll of that lost battle. One of those—a former school-mate of mine—who had brought that precious body walked beside the bier, with the stains of camp and battle on him from head to foot. The war was coming very near.

Out of the sea mists on the morning of April 18 appeared a Federal fleet under the command of David G. Farragut, an old sea dog who had been roaming the oceans since his appointment as a midshipman at the astonishing age of nine. Farragut now was in his early sixties; he was a lithe, square-built, hard-muscled man, painfully conscious of a bald head that he tried to cover by combing the side hair across the top of his head. Ordered to reduce the forts protecting New Orleans, seize the city and "hoist the American flag thereon," he had written his wife: "I have now obtained what I have been looking for all my life— a flag—and having obtained it, all that is necessary to complete the scene is victory."

On April 24 Farragut pounded his way past Forts St. Philip and Jackson. Doggedly he pressed ahead—undaunted by the boom of logs and hulks, the fire rafts, the rushing current of the Mississippi. Five days later, fingering the flag that he had come to hoist, he had gained possession of the gateway to the western Confederacy. Young Cable remembered the grief and hatred that swept through the proud old city:[9]

I shall not try to describe the day the alarm-bells told us the city was in danger and called every man to his mustering point. The children poured out from the school-gates and ran crying to their homes, meeting their sobbing mothers at their thresholds. The men fell into ranks. I was left entirely alone in charge of the store in which I was employed. Late in the afternoon, receiving orders to close it, I did so, and went home. But I did not stay. I went to the river-side. There until far into the night I saw hundreds of drays carrying cotton out of the presses and yards to the wharves, where it was fired. The glare of those sinuous miles of flame set men and women weeping and wailing thirty miles away on the farther shore of Lake Pontchartrain. But the next day was the day of terrors. During the night fear, wrath, and sense of betrayal had run through the people as the fire had run through the cotton. You have seen, perhaps, a family fleeing with lamentations and wringing of hands out of a burning house: multiply it by thousands upon thousands; that was New Orleans, though the houses were not burning. The firemen were out; but they cast fire on the waters, putting the torch to the empty ships and cutting them loose to float down the river.

Whoever could go was going. The great mass, that had no place to go to or means to go with, was beside itself. "Betrayed! betrayed!" it cried, and ran in throngs from street to street, seeking some vent, some victim for its wrath. I saw a crowd catch a poor fellow at the corner of Magazine and Common streets, whose crime was that he looked like a stranger and might be a spy. He was the palest living man I ever saw. They swung him to a neighboring lamp-post, but the Foreign Legion was patroling the town in strong squads, and one of its lieutenants, all green and gold, leaped with drawn sword, cut the rope, and saved the man. This was but one occurrence: there were many like it. I stood in the rear door of our store, Canal street, soon after reopening it. The junior of the firm was within. I called him to look toward the river. The masts of the cutter *Washington* were slowly tipping, declining, sinking—down she went. The gun-boat moored next to her began to smoke all over and then to blaze. My employers fell into ranks and left the city—left their goods and their affairs in the hands of one mere lad (no stranger would have thought I had reached fourteen) and one big German porter. I closed the doors, sent the porter to his place in the Foreign Legion, and ran to the levee to see the sights.

What a gathering! The riff-raff of the wharves, the town, the gutters. Such women—such wrecks of women! And all the juvenile rag-tag.

The lower steamboat landing, well covered with sugar, rice, and molasses, was being rifled. The men smashed; the women scooped up the smashings. The river was overflowing the top of the levee. A rainstorm began to threaten. "Are the Yankee ships in sight?" I asked of an idler. He pointed out the tops of their naked masts as they showed up across the huge bend of the river. They were engaging the batteries at Camp Chalmette—the old field of Jackson's renown. Presently that was over. Ah, me! I see them now as they come slowly round Slaughterhouse Point into full view, silent, grim, and terrible; black with men, heavy with deadly portent; the long-banished Stars and Stripes flying against the frowning sky. Oh, for the *Mississippi!* the *Mississippi!* Just then she came down upon them. But how? Drifting helplessly, a mass of flames.

The crowds on the levee howled and screamed with rage. The swarming decks answered never a word; but one old tar on the *Hartford,* standing with lanyard in hand beside a great pivot-gun, so plain to view that you could see him smile, silently patted its big black breech and blandly grinned.

And now the rain came down in sheets. About 1 or 2 o'clock in the afternoon (as I remember), I being again in the store with but one door ajar, came a roar of shoutings and imprecations and crowding feet down Common street. "Hurrah for Jeff Davis! Hurrah for Jeff Davis! Shoot them! Kill them! Hang them!" I locked the door on the outside, and ran to the front of the mob, bawling with the rest, "Hurrah for Jeff Davis!" About every third man there had a weapon out. Two officers of the United States navy were walking abreast, unguarded and alone, looking not to right or left, never frowning, never flinching, while the mob screamed in their ears, shook cocked pistols in their faces, cursed and crowded, and gnashed upon them. So through the gates of death those two men walked to the City Hall to demand the town's surrender. It was one of the bravest deeds I ever saw done.

III

Pudgy Ben Butler with his balding head, glittering eye and clownish moustache ruled New Orleans as its military administrator. Almost all of Butler's traits were distinctly individual. His New England conscience also stood apart, in the accepted sense; he was David Harum, Civil War general. The South nicknamed him "Beast" Butler, for reasons that Edward A. Pollard, editor of the Richmond Examiner, explained:[10]

The acts of the tyrant of New Orleans surpassed all former atrocities and outrages of the war. In frequent instances, citizens, accused by Butler of contumacious disloyalty, were confined at hard labor, with balls and chains attached to their limbs; and sometimes this degrading punishment was inflicted upon men whose only offence was that of selling medicines to the sick soldiers of the Confederacy. Helpless women were torn from their homes and confined in prison. One of these—a Mrs. Phillips—was accused of laughing as the funeral train of a Yankee officer passed her doors; she was seized, and with an ingenious and devilish cruelty, her sentence was pronounced by Butler —imprisonment on an island of barren sand under a tropical sun. Various pretexts were invented for plundering the inhabitants of the conquered city; men were forced to elect between starvation by the confiscation of all their property and taking an oath of allegiance to the invaders of their country; fines were levied at pleasure, and recusants threatened with ball and chain.

The conduct of the negroes in New Orleans became intolerable to their owners. They were fed, clothed, and quartered by the Yankees, who fraternized with them generally in a shameful way. The planters in the neighborhood of the city were required to share their crops with the commanding general, his brother, Andrew J. Butler, and other officers; and when this partnership was refused, the plantations were robbed of every thing susceptible of removal, and the slaves taken from their owners and compelled to work under the bayonets of Yankee guards.

It would occupy many pages to detail what the people of New Orleans suffered at the hands of the invaders whom they had so easily admitted into their city, in insult, wrongs, confiscation of property, seizure of private dwellings, and brazen robbery. The Yankee officers, from colonel to lieutenant, as the caprice of each might dictate, seized and took possession of gentlemen's houses, broke into their wine-rooms, forced open the wardrobes of ladies and gentlemen, and either used or sent away from the city the clothing of whole families. Some of the private residences of respectable citizens were appropriated to the vilest uses, the officials who had engaged them making them the private shops of the most infamous female characters.

But while Butler was thus apparently occupied with the oppression of "rebels," he was too much of a Yankee to be lost to the opportunity of making his pecuniary fortune out of the exigencies which he had created. The banker and broker of the corrupt operations in which he was engaged was his own brother, who bought confiscated property, shipped large consignments from New Orleans, to be paid for in cotton, and speculated largely in powder, saltpetre, muskets, and other war material sold to the Confederacy, surreptitiously sent out from the city and covered by permits for provisions. Of the trade in provisions for cotton, Butler received his share of the gains, while the robbery was covered up by the pretence of consumption in New Orleans "to prevent starvation," or by reported actual issue to troops. The Yankee general did not hesitate to deal in the very life-blood of his own soldiers.

Nothing that occurred during the entire war more outraged the South than Butler's "General Orders No. 28," which was answered with an impassioned plea:[11]

Head Quarters Western Department,
Corinth, Mississippi, May 19th, 1862

GENERAL ORDERS,
No. 44.

For the information of this army, the following General Orders No. 28, of the Federal Officer, Major General Butler, ("the Haynau of the North,") commanding at New Orleans, will be read on dress parade:

NOTICE.

Headquarters Department of the Gulf,
New Orleans, May 15, 1862.
General Orders, No. 28

As the officers and soldiers of the United States have been subject to repeated insults from the women (calling themselves ladies) of New Orleans, in return for the most scrupulous noninterference and courtesy on our part, it is ordered that hereafter when any female shall, by word, gesture or movement, insult or show contempt for any officer or soldier of the United States, she shall be regarded and held liable to be treated as a woman of the town plying her avocation.*

By command of

Major General Butler.

* "Avocation"—so the orders read. Had the women of New Orleans and their outraged defenders consulted a dictionary, they would have discovered that Butler had confused prostitution with crocheting, or playing backgammon, or any one of innumerable subsidiary occupations. The "Beast" should have omitted the phrase, "of the town," in the last sentence.

Geo. C. Strong, *A. A. G., Chief of staff.*

Men of the South! shall our mothers, our wives, our daughters and our sisters, be thus outraged by the ruffianly soldiers of the North, to whom is given the right to treat, at their pleasure, the ladies of the South as common harlots? Arouse friends, and drive back from our soil, those infamous invaders of our homes and disturbers of our family ties.

(Signed,)

G. T. Beauregard,
General Commanding

Pollard continued his bitter indictment of the Union general:[12]

The rule of Butler in New Orleans is especially memorable for the deliberate murder of William B. Mumford, a citizen of the Confederate States, against whom the tyrant had invented the extraordinary charge that he had insulted the flag of the United States.* The fact was, that before the city had surrendered, Mumford had taken down from the mint the enemy's flag. The ensign was wrongfully there; the city had not surrendered; and even in its worst aspects, the act of Mumford was simply one of war, not deserving death, still less the death of a felon. The horrible crime of murdering in cold blood an unresisting and noncombatant captive, was completed by Butler on the 7th of June. On that day, Mumford, the martyr, was publicly executed on the gallows. The Massachusetts coward and tyrant had no ear or heart for the pitiful pleadings made to save the life of his captive, especially by his unhappy wife, who in her supplications for mercy was rudely repulsed, and at times answered with drunken jokes and taunts. The execution took place in the sight of thousands of panic-stricken citizens. None spoke but the martyr himself. His voice was loud and clear. Looking up at the stars and stripes which floated high over the scene before him, he remarked that he had fought under that flag twice, but it had become hateful to him, and he had torn it and trailed it in the dust. "I consider," said the brave young man, "that the manner of my death will be no disgrace to my wife and child; my country will honor them."

* Mumford, head of a gambling ring, led a mob to the Mint and not only tore down the flag but afterward walked the streets wearing a piece of the flag in his buttonhole. Butler's flair for the dramatic led him to order Mumford hanged from a window of the Mint, so that the gambler could perish at the scene of his offense.

*Lincoln revoked General Orders No. 28; and Northern criticism of
Butler often became as heated as Pollard's angry strictures. In a letter
to J. G. Carney, a friend in Boston, the general defended his own behavior:*[13]

I am as jealous of the good opinion of my friends as I am careless
of the slanders of my enemies, and your kind expression in regard to
order No. 28, leads me to say a word to you on the subject.

That it ever could have been so misconceived as it has been by some
portion of the Northern Press is wonderful, and would lead one to exclaim with the Jew, "O Father Abraham, what these Christians are,
whose own hard dealings teach them to suspect the very thoughts of
others."

What was the state of things to which the women order applied? We
were two thousand five hundred men in a city seven miles long by two
to four wide, of a hundred and fifty thousand inhabitants, all hostile,
bitter, defiant, explosive, standing literally in a magazine, a spark only
needed for destruction. The devil had entered into the hearts of the
women of this town to stir up strife in every way possible. Every opprobrious epithet, every insulting question was made by these bejew-
elled, becrinolined, and laced creatures calling themselves ladies, toward my soldiers and officers, from the windows of houses and in the
street. How long do you suppose our flesh and blood could have stood
this without retort? That would lead to disturbance and riot from which
we must clear the streets by artillery, and then a howl that we had
murdered these fine women. I had arrested the men who *hurrahed*
for Beauregard,—could I arrest the women? No—what was to be
done? No order could be made save one that would execute itself. With
anxious, careful thought I hit upon this, "Women who insult my
soldiers are to be regarded and treated as common women plying
their vocation." *

Pray how do you treat a common woman plying her avocation in the
streets? You pass her by unheeded. She cannot insult you. As a gentleman you can and will take no notice of her. If she speaks, her words
are not opprobrious. It is only when she becomes a continuous and
positive nuisance that you call a watchman and give her in charge
to him.

But some of the Northern Editors seem to think that whenever one

* See footnote, page 254.

meets such a woman one must stop her, talk with her, insult her, or hold dalliance with her. And so from their own conduct they construed my order. The Editor of the Boston *Courier* may so deal with common women, and out of the abundance of the heart his mouth may speak, but so do not I.

Why, these she-adders of New Orleans themselves were at once shamed into propriety of conduct by the order, and from that day no woman has either insulted or annoyed my line soldiers or officers, and of a certainty no soldier has insulted any women. When I passed through Baltimore on the 23rd of February last, members of my staff were insulted by the gestures of the *ladies* there. Not so in New Orleans. One of the worst possible of all these women showed disrespect to the remains of gallant young De Kay, and you will see her punishment, a copy of the order for which I enclose is at once a vindication and a construction of my order.

Nor was Butler without a cynical sense of humor in his order concerning Mrs. Phillips:[14]

HEADQUARTERS DEPT. OF THE GULF, NEW ORLEANS, June 30th, 1862 SPECIAL ORDER No. 150

Mrs. Philipps, wife of Philipp Philipps, having been once imprisoned for her traitorous proclivities and acts at Washington, and released by the clemency of the Government, and having been found training her children to spit upon the Officers of the United States at New Orleans, for which act of one of those children both her husband and herself apologized and were again forgiven, is now found on the balcony of her house during the passage of the funeral procession of Lieut. De-Kay, laughing and mocking at his remains, and, upon being inquired of by the Com'd'g General, if this fact were so, contemptuously replies, "I was in good spirits that day."

It is therefore ordered that she be not "regarded and treated as a common woman," of whom no officer or soldier is bound to take notice, but as an uncommon, bad, and dangerous woman, stirring up strife and inciting to riot.

And that therefore she be confined at Ship Island in the State of Mississippi, within proper limits there, till further orders, and that she be allowed one female servant and no more, if she so choose. That one of the houses for Hospital purpose be assigned her as quarters, and a soldier's ration each day be served out to her with the means of cook-

ing the same, and that no verbal or written communication be allowed with her except through this office, and that she be kept in close
confinement until removed to Ship Island.

By Order of MAJ. GEN. BUTLER
R. S. DAVIS, *Capt. &* A. A. A. G.

*Butler was no less severe on foreign consuls in the captured city, sus-
pecting them of warm sympathy for the Confederacy, if not outright
collusion with it. Stung by the scandalous reports reaching England,
Charles Francis Adams told off the general:*[15]

FURNIVAL'S INN, LONDON, 15 July, 1862
B. F. BUTLER, *Esq., &c., &c.*

GENERAL: Altho' you have been invested with high honors and
power, it must not be supposed that you can act as the veriest despot
without being judged by the tribunal of the *Civilized World*. It is not
the rowdy press of New York that will recognize your actions, neither
can a suborned government, or a Congress impelled as it is by madness, who will assoilzie you in what you have done at New Orleans.
They are looking at it in Greece, in Turkey, in Austria, in France, in
Germany, and in England. The Consuls whom you have treated with
so much contumely *have rights* above those you describe, and their
despatches and journals will henceforth be brought forward as witnesses against you; in fact, neutrals have arrived in Europe to prove to
their respective Governments that you stole their money from Mr.
Smith's Bank and other places, *private property* in every sense of their
case.

Have foreign citizens no inalienable rights further than you choose
to grant them? Europe must see to this. Your authority will be called
in question seriously, and then will follow a system of reprisals, and
I need not tell you that friends will be sure to point out *your* property in New England for adjudication. Take warning in time. Conciliation is your forte instead of the reverse. I have been put to confusion
and shame on your account, and subscribe myself.

Your Sorrowing Countryman, and quondam friend,
C. F. ADAMS

*Butler remained in control of New Orleans until mid-December. "The
enemies of my country, unrepentant and implacable, I have treated*

with merited severity," declared an unabashed Ben on leave-taking. He advised the citizens of New Orleans to count their blessings: "You might have been smoked to death in caverns, as were the Covenanters of Scotland, by the command of a general of the royal household of England; or roasted like the inhabitants of Algiers during the French campaign; your wives and daughters might have been given over to the ravisher, as were the unfortunate dames of Spain in the Peninsular war; or you might have been scalped and tomahawked as our mothers were at Wyoming by the savage allies of Great Britain in our own revolution." In contrast, Butler described his enlightened administration:[16]

It is true I have levied upon the wealthy rebel, and paid out nearly half a million of dollars to feed forty thousand of the starving poor of all nations assembled here, made so by this war.

I saw that this rebellion was a war of the aristocrats against the middling men; of the rich against the poor; a war of the landowner against the laborer; that it was a struggle for the retention of power in the hands of the few against the many; and I found no conclusion to it save in the subjugation of the few, and the disenthralment of the many. I therefore felt no hesitation in taking the substance of the wealthy, who had caused the war, to feed the innocent poor who had suffered by the war. And I shall now leave you with the proud consciousness that I carry with me the blessings of the humble and loyal under the roof of the cottage and in the cabin of the slave, and so am quite content in incurring the sneers of the salon or the curses of the rich.

I found you trembling at the terrors of servile insurrection. All danger of this I have prevented by so treating the slave that he had no cause to rebel.

I found the dungeon, the chain and the lash your only means of enforcing obedience in your servants. I leave them peaceful, laborious, controlled by the laws of kindness and justice.

I have demonstrated that the pestilence can be kept from your borders.

I have added a million of dollars to your wealth, in the form of new land from the batture of the Mississippi.

I have cleansed and improved your streets, canals and public squares, and opened new avenues to unoccupied land.

I have given you freedom of elections, greater than you have ever enjoyed.

I have caused justice to be administered so impartially, that your own advocates have unanimously complimented the judges of my appointment.

You have seen, therefore, the benefit of the laws and justice of the government against which you have rebelled.

CHAPTER 12

UP THE
PENINSULA

O N THE THIRD of February, 1862, Lincoln wrote a tactful letter to Somdetch Phra Paramendr Maha Mongut, King of Siam: "I appreciate most highly Your Majesty's tender of good offices in forwarding to this government a stock from which a supply of elephants might be raised on our soil. This government would not hesitate to avail itself of so generous an offer if the object were one which could be made practically useful in the present condition of the United States. Our political jurisdiction, however, does not reach a latitude so low as to favor the multiplication of the elephant, and steam on land, as well as on water, has been our best and most efficient agent of transportation in internal commerce."

That same day Lincoln had quarreled with McClellan over whether steam on land or steam on water provided the better means for transporting the Army of the Potomac to within striking distance of Richmond. The President believed that the army should move directly to a point on the railroad southwest of Manassas, whereas McClellan favored a route "down the Chesapeake, up the Rappahannock to Urbanna, and across land to the terminus of the railroad on the York River." Lincoln asked needling questions. Did McClellan's plan save time or money? Did it make victory more certain or more valuable? Insofar as McClellan's route would break no great line of the enemy's communications, wouldn't it be *less* valuable? And the President asked, "In case of disaster, would not a safe retreat be more difficult by your plan than by mine?"

Everyone within Lincoln's official family knew that he was rapidly losing patience with McClellan. So also were senators like "Bluff Ben" Wade of Ohio and horse-faced, whiskey-scented Zachariah Chandler of Michigan. They had questioned if not challenged the President's authority by establishing an investigating committee for the principal purpose of discovering when, if ever, that old hen McClellan intended to hatch a little military action. Recognizing the colossal problems that had confronted the general in bringing discipline and proper organization to his ragtag army, Lincoln had pleaded for faith in McClellan. Hot summer, bright fall, chill winter, blossoming spring—McClellan was at an age when he should have known that even a honeymoon cannot endure forever.

In mid-February Grant had won at Donelson with an army not as well supplied as McClellan's. In early March the *Monitor* had checkmated the *Merrimack* and given the Federal Navy supremacy at Hampton Roads. Whether or not McClellan recognized the fact, destiny tapped his shoulder.

I

Nathaniel Hawthorne appeared at the White House on March 13, a member of a Massachusetts delegation that presented the President with an "elegant whip." "As we meet here socially," Mr. Lincoln said in a brief reply to Representative Charles R. Train, "let us not think only of whipping rebels, or of those who seem to think only of whipping Negroes, but of those pleasant days which it is to be hoped are in store for us, when, seated behind a good pair of horses, we can crack our whips and drive through a peaceful, happy and prosperous land."

The taste for a quick victory was strong in Lincoln's mouth. The evidence indicates that he composed the order which Stanton sent to McClellan that evening:[1]

The President having considered the plan of operations agreed upon by yourself and the commanders of army corps, makes no objection to same, but gives the following directions as to its execution:

1st. Leave such force at Manassas Junction as shall make it entirely certain that the enemy shall not repossess himself of that position and line of communication.*

* Eight months before, after the Battle of Manassas, the Confederates had held a line virtually on Washington's doorstep, but the steady build-up of the Army

2d. Leave Washington secure.

3d. Move the remainder of the force down the Potomac, choosing a new base at Fortress Monroe, or anywhere between here and there; or, at all events, move such remainder of the army at once in pursuit of the enemy by some route.

The italics and the exclamation points were lacking—Stanton relied on generals to remember his scowl. McClellan moved, overrunning Alexandria, Virginia, with his troops, whither the talented, talkative, observant George Alfred Townsend hastened to tell the story of war and its impact upon men, women and communal life:[2]

I rode through Washington Street, the seat of some ancient residences, and found it lined with freshly arrived troops. The grave-slabs in a fine old churchyard were strewn with weary cavalry-men, and they lay in some side yards, soundly sleeping. Some artillery-men chatted at doorsteps, with idle house-girls; some courtesans flaunted in furs and ostrich feathers, through a group of coarse engineers; some sergeants of artillery, in red trimmings, and caps gilded with cannon, were reining their horses to leer at some ladies, who were taking the air in their gardens; and at a wide place in the street, a provost-major was manoeuvring some companies, to the sound of the drum and fife. There was much drunkenness, among both soldiers and civilians; and the people of Alexandria were, in many cases, crushed and demoralized by reason of their troubles. One man of this sort led me to a sawmill, now run by Government, and pointed to the implements.

"I bought 'em and earned 'em," he said. "My labor and enterprise set 'em there; and while my mill and machinery are ruined to fill the pockets o' Federal sharpers, I go drunk, ragged, and poor about the streets o' my native town. My daughter starves in Richmond; God knows I can't get to her. I wish to hell I was dead."

Further inquiry developed the facts that my acquaintance had been a thriving builder, who had dotted all northeastern Virginia with evidences of his handicraft. At the commencement of the war, he took certain contracts from the Confederate government, for the construction of barracks at Richmond and Manassas Junction; returning inopportunely to Alexandria, he was arrested, and kept some time in

of the Potomac had so alarmed Joseph E. Johnston with the possibility of an attack on his right flank via the Potomac River that he had withdrawn to the line of the Rappahannock.

Capitol-Hill prison; he had not taken the oath of allegiance and consequently he could obtain no recompense for the loss of his mill property. Domestic misfortunes, happening at the same time, so embittered his days that he resorted to dissipation. Alexandria is filled with like ruined people; they walk as strangers through their ancient streets, and their property is no longer theirs to possess, but has passed into the hands of the dominant nationalists. My informant pointed out the residences of many leading citizens: some were now hospitals, others armories and arsenals, others offices for inspectors, superintendents, and civil officials. The few people that remained upon their properties obtained partial immunity by courting the acquaintance of Federal officers, and, in many cases, extending the hospitalities of their homes to the invaders. I do not know that any Federal functionary was accused of tyranny, or wantonness, but these things ensued, as the natural results of civil war; and one's sympathies were everywhere enlisted for the poor, the exiled, and the bereaved.

My dinner at the City Hotel was scant and badly prepared. I gave a Negro lad who waited upon me a few cents, but a burly Negro carver, who seemed to be his father, boxed the boy's ears and put the coppers into his pocket. The proprietor of the place had voluntarily taken the oath of allegiance, and had made more money since the date of Federal occupation than during his whole life previously. He said to me, curtly, that if by any chance the Confederates should reoccupy Alexandria, he could very well afford to relinquish his property. He employed a smart barkeeper, who led guests by a retired way to the drinking-rooms. Here, with the gas burning at a taper point, cobblers, cocktails, and juleps were mixed stealthily and swallowed in the darkness. The bar was like a mint to the proprietor; he only feared discovery and prohibition. It would not accord with the chaste pages of this narrative to tell how some of the noblest residences in Alexandria had been desecrated to licentious purposes; nor how, by night, the parlors of cosy homes flamed with riot and orgy. I stayed but a little time, having written an indiscreet paragraph in the Washington *Chronicle*, for which I was pursued by the War Department, and the management of my paper lacking heart, I went home in a pet.

II

The Federal troops poured onto the transports at Alexandria—with the Reverend K. J. Stuart watching and listening, then rushing to Richmond. Stuart answered the basic question; these Yankee rascals were headed for the lower Peninsula and not Norfolk. McClellan sailed off with 58,000 men—five infantry divisions, scattered cavalry, a hundred guns, and the gas-filled balloons perfected and supervised by Mr. S. T. C. Lowe, an aeronaut intent on revolutionizing military reconnaissance. McClellan expected another 90,000 troops to follow. The general's letters home recorded his changing spirits:[3]

STEAMER "COMMODORE," April 1, 1862, POTOMAC RIVER, 4.15 P.M.—As soon as possible after reaching Alexandria I got the *Commodore* under way and "put off." I did not feel safe until I could fairly see Alexandria behind us. I have brought a tug with us to take back despatches from Budd's Ferry, where I shall stop a few hours for the purpose of winding up everything. I found that if I remained at Alexandria I would be annoyed very much, and perhaps be sent for from Washington. . . . Officially speaking, I feel very glad to get away from that sink of iniquity. . . .

STEAMER "COMMODORE," April 3, HAMPTON ROADS, 1.30 P.M. — . . . I have been up to my eyes in business since my arrival. We reached here about four yesterday P.M.; ran into the wharf and unloaded the horses, then went out and anchored. Marcy * and I at once took a tug and ran out to the flag-ship *Minnesota* to see Goldsborough, where we remained until about nine, taking tea with him.

On our return we found Gen. Heintzelman, soon followed by Porter and Smith, all of whom remained here all night. I sat up very late arranging movements, and had my hands full. I have been hard at work all the morning, and not yet on shore. Dine with Gen. Wool to-day at four, and go thence to our camp. We move to-morrow A.M. Three divisions take the direct road to Yorktown, and will encamp at Howard's Bridge. Two take the James River road and go to Young's Mill. The reserve goes to Big Bethel, where my headquarters will be to-morrow night. . . .

Telegram—GREAT BETHEL, April 4, 1862, 6 P.M.—My advanced guard five miles from Yorktown. Some slight skirmishing to-day. Our people driving rebels. Hope to invest Yorktown to-morrow. All well and in good spirits.

BIG BETHEL, April 5, 2 A.M.— . . . Have just got through with

* General Randolph B. Marcy, McClellan's father-in-law and chief of staff; Townsend described him as "a fine specimen of man, with kindly features, dark, grayish, flowing hair, and slight marks of years upon his full, purplish face."

the orders for to-morrow; have been working very hard, and have
sent off officers and orderlies in every direction. I feel sure of to-morrow. I have, I think, provided against every contingency, and shall
have the men well in hand if we fight to-morrow. . . . I saw yesterday
a wonderfully cool performance. Three of our men had gone close

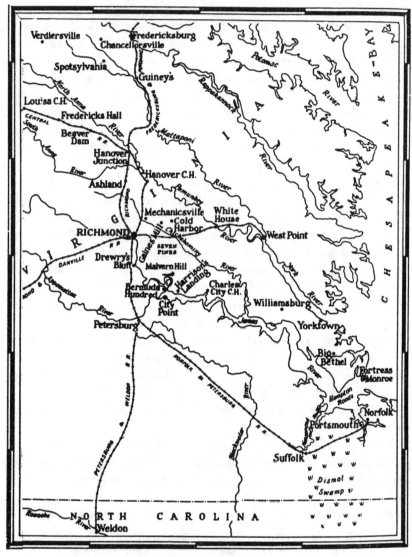

SOUTHEASTERN VIRGINIA, 1862

From *Atlas of American History*

down to the enemy's position after a sheep, which they killed, skinned, and started off with. They were, of course, fired at frequently, and in the course of their travels a 12-pound shot struck directly by them. They quietly picked up the shot, held on to the sheep, and brought the shot to me, yet warm. I never saw so cool and gallant a set of men; they do not seem to know what fear is. . . .

NEAR YORKTOWN, April 6, 1 A.M.— . . . While listening this P.M. to the sound of the guns I received an order detaching McDowell's corps from my command. It is the most infamous thing that history has recorded. I have made such representations as will probably induce a revocation of the order, or at least save Franklin to me. The idea of depriving a general of 35,000 troops when actually under fire! . . .

April 8, 8 A.M.—Raining hard all night, and still continues to do so. Am now encamped about five miles from Yorktown; have been here two or three days. Have now visited both the right and left, and, in spite of the heavy rain, must ride to Ship Point and our right immediately after breakfast. All I care for about the rain is the health and comfort of the men. They are more fond of me than ever; more enthusiastic than I deserve; wherever I go it seems to inspire the fullest confidence. . . .

I have raised an awful row about McDowell's corps. The President very coolly telegraphed me yesterday that he thought I had better break the enemy's lines at once! I was much tempted to reply that he had better come and do it himself. . . .

A Federal force under Nathaniel Banks had started across the Blue Ridge to reinforce Manassas Junction, when Jackson struck at Kernstown, encountering Shields's division. Stonewall's force was small and he earned no new laurels for the rough handling he received; still, Lincoln feared for Washington and thought Banks had better stay where he was, watching the wily Jackson. When the President counted the troops remaining to safeguard what McClellan called "the sink of iniquity," the aggregate was not reassuring. A Confederate army operating in the Valley had turned the tide at Bull Run; Lincoln could not forget that lesson. He had told McClellan not to move without leaving the capital secure; apparently he had wasted his breath. So Lincoln called McDowell's corps from Fredericksburg to cover this neglect. In a patient letter to McClellan Lincoln explained the reason for his action. Then he added the barb:[4]

I suppose the whole force which has gone forward for you, is with you by this time; and if so, I think it is the precise time for you to strike a blow. By delay the enemy will relatively gain upon you—that is, he will gain faster, by *fortifications* and *re-inforcements,* than you can by re-inforcements alone.

And, once more let me tell you, it is indispensable to *you* that you strike a blow. *I* am powerless to help this. You will do me the justice to remember I always insisted, the going down the Bay in search of a field, instead of fighting at or near Manassas, was only shifting, and not surmounting, a difficulty—that we would find the same enemy, and the same, or equal, intrenchments, at either place. The country will not fail to note—is now noting—that the present hesitation to move upon an intrenched enemy, is but the story of Manassas repeated.

The meddling of an unmilitary President, added to McClellan's other exasperations, came close to being the last straw. He had been prom-ised sandy roads, but along these highways of pure gumbo mud a mule sank one day until only his ears were visible! Try moving wagons, guns, men over that—in rain to boot! Proof that the gods conspired against McClellan was the calamity that almost befell General Fitz-John Porter when he went aloft in a balloon. Happily for posterity George Alfred Townsend witnessed this moment in war's travail:[5]

. . . It is needless to say that he [Porter] grew careless, and on this particular morning leaped into the car and demanded the cables to be let out with all speed. I saw with some surprise that the flurried as-sistants were sending up the great straining canvas with a single rope attached. The enormous bag was only partially inflated, and the loose folds opened and shut with a crack like that of a musket. Noisily, fit-fully, the yellow mass rose into the sky, the basket rocking like a feather in the zephyr; and just as I turned aside to speak to a comrade, a sound came from overhead, like the explosion of a shell, and some-thing striking me across the face laid me flat upon the ground.

Half blind and stunned, I staggered to my feet, but the air seemed full of cries and curses. Opening my eyes ruefully, I saw all faces turned upwards, and when I looked above, the balloon was adrift.

The treacherous cable, rotted with vitriol, had snapped in twain; one fragment had been the cause of my downfall, and the other trailed,

like a great entrail, from the receding car, where Fitz John Porter
was bounding upward upon a Pegasus that he could neither check nor
direct.

The whole army was agitated by the unwonted occurrence. From
battery No. 1, on the brink of the York, to the mouth of Warwick River,
every soldier and officer was absorbed. Far within the Confederate
lines the confusion extended. We heard the enemy's alarm-guns, and
directly the signal flags were waving up and down our front.

The General appeared directly over the edge of the car. He was tossing his hands frightenedly, and shouting something that we could not
comprehend.

"O—pen—the—valve!" called Lowe, in his shrill tones; "climb—
to—the—netting—and—reach—the—valve—rope."

"The valve!—the valve!" repeated a multitude of tongues, and all
gazed with thrilling interest at the retreating hulk that still kept straight
upward, swerving neither to the east nor the west.

It was a weird spectacle—that frail, fading oval, gliding against the
sky, floating in the serene azure, the little vessel swinging silently beneath, and a hundred thousand martial men watching the loss of their
brother in arms, but powerless to relieve or recover him. Had Fitz
John Porter been drifting down the rapids of Niagara, he could not
have been so far from human assistance. But we saw him directly, no
bigger than a child's toy, clambering up the netting and reaching for
the cord.

"He can't do it," muttered a man beside me; "the wind blows the
valve-rope to and fro, and only a spry, cool-headed fellow can catch it."

We saw the General descend, and appearing again over the edge of
the basket, he seemed to be motioning to the breathless hordes below
the story of his failure. Then he dropped out of sight, and when we
next saw him, he was reconnoitring the Confederate works through a
long black spy-glass. A great laugh went up and down the lines as this
cool procedure was observed, and then a cheer of applause ran from
group to group. For a moment it was doubtful that the balloon would
float in either direction; it seemed to falter, like an irresolute being,
and moved reluctantly southeastward, towards Fortress Monroe. A
huzza, half uttered, quivered on every lip. All eyes glistened, and some
were dim with tears of joy. But the wayward canvas now turned due
westward, and was blown rapidly toward the Confederate works. Its
course was fitfully direct, and the wind seemed to veer often, as if contrary currents, conscious of the opportunity, were struggling for the

possession of the daring navigator. The south wind held mastery for awhile, and the balloon passed the Federal front amid a howl of despair from the soldiery. It kept right on, over sharpshooters, rifle-pits, and outworks, and finally passed, as if to deliver up its freight, directly over the heights of Yorktown. The cool courage, either of heroism or despair, had seized upon Fitz John Porter. He turned his black glass upon the ramparts and masked cannon below, upon the remote camps, upon the beleaguered town, upon the guns of Gloucester Point, and upon distant Norfolk. Had he been reconnoitring from a secure perch at the tip of the moon, he could not have been more vigilant, and the Confederates probably thought this some Yankee device to peer into their sanctuary in despite of ball or shell. None of their great guns could be brought to bear upon the balloon; but there were some discharges of musketry that appeared to have no effect, and finally even these demonstrations ceased. Both armies in solemn silence were gazing aloft, while the imperturbable mariner continued to spy out the land.

The sun was now rising behind us, and roseate rays struggled up to the zenith, like the arcs made by showery bombs. They threw a hazy atmosphere upon the balloon, and the light shone through the network like the sun through the ribs of the skeleton ship in the *Ancient Mariner*. Then, as all looked agape, the air-craft "plunged, and tacked, and veered," and drifted rapidly toward the Federal lines again.

The allelujah that now went up shook the spheres, and when he had regained our camp limits, the General was seen clambering up again to clutch the valve-rope. This time he was successful, and the balloon fell like a stone, so that all hearts once more leaped up, and the cheers were hushed. Cavalry rode pell-mell from several directions, to reach the place of descent, and the General's personal staff galloped past me like the wind, to be the first at his debarkation. I followed the throng of soldiery with due haste, and came up to the horsemen in a few minutes. The balloon had struck a canvas tent with great violence, felling it as by a bolt, and the General, unharmed, had disentangled himself from innumerable folds of oiled canvas, and was now the cynosure of an immense group of people. While the officers shook his hands, the rabble bawled their satisfaction in hurrahs, and a band of music marching up directly, the throng on foot and horse gave him a vociferous escort to his quarters.

McClellan shuddered for Porter, berated Lincoln, and told his wife of the ordeal he suffered:[6]

April 11.—I am just recovering from a terrible scare. Early this morning I was awakened by a despatch from Fitz-John's headquarters stating that Fitz had made an ascension in the balloon this morning, and that the balloon had broken away and come to the ground some three miles southwest, which would be within the enemy's lines. You can imagine how I felt. I at once sent off to the various pickets to find out what they knew and try to do something to save him, but the order had no sooner gone than in walks Mr. Fitz just as cool as usual. He had luckily come down near my own camp after actually passing over that of the enemy. You may rest assured of one thing: you won't catch me in the confounded balloon, nor will I allow any other generals to go up in it. . . .

Don't worry about the wretches; they have done nearly their worst, and can't do much more. I am sure that I will win in the end, in spite of all their rascality. History will present a sad record of these traitors who are willing to sacrifice the country and its army for personal spite and personal aims. The people will soon understand the whole matter. . . .

April 19, 10.30 P.M.— . . . I can't tell you when Yorktown is to be attacked, for it depends on circumstances that I cannot control. It shall be attacked the first moment I can do it successfully. But I don't intend to hurry it; I cannot afford to fail. I may have the opportunity of carrying the place next week, or may be delayed a couple of weeks; much, of course, depends on the rapidity with which the heavy guns and ammunition arrive. Never mind what such people as ———— say; they are beneath contempt. . . . I will put in a leaf of holly from the bower some of the men have made in front of my tent to-day. They have made quite an artistic thing of it—holly and pine; it adds much, too, to my comfort, as it renders the tent more private and cool.

April 20, 7.30 A.M.— . . . It has been raining more or less all night, and if it were not for the men I would enjoy the rain, for I rather like to hear it patter on the tent.

I have a fire in my stove this morning, so it is quite comfortable. My tent is the same the aides use for an office; it has a floor of pine boughs —a carpet of boughs, I suppose I ought to say—a table in the middle, a desk in one corner, my bed in another, my saddle in another, a woodpile, etc., in the last. I have a splendid two-legged washstand which Charles's mechanical ingenuity devised. Then I have a clothes-rack, consisting of a sapling with the stumps of the branches projecting. So you see I am living quite *en prince*. . . .

Next morning (May 1).—Another wet, drizzly, uncomfortable sort of a day. Good deal of firing during the night. I shall be very glad when we are really ready to open fire, and then finish this confounded affair. I am tired of public life; and even now, when I am doing the best I can for my country in the field, I know that my enemies are pursuing me more remorselessly than ever, and "kind friends" are constantly making themselves agreeable by informing me of the pleasant predicament in which I am—the rebels on one side, and the abolitionists and other scoundrels on the other. I believe in my heart and conscience, however, that I am walking on the ridge between the two gulfs, and that all I have to do is to try to keep the path of honor and truth, and that God will bring me safely through. At all events I am willing to leave the matter in His hands, and will be content with the decision of the Almighty.

III

McClellan's huffiness stemmed from many sources. Montgomery Blair, the Postmaster General, wrote him: "I can see that the President thinks you are not sufficiently confident and it disturbs him." On May 1 Lincoln himself telegraphed: "Your call for Parrott guns from Washington alarms me—chiefly because it argues indefinite procrastination. Is anything to be done?" Those around McClellan were becoming unstrung. In a letter to Senator Ira Harris, General E. D. Keyes complained bitterly of the lack of co-operation from the Navy, and warned: "The Great Battle of the war is to come off here. If we win it, the rebellion will be crushed. If we lose it, the consequences will be more horrible than I care to foretell." A Rebel deserter led General Martindale to believe that there were fifty thousand Confederates inside Yorktown and thirty thousand more expected momentarily; both Keyes and Porter gravely endorsed Martindale's careful memorandum containing this ominous news.

Actually in the old town where Washington had "turned the world upside down" for the British, Confederate forces under John B. Magruder did not exceed twelve thousand. An amateur Shakespearean actor whom friends called "Prince John," Magruder had indulged his thespian talent by marching his forces around in a circle through trees close to the shore so that Federal observers concluded his army was many times stronger than it was. McClellan sensed neither his numerical nor psychological advantage. While he hesitated, Farragut captured New Orleans; a wave of abject pessimism swept through the

South. In Columbia, South Carolina, the worried Mary Boykin Chesnut confided to her diary:[7]

The news from New Orleans is fatal to us. Met Mr. Weston. He wanted to know where he could find a place of safety for two hundred Negroes. I looked in his face to see if he were in earnest, then to see if he were sane. He said there were a certain set of two hundred Negroes that had grown to be a nuisance. Apparently all the white men of the family had felt bound to stay at home to take care of them. There are, apparently, people who still believe Negroes to be property. They are like Noah's neighbors, who insisted that the deluge would only be a little shower after all. These Negroes were Plowden Weston's. He gave Enfield rifles to one of our companies, and forty thousand dollars to another, and he is away with our army at Corinth, so I said: "You may rely upon Mr. Chesnut * to assist you to his uttermost in finding a home for these people." Nothing belonging to that particular gentleman shall come to grief, not even if we have to take charge of them on our own place. Mr. Chesnut did get a place for them, as I said he would.

Another acquaintance of ours wanted his wife to go back home. They live in Charleston, and while he is in the army she could protect their property. "Would you subject me to the horrors of a captured and a sacked city?" she demanded. He answered, vacantly staring at her: "What are they?"

We had to go to the Governor's or they would think we had hoisted the Black Flag. They said we were going to be beaten as Cortez did the Mexicans, by superior arms. Mexican bows and arrows made a poor showing in the face of powder and shot. Our enemies have such superior weapons of war. We hardly have any but what we capture from them in the fray. The Saxons and Normans were in the same plight.

War seems a game of chess. We have knights, kings, queens, bishops, and castles enough, but not enough pawns; and our skillful generals whenever they cannot arrange the board to suit them exactly, burn up everything and march away. We want them to save the country. They seem to think their whole duty is to destroy ships and save the army. . . .

There is a report abroad that Richmond will be given up, that Jeff

---

* James Chesnut, Jr., who had been one of Beauregard's emissaries demanding the surrender of Sumter, now operated a nitre bureau; about this time he refused a place on President Davis's staff but later accepted.

Davis is expected here. Not he! He will be the last man to give up heart and hope! . . .

Men born Yankees are an unlucky selection as commanders for the Confederacy. They believe in the North in a way no true Southerner ever will, and they see no shame in surrendering to Yankees. They are half-hearted clear through; Stephens as Vice-President, Lovell, Pemberton, Ripley. A general must command the faith of his soldiers. These never will, be they ever so good and true.

Today the Courier pitches in, in the same vein; with the native talent, which we undoubtedly possess, to think of choosing Mallory and Walker for Navy and Army. "Whom the Gods would destroy they first make mad!"

On the fourth of May Yorktown surrendered to McClellan, plunging Virginia into deeper gloom:[8]

PELATIAH PERIT, *Esq., President Chamber of Commerce:*

The rebels evacuated this place at four o'clock this morning, keeping up a brisk cannonade to the last moment, leaving all their heavy guns, *eighty in number, with their ammunition.*

Also a large amount of material of war of every kind, which was abandoned, burnt, or sunk. Davis, Johnston and Lee were present, uniting in opinion that McClellan's disposition of his forces and artillery had made the place untenable.

Magruder furiously and publicly urged fight. The fortifications were very extensive and formidable, and the force of the enemy was very large. An assault upon them before bombarding would have cost us great carnage, and might have failed.

Our gunboat flotilla has passed up the river, followed by large bodies of troops in transports.

Several columns are moving rapidly along York River.

We hope to come up with them before they can reach West-Point. Our army is in the finest condition and best of spirits. The rebel army is much demoralized.   —J. J. ASTOR,
Colonel and A.D.C.

Edward A. Pollard, editor of the Richmond Examiner, *described the feelings within the capital of the Confederacy:*[9]

. . . The visible tremor of the Confederate authorities in that city was not a spectacle calculated either to nerve the army or assure the citizens. The fact is, that the Confederate authorities had shamefully neglected the defences of Richmond, and were now making preparations to leave it, which were called prudential, but which naturally inspired a panic such as had never before been witnessed in the history of the war. The destruction of the Virginia * had left the water avenue to Richmond almost undefended. The City Council had for months been urging upon the Confederate Government the necessity of obstructing the river, and failing to induce them to hurry on the work, had, with patriotic zeal, undertaken it themselves. A newspaper in Richmond— the *Examiner*—had in good time pointed out the necessity of obstructing the river with stone, but the counsel was treated with such conceit and harshness by the government, that it was only at the risk of its existence that that paper continued for weeks to point out the insecurity of Richmond and the omissions of its authorities. The government was at last aroused to a sense of danger only to fall to work in ridiculous haste, and with the blindness of alarm. The appearance of the Yankee gunboats in James river was the signal for Mr. Secretary Mallory to show his alacrity in meeting the enemy by an advertisement for "timber" to construct new naval defences. The only obstruction between the city and the dread Monitor and the gunboats was a half-finished fort at Drewry's Bluff, which mounted four guns. Some of the Confederate officers had taken a "gunboat panic," for the line of stone obstructions in the river was not yet complete. They seized upon schooners at the wharves loaded with plaster of paris, guano, and other valuable cargoes, carried them to points where they supposed the passage of the river was to be contested, and in some instances sunk them in the wrong places.

There is no doubt that about this time the authorities of the Confederate States had nigh despaired of the safety of Richmond. The most urgent appeals had been made to Congress by the press and the people to continue its session in Richmond while the crisis impended. But its members refused to give this mark of confidence to the government, or to make any sacrifice of their selfish considerations for the moral encouragement of their constituents. They had adjourned in haste and left Richmond, regarding only the safety of their persons or the convenience of their homes.†

* The *Merrimack*.
† War Clerk J. B. Jones noted in his diary for May 10: "The President's family have departed for Raleigh, and the families of most of the cabinet to their respective homes, or other places of refuge." Jones's own family left a day earlier since "No one, scarcely, supposes that Richmond will be defended."

Nor was the Executive more determined. In the President's mansion about this time all was consternation and dismay. A letter written by one of his family at a time when Richmond was thought to be imminently threatened, and intercepted by the enemy, afforded excessive merriment to the Yankees, and made a painful exhibition to the South of the weakness and fears of those intrusted with its fortunes. This letter, written with refreshing simplicity of heart, overflowed with pitiful sympathy for the President, and amused the enemy with references to the sore anxieties of "Uncle Jeff." and to the prospect of his sinking under the misfortunes of his administration. The authenticity of this letter was never called into question: it is a painful and delicate historical evidence, but one to which, in the interests of truth, allusion should not be spared.

In appending the letter, Pollard noted that "the reflections it makes upon the courage of our noble soldiers were probably hasty," and therefore the editor deleted them:[10]

". . . When I think of the dark gloom that now hovers over our country, I am ready to sink with despair. There is a probability of General Jackson's army falling back on Richmond, and in view of this, no lady is allowed to go up on the railroad to Gordonsville for fear, if allowed to one, that many others would wish to do it, which would incommode the army.

"General Johnston is falling back from the Peninsula, or Yorktown, and Uncle Jeff. *thinks we had better go to a safer place than Richmond.*

"We have not decided yet where we shall go, but I think to North Carolina, to some far off country town, or, perhaps, to South Carolina. If Johnston falls back as far as Richmond, all our troops from Gordonsville and 'Swift Run Gap' will also fall back to this place, and make one desperate stand against McClellan. If you will look at the map, you will see that the Yankees are approaching Richmond from three different directions—from Fredericksburg, Harrisonburg, and Yorktown. O God! defend this people with thy powerful arm, is my constant prayer. Oh, mother, Uncle Jeff. is miserable. He tries to be cheerful, and bear up against such a continuation of troubles, but, oh, I fear he cannot live long, if he does not get some rest and quiet.

"Our reverses distressed him so much, and he is so weak and feeble, it makes my heart ache to look at him. He knows that he ought to send his wife and children away, and yet he cannot bear to part with them, and we all dread to leave him too. Varina * and I had a hard cry about it to-day.

"Oh! what a blow the fall of New Orleans was. It liked to have set us all crazy here. Everybody looks depressed, and the cause of the Confederacy looks drooping and sinking; but if God is with us, who can be against us? Our troops are not doing as well as we expected. . . . The regiments that are most apt to run are from North Carolina and Tennessee. I am thankful to say that the Mississippi and Louisiana troops behave gloriously whenever called on to fight.

"Uncle Jeff. thinks you are safe at home, as *there will be no resistance at Vicksburg*, and the Yankees will hardly occupy it; and, even if they did, the army would gain nothing by marching into the country, and a few soldiers would be afraid to go so far into the interior.

"P.S. We all leave here to-morrow morning for Raleigh. Three gunboats are in James river, on their way to the city, and may probably reach here in a few hours; so we have no longer any time to delay. *I only hope that we have not delayed too long already.* I shall then be cut off from all communication with ———, and I expect to have no longer any peace.

"I will write again from Raleigh, and Fanny must write me a letter and direct it to Raleigh; perhaps I may get it. I am afraid that Richmond will fall into the hands of the enemy, as there is no way to keep back the gunboats. James river is so high that all obstructions are in danger of being washed away; so that there is no help for the city. She will either submit or else be shelled, and I think the latter alternative will be resorted to.

"Uncle Jeff. was confirmed last Tuesday in St. Paul's Church by Bishop Johns. He was baptized at home in the morning before church.†

"Do try to get a letter to me some way. Direct some to Raleigh and some to Richmond.   Yours, ever devotedly,

——— ———." ‡

IV

Suddenly McClellan's boys found themselves marching through the pages of history. In Yorktown the remnants of trenches and forts in

* Varina Davis, the President's wife.

† Davis was baptized on May 10, according to Jones, who had noted the President's intention to do so on April 18, commenting: "Some of his enemies allege that professions of Christianity have sometimes been the premeditated accompaniments of usurpations. It was so with Cromwell and with Richard III."

‡ The correspondent was Helen Keary, the President's niece.

which Washington's troops had fought were easily located. Like Lincoln, many of these Yankees had been raised on Weems's sentimental but intensely patriotic Life of Washington *and they marched over this hallowed ground with a sense of respectful awe. Ten miles up the Peninsula, as the crow flies, stood old Williamsburg, a rebel's roost that had given Colonial America such patriots as Thomas Jefferson, George Wythe, Edmund Pendleton, Richard Henry Lee, James Monroe, and a dozen others. On May 5 there was fighting in Williamsburg—bloody, brutal fighting in the rain, with the Confederate wounded left on the field. Thomas W. Hyde, serving with the Union's Sixth Army Corps, experienced his baptism of fire in the struggle for the historic old capital of Virginia where Jefferson had cried that slavery was a crime foisted by the king upon the colonies at a time when they were too weak to resist:[11]*

. . . I was at first sent out with some skirmishers into the woods on our right, and I went beyond the men to see if there was any one there. The day was over cast, the woods were wild and tangled, and it was rather gruesome looking from tree to tree to see if a foe lurked behind. Coming back I was fired on by our own men, very properly, as I came from the wrong direction. Returning to the regiment which was lying down in line in open field, I could see in front the 5th Wisconsin and 6th Maine skirmishing with the rebels, and Wheeler's battery firing for all it was worth upon some redoubts, and soon from beyond Fort Magruder some three or four thousand of the enemy appeared. I did not then know that the general with his staff so clearly seen with them was Jubal A. Early, called the late Mr. Early at West Point. . . . Our advance regiments fell back by General Hancock's order; on the Confederates came, and a fine picture of a charge they made. They were at the double-quick, and were coming over a ploughed field, diagonally across our front, to attack the troops that were retiring. They could not see us as we lay flat on the ground. From my place on the left of the regiment, I saw General Hancock galloping toward us, bareheaded, alone, a magnificent figure; and with a voice hoarse with shouting he gave us the order, "Forward! charge!" The papers had it that he said, "Charge, gentlemen, charge," but he was more emphatic than that: the air was blue all around him.

Well, up we started, and the long line of sabre bayonets came down together as if one man swayed them as we crossed the crest, and with a roar of cheers the 7th Maine dashed on. It was an ecstasy of excitement for a moment; but the foe, breathless from their long tug over the heavy ground, seemed to dissolve all at once into a quivering and disintegrating mass and to scatter in all directions. Upon this we halted and opened fire, and the view of it through the smoke was pitiful. They were falling everywhere; white handkerchiefs were held up in token of surrender; no bullets were coming our way except from a clump of a few trees in front of our left. Here a group of men, led by an officer whose horse had just fallen, were trying to keep up the unequal fight, when McK, the crack shot of Company D, ran forward a little and sent a bullet crashing through his brain. This was Lieutenant-Colonel J. C. Bradburn of the 5th North Carolina, and at his fall all opposition ceased. We gathered in some three hundred prisoners before dark. Then the rain came, though there is nothing specially remarkable about that, for it was always coming down. . . .

I went over the field and tried to harden myself to the sights of horror and agony. One gets accustomed to such things, just as doctors get accustomed to the dissecting table, but at this early day we were not much hardened. As it became dark we spread a lot of fence rails in the mud and sat on cracker boxes in our rubber blankets most of the night, for, between the excitement and the rain and the occasional shots of our picket just in front, we had no desire for sleep. Connor told stories and recited poetry, and we reiterated to each other our experiences of the battle with an enthusiasm that could not be quenched. Nor were the men much more sleepy. Beside their dim watch-fires murmurs of hushed conversation arose, and the phosphorescent glow on the faces of the dead in the fields beyond became more weird as the night sped on. Distant noises would have told older soldiers that the enemy was in retreat in the black darkness off toward Williamsburg, but we expected to attack Fort Magruder in the morning.

Our part of the battle was the beginning of Hancock's fame, and he always had a lively affection for the regiments who were in the "bayonet charge at Williamsburg."

The next day we did not move out of this rude bivouac. I went to see the doctors operate in a barn near by, and they had a pile of legs and arms that looked positively uncanny. We all wrote most exuberant letters home, and at night, while at dress parade, a great cavalcade was seen approaching, General McClellan at the head. He stopped before our colors, and in a graceful speech thanked us for the charge of the day before, which, he said, saved the day, and directed us to place "Williamsburg" upon our flag. We broke out into wild cheering, and no

British regiments were ever prouder of the emblazonments of Talavera
or Badajos than we, so recently from civil life, of the honors of our
maiden field.

*McClellan's private letters revealed a man of magic, who by a touch
electrified the world:*[12]

WILLIAMSBURG, May 6, 1862.—I telegraphed you this morning that
we had gained a battle. Every hour its importance is proved to be
greater. On Sunday I sent Stoneman in pursuit with the cavalry and four
batteries of horse-artillery. He was supported by the divisions of
Hooker, Smith, Couch, Casey, and Kearny, most of which arrived on
the ground only yesterday. Unfortunately I did not go with the advance
myself, being obliged to remain to get Franklin and Sedgwick started
up the river for West Point. Yesterday I received pressing private messages from Smith and others begging me to go to the front. I started
with half a dozen aides and some fifteen orderlies, and found things in
a bad state. Hancock was engaged with a vastly inferior force some two
miles from any support. Hooker fought nearly all day without assistance, and the mass of the troops were crowded together where they
were useless. I found everybody discouraged, officers and men; our
troops in wrong positions, on the wrong side of the woods; no system,
no co-operation, no orders given, roads blocked up. As soon as I came
upon the field the men cheered like fiends, and I saw at once that I
could save the day. . . .

WILLIAMSBURG, May 6, midnight.— . . . Am very tired; had but
little sleep last night, and have not had my clothes off; besides, was
pretty well wet last night. I have not a particle of baggage with me;
nothing but a buffalo-robe and horse-blanket, not even a hair-brush or
tooth-brush. . . .

Monday, 1 P.M. (8th).— . . . I have ordered up headquarters and
the accompanying paraphernalia at once, so I hope to get within a few
miles of my tooth-brush in a day or two. It is not very pleasant, this
going entirely without baggage, but it could not be helped. I find that
the results of my operations are beginning to be apparent. The rebels
are evacuating Norfolk, I learn. Your two letters of Sunday and Monday reached me last night. It would have been easy for me to have
sacrificed 10,000 lives in taking Yorktown, and I presume the world
would have thought it more brilliant. I am content with what I have
done. The battle of Williamsburg was more bloody. Had I reached the

field three hours earlier I could have gained far greater results and have saved a thousand lives. It is, perhaps, well as it is, for officers and men feel that I saved the day. . . .

On May 6, Lincoln, Stanton, and Chase arrived at Fortress Monroe. On learning that McClellan had done nothing to destroy the Merrimack, *the President threw his hat on the floor. He ordered troops to attack Norfolk and gunboats to shell the Confederate batteries at Sewall's Point. On May 8 Stanton notified the War Department:*[13]

The President is at this moment (two o'clock P.M.) at Fort Wool witnessing our gunboats—three of them besides the Monitor and Stevens—shelling the rebel batteries at Sewall's Point. At the same time, heavy firing up the James River indicates that Rodgers and Morris are fighting the Jamestown and Yorktown. . . . The boom of heavy cannonading strikes the ear every minute. The Sawyer gun in Fort Wool has silenced one battery on Sewall's Point. The James rifle mounted on Fort Wool also does good work. It was a beautiful sight to witness the boats moving on Sewall's Point, and one after another opening fire and blazing away every minute. The troops will be ready in an hour to move. . . .

Chase witnessed the occupation of Norfolk and on May 11 wrote his daughter Nettie:[14]

It was sundown when we left Norfolk . . . and near to 12 when we reached Ft. Monroe. The President had been greatly alarmed for our safety . . . and you can imagine his delight when we told him Norfolk was ours. Stanton soon came up to his room and was equally delighted. He fairly hugged General Wool.

For my part, I was very tired and glad to get to bed. . . .

So has ended a brilliant week's campaign of the President, for I think it quite certain that if he had not come down, it [Norfolk] would still have been in possession of the enemy and the Merrimac as grim and defiant and as much a terror as ever. The whole coast is now virtually ours. There is no port which the Monitor and Stevens cannot enter and take.

It was sad and pleasant to see the Union flag once more waving over Norfolk and the shipping in the harbor and to think of the destruction accomplished there a little more than a year ago.

Warmly McClellan telegraphed Stanton:[15]

I congratulate you from the bottom of my heart upon the destruction of the Merrimac. I would now most earnestly urge that our gunboats and the ironclad boats be sent as far as possible up the James River without delay. This will enable me to make our movements much more decisive.

But McClellan's letters home were little changed in tone:

May 12, Monday P.M.— . . . Are you satisfied now with my bloodless victories? Even the Abolitionists seem to be coming round; judging, at least, from the very handsome resolutions offered by Mr. Lovejoy in the House. I look upon that resolution as one of the most complimentary I know of, and that, too, offered by my bitterest persecutors. But the union of civic merit with military success is what pleases me most; to have it recognized that I have saved the lives of my men and won success by my own efforts is to me the height of glory. I hope that the result in front of Richmond will cause still greater satisfaction to the country. . . .

May 15, CUMBERLAND, 2.30 P.M.— . . . I am heartily tired of this life I am leading—always some little absurd thing being done by those gentry in Washington. I am every day more and more tired of public life, and earnestly pray that I may soon be able to throw down my sword and live once more as a private gentleman. . . . I confess I find it difficult to judge whether the war will soon be at an end or not. I think that the blows the rebels are now receiving and have lately received ought to break them up; but one can do no more than speculate. Yes, I *can* imagine peace and quietness reigning once more in this land of ours. It is just *that* I am fighting for! . . .

Telegram—May 16, 1862, WHITE HOUSE.—Have just arrived over horrid roads. No further movement possible until they improve. This house is where Washington's courtship took place and where he resided when first married. I do not permit it to be occupied by any one, nor the grounds around. It is a beautiful spot directly on the banks of the Pamunkey. All well and in fine spirits. Hope to get our baggage up by water, otherwise will fare badly to-night. . . .

With McClellan's army drawing nearer, the dismay in Richmond produced many repercussions; War Clerk J. B. Jones described one that angered him especially:[16]

May 12th.—I suggested to the Provost Marshal several days ago that there was an act of Congress *requiring* the destruction of tobacco, whenever it might be in danger of falling into the hands of the enemy. He ran to Gen. Winder, and he to some one else, and then a hundred or more negroes, and as many wagons, were "pressed" by the detectives. They are now gathering the weed from all quarters, and piling it in "pressed" warehouses, mixed with "combustibles," ready for the conflagration.

And now the consuls from the different nations are claiming that all bought on foreign account ought to be spared the torch. Mr. Myers, the little old lawyer, has been employed to aid them. He told me to-day that none ought to be burnt, that the Yankees having already the tobacco of Missouri, Kentucky, and Maryland, if we burn ours it will redound to their benefit, as it will enhance the price of that in their hands. That is a Benjamite * argument.

May 13th.—This morning I learned that the consuls had carried the day, and were permitted to collect the tobacco *alleged* to be bought on foreign account in separate warehouses, and to place the flags of their respective nations over them. This was saving the property claimed by foreigners whose governments refused to recognize us (these consuls are accredited to the United States), and destroying that belonging to our own citizens. I told the Provost Marshal that the act of Congress included *all* tobacco and cotton, and he was required by *law* to see it all destroyed. He, however, acknowledged only martial law, and was, he said, acting under the instructions of the Secretary of State. What has the Secretary of State to do with *martial law?* Is there really no Secretary of War?

May 14th.—Our army has fallen back to within four miles of Richmond. Much anxiety is felt for the fate of the city. Is there no turning point in this long lane of downward progress? Truly it may be said, our affairs at this moment are in a critical condition. I trust in God, and the chivalry and patriotism of the South *in the field.*

The enemy's fleet of gun-boats are ascending James River, and the obstructions are not completed. We have but one or two casemated guns in battery, but we have brave men there.

May 15th.—The enemy's gun-boats, Monitor, Galena, etc. are at Drewry's Bluff, eight miles below the city, shelling our batteries, and

* The reference is to Secretary of State Judah P. Benjamin, whom Jones never forgave for being a Jew.

our batteries are bravely shelling them. The President rode down to the vicinity this morning, and observed the firing.

The guns are heard distinctly in the city, and yet there is no consternation manifested by the people. If the enemy pass the obstructions, the city will be, it is true, very much at their mercy. They may shell us out of it, and this may occur any hour. South of the city the enemy have no forces, and we can find refuge there. I suppose the government would go to Lynchburg. I shall remain with the army, *and see that the tobacco be burnt, at all hazards, according to law.*

V

History still surrounded the Union troops wherever they turned. George Alfred Townsend, now representing the great and powerful New York Herald, told one day of an unusual experience:[17]

At White House, I met some of the mixed Indians and Negroes from Indiantown Island, which lies among the osiers in the stream. One of these ferried me over, and the people received me obsequiously, touching their straw hats, and saying, "Sar, at your service!" They were all anxious to hear something of the war, and asked, solicitously, if they were to be protected. Some of them had been to Richmond the previous day, and gave me some unimportant items happening in the city. I found that they had Richmond papers of that date, and purchased them for a few cents. They knew little or nothing of their own history, and had preserved no traditions of their tribe. There was, however, I understood, a very old woman extant, named "Mag," of great repute at medicines, pow-wows, and divination. I expressed a desire to speak with her, and was conducted to a log-house, more rickety and ruined than any of the others. About fifty half-breeds followed me in respectful curiosity, and they formed a semi-circle around the cabin. The old woman sat in the threshold, barefooted, and smoking a stump of clay pipe.

"Yaw's one o' dem Nawden soldiers, Aunt Mag!" said my conductor. "He wants to talk wid ye."

"Sot down, honey," said the old woman, producing a wooden stool; "is you a Yankee, honey? Does you want yo fauchun told by de old 'oman?"

I perceived that the daughter of the Delawares smelt strongly of fire-water, and the fumes of her calumet were most unwholesome. She was greatly disappointed that I did not require her prophetic services, and said, appealingly—

"Why, sar, all de gen'elmen an' ladies from Richmond has dere fauchuns told. I tells 'em true. All my fauchuns comes out true. Ain't dat so, chillen?"

A low murmur of assent ran round the group, and I was obviously losing caste in the settlement.

"Here is a dime," said I, "that I will give you, to tell me the result of the war. Shall the North be victorious in the next battle? Will Richmond surrender within a week? Shall I take my cigar at the Spotswood on Sunday fortnight?"

"I'se been a lookin' into dat," she said, cunningly; "I'se had dreams on dat ar'. Le'um see how de armies stand!"

She brought from the house a cup of painted earthenware containing sediments of coffee. I saw her crafty white eyes look up to mine as she muttered some jargon, and pretended to read the arrangement of the grains.

"Honey," she said, "gi' me de money, and let de ole 'oman dream on it once mo'! It ain't quite clar' yit, young massar. Tank you, honey! Tank you! Let de ole 'oman dream! Let de ole 'oman dream!"

She disappeared into the house, chuckling and chattering, and the sons of the forest, loitering awhile, dispersed in various directions. As I followed my conductor to the riverside, and he parted the close bushes and boughs to give us exit, the glare of the camp-fires broke all at once upon us. The ship-lights quivered on the water; the figures of men moved to and fro before the fagots; the stars peeped timorously from the vault; the woods and steep banks were blackly shadowed in the river. Here was I, among the aborigines; and as my dusky acquaintance sent his canoe skimming across the ripples, I thought how inexplicable were the decrees of Time and the justice of God. Two races united in these people, and both of them we had wronged. From the one we had taken lands; from the other liberties. Two centuries had now elapsed. But the little remnant of the African and the American were to look from their Island Home upon the clash of our armies and the murder of our braves.

Wherever Townsend rode, the past came forward to greet him:[18]

Hanover Court House is renowned as the birthplace of Patrick Henry, the colonial orator, called by Byron the "forest-born Demosthenes." In a little tavern, opposite the old Court House building, he began his humble career as a measurer of gills to convivials, and *in* the Court House—a small brick edifice, plainly but quaintly constructed—he gave the first exhibitions of his matchless eloquence. Not far away, on a by-road, the more modern but not less famous orator, Henry Clay, was born. The region adjacent to his father's was called the "Slashes of Hanover," and thence came his appellation of the "Mill Boy of the Slashes." I had often longed to visit these shrines; but never dreamed that the booming of cannon would announce me. The soldiers broke into both the tavern and courthouse, and splintered some chairs in the former to obtain relics of Henry.

The quarrels between McClellan and Washington continued. On May 14 the general wrote the President that he had received no reply from the War Department to repeated telegrams warning that "the enemy were concentrating all their available force to fight this army." Alarmed by the ridiculous reports Pinkerton's agents fed him, McClellan pictured his pitiable prospect of being able to throw only 80,000 men into battle against "a much larger force, perhaps double that number." He must be reinforced immediately. Lincoln responded tartly:[19]

. . . Have done, and shall do, all I could and can to sustain you— hoped that the opening of the James River, and putting Wool [at Fortress Monroe] and Burnside [in New Bern] in communication, with an open road to Richmond, or to you, had effected something in that direction. I am still unwilling to take all our force off the direct line between Richmond and here.

In his letters home, McClellan endeavored to be cheerful:

May 20, 12.30 A.M., TUNSTALL'S STATION.— . . . We are gradually drawing near the rascals. I think they intend to fight us in front of Richmond; if they do it will be a decisive battle. . . .

May 22, 6.30 P.M., CAMP NEAR CHICKAHOMINY.— . . . I have just returned from a ride to the front, where I have taken a good look at the rebel lines. I suppose I must have ridden some thirty miles or less to-day.

Some one just brought me a bouquet of wild white flowers—a negro at that. I clutched it most eagerly, as reminding me of one who two years ago became my wife. It is on the table in front of me as I write; in a tin tumbler, to be sure, but none the less pure and white. . . .

May 23, P.M.— . . . I have been within six miles of the rebel capital, and our balloonists have been watching it all day. The intentions of the enemy are still doubtful. I go on prepared to fight a hard battle, but I confess that the indications are not now that he will fight. Unless he has some deep-laid scheme that I do not fathom, he is giving up great advantages in not opposing me on the line of the Chickahominy. He could give me a great deal of trouble and make it cost me hundreds or thousands of lives. . . . God knows that I am sick of this civil war, although no feeling of the kind unsteadies my hand or ever makes me hesitate or waver. It is a cruel necessity. . . .

May 25, Sunday, 3.30 P.M., COLD HARBOR.— . . . I have this moment received a despatch from the President, who is terribly scared about Washington, and talks about the necessity of my returning in order to save it. Heaven save a country governed by such counsels! . . .

May 27, 11.45 P.M.— . . . I sent Fitz-John out this morning to "pick up" a large force of the enemy who were threatening my right and rear, also to burn the bridges of the two railways of the South Anna. The old fellow has done splendidly. Thrashed 13,000 badly, and I am momentarily expecting to hear the details of his second attack. We are getting on splendidly. I am quietly clearing out everything that could threaten my rear and communications, providing against the contingency of disaster, and so arranging as to make my whole force available in the approaching battle. The only fear is that Joe's [Johnston] heart may fail him. . . .

McClellan whistled to keep up his courage. The prospect of battle brought him wretched visions of the dead and wounded afterward; he had a warrior's training, but not a warrior's heart. Porter had fought at Hanover Court House on the twenty-seventh of May. For the good of the ordeal soon to confront McClellan it was fortunate that Townsend and not the general visited prison pens and hospitals next day:[20]

One person said that he enlisted for the honor of his family, that "fit in the American Revolution"; and another came out to "hev a squint et the fightin'." Several were Northern and foreign lads, that were working on Carolina railroads, and could not leave the section, and some labored under the impression that they were to have a "slice" of land and a "nigger," in the event of Southern independence. A few comprehended the spirit of the contest, and took up arms from principle; a few, also, declared their enmity to "Yankee institutions," and had seized the occasion to "polish them off," and "give them a ropein' in"; but many said it was "dull in our deestreeks, an' the niggers was runnin' away, so I thought I'ud jine the foces." The great mass said that they never contemplated "this box," or "this fix," or "these suckemstances," and all wanted the war to close, that they might return to their families.

Indeed, my romantic ideas of rebellion were ruthlessly profaned and dissipated. I knew that there was much selfishness, peculation, and "Hessianism" in the Federal lines, but I had imagined a lofty patriotism, a dignified purpose, and an inflexible love of personal liberty among the Confederates. Yet here were men who knew little of the principles for which they staked their lives; who enlisted from the commonest motives of convenience, whim, pelf, adventure, and foray; and who repented, after their first misfortune, with the salt rheum in their eyes. I think that all "great uprisings" resolve to this complexion. With due reverence for my own ancestry, I think that they sometimes stooped from greatness to littleness. I must confess that certain admissions in my revolutionary textbook are much clearer, now that I have followed a campaign. . . .

I rode across the fields to the Hogan, Curtis, and Gaines mansions; for some of the wounded had meantime been deposited in each of them. All the cow-houses, wagon-sheds, hay-barracks, hen-coops, Negro cabins, and barns were turned into hospitals. The floors were littered with "corn-shucks" and fodder; and the maimed, gashed, and dying lay confusedly together. A few, slightly wounded, stood at windows, relating incidents of the battle; but at the doors sentries stood with crossed muskets, to keep out idlers and gossips. The mention of my vocation was an "open sesame," and I went unrestrained into all the largest hospitals. In the first of these an amputation was being performed, and at the door lay a little heap of human fingers, feet, legs and arms. I shall not soon forget the bare-armed surgeons, with bloody instruments, that leaned over the rigid and insensible figure, while the comrades of the subject looked horrifiedly at the scene. The grating of murderous saw drove me into the open air, but in the second hospital which I visited, a wounded man had just expired, and I encountered his body at the threshold. Within, the sickening smell of mortality was almost insupportable, but by degrees I became accustomed to it.

The lanterns hanging around the room streamed fitfully upon the red eyes, and half-naked figures. All were looking up, and saying, in pleading monotone: "Is that you, doctor?" Men with their arms in slings went restlessly up and down, smarting with fever. Those who were wounded in the lower extremities, body, or head, lay upon their backs, tossing even in sleep. They listened peevishly to the wind whistling through the chinks of the barn. They followed one with their rolling eyes. They turned away from the lantern, for it seemed to sear them.

Soldiers sat by the severely wounded, laving their sores with water. In many wounds the balls still remained, and the discolored flesh was swollen unnaturally. There were some who had been shot in the bowels, and now and then they were frightfully convulsed, breaking into shrieks and shouts. Some of them iterated a single word, as, "doctor," or "help," or "God," or "oh!" commencing with a loud spasmodic cry, and continuing the same word till it died away in cadence. The act of calling seemed to lull the pain. Many were unconscious and lethargic, moving their fingers and lips mechanically, but never more to open their eyes upon the light; they were already going through the valley of the shadow.

I think, still, with a shudder, of the faces of those who were told mercifully that they could not live. The unutterable agony; the plea for somebody on whom to call; the longing eyes that poured out prayers; the looking on mortal as if its resources were infinite; the fearful looking to the immortal as if it were so far off, so implacable, that the dying appeal would be in vain; the open lips, through which one could almost look at the quaking heart below; the ghastliness of brow and tangled hair; the closing pangs; the awful *quietus*. I thought of Parrhasius, in the poem, as I looked at these things:

"Gods!
Could I but paint a dying groan——."

VI

In the Valley, Jackson smashed at Banks, sending his troops reeling back on Washington. At once McDowell began reducing his forces so that the approaches to the national capital could be guarded, but official Richmond mistook this movement and believed that McDowell had begun to extend his lines toward McClellan!

Panic seized the Confederate capital. McClellan's balloons, tied to trees, looked down on the city. Captured Northern newspapers boasted that Richmond must fall by not later than June 15. For good reason citizens of Richmond brushed aside such worries as tea at ten dollars a pound and boots at thirty dollars a pair.

On May 31, McClellan's army was spread along the east bank of the Chickahominy from Mechanicsville to Bottom's Bridge. Two corps had been thrown across the river, entrenching on a line from Seven Pines to Fair Oaks Station. Recent heavy rain had flooded the low grounds of the Chickahominy and endangered the Federal bridges. The situation held all the elements for a successful surprise attack against McClellan's exposed wing at Seven Pines (Fair Oaks); on the last day in May the Confederates struck. The first shock of battle hit the New Hampshire Fifth under command of Colonel E. E. Cross. "Charge them like hell, boys," Cross roared. "Show 'em you are damned Yankees!" * For a moment William Child feared for the life of his hard-swearing colonel:[21]

. . . Soon after the battle began on our left, with some skirmishing along in front of the Fifth, and to the left. The enemy's sharpshooters came very near killing Cross at this point, shooting one ball through his coat. The regiment remained in the woods near the railroad for some time. A regiment of Confederates, Sixth Virginia, advanced on us slowly through the woods. When near, the Fifth poured in a volley which broke their line, and the men came straggling in, and many were taken prisoners. The battle now increased, and Howard's Brigade was sent in. The Eighty-first Pennsylvania Volunteers ran at the first fire and left their commander, Colonel Miller, dead upon the field. Says Cross' personal journal, "Colonel Miller was a good soldier, and was the only field officer who could hold his regiment, which was partly Irish and partly American."

General French's Brigade was pressed very hard and the Fifty-third Regiment gave way. General Howard now entered the woods with the Sixty-first and Sixty-fourth New York Volunteers, together mustering about eight hundred men, and engaged the enemy with great fury. "Howard led his men with great gallantry close up to the enemy, and the heavy firing told that the stormy battle was at its height. General Howard had two horses killed and a third one wounded; then a ball struck him in the right arm, below the elbow, but he continued to cheer his men until hit in the same arm by another ball, which shattered the bone in a shocking manner." Word was at once sent to Colonel Cross to assume command of the brigade, as Howard was disabled. At the same time Cross had orders to move the Fifth into the battle.

---

* As reported in the Cincinnati *Commercial.*

Being senior colonel, Cross was now in command of the brigade. He left the woods with the Fifth, moved down the railroad track double-quick, until he arrived opposite the point where Howard's Brigade was engaged. By Adjutant Gregory of the Sixty-first New York Volunteers, Cross sent orders to the remains of the brigade to clear the front and form on the rear. While this was being done the Irish Brigade came up charging and yelling. The Sixty-ninth formed on Cross' right and the Eighty-eighth on the left.

The enemy's bullets came thick; and, finding Howard's Brigade out of the woods, Cross prepared to advance and open fire. The Fifth was along the railroad track; on the opposite side was a wood in which were the enemy; to the rear was the Irish Brigade, the Sixty-ninth on the right and the Eighty-eighth on the left. General Meagher was not present, nor any other general officer. Cross ordered an advance. "Forward in line, guide center!" and the Fifth New Hampshire Volunteers stepped off in noble style. Both the Irish Regiments stood still however. The Fifth moved on, both colors fluttering and the men steady. Cross gave orders for none to fire without the word, and though the bullets flew thick and struck down many a brave fellow, on they passed until in plain view of the enemy's line among the trees. That day the Confederates wore white bands around their hats, so that they were easily distinguished from the Federals.

When about thirty paces from the enemy, it was ordered to halt, kneel down and fire by battalion. At this close range the effect was awful. The bullets were heard to strike with a tearing sound into the close ranks of the enemy. Instantly moving forward, their first line gave way and the men encountered another, the Sixth Alabama—the first was the Second Alabama. Again the Fifth moved up and fought at short range, "behaving nobly."

Finding many men being injured by buckshot, Cross ordered another advance; and while shouting the command, "Forward in line," he received a Minie-ball in his left thigh, which made a very severe wound. He kept his feet for a few moments, and after falling rose up and gave orders, sustaining himself by a tree. While in this position three buckshot struck him in the left temple, a ball passed through his hat and one through the shoulder of his blouse; in all seven balls struck his person or clothing. He was finally carried out of the hottest of the fire by Lieutenant Parks and Corporal Towne, back to the railroad track, where was the Irish Brigade as it was left. Colonel Kelley sent some men off with him. Lieutenant-Colonel Langley soon brought out the regiment in good order, the firing having nearly ceased. The men brought out most of their wounded comrades, who were not able to walk. Thus ended the battle of Fair Oaks, the Fifth firing the first and the last shot on the 1st day of June.

The following account is . . . directly from the pen of Colonel Cross in his personal journal. Says Colonel Cross:—

"In this battle the generalship on the part of the Federals was wretched. Instead of shelling the woods with thirty pieces of artillery as we could readily have done, we allowed the rebels to choose their own ground, ambush themselves and wait for our attack. Nothing but the indomitable bravery of our men—the rank and file and line officers —saved us from defeat. Early in the morning I sent word to General Richardson that the artillery could be employed to great advantage in shelling the woods. He sent for me and desired me to point out the exact locality of the enemy. I did so, but nothing was done. Our lines of infantry ought also to have been formed back from the woods in order to draw the enemy out. As it was we entered a regular trap set for us the night before. I believe an Apache warrior would have arranged our men better. Everything was on the side of the enemy—position, numbers and knowledge of the ground. It is a wonder that we were not defeated."

Johnston was wounded and the command of the Confederate army defending Richmond passed to Lee—the climactic fact in the battle. Next day McClellan addressed his troops:[22]

HEADQUARTERS ARMY OF THE POTOMAC,
CAMP NEAR NEW-BRIDGE, VA., June 2, 1862
SOLDIERS OF THE ARMY OF THE POTOMAC! I have fulfilled at least a part of my promise to you. You are now face to face with the rebels, who are held at bay in front of their capital. The final and decisive battle is at hand. Unless you belie your past history, the result cannot be for a moment doubtful. If the troops who labored so faithfully and fought so gallantly at Yorktown, and who so bravely won the hard fights at Williamsburgh, West-point, Hanover Court-House, and Fair Oaks, now prove themselves worthy of their antecedents, the victory is surely ours.

The events of every day prove your superiority. Wherever you have met the enemy you have beaten him. Wherever you have used the bayonet he has given way in panic and disorder. I ask of you now one last crowning effort. The enemy has staked his all on the issue of the coming battle. Let us meet him, crush him here, in the very centre of the rebellion.

Soldiers! I will be with you in this battle, and share its dangers with you. Our confidence in each other is now founded upon the past. Let us strike the blow which is to restore peace and union to this distracted land. Upon your valor, discipline, and mutual confidence the result depends.

GEORGE B. McCLELLAN,
Major-General Commanding

Jefferson Davis also addressed his army:[23]

EXECUTIVE OFFICE, June 2, 1862

To THE ARMY OF RICHMOND:

I render to you my grateful acknowledgements for the gallantry and good conduct you displayed in the battles of the thirty-first of May, and first inst., and with pride and pleasure recognise the steadiness and intrepidity with which you attacked the enemy in position, captured his advanced intrenchments, several batteries of artillery and many standards, and everywhere drove them from the open field.

At a part of your operations it was my fortune to be present. On no other occasion have I witnessed more of calmness and good order than you exhibited while advancing into the very jaws of death, and nothing could exceed the prowess with which you closed upon the enemy when a sheet of fire was blazing in your faces!

In the renewed struggles in which you are on the eve of engaging, I ask and can desire but a continuance of the same conduct which now attracts the admiration and pride of the loved ones you have left at home.

You are fighting for all that is dearest to men; and, though opposed to a foe who disregards many of the usages of civilized war, your humanity to the wounded and the prisoners was the fit and crowning glory to your valor.

Defenders of a just cause, may God have you in his holy keeping!

JEFFERSON DAVIS

The general will cause the above to be read to the troops under his command.

In letters home McClellan could not conceal his mixture of military mind and unmilitary heart:[24]

June 2, 8 P.M., NEW BRIDGE.—It has been impossible for me to write to you for the last two or three days. I was quite sick on Friday and Saturday; on the last day rose from my bed and went to the field of battle; remained on horseback most of the time until Sunday evening. I came back perfectly worn out and exhausted; lay down at once, and, though I could not sleep much I got some rest. I think to-night will bring me quite up again; I am not anxious. The Chickahominy is now falling, and I hope we can complete the bridges to-morrow. I can do nothing more until that is accomplished. The enemy attacked on Saturday and Sunday with great ferocity and determination; their first attack alone was successful. Casey's division broke. As the other divisions came up they checked the enemy, and we gradually got the better of him; he was badly handled before night. On Sunday morning he renewed the attack and was everywhere repulsed in disorder and with heavy loss. We had regained all the ground lost, and more, last night; to-day we are considerably in advance of the field of battle. It is certain that we have gained a glorious victory; I only regret that the rascals were smart enough to attack when the condition of the Chickahominy was such that I could not throw over the rest of the troops to follow up the success; but the weather now seems settled, and I hope the river will be low enough to-morrow to enable me to cross. I am tired of the sickening sight of the battlefield, with its mangled corpses and poor suffering wounded! Victory has no charms for me when purchased at such cost. I shall be only too glad when all is over and I can return where I best love to be. . . .

CHAPTER 13

THE EMERGENCE
OF LEE

JEFFERSON DAVIS and Robert E. Lee watched the litter bearers carrying Joe Johnston from the field at Seven Pines. Two wounds had left the general in such excruciating pain that he could not stand a jostling ride in an ambulance. Davis and Lee rode back to Richmond through the darkness, each immersed in somber reflections. Then the President reached his decision: In the morning Lee would receive orders giving him command of the army.

For Lee, three months of the most exasperating kind of frustration were now ending. He had returned from rebuilding coastal defenses, to find a frightened Confederate capital under martial law; Davis and Congress had been snarling like angry dogs; and estimates reaching Richmond placed at between 120,000 and 150,000 the force that McClellan was mobilizing for his knockout punch against Virginia. Lee had studied his maps, had judged the personalities with whom he was dealing, and, keeping his head, had bolstered the defenses of Richmond.

Joe Johnston had been Lee's greatest personality problem—Johnston who believed he should have been ranked first in the Confederate military hierarchy and had been placed fourth by Davis; Johnston, a man thereafter of wounded dignity, who could match Davis with stubborn arguments and nervous irascibility under stress; Johnston, a classmate of Lee's at West Point and an affectionate comrade-in-arms in the Mexican War—a keen military strategist, a warmhearted man, generous by impulse. And suddenly frightened—when Lee called him

back to the lower Peninsula; when Lee more or less clandestinely kept
Jackson detached in the Valley for blows against the Federals that had
pinned down Banks and McDowell and brought Lincoln and McClellan to the point of mutual huffiness; when Lee, after Yorktown, then
after Williamsburg, kept pressing on Johnston the need to stand firm,
to fight, to keep the war from overrunning the streets of Richmond.

A headquarters general was Lee, and yet suddenly electric—the one
man determined that Richmond must not fall. Davis, Congress, the
people began to sense his magic; he was quiet, reserved, dignified,
intense. He was, unexpectedly, for Virginia, for the South, a passionate
lover, who had been devoted in turn to a sick mother and an invalid
wife and now embraced in his protective arms a stricken country.

Johnston had called his force the Army of the Peninsula. By morning, when orders came placing him in command, Lee renamed it the
Army of Northern Virginia.

I

Now Lee faced new problems. Robert E. Lee, A Great-Life-in-Brief
supplies this analysis of a major one:[1]

From this moment as Lee walked forward into history and into
legend—a great figure in one and an immortal symbol in the other—
he would suffer as have few men at the hands of biographers intent on
seeing their hero emerge full-grown like Minerva from the head of
Jupiter. The contention of Alexander Stephens that Lee was "child-like
in simplicity and unselfish in character" explained the man, but not the
general. As commander of the Army of Northern Virginia, it was Lee's
shrewdness, his fast thinking, his instinct for the counter punch, that
worked so well in his gamble on Jackson in the Valley, his ability to
learn by mistake and to improvise under the pressure of necessity, that
gave him dimension. Far from springing forth neatly packaged and pre-
shrunk, in the shining armor of Minerva, it was an intensely human
Lee, trusting in God that his blunders might not prove calamitous, that
somehow the Confederacy could muddle through, who came to deserve
the respect and affection of his countrymen. It was a Lee in doubt—and
severely doubted—who took command and set a course with such
mastery that every battle he fought became part of a single campaign.

Little of the awe and reverence with which two generations of
biographers have described Lee's rise to command was shared by his

subordinates. To the generals in the field Lee was at best untested if a charitable view was taken of his failure in western Virginia, and it remained a large question whether in battle he could meet the measure of Johnston. In time, to be sure, all would agree with Sir Frederick Maurice that whereas in the field Johnston was possibly as good as Lee, Old Joe "lacked that wider vision, that power to look calmly beyond the dangers and perils of his immediate front to the situation in the whole theatre of war, that power, in short, which takes Lee out of the ranks of the good ordinary and places him in the select band of the supreme generals."

At first critics tended to compare Johnston and his successor to the disparagement of Lee. Certainly it was in character for "Old Pete" Longstreet, with his blunt, rough, stolid, systematic nature, to wait and watch and ponder before his somewhat quarrelsome mind decided whether the army had gained or lost. Dan Hill, always sharp-tongued, always extreme in judgment, always edgy over when next his dyspepsia and a spine ailment would plague him, could swing the pendulum of his convictions one way or the other; and Gustavus Smith, the onetime street commissioner of New York City, invariably humphed and hawed and tugged at his enormous ears before relaxing the frown that came so naturally to his big, pompous face. Dick Ewell—"Old Baldhead"— squinting a pair of popeyes down a long beak, an enthusiastic amateur cook who complained almost constantly of indigestion, savored all sauces and personalities cautiously; and the other Hill—Ambrose Powell Hill, no relation to Dan—a good brigade leader despite poor health, a frail body, and previous experience limited to serving as superintendent of the United States Coast Survey, likewise would find apprehensions to mutter into his thick, auburn beard. Each liked Lee, the Virginia gentleman; each had been satisfied with Lee as the headquarters general; but Lee the commander of the Army of Northern Virginia they had yet to understand.

Lee's military brilliance rested in the fact that he never overestimated his fighting potential. On the Peninsula, for example, he must oppose 80,000 men to McClellan's 105,000, a circumstance as fixed as the necessity of cooking three days' rations before a battle. Thus from the beginning Lee realized that he was neither able to pay too high a price for his victories nor equipped to stand too long on the defensive. The Washington policy was to end the war as quickly as possible; and the Richmond policy, as Lee shaped and directed it, was to sustain the war through wit and maneuver to the point where the North grew thoroughly tired of a conflict that posed no immediate threat to its own basic way of life.

Lee, striding to the War Department on the morning after Seven Pines, passed scenes that Constance Cary Harrison, a Richmond resident, described:[2]

. . . The whole town was on the street. Ambulances, litters, carts, every vehicle that the city would produce, went and came with a ghastly burden; those who could walk limped painfully home, in some cases so black with gunpowder they passed unrecognized. Women with pallid faces flitted bareheaded through the streets searching for their dead or wounded. The churches were thrown open, many people visiting them for a sad communion-service or brief time of prayer; the lecture-rooms of various places of worship were crowded with ladies volunteering to sew, as fast as fingers could fly, the rough beds called for by the surgeons. Men too old or infirm to fight went on horseback or afoot to meet the returning ambulances, and in some cases served as escort to their own dying sons.

By afternoon of the day following the battle, the streets were one vast hospital. To find shelter for the sufferers a number of unused buildings were thrown open. I remember, especially, the St. Charles Hotel, a gloomy place, where two young girls went to look for a member of their family, reported wounded. We had tramped in vain over pavements burning with the intensity of the sun, from one scene of horror to another, until our feet and brains alike seemed about to serve us no further. The cool of those vast dreary rooms of the St. Charles was refreshing; but such a spectacle! Men in every stage of mutilation lying on the bare boards, with perhaps a haversack or an army blanket beneath their heads,—some dying, all suffering keenly, while waiting their turn to be attended to. To be there empty-handed and impotent nearly broke our hearts. We passed from one to the other, making such slight additions to their comfort as were possible, while looking in every upturned face in dread to find the object of our search. This sorrow, I may add, was spared, the youth arriving at home later with a slight flesh-wound.

The condition of things at this and other improvised hospitals was improved next day by the offerings from many churches of pew-cushions, which, sewn together, served as comfortable beds; and for the remainder of the war their owners thanked God upon bare benches for every "misery missed" that was "mercy gained." To supply food for the hospitals the contents of larders all over town were emptied into baskets; while cellars long sealed and cobwebbed, belonging to the old Virginia gentry who knew good Port and Madeira, were opened by the Ithuriel's spear of universal sympathy. There was not much going to bed that night, either; and I remember spending the greater part of it leaning from my window to seek the cool night air, while wondering as to the fate of those near to me.

There was a summons to my mother about midnight. Two soldiers came to tell her of the wounding of one close of kin; but she was already on duty elsewhere, tireless and watchful as ever. Up to that time the younger girls had been regarded as superfluities in hospital service; but on Monday two of us found a couple of rooms where fifteen wounded men lay upon pallets around the floor, and, on offering our services to the surgeons in charge, were proud to have them accepted and to be installed as responsible nurses, under direction of an older and more experienced woman. The constant activity our work entailed was a relief from the strained excitement of life after the battle of Seven Pines.

When the first flurry of distress was over, the residents of those pretty houses standing back in gardens full of roses set their cooks to work, or, better still, went themselves into the kitchen, to compound delicious messes for the wounded, after the appetizing old Virginia recipes. Flitting about the streets in the direction of the hospitals were smiling, white-jacketed negroes, carrying silver trays with dishes of fine porcelain under napkins of thick white damask, containing soups, creams, jellies, thin biscuit, eggs *à la crême,* boiled chicken, etc., surmounted by clusters of freshly gathered flowers. A year later we had cause to pine after these culinary glories when it came to measuring out, with sinking hearts, the meager portions of milk and food we could afford to give our charges.

II

The Confederate War Department Building at Ninth and Broad was an uncheerful place. War Clerk Jones shuddered every morning at the "smell of whiskey" in the tumbler by the water hydrant. In the basement, dead soldiers' garments, taken from hospitals and battle-fields, exhaled "a most disagreeable, if not deleterious, odor." But Lee passed these gloomy spectacles, not noticing; he was intent upon an idea. The Battle at Seven Pines, though seeming to prove nothing, con-

vinced him that the right wing of McClellan's army, north of the Chickahominy, was dangerously exposed. He called Jeb Stuart to his office.

Lee looked that morning, in the worshipful prose of John Esten

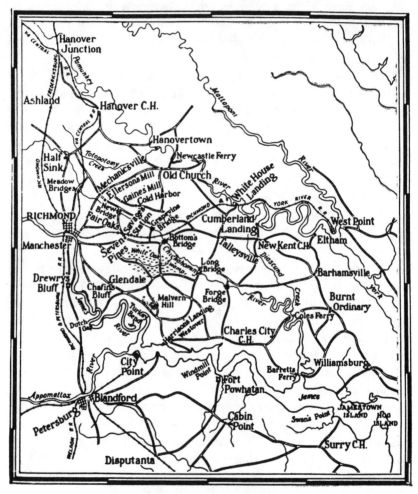

THE PENINSULA, 1862

From *Atlas of American History*

Cooke, at "blue eyes, flashing beneath a 'piled-up' forehead"; at a "joyous cavalier," not yet thirty, who "with his floating plume and splendid laughter" rode off to "the hottest battles humming a song." Lee explained his belief that McClellan's right wing was in the air; his orders, sending Stuart's cavalry on a reconnaissance in the rear of the

Federal army, stipulated that the "joyous cavalier" was to accomplish all he could without taking undue risk.

At two o'clock, on the morning of June 12, Stuart gave his boys ten minutes to be in their saddles. The first day, Stuart camped opposite Hanover Court House, twenty-two miles from Richmond; the next morning his "noiseless bivouac" was broken "without flag or bugle sound," and as the daylight brightened he was as far as Taliaferro's Mill on the road from Edom Church when Federal pickets were encountered. Stuart wrote an official report with gusto:[3]

. . . The regiment in front was the Ninth Virginia cavalry, Col. W. H. F. Lee,* whose advance-guard, intrusted to the command of Adjt.-Lieut. Rodins, did admirable service—Lieut. Rodins handling it in the most skilful manner, managing to clear the way for the march with little delay, and infusing, by a sudden dash at a picket, such a wholesome terror that it never paused to take a second look. Between Haws' shop and Old Church the advanced guard reported the enemy's cavalry in force in front. It proved to be the Fifth regular cavalry, (formerly the Second, commanded by yourself). The leading squadron was ordered forward at a brisk gait, the main body following closely, and gave chase to the enemy for a mile or two, but did not come up to him. We crossed the Totopotomy, a strong position of defence which the enemy failed to hold, confessing a weakness. In such places half a squadron was deployed afoot as skirmishers, till the point of danger was passed.

On, on dashed Rodins, here skirting a field, there leaping a fence or ditch, and cleaning the woods beyond, when, not far from Old Church, the enemy made a stand, having been reënforced. The only mode of attack being in column of fours along the road, I still preferred to oppose the enemy with one squadron at a time, remembering that he who brings on the field the last cavalry reserve wins the day. The next squadron, therefore, moved to the front, under the lamented Capt. Latane, making a most brilliant and successful charge, with drawn sabres, and upon the picket-guard, and after a hotly contested hand-to-hand conflict put him to flight, but not till the gallant Captain had sealed his devotion to his native soil with his blood. The enemy's rout (two squadrons by one of ours) was complete; they dispersed in terror and confusion, leaving many dead on the field, and blood in quantities

---

* William H. F. Lee, General Lee's son, known as "Rooney."

in their tracks. Their commander, Capt. Royall, was reported mortally wounded. Several officers and a number of privates were taken in this conflict, and a number of horses, arms, and equipments, together with five guidons. The woods and fields were full of the scattered and disorganized foe, straggling to and fro, and but for the delay and the great incumbrance which they would have been to our march, many more could and would have been captured.

Col. Fitz Lee, burning with impatience to cross sabres with his old regiment, galloped to the front at this point and begged to be allowed to participate with his regiment, the First Virginia cavalry, in the discomfiture of his old comrades—a request I readily granted—and his leading squadron pushed gallantly down the road to Old Church; but the fragments of Royall's command could not be rallied again, and Col. Lee's leading squadron charged, without resistance, into the enemy's camp, (five companies,) and took possession of a number of horses, a quantity of arms and stores of every kind, and several officers and privates. The stores, as well as the tents, in which everything had left, were speedily burned and the march resumed—whither?

Here was the turning-point of the expedition. Two routes were before me, the one to return by Hanover Court-House, the other to pass around through New-Kent, taking the chances of having to swim the Chickahominy, and make a bold effort to cut the enemy's lines of communication. The Chickahominy was believed by my guides to be fordable near Forge Bridge. I was fourteen miles from Hanover Court-House, which I would have to pass if I returned, the enemy had a much shorter distance to pass to intercept me there; besides, the South Anna River was impassable, which still further narrowed the chances of escape in that direction; the enemy, too, would naturally expect me to take that route. These circumstances led me to look with more favor to my favorite scheme, disclosed to you [Lee] before starting, of passing around. It was only nine miles to Tunstall's station, on the York River Railroad, and that point once passed, I felt little apprehension; beyond, the route was one of all others which I felt sure the enemy would never expect me to take. On that side of the Chickahominy infantry could not reach me before crossing, and I felt able to whip any cavalry force that could be brought against me. Once on the Charles City side, I knew you would, when aware of my position, if necessary, order a diversion in my favor on the Charles City road, to prevent a move to intercept me from the direction of White Oak Swamp. Beside this, the hope of striking a serious blow at a boastful and insolent foe, which would make him tremble in his shoes, made more agreeable the alternative I chose.

In a brief and frank interview with some of my officers, I disclosed my views, but while none accorded a full assent, all assured me a hearty support in whatever I did. With an abiding trust in God, and with such guarantees of success as the two Lees and Martin and their devoted followers, this enterprise I regarded as most promising. Taking care, therefore, more particularly after this resolve, to inquire of the citizens the distance and the route to Hanover Court-House, I kept my horse's head steadily toward Tunstall's station. There was something sublime in the implicit confidence and unquestioning trust of the rank and file in a leader guiding them straight apparently into the very jaws of the enemy; every step appearing to them to diminish the faintest hope of extrication. Reports of the enemy's strength at Garlick's and Tunstall's were conflicting, but generally indicated a small number. Prisoners were captured at every step, and included officers, soldiers and negroes.

Stuart was unique—as a personality and in his decision now to ride around McClellan's army! Invaluable military information he would most assuredly bring Lee; but there was much more to gain—an expression of impudence, of contempt for the enemy, of Southern self-confidence, to bolster wavering spirits within the Confederate capital. Continuing the narrative of Stuart's adventure, the Richmond Despatch lost none of this advantage:[4]

. . . The entire route from Ashland, by Hanover Court-House and Old Church, to Station No. 22, (Tunstall's, we believe,) on the York River Railroad, was naught else but a continuous scene of triumph and destruction. Commissary and quartermaster's stores were seized and burned at every turn; prisoners and horses were taken and sent to the rear, and by the time of their arrival at the railway station, more than one million dollars' worth of Federal property must have been captured and destroyed, besides scores of prisoners riding in the rear.

Upon approaching the railroad, cars were heard advancing, and the whistle sounded. By orders every man was instantly dismounted and ranged beside the track. Again the whistle blew, and thinking the force to be a friendly one perhaps, the steam was stopped, when the Caroline troop, opening fire, disclosed the ruse, and, putting on steam again, on sped the train towards the Chickahominy, and despite logs placed on the track, made good its escape, but the carriages being but uncovered freight-trucks, and having soldiers on them, the slaughter that ensued was frightful. Many of the enemy jumped from the train, and were afterwards captured or killed to the number of twenty or more. The engineer was shot dead by Lieut. Robinson.

Still adding to their conquests at every step, a detachment was immediately sent to the White House, on the Pamunkey, and discovering four large transports moored there, and some hundred wagons or more, with teams, etc., in a wagon-yard, all these were instantly seized, to the great fright and astonishment of the Federals, and the torch immediately applied to all things combustible. One of the transports escaped and floated down the river. The contents of the other three were chiefly valuable commissary and quartermaster's stores, vast quantities of army clothing, grain, fruits, and sutlers' stores. Tempting as they were, all things were laid in ashes, the horses led off and the prisoners secured. Thinking that the enemy would send out an overwhelming force in pursuit, an unlikely route was selected, and the whole command proceeded in triumph to New-Kent Court-House.

New-Kent Court-House being the rendezvous, the fourth squadron of the Ninth, under command of Capt. Knight, (consisting of the Lunenburgh troops and Lancaster cavalry,) having burned the transports and wagons, joined the column on its route thither. "Hab we got Richmon' yet, boss?" asked a darkey in a corn-field, turning up his eyeballs in admiration of the "Maryland cavalry;" "well, if we ain't, we soon shall, for McClellan and our boys is sure to fotch him." Others, however, proved keener-sighted than the negro: women ran to the wayside cottage-door; a flash of triumph mantled their cheek; and, as the eye kindles into a flame of admiration, tears trickle down, and "God bless you, boys," is all they say. Now and then an old man is met by the wayside, pensive and sad, but recognizing the horsemen, he stops, looks astonished, and throws up his hat for the "Maryland cavalry," just arrived. Others wave handkerchiefs—'tis useless to deceive them, for a woman instinctively discovers friends or foes at sight. "Our cavalry here!" exclaim they in wonder; and with hands clasped upon their breast, mutely, but eloquently, gaze. "Take care, men, take care. Heaven bless you; but take care—the enemy are everywhere." Such is their gentle warning, given to the weary, dusty, chivalric column dashing through the country in the enemy's rear.

The astonishing fact was that everything the Despatch *reported was true. So, too, were these incidents:*

The advance-guard having reached New-Kent, and found an extensive sutler's establishment, some dismount and enter. Every description of goods that taste or fancy might require are found in profusion here. Clothes of all descriptions and qualities, cutlery, sabres, pistols, shoes, preserves, conserves, boots, stationery, wines, liquors, tobacco, segars, tea, coffee, sugar, tapioca, maccaroni, champagne, sherry, and burgundy in great quantity; in fine, all that men could buy for money was there discovered, while round the store lolled Federal soldiers, and the sleek, fat proprietor eloquently holding forth upon McClellan's wonderful genius as a commander, and the speedy subjugation of the rebels.

Our wearied horsemen called for refreshments, which the sutler handed to the "Maryland cavalry" (!) with great alacrity; but when pay was demanded our troopers roared with laughter, told the proprietor who they were, and much to his surprise and indignation, pronounced them all prisoners of war. As the other troops arrived it was found that a magnificent Federal ambulance had been captured on the route, containing many valuable medical stores. The vehicle and contents were burned when overtaken, the driver, a good-looking, well-dressed doctor, and companions, being accommodated with a mule each, and were at the moment to be found among nearly two hundred other nondescripts—sailors, teamsters, negroes, sutlers, etc., etc., in the motley cavalcade at the rear.

Helping themselves liberally to all the store afforded, our troops remained at the sutler's till nearly midnight, (Friday,) when, being comparatively refreshed and all present, the head of the column was turned towards the Chickahominy and home. Champagne, we are told, flowed freely while any remained; wines, liquors, and segars were all consumed. Yankee products of every description were appropriated without much ado, and with light hearts all quietly journeyed by a lonely road, near the main body of the enemy, and a little before dawn of Sunday were on Chickahominy's bank, ready to cross.

Being far below all the bridges, and where deep water flows, they knew not how or where to cross! Here was an awful situation for a gallant band! Directed to Blind Ford, it was fifteen feet deep! The enemy had blocked up all the main roads, and had thousands scouring the country eager to entrap or slaughter them—but two miles from McClellan's quarters, within sound of their horse-pickets—and without means to cross! Quietly taking precautions against all surprise, strict silence being enjoined upon the prisoners, first one horseman plunged into the flood and then another, at different points—all too deep; no ford discoverable, no bridge! The horses, it was thought, would follow each other and swim the stream—it was tried, and the horses carried away by the current!

Breaking into small parties, the cavalrymen swam and re-swam the river with their horses, and when some fifty or more had been landed, a strange but friendly voice whispered in the dark: "The old bridge is a few yards higher up—it can be mended!" 'Twas found, and mended it could be! Quietly working, tree after tree was felled, earth, and twigs, and branches were carried and piled up on the main props —old logs were rolled and patched across the stream, yet after long and weary labor the bridge was built, and the long and silent procession of cavalry, artillery, prisoners, and spoils safely and quietly passed this frail, impromptu bridge, scarcely any sounds being heard but the rush of waters beneath. Once across and in the swamp, all was industry and expedition.

Artillery-axles sank low in the mire—ten Yankee horses were hitched to each piece, and as the first rays of morning crimsoned the tree-tops, the long line rapidly sought the shade of woods away from the Federal lines. Yet our troops had not proceeded far when the advance were halted. "Who comes there?" cried the Federal horsemen in the swamp. "Who goes there?" calls another, and quicker than thought our advance-guard (by order) dash away into the open ground; the Federals fire half a dozen shots, and rush in pursuit. Into the thicket some half-dozen Federal horsemen dart after our men, and quicker than lightning are surrounded and prisoners!

Once more within our lines, all went merry as a marriage-bell. Quickly the dirty, weary band sped along the Charles City road, dawn revealed them to our pickets, and they entered our camps faint and famished, but the noblest band of heroes that ever bestrode a charger, or drew a battle-blade for their birthright as freemen.

III

On June 14 Stuart returned to Richmond, a heroic symbol of an unconquerable South. His Federal prisoners numbered 165; his own casualties—one. Lee listened eagerly as Stuart sustained his hunch that McClellan's right wing was in the air. The roads behind the Federal lines, Stuart reported further, were in deplorable condition. Lee planned a trap—a thrust to turn Beaver Creek Dam, then a dash to White House from which McClellan was drawing his supplies by wagon train and railroad.

In the Valley, Lee already had set Jackson to playing a deft game of deception that bewildered both McClellan and Washington. With strict orders to his troops to answer all questions as to whither they were going with a stoical "I don't know," Jackson marched and counter-marched, and then on June 15 arrived at Ashland, fifteen miles from Richmond. Changing horses, Old Jack, now "red with the dust of three Virginia counties," pressed on to Lee's headquarters at Fair Oaks Station, where the cadaverous, haunting eyes of Dan Hill lighted in instant recognition:[5]

We went together into General Lee's office. General Jackson declined refreshments, courteously tendered by General Lee, but drank a glass of milk. Soon after, Generals Longstreet and A. P. Hill came in, and General Lee, closing the door, told us that he had determined to attack the Federal right wing and had selected our four commands to execute the movement. He told us that he had sent Whiting's division to re-enforce Jackson, and that at his instance the Richmond papers had reported that large re-enforcements had been sent to Jackson "with a view to clearing out the Valley of Virginia and exposing Washington." He believed that General McClellan received the Richmond papers regularly, and he [Lee] knew of the nervous apprehension concerning Washington. He then said that he would retire to another room . . . and would leave us to arrange the details among ourselves. The main point on his mind seemed to be that the crossings of the Chickahominy should be covered by Jackson's advance down the left bank, so that the other three divisions might not suffer in making a forced passage.

During the absence of General Lee, Longstreet said to Jackson: "As you have the longest march to make, and are likely to meet opposition, you had better fix the time for the attack to begin."

Jackson replied: "Daylight of the 26th."

Longstreet then said: "You will encounter Federal cavalry and roads blocked by felled timber, if nothing more formidable; ought you not to give yourself more time?"

When General Lee returned, he ordered A. P. Hill to cross at Meadow Hill, Longstreet at Mechanicsville Bridge, and me to follow Longstreet. The conference broke up about nightfall. . . .

On the eve of battle—June 25—a Prussian officer fighting with the Confederates told Pollard of a second meeting:[6]

. . . Assembled nearly all that was eminent in the Confederate army. There stood like a rock Gen. Lee, gazing cheerfully over the countenances of his comrades, for each of whom he had a part already assigned. Thoughtfully his eyes wandered from one to the other, as though he wished to stamp the features of each upon his memory, with the feeling that he, perhaps, should never behold many of them again. Close beside him towered the knightly form of Gen. Baldwin; at his left leaned pensively Stonewall Jackson, the idol of his troops, impatiently swinging his sabre to and fro, as though the quiet room were too narrow for him, and he were longing to be once more at the head of his columns. A little aside quietly stood the two Hills, arm in arm, while in front of them old Gen. Wise was energetically speaking. Further to the right stood Generals Huger, Longstreet, Branch, Anderson, Whiting, Ripley, and Magruder in a group. When all these generals had assembled, Gen. Lee laid his plans before them, and in a few stirring words pointed out to each his allotted task. The scheme had already been elaborated. It was compact, concentrated action, and the result could not fail to be brilliant.

When the conference terminated, all shook hands and hastened away to their respective army corps, to enter upon immediate activity.

Next day McClellan warned his wife that a battle was imminent:[7]

GEN. MCCLELLAN'S HEADQUARTERS, June 26, 1862—*Telegram, in cipher, care of Mr. Eckert, who will regard it as private and strictly confidential, and forward it privately to my wife.*—DEAR NELL: I may not be able to telegraph or write to you for some days. There will be a great stampede, but do not be alarmed. There will be severe fighting in a day or two, but you may be sure that your husband will not disgrace you, and I am confident that God will smile upon my efforts and give our arms success. You will hear that we are pursued, annihilated, etc. Do not believe it, but trust that success will crown our efforts. I tell you this, darling, only to guard against the agony you would feel if you trusted the newspaper reports. . . .

For Lee the Seven Days began badly. On the morning of June 26, Jackson was three hours late marching his men out of Ashland. A. P. Hill, waiting to hear from Jackson, saw the daylight fading away before he moved to the Mechanicsville Bridge. Meanwhile along Beaver Creek, unsupported, some raw troops panicking, Dan Hill suffered a

terrific pasting from intrenched Yankee guns. William D. Bickman
reported to the Cincinnati Commercial:[8]

. . . The fight was opened with artillery, at long range, but the enemy, finally discovering our superiority in this arm, foreshortened the
range, and came into close conflict. He was evidently provoked at his
own inefficiency, since his shells were not destructive in our intrenchments, while our gunners played upon his exposed ranks with fearful
effect. The fight seemed to increase in fury as it progressed, and it
finally became the most terrific artillery combat of the war. I had been
accustomed for months to the incessant roar of heavy guns, but until
that period I had failed to comprehend the terrible sublimity of a great
battle with field-pieces. The uproar was incessant and deafening for
hours. At times it seemed as if fifty guns exploded simultaneously, and
then ran off at intervals into splendid file-firing, if I may apply infantry
descriptive terms to cannonading. But no language can describe its
awful grandeur. The enemy at last essayed a combined movement.
Powerful bodies of troops plunged into the valley to charge our lines,
but our men, securely posted, swept them away ruthlessly. Again and
again the desperate fellows were pushed at the breastworks, only to be
more cruelly slaughtered than before. Meantime our force had been
strengthened by Griffin's brigade, which increased the volume of infantry fire, and Martindale's brigade came up to be ready for emergencies. At dark it was evident the rebels had enough, much more
than they bargained for.

Their infantry fire had entirely subsided, and it was obvious that
they were withdrawing under cover of their artillery. Our own batteries
which had opened in full cry at the start, had not slackened an instant.
Comprehending the situation fully now, the cannoneers plied themselves with tremendous energy to punish the retreating foe. We have
no sure means to determine how many were slaughtered, but prisoners
who were in the fight, and an intelligent contraband who escaped from
Richmond the next day, and who was all over the field, are confident
that three thousand fell. Our own loss was eighty killed and less than
one hundred and fifty wounded. The conduct of our troops was admirable, and the gallantry of the officers conspicuous. Gen. McClellan
was not in the battle, but was at Gen. Porter's headquarters until it
terminated.

On the night of June 26 the Prussian officer who was Pollard's confidant
knew how badly Lee had been hurt:[9]

. . . Although I, too, could scarcely keep in the saddle, so great was my fatigue, I hastened with one of my aids to that quarter of the field where the struggle had raged the most fiercely. The scene of ruin was horrible. Whole ranks of the enemy lay prone where they had stood at the beginning of the battle. The number of wounded was fearful, too, and the groans and imploring cries for help that rose on all sides had, in the obscurity of the night, a ghastly effect that froze the blood in one's veins. Although I had been upon so many battle-fields in Italy and Hungary, never had my vision beheld such a spectacle of human destruction.

The preparations for the transportation of the wounded were too trifling, and the force detailed for that purpose was either too feeble in numbers or had no proper knowledge of its duties. Even the medical corps had, by the terrors of the situation, been rendered incapable of attending to the wounded with zeal and efficiency. With inconceivable exertion I at length succeeded, with the assistance of some humane officers, in bringing about some kind of order amid this frightful confusion. By the happiest chance, I found some Union ambulances, had all our men who could drive and knew the way pressed into service, and set to work to get the wounded into Richmond. A most heart-rending task it was; for often the poor sufferer would expire just as we were about to extend him succor.

By midnight we had got the first train ready. It consisted of sixty wagons, with two hundred seriously wounded. I cautiously and slowly conducted this train with success to the city. The first hospital reached I was met with refusal. "All full," was the reply to my inquiry. "Forward to the next hospital," was my word of command. "All full," was again the answer. Just then a friend said to me that if I would wait he might be able to help me, as he would have a neighboring tenement, used as a tobacco warehouse, prepared for a hospital. So I had to make up my mind to wait there an hour and a half in the street with my dying charge. I did my best to supply the poor fellows with water, tea, and other refreshments, so as to alleviate their sufferings in some degree; but the late hour of the night and the agitation of the city prevented me from putting my design into more than half execution.

At length the so-called hospital was ready; but I could scarcely believe my eyes when I saw the dismal hole offered me by that name. There, in open lofts, without windows or doors, a few planks nailed together were to be the beds of the unfortunate defenders of our country. During those days of fate the soldier had endured all things—

hunger, thirst, heat. Nothing could rob him of his courage, his indifference to death, and now he lay there wounded to the death at the door of his friends, whose property he had defended, for whose welfare he had exposed his life; and these friends turn him away to an open barn, where, without dressing for his wounds or any care, he is left to perish.

And yet this city had a population of forty thousand souls, had churches admirably adapted to conversion into hospitals, had clergymen in numbers; but neither the doors of the churches opened, nor were the ministers of the gospel there to sweeten the last moments of the dying soldier. Sad and dispirited, I gave the order to carry in the wounded, cast one more glance at that house of death and horror, and then swung myself into my saddle and fled, with a quiet oath on my lips, back to my regiment.

IV

That night Lee sent Dan Hill's boys along the Upper Cold Harbor road to join Jackson's forces. Swinging to the east, Jackson flanked Mc-Clellan's position along Beaver Creek and threatened his base at White House. Repulse at nightfall, victory at dawn—thus Lee demonstrated that he could keep his head!

Fitz-John Porter, commanding the right wing, pulled back to a high bend on the Chickahominy near Gaines Mill or Cold Harbor. Lee went doggedly after Porter, but Powell Hill's troops became engaged before Longstreet could support them or Jackson could swing his flanking column to support their left. Lee sent Dan Hill to reinforce Jackson in a steady, stoical movement to the left. Powell Hill still fought furiously in the center. General E. M. Law, whose brigade was in the thick of the fighting that afternoon of June 27, remembered:[10]

. . . By 5 o'clock the battle was in full progress all along the line. Longstreet's and A. P. Hill's men were attacking in the most determined manner, but were met with a courage as obstinate as their own. After each bloody repulse the Confederates only waited long enough to reform their shattered lines or to bring up their supports, when they would again return to the assault. Besides the terrific fire in their front, a battery of heavy guns on the south side of the Chickahominy were in full play on their right flank. There was no opportunity for manoeuvering on flank attacks. The enemy was directly in front and could only be reached in that direction. If he could not be driven out before night it would be the equivalent to a Confederate disaster, and would involve the failure of General Lee's whole plan for the relief of Richmond. It was a critical moment for the Confederates.

A division under "Little Billy" Whiting came to the support of Powell Hill's remnant of a division. Law's heart lifted:

. . . As we moved forward to the firing we could see the straggling Confederate line lying behind a gentle ridge that ran across the field parallel to the Federal position. . . . Passing over the scattering line of Confederates on the ridge, we broke into a trot down the slope toward the Federal works. Men fell like leaves in the autumn wind; the Federal artillery tore gaps in the ranks at every step; the ground in the rear of the advancing column was strewn thickly with the dead and wounded. Not a gun was fired by us in reply; there was no confusion and not a step faltered as the two gray lines swept silently and swiftly on; the pace became more rapid every moment; when within thirty yards of the ravine, and the men could see the desperate nature of the work in hand, a wild yell answered the roar of Federal musketry and they rushed for the works. The Confederates were within ten paces of them when the Federals in the front line broke cover and, leaving their log breastworks, swarmed up the hill in their rear, carrying away their second line with them in their rout. . . . Anderson's brigade, till then in reserve, passed through on their right and led the way for Longstreet's division; while on the left the roll of musketry receded toward the Chickahominy, and the cheering of the victorious Confederates announced that Jackson, Ewell and D. H. Hill were sweeping that part of the field.

Lanky Sam Wilkeson, writing for the New York Tribune, did not minimize the extent of the Federal debacle:[11]

. . . A motley mob started pell-mell for the bridges. . . . Scores of gallant officers endeavored to rally and re-form the stragglers, but in vain; while many officers forgot the pride of their shoulder-straps and the honor of their manhood and herded with the sneaks and cowards. . . . The scene was one not to be forgotten. Scores of riderless, terrified horses dashing in every direction; thick flying bullets singing by, admonishing of danger; every minute a man struck down; wagons and ambulances and cannon blocking the way; wounded men limping and groaning and bleeding amid the throng; officers and civilians denouncing and reasoning and entreating, and being insensibly borne along with the mass; the sublime cannonading, the clouds of battle-smoke and the sun just disappearing, large and blood-red—I can not picture it, but I see it and always shall.

Crushed and over-wrought, at a little after midnight McClellan wrote a stinging letter:[12]

HEADQUARTERS, ARMY OF THE POTOMAC,
SAVAGE'S STATION, June 28, 1862, 12.20 A.M.
HON. E. M. STANTON, SECRETARY OF WAR:

I now know the full history of the day. On this side of the river (the right bank) we repulsed several strong attacks. On the left bank our men did all that men could do, all that soldiers could accomplish, but they were overwhelmed by vastly superior numbers, even after I brought my last reserves into action. The loss on both sides is terrible. I believe it will prove to be the most desperate battle of the war. The sad remnants of my men behave as men. Those battalions who fought most bravely and suffered most are still in the best order. My regulars were superb, and I count upon what are left to turn another battle in company with their gallant comrades of the volunteers. Had I twenty thousand (20,000), or even ten thousand (10,000), fresh troops to use to-morrow, I could take Richmond; but I have not a man in reserve, and shall be glad to cover my retreat and save the material and *personnel* of the army.

If we have lost the day we have yet preserved our honor, and no one need blush for the Army of the Potomac. I have lost this battle because my force was too small.

I again repeat that I am not responsible for this, and I say it with the earnestness of a general who feels in his heart the loss of every brave man who has been needlessly sacrificed to-day. I still hope to retrieve our fortunes; but to do this the government must view the matter in the same earnest light that I do. You must send me very large reinforcements, and send at once. I shall draw back to this side of the Chickahominy, and think I can withdraw all our material. Please understand that in this battle we have lost nothing but men, and those the best we have.

In addition to what I have already said, I only wish to say to the President that I think he is wrong in regarding me as ungenerous when I said that my force was too weak. I merely intimated a truth which to-day has been too plainly proved. If, at this instant, I could dispose of ten thousand (10,000) fresh men, I could gain the victory to-morrow.

I know that a few thousand more men would have changed this battle from a defeat to a victory. As it is, the government must not and cannot hold me responsible for the result.

I feel too earnestly to-night. I have seen too many dead and wounded comrades to feel otherwise than that the government has not sustained this army. If you do not do so now the game is lost.

If I save this army now, I tell you plainly that I owe no thanks to you or to any other persons in Washington.

You have done your best to sacrifice this army.

G. B. McClellan

V

Behind the grandeur of the flashing siege guns, beyond the military textbooks, above the pressure of political necessity, war was men who groaned and limped and became human wrecks—the luckless who had not died. This fact McClellan could never escape; it was the key to the man—perhaps the quality that gave him greatness as a human being while he failed as a general. McClellan loved his soldiers; when they died, sons were taken from him; when they were wounded, their cries haunted his dreams. He was soft, pitifully soft to be on the battle-field that young Bickman saw that morning:[13]

Saturday [June 28] . . . loomed upon us hotly and cheerlessly. Until nine o'clock not the sound of a hostile gun disturbed the dread silence. The profound stillness of morning became so oppressive that the dull report of a musket on the borders would have been comparative happiness. About nine o'clock this anxiety was relieved by an awful cannonade opened upon Smith's position from two forts in Garnett's field, a battery at Fitz-John Porter's old position, and another below it, on the left bank of the Chickahominy, raking his intrenchments and compelling him to abandon the strongest natural position on our whole line. The fire was terrible. I can describe its lines fairly by comparing it with the right lines and angles of a chess-board. Smith fell back to the woods, a few hundred yards, and threw up breastworks out of range. The enemy, content with his success, ceased firing, and quiet was not disturbed again that day. The silence of the enemy was explained to me that night by a negro slave, who had escaped from his master at headquarters in Richmond. He said a despatch had been sent by Jackson to Magruder, who remained in command in front of Richmond, expressed thus: *"Be quiet. Every thing is working as well as we could desire!"* Ominous words!

I now proceeded to Savage station. I shall not attempt to describe the sombre picture of gloom, confusion and distress, which oppressed me there. I found officers endeavoring to fight off the true meaning. Anxiety at headquarters was too apparent to one who had studied that branch of the army too sharply to be deluded by thin masks. Other external signs were demonstrative. The wretched spectacle of mangled men from yesterday's battle, prone upon the lawn, around the hospital, the wearied, haggard, and smoke-begrimed faces of men who had fought, were concomitants of every battle-field, yet they formed the sombre coloring of the ominous picture before me. Then there were hundreds who had straggled from the field, sprawled upon every space where there was a shadow of a leaf to protect them from a broiling sun; a hurry and tumult of wagons and artillery trains, endless almost, rushing down the roads towards the new base, moving with a sort of orderly confusion, almost as distressing as panic itself. But I venture that few of all that hastening throng, excepting old officers, understood the misfortune. Strange to say, that even then, almost eleven o'clock, communication with White House by railroad and telegraph was uninterrupted, but soon after eleven the wires suddenly ceased to vibrate intelligibly.

From headquarters I passed along our lines. The troops still stood at the breastworks ready for battle; but it was evident they had begun to inquire into the situation. Some apprehensive officers had caught a hint of the mysteries which prevailed. The trains were ordered to move, troops to hold themselves in readiness to march at any moment. So passed that day, dreadful in its moral attributes as a day of pestilence, and when night closed upon the dreary scene, the enterprise had fully begun. Endless streams of artillery-trains, wagons, and funereal ambulances poured down the roads from all the camps, and plunged into the narrow funnel which was our only hope of escape. And now the exquisite truth flashed upon me. It was absolutely necessary, for the salvation of the army and the cause, that our wounded and mangled braves, who lay moaning in physical agony in our hospitals, should be *deserted* and left in the hands of the enemy. . . .

Yet in McClellan's weakness as a general rested a resource of greatness. To save his army—his men—he could rise to shining heights, undaunted by risks, all at once clear-headed to the point of brilliance, ready to achieve miracles. This quality in McClellan fooled Lee; he lost a day before he accepted the fact that McClellan was moving to the James and the protection of the Federal gunboats, either to escape or recondition his army for another assault on Richmond. Lee wanted nothing less; now, while McClellan was reeling, he must catch and crush him! On the afternoon of the twenty-ninth, Magruder caught up with the Federals near Savage Station under circumstances that Bickman described in a fine piece of reporting:[14]

The advance column and all that mighty train had now been swallowed in the maw of the dreary forest. It swept onward, onward, fast and furious like an avalanche. Every hour of silence behind was ominous, but hours were precious to us. Pioneer bands were rushing along in front, clearing and repairing our single road; reconnoissance officers were seeking new routes for a haven of rest and safety. The enemy was in the rear pressing on with fearful power. He *could press down flankward to our front,* cutting off our retreat. Would such be our fate? The vanguard had passed White Oak bridge and had risen to a fine defensive post, flanked by White Oak swamps, where part of the train at least could rest. How sadly the feeble ones needed it, those who having suspected their friends were about to abandon them, trusted rather to the strength of fear to lead them to safety, than to the fate which might await them at the hands of the foe. But the march was orderly as upon any less urgent day, only swifter—and marvellous, too, it seemed that such caravans of wagons, artillery, horsemen, soldiers, camp-followers, and all, should press through that narrow road with so little confusion.

Two miles beyond the bridge the column suddenly halted. A tremor thrilled along the line. A moment more, and the dull boom of a cannon and its echoing shell fell grimly upon our ears. Were we beleaguered? An hour later, and there was an ominous roar behind. The enemy was thundering on our rear. I know that the moment was painful to many, but no soldier's heart seemed to shrink from the desperate shock. Back and forth dashed hot riders. Messengers here, orders there, *composure and decision where it should be,* with determination to wrest triumph from the jaws of disaster. As yet every thing had prospered, and at noon a brighter ray flashed athwart our dreary horizon. Averill—our dashing "Ashby"—had moved with the vanguard, met eight companies of rebel cavalry, charged them, routed them, pursued them miles beyond our reach, and returned in triumph with sixty prisoners and horses, leaving nine dead foes on the field. He explained it modestly, but I saw old generals thank him for the gallant exploit—not the first of his youthful career. Gen. Keyes had sent a section of artillery with the vanguard, Averill's cavalry escorting it. The rebels charged at the guns, not perceiving our cavalry, which was screened by thickets. The artillery gave them shell and canister, which checked their mad career. Averill charged, and horse, rider and all were in one red burial blend. Dead horses are scattered over that field, and dead men lie under the shadows of the forests. We lost but one brave trooper.

Bickman caught a glimpse of McClellan:[15]

Nothing struck me so keenly during all that gloomy day and more desolate night, as the thinly disguised uneasiness of those to whom the country had entrusted its fate. It was well that soldiers who carry muskets did not read the agony traced upon the face of that leader whom they had learned to love. A few in that gloomy bivouac folded their arms to sleep, but most were too exhausted to enjoy that blessed relief. That dreadful tumult, but a few short miles in the distance, raged till long after the whippoorwill had commenced his plaintive song. Late at night, couriers, hot from the field, dashed in with glad tidings. Sumner had beaten the enemy at every point, until they were glad to cease attack. The warrior was advised by Gen. McClellan to retire quietly to our main body; but the old man, game as a king-eagle, begged to be permitted to drive the rebels home. Said a General to me: "Old Bull Sumner didn't want to quit. The game old fellow had to be choked off.". . .

It was Sunday now . . . the day when McClellan must cross White Oak Swamp and Lee could win. He had hastened Jackson down the Chickahominy and into the swamp so that this gray-clad Joshua could wreak the vengeance belonging to a South betrayed. Once Robert Stiles, who fought with Jackson, said of his commander, "If he were not a very good man, he would be a very bad one." That Sunday Jackson was in a strange mood, writing his wife about how much sleep he had lost and how much money she should give to the church. He brushed aside a report that a ford had been found that would support a pontoon bridge and bring him onto the Federals where they could be smashed. He simply wouldn't fight. Stiles saw him next morning:[16]

Jackson and the little sorrel stopped in the middle of the road, probably not fifty feet off, while his staff halted perhaps a hundred and fifty yards in his rear. He sat stark and stiff in the saddle. Horse and rider appeared worn down to the lowest point of flesh consistent with effective service. His hair, skin, eyes and clothes were all one neutral dust tint, and his badges of rank so dulled and tarnished as to be scarcely perceptible. The "mangy little cadet cap" was pulled so low in front that the visor cut the glint of his eyeballs.

Troops of the Seventeenth and Twenty-first Mississippi, caught by the ambush of a Federal brigade, sprawled on the ground, and "a sickly summer rain" falling through the night had left the faces of the dead "bleached with more than death's pallor." Jackson looked briefly at the scene; no muscle quivered; then he glanced down the road toward Richmond:

A moment later and his gaze was rewarded. A magnificent staff approached from the direction of Richmond, and riding at its head, superbly mounted, a born king among men. At that time General Lee was one of the handsomest of men, especially on horseback, and that morning every detail of his dress and equipment of himself and horse was absolute perfection. When he recognized Jackson, he rode forward with a courier, his staff halting. . . .

The two generals greeted each other warmly, but wasted no time upon the greeting. They stood facing each other, some thirty feet from where I lay, Lee's left side and back toward me, Jackson's right and front. Jackson began talking in a jerky, impetuous way, meanwhile drawing a diagram on the ground with the toe of his right boot. He traced two sides of a triangle with promptness and decision; then, starting at the end of the second line, began to draw a third projected toward the first. This third line he traced slowly and with hesitation, alternately looking up at Lee's face and down at his diagram, meanwhile talking earnestly; and when at last the third line crossed the first and the triangle was complete, he raised his foot and stamped it down with emphasis, saying "We've got him"; then signalled for his horse and when he came, vaulted into the saddle and was off. Lee watched him a moment, the courier brought his horse, he mounted, and he and his staff rode away.

The third line was never drawn—so we never "got" McClellan.

VI

But McClellan "got" Lee—not decisively but viciously enough to take a good part of the sting away from the other discouragements of the Seven Days. While Jackson had slumbered, prayed, and meditated in White Oak Swamp, McClellan, escaping, had occupied Malvern Hill and protected his position by shrewdly placed artillery. Pollard's friend, the Prussian officer, described Lee's dilemma on July 1:[17]

The gray of morning was just beginning to appear upon the horizon when the roar of artillery was once more heard. A battery which, during the night, Gen. Anderson had placed nearer to the hostile lines was instantly noticed by the enemy and vigorously attacked by his field-pieces. Every shot struck, and the fragments were hurled in all directions. Of the twelve pieces in the battery five were quickly dismounted and the teams half destroyed, yet the commanding officer held his post. In the mean while our columns had formed without having tasted any strengthening or nourishing refreshment. Exhausted by the fatigues of the preceding days, they fairly reeled on their feet, yet not a man shrank back from duty. At length, as the sun rose in splendor, and we could better distinguish the enemy's position, an involuntary exclamation escaped me, for it was evident to me, from the denser ranks he exhibited, that McClellan had been considerably reinforced during the night, and could therefore withdraw his worn-out troops from the foremost lines, and have an easy struggle with fresh men against our famished and exhausted force.

Gen. Lee, convinced of the perilous position of affairs, at once issued orders to Stonewall Jackson to cover the retreat in case the army should be compelled to fall back, and directions were sent to Richmond to get all the public property ready for immediate removal. Then the divisions of Hill (second), Longstreet, Anderson, Cobb, and Whitcomb were ordered to storm the enemy's works.

And now again commenced one of the most desperate combats that ever took place in any war. The loss on our side was absolutely frightful. McClellan, observing the devastation his artillery was making among our troops, called up a division of reserves, and overwhelmed us with a terrific rain of musketry. His masses pressed forward, step by step, nearer and nearer, until at length some companies of ours threw their arms away and fled. McClellan availed himself of this panic, and ordered a flank movement of his cavalry. Quick as thought

Anderson placed himself at the head of our horse, and led three regiments to the charge. Their onset was magnificent. Our Texans burst with ringing huzzas into the ranks of the foe, who, without even giving us time to try our sabres, turned to the right-about; but here, too, the hostile field-pieces prevented further success, and we had to draw back from before that crushing fire.

The enemy, noticing our confusion, now advanced with the cry, "Onward to Richmond!" Yes, along the whole hostile front rang the shout, "Onward to Richmond!" Many old soldiers who had served in distant Missouri and on the plains of Arkansas wept in the bitterness of their souls like children. Of what avail had it been to us that our best blood had flowed for six long days?—of what avail all our unceasing and exhaustless endurance? Every thing, every thing seemed lost, and a general depression came over all our hearts. Batteries dashed past in headlong flight; ammunition, hospital, and supply wagons rushed along, and swept the troops away with them from the battle-field. In vain the most frantic exertion, entreaty, and self-sacrifice of the staff-officers. The troops had lost their foothold, and all was over with the Southern Confederacy.

"It was not war—it was murder," Dan Hill said afterward. And the Prussian officer knew why:

In this moment of desperation Gen. Hill came up with a few regiments he had managed to rally; but the enemy was continually pressing nearer and nearer, louder and louder their shouts, and the watchword, "On to Richmond!" could be heard. Cavalry officers sprang from their saddles, and rushed into the ranks of the infantry regiments, now deprived of their proper officers. Gen. Hill seized the standard of the 4th North Carolina regiment—which he had formerly commanded —and shouted to the soldiers: "If you will not follow me, I will perish alone!" Upon this a number of officers dashed forward to cover their beloved general with their bodies, the soldiers hastily rallied, and the cry, "Lead on, Hill, head your old North Carolina boys!" rose over the field. And now Hill charged forward with this mass he had thus worked up to the wildest enthusiasm.

The enemy halted when they saw these columns, in flight a moment before, now advancing to the attack, and Hill burst upon his late pursuers like a famished lion. A fearful hand-to-hand conflict now ensued, for there was no time to load and fire. The ferocity with which this combat was waged was incredible. It was useless to beg the exasperated men for quarter; there was no moderation, no pity, no compassion in that bloody work of bayonet and knife.

The son sank dying at his father's feet; the father forgot that he had a child—a dying child; the brother did not see that a brother was expiring a few paces from him; the friend heard not the last groans of a friend; all natural ties were dissolved; only one feeling, one thirst panted in every bosom—revenge. Here it was that the son of Major Peyton, but fifteen years of age, called to his father for help. A ball had shattered both his legs. "When we have beaten the enemy, then I will help you," answered Peyton; "I have here other sons to lead to glory. Forward!" But the column had advanced only a few paces further when the major himself fell to the earth a corpse. . . . Even the wounded, despairing of succor, collecting their last energies of life, plunged their knives into the bosoms of foemen who lay near them still breathing.

The success of Gen. Hill enabled other generals to once more lead their disorganized troops back to the fight, and the contest was renewed along the whole line, and kept up until deep into the night; for everything depended upon our keeping the enemy at bay, counting, too, upon their exhaustion at last, until fresh troops could arrive to reinforce us. At length, about half-past ten in the evening, the divisions of Magruder, Wise, and Holmes came up and deployed to the front of our army. Had the commanders of these divisions executed their orders with promptitude and skill, streams of blood would have been spared, and the foe would have been thrown back upon his reserves in the course of the forenoon; but they reached us fully seventeen hours behind time. The generals had been uncertain concerning the marching orders, their columns crossed each other and became entangled, and precious time was irremediably lost. Still, as it was, the remainder of our force had to thank the final arrival of these divisions for their rescue.

So soon as these reinforcements could be thrown to the front, our regiments were drawn back, and as far as possible reorganized during the night, the needful officers appointed, and after the distribution of provisions, which had also fortunately arrived, measures were adopted for the gathering up of the wounded and the burial of the dead.

On Tuesday, July first, at two o'clock in the morning, while the stars were still visible in the sky, Gen. Magruder again opened the battle, and very soon began a cannonade so fearful that the very earth trembled with the concussion. By twelve o'clock meridian McClellan had abandoned all his positions, leaving behind his wounded, his baggage, and many pieces of cannon. Magruder followed him, hot foot, but cautiously, as he had first to sweep the surrounding woods with artillery and sharpshooters.

Magruder was too late; McClellan, turning at Malvern Hill to gain second wind, had completed his escape. The Comte de Paris, who served as an officer on McClellan's staff and later wrote a thoughtful, authoritative history of the war, summarized the result:[18]

This time the Confederates had experienced a defeat unmitigated by any compensation. The great effort they had made to repair the errors committed on the preceding days had signally failed. Their divisions, exhausted and diminished by six days' marching and fighting, had been led to the assault of formidable positions without order or unity of action, and had paid dearly for the confidence of their generals —a confidence which, since the victory of Gaines' Mill, had become positive presumption. Their losses were enormous and out of all proportion to those they had inflicted upon their adversaries. So useless a sacrifice of life troubled and discouraged them. . . . Up to this time the Confederate army had labored under the conviction that the capitulation of McClellan and all his troops would be the inevitable result of the campaign. The soldier, unable to judge of the combined movements of the Federals, had seen nothing but success in all his encounters with them, and believed that as great advantages had been obtained at Frazier's Farm and Glendale as at Gaines' Mill; consequently, when on the evening of the 1st of July he found himself repulsed at all points by those very men whom he had supposed to be in full flight, discouragement took the place of the assurance which until then had imparted so much strength. The men still fit for service set themselves to numbering those present and those that were absent— the killed, the wounded, the sick and the stragglers; the latter were in frightful numbers. If Lee had desired at this moment to lead his army once more to the charge, he would not have been followed. He had to remain contented with the results obtained—results, indeed, of sufficient importance to satisfy any rational mind that had not been lulled into illusions. Lee could show, as substantial evidences of his success, fifty pieces of cannon—most of them damaged, it is true—which his soldiers had captured at the point of the bayonet or picked up on the field of battle, a considerable number of wagons, a large number of muskets, accoutrements of every description, provisions, tents, ammunition, together with six thousand prisoners, one-half of them wounded, and among them several generals. In a strategic point of view, the results were still more considerable. McClellan, who may be said to have been laying siege to Richmond, had been violently interrupted in that siege, conquered in open field, and compelled to undertake a perilous retreat in order to find a new base of operations at a much greater distance from the aim of all his efforts. He had sustained considerable losses, for the *matériel* which the enemy had taken from him was nothing compared with what he had himself been obliged to destroy. The wounded who had followed the army were far more numerous than those who had remained behind. No one had as yet counted the dead, who might be reckoned at many thousands. Finally, the thought that a campaign undertaken with so much perseverance had ended in a disaster, depressed the courage of every one, from the general-in-chief to the simple soldier.

The Federals, however, had achieved on the borders of the James the victory which had been denied them on the Chickahominy. If the first part of this short but sanguinary campaign was illustrated by the battle of Gaines' Mill, the second was by that of Malvern Hill. The enemy, therefore, could not compel them to fall back farther. But the motives which had decided McClellan to select a position below City Point for his army still existed; the vicinity of the right bank would always have rendered it difficult to provision Malvern Hill. The general-in-chief, therefore, adhered to the order issued before the battle, directing the evacuation of this position during the night of the 1st and 2d of July. The place he had designated as the quarters for the army near his new base was Harrison's Landing, formerly the property of President Harrison, situated twelve kilometres lower down in a direct line. . . .

VII

The balance that both armies had to strike after the Seven Days made grim reading:

	EFFECTIVES	KILLED	WOUNDED	MISSING
Union	91,169	1,734	8,062	6,053
Confederate	90,000	3,478	16,262	875

Indeed, Lee had paid highly to save Richmond, yet at least War Clerk Jones was immensely satisfied:[19]

. . . The serpent has been killed, though its tail still exhibits some spasmodic motions. It will die, so far as the Peninsula is concerned, after sunset, or when it thunders.

The commanding general neither sleeps nor slumbers. Already [July 4] the process of reorganizing Jackson's corps has been commenced for a blow at or near the enemy's capital. Let Lincoln beware the hour of retribution.

CHAPTER 14

TWO THOUSAND MILES OF WAR

ALONG THE CHICKAHOMINY and the James the guns were suddenly quiet; but along other rivers two thousand miles apart—the Mississippi, the Potomac, the Yellow Medicine—the war seemed carried by the wind. June brought the War Department in Washington the grim news of McClellan's failure on the Peninsula; but the Navy Department gave a shout of joy at the dispatches from Memphis.

I

In the early morning light of June 6, 1862, Union gunboats lay anchored in the Mississippi at the lower end of Island Number Forty-five, about a mile and a half above Memphis. At the city's levee lay eight Rebel rams and gunboats. "The engagement," Flag Officer C. H. Davis reported to Secretary Welles, "terminated in a running fight," which was a nice economy of language; but "C. D. M.," aboard the flagship Benton, *offered readers of the Cincinnati* Commercial *more of the stirring details:*[1]

At 6.05 A.M., "all hands to quarters" is Commodore Davis's order, throughout our fleet. In the mean time, the rebel fleet, comprising the Gen. Van Dorn, (flag-ship,) Gen. Price, Gen. Bragg, Jeff. Thompson, Gen. Lovell, Gen. Beauregard, Sumter, and Little Rebel, all rams, commanded by Commodore J. Ed. Montgomery, move up the river, the Little Rebel leading the van. Our fleet, in the mean time, advances to meet them, the Louisville and Cairo dropping below the Benton, the

Cairo "head on." The Benton is now signalled for, and takes the lead. The Little Rebel, on arriving opposite the upper end of the city, fires the first shot, the ball passing over our fleet and dropping into the river harmlessly in close proximity to our tugs, in the rear. The Benton instantly replies, when a general engagement ensues.

Your correspondent, taking his position on the upper deck and in front of the Benton's pilot-house, endeavors to see how the battle progresses. "Now comes the tug of war." Up come the rebel rams. Down go our ironclads, the Benton in advance. Thousands of people cover the Memphis bluffs. Another shot from the Benton, when the Louisville, Cairo, Carondelet, Mound City, and St. Louis all open out.

The scene is exciting, thrilling. The ram Queen of the West, under Col. Ellet, with a full head of steam and at her best speed, closely followed by the Monarch, Capt. D. M. Dryden, pass our fleet and go tearing down after the rebel fleet. In the mean time, an incessant fire is kept up on both sides. The rebel balls go chirping, whizzing, and zip, zip, zip! very close, but over and clear of our decks and heads. See! the rams Queen of the West and Monarch. On they go, each having selected her victim. Montgomery's fleet is firing and dropping back. Go in, Queen of the West. She is headed for the Beauregard. The latter is straightening up to meet her. They come together, the Queen of the West ramming Beauregard a glancing lick near the stern.

The Monarch is after another rebel ram and striking her a flanking blow, glances off, and for a moment is between two of the enemy's rams. Pop, pop, pop, pop, go the rifles of her unerring sharpshooters, who pick off the rebel gunners at their ports, thus preventing them from pouring broadside after broadside into the Queen and Monarch. Meantime, all our iron-clads are sending shell and shot after the other rebel gunboats out of the range of our bully rams. There goes our ram Switzerland a railing, followed by the Lancaster Number Three. She goes through all right, while the latter, in "backing," goes into the bank, and being disabled, too, by knocking off her rudder, retires from the scene of action.

The Monarch having got below the rebel fleet, is coming up, "head on." The Beauregard, while preparing to receive her, misses her mark, and goes chock into the side of one of her own fleet—the Price—taking off the starboard water-wheel of the latter. The shots from our gunboats tell with disastrous effect on the enemy's boats. The Gen. Price makes for the Arkansas shore, and, careening, sinks nearly out of sight. The Gen. Lovell now receives a heavy shot, and is the second rebel boat to go down.

The rams on both sides, and our iron-clads, are all in close quarters —the latter pouring in heavy shot with crushing effect. The Little Rebel is now crippled by one of our shot. She is making for the Arkansas shore, followed by one of our rams—the Switzerland. The Little Rebel reaches the shore, when Com. Montgomery and all his crew break for the timber, and by the tallest kind of swimming, escape. At one time, three of the rebel rams were, apparently, locked fast, foul, or perhaps, sympathizing with each other in their discomfiture. They receive no sympathy from our iron-clads, now pouring broadside after broadside into them, completely riddling their hulls and upper works. The hottest part of the engagement lasts some thirty minutes, when the Gen. Bragg, Sumter, Jeff. Thompson and Van Dorn, backing out with all possible speed, skedaddle off down the river, pursued by the Benton and the rest of the iron-clads, all sending shot after shot after the retreating rebels.

Succinctly, Flag Officer Davis ended his report to Welles:

The Mayor surrendered the city to me after the engagement. Col. Fitch came down at eleven o'clock, and has taken military possession.

But "C.D.M." could attest that the surrender had not been complete:

The following note, addressed "to any Federal Lincolnite," was found on the desk of the telegraph office:

"I leave this office to any Lincolnite successor, and will state that, although you can whip us on the water, if you will come out on land we'll whip you like hell.

[Signed]
"Operator"

II

Running down the list of Union vessels engaged in the action before Memphis, the knowing eye would have lighted with recognition at the mention of the Carondelet. *On an early April evening, with the moon hidden behind an oncoming thunderstorm, this sturdy vessel, looking in her skipper's phrase "like a farmer's wagon," had borne down on Island Number Ten below Columbus, Kentucky. Chain cable had been wrapped around her pilot house; a coal barge piled high with hay was lashed to her side. As lightning flecked the sky, shouts and bugles within the Confederate fort on Island Number Ten announced that the Rebels had spotted the boat. The guns of the Carondelet flashed, and an eerie scene followed with lightning striking down, guns belching ruin and death upon the fort, thunder rolling. Three days later, Union forces under John Pope found that the Carondelet had done her work so well the fort and island surrendered along with 7,000 prisoners.*

But Pope got most of the credit; that was why he appeared suddenly in Washington. Under Lincoln's orders Pope concentrated all the forces in the region of the Rappahannock and the Shenandoah into the Army of Virginia. While protecting the national capital, Pope was expected also to relieve the pressure on McClellan, still on the Peninsula. Pope's new corps commanders were all his seniors in rank, and one, John C. Frémont, had been Pope's commanding officer in Missouri. In a situation highly charged with wounded feelings, tact seemed an indispensable element.

"God damn McDowell!" cried Pope, no man to mince words. "He is never where I want him!" Profane and vulgar, full of bluff and bluster—that was Pope. "Let us look before and not behind," he addressed his troops. "Success and glory are in the advance. Disaster and shame lurk in the rear." In an astonishing order on July 23 he instructed his officers to consider all civilians who refused to take an oath of allegiance as "spies," to shoot "bushwhackers" who fired on troops and put private homes to the torch in retaliation, and to live off the country not wasting "force and energy . . . protecting private property of those most hostile to the Government." Enraged, Lee sent a blistering letter to Washington:[2]

The President also instructs me to inform you that we renounce our right of retaliation on the innocent, and will continue to treat the private enlisted soldiers of General Pope's army as prisoners of war; but if, after notice to your Government that we confine repressive measures to the punishment of commissioned officers, who are willing participants in these crimes, the savage practice threatened in the order alluded to be persisted in, we shall be reluctantly forced to the last resort of accepting the war on the terms chosen by our enemies, until the voice of an outraged humanity shall compel a respect for the recognized usages of war.

The "miscreant Pope," with a force of 43,000 on the line of the Rappahannock, threatened to squeeze Lee between this army and Mc-Clellan's 90,000 on the Peninsula. Jackson struck Pope at Cedar Run on August 9, then shied off from a general engagement next morning. From Harrison's Landing, McClellan screamed for reinforcements and insisted that "it is here on the banks of the James River that the fate of the Union should be decided." Washington disagreed, ordering Mc-Clellan to join Pope. Lee decided to get there first, and on August 19 looked down at Pope's army from Cedar Mountain. With the Federal forces was George Alfred Townsend, who thought he had been well instructed in military blunders on the Peninsula. He recalled a poignant incident:[3]

. . . At one time, a private soldier came out to me, presenting a scrap of paper, and asked me to scrawl him a line, which he would dictate. It was as follows:

"*My dear Mary, we are going into action soon, and I send you my love. Kiss baby, and if I am not killed I will write to you after the fight.*"

The man asked me to mail the scrap at the first opportunity; but the same post which carried his simple billet, carried also his name among the rolls of the dead.

Townsend drew a sketch of a pathetic figure:

We entered the beautiful lawn of the Springs' hotel, at ten o'clock, and a Negro came up to take our horses. By the lamplight and moon-light I saw McDowell's tent, a sentry pacing up and down before it, and the thick, powerful figure of the General seated at a writing-table within. Irvin McDowell was one of the oldest officers in the service, and when the war commenced he became a leading commander in the Eastern army. At Bull Run he had a responsible place, and the ill success of that battle brought him into unpleasant notoriety. Though he retained a leading position he was still mistrusted and disliked. None bore ingratitude so stolidly. He may have flinched, but he never replied; and though ambitious, he tried to content himself with subordinate commands. Some called him a traitor, others an incompetent, others a plotter. If McClellan failed, McDowell was cursed. If Pope blundered, McDowell received half the contumely. But he loosened no cord of discipline to make good will. Implacable, dutiful, soldierly, rigorous in discipline, sententious, brave—the most unpopular man in America went on his way. . . .

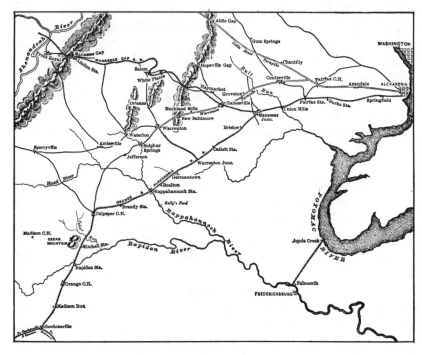

CEDAR MOUNTAIN AND SECOND BULL RUN

From John Codman Ropes, *The Army Under Pope*

Townsend was at Cedar Mountain, where the private fell before he could kiss the baby, and where the fortunes of combat still refused to smile on McDowell:

For a time, each party kept in the edges of the timber, firing at will, but the Confederates were moving forward in masses by detours, until some thousands of them stood in the places of the few who were at first isolated. Distinct charges were now made, and a large body of Federals attempted to capture the battery before Slaughter's house, while separate brigades charged by front and flank upon the impenetrable timber. The horrible results of the previous effort were repeated; the

Confederates preserved their position, and, at nightfall, the Federals fell back a mile or more. From fifteen hundred to two thousand of the latter were slain or wounded, and, though the heat of the battle had lasted no more than two hours, nearly four thousand men upon both sides were maimed or dead.

The valor of the combatants in either cause was unquestionable. But no troops in the world could have driven the Confederates out of the impregnable mazes of the wood. It was an error to expose columns of troops upon an open plain, in the face of imperceptible sharpshooters. The batteries should have shelled the thickets, and the infantry should have retained their concealment. The most disciplined troops of Europe would not have availed in a country of bog, barren, ditch, creek, forest, and mountain.

Compared to the bare plain of Waterloo, Cedar Mountain was like the antediluvian world, when the surface was broken by volcanic fire into chasms and abysses. In this battle, the Confederate batteries, along the mountainside, were arranged in the form of a crescent, and, when the solid masses charged up the hill, they were butchered by enfilading fires. On the Confederate part, a thorough knowledge of the country was manifest, and the best possible disposition of forces and means; on the side of the Federals, there was zeal without discretion, and gallantry without generalship.

During the action, Stonewall Jackson occupied a commanding position on the side of the mountain, where, glass in hand, he observed every change of position, and directed all the operations. General Banks was indefatigable and courageous; but he was left to fight the whole battle, and not a regiment of the large reserve in his rear came forward to succor or relieve him. As usual, McDowell was cursed by all sides, and some of Banks's soldiers threatened to shoot him. But the unpopular Commander had no defence to make, and said nothing to clear up the doubts relative to him. He exposed himself repeatedly, and so did Pope. The latter rode to the front at nightfall—for what purpose no one could say, as he had been in Culpeper during the whole afternoon—and he barely escaped being captured. The loss of Federal officers was very heavy. Fourteen commissioned officers were killed and captured out of one regiment. Sixteen commissioned officers only remained in four regiments. One general was taken prisoner and several were wounded. A large number of field-officers were slain.

During the progress of the fight I galloped from point to point along the rear, but could nowhere obtain a panoramic view. The common sentiment of civilians, that it is always possible to see a battle, is true of isolated contests only. Even the troops engaged know little of the occurrences around them, and I have been assured by many soldiers that they have fought a whole day without so much as a glimpse of an enemy. The smoke and dust conceal objects, and where the greatest execution is done, the antagonists have frequently fired at a line of smoke, behind which columns may or may not have been posted.

III

Lee intended to give Pope no respite. The Confederate's contempt for his adversary was hardly greater than that of Washington A. Roebling, an engineer with the Army of the Potomac. In a letter to the famous father with whom he would one day plan and build the Brooklyn Bridge, "Wash" told an ungilded story:[4]

For the last 10 days I have been on the trot constantly, scarcely ever out of the saddle and have lost one horse which I was compelled to abandon on the retreat, it being unable to get along. The day after I wrote you my last letter I surveyed a road out of Madison C.H. and returning late at night received orders to accompany an expedition to Louisa C.H., 20 miles within the enemy's lines. This trip was safely accomplished, . . . little was seen of the enemy during the trip and not more than 8 or ten stragglers captured. On the way out we took bye roads but returned on the main road, and here it was at 5 o'clock in the morning that we surprised the rebel Maj. General Stuart and staff at breakfast. The Gen. himself escaped through the stupidity of a Major, he being afraid to shoot him, but some of his staff were caught. This occurred only 2 miles from Stuart's cavalry camp and as he was escaping in that direction with lightning speed, we were certain of a speedy pursuit which our jaded horses could not stand. Therefore we made a straight cut in the direction of Fredricksburg, crossing the river some 15 miles from that place to Germanna Mills, before the enemy arrived there. Once over there, the hurry was over.

The information obtained and roads surveyed were quite valuable, or will be so whenever we get back there, if ever—which I doubt. Well, when I returned to where our camp was, behold it was gone; thinks I, what does this mean! I was too sleepy, however, to make any further enquiries that night, and went to sleep. Next day upon reaching Culpeper, I learned to my surprise that the whole army had retreated for no apparent cause whatever, and that I was about the last man left.

I was fortunate enough to get on the last train with my saddle, and so went to Rapp. Stat. on the Rapp. river. Here the army was posted on the North shore, ready to make a stand against an enemy who was perfectly justified in supposing that we had left from fear and on account of our smaller force. On the next day the enemy's cavalry made its appearance, whipped our cavalry, and drove in everything so that we retained nothing but two small hills on the South side of the river on which batteries were placed. Communication was held from the North shore with the one hill by the R. R. bridge and with the other by a low trestle bridge put up in one night.

The position was quite strong. Sigel had the right, McDowell the centre, next came Banks, then Reno. The next morning the enemy commenced feeling us. He opened light batteries at different points. I happened to be at Fruman's Ford when he opened first with 2 guns on a battery & regiment stationed to guard the Ford. The accuracy of his firing was such that in 15 minutes his 2 guns silenced our battery of 6 and drove away a regiment, (Maryland of course). All our troops were drawn up in line of battle. The enemy actually crossed at the Ford but was repulsed. The cannonading continued all day, the enemy being everywhere driven back by us. As Eng. officers are ex officio aids I acted as such to Gen. McDowell and have done so ever since. . . .

During that night it rained, which raised the river, carried off the trestle bridge which in turn endangered the R. R. bridge. Communication being cut off, one hill had to be abandoned, and the R. R. bridge, being in danger of going, the other side was evacuated and the R. R. bridge burned. This was done under a heavy fire from the enemy who immediately occupied those 2 hills. In the mean time the enemy crossed near Sigel who drove them back in a little fight in which he is reported by the papers to have taken 2000 prisoners. He took none at all. Our loss up to now was perhaps 200 killed & wounded in all.

Certain occurrences now gave rise to the suspicion that the enemy was merely fooling us with, say, one division here and that his main body was crossing some 20 miles further up. Our force was, say, 45,000 effectives and the question was shall we cross the river, whip this division and fall on the enemy's flank or shall we retreat and give up this point of the Rpphk. Pope decided on the latter course—the man, you remember, who snubbed McDowell about lines of retreat.

McDowell's corps, consisting of King's, Ricketts' & McCall's divisions, & 3000 cavalry, retired to around Warrenton. Sigel went to Sulphur Springs & Waterloo further up on the river. Banks & Reno also moved up on the river but camped some 5 miles from it.

When we retired from the river the enemy did not cross in force, showing the correctness of the supposition that he was there only in small force and that his main body was crossing further up. At Sulphur Springs & Waterloo the usual cannonading & skirmishing again commenced, which always takes place when troops are separated by a shallow creek of only 100 to 200 feet wide, the size of the Rpphk here. The day before our arrival at Warrenton our HdQurtr Trains, which had been sent to Catletts stat. for safety, were attacked by the advance guard of rebel cavalry. The things destroyed belonged principally to Pope. My things escaped. My nigger was taken but got off afterwards.

Rumours now began to circulate that a portion of McClellan's army was somewhere in the neighborhood, but where was not known. Communication between Warrenton & Washington was interrupted and Pope had neither the brains for devising any plan of operation, much less for executing it. A dozen orders were given & countermanded the same day and the troops subjected to a lot of useless marching which only fatigued them and lost 2 precious days and rations which were also running short. While waiting for dinner at the Warrenton Hotel, Houston & I got orders to rush down to the river and examine all fords, preparatory to all the troops crossing the Rpphk that night and falling in the enemy's rear. We returned at 1 o'clock in the morning, only to find the order countermanded. Pope in the meantime went to Catletts stat.

Morale ran high in Lee's army. The boys sensed that "Uncle Robert" was pushing hard, with Pope puzzled by the Confederate movements. In a cheery letter home, an unidentified Rebel lieutenant captured the spirit of Lee's troops:[5]

Now comes the great wonder. Starting up the bank of the river on Monday, the twenty-fifth, we marched through Amosville, in Rappahannock County—still further up, crossed the Rappahannock within ten miles of the Blue Ridge, marched across open fields, by strange country paths and comfortable homesteads, by a little town in Fauquier, called Orleans, on and on, as if we would never cease—to Salem, on the Manassas Gap Railroad, reaching there after midnight. Up again by day-dawn, and still on, along the Manassas Gap road, meeting crowds —all welcoming, cheering, staring with blank amazement. So all day Tuesday, through White Plains, Haymarket, Thoroughfare Gap, in Bull Run Mountains, Gainesville, to Bristow station, on the Orange and Alexandria Railroad—making the difference from Amosville to Bristow (between forty-five and fifty miles) within the forty-eight hours. We burned up at Bristow two or three railway-trains, and moved up to Manassas Junction on Wednesday, taking our prisoners with us. Ewell's division brought up the rear, fighting all the way a force Pope had sent up from Warrenton, supposing us a cavalry party.

Upon reaching Manassas Junction, we met a brigade—the First New-Jersey—which had been sent from Alexandria on the same supposition. They were fools enough to send a flag demanding our surrender at once. Of course we scattered the brigade, killing and wounding many, and among them the Brigadier-General, (Taylor,) who has since died. At the Junction was a large dépôt of stores, five or six pieces of artillery, two trains containing probably two hundred large cars loaded down with many millions of quartermaster and commissary stores. Beside these, there were very large sutlers' dépôts, full of every thing; in short, there was collected there, in the space of a square mile, an amount and variety of property such as I had never conceived of, (I speak soberly.) 'Twas a curious sight to see our ragged and famished men helping themselves to every imaginable article of luxury or necessity, whether of clothing, food, or what not. For my part, I got a toothbrush, a box of candles, a quantity of lobster salad, a barrel of coffee, and other things which I forget. But I must hurry on, for I have not time to tell the hundredth part, and the scene utterly beggars description.

A part of us hunted that New-Jersey brigade like scattered partridges over the hills just to the right of the battle-field of the eighteenth of July, 1861, while the rest were partly plundering, partly fighting the forces coming on us from Warrenton. Our men had been living on roasted corn since crossing the Rappahannock, and we had brought no wagons, so we could carry little away of the riches before us. But the men could eat for one meal at least. So they were marched up, and as much of every thing eatable served out as they could carry. To see a starving man eating lobster-salad and drinking Rhine wine, barefooted and in tatters, was curious; the whole thing was incredible.

Our situation now was very critical. We were between Alexandria and Warrenton—between the hosts of McClellan and Pope with over eighteen thousand jaded men, for the corps had not more than that. At nightfall, fire was set to the dépôt, storehouses, the loaded trains, several long, empty trains, sutlers' houses, restaurants, every thing. As the magnificent conflagration began to subside, the Stonewall or First division of Jackson's corps moved off toward the battle-field of Manassas, the other two divisions to Centreville, six miles distant.

As day broke [August 26], we came in sight of Centreville, rested a few hours, and toward evening the rear-guard of the corps crossed Bull Run at Stone Bridge—the scene of the great slaughter of last year—closely pursued by the enemy. A part of the force came up the Warrenton turnpike, and in a furious action of two hours—the last two daylight hours of Thursday, August twenty-eighth—disputed the possession of a ridge running from Sudley Church Ford to the Warrenton turnpike. We drove them off, and on Friday morning we held the ridge, in front of which runs an incomplete railroad-cut and embankment. Now, we had made a circuit from the Gap in Bull Run Mountains around to the Junction and Centreville, breaking up the railroad and destroying their stores, and returned to within six miles of the Gap, through which Longstreet must come. The enemy disputed his passage and delayed him till late in the day, and, meanwhile, they threw against our corps, all day long, vast masses of troops—Sigel's, Banks's, and Pope's own division. We got out of ammunition; we collected more from cartridge-boxes of fallen friend and foe; that gave out, and we charged with never-failing yell and steel. All day long they threw their masses on us; all day they fell back shattered and shrieking. When the sun went down, their dead were heaped in front of the incomplete railway, and we sighed with relief, for Longstreet could be seen coming into position on our right. The crisis was over; Longstreet never failed yet; but the sun went down so slowly.

The wonder to "Wash" Roebling was the fact that the Federals delayed anyone. He was with McDowell's troops when they left Warrenton on the main pike to Centreville, Gainesville and the battlefield at Bull Run:[6]

. . . We encamped that night 8 miles from Warrenton, being joined by Siegel & Raynolds with their Penn. reserves. Early next morning Rickets' Div. was dispatched west to Thoroughfare Gap in Bull Run mountain to prevent Longstreet's corps from passing through & reinforcing the rebels. But the rebels, finding him there, passed through

Hopewell gap 4 miles farther on and joined their main force. Rickets apparently knew nothing of Hopewell gap although laid down on every map. The main body of our army moved forward, crossing the Manassas gap road at Gainesville where Sigel turned off following the r.r. while King & Reynolds kept on (Hatch commanded King's Div., the later having had an epileptic fit some days previous). Suddenly a rebel battery opened on us in front with shells which came very near killing some of us, Gen. McDowell & staff as usual riding at the head of the column.

Our forces were deployed in line of battle, which took an hour, and then we proceeded to determine whether we had come up with the main body or only a portion of the enemy. By that time their battery had ceased firing and retired 2 miles. 5 men killed was the damage sustained. Well, after wasting 4 precious hours more, spent in robbing orchards & cornfields, and watching immense columns of dust in front of us, McDowell made a further division of force by leaving King there to march down the pike late in the afternoon and went himself down the R.R. towards Manassas in search of Pope, leaving Reynolds to follow him slowly.

We arrived at Manassas at dark and ascertained that Pope, with Hooker & Kearney, had gone in the direction of Centreville. We understood that Pope had been hunting McDowell & McDowell was likewise hunting Pope. While at Manassas that evening very heavy cannonading was heard about 2 miles in advance of where King had been left; it seems that King had advanced that afternoon, was attacked by the main body of the enemy, lost 500 killed & wounded in one brigade, retreated, and arrived at Manassas at 3 o'clock the next morning. McDowell, hearing that firing, wanted to get there by making a short cut across the country, but it was dark. We lost our way 3 times and finally at 1 o'clock encamped along the road side for a few hours. Getting under way again by 4½, we reached Reynolds by 6, took breakfast, found the rebels in front of Reynolds, and returned to Manassas where King & Rickets had arrived during the night, also Porter with the regulars.

Porter was pushed out in the same direction where King was . . . only not quite so far. McDowell went out with him, put him in position, and gave him his instructions, merely as superior officer, Pope being away. But Porter obeyed none, running off as soon as the enemy opened fire with a battery. McDowell then returned towards Manassas and led his two divisions of King & Rickets towards the old battle field of Bull Run where the main body of the enemy was. It was 1 or 2 o'clock on Friday afternoon when we got there. The fight had commenced a few hours before with Hooker, Kearney & Sigel. About 30 guns were in position then and firing as fast as possible, silencing most of the enemy's guns which were poorly handled and counterbalancing the poor result of Hooker's & Kearney's infantry attack in the afternoon.

It was a very interesting scene; much valuable ammunition was, however, thrown away, for which we paid dearly the next day. Sigel arranged most of the artillery; it was massed together very well, but was placed on two high elevations. Every shot lodged where it struck, in place of glancing and bounding off to do more mischief. The day was cloudy and windstill so that the battle field was covered with a dense, livid cloud of smoke. It was late in the day before McDowell's troops were deployed in line of battle and pushed forward to the proper place on the centre & left of the centre. Before Hatch's Brigade had arrived at its place it was pitch dark. Hatch had not the remotest idea where he was going, pushed too far ahead, got into a cross fire which the rebels suddenly opened on him, had half his men killed & wounded & the other half ran off. So ended that day.

IV

The battle of Second Manassas (August 28–30) is called one of Lee's masterpieces; it was Pope's finish. When on the thirtieth Lee readjusted his troops on the field, Pope decided that the Confederates were retreating. At about noon he ordered an attack. Fighting with Jackson that day, W. W. Blackford saw the Yankees handled roughly:[7]

Along so long a line these movements were not of course all at the same time nor alike. Sometimes a stand would be made and the first and even the second line would close in a hand-to-hand bayonet fight on the railroad where the conflict was deadly, but in no single instance that evening, I believe, did they penetrate our lines. The sides of the cuts and fills were covered with rounded stones as big as one's two fists, and these the Confederates collected in great numbers as reserved ammunition, particularly on the embankments. Breechloaders were not then in use among the infantry and when one of these determined charges was made there was no time to load after delivering fire; but the interval between their last shot and the time when they would come close enough for the bayonet was utilized by Jackson's men in showering down these stones on the heads of those climbing up the bank to them; and one such stone was as good as a cannon-ball so far as the man it hit on the head was concerned. After the battle little piles of these stones were left all along the top of the banks where each man had made his collection, and as the supply ran short after each repulse the men ran forward down the bank to recover those they had already used.

This contest went on about two hours, the intervals between the repulses becoming longer and longer and the tendency being to concentrate their attacks upon one spot at a time. Over broad spaces in our front the ground appeared, from where I stood, so thickly covered with the fallen that it looked like one vast blue carpet. I do not mean that the ground was really entirely covered, but at a distance, one body obstructing the vision of several yards of ground beyond, the effect was that described. All the fighting had been done by Jackson's corps alone up to this time, Longstreet's half of the army comprising the right wing not having fired a shot, except from the artillery under the command of S. D. Lee before mentioned, which did such splendid service. Longstreet's line was retired behind the hill out of sight and Pope probably did not know of his presence even then.

General Lee sat on his horse on the Warrenton Pike calmly watching the enemy exhausting his strength upon the impregnable position along the old railroad, and awaiting his time to order Longstreet to come down upon them. About five o'clock in the evening the order was given, and with a cheer that rang out for miles our right wing swept forward.

Seeing that the time had come for the cavalry I dashed off to rejoin General Stuart, who had been kept informed through frequent written reports of every event of the evening, sent by couriers detailed from cavalry headquarters to accompany me for this purpose. It was a grand sight to see our lines four miles in length with bayonets glittering in the evening sunlight and flags flying move rapidly forward, and before them in broken masses the enemy withdrawing. Pope had been prudent enough, however, to keep some of his force in reserve, and these Longstreet encountered and sharply engaged three-quarters of a mile from the field. They could not resist, however, the fury of the attack and in half an hour joined their comrades in retreat. This stand had given Pope, however, time to throw his shattered columns into the deep depression made by the Sudley Road at the very spot where the Zouave regiment we charged in the last year's battle had emerged upon the field, and here as the night came on Longstreet's advance terminated.

General Stuart with his cavalry covered Longstreet's right flank during his advance and soon encountered the cavalry of the enemy on the fields near Bull Run. Munford was in the advance and when the enemy first appeared, charged gallantly upon what he supposed to be only a regiment of about equal strength with his own; this he broke, but beyond were heavy reserves which came up at a charge and drove him back in some confusion. Then Stuart arrived with his reserves and swept them in turn, in utter discomfiture, driving them back pell-mell across Bull Run and killing and capturing a large number. This was the first time their cavalry had ever made any show of resistance and the sight of the charges and sabre fighting in the clear, open fields was very fine. Munford made a mistake in beginning his charge too soon and got his ranks opened too much before the shock came, while the enemy advanced at a trot and only took the charge pace when within a hundred yards of the meeting; his ranks were then solid and Munford's opened, strung-out force was dashed aside.

Blackford recounted a touching incident:[8]

In one place I heard through the darkness the shrill voice of a boy apparently not over fifteen or sixteen years old sobbing bitterly. I started towards the place to render him some assistance but as I reached the place his father, who it seems was the captain of his company, came up and said, "Hello, Charley, my boy, is that you?" "Oh, yes," said the boy, "Father, my leg is broken but I don't want you to think that is what I am crying for; I fell in a yellow-jackets' nest and they have been stinging me ever since. That is what makes me cry— please pull me out." The stings and the wound proved too much for the plucky boy and he died in his father's arms soon after.

Shaken to the core, Pope drew reserves from his center and right to stave off Longstreet. Jackson had exactly what he wanted—a chance to crash down on the weakened Federal right—and Blackford knew that Jackson did not intend to waste this opportunity:[9]

Many of our Generals and Colonels, as I have said, were on the ridge across which the enemy were now crossing, and these were watching Jackson's every movement with intense interest, for we could almost tell his thoughts by his movements. Sometimes he would halt, then trot on rapidly, halt again, wheel his horse and pass again along the front of the marching column, or rather along its flank. About a quarter of a mile off, troops were now opposite us. All felt sure Jackson could never resist the temptation, and that the order to attack would come soon, even if Longstreet was beyond the mountain.

Presently General Jackson pulled up suddenly, wheeled and galloped towards us. "Here he comes, by God," said several, and Jackson rode up to the assembled group as calm as a May morning and, touching his hat in military salute, said in as soft a voice as if he had been talking to a friend in ordinary conversation, "Bring out your men, gentlemen!" Every officer whirled round and scurried back to the woods at full gallop. The men had been watching their officers with as much interest as they had been watching Jackson, and when they wheeled and dashed towards them they knew what it meant, and from the woods arose a hoarse roar like that from cages of wild beasts at the scent of blood.

As the officers entered the woods, sharp, quick orders to fall in rang from rank to rank, followed by the din of clashing arms and accoutrements as the troops rapidly got under arms, and in an incredibly short time long columns of glittering brigades, like huge serpents, glided out upon the open field, to be as quickly deployed into lines of battle. Then all advanced in as perfect order as if they had been on parade, their bayonets sparkling in the light of the setting sun and their red battle flags dancing gayly in the breeze. Then came trotting out the rumbling artillery to positions on the flanks, where they quickly unlimbered and prepared for action. It made one's blood tingle with pride to see these troops going into action—as light-hearted and gay as if they were going to a dancing party, not with the senseless fun of a recruit who knew not what he had to expect, but with the confidence of veterans who had won every battle they ever fought.

As soon as the enemy saw what was coming they halted, came to a front face, advanced to meet our troops half way, and the battle opened. In a moment everything on the field was wrapped in smoke. The musketry became a roar, the individual shots merging into one continuous sound, broken upon by the rapid booming of the artillery accompaniment. In a few moments wounded men made their appearance, limping back as best they could, some still bearing their arms but some scarcely able to drag their bodies along.

John Dooley, a Confederate private, braced himself as the Yankees charged:[10]

Yes! Here they come! Four or five lines of fresh troops deploy in the open plain in our front and direct their charge directly against that copse of woods off to our right. Oh, this is a splendid sight and one which the disinterested might well go in raptures over. Line after line of the best of the Yankee army steadily advances—and as orderly as if on parade; and it seems as tho' there was a slight cessation in the frightful roar of the artillery and musketry as these well drilled troops press on over the blood red plain.

At every step they take they see the piles of wounded and slain and their feet are slipping in the blood and brains of their comrades. Shells burst among them and a desultory musketry fire helps to thin their ranks; but still on they press, closing up steadily, splendidly. Many of their officers may be plainly distinguished riding beside their Brigades and Divisions, while the Stars and Stripes boastfully flaunt out defiance in the advance of each Regt.

On they come over dead and dying right at the copse of woods. The order is given, "Charge!", and at a double quick the foremost lines charge against the woods. They are scarcely 50 or 80 yds. distant when a volume of smoke almost obscures the woods from our sight and volley after volley thunders against those ill fated columns. In vain does line after line advance at a run. Torn and bleeding they are hurled back, scattered, routed in confusion over the plain (blue with their slain). In vain do their officers dash in the midst of this storm of shell and bullets. The fugitives will not be rallied, but, broken and dismayed, are pursued by our victorious troops until darkness closes around.

Dooley saw the Federals thrown back, routed:

About 4 P.M., when we had given up the idea of our being wanted today, one of Genl. Longstreet's aides came over the field as if life and death depended on his speed, as verily it did. How well the men knew what his presence indicated; and he had scarcely been recognized before they had each one regained his musket and were arranging themselves in order along the line. We had driven the Yankee back on the left and also on the right, and it was for Longstreet's fresh troops (ourselves) to press the center.

Here we go—closing and double quick—now right in front marching by the flank so as to avoid the woods and other obstacles—now we are over a fence and the battery which we are to charge is right ahead. Ahead we form in line and now dashing thro' a cornfield; the bullets whistle thro' the leaves and ears and send many a brave comrade to his last account. But we have no time to think; such is the excitement, such the feeling with which I am inspired that I rush on with the rest, completely bewildered and scarcely heeding what takes place around. And now the bullets strike the ground in front of us and comrades are falling pretty fast all around. I catch a glimpse of *the battery;* it's on a hill (quite a hill), and as we approach at a double quick all along the line the very earth seems to open and belch forth fire and smoke and balls. Back! down the hill! rolls the Brigade which had immediately preceded us; back! in utter rout and confusion, some shouting for us to *go back*—others to advance—some to *lie down.*

Still on we went double quick all the time right over the flying broken Brigade and up the hill—volley after volley—broadside after broadside comes crashing thro' our thinned ranks. Our Col., the brave old Skinner, on this day the bravest of the brave, 40 or 50 yds. ahead is cutting down the Yankee gunners who defend their pieces to the last.

"Fire!" rings out along the brigade, our muskets rattle out a volley along the whole line, and I find myself among dismounted cannon, broken caissons, bleeding horses, the dead and the dying. Our gallant Col. (Skinner) comes reeling towards me bleeding profusely from three severe wounds. "Jack," said he, "bear me witness that I was the first man on that battery." "I will, Col.," replied I, and I set to work to bind up the flow of blood which was streaming from his arm which was torn from wrist to elbow by a bullet. The Col. is soon carried from the field and I turn to look for the brigade which had in the mean time borne away to the left.

I fall in with about 50 or 60 of ours who have become detached by that same leftward move. We all league together and drive thro' the woods a party of Yankees who keep up an annoying fire—and now we take possession of a rising knoll to the front and left where many of our men have gathered to play upon the advancing enemy. From this knoll, altho' constantly engaged, we have a splendid view of the Plain on our front and to the right. Some 500 or 600 yds. distant is a dense thicket or wood which must be filled by our troops. In front of this wood and directly in front of our position the whole plain, as far as the eye can reach, is covered with the blue of the enemy—some brigades flying in disorder, others advancing in serried lines with the Stars and Stripes innumerable floating in the breeze; officers vainly endeavoring to rally their wavering ranks furiously dashing up and down the lines.

Lee, with 48,527 effectives engaged, counted 1,481 killed, 7,627 wounded and 89 missing. The Federal strength had been 75,696 with

1,724 killed, 8,372 wounded and 5,958 missing. "Wash" Roebling could not contain his disgust:[11]

The running of our men had already commenced; at least 10,000 were on the full go. Many had not even heard the whistle of a shot before they ran. This was a most humiliating spectacle, showing the utterly demoralized condition of the men. A lot of reinforcements had come in, composed of raw troops. The mere sound of the firing sufficed to set them off. In the mean time the troops on our right had been brought over to the left; McDowell put himself at their head & succeeded in repulsing the rebels some distance. More troops came up in support, enabling us to hold our line with security.

It was also known that Franklin's Corps of fresh well tried troops was only 4 miles in the rear. By this time night had set in, the infantry firing had mostly ceased, & only 2 batteries continued a random firing. We were, in my opinion, in a good condition to recommence the fight in the morning with complete success. Rebel prisoners reported that they lived on mule & horse flesh for 2 days. They were so short of ammunition that we fired 20 cannon shots to their one and in place of lead they fired stones from their muskets.

Well, it was at this juncture that a certain * * * General by the name of P——e ordered a retreat; the rebels were, of course, so utterly surprised that they did not even offer to pursue . . . And remember this order was given only 2 hours after a flaming dispatch had been sent to Washington announcing a great victory, which had not been won. The retreat was conducted in perfect order. I noticed only 5 abandoned wagons, 15 guns were left on the field, the carriages being in too shattered a condition to admit of their being readily removed.

Of the subsequent events, the march to Centreville, to Fairfax and finally to Munson's hill where I am now encamped you are no doubt sufficiently familiar with through the papers. As for myself I am completely tired out and used up; I have not had one meal a day for the last 3 weeks, have slept on the ground every night generally without blankets, and been in the saddle constantly. I have also been lucky in not getting shot. McDowell is a brave and courageous man who don't hesitate a moment to expose himself when necessary, and I followed him closely. It is true there is something wrong about McDowell, but he is a jewel compared with the commander who was never to be found when wanted and did not even expose himself enough to get a general view of the battle ground and see how affairs went on. McDowell in many cases acted for him.

As for the future I have no hopes whatever; I assure you on Saturday night last I felt utterly sick, disgusted and tired of the war; being somewhat rested now, I feel more hopeful. Our men are sick of the war; they fight without an aim and without enthusiasm; they have no confidence in their leaders except one or two; I overheard Hooker give his opinion of McClellan and have little hopes of him. Sigel is physically unable to do much because he does everything himself so as to be certain; he is a shadow. . . . Franklin & Hooker are looked on with most favor, but Franklin lost his golden opportunity on Saturday when he might have marched up and changed the tide to victory, orders or no orders.

In the next place one Rebel is equal to 5 Union men in bravery— that is about the proportion.

Pope was sent west to fight Indians, and here he brooded on the evil that threatened the country. From St. Paul, Minnesota in mid-September he addressed a nine-page letter to Governor Richard Yates of Illinois, charging that a clique of officers in the Army of the Potomac were set on deposing Lincoln and establishing a dictatorship. His own defeat at Manassas he charged against Fitz-John Porter and McClellan, declaring that he had made only one error himself: ". . . I wished in earnestness and sincerity of purpose to make war on the rebels. I was from the West, and an interloper in the Army of the Potomac, neither to be bribed nor frightened and I must if possible be ruined." Pope warned Yates that unless McClellan was removed from command it would not be long before "the military factions (as in a thousand instances in history) demand another ruler, and then another until the seat of Washington shall be occupied by a military despot or by a creature of the military power."

Pope, warming to his letter writing, fixed the blame for his disaster in Virginia upon other villains in the missive he addressed to William Butler, state treasurer of Illinois and one of Lincoln's oldest friends:[12]

HEAD-QUARTERS, DEPARTMENT OF THE NORTHWEST,
SAINT PAUL, MINN., Sept. 26, 1862

MY DEAR SIR:

I send enclosed a letter to Gov Yates in view of the convention of Governors at Altoona.

I will not permit myself even in a letter to you to express the scorn and indignation with which the feeble cowardly & shameful conduct of Lincoln has impressed me. I would not have believed it of any respectable man, especially was it difficult to imagine any such conduct in a President of the U. S. He has sold himself or given himself away to the Devil or something worse. The letter I enclose will give you a mild statement of a part of the case, enough for you to imagine the depth of the degradation to which he has descended. How he can face his own people again is hard to say. The people in all this region are bitter against him. Is it not astonishing that knowing as well as he does the past record of McClellan, knowing McClellan's atrocious conduct during our battles in Virginia & his successful efforts to keep his accomplices from punishment he should have restored him & them to the command of the army? I do not like to trust myself to speak of these matters. Illinois is shamed and humiliated by her representative. I am a soldier and seek only to do my duty earnestly & zealously. If abuse of me will serve the Govt so be it. I never suffer my personal feelings to stand in the way of prompt & vigorous execution of my duty but I do feel shame & mortification that we should live under such a system of things as prevails at Washington. One comfort I have. This state of affairs cannot last long unless our Governors are weak & irresolute.

Look at the West. We have lost all we gained by hard fighting & immense sacrifice of life & treasure. Why? For the very same reason we have made no progress while McClellan has [been] Commander-in-Chief. *He* sought by making several Depts in the West to keep control of every body & manage all the details of the war from Washington. No man objected more loudly to this arrangement than Halleck when he was ordered to St. Louis. By persistent effort he finally got command of the whole Western Dept and the result was our rapid successes in the West. How is it now? No sooner does Halleck get to be commander in chief than he begins to do precisely what he blamed McClellan so much for doing. He has divided up the West into half a dozen separate and independent commands so that he can control all the details and of course under such a system we have lost all we gained.

Halleck feels that his position in Washington is insecure. He is trying to play trimmer and keep on the fence which no man can do in times like these. He keeps the West in its present condition thinking that if ousted at Washington he can come back to command us again. He is mistaken. He is indebted to me entirely for his position and to repay it he stands aloof when he knows that the grossest injustice is being done me which it is in his power to prevent. He wont do. He has neither pluck nor heart.

We must have the West again united in one Dept & commanded by a

Western man. Until that is done we are in constant danger. Urge this upon every one who has influence. Unless this is done we can have neither harmony of council nor unity of action. Wright has a separate command, Buell one, Grant one, Curtis one & myself one. It is absurd & wicked so to jeopardize the West to please any man.

Urge this by all means in your power. . . .

Very truly your friend,

JNO POPE

V

In Minnesota that September, along the Yellow Medicine River, Sioux warriors under the power-crazed Little Crow had embarked on an orgy of massacre and rape so terrible that the first reports were ridiculed as wildly exaggerated. Then the few survivors straggled in—frightfully mutilated children who somehow had wandered across the prairies for days, women who stared vacantly into space so that they would no longer see the brains of babies dashed out against wagon wheels, the sick burned in their beds, or, the ghastliest memory, frightened husbands who had deserted their families as they tried to flee to personal safety. Sioux warriors roared with contemptuous laughter at such men, abandoning their women and children without a backward glance, running to save their cowardly necks while a dozen naked, lustful Indians surrounded an adolescent daughter.

Four hundred settlers perished in a few days. Northern spokesmen charged the Confederates with instigating these outrages, and Secretary of the Interior Caleb Smith gave such allegations semiofficial endorsement, but no evidence supported the claim.

Henry H. Sibley, an ex-governor of the territory who had grown wealthy as an agent for the American Fur Company, commanded forces that outnumbered the Sioux two to one. While he dawdled, waiting for reinforcements and newspapers that would bring him up to date on events elsewhere in the country, Little Crow's vandals struck twice at New Ulm, a prosperous community established by German families from Chicago and Cincinnati. Two principal reasons, by later testimony, motivated these attacks—Indian resentment that the citizens of New Ulm jabbered in a language they could not comprehend and the town was full of pretty girls. What the Indians had not counted upon was the fighting quality of these German immigrants, who, though outnumbered and armed only with squirrel guns, beat off both assaults.

Still Sibley hesitated—one of his regiments was virtually wiped out in Birch Coulee—and then at Wood Lake in early September Sibley stumbled into the battle that broke the Sioux uprising. His report to Governor Ramsay gives no indication that he found the enemy by luck:[13]

SIR: I left the camp at Fort Ridgley on the nineteenth inst., with my command, and reached this point early in the afternoon of the twenty-second. There have been small parties of Indians each day in plain

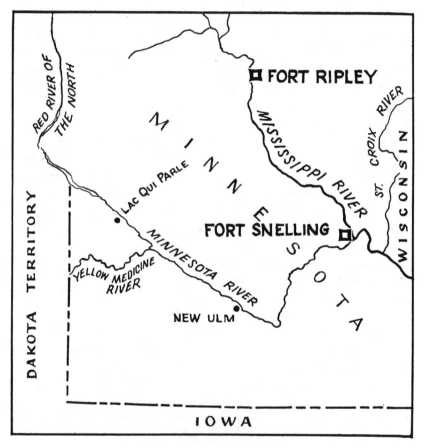

THE SIOUX WAR

sight, evidently acting as scouts for the main body. This morning I had determined to cross the Yellow Medicine River, about three miles distant, and there await the arrival of Capt. Rogers's company of the Seventh regiment, which was ordered by me from New-Ulm, to join me by a forced march, the presence of the company there being unnecessary by the arrival there of another company, a few days previous.

About seven o'clock this morning, the camp was attacked by about three hundred Indians, who suddenly made their appearance and dashed down toward us, whooping and yelling in their usual style, and firing with great rapidity.

The Renville Guards, under Lieutenant Gaman, were sent by me to check them, and Major Welch of the Third regiment, was instantly in line with his command, with his skirmishers in the advance, by whom the savages were gallantly met, and after a conflict of a serious nature, repulsed.

Meanwhile, another portion of the Indian force passed down a ravine on the right, with a view to outflank the Third regiment, and I ordered Lieut.-Colonel Marshall, who, with the five companies of the Seventh regiment, and who was ably seconded by Major Bradley, to advance to its support, with one six-pounder under the command of Captain Hendricks, and I also ordered two companies of the Sixth regiment to reënforce him.

Lieut.-Colonel Marshall advanced at a double-quick, amidst a shower of balls from the enemy, which fortunately did little damage to his command; and after a few volleys, he led his men to a charge, and cleared the ravine of savages.

Major McLaren, with Capt. Wilson's company, took position on the extreme left of the camp, where he kept at bay a party of the enemy who were endeavoring to gain the rear of the camp, and finally drove them back.

The battle raged for about two hours, the six-pounder and mountain howitzer being used with great effect, when the Indians—repulsed at all points with great loss—retired with great precipitation.

I regret to state that many casualties occurred on our side. The gallant Major Welch was badly wounded in the leg, and Captain Wilson, of the Sixth regiment, was severely bruised by a nearly spent ball in the shoulder. Four of our men were killed, and between thirty and forty wounded, most of them, I am rejoiced to say, not severely.

The loss of the enemy, according to the statement of a half-breed named Joseph Campbell, who visited the camp under a flag of truce, was thirty killed and a large number wounded. We found and buried fourteen of the bodies, and as the habit of the Indians is to carry off the bodies of their slain, it is not probable that the number told by Campbell was exaggerated.

The severe chastisement inflicted upon them has so far subdued their ardor that they sent a flag of truce into the camp to express the sentiment of the Wahpetons, composing a part of the attacking force, and to state that they were not strong enough to fight us and desired peace, with permission to take away their dead and wounded. I replied that when the prisoners were delivered up it would be time enough to talk of peace, and that I would not grant their permission either to take their dead or wounded.

I am assured by Campbell that there is serious depression in the Indian camp, many having been opposed to the war, but driven into the field by the more violent. He further stated that eight hundred Indians were assembled at the Yellow Medicine, within two miles of the camp, but that the greater part took no part in the fight. The intention of Little Crow was to attack us last night, but he was overruled by others, who told him if he was a brave man he ought to fight the white man by daylight. I am fully prepared against night attack, should it be attempted, although I think the lesson received by them to-day will make them very cautious for the future. . . .

I am very much in want of bread, rations, six-pounder ammunition, and shells for the howitzer, and unless soon supplied I shall be compelled to fall back, which, under present circumstances, would be a calamity, as it would afford time for the escape of the Indians with their captives. I hope a large body of cavalry is before this on their way to join us. If I had been provided with five hundred of this description of force to-day, I venture the assertion that I could have killed the greater part of the Indians, and brought the campaign to a successful close.

Not until December would the final act of the bloody drama in Minnesota unfold. On the fifteenth an agitated Sibley telegraphed Lincoln:

Your order of 6th Inst. for the Execution of 39 Indians just recd by Special messenger. They are imprisoned at Mankato 90 miles distant & the time fixed 19th is too short for preparation & for concentrating the troops necessary to protect the other Indians & preserve the peace. The excitement prevails [in] all sections of the state & secret combinations Exist Embracing thousands of citizens pledged to execute all the Indians. Matters must be managed with great discretion & as much secrecy as possible to prevent a fearful collision between the U. S. forces & the citizens. I respectfully ask authority to postpone the Execution one week . . .

Lincoln consented. On December 27 Sibley informed Washington:[14]

I have the honor to inform you that the 38 Indians and half-breeds ordered by you for execution were hung yesterday at Mankato, at 10 A.M. Everything went off quietly, and the other prisoners are well secured.

THE WAR'S BLOODIEST DAY

J AMES RYDER RANDALL was born in Baltimore on the first day of 1839. One of his early tutors was Joseph H. Clark, who had once taught Edgar Allan Poe. At Georgetown College, Randall held two distinctions—he was the smallest boy ever to enter the college, and he was its most promising poet. He traveled in the West Indies and South America before coming to Louisiana to teach English literature at Poydras College, a Creole institution at Pointe Coupée near New Orleans. In April, 1861, Randall read in the New Orleans *Delta* the news of the Baltimore riots when troops of the Sixth Massachusetts passed through that city; the first citizen to fall was an old college mate.

"This account excited me greatly," Randall remembered. "I had long been absent from my native city, and the startling event there inflamed my mind. That night I could not sleep, for my nerves were all unstrung, and I could not dismiss what I had read in the paper from my mind. About midnight I rose, lit a candle, and went to my desk. Some powerful spirit appeared to possess me, and almost involuntarily I proceeded to write the song of 'My Maryland.' . . . The whole poem was dashed off rapidly when once begun." Next morning the enthusiasm of the college boys for Randall's poem encouraged the young teacher to send his verses to the New Orleans *Delta;* soon hardly a journal existed in the South that had not copied it. Randall recalled: "I did not concern myself much about it, but very soon, from all parts of the country, there was borne to me, in my remote place of residence, evidence that I had made a great hit, and that, whatever might be the fate of the Confederacy, the song would survive it."

The poet's personal feelings were reflected most keenly in the second of the four spirited stanzas:

> Hark to an exiled Son's appeal,
> Maryland!
> My Mother State, to thee I kneel,
> Maryland!
> For life and death, for woe and weal,
> Thy peerless chivalry reveal,
> And gird thy beauteous limbs with steel,
> Maryland, my Maryland!

I

In early September, 1862, sixty thousand fresh troops were reported strengthening the Federal forces at Washington, so that if Lee lingered where he then stood he could be opposed by the most overwhelming odds he had yet encountered. To retreat to Richmond, one hundred and fifty miles away, meant marching hungry men and horses lacking

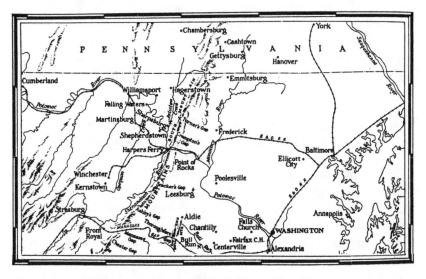

MARYLAND

From *Atlas of American History*

forage through country blighted in the past few months by two major battles. Lee made the bold choice—to carry the war into the North. While dusty Rebel bands played "Maryland, My Maryland," the Army of Northern Virginia began fording the Potomac. Then on September 8 Lee issued a proclamation "To the People of Maryland":[1]

. . . Under the pretense of supporting the Constitution, but in violation of its most valuable provisions, your citizens have been imprisoned upon no charge and contrary to all forms of law. The faithful and manly protest against this outrage made by the venerable and illustrious Marylanders—to whom in better days no citizen appealed for right in vain—was treated with scorn and contempt. The government of your chief city has been usurped by armed strangers; your Legislature has been dissolved by the unlawful arrest of its members; freedom of the press and of speech have been suppressed; words have been declared offences by the arbitrary desire of the Federal Executive, and citizens ordered to be tried by military commission for what they may dare to speak.

Clearly enjoying his new role as a propagandist, Lee told the people of Maryland that he marched into the state to aid them "in throwing off this foreign yoke," and concluded:

. . . Within the limits of this army, at least, Marylanders shall once more enjoy their ancient freedom of thought and speech. We know no enemies among you, and will protect all of every opinion. It is for you to decide your destiny, freely and without restraint. This army will respect your choice, whatever it may be; and, while the Southern people will rejoice to welcome you to your natural position among them, they will only welcome you when you come of your own free will.

In a fervent letter to Davis, Lee urged the President to propose peace contingent upon the recognition of Southern independence:

Such a proposition, coming from us at this time, could in no way be regarded as suing for peace; but, being made when it is in our power to inflict injury upon our adversary, would show conclusively to the world that our sole object is the establishment of our independence and the attainment of an honorable peace. The rejection of this offer would prove to the country that the responsibility for the continuance of war does not rest upon us, but that the party in power in the United States elect to prosecute it for purposes of their own. The proposal of peace would enable the people of the United States to determine at their coming elections whether they will support those who favor the prolongation of the war, or those who wish to bring it to a termination, which can be productive of good to both parties without affecting the honor of either.

Lee explained to Major General John G. Walker the Confederate plan of operations:[2]

"I wish you to return to the mouth of the Monocacy [Walker quoted Lee] and effectually destroy the aqueduct of the Chesapeake and Ohio canal. By the time that is accomplished you will receive orders to co-operate in the capture of Harper's Ferry, [and] will rejoin us at Hagerstown, where the army will be concentrated. My information is that there are between 10,000 and 12,000 men at Harper's Ferry, and 3,000 at Martinsburg. The latter may escape toward Cumberland, but I think the chances are that they will take refuge at Harper's Ferry and be captured. Besides the men and material of the war which we shall capture, the position is necessary to us, not to garrison and hold, but because in the hands of the enemy it would be a break in our new line of communication with Richmond.

"A few days' rest at Hagerstown will be of great service to our men. Hundreds of them are barefooted, and nearly all of them are ragged. I hope to get shoes and clothing for the most needy. But the best of it all will be that the short delay will enable us to get up our stragglers—not stragglers from a shirking disposition, but simply from an inability to keep up with their commands. I believe there are not less than from eight to ten thousand of them between here and Rapidan Station. . . .

"In ten days from now, if the military situation is then what I confidently expect it to be after the capture of Harper's Ferry, I shall concentrate the army at Hagerstown, effectually destroy the Baltimore and Ohio road, and march to this point," placing his finger at Harrisburg, Pennsylvania. "That is the objective point of the campaign. You remember, no doubt, the long bridge of the Pennsylvania Railroad over the Susquehanna, a few miles west of Harrisburg. Well, I wish effectually to destroy that bridge, which will disable the Pennsylvania Railroad for a long time. With the Baltimore and Ohio in our possession, and the Pennsylvania Railroad broken up, there will remain to the enemy but one route of communication with the West, and that very circuitous, by way of the Lakes. After that I can turn my attention to Philadelphia, Baltimore or Washington, as may seem best for our interests."

With "liberated" Marylanders rallying to the Rebel banner, Harpers Ferry seized, Northern communications snarled and three cities threatened, Lee hoped to count the end of the war in weeks if not in days. A negotiated peace then would save his beloved Virginia from further torment. Entranced by this vision, Lee planned boldly to divide his forces to strike west and north in a campaign that "very much astonished" General Walker. A Union Army surgeon watched the ragged Army of Northern Virginia march into Frederick:[8]

Their reception in Frederick was decidedly cool; all the stores shut, no flags flying, and every thing partook of a churchyard appearance. The troops had marched from Leesburgh, twenty-three miles distant, since two A.M., crossing at Hauling Ford—a swift march, and more than our men could do. They were the filthiest set of men and officers I ever saw; with clothing that was ragged, and had not been cleaned for weeks. They could be smelt all over the entire inclosure. Jackson I did not get a look at to recognize him, though I must have seen him, as I witnessed the passage of all the troops through the town.

The brigade in the grounds obtained some flour speedily, and commenced cooking rations for immediate use, and to be ready for a march. Their brigades were small, and horses and men all but starved. Every man seemed to have plenty of money, which they stated had been furnished to them freely to purchase whatever they wanted when they got to Philadelphia! The stores were entered, and the proprietors were either compelled to give their goods away or else take Confederate scrip.

Their behavior towards every one was very carefully managed—no bad treatment of any one was permitted. They broke into the *Examiner* office, but their Provost-Marshal caused every thing to be replaced and the offenders to be placed in the guard-house. No straggling was allowed, and although no discipline was observed, implicit obedience was maintained; for if a man declined or moved tardily, a blow from sabre or butt of a pistol enforced the order. It was stated by the men that four of the army had been shot for straggling since leaving Leesburgh. They were entirely in the dark as to their future movements, expecting, however, to go either to Baltimore or to Pennsylvania. . . .

By the Army surgeon's testimony, one day in Frederick must have depressed Lee with the realization that his appeal to the people of Maryland to throw off the "foreign yoke" had fallen on deaf ears:

Evening—Secesh belonging to the city were disgusted with their friends, and the Unionists unterrified and talking loudly. No rebel flags had yet been displayed. All the doctors slept at the hospital, as the streets were filled with soldiers who had been drinking freely, though, to their credit, when they commenced drinking they speedily became dead drunk and were then harmless. Did any one of them attempt to create a disturbance, a guard would slip up to him and say something to him, and the songster would immediately cease his brawling and go quietly to the guard-house. The next morning who should pass in but ——— ——— ———. They respectively belonged to the Eighth and Twelfth Virginia regiments, and Tenth Alabama. I asked them to dine with me, as they presented a rather more respectable appearance than the rest. So I gave them a good dinner, which they said they duly appreciated, on account of its rarity. To keep on good terms with the rebel doctors who kept coming in to see us during the day, I opened some bottles of brandy, and how they did seem to enjoy it and the iced water! They asked to look at a piece of ice, as a curiosity. Constant movements of the troops were all the time taking place, and we could not then at all estimate their number—afterwards we had a better chance.

On Sunday the churches were opened as usual, and Jackson attended the Presbyterian and German Reformed Church. At the latter place the minister, Dr. Zacharias, prayed for the President of the United States in a firm voice.

While at the hospital this day the United States telegraph operator from the Monocacy Junction was brought in. He had been engaged telegraphing on the night of the entrance of the rebels into Maryland on the business of the railroad, had failed to receive notice of the enemy's approach, and was notified of their arrival by the entrance of the confederate General Hill, with one or two aids. The General told him he was a prisoner, and desired him to telegraph to Baltimore to send up a large train of cars, signing his (the operator's) name. He, however, told the General that the wires had just been cut. He was then desired to telegraph (to test him) that the rebels had arrived and that he was a prisoner. He returned the same answer, and one of the men with Hill then stepped forward and tried the instrument and reported the same thing.

During the rebels' stay here, provisions became very scarce. All the stores were bought out. Coffee rose to one dollar per pound, and store-keepers increased their prices to a par with those of Richmond. The Confederates offered to pay double price for every thing. A Union man from whom they wished to purchase forage, told them that their scrip depreciated the paper on which it was printed.

All the while the enemy staid here we were continually excited by rumors of the approach of the Federal forces. At one time they were reported at Hanover; at another, to be within fifteen miles, etc. I took pains to learn the Star Spangled Banner on the piano, and played it with vim often during their stay here, greatly to the disgust of the passing soldiers.

II

Lincoln, having no other choice, restored McClellan to the command of the Army of the Potomac. "He is an able general, but a very cautious one," Lee told Walker. "His army is in a very demoralized and chaotic condition, and will not be prepared for offensive operations—or he will not think it so—for three or four weeks." Confidently Lee sent Jackson to capture Harpers Ferry, expecting to be on the Susquehanna by the time McClellan awoke to the Confederate plan. But on September 13, John M. Bloss of Company F, Twenty-seventh Indiana Infantry, serving that day on the skirmish line in front of his brigade, made an unusual discovery:[4]

. . . We moved forward rapidly and soon reached the suburbs of Frederick. It was a warm morning and we threw ourselves upon the grass to rest. While lying there I noticed a large envelope. It was not sealed, and when I picked it up two cigars and a paper fell out.

The cigars were divided and, while the needed match was being secured, I began to read the enclosed document. As I read, each line became more interesting. It was Lee's order to his army, giving his plans for the next four days from that time and, if true, was exceedingly important. I carried it back to Captain Kopp of our company, and together we took it to Colonel Colgrove. He was at that time talking to General Kimball. They read it, I imagine, with the same surprise I had felt, and immediately started with it to General McClellan.

The order made known not only Lee's position, but his intent. . . . It showed that Lee proposed to divide his army on the 10th and that at this time, the 13th, it was really separated into five divisions and that three divisions were far away. . . . McClellan's army was practically concentrated and could strike McLaws or Hill or both. . . .

How could such an order be lost? Confederate General G. Moxley Sorrel offered an explanation:[5]

. . . Perhaps two copies were sent [D. H.] Hill. Although Hill's was now an independent division, Jackson considered Hill under his command and sent him a copy of the order. One copy certainly reached him direct from General Lee. Jackson and Hill, although connected by marriage, had, it is said, no great personal liking for each other, and I can imagine the cross and dyspeptic Hill, with orders from Lee in his pocket, receiving another copy from Jackson with careless irritation. . . .

Bloss continued his story:

The time when I found the dispatch could not have been later than 10 o'clock on the 13th. I saw General Kimball start with it to McClellan's headquarters; he had a good horse, understood the importance of the dispatch, and has since told me that he carried it directly to General McClellan.

In about three-quarters of an hour after it was found, we noticed orderlies and staff officers flying in all directions, and soon the whole army was rapidly moving forward. . . .

McClellan had read the "lost order" in an exuberant mood. "If I don't crush Lee now," he declared, "you may call me whatever you please." To Lee, who knew nothing of Bloss's discovery, McClellan's sudden energy in marching over the Catoctin Mountain, threatening to isolate Lee from three of the five detachments co-operating with Jackson at Harpers Ferry, came as a bewildering surprise. Longstreet argued that Lee was in no position to fight and should fall back on Sharpsburg, but Lee believed that he could not yield the pass at South Mountain. Next day, when the armies clashed, Washington received a series of heady dispatches from McClellan:[6]

[To Halleck, September 14, 9:40 P.M.] After a very severe engagement, the corps of General Hooker and General Reno have carried the heights commanding the Hagerstown road by storm. The troops behaved magnificently—they never fought better. . . . It has been a glorious victory. I cannot yet tell whether the enemy will retreat during the night, or appear in increased force during the morning. . . .

[To Halleck, September 15, 8 A.M.] The enemy disappeared during the night. Our troops are now advancing in pursuit. I do not know where he will next be found.

[To Halleck, September 15, 8 A.M.] . . . I am hurrying every thing forward to endeavor to press their retreat to the utmost.

[To Halleck, September 15, 10 A.M.] Information this moment received, completely confirms the rout and demoralization of the rebel army.

General Lee is reported wounded, and Garland killed.

General Hooker, alone, has over a thousand more prisoners, seven hundred having been sent to Frederick. It is stated that Lee gives his loss as *fifteen thousand*. We are following as rapidly as the men can move.

III

By now Halleck had learned to view all field dispatches with a wary glance. In the first flush of victory, most generals talked through their hats. Lee's losses at South Mountain were about the same as McClellan's—eighteen hundred; and Lee, far from incapacitated, was falling back in good order on Sharpsburg. Meanwhile official Washington had to deal with the dispatches from Harpers Ferry, where Jackson had just raised hell. W. W. Blackford, who rode with Stuart, saw the vital action on a clear and sparkling Sunday morning:[7]

. . . The morning of the 15th opened with heavy cannonading from the Ferry five miles below us, where Jackson was beginning his bombardment. Up the valley we could see heavy masses of infantry bearing down upon us, their lines of skirmishers extending clear across from mountain to mountain as they came hastening down to the relief of the beleaguered garrison. If they had continued their advance with vigor they would inevitably have succeeded in relieving the place, but they halted and delayed. Ten o'clock found them only just beginning a skirmish fire with our dismounted cavalry, while since daylight the thunder of the guns told that Jackson was vigorously pressing his attack, and so long as this firing continued we knew our retreat in that direction was closed. Stuart was prepared to contest every foot of ground, but the disparity of numbers was fearful.

A little incident occurred just here which I must mention as an evidence of how the soldier snatches pleasure among the most trying scenes. The people occupying the pretty farmhouses around us, expecting a battle, had fled locking their doors, but leaving everything behind them. The staff had found their hasty early breakfast rather scant, and as the morning advanced a sharp appetite made itself felt in spite of the gravity of the situation. While reconnoitring the advance of the enemy my attention was attracted to a farmhouse near their lines, from which a good view could be had. It was a lovely cottage, all embowered in trees, with quantities of ripe grapes and peaches around but everything deserted. General Stuart coming up just then, I suggested that something more substantial might be had, and proposed that we should investigate, and to this proposition he eagerly agreed. Finding a lower window unfastened, I entered and found myself in a pantry richly stored with everything that could tempt the appetite. In the safe were cold meats and pies, bread, butter and milk and cheese in the greatest profusion, and handing them out of the window to my hungry comrades we made a glorious meal and stored our haversacks to their utmost capacity. The bullets were singing through the trees above us from the advancing enemy as we galloped back to our lines.

Their skirmishers were within two hundred yards of our lines when the roar of Jackson's guns suddenly ceased. There followed a few moments of painful suspense. The enemy halted, evidently arrested by the significant quiet. Then from away down the valley came rolling nearer and nearer, as the news reached the troops, ringing cheers and we knew the Ferry had surrendered and soon a courier came spurring in hot haste with the official information of the fact. A skirmisher of the enemy, as our cheers rang out in response, sprang up on a stone wall and called over to us, "What the hell are you fellows cheering for?" We shouted back, "Because Harpers Ferry is gone up, G—— d—— you." "I thought that was it," shouted the fellow as he got down off the wall. General Stuart, now at the head of his troops, rapidly withdrew to the south side of the river to march up and recross at Shepherdstown, to rejoin General Lee at Sharpsburg on the Antietam Creek where the battle was to be fought, as it turned out.

The ban that Halleck recently had slapped on correspondents neither kept them from the scenes of battle nor encouraged them to soften their accounts of a Federal disaster. The New York Times *told the Harpers Ferry story without pulling any punches:*[8]

Monday morning the rebels opened fire on Bolivar Heights at five o'clock, which was replied to until eight, when *our ammunition gave out.* The rebel batteries were so arranged as to enfilade us completely. To hold out longer seemed madness. Where is McClellan, that he does not send us reënforcements? Heavy firing is heard in the direction of

Martinsburgh and Sandy Hook, indicating the presence of Sigel and Banks, but *why are no reënforcements sent to us?* Fully one week and a half has elapsed since the enemy crossed into Maryland, evidently with the design of capturing this place. Are we to be left to our fate?

A few minutes after eight a council of war was held. The brave Col. D'Utassy, for one, *voted never to surrender,* and requested that he might have the privilege of cutting his way out. White flags were run up in every direction, and *a flag of truce was sent to inquire on what conditions a surrender would be accepted.* Gen. A. P. Hill sent back word that it must be unconditional. Further parleying resulted in our obtaining the following liberal conditions which were accepted:

The officers were to be allowed to go out with their side-arms and private effects; the rank and file with every thing save arms and equipments.

A murmur of disapprobation ran along the whole line when it became known that we had surrendered. Capt. McGrath burst into tears, exclaiming: "Boys, we have got no country now." Other officers exhibited a corresponding degree of grief, while the soldiers were decidedly demonstrative in their manifestations of rage. Yet, what could be done? Rebel batteries were opened on us *from seven different directions* and there was no hope of reënforcements reaching us.

As soon as the terms of surrender were completed, Gens. A. P. Hill and Jackson rode into town, accompanied by their staff, and followed by a troop of Loudon soldiers, who straightway commenced looking for "those d—— Loudon guerillas," referring to Capt. Means's Union company, who were fortunately not to be found. Gen. Hill immediately took up his headquarters in the tavern-stand, next to Col. Miles's. Old "Stonewall," after riding down to the river, returned to Bolivar Heights, the observed of all observers. He was dressed in the coarsest kind of homespun, seedy and dirty at that; wore an old hat which any Northern beggar would consider an insult to have offered him, and in his general appearance was in no respect to be distinguished from the mongrel, bare-footed crew who follow his fortunes. I had heard much of the decayed appearance of the rebel soldiers, but such a looking crowd! Ireland in her worst straits could present no parallel, and yet they glory in their shame.

IV

Through ten agonizing hours, Lee drew his army back to Sharpsburg over wagon-clogged roads; with daylight on September 16 his gray

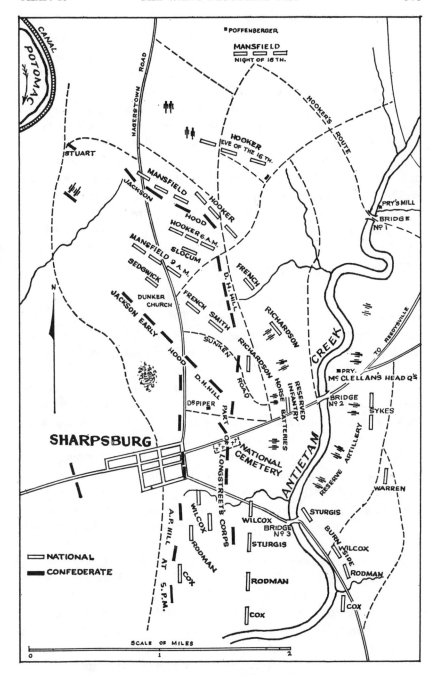

THE BATTLE OF ANTIETAM

From Lossing, *Pictorial History of the Civil War*

*columns crossed the stone bridge over Antietam Creek, forming a line
of battle along a range of hills between the town and the stream. A
courier, dashing down the road from Harpers Ferry, brought the news
that set Rebel troops to wild cheering—Jackson had captured 12,000
men, 70 pieces of artillery, 13,000 small arms!*

    *McClellan came up on September 16 and did what might have been
expected—he hesitated. That day Jackson arrived from Harpers Ferry
with Walker's troops and his own right behind. At nightfall Lee still
felt uncomfortable without the divisions of Powell Hill, Dick Anderson
and Lafayette McLaws, and yet he must have realized that he owed
McClellan no little gratitude for a day to entrench and gain such reinforcements as he had. The battle came exactly when he expected, in the
chill, damp morning of September 17, to be remembered thenceforth
as "the bloodiest day of the war." Battle-wise George W. Smalley, the
New York* Tribune's *top reporter now, saw it start:*[9]

    . . . Morning found both armies just as they had slept, almost close
enough to look into each other's eyes. The left of Meade's reserves
and the right of Ricketts's line became engaged at nearly the same moment, one with artillery, the other with infantry. A battery was almost
immediately pushed forward beyond the central woods, over a
ploughed field near the top of the slope where the corn-field began.
On this open field, in the corn beyond, and in the woods which stretched
forward into the broad fields like a promontory into the ocean, were
the hardest and deadliest struggles of the day.

    For half an hour after the battle had grown to its full strength, the
line of fire swayed neither way. Hooker's men were fully up to their
work. They saw their General every where in front, never away from
the fire, and all the troops believed in their commander, and fought
with a will. Two thirds of them were the same men who under McDowell
had broken at Manassas.

    The half-hour passed, the rebels began to give way a little—only a
little, but at the first indication of a receding fire, Forward, was the
word, and on went the line with a cheer and a rush. Back across the
corn-field, leaving dead and wounded behind them, over the fence, and
across the road, and then back again into the dark woods which closed
around them went the retreating rebels.

    Meade and his Pennsylvanians followed hard and fast—followed
till they came within easy range of the woods, among which they saw
their beaten enemy disappearing—followed still, with another cheer,
and flung themselves against the cover.

But out of those gloomy woods came suddenly and heavily terrible volleys—volleys which smote, and bent, and broke in a moment that eager front, and hurled them swiftly back for half the distance they had won. Not swiftly, nor in panic, any further. Closing up their shattered lines, they came slowly away; a regiment where a brigade had been; hardly a brigade where a whole division had been victorious. They had met at the woods the first volleys of musketry from fresh troops—had met them and returned them till their line had yielded and gone down before the weight of fire, and till their ammunition was exhausted.

In ten minutes the fortune of the day seemed to have changed; it was the rebels now who were advancing, pouring out of the woods in endless lines, sweeping through the corn-field from which their comrades had just fled. Hooker sent in his nearest brigade to meet them, but it could not do the work. He called for another. There was nothing close enough, unless he took it from his right. His right might be in danger if it was weakened, but his centre was already threatened with annihilation. Not hesitating one moment, he sent to Doubleday: "Give me your best brigade instantly."

The best brigade came down the hill to the right on the run, went through the timber in front through a storm of shot and bursting shell and crashing limbs, over the open field beyond and straight into the corn-field, passing as they went the fragments of three brigades shattered by the rebel fire and streaming to the rear. They passed by Hooker, whose eyes lighted as he saw these veteran troops, led by a soldier whom he knew he could trust. "I think they will hold it," he said.

Other correspondents, if they were lucky, found their initials at the end of a dispatch. Proudly the Tribune *signed "By George W. Smalley" to this account:*[10]

General Hartsuff took his troops very steadily, but, now that they were under fire, not hurriedly, up the hill from which the corn-field begins to descend, and formed them on the crest. Not a man who was not in full view—not one who bent before the storm. Firing at first in volleys, they fired then at will with wonderful rapidity and effect. The whole line crowned the hill and stood out darkly against the sky, but lighted and shrouded ever in flame and smoke. They were the Twelfth and Thirteenth Massachusetts and another regiment which I cannot remember—old troops all of them.

There for half an hour they held the ridge, unyielding in purpose, exhaustless in courage. There were gaps in the line, but it nowhere bent. Their General was severely wounded early in the fight, but they fought on. Their supports did not come—they determined to win without them. They began to go down the hill and into the corn; they did not stop to think that their ammunition was nearly gone; they were there to win that field, and they won it. The rebel line for the second time fled through the corn and into the woods. I cannot tell how few of Hartsuff's brigade were left when the work was done, but it was done. There was no more gallant, determined, heroic fighting in all this desperate day. General Hartsuff is very severely wounded, but I do not believe he counts his success too dearly purchased.

The crisis of the fight at this point had arrived. Ricketts's division, vainly endeavoring to advance and exhausted by the effort, had fallen back. Part of Mansfield's corps was ordered in to their relief, but Mansfield's troops came back again, and their General was mortally wounded. The left nevertheless was too extended to be turned, and too strong to be broken. Ricketts sent word he could not advance, but could hold his ground. Doubleday had kept his guns at work on the right, and had finally silenced a rebel battery that for half an hour had poured in a galling enfilading fire along Hooker's central line. There were woods in front of Doubleday's hill which the rebels held, but so long as those guns pointed toward them they did not care to attack.

With his left, then, able to take care of itself, with his right impregnable, with two brigades of Mansfield still fresh and coming rapidly up, and with his centre a second time victorious, Gen. Hooker determined to advance. Orders were sent to Crawford and Gordon—the two Mansfield brigades—to move forward at once, the batteries in the centre were ordered to advance, the whole line was called on, and the General himself went forward.

To the right of the corn-field and beyond it was a point of woods. Once carried and firmly held, it was the key of the position. Hooker determined to take it. He rode out in front of his furthest troops on a hill to examine the ground for a battery. At the top he dismounted and went forward on foot, completed his reconnoissance, returned, and re-mounted. The musketry-fire from the point of woods was all the while extremely hot. As he put his foot in the stirrup a fresh volley of rifle-bullets came whizzing by. The tall, soldierly figure of the General, the white horse which he rode, the elevated place where he was, all made him a most dangerously conspicuous mark. So he had been all day, riding often without a staff-officer or an orderly near him—all sent off on urgent duty—visible every where on the field. The rebel bullets had followed him all day, but they had not hit him, and he would not regard them.

Remounting on this hill, he had not ridden five steps when he was struck in the foot by a ball. Three men were shot down at the same moment by his side. The air was alive with bullets. He kept on his horse a few minutes, though the wound was severe and excessively painful, and would not dismount till he had given his last order to advance. He was himself in the very front. Swaying unsteadily on his horse, he turned in his seat to look about him. "There is a regiment to the right. Order it forward! Crawford and Gordon are coming up. Tell them to carry those woods and hold them—and it is our fight!"

It was found that the bullet had passed completely through his foot. The surgeon who examined it on the spot could give no opinion whether bones were broken, but it was afterward ascertained that though grazed they were not fractured. Of course the severity of the wound made it impossible for him to keep the field, which he believed already won, so far as it belonged to him to win it. It was nine o'clock. The fight had been furious since five. A large part of his command was broken, but with his right still untouched, and with Crawford's and Gordon's brigades just up; above all, with the advance of the whole central line, which the men had heard ordered with cheers, and with a regiment already on the edge of the woods he wanted, he might well leave the field, thinking the battle was won—that *his* battle was won, for I am writing only about the attack on the rebel left.

Antietam tortured the souls of those who fought there. W. W. Blackford told of an incident:[11]

Between our cavalry lines and the enemy stood a handsome country house in which, it seems, all the women and children in the neighborhood had assembled for mutual protection, not thinking that part of the country would be the scene of conflict. Between us and the house was a roughly ploughed field. When the cannonade began, the house happened to be right in the line between Pelham's battery and that of the enemy occupying the opposite hills, the batteries firing clear over the top of the house at each other. When the crossing shells began screaming over the house, its occupants thought their time had come, and like a flock of birds they came streaming out in "Mother Hubbards," and even less, hair streaming in the wind and children of all ages stretched out behind, and tumbling at every step over the clods of the ploughed field. Every time one would fall, the rest thought it was the result of a cannon shot and ran the faster. It was impossible to persuade them to return. I galloped out to meet them and represented to them that they were safe, probably, where they had been, but it was no use; so swinging up before and behind as many children as my horse could carry, I escorted them to our lines and quieted the fears of the party, assuring them that they were not in danger of immediate death. Seeing what was going on, the batteries on each side ceased firing until the little party was disposed of. . . .

Private John Dooley, who fought with the famous First Virginia regiment, caught Antietam's sense of dreadful immediacy:[12]

It is now noon, and we who have hitherto been inactive spectators of this scene must take our part, though small, in the action. Burnside's corps is moving against our position, the context having extended from left to right. We are moved to meet this attack almost between the advancing enemy and the town of Sharpsburg. A few of our men are in the orchard, and behind a stone wall, and the majority behind a rail fence on the borders of a cornfield. Two pieces of artillery are all that can be spared to keep the enemy back, and these are but very poor guns.

I might very readily omit what follows as reflecting but little credit on our gallant old brigade; but as I think it reflects no disgrace I shall tell the whole truth. When ordered into position to meet the enemy our brigade was again supposed to be able to do the duty of a full brigade or at least to try to do it. So depleted was it however that our Regt. had but 17 men rank and file, 8 officers and 9 men. With this brigade of about 200 men we covered a space of nearly as many yards, not presenting a skirmish line.

In the field below us the enemy are slowly but cautiously approaching, crouching low as they advance behind the undulating tracks in the rich meadows through which they are passing. From the numbers of their flags which are distinctly visible above the rising ground we judge them to be at least two thousand in number. As long as our little battery of two guns is served with tolerable precision the enemy, who appear to be new troops, do not dare to venture close or raise their heads. But in a few minutes the Yankee artillery, far superior to ours, dismounted one of our pieces, killed the horses; and the remaining gunner, fearing capture, hitched the only remaining horse to the other cannon and made away to the rear as hard as he could go.

I shall never forget poor Beckham on Kemper's staff. As soon as our first gun opened on the enemy, he gave a lusty cheer and rising in his stirrups flung his hat around his head, wild with enthusiasm. Almost instantly he was hurled from his horse by a shot and his foot terribly mangled. He was borne from the field cheering as he went and with him went General Kemper and his staff.

We were now left to oppose the numerous masses before us with a mere picket-line of musketry. There may have been other troops to our left and right but I did not see any. The Yankees, finding no batteries opposing them, approach closer and closer, cowering down as near to the ground as possible, while we keep up a pretty warm fire by file upon them as they advance. Now they are at the last elevation of rising ground and whenever a head is raised we fire. Now they rise up and make a charge for our fence. Hastily emptying our muskets into their lines, we fled back through the cornfield.

Oh, how I ran! or tried to run through the high corn, for my heavy belt and cartridge box and musket kept me back to *half* my speed. I was afraid of being struck in the *back*, and I frequently turned half around in running, so as to avoid if possible so disgraceful a wound. It never entered my head to throw away gun or cartridge box; but, encumbered as I was, I endeavored to keep pace with my captain, who with his long legs and unencumbered would in a little while have far outstripped me but that he frequently turned towards the enemy, and, running backwards, managed not to come out ahead in this our anything but creditable race. The enemy having taken our position appeared to think they had performed wonders, for instead of pursuing us and shooting us down, they began to give regular *methodical* cheers, as if they had gained a game of base ball.

Scarcely had we, breathless, reached the edge of the cornfield than we met Toombs' brigade of Georgians advancing in line of battle to our relief. Hastily forming in their rear we returned to our former line which by this time a well directed volley from this little brigade of Georgians had restored again to our possession. Still, even with this brigade, we were scarcely 800 men, and how were we to repulse the thousands that still threatened us, backed as they were by a terribly efficient artillery force?

General Toombs rides up and down the line like one frantic, telling the men to stand firm, etc., and sends off for reinforcements of artillery.

In less than ten minutes two pieces of the Washington Artillery are hurried rapidly forward to our support. They choose a pretty position, far safer and more advantageous than that of the other battery, and in a few minutes are playing with wonderful effect on the cowering lines of the enemy.

It was astonishing to witness the rapidity and coolness of these comrades, and with what admirable tact and skill they managed their pieces. . . .

The famous black-hatted Iron Brigade—Western troops—fought in the cornfield that bloody day. One of its rugged veterans, Rufus R. Dawes, remembered:[13]

The Fourteenth Brooklyn Regiment, red legged Zouaves, came into our line, closing the awful gaps. Now is the pinch. Men and officers of New York and Wisconsin are fused into a common mass, in the frantic struggle to shoot fast. Every body tears cartridges, loads, passes guns, or shoots. Men are falling in their places or running back into the corn. The soldier who is shooting is furious in his energy. The soldier who is shot looks around for help with an imploring agony of death on his face. After a few rods of advance, the line stopped and, by common impulse, fell back to the edge of the corn and lay down on the ground behind the low rail fence. Another line of our men came up through the corn. We all joined together, jumped over the fence, and again pushed out into the open field. There is a rattling fusillade and loud cheers. "Forward" is the word. The men are loading and firing with demoniacal fury and shouting and laughing hysterically, and the whole field before us is covered with rebels fleeing for life, into the woods. Great numbers of them are shot while climbing over the high post and rail fences along the turnpike. We push on over the open fields half way to the little church. The powder is bad, and the guns have become very dirty. It takes hard pounding to get the bullets down, and our firing is becoming slow. A long and steady line of rebel gray, unbroken by the fugitives who fly before us, comes sweeping down through the woods around the church. They raise the yell and fire. It is like a scythe running through our line. "Now, save, who can." It is a race for life that each man runs for the cornfield. A sharp cut, as of a switch, stings the calf of my leg as I run. Back to the corn, and back through the corn, the headlong flight continues. At the bottom of the hill, I took the blue color of the state of Wisconsin, and waving it, called a rally of Wisconsin men. Two hundred men gathered around the flag of the Badger state. Across the turnpike just in front of the haystacks, two guns of Battery "B," 4th U. S. Artillery were in action. The pursuing rebels were upon them. General John Gibbon, our brigade commander, who in regular service was captain of this battery, grimed and black with powder smoke in himself sighting these guns of his old battery, comes running to me, "Here, major, move your men over, we must save these guns." I commanded "Right face, forward march," and started ahead with the colors in my hand into the open field, the men following. As I entered the field, a report as of a thunderclap in my ear fairly stunned me. This was Gibbon's last shot at the advancing rebels. The cannon was double charged with canister. The rails of the fence flew high in the air. A line of Union blue charged swiftly forward from our right across the field in front of the battery, and into the corn-field. They drove back the rebels who were firing upon us. It was our own gallant 19th Indiana, and here fell dead their leader, Lieutenant Colonel A. F. Bachman; but the youngest captain in their line, William W. Dudley, stepped forward and led on the charge. I gathered my men on the turnpike, reorganized them, and reported to General Doubleday, who was himself there. He ordered me to move back to the next woods in the rear, to remain and await instruction. Bullets, shot, and shell, fired by the enemy in the corn-field, were still flying thickly around us, striking the trees in this woods, and cutting off the limbs. I placed my men under the best shelter I could find, and here we figured up, as nearly as we could, our dreadful losses in the battle. Three hundred and fourteen officers and men had marched with us into battle. There had been killed and wounded, one hundred and fifty-two. Company "C" under Captain Hooe, thirty-five men, was not in the fight in front of the corn-field. That company was on skirmish duty farther to our right. In this service they lost two men. Of two hundred and eighty men who were at the corn-field and turnpike, one hundred and fifty were killed or wounded. This was the most dreadful slaughter to which our regiment was subjected in the war. We were joined in the woods by Captain Ely, who reported to me, as the senior officer present, with the colors and eighteen men of the second Wisconsin. They represented what remained for duty of that gallant regiment.

Charles Francis Adams, Jr. would have a quite different recollection:[14]

. . . I was an officer in a regiment of cavalry; a mere subordinate, responsible only for obedience to orders. At Antietam, in the height of the engagement, the division to which my regiment belonged was hurried across the narrow stone bridge at the point where the little river intersects the Sharpsburg road, and deployed on its further side. We were then directly in front of Fitz-John Porter's corps, and between it and the Confederate line, covering Sharpsburg. A furious artillery duel was going on, to and fro, above our heads, between the batteries of Porter's command and those of the enemy, we being down in the valley of the river, they on the higher ground. The Confederate batteries we could not see; nor could they see us. When we first deployed on the further side of Antietam creek, it seemed as if we were doomed,—so deafening was the discharge of artillery on either side, and so incessant the hurtling of projectiles as they passed both ways over us. Every instant, too, we expected to be ordered to advance on the Confederate batteries. The situation was unmistakably trying. But no orders came; and no one was hurt. By degrees it grew monotonous. Presently, to relieve our tired horses, we were ordered to dismount, and, without breaking the ranks, we officers sat down on the sloping hill-side. No one was being struck; I was very tired; the noise was deadening; gradually it had on me a lulling effect; and so I dropped quietly asleep,— asleep in the height of the battle and between the contending armies! They woke me up presently to look after my horse, who was grazing somewhat wide; and, after a time, we were withdrawn, and sent elsewhere. I believe that day our regiment did not lose a man, scarcely a horse. Such is my recollection of that veritable charnel-house, Antietam. . . .

V

Smalley, Blackford, Dooley, Dawes, Adams each could tell something —a fragment of Antietam. The historian could describe in later years the little Dunkard Church around which the battle swirled; and the biographer could describe Powell Hill, in flowing auburn beard and flaming red shirt, bringing his exhausted division up from Harpers Ferry, striking Burnside's Federals in the flank, standing up hand to hand and carrying that terrible charge. Again, these were fragments. Later the military historian, combing the volumes of official records, tracing the movements and mistakes of every brigade, could tell why that hot September day cost the Confederates eight thousand casualties, the Union twelve thousand.

A grisly, horrible story it would all make; and yet somehow it would sound hollow, distorted, incomplete. Men, guns, generals, a battlefield —these were no longer the whole war. Generals needed telegraph wires between Richmond and Washington to tell what was happening at Antietam, but in Shepherdstown, across the Potomac, on Lee's route of escape, sensitive Mary Mitchell needed only the wind: [15]

On the 17th of September cloudy skies looked down upon the two armies facing each other on the fields of Maryland. It seems to me now that the roar of that day began with the light, and all through its long and dragging hours its thunder formed a background to our pain and terror. If we had been in doubt as to our friends' whereabouts on Sunday, there was no room for doubt now. There was no sitting at the windows now and counting discharges of guns, or watching the curling smoke. We went about our work with pale faces and trembling hands, yet trying to appear composed for the sake of our patients, who were much excited. We could hear the incessant explosions of artillery, the shrieking whistles of the shells, and the sharper, deadlier, more thrilling roll of musketry; while every now and then the echo of some charging cheer would come, borne by the wind, and as the human voice pierced that demoniacal clangor we would catch our breath and listen, and try not to sob, and turn back to the forlorn hospitals, to the suffering at our feet and before our eyes, while imagination fainted at thought of those other scenes hidden from us beyond the Potomac.

On our side of the river there were noise, confusion, dust; throngs of stragglers; horsemen galloping about; wagons blocking each other, and teamsters wrangling; and a continued din of shouting, swearing, and rumbling, in the midst of which men were dying, fresh wounded arriving, surgeons amputating limbs and dressing wounds, women going in and out with bandages, lint, medicines, food. An ever-present sense of anguish, dread, pity, and, I fear, hatred—these are my recollections of Antietam.

When night came we could still hear the sullen guns and hoarse, indefinite murmurs that succeeded the day's turmoil. That night was dark and lowering and the air heavy and dull. Across the river innumerable camp-fires were blazing, and we could but too well imagine the scenes that they were lighting. We sat in silence, looking into each other's tired faces. There were no impatient words, few tears; only silence, and a drawing close together, as if for comfort. We were almost hopeless, yet clung with desperation to the thought that we were hoping. But in our hearts we could not believe that anything human could have escaped that appalling fire. On Thursday the two armies lay idly facing each other, but we could not be idle. The wounded continued to arrive until the town was quite unable to hold all the disabled and suffering. They filled every building and overflowed into the country round, into farm-houses, barns, corn-cribs, cabins—wherever four walls and a roof were found together. Those able to travel were sent on to Winchester and other towns back from the river, but their departure seemed to make no appreciable difference. There were six churches, and they were all full; the Odd Fellows' Hall, the Freemasons', the little Town Council room, the barn-like place known as the Drill Room, all the private houses after their capacity, the shops and empty buildings, the school-houses,—every inch of space, and yet the cry was for room.

The unfinished Town Hall had stood in naked ugliness for many a long day. Somebody threw a few rough boards across the beams, placed piles of straw over them, laid down single planks to walk upon, and lo, it was a hospital at once. The stone warehouses down in the ravine and by the river had been passed by, because low and damp and undesirable as sanitariums, but now their doors and windows were thrown wide, and, with barely time allowed to sweep them, they were all occupied,—even the "old blue factory," an antiquated, crazy, dismal building of blue stucco that peeled off in great blotches, which had been shut up for years, and was in the last stages of dilapidation.

Lee expected to fight next morning, but the fight had gone out of Mc-Clellan. Mary Mitchell remembered:

General Lee crossed the Potomac under cover of the darkness, and when the day broke, the greater part of his force—or the more orderly portion of it—had gone on toward Kearneysville and Leetown. General McClellan followed to the river, and without crossing got a battery in position on Douglas's Hill, and began to shell the retreating army and, in consequence, the town. What before was confusion grew worse; the retreat became a stampede. The battery may not have done a very great deal of execution, but it made a fearful noise. It is curious how much louder guns sound when they are pointed at you than when turned the other way! And the shell, with its long-drawn screeching, though no doubt less terrifying than the singing minie-ball, has a way of making one's hair stand on end. Then, too, every one who has any experience in such things, knows how infectious fear is, how it grows when yielded to, and how, when you once begin to run, it soon seems impossible to run fast enough; whereas, if you can manage to stand your ground, the alarm lessens and sometimes disappears.

Some one suggested that yellow was the hospital color, and immediately everybody who could lay hands upon a yellow rag hoisted it over the house. The whole town was a hospital; there was scarcely a building that could not with truth seek protection under that plea, and the fantastic little strips were soon flaunting their ineffectual remonstrance from every roof-tree and chimney. When this specific failed the excitement became wild and ungovernable. It would have been ludicrous had it not produced so much suffering. The danger was less than it seemed, for McClellan, after all, was not bombarding the town, but the army, and most of the shells flew over us and exploded in the fields; but aim cannot be always sure, and enough shells fell short to convince the terrified citizens that their homes were about to be battered down over their ears. The better people kept some outward coolness, with perhaps a feeling of *"noblesse oblige"*; but the poorer classes acted as if the town were already in a blaze, and rushed from their houses with their families and household goods to make their way into the country. The road was thronged, the streets blocked; men were vociferating, women crying, children screaming; wagons, ambulances, guns, caissons, horsemen, footmen, all mingled—nay, even wedged and jammed together—in one struggling, shouting mass. The negroes were the worst, and with faces of a ghastly ash-color, and staring eyes, they swarmed into the fields, carrying their babies, their clothes, their pots and kettles, fleeing from the wrath behind them. The comparison to a hornet's nest attacked by boys is not a good one, for there was no "fight" shown; but a disturbed ant-hill is altogether inadequate. They fled widely and camped out of range, nor would they venture back for days.

Soldiers received bounties and were paid monthly wages for fighting; generals won fame, a place in history; but civilians like Mary Mitchell gained only memories:

Had this been all, we could afford to laugh now, but there was another side to the picture that lent it an intensely painful aspect. It was the hurrying crowds of wounded. Ah me! those maimed and bleeding fugitives! When the firing commenced the hospitals began to empty.

All who were able to pull one foot after another, or could bribe or beg comrades to carry them, left in haste. In vain we implored them to stay; in vain we showed them the folly, the suicide, of the attempt; in vain we argued, cajoled, threatened, ridiculed; pointed out that we were remaining and that there was less danger here than on the road.

There is no sense or reason in a panic. The cannon were bellowing upon Douglas's Hill, the shells whistling and shrieking, the air full of shouts and cries; we had to scream to make ourselves heard. The men replied that the "Yankees" were crossing; that the town was to be burned; that *we* could not be made prisoners, but they could; that, anyhow, they were going as far as they could walk, or be carried. And go they did. Men with cloths about their heads went hatless in the sun, men with cloths about their feet limped shoeless on the stony road; men with arms in slings, without arms, with one leg, with bandaged sides and backs; men in ambulances, wagons, carts, wheelbarrows, men carried on stretchers or supported on the shoulder of some self-denying comrade—all who could crawl went, and went to almost certain death.

They could not go far, they dropped off into the country houses, where they were received with as much kindness as it was possible to ask for; but their wounds had become inflamed, their frames were weakened by fright and over-exertion; erysipelas, mortification, gangrene set in; and long rows of nameless graves still bear witness to the results.

VI

No Marylanders had rallied to the Southern cause. Lee took his army and the war back to Virginia. General Walker saw his commander then:[16]

Detained in superintending the removal of a number of the wounded of my division, I was among the last to cross the Potomac. As I rode into the river I passed General Lee, sitting on his horse in the stream, watching the crossing of the wagons and artillery. Returning my greeting, he inquired as to what was still behind. There was nothing but the wagons containing my wounded, and a battery of artillery, all of which were near at hand, and I told him so. "Thank God!" I heard him say as I rode on.

CHAPTER 16

THE WAR AND THE NEGRO

In New York City on the twenty-first of February, 1862, occurred an execution unique in American history. "For forty years," reported *Harper's Weekly*, "the slave trade has been pronounced piracy by law, and to engage in it has been a capital offense. But the sympathy of the Government and its officials has been so often on the side of the criminal, and it has seemed so absurd to hang a man for doing at sea that which, in half the Union, is done daily without censure on land, that no one has ever been punished under the Act."

Steaming along the West Coast of Africa, about fifty miles outside the River Congo, the United States steamer *Mohican* in early August of 1860 had sighted a little vessel flying the American flag. Her name was the *Erie;* her captain, Nathaniel Gordon, a native of Maine. Beating hard to north with all sail set, the ship clearly wished to elude inspection. The gun on the *Mohican* quickly settled that argument. Aboard the *Erie* were eight hundred and ninety-seven Negroes. The New York *Times* reported: "They were half children, one-fourth men and one-fourth women, and so crowded when on the main deck that one could scarcely put his foot down without stepping on them." Gordon's vessel reeked with filth and disease. "Decency was unthought of," the *Times* added; "privacy was simply impossible—nastiness and wretchedness reigned supreme."

Gordon was arrested, convicted and sentenced to death. "His friends and the slave-trading interest," or so *Harper's Weekly* contended, exercised "immense exertions" to secure a pardon. Ralph Waldo Emerson, in Washington to lecture on "Civilization at a Pinch" before the Smithsonian Institution, called at the White House and recorded that Lincoln "argued to Sumner the whole case of Gordon, the slave-trader, point by point, and added that he was not quite satisfied yet, and meant to refresh his memory by looking again at the evidence." To Emerson, this caution on Mr. Lincoln's part revealed "a fidelity and conscientiousness very honourable to him"; Emerson would not be quite so charitable when later he called on Mr. Seward "in his dingy State Department" with Governor Andrew and John Murray Forbes:

". . . Sumner went into a corner, with Andrew, and Mr. Forbes seized the moment to say to the Secretary that he saw there was an effort making to get Gordon the slave-trader pardoned. He hoped the Government would show to foreign nations that there was a change and a new spirit in it, which would not deal with this crime as heretofore. Seward looked very cross and ugly at this; twisted his cigar, and I thought, twisted his nose also, and said coarsely, 'Well, perhaps you would be willing to stand in his place,' or something like that, and rather surprised and disconcerted Mr. Forbes . . ." *

In the end, neither Mr. Lincoln's scrupulous concern for the evidence nor Mr. Seward's rude manners saved Gordon. In New York City, at noon on the twenty-first of February he was led to the gallows where, in the estimate of the New York *Times*, he expired—"a lump of dishonored clay."

I

That same February, Salmon P. Chase, Secretary of the Treasury, received an unusual document. Its author was Edward Lillie Pierce, a native of Massachusetts with strong antislavery convictions, friend of Charles Sumner, onetime associate in Chase's Cincinnati law office, and now a special treasury agent.

With the capture of Port Royal the Federal government had gained control of the islands off the coast of South Carolina. Almost two hundred plantations, growing some of the finest cotton in the world, were located here. The owners had fled, the slaves remained. If the plantations could be kept in operation, they promised to yield a crop of two million five hundred thousand pounds of ginned long-staple Sea Island cotton, an unexpected source of revenue that Chase sorely wished to exploit. But Pierce's chief interest appeared to be in launching a social

* *Journals of Ralph Waldo Emerson*, Edward Waldo Emerson and Waldo Emerson Forbes, eds. (Boston, 1913), IX, 375, 377–78.

experiment to discover whether the Negroes on the islands could be "fitted for useful citizenship." He recounted a sermon that he had preached one Sunday to the slaves on Ladies' Island:[1]

. . . I told them that their masters had rebelled against the Government, and we had come to put down the rebellion; that we had now met them, and wanted to see what was best to do for them; that the great trouble about doing any thing for them was that their masters had always told us, and had made many people believe, that they were lazy, and would not work unless whipped to it; that Mr. Lincoln had sent us down here to see if it was so; that what they did was reported to him, or to men who would tell him; that where I came from all were free, both white and black; that we did not sell children or separate man and wife, but all had to work; that if they were to be free, they would have to work, and would be shut up or deprived of privileges if they did not; that this was a critical hour with them, and if they did not behave well now and respect our agents and appear willing to work, Mr. Lincoln would give up trying to do any thing for them, and they must give up all hope of any thing better, and their children and grandchildren a hundred years hence would be worse off than they had been. I told them they must stick to their plantations and not run about and get scattered, and assured them that what their masters had told them of our intention to carry them off to Cuba and sell them was a lie, and their masters knew it to be so, and we wanted them to stay on the plantations and raise cotton, and if they behaved well, they should have wages—small, perhaps, at first; that they should have better food, and not have their wives and children sold off; that their children should be taught to read and write, for which they might be willing to pay something; that by and by they would be as well off as the white people, and we would stand by them against their masters ever coming back to take them. . . .

Pierce admitted that the typical island slave possessed shortcomings. He often changed wives, because society did not legally protect his marriage. Other weaknesses Pierce excused by a simple rule of nature: "All races, as well as all animals, have their appropriate means of self-defence, and where the power to use physical force to defend one's self is taken away, the weaker animal, or man, or race, resorts to cunning and duplicity." Pierce tried to explain to Chase exactly what he meant:[2]

. . . On the plantations, I often found a disposition to evade the inquiry whether they wished to be free or slaves; and though a preference for freedom was expressed, it was rarely in the passionate phrases which would come from an Italian peasant. The secluded and monotonous life of a plantation, with strict discipline and ignorance enforced by law and custom, is not favorable to the development of the richer sentiments, though even there they find at least a stunted growth, irrepressible as they are. The inquiry was often answered in this way: "The white man do what he pleases with us; we are yours now, massa." One, if I understood his broken words rightly, said that he did not care about being free, if he only had a good master. Others said they would like to be free, but they wanted a white man for a "protector." All of proper age, when inquired of, expressed a desire to have their children taught to read and write, and to learn themselves. On this point they showed more earnestness than on any other. When asked if they were willing to fight, in case we needed them, to keep their masters from coming back, they would seem to shrink from that, saying that "black men have been kept down so like dogs that they would run before white men."

At the close of the first week's observation, I almost concluded that on the plantations there was but little earnest desire for freedom, and scarcely any willingness for its sake to encounter white men. But, as showing the importance of not attempting to reach general conclusions too hastily, another class of facts came to my notice the second week. I met then some more intelligent, who spoke with profound earnestness of their desire to be free, and how they had longed to see this day. Other facts, connected with the military and naval operations, were noted. At the recent reconnoissance toward Pulaski, pilots of this class stood well under the fire, and were not reluctant to the service. When a district of Ladies' Island was left exposed, they voluntarily took such guns as they could procure, and stood sentries. Also at Edisto, where the colony is collected under the protection of our gunboats, they armed themselves and drove back the rebel cavalry. An officer here high in command reported to me some of these facts, which had been officially communicated to him. The suggestion may be pertinent that the persons in question are divisible into two classes. Those who, by their occupation, have been accustomed to independent labor, and schooled in some sort of self-reliance, are more developed in this direction; while others, who have been bound to the routine of plantation life, and kept more strictly under surveillance, are but little awakened. But even among these last there has been, under the quickening inspiration of present events, a rapid development, indicating that the same feeling is only latent.

The island slave was not so eager for social reform as Pierce. The treasury agent confessed: "Here, as everywhere else, where our army has met them, they have been assured by their masters that we are going to carry them off to Cuba. There is probably not a rebel master, from the Potomac to the Gulf, who has not repeatedly made this assurance to his slaves." Pierce wanted doctors, nurses, teachers and social service workers to prepare the island Negroes for freedom.

But Secretary Chase could not use treasury funds for this social experiment. Private citizens, however, were quickly attracted to the idea. Boston organized an Educational Commission, New York a National Freedman's Relief Association and Philadelphia a Port Royal Relief Committee. On June 2, 1862, Pierce could report to Chase that these three groups now had sent to the islands seventy-four men and nineteen women, who were certainly hard at work:[3]

The superintendents have generally had five or six plantations in charge, sometimes one, aided by a teacher, having under him three, four, and even five hundred persons. The duty of each has been to visit all the plantations under him as often as practicable, some of which are one, two, three, and even four miles from his quarters—transport to them implements from the storehouses, protect the cattle and other public property upon them, converse with the laborers, explaining to them their own new condition, the purposes of the Government towards them, what is expected of them in the way of labor, and what remuneration they are likely to receive; procure and distribute among them clothing and food, whether issued in army rations or contributed by the benevolent associations; collecting the materials of a census; making reports of the condition and wants of the plantations and any peculiar difficulties to the Special Agent; drawing pay rolls for labor on cotton, and paying the amounts; going when convenient to the praise meetings, and reading the Scriptures; instructing on Sundays and other days those desirous to learn to read, as much as time permitted; attending to cases of discipline, protecting the negroes from injuries, and in all possible ways endeavoring to elevate them, and

prepare them to become worthy and self-supporting citizens. . . .
Many toiled beyond their strength, and nearly all did more than they
could persevere in doing.

*Pierce offered militant testimony to refute those who argued that the
Negro did not possess innate intelligence:*[4]

. . . One teacher on his first day's school, leaves in the room a
large alphabet card, and the next day returns to find a mother there
teaching her little child of three years to pronounce the first letters of
the alphabet she herself learned the day before. The children learn
without urging by their parents, and as rapidly as white persons of
the same age, often more so, the progress being quickened by the
eager desire.

One teacher reports that on the first day of her school only three
or four knew a part of their letters, and none knew all. In one week
seven boys and six girls could read readily words of one syllable, and
the following week there were twenty in the same class. The cases of
dulness have not exceeded those among the whites. The mulattoes, of
whom there are probably not more than five per cent of the entire
population on the plantations, are no brighter than the children of pure
African blood. In the schools which have been opened for some weeks,
the pupils who have regularly attended have passed from the alphabet,
and are reading words of one syllable in large and small letters. The
lessons have been confined to reading and spelling, except in a few
cases where writing has been taught.

There has been great apparent eagerness to learn among the adults
and some have progressed well. They will cover their books with care,
each one being anxious to be thus provided, carry them to the fields,
studying them at intervals of rest, and asking explanations of the superintendents who happen to come along. But as the novelty wore away,
many of the adults finding perseverance disagreeable, dropped off. Except in rare cases it is doubtful whether adults over thirty years, although appreciating the privilege for their children, will persevere in
continuous study so as to acquire the knowledge for themselves. Still,
when books and newspapers are read in negro houses, many, inspired
by the example of their children, will be likely to undertake the labor
again.

It is proper to state that while the memory in colored children is
found to be, if any thing, livelier than in the white, it is quite probable

that further along, when the higher faculties of comparison and combination are more to be relied on, their progress may be less. While their quickness is apparent, one is struck with their want of discipline. The children have been regarded as belonging to the plantation rather than to a family, and the parents, who in their condition can never have but a feeble hold on their offspring, have not been instructed to training their children into thoughtful and orderly habits. It has, therefore, been found not an easy task to make them quiet and attentive at the schools.

Through the schools, habits of neatness have been encouraged. Children with soiled faces or soiled clothing, when known to have better, have been sent home from the schools, and have returned in better condition.

II

The grotesque figure of Nathaniel Gordon hanging from a scaffold in New York City, and the enthusiasm of Edward Pierce and his voluntary workers for their social experiment were aspects of a staggering problem. In March, President Lincoln sent a special message to Congress:[5]

March 6, 1862

FELLOW-CITIZENS OF THE SENATE, AND HOUSE OF REPRESENTATIVES,

I recommend the adoption of a Joint Resolution by your honorable bodies which shall be substantially as follows:

"Resolved that the United States ought to co-operate with any state which may adopt gradual abolishment of slavery, giving to such state pecuniary aid, to be used by such state in its discretion, to compensate for the inconveniences public and private, produced by such change of system."

If the proposition contained in the resolution does not meet the approval of Congress and the country, there is the end; but if it does command such approval, I deem it of importance that the states and people immediately interested, should be at once distinctly notified of the fact, so that they may begin to consider whether to accept or reject it. The federal government would find its highest interest in such a measure, as one of the most efficient means of self-preservation. The leaders of the existing insurrection entertain the hope that this government will ultimately be forced to acknowledge the independence of some part of the disaffected region, and that all the slave states

North of such part will then say "the Union, for which we have struggled, being already gone, we now choose to go with the Southern section." To deprive them of this hope, substantially ends the rebellion;
and the initiation of emancipation completely deprives them of it, as
to all the states initiating it. The point is not that *all* the states tolerat-
ing slavery would very soon, if at all, initiate emancipation; but that,
while the offer is equally made to all, the more Northern shall, by such
initiation, make it certain to the more Southern, that in no event, will
the former ever join the latter, in their proposed confederacy. I say
"initiation" because, in my judgment, gradual, and not sudden emancipation, is better for all. In the mere financial, or pecuniary view, any
member of Congress, with the census-tables and Treasury-reports before him, can readily see for himself how very soon the current ex-
penditures of this war would purchase, at fair valuation, all the slaves
in any named State. Such a proposition, on the part of the general
government, sets up no claim of a right, by federal authority, to interfere with slavery within state limits, referring, as it does, the absolute
control of the subject, in each case, to the state and its people, immediately interested. It is proposed as a matter of perfectly free choice
with them.

In the annual message last December, I thought fit to say "The Union
must be preserved; and hence all indispensable means must be employed." I said this, not hastily, but deliberately. War had been
made, and continues to be, an indispensable means to this end. A
practical re-acknowledgement of the national authority would render
the war unnecessary, and it would at once cease. If, however, resistance
continues, the war must also continue; and it is impossible to foresee
all the incidents, which may attend and all the ruin which may follow
it. Such as may seem indispensable, or may obviously promise great
efficiency towards ending the struggle, must and will come.

The proposition now made, though an offer only, I hope it may be
esteemed no offence to ask whether the pecuniary consideration tendered would not be of more value to the States and private persons
concerned, than are the institution, and property in it, in the present
aspect of affairs.

While it is true that the adoption of the proposed resolution would
be merely initiatory, and not within itself a practical measure, it is
recommended in the hope that it would soon lead to important practical
results. In full view of my great responsibility to my God, and to my

country, I earnestly beg the attention of Congress and the people to the subject.

Contemptuously, Jefferson Davis attacked the President's message:[6]

This proposition of President Lincoln was wholly unconstitutional, because it attempted to do what was expressly forbidden by the Constitution.* It proposed a contract between the State of Missouri and the Government of the United States which, in the language of the act, shall be "irrepealable without the consent of the United States." The words of the Constitution are as follows:

"No State shall enter into any treaty, alliance, or confederation, grant letters of marque and reprisal, coin money, etc."

This is a prohibition not only upon the power of one State to enter into a compact, alliance, confederation, or agreement with another State, but also with the Government of the United States.

Again, if the State of Missouri could enter into an irrepealable agreement or compact with the United States, that slavery should not therein exist after the acceptance on the part of Missouri of the act, then it would be an agreement on the part of that State to surrender its sovereignty and make the State unequal in its rights of sovereignty with the other States of the Union. The other States would have the complete right of sovereignty over their domestic institutions while the State of Missouri would cease to have such right. The whole system of the United States Government would be abrogated by such legislation. Again, it is a cardinal principle of the system that the people in their sovereign capacity may, from time to time, change and alter their organic law; and a provision incorporated in the Constitution of Missouri that slavery should never thereafter exist in that State could not prevent a future sovereign convention of its people from reëstablishing slavery within its limits.

* Lincoln had not invented this political doctrine. On the question of war with England and Mexico, in April 1842, ex-President John Quincy Adams told the House of Representatives: "Whether the war be civil, servile, or foreign, I lay this down as the law of nations: I say that the military authority takes for the time the place of all municipal institutions, slavery among the rest. Under that state of things, so far from its being true that the states where slavery exists have the exclusive management of the subject, not only the President of the United States, but the commander of the army has the power to order the universal emancipation of the slaves."

"As He died to make men holy, let us die to make men free"—so sang the North now. Among the many who believed that Lincoln should boldly attack slavery by advocating emancipation in the District of Columbia was Horace Greeley, editor of the New York Tribune. *The President would not be stampeded:*[7]

. . . Of course I am anxious to see the policy proposed in the late special message, go forward; but you have advocated it from the first, so that I need to say little to you on the subject. If I were to suggest anything it would be that as the North are already for the measure, we should urge it *persuasively,* and not *menacingly,* upon the South. I am a little uneasy about the abolishment of slavery in this District, not but I would be glad to see it abolished, but as to the time and manner of doing it. If some one or more of the border-states would move fast, I should greatly prefer it; but if this can not be in a reasonable time, I would like the bill to have the three main features—gradual—compensation—and vote of the people—I do not talk to members of congress on the subject, except when they ask me. . . .

Nor would Lincoln be trapped by a headstrong general. In May the President issued a special proclamation:

Whereas there appears in the public prints, what purports to be a proclamation, of Major General Hunter, in the words and figures following, to wit:

HEADQUARTERS DEPARTMENT OF THE SOUTH,
HILTON HEAD, S. C., May 9, 1862

GENERAL ORDERS No. 11.—The three States of Georgia, Florida and South Carolina, comprising the military department of the south, having deliberately declared themselves no longer under the protection of the United States of America, and having taken up arms against the said United States, it becomes a military necessity to declare them under martial law. This was accordingly done on the 25th day of April, 1862. Slavery and martial law in a free country are altogether incompatible; the persons in these three States—Georgia, Florida and South Carolina—heretofore held as slaves, are therefore declared forever free.

(Official) DAVID HUNTER,
Major General Commanding
ED. W. SMITH, *Acting Assistant Adjutant General*

And whereas the same is producing some excitement, and misunderstanding: therefore

I, Abraham Lincoln, president of the United States, proclaim and declare, that the government of the United States, had no knowledge, information, or belief, of an intention on the part of General Hunter to issue such a proclamation; nor has it yet, any authentic information that the document is genuine. And further, that neither General Hunter, nor any other commander, or person, has been authorized by the Government of the United States, to make proclamations declaring the slaves of any State free; and that the supposed proclamation, now in question, whether genuine or false, is altogether void, so far as respects such declaration.

I further make known that whether it be competent for me, as Commander-in-Chief of the Army and Navy, to declare the Slaves of any state or states, free, and whether at any time, in any case, it shall have become a necessity indispensable to the maintainance of the government, to exercise such supposed power, are questions which, under my responsibility, I reserve to myself, and which I can not feel justified in leaving to the decision of commanders in the field. These are totally different questions from those of police regulations in armies and camps.

Lincoln referred to his special message to Congress on March 6, 1862, and concluded with an eloquent passage:

The resolution, in the language above quoted, was adopted by large majorities in both branches of Congress, and now stands an authentic, definite, and solemn proposal of the nation to the States and people most immediately interested in the subject matter. To the people of those states I now earnestly appeal. I do not argue. I beseech you to make the arguments for yourselves. You can not if you would, be blind to the signs of the times. I beg of you a calm and enlarged consideration of them, ranging, if it may be, far above personal and partizan politics. This proposal makes common cause for a common object, casting no reproaches upon any. It acts not the pharisee. The change it contemplates would come gently as the dews of heaven, not rending or wrecking anything. Will you not embrace it? So much good has not been done, by one effort, in all past time, as, in the providence of God, it is now your high privilege to do. May the vast future not have to lament that you have neglected it.

III

In late June a delegation of Quakers called on the President to present a memorial asking him to proclaim emancipation of the slaves. Mr. Lincoln received the Friends in good humor, confessing (as the New York Tribune *reported) that next to "applicants for office" slavery was his "most troublesome subject." The President, continued the* Tribune, *agreed that slavery was wrong. He said:*[8]

. . . If a decree of emancipation could abolish Slavery, John Brown would have done the work effectually. Such a decree surely could not be more binding upon the South than the Constitution, and that cannot be enforced in that part of the country now. Would a proclamation of freedom be any more effective?

Mr. Johnson replied as follows:

"True, Mr. President, the Constitution cannot now be enforced at the South, but you do not on that account intermit the effort to enforce it, and the memorialists are solemnly convinced that the abolition of Slavery is indispensable to your success."

The President further said that he felt the magnitude of the task before him, and hoped to be rightly directed in the very trying circumstances by which he was surrounded.

Wm. Barnard addressed the President in a few words, expressing sympathy for him in all his embarrassments, and an earnest desire that he might, under divine guidance, be led to free the slaves and thus save the nation from destruction. In that case, nations yet unborn would rise up to call him blessed, and, better still, he would secure the blessing of God.

The President responded very impressively, saying that he was deeply sensible of his need of Divine assistance. He had sometime thought that perhaps he might be an instrument in God's hands of accomplishing a great work and he certainly was not unwilling to be. Perhaps, however, God's way of accomplishing the end which the memorialists have in view may be different from theirs. It would be his earnest endeavor, with a firm reliance upon the Divine arm, and seeking light from above, to do his duty in the place to which he had been called.

Thomas T. Eckert, Superintendent of Military Telegraph in the Department of the Potomac, saw Mr. Lincoln often that summer:[9]

The President came to the office every day and invariably sat at my desk while there. Upon his arrival early one morning in June, 1862, shortly after McClellan's Seven Days' Battles, he asked me for some paper, as he wanted to write something special. I procured some foolscap and handed it to him. He then sat down and began to write. I do not recall whether the sheets were loose or had been made into a pad. There must have been at least a quire. He would look out of the window a while and then put his pen to paper, but he did not write much at once. He would study between times and when he had made up his mind he would put down a line or two, and then sit quiet for a few minutes. After a time, he would resume his writing, only to stop again at intervals to make some remark to me or to one of the cipher operators as a fresh dispatch from the front was handed to him.

Once his eye was arrested by the sight of a large spiderweb stretched from the lintel of the portico to the side of the outer window sill. This spiderweb was an institution of the cipher room and harbored a large colony of exceptionally big ones. We frequently watched their antics, and Assistant Secretary Watson dubbed them "Major Eckert's lieutenants." Lincoln commented on the web, and I told him that my lieutenants would soon report and pay their respects to the President. Not long after a big spider appeared at the crossroads and tapped several times on the strands, whereupon five or six others came out from different directions. Then what seemed to be a great confab took place, after which they separated, each on a different strand of the web. Lincoln was much interested in the performance and thereafter, while working at the desk, would often watch for the appearance of his visitors.

On the first day, Lincoln did not cover one sheet of his special writing paper (nor indeed on any subsequent day). When ready to leave, he asked me to take charge of what he had written and not allow any one to see it. I told him I would do this with pleasure and would not read it myself. "Well," he said, "I should be glad to know that no one will see it, although there is no objection to your looking at it; but please keep it locked up until I call for it tomorrow." I said his wishes would be strictly complied with.

When he came to the office on the following day he asked for the papers, and I unlocked my desk and handed them to him and he again sat down to write. This he did nearly every day for several weeks, always handing me what he had written when ready to leave the office each day. Sometimes he would not write more than a line or two, and once I observed that he had put question marks on the margin of what he had written. He would read over each day all the matter he had previously written and revise it, studying carefully each sentence.

On one occasion, he took the papers away with him, but he brought them back a day or two later. I became much interested in the matter and was impressed with the idea that he was engaged upon something of great importance, but did not know what it was until he had finished the document and then for the first time he told me that he had been writing an order giving freedom to the slaves in the South, for the purpose of hastening the end of the war.

On a Sunday in July Lincoln rode with Welles, Seward, and Mrs. Frederick Seward to the funeral of Stanton's infant child. "It was on this occasion and on this ride," Welles recorded in his diary, "that he [Lincoln] first mentioned to Mr. Seward and myself the subject of emancipating the slaves by proclamation in case the rebels did not cease to persist in their war on the government and the Union, of which he saw no evidence." The President's attitude, Welles said, "was a new departure." What had changed him? To Welles the logical answer seemed to be "the reverses before Richmond and the formidable power and dimension of the insurrection." Soon afterward, Lincoln broached the subject of an emancipation proclamation at a Cabinet meeting. Months later, while sitting for a painting by Francis B. Carpenter, the President recalled that occasion:[10]

This Cabinet meeting took place, I think, upon a Saturday. All were present, excepting Mr. Blair, the Postmaster-General, who was absent at the opening of the discussion, but came in subsequently. I said to the Cabinet that I had resolved upon this step, and had not called them together to ask their advice, but to lay the subject-matter of a proclamation before them; suggestions as to which would be in order, after they had heard it read. . . . Various suggestions were offered. Secretary Chase wished the language stronger in reference to the arming of the blacks. Mr. Blair, after he came in, deprecated the policy, on the ground that it would cost the Administration the fall elections. Nothing, however, was offered that I had not already fully anticipated and settled in my own mind, until Secretary Seward spoke. He said in substance: "Mr. President, I approve of the proclamation, but I question the expedience of its issue at this juncture. The depression of the public mind, consequent upon our repeated reverses, is so great that I fear the effect of so important a step. It may be viewed as the last measure of an exhausted government, a cry for help; the government stretching forth its hands to Ethiopia, instead of Ethiopia stretching forth her hands to the government." His idea was that it would be considered our last *shriek*, on the retreat. (This was his precise expression.) "Now," continued Mr. Seward, "while I approve the measure, I suggest, sir, that you postpone its issue, until you can give it to the country supported by military success, instead of issuing it, as would be the case now, upon the greatest disasters of the war!" The wisdom of the view of the Secretary of State struck me with very great force. It was an aspect of the case that, in all my thought upon the subject, I had entirely overlooked. The result was that I put the draft of the proclamation aside, as you do your sketch for a picture, waiting for a victory.

On July 12 Mr. Lincoln invited to the White House representatives and senators from the border states, and read to them this address:[11]

GENTLEMEN. After the adjournment of Congress, now very near, I shall have no opportunity of seeing you for several months. Believing that you of the border-states hold more power for good than any other equal number of members, I feel it a duty which I can not justifiably waive, to make this appeal to you. I intend no reproach or complaint when I assure you that in my opinion, if you all had voted for the resolution in the gradual emancipation message of last March, the war would now be substantially ended. And the plan therein proposed is yet one of the most potent, and swift means of ending it. Let the states which are in rebellion see, definitely and certainly, that, in no event, will the states you represent ever join their proposed Confederacy, and they can not much longer maintain the contest. But you can not divest them of their hope to ultimately have you with them so long as you show a determination to perpetuate the institution within your own states. Beat them at elections, as you have overwhelmingly done, and, nothing daunted, they still claim you as their own. You and I know what the lever of their power is. Break that lever before their faces, and they can shake you no more forever.

Most of you have treated me with kindness and consideration; and I trust you will not now think I improperly touch what is exclusively your own, when, for the sake of the whole country I ask "Can you, for your states, do better than to take the course I urge?" Discarding *punctillio*, and maxims adapted to more manageable times, and looking only to the unprecedentedly stern facts of our case, can you do better in any possible event? You prefer that the constitutional relation of the states to the nation shall be practically restored, without disturbance of the institution; and if this were done, my whole duty, in this respect, under the constitution, and my oath of office, would be performed. But it is not done, and we are trying to accomplish it by war. The incidents of the war can not be avoided. If the war continue long, as it must, if the object be not sooner attained, the institution in your states will be extinguished by mere friction and abrasion—by the mere incidents of the war. It will be gone, and you will have nothing valuable in lieu of it. Much of its value is gone already. How much better for you, and for your people, to take the step which, at once, shortens the war, and secures substantial compensation for that which is sure to be wholly lost in any other event. How much better to thus save the money which else we sink forever in the war. How much better to do it while we can, lest the war ere long render us pecuniarily unable to do it. How much better for you, as seller, and the nation as buyer, to sell out, and buy out, that without which the war could never have been, than to sink both the thing to be sold, and the price of it, in cutting one another's throats.

I do not speak of emancipation *at once*, but of a *decision* at once to emancipate *gradually*. Room in South America for colonization can be obtained cheaply, and in abundance; and when numbers shall be large enough to be company and encouragement for one another, the freed people will not be so reluctant to go.

I am pressed with a difficulty not yet mentioned—one which threatens division among those who, united, are none too strong. An instance of it is known to you. Gen. Hunter is an honest man. He was, and I hope, still is, my friend. I valued him none the less for his agreeing with me in the general wish that all men everywhere, could be free. He proclaimed all men free within certain states, and I repudiated the proclamation. He expected more good, and less harm from the measure, than I could believe would follow. Yet in repudiating it, I gave dissatisfaction, if not offence, to many whose support the country can not afford to lose. And this is not the end of it. The pressure, in this direction, is still upon me, and is increasing. By conceding what I now ask, you can relieve me, and much more, can relieve the country, in this important point. Upon these considerations I have again begged your attention to the message of March last. Before leaving the Capital,

consider and discuss it among yourselves. You are patriots and statesmen; and, as such, I pray you, consider this proposition; and, at the
least, commend it to the consideration of your states and people. As
you would perpetuate popular government for the best people in the
world, I beseech you that you do in no wise omit this. Our common
country is in great peril, demanding the loftiest views, and boldest
action to bring it speedy relief. Once relieved, its form of government
is saved to the world; its beloved history, and cherished memories,
are vindicated; and its happy future fully assured, and rendered inconceivably grand. To you, more than to any others, the privilege is
given, to assure that happiness, and swell that grandeur, and to link
your own names therewith forever.

*To Jefferson Davis this action, like everything else Lincoln had done
and would do, was another part of a calculated and devious plot to destroy the Southern way of life:*[12]

The reply of the majority, consisting of twenty of the twenty-nine
Senators and Representatives, subsequently made to the President, is
worthy of notice. They said that they were not of the belief that funds
would be provided for the object, or that their constituents would reap
the fruits of the promise held out. . . .

This measure of emancipation with compensation soon proved a
failure. A proposition to appropriate five hundred thousand dollars to
the object was voted down in the United States Senate with great
unanimity. The Government was, step by step, "educating the people"
up to a proclamation of emancipation, so as to make entire abolition
one of the positive and declared issues of the contest.

The so-called pressure upon the President was not organized for a
final onset. The Governors of fifteen States united in a request that
three hundred thousand more men should be called out to fill up the
reduced ranks, and it was done. The anti-slavery press then entered
the arena. . . .

The education of the conservative portion of the Northern people
up to emancipation was becoming more complete every day, notwithstanding the professed reluctance of the President. Another call for
three hundred thousand men was made, but enlistments were slow, so
that threats of a draft and most liberal bounties were required. The
champions of emancipation sought to derive an advantage from this
circumstance. They asserted that the reluctance of the people to enter

the army was caused by the policy of the Government in not adopting bold emancipation measures. If such were adopted, the streets and by-ways would be crowded with volunteers to fight for the freedom of the "loyal blacks," and thrice three hundred thousand could be easily obtained. They said that slavery in the seceded States should be treated as a military question; it contributed nearly all the subsistence which supported the Southern men in arms, dug their trenches, and built their fortifications. The watchword which they now adopted was, "The abolition of slavery by the force of arms for the sake of the Union."

On August 20, in an editorial entitled "The Prayer of Twenty Millions," Greeley spoke for those Republicans who were pained and disappointed by the President's failure to abolish slavery. Two days later, in a letter to the editor, Lincoln declared:[13]

I would save the Union. I would save it the shortest way under the Constitution. The sooner the national authority can be restored; the nearer the Union will be "the Union as it was." If there be those who would not save the Union, unless they could at the same time *save* slavery, I do not agree with them. If there be those who would not save the Union unless they could at the same time *destroy* slavery, I do not agree with them. My paramount object in this struggle *is* to save the Union, and *not* either to save or to destroy slavery. If I could save the Union without freeing *any* slave I would do it, and if I could save it by freeing *all* the slaves I would do it; and if I could save it by freeing some and leaving others alone I would also do that. What I do about slavery, and the colored race, I do because I believe it helps to save the Union; and what I forbear, I forbear because I do *not* believe it would help to save the Union. I shall do *less* whenever I shall believe what I am doing hurts the cause, and I shall do *more* whenever I shall believe doing more will help the cause. I shall try to correct errors when shown to be errors; and I shall adopt new views so fast as they shall appear to be true views.

I have here stated my purpose according to my view of *official* duty; and I intend no modification of my oft-expressed *personal* wish that all men every where could be free.

IV

Slavery had shaken more than the political foundations of the nation; Christian religion in America had broken apart. Southern Baptists, Presbyterians, and Methodists, among the larger denominations, apparently worshiped a different god from that of their Northern brethren.

In Chicago's Bryan Hall, on September 7, Northern Christians of all denominations adopted a memorial urging emancipation. Six days later a delegation called at the White House. In responding to the group, Lincoln argued as though the draft of a preliminary proclamation were not locked in his desk:[14]

The subject presented in the memorial is one upon which I have thought much for weeks past, and I may even say for months. I am approached with the most opposite opinions and advice, and that by religious men, who are equally certain that they represent the Divine will. I am sure that either the one or the other class is mistaken in that belief, and perhaps in some respects both. I hope it will not be irreverent for me to say that if it is probable that God would reveal his will to others, on a point so connected with my duty, it might be supposed he would reveal it directly to me; for, unless I am more deceived in myself than I often am, it is my earnest desire to know the will of Providence in this matter. *And if I can learn what it is I will do it!* These are not, however, the days of miracles, and I suppose it will be granted that I am not to expect a direct revelation. I must study the plain physical facts of the case, ascertain what is possible and learn what appears to be wise and right. The subject is difficult, and good men do not agree. For instance, the other day four gentlemen of standing and intelligence (naming one or two of the number) from New York called, as a delegation, on business connected with the war; but, before leaving, two of them earnestly beset me to proclaim general emancipation, upon which the other two at once attacked them! You know, also that the last session of Congress had a decided majority of anti-slavery men, yet they could not unite on this policy. And the same is true of the religious people. Why, the rebel soldiers are praying with a great deal more earnestness, I fear, than our own troops, and expecting God to favor their side; for one of our soldiers, who had been taken prisoner, told Senator Wilson, a few days since, that he met with nothing so discouraging as the evident sincerity of those he was among in their prayers. But we will talk over the merits of the case.

What *good* would a proclamation of emancipation from me do, especially as we are now situated? I do not want to issue a document that the whole world will see must necessarily be inoperative, like the Pope's bull against the comet! Would *my word* free the slaves, when I cannot even enforce the Constitution in the rebel States? Is there a single court, or magistrate, or individual that would be influenced by it there? And what reason is there to think it would have any greater effect upon the slaves than the late law of Congress, which I approved, and which offers protection and freedom to the slaves of rebel masters who come within our lines? Yet I cannot learn that that law has caused a single slave to come over to us. And suppose they could be induced by a proclamation of freedom from me to throw themselves upon us, *what should we do with them?* How can we feed and care for such a multitude? General Butler wrote me a few days since that he was issuing more rations to the slaves who have rushed to him than to all the white troops under his command. They *eat,* and that is all, though it is true General Butler is feeding the whites also by the thousand; for it nearly amounts to a famine there. If, now, the pressure of the war should call off our forces from New Orleans to defend some other point, what is to prevent the masters from reducing the blacks to slavery again; for I am told that whenever the rebels take any black prisoners, free or slave, they immediately auction them off! They did so with those they took from a boat that was aground in the Tennessee river a few days ago. And then *I am very ungenerously attacked for it!* For instance, when, after the late battles at and near Bull Run, an expedition went out from Washington under a flag of truce to bury the dead and bring in the wounded, and the rebels seized the blacks who went along to help and sent them into slavery, Horace Greeley said in his paper that the Government would probably do nothing about it. What *could* I do? . . .

Now, then, tell me, if you please, what possible result of good would follow the issuing of such a proclamation as you desire? Understand, I raise no objections against it on legal or constitutional grounds; for, as commander-in-chief of the army and navy, in time of war, I suppose I have a right to take any measure which may best subdue the enemy. Nor do I urge objections of a moral nature, in view of possible consequences of insurrection and massacre at the South. I view the matter as a practical war measure, to be decided upon according to the advantages or disadvantages it may offer to the suppression of the rebellion.

As though summing up for a jury, Lincoln answered other arguments advanced by the delegates:[15]

I admit that slavery is the root of the rebellion, or at least its *sine qua non.* The ambition of politicians may have instigated them to act, but they would have been impotent without slavery as their instrument. I will also concede that emancipation would help us in Europe, and convince them that we are incited by something more than ambition. I grant further that it would help *somewhat* at the North, though not so much, I fear, as you and those you represent imagine. Still, some additional strength would be added in that way to the war. And then unquestionably it would weaken the rebels by drawing off their laborers, which is of great importance. But I am not so sure we could do much with the blacks. If we were to arm them, I fear that in a few weeks the arms would be in the hands of the rebels; and indeed thus far we have not had arms enough to equip our white troops. I will mention another thing, though it meet only your scorn and contempt: There are fifty thousand bayonets in the Union armies from the Border Slave States. It would be a serious matter if, in consequence of a proclamation such as you desire, they should go over to the rebels. I do not think they all would—not so many indeed as a year ago, or as six months ago—not so many to-day as yesterday. Every day increases their Union feeling. They are also getting their pride enlisted, and want to beat the rebels. Let me say one thing more: I think you should admit that we already have an important principle to rally and unite the people in the fact that constitutional government is at stake. This is a fundamental idea, going down about as deep as any thing.

Lincoln knew what he would do—in God's good time, with God's help. The war and the Negro—the slave as property or a forgotten son of God—for months Lincoln had lived with the problem, seeking a just and practical answer:[16]

Do not misunderstand me, because I have mentioned these objections. They indicate the difficulties that have thus far prevented my action in some such way as you desire. I have not decided against a proclamation of liberty to the slaves, but hold the matter under advisement. And I can assure you that the subject is on my mind, by day and night, more than any other. Whatever shall appear to be God's will I will do. I trust that, in the freedom with which I have canvassed your views, I have not in any respect injured your feelings.

At Antietam the Army of the Potomac gave Lincoln the victory for which he waited. Secretary Chase recorded the historic Cabinet meeting that followed five days later:

Monday, Sept. 22, 1862

To Department about nine. State Department messenger came, with notice to Heads of Departments to meet at 12. Received sundry callers. Went to White House.

All the members of the Cabinet were in attendance. There was some general talk; President mentioned that Artemus Ward had sent him his book. Proposed to read a chapter which he thought very funny. Read it, and seemed to enjoy it very much—the Heads also (except Stanton), of course. The chapter was *High-handed Outrage at Utica*.

The President then took a graver tone and said:

"Gentlemen: I have, as you are aware, thought a great deal about the relation of this war to Slavery: and you all remember that, several weeks ago, I read to you an Order I had prepared on this subject, which, on account of objections made by some of you, was not issued. Ever since then, my mind has been much occupied with this subject, and I have thought all along that the time for acting on it might very probably come. I think the time has come now. I wish it were a better time. I wish that we were in a better condition. The action of the army against the rebels has not been quite what I should have best liked. But they have been driven out of Maryland, and Pennsylvania is no longer in danger of invasion. When the rebel army was at Frederick, I determined, as soon as it should be driven out of Maryland, to issue a Proclamation of Emancipation such as I thought most likely to be useful. I said nothing to any one; but I made the promise to myself, and (hesitating a little)—to my Maker. The rebel army is now driven out, and I am going to fulfill that promise. I have got you together to hear what I have written down. I do not wish your advice about the main matter for that I have determined for myself. This I say without intending anything but respect for any one of you. But I already know the views of each on this question. They have been heretofore expressed, and I have considered them as thoroughly and carefully as I can. What I have written is that which my reflections have determined me to say. If there is anything in the expressions I use, or in any other minor matter, which any one of you thinks had best be changed, I shall be glad to receive the suggestions. One other observation I will make. I know very well that many others might, in this matter, as in others, do better than I can; and if I were satisfied that the public confidence was more fully possessed by any one of them than by me, and knew of any Constitutional way in which he could be put in my place, he should have it. I would gladly yield it to him.

But though I believe that I have not so much of the confidence of the people as I had some time since, I do not know that, all things considered, any other person has more; and, however this may be, there is no way in which I can have any other man put where I am. I am here. I must do the best I can, and bear the responsibility of taking the course which I feel I ought to take."

The President then proceeded to read his Emancipation Proclamation, making remarks on the several parts as he went on, and showing that he had fully considered the whole subject, in all the lights under which it had been presented to him.

After he had closed, Governor Seward said: "The general question having been decided, nothing can be said further about that. Would it not, however, make the Proclamation more clear and decided, to leave out all reference to the act being sustained during the incumbency of the present President; and not merely say that the Government 'recognizes,' but that it will maintain the freedom it proclaims?"

I followed, saying: "What you have said, Mr. President, fully satisfies me that you have given to every proposition which has been made a kind and candid consideration. And you have now expressed the conclusion to which you have arrived clearly and distinctly. This it was your right, and, under your oath of office, your duty to do. The Proclamation does not, indeed, mark out exactly the course I should myself prefer. But I am ready to take it just as it is written, and to stand by it with all my heart. I think, however, the suggestions of Governor Seward very judicious, and shall be glad to have them adopted."

The President then asked us severally our opinions as to the modifications proposed, saying that he did not care much about the phrases he had used. Everyone favored the modification and it was adopted. Governor Seward then proposed that in the passage relating to colonization, some language should be introduced to show that the colonization proposed was to be only with the consent of the colonists, and the consent of the States in which colonies might be attempted. This, too, was agreed to; and no other modification was proposed. Mr. Blair then said that the question having been decided, he would make no objection to issuing the Proclamation; but he would ask to have his paper, presented some days since against the policy, filed with the Proclamation. The President consented to this readily. And then Mr. Blair went on to say that he was afraid of the influence of the Proclamation on the Border States and on the army, and stated at some length the grounds of his apprehensions. He disclaimed most expressly, however, all objection to emancipation per se, saying he had always been personally in favor of it—always ready for immediate emancipation in the midst of slave states, rather than submit to the perpetuation of the system.

V

That same day Lincoln issued the first, or preliminary, Proclamation of Emancipation, warning those states or parts of states then in rebellion that if they did not return to their allegiance by January 1, 1863, he would issue a second proclamation declaring their slaves to be "forever free." And what did it mean? Jefferson Davis took one view:[17]

For what honest purpose were these declarations made? They could deceive no one who was familiar with the powers and duties of the Federal Government; they were uttered in the season of invasion of the Southern States, to coerce them to obedience to the agent established by the compact between the States, for the purpose of securing domestic tranquility and the blessings of liberty. The power to coerce States was not given, and the proposition to make that grant received no favor in the Convention which formed the Constitution; and it is seen by the proceedings in the States, when the Constitution was submitted to each of them for their ratification or rejection as they might choose, that a proposition which would have enabled the General Government, by force of arms, to control the will of a State, would have been fatal to any effort to make a more perfect Union. Such declarations as those cited from the diplomatic correspondence, though devoid of credibility at home, might avail in foreign countries to conceal from their governments the real purpose of the action of the majority. Meanwhile, the people of the Confederacy plainly saw that the ideas and interests of the Administration were to gain by war the empire that would enable it to trample on the Constitution which it professed to defend and maintain.

It was by the slow and barely visible approaches of the serpent seeking its prey that the aggressions and usurpations of the United States Government moved on to the crimes against the law of the Union, the usages of war among civilized nations, the dictates of humanity and the requirements of justice, which have been recited. The performance of this task has been painful, but persistent and widespread misrepresentation of the cause and conduct of the South required the exposure of her slanderer. To unmask the hypocrisy of claiming devotion to the Constitution, while violating its letter and spirit for a purpose palpably hostile to it, was needful for the defense of the South. In the future progress of this work it will be seen how often we have been charged with the very offenses committed by our enemy—offenses of which the South was entirely innocent, and of which a chivalrous people would be incapable. There was in this the old trick of the fugitive thief who cries "Stop thief!" as he runs.

In Washington jubilant crowds, reading the proclamation in the newspapers, took another view. They paraded to the White House, serenaded the President, and persuaded him to speak briefly:[18]

FELLOW-CITIZENS: I appear before you to do little more than acknowledge the courtesy you pay me, and to thank you for it. I have not been distinctly informed why it is this occasion you appear to do me this honor, though I suppose [interruptions] it is because of the proclamation. [Cries of "Good," and applause.] I was about to say, I suppose I understand it. [Laughter—Voices: "That you do," "You thoroughly understand it."] What I did, I did after very full deliberation, and under a very heavy and solemn sense of responsibility. [Cries of "Good," "Good," "Bless you," and applause.]

I can only trust in God I have made no mistake. [Cries "No mistake —all right; you've made no mistakes yet. Go ahead, you're right."] I shall make no attempt on this occasion to sustain what I have done or said by any comment. [Voices—"That's unnecessary; we understand it."] It is now for the country and the world to pass judgment on it, and, may be, take action upon it. I will say no more upon this subject. In my position I am environed with difficulties. [A voice—"That's so."]

Yet they are scarcely so great as the difficulties of those who, upon the battle field, are endeavoring to purchase with their blood and their lives the future happiness and prosperity of this country. [Applause, long and continued.] Let us never forget them. On the 14th and 17th days of the present month there have been battles bravely, skillfully and successfully fought. [Applause.] We do not yet know the particulars. Let us be sure that in giving praise to particular individuals, we do no injustice to others. I only ask you, at the conclusion of these few remarks, to give three hearty cheers to all good and brave officers and men who fought those successful battles.

The editors of Harper's Weekly *asked and answered a very important question:*[19]

And how will negro emancipation be viewed at the North? There was a time, not very long since, when a large majority of the Northern people would have opposed it strenuously—not so much from any admiration for slavery, as from a belief that, under the Constitution, we had no right to meddle with it, and that its abolition involved dangers and inconveniences perhaps as formidable as those which were created by its existence. Even at the present time a mortal antipathy for the negro is entertained by a large class of persons at the North—as is evidenced by the recent vote against negroes in Illinois, the riots in Cincinnati and Brooklyn, and the unkind treatment of the negro fugitives at Hilton Head by the regiments of General Hunter's army. At the same time, the war has produced a remarkable change in the opinions of educated and liberal men at the North. Such leading men as General Wallace of Illinois, Daniel S. Dickinson of New York, General Butler of Massachusetts, and nine-tenths of the generals in the field—who, a year ago, really believed that slavery was the true station for the negro—have lately freely expressed what used to be called "abolition views." How long it will take for these liberal views to permeate society, and stamp themselves on the mind of the working-class, remains to be seen. We do not, for our part, apprehend any serious opposition at the North to the President's policy, except in circles whose loyalty to the country may well be questioned.

Demagogues will of course endeavor to excite our working-classes against the Government by threatening them with the competition of free negro labor. It seems hardly worth while to reply to so shallow and so mean an argument as this. Our laboring class in this country is intelligent enough to know that what we want in every part of this country is not fewer but more laborers. For years we at the North have been moving heaven and earth to get more labor from Europe, and we have succeeded in getting a very large number of men every year; yet wages have steadily advanced instead of falling. Who ever thought of opposing immigration for fear of the competition of the new Irishmen or Germans? So at the South. They have increased their stock of labor steadily by every means, lawful and unlawful, for thirty years, and yet the price of slaves has steadily risen from $400 to $1500 for adult field hands, and the cry—before the war—was still for more labor. The man who tries to frighten the North with threats of competition by emancipated negroes insults the understanding of our laboring class.

CHAPTER 17

GRANT COMES ON

I N THE WEST, Grant remained a discredited general. Reporters now called his victory at Donelson sheer luck and missed no chance to harp upon his disgraceful blundering at Shiloh. In early July after McClellan's failure on the Peninsula, Lincoln called Halleck to Washington as General in Chief. Grant, sent to Memphis to command the District of West Tennessee, was not taken seriously. He found his army scattered along railroads or performing garrison duties.

The movements that set Grant on the road to ultimate glory began in late July 1862. The Confederate Army of the Mississippi, now under the command of Braxton Bragg, was on the prowl toward Chattanooga and Buell's Union forces. Some fifteen thousand Rebels under Sterling Price remained to watch Grant while an equal Rebel force under Earl Van Dorn held the line of the Mississippi. As July ended, Grant started after Price, determined to drive him south. Halleck chose this time to play a muddleheaded game of war, detaching divisions from the District of West Tennessee. Within a month Grant's strength had been reduced from sixty-four thousand to forty-six thousand men. Meanwhile Bragg ordered Van Dorn to advance and co-operate with Price against Grant.

I

On September 12, 1862, Grant's forces were distributed as follows: seventeen thousand men under the hard-swearing William Starke Rosecrans were at Corinth, Rienzi, Jacinto and Danville; another ten thousand under Edward O. C. Ord were at Jackson and Bolivar; Sherman commanded seven thousand at Memphis. Six thousand troops

under Isaac F. Quinby near Columbus and six thousand under Ste-
phen A. Hurlbut near Brownsville constituted Grant's reserve.

By Grant's estimate, Van Dorn was about a four-day march to the
south; and Grant's "desire," to use his own word, was to attack Price
before Van Dorn could reach Corinth or go to Price's relief:[1]

General Rosecrans had previously had his headquarters at Iuka, where his command was spread out along the Memphis and Charleston railroad eastward. While there he had a most excellent map prepared showing all the roads and streams in the surrounding country. He was also personally familiar with the ground, so that I deferred very much to him in my plans for the approach. We had cars enough to transport all of General Ord's command, which was to go by rail to Burnsville, a point on the road about seven miles west of Iuka. From there his troops were to march by the north side of the railroad and attack Price from the north-west, while Rosecrans was to move east-ward from his position south of Corinth by way of the Jacinto road. A small force was to hold the Jacinto road where it turns to the northeast, while the main force moved on the Fulton road which comes into Iuka further east. This plan was suggested by Rosecrans.

Bear Creek, a few miles to the east of the Fulton road, is a formida-ble obstacle to the movement of troops in the absence of bridges, all of which, in September, 1862, had been destroyed in that vicinity. The Tennessee, to the north-east, not many miles away, was also a formidable obstacle for an army followed by a pursuing force. Ord was on the north-west, and even if a rebel movement had been pos-sible in that direction it could have brought only temporary relief, for it would have carried Price's army to the rear of the National forces and isolated it from all support. It looked to me that, if Price would remain in Iuka until we could get there, his annihilation was inevitable.

On the morning of the 18th of September General Ord moved by rail to Burnsville, and there left the cars and moved out to perform his part of the programme. He was to get as near the enemy as pos-sible during the day and intrench himself so as to hold his position until the next morning. Rosecrans was to be up by the morning of the 19th on the two roads before described, and the attack was to be from all three quarters simultaneously. Troops enough were left at Jacinto and Rienzi to detain any cavalry that Van Dorn might send out to make a sudden dash into Corinth until I could be notified. There was a telegraph wire along the railroad, so there would be no delay in communication. I detained cars and locomotives enough at Burnsville to transport the whole of Ord's command at once, and if Van Dorn had moved against Corinth instead of Iuka I could have thrown in reinforcements to the number of 7,000 or 8,000 before he could have arrived.

I remained at Burnsville with a detachment of about 900 men from Ord's command and communicated with my two wings by courier. Ord met the advance of the enemy soon after leaving Burnsville. Quite a sharp engagement ensued, but he drove the rebels back with considerable loss, including one general officer killed. He maintained his position and was ready to attack by daylight the next morning. I was very much disappointed at receiving a dispatch from Rosecrans after midnight from Jacinto, twenty-two miles from Iuka, saying that some of his command had been delayed, and that the rear of his column was not yet up as far as Jacinto. He said, however, that he would still be at Iuka by two o'clock the next day. I did not believe this possible because of the distance and the condition of the roads, which was bad; besides, troops after a forced march of twenty miles are not in a good condition for fighting the moment they get through. It might do in marching to relieve a beleaguered garrison, but not to make an assault. I immediately sent Ord a copy of Rosecrans' dispatch and ordered him to be in readiness to attack the moment he heard the sound of guns to the south or south-east. He was instructed to notify his officers to be on the alert for any indications of battle. During the 19th the wind blew in the wrong direction to transmit sound either towards the point where Ord was, or to Burnsville where I had remained.

Betrayed by the elements, Grant waited for reinforcements well past the appointed hour:[2]

A couple of hours before dark on the 19th Rosecrans arrived with the head of his column at Barnets [Barnett's Corners], the point where the Jacinto road to Iuka leaves the road going east. He here turned north without sending any troops to the Fulton road. While still moving in column up the Jacinto road he met a force of the enemy and had his advance badly beaten and driven back upon the main road. In this short engagement his loss was considerable for the number engaged, and one battery was taken from him.

The wind was still blowing hard and in the wrong direction to transmit sound towards either Ord or me. Neither he nor I nor any one in
either command heard a gun that was fired upon the battle-field. After
the engagement Rosecrans sent me a dispatch announcing the result.
This was brought by a courier. There was no road between Burnsville
and the position then occupied by Rosecrans and the country was impassable for a man on horseback. The courier bearing the message
was compelled to move west nearly to Jacinto before he found a road
leading to Burnsville. This made it a late hour of the night before I
learned of the battle that had taken place during the afternoon. I at
once notified Ord of the fact and ordered him to attack early in the
morning.

The next morning Rosecrans himself renewed the attack and went
into Iuka with but little resistance. Ord also went in according to orders, without hearing a gun from the south of town but supposing
the troops coming from the south-west must be up by that time.
Rosecrans, however, had put no troops upon the Fulton road, and the
enemy had taken advantage of this neglect and retreated by that road
during the night. Word was soon brought to me that our troops were
in Iuka. I immediately rode into town and found that the enemy was
not being pursued even by the cavalry. I ordered pursuit by the whole
of Rosecrans' command and went on with him a few miles in person.
He followed only a few miles after I left him and then went into camp,
and the pursuit was continued no further. I was disappointed at the
result of the battle of Iuka—but I had so high an opinion of General
Rosecrans that I found no fault at the time.

*Cautiously, Grant withdrew his advanced position to Bolivar on the
Mississippi Central Railroad. At first Van Dorn appeared to be endeavoring to strike above Memphis, then revealed his "deeper design"
—to attack Corinth in great force. Skirmishing outside Corinth on October 3 placed the Confederates in the northwest angle of two railroads—between Grant's troops at Corinth and his reserves. Faced
with this situation, Grant acted:*[3]

On the night of the 3d, accordingly, I ordered General McPherson,
who was at Jackson, to join Rosecrans at Corinth with reinforcements
picked up along the line of the railroad equal to a brigade. Hurlbut
had been ordered from Bolivar to march for the same destination; and
as Van Dorn was coming upon Corinth from the north-west some of

his men fell in with the advance of Hurlbut's and some skirmishing ensued on the evening of the 3d. On the 4th Van Dorn made a dashing attack, hoping, no doubt, to capture Rosecrans before his reinforcements could come up. In that case the enemy himself could have occupied the defences of Corinth and held at bay all the Union troops that arrived. In fact he could have taken the offensive against the reinforcements with three or four times their number and still left a sufficient garrison in the works about Corinth to hold them. He came near success, some of his troops penetrating the National lines at least once, but the works that were built after Halleck's departure enabled Rosecrans to hold his position until the troops of both McPherson and Hurlbut approached towards the rebel front and rear. The enemy was finally driven back with great slaughter: all their charges, made with great gallantry, were repulsed.

The loss on our side was heavy, but nothing to compare with Van Dorn's. McPherson came up with the train of cars bearing his command as close to the enemy as was prudent, debarked on the rebel flank and got in to the support of Rosecrans just after the repulse. His approach, as well as that of Hurlbut, was known to the enemy and had a moral effect. General Rosecrans, however, failed to follow up the victory, although I had given specific orders in advance of the battle for him to pursue the moment the enemy was repelled. He did not do so, and I repeated the order after the battle. In the first order he was notified that the force of 4,000 men which was going to his assistance would be in great peril if the enemy was not pursued.

Ord, joining Hurlbut on the fourth of October, took command as senior officer. To Grant's satisfaction, they caught the head of Van Dorn's retreating column as it crossed the Hatchie, about ten miles out of Corinth:[4]

. . . The bottom land here was swampy and bad for the operations of troops, making a good place to get an enemy into. Ord attacked the troops that had crossed the bridge and drove them back in a panic. Many were killed, and others were drowned by being pushed off the bridge in their hurried retreat. Ord followed and met the main force. He was too weak in numbers to assault, but he held the bridge and compelled the enemy to resume his retreat by another bridge higher up the stream. Ord was wounded in this engagement and the command devolved on Hurlbut.

Rosecrans did not start in pursuit till the morning of the 5th and then took the wrong road. Moving in the enemy's country he travelled with a wagon train to carry his provisions and munitions of war. His march was therefore slower than that of the enemy, who was moving towards his supplies. Two or three hours of pursuit on the day of battle, without anything except what the men carried on their persons, would have been worth more than any pursuit commenced the next day could have possibly been. Even when he did start, if Rosecrans had followed the route taken by the enemy, he would have come upon Van Dorn in a swamp with a stream in front and Ord holding the only bridge; but he took the road leading north and towards Chewalla instead of west, and, after having marched as far as the enemy had moved to get to the Hatchie, he was as far from battle as when he started. Hurlbut had not the numbers to meet any such force as Van Dorn's if they had been in any mood for fighting, and he might have been in great peril.

I now regarded the time to accomplish anything by pursuit as past and, after Rosecrans reached Jonesboro, I ordered him to return. He kept on to Ripley, however, and was persistent in wanting to go farther. I thereupon ordered him to halt and submitted the matter to the general-in-chief, who allowed me to exercise my judgment in the matter, but inquired "why not pursue?" Upon this I ordered Rosecrans back. Had he gone much farther he would have met a greater force than Van Dorn had at Corinth and behind intrenchments or on chosen ground, and the probabilities are he would have lost his army.

The battle of Corinth was bloody, our loss being 315 killed, 1,812 wounded and 232 missing. The enemy lost many more. Rosecrans reported 1,423 dead and 2,225 prisoners. We fought behind breastworks, which accounts in some degree for the disparity.

II

Van Dorn had lost over nine thousand men, and the battle, Grant believed, had been a "crushing blow to the enemy, and felt by him much more than it was appreciated in the North." Once more Grant had gained self-confidence.

The men who would bring ultimate victory to the North were beginning, slowly but irresistibly, to emerge in the West. Philip Henry Sheridan, a stump of an Irishman whose head sat so far forward of his ears that it was difficult for him to wear a hat, impressed the reporter for the Cincinnati Commercial as more than dynamic—"He was electric." Impulsive and hotheaded, the cut of Sheridan had been revealed one day at West Point when he fancied a cadet sergeant had given him an order in an offensive tone. Sheridan made for him with a bayonet before his "better judgment" prevailed.

Sheridan had won a reputation as an Indian fighter in the Far West when news of the Civil War brought him scampering east. His first action at Booneville, Missouri, disclosed an aggressive leader who fought Confederates as though they were redskins along the Rogue River—indecision could cost a man his scalp in either quarter. Grant and Sheridan met for the first time at Corinth when the campaign in Kentucky was drawing off divisions that Grant desperately needed. Sheridan wanted to go to Kentucky. Grant confessed that he felt "a little nettled" at Sheridan's desire to get away but did not detain him. Sheridan realized that Grant was "much hurt" at the inconsiderate way in which his command was being depleted; but Kentucky offered the better opportunity and Sheridan was as much on the make as any general.

Sheridan described the situation that he encountered on reaching Kentucky:[5]

During the interval from September 25 till October 1 there was among the officers much criticism of General Buell's management of the recent campaign, which had resulted in his retirement to Louisville; and he was particularly censured by many for not offering battle to General Bragg while the two armies were marching parallel to each other, and so near that an engagement could have been brought on at any one of several points—notably so at Glasgow, Kentucky, if there had been a desire to join issue. It was asserted, and by many conceded, that General Buell had a sufficient force to risk a fight. He was much blamed for the loss of Mumfordsville also. The capture of this point, with its garrison, gave Bragg an advantage in the race toward the Ohio River, which odds would most likely have ensured the fall of Louisville had they been used with the same energy and skill that the Confederate commander displayed from Chattanooga to Glasgow; but something always diverted General Bragg at the supreme moment, and he failed to utilize the chances falling to him at this time, for, deflecting his march to the north toward Bardstown, he left open to Buell the direct road to Louisville by way of Elizabethtown.

At Bardstown Bragg's army was halted while he endeavored to establish a Confederate government in Kentucky by arranging for the

installation of a provisional governor at Lexington. Bragg had been
assured that the presence of a Confederate army in Kentucky would so
encourage the secession element that the whole State could be forced
into the rebellion and his army thereby largely increased; but he had
been considerably misled, for he now found that though much latent
sympathy existed for his cause, yet as far as giving active aid was
concerned, the enthusiasm exhibited by the secessionists of Kentucky
in the first year of the war was now replaced by apathy, or at best by
lukewarmness. So the time thus spent in political machinations was
wholly lost to Bragg; and so little reinforcement was added to his army
that it may be said that the recruits gained were not enough to supply
the deficiencies resulting from the recent toilsome marches of the campaign.

*Reaching Louisville, Buell ordered an advance on October 1. Sheridan's
division, a part of the Third Corps commanded by C. C. Gilbert, expected a fight at Bardstown. Bragg, however, had retreated toward
Perryville with his eye on Louisville, which he hoped to attack as soon
as his "political projects were perfected." Sheridan had another idea:*[6]

Much time was consumed by Buell's army in its march on Perryville, but we finally neared it on the evening of October 7. During the
day, Brigadier-General Robert B. Mitchell's division of Gilbert's corps
was in the advance on the Springfield pike, but as the enemy developed
that he was in strong force on the opposite side of a small stream called
Doctor's Creek, a tributary of Chaplin River, my division was brought
up and passed to the front. It was very difficult to obtain water in this
section of Kentucky, as a drought had prevailed for many weeks, and
the troops were suffering so for water that it became absolutely necessary that we should gain possession of Doctor's Creek in order to relieve their distress. Consequently General Gilbert, during the night, directed me to push beyond Doctor's Creek early the next morning.

At daylight on the 8th I moved out Colonel Dan McCook's brigade
and Barnett's battery for the purpose, but after we had crossed the
creek with some slight skirmishing, I found that we could not hold the
ground unless we carried and occupied a range of hills, called Chaplin
Heights, in front of Chaplin River. As this would project my command
in the direction of Perryville considerably beyond the troops that were
on either flank, I brought up Laiboldt's brigade and Hescock's battery
to strengthen Colonel McCook. Putting both brigades into line we

quickly carried the Heights, much to the surprise of the enemy, I think, for he did not hold on to the valuable ground as strongly as he should have done. This success not only ensured us a good supply of water, but also, later in the day, had an important bearing in the battle of Perryville.

CENTRAL KENTUCKY, 1862

From *Atlas of American History*

After taking the Heights, I brought up the rest of my division and intrenched, without much difficulty, by throwing up a strong line of rifle-pits, although the enemy's sharpshooters annoyed us enough to make me order Laiboldt's brigade to drive them in on the main body. This was successfully done in a few minutes, but in pushing them back to Chaplin River, we discovered the Confederates forming a line of battle on the opposite bank, with the apparent purpose of an attack in force, so I withdrew the brigade to our intrenchments on the crest and there awaited the assault.

Gilbert kept signaling Sheridan not to bring on an engagement. Sheridan replied that he wasn't seeking an engagement but that the enemy evidently intended to bring one on. He was right:[7]

. . . Soon after returning to the crest and getting snugly fixed in the rifle-pits, my attention was called to our left, the high ground we occupied affording me in that direction an unobstructed view. I then saw General A. McD. McCook's corps—the First—advancing toward Chaplin River by the Mackville road, apparently unconscious that the Confederates were present in force behind the stream. I tried by the use of signal flags to get information of the situation to these troops, but my efforts failed, and the leading regiments seemed to approach the river indifferently prepared to meet the sudden attack that speedily followed, delivered as it was from the chosen position of the enemy. The fury of the Confederate assault soon halted this advance force, and in a short time threw it into confusion, pushed it back a considerable distance, and ultimately inflicted upon it such loss of men and guns as to seriously cripple McCook's corps, and prevent for the whole day further offensive movement on his part, though he stoutly resisted the enemy's assaults until 4 o'clock in the afternoon.

Seeing McCook so fiercely attacked, in order to aid him I advanced Hescock's battery, supported by six regiments, to a very good position in front of a belt of timber on my extreme left, where an enfilading fire could be opened on that portion of the enemy attacking the right of the First Corps, and also on his batteries across Chaplin River. But at this juncture he placed two batteries on my right and began to mass troops behind them, and General Gilbert, fearing that my intrenched position on the heights might be carried, directed me to withdraw Hescock and his supports and return them to the pits. My recall was opportune, for I had no sooner got back to my original line than the Confederates attacked me furiously, advancing almost to my intrenchments, notwithstanding that a large part of the ground over which they had to move was swept by a heavy fire of canister from both my batteries. Before they had quite reached us, however, our telling fire made them recoil, and as they fell back, I directed an advance of my whole division, bringing up my reserve regiments to occupy the crest of the hills; Colonel William P. Carlin's brigade of Mitchell's division meanwhile moving forward on my right to cover that flank. This advance pressed the enemy to Perryville, but he retired in such good order that we gained nothing but some favorable ground that enabled me to establish my batteries in positions where they could again turn their attention to the Confederates in front of McCook, whose critical condition was shortly after relieved, however, by a united pressure of Gilbert's corps against the flank of McCook's assailants, compelling them to retire behind Chaplin River.

The battle virtually ended about 4 o'clock in the afternoon, though more or less desultory firing continued until dark. Considering the severity of the engagement on McCook's front, and the reverses that had befallen him, I question if, from that part of the line, much could have been done toward retrieving the blunders of the day, but it did seem to me that, had the commander of the army been able to be present on the field, he could have taken advantage of Bragg's final repulse, and there would have remained in our hands more than the barren field. But no attempt was made to do anything more till next morning, and then we secured little except the enemy's killed and most severely wounded.

III

At Perryville the Union's effectives numbered 36,940 with 845 killed, 2,851 wounded and 515 missing; Confederate effectives numbered 16,-000 with 510 killed, 2,635 wounded and 251 missing. The battle by itself need not have depressed the South; but added to the defeat at Antietam and Grant's triumph at Corinth—the one driving Lee back into Virginia and the other opening the road to Vicksburg and complete control of the Mississippi—Bragg's subsequent retreat, sounding the end to an invasion of Kentucky, became doubly galling.

Plantation owner from South Carolina and farm boy from Iowa died side by side at Perryville; but that was only the military fact. Five hundred miles across the mountains in North Carolina a different set of circumstances prevailed. Zebulon B. Vance, soon to become governor of North Carolina, made an impassioned plea:[8]

The articles most needed, and which the State finds it most difficult to supply, are shoes, socks and blankets, though drawers, shirts, and pants would be gladly received. If every farmer who has hides tanning would agree to spare one pair of shoes, and if every mother in North-Carolina (knit) one strong pair of either thick cotton (or woolen) socks for the army, they would be abundantly supplied. A great lot of blankets also might yet be spared from private use, and thousands could be made from the carpets upon our parlor-floors. With good warm houses and cotton bed-clothing, we can certainly get through the winter much better than the soldiers can, with all the blankets we can give them.

The colonels of militia regiments throughout the State are hereby appointed agents for the purchase and collection of all such articles as can be spared by our people, who, through their respective captains, are ordered immediately to canvass every county and visit every citizen in their beats for this purpose. A liberal price will be paid for every thing where the owner feels that he or she is not able to donate it, and active agents will immediately forward them to our suffering regiments.

Expenses will be allowed the officers engaged in this duty, and transportation furnished the colonels or their agents to bring the articles to Raleigh.

And now, my countrymen and women, if you have any thing to spare for the soldier, in his name I appeal to you for it. Do not let the speculator have it, though he offer you enormous prices; spurn him from your door, and say to him that our brave defenders have need for it, and shall have it without passing through his greedy fingers. Do not place yourselves among the extortioners—they are the vilest and most cowardly of all our country's enemies; and when this war is ended, and people come to view the matter in its proper light, you will find that the most detested tories are more respected than they. When they tempt you with higher prices than the State offers, just think for a moment of the soldier, and what he is doing for you. Remember, when you sit down by the bright and glowing fire, that the soldier is sitting upon the cold earth; that in the wind which is whistling so fearfully over your roof, only making you feel the more comfortable because it harms you not, he is shivering in darkness on the dangerous outpost, or shuddering through the dreary hours of his watch. Remember that when you come forth in the morning well fed and warmly clad, leading your families toward the spot where the blessed music of the Sabbath bells tells you of the peaceful worship of the God of peace, the soldier is going forth at the same moment, perhaps, half fed, after a night of shivering and suffering, to where the roar of artillery and shout of battle announce that he is to die that your peace and safety may be preserved. Oh! remember these things, generous and patriotic people of North-Carolina, and give freely of your perishable goods to those who are giving all that mortal man can give for your safety and your rights.

From across the seas came heartening news for the South. Since early April, Charles Francis Adams had been protesting the building of a Rebel raider in Liverpool. The dockyard designation of No. 290 was changed subsequently to the Enrica, suggesting that the ship was being constructed for a Spanish firm, but the Spanish Legation denied that. By September 1 information reaching Benjamin Moran left no doubt of the game of guile the British had played:[9]

The British pirate vessel built and manned at Liverpool is now at its vile work on the ocean. A man by the name of Redden who went out in her has returned and tells the following story. It appears she made a trial trip in Liverpool bay with a number of rebels, male and female, on board, and then went down to Point Lynas. There she remained cruising about for a few days, and received additions to her crew from a L'pool tug boat. On the Sunday night following her departure from Birkenhead she ran down as far as Bardsey island, and . . . proceeded to the north of Ireland. She landed the pirate Bulloch * and the pilot off the entrance to Londonderry harbor, and at once struck boldly out to sea, being under British colors. . . . The vessel arrived in about ten days . . . at Terceira in the Bay of Angra in the Western Islands. Here she was met by a British bark from London from which she received six 32-pounder broadside guns and two 98-pounder swivels, one being rifled. And she also got 600 tons of coal, together with a supply of shot, shell, rifles and powder. The pirate Semmes † was awaiting her arrival, and the Englishman Butcher ‡ who took her out from Liverpool relinquished his command to the rebel. . . . In a few days the Bahama, a sister ship to the Bermuda, arrived from L'pool with the pirate Bulloch and some fifty English sailors and four more 32's. She also had two chests of gold to pay for the prizes the "290" might destroy . . . Semmes openly took command, the British flag was hauled down, and the rebel banner run up, the band playing Dixie's Land all the time. All hands were called aft, Semmes told them the ship was the Confederate vessel of war Alabama . . . said a good deal about the injuries of his country, talked about having had to steal out of Liverpool like a thief, and avowed his determination "to sink, burn & destroy" all American vessels he might fall in with. He offered prize money. About 40 men, among them Redden, refused to go. . . . To all intents and purposes she is a pirate, built, manned, armed and fitted out from England. But this Gov't quibbles out of responsibility. Posterity will decide the character of this proceeding and fix the guilt where it belongs. . . .

Earl Russell's "confessed negligence," young Henry Adams declared, had permitted the Alabama *to escape. In the bright summer of Con-*

---

* James Dunwoody Bulloch, a distinguished Georgian who was sent to England at the outbreak of the war to direct naval operations in Europe for the Confederacy; his half sister was the mother of Theodore Roosevelt.

† Raphael Semmes, who had served in the U. S. Navy since 1832; he joined the Confederacy immediately after his adopted state of Alabama seceded.

‡ Captain Mathew J. Butcher, whom Bulloch engaged to find a crew and take the *Alabama* to her rendezvous.

federate victory on the Peninsula and at Second Manassas, followed by news of Lee's invasion of Maryland, even Adams did not much blame Russell—or Palmerston—for expecting to hear next of the fall of Washington or Baltimore. But this disaster had not happened. Young Adams, grappling with the eccentricity of the British mentality and the idiosyncrasies of British diplomacy, came up completely baffled:[10]

By that time, October 3, news of Antietam and of Lee's retreat into Virginia had reached London. The Emancipation Proclamation arrived. Had the private secretary known all that Granville or Palmerston knew, he would surely have thought the danger past, at least for a time, and any man of common sense would have told him to stop worrying over phantoms. This healthy lesson would have been worth much for practical education, but it was quite upset by the sudden rush of a new actor upon the stage with a rhapsody that made Russell seem sane, and all education superfluous.

This new actor, as every one knows, was William Ewart Gladstone, then Chancellor of the Exchequer. If, in the domain of the world's politics, one point was fixed, one value ascertained, one element serious, it was the British Exchequer; and if one man lived who could be certainly counted as sane by overwhelming interest, it was the man who had in charge the finances of England. If education had the smallest value, it should have shown its force in Gladstone, who was educated beyond all record of English training. From him, if from no one else, the poor student could safely learn.

Here is what he learned! Palmerston notified Gladstone, September 24, of the proposed intervention: "If I am not mistaken, you would be inclined to approve such a course." Gladstone replied the next day: "He was glad to learn what the Prime Minister had told him; and for two reasons especially he desired that the proceedings should be prompt: the first was the rapid progress of the Southern arms and the extension of the area of Southern feeling; the second was the risk of violent impatience in the cotton-towns of Lancashire such as would prejudice the dignity and disinterestedness of the proffered mediation."

Had the puzzled student seen this letter, he must have concluded from it that the best educated statesman England ever produced did not know what he was talking about, an assumption which all the world would think quite inadmissible from a private secretary—but this was a trifle. Gladstone having thus arranged with Palmerston and Russell, for intervention in the American war, reflected on the subject for a fortnight from September 25 to October 7, when he was to speak on the occasion of a great dinner at Newcastle. He decided to announce the Government's policy with all the force his personal and official authority could give it. This decision was no sudden impulse; it was the result of deep reflection pursued to the last moment. On the morning of October 7, he entered in his diary: "Reflected further on what I should say about Lancashire and America, for both these subjects are critical." That evening at dinner, as the mature fruit of his long study, he deliberately pronounced the famous phrase:—

". . . We know quite well that the people of the Northern States have not yet drunk of the cup—they are still trying to hold it far from their lips—which all the rest of the world see they nevertheless must drink of. We may have our own opinions about slavery; we may be for or against the South; but there is no doubt that Jefferson Davis and other leaders of the South have made an army; they are making, it appears, a navy; and they have made, what is more than either, they have made a nation. . . ."

IV

Bitingly, Adams accused Gladstone. "No one knew so well as he that he and his own officials and friends at Liverpool were alone 'making' a rebel navy, and that Jefferson Davis had next to nothing to do with it." More than ever, Lincoln had needed Grant's success at Corinth and the victory at Perryville that had forced Bragg from Kentucky. With good reason the President had gone to Sharpsburg to urge McClellan to hasten his pursuit of Lee; again, Lincoln might have spared himself the effort.

In Tennessee, Grant busied himself for a movement toward Vicksburg, unmindful that Lincoln had told John A. McClernand, his friend in Springfield, that he could conduct a similar campaign. Stanton and Lincoln had cooked up for McClernand instructions that authorized him "to proceed to the States of Indiana, Illinois, and Iowa, and to organize the troops remaining in those states and to be raised by volunteering or draft," whereupon they were to be forwarded "with all dispatch" to "Memphis, Cairo, or such other points as may be designated by the General-in-Chief" and "when a sufficient force, not required by the operations of General Grant's command shall be raised, an expedition may be organized under General McClernand's command against Vicksburg and to clear the Mississippi River and open navigation to New Orleans."

These absurd orders were prudently marked "confidential." Grant, pushing forward his own forces for a campaign against Vicksburg, remembered crossly:[11]

. . . I was very much disturbed by newspaper rumors that General McClernand was to have a separate and independent command within mine, to operate against Vicksburg by way of the Mississippi River. Two commanders on the same field are always one too many, and in this case I did not think the general selected had either the experience or qualifications to fit him for so important a position. I feared for the safety of the new troops intrusted to him, especially as he was to raise new levies, raw troops, to execute so important a trust. But on the 12th [of November] I received a dispatch from General Halleck saying that I had command of all the troops sent to my department and authorizing me to fight the enemy where I pleased. The next day my cavalry was in Holly Springs . . .

Grant clearly was unnerved, and at Holly Springs issued an order that, in the judgment of the New York Times, *must be described as "one of the deepest sensations of the war":*[12]

The Jews, as a class violating every regulation of trade established by the Treasury Department and also department orders, are hereby expelled from the department within twenty-four hours from the receipt of this order.

Post commanders will see that all of this class of people be furnished passes and required to leave, and anyone returning after such notification will be arrested and held in confinement until an opportunity occurs of sending them out as prisoners, unless furnished with permit from headquarters.

No passes will be given these people to visit headquarters for the purpose of making personal application for trade permits.

Grant had stepped into a wasp's nest. In Memphis cotton dropped overnight to fifteen cents a pound. Newspapers blazed with angry editorials; in a dozen cities protest meetings were held; telegrams asked Lincoln to intervene. His only motivation for the "Jew order," Grant insisted, was a wish to free his army from the merchants, speculators and peddlers who were trading with the soldiers at exorbitant profits; but the reporter Sylvanus Cadwallader, in reminiscences written many years afterward, supplied another motivation for Grant's action:[13]

. . . He was surprised by a sudden visit from his father then living at Covington or Newport, Kentucky. The General was glad to see him; showed him every possible attention; and enjoyed his society for a day or two without unpleasant interruption. But several Cincinnati gentlemen of Hebrew persuasion soon appeared, and notably a Mr. Mack of the wealthy firm of Mack Brothers, and posed as the personal friends of "Uncle Jesse." These the General also treated handsomely for his father's sake until he learned the real object of their visit to be to obtain special permits and privileges to buy and ship cotton. It seems that playing upon "Uncle Jesse's" cupidity, these men had entered into a partnership with him for that purpose, they agreeing to furnish all the capital needed, and he to obtain the trade permits from his son, Gen. Grant. The impudence of these mercenaries was of course surprising, but the most astonishing feature of the whole transaction was that the father could have been so ignorant concerning his own son. The General's anger was bitter and malignant towards these men, and greatly intensified the mortification he felt at their having entrapped his old father into such an unworthy undertaking. The first train north bore them swiftly homeward, accompanied by "Uncle Jesse" with a stupendous flea in his ear. This was his last visit to the army. The order expelling all "Jews" from the department was issued immediately.

Ultimately Lincoln rescinded the order. In a tactful letter, Halleck told Grant: "The President has no objection to your expelling traitors and Jew peddlers, which I suppose was the object of your order; but, as it in terms proscribed an entire religious class, some of whom are fighting in our ranks, the President deemed it necessary to revoke it."

Meanwhile Grant had other worries—McClernand, principally, whose recruits were now pouring into Memphis. Grant had moved on to Oxford, Mississippi, whence on December 8 he wrote a remarkable letter to Sherman:[14]

You will proceed, with as little delay as possible, to Memphis, Tennessee, taking with you one division of your present command. On your arrival at Memphis you will assume command of all the troops there, and that portion of General Curtis's forces at present east of the Mississippi River, and organize them into brigades and divisions in your own army. As soon as possible move with them down the river to the vicinity of Vicksburg, and with the co-operation of the gunboat fleet under command of Flag-officer Porter proceed to the reduction of that place in such manner as circumstances, and your own judgment, may dictate.

In effect, Grant was telling Sherman to run off with another general's army. A gifted modern historian, Lloyd Lewis, explains how Sherman didn't need a second hint:[15]

Immediately Sherman returned to Memphis and began what he later described as "preparations hasty in the extreme." Grant in after years admitted that he had organized so hurried an attack to forestall McClernand:

"I feared that delay might bring McClernand who was his [Sherman's] senior. . . . I doubted McClernand's fitness; and I had good reason to believe that in forestalling him I was by no means giving offense to those whose authority to command was above both him and me."

Who those higher-ups might be, Grant never explained. In all likelihood he was not candid with Sherman in describing his new move as a "surprise attack." Grant was too good a militarist not to know how impossible it was for a flotilla bearing 40,000 men to steam down the river for days without its progress being described in many telegrams to Vicksburg and Pemberton.

In reality the only principal in the whole drama who could be surprised was McClernand, who was happily recruiting in the fields of war, politics, and marriage. At fifty-one years of age, he celebrated his approaching conquest of Vicksburg by marrying a lady whom Ellen Sherman later described in some scorn as his sister-in-law. On December 12 McClernand asked the War Department to send him to the front. He had his men transported to Memphis. He was ready. Silence hung on the wires. Knowing well the wiles of politicians and suspecting the cunning of Halleck, on the seventeenth McClernand telegraphed both Stanton and Lincoln, "I believe I am to be superseded." Stanton replied soothingly that McClernand was to command the expedition under the supervision of the departmental commander. This was not exactly what Lincoln had authorized in his private instructions—"a sufficient force, not required by the operation of General Grant's command." But McClernand's situation was worse than even Stanton's telegram had indicated. On December 18 Halleck telegraphed Grant:

"It is the wish of the President that General McClernand's corps shall constitute a part of the river expedition and that he shall have the immediate command under your directions." But Halleck did not send this word to McClernand until the twenty-second, and even so, did not send with it necessary orders directing the impatient man to quit his official recruiting station at Springfield, Illinois. It took McClernand another twenty-four hours to secure this.

At last on December 23 he entrained with his bride, the bridal party, and an accompanying rain of old shoes. On the twenty-sixth they steamed south from Cairo, and soon docked at Memphis, where the ladies thought to see the bridegroom take command of his legions. His men were gone! The whole expedition was gone! It had sailed off without him! Sherman had started with it on the nineteenth!

McClernand could never prove a conspiracy against him. Grant, he discovered, had tried to telegraph him on the eighteenth the information just received from Halleck, but Confederate cavalrymen had cut the wires and the message had not come through. However, such a telegram would have come too late to be of any use, with Sherman stealing out of Memphis on the nineteenth. McClernand believed that the guilt lay primarily in Washington. No Confederate cavalrymen had snipped wires between the capital and Springfield. The responsibility for his disappointment, he told Stanton, lay either with Halleck "or a strange occurrence of accidents." Sadly he left Memphis on December 30 and steamed after Sherman, his bride and her party still accompanying him.

Sherman had departed in such eagerness as to forget to take along necessary portions of pontoon bridges—a rare, almost unique instance in the career of a military leader whose memory and foresight were remarkable. His desire for secrecy on the trip had been unusually keen, even for him. He had commanded that his officers should seize "any unauthorized passenger and conscript him" into the military service for the unexpired term of the regiment that captured him. Not only had he excluded newspaper correspondents but he had also threatened to shoot Colonel A. H. Markland, regional superintendent for the United States Army mails, when that official had insisted upon joining the expedition. At length Sherman had relented and carried Markland with him as his guest on the Forest Queen. Markland's trustworthiness was soon apparent and Sherman made him a friend for life.

CHAPTER 18

A GRIM WINTER

IF LINCOLN COULD not escape a large share of the responsibility for the fiasco that found McClernand scurrying down the Mississippi after his "stolen" army, this blunder was far from the sum of the President's military mistakes. Butler in New Orleans and McClellan in Virginia were other problems pressing for immediate solution, and in both cases Lincoln guessed wrong. A crisp autumn that had brought to the North triumphs at Antietam, Corinth and Perryville ended abruptly; all at once the sparkling sunlight faded and winter winds chilled bone and heart.

I

It was not alone Butler's highhanded administration that led Lincoln to change his general in New Orleans, but rather the fact that in June Butler had failed to lend reasonable support to what, in theory, had been a combined land and naval assault on Vicksburg. Farragut's ships, passing Vicksburg's high, gun-laden bluffs, had proved that the Mississippi River provided a highway for future operations; but Butler, in sitting out the first dance, had convinced Stanton and Halleck as well as Lincoln that something better than a military wallflower was needed for the movements now developing in this theater of the war.

Why Lincoln selected Nathaniel P. Banks, former governor of Massachusetts, as Butler's successor is difficult to gauge. Banks in civilian life had worked his way up from a machinist to president of the Illinois Central; in politics, his agility had made him in turn a Democrat, a Know-Nothing and a Republican; and thus far in the war his record in the Shenandoah Valley and at Cedar Mountain had evoked no raptures among informed observers.

Before leaving for the Gulf, Banks sent the War Department a requisition for supplies. Stanton, probably among the first to enjoy the nickname of "Nothing Positive" that the Army attached to Banks, sent the requisition to Lincoln. The President could not conceal his irritation:[1]

EXECUTIVE MANSION,
WASHINGTON, Nov. 22, 1862

MY DEAR GENERAL BANKS:

Early last week you left me in high hope with your assurance that you would be off with your expedition at the end of that week, or early in this. It is now the end of this, and I have just been overwhelmed and confounded with the sight of a requisition made by you, which, I am assured, cannot be filled, and got off within an hour short of two months! I inclose you a copy of the requisition, in some hope that it is not genuine—that you have never seen it.

My dear General, this expanding, and piling up of *impedimenta*, has been, so far, almost our ruin, and will be our final ruin if it is not abandoned. If you had the articles of this requisition upon the wharf, with the necessary animals to make them of any use, and forage for the animals, you could not get vessels together in two weeks to carry the whole, to say nothing of your twenty thousand men; and, having the vessels, you could not put the cargoes aboard in two weeks more. And, after all, where you are going, you have no use for them. When you parted with me, you had no such idea in your mind. I know you had not, or you could not have expected to be off so soon as you said. You must get back to something like the plan you had then, or your expedition is a failure before you start. You must be off before Congress meets. You would be better off anywhere, and especially where you are going, for not having a thousand wagons, doing nothing but hauling forage to feed the animals that draw them, and taking at least two thousand men to care for the wagons and animals, who otherwise might be two thousand good soldiers.

Now dear General, do not think this is an ill-natured letter—it is the very reverse. The simple publication of this requisition would ruin you. Very truly your friend

A. LINCOLN

A telegram from Lincoln to McClellan late in October revealed how near the President had come to the limit of his patience with another general:

"I have just read your despatch about sore-tongued and fatigued horses. Will you pardon me for asking what the horses of your army have done since the Battle of Antietam that fatigues anything?"

The explanation McClellan offered didn't satisfy Lincoln, who on November 7 replaced him in command with Ambrose E. Burnside. Aside from the whiskers that made him famous, Burnside had other claims to distinction—as a successful gun manufacturer and railroad executive before the war, as the general who had captured Roanoke Island, as a creditable corps commander at South Mountain and Antietam. But Burnside insisted that he was not truly fitted to lead the Army of the Potomac, which gave him distinction also as a prophet.

In late November the President journeyed to Aquia Creek to present his own plan for beating Lee. Burnside and his generals did not agree, and Lincoln hurried a letter to his general in chief:[2]

STEAMER BALTIMORE
OFF ACQUIA CREEK, VA.
Nov. 27, 1862

MAJOR GENERAL HALLECK
SIR:

I have just had a long conference with Gen. Burnside. He believes that Gen. Lee's whole army, or nearly the whole of it is in front of him, at and near Fredericksburg. Gen. B. says he could take into battle now any day, about, one hundred and ten thousand men, that his army is in good spirit, good condition, good morale, and that in all respects he is satisfied with officers and men; that he does not want more men with him, because he could not handle them to advantage; that he thinks he can cross the river in face of the enemy and drive him away, but that, to use his own expression, it is somewhat risky. I wish the case to stand more favorable than this in two respects. First, I wish his crossing of the river to be nearly free from risk; and secondly, I wish the enemy to be prevented from falling back, accumulating strength as he goes, into his intrenchments at Richmond. I therefore propose that Gen. B. shall not move immediately; that we accumulate a force on the south bank of the Rappahannock—at, say, Port Royal, under protection of one or two gun-boats, as nearly up to twenty-five thousand strong as we can. At the same time another force of about the same strength as high up the Pamunkey, as can be protected by gunboats. These being ready, let all three forces move simultaneously, Gen. B.'s force in its attempt to cross the river, the Rappahannock force moving directly up the south side of the river to his assistance, and ready, if found admissible, to deflect off to the turnpike bridge over the Mattapony in the direction of Richmond. The Pamunkey force to move as rapidly as possible up the north side of the Pamunkey, holding all the bridges and especially the turnpike bridge immediately north of Hanover C.H.; hurry north, and seize and hold the Mattapony bridge before mentioned, and also, if possible, press higher up the streams and destroy the railroad bridges. Then, if Gen. B. succeeds in driving the enemy from Fredericksburg, he the enemy no longer has the road to Richmond, but we have it and can march into the city. Or, possibly, having forced the enemy from his line, we could move upon, and destroy his army. Gen. B.'s main army would have the same line of supply and retreat as he now provided; the Rappahannock force would have that river for supply, and gun-boats to fall back upon; and the Pamunkey force would have that river for supply, and a line between the two rivers—Pamunkey & Mattapony—along which to fall back upon its gun-boats. I think the plan promises the best results, with the least hazard, of any now conceivable.

Note—The above plan, proposed by me, was rejected by Gen. Halleck & Gen. Burnside, on the ground that we could not raise and put in position, the Pamunkey force without too much waste of time.

A. L.

On December 1, in his annual message to Congress, the President proposed three amendments to the Constitution: (1) to provide compensation to every state abolishing slavery before the year 1900; (2) to compensate loyal masters whose slaves had been freed by the exigencies of war; (3) to authorize Congress to appropriate money for colonizing free Negroes with their own consent. Boldly Lincoln faced the emotions that threatened any legislation to abolish slavery:[3]

The emancipation will be unsatisfactory to the advocates of perpetual slavery; but the length of time should greatly mitigate their dissatisfaction. The time spares both races from the evils of sudden derangement —in fact, from the necessity of any derangement—while most of those whose habitual course of thought will be disturbed by the measure will have passed away before its consummation. They will never see it. Another class will hail the prospect of emancipation, but will deprecate the length of time. They will feel that it gives too little to the now living slaves. But it really gives them much. It saves them from the vagrant destitution which must largely attend immediate emancipation in localities where their numbers are very great; and it gives the inspiring assurance that their posterity shall be free forever. The plan leaves to each state, choosing to act under it, to abolish slavery now, or at the end of the century, or at any intermediate time, or by degrees, extending over the whole or any part of the period; and it obliges no two states to proceed alike. It also provides for compensation, and generally the mode of making it. This, it would seem, must further mitigate the dissatisfaction of those who favor perpetual slavery, and especially of those who are to receive the compensation. Doubtless some of those who are to pay, and not to receive will object. Yet the measure is both just and economical. In a certain sense the liberation of slaves is the destruction of property—property acquired by descent, or by purchase, the same as any other property. It is no less true for having been often said, that the people of the South are not more responsible for the original introduction of this property, than are the people of the North; and when it is remembered how unhesitatingly we all use cotton and sugar, and share the profits of dealing in them, it may not be quite safe to say, that the South has been more responsible than the North for its continuance. If then, for a common object, this property is to be sacrificed is it not just that it be done at a common charge?

And if, with less money, or money more easily paid, we can preserve the benefits of the Union by this means, than we can by the war alone, is it not also economical to do it? Let us consider it then. Let us ascertain the sum we have expended in the war since compensated emancipation was proposed last March, and consider whether, if that measure had been promptly accepted, by even some of the slave states, the same sum would not have done more to close the war, than has been otherwise done. If so the measure would save money, and, in that view, would be a prudent and economical measure. Certainly it is not so easy to pay *something* as it is to pay *nothing;* but it is easier to pay a *large* sum than it is to pay a larger one. And it is easier to pay any sum *when* we are able, than it is to pay it *before* we are able. The war requires large sums, and requires them at once. The aggregate sum necessary for compensated emancipation, of course, would be large. But it would require no ready cash; nor the bonds even, any faster than the emancipation progresses. This might not, and probably would not, close before the end of the thirty-seven years. At that time we shall probably have a hundred millions of people to share the burden, instead of thirty-one millions, as now. And not only so, but the increase of our population may be expected to continue for a long time after that period, as rapidly as before; because our territory will not have become full. I do not state this inconsiderately. At the same ratio of increase which we have maintained, on an average, from our first national census, in 1790, until that of 1860, we should, in 1900, have a population of 103,208,415.*. . .

Lincoln came to the conclusion of his message. In his military judgments he had sometimes blundered; perhaps he would continue to blunder. But he knew, and could describe with rarely equaled eloquence, why the war must be fought:

Fellow-citizens, *we* cannot escape history. We of this Congress and this administration, will be remembered in spite of ourselves. No personal significance, or insignificance, can spare one or another of us. The fiery trial through which we pass, will light us down, in honor or dishonor, to the latest generation. We *say* we are for the Union. The world will not forget that we say this. We know how to save the Union. The world knows we do know how to save it. We—even *we here*—hold the power, and bear the responsibility. In *giving* freedom to the *slave*, we *assure* freedom to the *free*—honorable alike in what we give, and what we preserve. We shall nobly save, or meanly lose, the last, best hope of earth. Other means may succeed; this could not fail. The way is plain, peaceful, generous, just—a way which, if followed, the world will forever applaud, and God must forever bless.

II

In Virginia, as snow fell and cold winds blew during the first week of December, the Army of the Potomac began to move. At Aquia Creek a reporter for the Cincinnati Commercial *boarded a train to Fredericksburg:*[4]

. . . The country from the Potomac to the Rappahannock presented the usual features of Virginia scenery. Tall chimneys standing, monuments of departed peace, in the midst of wastes that had been farms. Not a cow, or chicken, or pig, or any living or movable thing that had been the property of the inhabitants. One nest of squalid children staring from a forlorn-looking cabin. A few dead horses and mules beside

* Census figures in 1900 gave the nation's population as 75,994,575; in 1920 it reached 105,710,620.

the roads. Six mule army wagons, with blaspheming drivers, whooping, lashing, and cursing their way through the mire, which is red as if it had all been soaked in blood. Long processions of cavalry winding their way like caravans, through the Virginian Sahara. The dismantled huts of deserted encampments, the camp-fires still smoking, showing that the troops were just put in motion. The tents and wigwams of the guards along the road, looking, in the chill wind that came down the ravines through hills spattered with snow, dismally uncomfortable. The bridge over Potomac Creek (the little Potomac) is a precarious thing in appearance, the track simply propped up on trestle-work of round logs, some seventy feet; and as the trains creep over the abyss, the impressions of the spectator are not, in the aggregate, comfortable. . . .

In the hills and along the quiet valleys surrounding old Fredericksburg, George Washington had played as a boy; the Commercial *man—"a stranger in a strange land and in a strange army"—could see the picket-fires of the Rebels across the Rappahannock River. The vast Army of the Potomac—"as difficult to learn as a great city"—which he had expected to find scattered along twenty miles of the river was "coiled up, within a space of six or seven miles." The day was Wednesday, December 10; the time, night—the eve of battle:*[5]

The men in our camps knew the task that was before them. There are certain indications that the old soldier well knows mean movements and battle. The orders issued had not told the men in so many words that they were going to fight without delay, but they knew it. They were in good spirits, too. The army of the Potomac never felt better than when, on the evening of Wednesday of last week, the men cooked their three days' rations and took the sixty rounds of cartridges. The smell of frying bacon and roasting coffee filled the air, and the men were jolly about their fires, full of the confidence, as I heard many of them express it, that "we'll whip them this time, sure."

I happened to inquire of the general, whose uninvited guest I had found myself, whether he knew the location of a certain regiment, whose colonel was one of my old personal friends. It was as surprising as agreeable to learn that he knew the colonel very well, and that his regiment was camped not more than a quarter of a mile distant. An orderly was despatched to conduct me to the colonel, and I surprised him in his tent, writing a few lines giving direction as to the disposition of his effects if he should be killed in the impending conflict. His duties for the day were over—every thing was in order for next day—the rations cooked, the cartridges distributed. . . .

The colonel was kind enough to invite me to attend a meeting of some [of] the officers of his brigade, who were to celebrate the arrival of the commissions of several good young fellows, who had been promoted for distinguished gallantry. . . . The company consisted of twenty or thirty young officers, four of them colonels. It assembled in a hut which an enterprising captain had erected for winter quarters, and it was really an excellent habitation. It was near twenty feet long and fifteen feet wide, with walls of pine logs, chinked and daubed six feet high, and roofed with tents, tacked upon sturdy rafters. They all felt that it was the night before battle, and in all probability the last of some of them on earth. . . . Whisky-punch was freely circulated but the conviviality did not become drunkenly uproarious. The punch seemed to cheer but not to inebriate. Many patriotic songs were sung with a fervor and melody most affecting and beautiful. I will never forget one, "The Hills of Old New-England," (the officers were, without exception, New-Englanders,) or "E Pluribus Unum," those not singing, shouting "Never, never," at the words of the song that the nation would fall if the banner of stars were trailed in the dust. There was a solemn, touching charm about the singing of a song, the leading words of which were: "Unfurl the glorious banner.". . . Another song, which I should not omit to name, was one which is a favorite in the army: "McClellan is our leader, so march along." This was given with great gusto, followed by a toast, "The health of Little Mac," and that received with "three times three." About one half of the officers thus engaged were wounded in the battles on the Peninsula and in Maryland. Three of the colonels had been wounded, one of them having been struck, during the various engagements of the war, eight times. . . .

Filled with the emotional strain of an impending battle, the reporter could not sleep that night:

. . . For hours I listened to the heavy rumble and deep metallic jar of the artillery trains moving forward, and the quick clatter of the horses' feet, bearing aids here and there. Once an officer came to the tent and told the colonel the precise hour at which his regiment was to move. Long before it was light, our bugles called the men from their slumbers, in notes as cheery and full of sweetness as if they summoned none to rise to march to bloody graves. The bugle-notes had hardly died away on the hills when the camps were astir and the hum of a vast busy multitude could be heard on every side.

An hour before daylight, or rather before the smoke-fog lifted so that the objects were visible distinctly a few rods distant, two heavy guns were heard in the direction of Fredericksburgh. They probably were signals that operations were commenced. For some time no other artillery-firing was heard, but there was an occasional snapping of musketry. The tents were struck, the knapsacks packed, the regimental property put in condition for removal, and breakfast was eaten. Day was fairly dawning when there was a rapid discharge of guns from our batteries, and the dull twang of exploding shells, and the deep roll of the echoes along the valley of the Rappahannock, came up to us a thunderous reveille.

The troops, taking up their haversacks, canteens, and cartridge-boxes, and muskets, fell in promptly at the call of the bugle, and the lean old regiments moved away, the men silent and tramping forward with sturdy ease. Not a cheer, not a word was heard. It was business, not a frolic, as the veterans well knew, that was meant by the deepening roar of the guns below. The column had moved about half a mile, when the heads of three other columns appeared, and a whole division was speedily massed in an open wood, perhaps half a mile back from the crest of the hill, on the north side of Fredericksburgh, and awaited orders.

The firing of artillery was, about eight o'clock, less rapid than an hour previous, and all sorts of stories came up from the front. The truth was, little could be seen of the action except by those engaged in it, and many of them could not see much. All that was visible of Fredericksburgh for some time, were two church spires, piercing the fog. At ten o'clock the enemy's sharp-shooters, having made a serious resistance to the laying of the bridges of pontoons, firing murderously out of houses, particularly from cellar-windows, to barricade which they used paving-stones, fire was opened upon the town from our whole line of batteries, one hundred and seventy guns playing. . . . It was difficult to mark the distinct reports. I attempted to count the guns by the watch for a minute, but could not be sure that I counted all, as there were at times volleys, so that you could not tell whether half a dozen or a dozen had been fired in the space of a second. The noise was prodigious. The thunder of the guns, the crack of the shells and the undercurrent of echoes shivering in incessant waves against the hillsides, made up an appalling concert. It seemed as if there was a vast flight of malignant

monsters, the surly whir of whose invisible and awful wings convulsed
all the air.

III

*Succinctly, Robert E. Lee reported to Richmond the situation he faced
that eleventh of December:*[6]

The plain on which Fredericksburgh stands is so completely commanded by the hills of Stafford, in possession of the enemy, that no effectual opposition could be offered to the construction of the bridges or
the passage of the river, without exposing our troops to the destructive
fire of his numerous batteries. Positions were, therefore, selected to oppose his advance after crossing. The narrowness of the Rappahannock,
its winding course and deep bed, afforded opportunity for the construction of bridges beyond the reach of our artillery, and the banks had to
be watched by skirmishers. The latter, sheltering themselves behind
the houses, drove back the working parties of the enemy at the bridges
opposite the city; but at the lowest point of crossing, where no shelter
could be had, our sharpshooters were themselves driven off, and the
completion of the bridge was effected about noon on the eleventh.

In the afternoon of that day the enemy's batteries opened upon the
city, and by dark had so demolished the houses on the river-bank as to
deprive our skirmishers of shelter—and, under the cover of his guns,
he effected a lodgment in the town.

*Volunteers of the Seventh Michigan finished laying the pontoons—"in
the glorious style," recorded the Cincinnati* Commercial *reporter, "that
becomes good boys from the West." The dash into town, in which he
joined, was "gallantly made":*[7]

Several houses were fired by our bombs, but for hours they burned
slowly, as they were nearly all composed of brick. Just before sundown
the fire in the town burned more briskly. The enemy opened a few batteries upon our men in the town and on the banks adjacent, throwing
shells at the troops whom they could see pressing on to the pontoons.
Our batteries, right and left, replied, and there was what Beauregard
calls an "artillery duel." The scene as the sun went down certainly had
the elements of sublimity. The horizon was hazy as on a day of Indian
summer. The sun, sinking in a sky of royal purple, looked like a big
drop of arterial blood. The quick rush of the smoke from our batteries

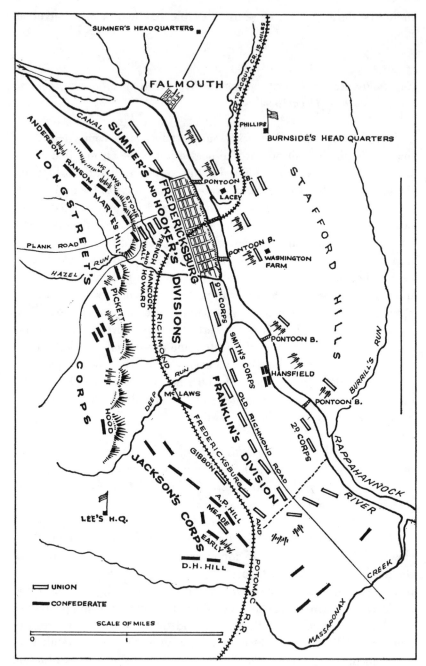

THE BATTLE OF FREDERICKSBURG

From Lossing, *Pictorial History of the Civil War*

on the hills, along a semi-circle miles in extent, was plainly visible, half a dozen fountains of sulphurous vapor playing horizontally.

The vehement vibration of the bombs in their flight could be felt in the air. The enemy's batteries responded, puffing curious masses of the prevailing powder-fog; and the sound of their guns throbbed in the hills, making them tremulous beneath our feet. As the shells burst in mid air, they formed little smoke-balloons, that quickly expanded and faded as they grew. As the air darkened, the red flashes of the guns gave a new effect—the roar of each report being preceded by a fierce dart of flame, and the explosion of each shell was announced by a gush of fire on the clouds, like a Mars of the first magnitude, created and extinguished in an instant. And, towering between us and the western sky, which was still showing its faded scarlet lining, was the huge sombre pillar of grimy smoke that marked the burning of Fredericksburgh. Ascending to a vast height, it bore away northward, shaped like a plume bowed in the wind.

The altogether different nature of events on December 12 gave rise to many speculations:[8]

On Friday morning those of us not fully posted, and not conversant with all the mysteries of "strategy," expected a battle. But the morning passed quietly, the smoke veiling all distant objects from observation. Our troops were crossing into Fredericksburgh. Some adventurers were straggling back bearing boxes of tobacco, which was as eagerly sought by our men as if it had been gold, or something more precious even than fine gold. I suppose it does rank in the army as one of the chief necessaries of life. The Town, in the afternoon, literally swarmed with troops. The enemy's batteries were ominously silent. If the rebel general had any particular objections to the presence of our troops in the town, why did he not open upon them from his batteries? What was to prevent the enemy from shelling the town, as we had done? I asked several military gentlemen the question, for the situation appeared to me to be one of the deepest peril. One said: "The enemy have not ammunition to spare." Another: "Oh! a bombardment don't amount to any thing any how." Another: "They don't care about bombing us, it is an inconsequential sort of business. We threw four thousand shells yesterday, and it amounted to nothing." Another: "They're afraid of our siege-guns this side." Another: "General Lee thinks he will have a big thing on us about the bombardment of this town. He proposes to rouse the indignation of the civilized world, as they call it. You'll see he won't throw a shell into it. He is playing for the sympathies of Europe." Another thought the enemy were skedaddling, and spoke of the laugh that would be raised at Burnside's expense in that case. But I think a private soldier came nearer the mark than any one else. He said, with the usual expletives: "They want us to get in. Getting out won't be quite so smart and easy. You'll see if it will."

On Saturday morning, December 13, the correspondent for the Richmond Enquirer awakened to the roar of Burnside's artillery and hastened to the front:[9]

Nothing but pale clouds of smoke struggling up through the undergrowth and forests on the right indicates the presence of our forces.

Now the fog has lifted, revealing the dark and heavy columns of the enemy moving down the opposite bank of the river. Far down, near the lower part of the valley, they are seen debouching. Whole fields are gleaming with bayonets. They continue to pour out upon the plain in a stream which seems to come from an inexhaustible fountain. The meadows are black with them, tens of thousands in solid columns. We can only vaguely conjecture at this distance the number. Old soldiers think there are sixty thousand. . . .

Readers of the Cincinnati Commercial approached the battle from the Union's side:[10]

. . . We had understood that the attack was to be made at daylight, and to consist of a movement by Franklin's grand division on our left. Franklin had thrown three bridges across the river, and passed it in force, three or four miles below (east of) Fredericksburgh. He was to turn the enemy's right. The attack in the centre, as it was called, or from Fredericksburgh, was to consist, first, of an advance upon the flanks to feel the enemy, and if they were found strong there, for a dash to be made, in heavy force, from the eastern portion of the town, or the left of our centre. Gen. Burns's division was deployed further to the left, to support Franklin's right. The main column of attack on the centre, was formed of Couch's corps.

Immediately at Fredericksburgh the Rappahannock valley proper is narrow. The ground rises on either side in terraces, or as we would say out West, in successive "bottoms." There are three terraces or steps before the crest is reached, these on the southern side being from a quarter to half a mile wide. The first is that upon which the town is situated, and has a steep slope to the river. The second formed the principal battle-ground. The third swells into the crest, so diligently and efficiently fortified by the enemy. The conformation of the ground on the north side of the river, is very like that on the south, but the steps are narrower. There are a number of little crooked valleys on this side convenient for hiding troops from shells, and many ravines so deep and rugged, that they resemble fissures caused by an earthquake.

Below Fredericksburgh about three miles, the hills press close to the river, from the north, and on the south there is a wide open plain wholly without the incumbrance of fences, grain, woods or bushes. This plain is fringed at the distance of a mile and a half or two miles from the river, by a continuous wood, which commences with the rise of the ground and thickens toward the crest of the ridge. In this wood, Saturday morning last, was Stonewall Jackson. In the plain was General Franklin, who had crossed the river at the point where it is approached by hills, on the north side, on the most advanced one of which was planted a battery of siege-guns to protect the bridges, and, if need be, shelter a retreat.

No one could accuse Lee of overstatement as he reported the events of the day:[11]

As soon as the advance of the enemy was discovered through the fog, Gen. Stuart, with his accustomed promptness, moved up a section of his horse-artillery, which opened with effect upon his flank, and drew upon the gallant Pelham a heavy fire, which he sustained unflinchingly for about two hours. In the mean time the enemy was fiercely encountered by General A. P. Hill's division, forming Gen. Jackson's right, and, after an obstinate combat, repulsed. During this attack, which was protracted and hotly contested, two of Gen. Hill's brigades were driven back upon our second line.

Gen. Early, with part of his division, being ordered to his support, drove the enemy back from the point of woods he had seized, and pursued him into the plain until arrested by his artillery. The right of the enemy's column extending beyond Hill's front, encountered the right of Gen. Hood, of Longstreet's corps. The enemy took possession of a small copse in front of Hood, but were quickly dispossessed and repulsed with loss.

During the attack on our right the enemy was crossing troops over the bridges at Fredericksburg, and massing them in front of Longstreet's line. Soon after his repulse on our right, he commenced a series of attacks on our left, with a view of obtaining possession of the heights immediately overlooking the town. These repeated attacks were repulsed in gallant style . . .

With Lee was a correspondent for the London Times, *who believed that he witnessed "a memorable day to the historian of the Decline and Fall of the American Republic":*[12]

At half-past eight A.M. Gen. Lee, accompanied by his full staff, rode slowly along the front of the confederate lines from left to right, and took up his station for a time beyond Hamilton's crossing, and in rear of the batteries on the extreme confederate right. It would be presumptuous in me to say one word in commendation of the serenity, or, if I may so express it, the unconscious dignity of Gen. Lee's courage, when he is under fire. No one who sees and knows his demeanor in ordinary life would expect any thing else from one so calm, so undemonstrative and unassuming. But the description applied after the battle of Alma to Lord Raglan, by Marshal St. Arnaud, and in which, noticing Lord Raglan's unconsciousness under fire, he speaks of his "antique heroism," seems to me so applicable to Gen. Lee, that I cannot forbear recalling it here. At a subsequent period of the day Gen. Lee assumed his station on the hill which takes its name from him, and thence, in company with Gen. Longstreet, calmly watched the repulse of the repeated Federal efforts against the heights on which he stood. Occasionally Gen. Jackson rode up to the spot and mingled in conversation with the other two leading generals. Once General Longstreet exclaimed to him, "Are you not scared by that file of Yankees you have before you down there?" to which Gen. Jackson replied: "Wait till they come a little nearer, and they shall either scare me or I'll scare them."

The battle opened when the sun had let in enough light through the mist to disclose the near proximity of the Federal lines and field-batteries. The first shot was fired shortly before ten A.M. from the batteries in the Federal centre, and was directed against Gen. Hood's division. The Pennsylvania reserves advanced boldly under a heavy fire against the confederates who occupied one of the copsewood spurs, and were for a time permitted to hold it; but presently the confederate batteries opened on them, and a determined charge of the Texans drove the

Yankees out of the wood in a confusion from which nothing could subsequently rally them.

Simultaneously a heavy fire issued from the batteries of General A. P. Hill's and General Early's divisions, which was vigorously replied to by the Federal field-batteries. The only advantage momentarily gained by the Federals in this quarter, and which is noticed in Gen. Lee's report, was on the occasion of the collapse of a regiment of North-Carolina conscripts, who broke and ran, but whose place was rapidly taken by more intrepid successors. The cannonading now became general along the entire line. Such a scene, at once terrific and sublime, mortal eye never rested on before, unless the bombardment of Sebastopol by the combined batteries of France and England revealed a more fearful manifestation of the hate and fury of man.

The thundering, bellowing roar of hundreds of pieces of artillery, the bright jets of issuing flame, the screaming, hissing, whistling, shrieking projectiles, the wreaths of smoke as shell after shell burst into the still air, the savage crash of round-shot among the trees of the shattered forest, formed a scene likely to sink forever into the memory of all who witnessed it, but utterly defying verbal delineation. A direct and enfilading fire swept each battery upon either side as it was unmasked; volley replied to volley, crash succeeded crash, until the eye lost all power of distinguishing the lines of combatants, and the plain seemed a lake of fire, a seething lake of molten lava, coursed over by incarnate fiends drunk with fury and revenge.

The London correspondent watched as twice Hill and Early broke charges of the Union troops:[13]

. . . The confederates drove them with horrid carnage across the plain, and only desisted from their work when they came under the fire of the Federal batteries across the river. Upon the extreme confederate right General Stuart's horse-artillery drove hotly upon the fugitives, and kept up the pursuit, subsequently understood to have been effective, until after dark. Upon the confederate right, where the antagonists fought upon more equal terms, the loss sustained by the confederates was greater than on the confederate left; the Federal loss in officers and men far outbalanced that of their opponents. . . .

Meanwhile the battle, which had dashed furiously against the lines of Gens. Hood, A. P. Hill, and Early, was little more than child's play as compared with the onslaught directed by the Federals in the immediate neighborhood of Fredericksburgh. The impression that the confederate batteries would not fire heavily upon the Federals advancing in this quarter, for fear of injuring the town of Fredericksburgh, is believed to have prevailed among the Northern generals. How bitterly they deceived themselves subsequent events served to show.

To the Irish division, commanded by Gen. Meagher, was principally committed the desperate task of bursting out of the town of Fredericksburgh, and forming, under the withering fire of the confederate batteries, to attack Marye's Heights, towering immediately in their front. Never at Fontenoy, Albuera, or at Waterloo was more undoubted courage displayed by the sons of Erin than during those six frantic dashes which they directed against the almost impregnable position of their foe. There are stories that General Meagher harangued his troops in impassioned language on the morning of the thirteenth, and plied them extensively with the whisky found in the cellars of Fredericksburgh. After witnessing the gallantry and devotion exhibited by his troops, and viewing the hill-sides for acres strewn with their corpses thick as autumnal leaves, the spectator can remember nothing but their desperate courage, and regret that it was not exhibited in a holier cause.

That any mortal men could have carried the position before which they were wantonly sacrificed, defended as it was, it seems to me idle for a moment to believe. But the bodies which lie in dense masses within forty yards of the muzzles of Col. Walton's guns are the best evidence what manner of men they were who pressed on to death with the dauntlessness of a race which has gained glory on a thousand battlefields, and never more richly deserved it than at the foot of Marye's Heights on the thirteenth day of December, 1862.

Eugene A. Cory of the Fourth New York remembered:[14]

. . . Our line was now formed at the foot of Marye's hill, which was crowned by earth-works, rifle-pits, and a stone wall, defended by both infantry and artillery, and completely commanded in the rear by an elevated plateau, red with the flashes of guns. Now the order came to advance, and up the hill moved French's division to one of the most desperate charges of the whole four years of war. Ranks torn by shot and shell; men falling from terrible grape and canister wounds; the very air lurid, and alive with the flashes of guns, and rent with the long shriek of solid shot and shell, and the wicked whistle of grape; with compressed lips and shortened breath, closing up shoulder to shoulder, at length we gained the brow; then while within a few yards of the rifle-pits and stone wall, up rose rank after rank of infantry, adding to the avalanche of artillery fire a perfect rain of the less noisy, but more destructive rifle ball. Here, almost blown off our feet, staggering as though against a mighty wind, the line for a few minutes held its ground; then (but not until orders to that effect had been given, more by the motions of the officers than by their voices), slowly and sullenly it gave way, and retiring a few paces below the brow of the hill, there lay down, panting for breath, and clinging to the ground so desperately attained. The division, (as later reports showed), had lost nearly one-half its numbers inside of fifteen or twenty minutes.

After a slight lull in the roar of battle, the ball again opened, and looking back, we saw the advance of Hancock's division, over the same ground that we had passed. The same tragedy re-occurred, and this splendid division, or what was left of it, lay immediately in our rear. Again was the charge repeated by another division, which we afterwards learned was Humphrey's, of the Fifth corps, but the result was the same. . . .

Atop Marye's Heights, where Confederate batteries behind a stone wall showered death upon six waves of Union soldiers ordered up that blood-stained slope, General James Longstreet could hardly believe what his eyes beheld:[15]

. . . From the moment of their appearance began the most fearful carnage. With our artillery from the front, right and left tearing through their ranks, the Federals pressed forward with almost invincible determination, maintaining their steady step and closing up their broken ranks. Thus resolutely they marched upon the stone fence behind which quietly waited the Confederate brigade of General Cobb. As they came within reach . . . a storm of lead was poured into their advancing ranks and they were swept from the field like chaff before the wind. A cloud of smoke shut out the scene for a moment, and, rising, revealed the shattered fragments recoiling from their gallant but hopeless charge. The artillery still plowed through their retreating ranks and searched the places of concealment into which the troops had plunged. A vast number went pell-mell into an old railroad cut to escape fire from the right and front. A battery on Lee's Hill saw this and turned its fire into the entire length of the cut, and the shells began to pour down upon the Federals with the most frightful destruction. . . .

Truthfully had Edward P. Alexander, Longstreet's engineer and super-
intendent of artillery, told Lee that morning, "General, we cover that
ground now so well that we will comb it as with a fine-tooth comb."
Stoically, as the battle raged, Longstreet told Lee, "Give me plenty of
ammunition, [and] I will kill them all before they reach my line." In
Longstreet's phrase, blue-clad boys fell "like the steady dripping of rain
from the eaves of a house"; and Lee said, "It is well that war is so ter-
rible—we should grow too fond of it!" Captain D. P. Conyngham of the
Irish Brigade did not disguise the appalling punishment that the Fed-
eral forces had suffered:[16]

A cold, bitter, bleak December night closed upon that field of blood
and carnage. Thousands lay along that hill-side, and in the valleys,
whose oozing wounds were frozen, and whose cold limbs were stiffened,
for they had no blankets; they had flung them away going into the fight.
Masses of dead and dying were huddled together; some convulsed in
the last throes of death; others gasping for water—delirious, writhing in agony, and stiffened with the cold frost. The living tried to shelter
themselves behind the bodies of the dead.

Cries, moans, groans, and shrieks of agony rang over that sad battle-
field. There was no one to tend them; no one to bring them a drop of
cold water to moisten their swollen tongues; for that field was still
swept with shot and shell, and in the hands of the enemy.

And this was war—"glorious war"—with all its pomp and parade—
all its glittering attractions. If we could see it in its true colors, it is the
most horrible curse that God could inflict upon mankind.

IV

Merciful darkness ended the slaughter. Reporters trying to leave the field
with stories of what they had seen were denied passage on the boats;
but by bribing a Negro in a rowboat and then the captain of a sailing
vessel, Henry Villard of the New York Tribune *finally managed to*
reach Washington. No one had cried louder than Greeley for Mc-
Clellan's removal. Now, reading Villard's account, the editor wielded a
blue pencil to tone down the almost unbelievable catastrophe.

Burnside had fought at Fredericksburg with 106,007 effectives;
now 1,284 were dead, 9,600 wounded, 1,769 missing. Lee, in contrast,
had fought with 72,497 effectives; his dead were 595, his wounded
4,061, his missing 653.

In reporting to Halleck, Burnside manfully placed the blame where it
belonged:[17]

For the failure in the attack I am responsible, as the extreme gallantry, courage, and endurance shown by them was never exceeded, and would have carried the points had it been possible.

To the families and friends of the dead I can only offer my heartfelt sympathies, but for the wounded I can offer my earnest prayers for their comfortable and final recovery.

The fact that I decided to move from Warrenton on to this line rather against the opinion of the President, Secretary of War, and yourself, and that you left the whole movement in my hands, without giving me orders, makes me the only one responsible.

Magnanimously the President replied:[18]

EXECUTIVE MANSION

WASHINGTON, December 23, 1862

To THE ARMY OF THE POTOMAC:

I have just read your Commanding General's preliminary report of the battle of Fredericksburgh. Although you were not successful, the attempt was not an error, nor the failure other than accident. The courage with which you on an open field maintained the contest against an intrenched foe, and the consummate skill and success with which you crossed and re-crossed the river in the face of the enemy, show that you possess all the qualities of a great army, which will yet give victory to the cause of the country and of popular government.

Condoling with the mourners of the dead, and sympathizing with the wounded, I congratulate you that the number of both is comparatively small.

I tender to you, officers and soldiers, the thanks of the nation.

A. LINCOLN

v

As the old year ended, the fighting quickened on many fronts. In the East the Union added to the major disaster at Fredericksburg the minor disappointment of repulse in an expedition against Goldsboro, North Carolina. Morgan was loose again in Kentucky. A small Federal victory at Prairie Grove, Arkansas, was counterbalanced by Van Dorn's raid on Holly Springs, Mississippi, and the destruction of $1,500,000 of supplies that Grant badly needed. By late December, the hustling Sherman had sailed up the Yazoo River, wishing to lose no time in an assault on Vicksburg. The result cooled his ardor:[19]

On the morning of December 29th all the troops were ready and in position. The first step was to make a lodgment on the foot-hills and bluffs abreast of our position, while diversions were made by the navy toward Haines's Bluff, and by the first division directly toward Vicksburg. I estimated the enemy's forces, then strung from Vicksburg to Haines's Bluff, at fifteen thousand men, commanded by the rebel Generals Martin Luther Smith and Stephen D. Lee. Aiming to reach firm ground beyond this bayou, and to leave as little time for our enemy to re-enforce as possible, I determined to make a show of attack along the whole front, but to break across the bayou at the two points named, and gave general orders accordingly. I pointed out to General Morgan the place where he could pass the bayou, and he answered, "General, in ten minutes after you give the signal I'll be on those hills." He was to lead his division in person, and was to be supported by Steele's division. The front was very narrow, and immediately opposite, at the base of the hills about three hundred yards from the bayou, was a rebel battery, supported by an infantry force posted on the spurs of the hill behind. To draw attention from this, the real point of attack, I gave instructions to commence the attack at the flanks.

I went in person about a mile to the right rear of Morgan's position, at a place convenient to receive reports from all other parts of the line; and about noon of December 29th gave the orders and signal for the main attack. A heavy artillery-fire opened along our whole line, and was replied to by the rebel batteries, and soon the infantry-fire opened heavily, especially on A. J. Smith's front, and in front of General George W. Morgan. One brigade (De Courcey's) of Morgan's troops crossed the bayou safely, but took to cover behind the bank, and could not be moved forward. Frank Blair's brigade, of Steele's division, in support, also crossed the bayou, passed over the space of level ground to the foot of the hills; but, being unsupported by Morgan, and meeting a very severe cross-fire of artillery, was staggered and gradually fell back, leaving about five hundred men behind, wounded and prisoners; among them Colonel Thomas Fletcher, afterward Governor of Missouri. Thayer's brigade, of Steele's division, took a wrong direction, and did not cross the bayou at all; nor did General Morgan cross in person. This attack failed; and I have always felt that it was due to the failure of General G. W. Morgan to obey his orders, or to fulfill his promise made in person. Had he used with skill and boldness one of his brigades, in addition to that of Blair's, he could have made a lodgment on the bluff, which would have opened the door for our whole force to follow. Meantime the Sixth Missouri Infantry, at heavy loss, had also crossed the bayou at the narrow passage lower down, but could not ascend the steep bank; right over their heads was a rebel battery, whose fire was in a measure kept down by our sharp-shooters (Thirteenth United States Infantry) posted behind logs, stumps, and trees, on our side of the bayou.

The men of the Sixth Missouri actually scooped out with their hands caves in the bank, which sheltered them against the fire of the enemy, who, right over their heads, held their muskets outside the parapet vertically, and fired down. So critical was the position, that we could not recall the men till after dark, and then one at a time. Our loss had been pretty heavy, and we had accomplished nothing, and had inflicted little loss on our enemy. At first I intended to renew the assault, but soon became satisfied that, the enemy's attention having been drawn to the only two practicable points, it would prove too costly, and accordingly resolved to look elsewhere for a point below Haines's Bluff, or Blake's plantation. That night I conferred with Admiral Porter, who undertook to cover the landing; and the next day (December 30th) the boats were all selected, but so alarmed were the captains and pilots, that we had to place sentinels with loaded muskets to insure their remaining at their posts.

So much for Sherman. Bragg and his Confederates remained—the year had still to write a sequel to Perryville.

In the last week of December Rosecrans, who had been refitting his Army of the Cumberland at Nashville, started after Bragg. He found the Confederates astride Stone's River, protecting Murfreesboro. General John Beatty, commanding a Union brigade, described the sparring that took place on December 30:[20]

A little after daylight the brigade moved and proceeded to within three miles of Murfreesboro, where we have been awaiting orders since 10 A.M.

The first boom of artillery was heard at ten o'clock. Since then there has been almost a continuous roar. McCook's corps is in advance of us, perhaps a mile and a half and, with divisions from other corps, has been gradually approaching the enemy all day, driving his skirmishers from one point to another.

About four o'clock in the afternoon the artillery firing became more vigorous, and, with Colonel Foreman, of the fifteenth Kentucky, I rode

to the front, and then along our advanced line from right to left. Our
artillery stationed on the higher points was being fired rapidly. The
skirmishers were advancing cautiously, and the contest between the
two lines was quite exciting. As I supposed, our army is feeling its way
into position. Tomorrow, doubtless, the grand battle will be fought, when
I trust the good Lord will grant us a glorious victory, and one that will
make glad the hearts of all loyal people on New Year's Day.

Next day there was style in Rosecrans' orders to his troops:[21]

HEADQUARTERS DEPARTMENT OF THE CUMBERLAND,
IN FRONT OF MURFREESBORO, TENN.,
December 31, 1862
ORDERS: The General Commanding desires to say to the soldiers
of the army of the Cumberland that he was well pleased with their con-

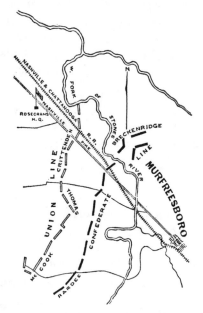

MURFREESBORO, MORNING, DECEMBER 31, 1862

From Lossing, *Pictorial History of the Civil War*

duct yesterday. It was all that he could have wished for. He neither
saw nor heard of any skulking. They behaved with the coolness and
gallantry of veterans. He now feels perfectly confident, with God's grace
and their help, of striking this day a blow for the country, the most

crushing perhaps which the rebellion has yet sustained. Soldiers! the eyes of the whole nation are upon you; the very fate of the nation may be said to hang on the issues of this day's battle. Be true, then, to yourselves, true to your own manly character and soldierly reputation, true to the love of your own dear ones at home, whose prayers ascend this day to God for your success. Be cool—I need not ask you to be brave. Keep ranks, do not throw away your fire; fire slowly, deliberately— above all, fire low, and be always sure of your aim. Close readily in upon the enemy, and when you get within charging distance, rush upon him with the bayonet. Do this and victory will certainly be yours. Recollect that there are hardly any troops in the world that will stand a bayonet charge, and that those who make it are sure to win.

By command of Major-General Rosecrans.

JULIUS P. GARESCHE,
Assistant Adjutant-General and Chief of Staff

Bragg, striking early on the thirty-first, rolled the Union's right against the turnpike and the river. The Louisville Journal *revealed how close Rosecrans' forces came to defeat:*[22]

. . . The rebels pressed up to the edge of the cedar forest and swarmed out into the open field. I saw the first few gray suits that dotted the dark green line of the cedars with their contrasted color thicken into a line of battle, and the bright glitter of their steel flashed like an endless chain of lightning amid the thick and heavy green of the thicket. This I saw before our fire, opening on them around the whole extent of our line, engirdled them with a belt of flame and smoke. After that I saw them no more, nor will any human eye ever see them more. Guenther, Loomis, and Stokes, with peal after peal, too rapid to be counted, mowed them down with double-shotted canister, the left of our line of infantry poured a continuous sheet of flame into their front, while the right of our line, posted in its remarkable position by the genius of Rousseau, enveloped their left flank and swept their entire line with an enfilading fire.

Thick smoke settled down upon the scene; the rim of the hill on which our batteries stood seemed to be surrounded by a wall of living fire; the turnpike road and the crest of the hill on the right were wrapped in an unending blaze; flames seemed to leap out of the earth and dance through the air. No troops on earth could withstand such a fire as that. One regiment of rebels, the boldest of their line, advanced to within seventy-five yards of our line, but there it was blown out of existence. It was utterly destroyed, and the rest of the rebel line, broken and decimated, fled like sheep into the depths of the woods.

Our centre still stood immovable as a rock, and the army was saved. The terrific firing ceased, the smoke quickly rolled away, and the sun shone out bright and clear on the scene that was lately so shrouded in smoke and moral gloom. How still every thing was! Every body seemed to be holding his breath. As soon as the firing ceased General Rousseau and his staff galloped forward to the ground the rebels had advanced over. Their dead lay there in frightful heaps, some with the life-blood not yet all flowed from their mortal wounds, some propped upon their elbows and gasping their last. The flag of the Arkansas regiment lay there on the ground beside its dead bearer. Every depression in the field was full of wounded, who had crawled thither to screen themselves from the fire, and a large number of prisoners came out of a little copse in the middle of the field and surrendered themselves to Gen. Rousseau in person. Among them was one captain. They were all that were left alive of the bold Arkansas regiment that had undertaken to charge our line. . . .

That night Bragg sent the first of a series of optimistic dispatches:[23]

MURFREESBORO, Dec. 31, 1862

GENERAL S. COOPER:

We assailed the enemy at seven o'clock this morning, and after ten hours' hard fighting have driven him from every position except his extreme left, where he has successfully resisted us. With the exception of this point, we occupy the whole field. We captured four thousand prisoners, including two brigadier-generals, thirty-one pieces of artillery and some two hundred wagons and teams. Our loss is heavy; that of the enemy much greater.

BRAXTON BRAGG,
General Commanding

On New Year's Day both armies were satisfied to rest, yet Beatty, like thousands of others, realized that grim fighting impended:[24]

At dawn we are all in line, expecting every moment the recommencement of the fearful struggle. Occasionally a battery engages a battery opposite, and the skirmishers keep up a continual roar of small arms;

but until nearly night there is no heavy fighting. Both armies want rest; both have suffered terribly. Here and there little parties are engaged burying the dead, which lie thick around us. Now the mangled remains of a poor boy of the Third is being deposited in a shallow grave. A whole charge of canister seems to have gone through him. Generals Rosecrans and Thomas are riding over the field, now halting to speak words of encouragement to the troops, then going on to inspect portions of the line.

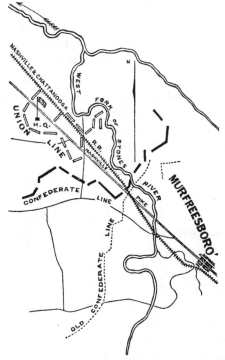

MURFREESBORO, EVENING, DECEMBER 31, 1862

From Lossing, *Pictorial History of the Civil War*

I have been supplied with a new horse, but one far inferior to the dead stallion. A little before sundown all hell seems to break loose again, and for about an hour the thunder of artillery and the volleys of musketry are deafening; but it is simply the evening salutation of the combatants. The darkness deepens; the weather is raw and disagreeable. Fifty thousand hungry men are stretched beside their guns again on the field. Fortunately I have a piece of raw pork and a few crackers in my pocket. No food ever tasted sweeter. The night is gloomy enough; but our spirits are rising. We all glory in the obstinacy with which Rosecrans has clung to his position. I draw closer to the campfire and, pushing the brands together, take out my little Bible, and as I open it my eyes fall on the XCIth Psalm:

"I will say of the Lord, He is my refuge and my fortress, my God; in Him will I trust. Surely He shall deliver thee from the snare of the fowler, and from the noisome pestilence. He shall cover thee with His feathers, and under His wings shall be thy trust. His truth shall be thy shield and buckler. Thou shalt not be afraid for the terror by night, nor for the arrow that flieth by day; nor for the pestilence that walketh in darkness, nor for the destruction that wasteth at noonday. A thousand shall fall by thy side, and ten thousand at thy right hand; but it shall not come nigh thee."

Campfires innumerable are glimmering in the darkness. Now and then a few mounted men gallop by. Scattering shots are heard along the picket line. The gloom has lifted, and I wrap myself in my blanket and lie down contentedly for the night.

Bragg, still the incurable optimist, wired Cooper again:[25]

MURFREESBORO, January 1, 1863

The enemy has yielded his strong point and is falling back. We occupy the whole field and shall follow. General Wheeler, with his cavalry, made a complete circuit of their army on the thirtieth and thirty-first. He captured and destroyed three hundred wagons loaded with baggage and commissary stores, and paroled seven hundred prisoners. He is again behind them, and has captured an ordnance train. Today he has secured several thousand stand of small arms. The body of Brigadier-Gen. Sill was left on the field, and three others are reported to have been killed. God has granted us a happy New Year.

BRAXTON BRAGG

On January 2, the more realistic Beatty got the fight he expected:

At sunrise we have a shower of solid shot and shell. The Chicago Board of Trade Battery is silenced. The shot roll up the Murfreesboro pike like balls on a bowling alley. Many horses are killed. A soldier near me, while walking deliberately to the rear to seek a place of greater safety, is struck between the shoulders by a ricocheting ball and instantly killed. We are ordered to be in readiness to repel an attack and form line of battle amid this fearful storm of iron. Gaunther and Loomis get their batteries in position and, after twenty or thirty minutes' active work, silence the enemy and compel him to withdraw. Then we have a lull until one or two o'clock, when Van Cleve's division on the left is attacked. As the volume of musketry increases, and the sound grows nearer, we understand that our troops are being driven back, and brigade after brigade double-quicks from the right and center, across the open field, to render aid. Battery after battery goes in the same direction on the run, the drivers lashing the horses to their utmost speed. The thunder of the guns becomes more violent; the volleys of musketry grow into one prolonged and unceasing roll. Now we hear the yell that betokens encouraged hearts; but whose yell? Thank God, it is ours! The conflict is working southward; the enemy has been checked, repulsed, and is now in retreat. So ends another day.

The hungry soldiers cut steaks from the slain horses, and with the scanty supplies that have come forward gather around the fires to prepare supper and talk over the incidents of the day. The prospect seems brighter. We have held the ground and in this last encounter have whipped the enemy. There is more cheerful conversation among the men. They discuss the battle, the officers, and each other, and give us now and then a snatch of song. Officers come over from adjoining brigades, hoping to find a little whisky, but learn, with apparent resignation and well-feigned composure, that the canteens have been long empty, that even the private flasks, which officers carry with the photographs of their sweethearts, in a side pocket next to their hearts, are destitute of even the flavor of this article of prime necessity. . . . Colonel Hobart stumbles up in the thick darkness to pay his respects. The sentinel, mistaking him for a private, tells him, with an oath, that this is neither the time nor the place for stragglers, and orders him back to his regiment; and so the night wears on, and fifty thousand men lay upon their guns again.

Bragg still did not understand what had happened:[26]

MURFREESBORO, January 2, 1863

The enemy retired last night but a short distance in rear of his former position. We had a short and sharp contest this evening. We drove his left flank from his position, but an attacking party again returned, with considerable loss to both sides.

Gens. Wheeler and Wharton were again in their rear yesterday, and

captured two hundred prisoners, one piece of artillery, and destroyed
two hundred loaded wagons.

-BRAXTON BRAGG

*Rosecrans, with 41,400 effectives, counted 1,667 killed, 7,543
wounded, 3,686 missing; Bragg, with 34,732 effectives, counted 1,294
killed, 7,945 wounded, 2,500 missing. The reporter for the Cincinnati
Commercial understood the futility of the stalemate:*[27]

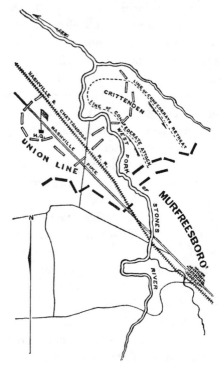

MURFREESBORO, JANUARY 2, 1863
From Lossing, *Pictorial History of the Civil War*

BATTLE-FIELD OF STONE RIVER, TENN.,
Saturday, Jan. 3, 1863—A week of horrors, a week of carnage, a
week of tremendous conflict—and battle still raging! At this moment
there is angry rattle of musketry and deep, sullen roar of cannon,
echoing in the forest within Minie range of our marquee. My God, when
will it end! A thousand gallant dead slumber in their bloody graves;
four thousand wounded and mangled patriots are moaning on this

sanguinary field. God knows how many rebel lives have spent during this fearful week, or how many desperate traitors suffer the agony of dreadful wounds.

Bragg at last faced the truth:

TULLAHOMA, January 5, 1863
Unable to dislodge the enemy from his intrenchments, and hearing of reenforcements to him, I withdrew from his front night before last. He has not followed. My cavalry are close on his front.

BRAXTON BRAGG

VI

So ended the year that had begun with the North mocking the stereo-typed report, "All quiet on the Potomac." Military reputations had been made and broken. No victory had endured, no defeat had pros-trated. With New Orleans captured, Lee back in Virginia, Kentucky won and Vicksburg threatened, the balance of field strategy belonged to the North; and with the Emancipation Proclamation to be signed on New Year's Day the political strategy also leaned toward Lincoln. Yet the South had gained enormously. Edward A. Pollard, Richmond editor and critic of Davis, proudly recorded that psychological triumph:[28]

Since the commencement of the war the North had had almost ex-clusive access to the ear of the world, and had poured into it whatever of slander or of misrepresentation human ingenuity could suggest. This circumstance, which was at first thought to be a great disadvantage to us, had not only proved a harmless annoyance, but had resulted in invaluable benefit. It had secured sympathy for us; it had excited the inquiries of the intelligent, who, after all, give the law to public opinion; and it had naturally tempted the North to such lying and bravado as to disgust the world.

At the beginning of the war the North had assured the world that the people of the South were a sensual and barbarous people, de-moralized by their institution of slavery, and depraved by self-will and licentiousness below the capacity for administrative government. The best reply to these slanders, was our conduct in this war. Even the little that was known in Europe of the patriotic devotion, the dignity and cultivated humanity of the people of the South, as shown in the war, had been sufficient to win unbounded encomiums for them. We had not only withstood for nearly two years a power which had put thirteen hundred thousand men in the field; but we had shown that we were a people able in public affairs, resolute, brave, and prudent.

Another characteristic Yankee misrepresentation, made to the world about this time on the subject of the war, was, that it was to be concluded at an early day by the force of destitution and suffering in the South. The delusion of conquering the "rebels" by famine easily caught the vulgar ear. The North made it a point to exaggerate and garble every thing it could find in Southern newspapers, of the ragged condition of our armies, the high prices of the necessaries of life, and the hardships of the war. The Yankees were pleasantly entertained with stories of our suffering. Their pictorials were adorned with caricatures of "secesh" in skeleton soldiers and gaunt cavalrymen with spurs strapped to their naked heels. Their perfumed fops and dainty ladies had the fashion of tittering at the rags of our prisoners. They had an overwhelming sense of the ludicrous in the idea of Southern women cutting up the carpets in their houses to serve for blankets and garments for the soldiers.

The fact was that our sufferings were great; but their mute eloquence, which the enemy misinterpreted as a prospect of craven submission, was truly the sign of self-devotion. Whatever was suffered in physical destitution was not to be regretted. It practised our people in self-denial; it purified their spirit; it brought out troops of virtues; it ennobled our women with offices of charity; it gave us new bonds of sympathy and love, and it trained us in those qualities which make a nation great and truly independent.

In the whirl of passing events, many strange things were daily happening around us that at a remoter period of history will read like romance. The directions of our industry were changed. Planters raised corn and potatoes, fattened hogs and cultivated garden vegetables, while cotton was by universal consent neglected. Our newspapers were of all sizes and colors, sometimes containing four pages, sometimes two, and not a few were printed on common brown wrapping paper. Politics were dead. A political enemy was a curiosity only read of in the records of the past. Our amusements had been revolutionized. Outside of Richmond, a theatre was remembered only as an institution of bygone times. Most of our people did their own playing and their own singing; and the ladies spent the mornings in sewing coarse shirts or pantaloons for the soldiers to wear, and sung in public at night to gain money for the soldiers' equipments.

The footprints of the enemy, in Virginia especially, had marked lines of desolation such as history seldom records. Starting from Fortress Monroe and running westward to Winchester, scarcely a house within fifty miles of the Potomac but bore evidence of Yankee greed and spoliation. In nearly every county the court-house in which the assizes for each county used to be held, was rudely demolished, doors and windows torn down; while within, upon the white walls in every phase of handwriting, were recorded the autographs of the vandals, whose handiwork surrounded the beholder.

While the people of the South suffered, the resources of the country were developed by harsh necessity; and . . . shortsighted expectations of peace were replaced by the policy of provision and an amassment of stores for a war of indefinite duration. Measures were adopted to afford adequate supplies of ordnance, arms, and munitions for the army. Of small-arms the supply was more adequate to the regiments of the army than at any other time. They had increased from importation and capture not less than eighty thousand. Establishments for making ordnance were founded in different parts of the South; a nitre corps was organized for service; and former dread of deficiency of the munitions of war no longer existed. The manufacturing resources of the country, especially in iron, were liberally patronized by the government, by large advances and liberal contracts; but in this the public service met great embarrassment from the temptations constantly offered to contractors to prefer the superior profits which they could command by supplying the general market. The quartermaster's department was under the direction of Gen. Myers, of South Carolina, whose contributions to the cause of the South, in the zeal and ability which he brought into his important office, must take a high rank in all the histories of the war. He contended against the great obstacles of the blockade, the difficulties of railroad transportation, and the constant losses in the enemy's ravages of the country, and performed wonders under the most unfavorable circumstances. Woollens and leather were imported from Europe through trains of difficulties, the most devoted exertions were made to replenish the scant supplies of blankets and shoes in the army; and by using to the utmost our internal resources, by the establishment of factories and the organization of workshops; and by greater economy in the use of our supplies, the sufferings of our soldiers were alleviated and their zeal refreshed for the campaign.

On frosty battlefields boys in blue and gray looked up at the star-studded heavens, waiting for the New Year. The wish, the melancholy they shared Walter Kittridge had captured:

> We're tenting tonight on the old camp ground,
>   Give us a song to cheer
> Our weary hearts, a song of home,
>   And friends we love so dear.
>
> Many are the hearts that are weary tonight,
>   Wishing for the war to cease;
> Many are the hearts that are looking for the right,
>   To see the dawn of peace.
> Tenting tonight, tenting tonight,
>   Tenting on the old camp ground.

1863

CHAPTER 19

WAR
ON THE WATER

O N THE LAST DAY of the year 1862 Senator Orville H. Browning
dined in distinguished company. By his careful and admiring computa-
tion the group included "seven Judges of the Supreme Court, and one
Ex Judge of the same Court—two cabinet Ministers, and six ex
cabinet ministers, one Senator and one representative in Congress."

Fifteen months earlier Browning, one of Lincoln's oldest friends, and
successor, by Lincoln's grace, to the seat of Stephen A. Douglas, had
berated the President for setting aside Frémont's headstrong proclamation emancipating slaves in Missouri. But on New Year's Eve, 1862,
Browning contemplated the President's own proclamation of emancipation with horror. Before retiring he wrote in his diary:

"Some days ago I said to Judge Thomas * that I thought he ought to
go to the President and have a full, frank conversation with him in
regard to the threatened proclamation of emancipation—that in my
opinion it was fraught with evil, and evil only and would do much injury; and that I thought his opinion would have influence with the
President—that he might possibly induce him to withhold, or at least to
modify it, so as to make it applicable to the slaves of those in armed
rebellion against the Government alone, and that even this would ease
the administration down, and get it in the way of regaining the lost confidence of the people. He informed me tonight that he had taken my advice, and had the talk but that it would avail nothing.

* Benjamin Franklin Thomas, former judge of the Massachusetts Supreme
Court; in 1862, a member of the House of Representatives from Massachusetts.

"The President was fatally bent upon his course, saying that if he should refuse to issue his proclamation there would be a rebellion in the north, and that a dictator would be placed over his head within the week. There is no hope. The proclamation will come—God grant it may not be productive of the mischief I fear."

I

Lincoln, who had never wavered in his determination to carry out the promise of his proclamation of September 22, 1862, saw no need to hurry. His secretaries described the fateful first of January, 1863:[1]

It is a custom in the Executive Mansion to hold on New Year's Day an official and public reception, beginning at eleven o'clock in the morning, which keeps the President at his post in the Blue Room until two in the afternoon. The hour for this reception came before Mr. Lincoln had entirely finished revising the engrossed copy of the proclamation, and he was compelled to hurry away from his office to friendly handshaking and festal greeting with the rapidly arriving official and diplomatic guests. The rigid laws of etiquette held him to this duty for the space of three hours. Had actual necessity required it, he could of course have left such mere social occupation at any moment; but the President saw no occasion for precipitancy. On the other hand, he probably deemed it wise that the completion of this momentous executive act should be attended by every circumstance of deliberation.

Vast as were its consequences, the act itself was only the simplest and briefest formality. It could in no wise be made sensational or dramatic. . . . No ceremony was made or attempted of this final official signing. The afternoon was well advanced when Mr. Lincoln went back from his New Year's greetings, with his right hand so fatigued that it was an effort to hold the pen. There was no special convocation of the Cabinet or of prominent officials. Those who were in the house came to the executive office merely from the personal impulse of curiosity joined to momentary convenience. His signature was attached to one of the greatest and most beneficent military decrees of history in the presence of less than a dozen persons; after which it was carried to the Department of State to be attested by the great seal and deposited among the archives of the Government.

The President had written:[2]

I do order and declare that all persons held as slaves within said designated States, and parts of States, are, and henceforward shall be free; and that the Executive government of the United States, including the military and naval authorities thereof, will recognize and maintain the freedom of said persons.

And I hereby enjoin upon the people so declared to be free to abstain from all violence, unless in necessary self-defence; and I recommend to them that, in all cases when allowed, they labor faithfully for reasonable wages.

And I further declare and make known, that such persons of suitable condition, will be received into the armed service of the United States to garrison forts, positions, stations, and other places, and to man vessels of all sorts in said service.

And upon this act, sincerely believed to be an act of justice, warranted by the Constitution, upon military necessity, I invoke the considerate judgment of mankind, and the gracious favor of Almighty God.

Nowhere were these words heard with more rejoicing than at Camp Saxton,* near Beaufort, South Carolina, which the Union forces had occupied since November 1861. There the First South Carolina Volunteers, first of the Federal Negro regiments, did garrison duty. Colonel Thomas W. Higginson, the former Unitarian minister who commanded the regiment, described the elation of soldiers and newly freed slaves:[3]

January 1, 1863 (evening)

A happy New Year to civilized people,—mere white folks. Our festival has come and gone, with perfect success, and our good General has been altogether satisfied. Last night the great fires were kept smouldering in the pit, and the beeves were cooked more or less, chiefly more, —during which time they had to be carefully watched, and the great spits turned by main force. Happy were the merry fellows who were permitted to sit up all night, and watch the glimmering flames that threw a thousand fantastic shadows among the great gnarled oaks. And such chattering as I was sure to hear whenever I awoke that night!

My first greeting today was from one of the most stylish sergeants, who approached me with the following little speech, evidently the result of some elaboration:—

"I tink myself happy, dis New Year's Day, for salute my own Cunnel. Dis day las' year I was servant to a Cunnel ob Secesh; but now I hab de privilege for salute my own Cunnel."

That officer, with the utmost sincerity, reciprocated the sentiment.

* Named for Brigadier General Rufus Saxton, Military Governor of the Department of the South.

About ten o'clock the people began to collect by land, and also by water,—in steamers sent by General Saxton for the purpose; and from that time all the avenues of approach were thronged. The multitude were chiefly colored women, with gay handkerchiefs on their heads, and a sprinkling of men, with that peculiarly respectable look which the people always have on Sundays and holidays. There were many white visitors also,—ladies on horseback and in carriages, superintendents and teachers, officers, and cavalrymen. Our companies were marched to the neighborhood of the platform, and allowed to sit or stand, as at the Sunday services; the platform was occupied by ladies and dignitaries, and by the band of the Eighth Maine, which kindly volunteered for the occasion; the colored people filled up all the vacant openings in the beautiful grove around, and there was a cordon of mounted visitors beyond. Above, the great live-oak branches and their trailing moss; beyond the people, a glimpse of the blue river.

The services began at half past eleven o'clock, with prayer by our chaplain, Mr. Fowler. . . . Then the President's Proclamation was read by Dr. W. H. Brisbane, a thing infinitely appropriate, a South Carolinian addressing South Carolinians; for he was reared among these very islands, and here long since emancipated his own slaves. Then the colors were presented to us by the Rev. Mr. French, a chaplain who brought them from the donors in New York. All this was according to the programme. Then followed an incident so simple, so touching, so utterly unexpected and startling, that I can scarcely believe it on recalling, though it gave the keynote to the whole day. The very moment the speaker had ceased, and just as I took and waved the flag, which now for the first time meant anything to these poor people, there suddenly arose, close beside the platform, a strong male voice (but rather cracked and elderly), into which two women's voices instantly blended, singing, as if by an impulse that could no more be repressed than the morning note of the song-sparrow:—

"My Country, 'tis of thee,
Sweet land of liberty,
Of thee I sing!"

People looked at each other, and then at us on the platform, to see whence came this interruption, not set down in the bills. Firmly and irrepressibly the quavering voices sang on, verse after verse; others of the colored people joined in; some whites on the platform began, but I motioned them to silence. I never saw anything so electric; it made

all other words cheap; it seemed the choked voice of a race at last un-
loosed. Nothing could be more wonderfully unconscious; art could not
have dreamed of a tribute to the day of jubilee that should be so affecting; history will not believe it; and when I came to speak of it, after it
was ended, tears were everywhere. If you could have heard how quaint
and innocent it was! Old Tiff and his children might have sung it; and
close before me was a little slave-boy, almost white, who seemed to
belong to the party, and even he must join in. Just think of it!—the first
day they had ever had a country, the first flag they had ever seen which
promised anything to their people, and here, while mere spectators
stood in silence, waiting for my stupid words, these simple souls burst
out in their lay, as if they were by their own hearths at home! When
they stopped, there was nothing to do for it but to speak, and I went on;
but the life of the whole day was in those unknown people's song.

Receiving the flags, I gave them into the hands of two fine-looking
men, jet black, as color-guard, and they also spoke, and very effectively,—Sergeant Prince Rivers and Corporal Robert Sutton. The regiment sang "Marching Along," and then General Saxton spoke, in his
own simple, manly way, and Mrs. Francis D. Gage spoke very sensibly
to the women, and Judge Stickney, from Florida, added something;
then some gentlemen sang an ode, and the regiment the John Brown
song, and then they went to their beef and molasses. Everything was
very orderly, and they seemed to have a very gay time. Most of the visitors had far to go, and so dispersed before dress-parade, though the
band stayed to enliven it. In the evening we had letters from home, and
General Saxton had a reception at his house, from which I excused myself; and so ended one of the most enthusiastic and happy gatherings I
ever knew. The day was perfect, and there was nothing but success.

*And nowhere were Lincoln's words read with more bitterness than in
the Confederate Capital where Jefferson Davis worked on the message that he would send to the Confederate Congress on January 12. In
that document he wrote:*[4]

The public journals of the North have been received, containing a
proclamation, dated on the 1st day of the present month, signed by
the President of the United States, in which he orders and declares all
slaves within ten of the States of the Confederacy to be free, except such
as are found within certain districts now occupied in part by the armed
forces of the enemy. We may well leave it to the instincts of that com-

mon humanity which a beneficent Creator has implanted in the breasts of our fellow-men of all countries to pass judgment on a measure by which several millions of human beings of an inferior race, peaceful and contented laborers in their sphere, are doomed to extermination, while at the same time they are encouraged to a general assassination of their masters by the insidious recommendation "to abstain from violence unless in necessary self-defense." Our own detestation of those who have attempted the most execrable measure recorded in the history of guilty man is tempered by profound contempt for the impotent rage which it discloses. So far as regards the action of this Government on such criminals as may attempt its execution, I confine myself to informing you that I shall, unless in your wisdom you deem some other course more expedient, deliver to the several State authorities all commissioned officers of the United States that may hereafter be captured by our forces in any of the States embraced in the proclamation, that they may be dealt with in accordance with the laws of those States providing for the punishment of criminals engaged in exciting servile insurrection. The enlisted soldiers I shall continue to treat as unwilling instruments in the commission of these crimes, and shall direct their discharge and return to their homes on the proper and usual parole. . . .

Both before and after the actual commencement of hostilities the President of the United States repeated in formal official communication to the Cabinets of Great Britain and France that he was utterly without constitutional power to do the act which he has just committed, and that in no possible event, whether the secession of these States resulted in the establishment of a separate Confederacy or in the restoration of the Union, was there any authority by virtue of which he could either restore a disaffected State to the Union by force of arms or make any change in any of its institutions. . . .

The people of this Confederacy, then, cannot fail to receive this proclamation as the fullest vindication of their own sagacity in foreseeing the uses to which the dominant party in the United States intended from the beginning to apply their power, nor can they cease to remember with devout thankfulness that it is to their own vigilance in resisting the first stealthy progress of approaching despotism that they owe their escape from consequences now apparent to the most skeptical. This proclamation will have another salutary effect in calming the fears of those who have constantly evinced the apprehension that this war might end by some reconstruction of the old Union or some renewal of close political relations with the United States. These fears have never been shared by me, nor have I ever been able to perceive on what basis they could rest. But the proclamation affords the fullest guarantee of the impossibility of such a result; it has established a state of things which can lead to but one of three possible consequences—the extermination of the slaves, the exile of the whole white population from the Confederacy, or absolute and total separation of these States from the United States.

This proclamation is also an authentic statement from the Government of the United States of its inability to subjugate the South by force of arms, and as such must be accepted by neutral nations, which can no longer find any justification in withholding our just claims to formal recognition. It is also in effect an intimation to the people of the North that they must prepare to submit to a separation, now become inevitable, for that people are too acute not to understand a restoration of the Union has been rendered forever impossible by the adoption of a measure which from its very nature neither admits of retraction nor can coexist with union.

II

At Galveston, Texas, fifteen hundred miles from Washington and Richmond, a starlit night and a sinking moon ushered in the first day of the new year. Three months earlier, lacking a few days, a Union naval squadron had forced the defenders to evacuate the town, one of the most important ports in the Confederacy. Since then it had remained unoccupied and intact, even to the long railroad bridge which connected the city and the island on which it stood with the mainland. Only the Harriet Lane, mounting eight guns, hovered offshore ready to throw shells into any Confederate force which might attempt repossession.

Late in December the Union command decided that the Texas port was vulnerable. Just before Christmas the Forty-second Massachusetts, the Twenty-third Connecticut and a Vermont battery, all stationed at Ship Island in the Gulf, were ordered to Galveston. Of these, only three companies of the Forty-second Massachusetts had arrived when the year ended, although the transports which carried the troops and several other ships of the blockading squadron had reinforced the Harriet Lane.

None of the defenders was aware that "Prince John" Magruder, recently transferred from Virginia to Texas, lay poised to strike at Galveston's defenders with a hastily gathered land force and a makeshift collection of tenders and packets padded with cotton.

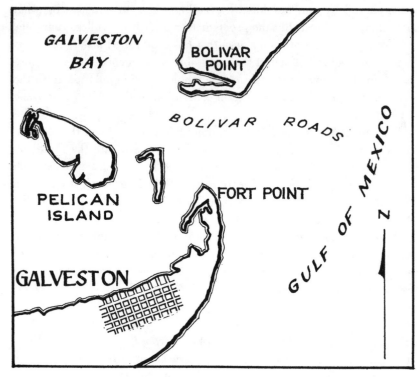

GALVESTON

The Houston Telegraph *described the sharp little battle that opened Galveston to blockade runners for the remainder of the war:*[5]

It was ordered that the boats should get in position by twelve o'clock, and await the signal from the land forces for the attack. They went down, and after midnight arrived close by the [Federal] fleet. They were discovered, and signal lights from the fleet at once showed that the enemy were awake and watching for them. They looked anxiously for the signal from shore.

Meanwhile the land forces, consisting of detachments from some four or five regiments . . . were moved at about dark from Virginia Point. This is on the mainland, and from it a bridge two miles in length crosses Galveston Bay to Galveston Island, being about five miles distant from the city. The battle took place at the city, the gunboats lying along in front of the city in the bay, on the landward side of the island. . . .

From the bridge they [the troops] moved down to the city, but met with unexpected delays, and did not reach their position until after four o'clock. In the meantime the boats had withdrawn to Half Moon Shoals, twelve miles distant, and awaited signal. At about five o'clock . . . , all things on shore being in readiness, the ball opened, Gen. Magruder firing the first gun. The boats at once put on steam and hurried to the scene. They must have been an hour or so on the way, during which time the artillery duel between the ships and the batteries was one of the most terrific on record. Darkness shut out everything but the flash of the guns.

The scene was at once sublime and appalling. Our men were once driven from their guns, but rallied and fought nobly on. As dawn approached the fire of the enemy appeared to increase in severity, and fearing that our men would be unable to withstand it after daylight gave the enemy a better view of our position, orders were prepared to withdraw. Just as they were about to be issued, however, at about six o'clock, the welcome announcement was made at headquarters that the *Bayou City* and *Neptune* had arrived, and opened on the *Harriet Lane*. Instantly new vigor was infused in our men; they played their pieces with redoubled energy, and seemed determined that the victory should be ours.

The gunboats paid their first attention to the *Harriet Lane*, the *Bayou City* leading the attack. The *Neptune*, being much the weaker, soon received such injuries as to disable her. The *Bayou City*, however, gallantly continued the fight, and, running aboard the *Harriet Lane*, swept her decks by boarding, and took possession of the ship. Captain Wainwright and his lieutenants having been killed, the ship was surrendered by the master's mate.

The *Westfield* now started off, apparently disabled, and made her way over to Bolivar Channel. . . . Here she was subsequently destroyed by the enemy during a truce. The propeller *Owasco* lay in the channel about three fourths of a mile from the *Bayou City* and *Harriet Lane*. As the *Lane* was boarded, the *Owasco* steamed up to within two or three hundred yards of them, firing into both. The force of the collision drove the *Bayou City's* stem so far into and under the wheel and gunwale of the *Lane* that she could not be got out. The *Lane* was also so careened that the guns could not be worked, and were consequently useless. They both lay, therefore, at the mercy of the *Owasco*. Herculean efforts were made to extricate them.

The *Owasco*, evidently fearing the *Lane's* guns, withdrew to a position about a mile distant. It became plainly evident that unless the

Bayou City and *Harriet Lane* could be separated, the enemy could escape if they wished. To gain time, therefore, a flag of truce was taken to the *Owasco* and *Clifton,* now lying close together, and a demand for a surrender. Time was asked to communicate with Com. Renshaw, who was on the *Westfield.* A truce of three hours was agreed upon. Previous to this, the Forty-second Massachusetts regiment, quartered on Kuhn's wharf, were charged. They were protected by barricades, and had taken up the planks from the wharf, rendering it impassable, and our forces withdrew.

During the truce with the vessels, the unconditional surrender of these men was demanded and complied with. Their colors consist of a United States flag of silk, and a white flag, having the coat of arms of Massachusetts painted on it, with the motto: "Ense petit placidum sub libertate quietam"—"Under freedom the sword seeks peaceful quiet." The appearance of the coat of arms is rather singular. In the center is an Indian with his bow; at the right corner of the shield is a single star, at which he is glancing askance. We might say the savage was coveting the Texas star. Unfortunately, the star is in the ascendant, and the result proved the vanity of his wishes. At any rate the sword of the Forty-second has found peaceful quiet by the aid of Texas freemen.

Before the truce expired, the Federal gunboats drew off, and escaped out of the harbor, utterly routed and defeated, leaving in our hands the city, the harbor, the *Harriet Lane,* the two barks and a schooner, and vast stores, and valuable artillery.

III

The loss of Galveston was only one of many naval reverses that marked the new year. In the long view, none was serious, but all tended to depress further a Northern morale already low.

Lieutenant R. G. Blake described how the U.S.S. Hatteras *met more than her match in the most famous of all Confederate raiders, the* Alabama. *His report was written to the Secretary of the Navy, Gideon Welles:*[6]

U. S. CONSULATE
KINGSTON, JAMAICA
January 31, 1863

DEAR SIR: It is my painful duty to inform the department of the destruction of the United States steamer *Hatteras,* recently under my command, by the rebel steamer *Alabama,* on the night of the eleventh instant, off the coast of Texas. The circumstances of the disaster are as follows:

On the afternoon of the eleventh inst., at half-past three o'clock, while at anchor in company with the fleet under Com. Bell, off Galveston, Texas, I was ordered by a signal from the United States flag-ship *Brooklyn* to chase a sail to the southward and eastward. I got under way immediately and steamed in the direction indicated. After some time the strange sail could be seen from the *Hatteras*, and was ascertained to be a steamer, which fact was communicated to the flag-ship by signal. I continued the chase and rapidly gained upon the suspicious vessel. Knowing the slow rate of the *Hatteras*, I at once suspected that deception was being practised, and at once ordered the ship to be cleared for action, with everything in readiness for a determined and vigorous defence. When within about four miles of the vessel I observed that she had ceased to steam, and was lying broadside on and awaiting us. It was nearly seven o'clock and quite dark, but notwithstanding the obscurity of the night I felt assured from the general character of the vessel and her manoeuvers that I should soon encounter the *Alabama*.

Being able to work only four guns on the side of the *Hatteras*, two short thirty-two pounders, one thirty-pounder rifled Parrott gun, and one twenty-pounder rifled gun, I concluded to close with her, so that my guns might be effective if necessary. I came within easy speaking distance, about seventy-five yards, and upon asking what steamer is that, received the answer: "Her Britannic Majesty's ship *Vixen*." I replied that I would send a boat aboard, and immediately gave the order. In the meantime, both vessels were changing their positions, the stranger endeavoring to gain a desirable position for a raking fire. Almost simultaneously with the piping away of the boat, the stranger craft again replied, "We are the Confederate steamer *Alabama*," which was accompanied with a broadside.

I at the same moment returned the fire. Being well aware of the many vulnerable points of the *Hatteras*, I hoped by closing with the *Alabama* to be able to board her, and thus rid the seas of this piratical craft. I steamed directly for the *Alabama*, but she was enabled by her great speed, and the foulness of the bottom of the *Hatteras* and consequently her diminished speed, to thwart my attempt when I had gained a distance of but thirty yards from her.

At this range musket and pistol-shots were exchanged. The firing continued with great vigor on both sides. At length a shell entered amidships in the hold, setting fire to it, and at the same instant—as I can hardly divide the time—a shell passed through the sick-bay and exploded in an adjoining compartment, also producing fire; another entered the cylinder, filling the engine-room and deck with steam, and depriving me of any power to manoeuver the vessel or to work the pumps, upon which the reduction of the fire depended.

With the vessel on fire in two places, and far beyond human power, a hopeless wreck upon the waters, with her walking-beam shot away, and her engines rendered useless, I still maintained an active fire, with the double hope of disabling the *Alabama* and attracting the attention of the fleet off Galveston, which was twenty-eight miles distant. It was soon reported to me that the shells had entered the *Hatteras* at the water-line, tearing off sheets of iron, and that the water was rushing in, utterly defying every attempt to remedy the evil, and that she was rapidly sinking.

Learning this melancholy truth, and seeing that the *Alabama* was on my port-bow, entirely beyond range of my guns, doubtless preparing for a raking fire across the deck, I felt I had no right to sacrifice uselessly, and without any desirable result, the lives of all under my command, and to prevent the blowing up of the *Hatteras* from the fire, which was making much progress, I ordered the magazine to be flooded, and afterward a lee-gun to be fired.

The *Alabama* then asked if assistance was desired, to which an affirmative answer was given. . . .

Clarence R. Tonge, paymaster on the Alabama, *described the condition of the* Hatteras *when the Confederates boarded her:*

None but an eye-witness can conceive the appearance of the wreck. With no standing rigging left, her entire broadside crushed in, and in one place under her guards an immense hole where our entire battery struck almost the same instant, presented a scene of confusion and destruction perfectly indescribable. Many of our shells struck and passed through both sides, tearing and smashing everything in its way, and exploding on the far side of the vessel. Six shells passed through the engine-room, five exploding and breaking everything to atoms; two others, entering and exploding in the coal-bunkers, set fire to her in different parts. Their condition was truly horrible, with the ship on fire and her bottom knocked out. We scarcely had time to clear the wreck after receiving the last man, when with a heavy lurch she went down, leaving visible a small portion of her top-gallant masts. The engagement lasted thirteen and a half minutes, and the entire time occupied in fighting and rescuing prisoners was fifty minutes. . . .

The most astonishing thing is, how little loss of life there was. Their loss was two killed, one severely wounded, and six slightly, with twelve missing. . . . Our calamities—one man wounded in the chest by a splinter from the smoke-stack. Not unto us, not unto us, O God, but unto Thee be all the praise! After receiving the prisoners on board, we immediately shaped our course for the island of Jamaica, at which place I mail this.

IV

Another raider, the Florida, *aggravated the wound inflicted by the* Alabama. *The* Florida's *commander, Lieutenant John N. Maffitt, made a diary record of his escape from the Federal squadron blockading Mobile, where he had completed the outfitting of his ship:*[7]

January 16.—Blowing with avidity from the westward—rain at night. Had up steam, but the pilot said it was too dark to see Light-House Island—in fact, nothing could be distinguished [at] twenty yards. At two I was called. The stars were out, but a light mist covered the surface of the water. Got underway—the wind puffy from W. N. W. Double reefs were taken in our topsails and balanced reefs in the fore and main trysails. The topsails I caused to be mastheaded, and the gaskets replaced by split rope-yarns which would give way when the sheets were hauled upon and the sail set without sending the topmen aloft. Everything was secured for bad weather, a double watch set, and the crew piped down. At 2:20 all hands were called, steam was up and we were heading for the bar. A night of bitter cold had doubtless caused the Federal lookouts to obtain partial shelter from the stinging blasts of winter, and consequently abate much of their acute vigilance. This was the presumption, as to our astonishment we passed quite near to a blockader inside the bar, and were not discovered until abreast of a third, when a flame from the coal dust caused our discovery. Then the alarm was given by drums beating the call, flashing lights and general commotion, as cables were slipped, and 'mid the confusion of a surprise, a general chase commenced in the wildest excitement.

All the steam and canvas that could be applied urged us swiftly over the rugged seas, as half a dozen rampant Federals followed with intense eagerness on the trail of the saucy Confederate—that "rebel" craft whose escape from thraldom was sorely dreaded at the North, in visions of burning vessels and commercial disasters.

From stormy morn to stormy eve the chase is vigilantly continued —but the *Florida* under sail and steam was too fast for the Federals. Just before day—when all hands were breathing with more freedom—a large sail was discovered right ahead and close aboard. It was a steam sloop-of-war under topsails and looked like the *Brooklyn*. We sheered slightly from her, and again went to quarters. For some fifteen minutes we were under all her starboard guns, and a broadside would have sunk us; but the only evidence she gave of seeing us was by showing a light over the starboard gangway—and continued gracefully on without further notice; taking us, I presume, for one of their own gunboats that are so numerous in this locality.

A large armed ship was seen to the eastward and a fast gunboat on the starboard beam. Our friends from the bar continued after us in hot haste. Heavy pitching springs the foretopsail yard; to fish and repair renders it necessary to unbend the sail and send the spar on deck. This is quickly done, but the reduction of canvas depletes our speed and the enemy shorten their distance with increased efforts to overhaul us. The *Cuyler* was within three miles of us. Their exertions are futile, for our damages repaired, the canvas again quickly swells to the storm, showing against the background of gathering darkness a white and fleecy guiding-mark for the persistent enemy.

Desirous of ending the chase, I determined to despoil them of their guiding facility for steering. All hands were called to shorten sail, and like snowflakes under a summer sun, our canvas melts from view and is secured in long low bunts to the yards. Thus shorn of her plumage, the engines at rest, between high toppling seas, clear daylight was necessary to enable them to distinguish the low hull of the "rebel."

In eager chase the Federals swiftly pass us, following with zeal the apparition of the Confederate that to their deluded fancy looms up far in the distance. Satisfied with this maneuver, we jubilantly bid the enemy good-night and merrily steer to the southward.

At daylight there was nothing in sight but a foamy sea and black clouds. The *Florida* ran under a pressure fourteen and a half knots. She was very wet but rode the sea like a pilot-boat.

The morning of the 17th was ushered in by a bright sun and moderate northwest wind that betokened a cessation of stormy weather. By the log we had made a run of one hundred and fifty miles to the southward and eastward since parting with our persistent fellow-traveler of the previous evening. An officer reported from aloft, "Nothing in sight but sky and water," so the customary duties of the day were resumed.

V

Confederate raiders were not always as lucky or as powerful as the Florida. In February the Federal blockading squadron off the north Georgia coast caught the cruiser Nashville, *Southern-built and un-armored, in the Ogeechee River a few miles south of Savannah. The cruiser moved upstream to gain the protection offered by the guns of Fort McAllister. The Federal ships went after her. The action that followed was related by an officer of the* Montauk, *a new monitor commanded by the same John L. Worden who, in the first* Monitor, *had fought the* Merrimack *to a standstill:*[8]

Friday, February 27, 1863

. . . This afternoon, at three o'clock and fifteen minutes, the United States steamer *Wissahickon,* lying three miles below us, signalled that there was a strange sail up the river. No strange sail could be in that vicinity except the *Nashville,* and we bent our eyes eagerly toward the point of woods, and from behind the trees we saw black smoke ascending as from a steamer's smoke-stack. In fifteen or twenty minutes the column of smoke began growing blacker and thicker, and to move rapidly by the trees. Intently we watched the point, and in a moment, from behind the trees, came the foremast, then the smoke-stack, then the main mast, and there indeed, with the thick black smoke arising from her funnel and filling the atmosphere, and steaming rapidly, was the famous blockade-runner, the rebel pirate *Nashville.*

She steamed a short distance by the point, and then very suddenly stopped, and we saw that in endeavoring to cut her way through the shoal she had been brought up aground hard and fast. Immediately we went to quarters, and the United States steamer *Seneca,* by permission from Capt. Worden, steamed up the river to reconnoitre. She went to within two miles of the *Nashville,* and by way of trial threw four or five shells at her, but doing no harm, and in half-an-hour came to her anchorage again. In the meantime, the smoke increased from the *Nashville,* coming up into the air from her funnel, and rolling and curling into great black clouds, and telling us, how plainly, that they were struggling to get away. But it was of no use. She did not move an inch; the tide at the ebb when she ran aground, was now falling, and her condition was every moment becoming worse and worse.

Captain Worden would have moved up to attack her if he had thought it judicious, but he saw she could not get off until morning. Night was fast coming on, and he chose to wait. . . .

Saturday, Feb. 28

At four o'clock this morning all hands were awake, and at five o'clock we were all ready for the work which we had been earnestly hoping the day might bring us to do. It was a mild, pleasant morning, and the surface of the river was scarcely broken by a ripple. At five o'clock and ten minutes we weighed anchor, and in ten minutes more we were steaming at the rate of six knots up the river. The morning was just breaking, and it was not yet light enough to discover whether the *Nashville* was still on the shoal where last 'evening's darkness found her. . . .

A little further, and there she is, swung by the tide, and now pointing down-stream, yet still there hard and fast. We see many on her forecastle and considerable bustle and confusion. We steam on by "Hardee's cut," by the range-target of Fort McAllister, which is one thousand five hundred yards from the Fort, to a point nine hundred yards from the Fort, and at seven o'clock we come to anchor with fifteen fathoms of chain from windlass. Fort McAllister is on our left, in the angle of the bend of the river; we are nine hundred yards below, lying close in to the marsh on our right hand, the *Nashville* is a mile and a half above the Fort, but only eleven hundred yards from us across the marshy peninsula, and lying with full, fair broadside toward us; and the gunboats *Wissahickon, Seneca,* and *Dawn* are lying a mile and a half below us.

From the level of our deck we can see nothing of the *Nashville* but the paddle-boxes, smoke-stack and masts; but from the inside of the pilot house we can see the whole steamer, below her guards, and nearly to the water. She looks clean and trim, and as though freshly painted, and is of that same light drab color as all of our national vessels of war. Her masts and spars look well, her rigging is taut, and her figurehead has been newly gilded. At seven minutes past seven o'clock we fire our first gun (the eleven-inch) at the *Nashville*, and immediately they let fly at us from the Fort three guns, but their shot all go by us. The smoke from our own gun rises slowly, and we cannot see the effect of its shell. In thirty seconds we see another puff from the Fort, and another shell flies by us.

The Montauk *blasts a shell at the* Nashville *every two or three minutes, ignoring Fort McAllister:*

At fifty-seven minutes past seven we discovered a small column of whitish-gray smoke coming from out of her fore-hatch, and in ten minutes more the flame accompanies the smoke from the same place. . . .

We fire our last shot at three minutes after eight, having fired fourteen times; and as soon as the smoke has cleared away, we see the flames bursting out around her paddle-boxes, issuing in great hot sheets from the fore-hatch, creeping up the foremast rigging, and gaining aft. The fog, which has been slowly gathering around us, now entirely shuts us in, and we cannot see thirty yards.

After half an hour, the Montauk *headed downstream:*

In a few minutes the fog and smoke had risen, revealing the *Nashville* enveloped in flames. The fire came out from her sides, from around her smoke-stack base and masts, from between the ribs and braces of her iron wheels, and indeed she was shrouded in fire.

At thirty-five minutes past nine she blew up with a smothered rumbling report like distant thunder. The explosion was amidships, and the column of flame and smoke, like the discharge of a great gun, shot up into the air high above the mastheads, carrying up with it the charred and broken timber, and the burning bales of cotton. . . .

In a few moments another explosion of less extent took place aft, shattering and opening the stern of the steamer. Her masts, which had stood like two black spectres through the whole of it, soon came down, the flames gradually grew less, the long black column of smoke wound its way up to the cloud which had grown until it overshadowed the heavens, and nothing remained but the stem and the iron wheels.

A mass of smouldering embers is all that remains of the noted blockade-runner, the terror of our northern merchants, the destroyer of the *Harvey Birch*, the rebel pirate *Nashville*.

VI

The raiders hit body blows; rabbit punches came from the blockaderunners. By 1863 the art and business of evading the Federal blockading fleet had been reduced to a system. Ships, mainly English-owned and English-manned, carried goods needed in the Confederacy to Nassau or Bermuda, where they were loaded into other bottoms for the short run to ports in the Gulf of Mexico or on the Atlantic coast. James Russell

Soley, writing naval history twenty years after the war, saw that the odds had favored the blockade-runners:[9]

The typical blockade-runner of 1863–64 was a long, low side-wheeler steamer of from four to six hundred tons, with a slight frame, sharp and narrow, its length perhaps nine times its beam. It had feathering paddles, and one or two raking telescopic funnels, which might be lowered close to the deck. The hull rose only a few feet out of the water, and was painted a dull gray or lead color, so that it could hardly be seen by daylight at two hundred yards. Its spars were two short lower-masts, with no yards, and only a small crow's-nest in the foremast. The deck forward was constructed in the form known as "turtle-back," to enable the vessel to go through a heavy sea. Anthracite coal, which made no smoke, was burned in the furnaces. This coal came from the United States, and when, in consequence of the prohibition upon its exportation enforced by the Government, it could not be obtained, the semi-bituminous Welsh coal was used as a substitute. When running in, all lights were put out, the binnacle and fire-room hatch were carefully covered, and steam was blown off under water. . . ..

The start from Nassau or Bermuda was usually made at such a time that a moonless night and a high tide could be secured for running in. A sharp lookout was kept for cruisers on the outside blockade, and the blockade-runner, by keeping at a distance, could generally pass them unobserved. If by accident or carelessness he came very close, he took to his heels, and his speed enabled him to get away. He never hove to when ordered; it was as hard to hit him as to overtake him; a stray shot or two he cared nothing for. Even if his pursuer had the advantage of him in speed, which was rarely the case, he still kept on, and, by protracting the chase for a few hours, he could be sure that a squall, or a fog, or the approach of night would enable him to escape. . . .

Having passed the outside blockade successfully, and arrived in the neighborhood of his destination, the blockade-runner would either lie off at a distance, or run in close to the land to the northward or southward of the port, and wait for the darkness. Sometimes vessels would remain in this way unobserved for a whole day. If they found the place too hot and the cruisers too active, one of the inlets at a little distance from the port of destination would give the needful shelter. Masonboro Inlet, to the north of Wilmington, was a favorite resort for this purpose. At night the steamers would come out of hiding and make a dash for the entrance. . . .

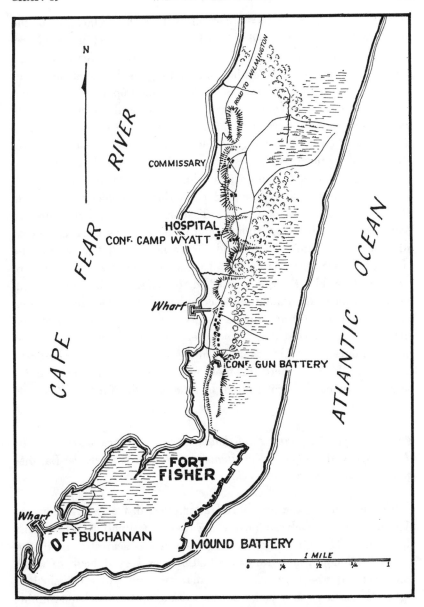

FORT FISHER AND THE APPROACH TO WILMINGTON

The run past the inshore squadron was always a critical moment, though by no means so dangerous as it looked. It was no easy matter on a dark night to hit, much less to stop, a small and obscure vessel, going at the rate of fifteen knots, whose only object was to pass by.

But the service nevertheless called into action all the faculties of the blockade-runner. It required a cool head, strong nerve, and ready resource. It was a combination of skill and pluck against force and vigilance. The excitement of fighting was wanting, as the blockade-runner must make no resistance; nor, as a rule, was he prepared to make any. But the chances, both outside and inshore, were all in his favor. He had only to make a port and run in, and he could choose time, and weather, and circumstances. He could even choose his destination. He always had steam up when it was wanted. He knew the critical moment, and was prepared for it; and his moments of action were followed by intervals of repose and relaxation. The blockader on the other hand, was in every way at a disadvantage. He had no objective point except the blockade-runner, and he never knew when the blockade-runner was coming. He could choose nothing, but must take the circumstances as they happened to come; and they were pretty sure to be unfavorable. He was compelled to remain in that worst of all situations, incessant watchfulness combined with prolonged inaction. There would be days and nights of anxious waiting, with expectation strained to the tensest point, for an emergency which lasted only as many minutes, and which came when it was least expected. There was no telling when or where the blow would need to be struck; and a solitary moment of napping might be fatal, in spite of months of ceaseless vigilance.

Thomas Taylor, a young Englishman lured into blockade-running by the prospect of profits and excitement, found both when the Banshee *made her first voyage early in 1863:*[10]

Wilmington was the first port I attempted; in fact with the exception of one run to Galveston it was always our destination. It had many advantages. Though furthest from Nassau it was nearest to headquarters at Richmond, and from its situation was very difficult to watch effectively. It was here, moreover, that my firm had established its agency as soon as they had resolved to take up the blockade-running business. The town itself lies some sixteen miles up the Cape Fear river, which falls into the ocean at a point where the coast forms the sharp salient angle from which the river takes its name. Off its mouth lies a delta, known as Smith's Island, which not only emphasizes the obnoxious formation of the coast, but also divides the approach to the port into two widely separated channels, so that in order to guard the approach to it a blockading force is compelled to divide into two squadrons.

At one entrance of the river lies Fort Fisher, a work so powerful that the blockaders instead of lying in the estuary were obliged to form roughly a semicircle out of range of its guns, and the falling away of the coast on either side of the entrance further increased the extent of ground they had to cover. The system they adopted in order to meet the difficulty was extremely well conceived, and, did we not know to the contrary, it would have appeared complete enough to ensure the capture of every vessel so foolhardy as to attempt to enter or come out.

Across either entrance an inshore squadron was stationed at close intervals. In the daytime the steamers composing this squadron anchored, but at night they got under weigh and patrolled in touch with the flagship, which, as a rule, remained at anchor. Further out there was a cordon of cruisers, and outside these again detached gun-boats keeping at such a distance from the coast as they calculated a runner coming out would traverse between the time of high water on Wilmington bar and sunrise, so that if any blockade-runner coming out got through the two inner lines in the dark she had every chance of being snapped up at daybreak by one of the third division.

Besides these special precautions for Wilmington there must not be forgotten the ships engaged in the general service of the blockade, consisting, in addition to those detailed to watch Nassau and other bases, of free cruisers that patrolled the Gulf-stream. From this it will be seen readily, that from the moment the *Banshee* left Nassau harbour till she had passed the protecting forts at the mouth of Cape Fear river, she and those on board her could never be safe from danger or free for a single hour from anxiety. But, although at this time the system was already fairly well developed, the Northerners had not yet enough ships at work to make it as effective as it afterwards became.

The *Banshee's* engines proved so unsatisfactory that under ordinary conditions nine or ten knots was all we could get out of her; she was therefore not permitted to run any avoidable risks, and to this I attribute her extraordinary success where better boats failed. As long as daylight lasted a man was never out of the cross-trees, and the moment a sail was seen the *Banshee's* stern was turned to it till it was dropped below the horizon. The lookout man, to quicken his eyes, had a dollar for every sail he sighted, and if it were seen from the deck first he was fined five. This may appear excessive, but the importance in blockade-running of seeing before you are seen is too great for any chance to be neglected; and it must be remembered that the pay of ordinary seamen for each round trip in and out was from £50 to £60.

Following these tactics we crept noiselessly along the shores of the Bahamas, invisible in the darkness, and ran on unmolested for the first two days out, though our course was often interfered with by the necessity of avoiding hostile vessels; then came the anxious moment on the third, when, her position having been taken at noon to see if she was near enough to run under the guns of Fort Fisher before the following daybreak, it was found there was just time, but none to spare for accidents or delay. Still the danger of lying out another day so close to the blockaded port was very great, and rather than risk it we resolved to keep straight on our course and chance being overtaken by daylight before we were under the Fort.

Now the real excitement began, and nothing I have ever experienced can compare with it. Hunting, pig-sticking, steeple-chasing, big-game shooting, polo—I have done a little of each—all have their thrilling moments, but none can approach "running a blockade"; and perhaps my readers can sympathise with my enthusiasm when they consider the dangers to be encountered, after three days of constant anxiety and little sleep, in threading our way through a swarm of blockaders, and the accuracy required to hit in the nick of time the mouth of a river only half a mile wide, without lights and with a coast-line so low and featureless that as a rule the first intimation we had of its nearness was the dim white line of the surf.

There were of course many different plans of getting in, but at this time the favourite dodge was to run up some fifteen or twenty miles to the north of Cape Fear, so as to round the northernmost of the blockaders, instead of dashing right through the inner squadron; then to creep down close to the surf till the river was reached: and this was the course the *Banshee* intended to adopt.

We steamed cautiously on until nightfall: the night proved dark, but dangerously clear and calm. No lights were allowed—not even a cigar; the engine-room hatchways were covered with tarpaulins, at the risk of suffocating the unfortunate engineers and stokers in the almost insufferable atmosphere below. But it was absolutely imperative that not a glimmer of light should appear. Even the binnacle was covered, and the steersman had to see as much of the compass as he could through a conical aperture carried almost up to his eyes.

With everything thus in readiness we steamed on in silence except for the stroke of the engines and the beat of the paddle-floats, which in the calm of the night seemed distressingly loud; all hands were on deck, crouching behind the bulwarks; and we on the bridge, namely, the captain, the pilot, and I, were straining our eyes into the darkness. Presently Burroughs made an uneasy movement—"Better get a cast of the lead, Captain," I heard him whisper. A muttered order down the engine-room tube was Steele's reply, and the *Banshee* slowed and then stopped. It was an anxious moment, while a dim figure stole into the fore-chains; for there is always a danger of steam blowing off when engines are unexpectedly stopped, and that would have been enough to betray our presence for miles around. In a minute or two came back the report, "sixteen fathoms—sandy bottom with black specks." "We are not as far in as I thought, Captain," said Burroughs, "and we are too far to the southward. Port two points and go a little faster." As he explained, we must be well to the northward of the speckled bottom before it was safe to head for the shore, and away we went again. In about an hour Burroughs quietly asked for another sounding. Again she was gently stopped, and this time he was satisfied. "Starboard and go ahead easy," was the order now, and as we crept in not a sound was heard but that of the regular beat of the paddle-floats still dangerously loud in spite of our snail's pace. Suddenly Burroughs gripped my arm—

"There's one of them, Mr. Taylor," he whispered, "on the starboard bow."

In vain I strained my eyes to where he pointed, not a thing could I see; but presently I heard Steele say beneath his breath, "All right, Burroughs, I see her. Starboard a little, steady!" was the order passed aft.

A moment afterwards I could make out a long low black object on our starboard side, lying perfectly still. Would she see us? that was the question; but no, though we passed within a hundred yards of her we were not discovered, and I breathed again. Not very long after we had dropped her Burroughs whispered—

"Steamer on the port bow."

And another cruiser was made out close to us.

"Hard-a-port," said Steele, and round she swung, bringing our friend upon our beam. Still unobserved we crept quietly on, when all at once a third cruiser shaped herself out of the gloom right ahead and steaming slowly across our bows.

"Stop her," said Steele in a moment, and as we lay like dead our enemy went on and disappeared in the darkness. It was clear there was a false reckoning somewhere, and that instead of rounding the head of the blockading line we were passing through the very center of it. However, Burroughs was now of opinion that we must be inside the squadron and advocated making the land. So "slow ahead" we went again, until the low-lying coast and the surf line became dimly visible. Still we could not tell where we were, and, as time was getting on alarmingly near dawn, the only thing to do was to creep down along the surf as close in and as fast as we dared. It was a great relief when we suddenly heard Burroughs say, "It's all right, I see the 'Big Hill'!"

The "Big Hill" was a hillock about as high as a full-grown oak tree, but it was the most prominent feature for miles on that dreary coast, and served to tell us exactly how far we were from Fort Fisher. And fortunate it was for us we were so near. Daylight was already breaking, and before we were opposite the fort we could make out six or seven gunboats, which steamed rapidly towards us and angrily opened fire. Their shots were soon dropping close around us: an unpleasant sensation when you know you have several tons of gunpowder under your feet. To make matters worse, the North Breaker shoal now compelled us to haul off the shore and steam further out. It began to look ugly for us, when all at once there was a flash from the shore followed by a sound that came like music to our ears—that of a shell whirring over our heads. It was Fort Fisher, wide awake and warning the gunboats to keep their distance. With a parting broadside they steamed sulkily out of range, and in half an hour we were safely over the bar. A boat put off from the fort and then—well, it was the days of champagne cocktails, not whiskies and sodas—and one did not run a blockade every day. For my part, I was mightily proud of my first attempt and my baptism of fire. Blockade-running seemed the pleasantest and most exhilarating of pastimes. I did not know then what a very serious business it could be.

The crew of a blockade-runner which had slipped into Wilmington found themselves in the most giddy—and corrupt—of Southern ports. A year after the war had ended "a late Confederate officer" wrote with aversion of a town that had placed profit above patriotism:[11]

. . . Through this port were brought till January '65 all the stores and material needed by the indefatigable Colonel Gorgas, the Confederate Chief of Ordnance, the most efficient bureau officer the Confederacy had. Through it came those famous Whitworth and Armstrong guns sent us by our English friends. Into Wilmington was brought by Mr. Commissary-General Northrup that rotten, putrid bacon called "Nassau," because it had spoiled on the wharves of that place before reshipped for Wilmington. . . .

But the cargoes of those white-painted, bird-like looking steamers that floated monthly into Wilmington, producing such excitement and joy among its population, unfortunately for the Confederates did not contain Government stores and munitions of war alone, bad as the bacon and much of the stuff bought abroad by worthless Confederate agents were. The public freight compared with the private was small. By them were brought in the cloth that made the uniforms of those gaily-decked clerks that swarmed the streets of Richmond with military titles, and read the battle bulletins and discussed the war news. From that source came the braid, buttons, and stars for that host of "Majors"—who were truly fifth wheels, and did not even have the labor of "following the Colonel around"—with which the Confederacy was afflicted. From it came the fine English brandies, choice foreign wines, potted meats, and conserves, jellies, and anchovy paste, etc., that filled the pantries and store-rooms of many of the officials at Richmond, and were spread out in such profusion at the dinners and suppers or *déjeuners* given by the "court circle" (as it was called) to officials when the "circle" wanted any of their pets promoted or assigned to good positions. From it came the loaf-sugar, coffee, tea, etc., that staff-officers, blockade-runners, and their relations and friends luxuriated in, while the ragged, dirty Confederate soldier, musket in hand, broiled or soaked in the trenches before Richmond and Petersburg. . . .

In fact there were numbers of Confederate officers, during the period blockade-running came under our view, whose sole business it seemed to be to lay in in that way stocks of groceries and dry-goods, and by speculating and shipping cotton from Wilmington and Charleston to lay by gold in case of an evil day. . . .

Talk about Yankees worshiping the almighty dollar! You should have seen the adoration paid the Golden Calf at Wilmington during the days of blockade-running. Everybody was engaged in it save the private soldiers and a few poor line and staff officers, who were not within the "ring," and possessed no influence or position there by which they could grant favors.

When a steamer came in, men, women, children rushed down to the wharves to see it, to buy, beg, or steal something. Everybody wanted to know if their "ventures"—the proceeds of the bales of cotton or boxes of tobacco sent out—had come in. No people were more excited than the women, expecting gloves, parasols, hoop-skirts, corsets, flannels, and bonnets, silks and calicoes; for these things became frightfully scarce and dear in the South during the last year of the war. The first people aboard of course were the agents—on such occasions very big men. Then swarmed officials and officers, "friends" and "bummers," hunting after drinks and dinners, and willing to accept any compliment, from a box of cigars or a bottle of brandy down to a bunch of bananas or a pocketful of oranges. Happy the man who knew well and intimately the steward of a blockade-runner, or could call the cook his friend, and get a part of the stealings from the pantry or the drippings from the kitchen!

How it made those bluff, coarse, vulgar Englishmen stare, who came in as pursers or officers, to see well-dressed gentlemen thus degrading themselves by sponging and loafing and disgracing their uniforms! We have seen many a fellow, bearing a commission, for hours eying from a stand-point on the wharf a blockade-runner as a cat would a mouse, and then just about lunch-time drop aboard to enjoy the champagne or porter, the sardines or Parmesan and English cheese. We have never heard them express it, but we can imagine the intense disgust that such men as John Wilkinson, Robert Carter, and other old navy officers, who occasionally commanded such ships, must have felt at this method some of their Confederate brethren had of living at other people's expense. . . .

Wilmington during that period swarmed with foreigners, Jews and Gentiles. In fact, going down the main street or along the river, you might well imagine you were journeying from Jerusalem to Jericho. As to the falling among thieves we will make no mention. The beggars at the gangways of the newly-arrived steamers were as thick as those in Egypt crying "bucksheesh."

At every turn you "met up," as our tar-heel friends say, with young Englishmen dressed like grooms and jockeys, or with a peculiar coachmanlike look, seeming, in a foreign land, away from their mothers, to indulge their fancy for the *outré* and extravagant in dress to the utmost. These youngsters had money, made money, lived like fighting-cocks, and astonished the natives by their pranks, and the way they flung the Confederate "stuff" about. Of course they were deeply interested in the Confederate cause, and at the same time wanted cotton. The Liverpool house of Alexander Collie and Co. had quite a regiment of these youngsters in their employ. Fine-looking fellows, with turned-up noses, blue eyes wide apart, and in their fluffy, straw-colored, mutton-chop whiskers floating in the wind, to the great admiration of their *chères amies*, the handsome quadroon washer-women, on whose man-telpieces and in whose albums were frequently to be found photographs strikingly resembling the aforesaid young foreigners. . . .

Of course there were many American houses, and American agents representing English houses, some of whom would fain have aped the hospitality of these young Britishers if they could; and others who upon no account would have done so. . . . Of course they all made fortunes—some at the expense of their country, some at the expense of their companies; which latter, in consequence, often had small divi-dends to make.

The residents of Wilmington were convinced that most blockade-runners made their destination. The reports of Federal naval commanders tell a different story:[12]

U. S. Schooner Matthew Vassar,
Off Little River Inlet,
January 11, 1863

Sir: I respectfully take the liberty of reporting to you the following: This morning at 9 when on my station, a sail hove in sight, bearing S. W. by S. I immediately got underway and gave chase. When they found what I was, they tacked and tried to run from me. When they found that I was gaining on them, they cut a hole in her port side with an ax, so that she might sink before I could capture her; and the cap-tain and crew took the boat and made for the land. I immediately sent an armed boat after them and captured them, while I pursued the vessel and boarded her and stopped the hole in her side from leaking. I found her to be the schooner *Florida*, of Nassau, Captain David Ireland, from Nassau, with a cargo of 400 sacks of salt, and was trying to get into some of the inlets on the coast of North or South Carolina. I made a seizure of her and put a prize master and four of a crew on board of her, and gave the prize master his proper instructions, with a detailed account of the seizure, to be forwarded to the flag officer at Hampton Roads and one for the Navy Department. . . .

Very respectfully, your obedient servant
Hugh H. Savage
Acting Master, Commanding, U. S. Navy.

U. S. Gunboat Chocura
At Sea, Lat. 33 24 N., Long. 78 05 W.,
January 21, 1863

Sir: I have the honor to inform you that this vessel, under my command, has this day seized for attempting to violate the blockade the British schooner *Pride*, from Nassau, New Providence, purporting to be bound to Baltimore, Md.

At the time of her capture she was about 15 miles S. E. from the outer end of Frying Pan Shoals, under a reefed mainsail and jib, with her head laying to the southward, the wind being west. As soon as she discovered this vessel to be in chase of her, she made sail, still standing to the southward, although the wind was fair for Baltimore.

The master, Thomas Phillips, on being asked why he was laying off the point of the shoals under easy sail with a fair wind blowing for his assumed port of destination, replied that he wished to keep to windward. The supercargo, James Brown, also told me that had he not been mistaken as to the character of this vessel we never would have caught him.

The *Pride* was built in Charleston, S. C., is loaded with 175 sacks salt, several cases drugs, shoes, etc.

I have sent her to Washington, D. C., for adjudication, in charge of Acting Master T. B. Sears. . . .

No other vessel was in sight at the time of the capture.

Very respectfully, your obedient servant,
W. T. Truxton,
Lieutenant-Commander

U. S. S. Cambridge
Off New Inlet, North Carolina,
January 24, 1863

Sir: The schooner *Time*, from Nassau, with an assorted cargo was taken as a prize by this vessel yesterday. I have put her in charge of a prize crew and ordered her to Beaufort, together with her papers.

From the course the schooner was steering when discovered, the nonappearance upon her manifest of soda, matches, and shoes, already found in her, the contradictory statements of her master, and his apparent anxiety, I have no hesitation in considering the schooner a legal prize, and also that it is my opinion her master (Poland), now on board the *Cambridge*, will, if released, endeavor again to run the blockade. . . .

I am, respectfully, your obedient servant,

WM. A. PARKER,

Commander

In spite of frequent losses, the owners of blockade-runners made fortunes:[13]

Until near the end of 1864, when the stringency of the blockade became extreme, the captures were not numerous enough to take up more than a slight margin of the enormous profits it [blockade-running] netted. These profits were made both on the outward and the inward voyages, and it is hard to say which were the more extraordinary. The inward cargoes consisted of all kinds of manufactured goods, and especially of "hardware," the innocent name under which arms and ammunition were invoiced. The sale of these brought in from five hundred to one thousand per cent of their cost. The return cargo was always cotton, and the steam-presses at Wilmington, reducing it to the smallest possible bulk, enabled the long, narrow, blockade-runners to carry six hundred, eight hundred, or even twelve hundred bales, of five or six hundred pounds each. Even the upper deck was piled up with two or three tiers of bales. As a clear profit of £30,000 each way was no uncommon result, it is easy to believe that owners could afford to lose a vessel after two successful trips. It was the current opinion in the squadron off Wilmington, in the early part of the last year, that two-thirds of the vessels attempting to enter were successful; and it has been estimated that out of the sixty-six blockade-runners making regular trips during the war, forty were captured or destroyed, but only after a successful career for a shorter or longer period. Gradually, in the last few months, too many vessels were caught to make the trade profitable; and it was slowly declining, though it did not cease altogether until the blockade was raised.

CHAPTER 20

OVER THE RIVER
AND UNDER
THE TREES

Georgia-born Montgomery C. Meigs was educated at the University of Pennsylvania and at West Point. An engineer by training, he built the Washington Aqueduct that brought a large part of the city's water supply from the Great Falls of the Potomac, and began the enlargement of the Capitol by adding wings and a new dome. In 1860, incurring the disfavor of Secretary of War Floyd through a disagreement over contracts, Meigs was "banished" to Tortugas and Key West to construct fortifications there, but soon after Lincoln took office he charged Meigs and Colonel Erasmus D. Keyes with the responsibility for drawing up plans for a secret expedition to Fort Pickens. In May 1861, the President named Meigs Quartermaster General.

Hitherto in American history no man had handled so much money so honestly. During the course of the war as Quartermaster General Meigs spent not less than $1,500,000,000, and he could produce a voucher for every penny of that sum. In later years he liked to boast that, beginning with John Quincy Adams, he had shaken hands with sixteen of twenty-one Presidents, but his favorite was clearly Lincoln. Meigs understood the President's problems in different terms from most frequent callers at the White House. At full strength, for example, the Army of the Potomac carried 200,000 men on its rolls and whether "idle or employed" this army cost the people of the United States $200,-000,000 a year.* When, therefore, McClellan dawdled on the Peninsula, growling over charges of intrigue that in Meigs's opinion "originated in his own typhoid fever," the Quartermaster General could put Lincoln's dilemma in entirely practical terms.

I

When the year 1862 had only a day to go, Meigs remained a fretful man. On this day, while Abraham Lincoln pondered the final wording of the Proclamation of Emancipation, and Magruder poised for an attack on Galveston, and Rosecrans and Bragg counted their thousands already dead along the banks of Stone River, the Quartermaster General wrote a long, impassioned letter. The recipient: a fellow West Pointer, Ambrose E. Burnside:[1]

WASHINGTON, December 30, 1862

MY DEAR GENERAL: You were good enough to say that you would be pleased to hear from me, and I venture to say a few words to you which neither the newspapers nor, I fear, anybody in your army is likely to utter.

In my position as Quartermaster-General much is seen that is seen from no other standpoint of the Army.

The Secretary of the Treasury has always felt the pressure of the difficulty of providing means to carry on the war, but he has thus far succeeded, so that the credit of the Government has not much suffered. Our contracts for supplies have not been made at prices higher than the consumption of the material might justify. Contractors have been content to wait a few weeks or months for their pay, and to receive it in certificates of debt, instead of in Treasury notes or gold. Hay and oats, two essentials for an army, have risen, however, until it is difficult to find men willing to undertake their delivery, and the prices are higher than ever before. A ton of hay costs not less than $30, and a bushel of oats costs $1 by the time it gets to Aquia. I begin to fear that

---

* Meigs was invited by the editors of *Battles and Leaders* to contribute a memoir of the war, and he wrote his account of planning the Fort Pickens expedition and the Cabinet meetings in January 1862 which finally prodded McClellan into the Peninsula campaign. The article was not published until years later when it came into the hands of the editors of the *American Historical Review*, where it appears in the issue for January 1921, pp. 285–303.

the supply will fail. Should this happen, your army would be obliged to retire, and the animals would be dispersed in search of food.

Every day's consumption of your army is an immense destruction of the natural and monetary resources of the country. The country begins to feel the effect of this exhaustion, and I begin to apprehend a catastrophe. Your army has, I suspect, passed its period of greatest efficiency, and, by sickness, disability, and discharge, is decreasing in numbers. The animals have been recruited by rest, and are in better condition than they will be a month hence. The weather and the roads will not in months be again as favorable as during the weeks which have elapsed since the battle of Fredericksburg, a battle which made veterans of your troops, and added more strength by this than it took from your army by losses in the field.

General Halleck tells me that you believe your numbers are greater than the enemy's, and yet the army waits! Some officers talk of having done enough; of going into winter quarters. This I do not understand to be your thought, but I am told that you probably find opinions differ as to the possibility of any proposed movement. In so great a matter, on which so much depends, there will be always differences of opinion. There are few men who are capable of taking the responsibility of bringing on such a great conflict as a battle between two such armies as oppose each other at Fredericksburg. So long as you consult your principal officers together, the result will be that proverbial of councils of war. Upon the commander, to whom all the glory of success will attach, must rest the responsibility of deciding the plan of campaign. Every day weakens your army; every day lost is a golden opportunity in the career of our country—lost forever. Exhaustion steals over the country. Confidence and hope are dying. While I have been always sure that ultimate success must attend the cause of freedom, justice and government sustained by 18,000,000 against that of oppression, perjury, and treason supported by 5,000,000, I begin to doubt the possibility of maintaining the contest beyond this winter, unless the popular heart is encouraged by victory on the Rappahannock. . . .

It seems to me that the army should move bodily up the Rappahannock, across the river, aim for a point on the railroad between the rebels and Richmond, and send forward cavalry and light troops to break up the road and intercept retreat. Your divisions marching within supporting distance, and ordered to march to the sound of battle, would concentrate upon any field, and compel a general engagement. The result would be with the God of battles, in whose keeping we believe our cause to rest. Will we ever have a better opportunity? Do not we grow weaker every day? Can you not adopt this movement, which, if successful, promises the greatest results, and even if unsuccessful, leaves a practicable route of retreat? If any other movement promises greater or readier results, let it be adopted; but rest at Falmouth is defeat to our nation—is defeat, border warfare, hollow truce, barbarism, ruin for ages, chaos! To any plan you will find objections. Address yourself to the great work. Decide upon your plan and give your orders to each general to march by a certain road at a certain hour, and to expect that on his right or left such another will cooperate with him if he meets the enemy. Whatever advice they may give, you have no general in your army who will fail to march promptly on your order or to fight gallantly when brought face to face with the enemy.

The gallantry of the attack at Fredericksburg made amends for its ill success, and soldiers were not discouraged by it. The people, when they understood it, took heart again. But the slumber of the army since is eating into the vitals of the nation. As day after day has gone, my heart has sunk, and I see greater peril to our nationality in the present condition of affairs than I have seen at any time during the struggle.

Forgive me if I have written freely and strongly. I cannot express myself as strongly as I feel our danger, and I know that you, as I hope myself, have only one object—the success of our cause and salvation of our country.

Truly and respectfully, your friend,
M. C. MEIGS

On the morning of January 1, 1863, Burnside made a hasty visit to the White House, spurred perhaps by Meigs's letter, perhaps by his own appraisal of the military situation. To Lincoln the Federal commander said that he wanted to order the Army of the Potomac across the Rappahannock but that his principal officers opposed the movement. Lincoln asked Halleck for advice, but so tactlessly that "Old Brains" huffily submitted his resignation. The President withdrew his request; Halleck withdrew his resignation. Burnside added to the confusion, and to Lincoln's trials, with a letter in which he stressed his differences with Halleck, Stanton, and his own commanders, and offered his resignation. If Lincoln received this distraught communication, he made no reply.

Four days later, at Headquarters of the Army of the Potomac, Burn-side wrote two more letters. The first he addressed to His Excellency the President of the United States:[2]

January 5, 1863

Since my return to the army I have become more than ever convinced that the general officers of this command are almost unanimously opposed to another crossing of the river, but I am still of the opinion that the crossing should be attempted, and I have accordingly issued orders to the engineers and artillery to prepare for it. There is much hazard in it, as there always is in the majority of military movements, and I cannot begin the movement without giving you notice of it, particularly as I know so little of the effect that it may have upon other movements of distant armies. . . .

In order to relieve you from all embarrassment in my case, I inclose, with this, my resignation of my commission as major-general of volunteers, which you can have accepted, if my movement is not in accordance with the views of yourself and your military advisers. . . .

I have the honor to be, very respectfully, your obedient servant,

A. E. BURNSIDE

The second letter went to Major General H. W. Halleck, General in Chief:

January 5, 1863

GENERAL: I have decided to move the army across the river again, and have accordingly given the directions to the engineers and artillery to make the necessary preparations to effect the crossing.

Since I last saw you it has become more apparent that the movement must be made almost entirely upon my own responsibility, so far as this army is concerned; and I do not ask you to assume any responsibility in reference to the mode or place of crossing, but it seems to me that, in making so hazardous a movement, I should receive some general directions from you as to the advisability of crossing at some point, as you are necessarily well informed of the effect at this time upon other parts of the army of a success or a repulse. You will readily see that the responsibility of crossing without the knowledge of this effect, and against the opinion of nearly all the general officers, involves a greater responsibility than any officer situated as I am ought to incur. . . .

I have the honor to be, very respectfully, your obedient servant,

A. E. BURNSIDE

The elementary tactical admonitions in Halleck's reply expressed the
General in Chief's lack of confidence in Burnside's capacity:[3]

WASHINGTON, January 7, 1863
MAJOR-GENERAL BURNSIDE, COMMANDING, &C., FALMOUTH:
GENERAL: Your communication of the 5th was delivered to me by your aide-de-camp at 12 M. today. . . .

In all our interviews I have urged that our first object was, not Richmond, but the defeat or scattering of Lee's army, which threatened Washington and the line of the Upper Potomac. I now recur to these things simply to remind you of the general views which I have expressed, and which I still hold.

The circumstances of the case, however, have somewhat changed since the early part of November. The chances of an extended line of operations are now, on account of the advanced season, much less than then. But the chances are still in our favor to meet and defeat the enemy on the Rappahannock, if we can effect a crossing in a position where we can meet the enemy on favorable or even equal terms. I therefore still advise a movement against him. The character of that movement, however, must depend upon circumstances which may change any day and almost any hour. If the enemy should concentrate his forces at the place you have selected for a crossing, make it a feint and try another place. Again, the circumstances at the time may be such as to render an attempt to cross the entire army not advisable. In that case theory suggests that, while the enemy concentrates at that point, advantages can be gained by crossing smaller forces at other points, to cut off his lines, destroy his communication, and capture his rear guards, outposts, etc. The great object is to occupy the enemy, to prevent his making large detachments or distant raids, and to injure him all you can with the least injury to yourself. If this can be best accomplished by feints of a general crossing and detached real crossings, take that course; if by an actual general crossing, with feints on other points, adopt that course. There seems to me to be many reasons why a crossing at some point should be attempted. It will not do to keep your large army inactive. As you yourself admit, it devolves on you to decide upon the time, place, and character of the crossing which you may attempt. I can only advise that an attempt be made, and as early as possible.

Very respectfully, your obedient servant,
H. W. HALLECK

To this letter the President added an indorsement:

January 8, 1863.

GENERAL BURNSIDE:

I understand General Halleck has sent you a letter of which this is a copy. I approve this letter. I deplore the want of concurrence with you by your general officers, but I do not see the remedy. Be cautious, and do not understand that the Government or country is driving you. I do not yet see how I could profit by changing the command of the Army of the Potomac, and if I did, I should not wish to do it by accepting the resignation of your commission.

A. LINCOLN

II

Thus encouraged—or at least not deterred—Burnside persisted in his determination to cross the Rappahannock and recoup the grievous loss his army had suffered at Fredericksburg. William Swinton, a correspondent of the New York Times, *writing from "Camp Near Falmouth, January 23, 1863," described the bad luck that dogged the apprehensive, ill-starred, but devoted commander:*[4]

On Tuesday [January 20] every preparation had been made. That day Gen. Burnside issued a general order, announcing that the Army of the Potomac was "about to meet the enemy once more," and that "the auspicious moment had arrived to strike a great and mortal blow to the rebellion, and to gain that decisive victory which is due to the country." This order was read to the men that evening, and night found the infantry encamped in the woods within easy speaking distance. The positions for the batteries had all been selected. The batteries were at hand. The pontoons were within reach, a short distance back of the river.

We were sitting, the editor in chief of the *Times* * and the present writer, in our tent at headquarters that evening, looking forward to a start on horseback for the scene of operations before daylight the following morning. About nine o'clock a light, ominous pattering was heard on the canvas roof. "It is rain!" was the exclamation, and, looking out from the tent, the heavens showed all the signs of a terrible storm. From that moment we felt that the winter campaign had ended.

* Henry J. Raymond had gone to Falmouth following an inaccurate report of the death of his younger brother James, who fought with the Twenty-fourth Michigan.

It was a wild Walpurgis night, such as Goethe paints in the "Faust" while the demons held revel in the forest of the Brocken. All hopes that it would be a "mere shower" were presently blasted. It was evident we were in for a regular north-easter, and among the roughest of that rough type. Yet there was hard work done that fearful night. One hundred and fifty pieces of artillery were to be planted in the position selected for them by Gen. Hunt, Chief of Artillery—a man of rare energy and of a high order of professional skill. The pontoons, also were drawn nearer toward the river, but it was dreadful work; the roads, under the influence of the rain, were becoming shocking; and by daylight, when the boats should all have been on the banks, ready to slide down into the water, but fifteen had been gotten up—not enough for one bridge, and five were wanted!

. . . The utmost effort was put forth to get pontoons enough into position to construct a bridge or two. Double and triple teams of horses and mules were harnessed to each pontoon-boat. It was in vain. Long powerful ropes were then attached to the teams, and one hundred and fifty men were put to the task on each boat. The effort was but little more successful. They would founder through the mire for a few feet —the gang of Lilliputians with their huge-ribbed Gulliver—and then give up breathless. Night arrived, but the pontoons could not be got up. The rebels had discovered what was up, and the pickets on the opposite bank called over to ours that they "would come over tomorrow and help us build the bridge."

That night the troops again bivouacked in the same position in the woods they had held the night before. You can imagine it must have been a desperate experience—and yet not by any means as bad as might be supposed. The men were in the woods, which afforded them some shelter from the wind and rain, and gave them a comparatively dry bottom to sleep on. Many had brought their shelter-tents; and making a flooring of spruce, hemlock, or cedar boughs, and lighting huge camp fires, they enjoyed themselves as well as the circumstances would permit. On the following morning a whisky ration, provided by the judicious forethought of Gen. Burnside, was on hand for them.

Thursday morning saw the light struggling through an opaque envelope of mist, and dawned upon another day of storm and rain. It was a curious sight presented by the army as we rode over the ground, miles in extent, occupied by it. One might fancy some new geologic cataclysm had overtaken the world; and that he saw around him the elemental wrecks left by another Deluge.

An indescribable chaos of pontoons, wagons, and artillery encumbered the road down to the river—supply wagons upset by the roadside—artillery "stalled" in the mud—ammunition trains mired by the way. Horses and mules dropped down dead, exhausted with the effort to move their loads through the hideous medium. One hundred and fifty dead animals, many of them buried in the liquid muck, were counted in the course of a morning's ride. And the muddle was still further increased by the bad arrangements, or rather the failure to execute the arrangements that had been made. It was designed that Franklin's column should advance by one road and Hooker's by another. But, by mistake, a portion of the troops of the left grand division debouched into the road assigned to the center, and cutting in between two divisions of one of Hooker's corps, threw everything into confusion. In consequence, the woods and roads have for the past two days been filled with stragglers, though every man of them were involuntary stragglers, and were evidently honestly seeking to rejoin their regiments.

It was now no longer a question of how to go on; it was a question of how to get back. . . .

III

Thus ended the career of Ambrose E. Burnside as commander of the Army of the Potomac. As if to insure his dismissal he confronted the President with a demand that four general officers of his command be discharged from the Army and that five others be relieved from duty. The alternative was the acceptance of his own resignation.

Lincoln did not hesitate. On January 25 he removed Burnside from command and appointed to his place Major General Joseph Hooker—the same Hooker whom Burnside had charged with being guilty of "unjust and unnecessary criticisms of the actions of his superior officers, and of the authorities," of having, "by the general tone of his conversation, endeavored to create distrust in the minds of officers who have associated with him," and of having made reports and statements "calculated to create incorrect impressions, and for habitually speaking in disparaging terms of other officers"—all of which made him "unfit to hold an important commission during a crisis like the present, when so much patience, charity, confidence, consideration, and patriotism are due from every soldier in the field."

Lincoln knew that Hooker was far from blameless, but the President hoped that wise counsel would curb his new commander's loose tongue and salvage for the Union his proved will to fight:[5]

EXECUTIVE MANSION,

WASHINGTON, January 26, 1863

MAJOR GENERAL HOOKER:

GENERAL.

I have placed you at the head of the army of the Potomac. Of course I have done this upon what appear to me to be sufficient reasons. And yet I think it best for you to know that there are some things in regard to which, I am not quite satisfied with you. I believe you to be a brave and a skilful soldier, which, of course, I like. I also believe you do not mix politics with your profession, in which you are right. You have confidence in yourself, which is a valuable, if not an indispensable quality. You are ambitious, which, within reasonable bounds, does good rather than harm. But I think that during Gen. Burnside's command of the Army, you have taken counsel of your ambition, and thwarted him as much as you could, in which you did a great wrong to the country, and to a most meritorious and honorable brother officer. I have heard, in such a way as to believe it, of your recently saying that both the Army and the Government needed a Dictator. Of course it was not *for* this, but in spite of it, that I have given you the command. Only those generals who gain successes, can set up dictators. What I now ask of you is military success, and I will risk the dictatorship. The government will support you to the utmost of its ability, which is neither more nor less than it has done and will do for all commanders. I much fear that the spirit which you have aided to infuse into the Army, of criticising their Commander, and withholding confidence from him, will now turn upon you. I shall assist you as far as I can, to put it down. Neither you, nor Napoleon, if he were alive again, could get any good out of an army, while such a spirit prevails in it.

And now, beware of rashness. Beware of rashness, but with energy, and sleepless vigilance, go forward, and give us victories.

Yours very truly

A. LINCOLN

Regis de Trobriand, French-born litterateur, volunteer colonel at the outbreak of the war, and in 1863 a seasoned brigade commander, added detail to the reservations which the President had expressed. Of the new commander of the Army of the Potomac, De Trobriand wrote:[6]

Towards the officers his manners were generally pleasant, familiar even to taking a glass of whiskey with those whom he liked. In the high position in which he was placed, a little more reserve would not have been out of place.

He was an easy talker, and was accustomed to criticise freely, with more sharpness than discretion, even in the presence of his inferiors, the conduct and acts of his superiors. On the other hand, when it concerned himself, he indulged in boastings, that one hearing could not accept as gospel truth, or reckon modesty in the number of his virtues.

Kind to his subordinates, his kindness would have been worth more if he had not extended it too indiscriminately to everybody. Prodigal of promises, his promises would have inspired more confidence if, after having made them, he had not often deprived himself of the power to fulfil them.

He had not acquired the cordial feeling of the generals as much as that of the troops. He had wounded some by openly criticising them; he had alienated others by putting himself forward at their expense. The friends of McClellan did not love him. They had against him the double grievance of his military judgments and of his political opinions, both equally opposed to those of their old idol, to whose overthrow he had contributed so much.

Captain Charles Francis Adams, Jr., son of the American Minister to England, saw in Hooker few virtues and many vices:[7]

A showy officer, and one capable of fairly good work in a limited command—that of a brigade or division—he was altogether devoid of character; insubordinate and intriguing when at the head of a corps, as a commander he was in nearly every respect lacking. It is true that after superseding Burnside he did some effective work towards organizing the Army of the Potomac. Nevertheless, that was a period in its history when, so far as character was concerned, the Army of the Potomac sank to its lowest point. It was commanded by a trio, of each of whom the least said the better. It consisted of "Joe" Hooker, "Dan" Sickles, and "Dan" Butterfield. All three were men of blemished character. During the winter (1862–63), when Hooker was in command, I can say from personal knowledge and experience, that the Headquarters of the Army of the Potomac was a place to which no self-respecting man liked to go, and no decent woman could go. It was a combination of barroom and brothel.

Yet even Major General Darius N. Couch, who became Hooker's bitterest critic, would write in retrospect that he had never known men "to change from a condition of the lowest depression to that of a healthy fighting state" as the Army of the Potomac changed under the new commander. Before the Committee on the Conduct of the War, Hooker described his methods:[8]

At the time the army was turned over to me, desertions were at the rate of about 200 a day. So anxious were parents, wives, brothers and sisters to relieve their kindred, that they filled the express trains to the army with packages of citizen clothing to assist them in escaping from service. At that time perhaps a majority of the officers, especially those high in rank, were hostile to the policy of the government in the conduct of the war. The emancipation proclamation had been published a short time before, and a large element of the army had taken sides antagonistic to it, declaring that they never would have embarked in the war had they anticipated this action of the government. When rest came to the army, the disaffected, from whatever cause, began to show themselves, and make their influence felt in and out of the camps. . . .

At the moment I was placed in command I caused a return to be made of the absentees of the army, and found the number to be 2,922 commissioned officers, and 81,964 non-commissioned officers and privates. These were scattered all over the country, and the majority were absent from causes unknown. . . .

My first object was to prevent desertion, and when this was accomplished, my whole attention was directed to securing the return of absentees, and rendering those present as comfortable and contented as circumstances would allow. I granted leaves of absence and furloughs to a limited extent, and in such manner as enabled all to be absent for a few days in the course of the winter. The disloyal officers were dismissed [from] the service as soon as evidence of the fact was brought to my knowledge. The express trains were examined by the provost marshal, and all citizens' clothing found was burned.

Important changes were introduced into the various staff departments, and especially in that of the inspector general, which was thoroughly organized and filled with the most competent officers I could select in the army. Believing idleness to be the great evil of all armies, every effort was made to keep the troops employed; and whenever the weather would permit it, they were engaged in field exercises. . . .

Early in April, though the roads were still heavy, and impractical for artillery and wagons, I believed that the army was in condition to march on the enemy, and, as I had about 40,000 nine-months and two-years men whose terms of service would soon expire, I felt it necessary to commence operations at the earliest practicable moment.

IV

Before Hooker could set his army in motion, Union spirits were dashed by the failure of a movement which everyone, Confederates included, had expected to succeed.

Ever since the surrender of Fort Sumter the North had dreamed of recapturing Charleston. The success of the Monitor *in battling the Merrimack to a draw led many naval officers to believe that monitors, low in the water, hard to hit, and even harder to sink, could reduce Sumter and the other forts that guarded Charleston harbor. As the new ships were commissioned they were sent one after the other to Admiral Samuel F. Du Pont, commanding the South Atlantic squadron. By early April, with eight monitors and his flagship, the heavily armored sloop* New Ironsides, *Du Pont was ready. On the sixth the flotilla crossed the Charleston bar and anchored off Morris Island to await a favorable tide and good weather. The combination came soon after noon the next day. Admiral Charles R. P. Rodgers, serving as Du Pont's chief of staff, saw the battle from the flagship:*[9]

It was a quarter-past one when the ironclads * left their anchorage. . . . The admiral had arranged to lead in the *Ironsides*, but, much against his will, after earnest persuasion from his captains, consented to occupy the center. As the fleet slowly passed near the beach of Morris Island, no shot was fired from ship or shore; Battery Wagner was also silent as it was passed; but as the leading monitor came within range of Fort Moultrie the Confederate and Palmetto flags were hoisted on the batteries, and a salute of thirteen guns was fired.

It was 3 o'clock when the first shot was fired from Moultrie and returned by the *Weehawken*. Then Sumter and Batteries Bee and Beauregard, Cumming's Point, and Wagner opened fire, and the action became general. The *Ironsides*, flat-bottomed and with greater draught than the monitors, found herself within one foot of the bottom, and under the influence of the current steered so badly that it became necessary to drop an anchor to bring her head to tide. The anchor was quickly raised, and she was again under way, but the delay threw the line into

* Rodgers' terminology is confusing. Only the *New Ironsides* was an armored ship of conventional design; the others were monitors, or floating batteries: revolving turrets mounted on low platformlike decks.

some unavoidable confusion, and two of the following monitors came in harmless collision with the flagship. They were directed to go on, disregarding the order of sailing, and the *Ironsides* quickly followed them; but when it was fifteen hundred yards or less from Sumter, the same difficulty in steering occurred, and the anchor was again dropped to prevent stranding and to bring the ship's head in the right direction. As the *Ironsides* swung to the tide into deeper water, she came directly over a huge torpedo, made from an old boiler, filled with gunpowder, and connected with Battery Wagner by an electric wire; but, fortunately for those on board, the electrician at Battery Wagner, to his great disgust, could not send the electric spark to the powder. . . .

In his order for the day, Admiral Du Pont had planned to deliver his first attack upon the north-west face of Sumter, passing inside the gorge of the harbor for that purpose, and lingering before the fort until he should have reduced it, or at least silenced its fire. The *Weehawken*, the leading monitor, pressing forward with this view, came to the floating obstructions between Sumter and Moultrie, and the probability of her screw being entangled and the vessel held immovable under a fire more deadly than any ship had ever before encountered led her commander to turn from the obstructions and begin the attack short of the place designated in the plan of battle. As he turned, a torpedo exploded under him, giving a shock but no serious injury to the monitor. In the whole navy there was no cooler, more gallant, more judicious man than John Rodgers. . . . No officer in the navy was better qualified to command its confidence when he decided not to attempt to force the obstructions. He was followed by Percival Drayton, Farragut's trusted and well-tried chief-of-staff, by John Worden, of monitor fame, and by that grim, true-hearted fighting man, Daniel Ammen. These, all turning short of the obstructions, threw the vessels following into some confusion, and caused the *Ironsides* to lose her steerageway and to anchor as already mentioned.

While the anchor was being lifted to move forward, Admiral Du Pont turned to his chief-of-staff and asked the time. Upon being told that it was nearly 5 o'clock he quietly said, "Make signal to the ships to drop out of fire; it is too late to fight this battle tonight; we will renew it early in the morning."

. . . The day on which this engagement took place was very beautiful; there was little wind and the sea was smooth. When the Confederate guns of 10-inch, 9-inch, 8-inch Columbiads and 7-inch Brooke rifles, with many other rifled and smooth-bore guns, were turned upon the ironclads, the sight was one that no one who witnessed it will ever forget; sublime, infernal, it seemed as if the fires of hell were turned upon the Union fleet. The air seemed full of heavy shot, and as they flew they could be seen as plainly as a baseball in one of our games. On board the *Ironsides*, the sense of security the iron walls gave those within was wonderful—a feeling akin to that which one experiences in a heavy storm when the wind and hail beat harmlessly against the windows of a well-protected house. This, however, was not equally felt in the monitors; for in their turrets the nuts that secured their laminated plates flew wildly, to the injury and discomfiture of the men at the guns, while the solid plates of the *Ironsides* gave no such trouble; and although she was reported to have been struck ninety-five times, she was uninjured except by the loss of a port shutter and the piercing of her unarmored ends. . . .

As the *Ironsides* lifted her anchor to drop down to the anchorage for the night . . . the other vessels, retiring from closer action in obedience to his signal, came near, some of them within hail. The first was the *Keokuk*, riddled like a colander, the most severely mauled ship one ever saw, and on her deck the daring and able Rhind, than whom no braver man ever commanded a ship, and who came limping forward, wounded, to tell in a few emphatic words that his ship was disabled. Then followed two or three of the monitors, their captains telling the story of disabled guns or crippled turrets. The others reported by signal. Orders were at once given to the mechanics of the squadron to work all night in repairing damages, and after dark the commanding officers, having made their ships secure, came on board the flagship to report in person.

Du Pont weighed the results of the day and came to a decision. The following morning Rodgers encountered an inflexible commander:

At daylight, when the chief-of-staff went on deck, he found the admiral already there, who said to him, with his usual straightforward frankness, "I have given careful thought during the night to all the bearings of this matter, and have come to a positive determination from which I shall not swerve. I ask no one's opinion, for it could not change mine. I have decided not to renew the attack. During the few minutes we were under the heaviest fire of the batteries we engaged, half of our turret-ships were in part or wholly disabled. We have only encountered the outer line of defense, and if we force our way into the harbor we have not men to occupy any forts we may take, and we can have no communication with our force outside except by running the gauntlet. In the end we shall retire, leaving some of our ironclads in the hands of the enemy, to be refitted and turned against our blockade with deplorable effect. We have met with a sad repulse; I shall not turn it into a great disaster."

And so it was announced to the fleet and to the army that the attack would not be renewed. The monitor *Patapsco* was sent at once to Port Royal to make that place secure, and the other monitors were ordered to be ready to sail as soon as the *Ironsides* could cross the bar.

V

The failure at Charleston made even more imperative a victory by the Army of the Potomac. Northern morale could not stand many more reverses. Hooker, supremely confident, embarked on the first phase of his plan to smash Lee's army in its lines around Fredericksburg, the scene of Burnside's disastrous defeat. Darius N. Couch, commanding the Second Corps, described the first moves:[10]

The weather growing favorable for military operations, on April 12th were commenced those suggestive preliminaries to all great battles, clearing out the hospitals, inspecting arms, looking after ammunition, shoeing animals, issuing provisions, and making every preparation necessary to an advance. The next day, the 13th, Stoneman was put in motion at the head of ten thousand finely equipped and well organized cavalry to ascend the Rappahannock and, swinging around, to attack the Confederate cavalry wherever it might be found, and "Fight! fight! fight!" At the end of two days' march Stoneman found the river so swollen by heavy rains that he was constrained to hold up, upon which Hooker suspended his advance until the 27th. This unexpected delay of the cavalry seemingly deranged Hooker's original plan of campaign. He had hoped that Stoneman would have been able to place his horsemen on the railroad between Fredericksburg and Richmond, by which Lee received his supplies, and make a wreck of the whole structure, compelling that general to evacuate his stronghold at Fredericksburg and vicinity and fall back toward Richmond.

Hooker had 120,000 men fit for duty, Lee no more than 60,000. The Union commander planned to cross the Rappahannock at three widely separated fords, concentrate one force at Fredericksburg on Lee's right and another at Chancellorsville, fifteen miles to the west, on the Confederate left; then converge with a pincers movement that would either crush the Army of Northern Virginia or force it to withdraw toward Richmond.

The river crossings met little opposition. By the evening of April 30 the troops were safely on the south side, and Hooker had set up his headquarters at Chancellorsville.

Meanwhile Lee had shown little concern. Captain James Power Smith of "Stonewall" Jackson's staff pictured the nonchalance of the Confederate commander on the eve of battle:[11]

At daybreak on the morning of the 29th of April, 1863, sleeping in our tents at corps headquarters, near Hamilton's Crossing, we were aroused by Major Samuel Hale, of Early's staff, with the stirring news that Federal troops were crossing the Rappahannock on pontoons under cover of a heavy fog. General Jackson had spent the night at Mr. Yerby's hospitable mansion near by, where Mrs. Jackson had brought her infant child for the father to see. He was at once informed of the news, and promptly issued to his division commanders orders to prepare for action. At his direction I rode a mile across the fields to army headquarters, and finding General Robert E. Lee still slumbering quietly, at the suggestion of Colonel Venable, whom I found stirring, I entered the General's tent and awoke him. Turning his feet out of his cot he sat upon its side as I gave him the tidings from the front. Expressing no surprise, he playfully said: "Well, I thought I heard firing, and was beginning to think it was time some of you young fellows were coming to tell me what it was all about. Tell your good general that I am sure he knows what to do. I will meet him at the front very soon."

May 1 was marked with hesitant, indecisive fighting. The right wing of the Army of the Potomac advanced, with little opposition, to a commanding position two miles east of Chancellorsville, and then, under the inexplicable but peremptory orders of its commander, was withdrawn. That night Lee and Jackson stayed at Catherine's Furnace, a mile and a half south of Hooker's headquarters at Chancellorsville. Early in the evening Captain Smith of Jackson's staff found both men asleep, Jackson on a pile of straw, Lee at the foot of a tree covered with his army cloak. Smith aroused Lee, who sat up on the ground and said:[12]

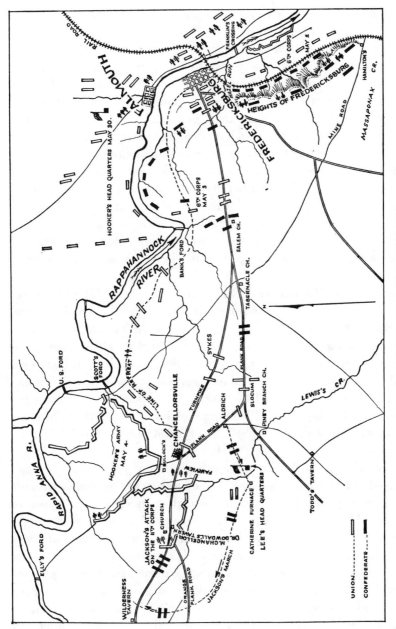

THE BATTLE OF CHANCELLORSVILLE

"Ah, Captain, you have returned, have you? Come here and tell me what you have learned on the right." Laying his hand on me he drew me down by his side, and, passing his arm around my shoulder, drew me near to him in a fatherly way that told of his warm and kindly heart. When I had related such information as I had secured for him, he thanked me for accomplishing his commission, and then said he regretted that the young men about General Jackson had not relieved him of annoyance, by finding a battery of the enemy which had harassed our advance, adding that the young men of that day were not equal to what they were when he was a young man. Seeing immediately that he was jesting and disposed to rally me, as he often did young officers, I broke away from the hold on me which he tried to retain, and, as he laughed heartily through the stillness of the night, I went off to make a bed of my saddle-blanket, and, with my head in my saddle, near my horse's feet, was soon wrapped in the heavy slumber of a wearied soldier.

Some time after midnight I was awakened by the chill of the early morning hours, and, turning over, caught a glimpse of a little flame on the slope above me, and sitting up to see what it meant, I saw, bending over a scant fire of twigs, two men seated on old cracker boxes and warming their hands over the little fire. I had but to rub my eyes and collect my wits to recognize the figures of Robert E. Lee and Stonewall Jackson. Who can tell the story of that quiet council of war between two sleeping armies? Nothing remains on record to tell of plans discussed, and dangers weighed, and a great purpose formed, but the story of the great day soon to follow.

It was broad daylight, and the thick beams of yellow sunlight came through the pine branches, when some one touched me rudely with his foot, saying: "Get up, Smith, the general wants you!" As I leaped to my feet the rhythmic click of the canteens of marching infantry caught my ear. Already in motion! What could it mean? In a moment I was mounted and at the side of the general, who sat on his horse by the roadside, as the long line of our troops cheerily, but in silence as directed, poured down the Furnace road. His cap was pulled low over his eyes, and, looking up from under the visor, with lips compressed, indicating the firm purpose within, he nodded to me, and in brief and rapid utterance, without a superfluous word, as though all were distinctly formed in his mind and beyond question, he gave me orders for our wagon and ambulance trains. From the open fields in our rear, at the head of the Catherine road, all trains were to be moved upon that road to Rodd's Tavern, and thence west by interior roads, so that our troops would be between them and the enemy at Chancellorsville. My orders having been delivered and the trains set in motion, I returned to the site of our night's bivouac, to find that General Jackson and his staff had followed the marching column.

What did it mean, this inexplicable forced march away from the enemy? Before the day was over, Private John O. Casler of the "Stonewall Brigade," and many thousand others, learned the answer:[18]

Three divisions of our corps under Jackson started on the march and moved south for a while, and we could hear skirmishing on our right. We could not imagine where we were going. We continued marching through fields and woods, until about three o'clock in the afternoon. The day was hot, and we marched fast—the men throwing away their overcoats and blankets.

The other two divisions were in front of ours and we began to think Jackson was on one of his flank movements, when one of his couriers came back and told our Gen. to hurry up his command as Gen. Jackson was waiting for it to form in line. We knew then there was business on hand. Our Pioneer Corps always marched in front of the division near the Gen. and staff, and was under directions from the engineers; consequently we heard and knew more of the movements of the army than generally falls to the lot of a private.

In a short time about three miles southwest of Chancellorsville we came to a road leading from Orange C. H. through Chancellorsville to Fredericksburg. We were halted and the three divisions formed in three lines of battle across the road to the right and left—one division in rear of the other. . . .

As yet not a gun had been fired; everything was still and quiet; the troops were tired and moved about noiselessly; there were thick woods and underbrush on each side of the road with an occasional field or farm. While resting in this position a courier came to us who was acquainted with some of our boys, and said we were in rear of the Yankees, and that he could not tell how it was, but we would soon see the greatest move of the war.

In a few moments Lieut. Heindrix, one of the engineers, came and said he wanted ten pioneers to go with him to remove a blockade in the road. I was one of the ten. We moved down the road in front and commenced clearing the road of trees that had been felled across it. There were four pieces of artillery there waiting to move forward. They unlimbered one piece, and we helped them to get it over the blockade before we had it cleared. They then fired a shot down the road, and moved on. At the same time the three lines of infantry moved forward at double quick with a yell. I learned afterwards that the firing of the gun was a signal for all to move; and move they did with a vengeance, and moved everything in front of them.

We soon got the blockade open and all the artillery through. We then came to another blockade and soon opened that. I heard two or three shells come tearing up the road from the enemy, but heard nothing else from them until we got to Chancellorsville after dark.

It was a running fight for three miles. We took them completely by surprise, and our three divisions got merged into one line of battle, all going forward at full speed. Our artillery did not have time to unlimber and fire, they had to keep in a trot to keep up with the infantry. We ran through the enemy's camps, where they were cooking supper. Tents were standing, and camp-kettles were on the fire full of meat. I saw a big Newfoundland dog lying in one tent as quietly as if nothing had happened. We had a nice chance to plunder their camps and search the dead; but the men were afraid to stop, as they had to keep with the artillery and were near a good many officers, who might whack them over the head with their swords if they saw them plundering; but the temptation was too great, and sometimes they would run their hands in some of the dead men's pockets as they hurried along, but seldom procured anything of value. . . .

It was the 11th U. S. Army Corps that we first attacked, and demoralized. Another corps was sent to their assistance, but were likewise repulsed. Our army did not halt until dark when we came to the enemy's fortified position in and around Chancellorsville.

Our officers then commenced forming the men in line, and getting them in some kind of order, but the men kept up a terrible noise and confusion, hollowing for this regiment and that regiment, until it seemed that there were not more than three or four of any regiment together. They were all mixed up in one confused mass. The enemy could hear us distinctly by the noise we made. They located us precisely, and immediately opened on us with twenty pieces of artillery, at short range, and swept the woods and road with the most terrific and destructive shelling that we were subjected to during the war. . . .

We could hear some one scream out every second in the agonies of death. Jake Fogle kept praying all the time. Every time a shell would pass directly over us Jake would say, "Lord, save us this time!" Sam Nunnelly, a wild reckless fellow, would laugh at him, and say, "Pray on, Jake!" "Pray on, Jake!" and the two kept that up as long as the shelling lasted. Cross and I tried to get Sam to hush, but it was no use.

Our infantry and artillery did not reply, as we did not have a piece in position. It stood in the road just where they left it when they drove up, and every man of them was laying as close to the ground as he could get. They dug "nose holes" to get closer. The Yankees soon ceased firing, however, and the men commenced calling for their commands again, making as much noise as ever. Immediately we were treated to another dose of shells as terrific as before, and with fearful effect, but for some reason it was not long continued.

If the enemy had known our situation, and the good range they had on us, they would literally have torn us to pieces and nearly annihilated our corps that night.

The Confederate victory—a victory despite the confusion in the attacking force—cost a high price. Captain Smith narrated the events that led to tragedy—the demoralization of the Confederate front, Jackson's order to throw in A. P. Hill's reserve division, Stonewall's impatience at the slowness of the maneuver:[14]

While this change was being effected . . . the general rode forward on the turnpike, followed by two or three of his staff and a number of couriers and signal sergeants. He passed the swampy depression and began the ascent of the hill toward Chancellorsville, when he came upon a line of the Federal infantry lying on their arms. Fired at by one or two muskets (two musket-balls from the enemy whistled over my head as I came to the front), he turned and came back toward his line, upon the side of the road to his left. As he rode near to the Confederate troops, just placed in position and ignorant that he was in the front, the left company began firing to the front, and two of his party fell from their saddles dead—Captain Boswell, of the Engineers, and Sergeant Cunliffe, of the Signal Corps. Spurring his horse across the road to his right, he was met by a second volley from the right company of Pender's North Carolina brigade. Under this volley, when not two rods from the troops, the general received three balls at the same instant. One penetrated the palm of his right hand and was cut out that night from the back of his hand. A second passed around the wrist of the left arm and out through the left hand. A third ball passed through the left arm half-way from shoulder to elbow. The large bone of the upper arm was splintered to the elbow-joint, and the wound bled freely. His horse turned quickly from the fire, through the thick bushes which swept the cap from the general's head, and scratched his forehead, leaving drops of blood to stain his face. As he lost his hold upon the bridle-rein, he reeled from the saddle, and was caught by the arms of Captain Wilbourn, of the Signal Corps. Laid upon the ground, there came at once to his succor General A. P. Hill and members of his staff. The writer reached his side a minute after, to find General Hill holding the head and shoulders of the wounded chief. Cutting open the coat-sleeve from wrist to shoulder, I found the wound in the upper arm, and with my handkerchief I bound the arm above the wound to stem the flow of blood. Couriers were sent for Dr. Hunter McGuire, the surgeon of the corps and the general's trusted friend, and for an ambulance. Being outside of our lines, it was urgent that he should be moved at once. With difficulty litter-bearers were brought from the line near by, and the general was placed upon the litter and carefully raised to the shoulder, I myself bearing one corner.

A moment after, artillery from the Federal side was opened upon us; great broadsides thundered over the woods; hissing shells searched the dark thickets through, and shrapnels swept the road along which we moved. Two or three steps farther, and the litter-bearer at my side was struck and fell, but, as the litter turned, Major Watkins Leigh, of Hill's staff, happily caught it. But the fright of the men was so great that we were obliged to lay the litter and its burden down upon the road. As the litter-bearers ran to the cover of the trees, I threw myself by the general's side and held him firmly to the ground as he attempted to rise. Over us swept the rapid fire of shot and shell—grape-shot striking fire upon the flinty rock of the road all around us, and sweeping from their feet horses and men of the artillery just moved to the front. Soon the firing veered to the other side of the road, and I sprang to my feet, assisted the general to rise, passed my arm around him, and with the wounded man's weight thrown heavily upon me, we forsook the road. Entering the woods, he sank to the ground from exhaustion, but the litter was soon brought, and again rallying a few men, we essayed to carry him farther, when a second bearer fell at my side. This time, with none to assist, the litter careened, and the general fell to the ground, with a groan of deep pain. Greatly alarmed, I sprang to his head, and, lifting his head as a stray beam of moonlight came through the clouds and leaves, he opened his eyes and wearily said: "Never mind me, Captain, never mind me." Raising him again to his feet, he was accosted by Brigadier-General Pender: "Oh, General, I hope you are not seriously wounded. I will have to retire my troops to re-form them, they are so much broken by this fire." But Jackson, rallying his strength, with firm voice said: "You must hold your ground, General Pender; you must hold your ground, sir!" and so uttered his last command on the field.

Again we resorted to the litter, and with difficulty bore it through the bush, and then under a hot fire along the road. Soon an ambulance was reached, and stopping to seek some stimulant at Chancellor's (Dowdall's Tavern), we were found by Dr. McGuire, who at once took charge of the wounded man. Passing back over the battlefield of the afternoon, we reached the Wilderness store, and then, in a field on the north, the field-hospital of our corps under Dr. Harvey Black. Here we found a tent prepared, and after midnight the left arm was amputated near the shoulder, and a ball taken from the right hand.

All night long it was mine to watch by the sufferer, and keep him warmly wrapped and undisturbed in his sleep. At 9 A.M., on the next day, when he aroused, cannon firing again filled the air, and all the Sunday through the fierce battle raged, General J. E. B. Stuart commanding the Confederates in Jackson's place. A dispatch was sent to the commanding general to announce formally his disability—tidings General Lee had received during the night with profound grief. There came back the following note:

"General: I have just received your note, informing me that you were wounded. I cannot express my regret at the occurrence. Could I have directed events, I should have chosen, for the good of the country, to have been disabled in your stead. I congratulate you upon the victory which is due to your skill and energy. Most truly yours, R. E. Lee, General."

When this dispatch was handed to me at the tent, and I read it aloud, General Jackson turned his face away and said, "General Lee is very kind, but he should give the praise to God."

Private John O. Casler, CSA, knew that a Federal attack on Jackson's corps would change Chancellorsville from a Union defeat to a victory; Major General Joseph Hooker, USA, did not. Couch described the Union commander's choice, and its result:[15]

After the day's mishaps Hooker judged that the enemy could not have spared so large a force to move around his front without depleting the defenses of Fredericksburg. According, at 9 P.M. [May 2], an imperative order was sent to the commander of the left wing to cross the river at Fredericksburg, march upon Chancellorsville, and be in the vicinity of the commanding general at daylight. But Sedgwick was already across the river and three miles below Fredericksburg. It was 11 P.M., May 2d, when he got the order, and twelve or fourteen miles had to be marched over by daylight. The night was moonlight, but any officer who has had experience in making night marches with infantry will understand the vexatious delays occurring even when the road is clear; but when, in addition, there is an enemy in front, with a line of fortified heights to assault, the problem which Sedgwick had to solve will be pronounced impossible of solution. However, that officer set his column in motion by flank, leaving one division that lay opposite the enemy, who were in force to his left. The marching column, being continually harassed by skirmishers, did not arrive at Fredericksburg until daylight. The first assault upon the heights behind the town failed. Attempts to carry them by flank movements met with no success. Finally a second storming party was organized, and the series of works were taken literally at the point of the bayonet, though at heavy loss. It was then 11 A.M. The column immediately started for Chancellorsville, being more or less obstructed by the enemy until its arrival near Salem Heights, 5 or 6 miles out, where seven brigades under Early, six of which had been driven from the defenses of Fredericksburg, made a stand in conjunction with supports sent from Lee's army before Chancellorsville. This was about the middle of the afternoon, when Sedgwick in force attacked the enemy. Though at first successful, he was subsequently compelled to withdraw those in advance and look to his own safety by throwing his own flanks so as to cover Banks's Ford, the friendly proximity of which eventually saved this wing from utter annihilation.

While Sedgwick's men struggled up the heights at Fredericksburg, the right wing of the Union army went into action a dozen miles to the west. Couch's story continues:

At about 5 A.M., May 3d, fighting was begun at Chancellorsville. . . . Soon . . . the battle ran along the whole line. The enemy's guns on the heights to our left, as well as at every point on the line where they could be established, were vigorously used, while a full division threw itself on Miles at Mott's Run. On the right flank our guns were well handled, those of the Twelfth Corps being conspicuous, and the opposing lines of infantry operating in the thicket had almost hand-to-hand conflicts, capturing and recapturing prisoners. The enemy appeared to know what he was about, for pressing the Third Corps vigorously he forced it back, when he joined or rather touched the left of Lee's main body, making their line continuous from left to right. Another advantage gained by this success was the possession of an open field, from which guns covered the ground up to the Chancellor House. Upon the south porch of that mansion General Hooker stood leaning against one of its pillars, observing the fighting, looking anxious and much careworn. After the fighting had commenced I doubt if any orders were given by him to the commanders on the field, unless, perhaps, "to retire when out of ammunition." None were received by me, nor were there any inquiries as to how the battle was going along my front. . . .

Not far from 8:30 A.M. the headquarters pennants of the Third and Twelfth corps suddenly appeared from the right in the open field of Chancellorsville; then the Third began to fall back, it was reported, for want of ammunition, followed by that portion of the Twelfth fighting on the same flank, and the division of the Second Corps on its right. . . . The open field seized by Jackson's old corps after the Third Corps drew off was shortly dotted with guns that made splendid practice through an opening in the wood upon the Chancellor House, and everything else, for that matter, in the neighborhood. Hooker was still at his place on the porch, with nothing between him and Lee's army but Geary's division of the Twelfth and Hancock's division and a battery of the Second Corps. But Geary's right was now turned, and that flank was steadily being pressed back along his intrenched line . . . when a cannon-shot struck the pillar against which Hooker was leaning and knocked him down. A report flew around that he was killed. I was at the time but a few yards to his left, and, dismounting, ran to the porch. The shattered pillar was there, but I could not find him or any one else. Hurrying through the house, finding no one, my search was continued through the back yard. All the time I was thinking, "If he is killed, what shall I do with this disjointed army?" * Passing through the yard I came upon him, to my great joy, mounted, and with his staff also in their saddles. Briefly congratulating him on his escape—

* Couch outranked all other officers on the field. Had Hooker been incapacitated, the command of the Army of the Potomac would have devolved on Couch.

it was no time to blubber or use soft expressions—I went about my own business. This was the last I saw of my commanding general in front.

Forty-five minutes later one of Hooker's aides informed Couch that the general wanted to see him:

Turning to General Hancock, near by, I told him to take care of things and rode to the rear. The Chancellor House was then burning, having been fired in several places by the enemy's shells.

At the farther side of an open field, half a mile in the rear of Chancellorsville, I came upon a few tents (three or four) pitched, around which, mostly dismounted, were a large number of staff-officers. General Meade was also present, and perhaps other generals. General Hooker was lying down I think in a soldier's tent by himself. Raising himself a little as I entered, he said: "Couch, I turn the command of the army over to you. You will withdraw it and place it on the position designated on this map," as he pointed to a line traced on a field-sketch. . . .

No time was to be lost, as only Hancock's division now held Lee's army. Dispatching Major John B. Burt with orders for the front to retire, I rode back to the thicket, accompanied by Meade, and was soon joined by Sickles, and after a little while by Hooker, but he did not interfere with my dispositions. Hancock had a close shave to withdraw in safety, his line being three-fourths of a mile long, with an exultant enemy as close in as they dared, or wished, or chose to be, firing and watching. But everything was brought off, except five hundred men of the Second Corps who, through the negligence of a lieutenant charged by Hancock with the responsibility of retiring the force at Mott's Run, were taken prisoners. . . .

VI

Throughout May 4 the two armies, exhausted, did little but glare at each other. That night Hooker summoned his corps commanders to a council of war. Couch reported:

Hooker stated that his instructions compelled him to cover Washington, not to jeopardize the army, etc. It was seen by the most casual observer that he had made up his mind to retreat. We were left by ourselves to consult, upon which Sickles made an elaborate argument, sustaining the views of the commanding general. Meade was in favor

of fighting, stating that he doubted if we could get off our guns.
Howard was in favor of fighting qualifying his views by the remark that
our present situation was due to the bad conduct of his corps, or words
to that effect. Reynolds, who was lying on the ground very much
fatigued, was in favor of an advance. I had similar views to those of
Meade as to getting off the guns, but said I "would favor of an advance
if I could designate the point of attack." Upon collecting the suffrages
Meade, Reynolds, and Howard voted squarely for an advance, Sickles
and myself squarely no; upon which Hooker informed the council that
he should take upon himself the responsibility of retiring the army to
the other side of the river. As I stepped out of the tent Reynolds,
just behind me, broke out, "What was the use of calling us together
at this time of night when he intended to retreat anyhow?"

*Lee issued a congratulatory order to his troops. The Confederate com-
mander's preamble was slightly askew—after all, it had been the
Union forces which had attacked, and the "strongly intrenched" forces
wore gray instead of blue—but no one could question the fact that the
South had won another sweeping victory:*[16]

GENERAL ORDERS   HDQRS. ARMY OF NORTHERN VIRGINIA,
   No. 59.   May 7, 1863.
With heartfelt gratification the general commanding expresses to the
army his sense of the heroic conduct displayed by officers and men
during the arduous operations in which they have just been engaged.
Under trying vicissitudes of heat and storm, you attacked the enemy,
strongly intrenched in the depths of a tangled wilderness, and again
on the hills of Fredericksburg, 15 miles distant, and, by the valor that
has triumphed on so many fields, forced him once more to seek
safety behind the Rappahannock. While this glorious victory entitles
you to the praise and gratitude of the nation, we are especially called
upon to return our grateful thanks to the only Giver of victory for the
signal deliverance He has wrought. It is, therefore, earnestly recommended that the troops unite on Sunday next in ascribing to the Lord of
Hosts the glory due unto His name.

*Captain James Power Smith told how, for Stonewall Jackson, the
battle continued after the guns had fallen silent:*[17]

On Monday [May 4] the general was carried in an ambulance,
by way of Spotsylvania Court House, to most comfortable lodging at

Chandler's, near Guinea's Station, on the Richmond, Fredericksburg and Potomac railroad. And here, against our hopes, notwithstanding the skill and care of wise and watchful surgeons, attended day and night by wife and friends, amid the prayers and tears of all the Southern land, thinking not of himself, but of the cause he loved, and for the troops who had followed him so well and given him so great a name, our chief sank, day by day, with symptoms of pneumonia and some pains of pleurisy, until, at 3:15 P.M. on the quiet of the Sabbath afternoon, May 10th, 1863, he raised himself from his bed, saying, "No, no, let us pass over the river, and rest under the shade of the trees"; and, falling again to his pillow, he passed away, "over the river, where, in a land where warfare is not known or feared, he rests forever 'under the trees.' "

Colonel G. F. R. Henderson, British military critic and author of the classic biography of Jackson, saw in the general's death a loss which the Confederacy could not replace:[18]

Jackson's fall left Lee alone, bereft of his *alter ego;* with none, save Stuart, to whom he could entrust the execution of those daring and delicate manoeuvers his inferior numbers rendered necessary; with none on whose resource and energy he could implicitly rely. Who shall say how far his own resolution had been animated and confirmed at other crises by the prompting and presence of the kindred spirit? "They supplemented each other," said Davis, "and together, with any fair opportunity, they were absolutely invincible."

Many a fierce battle still lay before the Army of Northern Virginia; marvellous was the skill and audacity with which Lee manoeuvered his ragged regiments in the face of overwhelming odds; fierce and unyielding were the soldiers, but with Stonewall Jackson's death the impulse of victory died away.

THE HOME FRONT

W ITH THE WAR costing the Lincoln Administration more than
$1,000,000 a day that it did not possess, the Federal government faced
with repugnance the two accepted means of raising money—either to
take it from the people or to borrow it. In a somewhat optimistic mood
Salmon P. Chase, Secretary of the Treasury, had estimated that the
deficit by July 1862 would reach $900,000,000; it amounted, in
fact, to $1,100,000,000.

Neither taxation nor a loan appealed to congressional leaders, who
invented, as an escape from both, the Legal Tender Act, putting the
Federal government into the paper-money business. In order to convince the public and themselves that they acted wisely, it became necessary for legislators to discredit the nation's bankers and brokers. Where
logic might be lacking, invective was not. Clubfooted old Thaddeus
Stevens of Pennsylvania rose in the Senate to stigmatize all dealers in
money as "sharks," adding, by way of afterthought, that they were also
"harpies"; the Honorable Samuel Shellabarger of Ohio damned all who
"out of the blood of their sinking country" would "coin the gains of
their infamy"; and Henry Wilson of Massachusetts saw the issue before the government as a practical choice between "brokers and
jobbers and money-changers on the one side, and the people of the
United States on the other."

I

*Spokesman for the Legal Tender Act in the House was Elbridge G.
Spaulding of New York, chairman of the all-powerful Ways and Means
Committee, whose bold voice rang out in deep emotion:*[1]

The bill before us is a war measure,—a measure of necessity, not of
choice. . . . Congress may judge of the necessity in the present exi-

gency. It may decide whether it will authorize the Secretary of the Treasury to issue demand Treasury notes, and make them a legal tender in payment of debts; or whether it will put its six or seven per cent bonds on the market, at ruinous rates of discount, and raise the money at any sacrifice the money-lenders may require, to meet the pressing demands upon the Treasury. In the one case the government will be able to pay its debts at fair rates of interest; in the other, it must go into the streets *shinning* for the means, like an individual in failing circumstances, and sure of being used up in the end by the avarice of those who may exact unreasonable terms. But, sir, knowing the power of money, and the disposition there is among men to use it for the acquisition of greater gain, I am unwilling that this government, with all its immense power and resources, should be left in the hands of any class of men, bankers or money-lenders, however respectable or patriotic they may be. The government is much stronger than any of them. Its capital is much greater. It has control of all the bankers' money and all the brokers' money, and all the property of the thirty millions of people under its jurisdiction. Why then should it go into Wall Street, State Street, Chestnut Street, or any other street, begging for money? Their money is not as secure as government money. All the gold they possess would not carry on the government for ninety days. They issue only promises to pay, which, if Congress does its duty, are not half so secure as United States Treasury notes based on adequate taxation of all the property of the country. *Why, then, go into the streets at all to borrow money?* I am opposed in our present extremities to all shifts of this kind. I prefer to assert the power and dignity of the government by the issue of its own notes.

By a vote of 93 to 59 the Legal Tender Act passed the House. The Senate was much more reluctant to go along with the measure, mustering a mere majority of five in its favor. Charles Sumner of Massachusetts spoke his misgivings:

. . . Is it necessary to incur all the unquestionable evils of inconvertible paper, forced into circulation by act of Congress; to suffer the stain upon our national faith; to bear the stigma of a seeming repudiation; to lose for the present that credit which in itself is a treasury; and to teach debtors everywhere that contracts may be varied by the will of the stronger? Surely, there is much in these inquiries which may make us pause. . . . It is hard, very hard, to think that such a country, so powerful, so rich, and so beloved, should be compelled to adopt a policy of even questionable propriety. . . . Surely we must all be against paper money,—we must all insist on maintaining the integrity of the government; and we must all set our faces against any proposition like the present, except as a temporary expedient rendered imperative by the exigency of the hour. . . . Others may doubt if the exigency is sufficiently imperative, *but the Secretary of the Treasury does not doubt.* . . . Reluctantly, painfully, I consent that the process should issue.

In early February 1863, the editors of Harper's Weekly *addressed themselves to "that famous mystic spot, Wall Street," then "going through one of those fevers which render it so terribly enchanting to persons of a speculative turn of mind." Ominously* Harper's Weekly *drew a picture of "a period which occurs but once in a century— perhaps but once in a couple of centuries":²*

History does but repeat itself. What England experienced in 1787– 1815 we are now going to attempt. There is this difference in our case. The Bank of England, under suspension, did not materially increase its paper issues. Our Bank—which is the United States Government—has already issued as much paper money as there was afloat in the whole country in 1860, and is going to issue an indefinite number of hundreds of millions more.

We are witnessing the commencement of the new era. Gold has risen to 155. Stocks have risen 100–200 per cent. The broker class has doubled in numbers. Instead of one board we have two, and each transacts far more business than was ever done in old times on the legitimate stock exchange. Speculators in stock have increased in the ratio of the square of the brokers. If the latter have doubled, the former have quadrupled. In this era of newspapers, railroads, and telegraphs, intelligence is transmitted rapidly throughout the country; our stock exchange represents not this city alone but the whole country.

One of the largest operators of the day lives in Wisconsin, and operates by telegraph. We deem him to be a quiet, thoughtful man, who never reads anything in the papers except the facts, and religiously declines to notice editorial comments and opinions. . . . He began business (in stocks) with a cargo of corn as his capital; he has already realized over a quarter of a million dollars. For, you see, he has this advantage over city operators—that he is not swayed by the temporary and deceptive currents of Wall Street, arrives at his conclusions on abiding principles of political economy, and steadily adheres to them until they are realized.

Harper's *editors offered practical advice:*

Nothing is more fatal in Wall Street than sympathies. Jones had a brother a Brigadier-General in the Army of the Potomac; was consequently confident of victory because he wanted victory; operated on the confidence, and was so thoroughly used up in August, 1862, after the battles of the seven days—which were not quite so brilliant things in victories as he expected—that he was glad to enter the office of Smith as a bookkeeper. Smith was a man of a different stamp. His father, his brothers, and his cousins were in the rebel army. He had a sister who was a rebel in New York, an aunt who was a rebel at Philadelphia, and an uncle who was a rebel at Baltimore. The uncle communicated, by rebel post, with a relative at Richmond—sent him letters, pins, needles, opium, and quinine—and received intelligence in return— Smith paying the bills. This intelligence was quickly transmitted to the female rebel relative at Philadelphia, and by her to the other female rebel relative at New York, and so Smith had a monopoly, the possession whereof tempted him so to operate that in a few months he smashed to pieces. His sympathies and his private exclusive information always led him to expect that Stonewall Jackson would be in New York, or at least in Washington, on the Monday morning following; and, operating accordingly, he met his fate.

The editors scratched their heads:

How will this end? Echo answers—how? To make money by buying stocks and selling them at an advance corresponding to the depreciation of the currency is really not to make any money at all. Prices must eventually adjust themselves to the gold standard, and the "purchasing power" of $100 of paper money with gold at par will ultimately prove the same as the purchasing power of $150 with gold at 150. . . . We must see, however, how the new financial scheme of Congress will affect Wall Street. That measure was designed to check speculation in gold and stocks, and was calculated to produce that end by creating a temporary stringency in the money market. If it succeeds, not a few of the *nouveaux riches* will realize the proverb about riches having wings. If the ingenuity of Congress can evade the inexorable law of political economy which declares that issues of irredeemable paper must cause that paper to depreciate steadily, and prices to advance in a corresponding ratio, a triumph of no mean import will have been won.

II

The financial worries of the editors of Harper's Weekly *still could not match the economic nightmares that had begun to disturb the slumbers of many in Richmond. At the outbreak of the war the gold in all Southern banks amounted to about $25,000,000, of which $10,000,000 was held by the banks in New Orleans where state laws made it virtually impossible to suspend specie payments. By April 1861, banks in New Orleans held over $17,000,000 in gold. Under Louisiana law, these banks could neither receive nor pay out Confederate notes. Not until mid-September was the Richmond government able to use this gold reserve. By then the Confederate Congress had authorized the issue of $100,000,000 in Confederate treasury notes and a levy of a tax on property to provide for their redemption. But the Confederacy had no taxgathering machinery of its own, and the collections fell upon the states. Charles W. Ramsdell, an incisive student of the Confederacy, tells how these policies and expediencies led to a rapid growth of state debts and an exhaustion of state credit:*[3]

. . . It was clearly a dangerous policy, as many Southerners well knew, and could be defended only as a necessary temporary expedient in the expectation of a short war. But, as the war dragged on and the Confederate treasury was driven by the scarcity of coin to the same paper money policy and began to issue huge amounts of unsalable bonds and irredeemable treasury notes, thoughtful men became alarmed. We shall see this depreciating currency aggravating every difficulty that beset both people and government.

Meanwhile, the course of business in general became erratic. The depression, which accompanied the futile discussions of compromise in the United States Congress and the secession movement in the Gulf states, caused southern merchants to cut down their orders for new goods. Whether there was much boycotting of northern-made articles is hard to say, though we know that there were threats of such reprisals. But when hostilities began, stocks of goods in many towns were already low. Then the blockade, while not yet very effective, discouraged importations. Business in the port towns fell off rapidly. On the other hand, there was a brisk demand for all sorts of army supplies—small arms, munitions, clothing, shoes, tents, blankets, cooking utensils, horses, wagons, leather goods, and foodstuffs. Agents and contractors for the army supply bureaus were busy; numbers of merchants whose ordinary business fell away became local quartermasters or purchasing agents for the army. Here and there men with an eye to profits in manufacturing articles needed for the army began to look about for capital with which to erect plants or enlarge existing establishments. The business of the railroads likewise suffered during the winter and many of them reduced their working force. Few were equipped for heavy business and, with the growth of government demands for transportation, they soon found themselves unable to handle the increased traffic. . . . In brief, while some lines of business were languishing, others were stimulated to great activity. Trade was suddenly shifted into new channels and the result was confusion.

By 1863, when the only certainty about the war was the fact that no one could predict how or when it would end, Jefferson Davis faced no problem more pressing than that of a dislocated Southern economy. In his message to the Confederate Congress that year the President did not disguise his alarm:[4]

. . . After great embarrassment, and more than three months of assiduous labor, you succeeded in framing the law of the twenty-fourth April, 1863, by which you sought to reach, so far as was practicable, every resource of the country, except the capital invested in real estate and slaves, and by means of an income-tax and a tax in kind on the product of the soil, as well as by the license on business occupations and professions, to command resources sufficient for the wants of the country. But a very large proportion of these resources could only be made available at the close of the present and the commencement of the ensuing year, while the intervening exigencies permitted no delay. In this state of affairs, superinduced almost unavoidably by the fortunes of the war in which we are engaged, the issue of treasury notes have been increased until the currency in circulation amounts to more than six hundred millions of dollars, or more than threefold the amount required by the business of the country.

I need not enlarge upon the evil effects of this condition of things. They are unfortunately but too apparent. In addition to the difficulty presented to the necessary operations of the government, and the effi-

cient conduct of the war, the most deplorable of all its results is undoubtedly its corrupting influence upon the morals of the people. The
possession of large amounts of treasury notes has naturally led to a
desire for investment, and with a constantly increasing volume of currency there has been an equally constant increase of price in all objects of investment. This effect has stimulated purchase by the apparent
certainty of profit, and a spirit of speculation has thus been fostered,
which has so debasing an influence and such ruinous consequences, that
it is our highest duty to remove the cause, and no measures directed
to that end can be too prompt or too stringent.

*Davis admitted that were it possible to take the census, taxation by
representation would be desirable "in exact compliance with the whole
letter and spirit of the Constitution"; but at the moment only a tax uniform throughout the Confederate states appeared possible. Under
these circumstances he was quite willing to put aside legal niceties:*

. . . With large portions of some of the States occupied by the
enemy, what justice would there be in imposing on the remainder the
whole amount of the taxation of the entire State in proportion to its
representation? What else would this be in effect than to increase the
burthen of those who are the heaviest sufferers by the war, and to make
our own inability to protect them from invasion, as we are required
to do by the Constitution, the ground for adding to their losses by an
attempted adherence to the letter, in violation of the spirit of that instrument? No such purpose could have been entertained, and no such
result contemplated by the framers of the Constitution. It may add
weight to these considerations, if we reflect that, although the Constitution provided that it should go into operation with a representation
temporarily distributed among the States, it expressly ordains, after
providing for a census within three years, that this temporary distribution of representative power is to endure "until such enumeration shall
be made." Would any one argue that, because the census cannot be
made within the fixed period, the government must, at the expiration of
that period, perish for want of a representative body? In any aspect in
which the subject can be viewed, I am led to the conclusion already
announced, and which is understood to be in accordance with a vote
taken in one or both houses at our last session. I shall, therefore, until
we are able to pursue the precise mode required by the Constitution,
deem it my duty to approve any law levying the taxation which you
are bound to impose for the defence of the country, in any other practi-

cable mode which shall distribute the burthen uniformly and impartially on the whole property of the people.

In your former legislation you have sought to avoid the increase in the volume of notes in circulation by offering inducements to voluntary funding. The measures adopted for that purpose have been but partially successful, and the evil has now reached such a magnitude as to permit no other remedy than the compulsory reduction of the currency to the amount required by the business of the country. This reduction should be accompanied by a pledge that, under no stress of circumstances, will that amount be exceeded. No possible mode of using the credit of the government can be so disastrous as one which disturbs the basis of all exchanges, renders impossible all calculations of future values, augments, in constantly increasing proportions, the price of all commodities, and so depreciates all fixed wages, salaries, and incomes, as to render them inadequate to bare subsistence. If to these be added the still more fatal influence on the morals and character of the people, to which I have already adverted, I am persuaded you will concur in the conclusion that an inflexible adherence to a limitation of the currency to a fixed sum is an indispensable element of any system of finance now to be adopted.

Members of the Confederate Congress found in the Richmond Dispatch *in late January a graphic lesson in the evils of inflation:*[5]

The state of affairs brought about by the speculating and extortion practiced upon the public cannot be better illustrated than by the following grocery bill for one week for a small family, in which prices before the war and those of the present are compared:

1860		1863	
Bacon, 10 lbs at 12½¢	$1.25	Bacon, 10 lbs at $1	$10.00
Flour, 30 lbs at 5¢	1.50	Flour, 30 lbs at 12½¢	3.75
Sugar, 5 lbs at 8¢	.40	Sugar, 5 lbs at $1.15	5.75
Coffee, 4 lbs at 12½¢	.50	Coffee, 4 lbs at $5	20.00
Tea (green) ½ lb at $1	.50	Tea (green) ½ lb at $16	8.00
Lard, 4 lbs at 12½¢	.50	Lard, 4 lbs at $1	4.00
Butter, 3 lbs at 25¢	.75	Butter, 3 lbs at $1.75	5.25
Meal, 1 pk. at 25¢	.25	Meal, 1 pk. at $1	1.00
Candles, 2 lbs at 15¢	.30	Candles, 2 lbs at $1.25	2.50
Soap, 5 lbs at 10¢	.50	Soap, 5 lbs at $1.10	5.50
Pepper and salt (about)	.10	Pepper and salt (about)	2.50
Total	$6.55	Total	$68.25

So much we owe the speculators, who have stayed at home to prey upon the necessities of their fellow-citizens.

On February 1, 1863, supporting a bill for the suppression of extortion, one of the members of the Virginia Legislature read a table of comparative prices:

Agricultural Produce	Before the War	Now
White Wheat, per bushel	$1.50	$ 4.50
Flour, per barrel	7.50	22.00
Corn, per bushel	.70	3.50
Hay, per hundred	1.00	3.50
Hides, per pound	.07	.40
Bacon, per pound	.13	.60
Beef, per pound	.08	.50
Lard, per pound	.15	1.00
Butter, per pound	.30	1.50
Irish potatoes	1.00	5.00
Sweet potatoes	1.00	6.00
Apple brandy	1.00	15.00
Wool, per pound	.30	2.00

Manufactures		
Bar iron, per pound	.04	.20
Nails, per pound	.04	.60
Leather, sole, per pound	.25	2.50
" , upper, per pound	.33	3.50

Cotton Goods		
Osnaburgs, per yard	.10	.75
Brown cotton, per yard	.10	.75
Sheeting, per yard	.15	1.25

Woolen Goods		
Coarse Jeans	.45	4.00
Crenshaw's gray	2.00	28.00

Miscellaneous		
Coarse shoes	1.50	15.00
High-quartered shoes	3.50	25.00
Boots	7.50	60.00
Wool hats, per dozen	7.00	50.00

Stocks

Dividends on stocks in cotton companies, worth in May, 1861, $25 to $50 per share, now from $112 to $140.

In large measure, these statistics were of academic interest. More and more the problem on the Confederate home front was becoming one of securing the necessities of life at any price. From Bladen County, on the Cape Fear River in the southern part of North Carolina, a citizen in no mood to fret over the Queen's English wrote to Governor Zebulon B. Vance:[6]

. . . The time has come that we the comon people has to hav bread or blood & we are bound boath men & women to hav it or die in the attempt Some of us has bin travling for the last month with the money in our pockets to buy corn & tyrd men that had plenty & has bin unable to buy a bushel holding on for a better price We are willing to gave . . . two Dollars a bushel but no more for the idea is that the Slave oner has the plantations & the hands to rais the brad stufs & the comon people is drove of[f] in the war to fight for the big mans negro & he at home making nearly all the corn that is made & then because he has the play in his own fingers he puts the price on his corn so as to take all the soldiers wages for a fiew bushels . . . it is not our desiar to organize & commence operations for if the precedent is laid it will be unanimous but if ther is not steps taken soon nessesity will drive us into measures that may prove awful   we dont ask meet on fair terms for we can live on bread   perhaps it would be better for you to esue your proclamation that no man should sell in the state at more than $2 per bushel   you no best & if you cant remedy Extosan [extortion] on the staff of life we will & we as your subjects will make Examples of all who Refuse to open there barn Doors & [will] appoint other men over there farms who perhaps will hav better harts we no that this is unlawful at a commontime but we are shut up   we cant trade with no body only Just those in the confedersy & they can perish [—] all those that has not [—] & it seems that all harts is turned to gizards. . . .

III

A war-weary North, confronted week after week by columns of reports and pen-and-ink sketches from the battlefields, found escape in two dazzling affairs of the heart. The marriage of the Prince of Wales to the Princess Alexandria in St. George's Chapel, Windsor, on March 10, found most newspapers reprinting in full the glowing account of the London Times and their readers sighing at the rapturous moment when the young bride appeared

"In gloss of satin and glimmer of pearls,
Queen lily and rose in one."

Harper's Weekly, *ready at the drop of a hat to reopen the* Trent *affair, noted that in the throng cheering the bridal party seven women were "crushed to death" and another hundred "wounded," and added cynically, "If such a thing occurred here, how our 'mobocracy' would be abused!"*

Yet this royal wedding could not compete in American interest with the nuptials on February 1, 1863, of Charles S. Stratton and Miss Lavinia Warren. Lee, stuck in the snow in Virginia, or Grant, stuck in the mud in Mississippi, could produce no headline that could equal for the tens of thousands of visitors to Barnum's Museum the captivating intelligence that cupid's arrow had pierced the heart of Tom Thumb! Miss Warren, a native of Middleboro, Massachusetts, now twenty years of age, thirty-two inches high, and twenty-nine pounds in weight, was herself an idol among habitués of Barnum's. The ceremony took place in Grace Church, with a breathless reporter for the New York Herald *not missing a trick:*[7]

We entered the sacred edifice. Grand, solemn, and silent dim aisles —"storied windows, richly dight" etc.—and here, indeed, was the show. . . . Never before was the scarlet lady seen to such advantage. Babylon was a rag fair to it. . . .

There were silks of every possible hue, and thus a rich variety of colors in the picture. There was, too, every possible species of toilet—dainty head-dresses, delicate bonnets, and whatever can make the sex beautiful and lead every body else into temptation.

But beautiful as they were they were not dwarfs. How many wished they were! How many regretted their "superb abundance!". . .

Commodore Nutt and Minnie Warren (the bride's sister) led the way, and the bride and bridegroom came after. . . .

Now Nutt, for size, is such a man as might be made after supper of a cheese paring. He is a full head shorter than Tom Thumb, but is self-possessed and easy to the most perfect extent. Tom Thumb is also considerably stouter than Nutt. He, a veteran in the show business, was also, of course, quite at ease.

Lavinia is a little lady of very fair proportions, decidedly of the plump style of beauty, with a well rounded arm and full bust, and all the appearance of *aimable embonpoint.* Her countenance is animated and agreeable; complexion decidedly brunette, black hair, very dark eyes, rounded forehead, and dimpled cheeks and chin.

Her little sister is, to our heretical taste, the prettier of the two.

Altogether they made, after all, a dainty little group.

It was the great moment of the great show; the ladies were in such extreme ecstasies that there was perfect silence, and the Rev. Mr. Wiley came forward and read the marriage rite. Thumb and Lavinia responded clearly and affirmatively at the proper places, and in due time a very tall and very slim gentleman in very black clothes, the very essence of respectability, ascended the steps of the dais with the measured tread of the Commander in "Don Juan," though he did not make so much noise about it, and gave the bride away.

Then they knelt for prayer, and the rich sunlight fell through the painted windows upon them—

> And threw warm gules upon the bride's fair breast,
>   As down she knelt for heaven's grace and boon;
> Rose bloom fell on her hands together prest,
>   And on her silver cross soft amethyst,
>   And on her hair a glory like a saint.

IV

On April 2, 1863, a shattering event occurred in Richmond but, for the sake of morale on the Confederate home front, no newspaper reported it. Fresh from the disconcerting scenes of the day, War Clerk Jones told the story in his diary:[8]

This morning early a few hundred women and boys met as by concert in the Capitol Square, saying they were hungry, and must have food. The number continued to swell until there were more than a thousand. But few men were among them, and these were mostly foreign residents, with exemptions in their pockets. About nine A.M. the mob emerged from the western gates of the square, and proceeded down Ninth Street, passing the War Department, and crossing Main Street, increasing in magnitude at every step, but preserving silence and (so far) good order.

Not knowing the meaning of such a procession, I asked a pale boy where they were going. A young woman, seemingly emaciated, but yet with a smile, answered that they were going to find something to eat. I could not, for the life of me, refrain from expressing the hope that they might be successful; and I remarked they were going in the right direction to find plenty in the hands of the extortioners.

I did not follow, to see what they did; but I learned an hour after that they marched through Cary Street, and entered diverse stores of the speculators, which they proceeded to empty of their contents. They impressed all the carts and drays in the street, which were speedily laden with meal, flour, shoes, etc. I did not learn whither these were driven; but probably they were rescued from those in charge of them. Nevertheless, an immense amount of provisions, and other articles, were borne by the mob, which continued to increase in numbers.

An eye-witness says he saw a boy come out of a store with a hat full of money (notes); and I learned that when the mob turned up into Main Street, when all the shops were by this time closed, they broke in the plate-glass windows, demanding silks, jewelry, etc. Here they were incited to pillage valuables, not necessary for subsistence, by the class of residents (aliens) exempted from military duty . . . Thus the work of spoliation went on, until the military appeared on the scene, summoned by Gov. Letcher . . . He had the Riot Act read (by the mayor), and then threatened to fire on the mob. He gave them five minutes' time to disperse in, threatening to use military force (the city battalion being present) if they did not comply with the demand. The timid women fell back, and a pause was put to the devastation, though but few believed he would venture to put his threat in execution. If he had done so, he would have been hung, no doubt.

About this time the President appeared, and ascending a dray, spoke to the people. He urged them to return to their homes, so that the bayonets there menacing them might be sent against the common enemy. He told them that such acts would bring *famine* upon them in the only form which could not be provided against, as it would deter people from bringing food to the city. He said he was willing to share his last loaf with the suffering people (his best horse had been stolen the night before), and he trusted we would all bear our privations with fortitude, and continue united against the Northern invaders, who were the authors of all our sufferings. He seemed deeply moved; and indeed it was a frightful spectacle, and perhaps an ominous one, if the government does not remove some of the quartermasters who have contributed very much to bring about the evil of scarcity. I mean those who have allowed transportation to forestallers and extortioners.

Gen. Elzey and Gen. Winder waited upon the Secretary of War in the morning, asking permission to call the troops from the camps near the city, to suppress the women and children by a summary process. But Mr. Seddon hesitated, and then declined authorizing any such absurdity. He said it was a municipal or State duty, and therefore he would not take the responsibility of interfering in the matter. Even in the moment of aspen consternation, he was still the politician.

I have not heard of any injuries sustained by the women and children. Nor have I heard how many stores the mob visited; and it must have been many.

All is quiet now (three P.M.); and I understand the government is issuing rice to the people.

The "bread riots" in Richmond were not an isolated incident; similar outbreaks occurred in Augusta, Columbus and Milledgeville, Georgia, in Salisbury, North Carolina, and in Mobile, Alabama. Aside from the speculative fever in stocks, the empty places at tables left by menfolk off to war, life in the North had not changed appreciably; whereas in the South the social patterns were almost entirely changed. A gifted Southern historian, Bell Irvin Wiley, traces some of the alterations:[9]

Education naturally suffered as a result of the impingements of war, particularly in the rural sections. Children often were required to forego school in the interest of the family livelihood. Books, slates and other supplies were expensive and scarce. The dearth of horses and carriages made transportation a difficult problem if not a downright impossibility. . . .

Most of the elementary schools seem to have been run on a subscription basis. Tuition was often paid in farm products or in cloth. The majority of schoolteachers were women, preachers, or old men, and few of them were well qualified for the role of instructor. Teacher compensation was miserly. A North Carolina woman in 1863 received $20 per month and board for teaching a school that opened at seven-thirty o'clock in the morning and closed at six in the evening. Sessions were generally shortened to two terms of three months or less—one in summer and the other after harvest. Educational facilities were discontinued in many border localities, but in most interior communities schools of some sort continued to function throughout the war.

Textbooks of Confederate imprint came into existence in considerable number. Some of these contained choice bits of propaganda. For instance, Johnson's Elementary Arithmetic set forth these problems: (1) "A Confederate soldier captured 8 Yankees each day for 9 succes-

sive days; how many did he capture in all?" (2) "If one Confederate
soldier can kill 90 Yankees, how many Yankees can 10 Confederate
soldiers kill?" (3) "If one Confederate soldier can whip 7 Yankees,
how many soldiers can whip 49 Yankees?". . .

Courting afforded considerable diversion for the young folk, though
the scarcity of eligible males created special problems. "I am still flying around with the girls," wrote a teen-age youngster to his bachelor
uncle in the army; "I tell you they keep me sterred up. I went to
meting . . . at Union and coming home I had to keep company with
about a dozen girls and you know that they keep me stirede up. I want
you to make haste and kill these old Yankies by Christmas and come
home and help me out for I tell you that I have my hands full." Another young beau indicated similar difficulties. "You said you wanted
me to keep the girls from going wild," he wrote his soldier cousin.
"That [is] hard to do with some of them . . . all they want is aman
So you must come hom with Hugh this fall and I will try to make arun
and we will have a fly around with the girls and have a big spree."

Much of the love-making was done at church functions, particularly
at summer revivals. A Virginia cavalryman wrote to a friend in Rock-
ingham County: "right to me a bout the big meating and how you in
joyed your self and how menny girls you Sqese." And a North Carolinian reporting to a soldier correspondent said: "At Camp meating the
boys an girls did not fly round the black stumps much they was a great
many wounded soldiers there the girls did not set back much this year
like they allways did . . . i reckon the reason of that was that the
boys did not Suit them."

When unattached soldiers went home on furlough they made the
rounds of picnics, singings, and parties; and often they found it impossible to meet all the social demands occasioned by their visits. "I did
not marrie whiles I was at home," wrote a young Alabaman in the
closing days of the conflict, "but you would have thought I would if
[you] had of seen me. . . . The gi[r]les was more friendly than ever
I saw them in my life they is getting very tired of this war, they all wants
it to end. I do too." In view of the concentrated social activity occasioned by circumstances such as these, it is not surprising that the Confederacy witnessed a series of marriage epidemics. . . .

Several factors contributed to the disheartening of the poorer classes.
Paramount among these was the feeling that privileged groups, particularly the planters, were shirking their military responsibilities. This
opinion derived mainly from the law exempting the owner of twenty

slaves from military service, and from the failure of planters to meet
the requisitions of army leaders for Negroes to work on fortifications.
Dissatisfaction on these scores gained currency from the airings of
local politicians who bore grievances against the Davis administration.
A Mississippian wrote his governor in the fall of 1862 that the twenty-
Negro law was "the handle at which most of the malcontents grind."
A soldier who wrote to Vance in June, 1863, asking for a furlough to
harvest his small crop of grain remarked significantly: "how can we
go in to battle and fight to keep the enemy back of[f] the rich who
beca[u]se he owns twenty negros is permitted to stay at home with his
family and save his grain but the [poor] man must suffer in the armmy
for something to eat his family suffering at home for something to eat."
    Another factor which depressed mightily the spirit of the poor was
the conviction that the "big folk" were using the war to enhance their
riches. A Georgian wrote his brother in 1862 that "lyeing, Swindling
and a Speculation is all that is goinge on here now thare is but littel
sade about war here all that has the means to go on is a trying to Seake
and devour every thing . . . there is a heap of Yankies here as well
as in [the] North.". . . Distress caused by suffering of loved ones in
the army was another depressing influence. A North Carolinian wrote
to his brother in 1863, urging him to desert. "I would advise you
to . . . go to the other side," he said, "whear you can get plenty and
not stay in this one horse barefooted naked and famine stricken Southern Confederacy."

V

*In this, as in all wars, more went on than met the average eye; and in
the North as well as in the South censorship was employed to keep from
the home front the seamy side of governmental activities. Certainly
Stanton was in no mood to release to the public the letter he received in
January 1863 from Charles A. Dana, a special agent he had sent to
Memphis:*[10]

    You will remember our conversations on the subject of excluding
cotton speculators from the regions occupied by our armies in the
South. I now write to urge the matter upon your attention as a measure of military necessity.
    The mania for sudden fortunes made in cotton, raging in a vast
population of Jews and Yankees scattered throughout this whole country, and in this town exceeding the numbers of the regular residents, has
to an alarming extent corrupted and demoralized the army. Every
colonel, captain, or quartermaster is in secret partnership with some

operator in cotton; every soldier dreams of adding a bale of cotton to his monthly pay. I had no conception of the extent of this evil until I came and saw for myself.

Besides, the resources of the rebels are inordinately increased from this source. Plenty of cotton is brought in from beyond our lines, especially by the agency of Jewish traders, who pay for it ostensibly in Treasury notes, but really in gold.

What I would propose is that no private purchaser of cotton shall be allowed in any part of the occupied region.

Let quartermasters buy the article at a fixed price, say twenty or twenty-five cents per pound, and forward it by army transportation to proper centers, say Helena, Memphis, or Cincinnati, to be sold at public auction on Government account. Let the sales take place on regular fixed days, so that all parties desirous of buying can be sure when to be present.

But little capital will be required for such an operation. The sales being frequent and for cash, will constantly replace the amount employed for the purpose. I should say that two hundred thousand dollars would be sufficient to conduct the movement.

I have no doubt that this two hundred thousand dollars so employed would be more than equal to thirty thousand men added to the national armies.

My pecuniary interest is in the continuance of the present state of things, for while it lasts there are occasional opportunities of profit to be made by a daring operator; but I should be false to my duty did I, on that account, fail to implore you to put an end to an evil so enormous, so insidious, and so full of peril to the country. . . .

Dana carried his point; on March 31, 1863, Lincoln issued a proclamation, declaring unlawful all commercial transactions with Confederate states except when regulated by the Secretary of the Treasury. Cotton, however, provided only one enticement to civilian, political and military seekers of a fast dollar. The authority upon the subject of "The War's Carnival of Fraud" was Colonel Henry S. Olcott, Stanton's watchdog over contracts. "Gladly would I leave my tale untold," wrote Olcott, who described the situation that he encountered:[11]

. . . We floated, on a sea of paper, into a fool's paradise. Contractors, bloated with the profits on shoddy, rode in emblazoned carriages, which, a little while before, they would have been glad to drive as hirelings; and vulgar faces and grimy fingers were made more vulgar and coarse with the glare of great diamonds. Intrigue held the key to the kitchen-stairs of the White House, shaped legislation, sat cheek by jowl with Congressmen, and seduced commissioned officers from the strict path of duty. Our sailors were sent to sea in ships built of green timber, which were fitted with engines good only for the junk-shop, and greased with "sperm" oil derived from mossbunkers and the fat of dead horses. For one pound of necessary metal, one yard of fabric, one gallon of liquid, the price of two was paid. Our soldiers were given guns that would not shoot, powder that would only half explode, shoes of which the soles were filled with shavings, hats that dissolved often in a month's showers, and clothing made of old cloth, ground up and fabricated over again.

In the navy yards there was a system of corrupt bargains between the public servants and contractors, under which goods of inferior quality and short quantity were accepted as of lawful standard and count; public property was purloined and carried off in open daylight; scores of superfluous men were quartered on the pay rolls by politicians; navy agents colluded with ring contractors for a fifteen per cent. commission, and clerks in the yard, for a consideration, would slip the pay requisitions of these ring thieves from the bottom to the top of the pile that awaited the official certificate . . .

In the military arsenals, the same rottenness prevailed. . . . Presents of horses, carriages, jewelry, wines, cigars, and friendly help toward promotion, though passing under a politer name than bribery, effected the same results . . . Every artifice that rascally ingenuity could devise, and clever men and women carry out, was resorted to to procure the brigadier's stars or the colonel's eagles for ambitious incompetents. The sacredest secrets of our government were sold to the enemy; loud-mouthed hypocrites trafficked across the lines; the very medicines for the sick were adulterated, and dishonest gains were made out of the transportation of the wounded. . . .

"This," sighed a disillusioned Olcott, "was the Augean stable to cleanse which the broom of authority was placed in my hands." No sooner had he been appointed than he was sumptuously dined at Delmonico's by one Solomon Kohnstamn, wealthy importer. Olcott scented a rat and found it:

Kohnstamn's crime consisted in his procuring from landlords—generally German saloon-keepers—their signatures to blank vouchers, which he would have filled up by his clerks for, say, one or two thousand dollars each, and then either get unprincipled commissioned officers to append their certificates for an agreed price, or, cheaper still, forge them. By this device he drew over three hundred thousand dollars from the "Mustering and Disbursing Office" in New York . . .

Army frauds followed a pattern—in the East and North the graft was in manufactured articles, in the West and Southwest in animals, forage and transportation. In mid-1863 Olcott was sent to Cincinnati to inspect the Quartermaster and Commissary Departments of the Military Department of Ohio:

. . . Upon reporting there my first care was to cause to be prepared by the chief quartermaster a complete list of all contracts awarded within a certain period, with the names of the bidders at each letting. With this as a guide it was a simple matter to learn what fraud had been practiced, for I had only to direct my orderlies to serve a summons upon each disappointed bidder to report at headquarters and testify, when the whole chicanery was invariably exposed. The regular dealers and responsible merchants were always to be found among this class, and, when satisfied the War Department was really in earnest, and would throw the market open to fair competition, they would tell the honest truth. Thus I discovered within forty-eight hours that by a corrupt conspiracy between a government purchasing agent, an inspector, a Cincinnati contractor, and an Indianapolis horse dealer and Republican politician the United States had been systematically robbed of one million dollars in the purchase of horses and mules, at the Cincinnati corral, during the preceding year. . . .

At Louisville frauds alike shameful had been perpetrated in the purchase of animals, while one Black—a captain and assistant quartermaster, who boasted much of his influence with Secretary Stanton, and whom I especially gratified that official by bringing before a court-martial—had not only connived at the fraudulent adulteration of grain by his contractors, but absolutely stood by to see it done and handled a shovel himself. . . .

Borrowed by the Navy Department, Olcott quickly discovered that "the same gang of scamps supplied the Washington, Philadelphia and New York Navy Yards":

. . . Their programme was simple, but effectual. Under the regulations, a contractor who had faithfully complied with the terms of a contract, was entitled to the first consideration of the navy agent (the purchaser of supplies in the open market at each station, the paying agent through whom all money passed to contractors) when extra supplies had to be obtained in the open market. The ring thief had only to collude, in each transaction, with three men to have everything as he could desire: 1. The master-workman, upon whose recommendation the Navy Department's annual estimate of the supplies that would be needed in that shop was based. 2. The inspector, who must pass upon the goods delivered, and was supposed to reject such articles as were scant in measure or weight, or inferior in quality. 3. The navy agent, dispenser of patronage, golden fountain of riches. Other minor potential obstructionists had, of course, to be disposed of; but a little money, a good deal of soft talk, unlimited liquor, and, occasionally, some pressure from superiors, went a long way.

Thus, practically, the master-workman would estimate for not above ten per cent. of the supplies he was morally certain would be required in his shop; the inspectors would see sperm oil in horse fat, two whole boxes of tin plates in the two halves of one box that had been sawed in two and fitted with an extra side each, pure "Banca" or "Lamb and Flag" tin in ingots of an equal mixture of tin and lead; and the benevolent navy agent, on a "divy" of fifteen per cent., would order of his pal the other ninety per cent. at open market prices, and throw in all additional orders that fortune might put it in his way to give out! And that was what I found in New York. The contractors were all arrested; arrests and removals were plentiful in the Brooklyn yard; Navy Agent Henderson was, December, 1864, indicted eight times by the grand jury . . .

Things were . . . if anything, worse at Philadelphia. Discovery was brought about by an honest dealer, named Barstow, sending to the Navy Department, for examination, four cases of thirty-two ounce sheathing copper, that he had bought, in good faith, of a responsible firm, but which was of the kind rolled at the Washington Navy Yard. The copper was easily traced back to one Harris, keeper of a sailors' boarding-house, and a man of bad repute at the time. He was arrested by General Cadwallader, for account of the Secretary of the Navy, and lodged in Fort Mifflin. A political striker named Anthony Hale— "Tony" Hale—employed as a boss carter in the yard, was next arrested, and then one thing brought on another until, before I was

through, thirty-three prisoners were in military custody. . . . Besides
the man Harris, the prisoners were the Naval Constructor, first assistant engineer, timber inspector, master plumber, caulker, joiner,
blacksmith, laborer and painter, the clerk of the yard, his chief clerk
and check clerk, three clerks of the storekeeper, a quarterman laborer,
a quarterman joiner, two quartermen plumbers, four receivers of
stolen property, six contractors, and one purser's steward. A pretty
lot of patriots and Republicans, indeed!

VI

In the cities of the North, as the war approached its third year, life
followed familiar, unbellicose patterns. In Chicago, in early 1863:[12]

The first free evening school under the Board of Education was
opened January 8 in the Dearborn School.

Frederick Douglass, former fugitive slave and later a welcomed
caller at the White House, lectured January 19. The recent Emancipation Proclamation whereby the President had freed three million of his
countrymen inspired him in his address.

During the two months of December and January the Illinois
Central sold farms to 422 persons, amounting to $262,787.

Erring Women's Refuge for Reform was opened February 13 in a
small house on the North Side.

Germans of the city in February reclaimed large quantities of soap
grease from the river. With axes, flat tin pans, long poles and old flour
barrels they secured the grease that had accumulated on the under surface of the ice.

At the meeting of the Board of Education [February 19] the English
Grammar of William H. Wells was dropped from the list of textbooks
on the ground that the recent city charter made it unlawful for the
superintendent to be financially interested in any book in the public
schools.

As the weather grew warmer, the New York Times *summarized the*
principal amusements awaiting pleasure-seeking visitors to the city:[13]

The stirring and excellent drama of the "Duke's Motto" continues to
attract overwhelming houses to Nicolo's Garden. It remains, of course,
on the bill until further notice. At Laura Keene's theatre the play of the
"Wives of Paris" is still the attraction. It shows a little of everything,

but exhibits the peculiar excellence of Mrs. English's company. At Barnum's Museum, in addition to the usual attractions, the new drama of the "Duke's Device" will be repeated.

We have on several occasions spoken of the Stereoptican now on exhibition at Irving Hall. The science of optics seldom comes to us in so acceptable a form. The instrument, indeed, has created a new pleasure, enabling the cosmopolitan to revisit the scenes of his travels, and the stay-at-home to see something of the world. . . . There is no trouble from the heat, the gas being turned down in the hall during the performance.

In more serious-minded Washington, a society of women organized "to abolish the use of foreign silks, satins, laces, indeed the whole family of millinery and feminine adornments, with a view to keep the gold in the country." The editor of the Washington Union *was not altogether happy:*[14]

A female, signing herself "Senex," has a communication in this morning's *Chronicle* relative to the idea of ladies dressing plainly. She and all other ladies have a right to dress as they please; but she has no right to force their fashions down the throats of those who are not inclined to dress as they want. A linsey-woolsey gown would be no discredit to any one, and those who desire to wear quarter calicoes have a perfect right to do so; but if a lady dresses in two-dollar silk, her character must not be impugned. This lady, "Senex," in winding up her effusion, says: "But let it be once understood that *respectable* ladies are to be known by the plainness of their attire, and the work will be done." She takes very broad ground relative to *respectability*, and we presume that if she gave out that females must wear breeches, they would not be considered *respectable* if they did not at once coincide with her. Her doctrines are like the abolitionist's—no one is loyal but a negro-worshipper.

The editors of the Philadelphia News *took a more charitable view:*

Whilst every one is complaining of the high cost of living and the speculation in gold, the ladies of Washington are adopting practical measures, with a view to remedy at least a portion of the evil. On Monday last, as we learn from the *Star*, nearly three hundred of the most prominent ladies of the city assembled in Dr. Sunderland's church, and formed a society, the object of which is to check the importation and consumption of foreign goods. A constitution was adopted, and the society was named the "Covenant." The constitution, which is to be signed by each member, contains the following pledge: "For three years or the war we pledge ourselves to purchase no foreign article or apparel when American articles can possibly be substituted." This is a good pledge, but might be made better. It will do, however, as a beginning; and if the men and women in all parts of the country will but act on the principle involved in it, much good will be accomplished. Economy should be the watchword in such times as these. There is no family that cannot reduce the consumption of goods now purchased for its use at least one-third, and this with entire regard to the health and comfort of all. Ignore the butterman when he demands an exorbitant price for it; reduce the supply of milk; substitute something else for coffee; live on plain food, and discard all luxuries; stop off one fire in the winter; watch the cook, that he or she does not waste; and in a thousand other ways pursue a system of strict and careful economy, and much, very much, will be done towards breaking down the conspirators who are robbing the people and the government.

In Cambridge, Massachusetts, a distinguished British visitor, Edward Dicey, attended commencement exercises at Harvard and only once was reminded that the nation was torn by a bitter civil strife:[15]

At the house of the acting President, the professors and the students were collected. . . . The fourth-year sophomores, who were the heroes of the day, were all assembled, arrayed in the glossiest of new black dress clothes and with the whitest of kid gloves. Evening dress somehow takes more kindly to American youths than to our own, and the students seemed to me a set of as good-looking gentlemanlike young men as it has been often my fortune to see. We formed a line, and marched two-and-two together through the grounds, with a band of music leading the way, and a sympathetic crowd of bystanders gazing at us, and following in our wake. I am afraid, as I think of it, that my friend and I must have rather marred the appearance of the procession, by being in coloured clothes. However, black is not a cool colour to wear in the dog-days, and so I hope we were pardoned. Our walk ended in the Unitarian church of Cambridge, which the University has a right to use for public ceremonies. Thanks to my being with the dons' party, I got a seat upon the raised platform at the end of the chapel, and sat there in glory and comparative coolness. The moment we were seated there was a rush of students through the doors, and a perfectly unnecessary fight was got up with the constables who guarded the entrance, which reminded me of wrestlings I had witnessed upon the staircase of the theatre at the Oxford Commemorations. In fact, the whole scene had an Oxford air about it. There were the ladies with bonnets of every colour, blue, white, and pink, fanning themselves in the crowded seats. There was a host of bright young faces, and the orations were strings of appropriate platitudes and decorous *facetiae* of the mildest character, such as most of us have heard often-times in college halls, and under no other circumstances. Of the speakers, I would only say, that they were two young men of six feet high and upwards— one the stroke of the Harvard boat—and as fine specimens of manhood as you would desire to see. We had a band, which played the overture to *Martha,* and other operatic music, with remarkable precision; a prayer full of the most apposite commonplaces; and an ode of a patriotic character. There were allusions to the war in plenty throughout the proceedings, but everything was too decorous for the exhibition of any ardent patriotism. Amongst the crowd, however, there was one poor lad, pale, worn, and limping upon crutches, who had lost his leg in the battle of Balls Bluff, and who had come to witness the gala day of the class which he had left to join the war. He was the hero of the day, and at every patriotic sentiment all eyes were turned towards him, as though he were the living embodiment of the country's struggle and defeats and victories. I have no doubt, according to the Yankee phrase, he had "a good time of it" that class-day at Cambridge, amongst his old friends and fellow-students; but I could not help feeling that there was a long hereafter before him, when the war is over, and the excitement has passed away; and when I, for my part, would sooner have both legs than have been a hero and be a cripple.

VII

Hoarder and extortioner in the South, speculator and grafter in the North—the difference was one of opportunity rather than character. The vast majority on the home front went off to an honest day's toil; and a few, like Walt Whitman, dedicated themselves unselfishly to the service of the less fortunate. Now a volunteer worker in the hospitals in Washington, Whitman witnessed the naked horror of war; most nights, from the effort he gave to aiding and comforting the wounded and dy-

ing, he fell into bed, exhausted; yet his soul heard poetry, without any
trace of bitterness—and in "Bivouac on a Mountainside" he sang:[16]

I see before me now a traveling army halting,
Below, a fertile valley spread, with barns and the orchards of summer,
Behind, the terraced sides of a mountain, abrupt, in places rising high,
Broken, with rocks, with clinging cedars, with tall shapes dingily seen,
The numerous camp-fires scattered near and far, some away up on the
    mountain,
The shadowy forms of men and horses, looming, large-sized, flickering,
And over all the sky—the sky! far, far out of reach, studded, breaking
    out, the eternal stars.

It was an age of caricature, of the broad humor of Artemus Ward that
Lincoln carried into his Cabinet meetings. The Emancipation Procla-
mation was followed by Negro recruiting, and Congress grew alarmed
and a great excitement spread over the country. For Charles Graham
Halpine, a literary light of the day now serving on the staff of General
David Hunter, the situation appealed to a native Irish wit. Under the
pseudonym of Private Miles O'Reilly, he published his verses in the
New York Herald:

Some tell us 'tis a burnin' shame
    To make the naygers fight;
An' that the thrade of bein' kilt
    Belongs but to the white:
But as for me, upon my sowl!
    So liberal are we here,
I'll let Sambo be murthered instead of myself
    On every day in the year.
        On every day of the year, boys,
            And in every hour of the day;
        The right to be kilt I'll divide wid him,
            An' divil a word I'll say.

The North chuckled. It understood slapstick. And sentimentality. Al-
most every parlor had its upright piano. One song, North and South,
swept the country; during the war it sold more than a million copies,
which, by comparative population figures, may make it America's

greatest song hit. Its author was Charles Carroll Sawyer; its title,
"Weeping, Sad and Lonely":

> Dearest love, do you remember,
> When we last did meet,
> How you told me that you loved me,
> Kneeling at my feet?
> Oh, how proud you stood before me,
> In your suit of blue,*
> When you vowed to me and country,
> Ever to be true.
> Weeping, sad and lonely,
> Hopes and fears how vain!
> Yet praying, when this cruel war is over,
> Praying that we meet again!

* Southerners sang "gray."

CHAPTER 22

THE DISLOYAL
OPPOSITION

THE THIRTY-SEVENTH CONGRESS met from December 1, 1862, until
March 4, 1863, in its third and final session. While Burnside's men
were dying on Marye's Heights at Fredericksburg, while they floundered on the "mud march" a few weeks later, while Rosecrans and
Bragg fought at Murfreesboro, while Grant, north of Vicksburg, contended against floods and an alert enemy, Senators and Representatives sparred, argued and passed laws that could be even more important to the Union than victories on land or sea.

I

The editors of Harper's Weekly *discussed the work of the Thirty-
seventh Congress:*[1]

The conscription bill enrolls all the males of the loyal States (including Indians and negroes) between the ages of 20 and 45 into a national
militia, and empowers the President to call them into the service of the
United States for three years or the war. The only exemptions are the
President and Vice-President, and one adult male in each family
where there are aged parents or infant children dependent upon
the labor of their adult relative for support. . . . There will remain,
in the loyal States, after deducting the army now in the field, some
3,500,000 liable to enrollment under this Act; and as it is quite certain
that under no circumstances can so large a number be required, Congress has wisely empowered the Executive to receive a sum of $300

from any drafted man who prefers paying to serving. This sum, it is believed, will always secure a substitute. Clergymen, professional men, large merchants and manufacturers, and others who are of more use to the country while prosecuting their various peaceful avocations than they would be if forced to carry a musket, will thus be exempted, while the class of men which take their place will receive money enough to keep their families as comfortably as if they had remained at home.

Under the operation of this Act the President will be enabled to recruit our armies to the full standard when the time of the nine months' men expires, and the hopes of the rebels—which have been re-echoed by the correspondents of disloyal journals—that our armies would melt away in the spring will be thoroughly defeated. Under this Act the President may keep a million of men in the field without difficulty. . . .

In another measure, Congress gave to the President what he had claimed as his constitutional right from the beginning of the conflict:

The purse and the sword of the country thus placed unconditionally in the President's hands, it only remained to invest him with power to protect the Government from attacks in the rear from invidious traitors at the North. For this purpose, in accordance with the purposes of old Rome, constitutional England, and of the United States themselves, Congress passed an Act empowering the President to suspend the Act of *habeas corpus* whenever and wherever he may deem it necessary. That this Act was necessary no one who has watched the treacherous movements of the Northern Copperheads, or reflected upon the mischief they might do if unrestrained, will venture to deny. At this very moment Southern emissaries and their sympathizers in Indiana are manoeuvering to wrest the control of the State troops out of the hands of the constitutional authorities; and individuals in New York and Connecticut are engaged in sending arms and supplies to the rebels, chiefly for the sake of gain, but also, in some degree, from love. It is quite evident that in the face of such a state of things, and when the nation is engaged in a death-grapple of which the issue is very doubtful, the slow and cautious remedies which the law provides for the redress of wrongs in time of peace would be out of place.

The editors added a comment:

When we undertook the war we tacitly agreed to accept it with all its evils. Prominent among these are a depreciated currency, a temporary deprivation of personal liberty, and a liability to be taken from one's business to carry a musket in the army. These are grave inconveniences. But they are temporary and bearable; whereas the evils which would result from the disruption of the Union are lasting and intolerable. We may suffer, but our children will benefit by our suffering. Whereas if this country is severed in twain the future which lies before us is plainly depicted in the history of Mexico and Central America: incessant wars, constant subdivisions, a cessation of honest industry and agriculture, a decay of trade, a disappearance of wealth and civilization, and in their stead chronic strife, rapine, bloodshed, and anarchy. To avoid these things we can well afford for a few years to have a strong government.

II

Not everyone in the country was as philosophical about the dictatorial powers given to the President as the editors of Harpers. While the bills were passing through Congress, many Democrats and conservative Union men denounced them as unnecessary or despotic. To Senator John S. Carlile, of Virginia,* conscription was a futile move:[2]

This is a general conscript law, asserting the power on the part of the Congress of the United States, without reference at all to the States of the Union, to give to the President the right to call the entire military force of the several States into the service of the United States, to provide how they shall be called in, to provide for enrolling and drafting them, and to make rules for their government, ignoring entirely the governments of the States. If this were a despotic Government, or if the people belonged to this Government, there might be some such assertion of power on the part of Congress; but, as I understand it, the Government belongs to the people, and the present war is an effort to preserve that Government. If the people do not feel interest enough in their own Government to preserve it, I doubt very much whether you can place power enough in the hands of their agents to make them do it.

William A. Richardson, who had succeeded Orville H. Browning as senator from Lincoln's own state of Illinois, went even further in his denunciation:

---

* In fact, of West Virginia, which was admitted to the Union on June 20, 1863, in accordance with an act of Congress signed by the President on December 31, 1862.

Mr. President, when I look at the measures that are proposed here, when I see the deep interest that is felt in the section of the country from which I come, I cannot forbear saying to the Senate of the United States, and to the country, if you pass this bill, if you pass the bill you had under consideration the other day to appropriate money to purchase slaves, and the bill to bring into your armies, side by side with our white race, an inferior race, the negro, I fear you will plunge the country into civil war.

To S. S. Cox ("Sunset" Cox) of Ohio, a Democrat but not an irresponsible partisan, the proposal to take Negroes into the Union armies—a section dropped before the conscription bill passed—would lead to irrevocable division of the country:

I say that I believe the object of gentlemen in forcing this bill here is to bring about, or rather make final and forever, a dissolution of the Union. . . .

The gentlemen from the border States here, gentlemen from Kentucky and Ohio—for there are two sides to the border—understand very well the hidden meaning and certain effect of this bill. Every man along the border will tell you that the Union is forever rendered hopeless if you pursue this policy of taking the slaves from their masters and arm them in this civil strife. It will only keep alive and aggravate this alienation of sections, which had its beginning in hate, and would have its end in vengeance.

III

But no denunciation of the conscription bill equaled that delivered by Clement L. Vallandigham, of Dayton, Ohio. This handsome, ardent, able Democrat, a member of the House of Representatives since 1858, had long been an advocate of restoration of the Union by compromise. By a speech entitled "The Great Civil War in America," delivered before the House on January 14, 1863, he had made himself the unrivaled champion of the "peace" wing of his party, and at the same time an archfiend in the eyes of all—still a large majority—who continued to believe in suppressing the rebellious South by force.

A sympathetic correspondent of the Cincinnati Gazette described a masterly performance:[3]

Finally the flow of motions ceases . . . and Mr. Vallandigham rises, leaves his usual seat on the extreme left and moves over to near the centre of the opposition benches.

There is a little flutter in the hall. This matter may require attention; it is well enough to lay aside the unfinished letters to constituents and drafts of new bills, and listen a little while. The wonderful old man from Pennsylvania [Thaddeus Stevens], who at 70 years of age retains all the fire and vigor of his earlier manhood, and, with the aid of a snuff-colored wig, makes everybody think him only fifty, still the imperious and sometimes wrong-headed leader of the House, faces about to the opposition side, braces himself back in his chair, and grimly eyes the member on the floor. Portly and good-natured Lovejoy bristles up, hitches his chair forward, and raises his hand to his ear to catch the opening sentences. Gray-headed, crabbed-faced, ruffle-shirted Wickliffe rears aloft his huge hulk of once-noble Kentucky proportions, and with the aid of crutch and cane hobbles his gouty way down the aisle, and seats himself just under his friend, the orator's extended hand, the better to catch the droppings from this sanctuary of Democracy, pure and undefiled. Colfax, with an attention to the business before the House that is never at fault, turns sharp and quick in his chair to listen. The Chairman of the Military Committee, black-whiskered Olin of New York, walks down the aisle to the Clerk's desk, and takes a position to hear distinctly. There is a general rising and turning on the Democratic and Border State side to get more favorable positions. The ladies on the front seats in the galleries lean over to catch a better view of the ogre from Ohio. The hitherto sleepy-looking occupants of the reporters' gallery shake off their indifference, exchange hurried remarks with each other, and lean over to notice how he opens, for this speech has been talked about and expected a long time. . . . He begins boldly, defiantly even, and is speedily preaching the very doctrine of devils. You can never subdue the seceded States. Two years of fearful experience have taught you that. Why carry on the war? If you persist it can only end in final separation between the North and South. And in that case, believe it now, as you did not my former warnings, the whole Northwest will go with the South!

He waxes more earnest as he approaches this key-note of his harangues and with an energy and force that makes every hearer, as his moral nature revolts from the bribe, acknowledge all the more the splendid force with which the tempter urges his cause, with flashing eye and livid features and extended hand, he hurls the climax of his threatening argument again upon the Republican side of the House: "Believe me, as you did not the solemn warning of years past, *the day which divides the North from the South, the self-same day decrees eternal divorce between the West and the East!*"

The group of Republicans standing in the open space between the Clerk's desk increases; they crowd down the aisles among the opposition and cluster around the speaker as he resumes. Even the eternal chattering in the ladies' galleries has ceased, the seats are all crowded, the correspondents and reporters have been attracted by the interest of the scene, and for a wonder the reporters' gallery is full and attentive.

An effort is making on the floor to get a joint session of the Military and Naval Committees, to hear a proposition from Cyrus W. Field, backed by the Secretary of War, about a submarine cable to New Orleans. One member after another flatly refuses to obey the call of the Committee and leave the debate. The eminent telegrapher waits an hour in the Committee-room, and finally gets to see three out of fourteen members. Such is the interest the discussion of treason's argument is arousing.

The speaker resumed: "There is not one drop of rain that falls over the whole vast expanse of the Northwest that does not find its home in the bosom of the Gulf. *We must and will follow it,* with travel and trade; not by treaty, but by right; freely, peaceably and without restriction or tribute, under the same Government and flag!"

It is eloquently spoken, and none are more willing to concede it than his opponents. . . .

He has spoken over an hour and a quarter, and has accomplished that rare feat, compelled the closest attention of the most disorderly deliberative body in the world, from the beginning to the end. . . .

There is a gradual relaxation, a sudden humming of conversation again on the floor and through the galleries. The Democrats and Border State men, with faces wreathed in smiles, crowd around their champion with their congratulations. At a single step the shunned and execrated Vallandigham has risen to the leadership of their party.

On February 23, Vallandigham attacked the conscription bill and the habeas corpus act:[4]

Talk to me, indeed, of the leniency of the Executive! too few arrests! too much forbearance by those in power! Sir, it is the people who have been too lenient. They have submitted to your oppressions and wrongs as no free people ought ever to submit. But the day of patient endurance has gone by at last. Mistake them not. They will be lenient no longer. Abide by the Constitution, stand by the laws, restore the Union, if *you* can restore it—not by force—you have tried that and failed. Try some other method now—the ancient, the approved, the reasonable way—the way in which the Union was first made. . . .

For what was the Union ordained? As a splendid edifice, to attract the gaze and admiration of the world? As a magnificent temple—a stupendous superstructure of marble and iron, like this Capitol, upon whose lofty dome the bronzed image—hollow and inanimate—of Freedom is soon to stand erect in colossal mockery, while the true spirit, the living Goddess of Liberty, veils her eyes and turns away her face in sorrow, because, upon the altar established here, and dedicated by our fathers to her worship—you, a false and most disloyal priesthood, offer up, night and morning, the mingled sacrifices of servitude and despotism? No, sir. It was for the sake of the altar, the service, the religion, the devotees, that the temple of the Union was first erected; and when these are all gone, let the edifice itself perish. Never—never—never will the people consent to lose their own personal and political rights and liberties, to the end that you may delude and mock them with the splendid unity of despotism.

Sir, what are the bills which have passed, or are still before the House? The bill to give the President the entire control of the currency—the purse—of the country. A tax-bill to clothe him with power over the whole property of the country. A bill to put all power in his hands over the personal liberties of the people. A bill to indemnify him, and all under him, for every act of oppression and outrage already consummated. A bill to enable him to suspend the writ of *habeas corpus*, in order to justify or protect him, and every minion of his, in the arrests which he or they may choose to make—arrests, too, for mere opinion's sake. Sir, some two hundred years ago, men were burned at the stake, subjected to the horrors of the Inquisition, to all the tortures that the devilish ingenuity of man could invent—for what? For opinions on questions of religion—of man's duty and relation to his God. And now, today, for opinions on questions political, under a free government, in a country whose liberties were purchased by our fathers by seven years' outpouring of blood, and expenditure of treasure—we have lived to see men, the born heirs of this precious inheritance, subjected to arrest and cruel imprisonment at the caprice of a President, or a secretary, or a constable. And, as if that were not enough, a bill is introduced here, today, and pressed forward to a vote, with the right of debate, indeed—extorted from you by the minority—but without the right to amend, with no more than the mere privilege of protest—a bill which enables the President to bring under his power, as Commander-in-chief, every man in the United States between the ages of twenty and forty-five—three millions of men. And, as if not satisfied with that, this bill provides, further, that every other citizen, man, woman, and child, under twenty years of age and over forty-five, including those that may be exempt between these ages, shall be also, at the mercy—so far as his personal liberty is concerned—of some miserable "provost-marshal" with the rank of a captain of cavalry, who is never to see service in the field; and every Congressional district in the United States is to be governed—yes, governed—by this petty satrap—this military eunuch—this Baba—and he even may be black —who is to do the bidding of your Sultan, or his Grand Vizier. Sir, you have but one step further to go—give him the symbols of his office— the Turkish bowstring and the sack.

What is it, sir, but a bill to abrogate the Constitution, to repeal all existing laws, to destroy all rights, to strike down the judiciary, and erect, upon the ruins of civil and political liberty, a stupendous superstructure of despotism. And for what? To enforce law? No, sir. It is admitted now, by the legislation of Congress, and by the two proclamations of the President; it is admitted by common consent, that the war is for the abolition of negro slavery, to secure freedom to the black man. You tell me, some of you, I know, that it is so prosecuted because this is the only way to restore the Union; but others openly and candidly confess that the purpose of the prosecution of the war is to abolish slavery. And thus, sir, it is that the freedom of the negro is to be purchased, under this bill, at the sacrifice of every right of the white men of the United States. . . .

What have we lived to hear in America daily, not in political harangues, or the press only, but in official proclamations and in bills in Congress! Yes, your high officials talk now of "treasonable practices," as glibly "as girls of thirteen do of puppy dogs." Treasonable practices! Disloyalty! Who imported these precious phrases, and gave them a legal settlement here? Your Secretary of War. He it was who, by command of our most noble President, authorized every marshal, every sheriff, every township constable, or city policeman, in every State in the Union, to fix, in his own imagination, what he might choose to call a treasonable or disloyal practice, and then to arrest any citizen at his discretion, without an accusing oath, and without due process, or any process of law. And now, sir, all this monstrous tyranny, against the whole spirit and the very letter of the Constitution, is to be deliberately embodied in an Act of Congress! Your petty provost-marshals are to determine what treasonable practices are, and "inquire into," detect, spy out, eavesdrop, ensnare, and then inform, report to the chief spy at Washington. These, sir, are now to be our American liberties under your Administration. There is not a crowned head in Europe who would venture on such an experiment.

IV

On March 5, the day after Congress adjourned, Vallandigham spoke at Philadelphia, where he advocated a convention of all the states, South as well as North, for the purpose of ending the war and restoring the Union. Next day he spoke in New York, then in Albany and several cities in New England. By late April he had returned to Ohio, where he denounced the policy of the administration in speeches at Dayton, Hamilton and Columbus.

Meanwhile General Ambrose E. Burnside, smarting from criticism over Fredericksburg, had been assigned to the command of the Department of the Ohio. On April 13, from his headquarters at Cincinnati, he issued General Order No. 38. Two paragraphs read:

"The habit of declaring sympathies for the enemy will not be allowed in this Department. Persons committing such offenses will be at once arrested, with a view to being tried as above stated, or sent beyond our lines into the lines of their friends.

"It must be distinctly understood that treason, expressed or implied, will not be tolerated in this department."

On May 1 Vallandigham spoke at Mount Vernon, a small town thirty-five miles northeast of Columbus. The Mt. Vernon Democratic Banner reported the meeting:[5]

Friday, May 1st, 1863, was a proud and glorious day for the faithful and unconquerable Democracy of old Knox, and one that will long be remembered by them with high and patriotic pleasure. Early in the morning the people began to come to town in wagons, carriages, and on horseback. Between ten and eleven o'clock the processions from the several townships arrived, and took the places assigned them by the Marshals. The processions were composed of wagons, carriages, buggies, &c., filled with people of both sexes and all ages, and of numerous horsemen. A remarkably large number of national flags, with *all* the flags of the Union as it was, on hickory poles, formed a very prominent and pleasing feature in each of these processions. A profusion of butternuts and liberty or copperhead pins, Union badges, and other appropriate emblems of Liberty and Union, were also distinguishable features.

Between eleven and one o'clock the township processions were united, and the grand procession filed through the principal streets of the city, making a splendid display. It was from four to five miles in length, and was over two hours in passing any one point. About 500 wagons, carriages, &c., came to town in the township processions, a number of which, however, dropped out of line before the grand procession was formed. The Democracy of the city displayed numerous flags on their private residences and places of business, and the processions heartily cheered them as they marched by them. The scene was beautiful and exciting, as well as vast, and caused all the good and true Union men who witnessed it to rejoice in their hearts with the fond hope for the salvation of their country, well knowing that it is by the Democracy that this most desirable object must and can be accomplished. The greatest enthusiasm was manifested throughout the entire line of procession. Cheers upon cheers rent the air in hearty acclaim. The hearts and consciences of those giving them were pure and clear, and the sounds were harmonious, peaceful, and patriotic.

One of the most noticeable and pleasing incidents of the procession and meeting, was a very large wagon drawn by six horses, from Wayne township, containing thirty-four young ladies representing the thirty-four States of the Union. The wagon was tastefully shaded with evergreens, in which the thirty-four young ladies were embowered.

The principal stand from which Messrs. Vallandigham, Cox, and Pendleton spoke, was canopied by large and beautiful American flags, and surrounded by various banners and emblems, all betokening the undying principles of the Democratic party.

The first speaker introduced to the audience was the bold and fearless patriot and statesman, Hon. C. L. Vallandigham, who was received with such a shout of applause as fairly made the welkin ring. He proceeded to deliver one of the ablest and most inspiring Union addresses ever made, in which he also evinced his unfaltering devotion to Liberty and the Constitution. Manliness, candor, genuine patriotism, and true statesmanship were manifested in the speaker throughout. If any of his lying detractors were present, it must have struck them with overwhelming force, and caused them to wince with a sense of their foul slanders. Mr. V. spoke for about two hours, and was listened to with the greatest attention, accompanied with tremendous shouts of applause.

Burnside struck at a tormentor whom he could no longer endure. Vallandigham's brother reported in melodramatic terms:[6]

On the evening of the 4th of May, Mr. Vallandigham and his family, consisting at that time of his wife, son, his wife's sister, and a young nephew of his own, and two domestics, females both, retired to rest at their accustomed hour. At half-past two o'clock in the morning they were rudely awakened from slumber by a violent knocking upon the front door. Arising, Mr. Vallandigham, who did not immediately suspect that it was a force coming to arrest him, went to the front window of the room over the parlor. As he approached it he heard the tramp of armed men, the low voice of command given by officers, the rattling of arms, and mutterings and whispering of many people. Looking out, lights were seen gleaming amidst the shrubbery in the yard below, and the glittering of many bayonets shone bright from the gas-light near the house. As he threw open the shutters the sounds struck upon his wife's ears, and she screamed with affright. He demanded what was wanted. Captain Hutton, an officer of General Burnside's staff, who was in command, answered that he had been sent by that General to arrest him, and that he might as well come down and surrender. Mr. Vallandigham replied that he would not; that he, Captain Hutton, had no right to arrest him, and that General Burnside had no right to issue an order for his arrest. To this a threat was made that unless he would come down he would be shot. He answered this in a defiant manner, and then shouted for the police. By this time the whole household was up; his wife and sister-in-law, both very nervous, timid women, were weeping, nearly crazed by terror, and begging him to come away from the window; the servant girls were equally alarmed. After repeated threats to shoot, intermingled with entreaties, the officer in command ordered the front door to be forced; but it was found too strong, and a door in the rear was then attacked. The house now shook with the violent blows of axes upon the door, and the horrid clamor filled the hearts of the women with an agony of fear. At last the door gave way, and the rattling of ramrods and bayonets, as well as the half-suppressed oaths of the men as they rushed into the back parlor, arose clearly and distinctly in the night air.

Mr. Vallandigham still determined he would not surrender whilst there was any hope of rescue. He desired to delay the soldiery until some organized effort could be made by his friends outside to drive off his assailants. He had dressed himself whilst the soldiers were burst-

ing upon the door below; and he arranged with his nephew, who had
served in the Union army, to open fire on the soldiers as soon as they
should be attacked from the outside. Another demand to surrender was
sternly refused, and the soldiers mounted the stair and commenced
battering away at the door of the room in which he stood. He then retired into another room which communicated with the one now attacked. In a few moments the second door was broken in, but lo! the
victim was not yet brought to bay. A short interval of silence followed,
and Mr. V. endeavored to soothe the affrighted ladies whilst he anxiously listened for the sound of footsteps coming to his aid; nothing,
however, but the measured tread of the sentinels could be heard on
the outside. The third door was now attacked, and as there was no
chance of successful resistance, he concealed his revolver and calmly
awaited the entry of the troops. The house was full of soldiers, though
the officer in command had not entered, and directly the third door
gave way the soldiers broke into the room where he stood, and half a
score of muskets were pointed instantly at him. Thereupon he said:
"You have now broken open my house and overpowered me by superior force, and I am obliged to surrender." The muskets were lowered, and hastily though not roughly he was torn from the arms of his
devoted wife and weeping child and hurried down stairs. Leaving his
wife stupefied in agony of grief and alarm, he passed through the shattered panels of his doors into the street. The bugles sounded the recall,
and surrounded by soldiery he was marched rapidly to the depot, and
thence carried by the special train to Cincinnati, where after daylight
he was taken to the military prison, Kemper Barracks.

*At Vallandigham's trial before a Military Commission at Cincinnati
Captain H. R. Hill, 115th Ohio Volunteer Infantry, gave the following
testimony:*[7]

Q. Were you present at a meeting of citizens held at Mount Vernon
on or about May 1, 1863?
A. I was.
Q. Did you hear the accused address this meeting?
A. I did.
Q. How near were you to him while speaking?
A. I was leaning on the end of the platform on which he was speaking.
I was about six feet from him.
Q. Was this your position during the whole of the time he was speak-
ing?

A. Yes.

Q. State what remarks he uttered in relation to the war now being waged, and any remarks he may have made in that connection.

A. The witness stated that, in order to state his remarks in the order in which they were made, he would refresh his memory from manuscript notes made on the occasion. These the witness produced, and held in his hands.

The speaker commenced by referring to the canopy under which he was speaking—the stand being covered by an American flag—"the flag which," he said, "had been rendered sacred by Democratic Presidents—the flag under the Constitution."

After finishing his exordium, he spoke of the designs of those in power being to erect a despotism; that "it was not their intention to effect a restoration of the Union; that previous to the bloody battle of Fredericksburg an attempt was made to stay this wicked, cruel, and unnecessary war." That the war could have been ended in February last. That, a day or two before the battle of Fredericksburg, a proposition had been made for the readmission of Southern Senators into the United States Congress, and that the refusal was still in existence over the President's own signature, which would be made public as soon as the ban of secrecy enjoined by the President was removed. That the Union could have been saved, if the plan proposed by the speaker had been adopted; that the Union could have been saved upon the basis of reconstruction; but that it would have ended in the exile or death of those who advocated a continuation of the war; that "Forney, who was a well-known correspondent of the *Philadelphia Press*, had said that some of our public men (and he, Forney, had no right to speak for any others than those connected with the Administration), rather than bring back some of the seceded States, would submit to a permanent separation of the Union." He stated that "France, a nation that had always shown herself to be a friend of our Government, had proposed to act as a mediator;" but "that her proposition, which, if accepted, might have brought about an honorable peace, was insolently rejected." It may have been "instantly rejected;" that "the people had been deceived as to the objects of the war from the beginning;" that "it was a war for the liberation of the blacks, and the enslavement of the whites. We had been told it would be terminated in three months—then in nine months, and again in a year—but that there was still no prospect of its being ended. That Richmond was still in the hands of the enemy; that Charleston was theirs, and Vicksburg was theirs; that the Mississippi was not opened, and would not be so long as there was cotton on its banks to be stolen, or so long as there were any contractors or officers to enrich." I do not remember which word, contractors or officers, he used.

He [Vallandigham] stated that a Southern paper had denounced himself and Cox, and the "Peace Democrats," as having "done more to prevent the establishing of the Southern Confederacy than a thousand Sewards." That "they proposed to operate through the masses of the people, in both sections, who were in favor of the Union." He said that "it was the purpose or desire of the Administration to suppress or prevent such meetings as the one he was addressing." That "military marshals were about to be appointed in every district, who would act for the purpose of restricting the liberties of the people;" but that "he was a freeman;" that he "did not ask David Tod, or Abraham Lincoln, or Ambrose E. Burnside for his right to speak as he had done, and was doing. That his final authority for so doing was higher than General Orders No. 38—it was General Orders No. 1—the Constitution. That General Orders No. 38 was a base usurpation of arbitrary power; that he had the most supreme contempt for such power. He despised it, spit upon it; he trampled it under his feet."

That only a few days before, a man had been dragged down from his home in Butler County, by an outrageous usurpation of power, and tried for an offense not known to our laws, by a self-constituted court-martial—tried without a jury, which is guaranteed to every one; that he had been fined and imprisoned. That two men had been brought over from Kentucky, and tried, contrary to express laws for the trial of treason, and were now under the sentence of death. That an order had just been issued in Indiana, denying to persons the right to canvass or discuss military policy, and that, if it was submitted to, it would be followed up by a similar order in Ohio. That he was resolved never to submit to an order of a military dictator, prohibiting the free discussion of either civil or military authority. "The sooner that the people informed the minions of this usurped power that they would not submit to such restrictions upon their liberties, the better." "Should we cringe and cower before such authority?" That "we claimed the right to criticise the acts of our military servants in power." That there never was a tyrant in any age who oppressed the people further than he thought they would submit to or endure. That in days of Democratic authority, Tom Corwin had, in face of Congress, hoped that our brave volunteers in Mexico "might be welcomed with bloody hands to hospitable graves," but that he had not been interfered with. It was never before thought necessary to appoint a captain of cavalry as Provost Marshal, as was now the case in Indianapolis, or military dictators, as were now exercising authority in Cincinnati and Columbus.

He closed by warning the people not to be deceived. That "an attempt would shortly be made to enforce the conscription act;" that "they should remember that this war was not a war for the preservation of the Union;" that "it was a wicked Abolition war, and that if those in authority were allowed to accomplish their purposes, the people would be deprived of their liberties, and a monarchy established; but that, as for him, he was resolved that he would never be a priest to minister upon the altar which his country was being sacrificed."

Q. Will you state what other flags or emblems decorated the platform than the American flag?

A. There were frames covered with canvas, all of which were decorated with "butternuts." One banner, which was borne at the head of a delegation, bore the inscription, "The Copperheads are coming."

Q. Did you see any badges worn by the citizens? How many, and what were those badges?

A. Yes: I saw hundreds of them wearing butternuts, and many of them wearing copperheads cut out of cents.

Q. Did you hear many, and how many, cheering for Jeff Davis, or expressing sympathy for him?

A. I heard no cheers for Jeff Davis, but I heard a shout in the crowd, that "Jeff Davis was a gentleman, and that was what the President was not."

On May 16 Vallandigham was found guilty of "publicly expressing, in violation of General Orders No. 38, from Head-quarters Department of the Ohio, sympathy for those in arms against the Government of the United States, and declaring disloyal sentiments and opinions, with the object and purpose of weakening the power of the Government in its efforts to suppress an unlawful rebellion." The commission sentenced the prisoner to imprisonment for the duration of the war. Three days later Lincoln commuted the sentence. At the President's order, Vallandigham was sent to Rosecrans' headquarters, then escorted beyond the Federal military lines. The Confederate authorities, embarrassed by the presence of a guest whom they did not quite want, and whom they did not quite know how to treat, finally solved their problem by sending the Ohioan on parole to Wilmington, North Carolina.

Many Northern Democrats held meetings protesting the action of the Federal Government. To Erastus Corning, president of the New York Central Railroad, who had presided over a meeting held in Albany, Lincoln sent a masterly justification of the government's action:[8]

Mr. Vallandigham avows his hostility to the war on the part of the Union; and his arrest was made because he was laboring, with some effect, to prevent the raising of troops, to encourage desertions from the army, and to leave the rebellion without an adequate military force to suppress it. He was not arrested because he was damaging the political prospects of the administration, or the personal interests of the commanding general; but because he was damaging the army, upon the existence, and vigor of which, the life of the nation depends. He was warring upon the military; and this gave the military constitutional jurisdiction to lay hands upon him. If Mr. Vallandigham was not damaging the military power of the country, then his arrest was made on mistake of fact, which I would be glad to correct, on reasonably satisfactory evidence.

I understand the meeting, whose resolutions I am considering, to be in favor of suppressing the rebellion by military force—by armies. Long experience has shown that armies can not be maintained unless desertion shall be punished by the severe penalty of death. The case requires, and the law and the constitution, sanction this punishment. Must I shoot a simple-minded soldier-boy who deserts, while I must not touch a hair of a wily agitator who induces him to desert? This is not the less injurious when effected by getting a father, or brother, or friend, into a public meeting, and there working upon his feelings, till he is persuaded to write the soldier boy, that he is fighting in a bad cause, for a wicked administration of a contemptible government, too weak to arrest and punish him if he shall desert. I think that in such a case, to silence the agitator, and save the boy, is not only constitutional, but, withal, a great mercy. . . .

I can no more be persuaded that the government can constitutionally take no strong measure in time of rebellion, because it can be shown that the same could not lawfully be taken in time of peace, than I can be persuaded that a particular drug is not good medicine for a sick man, because it can be shown to not be good food for a well one. Nor am I able to appreciate the danger, apprehended by the meeting, that the American people will, by means of military arrests during the rebellion, lose the right of public discussion, the liberty of speech and the press, the law of evidence, trial by jury, and habeas corpus, throughout the indefinite peaceful future which I trust lies before them, any more than I am able to believe that a man could contract so strong an appetite for emetics during temporary illness, as to persist in feeding upon them through the remainder of his healthful life. . . .

And yet, let me say that in my own discretion, I do not know whether I would have ordered the arrest of Mr. V. . . . I have to say it gave me pain when I learned that Mr. V. had been arrested . . . and that it will afford me great pleasure to discharge him so soon as I can, by any means, believe the public safety will not suffer by it.

The historian James Ford Rhodes devoted a long section of his History of the United States from the Compromise of 1850 *to the question of arbitrary arrests, including the Vallandigham case. Of Lincoln's letter to Corning, Rhodes wrote:*[9]

While he [Lincoln] was adroit and sincere in his reasoning, and went as far towards proving a bad case as the nature of things will permit, he did not take the view of the broad statesman we may note in his papers on compensation to the border States and on the emancipation of the slaves. He employed rather the arguments of the clever attorney and politician eager to seize the weak points of his adversary and bring out in shining contrast the strong features of his own case. We may wish, indeed, that the occasion which prompted these letters had not arisen, yet their tone demonstrated that the great principles of liberty would suffer no permanent harm while Abraham Lincoln was in the presidential chair. The mischief of the procedure lay in the precedent, even as his intimate friend and appointee, Justice David Davis, expressed it in the opinion of the court in the Milligan case: "Wicked men ambitious of power," he said, "with hatred of liberty and contempt of law, may fill the place once occupied by Washington and Lincoln, and if this right is conceded [that of a commander in time of war to declare martial law within the lines of his military district and subject citizens as well as soldiers to the rule of *his will*] and the calamities of war again befall us, the dangers to human liberty are frightful to contemplate."

V

Burnside next turned to two newspapers which he considered to be subversive. His General Order No. 84, issued on June 1, forbade the *circulation of the New York* World *and suppressed the publication of the Chicago* Times * *on account of "repeated expression of disloyal and incendiary sentiments."*

With public opinion in an inflamed state, the Times *had asked for trouble. Under Wilbur F. Storey it had criticized the Administration at every turn, attacking the President for dismissing McClellan, reviling him for issuing the Proclamation of Emancipation. By the end of 1862 the intemperate editor was calling for peace on any terms. "We believe the Union can be restored without another day of war," he wrote on December 4. "We do not believe slavery can be overthrown by endless war." Burnside's defeat at Fredericksburg was the result of "the same incompetency and folly and imbecility which have presided in Washington from the day Mr. Lincoln entered upon an office for which he had not a single qualification." The arrest of Vallandigham, Storey charged, was an "absolute violation of the plainest and most mandatory constitutional provisions," and signified the rule of a military despotism:*[10]

The officer refused to observe the order of the high civil authority [Judge Drummond], and forthwith returned to Camp Douglas, for the purpose of bringing down a squad of soldiers to take military possession of the office. Nevertheless, the preparations for getting out the morning edition continued. The first side went to press at half-past 11 o'clock [on the night of June 2], and at half-past 2 [on the morning of June 3] the forms of the second side were also locked up and put to press. At a quarter past 3 o'clock a military officer with a company surrounded the office and patrolled with fixed bayonets up and down the streets on each side of the block. The press was still working, and continued to work, throwing off the edition until nearly 5 o'clock, when the military burst in the rear door of the establishment, and ordered the press to be stopped. A large number of papers, fresh from the press, were seized and taken into the street, when the officer ordered his men to tear them into shreds. From this time until . . . 6½ o'clock on Thursday evening [June 5], the whole establishment was in possession of the military.

VI

Burnside had gone too far. Twenty thousand citizens of Chicago gathered in the Court House Square, listened to speeches by several of

* The present Chicago *Sun-Times* has no connection with the Chicago *Times* of 1863.

the city's most prominent men, and passed resolutions denouncing Burnside's action. The Chicago Tribune, *archenemy of the* Times, *admitted that a full half of the audience was made up of Republicans, and called them "strangely out of place" in a gathering which, "under the pretence of defending free speech, met to assail the Government and weaken its power." Undeterred by the* Tribune's *disapproval, Lyman Trumbull, the Republican Senator from Illinois, and Isaac N. Arnold, also a Republican and Lincoln's stanchest supporter in the House of Representatives, telegraphed the President to ask that he rescind Burnside's order. Lincoln immediately ordered the suspension revoked. Again James Ford Rhodes had an incisive comment:*

"Nothing can be a more striking condemnation of the President's course towards Vallandigham than his own action in the case of the Chicago Times. *Even in this he deserves no credit for the initiative in right doing; for he simply responded to the outburst of sentiment in Chicago, which was beginning to spread over the whole North. Nevertheless, in this censure of Lincoln it is well to remember that, over-weighted by the heavy misfortunes of the last year, he came to the consideration of the Vallandigham case oppressed with anxiety at the terrible defeat of the Army of the Potomac at Chancellorsville."*

While Chicagoans met to protest the suppression of the Times, *thousands of New Yorkers gathered to denounce the entire course of the Lincoln Administration. The occasion was a convention for "Peace and Reunion" which assembled at Cooper Institute on the early evening of June 3. The featured speaker was Fernando Wood, three times mayor of the city, a former Tammany leader who could advocate temperance and press for education yet blink at corruption and perhaps profit from it, a turnabout who could give secessionists his blessing and then urge the city council to appropriate a million dollars for equipping Union regiments. By 1863 Wood had adopted Vallandigham's position as his own. Although he did not approach most of the "blatant demagogues" (Rhodes' phrase) who held forth at four stands until midnight, Wood spoke with little restraint:*[11]

Fellow-Citizens: We have fallen upon evil times. We have lived too long if we have outlived our country. Indications admonish us that the American Union has been severed, and it may be forever. Disguise it as we may, candor compels the admission that our once proud Republic has fallen from its exalted height. It is now prostrate! Decried, insulted, and without a second-rate position abroad—rent asunder by fearful civil war at home—ruled by despotic power on principles of partisan hate—and upon theories of government utterly antagonistic to those upon which our institutions were founded—we stand before the world an object of wonder, contempt and ridicule. . . .

As the Almighty "tempers the wind to the shorn lamb," so has He heretofore provided the instrument by which great national results have been accomplished for the advantage of humanity. As yet, He has not vouchsafed this favor to us. No man equal to this crisis has appeared—neither in the field, nor in the Cabinet; nor in the many elevated spheres of private life has the man presented himself with the brain, the heart, and the courage to seize and work out the great political problem now to be solved in our case, and to utter efficiently the truths of reason with the force and power equal to the pending crisis. [Loud cheers.] Those who have the intellectual ability have lacked the nerve, and those with the nerve have lacked the ability. But there is another wonder: that in this civilized population of over thirty million —North and South—abounding with benevolence, purity, cultivation and enlightened Christianity, none are found to raise the Banner of Peace. Among the thousands of spires which rear their lofty turrets to a benignant God, but one covers a pulpit devoted to the principles of Christ, and proclaims: "On earth Peace: good will toward men." ["Who is it?"]—Mr. Pratt, of Staten Island. As if the opposite constituted the whole duty of man, war, bloodshed and rapine are encouraged, and "all uncharitableness" taught, as if to mock the spirit of the "meek and lowly Jesus." Those whose professions should instill the kindlier methods of settling human controversy have been foremost in the race for human sacrifice, forgetting that war and hate are the children of Satan, and that peace and love are the emanation of the Divine Spirit. . . .

I declare for peace [loud cheers], and as preparatory for peace, am in favor of a cessation of hostilities, that propositions may be made or accepted which shall conduce to, or result in, an amicable adjustment of the causes which led to this war. I am not for a peace based upon the final separation of the States—but for peace as the only means which will lead to restoration, and am opposed to, and until the popular voice of the country shall declare for it, shall continue to oppose any movement which has for its aim the breaking up of the glorious old Union under which we have lived and prospered for over three-quarters of a century. Upon this occasion I have not the time to go into an extensive analysis of the grounds upon which I can sustain my demand for a cessation of hostilities. . . . I will, however, submit ten propositions, each capable of elucidation, which, upon other occasions, I will attempt to maintain.

Wood's first six propositions embraced these major points: that the war should stop because the Federal government did not have, and never did have, the power to coerce a state; that the war had become a crusade for the abolition of slavery and the extinguishment of the Southern states; that it was being made "a pretext for the most outrageous and damnable crimes against the liberty of the citizen"; and that it was breeding a military despotism. Wood continued:

This night at this moment the city of Chicago may be in flames. There has been assembled this night one of the largest meetings ever held in Chicago in front of the office of that noble Democratic paper *The Chicago Times,* protesting with stentorian power against this military interference with the rights of a free press. [Cheers.] And if I know the character of the Western people—if I understand the character of the men at Chicago, they possess the spirit of the men of New York [cheers], and I dare and defy the Administration to send to the city of New York, their Gen. Burnside. [Groans. "Hang him!"] I, here in the name of assembled thousands and tens of thousands request the Administration to give Gen. Burnside this Department. [Great cheering and waving of hats.] Fellow-citizens, I may have uttered the language of treason. ["No, no."] I have certainly said more than the language uttered by our lamented friend Vallandigham, who was struck down by the Administration, and I may be the next glorious martyr upon the altar of my country's liberty.

Wood advanced his remaining propositions. The war should be stopped because no one in the North could match "the vastly superior statesmen and generals of the South"; because "the popular enthusiasm necessary to conduct the war and supply the failing armies has subsided" and a draft could not take its place; "and finally, because experience should admonish us that the over-ruling power of God is against us." Wood closed:

My friends, need I say more? Need I attempt the elucidation of these premises? The mere statement of these positions, without argument or illustration or reference, of itself proves the case. "Truth is mighty and will prevail," and hence let these facts, thus briefly though feebly expressed, go forth to the world as the avant courier of the American people. . . .

Fellow-citizens, be calm, prudent, and thoughtful! Liberty is cowering behind passion, and power is dallying with her there. Prejudice is dethroning reason and raising an oracular temple upon her ruins. Stupidity mocks at calamity and reproaches patriotism. Pandora's Box is opened. Men of New York, be firm. Define your position, and maintain it. Let no idle gasconade come from you to insult the hopes of your bleeding country. Liberty is the high mark, the first object—maintain that, and then restore the Union. A drowned man may be resuscitated; his friends will apply restoratives, and they will do it promptly, calmly, earnestly, and they will do it so long as there shall be the least indications of existing vitality, however feeble and doubtful. So with your country. If it is worth anything, it is worthy of every sacrifice we can make for its restoration, which must come speedily, or life is extinct. Let us hear no more about War Democrats. If this war is to go on, I want the Republican party to have the power and the responsibility. I tell you here, I speak to you advisedly, the thing that the South holds in utmost contempt, even greater than an Abolitionist, is a hypocritical, canting, lying, War Democrat. And if it be said that the South won't make peace with Lincoln's Administration, and if this war continues two years more the only apprehension I have is, that instead of our being in doubt about recognizing their independence, they will recognize our independence.

CHAPTER 23

MISSISSIPPI HIGH JINKS: VICKSBURG

Late in January 1863, Oliver P. Morton, Governor of Indiana, telegraphed Lincoln: "It is important that I see you for a few hours, but I cannot leave long enough to go to Washington. Can you meet me in Harrisburg?"

Morton believed that he had collected evidence of a conspiracy among Democratic politicians in Ohio, Indiana and Illinois to form a Northwest Confederacy, cast aside New England as an abolitionist's wilderness, and join with the South. Perhaps Lincoln never called Morton—as some said he did—"the skeerdest man I know of"; but, in any event, the President replied calmly:

"I think it would not do for me to meet you at Harrisburg. It would be known, and would be misconstrued a thousand ways. Of course if the whole truth could be told and accepted as the truth, it would do no harm, but that is impossible."

I

Governor Morton sent a courier to see Lincoln. Essential to the success of any Northwest Confederacy, the Governor stressed, was control of the Mississippi. Lincoln doubtless held his temper, though he might have inquired why a campaign against Vicksburg had been weeks in planning if he were not aware of the river's importance. Sherman's failure in December to take the city by frontal assault had increased Southern defiance and emboldened the Butternuts. Again, Lincoln didn't need Morton to tell him these facts of political life. His hope was that something of a happier nature would occur with the spirited bride-

groom, General John A. McClernand, now at Vicksburg to command his own troops.

What transpired principally was a clash of personalities, with Sherman declaring that he essayed the role of peacemaker between a huffy Admiral Porter and an arrogant McClernand. Eventually the admiral and the two generals agreed to put aside their own quarrels and concentrate upon the Confederates with an unexpected adventure into Arkansas. In McClernand's name, a glowing victory was claimed:[1]

HDQRS. ARMY OF THE MISSISSIPPI,
POST ARKANSAS, Jan. 12, 1863.

SOLDIERS OF THE ARMY OF THE MISSISSIPPI: I congratulate you. Within seven days you have sailed 250 miles, from Vicksburg to this Post, borne upon numerous transports, from time to time furnished with fuel cut by you from the forest. With ranks thinned by former battles and disease you have waded and cut your way through miles of swamps and timber in advancing to the attack. You have stormed the defenses of the enemy's position which both nature and art had combined to render extraordinarily strong, capturing after three and a half hours' hard fighting the whole hostile force opposed to you, numbering 7,000 men, together with 8,000 stand of arms, 20 cannon, and a large amount of commissary, quartermaster's, and ordnance stores.

A success so complete in itself has not hitherto been achieved during the war. It is an important step toward the restoration of our national jurisdiction and unity over the territory on the right bank of the Mississippi River. It reflects honor upon your courage and patriotism. It will challenge the grateful acclaim of your country.

Your and my only cause of regret is the loss of the brave men who have fallen or been wounded in the defense of a just and sacred cause. All honor to them! Their names and their memory will be cherished in the hearts of their countrymen.

Soldiers, let this triumph be but the precursor of still more important achievements. Win for the Army of the Mississippi an imperishable renown. Surmount all obstacles, and relying on the God of Battles wrest from destiny and danger the homage of still more expressive acknowledgments of your unconquerable constancy and valor.

By order of Maj. Gen. John A. McClernand, commanding Army of the Mississippi:

A. SCHWARTZ,
Major and Acting Assistant Adjutant-General

A somewhat different account of the battle was contained in the report of Brigadier General Thomas J. Churchill, the Confederate commander along the lower Arkansas and White Rivers:[2]

RICHMOND, VA., May 6, 1863

GENERAL: On the morning of the 9th of January I was informed by my pickets stationed at the mouth of the cut-off that the enemy, with his gunboats, followed by his fleet of seventy or eighty transports, were passing into the Arkansas River. It now became evident that their object was to attack the Arkansas Post. I immediately made every arrangement to meet him, and ordered out the whole force under my command, numbering about 3,000 effective men, to take position in some lower trenches about 1¼ miles below the fort. The Second Brigade, under Colonel Deshler, and the Third, under Colonel Dunnington, occupied the works, while the First Brigade, under Colonel Garland, was held in reserve.

Three companies of cavalry, under command of Captains Denson, Nutt, and Richardson, were sent in advance to watch the movements of the enemy. During the night the enemy effected a landing about 2 miles below, on the north side of the river.

The following day about 9 o'clock the gunboats commenced moving up the river and opened fire upon our position. Having but one battery of field pieces, of 6 and 12 pounders, I did not return their fire. It was here that I expected the co-operation of the guns from the fort, but owing to some defect in the powder they were scarcely able to throw a shell below the trenches much less to the fleet. About 2 o'clock P.M., discovering that I was being flanked by a large body of cavalry and artillery, I thought it advisable to fall back under cover of the guns of the fort to an inner line of intrenchments.

The enemy advanced cautiously, and as they approached our lines were most signally repulsed. They made no further attempt that evening to charge our works, and I employed the balance of the time till next morning in strengthening my position and completing my intrenchments. Discovering that a body of the enemy had occupied some cabins in our old encampment, I ordered Col. R. Q. Mills with his regiment to drive them from the position, which he did most successfully, capturing several prisoners. Just before dark Admiral Porter moved up with several of his iron-clads to test the metal of our fort. Colonel Dunnington, who commanded the fort, was ready in an instant to receive him. The fire opened and the fight lasted near two hours, and finally the gunboats were compelled to fall back in a crippled condition.

Our loss was slight; that of the enemy much heavier. During the night I received a telegraphic dispatch from you, ordering me "to hold out till help arrived or until all dead," which order was communicated to brigade commanders, with instructions to see it carried out in spirit and letter. Next morning I made every disposition of my forces to meet the enemy in the desperate conflict which was soon to follow. . . . It was near 12 o'clock before the enemy got fully into position, when he commenced moving upon my lines simultaneously by land and water. Four iron-clads opened upon the fort, which responded in gallant style with its three guns.

After a continuous fire of three hours they succeeded in silencing every gun we had with the exception of one small 6-pounder Parrott gun which was on the land side. Two boats passed up and opened a cross-fire upon the fort and our lines; still we maintained the struggle. Their attack by land was less successful; on the right they were repulsed twice in attempting to storm our works, and on the left were driven back with great slaughter in no less than eight different charges. To defend this entire line of rifle pits I had but one battery of small field pieces, under command of Captain Hart, to whom great credit is due for the successful manner in which they were handled, contending, as he did, with some fifty pieces in his front. The fort had now been silenced about an hour, most of the field pieces had been disabled, still the fire raged furiously along the entire line, and that gallant band of Texans and Arkansians having nothing to rely upon now save their muskets and bayonets, still disdained to yield to the overpowering foe of 50,000 men, who were pressing upon them from almost every direction. Just at this moment, to my great surprise, several white flags were displayed in the Twenty-fourth Regiment Texas Dismounted Cavalry, First Brigade, and before they could be suppressed the enemy took advantage of them, crowded upon my lines, and not being prevented by the brigade commander from crossing, as was his duty, I was forced to the humiliating necessity of surrendering the balance of the command. My great hope was to keep them in check until night, and then, if re-enforcements did not reach me, cut my way out. No stigma should rest upon the troops. It was no fault of theirs; they fought with a desperation and courage yet unsurpassed in this war, and I hope and trust that the traitor will yet be discovered, brought to justice, and suffer the full penalty of the law. My thanks are due to Colonels Anderson and Gillespie for the prompt measures taken to prevent the raising of the white flag in their regiments. In the Second Brigade, commanded by the gallant Deshler, it was never displayed.

So McClernand gave one version of the capture of the Arkansas Post and Churchill another; Sherman told a story that flattered neither McClernand nor Churchill, and by Porter's account the Navy had done most of the effective fighting. Meanwhile McClernand turned to the political arena, advising his neighbor from Springfield that the Emancipation Proclamation had been a sad mistake. McClernand had been talking to "a gentleman of the first respectability just arrived from the rebel army" who had been speaking with officers in that army "formerly my warm personal and political friends," and McClernand advised his old Springfield neighbor, "These officials desire the restoration of peace and are represented to be willing to wheel their columns into the line of that policy. They admit that the South West and the North West are geographically and commercially identified."

The old Springfield neighbor in this instance was Abraham Lincoln, who held an opinion of his own concerning the usefulness of the Emancipation Proclamation:[3]

EXECUTIVE MANSION,
WASHINGTON, January 8, 1863

MAJOR GENERAL McCLERNAND

MY DEAR SIR Your interesting communication by the hand of Major Scates is received. I never did ask more, nor ever was willing to accept less, than for all the States, and the people thereof, to take and hold their places, and their rights, in the Union, under the Constitution of the United States. For this alone have I felt authorized to struggle; and I seek neither more nor less now. Still, to use a coarse, but an expressive figure, broken eggs can not be mended. I have issued the emancipation proclamation, and I can not retract it.

After the commencement of hostilities I struggled nearly a year and a half to get along without touching the "institution"; and when finally I conditionally determined to touch it, I gave a hundred days fair notice of my purpose, to all the States and people, within which time they could have turned it wholly aside, by simply again becoming good citizens of the United States. They chose to disregard it, and I made the peremptory proclamation on what appeared to me to be a military necessity. And being made, it must stand. As to the States not included in it, of course they can have their rights in the Union as of old. Even the people of the states included, if they choose, need not to be hurt by it. Let them adopt systems of apprenticeship for the colored people, conforming substantially to the most approved plans of gradual emancipation; and, with the aid they can have from the general government, they may be nearly as well off, in this respect, as if the present trouble had not occurred, and much better off than they can possibly be if the contest continues persistently.

As to any dread of my having a "purpose to enslave, or exterminate, the whites of the South," I can scarcely believe that such dread exists. It is too absurd. I believe you can be my personal witness that no man is less to be dreaded for undue severity, in any case.

If the friends you mention really wish to have peace upon the old terms, they should act at once. Every day makes the case more difficult. They can so act, with entire safety, so far as I am concerned.

I think you would better not make this letter public; but you may rely confidently on my standing by whatever I have said in it. Please write me if any thing more comes to light. Yours very truly

A. LINCOLN

II

When later in January McClernand again wrote Lincoln, he had a new complaint—Grant had reduced him to a corps commander and he, McClernand, knew that Halleck was to blame for this mischief. Lincoln replied in part: "You are now doing well—well for the country, and well for yourself—much better than you could possibly be, if engaged in open war with Gen. Halleck. Allow me to beg, that for your sake, for my sake, & for the country's sake, you give your whole attention to the better work."

What Lincoln said between the lines was that Grant had taken personal command of the campaign against Vicksburg. On a bleak day, toward the end of January, Grant reached Young's Point, about seven miles above the fortified city on the river bluffs. He did not exaggerate the problems that confronted him:[4]

The real work of the campaign and siege of Vicksburg now began. The problem was to secure a footing upon dry ground on the east side of the river from which the troops could operate against Vicksburg. The Mississippi River, from Cairo south, runs through a rich alluvial valley of many miles in width, bound on the east by land running from eighty up to two or more hundred feet above the river. On the west side the highest land, except in a few places, is but little above the highest water. Through this valley the river meanders in the most tortuous way, varying in direction to all points of the compass. At places it runs to the very foot of the bluffs. After leaving Memphis, there are no such highlands coming to the water's edge on the east shore until Vicksburg is reached.

The intervening land is cut up by bayous filled from the river in high water—many of them navigable for steamers. All of them would be, except for overhanging trees, narrowness and tortuous course, making it impossible to turn the bends with vessels of any considerable length. Marching across this country in the face of an enemy was impossible; navigating it proved equally impracticable. The strategical way according to the rule, therefore, would have been to go back to Memphis; establish that as a base of supplies; fortify it so that the storehouses could be held by a small garrison, and move from there along the line of railroad, repairing as we advanced, to the Yallabusha, or to Jackson, Mississippi. At this time the North had become very much discouraged. Many strong Union men believed that the war must prove a failure. The elections of 1862 had gone against the party which was for the prosecution of the war to save the Union if it took the last man and the last dollar. Voluntary enlistments had ceased throughout the greater part of the North, and the draft had been resorted to to fill up our ranks. It was my judgment at the time that to make a backward movement as long as that from Vicksburg to Memphis, would be interpreted, by many of those yet full of hope for the preservation of the Union, as a defeat, and that the draft would be resisted, desertions ensue and the power to capture and punish deserters lost. There was nothing left to be done but to *go forward to a decisive victory*. This was in my mind from the moment I took command in person at Young's Point.

The winter of 1862–3 was a noted one for continuous high water in the Mississippi and for heavy rains along the lower river. To get dry land, or rather land above the water, to encamp the troops upon, took many miles of river front. We had to occupy the levees and the ground immediately behind. This was so limited that one corps, the 17th, under General McPherson, was at Lake Providence, seventy miles above Vicksburg.

It was in January the troops took their position opposite Vicksburg. The water was very high and the rains were incessant. There seemed no possibility of a land movement before the end of March or later, and it would not do to lie idle all this time. The effect would be demoralizing to the troops and injurious to their health. Friends in the North would have grown more and more discouraged, and enemies

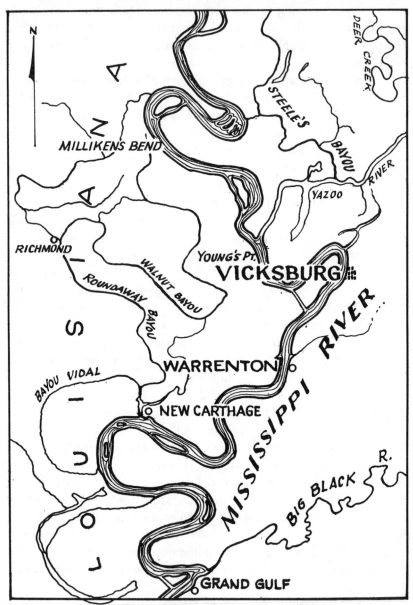

VICKSBURG: THE RIVER APPROACHES

in the same section more and more insolent in their gibes and denunciation of the cause and those engaged in it.

*One who could testify to how the flood waters of the Mississippi com-
plicated Grant's problems was the reporter Sylvanus Cadwallader:*[5]

For a few weeks after we arrived at Young's Point a large proportion of the dead were buried in a strip of bottom land laying between
the river bank and the levee. As the water rose to the level of the river
bank, in some places, this bottom was converted into a mud hole and
quagmire, until teams that were still contriving to drag through to the
transports for supplies would often strike the end of the box or coffin
and heave it clear out of the ground. Generally these were buried a
second time, a little deeper. For another period thereafter, the dead
were buried in the side of the levee (there being no other dry ground
for miles), until the levee was literally honeycombed by such excava-
tions.

On one occasion the father of a dead soldier came from the north
with a metallic casket, disinterred the remains of his son who had
died of smallpox from the bank, and left the empty box on the side of
the levee. That night one of the negro roustabouts on the *Magnolia* *
brought this discarded smallpox coffin to the lower deck of the vessel
and used it to sleep in for fully a week before he was detected. Singularly the contagion did not spread, but fumigations were in order for a
while.

*At Brokenburn, a large cotton plantation about thirty miles northwest
of Vicksburg, young Kate Stone recorded the discomforts produced by
the presence of Grant and his Yankees:*[6]

Jan. 25: Sunday. After three weeks of silence let me think of what
has happened. The Yankees, after an absence of more than a week
employed in taking Arkansas Post, have returned in large force, have
invested Vicksburg, and are cutting another ditch across the point
above DeSoto, or it may be deepening the first ditch. My Brother, Mr.
Hardison, Dr. Waddell, and several other Louisiana gentlemen were
in Vicksburg when the boats came in sight, and they had great trouble

* Grant's headquarters boat.

regaining their horses, just missing several encounters with scouting bands.

My Brother started off this morning with the best and strongest of the Negroes to look for a place west of the Ouachita. Only the old and sickly with the house servants are left here. He is sure we will all be forced to leave this place as the enemy intend going into camp at the Bend, and in the event of their defeat at Vicksburg which is certain, will lay this whole country waste, sending out bands of Negroes and soldiers to burn and destroy. My Brother thinks we had better leave at once, and we will commence packing tomorrow. The Negroes did so hate to go and so do we. . . .

Jan. 26: Preparing to run from the Yankees, I commit my book to the bottom of a packing box with only a slight chance of seeing it again.

March 2: Saturday [Monday] I think. We have not had an almanac for more than a year, and so I can only guess at the time until someone better posted comes along. The Yankees have not visited us yet, and so after more than a month's concealment I take my book out to write again.

The soldiers have been all around us but not on the place. At first we were frightened, expecting them all the time and preparing to start for the hills beyond the Macon, the Mecca for most of the refugeeing planters. Mamma had all the carpets taken up and the valuable clothes and everything but the furniture sent away or ready to send when My Brother came back from Delhi, where he left the Negroes waiting until they could be shipped on the train. Such a crowd was there that it will be several days before they can get off.

He gave such a disheartening account of the roads—they are impassable for anything but a six-mule team—that he and Mamma concluded it was impossible to move at this time and we would await further developments here. Mamma has had the house put in order, and we are again comfortable. I am so glad for I dreaded going into the back country, where we would never see or hear anything among total strangers, and to leave our pleasant home most probably to be destroyed by the Yankees, and we may be able to protect it if we are here. . . .

March 3: Last night it was reported that the Yankees were at Dr. Devine's, and we looked for them here today. My Brother and Mr. Hardison, who is conscript agent, went out early this morning to stay in the woods until nightfall, as they do not want to be captured and ornament a Yankee prison. It is My Brother's last day at home too, and we can see nothing of him because of those horrid Yankees. The fear of his imprisonment alone reconciles us to his departure. We are in hourly dread of his being taken. We will feel safe only when he is across the river again. . . .

Johnny who has been out scouting reports the Yankees at Rescue, the adjoining place, yesterday hunting horses and Negroes, and today they are scattered all through the lower neighborhood on the same quest. This band is said to be Kansas Jayhawkers, the very offscourings of the Northern Army. They say they will take by force all Negroes, whether they wish to go or not. A great number of Negroes have gone to the Yankees from this section. Mr. Watson and his father-in-law, Mr. Scott, living, I think, on Eagle Lake near Richmond got up one morning and found every Negro gone, about seventy-five, only three little girls left. The ladies actually had to get up and get breakfast. They said it was funny to see their first attempt at milking. Mr. Matt Johnson has lost every Negro off one place and a number from the other places. Keene Richards has lost 160 from Transylvania and fifty of them are reported dead. The Negroes at work on the canal have what they call black measles, and it is very fatal to them.

III

During those winter months along the flooded Mississippi, the campaign against Vicksburg followed neither military rule, rhyme nor reason. Grant's problem was to find a way—any way—to break through the natural obstacles of swamp, water and forest protecting the city; the schemes advanced—and tried—to achieve this end multiplied from week to week, and sometimes from day to day. The river in 1863 made a big bend in front of Vicksburg, and the purpose of the canal to which Kate Stone referred was to channel across this bend of land so that Union gunboats could approach the city out of range of the massed batteries. The canal failed; and names like Lake Providence and Yazoo Pass in newspaper headlines indicated bayous and complicated systems of waterways that were explored in an effort to get below the city, land troops, and swing back upon Vicksburg's defenses.

With flood waters permitting gunboats to sail in areas ordinarily unnavigable in a canoe, Admiral Porter was entranced by the possibilities. Among all the plans proposed for getting at Vicksburg through the back door, Porter's stood apart for dash and originality. Grant, believing that anything was better than idleness, sent troops under Sherman to co-operate in an expedition unique in naval history, as Porter cheerfully testified:[7]

When the fleet came to the pass into which it was to turn, after having ascended the Yazoo, the entrance could scarcely be made out, so dense was the growth of the overhanging bushes and trees, but these the men cut away with cutlasses and axes, and a pass wide enough for three vessels abreast, showed itself, lined out by heavy trees, and through this the gun-boats followed one another in line, their leadsmen singing out in melodious song, "quarter less three." There was no more channel here than elsewhere, as the water overflowed every place alike, but there was a long, straight pass opening through the forest, about 170 feet wide, which was, no doubt, a road cut through the woods for hauling cotton to some landing.

It was a novel scene. Thousands of crows flew from their perches, and broke the silence of the forest with their discordant notes, no doubt wondering what could have caused those great "mudturtles" to invade their hitherto inaccessible abode, where for centuries they had reared their young and digested their plunder without interruption.

On went the gun-boats, officers and sailors alike, delighted with the romantic scenery, which baffled description; every heart was cheered with the hope that the long sought for road to Vicksburg had been found, and that the great prize would soon be in their hands. Now and then, a stray tree as much as three feet in diameter would be found standing in the middle of the channel as if to dispute the way. The vessels might have passed on either side, but the desire to try the strength of these outlying sentinels proved so great that the flagship "Cincinnati" would run into them with her strong, broad bow, and topple them over, a feat rendered possible by the softening action of the water upon the earth about their roots. The vessels in the rear were told to haul them out of the way. This was good practice, and came into play before the expedition had proceeded many miles. It was all fair sailing at first, but became rough work in the end.

After some ten miles of easy progress through the woods, the fleet arrived at Black Bayou, a place about four miles long, leading into Deer Creek—and here the plain sailing ended. The gun-boats, being too wide to pass between the trees, had to go to work and knock them down, and pull them up by the roots. The line of vessels was broken, and each went to work to make her way through the tangle as best she

could. Saws and axes now came into use, and every means was resorted to for clearing the way. The narrow tugs and the mortar floats
had no difficulty in getting along, but the wider iron-clads were, for a
time, brought to a stand. The open roadway had vanished, and the pilot
confessed his ignorance of this locality. There was plenty of water,
and the stentorian voice of the leadsman was still heard singing out
"quarter less three!"

There is nothing that will daunt the American sailor but a lee shore
and no sea room. There was plenty of sea room here, but no room to
pass between the tangle. The obstruction was passed, after working
twenty-four hours consecutively, and that four miles overcome, leaving
a good road for those coming after, but a number of trees were moved
away, Titans of the forest that had reigned there for a century or more.

Sherman had arrived at Black Bayou with part of his force, another
part had started to march over from a point twenty miles above the
Yazoo River, on the Mississippi, following a ridge of land not inundated. The part of the Army embarked had been transported in small
stern-wheel steamers, which being very narrow, succeeded in passing
between the trees with only the loss of a few smoke-stacks. From Black
Bayou, the gun-boats turned again into Steele's Bayou, a channel just
one foot wider than the vessels, and here came the tug of war, such
as no vessels ever encountered before. The keel of the skiff was the
largest thing that had ever floated in waters now bearing vessels of
600 tons burthen. These had to break through bridges spanning this
muddy ditch, pass through the smoke and fire of burning cotton-bales
(which the enemy set in a blaze as soon as the fleet was discovered),
and work on, at the rate of half a mile an hour, through lithe willows
growing in the middle of the stream, which at intervals was choked up
with rafts that had been there for years. The pilot proved to be a fraud;
he had never seen the place before.

This bayou was bordered on both sides with overhanging trees,
whose Briarean arms would cling around the passing vessels and
sweep away boats and smoke-stacks, while the limbs of decayed trees
would fall upon the decks, smashing skylights to pieces, and injuring
the people.

It was dreadful to witness the infatuation of the Confederate Government agents, who, riding about on horseback, were setting fire to
the cotton far and near. They must have imagined the expedition sent
to gather cotton—a purpose never thought of.

Houses were often consumed with the cotton piles, and everything betokened a Moscow affair. It was the cotton of the Confederate government, and they were allowed to burn it. It was the Confederate sinews of war they were destroying; they were burning up their cash with which they had expected to carry on the struggle.

The leaders of the expedition soon saw they were discovered; the move was certainly known in Vicksburg, and the whole Confederacy would be at work to defeat this measure. . . . The expedition hurried on to get into the Rolling Fork, and thence into the Sunflower, whence it could reach the Yazoo above Haines' Bluff. It seemed insane to proceed, there were so many dreadful obstacles in the way, yet no one apparently minded them. The work was hard on the sailors, nevertheless they only made a lark of it.

Vicksburg was never so aroused as on hearing of the raid right into the heart of her preserves. The expedition had struck that city's storehouse: here were the fleshpots that would make any people glad; cattle, corn, "hog and hominy" enough to subsist a great Army.

Porter was ahead of Sherman's troops, with his gunboats stuck in willow withes and an armed Confederate force soon appearing to contest his escape. By courier the admiral dispatched to the general "somewhere in the bayous" an urgent plea:

"Dear Sherman: Hurry up, for Heaven's sake. I never knew how helpless an ironclad could be steaming around through the woods without an army to back her."

Porter continued his tale of how not to fight in an ironclad:[8]

As night came on, the gun-boats were ordered to unship their rudders and drop down with the current; and, the water now running rapidly into the bayou, owing to the cut at Delta—which was overflowing the whole country—the vessels bumped along at double the rate they had ascended, bounding from tree to tree, and bringing down the dead branches on the decks, to the destruction of everything around —boats were smashed, and more or less injury done to everything.

As the gun-boats departed, the enemy . . . kept the fleet under fire without the latter being able to fire more than an occasional gun until nightfall, when it was found necessary to tie up. A watch of armed men and all the howitzers were put ashore in preparation for emergencies.

In the night the patrolling parties captured two of the enemy's officers and some men, who stated that two batteries had been landed, and three thousand sharpshooters, and that they were quite satisfied they would capture the gun-boats in twenty-four hours. They were not aware that an army was with the fleet; they took this for a raid of gun-boats only, and, as one of them remarked, "a crazy one at that."

At daylight the fleet started down stream again, stern foremost, hoping to meet the army by noon, but at 8 A.M., they were surrounded by sharpshooters, who kept up such a fire that it was almost impossible for any one to show himself on deck. The riflemen on board, lying behind defences, kept up a brisk fire whenever they saw a curl of smoke. The howitzers were kept at work from behind the deck-houses, and the mortars, which were fired with small charges, landed their shells in amongst the enemy, and kept them at a distance. Now and then a mortar shell, landing at the foot of a tree behind which was a sharpshooter, would overthrow the tree as it exploded—making trees unsafe as a protection. Still, the sharpshooters increased in numbers, when, suddenly, the fleet had to come to a stand. Eight or ten large trees, some three feet in diameter, had been felled right across their track, from either side of the bayou, thus completely blocking the way, and the loud cheers of the Confederates as they rang through the woods showed they thought their prey entrapped.

The officers and men of the fleet, undaunted by this state of things, went to work to surmount the difficulty and remove the trees. Five hundred armed men were put on shore, and took to the trees to meet the enemy's sharpshooters, while howitzers and mortars kept up a rapid fire which was more than the enemy cared to face.

The working party from the vessels commenced operations below the banks, out of reach of the enemy's fire, and by using hawsers, tackles, and that powerful adjunct, steam, in six hours the trees were all removed, and the fleet went on its way down rejoicing.

Sherman had heard the firing, and had pushed on to get to the aid of the gun-boats. In the meantime, the enemy had landed more infantry —there were about four thousand in all. Pemberton, at Vicksburg, was well posted in all that was going on, and was determined to leave nothing undone to capture the venturesome fleet.

Again the fleet came to a stand-still, but this time only two large . trees had been felled. The crews of the vessels commenced the work of removal, when a large body of Confederate troops were seen advancing directly through the woods upon the steamers, while the sharpshooters in redoubled numbers opened fire on the fleet from behind trees not more than fifty yards distant.

The working parties were called on board to defend the vessels, but before they could get to their arms, there was a rattle of musketry in the woods, a cheering of the crews, and a rapid retreat by the Confederates. They had fallen in with the head of Sherman's column, which was a great surprise to them, and after one or two volleys, they broke and fled back to their steamers. Sherman arrived just in the nick of time. Whether the gun-boats could have held their own under the circumstances is impossible to say. They were well prepared for a brave fight, and from behind the banks they could have mown down the enemy as they rushed on, but it was better as it was, and they were not subjected to the trial. . . . No set of people were ever so glad to see the soldiers as the men of that fleet were to see Sherman and his Army; and, as the gallant general rode up to the gun-boats, he was received with the warmest cheers he ever had in his life.

IV

Cries arose that the Union forces under Grant were hopelessly stuck in the mud before Vicksburg. To judge the situation at first hand, Secretary of War Stanton sent Charles A. Dana as a special emissary from Washington. Sylvanus Cadwallader described a threatened crisis:[9]

Gen. Grant had been apprized by friends of Mr. Dana's visit and its probable object. A conference of Staff officers was held, the situation was explained by Rawlins, and a line of procedure agreed upon. The paramount object was to keep Mr. Dana quiet until Grant could work out his campaign. Several of the staff could scarcely be restrained from open manifestations of their hostility, but wiser counsel prevailed. Col. Duff, chief of artillery, pronounced him a government spy, and was more inclined to throw him in the river, than to treat him with common civility. But Rawlins took a sensible, practical view of the situation, and said: "I am surprised, Col. Duff, at your discourteous and unmilitary remarks. Mr. Dana is the First Assistant Secretary of War,* and an official representative of the government. He should not be left in a moment's doubt as to the cordiality of his reception. He is entitled to as much official recognition as Mr. Stanton, or any other high

---

* Previously Dana, as editor of the New York *Tribune*, had stanchly supported Stanton as Cameron's successor in the War Department, one of the many points of disagreement between Dana and Greeley. When finally publisher and editor parted, Dana said: "While he was for peace I was for war . . . and there was a spirit that was not his spirit—that he did not like."

public functionary. I shall expect you to see that a tent is always pitched alongside Gen. Grant's, for Mr. Dana's use as long as he remains at headquarters—that sentries are placed in front of it—that orderlies are detailed for his service—and a place at mess-table specially reserved for him."

A suitable horse and equipments were provided for Mr. Dana's use and the entire staff, including Col. Duff, were properly deferential. Dana was not long in becoming an enthusiastic admirer of Gen. Grant's military ability, and remained his staunch friend till the war ended. Thus again was imminent danger averted by the wisdom and tact of Rawlins, and Grant spared to become the greatest military chieftain his generation produced.

Dana's own story bore out Cadwallader's claims:[10]

As soon as I arrived at Milliken's Bend, on April 6th, I had hunted up Grant and explained my mission. He received me cordially. Indeed, I think Grant was always glad to have me with his army. He did not like letter writing, and my daily dispatches to Mr. Stanton relieved him from the necessity of describing every day what was going on in the army. From the first neither he nor any of his staff or corps commanders evinced any unwillingness to show me the inside of things. In this first interview at Milliken's Bend, for instance, Grant explained to me so fully his new plan of campaign—for there was now but one—that by three o'clock I was able to send an outline of it to Mr. Stanton. From that time I saw and knew all the interior operations of that toughest of tough jobs, the reopening of the Mississippi.

The new project, so Grant told me, was to transfer his army to New Carthage, and from there carry it over the Mississippi, landing it at or about Grand Gulf; to capture this point, and then to operate rapidly on the southern and eastern shore of the Big Black River, threatening at the same time both Vicksburg and Jackson, and confusing the Confederates as to his real objective. If this could be done he believed the enemy would come out of Vicksburg and fight.

The first element in this plan was to open a passage from the Mississippi near Milliken's Bend, above Vicksburg, to the bayou on the west side, which led around to New Carthage below. The length of navigation in this cut-off was about thirty-seven miles, and the plan was to take through with small tugs perhaps fifty barges, enough, at least, to transfer the whole army, with artillery and baggage, to the other side of the Mississippi in twenty-four hours. If necessary, troops were to be transported by the canal, though Grant hoped to march them by the road along its bank. Part of McClernand's corps had already reached New Carthage overland, and Grant was hurrying other troops forward. The canal to the bayou was already half completed, thirty-five hundred men being at work on it when I arrived.

The second part of the plan was to float down the river, past the Vicksburg batteries, half a dozen steamboats protected by defenses of bales of cotton and wet hay; these steamboats were to serve as transports of supplies after the army had crossed the Mississippi.

Perhaps the best evidence of the feasibility of the project was found in the fact that the river men pronounced its success certain. General Sherman, who commanded one of the three corps in Grant's army, and with whom I conversed at length upon the subject, thought there was no difficulty in opening the passage, but that the line would be a precarious one for supplies after the army was thrown across the Mississippi. Sherman's preference was for a movement by way of Yazoo Pass, or Lake Providence, but it was not long before I saw in our daily talks that his mind was tending to the conclusion of General Grant. As for General Grant, his purpose was dead set on the new scheme. Admiral Porter cordially agreed with him.

In early February the Union ram, Queen of the West, *had run past the Vicksburg batteries, giving Grant his idea for transporting his army below the city via the same route. Julia Grant arrived to be with the general on the appointed night. James H. Wilson, an aide on Grant's staff, described the scene:*[11]

On the night of the first passage Grant with his staff and family moved down the river on his headquarters steamboat to a favorable point of observation just beyond the range of the enemy's guns and witnessed the whole extraordinary pageant. The fleet started after dark, between nine and ten o'clock, but before it got abreast of the enemy's guns all engines were stopped and all lights concealed, and for a few minutes it was hoped that the rapid current might carry the boats by unperceived, but this hope was fallacious. By the time they were abreast of the upper part of the bend, where the river was narrowest, the enemy discovered them and opened fire upon them with all the guns they could bring to bear. A small outhouse near the water was set on fire, lighting up the whole river and the opposite shore.

The roar of the heavy guns both from the batteries and the fleet was incessant and impressive, but without starting the engines the fleet drifted by and out of danger, lighted in its lower course by the transport which had been set on fire, abandoned by the crew, and burned to the water's edge.

It was an anxious hour for all, and especially for me. It was a brilliant moonlight night, and during the firing the point opposite the front of the city, as well as the surface of the river, in this bend only eight hundred yards wide, were further lighted up by the burning buildings on the banks. The roar of the enemy's heavy guns, twenty-five in number, from six-inch to ten-inch caliber, was deafening, and the whole scene was grand and awe-inspiring. One of the Grant children sat on my knees with its arms around my neck, and as each crash came, it nervously clasped me closer, and finally became so frightened that it was put to bed. Mrs. Grant sat by the General's side with the other children near, while the staff and clerks looked on in silence and wonder, if not in doubt. It was not till after midnight that the roar of artillery ceased and silence rested on the scene, and it was not till the next morning that the details became fully known. . . .

Dana witnessed the passage of the batteries:[12]

Just before ten o'clock on the night of April 16th the squadron cast loose its moorings. It was a strange scene. First a mass of black things detached itself from the shore, and we saw it float out toward the middle of the stream. There was nothing to be seen except this big black mass, which dropped slowly down the river. Soon another black mass detached itself, and another, then another. It was Admiral Porter's fleet of ironclad turtles, steamboats, and barges. They floated down the Mississippi darkly and silently, showing neither steam nor light, save occasionally a signal astern, where the enemy could not see it.

The vessels moved at intervals of about two hundred yards. First came seven ironclad turtles and one heavy armed ram; following these were two side-wheel steamers and one stern-wheel, having twelve barges in tow; these barges carried the supplies. Far astern of them was one carrying ammunition. The most of the gunboats had already doubled the tongue of land which stretches northeasterly in front of Vicksburg, and they were immediately under the guns of nearly all the Confederate batteries, when there was a flash from the upper forts, and then for an hour and a half the cannonade was terrific, raging incessantly along the line of about four miles in extent. I counted five hundred and twenty-five discharges. Early in the action the enemy put the torch to a frame building in front of Vicksburg to light up the scene and direct his fire.

About 12:45 A.M. one of our steamers, the *Henry Clay*, took fire, and burned for three quarters of an hour. The *Henry Clay* was lost by being abandoned by her captain and crew in a panic, they thinking her to be sinking. The pilot refused to go with them, and said if they would stay they would get her through safe. After they had fled in the yawls, the cotton bales on her deck took fire, and one wheel became unmanageable. The pilot then ran her aground, and got upon a plank, on which he was picked up four miles below.

The morning after Admiral Porter had run the Vicksburg batteries I went with General Grant to New Carthage to review the situation. We found the squadron there, all in fighting condition, though most of them had been hit. Not a man had been lost.

Porter explained why the maneuver had succeeded:[13]

The danger to the vessels was more apparent than real. Their weak points on the sides were mostly protected by heavy logs which prevented many shot and shells going through the iron. Some rents were made but the vessels stood the ordeal bravely and received no damage calculated to impair their efficiency.

The management of the vessels on this occasion was virtually in the hands of the pilots, who handled them beautifully and kept them in line at the distance apart ordered.

The enemy's shot was not well aimed; owing to the rapid fire of shells, shrapnel, grape and canister from the gun-boats, the sharpshooters were glad to lay low, and the men at the great guns gave up in disgust when they saw the fleet drift on apparently unscathed.

V

Elsewhere Mississippians were experiencing a different kind of shock. On the morning Porter's fleet moved below Vicksburg a one-time teacher of music and greengrocer named Benjamin H. Grierson set off at Grant's bidding on a series of lightning-fast cavalry raids. Some seventeen hundred horse soldiers rode with Grierson into the heart of enemy country. In late April the Jackson, Mississippi, Appeal told this story:[14]

From various sources we have particulars of the enemy's movements from the north line of Mississippi, through the eastern portion of the State, almost to the Louisiana line. The route chosen for his daring dash was through the line of counties lying between the Mobile and Ohio, and New Orleans, Jackson and Great Northern Railroads, in which, as they anticipated, there was no organized force to oppose them.

The penetration of an enemy's country, however, so extensively, will be recorded as one of the gallant feats of the war, no matter whether the actors escape or are captured. The expedition, we learn, was under command of Col. Grierson, of Illinois, who has already acquired considerable reputation as a dashing leader in West Tennessee. He boasted that he had no fears of his ability to extricate his command from the dangerous position it seemed to be in, but gave no indication as to the route he should take to get out of the country. . . . After crossing Leaf river, the bridges behind them were burned. Last night, it appears to be authentically reported, they camped near Westville, in the southern part of Simpson county. Whether they will move thence to Natchez, *via* Monticello and Holmesville, can only be conjectured; but we still incline to the opinion so confidently expressed some days ago, on first being advised of their presence at Newton, that Baton Rouge will be their haven, if undisturbed.* The crossing of Pearl river is the only natural difficulty they will encounter, and as we have no doubt they are advised as to the facilities they can secure at the different prominent fords, we presume they will act accordingly. Monticello and Holmesville may expect a visit.

The damage to the Southern railroad extends over a distance of four and a half miles, commencing a mile west of Newton, and running east. Two bridges, each about 150 feet long, seven culverts and one cattle gap, constitute the injury done. . . . Twenty freight cars were burned at Newton, and the depot buildings and two commissary buildings. The telegraph wire was taken down for miles, and cut in pieces. In many instances the wire was rolled up and put into ditches and pools. But few poles were destroyed. We can hear of but little outrage having been committed upon the persons of non-combatants or upon their property, except by the seizure of every good horse, and of the necessary forage and provisions. They had to depend upon the country for these. . . . The safe at the railroad depot was broken

* The editor guessed correctly.

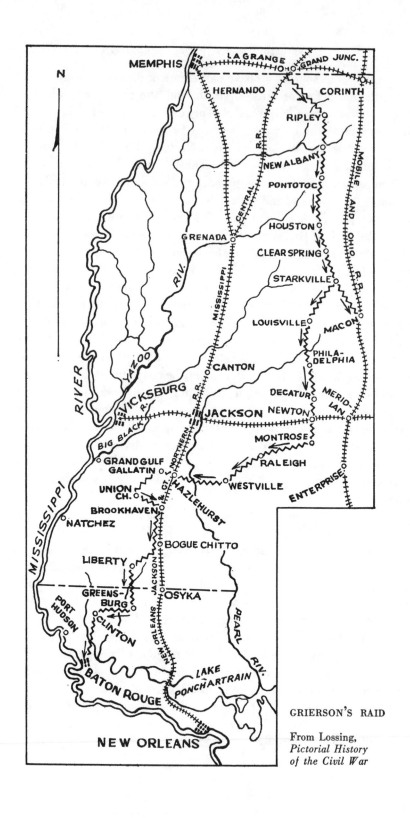

GRIERSON'S RAID

From Lossing,
*Pictorial History
of the Civil War*

open and the funds abstracted. The money was returned, however, by their commanding officer, with the exception of fifteen hundred dollars that, it was claimed, some of the men had stolen. The main body of the party in the movement upon Enterprise was halted at Hodge's residence, about five miles out, where they remained several hours. A detachment was sent to take the place [Company B, Seventh Illinois], and they advanced with the greatest confidence. Fortunately, the Thirty-fifth Alabama, under Lieutenant-Colonel Goodman, arrived about the same time and met the advancing party as they were approaching the bridge. As our men were about to open fire a flag of truce was raised, when a parley ensued and a demand for a surrender was made. Colonel G. was expecting reinforcements every moment and asked time to consider. The Yankees then fell back and, Colonel Loring arriving with the Twelfth Louisiana, Colonel Scott, and the Seventh Kentucky, Major Bell, pursuit was commenced, when it was found the advance had fallen back to the main body and all had gone. A fruitless effort to come up with them was made some miles further, but they had evidently become alarmed and feared an encounter.

At Doctor Hodge's the main body halted several hours. . . . Some of them entered the doctor's enclosure and required his daughters to furnish them provisions, which was done to the extent of cooked articles on hand. The rose bushes and flower beds of the young ladies were also sadly despoiled by the unwelcome visitors, but beyond this our informant says they did no damage, nor did they insult the ladies. The doctor was absent.

The Columbus, Mississippi, Republic drew a bitter conclusion from the success of Grierson and his Yankee raiders:[15]

The past week has been an eventful one. The boldest, and we may say one of the most successful, raids of cavalry that has been known since the war began, has been made (we say it with shame) through the very center of Mississippi, and at the time of this writing we fear have escaped without the loss of a man. We are almost inclined to believe the words of a correspondent, that the manhood of Mississippi had gone to the wars; women only were left, although some of them wore the garb of men. We do not know where the responsibility rests, but wherever it is, if it is not a fit and proper subject for court martial, we are afraid there are none. . . . It is reported that between four and five thousand federal cavalry started on this raid. They divided; some fifteen hundred, or perhaps a few more, stopped and gave Colonel Barteau battle, while the remainder, three thousand strong, marched directly south, scouring the country, from eight to ten miles wide, leaving the railroad, south of West Point, on their left. They encamped one night within twenty-five miles of this place. They destroyed the hospital at Okolona and a few other buildings, passing south through Houston, Siloam and Starkville, to within one mile of Macon, and thence south to Newton Station, on the Southern road, which we learn they destroyed. We can learn of no serious damage done or any ill treatment to the inhabitants personally. Their main objects seem to have been to examine the country and robbery—taking horses, mules and a few negroes.

At Starkville they robbed the inhabitants of horses, mules, negroes, jewelry and money; went into the stores and threw their contents (principally tobacco) into the street or gave it to the negroes; caught the mail boy and took the mail, robbed the postoffice, but handed back a letter from a soldier to his wife, containing $50.00, and ordered the postmaster to give it to her. Doctor Montgomery was taken prisoner and kept in camp all night, six miles from town, and allowed to return home next morning, after relieving him of his watch and other valuables. Hale & Murdock's hat wagon, loaded with wool hats, passing through at the time was captured. They gave the hats to the negroes and took the mules. Starkville can boast of better head covering for its negroes than any other town in the state.

They left quite a number of broken down horses all along their route, supplying themselves as they went. They stated that they were not destroying property; that they were gentlemen.

VI

While Grierson and his raiders disrupted Confederate communications, Grant pushed on. To reach the crossing point from Louisiana to Mississippi that he had selected, the next obstacle to overcome was the Confederate bastion at Grand Gulf called Bald Head, which, set on a promontory at the bend of the river, enabled its gunners to sight for miles along the Mississippi. Porter believed that Grand Gulf was too strong for a direct assault; Grant, convinced that the admiral overestimated the strength of the rebel batteries, ordered the attack. The battle raged for five and a half hours. Porter never forgot its flaming intensity:[16]

When the troops arrived at the point abreast of Bald Head, and the soldiers on the transports were ready to land as soon as the batteries should be silenced, Admiral Porter got under way with the squadron and commenced the attack at 8 A.M., on the 29th of April, 1863.

The "Pittsburg," "Louisville," "Mound City," and "Carondelet" attacked the lower batteries, while the "Benton," "Tuscumbia," and "Lafayette" attacked Bald Head battery, the two former as close as they could get, and the "Lafayette" lying in an eddy four hundred yards above the fort where she could enfilade it.

As the vessels approached the works the enemy opened fire and in ten minutes the battle was raging all along the line. The fight was severely contested, and it was not until three hours after the first gun was fired, that the enemy deserted his guns at the lower batteries, and then only after the "Lafayette" had been ordered from her first position to reinforce the gun-boats below.

In the meantime the flag-ship "Benton," and the "Tuscumbia" were doing their best to silence the upper battery, getting close *under* the guns and endeavoring to knock off their muzzles, when they were run out to fire. The current was so strong, however, that it was impossible to keep the two vessels in position and they sheered about very much. In one of these sheers, a shot entered the "Benton's" pilot house, disabled the wheel and cut Pilot Williams' foot nearly off. Though the brave pilot never left his post it was impossible to manage the vessel and she was accordingly run into the bank to repair damages.

The gun-boats at the lower batteries had been signalled to double up on Bald Head, the "Lafayette" to resume her old position, and the "Pittsburg," Volunteer-Lieutenant Hoel, arrived opportunely to take the "Benton's" place. During the time the latter vessel was out of action—twenty-five minutes—the "Pittsburg" lost six killed and had twelve wounded.

After all the vessels concentrated their fire on Bald Head, there was less resistance, although the Confederates still stood to their guns. When the battle had lasted more than five hours, General Grant, who from a tug up the river, was looking on, made signal to the Admiral that he wished to communicate, and the "Benton" joined him two miles above the forts. The Confederates had now ceased firing, but the gun-boats maintained their position around Bald Head, occasionally firing a shell to keep the enemy out of the works.

When General Grant went on board the flag-ship, he decided that it would be too hazardous to attempt to land troops, as it did not appear that the guns in the enemy's works were dismounted and the gunners would therefore jump to their batteries again, open on the unprotected transports and destroy many of the troops. For the same reason the general concluded not to send the transports past the batteries with the soldiers on board but to march the latter around by land. In this he was quite right, as afterwards appeared.

As there was no longer any object in keeping the gun-boats under the batteries, all but the "Lafayette" were recalled, and the latter was left in her old position to keep the enemy from reoccupying the works and repairing damages. This duty Commander Walke effectually performed, firing a shell every five minutes into the works until darkness set in.

The engagement was fought under great disadvantages; the current around the promontory of Bald Head ran with great rapidity, and it was as much as the gun-boats could do to stem it. Clumsy vessels at best, the ironclads would frequently be turned completely round, presenting their weak points to the enemy, of which the expert Confederate gunners were not slow to take advantage, and seldom missed their mark so close were the vessels to the forts. The light armor plates of most of the vessels offered but an imperfect resistance to the heavy missiles of the enemy, and, in consequence, the list of killed and wounded in the squadron was large.

Porter offered harrowing statistics to show the damage his river fleet had suffered—eighty-one hits on the Tuscumbia, *forty-five on the* Lafayette, *forty-seven on the flagship* Benton, *as examples. The admiral concluded: "Then came the melancholy duty of burying the dead, who were followed mournfully to their graves by their messmates and friends." Meanwhile Grant accepted the failure of the assault in good spirit and revised his plans to take advantage of an unexpected opportunity:*[17]

When the troops debarked, the evening of the 29th, it was expected that we would have to go to Rodney, about nine miles below, to find a landing; but that night a colored man came in who informed me that a good landing would be found at Bruinsburg, a few miles above Rodney, from which point there was a good road leading to Port Gibson some twelve miles in the interior. The information was found correct, and our landing was effected without opposition.

Sherman had not left his position above Vicksburg yet. On the morning of the 27th I ordered him to create a diversion by moving his corps up the Yazoo and threatening an attack on Haines' Bluff. My object was to compel Pemberton to keep as much force about Vicksburg as I could, until I could secure a good footing on high land east of the river. The move was eminently successful and, as we afterwards learned, created great confusion about Vicksburg and doubts about our real design. Sherman moved the day of our attack on Grand Gulf, the 29th, with ten regiments of his command and eight gunboats which Porter had left above Vicksburg.

He debarked his troops and apparently made every preparation to attack the enemy while the navy bombarded the main forts at Haines' Bluff. This move was made without a single casualty in either branch of the service. On the first of May Sherman received orders from me (sent from Hard Times the evening of the 29th of April) to withdraw from the front of Haines' Bluff and follow McPherson with two divisions as fast as he could.

I had established a depot of supplies at Perkins' plantation. Now that all our gunboats were below Grand Gulf it was possible that the enemy might fit out boats in the Big Black with improvised armament and attempt to destroy these supplies. McPherson was at Hard Times with a portion of his corps, and the depot was protected by a part of his command. The night of the 29th I directed him to arm one of the transports with artillery and send it up to Perkins' plantation as a guard; and also to have the siege guns we had brought along moved there and put in position.

The embarkation below Grand Gulf took place at De Shroon's, Louisiana, six miles above Bruinsburg, Mississippi. Early on the morning of 30th of April McClernand's corps and one division of McPherson's corps were speedily landed.

When this was effected I felt a degree of relief scarcely ever equalled since. Vicksburg was not yet taken it is true, nor were its defenders demoralized by any of our previous moves. I was now in the enemy's country, with a vast river and the stronghold of Vicksburg between me and my base of supplies. But I was on dry ground on the same side of the river with the enemy. All the campaigns, labors, hardships and exposures from the month of December previous to this time that had been made and endured, were for the accomplishment of this one object.

Grant now was sixty miles south of Vicksburg. He moved swiftly to-
ward Port Gibson, and at a point about five miles west of that place
collided with a force of Missourians and Mississippians under General
John S. Bowen. The Battle of Thompson's Hill, bitter and brief, served
notice that the Yankees were across the river to stay. Grant pushed
through Port Gibson to Grand Gulf. Once more confronted with unex-
pected circumstances, he readjusted his plans:[18]

When I reached Grand Gulf May 3d I had not been with my baggage
since the 27th of April and consequently had had no change of underclothing, no meal except such as I could pick up sometimes at other
headquarters, and no tent to cover me. The first thing I did was to
get a bath, borrow some fresh underclothing from one of the naval
officers and get a good meal on the flag-ship. Then I wrote letters to the
general-in-chief informing him of our present position, dispatches to be
telegraphed from Cairo, orders to General Sullivan commanding above
Vicksburg, and gave orders to all my corps commanders. About twelve
o'clock at night I was through my work and started for Hankinson's
ferry, arriving there before daylight. While at Grand Gulf I heard from
Banks, who was on the Red River, and who said that he could not be at
Port Hudson before the 10th of May and then with only 15,000 men.
Up to this time my intention had been to secure Grand Gulf, as a base
of supplies, detach McClernand's corps to Banks and co-operate with
him in the reduction of Port Hudson.

The news from Banks forced upon me a different plan of campaign
from the one intended. To wait for his cooperation would have detained
me at least a month. The reinforcements would not have reached ten
thousand men after deducting casualties and necessary river guards at
all high points close to the river for over three hundred miles. The
enemy would have strengthened his position and been reinforced by
more men than Banks could have brought. I therefore determined to
move independently of Banks, cut loose from my base, destroy the rebel
force in rear of Vicksburg and invest or capture the city.

Grand Gulf was accordingly given up as a base and the authorities
at Washington were notified. I knew well that Halleck's caution would
lead him to disapprove of this course; but it was the only one that
gave any chance of success. The time it would take to communicate with
Washington and get a reply would be so great that I could not be interfered with until it was demonstrated whether my plan was practicable. Even Sherman, who afterwards ignored bases of supplies other

than what were afforded by the country while marching through four States of the Confederacy with an army more than twice as large as mine at this time, wrote me from Hankinson's ferry, advising me of the impossibility of supplying our army over a single road. He urged me to "stop all troops till your army is partially supplied with wagons, and then act as quick as possible; for this road will be jammed, as sure as life." To this I repied: "I do not calculate upon the possibility of supplying the army with full rations from Grand Gulf. I know it will be impossible without constructing additional roads. What I do expect is to get up what rations of hard bread, coffee and salt we can, and make the country furnish the balance." We started from Bruinsburg with an average of about two days' rations, and received no more from our own supplies for some days; abundance was found in the mean time. A delay would give the enemy time to reinforce and fortify.

VII

Grant was in camp now at Hankinson's Ferry, whence Charles A. Dana wrote a cheerful letter to a young relative:[19]

All of a sudden it is very cold here. Two days ago it was hot like summer, but now I sit in my tent in my overcoat, writing, and thinking if I only were at home instead of being almost two thousand miles away.

Away yonder, in the edge of the woods, I hear the drum-beat that calls the soldiers to their supper. It is only a little after five o'clock, but they begin the day very early and end it early. Pretty soon after dark they are all asleep, lying in their blankets under the trees, for in a quick march they leave their tents behind. Their guns are all ready at their sides, so that if they are suddenly called at night they can start in a moment. It is strange in the morning before daylight to hear the bugle and drums sound the reveille, which calls the army to wake up. It will begin perhaps at a distance and then run along the whole line, bugle after bugle and drum after drum taking it up, and then it goes from front to rear, farther and farther away, the sweet sounds throbbing and rolling while you lie on the grass with your saddle for a pillow, half awake, or opening your eyes to see that the stars are all bright in the sky, or that there is only a faint flush in the east, where the day is soon to break.

Living in camp is queer business. I get my meals in General Grant's mess, and pay my share of the expenses. The table is a chest with a double cover, which unfolds on the right and the left; the dishes, knives and forks, and caster are inside. Sometimes we get good things, but generally we don't. The cook is an old negro, black and grimy. The cooking is not as clean as it might be, but in war you can't be particular about such things.

The plums and peaches here are pretty nearly ripe. The strawberries have been ripe these few days, but the soldiers eat them up before we get a sight of them. The figs are as big as the end of your thumb, and the green pears are big enough to eat. But you don't know what beautiful flower gardens there are here. I never saw such roses; and the other day I found a lily as big as a tiger lily, only it was a magnificent red.

The apparent calm was deceptive. Grant, like a panther tensing for a spring, moved his headquarters to Rocky Springs on May 7. Grant knew where he would strike—the state capital at Jackson, thus getting astride the railroad that supplied Vicksburg. Pemberton thought he divined Grant's intentions, and guessed wrong.

Some critics of John C. Pemberton would have said that guessing wrong was one of his chief traits, but at the base of all criticisms of "Old Pem" was the fact that he was one of those Southern generals who carried the heavy burden of being Northern-born. Pemberton's first war service had been in Charleston where his refusal to permit trading with the enemy in cotton had earned him a reputation as an "unfeeling brute," but that great student of character, Rhett of the Charleston Mercury, had called Pemberton "a thorough soldier" although "not a 'popular man.'" The Vicksburg paper at least had been happy to see Pemberton take command, and had rejoiced that at last Mississippians no longer were "to be put off" with "one-horse Generals."

Moods had shifted since then—most of all since Grant had started to change his campaign whenever the fancy took him. No one was more aware of the confusion that consumed Pemberton than Samuel H. Lockett, chief engineer of Vicksburg's defenses:[20]

. . . General Pemberton first thought that Grant would turn north from Port Gibson and try to force a passage across Big Black River at one of the ferries. He accordingly sent about a brigade each to Hankinson's, Hall's, and Baldwin's ferries, and ordered field-works to be thrown up at these crossings. . . .

At last General Pemberton became convinced that General Grant's intention was to march up the east bank of the Big Black River, to strike the railroad at or near Edwards's depot, and thus cut his communications with Jackson. To prevent this, and at the same time to defeat Grant, if possible, he concentrated all of his forces at Edwards's depot, excepting General Forney's division which was left in Vicksburg, and General Smith's which was posted at and near the railroad bridge. On the 12th of May, under the orders of General Pemberton, I went to Edwards's depot to put the Confederate forces in position upon the ground selected for them to occupy, covering all the approaches from the south and east. The army here assembled consisted of three divisions: Bowen's on the right, Loring's in the center, and C. L. Stevenson's on the left, numbering about 18,000 men. Some slight field-works had been thrown up at favorable points. The position was naturally a strong one, on high ground, with the cultivated valley of Baker's Creek in its front. Here General Pemberton wished to wait to be attacked by Grant. There can be no doubt that if he had been allowed to do so a desperate and bloody battle would have been fought on that ground, the issue of which might have been different from that of the two unfortunate engagements which did actually occur. The army remained at Edwards's depot from the 13th to the 15th. During this time General Pemberton received numerous dispatches from President Davis, and from General J. E. Johnston, who had recently arrived at Jackson. I saw, or heard read, most of these dispatches. They were very conflicting in their tenor, and neither those of Mr. Davis nor those of General Johnston exactly comported with General Pemberton's views. He then made the capital mistake of trying to harmonize instructions from his superiors diametrically opposed to each other, and at the same time to bring them into accord with his own judgment, which was adverse to the plans of both. . . .

Grant's great advantage was not only that he knew whither he was going, but also that Washington couldn't possibly argue the decision beforehand. By May twelfth a Federal column approached Raymond, eighteen miles west of Jackson, where a small Confederate force offered brisk, if hopeless, opposition. Sylvanus Cadwallader drew a picture of another type of difficulty Grant's forces encountered:[21]

That afternoon and night refugee "contrabands" came swarming into our lines by hundreds. They were of all ages, sexes and conditions, and came on foot, on horses and mules, and in all manner of vehicles, from the typical southern cart, to elegant state carriages and barouches.

Straw collars and rope harness alternated with silver plate equipments, till the moving living panorama became ludicrous beyond description.

The runaway darkies who had made sudden and forcible requisition upon their old masters for these varied means of transportation, generally loaded their wagons and carriages with the finest furniture left in the mansions when their owners had abandoned them at our approach. Feather beds and tapestried upholstery seemed to possess a peculiar charm and value to the dusky runaways. A black boy named Jerry, probably fourteen years old, who came to headquarters at that time, was taken by Rawlins as a body servant, and attended him till the war ended. On settling in Washington City in 1865, Rawlins kept him in his family, gave him quite a fair education, and had no more sincere mourner at his funeral than this faithful black boy Jerry.

Another boy named Willis attached himself in the same capacity to Col. Duff and remained with him till his expiration of service at City Point. He then became mine by adoption, as he claimed; but he certainly adopted me instead of my adopting him; and would doubtless be with me today,* had not Count Saldatankoff of the Grand Duke Alexis' retinue during his visit to the U. S. over a quarter of a century ago, taken an especial fancy to him and prevailed on Willis to accompany him to Russia.

"Cad" witnessed another side of Grant:[22]

The night of May 12th was spent by me on an army cot in Col. Duff's tent. About midnight, or soon thereafter, Gen. Grant came into the tent alone, in the dark, and requested a drink of whiskey. Col. Duff drew a canteen from under his pillow and handed it to him. The general poured a generous potation into an army tin cup and swallowed it with great apparent satisfaction. He complained of extraordinary fatigue and exhaustion as his excuse for needing the stimulant, and took the second, if not the third drink, before retiring.

A light was struck upon his entrance, so that he knew of my presence; but he made his request, and drank the whiskey in an ordinary manner, as if it was a matter of fact procedure which required no particular apology. His stay in the tent did not exceed twenty or thirty minutes. He

* Cadwallader's reminiscences were written "very near to the close of a busy life"; notations on the manuscript by General James H. Wilson are dated February, 1905.

sat on the edge of Duff's cot, facing mine, and apparently addressed himself to me as much as to Duff.

This was the first time I ever saw Gen. Grant use any spirituous liquor, and I was a little surprised by his openness in asking for it, and drinking it, before me. My intercourse with him to that time had been casual or accidental rather than intimate and confidential as it afterwards became; yet there was nothing evinced in word or behavior, from which I could infer that he desired the slightest secrecy or concealment concerning the object of his midnight call. The occurrence was never mentioned by me, excepting perhaps to Rawlins, until after the close of the rebellion. I think Col. Duff did suggest to me after the general's exit from the tent, that in view of Grant's reputation for excessive drinking, and his peculiar surroundings at the time, the affairs of state as well as my personal interests, might be best promoted by discreet silence, inasmuch as the general did not know that anyone occupied the tent with him until concealment was out of the question.

But I put a different construction upon his indifference, which was fully borne out by after events. The general knew that Gov. Oglesby * had left nearly a half barrel of whiskey in the joint care of Col. Duff and myself on taking his departure from headquarters a few days before. I also subsequently learned that Duff had catered to Grant's inordinate desire for stimulants long before this, and continued to do so till his "muster-out" at City Point. Rawlins suspected him of doing so, but had no positive proof of the fact for more than a year after this. Duff did not rise from his cot during Grant's stay that night, but lay stretched out at full length, except when he half rose on one elbow to join the General in his drinks, and to volunteer "success to our campaign, and confusion to the Whole Confederacy." But little was said by Grant in response to these sentiments, beyond an expression of satisfaction at what he had thus far accomplished, and a cheerful hope and belief that Vicksburg would soon be ours.

VIII

Whatever the brand of whisky Duff served, it was not clouding Grant's judgment. One who could testify to that fact was General Joseph E. Johnston, whom Richmond ordered from Tennessee to Mississippi in the prayerful hope that he could avert a Confederate disaster. John-

* Should read Yates; Oglesby was not elected governor of Illinois until late 1864.

ston reached the state capital on the thirteenth of May; the news that he received was hardly cheering:[23]

I arrived in Jackson at nightfall, exhausted by an uninterrupted journey of four days, undertaken from a sickroom; in consequence of which Major Mims, chief quartermaster of the department, the first officer who reported to me, found me in bed. He informed me, among other military occurrences, that two brigades had marched into the town an hour or two before. Brigadier-General Gregg, their senior officer, reported to me soon after that he had been ordered from Port Hudson to Raymond by General Pemberton, but had been driven from that place the day before by the Federal Seventeenth Corps; and, in obedience to the general's instructions for such an event, had fallen back to Jackson, accompanied by Brigadier-General W. H. T. Walker, whom he had met on the way, marching to join him with his brigade. The latter had just come from General Beauregard's department [South Carolina, Georgia, and Florida]. There were about six thousand men in the two brigades.

He said further that Colonel Wirt Adams, of the cavalry, had informed him that General Pemberton's forces were at Edwards's depot, 20 miles from Vicksburg, and his headquarters at Bovina, 8 miles from that place; that the Seventeenth Corps (McPherson's) had moved that day from Raymond to Clinton 9 or 10 miles from Jackson, on the road to Vicksburg. He added that General Maxey's brigade from Port Hudson was expected in Jackson next day. I had passed General Gist's during that day, on its way from Charleston. The arrival of these troops, and, as I hoped, 3000 from Tennessee, would increase the force in Jackson to near 15,000 men. The most important measure to be executed then was the junction of these reënforcements with the army. For that object, an order in writing was sent without delay to General Pemberton by Captain Yerger, who volunteered to bear it, to move to Clinton at once and attack a Federal corps there, the troops in Jackson to coöperate; to beat that detachment and establish communication, that he might be reënforced. It was delivered at Bovina early next morning, and General Pemberton replied promptly that he "moved at once with his whole available force"; but in the ride of ten or twelve miles to his camp at Edwards's depot he determined to disobey my order, and on his arrival assembled a council of war, which he informed of that intention, and consulted upon the measure to be substituted for the movement to Clinton. It was decided to move southward to a point on the road by which General Grant's forces had advanced, which would have made it impossible for the troops then in Jackson and other expected reënforcements to join Pemberton's army.

Grant, reaching Jackson, recalled, "I slept that night in the room that Johnston was said to have occupied the night before." Sylvanus Cadwallader supplied other details of the Federal occupation of the capital of Jefferson Davis' home state:[24]

As soon as the fire of the Confederate batteries was silenced, Fred Grant (a stout, good-natured son of the General who accompanied the army all through the campaign) and myself, started for the Capitol at full speed to secure the large Confederate flag which waved from a staff on the roof. We supposed ourselves far in advance of anyone connected with the Union army. We dismounted hurriedly in front of the building, ran upstairs till we reached those leading from the garret to the roof, where we met a ragged, muddy, begrimed cavalryman descending with the coveted prize under his arm. To say that our disappointment was extreme but mildly expresses the state of our feelings. We were beaten and compelled to admit that to the victor belongs the spoils.

I pushed on to the Bowman House, then the principal hotel in the city, and found its office and corridors filled with Confederate officers and soldiers, some of whom were wounded and disabled men from convalescent hospitals; others who were doubtless bummers, skulkers and deserters who fell out of the Confederate ranks as Johnston's army retreated across the river; and a large concourse of townspeople and civilians who chanced to be there from other parts of the state. I ran the gauntlet of unfriendly observation; secured a room at once; and wrote dispatches for the Chicago *Times*, with scarcely a moment's relaxation, till Gen. Grant's courier was ready to take the road for Grand Gulf, with government dispatches, announcing his victories at the capital of Mississippi.

Grant and staff arrived at the Bowman House soon after I did, which diverted attention from me. . . . Many calls were made upon him by citizens asking for guards to protect their private property, some of which perhaps were granted, but by far the greater number were left to the tender mercies of Confederate friends.

Gen. Sherman was charged with the provost duty of the city and was directed to remain with his corps till all the public property used by the Confederacy had been destroyed and its usefulness as a great Confederate railroad center put past the possibility of being speedily re-established. Foundries, machine-shops, warehouses, factories, arsenals and public stores were fired as fast as flames could be kindled. Many citizens fled at our approach, abandoning houses, stores, and all their personal property, without so much as locking their doors.

The negroes, poor whites—and it must be admitted—some stragglers and bummers from the ranks of the Union army—carried off thousands of dollars worth of property from houses, homes, shops and stores, until some excuse was given for the charge of "northern vandalism," which was afterward made by the South. The streets were filled with people, white and black, who were carrying away all the stolen goods they could stagger under, without the slightest attempt at concealment, and without let or hindrance from citizens or soldiers. Of course this was mainly stopped as soon as Sherman had fairly and formally assumed control of affairs; but the era of stealing and plundering lasted through the evening and night of the 14th, I believe. In addition to destruction of property by Gen. Sherman's orders, the convicts of the penitentiary, who had been released by their own authorities, set all the buildings connected with that prison on fire, and their lurid flames added to the holocaust elsewhere prevailing. . . .

CHAPTER 24

SEESAW:
VICKSBURG AND
GETTYSBURG

O N MAY 15, 1863, Grant moved out of Jackson, Mississippi. Now that he was securely wedged between Confederate armies under Johnston and Pemberton, Grant proposed to lose no time in disposing of each in detail. Soon his blue-clad columns were marching back toward Vicksburg, seeking to find Pemberton for the kill.

In Richmond, Virginia, there were grave conflicts of heart and mind. War Clerk Jones wrote in his diary on May 15:

"Gens. Lee, Stuart and French were all at the War Department today. Lee looked thinner, and a little pale. Subsequently he and the Secretary of War were long closeted with the President."

Mounting Confederate disasters in Mississippi weighed heavily in the gloomy speculations of Richmond. If the situation worsened in the West, should Lee detach part of his forces in an effort to rescue Pemberton? Lee responded in character—passionately a Virginian. The best way—the only way—that Lee saw to help Pemberton was by creating a diversion in the East. Moreover, Virginia's proud defenders weren't going to be of much assistance anywhere unless they could obtain food, shoes, horses, forage. Lee thought he knew exactly where he could find these provisions. The magic word that he mentioned was Pennsylvania.

I

Lee hurried back to his base at Culpeper, where, as he should have expected, Longstreet disagreed with the plan of invasion. To save Pemberton and ease the strain on Virginia, in Longstreet's opinion, Lee should help Bragg stand off Rosecrans in Tennessee. Lee shook his head. Bragg like Pemberton must take comfort from the strike into Pennsylvania.

Nonetheless misgivings gnawed at Lee. "We should not conceal from ourselves," he wrote Davis, "that our resources in men are constantly diminishing, and the disproportion in this respect between us and our enemies, is steadily augmenting." Burnside's arrest of Vallandigham had encouraged many Confederates to believe that Lincoln and his cronies were quaking in their boots at the growing force of Copperhead opposition to the war. Lee apparently had indulged in the same wishful thinking, for his letter to Jefferson Davis continued:[1]

Nor do I think we should, in this connection, make nice distinctions between those who declare for peace unconditionally and those who advocate it as a means of restoring the Union, however much we may prefer the former.

We should bear in mind that the friends of peace at the North must make concessions to the earnest desire that exists in the minds of their countrymen for a restoration of the Union, and that to hold out such an inducement is essential to the success of their party.

Should the belief that peace will bring back the Union become general, the war would no longer be supported, and that, after all, is what we are interested in bringing about. When peace is proposed to us, it will be time enough to discuss its terms, and it is not the part of prudence to spurn the proposition in advance, merely because those who wish to make it believe, or affect to believe, that it will result in bringing us back into the Union. We entertain no such apprehensions, nor doubt that the desire of our people for a distinct and independent national existence will prove as steadfast under the influence of peaceful measures as it has shown itself in the midst of war.

If the views I have indicated meet the approval of Your Excellency, you will best know how to give effect to them. Should you deem them inexpedient or impracticable, I think you will nevertheless agree with me that we should at least carefully abstain from measures or expressions that tend to discourage any party whose purpose is peace.

This was "Butternut talk," pure and simple, comforting alike to Peace Democrats and wearied, worried Confederates. If Davis failed to respond to Lee's somewhat crafty suggestions, perhaps two items for May 19 in the diary of War Clerk Jones explained why:[2]

A despatch from Gen. Johnston says a battle has been fought between Pemberton and Grant, between Jackson and Vicksburg, Mississippi. Pemberton was *forced back.* That is all we know yet. . . .

The President is too ill again to come to the Executive Office. His messenger, who brought me some papers this morning, says he is in a "decline." I think he has been ill every day for several years, but this has been his most serious attack. No doubt he is also worried at the dark aspects in his own State—Mississippi.

Grant's army had collided with Pemberton's at the Battle of Champion's Hill on May 16. The Rebels, dug in along a ridge with a ravine and creek protecting one flank and a narrow belt of timber screening the other, in Grant's phrase "commanded all the ground in range." The fighting was opened by troops under Brigadier General Alvin P. Hovey, an Indiana lawyer who had taught himself as much about war as most West Pointers learned. He threw his troops in waves up the hill, trying to gain a foothold on the ridge, and his boys seemed to melt away under the broiling Mississippi sun. That morning Sergeant Charles L. Longley had eaten a "hasty and slender breakfast" as he awaited "a pregnant day." Hours went by as Longley and his comrades in the Twenty-fourth Iowa wondered if Hovey had forgotten them. Longley needn't have fretted; his turn was coming:[3]

. . . The grim chorus of battle has been nearing, rising and swelling on the air until its angry roar seems to have filled the earth; then, at a little after twelve comes the dreaded and impatiently expected command, "Fall in.". . . The lines are formed and dressed with an absolute sense of relief. See them now, stretching away to the length of nine companies of about forty-five men each, and prolonged by the rest of the brigade on the right. Now we are advancing over rough ground, but steadily touching elbows, while the warming blood begins to be felt bounding through the veins and throbbing at the temples. Now we pass through the first brigade, lying at the foot of the long wooded hill, and for the first time begin to hear the wicked *zipping* of the hostile lead. Soon it tells its errand—the first man falls. . . .

Onward and upward you go; thicker and faster falls the hissing hail. At last the timber grows larger and you begin to locate the flaming line whence the trouble comes. Suddenly the added elevation brings into view a battery, and at the same instant the horrid howling of grape and

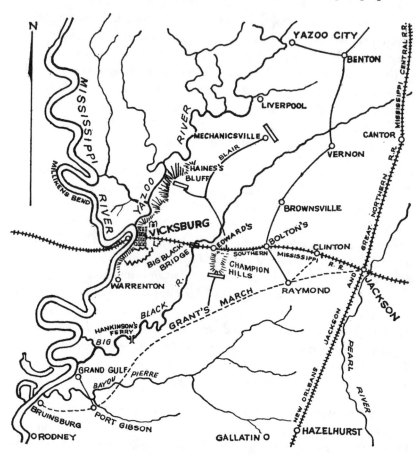

VICKSBURG: THE APPROACHES FROM SOUTH AND EAST

From Lossing, *Pictorial History of the Civil War*

canister is about us. A halt is made and the Enfields of the 24th add their clamor to the hell of sound, and their missiles to the many that make the very air writhe. The more accustomed eye now detects here and there a gray-clad enemy marking their line at but a few rods distant. You note one, perhaps, striving to find shelter behind a slender tree—he is reloading, and, hastily withdrawing his rammer, uncovers the upper part of his body—instantly you aim and fire, and when he falls backward, throwing the useless gun over his head, you forget that other bullets than your own have sped and scream aloud in the very frenzy of self-congratulation.

At this moment, while every human instinct is carried away by a torrent of passion, while kill, KILL, KILL, seems to fill your heart and be written over the face of all nature—at this instant you hear a command (it may have come from the clouds above, you know not) to "Fix bayonets, forward, charge!" and away you go with a wild yell in which all mouths join. . . .

Their backs are toward you—they fly—the line becomes a crowd—you pause only to fire—from one end of the regiment to the other the leaden hail converges upon that fated band; you see them plunging down in all directions, and shout with unnatural glee. They pass through the Rebel battery, and that too is swept with the besom of destruction. As it runs parallel with the line, a full artillery team catches the eye just long enough to see a leader fall and the six horses almost stand on end as they go over and down in struggling confusion—now the battery itself is ours, and fairly won, and cheer follows cheer!

What next? Alas, there is no leader, Wilds is wounded, and so is Wright. . . . You had seen no one fall but enemies since your own work began. But so it is; they, with brave Carbee, Johnson, Lawrence, and many more. Confusion reigns. . . . There comes a new line of gray. Its head of column is already in our rear. See that orderly sergeant in advance making the ins and outs of the fence he is following. Shoot at him? Yes; and all the rest while you may, for now they halt, front, and enfilade that road with a fire that patters in the dust like the big drops of a summer shower and makes the wounded wretches lying there writhe again in impotent agony and terror.

Grant understood this battle, as critical and as desperate as any he would ever fight:[4]

From Raymond there is a direct road to Edward's station, some three miles west of Champion's Hill. There is one also to Bolton. From this latter road there is still another, leaving it about three and a half miles before reaching Bolton and leads direct to the same station. It was along these two roads that three divisions of McClernand's corps, and Blair of Sherman's, temporarily under McClernand, were moving. Hovey of McClernand's command was with McPherson, farther north on the road from Bolton direct to Edward's station. The middle road

comes into the northern road at the point where the latter turns to the
west and descends to Baker's Creek; the southern road is still several
miles south and does not intersect the others until it reaches Edward's
station. Pemberton's lines covered all these roads, and faced east.
Hovey's line, when it first drove in the enemy's pickets, was formed
parallel to that of the enemy and confronted his left.

By eleven o'clock the skirmishing had grown into a hard-contested
battle. Hovey alone, before other troops could be got to assist him, had
captured a battery of the enemy. But he was not able to hold his position and had to abandon the artillery. McPherson brought up his
troops as fast as possible, Logan in front, and posted them on the right
of Hovey and across the flank of the enemy. Logan reinforced Hovey
with one brigade from his division; with his other two he moved farther
west to make room for Crocker, who was coming up as rapidly as the
roads would admit. Hovey was still being heavily pressed, and was calling on me for more reinforcements. I ordered Crocker, who was now
coming up, to send one brigade from his division. McPherson ordered
two batteries to be stationed where they nearly enfiladed the enemy's
line, and they did good execution.

From Logan's position now a direct forward movement carried him
over open fields, in rear of the enemy and in a line parallel with them.
He did make exactly this move, attacking, however, the enemy through
the belt of woods covering the west slope of the hill for a short distance.
Up to this time I had kept my position near Hovey where we were the
most heavily pressed; but about noon I moved with a part of my staff by
our right around, until I came up with Logan himself. . . .

Grant's composure was no pose. S. H. M. Byers saw him that day:[5]

We were in that most trying position of soldiers, for regulars even—
being fired on without permission to return the shots. We were standing two files deep, bearing as patiently as we could not a heavy, but a
steady fire from infantry, while an occasional cannon-ball tore up the
turf in front or behind us. A good many men were falling, and the
wounded were being borne to the rear of the brigade, close to an old
well, whose wooden curb seemed to offer the only protection from bullets on the exposed line. "Colonel, move your men a little by the left
flank," said a quiet, though commanding voice. On looking round, I
saw immediately behind us Grant, the commander-in-chief, mounted on
a beautiful bay mare, and followed by perhaps a half dozen of his staff.

For some reason he dismounted, and most of his officers were sent off, bearing orders, probably, to other quarters of the field. It was Grant under fire. . . . He now stood leaning complacently against his favorite steed, smoking—as seemed habitual with him—the stump of a cigar. . . . In front of us was an enemy; behind us, and about us, and liable to overcome and crush us, were his reinforcements. For days we had been away from our base of supplies, and marching inside the enemy's lines. What if Grant should be killed, and we be defeated here—in such a place, and at such a time? I am sure everyone who recognized him wished him away; but there he stood—clear, calm, and immovable.

What manner of man was Grant? Pondering this question, Byers watched a comrade with a fractured leg being helped to the rear:

. . . His cries of pain attracted the attention of Grant, and I noticed the half-curious, though sympathizing shades, that crossed his quiet face as the bleeding soldier seemed to look toward him for help. Men have often asked if Grant were personally brave in battle. Bravery, like many other human qualities, is comparative. . . . Where duty was, imposed or assumed, Grant feared not to stand . . . He was eminently and above all things a cool man, and that, I take it, was, in the exciting times in which he lived, the first great key to his success. . . . He was called a born soldier, but was, in fact, nothing of the kind. He was simply a man of correct methods and a fixed will. The same methods and the same will would have led men to call him a born railway director, or a born anything to which he had once in good earnest turned his hand. As a young soldier he had lacked opportunity. He lived in a land where neither soldiers nor poets were wanted. There were no wars, no romances, and little history. If he had tried business a little as a farmer, a tanner, a surveyor, or what not, it was not in good earnest. It was a makeshift for the occasion. The war was Grant's opportunity, and he was at the age and had the disposition to seize it. But his military renown was not of luck alone. It was earned blow by blow.

One of the hardest blows—Champion's Hill—soon mounted to its climax, and Byers was in the thick of that action:

We had not waited many minutes at the meadow when an orderly dashed up to Grant, and handed him a communication. Then followed an order to move rapidly to the left, and into the road. The fire grew heavier, and the air seemed too hot to be borne. "Forward!" came a second order, all along the line—"Forward! double quick!" Everybody shouted "double quick," as the noise was becoming terrific. We had forgotten to fix bayonets! what forgetfulness! and again the screaming was, "Fix bayonets! fix bayonets!" I had been selected by the colonel, just as we entered the road, to act as sergeant major, and I now ran behind and along the line, shouting at the top of my voice, "Fix bayonets!" The orders were not heard, and we were charging the enemy's position with bare muskets. A moment more and we were at the top of the ascent, and among thinner wood and larger trees. The enemy had fallen back a few rods, forming a solid line parallel with our own; and now commenced, in good earnest, the fighting of the day. For half an hour we poured the hot lead into each others' faces. We had forty rounds each in our cartridge-boxes, and, probably, nine-tenths of them were fired in that half hour. For me it was the first real "stand up and fight," as the boys called it, of my life. Of skirmishes, I had seen many, and had been under fire; but this was a real battle, and what Grant himself might have called the "business." I tried to keep cool, and determined to fire no shot without taking aim; but a slight wound in the hand ended my coolness, and the smoke of the battle soon made aim-taking mere guessing. One rebel officer I noticed, through the smoke, directly in front of me on horseback. That was my mark, and I must have fired twenty times at him before his form disappeared. I remember how, in the midst of it all, a young lad—he could not have been more than sixteen—came running up to me, and weeping, cried: "My regiment—my regiment is gone—has run! What shall I do?" "Here's the place," I said, "pitch in!" and pitch in he did. He was of metal, that boy, and kept his place with the bravest veteran in the line. Hotter and hotter grew the fight, and soon this same boy cried: "Look —look behind us," and sure enough, the regiment to our left had disappeared, and we were flanked.

"Stop! halt! surrender!" cried a hundred rebels, whose voices seem to ring in my ears to this very day. But there was no stopping, and no surrender. We ran, and ran manfully. It was terribly hot, a hot afternoon under a Mississippi sun, and an enemy on flank and rear, shouting and firing. The grass, the stones, the bushes, seemed melting under the shower of bullets that was following us to the rear. We tried to halt, and tried to form. It was no use. Again we ran, and harder, and farther, and faster. We passed over the very spot where, half an hour before, we left Grant leaning on his bay mare and smoking his cigar. Thank

God! he was gone. The dead were still there, and the wounded called pitiably to us to halt and help them as we ran headlong to the rear. Like ten thousand starving and howling wolves the enemy pursued, closer and closer, and we scarcely dared look back to face the fate that seemed certain. Grant had seen it all, and in less time than I can tell it a line of cannon had been thrown across our path, which as soon as we had passed, belched grape-shot and canister into the faces of our pursuers. They stopped, they turned, and they, too, ran, and left their dead side by side with our own. Our lines, protected by the batteries, rallied and followed, and Champion hills was won, and with it was won the door to Vicksburg. . . .

Byers overstated the situation. Considerable fighting still faced Grant before the door to Vicksburg would be open to him. In fact, the Union general left the field at Champion's Hill nourishing a bitter grievance:[6]

McClernand, with two divisions, was within a few miles of the battle-field long before noon, and in easy hearing. I sent him repeated orders by staff officers fully competent to explain to him the situation. These traversed the wood separating us, without escort, and directed him to push forward; but he did not come. It is true, in front of McClernand there was a small force of the enemy and posted in a good position behind a ravine obstructing his advance; but if he had moved to the right by the road my staff officers had followed the enemy must either have fallen back or been cut off. Instead of this he sent orders to Hovey, who belonged to his corps, to join on to his right flank. Hovey was bearing the brunt of the battle at the time. To obey the order he would have had to pull out from the front of the enemy and march back as far as McClernand had to advance to get into battle, and substantially over the same ground. Of course I did not permit Hovey to obey the order of his immediate superior.

We had in this battle about 15,000 men absolutely engaged. This excludes those that did not get up, all of McClernand's command except Hovey. Our loss was 410 killed, 1,814 wounded and 187 missing. Hovey alone lost 1,200 killed, wounded and missing—more than one-third of his division.

Had McClernand come up with reasonable promptness, or had I known the ground as I did afterwards, I cannot see how Pemberton could have escaped with any organized force. As it was he lost over three thousand killed and wounded and about three thousand captured in battle and in pursuit.

II

Pemberton reported the number of Confederates engaged at Champion's Hill at 17,400 and his casualties at 3,624. That night he fell back to the Big Black River, and after a sharp struggle here, crossed the bridge and gained the security of his prepared defenses. His official report told of his conflict behind the scenes with Johnston:[7]

. . . About noon of the eighteenth May, whilst engaged in an inspection of the intrenchments, with Major Lockett, my Chief Engineer, and several of my General officers, the enemy was reported to be advancing by the Jackson road. Just at this moment the following communication was received by courier:

"CAMP BETWEEN LIVINGSTON AND BROWNSVILLE,
"May 17, 1863
"LIEUTENANT-GENERAL PEMBERTON:
"Your dispatch of to-day, by Captain Henderson, was received. If Haines' Bluff is untenable, Vicksburg is of no value, and cannot be held. If, therefore, you are invested in Vicksburg, you must ultimately surrender. Under such circumstances, instead of losing both troops and place, we must, if possible, save the troops. If it is not too late, evacuate Vicksburg and its dependencies, and march to the north-east.
"Most respectfully,
    "Your obedient servant,
"(Signed)   J. E. JOHNSTON,
                                                          "General"

The evacuation of Vicksburg! It meant the loss of the valuable stores and munitions of war collected for its defence; the fall of Port Hudson; the surrender of the Mississippi River, and the severance of the Confederacy.

These were mighty interests, which, had I deemed the evacuation practicable, in the sense in which I interpreted General Johnston's instructions, might well have made me hesitate to execute them. I believed it to be in my power to hold Vicksburg. I knew and appreciated the earnest desire of the government and of the people that it should be held. I knew, perhaps better than any other individual, under all the circumstances, its capacity for defence.

As long ago as the seventeenth of February last, in a letter addressed to his Excellency the President, I had suggested the possibility of the investment of Vicksburg by land and water, and for that reason the necessity of ample supplies of ammunition, as well as of subsistence, to stand a siege. My application met his favorable consideration, and additional ammunition was ordered. With proper economy of subsistence and ordnance stores, I knew that I could stand a siege. I had a firm reliance on the desire of the President and of General Johnston to do all that could be done to raise a siege. I felt that every effort would be made, and I believed it would be successful. With these convictions in my own mind, I immediately summoned a council of war, composed of all my General officers. I laid before them General Johnston's communication, but desired them to confine the expression of their opinions to the question of practicability. Having obtained their views, the following communication was addressed to General Johnston:

"HEADQUARTERS DEPARTMENT OF MISSISSIPPI
"AND EAST LOUISIANA,
"VICKSBURG, May 18, 1863
"GENERAL J. E. JOHNSTON:

"GENERAL: I have the honor to acknowledge receipt of your communication in reply to mine, by the hands of Captain Henderson. In a subsequent letter of same date as this letter, I informed you that the men had failed to hold the trenches at Big Black Bridge, and that, as a consequence, Snyder's Mills was directed to be abandoned.

"On the receipt of your communication, I immediately assembled a council of war of the General officers of this command, and having laid your instructions before them, asked the free expression of their opinions as to the practicability of carrying them out. The opinion was unanimously expressed that it was impossible to withdraw the army from this position with such *morale* and material as to be of further service to the Confederacy. While the council of war was assembled, the guns of the enemy opened on the works, and it was at the same time reported that they were crossing the Yazoo River at Brandon's Ferry, above Snyder's Mills. I have decided to hold Vicksburg as long as is possible, with the firm hope that the government may yet be able to assist me in keeping this obstruction to the enemy's free navigation of the Mississippi River. I still conceive it to be the most important point in the Confederacy.

"Very respectfully,
"Your obedient servant,

"J. C. PEMBERTON,
"Lieutenant-General"

On May 19 Grant ordered an assault which, in an optimistic view, he declared "resulted in securing more advanced positions for all our troops where they were fully covered from the fire of the enemy." What, really, Grant was gleaning he probably didn't care to admit. Could he take Vicksburg by a direct assault? He calculated the risks—and the stakes:[8]

The 20th and 21st were spent in strengthening our position and in making roads in rear of the army, from Yazoo River or Chickasaw Bayou. Most of the army had now been for three weeks with only five days rations issued by the commissary. They had an abundance of food, however, but began to feel the want of bread. I remember that in passing around to the left of the line on the 21st, a soldier, recognizing me, said in rather a low voice, but yet so that I heard him, "Hard tack." In a moment the cry was taken up all along the line, "Hard tack! Hard tack!" I told the men nearest to me that we had been engaged ever since the arrival of the troops in building a road over which to supply them with everything they needed. The cry was instantly changed to cheers. By the night of the 21st all the troops had full rations issued to them. The bread and coffee were highly appreciated.

I now determined on a second assault. Johnston was in my rear, only fifty miles away, with an army not much inferior in numbers to the one I had with me, and I knew he was being reinforced. There was danger of his coming to the assistance of Pemberton, and after all he might defeat my anticipations of capturing the garrison if, indeed, he did not prevent the capture of the city. The immediate capture of Vicksburg would save me sending the reinforcements which were so much wanted elsewhere, and would set free the army under me to drive Johnston from the State. But the first consideration of all was—the troops believed they could carry the works in their front, and would not have worked so patiently in the trenches if they had not been allowed to try.

The attack was ordered to commence on all parts of the line at ten o'clock A.M. on the 22d with a furious cannonade from every battery in position. All the corps commanders set their time by mine so that all might open the engagement at the same minute. The attack was gallant, and portions of each of the three corps succeeded in getting up to the very parapets of the enemy and in planting their battle flags upon them; but at no place were we able to enter. . . .

General McClernand claimed otherwise. At 11:15 A.M. his courier brought Grant a note:[9]

GENERAL,

I am hotly engaged with the enemy. He is massing on me from the right and left. A vigorous blow by McPherson would make a diversion in my favor.

At noon McClernand sent Grant another message:

GENERAL,

We are hotly engaged with the enemy. We have part possession of two forts, and the Stars and Stripes are floating over them. A vigorous push ought to be made all along the line.

"I did not see the success he reported," Grant said; still, Grant sent the reinforcements and at 3:15 P.M. McClernand dispatched another message.

GENERAL,

I have received your dispatches in regard to Gen. Quinby's division and Gen. MacArthur's. As soon as they arrive I will press the enemy with all possible dispatch, and doubt not that I will force my way through. I have lost no ground. My men are in two of the enemy's forts, but they are commanded by rifle pits in the rear. Several prisoners have been taken who intimate that the rear is strong. At this moment I am hard pressed.   J. A. McC.

Sylvanus Cadwallader claimed that he witnessed McClernand's troops in action on that twenty-second of May:[10]

As McClernand's advance neared the rebel works, it came into plain view from my place of shelter. It had been so mercilessly torn to pieces by Confederate shot and shell that it had lost nearly all resemblance to a line of battle, or the formation of a storming column. Officers and men were rushing ahead pell-mell without much attention to alignment. The small number in sight could no longer be mown down by artillery, as the guns of the forts could not be depressed sufficiently.

When they crossed the deep ditch in front of the earthworks and began to ascend the glacis, they were out of musketry range for the same reason, excepting from one or two salients within reach. A straggling line, continually growing thinner and weaker, finally reached the summit, when all who were not instantly shot down were literally pulled over the rebel breastworks as prisoners. One stand of our colors was planted half way up the embankment and remained there till they could crawl away covered by darkness. I cannot pretend to say how much time was consumed in what I have been describing. But it seemed to me hours before firing subsided enough to warrant my crossing the field and returning to headquarters.

I then learned that McClernand signalled Gen. Grant that he had carried the rebel works on his front—asked for reinforcements to hold them—and also requested the attack to be vigorously pressed at all points, to prevent concentration on him. Grant was somewhat incredulous, and had the dispatch repeated, fearing some mistake in its transmission. He then ordered Quinby's brigade lying near McClernand's right to be moved to his support at once. This was done quickly as possible.

But instead of using Quinby as a support to his own troops, McClernand ordered them to the front in the forlorn hope of retrieving the fortunes of the day, and attempted to make a second assault, with some of his own demoralized troops on Quinby's flank. One of his Colonels flatly refused to obey this order and declared that he would take the consequences of his disobedience rather than lead his men to certain death. . . . I remember distinctly that I gave to Grant and Rawlins the first complete account of its failure—stated that I was within plain view of the rebel earthworks—that McClernand never gained a footing inside of them—and that the small number of his men who actually reached the crest, or scrambled over it, were there yet as prisoners. I was questioned closely concerning it; and shall never forget the fearful burst of indignation from Rawlins, and the grim glowering look of disappointment and disgust which settled down on Grant's usually placid countenance, when he was convinced of McClernand's duplicity, and realized its cost in dead and wounded.

III

Clearly, Grant had approached the breaking point with McClernand. Bitter charges and countercharges remained to be exchanged, and when shortly thereafter Grant relieved McClernand of his command, stinging protests would be addressed to the Governor of Illinois, influential politicians in Washington, and the President. But McClernand, shrewd politician though he was, should have realized that he was involved in a losing argument. Grant had success on his side.

True, after the failure of the assault on May 22 Grant must call his situation anything but a complete success. Except at perhaps fatal cost, he was not going to oust Pemberton from Vicksburg by conventional methods.

Grant's Vicksburg campaign continued to be without parallel in American history. Lieutenant Cyrus E. Dickey wrote to his sister in Ottawa, Illinois:[11]

> HEADQUARTERS,
> 2ND BRIGADE, 6TH DIVISION,
> 17TH CORPS,
> WALNUT HILLS, NEAR VICKSBURG
> May 29, 1863

MY DEAR SISTER,

This evening closes the tenth day of our siege of Vicksburg. I am sitting in my booth, made of a tent fly, concealed by clippings from a cane-brake, and located on the eastern slope of a ridge 500 yards from the enemy. . . . General Grant has ridden out to McPherson's quarters and I am sitting up to wait for him. Things are remarkably quiet. An occasional shell from one of our gunboats, or from a battery, breaks the stillness of the night, then a long silence, and another gun.

I have been over to the picket lines for an hour tonight; the lines of the picket are so close together that the sentries talk together in ordinary tones and spend the whole night in "poking jokes" at each other, and they are not much disposed to deal in compliments. We have them thoroughly invested, and unless a stray force attacks us in the rear, we will keep them caged until they surrender. Our brigade has made two assaults upon the works, but were both times repulsed with heavy loss; the first was on the 19th the second on the 22nd.

. . . We are apt to go into almost any kind of a fight any day, or any hour. . . . There is a part, at least, of the 6th Texas in our Vicksburg pen and I have hopes of capturing our cousin alive.

> INCONVENIENTLY NEAR THE REBEL
> WORKS, IN VIEW OF VICKSBURG
> June 17th 1863

MY DEAR SISTER,

It will be one month tomorrow since we invested this rebel Sebastapol, and still it holds out against us.

For the first week I looked daily for a surrender; for the next two weeks we daily expected an attack in our rear; for the past week new

614 TRAGIC YEARS 1863

reenforcements have been rapidly arriving, we feel secure against all outside assaults. The excitement attending the commencement of our intimate relations with the Vicksburg garrison has worn away, and we have settled down to our work as quietly and regularly as if we were hoeing corn or drawing bills in chancery. We are drawing closer day by day in regular approaches. General Ransom got a battery in position last night, so close that I threw a clod of dirt into the rebel entrenchments from it. The rebels do not submit to this quietly. They have been throwing 9-inch shells from mortars at us all day today, several of which have exploded very uncomfortably close to our quarters.

I have gathered up about a peck of fragments that fell close to our tent, yesterday and today.

Our brigade has been exceedingly fortunate during the siege, having lost about a dozen men since the charges of the 22d.

This is a queer phase of war to us all; the ground around Vicksburg is a network of ravines running parallel to the rebel works. Our troops are occupying these ravines, have terraced the slopes, and dug caves for tents. During a bombardment from the enemy these caves are at a premium. The timid boys who have not dug caves for themselves try to buy out others who have dug their holes. Good caves today run up to $250 this afternoon, but are at a discount this evening since the line has become quiet.

Private Francis W. Tupper, Fifteenth Illinois Cavalry, gave his parents an unretouched picture of what life could be like "in the ditches" before Vicksburg:[12]

Some two weeks ago I went out into the trench and tried my hand at sharpshooting. The men are mostly detailed for this work, but I went into an advanced place where no one went—only those that volunteered.

One of the boys gave me his gun, but I couldn't see any heads in sight above their works, yet I could hear balls whistle over, every minute, and some of them very close. At last we discovered that they had a hole through the embankment about two feet from the top, and by knowing where it was, and looking sharp, you could see the sky beyond it. I fired a few times to get the range. The boys told me where my shots struck. After that every time we couldn't see through the hole we would all fire and the firing from the hole soon ceased. There are several such places along the line, and I am told that at one of them the rebs have had over a dozen men killed. We also have a lookout and sharpshooter post, on the highest point of the ridge, the lookout is 20 or 25 feet high, and is built of heavy timber and protects a man on three sides and has three loop-holes in it. Hole #1 has five large bullet holes in the exposed side of it; this was named "Coonskin Tower," I believe, in honor of one of our men that used it.* The outside is more than spotted full of holes. An ingenious plan was devised to watch their operations and not be exposed at the loopholes, which was for the time being closed up. A looking-glass was put up on top, and to the back side of the tower. You could just stand in the tower and look into the glass and see all that was to be seen of their operations. They soon discovered this and commenced firing at it and broke it all to smash after about 100 rounds had been fired at it. It was in the morning when I was there, and the sun shone just right. I had an excellent view of their works: . . . their yellow flags,† the court house and part of the town, the river, and in the distance the Louisiana shore. At one battery we had two 9-inch guns and two Parrots 30-pounders, the first two are from the gunboats and are smooth, the latter are siege-pieces and rifled. They all sighted nearly as fine as a rifle, and they can put a shot right where they want it every time. You can see the balls plainly from these pieces as they go screaming through the air, and see them when they strike, they make the dust fly at a terrible rate sometimes. The army is a great place for jokes and they always have a joke no matter what the circumstances are.

Our 6th Missouri regiment is in the trenches opposite the rebel 6th Missouri, and the boys call them the "bogus six" to distinguish them from ours. At night firing ceases as a general thing, except at or near their forts where we will not allow them to come out. At the other points on the line they post their pickets outside of the works and ours are advanced and posted near them. They have great times talking together. They know every regiment of ours that has ever been in a fight and are always asking where they are and they also know the numbers of the regiments that have fought them the hardest.

* "Coonskin" was Lieutenant Henry C. Foster, Company B, Twenty-third Indiana Volunteers, who built his tower from railroad iron and cross-ties. A contemporary said: "Learned in backwoods lore, he knew how to construct the genuine pioneer log-cabin." Height was what Coonskin wanted, and in time he was able to look down into the Confederate parapets, giving credence to the report that he was the "terror" among all Yankee sharpshooters.
† In the Civil War, hospitals flew yellow flags.

The reporters make some big yarns out of whole cloth. They stay mostly on the boats at the landing, eight or ten miles off. They fill a whole column and have it headed with large type about something that no one here would cross the road to see. They send to their respective papers for publication any report they may hear without ascertaining whether it is true or not. That is the way Vicksburg and other places come to be captured so often.

We have on our table a 3-inch shot weighing 8¼ pounds, which was dug up three-quarters of a mile beyond our camp. We use it for a paperweight and ornament. Some of the rebel ladies that have had to come to us for rations lately don't feel exactly comfortable while here after they are informed that such rebel messengers pass over camp repeatedly. . . .

I have just seen a sketch by Frank Leslie's artist which shows the manner in which the secesh ladies make their appearance here at our office to get an order on the commissary for rations. In case the picture is published I can inform you that it is a facsimile of the scene. The commissary's quarters represented in the picture is just on the left of us. When we came here we had nothing to eat and the soldiers ate up everything the folks had for ten miles around. They are now of necessity compelled to come here and ask for something to live upon, and they have also discovered that they have the best success when the youngest and best-looking one in the family comes to plead their case and they have some very handsome women here. They are well educated and were rich before their niggers ran away. If I was to meet them in Illinois I should think they were born and brought up there. . . .

IV

Besieged Vicksburg had only one hope—relief from Johnston—but by late May Pemberton knew that the hope was vain:[13]

. . . Two couriers had arrived from General Johnston on the twenty-eighth and twenty-ninth, respectively. The former brought eighteen thousand caps, the latter twenty thousand, and the following dispatch, the first received since the eighteenth:

"May 25, 1863
"LIEUTENANT-GENERAL PEMBERTON:

"My last note was returned by the bearer. Two hundred thousand caps have been sent. It will be continued as they arrive. Bragg is sending a division; when it comes I will move to you. Which do you think the best route? How and where is the enemy encamped? What is your force?

"(Signed)   J. E. JOHNSTON"

The two hundred thousand caps mentioned in the above dispatch were captured by the enemy. I dispatched the following in reply: "Your dispatch of twenty-fifth received this morning, with twenty thousand caps; Fontaine yesterday with eighteen thousand. No messenger from you since the eighteenth. I have eighteen thousand men to man the lines and river-front; no reserves. I do not think you should move with less than thirty or thirty-five thousand men, and then, if possible towards Snyder's Mills, giving me notice of the time of your approach. The enemy encompasses my lines from right to left flank, occupying all roads. He has three corps: Sherman on my left; McPherson, centre; McClernand on my right; Hurlbut's division from Memphis, and Ellett's marine brigade (the last afloat). Enemy has made several assaults. My men are in good spirits, awaiting your arrival. Since investment we have lost about one thousand men, many officers. You may depend on my holding the place as long as possible. On the twenty-seventh we sunk one of their best iron-clad gunboats."

On the thirtieth, I again dispatched as follows: "Scouts report the enemy to have withdrawn most of his forces from our right yesterday, leaving Hall's Ferry road open, I apprehend, for a movement against you. I expect this courier to return to me."

The meat ration having been reduced one-half, that of sugar, rice, and beans, was largely increased. It was important, above all things, that every encouragement should be given to the troops. With this object in view, I ordered the impressment of chewing-tobacco, and its issue to the troops. This had a very beneficial influence. The enemy kept steadily at work, day and night, and, taking advantage of the cover of the hills, had run his parallels up to within seventy-five yards of our works. He was also mining at different points, and it required the active and constant attention of our engineers to repair at night the damage inflicted upon our works during the day, and to meet his different mines by countermining. Orders were issued to prepare thunder-barrels and petards for the defence of near points, and every precaution taken to check the enemy in his operations, and to delay them as far as possible. On the seventh of June, the following dispatch was sent to General Johnston: "I am still without information from you later than your dispatch of twenty-fifth. The enemy continues to intrench his position around Vicksburg. I have sent out couriers to you almost daily. The same men are constantly in the trenches, but are still in good spirits, expecting your approach. The enemy is so vigilant that it is impossible to obtain reliable information. When may I expect you to move, and in what direction? My subsistence may be put down for about twenty days." On the tenth, I again dispatched as follows: "The enemy bombards day and night from seven mortars on opposite side of peninsula. He also keeps up constant fire on our lines with artillery and sharpshooters. We are losing many officers and men. I am waiting most anxiously to know your intentions. Have heard nothing of you or from you since twenty-fifth of May. I shall endeavor to hold out as long as we have anything to eat. Can you not send me a verbal message by a courier crossing the river above or below Vicksburg, and swimming across again opposite Vicksburg?" Again, on the twelfth, I dispatched as follows: "Courier Walker arrived this morning, with caps. No message from you. Very heavy firing yesterday from mortars and on lines." About this time our provisions, particularly of meat, having become exhausted, General Stevenson was instructed to impress all the cattle in the city, and the Chief Commissary directed to sell only one ration per diem to any officer. He was also instructed to issue for bread equal portions of rice and flour—four ounces each. About the thirteenth, Captain Saunders arrived from Jackson, via Steele's Bayou, with two hundred thousand percussion-caps, and a day or two subsequently I received the following dispatch from General Johnston:

"May 29, 1863

"I am too weak to save Vicksburg; can do no more than attempt to save you and your garrison. It will be impossible to extricate you unless you co-operate, and we make mutually supporting movements. Communicate your plans and suggestions, if possible."

Meanwhile, within Vicksburg, men, women and children shared the terrors of the siege, praying that Johnston would soon come to their rescue. Among them was one whom George W. Cable described simply as "a young lady of New Orleans." In time "a betrothed lover came suddenly from a neighboring state . . . and bore her away, a happy bride. . . . In the south, those days, all life was romantic. Theirs was full of adventure. At length they were shut up in Vicksburg." So the "young lady of New Orleans" watched the war approach the city—in

January, when "paper is a serious want"; in February, when "an egg is a rare and precious thing"; in March, when "the slow shelling of Vicksburg goes on all the time, and we have grown indifferent"; in April, when "the owner of the house suddenly returned and notified us that he intended to bring his family back; didn't think there'd be any siege." In late May both the "young lady from New Orleans" and her landlord realized how far wrong they had guessed:[14]

May 28th: "We are utterly cut off from the world, surrounded by a circle of fire. Would it be wise like the scorpion to sting ourselves to death? The fiery shower of shells goes on day and night. H——'s occupation, of course, is gone, his office closed. Every man has to carry a pass in his pocket. People do nothing but eat what they can get, sleep when they can, and dodge the shells. There are three intervals when the shelling stops, either for the guns to cool or for the gunners' meals, I suppose—about eight in the morning, the same in the evening, and at noon. In that time we have both to prepare and eat ours. Clothing cannot be washed or anything else done. On the 19th and 22nd, when the assaults were made on the lines, I watched the soldiers cooking on the green opposite. The half-spent balls coming all the way from those lines were flying so thick that they were obliged to dodge at every turn. At all the caves I could see from my high perch, people were sitting, eating their poor suppers at the cave doors, ready to plunge in again. As the first shell again flew they dived, and not a human being was visible. The sharp crackle of the musketry-firing was a strong contrast to the scream of the bombs. I think all the dogs and cats must be killed or starved, we don't see any more pitiful animals prowling around."

Friday, June 5th: In the cellar.

"Wednesday evening H—— said he must take a little walk, and went while the shelling had stopped. He never leaves me alone for long, and when an hour had passed without his return I grew anxious; and when two hours, and the shelling had grown terrific, I momentarily expected to see his mangled body. All sorts of horrors fill the mind now, and I am so desolate here; not a friend. When he came he said that passing a cave where there were no others near, he heard groans, and found a shell had struck above and caused the cave to fall in on the man within. He could not extricate him alone, and had to get help and dig him out. He was badly hurt, but not mortally, and I felt fairly sick from the suspense. . . ."

June 7th: In the cellar.

"There is one thing I feel especially grateful for, that amid these horrors, we have been spared that of suffering for water. The weather has been dry a long time, and we hear of others dipping up the water from the ditches and mud-holes. This place has two large underground cisterns of good cool water, and every night in my subterranean dressing-room a tub of cold water is the nerve-calmer that sends me to sleep in spite of the roar. . . ."

June 9th: "The churches are a great resort for those who own no caves. People fancy they are not shelled so much, and they are substantial and the pews good to sleep in. . . ."

June 13th: "Shells burst just over the roof this morning. Pieces tore through both floors down into the dining-room. The entire ceiling of that room fell in a mass. We had just left it. Every piece of crockery on the table was smashed up. The 'Daily Citizen' to-day is a foot and a half long and six inches wide. The editorial says, '. . . The undaunted Johnston is at hand.' "

June 18th: "To-day the 'Citizen' is printed on wall paper; therefore has grown a little in size. It says, 'But a few days more and Johnston will be here'; also that 'Kirby Smith has driven Banks from Port Hudson'; and that 'the enemy are throwing incendiary shells in.' "

June 20th: "The gentleman who took our cave came yesterday to invite us to come to it, because he said, 'It's going to be very bad today!' I don't know why he thought so. We went, and found his own and another family in it; sat outside and watched the shells till we concluded the cellar was as good a place as that hill-side. I fear the want of good food is breaking down H——. I know from my own feelings of weakness, but mine is not an American constitution, and has a recuperative power that his has not."

June 21st: "I had gone upstairs to-day during the interregnum to enjoy a rest on my bed and read the reliable items in the 'Citizen' when a shell burst right outside the window in front of me. Pieces flew in, striking all round me, tearing down masses of plaster that came tumbling over me. When H—— rushed in I was crawling out of the plaster, digging it out of my eyes and hair. When he picked up a piece large as a saucer beside my pillow, I realized my narrow escape. The window-frame began to smoke, and we saw the house was on fire. H——— ran for a hatchet and I for water, and we put it out. Another [shell] came crashing near, and I snatched up my comb and brush and ran down here. It has taken all afternoon to get the plaster out of my hair, for my hands were rather shaky. . . ."

June 25th: "A horrible day. The most horrible yet to me, because I've lost my nerve. We were all in the cellar when a shell came tearing through the roof, burst upstairs, tore up that room, and the pieces coming through both floors down into the cellar. One of them tore open the leg of H———'s pantaloons. This was tangible proof the cellar was no place of protection from them. . . ."

Mrs. W. W. Lord and her four children were among the unhappy horde who "literally lived in the dens and caves of the earth." She remembered that, when she had heard the news of Johnston's evacuating Jackson and of Pemberton's moving toward the Big Black River, she had accepted the two movements as "parts of a great plan . . . to surround Grant's army." Now, "sadly undeceived," she lived on numbly:[15]

. . . Imagine one of these Vicksburg hills in the very heart of the city—caves underlay even the very heart of it and intersecting each other reaching again to the front, forming in that way several passages and fire openings. In this cave were gathered 8 families besides other single persons . . . The firing began to be very steady and severe and the whole hill shook—a large piece of earth fell upon Mrs. McRoas's little daughter and almost killed her . . . You can imagine our feelings all shut up in this cave—the horrible shells roaring and bursting all around us and the concussion making our heads feel like they would burst. Poor Mrs. Gunn with her little baby only ten days old!

The next day, Friday, the most terrible battle took place between our batteries and the gunboats,—but we were successful, by the mercy of God, and drove them back. The same day a shell burst at the opening and almost closed it. Mr. Ford and Mr. Merriam were standing almost at the place—such screaming and rushing you never heard. Mr. Merriam exclaimed, "Great God! Out of these caves, out of these caves!"

. . . I have not been undressed now for nearly two weeks and we all live on the plainest food. . . . the children bear themselves like little heroes. At night when the balls begin to fly like pigeons over our tent and I call them to run to the caves, they spring up, even to little Louli, like soldiers, slip on their shoes without a word and run up the hill to the cave.

Mrs. Lord described her cave:

. . . Imagine to yourself in the first place a good sized parapet, about 6 feet high, a path cut through, and then the entrance to the cave —this is secured strong with boards; it is dug the height of a man and about 40 feet under the hill. It communicates with the other cave which is about the same length opening out on the other side of the hill,—this gives us a good circulation of air. . . . I have a little closet dug for provisions, and niches for flowers, lights and books—inside just by the little walk is our eating table with an arbor over it and back of that our fireplace and kitchen with table &c. In the valley beneath is our tent and back of it the tents of the generals. This is quite picturesque and attractive to look at but Oh! how wearisome to live.

Even in these surroundings of common suffering, according to the Vicksburg *Daily Citizen, that great foe of the Southern cause—the extortioner—was not to be denied his pound of flesh:*[16]

If aught would appeal to the heart of stone of the extortioner with success, the present necessities of our citizens would do so. It is needless to attempt to disguise from the enemy of our people that our wants are great. . . . We are satisfied that there are numerous persons within our city who have bread secreted, and are doling it out, at exorbitant prices, to those who had not the foresight or means at their command to provide for the exigencies now upon us. A rumor has reached us that parties in our city have been, and are now, selling flour at $5 per pound! molasses at $10 per gallon! and corn at $10 per bushel! We have not as yet proved the facts upon the parties accused, but this allusion to the subject may induce some of our citizens to ascertain whether such prices have been paid, and to whom; and if so, may a brand not only be placed upon their brows, but seared into their very brains, that humanity may scorn and shun them as they would the portals of hell.

The great historian of the old river, Sam Clemens, added his chapter on "Vicksburg during the trouble"—perhaps the best, most perceptive chapter on the subject ever written. Sam found a couple who had lived through the siege and let them tell the story:[17]

A week of their wonderful life there would have made their tongues eloquent forever perhaps; but they had six weeks of it, and that wore the novelty all out; they got used to being bombshelled out of home and into the ground; the matter became commonplace. After that, the possibility of their ever being startlingly interesting in their talks about it was gone. What the man said was to this effect:

It got to be Sunday all the time. Seven Sundays in the week—to us, anyway. We hadn't anything to do, and time hung heavy. Seven Sundays, and all of them broken up at one time or another, in the day or in the night, by a few hours of the awful storm of fire and thunder and iron. At first we used to shin for the holes a good deal faster than we did afterward. The first time I forgot the children, and Maria fetched them both along. When she was all safe in the cave she fainted. Two or three weeks afterward, when she was running for the holes, one morning, through a shell-shower, a big shell burst near her and covered her all over with dirt, and a piece of iron carried away her game-bag of false hair from the back of her head. Well, she stopped to get that game-bag before she shoved along again! Was getting used to things already, you see. We all got so that we could tell a good deal about shells; and after that we didn't always go under shelter if it was a light shower. Us men would loaf around and talk; and a man would say, "There she goes!" and name the kind of shell it was from the sound of it, and go on talking—if there wasn't any danger from it. If a shell was bursting close over us, we stopped talking and stood still; uncomfortable, yes, but it wasn't safe to move. When it let go, we went on talking again, if nobody was hurt—maybe saying, "That was a ripper!" or some such commonplace comment before we resumed; or, maybe, we would see a shell poising itself away high in the air overhead. In that case, every fellow just whipped out a sudden "See you again, gents!" and shoved. Often and often I saw gangs of ladies promenading the streets, looking as cheerful as you please, and keeping an eye canted up watching the shells; and I've seen them stop still when they were uncertain about what a shell was going to do, and wait and make certain; and after that they sa'ntered along again, or lit out for shelter, according to the verdict. Streets in some towns have a litter of pieces of paper, and odds and ends of one sort or another lying around. Ours hadn't; they had *iron* litter. Sometimes a man would gather up all the iron fragments and unbursted shells in his neighborhood, and pile them into a kind of monument in his front yard—a ton of it, sometimes. No glass left; glass couldn't stand such a bombardment; it was all shivered out. Windows of the houses vacant—looked like eyeholes in a skull. *Whole* panes were as scarce as news.

We had church Sundays. Not many there, along at first; but by and by pretty good turnouts. I've seen service stop a minute, and everybody sit quiet—no voice heard, pretty funeral-like then—and all the more so on account of the awful boom and crash going on outside and overhead; and pretty soon, when a body could be heard, service would go on again. Organs and church music mixed up with a bombardment is a powerful queer combination—along at first. Coming out of church, one morning, we had an accident—the only one that happened around me on a Sunday. I was just having a hearty hand-shake with a friend I hadn't seen for a while, and saying, "Drop into our cave to-night, after bombardment; we've got hold of a pint of prime wh—" Whisky, I was going to say, you know, but a shell interrupted. A chunk of it cut the man's arm off, and left it dangling in my hand. And do you know the thing that is going to stick the longest in my memory, and outlast everything else, little and big, I reckon, is the mean thought I had then? It was, "the whisky *is saved*." And yet, don't you know, it was kind of excusable; because it was as scarce as diamonds, and we had only just that little; never had another taste during the siege.

Sometimes the caves were desperately crowded, and always hot and close. Sometimes a cave had twenty or twenty-five people packed into it; no turning-room for anybody; air so foul, sometimes, you couldn't have made a candle burn in it. A child was born in one of those caves one night. Think of that; why, it was like having it born in a trunk.

Twice we had sixteen people in our cave; and a number of times we had a dozen. Pretty suffocating in there. We always had eight; eight belonged there. Hunger and misery and sickness and fright and sorrow, and I don't know what all, got so loaded into them that none of them were ever rightly their old selves after the siege. They all died but three of us within a couple of years. One night a shell burst in front of the hole and caved it in and stopped it up. It was lively times, for a while, digging out. Some of us came near smothering. After that we made two openings—ought to have thought of it at first.

Mule meat? No, we only got down to that the last day or two. Of course it was good; anything is good when you are starving.

This man had kept a diary during—six weeks? No, only the first six days. The first day, eight close pages; the second, five; the third, one —loosely written; the fourth, three or four lines; a line or two the fifth and sixth days; seventh day, diary abandoned; life in terrific Vicksburg having now become commonplace and matter of course.

V

For Grant's soldiers, cooped up "in the ditches" before Vicksburg, the days dragged slowly. But generals also were depressed by the tedium of the siege, as William Ward Orme could testify:[18]

> BRIGADE HEADQUARTERS
> CAMP 2½ MILES S. OF VICKSBURG
> June 20th 1863—
> Saturday night

MY DEAR GOOD WIFE—

On account of the delay in forwarding letters from here I have not written for two days— Since I wrote you the other day I received your nice letter of the 9th— How glad I was to hear from you & of your safe arrival at home;—that home at which before very long I hope to arrive safe & sound myself— Once more there, my dear Nannie, I pledge you never again to leave you, our dear sweet children and our happy happy homestead.— O! for its cool recesses and shady trees, now! for its comforts & luxuries—

This is an awful hot country here full of bugs of all sorts.— The heat is very oppressive indeed— Yesterday morning I was taken with a slight attack of bilious diarrhea, but it wore off without proving serious; and this evening I am as well as usual. We have blackberries here in abundance; they are nice & ripe.— Peaches will be ripe in four or five days.

I am now suffering terribly from the effects of mosquitos & other bugs— I am full of bites all over. There is a small insect about the size of a pin's point which bites its way into the flesh & makes a very sore place— This insect is called a "chicker" or "jigger."— We are all suffering from its depredations. They are much worse than the "wood tick"— I have to stop after every sentence I write to scratch myself & drive off the bugs.— . . .

. . . I have no news to send you from here. We are still closely investing the city and digging our way nearer to the enemy's forts every night.— This morning at four O'Clock a general cannonade opened all around the line; and the enemy replied throwing their shell in every direction, but doing no damage to us— Our cannonade was kept up for about four hours.— I don't know what the prospect of a surrender is— The rebels hold out well, & it may be a month before they give up, or it may be a week.— So you see there is nothing new & everything is comparatively quiet & dull.—

Kiss the children for me very often— Tell Willy & Berny they each owe me a letter— I think I wrote them last. Lucy's letter will come soon tell her. Remember me to all friends & much love to Fanny & your mother.—

Keep me in constant remembrance & be assured dear Nannie of my increasing love for you & home—

Your devoted husband
Wm. W. O.

No one chafed more than Grant under the strain of the siege. Toward mid-June his hope for ending the ordeal rested in a scheme to tunnel under the Vicksburg defenses and blow them into eternity. Major Andrew Hickenlooper, Grant's chief engineer, explained how a trap was set:[19]

The general plan of conducting the work with flying-sap by night and deepening and widening by day was pushed forward with the utmost energy until June 22d, when the head of the sap * reached the outer ditch surrounding the fort. A few days previous an order had been issued for all men in the corps having a practical knowledge of coal-mining to report to the chief engineer. Out of those reporting thirty-six of the strongest and most experienced were selected and divided into two shifts for day and night duty, and each shift was divided into three reliefs. On the night of the 22d these men, properly equipped with drills, short-handled picks, shovels, etc., under the immediate command of Lieutenant Russell of the 7th Missouri and Sergeant Morris of the 32d Ohio, commenced the mining operations by driving a gallery, four feet in width by five feet in height, in at right angles to the face of the parapet of the fort. Each relief worked an hour at a time, two picking, two shoveling, and two handing back the grain-sacks filled with earth, which were deposited in the ditch

* A sap-roller, used to protect the diggers against the enfilading fire of the enemy, was a wicker casing, five feet in diameter and ten feet in length, compactly filled with cotton.

until they could be carried back. The main gallery was carried in 45 feet, and then a smaller gallery extended in on the same line 15 feet, while from the end of the main gallery two others were run out on either side at angles of 45 degrees for a distance of 15 feet. The soil through which this gallery was driven was a reddish clay of remarkable tenacity, easily cut and requiring but little bracing. So rapidly was this work executed that on the morning of the 25th the miners commenced depositing the powder, 800 pounds at the extreme end of the main gallery and 700 pounds at the end of each of the lateral galleries, making a total of 2,200 pounds. From each of these deposits there were laid two strands of safety fuse,—obtained, as was the powder, from the navy,—this duplication being made to cover the possible contingency of one failing to burn with the desired regularity and speed. These six strands were cut to exactly the same length, and having been carefully laid, the earth, which had been previously removed in grain-sacks, was carried back and deposited in the most compact manner possible, and well braced by heavy timbers, beyond the junction point of the three galleries. From this point out to the entrance it was more loosely packed in. The Confederate garrison, surmising the object in view, were active in efforts to thwart the purpose of the Union forces by throwing hand-grenades and rolling shells with lighted fuses over their parapet down into the trench in front of the fort. They also counter-mined in hopes of tapping the gallery. So near were they to the attainment of this object that during the last day the miners could distinctly hear the conversation and orders given in the counter-mine.

The powder was brought up in barrels and kept in the main sap at a safe distance from the enemy's hand-grenades and shells, and there opened and placed in grain-sacks, each one of which contained about 25 pounds. These were taken upon the backs of the miners, who made the run over the exposed ground during the intervals between the explosion of the enemy's shells; and so well timed were these movements that, although it required nearly one hundred trips with the dangerous loads, all were landed in the mine without a single accident.

The commanding general having been advised on the day previous that the work would be completed before 3 P.M. of the 25th, general orders were issued directing each corps commander to order up the reserves and fully man the trenches, and immediately following the explosion to open with both artillery and musketry along the entire twelve miles of investing line; under cover of which the assaulting columns, composed of volunteers from the 31st and 45th Illinois, preceded by ten picked men from the pioneer corps under charge of the chief engineer, were to move forward and take possession of the fort. For an hour or two previous to the time of the explosion the scene from "Battery Hickenlooper," where General Grant and his subordinate commanders had taken their positions, was one of the most remarkable ever witnessed. As far as the eye could reach to the right and left could be seen the long winding columns of blue moving to their assigned positions behind the besiegers' works. Gradually as the hour of 3 approached the booming of artillery and incessant rattle of musketry, which had been going on day and night for thirty days, suddenly subsided, and a deathlike and oppressive stillness pervaded the whole command. Every eye was riveted upon that huge redoubt standing high above the adjoining works. At the appointed moment it appeared as though the whole fort and connecting outworks commenced an upward movement, gradually breaking into fragments and growing less bulky in appearance until it looked like an immense fountain of finely pulverized earth, mingled with flashes of fire and clouds of smoke, through which could occasionally be caught a glimpse of some dark objects,—men, gun-carriages, shelters, etc. Fire along the entire line instantly opened with great fury, and amidst the din and roar of 150 cannon and the rattle of 50,000 muskets the charging column moved forward to the assault. . . .

With that assaulting column went Wilbur F. Crummer of the Forty-fifth Illinois, who remembered:[20]

. . . When the smoke and dust had cleared away partly, a great saucer-shaped crater was seen, where before was the A-shaped Fort Hill. It was large enough to hold about 60 or 80 men. The 23rd Indiana and the 45th Illinois were in the trenches ready to charge; the command was given before the dust had fully settled; the 23rd Indiana charging to the left of the crater to the top of the works; the 45th Illinois up and into the crater. The enemy had come up behind the big pile of earth thrown out by the explosion, and as we went into the crater, they met us with a terrible volley of musketry, but on the boys went, up and over the embankment with a cheer, the enemy falling back a few paces to an inner or second line of breastworks, where are placed cannon loaded with grape and canister, and these cannon belched forth their death-dealing missiles, in addition to the heavy musketry fire, with such telling effect that many of the brave boys fall to rise no more; the line wavers, staggers, and then falls back into the crater. The enemy charge on us, but we repel them at the west bank of the crater; and a hand-to-hand conflict rages for hours; hand grenades and loaded shells are lighted and thrown over the parapet as you would play ball. These shells and hand grenades carry death, as many as a dozen men being killed and wounded at one explosion. . . . Many a brave hero laid down his life in that death hole, or, as we most appropriately called it, "Fort Hell.". . .

We fought at close range with the enemy over that embankment of earth, many of the men receiving bayonet wounds. . . . What a terrible sacrifice it was to hold that little piece of ground. It probably was all right to have made the charge into the crater after the explosion and try to make a breech inside the enemy's lines, but it was a serious mistake, either of Gen. Grant or Gen. McPherson, to cause that crater to be held for over 48 hours with the loss of brave men every hour. I remember, upon returning to the trenches, after having been relieved in the crater, of passing Gen. John A. Logan, surrounded by some of his aid-de-camp, and as they bore past him some wounded hero, he broke forth with vehemence, saying: "My God! they are killing my bravest men in that hole.". . . The crater was at last given up and we resumed the ordinary duties of everyday life in the trenches and in camp.

VI

Grant's troops settled back to the tedium of life in the ditches before the besieged city. Meanwhile there were persistent rumors from the East that Lee's Army of Northern Virginia had crossed the Potomac and was invading Maryland and Pennsylvania.

The reports were true. On June 22 Ewell's corps had crossed in two columns at Shepherdstown and Williamsport, converged at Hagerstown and struck up the valley toward Chambersburg, Pennsylvania. On the twenty-fourth A. P. Hill's corps crossed a mile above Shepherdstown; and Longstreet moved up to follow.

In the sleepy town of Gettysburg the Reverend Dr. Michaels Jacobs taught mathematics and chemistry at little Pennsylvania College. The mine that Grant had exploded under Fort Hill, or the agony with which Wilbur Crummer's comrades died as they tried to wrest that crater from the rebels, were part of a fantastic military seesaw that historians

would comprehend long years afterward; what Professor Jacobs re-
membered on June twenty-six was a sudden disruption in his academic
life:[21]

The advance guard of the enemy, consisting of 180 to 200 cavalry,
rode into Gettysburg at 3¼ P.M., shouting and yelling like so many
savages from the wilds of the Rocky Mountains; firing their pistols, not
caring whether they killed or maimed man, woman, or child; and rush-

GETTYSBURG AND VICINITY

From *Atlas of American History*

ing from stable to stable in search of horses, the most of which, however, had fortunately a few hours before been sent forward to Hanover
and York.

This advance party was soon followed by 5,000 infantry, being General Gordon's brigade of Early's division of Ewell's corps. Most of the
men were exceedingly dirty, some ragged, some without shoes, and
some surmounted by the skeleton of what was once an entire hat, affording unmistakable evidence that they stood in great need of having
their scanty wardrobe replenished; and hence the eagerness with which
they inquired after shoe, hat, and clothing stores, and their disappointment when they were informed that goods of that description were not
to be had in town; and it ought not to have surprised us that they actually took shoes and hats from the persons of some of our Franklin
county cousins whom they considered more able to endure the loss

than we, whilst they permitted us to escape that infliction. Being wet from the rain which had fallen during the most of the day, and considerably heated by a long march, there was found, by a person near them as they passed, to have been more truth than fiction in the remark of a friend, that "the air was filled with the filthy exhalations from their bodies." Whether this was a judgment dictated by prejudice or not, it was difficult for us to recognize, in the great body of them, the character previously heralded in our community by a lady sympathizer, of "chivalrous Southerners, all from the first families of the South." But we do not intend to reproach them for not presenting a better appearance; they doubtless did the best they could, and had come a long journey for the express purpose of supplying their pressing wants.

General Early, who accompanied this brigade and remained in town over Friday night, demanded of the authorities of our borough 1,200 pounds of sugar, 600 pounds of coffee, 60 barrels of flour, 1,000 pounds of salt, 7,000 pounds of bacon, 10 barrels of whisky, 10 barrels of onions, 1,000 pairs of shoes, and 500 hats, amounting in value to $6,000; or, in lieu thereof, $5,000 cash. To this demand Messrs. D. Kendlehart and A. D. Buehler, as representatives of the town council, replied in substance, that it was impossible to comply with their demands; that the goods were not in town or within reach; that the borough had no funds, and the council had no authority to borrow either in the name of the borough or county; and that, as we were at the mercy of the General and his men, they could search, and take from citizens and the empty stores whatsoever they might be able to find. No attempt was made to enforce the requisition, and but few of the houses of citizens were robbed. Whether this forbearance was owing to the evident fact that he was outwitted by our citizens, or from his generosity to our apparent poverty, we will permit our York friends to judge, to whom he is reported to have replied, when, as a reason why he should not insist on the enforcement of the large demand he had made of them, they reminded him of his leniency towards us, "Why, gentlemen, there was nothing there to take." Be it so: Gettysburg escaped; and York paid a premium of $28,000. During the evening of Friday, however, the Rebels burned the railroad bridge and a few cars, took from the few articles that our merchants had not sent away such as suited them, and divested the taverns and liquor stores of their liquors. Besides this, they did not do much damage in the town. In the country, however, they treated the farmers less gently. They there re-enacted their old farce of professing to pay for what they took by offering freely their worthless "Confederate" scrip; which, they said, would, in a few days, be better than our own currency. In the town they obtained but little booty, because all the valuables of the Bank, and nearly all those of the merchants, had been previously sent for safety to Philadelphia. This proved a great disappointment to them; and they acknowledged that, for this time, they had been too slow in their movements. They consequently hurried forward, that night and the next morning, towards Hanover and York. A portion of them passed through Hanover at 11 A.M., reaching the Northern Central Railroad at Hanover Junction, early in the afternoon, whilst another portion went to East Berlin, and on the next day, Sunday, reached York.

Our citizens, with a few exceptions, kept at a respectful distance from them during their stay amongst us, avoiding as much as possible communicating any information which might prove advantageous to them; so much so, that they said: "It is a very strange thing that you people know so little."

CHAPTER 25

FATEFUL JULY

On June 16, 1863, Lincoln had written to his wife, who was visiting in Philadelphia: "It is a matter of choice with yourself whether you come home. There is no reason why you should not, that did not exist when you went away. As bearing on the question of your coming home, I do not think the raid into Pennsylvania amounts to anything at all."

A week later "the raid" had proved the precursor of a full-scale invasion. On June 27 residents of Philadelphia read an ominous proclamation:

"CITIZENS OF PHILADELPHIA: Prepare to defend your homes. The traitors who have spread desolation in the southern counties of your State, and carried into captivity free men and women, because they were black and under your protection, approach your city. Their strategy is sufficiently well understood to make it certain that their object is Philadelphia. Do the citizens of the Quaker City expect more favorable treatment at their hands than others? Arise now in your might; shake off your apathy, meet the enemy and drive him back, that you may deserve the blessings of a home. To stand idly now would invite suspicion either of treachery or cowardice. I urge upon the citizens of Philadelphia that they close all places of manufacture by noon, and all other places of business at three o'clock P.M. of each day, devoting the remainder of the day to military organization and instruction. Let companies of from sixty to a hundred men each be rapidly organized, and having chosen their officers, stand ready at a moment's notice. There is not a moment to be lost, and therefore let us not squander away valuable time.

N. J. T. Dana, *Major-Gen. Commanding.*"

I

Marching his troops through the abundant farm lands of Pennsylvania,
Confederate General Richard S. Ewell was delighted by the scene
around him. "It's like a hole of blubber to a Greenlander," he wrote
home. On Sunday, June 22, Gettysburg had not yet seen a rebel, but
Sallie Robbins Broadhead, a schoolteacher in the village, filled her
diary with disquieting news:[1]

The report now is that a large [Rebel] force is in the mountains
about eighteen miles away, and a call is made for a party of men to go
out and cut down trees to obstruct the passages of the mountains.

About fifty, among them my husband, started.

I was very uneasy lest they might be captured, but they had not gone
halfway when the discovery was made that it was too late; that the
Rebels were on this side of the mountain, and coming this way. Our
men turned back, uninjured, though their advance, composed of a
few men, was fired upon. About seventy of the Rebels came within
eight miles, and then returned by another road to their main force.

They stole all the horses and cattle they could find, and drove them
back to their encampment.

We did not know but that the whole body would be down upon us,
until eleven o'clock, when a man came in and said that he had seen
them, and that they had recrossed. I shall now retire, and sleep much
better than I had expected an hour since.

Another resident of Gettysburg, Tillie Alleman, remembered:[2]

. . . It was amusing to behold the conduct of the colored people of
the town. Gettysburg had a goodly number of them. They regarded the
Rebels as having an especial hatred toward them, and believed that if
they fell into their hands, annihilation was sure.

These folks mostly lived in the southwestern part of town, and their
flight was invariably down Breckenridge Street and Baltimore Street,
and toward the woods on and around Culp's Hill.

I can see them yet; men and women with bundles as large as old-
fashioned feather ticks slung across their backs, almost bearing them
to the ground. Children also, carrying their bundles, and striving in
vain to keep up with their seniors. The greatest consternation was
depicted on all their countenances as they hurried along; crowding,
and running against each other in their confusion; children stumbling,

falling, and crying. Mothers, anxious for their offspring, would stop for a moment to hurry them up, saying:

"Fo' de Lod's sake, you chillen, cum right long quick! If dem Rebs dun kotch you, day tear you all up." These terrible warnings were sure to have the desired effect; for, with their eyes open wider than ever, they were not long in hastening their steps.

On the other side of town thirteen-year-old Billy Bayly was having the time of his life, running horses into the foothills where the Rebs couldn't find them:[3]

Along the wood-bordered ridge which constituted the west boundary of the farm we could see soldiers moving at a rapid pace in an easterly direction—the general direction in which we were going. The afternoon being cloudy and dark, with rain still falling, made it impossible for us to distinguish uniforms, and we knew not whether the soldiers were friends or foes. But we took no chance and rode off at a John Gilpin rate, I using my coat and shoes forcibly to urge "Nellie" to more rapid motion. One of my uncles living in the vicinity and other neighbors had ridden up to the barn while father was saddling the horses, but seeing the "Rebs," as they supposed, only a quarter of a mile distant, hastily fled leaving us to follow. As we were well mounted, we soon overtook the party and remained with them three or four days.

Our first purpose was to go toward Harrisburg, but fearing the enemy had cut us off in that direction, we turned toward Hanover.

On crossing one of the roads radiating from Gettysburg, I noticed a horseman coming over the hill toward us and being anxious for information about the enemy, I hung back and let my party go on, having every confidence in the fleetness of my mount. The horseman, covered with a rubber poncho splashed with mud, rode up to where my horse was standing, and I recognized him as a recruit in Bell's Cavalry whom I knew, so I said, "Hello, Bill! What's up?"

Bill replied, "If you don't get out of here pretty quick you'll find out what's up. The Rebel Cavalry chased me out of town about fifteen minutes ago, and must now be close on my heels."

My desire for information not being satisfied however, I said, "But where is the rest of your company?"

"Oh hell," said the trooper, "I don't know; they ran long before I did. But you git or you'll be got." And away he rode toward Harrisburg and I after my party.

Our riding party continued for about fifteen miles, and darkness approaching, concluded that the Rebels would not overtake us that night so we put up with a farmer who fed us abundantly, and I was tired enough to sleep soundly regardless of what the morrow might bring forth.

II

Lincoln, who had doubted from the start whether Hooker could "keep tavern" for an entire army, faced the truth that Chancellorsville had revealed. On June 27—that Saturday when Philadelphians were being roused to defend their city—the command of the Army of the Potomac was given to Pennsylvania-born George G. Meade, whose childhood playmates had included George B. McClellan and John C. Pemberton. Some described this West Pointer as a quiet man without much sense of humor; others insisted that in Meade's case still water ran deep. Next day none could deny the manly tone of Meade's address to his army:[4]

By direction of the President of the United States, I hereby assume command of the Army of the Potomac. As a soldier, in obeying this order—an order totally unexpected and unsolicited—I have no promises or pledges to make. The country looks to this army to relieve it from the devastation and disgrace of the hostile invasion. Whatever fatigues and sacrifices we may be called upon to undergo, let us have in view constantly the magnitude of the interests involved, and let each man determine to do his duty, leaving to an all-controlling Providence the decision of the contest. It is with just diffidence that I relieve, in the command of this army, an eminent and accomplished soldier, whose name must ever appear conspicuous in the history of its achievements; but I rely upon the hearty support of my companions in arms to assist me in the discharge of the duties of the important trust which has been confided to me.

GEORGE G. MEADE
Major-General Commanding

As the Army of the Potomac marched toward Gettysburg under a new chief, at Cashtown, only eight miles away, Lee set up temporary quarters and wondered what had happened to Jeb Stuart. After the affair at Brandy Station in early June, Lee had reason to expect results from Jeb. A surprise raid of the Yankees at Brandy Station had caught Stuart and his officers at a dance and cost 523 Confederate casualties. The Richmond Examiner *had sneered—"If the war was a tournament, invented and supported for the pleasure of a few vain and weak-headed officers, these disasters might be dismissed with compassion." Cut to the quick, Stuart listened perfunctorily to orders to screen the movements of Hill and Longstreet, then to join Ewell and act as "the eyes" of the army. On that twenty-seventh of June when Philadelphians read an ominous proclamation and Hooker stepped down from command, Stuart rested on the shores of the Potomac at Rockville, Maryland. Lieutenant Colonel W. W. Blackford remembered:[5]*

. . . A long wagon train of a hundred and fifty wagons appeared on the road slowly approaching from the direction of Washington, and a detail from Hampton's brigade was at once sent to capture it, which I accompanied. Galloping full tilt into the head of the train, we captured a small guard and a lot of gayly dressed quartermasters, and over half the wagons, before they could turn round; but then those beyond took the alarm, turned and fled as fast as their splendid mule teams could go. After them we flew, popping away with our pistols at such drivers as did not pull up, but the more we popped the faster those in front plied the whip; finally, coming to a sharp turn in the road, one upset and a dozen or two others piled up on top of it, until you could see nothing but the long ears and kicking legs of the mules sticking above the bags of oats emptied from the wagons upon them. . . . Half a dozen wagons had made the turn . . . and after them two or three of us dashed. It was as exciting as a fox chase for several miles, until when the last was taken I found myself on a hill in full view of Washington. . . . Here was a godsend to our poor horses, for every wagon was loaded with oats intended for Meade's army and it did one's heart good to see the way the poor brutes got on the outside of those oats. . . .

Stuart's horsemen returned to Rockville. Girls cheered them and cut buttons from their uniforms for souvenirs. While Lee waited at Cashtown, eager to learn whither Meade had taken the Army of the Potomac, Stuart continued to play hare and hounds with detachments of the Yankee cavalry protecting railroads and supply convoys.

Meanwhile Pickett's division, the rearmost of Lee's army, reached Chambersburg, Pennsylvania. Private John E. Dooley railed in his journal against the "dashing" Stuart who had left "our infantry and artillery unguarded in flank and rear" and had stripped "our cautious Lee of sufficient force to explore the exact position of his enemy." Pickett's boys were protecting "the spoils of our invasion, which with very frail guards were being constantly sent across the Potomac." For Dooley the situation was discomfiting:[6]

In and around the town of Chambersburg we found the people very sullen and maliciously disposed, and not a few maledictions were hurled at us from garret windows by croaking croans; and many young but frowning brows and pouting lips we saw in doorways and even on the sidewalks. But our boys laughed cheerfully, and when contempt and scorn were shewn them answered by jests and witticisms rather than with the bayonet, as often did those Yankee ruffians in our Southern Cities. . . . Here any where may be seen young ladies in silks padding along the pavement without *shoes or stockings.* Such sights are worthy of note as manifesting one of the peculiar customs of this *race of people,* if indeed it be not a peculiarity arising from the war. . . . We know how straight into the very jaws of destruction and death leads this road of Gettysburg; and none of us are yet aware that a battle is before us; still there pervades our ranks a solemn feeling, as if some unforeseen danger was ever dropping darksome shadows over the road we unshrinkingly tread.

III

On July 1 Lee agreed that General Henry Heth could take his division to Gettysburg in the hope of securing shoes for the barefooted men of the Third Corps. On the Chambersburg Pike, about a mile and a half from the village near a sluggish little stream called Willoughby Run, Yankee vedettes were encountered. So, unexpectedly, began one of the world's classic battles. Thus war overtook Tillie Alleman:[7]

We were having our regular literary exercises on Friday afternoon, at our Seminary, when the cry reached our ears. Rushing to the door, and standing on the front portico we beheld a dark, dense mass, moving toward town. Our teacher, Mrs. Eyster, at once said:

"Children, run home as quickly as you can."

It did not require repeating. I am satisfied some of the girls did not reach their homes before the Rebels were in the streets.

As for myself, I had scarcely reached the front door, when, on looking up the street, I saw some of the men on horseback. I scrambled in, slammed shut the door, and hastening to the sitting room, peeped out between the shutters.

Already at home, Sallie Robbins Broadhead remembered:[8]

I had just put my bread in the pans when the cannons began to fire
. . . About ten o'clock the shells began to "fly around quite thick," and I took my child and went to the house of a friend up town. As we passed up the street we met wounded men coming in from the field. When we saw them, we, for the first time, began to realize our fearful situation, and anxiously to ask, "Will our army be whipped?" Some said there was no danger of that yet, and pointed to Confederate prisoners who began to be sent through our streets to the rear.

Such a dirty, filthy set, no one ever saw. They were dressed in all kinds of clothes, of all kinds and no kind of cuts. Some were barefooted and a few wounded. Though enemies, I pitied them. I, with others, was sitting at the doorstep bathing the wounds of some of our brave soldiers, and became so much excited as the artillery galloped through the town, and the infantry hurried out to reinforce those fighting, that for a time we forgot our fears and our danger.

Young Billy Bayly was up on a ridge outside Gettysburg, picking raspberries with two chums:[9]

. . . The discharge of a cannon . . . made us jump, as it seemed to be just beyond the bushes concealing us. This was instantly followed by a rapid succession of discharges, and we three boys broke for the open and back to the blacksmith's shop. . . . The blacksmith's shop was deserted by all but its owner; his anvil was silent and his forge dead . . . so we perched ourselves on the topmost rail of the road fence and drank in the melody of the battle.

But our gallery seats, although good for the whole show, began to have features of discomfort when we noticed up the road, coming over the nearest hill, great masses of troops and clouds of dust; how the first wave swelled into successive waves, gray masses with the glint of steel as the sun struck the gun barrels, filling the highway, spreading out into the fields, and still coming on and on, wave after wave, billow after billow. We waited not until we could "see the whites of their eyes" but until they were a few hundred yards between us and the advance column, and then we departed. . . .

*Among the first Union casualties was General John F. Reynolds, who
was shot through the back of the head by a Rebel sharpshooter. Yankee
cavalry under General John Buford and a corps under General Abner
Doubleday managed at first to throw back the Rebels at Willoughby
Run. Meanwhile General Oliver Otis Howard reached Gettysburg,
climbed to the top of an observatory, and "with maps and field glasses"
looked down on the battle:*[10]

. . . Wadsworth's infantry, Buford's cavalry and one or two batteries were nearest, and their fighting was manifest. Confederate prisoners were just then being sent to the rear in large groups from Seminary Ridge down the street past my post of observation. . . .

Under my order Osborn's batteries were placed on Cemetery Ridge.
. . . General Steinwehr's division I put on the same heights near the
Baltimore Pike. Dilger's Ohio Battery preceded the corps, and soon
after Wheeler's, the two pacing through the town at a trot, to take their
places on the right of the First Corps. Schurz ordered General Schim-
melfennig (who had Schurz's division now) to advance briskly
through Gettysburg and form on the right of the First Corps in two
lines. Shortly after that the first division under Barlow arrived by the
Emmitsburg Road proper, and advanced through the town on the right
of the third division. I rode with Barlow through the city and out to
what is now Barlow Hill.

The firing at the front was now severe and an occasional shell burst
over our heads or among the houses. When I think of this day, I shall
always recall one incident which still cheers my heart: it was that a
young lady, after all other persons had disappeared for safety, remained behind on her porch and waved her handkerchief at the soldiers
as they passed. . . . How heartily they cheered her!

*Meade had reached Taneytown, about thirteen miles south of Gettys-
burg. Around two o'clock the first reports reached him and "he rode
at a rapid gallop." Meanwhile at Cashtown, Lee heard the sound of
battle and hurried forward. His immediate plan was to avoid a major
engagement until his entire army had reached the vicinity. By luck a
courier overtook Ewell, who was marching the Second Corps from
Fayetteville to Cashtown, and wheeled him around toward Gettysburg.
More or less the power of Federal troops had been split in two, with
Doubleday's First Corps occupying the Rebels along Willoughby Run
and Howard's Eleventh Corps fighting along Seminary Ridge. A railroad cut drew both armies toward the bitterest, climactic contest of*

the day. In the thickest of the fray were "those damned black-hatted fellows," the Iron Brigade. Sergeant George Eustice remembered:[11]

It must have been about noon when I saw a little old man coming up in the rear of Company F. In regard to the peculiarities of his dress, I remember he wore a swallowed-tailed coat with smooth brass buttons. He had a rifle on his shoulder. We boys began to poke fun at him as soon as he came amongst us, as we thought no civilian in his senses would show himself in such a place. . . . Bullets were flying thicker and faster, and we hugged the ground about us as close as we could. Burns got behind a tree and surprised us all by not taking a double-quick to the rear. He was as calm and collected as any veteran.

Bret Harte immortalized old John Burns, standing firm with the Iron Brigade:[12]

'Twas but a moment, for that respect
Which clothes all courage their voices checked;
And something the wildest could understand
Spake in the old man's strong right hand,
And his corded throat, and the lurking frown
Of his eyebrows under his old bell-crown;
Until, as they gazed, there crept an awe
Through the ranks in whispers, and some men saw,
In the antique vestments and long white hair,
The Past of the Nation in battle there;
And some of the soldiers since declare
That the gleam of his old white hat afar,
Like the crest plume of the brave Navarre,
That day was their oriflamme of war.

Yet an old man's courage does not win battles. Charles Coffin, reporting for the Boston Journal, *understood how Ewell's forces, deploying on the York Road, won the day for Lee:*[13]

. . . The [Rebel] batteries were wheeled into position and opened on the Union forces. Weiderick's battery in the cemetery replied. . . .

"I sent again to General Slocum, stating that my right flank was attacked; that it was in danger of being turned, and asking him if he was coming up," said General Howard. . . . But General Slocum did not move. . . .

Sickles was too far off to render assistance. Meanwhile Ewell was pressing on towards the college. Another division of Rebels under General Pender came in from the southwest, and began to enfold the left of Howard's line. . . .

An hour passed of close, desperate fighting. It wanted a quarter to four. Howard, confronted by four times his own force, was still holding his ground, waiting for Slocum. Another messenger rode to the Two Taverns [Slocum's fieldquarters on the Baltimore Pike], urging Slocum to advance.

"I must have reinforcements!" was the message Howard received from Doubleday on the left. "You must reinforce me!" was the word from Wadsworth in the center.

"Hold out a little longer, if possible; I am expecting General Slocum every moment" was Howard's reply. Still another dispatch was sent to the Two Taverns, but General Slocum had not moved. The Rebel cannon were cutting Wadsworth's line. Pender was sweeping round Doubleday; Ewell was enclosing Schurz [part of Howard's own Eleventh Corps]. Sickles was five miles distant, advancing as fast as he could. . . . For six hours the ground had been held against a greatly superior force.

Major Howard, the general's brother, a member of his staff, dashed down the pike in search of Slocum, with a request that he move at once and send one division to the right and the other to the left of Gettysburg. Slocum declined to go up to the front himself and take any responsibility, as he understood that General Meade did not wish to bring on a general engagement. He was willing, however, to send forward his troops as General Howard desired, and issued his orders accordingly. . . .

But before the divisions of the Twelfth Corps could get in motion, the Confederates had completely enfolded both flanks of Howard's line. The order to retreat was given. . . . The enemy pressed on with cheers. . . .

Sallie Broadhead hated what she saw—"The town was full of filthy rebels." Tillie Alleman was more struck by the terrible consequences of a battle:[14]

The first wounded soldier whom I met had his thumb tied up. This I thought was dreadful, and told him so.

"Oh," said he, "this is nothing; you'll see worse than this before long."

Soon two officers carrying their arms in slings made their appearance, and I more fully began to realize that something terrible had taken place.

Now the wounded began to come in greater numbers. Some limping, some with their heads and arms in bandages, some crawling, others carried on stretchers or brought in ambulances. Suffering, cast down and dejected, it was a truly pitiable gathering. Before night the barn was filled with shattered and dying heroes of this day's struggle.

That evening Beckie Weikert, the daughter at home, and I went out to the barn to see what was transpiring there. Nothing before in my experience had ever paralleled the sight we then and there beheld. There were the groaning and the crying, the struggling and dying, crowded side by side, while attendants sought to aid and relieve them as best they could.

We were so overcome by the sad and awful spectacle that we hastened back to the house weeping bitterly.

As we entered the basement or cellar-kitchen of the house, we found many nurses making beef tea for the wounded. Seeing that we were crying . . . they at once endeavored to cheer us by telling funny stories, and ridiculing our tears. They soon dispelled our terror and caused us to laugh so much that many times when we should have been sober minded we were not; the reactions having been too sudden for our overstrung nerves.

Ewell led the Confederate pursuit of the fleeing Yankees. Tired obviously from handling his new artificial limb, depressed in mind and spirit, surrounded by joyous soldiers toasting their victory with wine pilfered from Gettysburg cellars, Ewell decided to wait until morning to renew the battle. The Federals escaped into Cemetery Ridge beyond the town, falling exhausted among the tombstones. Frank Aretas Haskell, who served with the Iron Brigade as aide-de-camp to General Gibbon, had learned that the night before a battle was not a time for generals and their staff officers to sleep:[15]

. . . This war makes strange confusion of night and day! . . . At midnight Gen. Meade and staff rode by Gen. Gibbon's headquarters, on their way to the field; and in conversation with Gen. Gibbon, Gen. Meade announced that he had decided to assemble the whole army before Gettysburg, and offer the enemy battle there. The Second Corps would move at the earliest daylight, to take up its position.

At three o'clock, A.M., of the second of July, the sleepy soldiers of the Corps were aroused; before six the Corps was up to the field, and halted temporarily by the side of the Taneytown Road, upon which it had marched, while some movements of the other troops were being made, to enable it to take position in the order of battle. The morning was thick and sultry, the sky overcast with low, vapory clouds. As we approached all was astir upon the crests near the Cemetery, and the work of preparation was speedily going on. Men looked like giants there in the mist, and the guns of the frowning batteries so big that it was a relief to know that they were our friends.

. . . The line of battle as it was established, on the evening of the first, and morning of the second of July was in the form of the letter "U," the troops facing outwards, and the "Cemetery," which is at the point of the sharpest curvature of the line, being due South of the town of Gettysburg. "Round Top," the extreme left of the line, is a small, woody, rocky elevation, a very little West of South of the town, and nearly two miles from it. . . . A short distance North . . . is a smaller elevation called Little Round Top. . . . Near the right of the line is a small, woody eminence, named Culp's Hill. . . .

On arriving upon the field, Gen. Meade established his headquarters at a shabby little farmhouse on the left of the Taneytown Road, the house nearest the line, and a little more than five hundred yards in the rear of what became the center of the position of the Second Corps, a point where he could communicate readily and rapidly with all parts of the army. The advantages of the position, briefly, were these: the flanks were quite well protected by the natural defences there, Round Top up the left, and a rocky, steep, untraversable ground up the right. Our line was more elevated than that of the enemy, consequently our artillery had a greater range and power than theirs. On account of the convexity of our line, every part of the line could be reinforced by troops having to move a shorter distance than if the line were straight; further, for the same reason, the line of the enemy must be concave, and, consequently, longer, and with an equal force, thinner and so weaker than ours. Upon those parts of our line which were wooded, neither we nor the enemy could use artillery; but they were so strong by nature, aided by art, as to be readily defended by a small, against a very large, body of infantry. When the line was open, it had the advantage of having open country in front, consequently, the enemy here could not surprise, as we were on a crest, which besides the other advantages that I have mentioned, had this: the enemy must advance to the attack up an ascent, and must therefore move slower, and be, before coming upon us, longer under our fire, as well as more exhausted. These and some other things, rendered our position admirable—for a defensive battle.

IV

Longstreet liked nothing about the Confederate situation. With Meade up on those heights, Lee faced Fredericksburg in reverse. Common sense to Longstreet would be to move Lee's right to the left of Meade, putting the Army of Northern Virginia between Meade and Washington, "and thus force him to attack us in such position as we might select." Longstreet, full of arguments proving how foolhardy it was to fight here, recalled them all long years afterward—and also the strange mood that had fallen upon Lee:[16]

General Lee was impressed with the idea that by attacking the Federals he could whip them in detail. I reminded him that if the Federals were there in the morning, it would be proof that they had their forces well in hand, and that with Pickett in Chambersburg and Stuart out of reach we should be somewhat in detail. He, however, did not seem to abandon the idea of attack on the next day. He seemed under a subdued excitement, which occasionally took possession of him when "the hunt was up," and threatened his severe equipoise. The sharp battle fought by Hill and Ewell on that day had given him a taste of victory. . . .

On the morning of the second, I went to General Lee's headquarters and renewed my views against making an attack. He seemed resolved, however, and we discussed the probable results. We observed the position of the Federals and got a general idea of the nature of the ground. About sunrise General Lee sent Colonel Venable, of his staff, to General Ewell's headquarters, ordering him to make a reconnaissance of the ground in his front with a view of making the main attack on his left. A short time afterward he followed Colonel Venable in person. He returned about nine o'clock and informed me that it would not do to have Ewell open the attack. He finally determined that I should make the main attack on the extreme right. It was fully eleven o'clock when General Lee arrived at this conclusion and ordered the movement.

Under overcast skies, with a mizzling effort at rain, the morning wore on. Haskell watched the waiting Union soldiers—"Some loitered, some

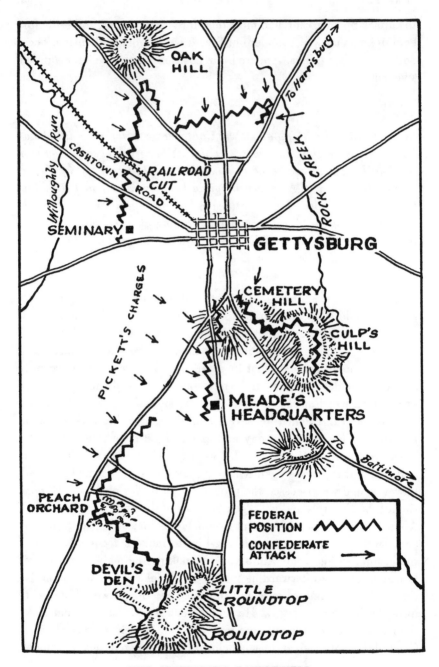

THE GETTYSBURG BATTLEFIELD

*went to sleep on the ground, some, a single man, carrying twenty can-
teens slung over the shoulder, went for water. Some made a fire and
boiled a dipper of coffee. Some with knees cocked up enjoyed the soldier's peculiar solace, a pipe of tobacco." In town Sallie Broadhead
could not hide her amusement at her husband, going into the garden to
pick "a mess of beans, though stray bullets from sharpshooters or others
whizzed about his head in a way I would not have liked. He persevered
until he had picked all, for he declared the Rebels should not have
one." Young Billy Bayly, tasting high adventure, helped conceal a
deserter on the farm—"He was added to the cherry picking brigade and
broke off branches and threw them down to his late comrades in arms."
Poor Tillie Alleman faced a grimmer experience:*[17]

During the early part of the forenoon my attention was called to
numerous rough boxes which had been placed outside the garden fence.
Ominous and dismal as was the sight presented, it nevertheless did not
prevent some of the soldiers from passing jocular expressions. One of
the men near by, being addressed with the remark that there was no
telling how soon he would be put in one of them, replied:

"I will consider myself very lucky if I *get* one."

This forenoon another incident occurred which I shall ever remember. While the infantry were passing, I noticed a poor, worn-out soldier
crawling along on hands and knees. An officer yelled at him, with cursing, to get up and march. The poor fellow said he could not, whereupon
the officer, raising his sword, struck him down three or four times. The
officer passed on, little caring what he had done. Some of his comrades
at once picked up the prostrate form and carried the unfortunate man
into the house. After several hours of hard work the sufferer was
brought back to consciousness. He seemed quite a young man, and
was suffering from sunstroke received on the forced march. As they
were carrying him in, some of the men who had witnessed this act of
brutality remarked:

"We will mark that officer for this."

It is a pretty well established fact that many a brutal officer fell in
battle, from being shot other than by the enemy.

*Lee's plan was for Longstreet to attack on the right as quickly as pos-
sible; and for Ewell, on the extreme left opposite Culp's Hill, to assault
when he heard Longstreet's guns. The morning passed; then one
o'clock, two o'clock. Pickett's division had not come up, a source of*

fretfulness to Longstreet, who with a force of hardly 13,000 men believed that "the proposition for our inferior forces to assault and drive out the masses of troops on the heights was a very problematical one." Colonel James Freemantle of the Coldstream Guards, serving as an observer with Lee's army, judged that the time was about two o'clock:[18]

. . . General Longstreet advised me if I wished to have a good view of the battle to return to my tree of yesterday. I did so, and remained there with Lawly and Captain Schreibert [of the Prussian Army] during the rest of the afternoon. But until four forty-five P.M. all was profoundly still and we began to doubt whether a fight was coming off today at all. At that time, however, Longstreet suddenly commenced a heavy cannonade on the right. Ewell immediately took it up on the left. The enemy replied with at least equal fury. . . . A dense smoke rose for six miles . . . [and] so soon as the firing began, General Lee joined Hill just below our tree, and he remained there nearly all the time looking through his field glasses—sometimes talking to Hill and sometimes to Colonel Long of his staff. But generally he sat quite alone on the stump of a tree. . . . When the cannonade was at its height, a Confederate band of music, between the cemetery and ourselves, began to play polkas and waltzes, which sounded very curious accompanied by the hissing and bursting of shells.

Meanwhile across the 1,400 yards that separated the two armies, a Union general, Dan Sickles, headstrong, rash, an egotistic product of the hard school of Tammany politics, decided he knew more about war than Meade. The ground in front of him, strewn in places with boulders, he described as "unfit for infantry, impracticable for artillery"; if Lee planted enough guns along the higher ground of the Emmitsburg Road, then Gettysburg could become another Chancellorsville! So reasoned Sickles, who might have been a presidential candidate had he not killed a man for an affair with Mrs. Sickles. He decided to move within reach of the Emmitsburg Road. Astonished, Frank Haskell described what followed:[19]

It was magnificent to see those ten thousand or twelve thousand men —they were good men—with their batteries, and some squadrons of cavalry upon the left flank . . . sweep steadily down the slope, across the valley, and up the next ascent toward their destined position! . . . The Third Corps now became the absorbing object of interest of all eyes. The Second Corps took arms, and the 1st Division of this Corps was ordered to be in readiness to support the Third Corps, should circumstances render support necessary. The Third Corps was the extreme left of our line, as it advanced, and if the enemy was assembling to the West of Round Top with a view to turn our left, as we had heard, there would be nothing between the left flank of the corps and the enemy, and the enemy would be square upon its flank by the time it had attained the road. So when this advance line came near the Emmitsburg Road, and we saw . . . the smoke of some guns, and we heard the reports away to Sickles' left, anxiety became an element in our interest in these movements. The enemy opened slowly at first, and from long range; but he was square upon Sickles' left flank.

General Caldwell pulled back the first division of the Second Corps to the woods at the west slope of Round Top, thus attempting to cover Sickles in flank and rear. A reserve corps came up the Baltimore Pike, heading to the support of Caldwell. Another corps came up and halted on the Baltimore Pike. As Haskell said, "the plot thickened":

. . . The enemy seem to be fearfully in earnest this time. And what is more ominous than the thunder or the shot of his advancing guns . . . far to Sickles' left, appear the long lines and the columns of the Rebel infantry, now unmistakably moving out to the attack. The position of the Third Corps becomes at once one of great peril, and it is probable that its commander by this time began to realize his true situation. All was astir now on our crest. Generals and their Staffs were galloping hither and thither—the men were all in their places, and you might have heard the rattle of ten thousand ramrods as they drove home and "thugged" upon the little globes and cones of lead. As the enemy was advancing upon Sickles' flank, he commenced a change, or at least a partial one, of front, by swinging back his left and throwing forward his right, in order that his lines might be parallel to those of his adversary, his batteries meantime doing what they could to check the enemy's advance; but this movement was not completely executed before new Rebel batteries opened upon Sickles' right flank—his former front—and in the same quarter appeared the Rebel infantry also.

Now came the dreadful battle picture, of which we for a time could be but spectators. Upon the front and right flank of Sickles came sweeping the infantry of Longstreet and Hill. Hitherto there had been skirmishing and artillery practice—now the battle began; for amid the heavier smoke and larger tongues of flame of the batteries, now began to appear the countless flashes, and the long fiery sheets of the muskets, and the rattle of the volleys, mingled with the thunder of the guns. We see the long gray lines come sweeping upon Sickles' front, and mix with the battle smoke; now the same colors emerge from the bushes and orchards upon his right, and envelope his flank in the confusion of the conflict. O, the din and the roar, and these thirty-thousand Rebel wolf cries! What a hell is there down that valley!

Through the Peach Orchard, the Wheat Field—names that by nightfall would forever be inscribed in blood in American history—came the howling Rebels who would make July 2, 1863, "Longstreet's greatest day." Haskell watched mutely:[20]

These ten or twelve thousand men of the Third Corps fight well, but it soon becomes apparent that they must be swept from the field, or perish there where they are doing so well, so thick and overwhelming a storm of Rebel fire involves them. It was fearful to see, but these men, such as ever escape, must come from that conflict as best they can. To move down and support them with other troops is out of the question, for this would be to do as Sickles did, to relinquish a good position, and advance to a bad one. There is no other alternative—the Third Corps must fight itself out of its position of destruction! . . .

The Rebel, as anticipated, tries to gain the left of the Third Corps, and for this purpose is now moving into the woods at the west of Round Top. We knew what he would find there. No sooner had the enemy gotten a considerable force into the woods mentioned, in the attempted execution of his purpose, than the roar of the conflict was heard there also. The Fifth Corps and the First Division of the Second were there at the right time, and promptly engaged him; and there, too, the battle soon became general and obstinate.

Now the roar of battle has become twice the volume that it was before, and its range extends over more than twice the space. The Third Corps has been pressed back considerably, and the wounded are streaming to the rear by hundreds, but still the battle there goes on, with no considerable abatement on our part. The field of actual conflict extends now from a point to the front of the left of the Second Corps, away down to the front of Round Top, and the fight rages with the greatest fury. The fire of artillery and infantry and the yells of the

Rebels fill the air with a mixture of hideous sounds. When the First Division of the Second Corps first engaged the enemy, for a time it was pressed back somewhat, but under the able and judicious management of Gen. Caldwell, and the support of the Fifth Corps, it speedily ceased to retrograde, and stood its ground; and then there followed a time, after the Fifth Corps became well engaged, when from appearances we hoped the troops already engaged would be able to check entirely, or repulse the further assault of the enemy. . . .

Private John W. Plummer, sent to support the left of the beleaguered Third Corps, found that men in battle act strangely:[21]

We were marched up there about a quarter of a mile, and ordered to lie down in front of the batteries, as the shot and shell were coming over pretty plentifully. From there we could look all over the field, see our lines, the rebel lines, and their batteries very plainly. As I saw our men fall back, rally, and fall back again, skedaddlers rushing to the rear in squads, I never felt so bad in my life. I thought sure the day was gone for us, and felt that I would prefer to die there, rather than live and suffer the disgrace and humiliation a defeat of our army there would entail on us; and if ever I offered a sincere prayer in my life, it was then, that we might be saved from defeat. We all felt bad, but resolved, when our chance came, to do our best to retrieve the fortunes of the day, hardly expecting to come out of the conflict unharmed. Our turn soon came. We were ordered forward against the enemy, who were then within musket range of us; and if any ever were willing and anxious to go forward into what we all could see was a deadly place, our boys were. We had two open fields to advance over, while the rebels were coming down over another open field, and the Third corps falling back before. We went forward on a run, and with a yell, till about half way across the second field, when we were ordered, for some unaccountable reason to us, to halt, and the bullets were coming like hail-stones, and whittling our boys like grain before the sickle. "Why don't they let us charge?" cried all of us. "Why do they stop us here to be murdered?" Every one seemed anxious to go forward, and some run way out ahead and beckoned for us to come on. We have always believed that a determined charge would break any line, and that more would be accomplished and less life lost, than by lying down and firing two or three hours. We felt that we could check and force them to retreat, and we wanted to go against them with a vengeance and get over the deadly ground as soon as possible. We were halted again when across the second field; and though by this time few were left, we were just as anxious to go forward. We were almost together, and the rebels had nearly flanked the right of the regiment. But what surprised me most was to see some of the rebels, not fifty yards from us, standing out openly and loading and firing as deliberately as though they were in no danger whatever. Ah! there is no mistake but what some of those rebels are just as brave as it is possible for human beings to be. . . .

The afternoon shadows lengthened, the battle roared on, and then with a sense of shock both North and South realized that the key to the entire field, the Round Tops, had been ignored. How close the Rebels came to winning this prize lived in the memory of William Colvin Oates, who led the Fifteenth Alabama up those rocky slopes:[22]

I now ordered my regiment to drive the Federals from the ledge of rocks and from the hill. My men advanced about halfway to the enemy's position, but the fire was so destructive that my line wavered like a man trying to walk against a strong wind, and then slowly, doggedly, gave back a little; then, with no one on the left or right of me, to stand there and die was sheer folly; either to advance or retreat became a necessity.

I again ordered the advance . . . I passed through the line waving my sword, shouting, "Forward, men, to the ledge!" and was promptly followed by the command in splendid style. . . . Five times they rallied and charged us, twice coming so near that some of my men had to use the bayonet. . . . It was our time now to deal death. . . .

Colonel W. F. Perry of the Forty-eighth Alabama thought that "the view was imposing. Little Round Top, crowned with artillery, resembled a volcano in eruption; while a hillock near Devil's Den resembled a smaller one." Perry's line emerged from a woods:

A sheet of flame burst from the rocks less than fifty yards away. A few scattering shots in the beginning gave warning in time for my men to fall down, and thus largely to escape the effect of the main volley. They doubtless seemed to the enemy to be all dead, but the volley of the fire which they immediately returned proved that they were very much alive. . . . Before the enemy had time to load their guns a decision was made. Leaping over the prostrate line before me, I shouted the order, "Forward!" and started for the rocks. The response was a bound, a yell, and a rush, and in ten seconds my men were pouring into the Den, and the enemy were escaping from the opposite side. . . . In the charge the left wing of the regiment struck the hill on which the artillery were stationed, and the center and right swept into the rocks east of it. Major George W. Carey led the left wing up the hill, and bounding over the rocks on its crest, landed among the artillery-men ahead of the line, and received their surrender. . . . The Major a few moments later found me near the foot of the hill, completely prostrated by heat and excessive exertion.

To the little band of the Twentieth Maine fell the brunt of saving the Round Tops for the Union. For Captain Howard L. Prince the sight of those hostile slopes was etched on his memory:[23]

The front surged backward and forward like a wave. At times our dead and wounded were in front of our line, and then by a superhuman effort our gallant lads would carry the combat forward beyond their prostrate forms. Continually the gray lines crept up by squads under protecting trees and boulders, and the firing became at closer and closer range. And even the enemy's line essayed to reach around the thin front of blue that stretched out in places in single rank and could not go much farther without breaking. So far had they extended, that their bullets passed beyond and into the ranks farther up the hill, and Captain Woodward, commanding the Eighty-third, sent his adjutant to ask if the Twentieth had been turned. . . . Meanwhile the brigade in front of the hill was hard pushed to hold its own, and the heavy roar of musketry in the fitful lulls of our guns came to the anxious ears of our commander and told too plainly what would be the result if our line gave way. Not a man in that devoted band but knew that the safety of the brigade, and perhaps of the army, depended on the steadfastness with which that point was held, and so fought on and on, with no hope of assistance, but not a thought of giving up. Already nearly half of the little force is prostrate. The dead and the wounded clog the footsteps of the living.

The countercharges of the Twentieth Maine broke the Rebel attack; Oates described the retreat: "We ran like a herd of wild cattle." Many times that day on those slopes an exhausted Ziba B. Graham of the

Sixteenth Michigan turned his head and saw the Third Corps in the peach orchard and the wheat field:

We could see line after line of Longstreet's men forming and advancing; also the close contact, the repulses, the fierce havoc of artillery, the close range of the musketry, the break of the lines, the gallant unbroken line still pushing forward, the gradual pressure upon Sickles, his stubborn falling back, the hand-to-hand conflict in the wheatfield where the gallant Fourth Michigan fought so stubbornly, and where their brave and noble Colonel Jefferds lost his life by a bayonet thrust, still holding to the flag. All this and more passed before our eyes. So fierce was our own fight that we could spare no men to take off the field our own wounded. I engaged part of my time in securing from them the ammunition they had not used.

On Cemetery Ridge, Haskell now discovered that a battle raged furiously:[24]

All senses for the time are dead but the one of sight. The roar of the discharges and the yells of the enemy all pass unheeded; but the impassioned soul is all eyes, and sees all things, that the smoke does not hide. How madly the battery men are driving home the double charges of canister in those broad-mouthed Napoleons, whose fire seems almost to reach the enemy. How rapidly these long, bluecoated lines of infantry deliver their file fire down the slope.

But there is no faltering—the men stand nobly to their work. Men are dropping dead or wounded on all sides, by scores and by hundreds, and the poor mutilated creatures, some with an arm dangling, some with a leg broken by a bullet, are limping and crawling towards the rear. They make no sound of complaint or pain, but are as silent as if dumb and mute. . . . The fire all along our crest is terrific, and it is a wonder how anything human could have stood before it, and yet the madness of the enemy drove them on, clear up to the muzzle of the guns, clear up to the lines of our infantry—but the lines stood right in their places. Gen. Hancock and his Aides rode up to Gibbon's Division under the smoke. Gen. Gibbon, with myself, was near, and there was a flag dimly visible, coming toward us from the direction of the enemy.

"Here, what are these men falling back for?" said Hancock.

The flag was no more than fifty yards away, but it was the head of a Rebel column, which at once opened fire with a volley. . . . The 1st Minn. . . . the less than three hundred that are left out of fifteen hundred that it has had, swings around upon the enemy, gives them a volley in their faces, and advances upon them with the bayonet. . . .

Such fighting as this cannot last long. It is now near sundown, and the battle has gone on wonderfully long already. But if you will stop to notice it, a change has occurred. The Rebel cry has ceased, and the men of the Union begin to shout there, under the smoke, and their lines to advance. See, the Rebels are breaking! They are in confusion in all our front! The wave has rolled upon the rock, and the rock has smashed it. Let us shout, too!

First upon their extreme left the Rebels broke, where they had almost pierced our lines; thence the repulse extended rapidly to their right. They hung longest about Round Top . . . but in a space of time incredibly short, after they first gave signs of weakness, the whole force of the Rebel assault along the whole line, in spite of waving red flags, and yells, and the entreaties of officers, and the pride of the chivalry, fled like chaff before the whirlwind, back down the slope, over the valley, across the Emmitsburg Road, shattered, without organization in utter confusion, fugitive into the woods, and victory was with the arms of the Republic.

V

Fields beautiful this morning and desolate now—in the last glimmering light of that second of July Haskell noted the "haversacks, yawning with the rations the owners will never call for; canteens of cedar of the Rebel men of Jackson, and of cloth-covered tin of the men of the Union; blankets and trousers, and coats and caps, and some are blue and some are gray; muskets and ramrods, and bayonets, and swords, and scabbards and belts, some bent and cut by the shot or shell; broken wheels, exploded caissons, and limber-boxes, and dismantled guns, and all of these are sprinkled with blood; horses, some dead, a mangled heap of carnage, some alive, with a leg shot clear off, or other frightful wounds, appealing to you with almost more than brute gaze as you pass; and last, but not least numerous, many thousands of men . . . sleeping the last sleep." The wounded Sickles ordered a special casket made for his amputated leg so that he could carry it with pride to Washington; and General Birney, who took over his command, whispered to a lieutenant, "I wish I were already dead!" Sallie Broadhead could not sleep; she washed a few pieces for her child and fretted over rumors that the Rebels would shell the town in the morning. Billy Bayly was tempted to steal the scabbards of two officers who slept at the farm, but then "feared for the rest of the family."

For Meade it had been a long day. Earlier to Colonel Thomas Rafferty, who fought under Sickles, Meade had seemed "utterly worn out and hollow-eyed. Anxiety and want of sleep were evidently telling on him." Later, when a shell frightened his horse, Meade had clung to the runaway, and, in the testimony of Henry Tremain of Sickles' staff, "was apparently ingloriously and temporarily carried from the front at the formal opening of the furious engagement of July 2, 1863." But now that day had ended, at least in a draw for Meade, and he called his generals to a council of war. Haskell's portrait of Meade, with his Romanish face, large nose, white forehead and wide, bespectacled eyes, was sympathetic; "His fibres are all of the long and sinewy kind." Yet for General John Gibbon the meeting produced an uneasy mood:[25]

I had never been a member of a council of war before (nor have I since) and did not feel very confident that I was properly a member of this one; but I was engaged in the discussion and found myself (Warren being asleep) the junior member in it. By the customs of war the junior member votes first, as on courts-martial; and when Butterfield read off his question, the substance of which was: "Should the army remain in its present position or take up some other?" he addressed himself first to me. To say "Stay and fight" would be to ignore the objections made by General Newton [an officer of engineers, who had argued "this was no place to fight a battle"], and I therefore answered somewhat in this way: "Remain here, and make such correction in our position as may be deemed necessary, but take no step which even looks like retreat." The question was put to each member and his answer taken down, and when it came to Newton who was first in rank, he voted pretty much the same way I did, and we had some playful sparring as to whether he agreed with me or I with him; the rest voted to remain.

The next question put by Butterfield was: "Should the army attack or await the attack of the enemy?" I voted not to attack, and all the others voted substantially the same way; and on the third question, "How long shall we wait?" I voted "Until Lee moves." The answer to this last question showed the only material variation in the opinion of the members.

When the meeting was over, General Meade said, quietly but decidedly, "Such then is the decision" and certainly he said nothing which produced a doubt in my mind as to his being in accord with the members of the council.

The night, sultry and starless, stretched on; the slopes between the contending armies flickered with the twinkling lanterns of the litter-bearers. Then daylight—the work of the ambulance corps has been suspended—and General George Pickett tries to explain what this day must mean to him in a letter to his wife:[26]

. . . A summons came from Old Peter, and I immediately rode to the top of the ridge where he and Marse Robert were making a reconnaissance of Meade's position. "Great God!" said Old Peter as I came up. "Look, General Lee, at the insurmountable difficulties between our line and that of the Yankees—the steep hills, the tiers of artillery, the fences, the heavy skirmish line—and then we'll have to fight our infantry against their batteries. Look at the ground we'll have to charge over, nearly a mile of that open ground there under the rain of their canister and shrapnel."

"The enemy is there, General Longstreet, and I am going to strike him," said Marse Robert in his firm, quiet, determined voice.

About 8 o'clock I rode with them along our line of prostrate infantry. They had been told to lie down to prevent attracting attention, and though they had been forbidden to cheer they voluntarily arose and lifted in reverential adoration their caps to our beloved commander as we rode slowly along. Oh, the responsibility for the lives of such men as these! Well, my darling, their fate and that of our beloved Southland will be settled ere your glorious brown eyes rest on these scraps of penciled paper—your Soldier's last letter, perhaps. . . .

I closed my letter to you a little before three o'clock and rode up to Old Peter for orders. I found him like a great lion at bay. I have never seen him so grave and troubled. For several minutes after I had saluted him he looked at me without speaking. Then in an agonized voice, the reserve all gone, he said:

"Pickett, I am being crucified at the thought of the sacrifice of life which this attack will make. I have instructed Alexander to watch the effect of our fire upon the enemy, and when it begins to tell he must take the responsibility and give you your orders, for I can't."

While he was yet speaking a note was brought to me from Alexander. After reading it I handed it to him, asking if I should obey and go forward. He looked at me for a moment, then held out his hand. Presently, clasping his other hand over mine without speaking he bowed his head upon his breast. I shall never forget the look in his face nor the clasp of his hand when I said:—"Then, General, I shall lead my Division on.". . .

From the start the day went badly for Lee. Ewell, who was to open with an assault on Culp's Hill in co-ordination with Longstreet's attack, received too late an order to delay his action. Ewell fought with spirit, yet his failure was complete. Stuart, who finally had reached Gettysburg the night before, was expected to get behind the Union lines and disrupt their concentration but the Yankee cavalry under Alfred Pleasonton had been waiting for Stuart and handled him roughly. Meanwhile Pickett's boys moved up—with them, Private John Dooley:[27]

How long we take to gain our position, what delays, what suspense! We are soon passing over the battlefield of yesterday, and the details of burying parties are digging graves to receive the freshly fallen comrades, and, in many instances, they have only the ghastly and mangled remnants of their gallant friends to deposit in these hastily dug pits. I press very close to a headless body; the boy's head being torn off by a shell is lying around in bloody fragments on the ground.

A little further we take temporary position in the hollow of a field. Before us is a rising slope which hides the Yankee position from view. To the right of our front some quarter of a mile is a brick house near which one of our batteries now and then opens on the enemy who are generally ready to respond to the harsh greeting. Around us are some trees with very small green apples; and while we are resting here we amuse ourselves by pelting each other with green apples.

Even the debonair Colonel Freemantle was nonplused to discover that Longstreet, having his deployments completed by noon, "then dismounted and went to sleep for a short time." Over on Cemetery Ridge —across those fateful 1,400 yards, where Pickett has been ordered to charge—Haskell looked at the men dozing in the heat and lolling upon the ground: "I yawned and looked at my watch. It was five minutes before one o'clock." Then Lee was ready—all along his line the guns opened, outdoing anything at Second Bull Run, at Antietam, at Fredericksburg. In Haskell's judgment:[28]

A hundred and twenty-five rebel guns, we estimate, are now active, firing twenty-four pound, twenty, twelve, and ten pound projectiles, solid shot and shells, spherical, conical, spiral. The enemy's fire is chiefly concentrated upon the position of the Second Corps. From the Cemetery to Round Top, with over a hundred guns, and to all parts of the enemy's line, our batteries reply . . .

Who can describe such a conflict as is raging around us? To say that it was like a summer storm, with the crash of thunder, the glare of lightning, the shrieking of the wind, and the clatter of hailstones, would be weak. The thunder and lightning of these two hundred and fifty guns and their shells, whose smoke darkens the sky, are incessant, all pervading, in the air above our heads, on the ground at our feet, remote, near, deafening, ear-piercing, astounding; and these hailstones are massy iron, charged with exploding fire. And there is little of human interest in a storm; it is an absorbing element of this. . . . These guns are great infuriate demons, not of the earth, whose mouths blaze with smoky tongues of living fire, and whose murky breath, sulphur-laden, rolls around them and along the ground, the smoke of Hades. These grimy men, rushing, shouting, their souls in frenzy, plying the dusky globes and the igniting spark, are in their league, and but their willing ministers.

. . . The projectiles shriek long and sharp. They hiss, they scream, they growl, they sputter; all sounds of life and rage; and each has its different note, and all are discordant. . . . We see the solid shot strike axle, or pole, or wheel, and the tough iron and heart of oak snap and fly like straws. The great oaks there by Woodruff's guns heave down their massy branches with a crash, as if the lightning smote them. The shells swoop down among the battery horses standing there apart. A half a dozen horses start, they tumble, their legs stiffen, their vitals and blood smear the ground. And these shot and shells have no respect for men either. We see the poor fellows hobbling back from the crest, or unable to do so, pale and weak, lying on the ground with the mangled stump of an arm or leg, dripping their life-blood away; or with a cheek torn open, or a shoulder mashed. And many, alas! hear not the roar as they stretch upon the ground with upturned faces and open eyes, though a shell should burst at their very ears. Their ears and their bodies this instant are only mud. We saw them but a moment since there among the flame, with brawny arms and muscles of iron wielding the rammer and pushing home the cannon's plethoric load.

A shell tears off a man's knapsack but does not tear his coat. Like a pagan worshiper, a man sits with his head bowed to a stone; a shell smashes the stone into a thousand fragments, but does not touch the man. These are freak incidents. Haskell watches the shells bursting in the air:

. . . Their flash was a bright gleam of lightning radiating from a point, giving place in the thousandth part of a second to a small, white, puffy cloud, like a fleece of the lightest, whitest wool. These clouds were very numerous. We could not often see the shell before it burst; but sometimes, as we faced towards the enemy, and looked above our heads, the approach would be heralded by a prolonged hiss, which always seemed to me to be a line of something tangible, terminating in a black globe, distinct to the eye, as the sound had been to the ear. The shell would seem to stop, and hang suspended in the air an instant, and then vanish in fire and smoke and noise.

VI

Stretched flat on the ground, hands pointed toward the firing, Captain W. W. Wood waited with the men in Pickett's division. Not a breath of air stirred; in Wood's company of fifty men, the shells had killed four and wounded fifteen; all around heads of clover had been clipped off. Then the guns both North and South slackened their fire; soon a silence as oppressive as the heat crept over the field. Wood scrambled up and called his men into line:[29]

The order to go forward was given and obeyed with alacrity and cheerfulness, for we believed that the battle was practically over, and we had nothing to do but march unopposed to Cemetery Heights and occupy them. The ascent of the crest of the hill, which had hitherto concealed us from the enemy's view, was made speedily and in good order. While making the ascent it was seen that the supports to our left and right flanks were not coming forward, as we had been told they would. Mounted officers were dashing frantically up and down their line, apparently endeavoring to get them to move forward, but we could see that they could not move. Their failure to support us was discouraging, but did not dishearten us. Some of our men cursed them for being cowards but still our charge was kept up and no man fell out.

Soon we were past the crest of the hill and out of sight of them. Before us stood Cemetery Heights, of which we could get glimpses through rifts in the clouds of powder-smoke. We could not see whether or not there were troops there to defend them against us.

Somewhere further on, perhaps a hundred and fifty yards beyond the crest of the hill we had just passed, a post-and-rail fence some five feet high was encountered. This fence was quickly mounted . . . a shot, fired from somewhere to our left, struck the center company of my regiment, and . . . the smoke now lifted from our front and there, right before us stood Cemetery Heights in awful grandeur. At their base was a double line of Federal infantry and several pieces of artillery planted behind stone walls, and infantry supports were hurriedly coming up. We fully realized that Pickett's three little brigades, already greatly reduced by heavy casualties, were making alone and without possibility of succor, a desperate charge against the whole power of the Federal army.

Haskell, watching, almost unable to believe, saw "an overwhelming restless tide of an ocean of armed men sweeping upon us":[30]

. . . More than half a mile their front extends; more than a thousand yards the dull gray masses deploy, man touching man, rank pressing rank, and line supporting line. The red flags wave, their horsemen gallop up and down; the arms of eighteen thousand men, barrel and bayonet, gleam in the sun, a sloping forest of flashing steel. Right on they move, as with one soul, in perfect order without impediment of ditch, or wall or stream, over ridge and slope, through orchard and meadow, and cornfield, magnificent, grim, irresistible.

All was orderly still upon our crest; no noise and no confusion. . . . The click of the locks as each man raised the hammer to feel with his fingers that the cap was on the nipple; the sharp jar as a musket touched a stone upon the wall when thrust in aiming over it, and the clicking of the iron axles as the guns were rolled up by hand a little further to the front, were quite all the sounds that could be heard. Cap-boxes were slid around to the front of the body; cartridge boxes opened, officers opened their pistol-holsters. Such preparations, little more was needed. . . .

Doggedly up those slopes toward the waiting Yankees marched Private John Dooley:[31]

. . . Directly in front of us, breathing flame in our very faces, the long range of guns which must be taken thunder on our quivering

melting ranks. . . . The line becomes unsteady because at every step
a gap must be closed and thus from left to right much ground is
lost. . . . Capt. Hallinan has fallen and I take his place. So many
men have fallen now that I find myself within a few yards of my old
Captain. His men are pressing mine out of place. I ask him to give way
a little to the left, and scarcely has he done so, than he leaps into the air,
falling prostrate. . . . Our men are falling faster now, for the deadly
musket is at work. Volley after volley of crushing musket balls sweeps
through the lines and mows us down like wheat before the scythe.

On! men, on! Thirty yards more . . . but who can stand such a
storm of hissing lead and iron? . . . Just here—from right to left the
remnants of our braves pour in their long reserved fire; until now no
shot has been fired, no shout of triumph has been raised; but as the
cloud of smoke rises over the heads of the advancing divisions the
well-known Southern battle cry which marked the victory gained or
nearly gained bursts wildly over the blood stained field and *all that line
of guns is ours.*

Shot through both thighs, I fall.

*Haskell couldn't believe it. "Were my senses mad?" he wondered.
Yet:*[32]

. . . The larger portion of Webb's brigade—my God, it was true—
there by the group of trees and the angles of the wall, was breaking
from the cover of their works, and, without orders or reason, with no
hand lifted to check them, was falling back, a fear-stricken flock of
confusion! * The fate of Gettysburg hung upon a spider's single thread!

A great magnificent passion came on me at the instant, not one that
overpowers and confounds, but one that blanches the face and sublimes
every sense and faculty. . . . I ordered these men to "halt," and
"face about," and "fire," and they heard my voice and gathered my
meaning, and obeyed my commands. On some unpatriotic backs of
those not quick of comprehension, the flat of my sabre fell not lightly,
and, at its touch their love of country returned, and with a look at me as
if I were the destroying angel, as I might have become theirs, they
again faced the enemy. . . . This portion of the wall was lost to us,

---

* General Webb insisted: "What Haskell wrote, he wrote in ignorance." Bruce
Catton, editing a modern edition of Haskell's narrative, believes that Webb's
men were overpowered rather than routed.

and the enemy had gained the cover of the reverse side, where he now stormed with fire.

But Webb's men, with their bodies in part protected by the abruptness of the crest, now sent back in the enemies' faces as fierce a storm. Some scores of venturesome Rebels, that in their first push at the wall had dared to cross at the further angle, and those that had desecrated Cushing's guns, were promptly shot down, and speedy death meet him who should raise his body to cross it again. At this point little could be seen of the enemy, by reason of his cover and the smoke, except the flash of his muskets and his waving flags.

These red flags were accumulating at the wall every moment, and they maddened us as the same color does the bull. Webb's men are falling fast, and he is among them to direct and encourage; but, however well they may now do, with that walled enemy in front, with more than a dozen flags to Webb's three, it soon becomes apparent that in not many minutes they will be overpowered, or that there will be none alive for the enemy to overpower.

Webb has but three regiments, all small, the 69th, 71st and 72nd Pennsylvania . . . and he must have assistance, or this crest will be lost. Oh, where is Gibbon? where is Hancock?—some general—anybody with the power and the will to support that wasting, melting line? No general came, and no succor! I thought of Hayes upon the right, but from the smoke and war along his front, it was evident that he had enough upon his hands, if he stayed the in-rolling tide of the Rebels there. Doubleday upon the left was too far off and too slow. . . . As a last resort I had resolved to see if Hall and Harrow could not send some of their commands to reinforce Webb. . . .

Hall agreed to send his brigade, and five new colors joined Webb's embattled three. Webb had been pressed back so that he was not far from Hall's right; still, Haskell recounted:

The movement, as it did, attracting the enemy's fire, and executed in haste, as it must be, was difficult; but in reasonable time, and in order that is serviceable, if not regular, Hall's men are fighting gallantly side by side with Webb's before the all important point. I did not stop to see all this movement of Hall's, but from him I went at once further to the left, to the 1st brigade. . . . All men that I could find I took over to the right at the *double quick.*

As we were moving to, and near the other brigade of the division, from my position on horseback I could see that the enemy's right, under Hall's fire, was beginning to stagger and to break.

"See," I said to the men, "See the *chivalry!* See the gray-backs run!"

The men saw, and as they swept to their places by the side of Hall and opened fire, they roared, and this in a manner that said more plainly than words—for the deaf could have seen it in their faces, and the blind could have heard it in their voices—*the crest is safe!*

In Haskell's vivid description, "Now it was as if a new battle, deadlier, stormier than before, had sprung from the body of the old—a young Phoenix of combat, whose eyes stream lightning, shaking his arrowy wings over the yet glowing ashes of his progenitor." Wounded on the field thirty yards from the wall, Private Dooley knew—"That huzza never broke from southern throats. Oh God!" Lee saw them coming back—broken, frightened, bleeding, crippled, exhausted, crying—and more like a father than a general said gently, "Don't be discouraged. It was my fault this time." Colonel Freemantle told Longstreet, "I wouldn't have missed this for anything," and Old Pete answered, "I would have liked to have missed it very much." This was the end, yet in town Sallie Broadhead didn't know:[33]

The time we sat in the cellar seemed long, listening to the terrific sound of the strife; more terrible never greeted human ears. We knew that with every explosion, and the scream of each shell, human beings were hurried through excruciating pain into another world, and that many more were torn, and mangled, and lying in torment worse than death, and no one able to extend relief. The thought made me very sad, and feel that, if it was God's will, I would rather be taken away than remain to see the misery that would follow. Some thought this afternoon would never come to a close.

We knew that the Rebels were putting forth all their might, and it was a dreadful thought that they might succeed.

Who is victorious, or with whom the advantage rests, no one here can tell. It would ease the horror if we knew our arms were successful. Some think the Rebels were defeated, as there has been no boasting as on yesterday, and they look uneasy and by no means exultant. I hope they are correct, but I fear we are too hopeful. We shall see tomorrow. It will be the Fourth of July, and the Rebels have promised us a glorious day. If it only ends the battle and drives them off it will be glorious.

Tillie Alleman, who had taken refuge on a farm, returned to the Weikert home:[34]

I fairly shrank back aghast at the awful sight presented. The approaches were crowded with wounded, dying and dead. The air was filled with moanings, and groanings. As we passed on toward the house, we were compelled to pick our steps in order that we might not tread on the prostrate bodies. . . .

Amputating benches had been placed about the house. I must have become inured to seeing the terrors of battle, else I could hardly have gazed upon the scenes now presented. I was looking out one of the windows facing the front yard. Near the basement door, and directly under the window I was at, stood one of these benches. I saw them lifting the poor men upon it, then the surgeons cutting and sawing off legs, then again probing and picking bullets from the flesh.

Some of the soldiers fairly begged to be taken next, so great was their suffering, so anxious were they to obtain relief.

I saw the surgeons hastily put a cattle horn over the mouths of the wounded ones, after they were placed upon the bench. At first I did not understand the meaning of this, but upon inquiry, soon learned that that was their mode of administering chloroform, in order to produce unconsciousness. But the effect in some instances was not produced; for I saw the wounded throwing themselves wildly about, and shrieking with pain while the operation was going on.

To the south of the house, and just outside of the yard, I noticed a pile of limbs higher than the fence. It was a ghastly sight! Gazing upon these, too often the trophies of the amputating bench, I could have no other feeling, than that the whole scene was one of cruel butchery.

That night General Pickett wrote his wife another letter:[35]

My brave boys were full of hope and confident of victory as I led them forth, forming them in column of attack, and though officers and men alike knew what was before them—knew the odds against them— they eagerly offered up their lives on the altar of duty, having absolute faith in their ultimate success. Over on Cemetery Ridge the Federals beheld a scene never before witnessed on this continent—a scene which has never previously been enacted and can never take place again—an army forming in line of battle in full view, under their very eyes— charging across a space nearly a mile in length over fields of waving grain and anon of stubble and then a smooth expanse—moving with the steadiness of a dress parade, the pride and glory soon to be crushed by an overwhelming heartbreak. . . .

Well, it is all over now. The battle is lost, and many of us are prisoners, many are dead, many wounded, bleeding and dying. Your Soldier lives and mourns and, but for you, my darling, he would rather, a million times rather, be back there with his dead, to sleep for all time in an unknown grave.

After three days young Billy Bayly had learned the Rebel way:[36]

The tempers of our guests changed materially; while they insisted that the Yanks were being whipped and driven from their defensive position we knew to the contrary and told them so. Then the drift of the wagon trains, stragglers and camp followers in general was back in the direction whence they came, and inquiries as to the most direct route to Chambersburg and Hagerstown highways were of promising portent.

History, coming to Gettysburg quite by accident, moved on. Bret Harte wrote:

So raged the battle. You know the rest:
How the rebels, beaten and backward pressed,
Broke at the final charge and ran.
At which John Burns—a practical man—
Shouldered his rifle, unbent his brows,
And then went back to his bees and cows.

VII

Lee, who had invaded Pennsylvania to counterbalance Grant's invasion of Mississippi, had failed. What now in Vicksburg? On that third of July, as Pickett's shattered forces reeled back from their futile charge at Gettysburg, Grant sent a message to Pemberton:[37]

Your note of this date is just received, proposing an armistice for several hours, for the purpose of arranging terms of capitulation through commissioners to be appointed, etc. The useless effusion of blood you propose stopping by this course can be ended at any time you may choose, by the unconditional surrender of the city and garrison.

Men who have shown so much endurance and courage as those now in Vicksburg, will always challenge the respect of an adversary, and I can assure you will be treated with all the respect due to prisoners of war. I do not favor the proposition of appointing commissioners to arrange the terms of capitulation, because I have no terms other than those indicated above.

At three o'clock that afternoon occurred a historic meeting:

. . . Pemberton appeared at the point suggested in my verbal message, accompanied by the same officers who had borne his letter of the morning. Generals Ord, McPherson, Logan and A. J. Smith, and several officers of my staff, accompanied me. Our place of meeting was on a hillside within a few hundred feet of the rebel lines. Near by stood a stunted oak-tree, which was made historical by the event. It was but a short time before the last vestige of its body, root and limb had disappeared, the fragments taken as trophies. Since then the same tree has furnished as many cords of wood, in the shape of trophies, as "The True Cross."

Pemberton and I had served in the same division during part of the Mexican War. I knew him very well therefore, and greeted him as an old acquaintance. He soon asked what terms I proposed to give his army if it surrendered. My answer was the same as proposed in my reply to his letter. Pemberton then said, rather snappishly, "The conference might as well end," and turned abruptly as if to leave. I said, "Very well." General Bowen, I saw, was very anxious that the surrender should be consummated. His manner and remarks while Pemberton and I were talking, showed this. He now proposed that he and one of our generals should have a conference. I had no objection to this, as nothing could be made binding upon me that they might propose. Smith and Bowen accordingly had a conference, during which Pemberton and I, moving a short distance away towards the enemy's lines were in conversation. After awhile Bowen suggested that the Confederate army should be allowed to march out with the honors of war, carrying their small arms and field artillery. This was promptly and unceremoniously rejected. The interview here ended, I agreeing, however, to send a letter giving final terms by ten o'clock that night.

Grant amended his terms in the end, allowing side arms and clothing to officers, one horse each to field, staff and cavalry officers, and to "the rank and file . . . all their clothing, but no other property." Nor was his change of heart a device for saving Pemberton's face—"Had I insisted upon an unconditional surrender there would have been over thirty thousand men to transport to Cairo very much to the inconvenience of the army on the Mississippi." Pemberton "promptly accepted these terms," and on July 4 Grant and his troops had the last laugh on an old tormentor:

During the siege there had been a good deal of friendly sparring between the soldiers of the two armies, on picket and where the lines were close together. All rebels were known as "Johnnies," all Union troops as "Yanks." Often "Johnny" would call: "Well, Yank, when are you coming into town?" The reply was sometimes: "We propose to celebrate the 4th of July there." Sometimes it would be: "We always treat our prisoners with kindness and do not want to hurt them"; or, "We are holding you as prisoners of war while you are feeding yourselves." The garrison, from the commanding general down, undoubtedly expected an assault on the fourth. They knew from the temper of their men it would be successful when made; and that would be a greater humiliation than to surrender. Besides it would be attended with severe loss to them.

The Vicksburg paper, which we received regularly through the courtesy of the rebel pickets, said prior to the fourth, in speaking of the "Yankee" boast that they would take dinner in Vicksburg that day, that the best receipt for cooking a rabbit was "First ketch your rabbit.". . . The last number was issued on the fourth and announced that we had "caught our rabbit." *

* July 3, 1863—Lee defeated at Gettysburg with 3,903 dead, 18,735 wounded and 5,425 missing against Union losses of 3,155 dead, 14,529 wounded and 5,365 missing.

July 4, 1863—Vicksburg surrendered to Grant along with 29,491 prisoners of war.

CHAPTER 26

THE ROCK OF CHICKAMAUGA

EARLY IN THE YEAR 1863 the editors of *Harper's Weekly* asked a question which had been worrying all thoughtful Northerners —"Have We a General Among Us?" The lead editorial for January 17 began: "They say at Washington that we have some thirty-eight to forty Major-Generals, and nearly three hundred Brigadiers; and now the question is, have we one man who can fairly be called a first-class General in the proper meaning of the term?"

One by one the editors ticked them off. McDowell: "respectable . . . but no claim to the first place." McClellan: "prone rather to exaggerate than to underrate an enemy's strength; a man . . . of more science than genius." Burnside: "place . . . undetermined." Grant: will his record at Shiloh "bear the test of inquiry"? Sherman: "a capable officer and a far-seeing man." And so on through Samuel R. Curtis, James G. Blunt and Nathaniel P. Banks.

I

Only one officer drew unqualified praise:[1]

At this present moment . . . the most promising of our soldiers is William S. Rosecrans. This officer was selected by General McClellan at the outbreak of the war, and served under him in Western Virginia. He, like McClellan, had served in the army, resigned, and engaged in scientific and business pursuits. When McClellan was ordered to Washington Rosecrans succeeded him, and thoroughly accomplished his work. He drove the rebels out of Western Virginia, and enabled the people of that State to organize a State government in peace. . . . After a period of idleness, he was sent to Corinth, where he spent some weeks in necessary preparations, knowing that the enemy must attack him if he remained still. The attack came, and resulted not only in the repulse, but in the destruction of the rebel army,* and enabled General Grant to move forward to Oxford. Promoted then to the command of the Army of the Ohio, he spent six weeks at Nashville in concentrating his forces, and accumulating equipments and supplies for the campaign. He moved on 29th December, and after five days' desperate fighting, completely defeated, and "drove" the rebel army under Bragg, which, according to Richmond papers, was "to repossess Nashville within a week."

As a strategist Rosecrans has proved himself second to none. In Western Virginia his combinations were most ingenious, and his foresight wonderful. So at Corinth, where he alone of his officers foresaw the battle, and how it would end. His wonderful mathematical ability, which was remarked at West Point, stood him in good stead. At Murfreesboro he seems to have developed personal gallantry of the Grant order. Twice, at least, in the course of those five days' battles, he saved the day, and repelled the enemy, by galloping into the thick of the fight, and reanimating his troops by the spectacle of his courage. He is a man of enthusiasm, as well as a man of calculation: when his army fights, he is with them. If he pursues the enemy as briskly as he attacked them, none of our Generals will stand higher than Rosecrans.

II

But Rosecrans did not "pursue the enemy." Instead, he held the battered Army of the Cumberland in its camps at Murfreesboro. Against the proddings of the Administration he advanced a succession of arguments—he needed more supplies and forage, more cavalry, more repeating rifles for his mounted troops. Spring came, with green grass for horses and soft winds that dried up the roads; still the Federal commander waited.

Braxton Bragg, commanding the Confederate Army of Tennessee, was equally reluctant to move. Encamped at Tullahoma and Shelbyville, some thirty-five miles south of the Federal position, Bragg trained

---

* The Battle of Corinth, October 3–4, 1862, was a Confederate defeat, but Van Dorn's army was not demolished. Losses are given as follows: Union, 2,520; Confederate, 4,838.

and drilled his men—and at the same time smarted under the distrust of subordinates who, he well knew, dreaded another battle under his command.

By late June 1863, Rosecrans was at last ready. He planned to threaten Bragg's position at Shelbyville, which Rosecrans knew to be strongly fortified, and then slip around the right of the Confederate army—a move which would force Bragg either to fight on ground selected by the enemy, or to retreat.

Major James A. Connolly of the 123rd Illinois Regiment of Mounted Infantry, one of the four regiments that led the advance, described the beginning of the campaign:[2]

On the morning of June 24th, at 3 o'clock, we left camp 5 miles north of Murfreesboro, and started to the "front," in advance of everything. As we passed through the camps in Murfreesboro, the rattle of drums, sounding of bugles, and clatter of wagons, told us plainly that the whole army was to follow in our wake, and we knew full well, from the direction we were taking, that a few hours' march would bring the brigade to some of the strongholds of the enemy, so there was silence in the column as we moved along through the mud, and every ear was strained to catch the sound of the first gun of our advance guard that would tell us of the presence of the enemy.

The report of the first gun echoed through the hills at noon, when the 123rd Illinois found itself a dozen miles southeast of Murfreesboro. Connolly told the story of a sharp engagement:

We pushed ahead rapidly, for we were nearing the formidable "Hoover's Gap," which it was supposed would cost a great many lives to pass through, and our brigade commander determined to surprise the enemy if possible, by a rapid march, and make a bold dash to pass through the "Gap" and hold it with our brigade alone until the rest of the army could get up. We soon came into the camp of a regiment of cavalry which was so much surprised by our sudden appearance that they scattered through the woods and over the hills in every direction, every fellow for himself, and all making the best time they could bareback, on foot and every other way, leaving all their tents, wagons, baggage, commissary stores and indeed everything in our hands, but we didn't stop for anything, on we pushed, our boys, with their Spencer rifles, keeping up a continual popping in front. Soon we reached the celebrated "Gap" on the run.

This "Gap" is formed by a range of hills that run westwardly from the Cumberland Mountains, and the pike runs for about two miles through between these hills; the valley is barely wide enough to admit the passage of two wagons side by side, and the hills upon either side command the valley completely; as we swept through the valley with our 1,500 horsemen on a gallop we noticed the lines of entrenchments crowning the hills, but they were deserted; the enemy was surprised and flying before us, so we pushed onward until we passed entirely through the "Gap," when a puff of white smoke from a hill about half a mile in front of us, then a dull heavy roar, then a shrieking of a shell told us we could advance no further as we had reached their infantry and artillery force. But we had done enough, had advanced 6 miles further than ordered or expected possible, and had taken a point which it was expected would require a large part of the army to take; but the serious question with us now was: "Could we alone hold it in the presence of superior force?" We were at least 12 miles in advance of our army, and from prisoners we learned that we were confronted with 4 brigades of infantry and 4 batteries. . . .

As soon as the enemy opened on us with their artillery we dismounted and formed line of battle on a hill just at the south entrance to the "Gap," and our battery of light artillery was opened on them, a courier was dispatched to the rear to hurry up reinforcements, our horses were sent back some distance out of the way of bursting shells, our regiment was assigned to support the battery, the other three regiments were properly disposed, and not a moment too soon, for these preparations were scarcely completed when the enemy opened on us a terrific fire of shot and shell from five different points, and their masses of infantry, with flags flying, moved out of the woods on our right in splendid style; there were three or four times our number already in sight and still others came pouring out of the woods beyond. Our regiment lay on the hill side in mud and water, the rain pouring down in torrents, while each shell screamed so close to us as to make it seem that the next would tear us to pieces.

Presently the enemy got near enough to us to make a charge on our battery, and on they came; our men are on their feet in an instant and a terrible fire from the "Spencers" * causes the advancing regiment to

* The Spencer repeating rifle—which Lincoln had tested in person, and for which he had suggested an improved sight—began to find its way westward more abundantly after its young inventor, Christopher Spencer, dined in April 1863 with Grant. Morgan, the Rebel raider, had been an enthusiastic champion of the Spencer even earlier.

reel and its colors fall to the ground, but in an instant their colors are up again and on they come, thinking to reach the battery before our guns can be reloaded, but they "reckoned without their host," they didn't know we had the "Spencers," and their charging yell was answered by another terrible volley, and another and another without cessation, until the poor regiment was literally cut to pieces, and but few men of that 20th Tennessee that attempted the charge will ever charge again. During all the rest of the fight at "Hoover's Gap" they never again attempted to take that battery. After the charge they moved four regiments around to our right and attempted to get in our rear, but they were met by two of our regiments posted in the woods, and in five minutes were driven back in the greatest disorder, with a loss of 250 killed and wounded. . . .

We held our ground with continual fighting until 7 o'clock in the evening, when we discovered a battery coming up to our support as fast as the horses could run, and such a cheer as was sent up does one good to hear. In a few minutes our new battery was opened and we all felt better. We were nearly exhausted with the rapid march since before daylight in the morning, yet the prospect of assistance nerved the men to maintain the unequal conflict a little longer. About half past seven in the evening along came a weary, jaded regiment of infantry, trying to double quick, but it was all they could do to march at all; we greeted them with such lusty cheers as seemed to inspire them with new vigor, and they were soon in position; then came two more regiments of infantry, weary and footsore, but hurrying the best they could to the dance of death; then just at dark came our Division Commander, with his staff, and riding along our lines gave words of cheer to his brigade that had fought so long and well. In a few minutes up came General Thomas, our corps commander, his grave face beaming with delight as he grasped our brigade commander by the hand and said: "You have saved the lives of a thousand men by your gallant conduct today. I didn't expect to get this Gap for three days."

III

In nine days Rosecrans forced Bragg from his strongly fortified positions in central Tennessee to Chattanooga—and lost fewer than 600 men (killed, wounded, and missing) out of almost 60,000.

Rosecrans' achievement was a masterpiece of both strategy and tactics, yet his success was due in part to the Confederate commander. Bragg had never really intended to fight unless he was attacked behind the breastworks at Shelbyville. Expecting to retreat, but expecting also

*to fight a battle somewhere in the vicinity of Chattanooga, he planned
to draw a part of the Federal army away from his front by permitting
brash John Hunt Morgan, now a brigadier general commanding a
cavalry division, to make a raid into Kentucky.*

*For the last three weeks in June, Morgan lay poised in southern
Kentucky, about seventy-five miles northeast of Nashville, Tennessee.
On July 2, as Bragg was nearing Chattanooga, Morgan, with 2,460 men
and four pieces of artillery, crossed the Cumberland River and headed
north. On the Fourth his troopers ran into a stubborn Federal regiment
stationed at Columbia near the Green River. In half an hour Morgan's
men took a sound licking, drew off, found a ford at some distance from
the town, and swung around it. Next day they had a sharp skirmish at
Lebanon but drove back the Union defenders and captured a large
quantity of rifles, ammunition, and supplies.*

*Bragg had ordered Morgan to confine his operations to Kentucky,
but the Confederate cavalryman had other ideas. Indiana and Ohio
were his real goals. A raid into Kentucky would take some of the
pressure off the retreating Bragg, but it would not help him in the battle
that would soon follow. Morgan reasoned that an invasion of the
North would create panic, and force Rosecrans to send thousands of
troops in pursuit. And what a hell of an adventure it would be!*

*After the skirmish at Lebanon, Morgan raced toward the Ohio River.
On July 8 he reached the town of Brandenburg on the Kentucky side.
An advance party had already captured two river steamers. The Confederates began to embark. A Federal gunboat tried to impede the
crossing but did little damage. By midnight Morgan's two brigades
were across.*

*Morgan headed north toward Corydon, some fifteen miles from the
river. Basil W. Duke, Morgan's brother-in-law who commanded the
Second Kentucky Cavalry, described the invasion of Indiana:*[3]

A "great fear" had fallen upon the inhabitants of that part of the
State of Indiana. They had left their houses, with open doors and unlocked larders, and had fled to the thickets and "caves of the hills." At
the houses at which I stopped, everything was just in the condition in
which the fugitive owners had left it, an hour or two before. A bright
fire was blazing upon the kitchen hearth, bread half made up was in the
tray, and many indications convinced us that we had interrupted preparations for supper. The chickens were strolling before the door with a
confidence that was touching, but misplaced. General Morgan rode by

soon afterward, and was induced to "stop all night." We completed the preparations, so suddenly abandoned, and made the best show for Indiana hospitality that was possible under the disturbing circumstances.

MORGAN'S RAID

Morgan occupied Corydon on July 9. A local newspaper revealed how Colonel Duke took advantage of Indiana hospitality:

His men commenced pillaging the stores of Douglass, Denbo & Co., and Samuel J. Wright. Mr. W. was not at home, and they took what they pleased without let or hindrance. Mr. Denbo was sent for by Captain Charlton Morgan, the General's brother, and compelled to open his store. Everything in the shape of ready-made clothing, hats, caps, boots, shoes, etc., was taken, Captain Morgan taking a piece of fine gray cassimere, out of which to make a suit for "John." For all these goods, amounting in value to about $3,500, Mr. Denbo received the sum of $140 in Confederate scrip, some of which was dated as late as May, 1863. Mr. Wright's loss was probably somewhat larger than that of Mr. Denbo. The drug store of Dr. Reader, and several other establishments, were also relieved of portions of their contents. The hardware and drug store of Slaughter & Slemmons was saved, and is said to have been guarded, owing to the influence of a relative of Mr. Slaughter in the rebel command.

The store of the late Mr. Vance was spared, on the representation that the proprietor had been buried the day before, and nothing was taken from it.

Upon each of the three flouring-mills in Corydon a levy was made of $1,000, to be paid in consideration of Morgan's refraining to burn them. The chivalry, however, graciously condescended to receive 2,100 in greenbacks in liquidation of their claim upon the mill property.

The rebels paid no attention to the rights of private citizens or families. They robbed Mr. Hisey, Treasurer, of $750 in money; stole all the clothing of Judge F. W. Matthis, except what he had on; stole a pair of fine boots from Mr. P. B. Douglass, and committed numerous other petty thefts of a similar character. They entered private houses with impunity, ate all the victuals the ladies had cooked for the Home Guards, and compelled them to cook more.

Morgan made a feint at Cincinnati, which he had no intention of taking even had he been able, and then headed east. A correspondent of a Cincinnati newspaper recorded the raider's progress:

EAST SYCAMORE, HAMILTON COUNTY, OHIO. . . . On Tuesday, the 14th instant, at early dawn, the inhabitants hereabout were aroused from slumber by the clattering of hoofs upon the stony pike, and the clanking of *stirrups* (I suppose, as I didn't see any sabers or the like). On peeping through the window, I recognized them immediately as secesh, from their hard looks, their clothes of many colors and fashions, and their manner of riding. They did not ride in any kind of order, unless it was *disorder*. As many as could, rode abreast. Some galloped, some trotted, and others allowed their horses to walk slowly while they slept in the saddles. They were not uniformly dressed. Some wore a whole suit of the well-known blue which designates our soldiers; others had part of a suit, but most of them were arrayed in citizens' garb. Some were barefooted, some bareheaded, and one, I noticed, wore a huge green veil . . . Some wore jackets outside of their coats, as though they had dressed in a hurry. . . . Some had ladies' gaiters, dress-patterns, and the like, protruding from their pockets; and one bootless, hatless, shirtless being held his *suspenderless* pants with one hand, while he held the bridle with the other, and heeled his horse to a gallop. . . .

They were evidently very tired and sleepy, and, judging from their questions to each other, "How far do you think the blue-jackets are behind?" I should say as much frightened as we were. "How far is it to Cincinnati?" and "Have you yesterday's paper?" were the principal questions asked. In some houses of this vicinity, they turned over beds, peeped into cellars, cupboards, drawers, closets, and even babies' cradles, in search of arms, ammunition, "greenbacks," and *sich*, while others were not disturbed. They helped themselves very liberally to such eatables as could be found, besides ordering the women to prepare more. Of course, they took horses. They just *gobbled* up everybody's, except—well, perhaps his were lame, blind, or fractious. Generally, they made no distinction between the property of Copperheads and that of "Abolitionists," as they call all unconditional Union men. 'Cause why? They either did not *know* their friends, or else they considered the Northern Butternuts beneath the respect of Southern rebels, horse-thieves, freebooters, guerillas, or whatever else they may call themselves. . . .

Most persons in this part of the world considered discretion the better part of valor, and held their temper until the last invader had vanished. Like a sudden clap of thunder Morgan came among us, and passed off to the east like a meteor, leaving the natives gazing after him in stupefied horror, rubbing their eyes, and wondering whether it was all the dream of a nightmare, or a reality.

On July 19 two Federal forces, numbering 8,000, caught up with Morgan at Buffington on the Ohio River. Seven hundred Confederates were taken prisoner, but Morgan with the remaining 1,200 scurried northward on a hopeless expedition. Six days later all were captured.

Basil W. Duke, historian and apologist of the expedition, called the raid "incomparably the most brilliant of the entire war":[4]

It was not an expedition started from a point impregnably garrisoned, to dash by a well marked path to another point occupied by a friendly army. It differed from even the boldest of Confederate raids, not only in that it was vastly more extended, but also in the nerve with which the great natural obstacles were placed between the little band with which it was undertaken and home, and the unshrinking audacity with which that slight force penetrated into a populous and intensely hostile territory, and confidently exposed itself to such tremendous odds, and such overwhelming disadvantages. Over one hundred thousand men were in arms to catch Morgan (although not all employed at one time and place), and every advantage in the way of transporting troops, obtaining information, and disposing forces to intercept or oppose him, was possessed by his enemy, and yet his wily strategy enabled him to make his way to the river, at the very point where he had contemplated recrossing it when he started from Tennessee; and he was prevented from recrossing and effecting his escape (which would then have been certain) only by the river having risen at a season at which it had not risen for more than twenty years before.

The objects of the raid were accomplished. General Bragg's retreat was unmolested by any flanking forces of the enemy, and I think that military men . . . will pronounce that this expedition delayed for weeks the fall of East Tennessee, and prevented the timely reinforcement of Rosecrans by troops that would otherwise have participated in the battle of Chickamauga. . . .

To have, in our turn, been invaders, to have carried the war north of the Ohio, to have taught the people, who for long months had been pouring invading hosts into the South, something of the agony and terror of invasion—to have made them fly in fear from their homes, although they returned to find those homes not laid in ashes; to have scared them with the sound of hostile bugles, although no signals were sounded for flames and destruction—these luxuries were cheap at almost any price. It would have been an inexpiable shame if, in all the Confederate army, there had been no body of men found to carry the war, however briefly, across the Ohio, and Morgan by this raid saved us, at least, that disgrace.

Three-quarters of a century later Stanley Horn, a Southern historian justly proud of Confederate prowess, made a more realistic comment:[5]

The raid north of the Ohio was a showy affair and struck terror into Hoosier and Buckeye communities, but it was without military significance or possibilities. . . . Before the month was over Morgan and practically all his men had been captured and were locked up in various Northern prisons—Morgan himself and most of his officers in the Ohio State Penitentiary at Columbus. He escaped from prison in

late November and made his way back to the Confederacy, but his days
of usefulness to the Army of Tennessee were over.

IV

*Morgan jabbed at the North. New York City took a belly blow that
staggered the Lincoln Administration.*

*Behind four days of bloody rioting lay a deep, bitter resentment over
the draft. The government, nevertheless, drove ahead with its conscription program. The first drawing of names took place on Saturday,
July 11. Crowds gathered at the office of the provost marshal, but the
people were good-natured, even jocular. Over Sunday their temper
changed. As men read their names in the lists of those drawn for
service, and realized that they faced three years of hardship and
danger, they gave themselves up to excitement and rage.*

*Monday, July 13, brought the incident that led to the four bloody
days. At the draft office of the ninth district, 677 Third Avenue, the
drawing was resumed. Reporters for* Frank Leslie's Illustrated Newspaper *were on hand:*[6]

A crowd had meanwhile assembled, and towards eleven o'clock, as
the name of Z. Shay, 633 West 42 street, was called, a stone was thrown
through the window, and the crowd pouring in almost in a moment
destroyed the wheel, the papers, books, everything connected with the
draft, and everything in the rooms, the officers barely escaping with
their lives. . . .

Had it stopped here, the riot might have been regarded as a kind of
spontaneous ebullition of excited men; but they proceeded to fire the
building, the upper stories of which were occupied by many families,
thus perilling hundreds of lives. They then cut the telegraph wires, and
when the firemen arrived prevented them from extinguishing the fire.
The house, with one on each side, was soon in ruins. The small force of
police was powerless, and the only force sent was a squad of 40 soldiers,
who were speedily attacked, and, after they had fired a volley of blank
cartridges, disarmed and routed, many of them horribly beaten. The
police were then attacked and, although they fought well, were similarly
treated. . . .

A reporter for Harper's Weekly *captured the terrible immediacy of
the riot:*[7]

MASSACRE OF A NEGRO IN CLARKSON STREET

One of the first victims to the insane fury of the rioters was a negro cartman residing in Carmine Street. A mob of men and boys seized this unfortunate man on Monday evening, and having beaten him until he was in a state of insensibility, dragged him to Clarkson Street, and hung him from a branch of one of the trees that shade the sidewalk by St. John's Cemetery. The fiends did not stop here, however. Procuring long sticks, they tied rags and straw to the ends of them, and with these torches they danced round their victim, setting fire to his clothes, and burning him almost to a cinder. The remains of the wretched negro hung there till near daylight on Tuesday morning, when they were removed by the police. This atrocious murder was perpetrated within ten feet of consecrated ground, where the white headstones of the cemetery are seen gleaming through the wooden railing.

THE MURDER OF COLONEL O'BRIEN

As I arrived at the corner of Thirty-fourth Street and Second Avenue, the rioters were dragging the body of a man along the sidewalk with a rope. It was difficult to obtain any information from the bystanders, who were terror-struck by the savage fury of the mob. I ascertained, however, that the body was that of Colonel O'Brien of the Eleventh New York. There was not a policeman or soldier within view of whom inquiry could be made. "What did they kill him for?" I asked a man leaning against a lamp-post. "Bedad I suppose it was to square accounts," replied he. "There was a woman and child kilt there below a while ago by the sojers, and in coorse a sojer had to suffer." The brutal roughs who surrounded the body fired pistols at it occasionally, and pelted it with brickbats and paving-stones. The tenacity of life of this unfortunate victim is said to have been remarkable, and those who entered the yard where the body lay some hours later state that breathing was even then perceptible.

SACKING OF A DRUG-STORE

Sated with blood, the rioters now turned their attention to plunder. A drug-store close by where Colonel O'Brien lay was completely riddled by them, the doors and windows being smashed in with clubs and stones. Women hovered upon the skirts of the crowd, and received the articles as they were thrown or handed from the store. One fellow rushed out with a closely-packed valise, which he opened in the street.

The clothes and other things contained in it were eagerly seized and contended for by boys and women standing around. There were a number of letters in it, and some documents with seals, which were probably of value to the owner; but these were savagely torn and trampled under foot by the disappointed plunderers. A woman sat upon the steps near by, and read out portions of one of the letters amidst the jeers of her ribald companions. Another passed me waving in triumph a large parchment manuscript of many pages.

ATTACK UPON THE CLOTHING-STORE OF MESSRS. BROOKS BROTHERS

From the first of the riot clothing appeared to be a great desideratum among the roughs composing the mob. On Monday evening a large number of marauders paid a visit to the extensive clothing-store of Messrs. Brooks Brothers, at the corner of Catharine and Cherry streets. Here they helped themselves to such articles as they wanted, after which they might be seen dispersing in all directions, laden with their ill-gotten booty.

THE GERMAN TAILORS

Away up in the Avenues the German tailors were sad sufferers, in consequence of the demand for confiscable apparel. I saw an able-bodied ruffian emerging from a tailor's shop with the breast of his shirt crammed full of pieces of dry-goods of all colors. His arms and shoulders were laden with clothing. He had a new soft hat stuck upon the top of his greasy cap, while in one hand he carried a "nest" of hats of assorted sizes, and a bunch of gorgeous, many-colored ties fluttered from his arm as he ran. "Why did they riddle that shop?" I asked of a woman who was standing by. "Sure the owner is a Jarman," was the reply. Here an Irishman of the non-combative type chimed in, saying, "No, it wasn't that at all; it's becase the boys wanted the clothes. But it's a shame to stale them, any how, and no good ever come of the likes." "Begorra that's thrue for you, Frank Tully," remarked his companion; and thereupon they both expressed themselves greatly in favor of virtue, and opposed to the scenes of violence passing around us. On returning down the Avenue, a quarter of an hour later, I recognized the virtuous Frank Tully and his friend, in an alley-way, busily engaged in trying on some new trowsers, which did not look as if they had been just bought and paid for.

A GORILLA AT LARGE

During the entire withdrawal of the police and military from large districts of the city many highway robberies must have been perpetrated. Coming down Third Avenue, I passed a group of young rowdies who were amusing themselves with snapping their pistols. One threw his revolver high into the air, and caught it by the barrel as it came down, bragging at the same time that it was both loaded and cocked. A few steps further on I found myself face to face with a fearful-looking desperado, who came suddenly upon me round a corner.

"Hello me buck!" cried he; "don't be in a hurry, now. Hand over your cane; and fork out all you've got."

Fortunately he was somewhat drunk, and he grasped in his right hand a bundle of "greenbacks," which seemed to embarrass him a little. As he still pressed upon me, however, I turned to the young pistoliers, saying,

"Boys, here's a fellow wants to draft me; are we going to stand that?"

This created a diversion in my favor; and when I saw that the attention of the young rowdies was attracted to the money in the desperado's hand I improved the opportunity and proceeded up a by-street, at an accelerated pace. Had I struck him with my stick, which was my first impulse, I should most assuredly have fallen a victim to the blind fury of the young pistoliers. Probably the right owner of the "greenbacks" fared much worse than I did, independent of the loss of his money.

On Tuesday, July 14, a larger, bolder mob continued the depredations of the day before. Governor Seymour hurried to the city from Long Branch, New Jersey, and from the steps of the City Hall pleaded with the crowd to disperse. At the same time, troops were ordered in—the garrisons of the forts in the harbor, a company from West Point. The police, infuriated, shot to kill. On Wednesday the suspension of the draft was announced, and New York militia regiments from the Army of the Potomac began to patrol the streets. Chaos came to an end; streetcars and omnibuses covered their routes, men returned to work. The riot had taken many lives—the estimate in killed and wounded was 1,000—and had damaged property to the extent of $1,500,000.

To what end? James Ford Rhodes answered the question:[8]

The draft was only temporarily interrupted. Strenuous precautions were taken to insure order during its continuance. Ten thousand infantry and three batteries of artillery—"picked troops including the regulars"—were sent to New York City from the Army of the Potomac; the First Division of the New York State National Guard was ordered upon duty; and the governor by proclamation counselled and admonished the citizens to submit to the law of Congress. August 19 the draft was resumed and proceeded with entire peacefulness. It went on generally throughout the country, and while it did not actually furnish many soldiers to the army, owing to the numerous exemptions under the statute and the large number of those drafted who paid the commutation money, it stimulated enlistments by inducing States, counties, cities, and towns to add to the government bounty other bounties sufficient to prevail upon men to volunteer and fill their respective quotas.

V

A month later the North suffered another brutal blow. At dawn on August 21, 1863, the guerrilla chieftain William Clarke Quantrill rode into Lawrence, Kansas, with a band of four hundred men. In his twenty-six years Quantrill had been schoolteacher, horse thief, and murderer. In 1863 he was a regularly commissioned Confederate captain, but the Union authorities had formally branded him an outlaw. Ardently proslavery, Quantrill had a grudge against Kansas, especially the antislavery center of Lawrence.

J. S. Boughton, Lawrence publisher, collected eyewitness accounts of the "massacre" for a brief history that suffers nothing in realism for having been published twenty years after the event:[9]

After . . . all fears of resistance were removed, the ruffians scattered in small gangs to all parts of the town in search of plunder and blood. The order was "to burn every house, and kill every man." Almost every house was visited and robbed, and the men found in them killed or left, according to the character or whim of the captors. Some of these seemed completely brutalized, while others showed some signs of remaining humanity. One lady said that as gang after gang came to her house, she always met them herself, and tried to get them to talking. If she only got them to talking, she could get at what little humanity was left in them. . . .

It is doubtful whether the world has ever witnessed such a scene of horror—certainly not outside the annals of savage warfare. . . . The carnage was much worse from the fact that the citizens could not believe that men could be such fiends. . . . Few expected a wholesale murder. Many who could have escaped, therefore, remained and were slain. . . .

We can only give a few of the incidents of the massacre as specimens of the whole. The scenes of horror we describe must be multiplied till the amount reaches one hundred and eighty, the number of killed and wounded.

Gen. Collamore, Mayor of the city, was awakened by their shouts around the house. His house was evidently well known, and they struck for it to prevent his taking measures for defense. When he looked out, the house was surrounded. Escape was impossible. There was but one hiding place—the well. He at once went into the well. The enemy went into the house and searched for the owner, swearing and threatening all the while. Failing to find him, they fired the house and waited round to see it burn. Mrs. Collamore went out and spoke to her husband while the fire was burning. But the house was so near the well that when the flames burst out they shot over the well, and the fire fell in. When the flames subsided, so that the well could be approached, nothing could be seen of Mr. Collamore or the man who descended into the well with him. After the rebels had gone, Mr. Lowe, an intimate friend of Gen. Collamore, went at once down the well to seek for him. The rope supporting him broke, and he also died in the well, and three bodies were drawn from its cold water.

At Dr. Griswold's there were four families. The doctor and his lady had just returned the evening before from a visit east. Hon. S. M. Thorp, State Senator, Mr. J. C. Trask, Editor of State Journal, Mr. H. W. Baker, grocer, with their wives, were boarding in Dr. Griswold's family. The house was attacked about the same time as Gen. Collamore's. They called for the men to come out. When they did not obey very readily, they assured them "they should not be harmed—if the citizens quietly surrender, it might save the town." This idea brought them out at once. Mr. Trask said, "if it will help save the town, let us go." They went down stairs and out of doors. The ruffians ordered them to get in line, and to march before them towards town. They had scarcely gone twenty feet from the yard before the whole four were shot down. Dr. Griswold and Mr. Trask were killed at once. Mr. Thorp and Mr. Baker wounded, but apparently dead. The ladies attempted to reach their husbands from the house, but were driven back. A guard was stationed just below, and every time any of the ladies attempted to go from the house to their dying friends, this guard would dash up at full speed, and with oaths and threats drive them back. After the bodies had lain about half an hour, a gang rode up, rolled them over, and shot them again. . . .

The most brutal murder was that of Judge Carpenter. Several gangs called at his house and robbed him of all he had—but his genial manner was too much for them, and they all left him alive and his house standing. Towards the last, another gang came, more brutal than the rest. They asked him where he was from. He replied, "New York." "It is you New York fellows that are doing all the mischief," one replied, and drew his revolver to shoot him. Mr. Carpenter ran into the house, up stairs, then down again, the ruffian after him and firing at him at every turn. He finally eluded them and slipped into the cellar. He was already badly wounded, so that the blood lay in pools in the cellar where he stood for a few minutes. His hiding place was soon discovered, and he was driven out of the cellar into the yard and shot again. He fell mortally wounded. His wife threw herself on to him and covered him with her person to shield him from further violence. The ruffian deliberately walked around her to find a place to shoot under her, and finally raised her arm and put his revolver under, and fired so that she could see the ball enter his head. They then fired the house. . . .

The rebels were in town from about five o'clock until nine. . . . The whole number killed was about one hundred and fifty.

VI

By holing up in Chattanooga, Bragg made that point the target of the Army of the Cumberland. Characteristically, Rosecrans planned carefully. While he threatened the Confederate position from the northwest he would put the main body of his army across the Tennessee River to the southwest. If he succeeded, Bragg would be compelled to retreat, and Rosecrans could pounce on the Confederate flank and fight a battle under conditions of his choice.

The strategy worked. The Army of the Cumberland moved forward on August 16, and Bragg acted as Rosecrans hoped he would. As the Federal army closed in, Bragg pulled out of Chattanooga, but instead of running away, he halted a few miles south of the town and gave every indication of offering battle. Rosecrans suddenly realized that his army was widely dispersed and in no position to fight a major battle. Frantically he tried to pull the scattered corps together.

Charles A. Dana, newly appointed Assistant Secretary of War and on the ground to prod Rosecrans into action—unnecessarily as it happened —described the situation of the Army of the Cumberland on the day before a bloody conflict:[10]

By noon of September 18th the concentration was practically complete. Our army then lay up and down the valley, with West Chicka-

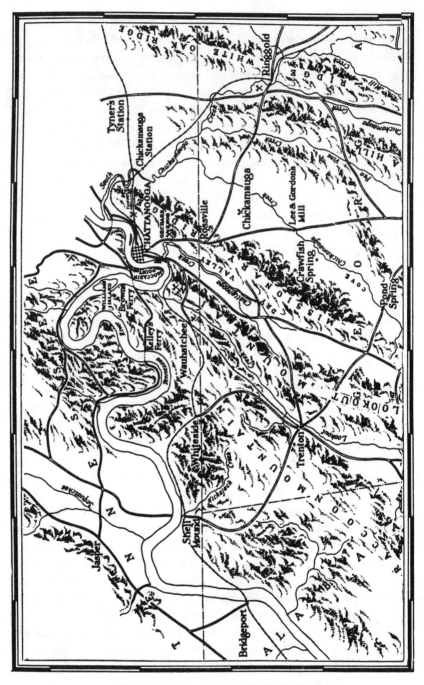

CHATTANOOGA AND CHICKAMAUGA

From *Atlas of American History*

mauga Creek in front of the greater part of the line. The left was held by Crittenden, the center by Thomas, and the right by McCook, whose troops were now all in the valley except one brigade. The army had not concentrated any too soon, for that very afternoon the enemy appeared on our left, and a considerable engagement occurred. It was said at headquarters that a battle was certain the next day. The only point Rosecrans had not determined at five o'clock on the afternoon of the 18th was whether to make a night march and fall on Bragg at daylight or to await his onset.

But that night it became pretty clear to all that Bragg's plan was to push by our left into Chattanooga. This compelled another rapid movement by the left down the Chickamauga. By a tiresome night march Thomas moved down behind Crittenden and below Lee and Gordon's Mills, taking position on our extreme left. Crittenden followed, connecting with Thomas's right, and thus taking position in the center. McCook's corps also extended downstream to the left. . . . These movements were hurriedly made, and the troops, especially those of Thomas, were very much exhausted by their efforts to get into position.

On the next day—September 19—the battle began in earnest. Dana summarized the fighting as it affected the Army of the Cumberland:

About nine o'clock . . . at Crawfish Spring, where the general headquarters were, we heard firing on our left, and reports at once came in that the battle had begun there, Bragg being in command of the enemy. Thomas had barely headed the Confederates off from Chattanooga. We remained at Crawfish Springs on this day until after one o'clock, waiting for the full proportions of the conflict to develop. When it became evident that the battle was being fought entirely on our left, Rosecrans removed his headquarters nearer to the scene, taking a little house near Lee and Gordon's Mills, known as the Widow Glenn's. Although closer to the battle, we could see no more of it here than at Crawfish Springs, the conflict being fought altogether in a thick forest, and being invisible to outsiders. . . .

It was not until after dark that firing ceased and final reports began to come in. From these we found that the enemy had been defeated in his attempt to turn and crush our left flank and secure possession of the Chattanooga roads, but that he was not wholly defeated, for he still held his ground in several places, and was preparing, it was believed, to renew the battle the next day.

That evening Rosecrans decided that if Bragg did not retreat he would renew the fight at daylight, and a council of war was held at our headquarters at the Widow Glenn's, to which all the corps and division commanders were summoned. . . . Rosecrans began by asking each of the corps commanders for a report on the condition of his troops and of the position they occupied; also for his opinion of what was to be done. Each proposition was discussed by the entire council as it was made. General Thomas was so tired—he had not slept at all the night before, and he had been in battle all day—that he went to sleep every minute. Every time Rosecrans spoke to him he would straighten up and answer, but he always said the same thing, "I would strengthen the left," and then he would be asleep, sitting up in his chair. General Rosecrans, to the proposition to strengthen the left, made always the same reply, "Where are we going to take it from?"

After the discussion was ended, Rosecrans gave his orders for the disposition of the troops on the following day. Thomas's corps was to remain on the left with his line somewhat drawn in, but substantially as he was at the close of the day. McCook was to close on Thomas and cover the position at Widow Glenn's, and Crittenden was to have two divisions in reserve near the junction of McCook's and Thomas's lines, to be able to succor either. These orders were written for each corps commander. They were also read in the presence of all, and the plans fully explained. Finally, after everything had been said, hot coffee was brought in, and then McCook was called upon to sing the Hebrew Maiden. McCook sang the song, and then the council broke up and the generals went away.

This was about midnight, and, as I was very tired, I lay down on the floor to sleep, beside Captain Horace Porter, who was at that time Rosecrans' chief of ordnance. There were cracks in the floor of the Widow Glenn's house, and the wind blew up under us. We would go to sleep, and then the wind would come up so cold through the cracks that it would wake us up, and we would turn over together to keep warm.

General J. S. Fullerton, chief of staff to General Gordon Granger, commanding the Federal reserve, described the climactic fighting of September 20—a day of wild but unco-ordinated charges and counter-charges, a day of slaughter fatal to the careers of both commanding generals, a day when a Virginian who had remained loyal to the Union won the sobriquet by which he is still known:[11]

The morning of Sunday, the 20th, opened with a cloudless sky, but a fog had come up from the warm water of the Chickamauga and hung over the battle-field until 9 o'clock. A silence of desertion was in the front. This quiet continued till nearly 10 o'clock; then, as the peaceful tones of the churchbells, rolling over the land from the east, reached the meridian of Chickamauga, they were made dissonant by the murderous roar of the artillery of Bishop Polk, who was opening the battle on Thomas's front [the left or northern flank of the Federal line]. Granger, who had been ordered at all hazards to hold fast where he was, listened and grew impatient. Shortly before 10 o'clock, calling my attention to a great column of dust moving from our front toward the point from which came the sound of battle, he said, "They are concentrating over there. That is where we ought to be." The corps flag marked his headquarters in an open field near the Ringgold road. He walked up and down in front of his flag, nervously pulling his beard. Once stopping, he said, "Why the hell does Rosecrans keep me here? There is nothing in front of us now. There is the battle"—pointing in the direction of Thomas. Every moment the sounds of battle grew louder, while the many columns of dust rolling together here mingled with the smoke that hung over the scene.

At 11 o'clock, with Granger, I climbed a high hayrick nearby. We sat there for ten minutes listening and watching. Then Granger jumped up, thrust his glass into its case, and exclaimed with an oath:

"I am going to Thomas, orders or no orders!"

"And if you go," I replied, "it may bring disaster to the army and you to a court-martial."

"There's nothing in our front now but ragtag, bobtail cavalry," he replied. "Don't you see Bragg is piling his whole army on Thomas? I am going to his assistance."

. . . Thomas was nearly four miles away. The day had now grown very warm, yet the troops marched rapidly over the narrow road, which was covered ankle-deep with dust that rose in suffocating clouds. Completely enveloped in it, the moving column swept along like a desert sandstorm. Two miles from the point of starting, and three-quarters of a mile from the left of the road, the enemy's skirmishers and a section of artillery opened fire on us from an open wood. This force had worked round Thomas's left, and was then partly in his rear. Granger halted to feel them. Soon becoming convinced that it was only a large party of observation, he again started his column and pushed rapidly forward. . . .

A little farther on we were met by a staff-officer sent by General Thomas to discover whether we were friends or enemies; he did not know whence friends could be coming, and the enemy appeared to be approaching from all directions. All of this shattered Army of the Cumberland left on the field was with Thomas; but not more than one-fourth of the men of the army who went into battle at the opening were there. Thomas's loss in killed and wounded during the two days had been dreadful. As his men dropped out his line was contracted to half its length. Now its flanks were bent back, conforming to ridges shaped like a horse-shoe.

On the part of Thomas and his men there was no thought but that of fighting. He was a soldier who had never retreated, who had never been defeated. He stood immovable, the "Rock of Chickamauga." Never had soldiers greater love for a commander. He imbued them with his spirit, and their confidence in him was sublime.

To the right of Thomas's line was a gorge, then a high ridge, nearly at right angles thereto, running east and west. . . . Confeder-ates . . . were passing through the gorge . . . ; divisions were forming on this ridge for an assault; to their left the guns of a battery were being unlimbered for an enfilading fire. There was not a man to send against the force on the ridge, none to oppose this impending as-sault. The enemy saw the approaching colors of the Reserve Corps and hesitated.

At 1 o'clock Granger shook hands with Thomas. Something was said about forming to fight to the right and rear.

"Those men must be driven back," said Granger, pointing to the gorge and ridge. "Can you do it?" asked Thomas.

"Yes. My men are fresh, and they are just the fellows for that work. They are raw troops, and they don't know any better than to charge up there."

Granger quickly sent Aleshire's battery of 3-inch rifle guns which he brought up to Thomas's left to assist in repelling another assault about to be made on the Kelly farm front. Whitaker's and Mitchell's brigades under Steedman were wheeled into position and projected against the enemy in the gorge and on the ridge. With ringing cheers they advanced in two lines by double-quick—over open fields, through weeds waist-high, through a little valley, then up the ridge. The enemy opened on them first with artillery, then with a murderous musketry fire. When well up the ridge the men, almost exhausted, were halted for breath. They lay on the ground two or three minutes, then came the command, "Forward!" Brave, bluff old Steedman, with a regimental flag in his hand, led the way. On went the lines, firing as they ran and bravely receiving a deadly and continuous fire from the enemy on the summit. The Confederates began to break and in another minute were flying down the southern slope of the ridge. In twenty minutes from the beginning of the charge the ridge had been carried. . . .

The enemy massed a force to retake the ridge. They came before our men had rested; twice they assaulted and were driven back. During one assault, as the first line came within range of our muskets, it halted, apparently hesitating, when we saw a colonel seize a flag, wave it over his head, and rush forward. The whole line instantly caught his enthusiasm, and with a wild cheer followed, only to be hurled back again. Our men ran down the ridge in pursuit. In the midst of a group of Confederate dead and wounded they found the brave colonel dead, the flag he carried spread over him where he fell.

Soon after 5 o'clock Thomas rode to the left of his line, leaving Granger the ranking officer at the center. The ammunition of both Thomas's and Granger's commands was now about exhausted. . . . The cartridge-boxes of both our own and the enemy's dead within reach had been emptied by our men. When it was not yet 6 o'clock, and Thomas was still on the left of his line, Brannan rushed up to Granger, saying, "The enemy are forming for another assault; we have not another round of ammunition—what shall we do?" "Fix bayonets and go for them," was the reply. Along the whole line ran the order, "Fix bayonets." On came the enemy—our men were lying down. "Forward," was sounded. In one instant they were on their feet. Forward they went to meet the charge. The enemy fled. So impetuous was this countercharge that one regiment, with empty muskets and empty cartridge-boxes, broke through the enemy's line, which, closing in their rear, carried them off as in the undertow.

One more feeble assault was made by the enemy; then the day closed, and the battle of Chickamauga was over.

Granger, proudly recording victory, was speaking for only the fragment commanded by the intrepid Thomas. The bulk of the Army of the Cumberland had been routed. General John Beatty, whose brigade was in line not far from Granger's troops, told a different story:[12]

About four o'clock we saw away off to our rear the banners and glittering guns of a division coming toward us, and we became agitated by doubt and hope. Are they friends or foes? The thunder, as of a thousand anvils, still goes on in our front. Men fall around us like leaves in autumn. Thomas, Garfield, Wood, and others are in consultation below the hill just in rear of Harker. The approaching troops are said to be ours, and we feel a throb of exultation. Before they arrive we ascertain that the division is Steedman's; and finally, as they come up, I recognize my old friend Colonel Mitchell, of the One Hundred and Thirteenth. They go into action on our right, and as they press forward the roar of musketry redoubles; the battle seems to be working off in that direction. There is now a comparative lull in our front, and I ride over to the right and become involved in a regiment that has been thrown out of line and into confusion by another regiment that retreated through it in disorder. I assist Colonel Mitchell in rallying it, and it goes into the fight again. Returning to my old place, I find that disorganized bodies of men are coming rapidly from the left, in regiments, companies, squads, and singly. I meet General Wood and ask if I shall not halt and reorganize them. He tells me to do so; but I find the task impossible. They do not recognize me as their commander, and most of them will not obey my orders. Some few, indeed, I manage to hold together; but the great mass drift by me to the woods in the rear. The dead are lying everywhere; the wounded are continually passing to the rear; the thunder of the guns and roll of musketry are unceasing and unabated until nightfall. Then the fury of the battle gradually dies away, and finally we have a silence, broken only by a cheer here and there along the enemy's line.

"Old Pete" Longstreet, who had arrived on the field the day before with 5,000 men from the Army of Northern Virginia, also saw the battle end. His emotions were different from Beatty's:[13]

The last of my reserve, Trigg's brigade, gave us new strength, and Preston gained Snodgrass Hill. The trampled ground and bushy woods were left to those who were too much worn to escape the rapid strides of the heroic Confederates. The left wing swept forward, and the right sprang to the broad Chattanooga highway. Like magic the Union army had melted away in our presence. A few hundred prisoners were picked up by both wings as they met, to burst their throats in loud huzzas. The Army of Tennessee knew how to enjoy its first grand victory. The dews of twilight hung heavy about the trees as if to hold down the voice of victory; but the two lines nearing as they advanced joined their continuous shouts in increasing volume, not as the burstings from the cannon's mouth, but in a tremendous swell of heroic harmony that seemed almost to lift from their roots the great trees of the forest.

Before greetings and congratulations upon the success had passed it was night, and the mild beams of the quartering moon were more suggestive of Venus than of Mars. The haversacks and ammunition supplies were ordered replenished, and the Confederate army made its bivouac on the ground it had gained in the first pronounced victory in the West, and one of the most stubbornly contested battles of the war.

In midafternoon, convinced that Chickamauga was lost, Rosecrans rode off the field to Chattanooga to prepare to receive the remnants of his shattered army. To Halleck, Rosecrans sent a dismal dispatch: "We have met with a serious disaster. . . . Enemy overwhelmed us, drove our right, pierced our centre, and scattered troops there." Dana, also in Chattanooga, wired Washington: "Chickamauga is as fatal a name in our history as Bull Run."

A few hours later a future President of the United States, General James A. Garfield, Rosecrans' chief of staff, who had kept his head while his commander had panicked, put the day's fighting in proper perspective. Casualty figures confirmed Garfield's estimate of the situation. Union losses were: killed, 1,657; wounded, 9,756; missing, 4,757. Confederate losses were: killed, 2,312; wounded, 14,674; missing, 1,468:[14]

HEADQUARTERS DEPT. OF THE CUMBERLAND.
ROSSVILLE, GEORGIA, 8:40 P.M., Sept. 20, 1863

MAJOR GENERAL ROSECRANS:

I have this moment returned from the front. I wrote you a long despatch as I arrived on the field and while the battle was in progress, but it was so difficult to get communication to the rear that I fear you have not yet received it. Thomas has kept Baird's, Brannan's Raynolds' Woods' and Palmer's divisions in good order and has maintained almost the exact position he occupied this morning, except that his right has swung back nearly at right angles with the Gordon's Mills and Rossville road. Negley has stopped about six thousand men at this place. Sheridan gathered fifteen hundred of his division and reached a point three miles south of here at sunset; Davis is here with his brigade.

General Thomas has fought a most terrific battle and has damaged the enemy badly. General Granger's troops moved up just in time and fought magnificently. From the time I reached the battle-field, 3:45 P.M., till sunset the fight was by far the fiercest I have ever seen; our men not only held their ground, but at many points drove the enemy splendidly. Longstreet's Virginians have got their bellies full. Nearly every division of the field exhausted its ammunition—got supplies and exhausted it again. Turchin's brigade charged the rebel lines and took five hundred prisoners, became enveloped, swept around behind their lines and cut its way out in another place but abandoned his prisoners. Another brigade was attacked just at the close of the fight, and its ammunition being exhausted, it went in with the bayonet and drove the rebels, taking over two hundred prisoners and have got them yet. On the whole General Thomas and General Granger have done the enemy fully as much injury today as they have suffered from him, and they have successfully repelled the repeated combined attacks, most fiercely made, of the whole rebel army, frequently pressing the front and both our flanks at the same time.

The disaster on the right cannot of course be estimated now; it must be very considerable in men and material, especially the latter. The rebels have, however, done their best today, and I believe we can whip them tomorrow. I believe we can now crown the whole battle with victory. Granger regards them as thoroughly whipped tonight, and thinks they would not renew the fight were we to remain on the field. Clouds of dust to the eastward and northward seem to indicate some movements to our left. Sheridan thinks they may be projecting to come in directly on Chattanooga. I don't think so. Your order to retire on this place was received a little after sunset and communicated to Generals Thomas and Granger. The troops are now moving back and will be here in good shape and strong position before morning. I hope you will not budge an inch from this place but come up early in the morning, and if the rebels try it, accommodate them. . . .

If I am not needed at headquarters tonight, I will stay here; I am half dead with fatigue. . . .

But Rosecrans was still as thoroughly defeated as he had been in mid-afternoon. He had no stomach for the fight that might very well have turned defeat into triumph.

Braxton Bragg was in the same state of mind as the Federal commander. In fact, for most of September 20 Bragg was firmly convinced that the Army of Tennessee was being beaten. In a funk he ceased to give orders, allowing division and brigade commanders to fight their own unco-ordinated battles.

Lieutenant General D. H. Hill, Confederate corps commander, saw
Chickamauga for what it was—a worthless victory:[15]

Whatever blunders each of us in authority committed before the battles of the 19th and 20th, and during their progress, the great blunder of all was that of not pursuing the enemy on the 21st. The day was spent in burying the dead and gathering up captured stores. Forrest, with his usual promptness, was early in the saddle, and saw that the retreat was a rout. Disorganized masses of men were hurrying to the rear; batteries of artillery were inextricably mixed with trains of wagons; disorder and confusion pervaded the broken ranks struggling to get on. Forrest sent back word to Bragg that "every hour was worth a thousand men." But the commander-in-chief did not know of the victory until the morning of the 21st, and then he did not order a pursuit. Rosecrans spent the day and the night of the 21st in hurrying his trains out of town. A breathing-space was allowed him; the panic among his troops subsided, and Chattanooga—the objective point of the campaign—was held. There was no more splendid fighting in '61, when the flower of the Southern youth was in the field, than was displayed in those bloody days of '63. But it seems to me that the *élan* of the Southern soldier was never seen after Chickamauga—that brilliant dash which had distinguished him was gone forever. . . . He fought stoutly to the last, but, after Chickamauga, with the sullenness of despair and without the enthusiasm of hope. That "barren victory" sealed the fate of the Southern Confederacy.

VII

In Richmond, J. B. Jones, the "Rebel War Clerk," made a jubilant entry
in his diary:
"September 22d. . . . The effects of this great victory will be elec-
trical. The whole South will be filled with patriotic fervor, and in the
North there will be a corresponding depression . . . Surely the Gov-
ernment of the United States must now see the impossibility of sub-
jugating the Southern people, spread over such a vast extent of terri-
tory; and the European governments ought now to interpose to put an
end to this cruel waste of blood and treasure."
Had Jones known of a decision of the British government, not yet
made public, he would not have looked so hopefully to European in-
tervention in behalf of the Confederacy.
The decision was the culmination of a train of events which began
in the spring of 1862, when the Confederate Navy Department ordered

*its agent in England, James D. Bulloch, to contract for at least two
armored vessels for delivery at the earliest possible moment. The instructions, delayed in transmission, did not reach Bulloch until June 10.
By that time he was ready with plans and specifications for two powerful armored ships which, when equipped with rams and rifles of the
latest type, would be superior to anything in the Federal Navy. Bulloch
acted at once and reported to his Department:*[16]

On the day after the receipt of your * letter I requested the parties
who had been assisting me all along to make a tender for the contract,
having previously provided myself with estimates from other builders
who competed for Admiralty contracts. In a few days the price was
agreed upon, and I gave a verbal order for two vessels, so that no time
should be lost in contracting for the large quantity of armour plate required. By giving the order for both vessels to the same builders I got
a reduction of £1,250 on the cost of each, and by adopting the same
size and model of ship, and a like form of engines, they can both be completed in very nearly the same time. Besides this, experience has taught
me that it is far safer to keep our business as little extended as possible,
as otherwise the chance of our transactions being ferreted out by the
Federal spies, who abound even in this country, is greatly increased.

Later, Bulloch amplified this brief account:

I added that the contracting parties had shown great confidence in
me by taking this large contract upon my assurance that the money
would be forthcoming, and I hoped that the remittances would be
forwarded so as to ensure prompt payment of the several instalments
as they fell due. The builders with whom I contracted for the above
ships were Messrs. Laird Brothers, of Birkenhead, and the whole of the
arrangements were made in the same way as those for the building of
the *Alabama.* They treated with me as a private individual, and the
contract was a purely "commercial transaction," the agreement being
that they should build and deliver the two vessels to me in the port of
Liverpool, finished according to the stipulated specifications, but
furnished only with such fittings and outfit as were required for an ordinary sea-voyage. In order to avoid every possible appearance of an intent to arm them within British jurisdiction, it was arranged that no

* Stephen R. Mallory, the Confederate Secretary of the Navy.

magazines were to be placed in either ship, nor any special places for stowing shells and ordnance stores.

Bulloch underestimated the astuteness of Charles Francis Adams, American Minister to England. Adams soon knew of the building of the rams, and began to present proof to the Foreign Secretary that they were intended for the Confederate service. Earl Russell, uneasy, instituted his own investigation. Bulloch made a shrewd move—he sold the ships to a French firm which engaged to resell them to him when they should be beyond British jurisdiction. So certain was he of the success of his ruse that he indulged in dreams of the destruction the rams would cause once they sailed under the Stars and Bars. On July 9, 1863, he advised the Confederate Secretary of the Navy:

I respectfully propose . . . that the ships, when ready for sea, should be ordered to proceed as quickly as possible to Wilmington, North Carolina. One could fall in with the land at New Inlet, and the other at the main "ship bar" at the mouth of Cape Fear river.

By steaming quietly in at early daylight, they might entirely destroy the blockading vessels—not one should be left to steal away and make known the fact that the iron-clads were on the coast. Crews might be ready at Smithville or Fort Caswell, to be put on board the ships as soon as they had destroyed or dispersed the blockaders, and in a very few hours afterwards the two vessels would be ready to strike a decisive blow in any direction, north or south. . . .

The Atlantic coast offers enticing and decisive work in more than one direction. Without a moment's delay, after getting their crews on board off Wilmington, our vessels might sail southward, sweep the blockading fleet from the sea-front of every harbour from the Capes of Virginia to Sabine Pass, and cruising up and down the coast, could prevent anything like permanent systematic interruption of our trade for the future. Again, should Washington still be held by the enemy, our iron-clads could ascend the Potomac, and after destroying all transports and gun-boats falling within their reach, could render Washington itself untenable, and could thus create a powerful diversion in favour of any operations General Lee might have on foot. Third, Portsmouth, New Hampshire . . . is a wealthy city in itself, and opposite the town is an important national dock and building-yard. The whole lies invitingly open to attack and destruction. Suppose our two iron-clads should steam, unannounced, into that harbour on some fine October

morning, and while one proceeded to demolish the navy-yard and all it
contained, the other should send a flag of truce to the mayor, to say that
if $1,000,000 in gold or $5,000,000 in greenbacks were not sent on
board in four hours the city would be destroyed. . . . Portsmouth
could afford to pay for its existence. Philadelphia is another point open
to such an attack. The river is navigable, the banks comparatively
low, so that no plunging fire could be brought to bear upon the ships,
and once in front of the city they could dictate their own terms. Such
operations as are thus hastily sketched would inflict great damage upon
the enemy, besides creating a striking effect in Europe.

*Two days after Bulloch recorded his vision of conquest and ransom,
William H. Seward, Secretary of State, wrote a long letter of instruction
to Minister Adams. Seward granted that the officers of the crown
might have interpreted British law correctly in the cases of the* Alabama, Florida *and, more recently, the* Alexandra,* *but the United
States still had an intolerable grievance:*[17]

If the law of Great Britain must be left without amendment, and be
construed by the government in conformity with the rulings of the Chief
Baron of the Exchequer, then there will be left for the United States no
alternative but to protect themselves and their commerce against armed
cruisers proceeding from British ports, as against the naval forces
of a public enemy; and also to claim and insist upon indemnities for
the injuries which all such expeditions have hitherto committed or shall
hereafter commit against this government and the citizens of the United
States. To this end this government is now preparing a naval force with
the utmost vigor; and if the national navy, which it is rapidly creating,
shall not be sufficient for the emergency, then the United States must
bring into employment such private armed naval forces as the mer-
cantile marine shall afford. British ports, domestic as well as colonial,
are now open, under certain restrictions, to the visits of piratical vessels, and not only furnish them coals, provisions, and repairs, but
even receive their prisoners when the enemies of the United States
come in to obtain such relief from voyages in which they have either
burned ships they have captured, or have even manned and armed them
as pirates and sent them abroad as auxiliaries in the work of destruc-

---

* A gunboat constructed by the Lairds which the British government had seized
on April 5, 1863. The lawsuits resulting from the seizure dragged on so long that
the *Alexandra* was still the subject of litigation when the war ended.

tion. Can it be an occasion for either surprise or complaint that if this condition of things is to remain and receive the deliberate sanction of the British government, the navy of the United States will receive instructions to pursue these enemies into the ports which thus, in violation of the law of nations and the obligations of neutrality, become harbors for the pirates? The President very distinctly perceives the risks and hazards which a naval conflict thus maintained will bring to the commerce and even to the peace of the two countries. But he is obliged to consider that in the case supposed the destruction of our commerce will probably amount to a naval war waged by a portion at least of the British nation against the government and people of the United States—a war tolerated though not declared or avowed by the British government. If, through the necessary employment of all our means of national defence, such a partial war shall become a general one between the two nations, the President thinks that the responsibility for that painful result will not fall upon the United States.

Adams, aware that the presentation of this document to the British Foreign Secretary would be considered a declaration of war, kept it in his desk and continued to gather proof of the real ownership of the rams. The London Times *remarked that "ninety-nine people out of a hundred believe that these steam rams are 'intended to carry on hostilities sooner or later against the Federals,'" yet Her Majesty's law officers persisted in their refusal to advise Russell to detain the ships. On September 1 the Foreign Secretary informed Adams that the British government, though unable to interfere with the rams, would watch vigilantly for any action which could be construed as a violation of neutrality.*

Replying on September 5, Adams relied on his instructions from Seward, though he still refrained from communicating them to Russell:[18]

My Lord,

At this moment, when one of the iron-clad war-vessels is on the point of departure from this kingdom on its hostile errand against the United States, I am honoured with the reply of your Lordship to my notes of the 11th, 16th, and 25th of July and of the 14th of August. I trust I need not express how profound is my regret at the conclusion to which Her Majesty's Government have arrived. I can regard it no otherwise than as practically opening to the insurgents free liberty in this kingdom to execute a policy described in one of their late publications in the following language:—

"In the present state of the harbour defences of New York, Boston, Portland, and smaller Northern cities, such a vessel as the 'Warrior' would have little difficulty in entering any of those ports, and inflicting a vital blow upon the enemy. The destruction of Boston alone would be worth a hundred victories in the field. It would bring such a terror to the 'blue-noses' as to cause them to wish eagerly for peace, despite their overweening love of gain which has been so freely administered to since the opening of this war. Vessels of the 'Warrior' class would promptly raise the blockade of our ports, and would, even in this respect, confer advantages which would soon repay the cost of their construction."

It would be superfluous in me to point out to your Lordship that this is war. No matter what may be the theory adopted of neutrality in a struggle, when this process is carried on in the manner indicated from a territory and with the aid of the subjects of a third party, that third party, to all intents and purposes, ceases to be neutral. Neither is it necessary to show that any Government which suffers it to be done fails in enforcing the essential conditions of international amity towards the country against whom the hostility is directed. In my belief it is impossible that any nation retaining a proper degree of self-respect could tamely submit to a continuance of relations so utterly deficient in reciprocity. I have no idea that Great Britain would do so for a moment.

After a careful examination of the full instructions with which I have been furnished in preparation for such an emergency, I deem it inexpedient for me to attempt any recurrence to arguments for effective interposition in the present case. The fatal objection of impotency which paralyzes Her Majesty's Government seems to present an insuperable barrier against all further reasoning. Under these circumstances I prefer to desist from communicating to your Lordship even such further portions of my existing instructions as are suited to the case, lest I should contribute to aggravate difficulties already far too serious. I therefore content myself with informing your Lordship that I transmit by the present steamer a copy of your note for the consideration of my Government, and shall await the more specific directions that will be contained in the reply.

Adams had issued an unnecessary ultimatum. Whether Earl Russell had finally decided to rely on what he knew but could not prove, whether the import of the smashing Union victories of Gettysburg and Vicksburg had convinced him, as they had convinced many leaders of opinion in England, that the cause of the South was hopeless, may never be known. Whatever his reason, Russell had written to his Prime Minister two days before Adams had threatened England with war:

My dear Palmerston,—The conduct of the gentlemen who have contracted for the two iron-clads at Birkenhead is so very suspicious that I have thought it necessary to direct that they should be detained. The Solicitor-General has been consulted, and concurs in the measure, as one of policy, though not of strict law. We shall thus test the law, and, if we have to pay damages, we have satisfied the opinion, which prevails here as well as in America, that that kind of neutral hostility should not be allowed to go on without some attempt to stop it. If you do not approve, pray appoint a Cabinet for Tuesday or Wednesday next.

Palmerston did not dissent. Henry Adams, the Minister's son and secretary, wrote from London on September 16:[19]

Undoubtedly to us this is a second Vicksburg. It is our diplomatic triumph, if we manage to carry it through. . . . Whether we shall succeed, I am not yet certain. The vessels are only detained temporarily, but the signs are that the gale that has blown so long is beginning to veer about. . . . I think the discussion which is now taking place has pretty much convinced most people that this war-vessel matter is one that ought to be stopped. And if so, the mere fact that they have managed to take the first step is to me reasonable ground for confidence that they will take the others as the emergencies arise.

On October 20 Bulloch reported from Liverpool to the Confederate Secretary of the Navy:[20]

The two rams building by Messrs Laird have been virtually seized by orders from the Foreign Office, and are now in the possession of the customs officers of this port, assisted by one of her Majesty's gunboats, and a guard of marines from her Majesty's ship *Majestic*. The actual seizure took place only about a fortnight ago (October 9th), although the public has been prepared for such an event by intimations in the so-called Government organs, and discussions upon the matter in all the newspapers of the kingdom. . . .

Bulloch concluded ruefully:

Now, sir, the final issue of this affair is no longer a practical question. No amount of discretion or management on my part can effect the release of the ships.

CHAPTER 27

"THE YEAR OF THE PROCLAMATION"

AFTER CHICKAMAUGA, Rosecrans fortified Chattanooga. Bragg saw an opportunity for the kind of bloodless conquest that was his concept of war. Chattanooga lies on the south side of the tortuous Tennessee River, which at this point flows from west to east. East of the city, five miles away at the closest point, Missionary Ridge extends north and south. An equal distance to the southwest lies Lookout Mountain with its northernmost shoulder touching the Tennessee. The one railroad coming in from the north—the Nashville and Chattanooga—ran so close to Lookout Mountain that, like the Tennessee River, it could be controlled by a force on the mountain. Bragg distributed his troops on Missionary Ridge, on Lookout and in the Chattanooga Valley between the two elevations, closed off the Federal communications, and waited for starvation to force his opponent to surrender.

Rosecrans, strangely bereft of the dash he had formerly shown, seemed to see as the alternative to this fate a retreat toward Nashville. Washington refused to consider the possibility. Rosecrans was relieved, and Thomas was put in command of the Army of the Cumberland. Sherman with the Army of the Tennessee was ordered to Chattanooga; Hooker brought two corps from the Army of the Potomac; and Grant was given supreme command.

I

*Stanton, meeting Grant at Louisville, gave the general his orders. Grant
hurried to Chattanooga, reaching there on October 23. He found the
army in deplorable condition:*[1]

Owing to the position of Bragg, all supplies for Rosecrans had to be
hauled by a circuitous route north of the river and over a mountainous
country. . . .

This country afforded but little food for his animals, nearly ten thousand of which had already starved, and not enough were left to draw a
single piece of artillery or even the ambulances to convey the sick. The
men had been on half rations of hard bread for a considerable time,
with but few other supplies except beef driven from Nashville across
the country. The region along the road became so exhausted of food for
the cattle that by the time they reached Chattanooga they were much
in the condition of the few animals left alive there—"on the lift." Indeed, the beef was so poor that the soldiers were in the habit of saying,
with a faint facetiousness, that they were living on "half rations of hard
bread and *beef dried on the hoof.*"

Nothing could be transported but food, and the troops were without
sufficient shoes or other clothing suitable for the advancing season.
What they had was well worn. The fuel within the Federal lines was exhausted, even to the stumps of trees. There were no teams to draw it
from the opposite bank, where it was abundant. The only way of supplying fuel, for some time before my arrival, had been to cut trees on the
north bank of the river at a considerable distance up the stream, form
rafts of it and float it down with the current, effecting a landing on the
south side within our lines by the use of paddles or poles. It would then
be carried on the shoulders of the men to their camps.

*At Chattanooga, Grant found General William F. Smith, recently trans-
ferred from the Army of the Potomac. Smith, an outstanding engineer,
had already made plans to break Bragg's hold on the Union supply
lines. Hooker, at Bridgeport on the Tennessee River twenty-five miles
west of Chattanooga, would cross to the south side and fight his way if
necessary to Brown's Ferry, only three miles across country from
Chattanooga. There he would be met by a force which would cross the
river on ferries and a pontoon bridge. Nearby heights, when seized,
would cover the position.*

Hooker started on October 26. The Confederates were caught nap-ping, and put up little resistance. Two days later the Union right was firmly based on Lookout Valley, south of the Tennessee, and Grant had a supply line—a "cracker line" the troops called it—by steamer and road to Bridgeport. The effect was miraculous. Grant described it:[2]

On the way to Chattanooga I had telegraphed back to Nashville for a good supply of vegetables and small rations, which the troops had been so long deprived of. Hooker had brought with him from the east a full supply of land transportation. His animals had not been subjected to hard work on bad roads without forage, but were in good condition. In five days from my arrival in Chattanooga the way was open to Bridgeport and, with the aid of steamers and Hooker's teams, in a week the troops were receiving full rations. It is hard for any one not an eye-witness to realize the relief this brought. The men were soon reclothed and also well fed; an abundance of ammunition was brought up, and a cheerfulness prevailed not before enjoyed in many weeks. Neither officers nor men looked upon themselves any longer as doomed. The weak and languid appearance of the troops, so visible before, disap-peared at once. I do not know what the effect was on the other side, but assume it must have been correspondingly depressing. Mr. Davis had visited Bragg but a short time before, and must have perceived our condition to be about as Bragg described it in his subsequent report. "These dispositions," he said, "faithfully sustained, insured the enemy's speedy evacuation of Chattanooga for want of food and forage. Pos-sessed of the shortest route to his depot, and the one by which rein-forcements must reach him, we held him at our mercy, and his destruc-tion was only a question of time."

Bragg made only one effort to "faithfully sustain" his position. Grant described a sharp engagement in which the much-abused mule played an important part:[3]

The enemy was surprised by the movements which secured to us a line of supplies. He appreciated its importance, and hastened to try to recover the line from us. His strength on Lookout Mountain was not equal to Hooker's command in the valley below. From Missionary Ridge he had to march twice the distance we had from Chattanooga, in order to reach Lookout Valley; but on the night of the 28th and 29th [of October] an attack was made on Geary * at Wauhatchie by Long-street's corps. When the battle commenced, Hooker ordered Howard up from Brown's Ferry. He had three miles to march to reach Geary. On his way he was fired upon by rebel troops from a foot-hill to the left of the road and from which the road was commanded. Howard turned to the left, charged up the hill and captured it before the enemy had time to intrench, taking many prisoners. Leaving sufficient men to hold this height, he pushed on to reinforce Geary. Before he got up, Geary had been engaged for about three hours against a vastly superior force. The night was so dark that the men could not distinguish one from another except by the light of the flashes of their muskets. In the darkness and uproar, Hooker's teamsters became frightened, and breaking loose from their fastenings stampeded directly towards the enemy. The latter, no doubt, took this for a charge, and stampeded in turn. By four o'clock in the morning the battle had entirely ceased, and our "cracker line" was never afterward disturbed.

II

Before Grant assumed command at Chattanooga, Burnside had been sent with 25,000 men to east Tennessee. The purpose of the expedition —to "protect" the loyal people of the region—was one which Lincoln cherished and continually pressed, though no important military result could be expected. Early in November, Bragg ordered Longstreet, with 20,000 troops, to follow Burnside and take care of him. Even without the menace of Longstreet, the Federal commander was in critical condition, having neither adequate supplies nor ammunition. Lincoln and Halleck urged Grant to do something, anything, for Burnside's relief. As Grant saw the situation, he could help Burnside only by attacking Bragg. If the Confederate commander could be driven from his seemingly impregnable position, he would have to recall Longstreet, and Burnside would be saved.

Yet Grant would not be strong enough to attack until Sherman and the Army of the Tennessee reached Chattanooga. While Grant waited, the President of the United States, a thousand miles away, slowly wrote the remarks he had promised to make at the dedication of the Gettysburg military cemetery on November 19. When the day came, John Hay, Lincoln's twenty-five-year-old secretary, made a short entry in his diary:[4]

* John W. Geary commanded a division in the Twelfth Corps from the Army of the Potomac.

In the morning I got a beast and rode out with the President's suite to the Cemetery in the procession. The procession formed itself in an orphanly sort of way & moved out with very little help from anybody & after a little delay Mr. Everett took his place on the stand—and Mr. Stockton made a prayer which thought it was an oration; and Mr. Everett spoke as he always does, perfectly—and the President, in a fine, free way, with more grace than is his wont, said his half dozen words of consecration, and the music wailed and we went home through crowded and cheering streets. And all the particulars are in the daily papers.

The President had said:

Four score and seven years ago our fathers brought forth on this continent, a new nation, conceived in Liberty, and dedicated to the proposition that all men are created equal.

Now we are engaged in a great civil war, testing whether that nation, or any nation so conceived and so dedicated, can long endure. We are met on a great battle-field of that war. We have come to dedicate a portion of that field, as a final resting place for those who here gave their lives that that nation might live. It is altogether fitting and proper that we should do this.

But, in a larger sense, we can not dedicate—we can not consecrate—we can not hallow—this ground. The brave men, living and dead, who struggled here, have consecrated it, far above our poor power to add or detract. The world will little note, nor long remember what we say here, but it can never forget what they did here. It is for us the living, rather, to be dedicated here to the unfinished work which they who fought here have thus far so nobly advanced. It is rather for us to be here dedicated to the great task remaining before us—that from these honored dead we take increased devotion to that cause for which they gave the last full measure of devotion—that we here highly resolve that these dead shall not have died in vain—that this nation, under God, shall have a new birth of freedom—and that government of the people, by the people, for the people, shall not perish from the earth.

III

Sherman's advance units reached Brown's Ferry on November 20, but heavy rains forced Grant to postpone his attack until the twenty-third.

Major James A. Connolly, now on the staff of division commander Absalom Baird, described three stirring days in a letter to his wife:[5]

On Monday, Nov. 23rd our Division was ordered to move out just in front of the fortifications. We did so, and the rebels, as they looked down on us from Lookout Mountain and Mission Ridge, no doubt thought we had come out for a review. But Sheridan's Division followed us out and formed in line with us. Wonder what the rebels thought then? "Oh, a Yankee review; we'll have some fun shelling them directly." But out came Wood's Division, then Cruft's Division, then Johnson's Division, then Howard's entire Corps of "Potomacs." "What can those Yankee fools mean," Bragg must have thought, as he sat at the door of his tent on Mission Ridge and watched the long lines of blue coats and glistening guns marching around in the valley below him, almost within gun shot of his pickets, and yet not a gun fired. All was peace in Chattanooga valley that day.

The sun shone brightly, the bands played stirring airs; tattered banners that had waved on battle fields from the Potomac to the Mississippi streamed out gaily, as if proud of the battle scars they wore. Generals Grant and Hooker, and Sherman and Thomas and Logan and Reynolds and Sheridan and scores of others, with their staffs, galloped along the lines, and the scene that spread out around me like a vast panorama of war filled my heart with pride that I was a soldier and member of that great army. But what did it all mean? Bragg, from his mountain eyrie, could see what we were doing just as well as Grant who was riding around amongst us. The rebels thought they had us hemmed in so that we dared not move. Two o'clock came, and all was yet quiet and peaceful, gay as a holiday review; we could see crowds of rebels watching us from Mission Ridge and Lookout Mountain, but three o'clock came, and a solitary shot away over on our left, among Wood's men, made every fellow think: "Hark!" A few moments and another shot, then a rat-tat-tat-tat made almost every one remark: "Skirmishing going on over there." Wood's line moved forward, a few volleys, still Wood's line moved forward, and Sheridan's started forward, heavy work for a few minutes then all was quiet; two important hills were gained; cheer after cheer rang out in the valley and echoed and reverberated through the gorges of Lookout and Mission Ridge; still it was only 5 o'clock Monday afternoon. The bands commenced playing and the valley was again peaceful, but we all knew there was "something up," and Bragg must have thought so too.

The men stayed where nightfall found them, sleeping on their arms.
Connolly continued:[6]

Tuesday morning, Nov. 24th, broke bright and beautiful; the sun
rose clear. . . . Daylight revealed the hills which Wood and Sheridan
had won the day before, bristling with cannon of sufficient caliber to
reach Bragg's eyrie on Mission Ridge. About 9 o'clock in the morning
some 30 heavy guns opened on Mission Ridge. It appeared then that
we were to advance right down the valley and attack the rebel centre,
but, hark! Away off on our right—3 miles away, on the opposite side
of Lookout—we hear firing. What can that mean? Suddenly the cannon, with which we have been pounding away at Mission Ridge, are
silent, and all eyes are turned westward toward Lookout Mountain.
The sounds of battle increase there but it is on the other side of the
mountain from us and we can see nothing, but the word passes
around: "Hooker is storming Lookout!" My heart grows faint. Poor
Hooker, with his Potomac boys are to be the forlorn hope! What?
Storm that mountain peak 2400 feet high, so steep that a squirrel could
scarcely climb it, and bristling all over with rebels, bayonets and cannon? Poor boys! Far from your quiet New England homes, you have
come a long way only to meet defeat on that mountain peak, and find
your graves on its rugged sides! Lookout Mountain will only hereafter
be known as a monument to a whole Corps of gallant New Englanders
who died there for their country! But hold! Some one exclaims: "The
firing comes nearer, our boys are getting up!" All eyes are turned toward the Mountain, and the stillness of death reigns among us in the
valley, as we listen to the sounds of battle on the other side of the Mountain while all was quiet as a Puritan sabbath on our side of it. How hope
and despair alternated in our breasts! How we prayed for their success
and longed to assist them, can only be known by those of us who, in that
valley, stood watching that afternoon and listening to the swelling dia-
pason of their battle. But the firing actually did grow nearer, manifestly
our men were driving them; Oh! now if they only can continue it,
but we fear they cannot! I have a long telescope with which I can distinctly see everything on our side of the mountain. I scan the mountain
with it closely and continuously, but not a soul can I see. After hours
of anxious suspense I see a single rebel winding his way back from the
firing and around to our side of the mountain.

I announce to the crowd of Generals standing around: "There goes
a straggler!" and in an instant everybody's glass is to his eye, but no

more stragglers are seen, still the battle rages, and the little gleam of hope, that solitary straggler raised in our breasts, dies out. Minutes drag like hours, the suspense is awful, but look! look! Here comes a crowd of stragglers! here they come by hundreds, yes by thousands! The mountain is covered with them! They are broken, running! There comes our flag around the point of the mountain! There comes one of our regiments on the double quick! Oh! such a cheer as then went up in the valley! Manly cheeks were wet with tears of joy, our bands played "Hail to the Chief," and 50 brazen throated cannon, in the very wantonness of joy, thundered out from the fortifications of Chattanooga, a salute to the old flag which was then on the mountain top. The work was done. Lookout was ours, never again to be used as a perch by rebel vultures. Didn't we of the old Army of the Cumberland feel proud though? It was one of the regiments that fought at Chickamauga that carried that first flag to the mountain top. It was a brigade of the old Chickamauga army that led the storming party up the mountain. A straggling skirmish fire was kept up along our (eastern) side of the mountain, which we could trace by the flashes of the guns, until 11 o'clock at night, but then all became quiet, and again we passed the night in line of battle, sleeping on our arms.

Bragg expected Hooker to press forward against the Confederate left at the south end of Missionary Ridge. During the night of the twenty-fourth Bragg shifted troops from the northern end of the Ridge to meet the onslaught. The Confederate commander did not know that Sherman with his Vicksburg veterans lay concealed north of the Tennessee River ready to strike at the very point which Bragg had weakened.

This day in the thick of the fighting, Connolly continued his account:[7]

Before daylight of Wednesday, Nov. 25th, Sherman had his pontoons across the river, about 3 miles north of Chattanooga, and under cover of a dense fog, crossed his whole Corps and took possession of the northern extremity of Mission Ridge, finding nothing there but a few pickets, and there he fell to work fortifying. By this time Bragg saw his mistake. The attack of Wednesday was to be on his right, at the north end of Mission Ridge, instead of his left at the south end of the Ridge, so he hurriedly countermarched his troops back from his left to his right. When the fog rose, about ten o'clock in the morning, Sherman attempted to carry the summit of the Ridge but was repulsed; again he tried it but was again repulsed, still again he tried it and was repulsed. . . .

An order came for our Division to move up the river to his support. We started. The enemy could see us from the top of the Ridge, and quickly understood (or thought they did) our design, so they commenced shelling us, as our long line of 20 regiments filed along, but we moved along until we came to where a thin strip of woodland intervened between us and the Ridge. Sheridan's Division followed us and did the same. The enemy supposed of course that we were moving on up the river to the support of Sherman, but we were not; we halted and formed line of battle in that strip of woodland, facing Mission Ridge. This, I confess, staggered me; I couldn't understand it; it looked as though we were going to assault the ridge, and try to carry it by storm, lined and ribbed as it was with rifle pits, and its topmost verge crowded with rebel lines, and at least 40 cannon in our immediate front frowning down on us; we never could live a moment in the open spaces of 600 yards between the strip of woods in which we were formed, and the line of rifle pits at the base of the mountain, exposed as we would be to the fire of the 40 cannon massed, and from five to eight hundred feet immediately above us, also to the infantry fire from the rifle pits.

I rode down along the line of our Division, and there I found Wood's Division formed on our right and facing the Ridge just as we were; I rode on and came to Sheridan's Division formed on Wood's right and facing the same. Here was a line of veteran troops nearly two miles long, all facing Mission Ridge, and out of sight of the enemy. The purpose at once became plain to me, and I hurried back to my own Division, and on asking Gen. Baird he replied: "When 6 guns are fired in quick succession from Fort Wood, the line advances to storm the heights and carry the Ridge if possible. Take that order to Col. Phelps" (commanding the third brigade of our Division) "and tell him to move forward rapidly when he hears the signal." I communicated the order at once and that was the last I saw of the brigade commander, for he was killed just as he reached the summit of the Ridge.

A few moments elapse, it is about half past three o'clock P.M., when suddenly, 6 guns are rapidly fired from Fort Wood. "Forward!" rings out along that long line of men, and forward they go, through the strip of woods, we reach the open space, say 600 yards, between the edge of the woods and the rifle pits at the foot of the Ridge. "Charge!" is shouted wildly from hundreds of throats, and with a yell such as that valley never heard before, the three Divisions (60 regiments) rushed forward; the rebels are silent a moment, but then the batteries on top of the Ridge, open all at once, and the very heavens above us seem to be rent asunder; shells go screaming over our heads, bursting above and behind us, but they hurt nobody and the men don't notice them; about midway of the open space a shell bursts directly over my head, and so near as to make my horse frantic and almost unmanageable; he plunges and bursts breast strap and girth and off I tumble with the saddle between my legs. My orderly catches my horse at once, throws the blanket and saddle on him, gives me a "leg lift" and I am mounted again, without girth, but I hold on with my knees and catch up with our madcaps at the first rifle pits, over these we go to the second line of pits, over these we go, some of the rebels lying down to be run over, others scrambling up the hill which is becoming too steep for horses, and the General and staff are forced to abandon the direct ascent at about the second line of rifle pits; the long line of men reach the steepest part of the mountain, and they must crawl up the best way they can 150 feet more before they reach the summit, and when they do reach it, can they hold it? The rebels are there in thousands, behind breastworks, ready to hurl our brave boys back as they reach their works.

One flag bearer, on hands and knees, is seen away in advance of the whole line; he crawls and climbs toward a rebel flag he sees waving before him; he gets within a few feet of it and hides behind a fallen log while he waves his flag defiantly until it almost touches the rebel flag; his regiment follows him as fast as it can; in a few moments another flag bearer gets just as near the summit at another point, and his regiment soon gets to him, but these two regiments dare not go the next twenty feet or they would be annihilated, so they crouch there and are safe from the rebels above them, who would have to rise up to fire down at them, and so expose themselves to the fire of our fellows who are climbing up the mountain.

The suspense is greater, if possible, than that with which we viewed the storming of Lookout. If we can gain that Ridge, if we can scale those breastworks, the rebel army is routed, everything is lost for them, but if we cannot scale the works few of us will get down this mountain side and back to the shelter of the woods. But a third flag and regiment reaches the other two; all eyes are turned there; the men away above us look like great ants crawling up, crouching on the outside of the rebel breastworks. One of our flags seems to be moving; look! look! look! Up! Up! Up! it goes and is planted on the rebel works; in a twinkling the crouching soldiers are up and over the works; apparently quicker than I can write it the 3 flags and 3 regiments are up, the close fighting is terrific; other flags go up and over at different points along the mountain top—the batteries have ceased, for friend and foe are mixed in a surging mass; in a few moments the flags of 60 Yankee regiments float along Mission Ridge from one end to the other, the enemy are plunging down the eastern slope of the Ridge and our men are in hot pursuit, but darkness comes too soon and the pursuit must cease; we go back to the summit of the Ridge and there hold our trophies—dead and wounded rebels under our feet by hundreds, cannon by scores scattered up and down the Ridge with yelling soldiers astraddle them, rebel flags laying around in profusion, and soldiers and officers completely and frantically drunk with excitement. Four hours more of daylight, after we gained that Ridge would not have left two whole pieces of Bragg's army together.

Our men, stirred by the same memories, shouted "Chickamauga!" as they scaled the works at the summit, and amid the din of battle the cry "Chickamauga!" "Chickamauga!" could be heard. That is not *fancy* it is *fact*. Indeed the plain unvarnished facts of the storming of Mission Ridge are more like romance to me now than any I have ever read in Dumas, Scott or Cooper. On that night I lay down upon the ground without blankets and slept soundly, without inquiring whether my neighbors were dead or alive, but, on waking found I was sleeping among bunches of dead rebels and Federals, and within a few rods of where Bragg slept the night before, if he slept at all.

Private Sam Watkins of Company H, First Tennessee, saw the battle as a Confederate:[8]

About two or three o'clock, a column of Yankees advancing to the attack swept right over where I was standing. I was trying to stand aside to get out of their way, but the more I tried to get out of their way, the more in their way I got. I was carried forward, I know not whither. We soon arrived at the foot of the ridge, at our old breastworks. I recognized Robert Brank's old corn stalk house, and Alf Horsley's fort, an old log house called Fort Horsley. I was in front of the enemy's line, and was afraid to run up the ridge, and afraid to surrender. They were ordered to charge up the hill. There was no firing from the Rebel lines in our immediate front. They kept climbing and pulling and scratching until I was in touching distance of the old Rebel breastworks, right on the very apex of Missionary Ridge. I made one jump, and I heard Captain Turner, who had the very four Napoleon guns we had captured at Perryville, halloo out, "Number Four, solid!" and then a roar. The next order was, "Limber to the rear." The

Yankees were cutting and slashing, and the cannoneers were running in every direction. I saw Day's brigade throw down their guns and break like quarter horses. Bragg was trying to rally them. I heard him say, "Here is your commander," and the soldiers hallooed back, "Here is your mule."

Braxton Bragg was as befuddled as Private Sam Watkins:[9]

A panic which I had never before witnessed seemed to have seized upon officers and men, and each seemed to be struggling for his personal safety, regardless of his duty or his character. . . . No satisfactory excuse can possibly be given for the shameful conduct of our troops on the left in allowing their line to be penetrated. The position was one which ought to have been held by a line of skirmishers against any assaulting column, and whenever resistance was made the enemy fled in disorder after suffering heavy loss. Those who reached the ridge did so in a condition of exhaustion from the great physical exertion in climbing which rendered them powerless, and the slightest effort would have destroyed them. Having secured much of our artillery, they soon availed themselves of our panic, and turning our guns upon us enfiladed the lines, both right and left, rendering them entirely untenable. Had all parts of the line been maintained with equal gallantry and persistence, no enemy could ever have dislodged us, and but one possible reason presents itself to my mind in explanation of this bad conduct in veteran troops who never before failed in any duty assigned them, however difficult and hazardous: They had for two days confronted the enemy, marshaling his immense forces in plain view, and exhibiting to their sight such a superiority in numbers as may have intimidated weak-minded and untried soldiers. But our veterans had so often encountered similar hosts when the strength of position was against us, and with perfect success, that not a doubt crossed my mind.

Perhaps Private Watkins knew more about Braxton Bragg than Bragg knew about himself. Recalling Missionary Ridge, Watkins wrote:[10]

I felt sorry for General Bragg. The army was routed, and Bragg looked so scared. Poor fellow, he looked so hacked and whipped and mortified and chagrined at defeat, and all along the line, when

Bragg would pass, the soldiers would raise the yell, "Here is your mule;" "Bully for Bragg, he's h--l on retreat."

IV

When Jefferson Davis sent his annual message to the Confederate Congress on December 7, 1863, he adopted Bragg's explanation for the defeat at Missionary Ridge:[11]

This signal defeat of General Rosecrans [at Chickamauga] was followed by his retreat into Chattanooga, where his imperiled position had the immediate effect of relieving the pressure of the invasion at other points, forcing the concentration for his relief of large bodies of troops withdrawn from the armies in the Mississippi Valley and in Northern Virginia. The combined forces thus accumulated against us in Tennessee so greatly outnumbered our army as to encourage the enemy to attack. After a long and severe battle, in which great carnage was inflicted on him, some of our troops inexplicably abandoned a position of great strength, and by a disorderly retreat compelled the commander to withdraw the forces elsewhere successful, and finally to retreat with his whole army to a position some twenty or thirty miles to the rear. It is believed that if the troops who yielded to the assault had fought with the valor which they had displayed on previous occasions, and which was manifested in this battle on the other parts of the line, the enemy would have been repulsed with very great slaughter, and our country would have escaped the misfortune and the Army the mortification of the first defeat that has resulted from misconduct by the troops.

Davis had other reverses to account for. Gettysburg he blamed on a flooded river:[12]

The able commander who conducted the campaign in Virginia determined to meet the threatened advance on Richmond, for which the enemy had made long and costly preparations, by forcing their armies to cross the Potomac and fight in defense of their own capital and homes. Transferring the battlefield to their own soil, he succeeded in compelling their rapid retreat from Virginia, and in the hard-fought battle of Gettysburg inflicted such severity of punishment as disabled them from early renewal of the campaign as originally projected. Unfortunately the communications on which our general relied for receiving his supplies of munitions were interrupted by extraordinary floods, which so swelled the Potomac as to render impassable the fords by which his advance had been made, and he was thus forced to a withdrawal, which was conducted with deliberation after securing large trains of captured supplies, and with a constant and unaccepted tender of battle. On more than one occasion the enemy has since made demonstrations of a purpose to advance, invariably followed by a precipitate retreat to intrenched lines on the approach of our forces.

The major diplomatic failure of the year—Great Britain's refusal to release the Laird rams—Davis blamed on the obstinacy and partiality of a haughty nation:[13]

I regret to inform you that there has been no improvement in the state of our relations with foreign countries since my message in January last. On the contrary, there has been a still greater divergence in the conduct of European nations from that practical impartiality which alone deserves the name of neutrality, and their action in some cases has assumed a character positively unfriendly. . . .

For nearly three years this Government has exercised unquestioned jurisdiction over many millions of willing and united people. It has met and defeated vast armies of invaders, who have in vain sought its subversion. Supported by the confidence and affection of its citizens, the Confederacy has lacked no element which distinguishes an independent nation according to the principles of public law. Its legislative, executive, and judicial Departments, each in its sphere, have performed their appropriate functions with a regularity as undisturbed as in a time of profound peace, and the whole energies of the people have been developed in the organization of vast armies, while their rights and liberties have rested secure under the protection of courts of justice. This Confederacy is either independent or it is a dependency of the United States; for no other earthly power claims the right to govern it. Without one historic fact on which the pretension can rest, without one line or word of treaty or covenant which can give color to title, the United States have asserted, and the British Government has chosen to concede, that these sovereign States are the dependencies of the Government which is administered at Washington. Great Britain has accordingly entertained with that Government the closest and most intimate relations, while refusing, on its demands, ordinary amicable intercourse with us, and has, under arrangements made with the other nations of Europe, not only denied our just claim of admission into the family of nations, but interposed a passive though effectual bar to the knowledge of our rights by other powers. So soon as it had become apparent by the declarations of the British Ministers in the debates of the British Parliament in July last that Her Majesty's Government was determined to persist indefinitely in a course of policy which under professions of neutrality had become subservient to the designs of our enemy, I felt it my duty to recall the Commissioner formerly accredited to that Court, and the correspondence on the subject is submitted to you.

Davis could see no early end to the war, which continued only because of Northern perversity and degradation:[14]

The hope last year [1862] entertained of an early termination of the war has not been realized. Could carnage have satisfied the appetite of our enemy for the destruction of human life, or grief have appeased their wanton desire to inflict human suffering, there has been bloodshed enough on both sides, and two lands have been sufficiently darkened by the weeds of mourning to induce a disposition for peace.

If unanimity in a people could dispel delusion, it has been displayed too unmistakably not to have silenced the pretense that the Southern States were merely disturbed by a factious insurrection, but it must long since have been admitted that they were but exercising their reserved right to modify their own Government in such manner as would best secure their own happiness. But these considerations have been powerless to allay the unchristian hate of those who, long accustomed to draw large profits from a union with us, cannot control the rage excited by the conviction that they have by their own folly destroyed the richest sources of their prosperity. They refuse even to listen to proposals for the only peace possible between us—a peace which, recognizing the impassable gulf which divides us, may leave the two peoples separately to recover from the injuries inflicted on both by the causeless war now waged against us. Having begun the war in direct violation of their Constitution, which forbade the attempt to coerce a State, they have been hardened by crime until they no longer attempt to veil their purpose to destroy the institutions and subvert the sovereignty and independence of these States. We now know that the only reliable hope for peace is in the vigor of our resistance, while the cessation of their hostility is only to be expected from the pressure of their necessities.

The patriotism of the people has proved equal to every sacrifice demanded by their country's need. We have been united as a people never were united under like circumstances before. God has blessed us with success disproportionate to our means, and under His divine favor our labors must at last be crowned with the reward due to men who have given all they possessed to the righteous defense of their inalienable rights, their homes, and their altars.

V

One day after Davis' message was read, the Congress of the United States heard Abraham Lincoln's annual report on the state of the Union. The document was a calm recital of progress in many fields. Of one subject the President wrote with particular satisfaction:[15]

When Congress assembled a year ago the war had already lasted nearly twenty months, and there had been many conflicts on both land and sea, with varying results.

The rebellion had been pressed back into reduced limits; yet the tone of public feeling and opinion, at home and abroad, was not satisfactory. With other signs, the popular elections, then just past, indicated uneasiness among ourselves, while amid much that was cold and menacing the kindest words coming from Europe were uttered in accents of pity, that we were too blind to surrender a hopeless cause. Our commerce was suffering greatly by a few armed vessels built upon and furnished from foreign shores, and we were threatened with such additions from the same quarter as would sweep our trade from the sea and raise our blockade. We had failed to elicit from European governments anything hopeful upon this subject. The preliminary emancipation proclamation, issued in September, was running its assigned period to the beginning of the new year. A month later the final proclamation came, including the announcement that colored men of suitable condition would be received into the war service. The policy of emancipation, and of employing black soldiers, gave to the future a new aspect, about which hope, and fear, and doubt contended in uncertain conflict. According to our political system, as a matter of civil administration, the general government had no lawful power to effect emancipation in any State, and for a long time it had been hoped that the rebellion could be suppressed without resorting to it as a military measure. It was all the while deemed possible that the necessity for it might come, and that if it should, the crisis of the contest would then be presented. It came, and as was anticipated, it was followed by dark and doubtful days. Eleven months having now passed, we are permitted to take another review. The rebel borders are pressed still further back, and by the complete opening of the Mississippi the country dominated by the rebellion is divided into distinct parts, with no practical communication between them. Tennessee and Arkansas have been substantially cleared of insurgent control, and influential citizens in both, owners of slaves and advocates of slavery at the beginning of the rebellion, now declare openly for emancipation in their respective States. Of those States not included in the emancipation proclamation, Maryland, and Missouri, neither of which three years ago would tolerate any restraint upon the extension of slavery into new territories, only dispute now as to the best mode of removing it within their own limits.

Of those who were slaves at the beginning of the rebellion, full one hundred thousand are now in the United States military service, about one-half of which number actually bear arms in the ranks; thus giving the double advantage of taking so much labor from the insurgent cause, and supplying the places which otherwise must be filled with so many white men. So far as tested, it is difficult to say they are not as good soldiers as any. No servile insurrection, or tendency to violence or cruelty, has marked the measures of emancipation and arming the blacks. These measures have been much discussed in foreign countries, and contemporary with such discussion the tone of public sentiment there is much improved. At home the same measures have been fully discussed, supported, criticised, and denounced, and the annual elections following are highly encouraging to those whose official duty it is to bear the country through this great trial. Thus we have the new reckoning. The crisis which threatened to divide the friends of the Union is past.

Jefferson Davis had been unable to see an end to the conflict; Lincoln could look forward to an increasing extension of the Federal authority as the Union armies pushed into Confederate territory. Accordingly, the President had issued a proclamation, dated the same day as his message,* providing a plan for reunion. The proclamation had two basic features. The first was an oath of allegiance offered to all except those "who are, or shall have been, civil or diplomatic officers or agents of the so-called confederate government; all who have left judicial stations

---

* That is, December 8, 1863.

under the United States to aid the rebellion; all who are, or shall have been, military or naval officers of said so-called confederate government above the rank of colonel in the army, or of lieutenant in the navy; all who left seats in the United States Congress to aid the rebellion; all who resigned commissions in the army or navy of the United States, and afterwards aided the rebellion; and all who have engaged in any way in treating colored persons or white persons, in charge of such, otherwise than lawfully as prisoners of war, and which persons may have been found in the United States service, as soldiers, seamen, or in any other capacity."

The oath read: "I, ———, do solemnly swear, in presence of Almighty God, that I will henceforth faithfully support, protect and defend the Constitution of the United States, and the Union of the States thereunder; and that I will, in like manner, abide by and faithfully support all acts of Congress passed during the existing rebellion with reference to slaves, so long and so far as not repealed, modified or held void by Congress, or by decision of the Supreme Court; and that I will, in like manner, abide by and faithfully support all proclamations of the President made during the existing rebellion having reference to slaves, so long and so far as not modified or declared void by decision of the Supreme Court. So help me God."

The second feature of the proclamation provided for re-establishing state governments: "Whenever, in any of the States of Arkansas, Texas, Louisiana, Mississippi, Tennessee, Alabama, Georgia, Florida, South Carolina, and North Carolina, a number of persons, not less than one-tenth in number of the votes cast in such State at the Presidential election of the year of our Lord one thousand eight hundred and sixty, each having taken the oath aforesaid and not having since violated it, and being a qualified voter by the election law of the State existing immediately before the so-called act of secession, and excluding all others, shall re-establish a State government which shall be republican, and in no wise contravening said oath, such shall be recognized as the true government of the State, and the State shall receive thereunder the benefits of the constitutional provision which declares that 'The United States shall guaranty to every State in this union a republican form of government, and shall protect each of them against invasion; and, on application of the legislature, or the executive, (when the legislature cannot be convened,) against domestic violence.' "

Lincoln closed on a note of caution—and gratitude:

In the midst of other cares, however important, we must not lose sight of the fact that the war power is still our main reliance. To that power alone can we look, yet for a time, to give confidence to the people in the contested regions, that the insurgent power will not again overrun them. Until that confidence shall be established, little can be done anywhere for what is called reconstruction. Hence our chiefest care must still be directed to the army and navy, who have thus far borne their harder part so nobly and well. And it may be esteemed fortunate that in giving the greatest efficiency to these indispensable arms, we do also honorably recognize the gallant men, from commander to sentinel, who compose them, and to whom, more than to others, the world must stand indebted for the home of freedom disenthralled, regenerated, enlarged, and perpetuated.

VI

While Lincoln worked on his annual message J. T. Fields, editor of the Atlantic Monthly, *or some member of his staff, was composing a long review of the year 1863. The article, entitled "The Beginning of the End," appeared in the issue for January 1864. After reciting the record of military and domestic events and describing the diplomatic successes of the Union, the author closed with a paragraph contradicting Jefferson Davis' assumption of divine favor:*[16]

Such was the year of the Proclamation, and its history is marvellous in our eyes. It stands in striking contrast to the other years of the war, both of which closed badly for us, and left the impression that the enemy's case was a good one, speaking militarily. Our improved condition should be attributed to the true cause. When, in the Parliament of 1601, Mr. Speaker Croke said that the kingdom of England "had been defended by the mighty arm of the Queen," Elizabeth exclaimed from the throne, "No, Mr. Speaker, but rather by the mighty hand of God!" So with us. We have been saved "by the mighty hand of God." Neither "malice domestic" nor "foreign levy" has prevailed at our expense. Whether we had the right to expect Heaven's aid, we cannot undertake to say; but we know that we should not have deserved it, had we continued to link the nation's cause to that of oppression, and had we shed blood and expended gold in order to restore the system of slavery and the sway of slaveholders.

THE DEPTHS
OF SUFFERING

AT MISSIONARY RIDGE, for almost the only time between 1861 and 1865, war became the romantic adventure pictured by the artists of *Leslie's* and *Harper's*, with bands blaring, color-bearers advancing flags, and lines of cheering men following sword-waving officers. Much of the time war was nasty, nameless little fights. Yet the two or three men killed in such encounters were just as dead as the 1,114 (Federal, 753; Confederate, 361) who lost their lives in the spectacular storming of the heights south and east of Chattanooga.

I

Confederate Cavalry Sergeant Edwin H. Fay described a brush with the enemy which took place in western Mississippi in mid-October 1863:[1]

Last Thursday morning our scouts announced the enemy coming and all was bustle and confusion loading up our wagons and sending them to the rear. We saddled up and drew up in line of battle across our camp. Capt. Bowie of Adams Regt. was on picket and held them at bay all day but lost one man, an old Ala. acquaintance of mine, Charley Drummond from Greenville, Ala. a mess mate of Zeb. Rudulph. Poor fellow he was a good soldier and the bravest among the brave. We lay in line of battle that night and next morning the pickets falling back the enemy advanced and planted a battery within 1000 yards of ours and one of the fiercest artillery duels of the war commenced. We silenced the enemy's battery and they commenced flanking us on the right and left when we fell back about a mile and waited their approach. About 100 skirmishers held the column at bay all the rest of the day. We fell back at night some two miles and the enemy, 10,000 strong, only advanced 2 miles in two days though only opposed by 1000 cavalry and a battery of four guns. They had 30 pieces of artillery and 2500 cavalry. They took (Saturday Morn.) another road and found Gen'l John W. Whitfield and his Texans on it supported by Col. Logan's command. They skirmished all day near Livingston while we went to Canton and next morning started early to reinforce them. Loring's Division of Infantry was waiting near Canton but Sunday morning or rather Saturday night the Yanks got wind of it and started back towards Vicksburg at a double quick. We cut them off at their right flank at the Baker Creek ground but they had their wagons guarded on both sides with a double file of Infantry and our officers deemed it not prudent to attack them, so we lay still and let them pass by unmolested.

There were murmurings loud and deep from the soldiers of the brigade because the Yanks escaped us. They brought out 300 wagons some loaded with entrenching tools and telegraph wires evidently intending to take Canton and occupy it, but they met such stubborn resistance from our cavalry that they concluded west of Big Black was a safer place. They told citizens on their retreat that we had 30 thousand infantry fighting them. We lost four killed and ten wounded in our brigade, and ten or 15 graves of Yankees we have found on our battle field.

Lieutenant John Merrilies, Battery E, Illinois Light Artillery, described another of the thousands of minor expeditions in which the armies were engaged in the intervals between big battles:[2]

Dec. 2nd. 1863. Turned out at 3 o.c. Ordered to draw three days' rations of coffee and hard bread and be ready to march at daylight. Forrest reported to be in the neighborhood, evidently contemplating another raid on the R. R. Marched at 6 o.c., a brigade of cavalry and the 2nd Brigade of our division composing the expedition, Tuttle and Mowrer commanding. Followed the railroad east, marching quick. Passed thro Grand Junction and Salisbury in the forenoon, Middleton in the afternoon and by dark were within five miles of Pocahontas, which was to be our destination, the track having been torn up there yesterday. Halted here till word was brought back by the cavalry that there was no enemy in town or near it. Lay in the road all night, the horses hitched up, ordered to be in readiness at a moment's notice, notwithstanding which the men dropped asleep around the fires, worn out by the forced marching. At 2 in the morning turned out again, reversed the battery, and started back by 6 o.c. getting safely across the terrible Hatchie bottoms, which at present may be called bottomless.

Dec. 3. Reports of the rebs having got behind us last night, struck the R. R. at Salisbury, and destroyed the track. The story did not appear probable at first, but about noon skirmishing commenced ahead and the people along the road say there are about 3000 in the neighborhood of Salisbury. Marched ahead lively, but we failed to come in range, the cavalry driving them. Some artillery skirmishing commenced, continuing about an hour. Their cavalry had drawn up in two lines, but our mountain howitzers made it too hot for them, and the appearance of our column coming over the hill, admonished them to leave which they did in different directions, our cavalry pursuing. Reached La Grange at 5 o.c., horses and men badly used up, having marched over 40 miles since we left camp yesterday morning, with no better result from our journey than having the enemy double on us very handsomely, tear up our railroad six miles from camp, and get away again with little or no punishment.

II

Oftener even than little scouts and skirmishes, war was boredom, aimless marching, drudgery, disgust. Witness the diary of James Daniels, Fifth New Hampshire Volunteers, for two weeks in May 1863:[3]

May 7th. In camp near Falmouth. Fixed up our old tents. Dress-parade at night. Rained.

May 8th. In camp. Pleasant. Dress-parade.

May 9th. In camp. Pleasant.

May 10th. In camp. Inspection.

May 11th. In camp. Inspection. Dress-parade.

May 12th. In camp. Two hours' drill in forenoon. Dress-parade. Pleasant.

May 13th. In camp. No drill. Pleasant.

May 14th. In camp. Squad drill. Some rain. Dress-parade.

May 15th. In camp. Pleasant. Battalion drill in the afternoon. Dress-parade.

May 16th. In camp. Dress-parade. Pleasant.

May 17th. In camp. Was detailed on picket; was excused from duty by the doctor; abscess in the groin. Pleasant. Dress-parade.

May 18th. In camp, sick. Pleasant. Dress-parade. The colonel came back from Washington.

May 19th. Sick. Drill. Dress-parade. Pleasant.

May 20th. In camp. Moved from the old camp to a new one about a half mile in the rear. Pleasant all day.

May 21st. In camp. Detailed to dig a spring; made a good one. Pleasant all day.

In the fall of 1863 Albert Dickinson, of Taylor's Battery, Illinois Artillery, floundered around in northern Alabama:[4]

Oct. 28th. 22 years old today. Left Tuscumbia in morn & arrived at Cherokee at sundown.

29th. Heavy skirmishing Osterhaus front. We harnessed up. About noon we harnessed & went out about 2 miles & staid afternoon. Skirmishing all day in front.

30th. Started for Tennessee river, was stopped on act bad roads in front. Made about 3 or 4 miles & camped. Rained very hard during the day. . . .

31st. Marched through to Chickasaw Landing about 7 miles. Arrived in camp about 10 P.M. It was the most disagreeable days march we ever made. Marched few yards then stopped, all day long. Very cold at night. No hard bread. . . .

Nov. 1st. Stopped in Chickasaw all day. Charles B. Andrews was appointed Sergeant of Squad 4. Bill Turner appointed artificer.

Nov. 2nd. Got up at 1 A.M. & crossed Tenn River. Marched to Waterloo. Splendid springs all along the road.

Nove. 3rd. Marched to Florence. Camped mile beyond town. Splendid country. Cypress Mills. Seminary. Nice town. Had good dinner at house.

At the same time Florison D. Pitts, also an Illinois artilleryman, did nothing in Louisiana:[5]

Sunday, Nov. 1st, 1863. Put on a clean shirt. Had a pow wow in the evening. Day cloudy & rainy. Read all day.

Nov. 2nd. Had a drill in the morning. Went out as cannoneer. Mouth sore could not blow the bugle. Got a pass and went down town in afternoon. Played three games with Hugh Wilson. Day very warm. . . . Went to town in evening on my horse.

Nov. 3rd. Drilled in the morning, Cone drill master. Went out on my horse, again played coming through town. Got every body out to see what was the row. Went out and practiced Bugle in afternoon. Evening Deacon & myself took a walk in vicinity of the camp. Played flute with Roe in afternoon. Had a sing in the evening.

Nov. 4th. Drilled in the morning. Day clear & quite warm. Throop drill master. Drilled principally in the Bugle calls, fooled the Boys a good deal on them. Mail came in, got a paper from Mother & a letter from Jennie. Boys went out after cattle.

Nov. 5th. Got up at 6 o'clock in time for Breakfast. Cloudy & some rain. After Breakfast greased my Saddle & Boots. Rain came down all the afternoon. Wrote a letter to Jennie. Evening played whist with Throop & Roe. . . .

Nov. 6th. Day warm & Sultry. Read abt all day, finished *Frank Fowleigh*. In evening wrote to Mother & Charlie Pitts. No drill today, practiced Bugle in afternoon. . . .

Nov. 7th. Drilled in morning under Cone. . . . Went down town in evening. Practiced Bugle in afternoon. Day bright & warm.

A year of inactivity had reduced the Texas cavalryman Edwin H. Fay to a state of complete disgust. From Raymond, Mississippi, he wrote to his wife on September 19, 1863:[6]

This Cavalry has done nothing since a year ago. Our Co. has done nothing and worse than nothing since the fight at Corinth last Oct. Do you wonder then that I am dissatisfied when I see the Confed. losing ground daily and feel that I am so situated that I can do nothing. Our Cavalry wastes its time in grand Reviews before Hardee & Stephen D. Lee and dress parades for a few lonesome and garish young ladies. Noble employment for a band of men.

III

The soldier who had to endure only boredom and drudgery was fortunate; the wounded and the prisoners were war's pitiable victims. Sergeant Joseph F. Johnston, Company K, Nineteenth Illinois Infantry, described an experience shared by many thousands, on both sides:

FIELD HOSPITAL OPPOSITE
CHATTANOOGA TENN. Oct 1st

DEAR MOTHER

I am wounded through the left shoulder, the ball entering below the joint of the shoulder blade & coming out just below the collar bone, thus passing through the top of the left lung. I have to lie on my back the only position in which I can breathe with ease. I can walk a little ways but it makes me breathe hard. I was hit Sunday between 12 & 2 o'clock and as the regt was falling back I was carried off the field by some of my own boys. I was left at a shanty about 7 miles from Chattanooga & two boys of my own company stayed with me to take care of me. They did all they could until 11 AM Monday when the secesh cavalry took them prisoners. The rebs left six nurses for 53 wounded & the nurse who took care of me was very kind. I had cold water constantly by my side & I kept the wound cool all the time. I was bilious & could eat little & what hunger I had was relieved by bran biscuit. There was one small one for each meal. On Sunday the 27th the rebs came with army wagons & moved on to Cloud Springs 5 miles. Tuesday Rosecrans sent 200 ambulances & took 800 wounded from Cloud Springs to Chattanooga. I was dumped in an old grocery store late at night & did not sleep a wink on the hard floor. Wednesday a lot of my boys came to see me. One of them spoke to Dr Bogue & he sent me over here. With so much riding I was very tired. I will not move an inch now till I get strong enough. I am here with the wounded of our own regt, with our own boys to wait on us & our own surgeon. I will now get the best care the place will afford. . . .

Your affectionate son
J. S. JOHNSTON

A month later Sergeant Johnston was still in the hospital (he was not to be discharged until early January 1864):

FIELD HOSP OPP CHATT
TENN. Nov 1st 1863

DEAR FATHER

The chills I spoke of in my last have gone away. The Dr ascribed it to biliousness & gave me some "Cathartic Pills" which helped me very much. Yesterday & the day before were cold & made me a little bilious but today the sun shone pleasant and I put on a jacket Fred Temple gave me and made a journey of over a quarter of a mile & back which fatigued me and gave me a little appetite.

But alas! we are reduced on rations. While the army received nothing we have half rations—*mouldy* crackers. I will have to come pretty near starving before I eat them.

The Dr says it is the diet that makes me bilious & he will send me off the first chance. The ambulance train is here but they seem to be waiting to send us *"down the river.".* . . . I have seen Elder Raymond again. He brought me a can of milk. I can get nothing of that sort after this. Army half rations is my lot. . . .

Your Aff. Son

J. S. JOHNSTON

Field hospitals were shambles. A correspondent of the Cincinnati Gazette, *writing from headquarters of the Army of the Cumberland on September 23, 1863, described the Union wounded and the treatment they received at Chickamauga:*[7]

A few miles' riding brought us so far on the way that we began to get glimpses of that stream of wreck, debris, mingled life and mangled humanity which always flows from a battle-field. . . .

Here is a man with an arm roughly bandaged and very bloody. The blood has dried upon it and hangs to it in great black clots. "Who are you?" "Private ———, of the Thirty-eighth Indiana." "What news have you?" "Bad enough." "Has your regiment been in the fight?" "If it has not no one has." "With what result?" "One third of its members are killed and wounded." "Were you whipped?" "Our brigade was left unsupported, overpowered by numbers, and compelled for a time to give way." "Is Colonel Scribner safe?" "So far as I know, he is."

Another with a ghastly wound in his head has upon his jacket the red stripes which show him to be an artilleryman. "Whose battery do you belong to?" "Guenther's." "Why, that is the regular battery belonging to General King's brigade; what has it been doing?" "It has been taken by the enemy." "Can that be possible?" "It is, but I have heard since that it was retaken." "How came it to be lost?" "The infantry supports gave way, and the horses being nearly all killed, of course the guns were captured."

The stream grew stronger and stronger. Stragglers were run over by wagons dashing back toward the rear. Ambulances, filled with wounded, came in long procession from toward where the battle was raging. Men with wounds of every imaginable description not affecting their locomotion, came staggering by on foot, and scores even of those who had been shot in their lower limbs, hobbled slowly on through blinding masses of dust, which at times concealed every thing from view.

At length we reached the hospital for General Brannan's division. The house had already been filled. The outhouses had been brought into requisition, and large numbers of sufferers were lying on the ground in the yard. In one corner was an operating table, beneath which lay the usual quantity of legs, arms, hands, feet, fingers, and toes. Here and there among the wounded were some cold and stiff, the seal of death upon their countenances. These had died after being carried to the yard.

Major General Carl Schurz, who commanded the Eleventh Corps at Gettysburg, watched the surgeons at work immediately after the battle:[8]

The wounded—many thousands of them—were carried to the farm-steads behind our lines. The houses, the barns, the sheds, and the open barnyards were crowded with the moaning and wailing human beings, and still an unceasing procession of stretchers and ambulances was coming in from all sides to augment the number of the sufferers. A heavy rain set in during the day—the usual rain after a battle—and large numbers had to remain unprotected in the open, there being no room left under roof. I saw long rows of men lying under the eaves of the buildings, the water pouring down upon their bodies in streams. Most of the operating tables were placed in the open where the light was best, some of them partially protected against the rain by tarpau-lins or blankets stretched upon poles.

There stood the surgeons, their sleeves rolled up to the elbows, their bare arms as well as their linen aprons smeared with blood, their knives not seldom held between their teeth, while they were helping a patient on or off the table, or had their hands otherwise occupied; around them pools of blood and amputated arms or legs in heaps, sometimes more than man-high. Antiseptic methods were still unknown at that time. As a wounded man was lifted on the table, often shrieking with pain as the attendants handled him, the surgeon quickly examined the wound and resolved upon cutting off the injured limb. Some ether was administered and the body put in position in a moment. The surgeon snatched his knife from between his teeth, where it had been while his hands were busy, wiped it rapidly once or twice across his blood-stained apron, and the cutting began. The operation accomplished, the surgeon would look around with a deep sigh, and then— "Next!"

And so it went, hour after hour, while the number of expectant patients seemed hardly to diminish. Now and then one of the wounded men would call attention to the fact that his neighbor lying on the ground had given up the ghost while waiting for his turn, and the dead body was then quietly removed. Or a surgeon, having been long at work, would put down his knife, exclaiming that his hand had grown unsteady, and that this was too much for human endurance—not seldom hysterical tears streaming down his face. Many of the wounded men suffered with silent fortitude, fierce determination in the knitting of their brows and the steady gaze of their bloodshot eyes. Some would even force themselves to a grim jest about their situation or about the "skedaddling of the rebels." But there were, too, heart-rending groans and shrill cries of pain piercing the air, and despairing exclamations, "Oh, Lord! Oh, Lord!" or "Let me die!" or softer murmurings in which the words "mother" or "father" or "home" were often heard.

From battlefield stations the badly wounded and gravely ill flowed into general hospitals. Cornelia Hancock, a young Quaker woman serving as a government nurse at Letterman General Hospital, Gettysburg, wrote of her life there in letters to members of her family:[9]

Aug. 8th, 1863

. . . Our hospital is on rising ground, divided off into six avenues, and eighteen tents holding twelve men each on each avenue. We call four tents a ward and name them by a letter; mine is ward E. The water is excellent and there is order about everything. I like it a great deal better than the battlefield, but the battlefield is where one does most good. . . .

It is now about nine o'clock, every tent has a light in it, and a lot of groaning sick men. Our cook-house alone is a sight; they have meals cooked for thirteen hundred men, so you may know that they have to have the pots middling size. If you ever saw anything done on a large scale, it is done so here. There are many sights here, but the most melancholy one is to see the wounded come in in a long train of ambulances after night fall. I must be hardhearted though, for I do not feel these things as strangers do. . . .

I think we have some excellent nurses; we must have at least thirty women in the whole hospital. I have one tent of Johnnies in my ward, but I am not obliged to give them anything but whiskey. . . .

Aug. 17, 1863

. . . I do think military matters are enough to aggravate a saint. We no sooner get a good physician than an order comes to remove, promote, demote or *something*. Everything seems to be done to aggravate the wounded. They do not get any butter; there is certainly a want of generalship somewhere for there is surely enough butter in the United States to feed these brave wounded. There are many hardships that soldiers have to endure that cannot be explained unless experienced. I have nothing to do in the hospital after dark which is well for me—all the skin is off my toes, marching so much. I am not tired of being here, feel so much interest in the men under my charge. The friends of men who have died seem so grateful to me for the little that it was in my power to do for them. I saw a man die in half a minute from the effects of chloroform; there is nothing that has affected me so much since I have been here; it seems almost like deliberate murder. His friends arrived today but he had to be buried before they came. Every kind of distress comes upon the friends of soldiers. . . .

Aug. 31st, 1863

. . . All the men in my ward are doing well but two. Rufus M. is in process of dying. He belongs to the 111th New York, has keen black eyes and laid in the upper tent where thee saw him. I have taken every care of him that is possible; was determined to save him, his leg has commenced bleeding and he cannot last long. . . .

We had the medical director around yesterday, had a big inspection; he was a real alive man, went with the surgeon in charge of this hospital, went into every tent, pointed to every man, asked him the point blank question "Do you get enough to eat?" The men, of course, answered in the negative. Then in the presence of Chamberlain said: "The first thing to set your self about is feeding these men; there is nothing better, *feed them*, I say, feed them. Feed them till they can't complain." Said he had been in the service twenty-five years. Said *he* could feed men till they would not complain. Said clean avenues and clean tents would not cure a man. Things were better today and they will be, I know. The old gentleman stuck his head in every oven, in the barrels, into everything and is still on hand. . . .

Southern hospitals differed little from those in the North. Mrs. Thomas Pember, superintendent of a wing in Chimborazo Hospital, Richmond, described some of her duties in a way that throws light on the medical practices of the time:[10]

The duty which of all others pressed most heavily upon me and which I never did perform voluntarily was that of telling a man he could not live, when he was perhaps unconscious that there was any danger apprehended from his wound. The idea of death so seldom occurs when disease and suffering have not wasted the frame and destroyed the vital energies, that there is but little opening or encouragement to commence such a subject unless the patient suspects the result ever so slightly. In many cases too, the yearning for life was so strong that to destroy the hope was beyond human power. Life was for him a furlough, family and friends once more around him; a future was all he wanted, and he considered it cheaply purchased if only for a month by the endurance of any wound, however painful or wearisome.

There were long discussions among those responsible during the war, as to the advisability of the frequent amputations on the field, and often when a hearty, fine-looking man in the prime of life would be brought in minus an arm or leg, I would feel as if it might have been saved, but experience taught me the wisdom of prompt measures. Poor food and great exposure had thinned the blood and broken down the system so entirely that secondary amputations performed in the hospital almost invariably resulted in death, after the second year of the war. The blood lost on the battlefield when the wound was first received would enfeeble the already impaired system and render it incapable of further endurance.

Once we received a strong, stalwart soldier from Alabama, and after five days' nursing, finding the inflammation from the wound in his arm too great to save the limb, the attending surgeon requested me to feed him on the best I could command; by that means to try and give him strength to undergo amputation. Irritability of stomach as well as indifference to food always accompanying gun-shot wounds, it was necessary, while the fever continued, to give him as much nourishment in as small a compass as possible, as well as easily digestible food, that would assimilate with his enfeebled condition. Beef tea he (in common with all soldiers and I believe men) would not, or could not take, or anything I suggested as an equivalent, so getting his consent to drink some "chemical mixture," I prepared the infusion. Chipping up a pound of beef and pouring upon it a half pint of water, the mixture was stirred until all the blood was extracted, and only a tea-spoonful of white fibre remained; a little salt was added, and favored by the darkness of the corner of the ward in which he lay, I induced him to swallow it. He drank without suspicion, and fortunately liked it, only complaining of its being too sweet; and by the end of ten days his pulse was fairly good, and there had been no accession of fever. Every precaution was taken, both for his sake and the benefit of the experiment, and the arm taken off by the most skillful surgeon we had. After the amputation, which he bore bravely, he looked as bright and well as before, and so on for five days—then the usual results followed. The system proved not strong enough to throw out the "pus" or inflammation; and this, mingling with the blood, produced that most fatal of all diseases, pyaemia, from which no one ever recovers.

He was only one of numerous cases, so that my heart beat twice as rapidly as ordinarily whenever there were any arrangements progressing for amputation, after any length of time had elapsed since the wound, or any effort made to save the limb. The only cases under my observation that survived were two Irishmen, and it was really so difficult to kill an Irishman that there was little cause for boasting on the part of the officiating surgeons.

In the light of modern practice the surgical and hospital records of the Civil War look barbarous. Yet George Worthington Adams, whose book, Doctors in Blue, *is an able study of the medical history of the Union Army, concludes: "The medical and sanitary record of the Civil War was on the whole a good one. That this has not been generally realized is partly due to the fact that the Civil War took place at the very end of the medical 'middle ages'—immediately before bacteriology and aseptic surgery made some of the war generation's triumphs seem piddling or irrelevant." H. H. Cunningham in a companion work,* Doctors in Gray, *offers a similar but more detailed appraisal:*[11]

Confederate medical officers met the demands imposed upon them as courageously and as effectively as could have been expected. Visits to hospitals other than their own for purposes of investigation, the

formation of medical societies, quiz classes, and the like all would appear to indicate the presence of a desire to improve themselves pro-
fessionally; and while there was much that they did not know the restrictions to which they were sometimes subjected made it impossible
for them to apply what they did know. "We did not do the best we
would," explained one, "but the best we could." Some of the disadvantages under which Confederate medical officers worked was set forth
concisely by one of their number: "The surgeon-general issued some
valuable and useful publications, but we had no 'Medical and Surgical
History of the Confederate States'; we had scarcely a journal; we had
no 'Army Medical Museum'; we had no men of science and leisure to
produce original work, or to record, classify and arrange the rich
and abundant material gathered in the departments of either medicine
or surgery. . . ."

Neither, it might be added, did they have blood plasma, x-rays, anti-
biotics, vitamin concentrates, vaccine to prevent typhoid fever and
tetanus, and other products of recent medical and surgical research
considered so essential today to the military medical officer. Nor did
they have in the latter part of the war—perhaps after the battle of
Chickamauga—patients whose physical condition was favorably
influenced by a confident mental outlook. The men became less and
less sanguine as the war entered its final stages, and the surgeons' task
was rendered more difficult by the ensuing mental depression. Yet
available records for the war years appear to indicate that the annual
mortality and disease mortality rates throughout the conflict were less
than those of other armies (except for those of the Union forces which
were also relatively low) that took the field in the nineteenth century.

IV

*On the morning of April 8, 1862, the day after the Battle of Shiloh,
Willie Barrow, a young Confederate soldier from St. Francisville,
Louisiana, found himself a prisoner of war. In the next two weeks he
experienced hardships which were the common lot of hundreds of thousands, Union and Confederate, between 1862 and 1865:*[12]

Wednesday, 9th. This morning I awoke early after setting up half
the night with the wounded. They were all much better. They began
moving them about nine o'clock to the river; about one I went with one
load. Got to the river at two o'clock and a man separated me from the

wounded and carried me to General Buell's quarters on the *Empress*. He had me sent to the provost-marshal and from there I went where the rest of the prisoners were.

Thursday, 10th. This morning I was up early as there was no use to attempt to sleep. We had nothing to eat until nine o'clock when they brought us a barrel of crackers and some bacon. We fried the bacon on sticks. Lord deliver me from such hardships. Sitting on the ground trying to keep warm our eyes filled with smoke and no handkerchief to blow my nose on. Sky cloudy.

Friday, April 11th. This morning it commenced to rain. We had nothing to eat but what was given to us the day before. We staid in the rain trying to keep as dry as possible before the fires. About two o'clock the provost marshal came and called us out in two ranks and called the roll to see if we were all there; they then marched us between two rows of Wisconsin troops to the river where we got aboard the *Woodford*. I slept on some straw; went to bed without anything to eat, but slept pretty sound notwithstanding the poor accommodations.

Saturday, April 12th. This morning I awoke early after a pretty sound sleep. Had for breakfast a piece of bacon, a hard cracker and a little coffee. We got out of the Tennessee in to the Ohio river about twelve o'clk. Got to Paducah about one o'clk. For dinner I had a piece of bacon and a hard cracker. This afternoon I got a paper of the 10th giving an account of the battle of Pittsburgh [Landing]. We got to Cairo about four o'clk in the morning where we staid until 10 o'clk. Weather sultry.

Sunday, April 13th. This morning I awoke bright and early as usual. Had for breakfast a hard cracker and some coffee. Got a little soap and succeeded in getting a little dirt off my hands. For dinner I had the same as for breakfast, a hard biscuit and some coffee. We were in the Mississippi river running five miles an hour. Weather cool but pleasant. I changed my bed from the straw to some hard boards.

Monday, April 14th. This morning I awoke and found myself in St. Louis, Mo.

April 23rd. We staid in St. Louis for two or three days and from there came to Chicago, Camp Douglas, where they keep all their prisoners. The reason I have not kept up my regular journal is that I have been suffering from dysinterry. The weather here is very cold and goes very hard with the boys from the south.

At Camp Douglas, Barrow found no serious cause for complaint:

Chicago, Sunday, April 27th, 1862. I am now getting over my attack of dysinterry and will commence my journal again. We are very well fixed off for prisoners. Our quarters are plenty large enough and we are permitted to go out and walk in the inclosure. Today I read and slept the day away. . . .

April 28th. This morning I was up early. After breakfast which consisted of a piece of toast and some arrow root, I read and played a game of eucre. They treat us as if we were their own soldiers, give us the same rations and everything that is necessary: for dinner we had irish potatoes and hominy. In the evening I passed the time by sleeping and reading. The weather is moderating and getting quite pleasant. . . .

Thursday, May 1st. I was up early this morning and learnt that I was to be the cook for the day. I started and made coffee for breakfast; for dinner I had beans, fried beef, and irish potatoes. After dinner I cleaned the pots and then past some of my time reading. For supper we had coffee and bread. I past the rest of my time playing whist. Weather is a little rainy. My imprisonment is beginning to pass away a little better than when I was sick. . . .

May 4th. This morning I was up a little later than usual. Blacked my shoes as it was sunday and fixed myself as nice as possible. After breakfast I read six chapters in the New Testament. Afterwards I lounged around until dinner time. After dinner I walked down in camp. . . .

May 14th. This morning after breakfast I read "Travels in Denmark & Sweden"; we got some books through the kind ladies in St. Louis, and we get books at this place through a parson (Presby) by the name of Tutle. Our dinner today was very good for prisoners-of-war; we had beef-steak, mashed-irish-potatoes, and a bread-pudding with a nice sauce. The beef-steak and potatoes was the ration but the sauce was not. . . .

June 1st. Today was a miserable day, rain, a cold wind, muddy, in fact, I have never experienced a worse one—I had to go to bed to keep warm. I tried to read—but it was too cold and disagreeable. How people can live in such a climate I cannot conceive. We received the news of the evacuation of Corinth by Beauregard. I am reading the Count of Monte Christo which is very interesting. . . .

June 4th. This morning the first thing I caught was a body louse, Ugh! Well that was strange, I did not know what kind of a louse it was. All night I was restless, scratching away at what I supposed to be the *rash*. The doctor had gave me an ointment for it but it had got no better.

In the evening I thought I would wash my neck and put on a clean undershirt. I got everything ready. I looked in my unclean shirt and lo! & behold! it was filled with lice, horrid! The whole mess profiting by my discovery we soon had a tub full of the varmints. . . .

June 13. This morning after breakfast I went to the post office. Came back and read and played a few games of draughts. After dinner I read and went to sleep; the weather is very pleasant, a little cold from the rain of last night. Reports keep coming about the exchange of prisoners. I only hope and pray that it is true and that I may soon be in my native land once again.

June 23rd. Today we had a strange proceeding. We were ordered to be in front of our quarters at one o'clock. We obeyed the cowards' orders, and were marched all into two squares, and guards placed all around us while we were in the squares. Guards around us with loaded guns. Then the brave *yanks* came with Police from Chicago, went around in the prisoners' quarters, took watches, money, Guata Percha rings, sigars, clothes etc. Then the Police robbers came through our ranks and searched us, taking pocket knives & money. The once United states giving commissions to officers who are afraid of prisoners' pocket knives. One incident is worthy of note. There was a company of Tennesseans who were thinking of taking the oath but after the proceedings of this evening they concluded that the Confederacy was the best government. . . .

June 29th . . . In the evening we received the news of our successes in Virginia.* The whole encampment was filled with the greatest enthusiasm. The men were running all over the camp for papers—but the yankees would not permit the paper boys to come in the camp. However we succeeded in getting one or two papers and received the news. Hurrah! for Seceshindom. Good! for Jackson.

A year later a prisoner, wherever confined, faced an existence far grimmer than that which Willie Barrow had endured. The South, whatever its will, lacked the resources to feed and house its prisoners in the comparative comfort which, as Union soldiers, they had enjoyed. Besides, constant contact with suffering had made even humane men callous. One result was Libby Prison, Richmond. Lieutenant Colonel F. F. Cavada, captured on the second day of Gettysburg, described the prison as he saw it on the eighteenth of July, 1863:[13]

---

* Confederate victories in Stonewall Jackson's Valley campaign.

The gloomy and forbidding exterior of the prison, and the pale, emaciated faces staring vacantly at us through the bars, were repulsive enough, but it was at least a haven of rest from the weary foot-march, and from the goad of the urging bayonet. . . .

We are now fairly launched upon the mysterious ocean of Libby life. . . . The room we are in is long, low, dingy, gloomy, and suffocating. Some two hundred officers are lying packed in rows along the floor, sleeping the heavy, dreamless sleep of exhaustion. But there are some who cannot sleep; they are thinking of the camp, of home, and of friends; they are quarreling with the fortune of war; they are longing for the termination of a loathsome and hateful captivity, which has only just begun. By-and-by even the most wakeful yield to the imperative demand for rest, and with one arm for a pillow, have stretched themselves out on the bare floor. . . .

Now for the Libby itself. It stands close by the Lynchburg canal, and in full view from the river. It is a capacious warehouse, built of brick and roofed with tin. It was a busy place previous to the Rebellion; barrels and bales obstructed the stone side-walk which surrounds the building on all four of its sides; barrels and boxes were being constantly hoisted in and hoisted out; numberless boats lined the canal in front of it, and loaded drays rattled over the cobbled pavement of Carey street. There was a signboard at an angle of the building, whereon you might have read in black letters on a white ground: "Libby & Sons, Ship Chandlers and Grocers." This signboard is still at its post; but a wondrous change has come over the place. There are now no bales and boxes coming in at one end, and going out at the other; no laden boats on the canal; no drays rattling over the stone pave. There is something about it indicative of the grave, and, indeed, it *is* a sort of unnatural tomb, whose pale, wan inhabitants gaze vacantly out through the barred windows on the passer-by, as if they were peering from the mysterious precincts of another world.

The building has a front of about one hundred and forty feet, with a depth of about one hundred and five. There are nine rooms, each one hundred and two feet long by forty-five wide. The height of ceilings from the floor, is about seven feet; except in the upper story, which is better ventilated owing to the pitch of the roof. At each end of these rooms are five windows.

Nothing but bread has, as yet, been issued to us, half a loaf twice a day, per man. This must be washed down with James River water, drawn from a hydrant over the wash-trough. Tomorrow, we are to be indulged with the luxury of bacon-soup.

There are some filthy blankets hanging about the room; they have been used time and again by the many who have preceded us; they are soiled, worn, and filled with vermin, but we are recommended to help ourselves in time; if we do so with reluctance and profound disgust it is because we are now more particular than we will be by-and-by.

We have tasted of the promised soup; it is boiled water sprinkled with rice, and seasoned with the rank juices of stale bacon; we must shut our eyes to eat it; the bacon, I have no doubt, might have walked into the pot of its own accord. It is brought up to us in wooden buckets, and we eat it, in most cases without spoons, out of tin cups.

Henry H. Eby, Seventh Illinois Cavalry, was captured during the battle of Chickamauga. Ten days later he and several hundred other prisoners were herded into the prison pen on Belle Isle, in the James River near Richmond:[14]

The train stopped on the south side of the river and we were ordered to alight and were conducted down to the bridge and across it to the island. The Confederate iron works were located on the island, near the bridge, it was now getting dark and as we passed them they seemed to be all aglow from the light of the fires within, and one of the boys remarked in a joking way: "Here are the iron works, and the next place will be worse." I guess the prison pen on the island, into which we were placed a few moments later, about filled the bill.

We soon arrived at the place where we were to be confined, and found it to consist of several acres of ground, surrounded by a ditch about two feet deep and three feet wide, with the soil thrown up on the outside, which formed the deadline. Outside of this the guards paced back and forth. Any person stepping upon this line would be shot down without a moment's warning. There were 7,000 or 8,000 prisoners confined on this small area of ground. Nearly one-half of them were without any shelter whatever, and many had no blankets or overcoats.

We arrived at our new quarters in the evening, and after partaking of a scanty meal looked about for a spot large enough to lie down upon to sleep. I found a place that reminded me of the garden beds we used to make at home, it being slightly raised, with a path around it. Probably this had been made by some of the prisoners, to keep the water off in case of heavy rains. We now made preparations to retire, which were very simple. As many as could crowd upon this small space of ground lay down, in spoon fashion; that is, all lying with our faces turned in the same direction, and fitted together as one would spoons in packing them away, in order to have sufficient room and keep as warm as possible. We had nothing under us except the cold, bare earth, and nothing over us except a pup tent (a piece of muslin six feet square) and the blue sky, which was rather light covering. We had advantages on the island in some respects that we did not possess at home, we were not obliged to open the windows to air our beds. My outfit of clothing consisted of shirt, pants, cavalry jacket, boots and hat. I used my hat in place of a nightcap, to keep my head from coming in contact with the ground. I generally felt quite chilly during the night, and did not sleep soundly. Got up in the morning and found that the surroundings looked very discouraging. Did not see a soul that I knew, but saw many prisoners, some of whom had been confined here for months. These appeared ragged, dirty, and discouraged to the last degree. Rations were very small, and we were hungry continually, but had plenty of river water to drink.

After six days at Belle Isle, Eby was transferred to Smith Prison, Richmond:

It had formerly been used as a tobacco factory. . . . I was confined on the third floor. . . . This was a large room, but after lying down at night the floor was about covered with men. There was scarcely room enough for a person to walk through between the rows of men. Here we were well sheltered, but suffered another extreme, being nearly suffocated on account of not having proper ventilation; not even being allowed to open a window wide enough to admit sufficient fresh air to supply the number of prisoners within. . . .

There were about three hundred of us confined within this room, for a term of about two months, and during all that time we were hardly allowed to draw a breath of fresh air. . . . This and starvation, together, weakened us to an alarming degree. Our rations were issued once a day, and we generally devoured them at one meal, and still felt hungry. It was really just enough to make one meal a day. The order to draw rations generally came in the following manner. The Confederate orderly would enter the room and cry out: "Sargin ob de floor, four men and four blankets." This announcement in the southern dialect soon became a proverb among the boys. The "sargin ob de floor" would then detail four men and four blankets (blankets were a scarce article but generally enough were found to carry the rations) to carry the rations to our room. They would hasten down the stairs, and then those left behind anxiously crowded around the windows, pale, hungry, and each one eager to catch the first glimpse of the returning four men and four blankets with the morsel of bread, and soup (the soup being carried in buckets). This was composed of small beans, some being black and others red, and nearly every one was hollow and contained several black bugs enclosed, with hard shells. When the beans were boiled the bugs separated from them, and became mixed all through the soup, and while eating it we were obliged to grind the bugs between our teeth, which made me think of chewing parched corn or grinding coffee. The ingredients of the soup except the beans and bugs were unknown to us. Some declared that there was mule meat in it, judging from the bones found in the soup. I was almost famished for a meat diet, but did not care to have it in bug form. The bread rations consisted of brown bread, which tasted good to me, but we could not tell of what it was composed. The quantity was so small that it failed to satisfy our hunger. Part of the time while in this building we received corn-bread instead of the brown bread, and occasionally a small piece of meat, the quantity being too small to be mentioned. The soup was named by some of the men "bug soup," and it was a very appropriate name, as the bugs seemed to make the biggest show.

Our beds consisted of the bare floor. For covering I had my indispensable pup tent. We remained in this building during the months of October and November, and during that time there was no fire in the room, but any quantity of foul air, which at times was so terrible that I believe it was poison to us. The closet was located at or in one corner of the room. It was nothing more than a space about six or eight feet in length and several feet wide, and extended down to the basement to the depth of twenty or twenty-five feet. It was enclosed on three sides, and the side which opened into our room or prison had no door. It remained open all the time that we were confined in this place. I do not know whether there was sufficient water at the closet to carry away all the refuse or not, but by what we saw I think not. The condition of the atmosphere was simply horrible beyond description. At times it seemed as if we would certainly suffocate. In this condition about three hundred of us lived, slept, and dined for a period of about two months.

Of all Southern prisons, Andersonville was the most feared. Sergeant S. S. Boggs, Twenty-first Illinois Infantry, described his experiences there:[15]

We learned that this was Andersonville. We were taken from the cars to an open piece of ground just east of the station, looking east about a quarter of a mile, we could see an immense stockade. The last few days of our journey we had no water, and were suffering from thirst. The car that I was in had been used as a lime car, and had a half-inch of lime dust on the floor when they loaded us in at Petersburg; they put about seventy-five men in each car; any moving around would stir up the dust. Our lips and tongues seemed parched and cracked. Two died in our car on the trip. There was a small brook within two rods of us; the guard line was between us and the water. I was pleading with the guard to let us to the water, when a little grinny-faced Rebel captain, on a sway-backed gray horse, rode up and shook a revolver in my face and said: "You Got tam Yankee! you youst vait, and you got so much vater voy you drown in booty quick!" He rode around us several times, bouncing high in his saddle, flourishing a revolver and swearing at the guards and us alternately. After satisfying himself that we did not have any thing worth robbing us of, he proceeded to form us into nineties and detachments. One of our sergeants was put over each ninety, and one over each detachment. By this time we learned that this was Captain Wirz, the commander of the interior of the prison.

We were ordered forward toward the big stockade, moving quietly and painfully along, our spirits almost crushed within us, urged on by the double file of guards on either side of our column of ragged, lousy, skeletons, who scarce had strength to run away if given the opportunity. We neared the wall of great squared logs and the massive wooden gates that were to shut out hope and life from nearly all of us forever. The uncheerful sight, near the gate, of a pile of ghastly dead—the eyes of whom shone with a stony glitter, the faces black with a smoky grime, and pinched with pain and hunger, the long matted hair and almost fleshless frame swarming with lice—gave us some idea that a like fate awaited us on the inside. The rebels knowing our desperation, used every precaution to prevent a break; the artillerymen stood with lanyard in hand at their cannister-shotted guns, which were trained to sweep the gates. All being ready, the huge bolts were drawn, the gate swung open on its massive iron hinges, and as we moved into that hell on earth we felt that we were cut off from the world and completely at the mercy of our cruel keepers.

The creek which ran through the pen was pointed out to us. A rush was made for it, as we were famishing from thirst. The water soon became cloudy; two comrades, to get the water just above the "dead line," and not knowing the danger, reached beyond it, and both dropped dead in the water, shot by the guards on the wall. We dared not move their bodies until ordered to do so by a Rebel officer, who was some time in getting around. The water running red with our comrades' blood, stopped the drinking until the bodies were removed. We had not been in the stockade ten minutes until two of our number were ready to be put on the dead pile we had seen just outside the gate, but the poor fellows missed the horrible torture which was planned for them and us, and which if I knew I had to pass through again I would cross the "dead line" and ask the guard to show me mercy by tearing my body through with the ball and buckshot from his old Queen Anne musket. . . .

The spot of ground we were to occupy was pointed out to the sergeant of our detachment, who guided us to near the northeast corner of the pen, where we arranged in rows, north and south, leaving a narrow alley between each ninety. We then commenced fixing our bedding-place, or, rather, "spooning-ground." There was yet some debris left from cutting and hewing the palisade timbers. The prisoners who had been there, some of them more than a month, had consumed nearly all of the refuse for fuel, for making huts and "dug outs." Some, with a view of speculation, had stored by many of the best poles and sticks. However, there were yet some small poles and sticks to be had along the edge of the swamp; with these, and sun-dried bricks, we made a temporary shelter, which would do in dry weather, but when it rained it seemed to rain more in the hut than it did outside, and our brick generally had to be made anew.

Our rations now consisted of a pint of coarse corn-meal and about a *gill* of stock peas per day. . . .

We tried to occupy our time in bettering our shelter and killing the lice, which had gotten a good start on us while we were being moved. When the sun shone out warm, we would take off our rags, and sitting along in a row, our hands soon were in motion, which would lead a distant observer to believe that we were having a knitting frolic, in which he might not be mistaken, and "nits" were part of the game we were after. . . .

Each detachment and ninety was counted by a Rebel sergeant every morning at eight o'clock, and about the middle of the afternoon a four-mule team drove in with a wagon-body full of coarse, chaffy corn meal. The sergeant would call for two men from each ninety to draw rations, then the man who had a pair of pants or drawers, which could be made to hold meal by tying the legs at the bottom, loaned them to the sergeant for the consideration of a spoonful of meal. The rations would be drawn in proportion to the number found in each ninety—then carried to their respective grounds, divided out, each man getting for a day's allowance nearly a pint of the meal, a tablespoonful of peas, or, instead, about one ounce of beef; a piece of bone weighing six or eight ounces being considered equal to an allowance of beef. Nearly all would eat their rations as soon as issued. Many for want of means to cook them would eat their rations raw. In all my eighteen months' prison experience, the Rebels never furnished us one item in the way of cups, cooking vessels or clothing (except water pails at Danville, Va.).

Confederate prisoners could match the Northern stories of hardship and maltreatment. This is the account of a captured Virginia infantryman:[16]

The military prison, or rather prisons, at Point Lookout [Maryland], consisted of two inclosures, the one containing about thirty, the other about ten acres of flat sand, on the northern shore of the Potomac at its mouth, but a few inches above high tide, and utterly innocent of tree, shrub, or any natural equivalent for the same. Each was surrounded by a fence about fifteen feet high, facing inwards, around the top of which on the outer face, and about twelve feet from the ground, ran a platform on which twenty or thirty sentinels were posted, keeping watch and ward, night and day, over the prisoners within. Besides these precautions, a strongly fortified palisade stretched across the tongue of land on which the prisons stood, from the bay on the northeast to the Potomac on the southwest. Within this palisade, but of course outside of the "pens," were usually two regiments of infantry, and a couple of batteries of artillery, and without the fortification two or three companies of cavalry, while, riding at anchor in the bay, one gunboat at least was always to be seen. One face of each of these "pens," the eastern, fronted the bay, and gates led from the inclosures to a narrow belt of land between the fence and the water, which was free to the prisoners during the day, piles being driven into the bay on either hand to prevent any dexterous "reb" from *flanking out.* A certain portion of the water was marked off by stakes driven into the bottom, for bathing purposes, and most of the prisoners gladly availed themselves of the privilege thus afforded; although, as the same locality precisely and exclusively was devoted to the reception of all the filth of the camp, I admit a squeamishness which deprived me of sea-bathing as long as I stayed there. . . .

I now began prison life in earnest, and none but those who have experienced it can approximate an idea of its wretchedness. This does not consist in loss of liberty, in absence from home, in subjection to others' control, in insufficient food, in scant clothing, in loss of friends, in want of occupation, in an exposed life, in the absence of all conveniences of living. God knows, all these are bad enough, and contribute in the aggregate greatly to the enhancement of the misery of a prisoner. I think, however, that the great overshadowing agony of imprisonment, to persons of any culture, is isolation—

> "———— the dreary void,
> The leafless desert of the mind,
> The waste of feelings unemployed."

The world, friends, fellow-citizens, home, are things as remote as though in another sphere. Death brings its compensation, aside from the consolations of religion, in the remembrance that it is irreversible, and we choke down and eradicate, if we cannot exalt and purify those emotions, whereof the lost were the objects, insensibly changing our social schedule to meet the new order of things. But the prisoner preserves affections and interests without being able to indulge them, and thus with straining eyes and quickening pulse, he dismisses continually the dove for the expected emblem, but it returns forever with flagging wing and drooping head, not having found whereon to rest its weary foot. Thus, there comes that despair which is the aggregate of many, or the supremacy of one disappointment—and from despair comes always degradation. Men become reckless, because hopeless—brutalized, because broken-spirited, until from disregard of the formalities of life, they become indifferent to its duties, and pass with rapid though almost insensible steps from indecorum to vice—until a man will pick your pocket in a prison, who would sooner cut his own throat at home.

From Point Lookout, the Virginian was transferred to a Federal prison at Elmira, New York:

The chief of the [medical] department was a clubfooted little gentleman, with an abnormal head and a snaky look in his eyes, named Major E. L. Sanger. On our arrival in Elmira, another surgeon, remarkable chiefly for his unaffected simplicity and virgin innocence of everything appertaining to medicine, played doctor there. But as the prisoners increased in numbers, a more formal and formidable staff was organized, with Sanger at the head.

Sanger was simply a brute. . . . He was assisted by Dr. Rider, of Rochester, one of the few "copperheads" whom I met in any office, great or small, at the North. My association was rather more intimate with him than with any of the others, and I believe him to have been a competent and faithful officer. . . . The rest of the "meds" were, in truth, a motley crew in the main, most of them being selected from the impossibility, it would seem, of doing anything else with them. I remember one of the worthies, whose miraculous length of leg and neck suggested "crane" to all observers, whose innocence of medicine was quite refreshing. On being sent for to prescribe for a prisoner, who was said to have bilious fever, he asked the druggist, a "reb," in the most *naive* manner, what was the usual treatment for that disease! Fortunately, during his stay at Elmira, which was not long, there were no drugs in the dispensary, or I shudder to picture the consequences. . . .

The whole camp was divided into wards, to which physicians were assigned. . . . These ward physicians treated the simplest cases in their patients' barrack, and transferred the more dangerous ones to the hospitals, of which there were ten or twelve, capable of accommodating about eighty patients each. Here every arrangement was made that *carpenters* could make to insure the patients against unnecessary mortality, and, indeed, a *system* was professed which would have delighted the heart of a Sister of Charity; but, alas! the practice was quite another thing. The most scandalous neglect prevailed even in so simple a matter as providing food for the sick, and I do not doubt that many of those who died perished from actual starvation.

One of the Petersburg prisoners having become so sick as to be sent to the hospital, he complained to his friends who visited him that he could get nothing to eat, and was dying in consequence, when they made application for leave to buy him some potatoes and roast them for him. Dr. S. not being consulted, the request was granted, and when, a few hours afterwards, the roasted potatoes were brought in, the poor invalids on the neighboring cots crawled from their beds and begged the peelings to satisfy the hunger that was gnawing them.

When complaint was made of this brutality to the sick, there was always a convenient official excuse. Sometimes the fault would be, that a lazy doctor would not make out his provision return in time, in which case his whole ward must go without food, or with an inadequate supply until the next day. Another time there would be a difficulty between the chief surgeon and the commissary, whose general relations were of the stripe characterized by S. P. Andrews as "cat-and-dogamy," which would result in the latter refusing to furnish the former with bread for the sick! In almost all cases the *"spiritus frumenti"* failed to get to the patients, or in so small a quantity after the various *tolls,* that it would not quicken the circulation of a canary.

But the great fault, next to the scant supply of nourishment, was the inexcusable deficiency of medicine. During several weeks, in which dysentery and inflammation of the bowels were the prevalent diseases in prison, there was not a grain of any preparation of opium in the dispensary, and many a poor fellow died for the want of a common medicine, which no family is ordinarily without—that is, if men ever die for want of drugs.

There would be, and is much excuse for such deficiencies in the South—and this is a matter which the Yankees studiously ignore— inasmuch as the blockade renders it impossible to procure any luxuries even for our own sick, and curtails and renders enormously expensive the supply of drugs, of the simplest kind, providing they are exotics; but in a nation, whose boast it is that they do not feel the war, with the world open to them, and supplies of all sorts wonderfully abundant, it is simply infamous to starve the sick as they did there, and equally discreditable to deny them medicines—indispensable according to Esculapian traditions. . . .

I ascend from pills to provender.

The commissary department was under the charge of a cute, active ex-bank officer, Captain G. C. Whiton. The ration of bread was usually a full pound *per diem,* forty-five barrels of flour being converted daily into loaves in the bake-shop on the premises. The meat-ration, on the other hand, was invariably scanty; and I learned, on inquiry, that the fresh beef sent to the prison usually fell short from one thousand to twelve hundred pounds in each consignment. Of course, when this happened, many had to lose a large portion of their allowance; and sometimes it happened that the same man got bones only for several successive days. The expedients resorted to by the men to supply this want of animal food were disgusting. Many found an acceptable substitute in rats, with which the place abounded; and these Chinese delicacies commanded an average price of about four cents apiece—in greenbacks.

I have seen scores of them in various states of preparation, and have been assured by those who indulged in them that worse things have been eaten—an estimate of their value that I took on trust.

Others found in the barrels of refuse fat, which were accumulated at the cook-house, and in the pickings of the bones, which were cut out of the meat and thrown in a dirty heap back of the kitchen, to be removed once a week, the means of satisfying the craving for meat, which rations would not satisfy. I have seen a mob of hungry "rebs" besiege the bone-cart, and beg from the driver fragments on which an August sun had been burning for several days, until the impenetrable nose of a Congo could hardly have endured them.

Twice a day the camp poured its thousands into the mess-rooms, where each man's ration was assigned him; and twice a day the aforesaid rations were characterized by disappointed "rebs" in language not to be found in a prayer-book. Those whose appetite was stronger than their apprehensions frequently contrived to supply their wants by "flanking"—a performance which consisted in joining two or more companions as they successively went to the mess-rooms, or in quietly sweeping up a ration as the company filed down the table. As every ration so flanked was, however, obtained at the expense of some helpless fellow-prisoner, who must lose that meal, the practice was almost universally frowned upon; and the criminal, when discovered, as was frequently the case, was subjected to instant punishment.

This was either confinement in the guard-house, solitary confinement on bread and water, the "sweat box," or the barrel-shirt. The war has made all these terms familiar, except the third, perhaps; by it I mean a wooden box, about seven feet high, twenty inches wide, and twelve deep, which was placed on end in front of the major's tent. Few could stand in this without elevating the shoulders considerably; and when the door was fastened all motion was out of the question. The prisoner had to stand with his limbs rigid and immovable until the jailer opened the door, and it was far the most dreaded of the *peines fortes et dures* of the pen. In midsummer, I can fancy that a couple of hours in such a coffin would inspire Tartuffe himself with virtuous thoughts, especially if his avoirdupois was at all respectable.

Jefferson Davis, in his message of December 7, 1863 to the Confederate Congress, lashed out at the North for its treatment of Confederate prisoners, ignoring the fact that conditions were at least as bad in the South. All was the fault of the Federal government's refusal to continue the exchange of prisoners under a cartel agreed upon in 1862:[17]

A systematic and concerted effort has been made to quiet the complaints in the United States of those relatives and friends of the prisoners in our hands, who are unable to understand why the cartel is not executed in their favor, by the groundless assertion that we are the parties who refuse compliance. Attempts are also made to shield themselves from the execration excited by their own odious treatment of our officers and soldiers, now captive in their hands, by misstatements, such as that the prisoners held by us are deprived of food. To this last accusation the conclusive answer has been made that, in accordance with our law and the general orders of the Department, the rations of the prisoners are precisely the same, in quantity and quality, as those served out to our own gallant soldiers in the field, and which have been found sufficient to support them in their arduous campaigns, while it is not pretended by the enemy that they treat prisoners by the same generous rule. By an indulgence, perhaps unprecedented, we have even allowed the prisoners in our hands to be supplied by their friends at home with comforts not enjoyed by the men who captured them in battle. In contrast to this treatment the most revolting inhumanity has characterized the conduct of the United States toward prisoners held by them. One prominent fact, which admits no denial or palliation, must suffice as a test. The officers of our Army, natives of southern and semi-tropical climates, and unprepared for the cold of a northern winter, have been conveyed for imprisonment during the rigors of the present season to the most northern and exposed situation that could be selected by the enemy. There, beyond the reach of comforts, and often even of news from home and family, exposed to the piercing cold of the northern lakes, they are held by men who cannot be ignorant of, even if they do not design, the probable result. How many of our unfortunate friends and comrades, who have passed unscathed through numerous battles, will perish on Johnson's Island, under the cruel trial to which they are subjected, none but the Omniscient can foretell.

Clement Eaton, a present-day Southern historian, willingly admits the existence of conditions which the Confederate President denied:[18]

The prison camps in the South were undoubtedly places of great suffering and death. . . . The worst condition prevailed at the huge prison camp at Andersonville, established early in 1864 and abandoned in September of that year as Sherman's army threatened to capture it. In July, 31,000 prisoners were crowded into the Andersonville stockade. The Confederate guards were young boys and old men who at times were afraid to go into the stockade and police it properly. Some criminals, called "raiders," from New York terrorized their fellow prisoners; but finally the Federals erected a gallows and hung six ringleaders. The food allowance was the same as that of the guards; but Northern soldiers, who came from the wheat country, were unaccustomed to a monotonous diet of corn-bread. They had to cook their rations, and often the pones would be baked so hard that they were used as footballs. Furthermore, the corn meal was coarse and unsifted, resulting in widespread diarrhea. Sanitation and hospital facilities were extremely bad. A stream flowing through the stockade became a source of great pollution; nearly all the prisoners became sick, and the mortality was frightful. By the end of the war there were 12,912 prisoners' graves at Andersonville.

Southerners have apologized for the Andersonville prison camp by pointing out that the Confederacy did not have the proper medical supplies even for its own army, and that the policy of Secretary of War Stanton and Grant of no exchange of prisoners was partly responsible for the suffering of Northern captives. Although the mortality rate of Northerners in Southern prisons was somewhat greater than that of Confederate soldiers in Northern prisons, the difference was not striking.

Fifty years before Eaton wrote, the Northern historian James Ford Rhodes reached the same conclusion:[19]

All things considered the statistics show no reason why the North should reproach the South. If we add to one side of the account the refusal to exchange the prisoners and the greater resources, and to the other the distress of the Confederacy the balance struck will not be far from even. Certain it is that no deliberate intention existed either in Richmond or Washington to inflict suffering on captives more than inevitably accompanied their confinement. Rather than to charge either section with inhumanity it were truer to lay the burden on war, recalling in sympathy with their import the words of Sophocles:—

"From wars unnumbered evils flow
The unexhausted source of every human woe."

1864

CHAPTER 29

"A HIDEOUS FAILURE"

EHIND THE SCENES in Richmond and Washington, as the year 1864 began, forces were unleashed that would bring the war into a new and final phase. North and South, men now thought and wrote as seasoned practitioners of the brutal art of killing. The blacksmith's son from Michigan on a raid up the Neuse River, or the farmer's son from Vermont riding with Averell in West Virginia, killed, plundered, and burned as matter-of-factly as in 1861 one would have shod a horse and the other plowed a field. The elation of battle had dulled; brutality had become commonplace.

I

Jefferson Davis, in his message of December 7, 1863, to the Confederate Congress, emphasized a Southern conviction that would affect the war profoundly in coming months:[1]

I cannot close this message without again adverting to the savage ferocity which still marks the conduct of the enemy in the prosecution of the war. After their repulse from the defences before Charleston, they first sought revenge by an abortive attempt to destroy the city with an incendiary composition, thrown by improved artillery from a distance of four miles. Failing in this, they changed their missiles, but fortunately have thus far succeeded only in killing two women in the city. Their commanders, Butler, McNeil, and Turchin, whose horrible barbarities have made their names widely notorious and everywhere execrable, are still honored and cherished by the authorities at Washington. The first-named, after having been withdrawn from the scenes of his cruelties against women and prisoners of war (in reluctant concession to the demands of outraged humanity in Europe,) has just been put in a new command at Norfolk, where helpless women and children are again placed at his mercy.

Nor has less unrelenting warfare been waged by these pretended friends of human rights and liberties against the unfortunate negroes. Wherever the enemy have been able to gain access, they have forced into the ranks of their army every able-bodied man that they could seize, and have either left the aged, the women, and the children to perish by starvation, or have gathered them into camps, where they have been wasted by a frightful mortality. Without clothing or shelter, often without food, incapable, without supervision, of taking the most ordinary precaution against disease, these helpless dependents, accustomed to have their wants supplied by the foresight of their masters, are being rapidly exterminated wherever brought in contact with the invaders. By the Northern man, on whose deep-rooted prejudices no kindly restraining influence is exercised, they are treated with aversion and neglect. There is little hazard in predicting that, in all localities where the enemy have gained a temporary foothold, the negroes, who under our care increased six fold in number since their importation into the colonies of Great Britain, will have been reduced by mortality during the war to not more than one half their previous number. . . .

The frontier of our country bears witness to the alacrity and efficiency with which the general orders of the enemy have been executed in the devastation of the farms, the destruction of the agricultural implements, the burning of the houses, and the plunder of every thing movable. Its whole aspect is a comment on the ethics of the general order issued by the United States on the twenty-fourth of April, 1863, comprising "instructions for the government of armies of the United States in the field," and of which the following is an example:

"Military necessity admits of all direct destruction of life or limb of armed enemies, and of other persons whose destruction is incidentally unavoidable in the armed contests of the war; it allows of the capturing of every armed enemy, and of every enemy of importance to the hostile government, or of peculiar danger to the captor; it allows of all destruction of property and obstructions of the ways and channels of traffic, travel, or communication, and of all withholding of sustenance or means of life from the enemy; of the appropriation of whatever an enemy's country affords necessary for the subsistence and safety of the army, and of such deception as does not involve the breaking of good faith, either positively pledged regarding agreements entered into during the war, or supposed by the modern law of war to exist. Men who take up arms against one another in public war do not cease on this account to be moral beings, responsible to one another and to God."

The striking contrast to these teachings and practices, presented by our army when invading Pennsylvania, illustrates the moral character of our people. Though their forbearance may have been unmerited and unappreciated by the enemy, it was imposed by their own self-respect, which forbade their degenerating from Christian warriors into plundering ruffians, assailing the property, lives, and honor of helpless noncombatants. If their conduct, when thus contrasted with the inhuman practices of our foe, fail to command the respect and sympathy of civilized nations in our day, it cannot fail to be recognized by their less deceived posterity.

Southern newspapers could always find stories and letters to support the President's charges of Yankee cruelty. One certain to inflame all Southerners came from a Confederate colonel early in 1864:[2]

HEADQUARTERS FORCES ON BLACKWATER,
FRANKLIN, VA., January 1864
GENERAL WILD, COMMANDING COLORED BRIGADE, NORFOLK, VA.:
SIR: Probably no expedition, during the progress of this war, has been attended with more utter disregard for the long-established usages of civilization or the dictates of humanity, than your late raid into the country bordering the Albemarle. Your stay, though short, was marked by crimes and enormities. You burned houses over the heads of defenceless women and children, carried off private property of every description, arrested non-combatants, and carried off ladies in irons, whom you confined with negro men.

Your negro troops fired on confederates after they had surrendered, and they were only saved by the exertions of the more humane of your white officers. Last, but not least, under the pretext that he was a guerrilla, you hanged Daniel Bright, a private of company L, Sixty-second Georgia regiment, (cavalry,) forcing the ladies and gentlemen whom you held in arrest to witness the execution. Therefore, I have obtained an order from the General Commanding, for the execution of Samuel

Jones, a private of Company B, Fifth Ohio, whom I hang in retaliation. I hold two more of your men—in irons—as hostages for Mrs. Weeks and Mrs. Mundin. When these ladies are released, these men will be relieved and treated as prisoners of war.

JOEL R. GRIFFIN,
Colonel

II

Whether General Edward A. Wild, commanding the district of Norfolk and Portsmouth, ever replied to Colonel Griffin's letter is of little importance. (No answer can be found in the Official Records.*) The material fact is the animosity toward Negro troops that Griffin revealed. In less than three months that attitude, widely prevalent in the South, would come to a point where it could be satisfied only by blood.*

On the east bank of the Mississippi River, forty miles north of Memphis in a direct line, twice that far by the meandering river, stood Fort Pillow. Originally erected by the Confederates, the fort had been in Federal hands since the early summer of 1862. In the spring of 1864 it was garrisoned by the Thirteenth Tennessee Cavalry (Union) and four companies of colored artillery—557 officers and men.

On April 12 Forrest,* with 1,500 men, attacked the fort. Striking just before dawn, his men slowly drove in the pickets. By midafternoon, after advancing cautiously and with small loss of life, they had succeeded in investing the fort on its three land sides. Under a flag of truce, Forrest sent in a demand for surrender. The defenders refused to give up. Forrest ordered an assault.

Lieutenant Mack J. Leaming, adjutant of the Thirteenth Tennessee Cavalry, described what followed:[3]

The rebel charge was immediately sounded; when, as if rising from out [of] the very earth on the center and north side, within 20 yards of our works, the rebels received our first fire, wavered, rallied again and finally succeeded in breaking our lines, and in thus gaining possession

---

* Nathan Bedford Forrest, a onetime slave dealer in Memphis, began as a private in the Confederate Army, equipped a battalion of cavalry troops at his own expense, and soon rose in reputation and rank as the best, most daring cavalry leader in the South. He escaped from Donelson and fought at Shiloh. By then neither Grant nor Sherman ever referred to him except in terms of respect for his military ability. Some credit him with originating the phrase that he who "gets there firstest with the mostest" wins the battle.

of the fort. At this juncture, one company of the Sixth U. S. Heavy Artillery, colored troops, rushed down the bluff, at the summit of which were our works, and many of them jumped into the river, throwing away their arms as they fled.

Seeing that . . . the enemy had now gained possession of our works, and in consequence that it would be useless to offer further resistance, our men threw down their arms and surrendered. For a moment the fire seemed to slacken. The scene which followed, however, beggars all description. The enemy carried our works at about 4 P.M., and from that time until dark, and at intervals throughout the night, our men were shot down without mercy and almost without regard to color. This horrid work of butchery did not cease even with the night of murder, but was renewed again the next morning, when numbers of our wounded were basely murdered after a long night of pain and suffering on the field where they had fought so bravely. . . .

Of the commissioned officers of the Thirteenth West Tennessee Cavalry . . . all were killed save First Lieut. Nicholas D. Logan, of C Company, . . . and myself, the adjutant of the regiment.

The rebels were very bitter against these loyal Tennesseans, terming them "home-made Yankees," and declaring they would give them no better treatment than they dealt out to the negro troops with whom they were fighting. . . .

Of the number, white and black, actually murdered after the surrender I cannot say positively; however, from my own observation, as well as from prisoners who were captured at Fort Pillow and afterward made their escape, I cannot estimate that number at anything less than 300.

Survivors added gruesome details. Hardy N. Revelle, a storekeeper at Fort Pillow, testified under oath:[4]

When we found there was no quarter to be shown, and that (white and black) we were to be butchered, we . . . gave up our arms and passed down the hill. . . . We were followed closely and fiercely by the advancing rebel forces, their fire never ceasing at all. Our men had given signals themselves that they surrendered, many of them throwing up their hands to show they were unarmed, and submitted to overwhelming odds.

I was about half-way down the hill, partially secreted in a kind of ravine with Dr. Fitch, when I saw 2 men (white men) belonging to the

Thirteenth Tennessee Cavalry standing behind a stump on which they had fixed a white handkerchief, their hands thrown up. They asked for quarter. When they stood on their feet they were exposed, and I saw them shot down by rebel soldiers and killed.

A captain of the rebel troops then came where we were and ordered all the Federals (white and black) to move up the hill or he would "shoot their God-damned brains out." I started up the hill with a number of others, in accordance with the order. I was surrendered with our men. While going up I saw white men fall on both sides of me, who were shot down by rebel soldiers who were stationed upon the brow of the hill. We were at the time marching directly at the men who fired upon us. I do not know how many fell, but I remember of seeing 4 killed in this way. I also saw negroes shot down with pistols in the hands of rebels. One was killed at my side. I saw another negro struck on the head with a saber by a rebel soldier. I suppose he was also killed. One more just in front of me was knocked down with the butt of a musket.

William J. Mays, Company B, Thirteenth Tennessee Cavalry, related his experiences after the surrender. He too testified under oath:[5]

We all threw down our arms and gave tokens of surrender, asking for quarter (I was wounded in the right shoulder and muscle of the back and knocked down before I threw down my gun). But no quarter was given. Voices were heard upon all sides, crying, "Give them no quarter; kill them; kill them; it is General Forrest's orders." I saw 4 white men and at least 25 negroes shot while begging for mercy, and I saw 1 negro dragged from a hollow log within 10 feet of where I lay, and as 1 rebel held him by the foot another shot him. These were all soldiers. There were also 2 negro women and 3 little children standing within 25 steps from me, when a rebel stepped up to them and said, "Yes, God damn you, you thought you were free, did you?" and shot them all. They all fell but 1 child, when he knocked it in the head with the breech of his gun. They then disappeared in the direction of the landing, following up the fugitives, firing at them wherever seen. They came back in about three-quarters of an hour, shooting and robbing the dead of their money and clothes. I saw a man with a canteen upon him and a pistol in his hand. I ventured to ask him for a drink of water. He turned around, saying, "Yes, God damn you, I will give you a drink of water," and shot at my head three different times, covering my face with dust, and then turned from me—no doubt thinking he had killed me—remarking, "God damn you, it's too late to pray now"; then went on with his pilfering. I lay there until dark, feigning death, when a rebel officer came along, drawing his saber, and ordered me to get up, threatening to run his saber into me if I did not, saying I had to march 10 miles that night. I succeeded in getting up and got among a small squad he had already gathered up, but stole away from them during the night and got among the dead, feigning death for fear of being murdered.

Some of the survivors may have exaggerated the brutality of the captors, yet Forrest's official report gives proof that there was savagery at Fort Pillow. On April 15 the General wrote:[6]

Arrived there [Fort Pillow] on the morning of the 12th and attacked the place with a portion of McCulloch's and Bell's brigades, numbering about 1,500 men, and after a sharp contest captured the garrison and all of its stores. A demand was made for the surrender, which was refused. The victory was complete, and the loss of the enemy will never be known from the fact that large numbers ran into the river and were shot and drowned. The force was composed of about 500 negroes and 200 white soldiers (Tennessee Tories). The river was dyed with the blood of the slaughtered for 200 yards. . . .

It is hoped that these facts will demonstrate to the northern people that negro soldiers cannot cope with Southerners.

The reports from Fort Pillow inflamed the North. Lincoln, who took the news more calmly than most, was deeply concerned. Speaking at the Baltimore Sanitary Fair on April 18, he said:[7]

A painful rumor, true I fear, has reached us of the massacre, by the rebel forces, at Fort Pillow, in the west end of Tennessee, on the Mississippi River, of some three hundred colored soldiers and white officers, who had just been overpowered by their assailants. . . . We do not today *know* that a colored soldier, or white officer commanding colored soldiers, has been massacred by the rebels when made a prisoner. We fear it, believe it, I may say, but we do not *know* it. To take the life of one of their prisoners, on the assumption that they murder ours, when it is short of certainty that they do murder ours, might be too serious, too cruel a mistake. We are having the Fort Pillow affair thoroughly investigated; and such investigation will probably show conclusively how the truth is. If, after all that has been said, it shall turn out that there has been no massacre at Fort Pillow, it will be almost safe to say that there has been none, and will be none elsewhere. If there has been the massacre of three hundred there, or even the tenth part of three hundred, it will be conclusively proved; and being so proved, the retribution shall as surely come.

Two weeks later Lincoln informed the members of his Cabinet:

"It is now quite certain that a large number of our colored soldiers, with their white officers, were, by the rebel force, massacred after they had surrendered, at the recent capture of Fort Pillow. So much is known, though the evidence is not yet quite ready to be laid before me. Meanwhile I will thank you to prepare, and give me in writing your opinion as to what course, the government should take in the case."

Some Secretaries favored retributive measures; others thought that any punitive action would backfire against the North. In the end Lincoln did nothing, perhaps because he became engrossed in the Wilderness campaign, perhaps because he became convinced that the excesses were the inevitable result of hatreds described years later by Forrest's biographer, John A. Wyeth:[8]

Everything considered, it may well be a matter of surprise that the slaughter was not greater. Human life was held exceedingly cheap in 1864, and especially in west Tennessee; the scenes of bloodshed which stained this section of the South may well suggest the reddest days of the French Revolution.

It is difficult for those who did not live through this unhappy period, and in this immediate section, to appreciate the bitterness of feeling which then prevailed. Three years of civil war had passed, not without a deplorable effect upon the morals of the rank and file of either army. War does not bring out the noblest traits in the majority of those who from choice or necessity follow its blood-stained paths. Too often the better qualities hide away, and those that are harsh and cruel prevail. Some of Forrest's men treasured a deep resentment against some of the officers and soldiers of this garrison. They had been neighbors in times of peace, and had taken opposite sides when the war came on. These men had suffered violence to person and property, and their wives and children, in the enforced absence of their natural protectors, had suffered various indignities at the hands of the "Tennessee Tories," as the loyal Tennesseeans were called by their neighbors who sided with the South. When they met in single combat, or in scouting parties, or in battle, as far as these individuals were concerned, it was too often a duel to the death. Between the parties to these neighborhood feuds the laws of war did not prevail. Here, in this melee, in the fire and excitement of the assault, they found opportunity and made excuse for bloody vengeance. No official surrender; their flag still flying; some of the Federals, no matter how few, still firing back, and they shot them down regardless of the cry for quarter.

Moreover, Fort Pillow was the first prominent occasion on which Negro troops, whose free status the Confederates would not admit, came into conflict with their former owners.

But was Fort Pillow a massacre? Wyeth, a Southerner who had served two years under Forrest (though not at Fort Pillow), approached the question objectively:

To the rational mind, capable of carefully weighing the evidence on both sides, and arriving at a conclusion unbiased by prejudice, it must be clear that there was no massacre as charged. Had a wholesale and merciless slaughter been intended by General Forrest and his subordinates, it could and would have been carried out, as there was nothing to prevent it. The fact that so many escaped death is of itself a proof that a massacre was not premeditated or permitted.* It is true that more of the garrison were shot after the Southern troops were in possession of the breastworks than was necessary for the full success of the assault, but under the conditions which prevailed during the attack, it is clearly shown that an unusually large loss in killed and wounded was inevitable, even had no excesses been indulged in by the captors.

From a careful study of the subject, I am convinced that a few desperate or insanely intoxicated soldiers of the garrison resisted to the very last, and even after escape was hopeless continued to fire at the Confederates. On the other hand, notwithstanding this extreme provo-

---

* "It appears then that of the garrison of 557 there were at least 336 survivors, of whom 226 were unwounded or only slightly wounded and approximately 100 seriously wounded. The dead of the garrison may be calculated as not more than 231, which accords with the burial reports. . . . The loss of life approximated forty percent of the garrison—by no means an extraordinarily high rate for a place carried by assault as Fort Pillow was."—Robert S. Henry, *"First With the Most" Forrest,* 259.

cation, there were a number of men, both white and black, shot down, who were trying to surrender and should have been spared. About an hour before the assault was made a detachment of Forrest's command posted at the extreme left of his line broke into the quartermaster's stores which had been captured at this time, and before they could be compelled to quit the building had had access to a supply of whiskey which they discovered there. The moment Forrest learned that his men were pillaging the captured stores he rode there rapidly and put a stop to it in person.

III

While Forrest was engaged in the brief campaign that culminated in the horror of Fort Pillow, an ambitious Union expedition west of the Mississippi bogged down in the greatest fiasco of the war.

Early in 1864 Halleck ordered General Nathaniel P. Banks, then commanding at New Orleans, to invade northwestern Louisiana and nearby Arkansas and Texas. The purpose of the expedition was threefold: to seize the great stores of cotton which the farmers of the region had been unable to market; to nurture nascent reconstruction movements in Louisiana and Arkansas; and to warn the French in Mexico, by planting the Stars and Stripes in Texas, that there would come a day when the United States would be able to enforce the Monroe Doctrine.

Banks, former congressman and governor of Massachusetts, had hardly distinguished himself since he had been commissioned a major general of volunteers in the spring of 1861. Yet even he had had experience enough to realize that Halleck's venture was a hazardous one. Banks remonstrated, but Halleck overrode his objections and proceeded to put an invading army together. Banks would bring up a force from the Bayou Teche; A. J. Smith would come over from Vicksburg with 10,000 men; Frederick Steele, commanding in Arkansas, would march down from Little Rock; and Admiral D. D. Porter would ascend the Red River with a powerful fleet of gunboats. All would converge at Alexandria, Louisiana, on March 17 and then go up river to Shreveport in the northwestern corner of the state. When the expedition reached this point, Halleck apparently believed, its purposes would be achieved.

When Smith's troops arrived at the mouth of the Red River on March 11 they found Porter's flotilla already there. Two days later the soldiers disembarked from their transports and assaulted Fort de Russy, taking 260 prisoners and ten guns. Porter moved on to Alexandria, arriving there on March 14; Smith's ten thousand came in the next day. But

Banks's contingent, sent ahead under the command of W. B. Franklin, did not reach the concentration point until March 25. Steele, faced with many difficulties, never even came close to the Louisiana border.

Meanwhile, the Confederate commander, General Richard Taylor, erudite and peppery son of old Zachary, kept withdrawing ahead of the

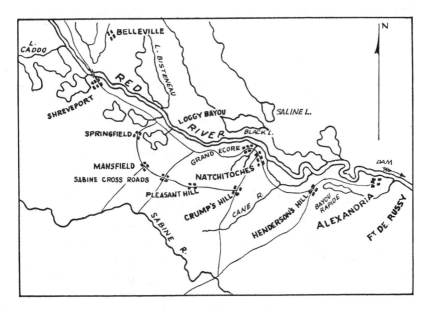

RED RIVER CAMPAIGN

advancing Federals, harassing the invaders with frequent skirmishes and complaining that he was expected to stop 27,000 men with hardly more than half that number. His dispatches to Kirby Smith describe the progress of the campaign:[9]

IN THE FIELD, March 26, 1864.

GENERAL: . . . I am still ignorant of what disposition the enemy has made or is making of his large force, and have no news of Green * since I last wrote you. The difficulty of obtaining accurate intelligence is greatly enhanced by jayhawkers.† The whole country between this and Alexandria swarms with these outlaws, who are allied with the

---

* General Thomas Green, who commanded the trans-Mississippi Confederate cavalry.

† "During the Civil War, a free-lance soldier, freebooter, or guerilla operating in Kansas; any lawless marauder or robber." —Mathews, *A Dictionary of Americanisms.*

enemy and acting in his interests. Several of our scouts have been murdered, and it is more dangerous for small parties to pass through the pine woods than it would be to penetrate the enemy's lines. Besides, the intimate acquaintance of the country possessed by these people renders it impossible to escape their vigilance. The arrival of one, or two even, of Green's regiments will change the whole aspect of affairs.

NATCHITOCHES, March 30, 1864—9 P.M.

GENERAL: I reached this place some two hours since. The enemy is within 12 or 14 miles in full force. He will occupy the place in the morning if he sees proper. Only one of General Green's regiments has reached here. It will go to the front in the morning. The regiment numbers 250—no very heavy re-enforcement. The next regiment numbers 350, with more than half the men reported unarmed. It will reach here tomorrow. . . .

Your dispatch of the 29th instant (No. 2460) has just come to hand. I respectfully suggest that the only possible way to defeat Steele's movement is to whip the enemy now in the heart of the Red River Valley. Price's * command could have been here on the 28th, and I could have fought a battle for the department today. To decline concentration when we have the means, and when the enemy is already in the vitals of the department, is a policy I am too obtuse to understand. There is no position short of the head of Spanish Lake, 18 miles from here, where I can undertake to do anything with my present means. In fact, Pleasant Hill, with an effort to hold the country to Blair's Landing, is the only position where I can await Green's forces and secure subsistence and forage. The enemy is in formidable numbers, prepared to overrun the Red River Valley, and he must and will succeed unless all the means at our disposal are used energetically to prevent him. I most respectfully call attention to the fact that sixteen days after the fall of Fort de Russy and the opening of the campaign by the enemy only 250 re-enforcements have reached me.

CAMPTI, March 31, 1864

GENERAL: I have the honor to report that I left Natchitoches today at 11:00 A.M., just before the head of the enemy's column reached the place. I am on the steamer *Frolic,* and shall proceed to Blair's to inspect

* General Sterling Price, whom Kirby Smith had ordered to oppose Steele's advance in Arkansas.

the road to Pleasant Hill, at which place the main body of my troops will encamp tonight. . . .

From all I can learn, it will be ten days before Green's command will reach me, one regiment under Major McPhaill having alone come up. The troops ordered here from Texas, excepting Green's original division, have been directed to halt in Polk County until further orders, so I am informed by Lieutenant-Colonel Herbert. If this be true, Green will bring me less than 2,000 men. Had I conceived for an instant that such astonishing delay would ensue before re-enforcements reached me I would have fought a battle even against the heavy odds. It would have been better to lose the State after a defeat than surrender it without a fight. The fairest and richest portion of the Confederacy is now a waste. Louisiana may well know her destiny. Her children are exiles; her labor system is destroyed. Expecting every hour to receive the promised re-enforcements, I did not feel justified in hazarding a general engagement with my little army. I shall never cease to regret the error.

On the day after Taylor wrote his gloomy report two divisions of infantry reached him. Green's cavalry arrived on April 6. The Confederate commander believed that he was now strong enough to offer battle. From Pleasant Hill he withdrew twenty miles in the direction of Shreveport, disposed his troops at Sabine Cross Roads near Mansfield, and waited for Banks.

The two armies probed each other on the morning of April 8, but a full-scale engagement did not take place until 4:00 P.M., when Taylor ordered his whole line forward. The Confederate cavalry advance coincided with a fainthearted Union cavalry charge. J. Russell Young, correspondent of the Philadelphia Press, described an hour of bloody fighting:[10]

. . . The attack of our cavalry was weak and spiritless. The firing lasted for a few minutes, the discharges of musketry became incessant, the long, thin line of clay-colored rebels began to emerge slowly from the woods, firing constantly, but always advancing at a pace that seemed like an uncertain, shuffling run. Their fire was too strong for our cavalry, and it fell back with precipitation—too much precipitation it proved; for before Ransom had his line properly formed, he was compelled to meet the onset of the whole rebel force. The retreating cavalry had partly demoralized his men, for in the heat of action, and being where they could not see the field, they could not understand why this multitude of flushed and frightened men should thus be running from the scene of battle. Many who wanted nothing but a cheerful look or nod to make them brave men, turned around without having seen a rebel, and ran likewise, so that before the battle had really opened the road presented the strange sight of hundreds of armed and unarmed men hastening to the rear, some the pictures of fright, others of abject fear, and carrying exaggerated stories to all who troubled them for information.

Four o'clock had passed, and the long shadows of the evening were darkening the pine woods. Ransom's division fought with intrepid bravery, all things considered—the sudden attack, the panic-stricken cavalry, and the number of the enemy—with a bravery that cannot be too highly commended. The rebels, however, saw their advantage, and pressed it. In the beginning of the fight General Ransom was struck in the knee, and carried from the field. This dispirited the men, for they all loved the young commander, and rejoiced to speak his praise. The fight became furious, and for a few minutes there was doubt, and gloom, and anxiety among the Federal commanders. Aid after aid galloped down the road to bring up the Third division of the Thirteenth corps, commanded by General Cameron. It was doubtful if even Cameron's men would be successful. But other troops were behind— Emory and his splendid division—and we knew that the day was ours if time only permitted us to make a proper disposition of our forces.

At three o'clock in the afternoon General William H. Emory, commanding the First Division of the Nineteenth Corps, bivouacked a mile and a half behind the Thirteenth Corps. At 3:50—Emory noted the time exactly—Franklin, the corps commander, ordered Emory to bring his infantry to the front immediately. Within fifteen minutes Emory had his men in motion:[11]

About forty minutes after commencing the march I met an aide-de-camp from the front with orders to hurry up, that the battle had commenced. After going about a mile further I met General Ransom coming back, wounded, in an ambulance, who told me that they had a pretty tough fight in front, but he did not give any very sad picture of the condition of affairs; but I thought there were a great many more men about that ambulance than looked well following him to the rear. I ordered the men to double-quick; to take a slow trot. After going about a mile further, in all, four miles from the point of starting, I met a parcel of servants, men and women, mounted on horses, who told us that the day was all gone, and hallooed out to my men to turn back. There were also a great deal of cavalry scattered among these people. At almost the next moment a crowd of perfectly disorganized cavalry, wagons, ambulances, and loose animals came right down the road upon us, and all said the day was gone. I directed the leading regiments and the flankers on each side, without halting, to fix their bayonets, and I ordered the bands to strike up, and we had to use violence to get along the road. There was scarcely a staff officer who did not have his sabre bent beating people out of the road. It soon became apparent to me that the whole cavalry was driven back and in disorder. We continued our march; the men never broke a step, and not a man fell out of the ranks.

In a short time we began to meet the infantry going to the rear in disorder. About this time I received a message from either General Banks or General Franklin, I do not remember which, to take as good a position as I could, and form across the road, for the purpose of checking the enemy, informing me that the advance was routed. There was no good place where I was, and I had to continue to advance. The ground there was not favorable for forming a line. I continued to advance for about half a mile further, still pressed on each side by infantry and some cavalry going to the rear. Every effort to halt them or reorganize them was impossible. I threw out regiments on each flank to try to stop them, but they ran around them.

After marching from half a mile to a mile further I found a place that I thought was favorable for forming a line. We also began to feel pretty smartly the bullets of the enemy, which began to drop around us thickly, and some of our men fell. For a moment I was afraid I had put off forming my line too late. So I took my leading regiment, the 161st New York, under Colonel Kinsley, and led them to the front and deployed them as skirmishers to cover my line while it was being formed. We then found the enemy in sight and firing upon us very rapidly. I put the first brigade directly across the road at right angles, the second brigade on the right and a little in reserve, and the third brigade on the left. I was still to the front with this regiment holding the enemy. Seeing the line was formed, or nearly formed, I directed Colonel Kinsley to rally his skirmishers and come in behind the line. It was with great difficulty that he did so; his loss was very severe. They had no sooner got in than the enemy appeared in three columns of attack, one coming directly up the road, one on our right, and one on our left.

I directed my men to lie down and hold their fire until the enemy had got close up. The enemy came on, apparently not expecting to meet anything there. When the enemy got within about 100 yards my line opened on them. In about fifteen minutes the enemy were driven from the field with very considerable loss. By this time it was dark, and we could hear nothing in our front, except the noise of wheels, perhaps artillery or wagons going to the rear of the enemy, and the cries of the wounded men calling for water.

The stubborn stand of Emory's division had only staved off a Union rout; Mansfield would stand as a Confederate victory. Banks, convinced that he could not fight his way to Shreveport, ordered a retreat to Pleasant Hill. J. Russell Young described the Union army and its principal commanders as it lay in its new position on April 9:[12]

Pleasant Hill . . . is a clearing in the midst of these vast pine woods, about thirty-five miles from the Red River, on the road that leads from Natchitoches. It forms a plateau that rises to a noticeable elevation above the country around. It was probably intended as a settlement of more than usual importance, for I noticed an unfinished seminary, a church, a sawmill, many fine houses, and one or two that would have done credit to our Northern towns. The land was in a high state of cultivation, and every acre seemed to be traversed by ridges of ploughed soil. On the elevation where the unfinished seminary stands, a complete view of the whole field could be obtained, and with a glass, the features and the rank of men . . . could be readily seen. Here we determined to make a stand.

The day was as bright and clear and fresh as a May day in the North, and the air was so bracing that the officers found their great-coats grateful. The morning passed on. The plateau had the appearance of a parade-ground on a holiday. . . . Regiments marching to the right, and regiments marching to the left, batteries being moved and shifted, cavalry squads moving in single file through the brush, now and then an aid galloping madly, or an orderly at full speed, driving his spurs, and holding an order or despatch between his teeth, bugles sounding the different cavalry calls, and drums repeating the orders of the captains, all passed and repassed, and controlled the vision, making very much the impression that a spectator in the theatre receives as he looks upon a melodrama.

In an inclosure near the roadside was a small cluster of gentlemen to whom all this phantasmagoria had the meaning of life, and death, and power, and fame. General Banks, with his light blue overcoat buttoned closely around his chin, was strolling up and down, occasionally conversing with a member of his staff, or returning the salute of a passing subaltern. Near him was General William B. Franklin, his face as rough and rugged as when he rode through the storms of the Peninsula, the ideal of a bold, daring, imperturbable soldier. There are few braver men than this Charles O'Malley of major generals.* He had two horses shot under him the day before. His face was very calm that morning, and occasionally he pulls his whiskers nervously, as though he scented the battle afar off, and was impatient to be in the midst of the fray. General Charles P. Stone, the chief of staff, a quiet, retiring man, who is regarded, by the few that know him, as one of the finest soldiers of the time, was sitting on a rail smoking cigarettes, and apparently more interested in the puffs of smoke that curled around him, than in the noise and bustle that filled the air. There was General Smith, with his bushy, grayish beard, and his eager eye, as it looks through spectacles, giving him the appearance of a schoolmaster. General Arnold, the chief of artillery, with his high boots, and his slouched hat thrown over his head, seemed the busiest of all. The other members of the staff, colonels, and majors, and captains, completed the group; with orderlies in the distance, and servants chiding or soothing their masters' restless horses, and the body-guard dismounted and dozing under the trees. . . .

The General called for his horse and proposed to go to the front. . . . It was now eleven o'clock, and our whole army was prepared for action. The generals had determined to await the attack of the enemy, and finding it impossible to subsist the army in a country without water or forage, concluded to move the trains back to Grand Ecore, there concentrate our army, and await news from the cooperating column of General Steele, which is known to be moving through Arkansas on Shreveport. Accordingly, before our lines were formed, the trains were ordered to move, and before noon we had a clear field,

---

* An allusion far more familiar a hundred years ago than today. Charles O'Malley was the hero of Charles J. Lever's romantic novel of the same name, a story of the Peninsular War. Published in 1841, the book retained its popularity for two generations.

and were ready for the attack. . . . Noon came and passed; but beyond the slow shelling of the woods, and a stray shot from some impetuous picket, there was no sign of an engagement. Our men remained in line all day, and passed the hours by their guns; some lying down, some sleeping and dozing, others reading and eating the remnants of yesterday's ration; but all ready for the signal that would bring on the action. The day remained bright, and warm, and clear, and it began to be thought that it would close without an action, and that the enemy had withdrawn with their booty. Those in the front knew better. The rebels were there, making their dispositions and preparing for the onset.

Late in the afternoon hesitant, halfhearted sparring suddenly turned into vicious battle. Young's account continues:

On our left centre, far in the advance, was a battery of four guns, belonging to a New York regiment. It occupied an exposed position, and it had been suggested by some of the staff officers that there was danger of its capture. This battery had been making itself an object of interest to the rebels, for every ten minutes it sent a shot into their midst. About half-past four in the afternoon, a sharp volley of musketry was heard, and all eyes turned toward this battery, for over it circles of smoke were ascending, and around it men were engaged in battle. The rebel line rushed from the woods and charged the battery. The contest was sharp. The smoke obscured the sight, and for a few minutes we could only guess how the struggle was going. Finally our line was seen to retreat, but we had no fear. We knew that the men composing that line were men of the Nineteenth corps. We had seen their valor on the day before, and, although there, before our eyes, they were falling back, we felt assured it was with a purpose. So it proved. The temporary retreat was a feint, intended to draw the rebels from the woods. They came, rushed upon the battery, and surrounded it. This success brought another line of clay-colored rebels, and they cheered as though they had gained a victory. The time had come. The enemy was before us. Emory's division rallied; and one of Smith's divisions, which had been lying on the ground, arose, and sent volley after volley into the enemy's midst. This was something different from fighting an exposed division in pine woods, in the midst of baggage trains, and so the poor rebels found. Again and again they rallied, but only to fall back again and again, and finally to retreat and scamper through the woods. The battery which tempted them from their covert was retaken, and its shot and shell went plunging through their retreating column. . . .

The battle was extended along the whole line; it was nothing but charge and rally, to charge and rally again. In every point our men gained the day. The lines of Smith's division stood like the stone walls that Virginian *patois* has contributed to our military language, and every effort of the enemy to force them was futile. Thus it continued for an hour. . . . The rebels, toward the end of the engagement, tried to flank our left by sending a column over the ridge, upon which the unfinished seminary stood. The effort was more disastrous than the attempt upon the battery. They were driven back with fearful slaughter, routed from the field, leaving many hundreds of prisoners in our hands.

On April 11 General Taylor issued a flamboyant address to his troops. "Never in war," he told them, was there "a more complete victory" than Mansfield. Pleasant Hill "was emphatically the soldier's victory," where "valor and devotion triumphed over all." Kirby Smith made a more realistic evaluation. "Our repulse at Pleasant Hill," he wrote, "was so complete and our command was so disorganized that had Banks followed up his success vigorously he would have met but feeble opposition to his advance on Shreveport."

Banks, in fact, wanted to turn about and strike for Shreveport but his generals dissuaded him. Grant had stipulated that Smith's troops must be on the east side of the Mississippi by May 1. Equally important, the Red River was at an unprecedented low level and still falling. If Porter did not draw off his gunboats quickly he might well lose them. Banks gave in, and ordered a return to the starting point of the expedition.

As it was, the fleet had trouble enough in the next few days. Porter described the running battle, without equal in the war, that took place between a Confederate army and gunboats and transports:[13]

We had every reason to suppose that our return would be interrupted in every way and at every point by the enemy's land forces, and we were not disappointed. They commenced on us from high banks, at a place called Coushatta, and kept up a fire of musketry whenever an opportunity was offered them. By a proper distribution of the gunboats I had no trouble in driving them away, though from the high banks they could fire on our decks almost with impunity. As we proceeded down the river they increased in numbers, and as we only made thirty miles a day, they could cross from point to point and be ready to meet us on our arrival below. On the left bank of the river a man by the name of Harrison, with one thousand nine hundred cavalry and four or five pieces of artillery, was appointed to follow us down and annoy us. It was very fortunate for us that this person and his command were lately severely handled by a gunboat (a few weeks ago) which made them careful about coming within range. On the evening of the twelfth instant we were attacked from the right bank of the river by a detachment of men of quite another character. They were a part of the army which two or three days previous had gained success over our army, and flushed with victory, or under the excitement of liquor, they appeared suddenly upon the right bank, and fearlessly opened fire on the *Osage*, Lieutenant Commander T. O. Selfridge, (iron-clad), she being hard aground at the time with a transport (the *Black Hawk*) alongside of her, towing her off. The rebels opened with two thousand muskets, and soon drove everyone out of the *Black Hawk* to the safe casemates of the monitor. Lieutenant Bache had just come from his vessel (the *Lexington*) and fortunately was enabled to pull up to her again, keeping close under the bank, while the *Osage* opened a destructive fire on these poor deluded wretches, who, maddened with liquor and led on by their officers, were vainly attempting to capture an iron vessel. I am told that their hootings and actions baffle description. Force after force seemed to be brought up to the edge of the bank, where they confronted the guns of the iron vessel, only to be cut down by grape-shot and cannister. In the meantime Lieutenant Bache had reached his vessel, and widening the distance between him and the *Osage*, he opened a cross-fire on the infuriated rebels, who fought with such desperation and courage against certain destruction, that it could only be accounted for in one way. Our opinions were verified on inspection of some of the bodies of the slain—the men actually smelling of Louisiana rum! This affair lasted nearly two hours before the rebels fled. They brought up two pieces of artillery, one of which was quickly knocked over by the *Lexington's* guns, the other they managed to carry off. The cross-fire of the *Lexington* finally decided this curious affair of a fight between infantry and gunboats. The rebels were mowed down by her canister, and finally retreated in as quick haste as they had come to the attack, leaving a space of a mile covered with the dead and wounded, muskets and knapsacks. . . .

Night coming on, we had no means of ascertaining the damage done to the rebels. We were troubled no more from the right bank of the river, and a party of five thousand men who were marching to cut us off were persuaded to change their mind after hearing of the unfortunate termination to the first expedition. That same night I ordered the transports to proceed on, having placed the gunboats at a point where the rebels had a battery. All the transports were passed safely, the rebels not firing a shot in return to the many that were bursting over the hills. The next morning, the thirteenth instant, I followed down myself, and finding at Compte, six miles from Grand Ecore by land, that they had got aground, and would be some time in getting through, I proceeded down in this vessel [*Cricket*] to Grand Ecore, and got General Banks to send up troops enough to keep the guerillas away from the river. We were fired on as usual after we started down, but when I had the troops sent up, the transports came along without any trouble.

At Alexandria, the fleet encountered a more formidable opponent than Dick Taylor's artillery and sharpshooters—low water. Only the ingenuity of a landsman and the mighty labor of several thousand soldiers prevented an almost irreparable disaster. Admiral Porter, blithely concealing the fact that he had been the first to scoff at the expedient by which his beloved gunboats were saved, reported to Secretary of the Navy Gideon Welles:[14]

FLAG SHIP *Black Hawk*, MISSISSIPPI SQUADRON
MOUTH OF RED RIVER, May 16, 1864

SIR: I have the honor to inform you that the vessels lately caught by low water above the falls at Alexandria have been released from their unpleasant position. The water had fallen so low that I had no hope or expectation of getting the vessels out this season, and as the army had made arrangements to evacuate the country, I saw nothing before me but the destruction of the best part of the Mississippi squadron.

There seems to have been an especial providence looking out for us in providing a man equal to the emergency. Lieutenant-Colonel Bailey, Acting Engineer of the Nineteenth army corps, proposed a plan of building a series of dams across the rocks at the falls, and raising the water high enough to let the vessels pass over. This proposition looked like madness, and the best engineers ridiculed it; but Colonel Bailey was so sanguine of success that I requested General Banks to have it done, and he entered heartily into the work. Provisions were short and forage was almost out, and the dam was promised to be finished in ten days, or the army would have to leave us. I was doubtful about the time, but had no doubt about the ultimate success, if time would only permit. General Banks placed at the disposal of Colonel Bailey all the force he required, consisting of some three thousand men and two or three hundred wagons. All the neighboring steam-mills were torn down for material, two or three regiments of Maine men were set to work felling trees, and on the second day after my arrival in Alexandria from Grand Ecore the work had fairly begun. Trees were falling with great rapidity; teams were moving in all directions, bringing in brick and stone; flatboats were built to bring stone down from above; and every man seemed to be working with a vigor I have seldom seen equalled, while perhaps not one in fifty believed in the success of the undertaking.

These falls are about a mile in length, filled with rugged rocks, over which, at the present stage of water, it seemed to be impossible to make a channel.

The work was commenced by running out from the left bank of the river a tree dam, made of the bodies of very large trees, brush, brick, and stone, cross-tied with other heavy timber, and strengthened in every way which ingenuity could devise. This was run out about three hundred feet into the river; four large coal-barges were then filled with brick and sunk at the end of it. From the right bank of the river cribs filled with stone were built out to meet the barges. All of which was successfully accomplished, notwithstanding there was a current running of nine miles an hour, which threatened to sweep everything before it.

It will take too much time to enter into the details of this truly wonderful work. Suffice it to say, that the dam had nearly reached completion in eight days' working time, and the water had risen sufficiently on the upper falls to allow the *Fort Hindman, Osage,* and *Neosho* to get down and be ready to pass the dam. In another day it would have been high enough to enable all the other vessels to pass the upper falls. Unfortunately, on the morning of the ninth instant, the pressure of water became so great that it swept away two of the stone barges, which swung in below the dam on one side. Seeing this unfortunate accident, I jumped on a horse and rode up to where the upper vessels were anchored, and ordered the *Lexington* to pass the upper falls, if possible, and immediately attempt to go through the dam. I thought I might be able to save the four vessels below, not knowing whether the persons employed on the work would ever have the heart to renew their enterprise.

The *Lexington* succeeded in getting over the upper falls just in time, the water rapidly falling as she was passing over. She then steered directly for the opening in the dam, through which the water was rushing so furiously that it seemed as if nothing but destruction awaited her. Thousands of beating hearts looked on, anxious for the result. The silence was so great as the *Lexington* approached the dam that a pin might almost be heard to fall. She entered the gap with a full head of steam on, pitched down the roaring torrent, made two or three spasmodic rolls, hung for a moment on the rocks below, was then swept into deep water by the current, and rounded to safety into the bank. Thirty thousand voices rose in one deafening cheer, and universal joy seemed to pervade the face of every man present.

The *Neosho* followed next; all her hatches battened down, and every precaution taken against accident. She did not fare as well as the *Lexington*, her pilot having become frightened as he approached the abyss and stopped her engine, when I particularly ordered a full head of steam to be carried; the result was that for a moment her hull disappeared from sight under the water. Everyone thought she was lost. She rose, however, swept along over the rocks with the current, and fortunately escaped with only one hole in her bottom, which was stopped in the course of an hour.

The *Hindman* and *Osage* both came through beautifully without touching a thing, and I thought if I was only fortunate enough to get my large vessels as well over the falls, my fleet once more would do good service on the Mississippi.

The accident to the dam, instead of disheartening Colonel Bailey, only induced him to renew his exertions, after he had seen the success of getting four vessels through.

The noble-hearted soldiers, seeing their labor of the last eight days swept away in a moment, cheerfully went to work to repair damages, being confident now that all the gunboats would be finally brought over. These men had been working for eight days and nights up to their necks in water in the boiling sun, cutting trees and wheeling bricks, and nothing but good humor prevailed among them. On the whole, it was very fortunate that the dam was carried away, as the two barges that were swept away from the centre swung around against some rocks on the left, and made a fine cushion for the vessels, and prevented them, as it afterward appeared, from running on certain destruction.

The force of the water and the current being too great to construct a continuous dam of six hundred feet across the river in so short a time, Colonel Bailey determined to leave a gap of fifty-five feet in the dam, and build a series of wing dams on the upper falls. This was accomplished in three days' time, and on the eleventh instant the *Mound City, Carondelet,* and *Pittsburgh* came over the upper falls, a good deal of labor having been expended in hauling them through, the channel being very crooked, and scarcely wide enough for them. Next day the *Ozark, Louisville,* and *Chillicothe,* and two tugs also succeeded in crossing the upper falls. Immediately afterward the *Mound City, Carondelet,* and *Pittsburgh* started in succession to pass the dam, all their hatches battened down, and every precaution taken to prevent accident. The passage of these vessels was a most beautiful sight, only to be realized when seen. They passed over without an accident, except the unshipping of one or two rudders. This was witnessed by all the troops, and the vessels were heartily cheered when they passed over. Next morning, at ten o'clock, the *Louisville, Chillicothe, Ozark,* and two tugs passed over without any accident, except the loss of a man, who was swept off the deck of one of the tugs. By three o'clock that afternoon the vessels were all coaled, ammunition replaced, and all steamed down the river, with the convoy of transports in company. A good deal of difficulty was anticipated in getting over the bars in lower Red River; depth of water reported only five feet; gunboats were drawing six. Providentially, we had a rise from the back-water of the Mississippi, that river being very high at that time; the back-water extending to Alexandria, one hundred and fifty miles distant, enabling us to pass all the bars and obstructions with safety.

Union Private Larry Van Alystyne, who had come out of the peaceful Catskills to fight with New York's "Bostwick's Tigers," was aghast at the bitterness and cruelty of the war as border people knew it:[15]

Eight miles below Alexandria. The Jay-hawkers kept their promise to burn the place rather than have it go into the hands of the enemy again. About daylight this morning cries of fire and the ringing of alarm bells were heard on every side. I think a hundred fires must have been started at one time. We grabbed the few things we had to carry and marched out of the fire territory, where we left them under guard and went back to do what we could to help the people. There was no such thing as saving the buildings. Fires were breaking out in new places all the time. All we could do was to help the people get over the levee, the only place where the heat did not reach and where there was nothing to burn. There was no lack of help, but all were helpless to do more than that. Only the things most needful, such as beds and eatables, were saved. One lady begged so for her piano that it was got out on the porch and there left to burn. Cows ran bellowing through the streets. Chickens flew out from yards and fell in the streets with their feathers scorching on them. A dog with his bushy tail on fire ran howling through, turning to snap at the fire as he ran. There is no use trying to tell about the sights I saw and the sounds of distress I heard. It cannot be told and could hardly be believed if it were told. Crowds of people, men, women, children and soldiers, were running with all they could carry, when the heat would become unbearable, and dropping all, they would flee for their lives, leaving everything but their bodies to burn. Over the levee the sights and sounds were harrowing. Thousands of people, mostly women, children and old men, were wringing their hands as they stood by the little piles of what was left of all their worldly possessions. Thieves were everywhere, and some of them were soldiers. I saw one knocked down and left in the street, who had his arms full of stolen articles. The provost guards were everywhere, and, I am told, shot down everyone caught spreading the fire or stealing. Nearly all buildings were of wood; great patches of burning roofs would sail away, to drop and start a new fire. By noon the thickly settled portion of Alexandria was a smoking ruin. The thousands of beautiful shade trees were as bare as in winter, and those that stood nearest the houses were themselves burning. An attempt was made to save one section by blowing up a church that stood in an open space, but the fuse went out and the powder did not explode until the building burned down to it, and then scattered the fire instead of stopping it, making the destruction more complete than if nothing of the kind had been attempted.

The campaign ended. Transports took Smith's army back to Sherman, Banks turned over the remaining troops to General E. R. S. Canby (recently put in charge of the Military Division of the West Mississippi), Porter resumed the Mississippi patrol. The Union wrote off an inglorious failure.

At least one Confederate was no happier with the results than Washington. General Richard Taylor had protested strongly when his superior, Kirby Smith, had drawn off a part of the Confederate forces after Mansfield and Pleasant Hill and marched north to join Price in southern Arkansas. There, on April 30, the combined force had won an indecisive victory (Jenkins' Ferry) over the army which Steele was to have had at Shreveport six weeks earlier. As weeks passed, Taylor's resentment mounted, until he ended an acrimonious correspondence with as bitter and insubordinate a letter as the war produced:[16]

NEAR ALEXANDRIA, June 5, 1864

GENERAL: . . . You are mistaken in supposing that my communications were intended as complaints. I have no complaints to make. My communications were statements of facts, necessary, in my judgment, to the proper understanding of the campaign. I have not read the story of Gil Blas and the Archbishop to so little purpose as not to know that truth is often considered "objectionable by superiors," but I have not drawn the moral that it is therefore "improper in subordinates to state it."

. . . You state that the fruits of the victory of Mansfield were secured by the march of the column against Steele, and that the complete success of the campaign was determined by his overthrow at Jenkins' Ferry. After a series of engagements Banks was driven into his works at Alexandria on April 28, two days before the fight at Jenkins' Ferry, and on the day of that fight the river was completely blockaded below Alexandria against both transports and gun-boats. I am at a loss to conceive what connection the fruits of Mansfield have with the fight at Jenkins' Ferry. . . .

At Jenkins' Ferry you lost more heavily in killed and wounded than the enemy. This appears from the official report of Steele, confirmed by our officers who were present. You lost two pieces of artillery, which the enemy did not carry off because he had previously been deprived of means of transportation. . . . He burned his pontoon for the same reason, and because after crossing the Saline he had no further use for it. He marched to Little Rock after the fight entirely unmolested. He would unquestionably have gone there had the fight never occurred. We do not today hold one foot more of Arkansas than if Jenkins' Ferry had never been, and we have a jaded army and 1,000 less soldiers. How, then, was the "complete success of the campaign determined by Steele's overthrow at Jenkins' Ferry"? In truth, the campaign as a whole has been a hideous failure. The fruits of Mansfield have been turned to dust and ashes. Louisiana, from Natchitoches to the Gulf, is a howling wilderness and her people are starving. Arkansas is probably as great a sufferer. In both States abolition conventions are sitting to overthrow their system of labor. The remains of Banks' army have already gone to join Grant or Sherman, and may turn the scale against our overmatched brethren in Virginia and Georgia.

On April 24 the affair of Monett's Ferry * took place. The Federals admit that a few hours' more delay would have led to the destruction of their army. Admiral Porter in his official report states this army to be 35,000 strong. The destruction of the army would have led, of necessity, to the destruction of the fleet. These advantages were all thrown away, to the utter destruction of the best interests of the country, and in their place we have Jenkins' Ferry. Our material of war is exhausted, our men are broken down with long marches from Red River to Arkansas and from Arkansas back to Red River. About 1,000 of the best officers and men were sacrificed and no result attained. The roads to Saint Louis and New Orleans should now be open to us. Your strategy has riveted the fetters on both. . . . The grave errors you have committed in the recent campaign may be repeated if the unhappy consequences are not kept before you. After the desire to serve my country, I have none more ardent than to be relieved from longer serving under your command.

* A sharp engagement in which the Confederates tried unsuccessfully to prevent the Union forces from crossing the Cane River. The battle, which is sometimes called Cane River Crossing, took place on April 23, rather than 24, as Taylor stated.

CHAPTER 30

"CRIES AROSE
OF GRANT!"

BLACKS AND WHITES slaughtered heedlessly at a minor outpost along the Mississippi, infantry and artillery fighting gunboats along the distant Arkansas—these were new aspects of a war now three years old. But the climactic event of that spring took place in Washington.

I

Horace Porter was a guest at the White House:[1]

On the evening of March 8 the President and Mrs. Lincoln gave a public reception at the White House, which I attended. The President stood in the usual reception-room, known as the "Blue Room," with several cabinet officers near him, and shook hands cordially with everybody, as the vast procession of men and women passed in front of him. He was in evening dress, and wore a turned-down collar a size too large. The necktie was rather broad and awkwardly tied. He was more of a Hercules than an Adonis. His height of six feet four inches enabled him to look over the heads of most of his visitors. His form was ungainly, and the movements of his long, angular arms and legs bordered at times upon the grotesque. His eyes were gray and disproportionately small. His face wore a general expression of sadness, the deep lines indicating the sense of responsibility which weighed upon him; but at times his features lighted up with a broad smile, and there was a merry twinkle in his eyes as he greeted an old acquaintance and exchanged a few words with him in a tone of familiarity. He had sprung from the common people to become one of the most uncommon of men. Mrs. Lincoln occupied a position on his right. For a time she stood on a line with him and took part in the reception, but afterward stepped back and conversed with some of the wives of the cabinet officers and other personal acquaintances who were in the room. At about half-past nine o'clock a sudden commotion near the entrance to the room attracted general attention, and, upon looking in that direction, I was surprised to see General Grant walking along modestly with the rest of the crowd toward Mr. Lincoln. He had arrived from the West that evening, and had come to the White House to pay his respects to the President. He had been in Washington but once before, when he visited it for a day soon after he had left West Point.* Although these two historical characters had never met before, Mr. Lincoln recognized the general at once from the pictures he had seen of him. With a face radiant with delight, he advanced rapidly two or three steps toward his distinguished visitor, and cried out: "Why, here is General Grant! Well, this is a great pleasure, I assure you," at the same time seizing him by the hand, and shaking it for several minutes with a vigor which showed the extreme cordiality of the welcome.

The scene now presented was deeply impressive. Standing face to face for the first time were the two illustrious men whose names will always be inseparably associated in connection with the war of the rebellion. Grant's right hand grasped the lapel of his coat; his head was bent slightly forward, and his eyes upturned toward Lincoln's face. The President, who was eight inches taller, looked down with beaming countenance upon his guest. Although their appearance, their training, and their characteristics were in striking contrast, yet the two men had many traits in common, and there were numerous points of resemblance in their remarkable careers. Each was of humble origin, and had been compelled to learn the first lessons of life in the severe school of adversity. Each had risen from the people, possessed an abiding confidence in them, and always retained a deep hold upon their affections. Each might have said to those who were inclined to sneer at his plain origin what a marshal of France, who had risen from the ranks to a dukedom, said to the hereditary nobles who attempted to snub him in Vienna: "I am an ancestor; you are only descendants."

. . . The statesman and the soldier conversed for a few minutes, and then the President presented his distinguished guest to Mr. Seward. The Secretary of State was very demonstrative in his welcome, and

* 1843.

after exchanging a few words, led the general to where Mrs. Lincoln was standing, and presented him to her. Mrs. Lincoln expressed much surprise and pleasure at the meeting, and she and the general chatted together very pleasantly for some minutes. The visitors had by this time become so curious to catch a sight of the general that their eagerness knew no bounds, and they became altogether unmanageable. Mr. Seward's consummate knowledge of the wiles of diplomacy now came to the rescue and saved the situation. He succeeded in struggling through the crowd with the general until they reached the large East Room, where the people could circulate more freely. This, however, was only a temporary relief. The people by this time had worked themselves up to a state of uncontrollable excitement. The vast throng surged and swayed and crowded until alarm was felt for the safety of the ladies. Cries now arose of "Grant! Grant! Grant!" Then came cheer after cheer. Seward, after some persuasion, induced the general to stand upon a sofa, thinking the visitors would be satisfied with a view of him, and retire; but as soon as they caught sight of him their shouts were renewed, and a rush was made to shake his hand. The President sent word that he and the Secretary of War would await the general's return in one of the small drawing-rooms, but it was fully an hour before he was able to make his way there, and then only with the aid of several officers and ushers.

On the following day, March 9, General Grant returned to the White House, accompanied by Fred, his eldest son. Lincoln and the members of his Cabinet greeted the distinguished visitor. The President said:

"General Grant, the nation's appreciation of what you have done, and its reliance upon you for what remains to be done in the existing great struggle, are now presented, with this commission constituting you lieutenant-general in the Army of the United States.* With this high honor, devolves upon you, also, a corresponding responsibility. As the country herein trusts you, so, under God, it will sustain you. I scarcely need to add, that, with what I here speak for the nation, goes my own hearty personal concurrence."

Grant responded:

"Mr. President, I accept the commission, with gratitude for the high honor conferred. With the aid of the noble armies that have fought

---

* The grade of lieutenant general, bestowed previously only on George Washington and Winfield Scott, was revived by act of Congress in February. Grant was nominated for this office on March 1 and confirmed by the Senate next day.

*in so many fields for our common country, it will be my earnest
endeavor not to disappoint your expectations. I feel the full weight of
the responsibilities now devolving upon me; and I know that if they are
met, it will be due to those armies, and above all, to the favor of that
Providence which leads both nations and men."*

II

In character, Grant moved swiftly:[2]

. . . My commission as lieutenant-general was given to me on the
9th of March, 1864. On the following day . . . I visited General
Meade, commanding the Army of the Potomac, at his headquarters at
Brandy Station, north of the Rapidan. I had known General Meade
slightly in the Mexican war, but had not met him since until this visit.
I was a stranger to most of the Army of the Potomac, I might say to all
except the officers of the regular army who had served in the Mexican
war. There had been some changes ordered in the organization of that
army before my promotion. One was the consolidation of five corps
into three, thus throwing some officers of rank out of important commands. Meade evidently thought that I might want to make still one
more change not yet ordered. He said to me that I might want an
officer who had served with me in the West, mentioning Sherman specially, to take his place. If so, he begged me not to hesitate about making the change. He urged that the work before us was of such vast
importance to the whole nation that the feeling or wishes of no one person should stand in the way of selecting the right men for all positions. For himself, he would serve to the best of his ability where placed.
I assured him that I had no thought of substituting any one for him.
As to Sherman, he could not be spared from the West.

This incident gave me even a more favorable opinion of Meade than
did his great victory at Gettysburg the July before. It is men who wait
to be selected, and not those who seek, from whom we may always expect the most efficient service.

Meade's position afterwards proved embarrassing to me if not to him.
He was commanding an army and, for nearly a year previous to
my taking command of all the armies,* was in supreme command of the
Army of the Potomac—except from the authorities at Washington. All
other general officers occupying similar positions were independent in

* The official order, placing Grant in command of all armies, was issued on
March 12.

their commands so far as any one present with them was concerned.
I tried to make General Meade's position as nearly as possible what it
would have been if I had been in Washington or any other place away
from his command. I therefore gave all orders for the movements of the
Army of the Potomac to Meade to have them executed. To avoid the
necessity of having to give orders direct, I established my headquarters
near his, unless there were reasons for locating them elsewhere. . . .

A quick trip to the West gave Grant a chance to confer with Sherman:

. . . We left Nashville together for Cincinnati. I had Sherman accompany me that far on my way back to Washington so that we could
talk over the matters about which I wanted to see him, without losing any more time from my new command than was necessary. The
first point which I wished to discuss was particularly about the co-operation of his command with mine when the spring campaign should commence. . . .

Some time in the winter of 1863–64 I had been invited by the general-in-chief to give my views of the campaign I thought advisable for
the command under me—now Sherman's. General J. E. Johnston was
defending Atlanta and the interior of Georgia with an army, the largest
part of which was stationed at Dalton, about 38 miles south of Chattanooga. Dalton is at the junction of the railroad from Cleveland [Ten-
nessee] with the one from Chattanooga to Atlanta.

There could have been no difference of opinion as to the first duty of
the armies of the military division of the Mississippi. Johnston's army
was the first objective, and that important railroad centre, Atlanta, the
second. . . . The plan therefore was for Sherman to attack Johnston
and destroy his army if possible, to capture Atlanta and hold it, and
with his troops and those of Banks * to hold a line through to Mobile,
or at least to hold Atlanta and command the railroad running east and
west, and the troops from one or other of the armies to hold important
points on the southern road, the only east and west road that would be
left in the possession of the enemy. This would cut the Confederacy in
two again, as our gaining possession of the Mississippi River had done
before. . . .

*On the twenty-third of March, Grant was back in Washington. Three
days later he established his headquarters at Culpeper Court House. He
believed that he understood both Lincoln and Stanton now:*

---

* Still commanding the Department of the Gulf.

Although hailing from Illinois myself, the State of the President, I never met Mr. Lincoln until called to the capital to receive my commission as lieutenant-general. I knew him, however, very well and favorably from the accounts given by officers under me at the West who had known him all their lives. I had also read the remarkable series of debates between Lincoln and Douglas a few years before, when they were rival candidates for the United States Senate. I was then a resident of Missouri, and by no means a "Lincoln man" in that contest; but I recognized then his great ability.

In my first interview with Mr. Lincoln alone he stated to me that he had never professed to be a military man or to know how campaigns should be conducted, and never wanted to interfere in them; but that procrastination on the part of commanders, and the pressure from the people of the North and Congress, *which was always with him,* forced him into issuing his series of "Military Orders"—one, two, three, etc. He did not know but they were all wrong, and did know that some of them were. All he wanted or had ever wanted was some one who would take the responsibility and act, and call on him for all the assistance needed, pledging himself to use all the power of the government in rendering such assistance. Assuring him that I would do the best I could with the means at hand, and avoid as far as possible annoying him or the War Department, our first interview ended.

The Secretary of War I had met once before only, but felt that I knew him better.

While commanding in West Tennessee we had occasionally held conversations over the wires, at night, when they were not being used. He and General Halleck both cautioned me against giving the President my plans of campaign, saying that he was so kind-hearted, so averse to refusing anything asked of him, that some friend would be sure to get from him all he knew. I should have said that in our interview the President told me he did not want to know what I proposed to do. But he submitted a plan of campaign of his own which he wanted me to hear and then do as I pleased about. He brought out a map of Virginia on which he had evidently marked every position occupied by the Federal and Confederate armies up to that time. He pointed out on the map two streams which empty into the Potomac, and suggested that the army might be moved on boats and landed between the mouths of these streams. We would then have the Potomac to bring our supplies, and the tributaries would protect our flanks while we moved out. I listened respectfully, but did not suggest that the same streams would protect Lee's flanks while he was shutting us up.

I did not communicate my plans to the President, nor did I to the Secretary of War or to General Halleck.

III

All was not sweetness and light. Grant called Sheridan east to command the Federal cavalry in the approaching campaign against Lee. "Little Phil" had definite notions about how he wished to operate. He would not be as gratified as Grant by an early interview:[3]

At first General Meade would hardly listen to my proposition [that cavalry should be used to fight cavalry], for he was filled with the prejudices that, from the beginning of the war, had pervaded the army regarding the importance and usefulness of cavalry, General Scott then predicting that the contest would be settled by artillery, and thereafter refusing the services of regiment after regiment of mounted troops. General Meade deemed cavalry fit for little more than guard and picket duty, and wanted to know what would protect the transportation trains and artillery reserve, cover the front of moving infantry columns, and secure his flanks from intrusion, if my policy was pursued. I told him that if he would let me use the cavalry as I contemplated, he need have little solicitude in these respects, for, with a mass of ten thousand mounted men, it was my belief that I could make it so lively for the enemy's cavalry that, so far as attacks from it were concerned, the flanks and rear of the Army of the Potomac would require little or no defense, and claimed, further, that moving columns of infantry should take care of their own fronts. I also told him that it was my object to defeat the enemy's cavalry in a general combat, if possible, and by such a result establish a feeling of confidence in my own troops that would enable us after a while to march where we pleased, for the purpose of breaking General Lee's communications and destroying the resources from which his army was supplied.

The idea as here outlined was contrary to Meade's convictions, for though at different times since he commanded the Army of the Potomac considerable bodies of the cavalry had been massed for some special occasion, yet he had never agreed to the plan as a permanency, and could not be bent to it now. He gave little encouragement, therefore, to what I proposed, yet the conversation was immediately beneficial in one way, for when I laid before him the true condition of the cavalry, he promptly relieved it from much of the arduous and harassing picket service it was performing, thus giving me about two weeks in which to nurse the horses before the campaign opened.

While Sheridan and Meade were each gauging the other's peppery temper, disaster almost overtook Grant:[4]

. . . I generally visited Washington once a week to confer with the Secretary of War and President. On the last occasion, a few days before moving [from Culpeper], a circumstance occurred which came near postponing my part in the campaign altogether. Colonel John S. Mosby had for a long time been commanding a partisan corps, or regiment, which operated in the rear of the Army of the Potomac. On my return to the field on this occasion, as the train approached Warrenton Junction, a heavy cloud of dust was seen to the east of the road as if made by a body of cavalry on a charge. Arriving at the junction the train was stopped and inquiries made as to the cause of the dust. There was but one man at the station, and he informed us that Mosby had crossed a few minutes before at full speed in pursuit of Federal cavalry. Had he seen our train coming, no doubt he would have let his prisoners escape to capture the train. I was on a special train, if I remember correctly, without any guard.

IV

With the Virginia dogwoods all in bloom, Grant selected May 4 as the day to begin the movement to knock Lee out of the war. Federal effectives amounted to over 100,000, not counting Burnside's Ninth Corps held near the Rappahannock railroad bridge. Lee's army, lying west of the Rapidan, counted about 64,000 effectives. The Confederate commander knew that the hour of desperate decision approached rapidly, and tallied the tell-tale signs for his son Custis:[5]

CAMP 30 Apl '64

MY DEAR CUSTIS:

Nothing of much interest has occurred during the past week. The reports of scouts all indicate large preparations on the part of the enemy and a state of readiness for action. The 9th Corps is reported to be encamped (or rather was on the 27th) on the O & A RR between Fairfax CH and Alexandria. This is corroborative of information sent the President yesterday, but there may be some mistake as to the fact or number of corps. All their troops north of Rappahannock have been moved South, their guards called in, etc. The garrisons, provost guards, etc., in Northern cities have been brought forward and replaced by state troops. A battalion of heavy artillery is said to have recently arrived in Culpeper, numbering 3,000. I presume these are the men stated in their papers to have been drawn from the forts in N. Y. Harbour.

I wish we could make corresponding preparations. If I could get back Pickett, Hoke and R. Johnston I would feel strong enough to operate.* I have been endeavouring for the last eight or ten days to move Imboden against the B. & O. RR in its unprotected state, but have not been able. I presume he has his difficulties as well as myself. I am afraid it is too late now. I can not yet get the troops together for want of forage and am hoping for grass. Endeavour to get accurate information from Peninsula, James river, etc. My scouts have not returned from Annapolis and may get back too late.

Very affectionately your father,
R. E. LEE

GEN. G. W. CUSTIS LEE

Confederate General G. Moxley Sorrel described the real problem that confronted Lee:[6]

We were at no loss to understand Grant's intention. The Northern papers, as well as himself, had boldly and brutally announced the purpose of "attrition"—that is, the Federals could stand the loss of four or five men to the Confederates' one, and throw nice strategy into the background. It was known that we were almost past recruiting our thin ranks, and the small figures of the army as it now stood; while the double numbers of the Federals could be reproduced from the immense resources in population, not to speak of their foreign field of supplies under inducement of liberal bounties.

Grant started his march the night of May 3d [4th], via Germanna and Ely's Fords, Wilson's and Gregg's cavalry leading. Burnside also was ordered to him.

The wilderness was a wild, tangled forest of stunted trees, with in places impassable undergrowth, lying between Fredericksburg and Orange Court House, probably sixteen or seventeen miles square. Some farm clearings and a shanty or two for a few poor inhabitants might oc-

---

* Pickett was still in the Petersburg field; Hoke was in North Carolina on recruiting duty; Robert D. Johnston was with Early in the Valley.

casionally be seen. Two principal roads penetrated this repulsive district, the Orange Plank Road and the turnpike. The ground generally
lay flat and level.

And now was to begin the last and greatest of the campaigns of the
Army of Northern Virginia. The campaign of *attrition* on one side met
and foiled by the fine flower of the ablest strategy of the other. It was
Grant's stubborn perseverance, indifferent to the loss of life, against
Lee's clear insight and incessant watchfulness. . . .

v

From a signal station on Clark's Mountain, the Confederates watched
the advance of Grant's columns. A shrewd flanking movement by Lee
threatened to drive a wedge between Hancock's Second Corps and the
Fifth under Warren and the Sixth under Sedgwick. The skirmishing
was heavy on the morning of May 5 when Meade, Warren, and
Sedgwick met at Old Wilderness Tavern and decided they must attack
without waiting for Hancock. By eleven o'clock the battle was becom-
ing a bloody page in history—especially at the front where Sedgwick,
coming up, soon found rebels pounding his lines. With Sedgwick
traveled an unidentified eyewitness:[7]

"Forward! by the right flank; forward!" rings along the lines. Yonder
in front are the gleaming bayonets of our first line of battle; back, just
in rear, is the second line, the anxious eyes of the soldiers peering
through the trees.

Was it a sadder wind than usual that swept down from the front that
moment, bearing the first earnest clangor of the combat? Else why, as
that wind touched the faces of the men, did such a mournful fervor
blend with, but not blight the resolute curves of lips that pride forbade
to tremble?

"Forward! by the right flank; forward!" again and again repeated
far to right and left, until it becomes an echo.

And through a thicket, blind and interminable; over abattis of fallen
trees; through swamps, and ditches, and brush-heaps; and once—a
glorious breathing-space—across a half acre of open field, the obedient
troops move on. . . . Sometimes the eyes of the men sink to note a by-
path in the forest, like that which many a one has travelled in old days
to some old spring of home-like memory. And here is the "birr" of a
bullet, like that which startled one who heard it one summer afternoon,
when a brother hunter was careless, and fired at a partridge as he stood

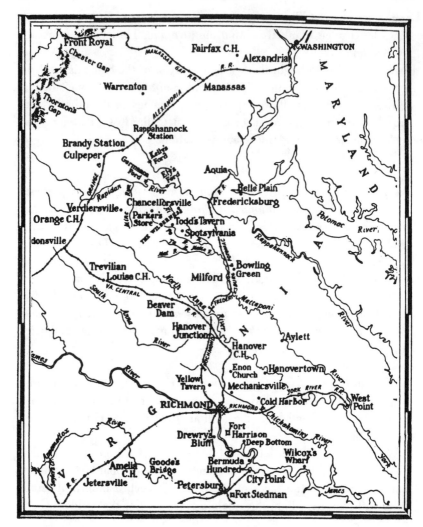

RICHMOND AND VICINITY, 1864
From *Atlas of American History*

in range. The bee-like sounds are thicker on this ridge; in the forest, a little way ahead, there is a crackling, roaring tumult, seasoned with wild cheers.

The Fifth corps has begun the fight in earnest—Griffin is pressing on. Wadsworth, and Robinson, and Crawford are going in; the latter on the left, supported by Getty, is advancing toward the enemy at Parker's store. Behind Crawford and Getty, who are on the Orange Court-house road, is the junction of that and the Brock road, up which, from the direction of Chancellorsville, Hancock is advancing to make connection. *That* is the vital point—that junction; to be held against all odds unto the death, else the army is severed. . . .

Here, marching through the forest with General John Sedgwick and his officers, between the first and second lines of battle of that grand old corps, which has left its mark in blood on every great battle-field in Virginia, we can hear but not see the progress of the contest in front and on the left. We hear that Griffin and Wadsworth, after gallantly charging the enemy, advancing over two lines of works, have met with superior numbers, have fought courageously, but have been pushed back. The cannon that spake a moment ago are silent. They were two guns of Captain Winslow's (Second Massachusetts) battery, the horses of which have been killed, the men of which have been sorely pressed, and which have been spiked and abandoned. We hear that Crawford's division of Pennsylvania Reserves, sent forward to Parker's store to check the surging tide of Hill's troops, pouring on to attack that junction of two roads on which so much depends, have been hurled back by the same overwhelming pressure that forces Wadsworth, and that the Seventh Pennsylvania regiment has been captured. We hear that everywhere the enemy is strongly posted, everywhere; on height, in the dense forest, using occasional open fields in the rear for artillery, but forcing us to attack in positions where the use of our own artillery is impossible. A cunning and a deceitful foe, knowing of old the splendid aim and discipline of our batteries, now compelled to silence.

The air is stifling, the sun sends its rays down through the jagged limbs of the chapparal around like red hot spears. This march is long, these bullets from an unseen foe are staining some sleeves and jackets too soon. . . .

They are there at last; the bushwhackers, thick as the sprigs and leaves that partly hide their treacherous faces. As the ponderous battle-line of the Sixth corps swings into level in their front, it sends a volley in greeting that thins those faces even as a wind of autumn rushing through an oak. General Ricketts is on the left, General Wright next, General Neill, of the Second division, whose iron brigade is made up of men who never flinched a desperate strait, holds the right of the line in support.

The fighting—who shall describe it? Not a thousand men can be seen at once, yet for miles in the front thousands are engaged. The volleyed thunders of the combat roll among the glens and ravines hoarser and higher than the voices of an Eastern jungle. The woods are alive with cries and explosions, and the shrill anvil-clatter of musketry. One cannon, pitched afar, times the wild tumult like a tolling bell. The smoke is a shroud about our heroes; there is not wind enough to lift it into a canopy.

And now, out of the concealed and awful scenery where the fight goes on, there come the ruins it has wrought, in shapes borne in blankets and on litters—maimed, tortured, writhing; with eyes dull with the stupor of coming death, or bright with delirious fire. Listen to the hell raging beyond and below; behold this silent, piteous procession, that emerges ceaselessly, and passes on. . . .

Two o'clock. In the momentary calm that sinks upon the forest in front we can hear a louder conflict gathering and growing on the left. There Crawford has been driven back; there the enemy are pressing in hordes down the turnpike, to gain the junction of the Brock road. Getty has advanced and met them. Hancock has come up at last, and Birney is going in on Getty's right. Mott and Barlow are forming on the left of the line, and Gibbon's division is coming up as a reserve. The enemy are checked, but their concentration continues. Troops are sent to the left from the Fifth corps, and by four o'clock General Hancock is in command of half the army in action.

And now, from left to right the sound of the shock of battle arises anew. Hancock is advancing, Sedgwick is advancing, Warren is in partial wait. Along the left a guttural, oceanic roar prevails, without an interval of rest. Like a great engine, dealing death, the Second corps and its supports move forward, taking equal death in return. Companies fall, regiments are thinned, brigades melt away. Stricken in the head by a bullet, General Alexander Hays, commanding the Second brigade of Birney's division, has rolled from his horse, dead. General Getty is wounded; Colonel Carroll, commanding the Third brigade of the Second division, is wounded; a host of line officers are stricken low; the enemy fights like a demon, but the fight moves on.

Sedgwick moves on, breaking the enemy's line for a moment, and taking four or five hundred prisoners. There are ripples of disaster on all the line, but they are quickly repaired.

Slowly, for the enemy is stubborn; slower yet on the extreme right, toward the river, for the enemy there has massed another force, and strives to break our flank. He finds a rock, and though he checks our advance, though hundreds of soldiers make the obeisance of death before him, he does not come on.

And as the day dies, and the darkness creeps up from the west, although no cheer of victory swells through the Wilderness from either side, we have accomplished this much at least, with much sore loss: the concentration of our army, the holding of the junction of the Orange Court-house and Brock roads; the turning back of the enemy's right flank from our path toward Richmond, and the average gain of a half mile of ground.

Colonel Theodore Lyman, who served on Meade's staff, watched his new general-in-chief that day:[8]

. . . General Grant had his station with us (or we with him); there he took his seat on the grass, and smoked his briarwood pipe, looking sleepy and stern and indifferent. His face, however, may wear a most pleasing smile, and I believe he is a thoroughly amiable man. That he believes in his star and takes a bright view of things is evident. At 4:15 P.M. General Meade ordered me to take some orderlies, go to General Hancock (whose musketry we could now hear on the left) and send him back reports, staying there till dark. Delightful! At the crossing of the dotted cross-road with the plank sat Hancock, on his fine horse—the *preux chevalier* of this campaign—a glorious soldier, indeed! The musketry was crashing in the woods in our front, and stray balls—too many to be pleasant—were coming about. It's all very well for novels, but *I* don't like such places and go there only when ordered. "Report to General Meade," said Hancock, "that it is very hard to bring up troops in this wood, and that only a part of my Corps is up, but I will do as well as I can." Up rides an officer: "Sir! General Getty is hard pressed and nearly out of ammunition!" "Tell him to hold on and General Gibbon will be up to help him." Another officer: "General Mott's division has broken, sir, and is coming back." "Tell him to stop them, sir!!" roared Hancock in a voice of a trumpet. As he spoke, a crowd of troops came from the woods and fell back into the Brock road. Hancock dashed among them. "Halt here! halt here! Form behind this rifle-pit. Major Mitchell, go to Gibbon and tell him to come up on the double-quick!" It was a welcome sight to see Carroll's brigade coming along that Brock road, he riding at their head as calm as a May morning. "Left face—prime—forward," and the line disappeared in the woods to waken the musketry with double violence. Carroll was brought back wounded. Up came Hays's brigade, disappeared in the woods, and, in a few minutes, General Hays was carried past me, covered with blood, shot through the head.

Horace Porter, on Grant's staff, found that the general, upon occasion, could lose his patience:[9]

. . . Darkness had set in, but the firing still continued. Aides came galloping in from the right, laboring under intense excitement, talking wildly, and giving the most exaggerated reports of the engagement. Some declared that a large force had broken and scattered Sedgwick's entire corps. Others insisted that the enemy had turned our right completely, and captured the wagon-train. It was asserted at one time that both Sedgwick and Wright had been captured. Such tales of disaster would have been enough to inspire serious apprehension in daylight and under ordinary circumstances. In the darkness of the night, in the gloom of a tangled forest, and after men's nerves had been racked by the strain of a two days' desperate battle, the most immovable commander might have been shaken.

But it was in just such sudden emergencies that General Grant was always at his best. Without the change of a muscle of his face, or the slightest alteration in the tones of his voice, he quietly interrogated the officers who brought the reports; then, sifting out the truth from the mass of exaggerations, he gave directions for relieving the situation with the marvelous rapidity which was always characteristic of him when directing movements in the face of an enemy. Reinforcements were hurried to the point attacked, and preparations made for Sedgwick's corps to take up a new line, with the front and right thrown back. General Grant soon walked over to his own camp, seated himself on a stool in front of his tent, lighted a fresh cigar, and there continued to receive further advices from the right.

A general officer came in from his command at this juncture, and said to the general-in-chief, speaking rapidly and laboring under considerable excitement: "General Grant, this is a crisis that cannot be looked upon too seriously. I know Lee's methods well by past experience; he will throw his whole army between us and the Rapidan, and cut us off completely from our communications." The general rose to his feet, took his cigar out of his mouth, turned to the officer, and replied, with a degree of animation which he seldom manifested: "Oh, I am heartily tired of hearing about what Lee is going to do. Some of you always seem to think he is suddenly going to turn a double somersault, and land in our rear and on both of our flanks at the same time. Go back to your command, and try to think what we are going to do ourselves, instead of what Lee is going to do."

VI

The battle, by Theodore Lyman's account, opened smartly next morning, the sixth of May:[10]

. . . General Grant ordered the attack all along the line, the next morning at 4:30; but put it off to 5 o'clock on the representation that Burnside could not get up in time. He was ordered to get in position by day-light and to go in on Hill's left flank . . . nearly parallel to the Parker's Store road. We were all up right early on that Friday the 6th of May, you may depend. "Lyman," said the General [Meade], "I want you to take some orderlies and go to General Hancock and report how things go there during the day."

It was after five when I mounted, and already the spattering fire showed that the skirmishers were pushing out; as I rode down the cross-road, two or three crashing volleys rang through the woods, and then the whole front was alive with musketry. I found General Hancock at the crossing of the plank: he was wreathed with smiles. "We are driving them, sir; tell General Meade we are driving them most beautifully. Birney has gone in and he is just cleaning them out be-au-ti-fully!" This was quite apparent from the distance of the receding firing and the absence of those infernal minié balls. "I am ordered to tell you, sir, that only one division of General Burnside is up, but that he will go in as soon as he can be put in position." Hancock's face changed. "I knew it!" he said vehemently. "Just what I expected. If he could attack *now*, we would smash A. P. Hill all to pieces!" And very true were his words.

Meantime, some hundreds of prisoners were brought in; all from Hill's troops. Presently, however, the firing seemed to wake again with renewed fury; and in a little while a soldier came up to me and said: "I was ordered to report that this prisoner here belongs to Longstreet's Corps." "Do you belong to Longstreet?" I hastened to ask. "Ya-as, sir," said grey-back, and was marched to the rear. It was too true! Longstreet, coming in all haste from Orange Court House, had fallen desperately on our advance; but he had uphill work. Birney's and Getty's men held fast and fought with fury, a couple of guns were put in the plank road and began to fire solid shot over the heads of our men, adding their roar to the other din. The streams of wounded came faster and faster back; here a field officer, reeling in the saddle; and there another, hastily carried past on a stretcher. I stood at the crossing and assisted in turning back stragglers or those who sought to go back, under pretext of helping the wounded. To some who were in great pain I gave some opium, as they were carried past me.

General Sorrel explained how the Confederates managed to spring this surprise:[11]

Longstreet had moved at 1 A.M., the march being difficult and slow in the dense forest by side tracks and deep furrowed roadways. At daylight he was on the Plank Road and in close touch with Lee when Hancock struck the two unprepared divisions [Heth's and Wilcox's of the Third Corps]. The situation when we came on the scene, that of May 6th, was appalling. Fugitives from the broken lines of the Third Corps were pouring back in disorder and it looked as if things were past mending.

But not so to James Longstreet; never did his great qualities as a tenacious, fighting soldier shine forth in better light. He instantly took charge of the battle, and threw his two divisions across the Plank Road, Kershaw on the right, Field on the left. None but seasoned soldiers like the First Corps could have done even that much. . . . Hill's men were prompt to collect and reform in our rear and soon were ready for better work.

General Lee was under great excitement immediately on the left. He wanted to lead some of our troops into action, but the Texas brigade was about him and swore they would do nothing unless he retired. A confident message from Longstreet through Colonel Venable that his line would be restored within an hour also helped him to regain his calm; and then at it we went in earnest, on both sides of the road.

Hancock's success had loosened his ranks somewhat, which helped us when we fell on him. It was a hard shock of battle by six of our brigades, three on each side of the road. No artillery came into play, the ground not being fit for it. . . .

Lyman saw that events had taken an ugly turn for Hancock:[12]

. . . Longstreet knew full well (they know everything, those Rebels) that Burnside was coming up with two divisions, on his flank; and knew too that he was late, very late. If Hancock could first be paralyzed, the day was safe from defeat, which now impended. Gathering all his forces, of both corps, he charged furiously. At a little after eleven Mott's left gave way. On the right the brigade of Stevenson, consisting of three raw Massachusetts regiments miscalled "Veterans," broke, on being brought under a tremendous fire. . . .

The musketry now drew nearer to us, stragglers began to come back, and, in a little while, a crowd of men emerged from the thicket in full retreat. They were not running, nor pale, nor scared, nor had they thrown away their guns; but were just in the condition described by the Prince de Joinville, after Gaines's Mill. They had fought all they meant to fight for the present, and there was an end of it! If there is anything that will make your heart sink and take all the backbone out of you, it is to see men in this condition! I drew my sword and rode in among them, trying to stop them at a little rifle-pit that ran along the road. I would get one squad to stop, but, as I turned to another, the first would quietly walk off.

There was a German color-bearer, a stupid, scared man (who gave him the colors, the Lord only knows!), who said, "Jeneral Stavenzon, he telled me for to carry ze colors up ze road." To which I replied I would run him through the body if he didn't plant them on the rifle-pit. And so he did, but I guess he didn't stick. Meanwhile there was no danger at all; the enemy did not follow up—not he. He was busy swinging round to oppose Burnside, and was getting his men once more in order. At half-past one I rode to General Meade and reported the state of affairs. The Provost-General went out at once and stopped and organized the stragglers. At two o'clock Burnside, who had been marching and countermarching, *did* attack. He made some impression, but it was too late, and he had not enough force to follow on. About this time I returned to General Hancock. His men were rallied along the road; but regiments and brigades were all mixed up; and we were obliged to listen to Burnside's fighting without any advance on our part. . . .

An eyewitness to the clash between Longstreet's forces and Hancock's was not surprised when shocked Federals came stumbling down the road:[13]

There, in the depths of those ravines, under the shadows of those trees, entangled in that brushwood, is no pomp of war, no fluttering of banners in an unhindered breeze, no solid tramp of marching battalions, no splendid strategy of the fields Napoleon loved to fight on. There a Saturnalia, gloomy, hideous, desperate, rages confined. That metallic, hollow rack of musketry is like the clanking of great chains about the damned; that sullen yell of the enemy, a fiendish protest and defiance. How the hours lag; how each minute is freighted with a burden that the days would have groaned to bear in other times! Still the sad, shuddering procession, emerging out of the smoke and tumult and passing on. Still the appealing eyes and clenched hands and quivering limbs of human creatures, worse than helpless, whose fighting is over. The paths are full of them; the woods are thick with them; the forest seems to take up the slow movement, and move with them, like giants hovering over the funeral of Liliputians.

Piled in ambulances, they move on further yet, while the torture of battle plies on below, making more victims. Here and there, beside some path, you shall see a heaped blanket, labelled by some thoughtful bearer with the name the corpse beneath it bore in life; here and there you shall come across a group of men bending over one wounded past help, and dying an agonized death. And often—too often—the shameful spectacle of one bearing a weapon, unhurt, pallid and fear-stricken, flits through an opening toward the rear and is gone. You shall meet with soldiers in groups of one, or two, or three, hidden in some thicket or, coolly making coffee by the roadside. And hearing the roar of the battle below, and seeing the bloody trails of the battle behind, it shall be a glad thing to see these men hunted by officers back with curses to the ranks, to share the dangers of their nobler comrades.

About this battle there is a horrible fascination. It is like a maelstrom. You feel it sucking you in, and you go nearer to see men fall like those you have seen fallen. Down through the break, underneath the edges of the smoke, where the bullets are thick and the trunks of trees, like the ranks of men, sway and fall with the smiting of shells, you have a little view of the courage and the carnage of this fight. There are the enemy, retreated to the breastworks—a ragged pile of fallen trees and heaped-up earth—hiding their heads, spitting lead and flame. Here is the Sixth corps—what you can see of it—plunging on, firing continually, tumbling over branches and limbs, sinking waist deep in swamps, fighting with its might and bleeding at every pore. The troops of the First division, under Wright, are martyred for a time in a ravine swept by musketry in front, and by a cross-fire of artillery from right and left. The few guns that we have posted to the left have funeral voices for our enemy on the ridge, perishing beneath their fire in scores.

The ridge is taken, the division breathes once more, but on come the enemy, an avalanche of greater numbers, pushing us back. . . .

As the Confederate assault gathered momentum, Sorrel heard Longstreet calling him:[14]

"Colonel, there is a fine chance of a great attack by our right. If you will quickly get into those woods, some brigades will be found much scattered from the fight. Collect them and take charge. Form a good line and then move forward and turning as much as possible to the left. Hit hard when you start, but don't start until you have everything ready. I shall be waiting for your gun fire, and be on hand with fresh troops for further advance."

. . . The brigades of Anderson, Mahone, and Wofford were lined up in fair order and in touch with each other. It was difficult to assemble them in that horrid Wilderness, but in an hour we were ready. The word was given, and then with heavy firing and ringing yells we were upon Hancock's exposed left, the brigades being ably commanded by their respective officers. It was rolled back line after line. I was well mounted, and despite the tangled growth could keep with our troops in conspicuous sight of them, riding most of the charge with Mahone's men of the Eighteenth Virginia. . . .

A stand was attempted by a reserve line of Hancock's, but it was swept off its feet in the tumultuous rush of our troops, and finally we struck the Plank Road lower down. On the other side of it was James S. Wadsworth's corps in disorder. . . . Though the old General was doing all possible to fight it, his men would not stay. A volley from our pursuing troops mortally wounded the gallant New Yorker and killed his horse.

Every care was given to General Wadsworth by our surgeon. Before they could get to him, however, some of his valuables—watch, sword, glasses, etc.—had disappeared among the troops. One of the men came up with, "Here, Colonel, here's his map." It was a good general map of Virginia, and of use afterwards.

We were then so disorganized by the chase through the woods that a halt was necessary to reform, and I hastened back to General Longstreet to press for fresh troops. There was no need with him. He had heard our guns, knew what was up, and was already marching, happy at the success, to finish it with the eager men at his heels.

There was quite a party of mounted officers and men riding with him

—Generals Kershaw and Jenkins, the staff, and orderlies. Jenkins, always enthusiastic, had thrown his arm around my shoulder, with "Sorrel, it was splendid; we shall smash them now." And turning back I was riding by Longstreet's side, my horse's head at his crupper, when firing broke out from our own men on the roadside in the dense tangle.

The Lieutenant General * was struck. He was a heavy man, with a very firm seat in the saddle, but he was actually lifted straight up and came down hard. Then the lead-torn coat, the orifice close to the right shoulder pointed to the passage of the heavy bullet of those days. His staff immediately dismounted him, at foot of a branching tree, bleeding profusely.

The shot had entered near the throat and he was almost choked with blood. Doctor J. S. D. Cullen, his medical director, was quickly on the spot. Even then the battle was in the leader's mind, and he sent word to Major General Charles W. Field to go straight on. He directed me to hasten to General Lee, report what had been accomplished, and urge him to continue the movement he was engaged on; the troops being all ready, success would surely follow, and Grant, he firmly believed, be driven across the Rapidan. . . .

My report to General Lee was, as instructed, immediate. I found him greatly concerned by the wounding of Longstreet and his loss to the army. . . . A new attack with stronger forces was settled on. It was to be made direct on the enemy's works, lower down the Plank Road, in the hope of dislodging him.

But meantime the foe was not idle. He had used the intervening hours in strengthening his position and making really formidable works across the road. When the Confederate troops assaulted them late in the afternoon they met with a costly repulse, and with this the principal operations on our part of the field ceased for the day; it was coming on dark.

In two days Grant's assault against Lee had cost the Union 2,246 killed, 12,037 wounded, and 3,383 missing; Confederate losses in killed and wounded were estimated at 7,750. Still, Theodore Lyman reckoned that the engagements could not be judged by comparative casualties:[15]

---

* Whereas lieutenant general was the highest rank in the U. S. Army, the Confederacy bestowed the rank of full general on Samuel Cooper, Albert Sidney Johnston, Robert E. Lee, Joseph E. Johnston, and P. G. T. Beauregard. On February 6, 1865 the Confederate Congress created the post of general in chief for Lee.

The result of this great Battle of the Wilderness was a drawn fight, but strategically it was a success, because Lee marched out *to stop our advance on Richmond,* which, at this point, he did not succeed in doing. We lost a couple of guns and took some colors. On the right we made no impression; but, on the left, Hancock punished the enemy so fearfully that they, that night, fell back entirely from his front and shortened their own line, as we shortened ours, leaving their dead unburied and many of their wounded on the ground. The Rebels had a very superior knowledge of the country and had marched shorter distances. Also I consider them more daring and sudden in their movements; and I fancy their discipline on *essential* points is more severe than our own—that is, I fancy they shoot a man when he ought to be shot, and we do not. As to *fighting,* when two people fight without cessation for the best part of two days, and then come out about even, it is hard to determine.

VII

Grant decided that he had enough of fighting Lee in this jungle. On the night of May 6 he issued new orders—with surprising results, as Horace Porter explained:[16]

Soon after dark, Generals Grant and Meade, accompanied by their staffs, after having given personal supervision to the starting of the march, rode along the Brock road toward Hancock's headquarters, with the intention of waiting there till Warren's troops should reach that point. While moving close to Hancock's line, there occurred an unexpected demonstration on the part of the troops, which created one of the most memorable scenes of the campaign. Notwithstanding the darkness of the night, the form of the commander was recognized, and word was passed rapidly along that the chief who had led them through the mazes of the Wilderness was again moving forward with his horse's head turned toward Richmond.

Troops know but little about what is going on in a large army, except the occurrences which take place in their immediate vicinity; but this night ride of the general-in-chief told plainly the story of success, and gave each man to understand that the cry was to be "On to Richmond!" Soldiers weary and sleepy after their long battle, with stiffened limbs and smarting wounds, now sprang to their feet, forgetful of their pains, and rushed forward to the roadside. Wild cheers echoed through the forest, and glad shouts of triumph rent the air. Men swung their hats, tossed up their arms, and pressed forward to within touch of their chief, clapping their hands, and speaking to him with the familiarity of comrades. Pine-knots and leaves were set on fire, and lighted the scene with their weird, flickering glare.

The night march had become a triumphal procession for the new commander. The demonstration was the emphatic verdict pronounced by the troops upon his first battle in the East. The excitement had been imparted to the horses, which soon became restive, and even the general's large bay, over which he possessed ordinarily such perfect control, became difficult to manage. Instead of being elated by this significant ovation, the general, thoughtful only of the practical question of the success of the movement, said: "This is most unfortunate. The sound will reach the ears of the enemy, and I fear it may reveal our movement." By his direction, staff-officers rode forward and urged the men to keep quiet so as not to attract the enemy's attention; but the demonstration did not really cease until the general was out of sight.

With cynicism, Theodore Lyman commented on the false optimism in the North:[17]

The newspapers would be comic in their comments, were not the whole thing so tragic. More absurd statements could not be. Lee is *not* retreating: he is a brave and skilful soldier and he will fight while he has a division or a day's rations left. These Rebels are not half-starved and ready to give up—a more sinewy, tawny, formidable-looking set of men could not be. In education they are certainly inferior to our native-born people; but they are usually very quick-witted within their own sphere of comprehension; and they know enough to handle weapons with terrible effect. Their great characteristic is their stoical manliness; they never beg, or whimper, or complain; but look you straight in the face, with as little animosity as if they had never heard a gun.

With equal cynicism, Lyman listened to Grant:

As General Grant sat under a pine tree, stoically smoking his briarwood pipe, I heard him say: "To-night Lee will be retreating south." Ah! General, Robert Lee is not Pemberton; he will retreat south, but only far enough to get across your path, and then he will retreat no more, if he can help it. In fact, orders were out for the whole army to move at dark on Spotsylvania Court House. But Lee knew it all: he could see the waggons moving, and had scouts besides. As night fell, his troops left their works and were crowding down the Parker's Store road, towards Spotsylvania—each moment worth untold gold to them! Grant had no longer a Pemberton! "His best friend," as he calls him. And we marched also. . . .

VIII

Lee guessed correctly; Grant would not retreat, but would strike for Spotsylvania Court House, on the edge of the Wilderness five miles to the southeast. On May 7 Lee began to pull back his troops; he would choose the ground where he would make a stand instead of leaving the initiative to Grant.

As the two armies converged on Spotsylvania and dug in for the coming battle, Phil Sheridan had a chance at last to use his cavalry in the way he wanted—to force Stuart to a duel in the open country behind Lee's lines. Sheridan started on May 9. For two days Stuart's troopers harassed Sheridan's long column. Then, changing tactics, Stuart swung from Sheridan's rear to his front, hoping to intercept the Union cavalry before it could ride into Richmond and commit God knew what devilry. Stuart's point of concentration was Yellow Tavern, six miles north of the Confederate capital.

Sheridan described the climax of the fighting:[18]

By forced marches General Stuart succeeded in reaching Yellow Tavern ahead of me on May 11; and the presence of his troops on the Ashland and Richmond road becoming known to Merritt as he was approaching the Brock turnpike, this general pressed forward at once to the attack. Pushing his division to the front, he soon got possession of the turnpike and drove the enemy back several hundred yards to the east of it. This success had the effect of throwing the head of my column to the east of the pike, and I quickly brought up Wilson and one of Gregg's brigades to take advantage of the situation by forming a line of battle on that side of the road. Meanwhile the enemy, desperate but still confident, poured in a heavy fire from his line and from a battery which enfiladed the Brock road, and made Yellow Tavern an uncomfortably hot place. Gibbs's and Devin's brigades, however, held fast there, while Custer, supported by Chapman's brigade, attacked the enemy's left and battery in a mounted charge.

Custer's charge, with Chapman on his flank and the rest of Wilson's division sustaining him, was brilliantly executed. Beginning at a walk, he increased his gait to a trot, and then at full speed rushed at the enemy. At the same moment the dismounted troops along my whole front moved forward, and as Custer went through the battery, capturing two of the guns with their cannoneers and breaking up the enemy's left, Gibbs and Devin drove his centre and right from the field. Gregg meanwhile, with equal success, charged the force in his rear—Gordon's brigade—and the engagement ended by giving us complete control of the road to Richmond.

Sheridan exaggerated his success at Yellow Tavern, for Stuart's stand had given Richmond's defenders time to man the fortifications and save the city. But the Confederates paid a high price. H. B. McClellan, Stuart's chief of staff, assessed it:[19]

We reached the vicinity of the Yellow Tavern that morning about ten o'clock, and found that we were in advance of the enemy's column, and in time to interpose between it and Richmond. Not knowing what force we had there, the General was uncertain whether to place himself at once between the enemy and the city, or to take a position on his flank, near the Yellow Tavern—the latter he preferred if he could be satisfied that we had a sufficient force in the trenches to defend Richmond. To ascertain this he sent me to see General Bragg. When I returned to him about two o'clock, I found that a heavy engagement had taken place, and, that after driving in a portion of our line, the enemy had been heavily repulsed. When I found the General there was a lull in the fight, and we sat quietly near one of our batteries for more than an hour, resting and talking. About four o'clock the enemy suddenly threw a brigade of cavalry, mounted, upon our extreme left, attacking our whole line at the same time. As he always did, the General hastened to the point where the greatest danger threatened—the point against which the enemy directed the mounted charge. My horse was so much exhausted by my severe ride of the morning that I could not follow him, but Captain Dorsey gave the particulars that follow.

The enemy's charge captured our battery on the left of our line, and drove back almost the entire left. Where Captain Dorsey was stationed —immediately on the Telegraph road—about eighty men had collected together, and among these the General threw himself, and by his personal example held them steady while the enemy charged entirely past their position. With these men he fired into their flank and rear, as they passed him, in advancing and retreating, for they were met by a mounted charge of the First Virginia cavalry and driven back some distance. As they retired, one man, who had been dismounted in the charge and was running out on foot, turned, as he passed the General, and, discharging his pistol, inflicted the fatal wound. When Captain Dorsey discovered that he was wounded, he came at once to his assistance and endeavored to lead him to the rear; the General's horse became so restive and unmanageable that he insisted upon being taken down and allowed to rest against a tree. When this was done Captain Dorsey sent for another horse. While waiting for this horse, the General ordered him to leave him alone and return to his men and drive back the enemy; said that he feared he was mortally wounded and could be of no more service. Captain Dorsey told him that he could not obey that order—that he would sacrifice his life rather than leave him until he had placed him out of all danger. The situation was a dangerous one. Our men were sadly scattered, and there was hardly a handful of men between that little group and the advancing enemy. But the horse arrived in time; the General was lifted onto him and led by Captain Dorsey to a safer place. There, by the General's order, he gave him into charge of Private Wheatly, of his company, and returned to rally our scattered men. Wheatly procured an ambulance, placed the General in it with the greatest care, and supporting him in his arms, he was driven from the field. As he was being brought off, he spoke to our men, whom he saw retreating, and said: "Go back! go back! and do your duty as I have done mine, and our country will be safe. Go back! go back! I had rather die than be whipped."

Stuart, mortally wounded, was carried to Richmond, where he lingered only a day. The Richmond Examiner *described his last hours:*[20]

Major-General J. E. B. Stuart, the model of Virginian cavaliers and dashing chieftain, whose name was a terror to the enemy, and familiar as a household word in two continents, is dead—struck down by a bullet from the foe, and the whole Confederacy mourns him. He breathed out his gallant spirit resignedly, and in the full possession of all his remarkable faculties of mind and body, at twenty-two minutes to eight o'clock Thursday night. . . .

We learn from the physicians in attendance upon the General, that his condition during the day was very changeable, with occasional delirium and other unmistakable symptoms of speedy dissolution. In the moments of delirium the General's mind wandered, and, like the immortal Jackson (whose spirit, we trust, his has joined) in the lapse of reason his faculties were busied with the details of his command. He reviewed, in broken sentences, all his glorious campaigns around McClellan's rear on the Peninsula, beyond the Potomac, and upon the Rapidan, quoting from his orders and issuing new ones to his couriers, with a last injunction to "make haste."

About noon, Thursday, President Davis visited his bedside, and spent some fifteen minutes in the dying chamber of his favorite chieftain. The President, taking his hand, said, "General, how do you feel?" He replied, "Easy, but willing to die, if God and my country think I have fulfilled my destiny and done my duty." As evening approached the General's delirium increased, and his mind again wandered to the battlefields over which he had fought, then off to wife and children, and off again to the front. . . .

As the evening wore on, the paroxysms of pain increased. . . . Though suffering the greatest agony at times, the General was calm, and applied to the wound with his own hand the ice intended to relieve the pain. During the evening he asked Dr. Brewer how long he thought he could live, and whether it was possible for him to survive through the night. The Doctor, knowing he did not desire to be buoyed by false hopes, told him frankly that death, that last enemy, was rapidly approaching. The General nodded and said, "I am resigned if it be God's will; but I would like to see my wife. But God's will be done." Several times he roused up and asked if she had come. . . .

At half-past seven o'clock it was evident to the physicians that death was setting its clammy seal upon the brave, open brow of the General, and told him so; asked if he had any last messages to give. The General, with a mind perfectly clear and possessed, then made dispositions of his staff and personal effects. To Mrs. General R. E. Lee he directed that his golden spurs be given as a dying memento of his love and esteem of her husband. To his staff officers he gave his horses. So particular was he in small things, even in the dying hour, that he emphatically exhibited and illustrated the ruling passion strong in death. To one of his staff, who was a heavy-built man, he said, "You had better take the larger horse; he will carry you better." Other mementoes he disposed of in a similar manner. To his young son he left his glorious sword.

His worldly matters closed, the eternal interest of his soul engaged his mind. Turning to the Rev. Mr. Peterkin, of the Episcopal Church, and of which he was an exemplary member, he asked him to sing the hymn commencing—

> Rock of ages cleft for me,
> Let me hide myself in thee—

he joined in with all the voice his strength would permit. He then joined in prayer with the ministers. To the Doctor he again said, "I am going fast now; I am resigned; God's will be done." Thus died General J. E. B. Stuart.

IX

On May 12, the day when "Jeb" Stuart's gay spirit struggled for release, the storm broke at Spotsylvania, staggering those who witnessed and survived it. At a salient in Lee's line, the "Bloody Angle," Horace Porter saw the conflict reach its peak:[21]

The battle near the "angle" was probably the most desperate engagement in the history of modern warfare, and presented features which were absolutely appalling. It was chiefly a savage hand-to-hand fight across the breastworks. Rank after rank was riddled by shot and shell and bayonet-thrusts, and finally sank, a mass of torn and mutilated corpses; then fresh troops rushed madly forward to replace the dead, and so the murderous work went on. Guns were run up close to the parapet, and double charges of canister played their part in the bloody work. The fence-rails and logs in the breastworks were shattered into splinters, and trees over a foot and a half in diameter were cut completely in two by the incessant musketry fire. . . .

We had not only shot down an army, but also a forest. The opposing flags were in places thrust against each other, and muskets were fired with muzzle against muzzle. Skulls were crushed with clubbed muskets, and men stabbed to death with swords and bayonets thrust between the logs in the parapet which separated the combatants. Wild cheers, savage yells, and frantic shrieks rose above the sighing of the wind and the pattering of the rain, and formed a demoniacal accompaniment to the booming of the guns as they hurled their missiles of death into the contending ranks. Even the darkness of night and the pitiless storm failed to stop the fierce contest, and the deadly strife did not cease till after midnight. Our troops had been under fire for twenty hours, but they still held the position which they had so dearly purchased.

X

*The fighting at Spotsylvania cost Grant casualties of perhaps 17,000;
Lee's loss may have been as many as 12,000. Again, Grant "sidled to
the left," with Lee in dogged pursuit. As the Wilderness campaign
moved into its third phase, Theodore Lyman noted with wonder the
adjustments people made to the rigors of war:*[22]

. . . There is, and can be, no doubt of the straits to which these
people are now reduced; particularly, of course, in this distracted region; there is nothing in modern history to compare with the conscription they have. They have swept this part of the country of all persons
under 50, who could not steal away. I have just seen a man of 48, very
much crippled with rheumatism, who said he was enrolled two days
ago. He told them he had thirteen persons dependent on him, including
three grandchildren (his son-in-law had been taken some time since);
but they said that made no difference; he was on his way to the rendezvous, when our cavalry crossed the river, and he hid in the bushes, till
they came up. I offered him money for some of his small vegetables;
but he said: "If you have any bread, I would rather have it. Your cavalry have taken all the corn I had left, and, as for meat, I have not tasted
a mouthful for six weeks." If you had seen his eyes glisten when I gave
him a piece of salt pork, you would have believed his story. He looked
like a man who had come into a fortune. "Why," said he, "that must
weigh four pounds—that would cost me forty dollars in Richmond!
They told us they would feed the families of those that were taken;
and so they did for two months, and then they said they had no more
meal."

What is even more extraordinary than their extreme suffering, is
the incomprehensible philosophy and endurance of these people. Here
was a man, of poor health, with a family that it would be hard to support in peacetimes, stripped to the bone by Rebel and Union, with no
hope from any side, and yet he almost laughed when he described his
position, and presently came back with a smile to tell me that the only
two cows he had, had strayed off, got into a Government herd, and
"gone up the road"—that's the last of *them*. In Europe, a man so situated would be on his knees, tearing out handfuls of hair, and calling
on the Virgin and on several saints. There were neighbors at his house;
and one asked me if I supposed our people would burn his tenement?
"What did you leave it for?" I asked. To which he replied, in a concise

way that told the whole: "Because there was right smart of bullets over thaar!"

The poorest people seem usually more or less indifferent or adverse to the war, but their bitterness increases in direct ratio to their social position. Find a well-dressed lady, and you find one whose hatred will end only with death—it is unmistakable, though they treat you with more or less courtesy. Nor is it extraordinary: there is black everywhere; here is one that has lost an only son; and here another that has had her husband killed. People of this class are very proud and spirited; you can easily see it; and it is the officers that they supply who give the strong framework to their army. They have that military and irascible nature so often seen among an aristocracy that was once rich and is now poor; for you must remember that, before the war, most of these land-owners had ceased to hold the position they had at the beginning of this century.

Sometimes Lyman was exasperated by foes who thought they were friends:[23]

To-day has been entirely quiet, our pickets deliberately exchanging papers, despite orders to the contrary. These men are incomprehensible —now standing from daylight to dark killing and wounding each other by thousands, and now making jokes and exchanging newspapers! You see them lying side by side in the hospitals, talking together in that serious prosaic way that characterizes Americans. The great staples of conversation are the size and quality of rations, the marches they have made, and the regiments they have fought against. All sense of personal spite is sunk in the immensity of the contest.

Yet when the call to battle came, they were once more bitter, unremitting enemies—a fact that Horace Porter understood:[24]

Everything was now in readiness for the memorable battle of Cold Harbor. Headquarters had been moved two miles farther to our left, and established near Old Cold Harbor, so as to be within easy reach of the main point of attack. It has been stated by inimical critics that the men had become demoralized by the many assaults in which they had been engaged; that they had lost much of their spirit, and were even insubordinate, refusing to move against the earthworks in obedience to the orders of their immediate commanders. This is a gross slander upon the troops, who were as gallant and subordinate as any forces in the history of modern warfare, although it is true that many of the veterans had fallen, and that the recruits who replaced them were inferior in fighting qualities.

In passing along on foot among the troops at the extreme front that evening while transmitting some of the final orders, I observed an incident which afforded a practical illustration of the deliberate and desperate courage of the men. As I came near one of the regiments which was making preparations for the next morning's assault, I noticed that many of the soldiers had taken off their coats, and seemed to be engaged in sewing up rents in them. This exhibition of tailoring seemed rather peculiar at such a moment, but upon closer examination it was found that the men were calmly writing their names and home addresses on slips of paper, and pinning them on the backs of their coats, so that their dead bodies might be recognized upon the field, and their fate made known to their families at home.

It was a wise precaution. William Swinton, historian of the Army of the Potomac, understood why Cold Harbor was unique:[25]

Next morning, with the first gray light of dawn struggling through the clouds, the preparations began: from behind the rude parapets there was an upstarting, a springing to arms, the muffled commands of officers forming the line. The attack was ordered at half-past four, and it may have been five minutes after that, or it may have been ten minutes, but it certainly was not later than forty-five minutes past four, when the whole line was in motion, and the dark hollows between the armies were lit up with the fires of death.

It took hardly more than ten minutes of the figment men call time to decide the battle. There was along the whole line a rush—the spectacle of impregnable works—a bloody loss—then a sullen falling back, and the action was *decided*. Conceive of this in the large, and we shall then be able to descend to some of the points of action as they individualize themselves along the line.

Colonel William Oates of the Fifteenth Alabama Infantry saw Union troops sacrificed on a scale unparalleled since Burnside's bumbling charges on Marye's Heights at Fredericksburg:[26]

. . . Just before I could see the sun, I heard a volley in the woods, saw the Major running up the ravine in the direction of Anderson's brigade, which lay to the right of Law's, and the skirmishers running in, pursued by a column of the enemy ten lines deep, with arms at a trail, and yelling "Huzzah! huzzah!" I ordered my men to take arms and fix bayonets. Just then I remembered that not a gun in the regiment was loaded. I ordered the men to load and the officers each to take an ax and stand to the works. I was apprehensive that the enemy would soon be on our works before the men could load.

As Capt. Noah B. Feagin and his skirmishers crawled over the works I thought of my piece of artillery. I called out: "Sergeant, give them double charges of canister; fire, men, fire!" The order was obeyed with alacrity. The enemy were within thirty steps. They halted and began to dodge, lie down, and recoil. The fire was terrific from my regiment, the Fourth Alabama on my immediate right, and the Thirteenth Mississippi on my left, while the piece of artillery was fired more rapidly and better handled than I ever saw one before or since. The blaze of fire from it at each shot went right into the ranks of our assailants and made frightful gaps through the dense mass of men. They endured it but for one or two minutes, when they retreated, leaving the ground covered with their dead and dying. There were 3 men in my regiment killed, 5 wounded. My piece of artillery kept up a lively fire on the enemy where they halted in the woods, with shrapnel shell.

After the lapse of about forty minutes another charge was made by the Twenty-third and Twenty-fifth Massachusetts regiments, in a column by divisions, thus presenting a front of two companies only. Bryan's Georgia brigade came up from the rear and lay down behind Law's. The charging column, which aimed to strike the Fourth Alabama, received the most destructive fire I ever saw. They were subjected to a front and flank fire from the infantry, at short range, while my piece of artillery poured double charges of canister into them. The Georgians loaded for the Alabamians to fire. I could see the dust fog out of a man's clothing in two or three places at once where as many balls would strike him at the same moment. In two minutes not a man of them was standing. All who were not shot down had lain down for protection. One little fellow raised his head to look, and I ordered him to come in. He came on a run, the Yankees over in the woods firing at him every step of the way, and as he climbed over our works one shot took effect in one of his legs. They evidently took him to be a deserter. I learned from him that there were many more out there who were not wounded. This I communicated to Colonel Perry, who was again in command, General Law having been wounded in the head during the first assault; and thereupon Perry sent a company down a ravine on our right to capture them; they soon brought the colonel who led the charge, and about one hundred other prisoners. The colonel was a brave man. He said he had been in many places, but that was the worst.

Grant knew that he had made a mistake. Years later he confessed:[27]

I have always regretted that the last assault at Cold Harbor was ever made. . . . No advantage whatever was gained to compensate for the heavy loss we sustained. Indeed, the advantages other than those of relative losses, were on the Confederate side. Before that, the Army of Northern Virginia seemed to have acquired a wholesome regard for the courage, endurance, and soldierly qualities generally of the Army of the Potomac. They no longer wanted to fight them "one Confederate to five Yanks." Indeed, they seemed to have given up any idea of gaining any advantage of their antagonist in the open field. They had come to much prefer breastworks in their front to the Army of the Potomac. This charge seemed to revive their hopes temporarily; but it was of short duration. . . . When we reached the James River . . . all effects of the battle of Cold Harbor seemed to have disappeared.

Cold Harbor cost Grant 12,000 in killed and wounded against casualties for Lee of not more than 1,500. And when it was all over? Lyman found that again foes were virtually friends:[28]

To-night all the trenching tools were ordered up and the lines were strengthened, and saps run out, so as to bring them still closer to the opposing ones. And there the two armies slept, almost within an easy stone-throw of each other; and the separating space ploughed by cannon-shot and clotted with the dead bodies that neither side dared to bury! I think nothing can give a greater idea of deathless tenacity of purpose, than the picture of these two hosts, after a bloody and nearly continuous struggle of thirty days, thus lying down to sleep, with their heads almost on each other's throats! Possibly it has no parallel in history. So ended the great attack at Cool Arbor.*. . .

* Another designation of Cold Harbor.

"BOLD OFFENSIVE"

I
N MID-MARCH 1864 Grant had turned over to Sherman command
of the Army of the Cumberland, the Army of the Tennessee, and the
Army of the Ohio. Sherman met Grant in Cincinnati that month.

"Amidst constant interruptions of a business and social nature, we
reached the satisfactory conclusion that, as soon as the season would
permit, all the armies of the Union would assume the 'bold offensive'
by 'concentric lines' on the common enemy, and would finish up the
job in a single campaign if possible. The main 'objectives' were Lee's
army behind the Rapidan in Virginia, and Joseph E. Johnston's army
at Dalton, Georgia."

I

*Sherman made clear his enthusiasm for Grant and his plan of opera-
tions.*[1]

. . . There never was and never can be raised a question of rivalry
or claim between us as to the relative merits of the manner in which
we played our respective parts. We were as brothers—I the older man
in years, he the higher in rank. We both believed in our heart of hearts
that the success of the Union cause was not only necessary to the then
generation of Americans, but to all future generations. We both professed to be gentlemen and professional soldiers, educated in the science of war by our generous Government for the very occasion which

had arisen. Neither of us by nature was a combative man; but with honest hearts and a clear purpose to do what man could we embarked on that campaign, which I believe, in its strategy, in its logistics, in its grand and minor tactics, has added new luster to the old science of war. Both of us had at our front generals to whom in early life we had been taught to look up,—educated and experienced soldiers like ourselves, not likely to make any mistakes, and each of whom had as strong an army as could be collected from the mass of the Southern people,—of the same blood as ourselves, brave, confident, and well equipped; in addition to which they had the most decided advantage of operating in their own difficult country of mountain, forest, ravine, and river, affording admirable opportunities for defense, besides the other equally important advantage that we had to invade the country of our unqualified enemy and expose our long lines of supply to the guerrillas of an "exasperated people." Again, as we advanced we had to leave guards to bridges, stations, and intermediate depots, diminishing the fighting force, while our enemy gained strength by picking up his detachments as he fell back, and had railroads to bring supplies and reenforcements from his rear. I instance these facts to offset the common assertion that we of the North won the war by brute force, and not by courage and skill.

In contrast, Confederate General John Bell Hood recalled the circumstances under which he transferred from Virginia to "the Western Army":[2]

The War Department [in Richmond] had been anxious that an offensive campaign into Tennessee and Kentucky be initiated in the early Spring of 1864, and made a proposition to General Johnston to reinforce him with Polk's troops, then in Mississippi, and Longstreet's Corps, in East Tennessee. Johnston, at the appointed time, was expected to move forward and form a junction with these troops. The President and General Bragg, and also General Lee, were desirous that the offensive be assumed, and an attempt be made to drive the Federals to the Ohio river, before a large Army could be concentrated to move against us. . . .

Contending that 75,000 Confederate forces could have been mustered for this campaign, Hood told how he had come to northern Georgia under a misconception:

The President had thus agreed to afford General Johnston every facility in his power for the execution of the proposed plan of operations; and it was with the understanding we were to enter upon an active campaign that I consented to leave the Army of Northern Virginia, with which I had served since the outbreak of the war.

On the evening of my arrival at Dalton, on or about the 4th of February, I repaired to General Johnston's headquarters, and reported to him for duty. During our interview, in his room alone, he informed me that General Thomas was moving forward, and he thought it might be best for us to fall back and take up some position in rear of Dalton. I at once told him that I knew nothing of the situation or the object of General Thomas's move from Ringgold, but that we could, at least, hold our position a sufficient length of time to compel the enemy to develop his plan. The Federals, in a few days, fell back to Ringgold, having merely made a feint, in order to cover some movement then being made in Mississippi.

This was my introduction to the Army of Tennessee; albeit not calculated to inspire or encourage military ardor,—since it was proposed to retreat even before the enemy became in earnest—I nevertheless laid before General Johnston the plan to join Polk's Army and Longstreet's Corps on the march into Tennessee, gave him assurance that the authorities in Richmond would give him every assistance, and informed him, moreover, that General Lee favored the projected campaign.

General Johnston immediately took the ground that he did not very well know the country through which it was proposed to pass to the rear of the enemy; that there were difficulties to be encountered, etc., etc.; he desired Polk's and Longstreet's forces to join him at Dalton, where, this large Army being concentrated, he considered he should be left to decide and act for the best; in other words, be left to move forward, stand his ground or retreat, as might seem most expedient.

To this demand, General Lee was unwilling to accede; he was reluctant to give up Longstreet's Corps, unless for the purpose of active work and dealing hard blows, in the performance of which task it had already so often distinguished itself. The War Department objected to the withdrawal of Polk's Army from Mississippi, until active operations were to commence, as by such a movement one of the best regions of country for supplies would be abandoned to the enemy. . . .

April passed with Johnston refusing to budge from Dalton and with Hood still insisting in a letter to Braxton Bragg, who now served as military adviser to Jefferson Davis, that "to regain Tennessee would be of more value to us than a half a dozen victories in Virginia." In later years Hood retained his intense bitterness:

I cannot name one of Lee's Lieutenant Generals who would not have met this proposition from the War Department with that spirit of co-operation which is so essential in time of war. Moreover, any officer possessed of even a part of that heroic self-reliance so characteristic of Lee and Jackson, would not only have gladly accepted the ninety-one thousand (91,000) men, but, having secured a competent Quarter Master, would soon have found the necessary transportation; would have sent a dispatch to Richmond that he was moving forward, and, God willing, would take from the enemy all else needed to equip the army. Such might have been the result, instead of unremitting demands, upon the part of General Johnston, for an outfit equal to that of the United States troops, visions of insuperable difficulties, and vacillations unending.

"With the month of May," wrote an exuberant Sherman, "came the season for action." The three Western armies that he commanded—in round figures, 98,000 men and 250 guns—marched from Chattanooga without any intention of attacking Johnston at Dalton. Rather, Sherman's plan was to feint at Johnston's front and to make a lodgment in Resaca, eighteen miles to his rear, on the line of his communication and supply. The movement, Sherman admitted, was "partly, not wholly, successful"; still, Johnston was compelled "to let go Dalton and fight us at Resaca." This action, beginning on the thirteenth of May and continuing through the sixteenth, was a standoff with casualties practically even on each side. "I fought offensively and he defensively, aided by earth parapets," Sherman said succinctly. Major James Austin Connolly of the 123rd Illinois wrote his wife from the field of battle:[3]

May 15, 1864

Just as I had written the date above, I said: "Hello, the enemy are shelling us.". . . It is now about nine o'clock at night, the moon is shining with a misty light through the battle smoke that is slowly settling down like a curtain, over these hills and valleys; the mournful notes of a whippoorwill, near by, mingle in strange contrast with the exultant shouts of our soldiers—the answering yells of the rebels—the rattling fire of the skirmish line, and the occasional bursting of a shell.

Today we have done nothing but shift positions and keep up a heavy skirmish fire. Yesterday our Division and Judah's Division of Schofield's Corps, had some hard fighting. We drove the enemy about a mile and entirely within his fortifications, several of our regiments planting their colors on his fortifications, but were compelled to withdraw under a terrible fire. We, however, fell back but a short distance to the cover of the woods, where we still are, and the enemy have not ventured outside their works since. A report has just reached us that Hooker drove the enemy about a mile today. . . . We have men enough here to whip Johnston, and if he don't escape pretty soon he never will. . . .

Johnston "let go" next day, and on the twentieth of May Major Connolly wrote his wife from Kingston, Georgia:

If you will look at a map you will see that "we all" are still pushing southward, but a look at the map will give you little idea of the country we are passing through—will fail to point out to you the fields that are being reddened by the blood of our soldiers, and the hundreds of little mounds that are rising by the wayside day by day, as if to mark the footprints of the God of War as he stalks along through this beautiful country. This point is where the railroad from Rome forms a junction with the main line from Chattanooga to Atlanta. Rome is in our possession, and such has been the extraordinary rapidity with which the railroad has been repaired, as we have pushed along, that a train from Chattanooga ran into Kingston this morning about daylight, while at the same time a rebel train from Atlanta was whistling on the same road, and only two miles distant, but it is now about 9 o'clock in the morning, and the last whistle of the rebel train, north of the Etowah River, sounded some hours ago, the last rebel has undoubtedly crossed the river, the bridge across the river has been burned, I suppose, and the rebel army is wending its way, weary and dispirited, toward that mythical ditch of which we have heard so much.

General Johnston nursed a deepening resentment as he fell back across the Etowah:[4]

. . . When Brig.-General Jackson's reports showed that the head of the Federal column following the railroad was near Kingston, Lieutenant-General Hood was directed to move with his corps to a country

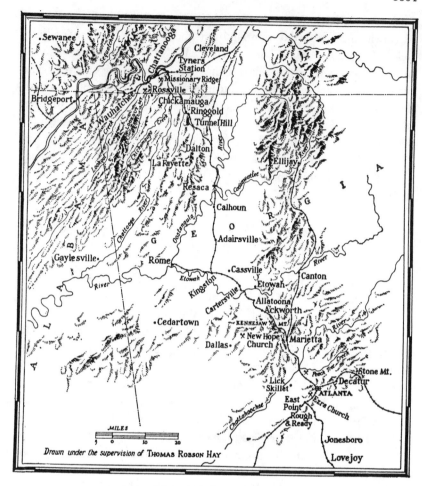

CHATTANOOGA TO ATLANTA

From *Atlas of American History*

road about a mile to the east of that from Adairsville, and parallel to it, and to march northward on that road, right in front. Polk's corps, as then formed, was to advance to meet and engage the enemy approaching from Adairsville; and it was expected that Hood's would be in position to fall upon the left flank of those troops as soon as Polk attacked them in front. An order was read to each regiment, announcing that we were about to give battle to the enemy. It was received with exultation.

When General Hood's column had moved two or three miles, that officer received a report from a member of his staff, to the effect that the enemy was approaching on the Canton road, in rear of the right of the position from which he had just marched. Instead of transmitting this report to me, and moving on in obedience to his orders, he fell back to that road and formed his corps across it, facing to our right and rear, toward Canton, without informing me of this strange departure from the instructions he had received. I heard of this erratic movement after it had caused such loss of time as to make the attack intended impracticable; for its success depended on accuracy in timing it.

Hood told another story:[5]

The three Corps Commanders, especially General Polk and myself, urged General Johnston, soon after our arrival at Cassville, to turn back and attack Sherman at Adairsville, as we had information of a portion of his Army having been sent to cross the Etowah, in order to threaten our communications south of that river. The opportunity was the more favorable, because of an open country and good roads, which would have enabled the Army to move rapidly and force the Federals, whilst divided in their forces, to accept a pitched battle, with rivers in their rear. This he declined to do. . . .

On the following day, Howard's Corps having been reported on the Ironton road (the country road referred to), I asked his authorization to march my command across an open field, and attack this detachment of the enemy, in case the report was correct. He consented.

I received no orders for battle as related by General Johnston, nor were the Corps Commanders brought together and given explicit instructions, verbal or written, as is usual and necessary upon the eve of a general engagement, although he had published, soon after our arrival at Cassville, a general order to the effect that he intended to fight. I was merely granted the privilege of doing what I had requested; the assertion, therefore, of General Johnston, that I had been ordered to move to the country road and be in readiness to attack in flank when Polk engaged the enemy in front is as erroneous as it is inexplicable.

II

Sherman, in pursuit of Johnston, could know nothing of the animosity developing between Hood and his superior, but of another source of animosity Sherman was well informed:[6]

. . . The newspapers of the South, many of which we found, were also loud in denunciation of Johnston's falling back before us without a serious battle, simply resisting by his skirmish-lines and by his rear-guard. But his friends proclaimed that it was all *strategic;* that he was deliberately drawing us farther and farther into the meshes, farther and farther away from our base of supplies, and that in due season he would not only halt for battle, but assume the bold offensive. Of course it was to my interest to bring him to battle as soon as possible, when our numerical superiority was at the greatest; for he was picking up his detachments as he fell back, whereas I was compelled to make similar and stronger detachments to repair the railroads as we advanced, and to guard them. . . .

Johnston's plan was to screen himself behind the Allatoona range. Sherman explained how a youthful experience saved him from a possible trap:

In early days (1844), when a lieutenant of the Third Artillery, I had been sent from Charleston, South Carolina, to Marietta, Georgia, to assist Inspector-General Churchill to take testimony concerning certain losses of horses and accoutrements by the Georgia Volunteers during the Florida War; and after completing the work at Marietta we transferred our party over to Bellefonte, Alabama. I had ridden the distance on horseback, and had noted well the topography of the country, especially that about Kenesaw, Allatoona, and the Etowah River. On that occasion I had stopped . . . to see some remarkable Indian mounds on the Etowah River, usually called the "Hightower." I therefore knew that the Allatoona Pass was very strong, would be hard to force, and resolved not even to attempt it, but to turn the position, by moving from Kingston to Marietta *via* Dallas; accordingly I made orders on the 20th to get ready for the march to begin on the 23d. . . .

Telegraphic communications told Sherman that Grant and Lee had met in "the bloody and desperate" battles of the Wilderness. The western armies moved from Kingston. At New Hope Church—so named from the Methodist meetinghouse there—an "accidental intersection" of the road from Allatoona to Dallas with the road from Van Wert to Marietta provided the setting for bloody fighting May 25 through 28. Sherman understood why his boys renamed New Hope the "Hell-Hole":

The night [May 25] was pitch-dark, it rained hard, and the convergence of our columns toward Dallas produced much confusion. I am sure similar confusion existed in the army opposite to us, for we were all mixed up. I slept on the ground, without cover, alongside of a log, got little sleep, resolved at daylight to renew the battle, and to make a lodgment on the Dallas and Allatoona road if possible, but the morning revealed a strong line of intrenchments facing us, with a heavy force of infantry and guns. The battle was renewed, and without success. . . .

Satisfied that Johnston in person was at New Hope with all his army, and that it was so much nearer my "objective," the railroad, than Dallas, I concluded to draw McPherson from Dallas to Hooker's right. . . . On the morning of the 28th he was fiercely assailed [and] a bloody battle ensued. . . . Meantime Thomas and Schofield were completing their deployments, gradually overlapping Johnston on his right, and thus extending our left nearer and nearer to the railroad, the nearest point of which was Acworth, about eight miles distant. All this time a continual battle was in progress by strong skirmish-lines, taking advantage of every species of cover, and both parties fortifying each night by rifle-trenches, with head-logs, many of which grew to be as formidable as first-class works of defense. Occasionally one party or the other would make a dash in the nature of a sally, but usually it sustained a repulse with great loss of life. I visited personally all parts of our lines nearly every day, was constantly within musket-range, and though the fire of musketry and cannon resounded day and night along the whole line, varying from six to ten miles, I rarely saw a dozen of the enemy at any one time; and these were always skirmishers dodging from tree to tree, or behind logs on the ground, or who occasionally showed their heads above the hastily constructed but remarkably strong rifle-trenches. . . .

By Johnston's account, Sherman's troops were roughly handled on May 27. He described an incident that revealed the stubborn nature of the combat:[7]

When the United States troops paused in their advance, within fifteen paces of the Texan front rank, one of their color-bearers planted his colors eight or ten feet in front of his regiment, and was instantly shot dead; a soldier sprang forward to his place, and fell also, as he grasped the color-staff; a second and third followed successively, and each received death as speedily as his predecessors; a fourth, however, seized and bore back the object of soldierly devotion.

Johnston saw the Federal dead piling up. Yet Major Connolly, writing his wife next day, May 28, from "in the woods, near Dallas," was singularly composed and confident:[8]

I have just sat down with my back to a sapling, to write this with pencil, on this soiled piece of paper, with a shingle on my lap, for writing desk. The adjutant of my regiment got into the enemy's lines, by some kind of mistake, a few days since, and was captured. . . . For several days our Division has not been in the front, and I have only heard the enemy's guns in the distance. . . . The weather is delightful for campaigning, and I am quite sure we will be in Atlanta by the middle of June, and we are all strongly in hope of celebrating the 4th of July at the "last ditch" of the rebellion. Some of the half hearted in our army (for we have such) are gloomy because, they say, Grant can't whip Lee, and point to the fact that gold has been rising in value ever since Grant first engaged Lee. I don't know how you folks at home feel about it, but I feel sure Grant *will* defeat Lee and that we will defeat Johnston, and that our flag will float over Richmond and Atlanta by the 4th of July, but if not by that time it will *sometime.*

We passed about 200 rebels going to the rear, this morning. They were captured in a sharp engagement last evening. We are now in the region of the Georgia gold mines, and I am told that the cripples and poor men who have not been conscripted, are out gold washing over the mountain streams, to get gold dust enough to buy corn with.

III

While Grant fought Lee and Sherman pressed Johnston closer to Atlanta, the North turned to another arena of conflict, for 1864 was a presidential election year.

By the spring of 1864 the glow of the great Union victories at Gettysburg and Vicksburg had faded. Radical dissatisfaction with the President's "soft" policy on reconstruction had mounted; conservatives looked with increasing dismay on the violation of civil rights. The distribution of patronage, always a source of trouble, had made many enemies. In some states—Missouri and New York particularly—local politicians had come to believe that their own chances of survival would be better if someone other than Lincoln headed the national ticket.

All this was political opposition. Lincoln still held the confidence of the masses, and the politicians knew it. Therefore they resorted to a flank attack—postpone the national convention from June 7, the date set by the National Committee, to September, and let the forces of discontent have time to mount.

While most of the manipulators contented themselves with behind-the-scenes maneuvering, one group of New Yorkers spoke out. The signers of an open letter to the Republican National Committee included William Cullen Bryant, editor of the New York Evening Post *(better known today as the author of "Thanatopsis" and "To a Waterfowl"); George P. Putnam, publisher; George Opdyke, millionaire merchant and former mayor of New York; William Curtis Noyes, eminent lawyer; and sixteen Union members of the New York State Senate. Calling themselves "friends of the Government and supporters of the present Administration" the signers argued:*[9]

NEW YORK, March 25

. . . The country is not now in position to enter into a presidential contest. It is very important that all parties friendly to the Government shall be united in support of a single candidate, and that, when a selection shall be made, it shall be acquiesced in by all loyal sections of the country, and by all branches of the loyal party. It is equally clear that such unanimity cannot at present be obtained, and it is not believed that it can be reached as early as the day named by you for the national convention.

Upon the result of the measures adopted by the Administration to finish the war during the present spring and summer, will depend the wish of the people to continue in power their present leaders, or to change them for those from whom they may expect other and more favorable results.

Whatever time may be gained will be an advantage to the country, inasmuch as it will allow the forming of a better informed opinion on these subjects. . . .

With a pure and patriotic desire to serve the best interests of the country, and in the belief that they will be best served by a postponement of a political convention to the latest day possible, we respectfully ask that you will reconsider your action, and name a day for the assembling of the national convention not earlier than the first day of September next.

James G. Randall, after a patient, exhaustive examination of thousands of letters exchanged by Republican politicians at this time, came to the conclusion that "a book could be made up of letters expressing distrust of the President." Thus Joseph Medill, whose Chicago Tribune continued to support Lincoln stanchly, wrote in confidence to Elihu B. Washburne, Republican Congressman from the Galena, Illinois, district:[10]

CHICAGO April 12.

FRIEND WASHBURNE

. . . I don't care much if the convention is put off till Aug. I oppose it in the paper moderately, but will not be distressed if the Com. postpone it a couple of months. I was opposed to calling it so early as June 7. If it should happen that Lincoln loses the nomination thereby he will have no body but himself to blame for it. If he prefers the Blairs to the Presidency why should he be deprived of his choice? I am free to say to you that if it shall be known to be his intention to continue his present cabinet I don't believe we could elect him if nominated. . . . Lincoln has some very weak and foolish traits of character. . . . If he had reasonable political sagacity and would cut loose from the semi-copperheads in his cabinet and about him, if he would put live bold vigorous radicals in their places no human power could prevent his nomination or election. The game is in his own hands: will he play it right? or has he Blair on the brain so badly that he is blinded to the true state of public feeling?

If he should be thrown overboard at Baltimore the party will in my judgment take up Grant—if he continues to be successful in battle-field. . . .

And Charles Sumner, personally friendly to the President though opposed to his reconstruction policy, could write to Charles Eliot Norton of Boston, loyal Lincoln supporter:[11]

Private, SENATE CHAMBER, 2nd May, 1864

MY DEAR NORTON,—I regret very much that the Baltimore Convention is to be at so early a day. I see nothing but disaster from mixing our politics with battle and blood. The Presidential Question should be kept back as long as possible—at least until the end of summer. On this point I have no doubt. Do not regard me as dogmatical. I should not write on this point, if you had not expressly asked my opinion.

Unless the Convention is postponed, the future seems to me uncertain. . . .

Lincoln's supporters, who dominated the Republican National Committee, had no intention of playing the game of the disaffected. On June 7, as planned, the National Union convention met at Baltimore. Here War Democrats and Republicans could join in a common cause. The official reporter noted that "a splendid band, from Fort McHenry, animated the crowded theatre with national airs, and the assemblage was graced by the presence of many ladies, who were accommodated in one of the tiers of boxes."

On the second day of the convention B. C. Cook of Illinois won the floor. "Mr. President," he said, "the State of Illinois again presents to the loyal people of this Nation, for President of the United States, Abraham Lincoln. God bless him."

William M. Stone of Iowa leaped to his feet. "In the name of the great West," he shouted, "I demand that the roll be called."

When the secretary intoned the names of the states a few minutes later, the delegations revealed the difference between private convictions and public acts:[12]

MAINE.—Maine casts her entire vote for Abraham Lincoln, of Illinois.—14 votes.

NEW HAMPSHIRE.—New Hampshire, the Granite State, in her convention on the 6th of January last, unanimously passed a resolution, nominating Abraham Lincoln for re-election as President of the United States. New Hampshire today, by her delegates, casts her ten votes, first and last, for Abraham Lincoln, of Illinois.

VERMONT.—The Green Mountain State casts her small but entire vote of ten for Abraham Lincoln, of Illinois.

MASSACHUSETTS.—Massachusetts gives her entire vote, twenty-four, to Abraham Lincoln.

RHODE ISLAND.—Rhode Island casts her entire eight votes for Abraham Lincoln.

CONNECTICUT.—Connecticut gives her twelve votes to that pure and patriotic statesman, Abraham Lincoln, of Illinois.

NEW YORK.—New York casts sixty-six votes, her entire vote, for Abraham Lincoln, of Illinois, for President of the United States.

NEW JERSEY.—New Jersey gives fourteen votes for Abraham Lincoln.

PENNSYLVANIA.—Pennsylvania gives her entire vote, fifty-two, for Abraham Lincoln, "nigger" troops, and all.

DELAWARE.—Delaware gives her vote, six, for Abraham Lincoln.

MARYLAND.—Maryland casts fourteen votes for Abraham Lincoln, of Illinois.

LOUISIANA.—Louisiana gives her fourteen votes for Abraham Lincoln.

ARKANSAS.—Arkansas casts all her votes, ten, for Abraham Lincoln.

When Missouri was called, the machinery faltered:

MISSOURI.—Mr. J. F. HUME.—Missouri comes into the Convention purified by its action, and her delegates will support the nominees made here, and do the utmost in our power to secure for them the electoral vote of the State. It is but right and proper, however, that I should state that, in the convention which designated us as delegates to this Convention, we were instructed, and we cannot, upon the first ballot, give our votes in unanimity with those who have already cast their votes. ["Order," "order."]

Mr. J. H. LANE, of Kansas.—I appeal to the Convention to hear Missouri.

The PRESIDENT.—The gentleman from Missouri is not in order unless by consent of the House.

Mr. J. H. LANE, of Kansas.—I move that consent be given.

The motion was agreed to unanimously.

Mr. J. F. HUME, of Missouri.—It is a matter of much regret that we now differ from the Convention which has been so kind to the Radicals of Missouri; but we come here instructed. We represent those who are behind us at home, and we recognize the right of instruction, and intend to obey our instructions; but in doing so, we declare emphatically that we are with the Union party of this Nation, and we intend to fight the battle through with it, and assist in carrying its banner to victory in the end, and we will support your nominees, be they who they may. [Great applause.] I will read the resolution adopted by the convention which sent us here:

"That we extend our heartfelt thanks to the soldiers of Missouri, who have been, and are now, baring their breasts to the storm of battle for the preservation of our free institutions. That we hail them as the practical Radicals of the Nation, whose arguments are invincible, and whose policy for putting down the rebellion is first in importance and effectiveness."

Mr. President, in the spirit of that resolution, I cast the twenty-two votes of Missouri for the man who stands at the head of the fighting Radicals of the nation, Ulysses S. Grant.

The roll call continued:

TENNESSEE.—The convention that sent us here instructed us to say that, in their opinion, the election by the American people to the office of President of any other man than he who now fills the Executive Chair, would be regarded both at home and abroad as a concession of something to the Rebellion, and instructed us, by all means in our power, to secure the nomination of Abraham Lincoln, and I now give him the fifteen votes of Tennessee.

KENTUCKY.—Kentucky casts her twenty-two votes for Abraham Lincoln, and will ratify that nomination in November.

OHIO.—Ohio gives her forty-two votes for "Old Abe" for President.

INDIANA.—Indiana casts her twenty-six votes for Abraham Lincoln.

ILLINOIS.—Illinois gives thirty-two votes for Abraham Lincoln.

MICHIGAN.—Michigan gives sixteen votes for Abraham Lincoln.

WISCONSIN.—Wisconsin casts sixteen votes for Abraham Lincoln, of Illinois.

IOWA.—Iowa casts sixteen votes for Abraham Lincoln.

MINNESOTA.—Minnesota casts eight votes for Abraham Lincoln.

CALIFORNIA.—California casts ten votes, all for Abraham Lincoln.

OREGON.—Oregon casts six votes, all of them, first, last, and all the time for Abraham Lincoln, of Illinois.

KANSAS.—Radical Kansas casts her six votes for "Honest Old Abe."

WEST VIRGINIA.—West Virginia remembers her friends. She casts her ten votes in this Convention, the entire vote of the State of West Virginia, representing almost the entire loyal vote of the State, for Abraham Lincoln.

NEBRASKA.—Nebraska has one man in her delegation who was never a Lincoln man, but who belongs to that proud party called the War Union Democrats, and I am requested by that delegate to say, that he submits to the Convention, and I give the six votes of Nebraska for Abraham Lincoln, whom we regard as the second saviour of the world.

COLORADO.—Colorado casts her six votes for Abraham Lincoln.

NEVADA.—Nevada gives six votes for Abraham Lincoln, of Illinois.

The PRESIDENT.—The call of the States and Territories has now been completed.

Mr. J. F. HUME, of Missouri.—The vote has not been announced, but I wish to make a motion now, without waiting for the announcement, inasmuch as it is well understood what the result of the ballot just given is. I move that the nomination of Abraham Lincoln, of Illinois, be declared unanimous.

SEVERAL DELEGATES.—Change your votes.

Mr. J. F. HUME, of Missouri.—Our vote was given under instructions, and therefore I do not know that we can change it.

The PRESIDENT.—The gentleman's motion is not in order until the vote shall have been announced.

The Secretary proceeded to announce the vote as follows: Lincoln, 484; Grant, 22.

The PRESIDENT.—The total number of votes cast is 506, of which 484 have been cast for Abraham Lincoln, and 22 for Ulysses S. Grant.

Mr. J. F. HUME, of Missouri.—I now move that the nomination of Abraham Lincoln be declared unanimous; and I do not care whether the vote of Missouri is changed or not.

SEVERAL DELEGATES.—Change the vote.

Mr. J. F. HUME.—I am authorized now to change the vote of Missouri to Abraham Lincoln, of Illinois.

The Secretaries announced that the vote was unanimous—506 for Abraham Lincoln.

The official reporter recorded that "the delegates and the audience simultaneously rose to their feet, and greeted the announcement with vociferous applause. The band struck up 'Hail Columbia' and 'Yankee Doodle,' which were rapturously received." Later in the day the convention completed its work by nominating Andrew Johnson of Tennessee for Vice President, discarding Hannibal Hamlin in favor of a War Democrat from a loyal section of the South.

Two days after the convention adjourned, crusty Edward Bates, Lincoln's Attorney General, made an entry in his diary:[13]

June 10. The Baltimore Convention (*National Union* I believe, it's called itself) has surprised and mortified me greatly. It did indeed nominate Mr. Lincoln, but in a manner and with attendant circumstances, as if the object were to defeat their own nomination. They were all (nearly) instructed to vote for Mr. Lincoln, but many of them hated to do it, and only "kept the word of promise to the ear" doing their worst to break it to the hope. They *rejected* the only delegates from Mo. who were instructed and pledged for Lincoln, and admitted the *destructives*, who were *pledged against Lincoln*, and, in fact, voted against him, *falsely alleging* that they were instructed to vote for Grant!

. . . I shall tell the Prest: in all frankness, that his best nomination is not that at Baltimore, but his nomination spontaneously, by the People, by which the convention was constrained to name him.

IV

One small segment of the Republican party—the extreme Radicals—had the courage of their convictions. In response to three calls—one representing German liberals, another disgruntled New Yorkers, a third Eastern abolitionists—the "Radical Men of the Nation" had assembled at Cleveland on May 31 for the avowed purpose of nominating John C. Frémont. Wendell Phillips, unable to attend, had sent a letter which expressed the opinions of most of the delegates:[14]

BOSTON, May 27, 1864.

. . . We have three tools with which to crush the rebellion—men, money, and the emancipation of the negro. We were warned to be quick and sharp in the use of these, because every year the war lasted hardened the South from a rebellion into a nation, and doubled the danger of foreign interference. Slavery has been our great trouble in the past, and, as every man saw, was our great danger in the future. Statesmanship said, therefore, seize at once the God-given opportunity to end it, at the same time that you, in the quickest, shortest, and cheapest manner, annihilate the rebellion.

For three years the Administration has lavished money without stint, and drenched the land in blood, and it has not yet thoroughly and heartily struck at the slave system. Confessing that the use of this means is indispensable, the Administration has used it just enough to irritate the rebels and not enough to save the State. In sixty days after the rebellion broke out the Administration suspended *habeas corpus* on the plea of military necessity—justly. For three years it has poured out the treasure and blood of the country like water. Meanwhile slavery was too sacred to be used; that was saved lest the feelings of the rebels should be hurt. The Administration weighed treasure, blood, and civil liberty against slavery, and, up to the present moment, has decided to exhaust them all before it uses freedom, heartily, as a means of battle. . . .

The Administration, therefore, I regard as a civil and military failure, and its avowed policy ruinous to the North in every point of view. Mr. Lincoln may wish the end—peace and freedom—but he is wholly unwilling to use the means which can secure that end. If Mr. Lincoln is re-elected I do not expect to see the Union reconstructed in my day, unless on terms more disastrous to liberty than even disunion would be. If I turn to General Fremont, I see a man whose first act was to use the freedom of the negro as his weapon, I see one whose thorough loyalty to democratic institutions, without regard to race, whose earnest and decisive character, whose clear-sighted statesmanship and rare military ability justify my confidence that in his hands all will be done to save the State that foresight, skill, decision, and statesmanship can do.

I think the Convention should incorporate in its platform the demand for an amendment to the Constitution prohibiting slavery everywhere within the Republic, and forbidding the States to make any distinction among their citizens on account of color or race. I think it should demand a reconstruction of States as speedily as possible on the basis of every loyal man, white or black, sharing the land and the ballot. . . .

If the Baltimore Convention shall nominate Mr. Lincoln, then I hope we shall fling our candidate's name, the long-honored one of J. C. Fremont, to the breeze, and appeal to the patriotism and common sense of the people to save us from another such three years as we have seen. If, on the contrary, the Baltimore convention shall give us the name of any man whom the Radicals of the Loyal States can trust, I hope we shall be able to arrange some plan which will unite all on a common basis and carry our principles into the Government.

In one day the Cleveland convention adopted a platform and nominated Frémont for President and John Cochrane, Attorney General of New York, for Vice President.

In Washington, Lincoln laughed. Nicolay and Hay recorded:[15]

The whole proceeding, though it excited some indignation among the friends of Mr. Lincoln, was regarded by the President himself only with amusement. On the morning after the Convention, a friend, giving him an account of it, said that, instead of the many thousands who had been expected, there were present at no time more than four hundred men. The President, struck by the number mentioned, reached for the Bible which commonly lay on his desk, and after a moment's search read these words: "And every one that was in distress, and every one that was in debt, and every one that was discontented, gathered themselves unto him; and he became a captain over them: and there were with him about four hundred men."

V

The eyes of the North focused on Grant in Virginia and Sherman in Georgia, but bloody fighting continued in other parts of the country. Nathan Bedford Forrest harried the Union forces in Tennessee and Mississippi. To dispose of the audacious Confederate cavalryman, Sherman ordered General Samuel D. Sturgis, at Memphis, to fit out an expedition, corner Forrest, and destroy him. Sturgis started in early June with nearly 9,000 men—3,300 cavalry under the now famous Grierson, 5,000 infantry (including 1,200 colored troops), 250 wagons, and 22 guns—a force three times as strong as Forrest could muster.

Rain roiled the roads and sent the creeks out of their banks. On June 8 Sturgis, oppressed by the obstacles which a perverse nature placed in his way, called a council of his senior officers to decide whether to turn back or not. All agreed that success was unlikely, but Sturgis could not forget that only a few weeks earlier he had abandoned another expedition under similar circumstances. His pride raw, he determined to move forward.

Two days later, in northern Mississippi a hundred miles southeast of Memphis, Sturgis and Forrest collided. In a few hours Sturgis's worst forebodings were realized. Lieutenant John Merrilies of Battery E, Illinois Light Artillery, recorded the Federal disaster in his diary:[16]

Friday June 10th. . . . The cavalry took the road . . . and about noon came on the enemy in force near Tishomingo Creek, bringing on heavy skirmishing. After finding the strength of the enemy Grierson sent word back to Sturgis who immediately hurried up our column, double-quicking the infantry for two miles under a broiling sun, after a march of ten miles. The 2nd Brigade got up about two o. c., or what was left of it after falling out exhausted and sun struck in squads for two miles along the road—and were immediately sent in to support the cavalry, who were being driven back and suffering from a very heavy artillery fire. Their arrival checked the advance of the enemy who had already gained the hill, and endeavored to hold Brice's Cross Roads and after severe skirmishing they succeeded in driving them [the Confederates] some distance, and holding the position.

By this time our Brigade came up, in little better plight than the 2nd, the men perfectly exhausted and entirely unfit to go into action, but there was no time to rest now, and as fast as a regiment came up it was formed and sent in—one at a time—the fighting all the time becoming harder and harder. The cavalry were now withdrawn having been fighting almost constantly since 11 o. c. and the last of our Brigade went in, by which time the 2nd Brigade was used up, or nearly so, leaving the brunt of the work to be borne by ours, for the nigger Brigade having the train to guard could not be used in front. After half an hours fighting, our 1st piece was ordered in and took position on the right, in time to assist with canister in repelling the charge the enemy soon after made in front. The ground however was not eligible for artillery, more being in position than could be used to advantage. A second time the enemy tried to carry the ridge in front, causing us severe loss, especially in the 93rd Indiana, which got into considerable confusion, a perfect storm of bullets sweeping thro them, but McMillan rallied them with great gallantry, and succeeded in again repulsing the enemy and holding his ground.

There was now a short lull in the firing, but it boded no good for us, soon springing up again, not only in front, but the bullets beginning to come over from both flanks crossing the road at almost right angles, and taking our line of battle directly in flank. It was evident now that the enemy, unable to force our position in front, were going to try their success at turning it. The Brigade was swung round as well as possible to meet this new emergency, but the nature of the ground prevented anything like a good position being obtained, and it had to fight at a great disadvantage, the enemy gradually moving round slackening their fire in front and increasing it on the flanks, their line advancing steadily and ours falling back. All hope of our being able to hold our position was given up, and the order was issued to move the artillery to the rear as fast as possible. It was not given a minute too soon, for before we could limber up our two pieces and get down the road, the enemy were on it, and one of the pieces had to go through a field, in order to get around them. The cavalry however were formed in line on one flank, and the Colored Brigade on the other, checking the onward rush of the enemy until the artillery had passed and then covering the rear of that and the ammunition train.

The supply train of over 200 wagons, with nine days' rations, had been, with astonishing carelessness, corraled within a quarter of a mile of the battle field and no effort made to get it to the rear till the troops retreating filled the road, and it became impossible to remove it. Most of the mules were unhitched at the last moment and ridden off, but not a single wagon was brought away. The column now continued moving slowly forward [away from the enemy], hard fighting going on in rear, and the enemy shelling us vigorously till darkness began to fall, when the fighting gradually ceased. The column, which had been hitherto a mass of confusion, commands being mixed up all through it, was now put in comparative order, commands united, and we continued our march steadily. All our Battery was safe with the exception of the 5th Caisson, which had the wheel horses shot and upset in the road, when there was no time left to right it.

But for Merrilies the worst was yet to come:

About 9 o. c. [on the night of June 10] the column came to a halt, and going ahead to see what the matter was, the scene that met the eye was little less than appalling. The head of the column had reached the big swamp we crossed in the morning and had commenced passing over, but no one being there to give orders, or no orders being attended to, a general rush of carriages had been made for the road which with the late rains, was in very bad order, and now after crossing it this morning was nothing but a gulf of mud and water. The whole passage soon became jammed with a confused mass of men, horses, wagons, ambulances, and artillery, plunging and floundering in the abyss, carriages dashing recklessly into each other in their frantic attempts to get away, getting smashed up and turned over, the drivers yelling, lashing, swearing, and making night hideous and soon getting the passage so hopelessly blockaded that it was impossible to get either one way or the other, except on foot or on horseback. All this was taking place long after dark, but numberless lanterns and candles twinkled all the way across, where the line of men were eagerly picking a way out, the imperfect light adding to the dismal character of the scene.

Here we lay waiting orders till half past 12, when a general council of officers was held, and it was decided—all hope of getting the column across being cut off and Sturgis having gone nobody knew where, and left us to shift for ourselves—to destroy as quickly and effectually as possible the artillery and ammunition, abandon everything and endeavor to save ourselves while the two remaining hours of darkness favored us. Accordingly after an hour spent in cutting up cartridges, chopping wheels, spiking the guns, and rendering the battery generally unserviceable, we unhitched, mounted the horses, and with some little difficulty all got safely across the dismal swamp, and followed the main column which had not three or four hours start of us. The wounded begged hard to be taken along, but that was impossible and they were left in the ambulances, with a sufficient supply of medicines. We travelled all night without being molested, but just at grey dawn while our detachment was passing a creek, where a good many of the infantry were resting and filling their canteens, a party of the enemy's cavalry dashed out of the woods and across the road, calling out Halt! Halt! and firing their pieces among the crowd. This caused considerable of a scattering, but a good many of the men had their guns loaded and returned the fire, soon making the place too hot for them, and forcing them to leave as suddenly as they had come on us.

Soon after a rear guard of cavalry was sent us, who fell in behind after we had passed, and did good service in the constant skirmishing which continued without intermission. The 59th U. S. C. was also detached to cover the rear and altho the first fighting they had seen they behaved, under very trying circumstances, with a coolness and confidence worthy of old troops. The indifference of the niggers to wounds was perfectly astonishing, numbers shot in the arms, hands, legs, their clothing soaked with blood, marching along with the rest, without a sign of pain.

VI

Brice's Cross Roads cost Sturgis 2,240 men, sixteen cannon, and his military reputation. The rumors said that Sturgis had been hoot-owl drunk; there was talk also of women—one, anyhow—over whom the general's strategy had brought tactical success. Meanwhile Sherman's solemn, plodding columns drew nearer to Atlanta as Johnston fell back into a chain of isolated hills—Pine Mountain, Lost Mountain, Kenesaw Mountain. In those June days Samuel G. French, a New Jersey Quaker turned Confederate general, was a faithful diarist:[17]

June 18.—This morning pickets and skirmishers on my left (Walker's division) gave way and let the enemy in behind Cockrell's skirmishers, and enabled them to gain the Latimer house, four hundred yards distant. Ector's skirmishers also came in. Enemy soon advanced in line of battle, and with batteries opened on the salient an enfilading and reverse fire; and all day long this fire never ceased. They could not carry my lines successfully, and we would not attack them by leaving the trenches; and so the firing went on. My loss was severe, amounting to one hundred and eighty, and as an instance of the severity of the fire on the salient, Captain Guibor had served with his battery throughout the siege of Vicksburg, yet his loss this day of thirteen men is greater than that sustained during the whole siege. Toward evening ordered to withdraw and assume a new line on Kenesaw Mountain.

June 19.—The enemy made rapid pursuit, and before my line was established on Kenesaw Mountain, skirmishing commenced, and by 12 M. artillery fire from the enemy was rapid. It ranged up and over the spur of the mountain with great fury, and wounded General Cockrell, and put thirty-five of his men *hors du combat.*

The position of our army to-day is: Hood on the right, covering Marietta on the northwest. From his left, Polk's corps (now Loring's) extends over both Big and Little Kenesaw Mountains, with the left on the road from Gilgal church to Marietta. From this road Hardee extended the line nearly south, covering Marietta on the west, the left of my division was fixed on the Marietta road; thence it ran up to the spur of the mountain called Little Kenesaw, and thence to the top of same and on up to the top of Big Kenesaw, connecting with General Walthall. Featherston was on the right of Walthall, and joined Gen. Hood's left; Walker, of Hardee's corps, was on my left; then in order came Bate, Cleburne and Cheatham.

Kenesaw Mountain is about four miles northwest of Marietta. It is over two-and-a-half miles in length, and rises abruptly from the plain, solitary and alone, to the height of perhaps 600 or 700 feet. Its western side is rocky and abrupt. Its eastern side can, in a few places, be gained on horseback, and the west of Little Kenesaw, being bald and destitute of timber, affords a commanding view of all the surrounding country as far as the eye can reach, except where the view is interrupted by the higher peak.

June 20.—Busy this morning in establishing batteries on the road, on the spur of the mountain and on the top of Little Kenesaw. In the afternoon changed the line lower down the mountain side, so as to command the ascent as far as possible. Heavy cannonading on the left of my line. Lost ten horses and a few men.

Two days later the rain ceased and Sherman established a headquarters camp close to the base of Kenesaw Mountain. Next day the cannonade was "fast and furious"; the following day nothing happened. But Sherman was getting set—French wasn't fooled:

June 25.—The everlasting "pop," "pop," on the skirmish line is all that breaks the stillness of the morning. Went early to the left of my line; could not ride in rear of Hoskins' Battery, on account of the trees and limbs felled by the shells. From top of the mountain the vast panorama is ever changing. There are now large trains to the left of Lost Mountain and at Big Shanty, and wagons are moving to and fro everywhere. Encampments of hospitals, quartermasters, commissaries, cavalry and infantry whiten the plain here and there as far as the eye can reach. Our side of the line looks narrow, poor and lifeless, with but little canvas in spots that contrasts with the green foliage.

The usual flank extension is going on. Troops on both sides move to left, and now the blue smoke of the musket discloses the line by day, trending away, far away south toward the Chattahoochee, and by night it is marked, at times by the red glow of the artillery, amidst the spark-like flash of small arms that looks in the distance like innumerable fireflies.

At 10 A.M. opened fire on the enemy from the guns on Kenesaw. Enemy replied furiously, and for an hour the firing was incessant. Received an order to hold Ector's brigade in reserve. In the afternoon considerable firing, and all the chests of one of my caissons were blown up by a shell from the enemy, and a shell from one of the chests killed a gunner. They have now about forty guns in my fronts, and when they concentrate their fire on the mountain at any one place, it is pretty severe, but owing to our height nearly harmless. Thousands of their parrott-shells pass high over the mountain, and exploding at a great elevation, the after-part of the shell is arrested in its flight, and falling perpendicularly, comes into camp, and they have injured our tents. Last night I heard a peculiar "thug" on my tent, and a rattle of tin pans, and this morning my negro boy cook put his head into my tent and said: "See here, Master Sam, them 'fernal Yanks done shot my pans last night. What am I going to do 'bout it?" A rifle ball coming over the mountain had fallen from a great height, and, perforating the pans, had entered the ground.

Except for one artillery duel, Sunday, June 26, was quiet. Flank Kene-saw or attack the center where Johnston's lines were thin—that was Sherman's problem. General Logan said that the attention the papers were giving Grant in Virginia led Sherman to remark "that his army was entirely forgotten" but "now it would fight." Up on Kenesaw, French didn't know why Sherman attacked, but French's diary made clear why, afterward, Sherman wished he had run the Rebel ends once more:

June 27.—This morning there appeared great activity among staff officers and Generals all along my front and up and down the line. The better to observe what it portended, myself and staff seated ourselves on the brow of the mountain, sheltered by a large rock that rested between our guns and those of the enemy, the infantry being still lower down the side of the mountain.

Artillery firing was common on the line at all times, but now it swelled in volume and extended down to the extreme left, and then from fifty guns burst out in my front, and thence, battery after battery following on the right, disclosed a general attack on our entire line. Presently, and as if by magic, there sprung from the earth a host of men, and in one long waving line of blue the infantry advanced and the battle of Kenesaw Mountain began.

I could see no infantry on my immediate front, owing to the woods at the base of the mountain, and therefore directed the guns from their elevated position to enfilade Walker's front. In a short time the flank fire down the line drove them back, and Walker was relieved from the attack.

We sat there, perhaps an hour, enjoying a bird's-eye view of one of the most magnificent sights ever allotted to man—to look down upon an hundred and fifty thousand men arrayed in the strife of battle on the plain below.

As the infantry closed in, the blue smoke of the musket marked out our line for miles, while over it rose in cumuli-like clouds the white smoke of the artillery. Through the rifts of smoke, or, as it was wafted aside by the wind, we could see the assault made on Cheatham, and there the struggle was hard, and there it lasted longest. So many guns were trained on those by our side, and so incessant was the roar of cannon and sharp the explosion of shells, that naught else could be heard. From the fact that I had seen no infantry in my front, and had heard no musketry near, and the elevation of my line on the mountain, I thought I was exempted from the general infantry attack; I was therefore surprised and awakened from my dreams when a courier came to me about 9 o'clock and said General Cockrell wanted assistance, that his line had been attacked in force. General Ector was at once directed to send two regiments to report to him. Soon again a second courier came and reported the assault on the left of my line. I went immediately with the remainder of Ector's brigade to Cockrell, but on joining him found the Federal forces had been repulsed. The assaulting column had struck Cockrell's works near the centre, recoiled under the fire, swung around into a steep valley where—exposed to the fire of the Missourians in front and right flank and of Sears' men on the left—it seemed to melt away or sink to the earth to rise no more.

The assault on my line repulsed, I returned to the mountain top. The intensity of the fire had slackened and no movement of troops was visible; and although the din of arms yet resounded far and near, the battle was virtually ended.

From prisoners and from papers on their persons shown us, I learned my line had, from its position, been selected for assault by General McPherson, as that of Cheatham's had been by General Thomas. . . .

The battle, in its entirety, became a pageantry on a grand scale, and barren of results, because the attacking columns were too small in numbers, considering the character of the troops they knew they would encounter.

General Cheatham's loss was one hundred and ninety-five (195); mine (French's) one hundred and eighty-six (186); all other Confederate losses were one hundred and forty-one (141), being a total of five hundred and twenty-two. What the Federal loss was I do not know. It has been variously estimated from three to eight thousand.

As nothing decisive was obtained by Sherman's attack, the firing slackened except on the skirmish line. After dark the enemy withdrew to their main trenches, the roar of guns died gradually away, and the morning of the 28th dawned on both armies in their former positions. The battle of Kenesaw, then, was a display of force and advance of troops by the enemy on the entire length of our line, that opened a furious fire of artillery and musketry, under cover of which two grand attacks were made by assaulting columns—the one on my line and the other on Cheatham's.

FROM CHERBOURG
HARBOR TO PEACH
TREE CREEK

S HERMAN WOULD NOT ADMIT that his frontal attack on Kenesaw
Mountain, which cost him 2,000 casualties as against 432 for the Confederates, was a mistake. Perhaps he was concerned about Northern
morale. He need not have worried. Eight days earlier the U. S. S. *Kearsarge* had sent the Confederate raider *Alabama* to the bottom of the
English Channel. When news of the victory reached the North, Sherman's one serious reverse in the Atlanta campaign was forgotten.

I

The Alabama, *commissioned by the Confederate government and built
at Liverpool, slipped out of the Mersey in the early summer of 1862.
During the next two years, under the command of Captain Raphael
Semmes, she sank, burned or captured more than sixty ships flying
the flag of the United States. In early June 1864 the* Kearsarge, *Captain
John A. Winslow, caught the* Alabama *in the harbor of Cherbourg,
France. Semmes's account of the battle that followed disclosed that he
was living, in imagination if not in fact, in the days of chivalry:*[1]

When the *Alabama* arrived in Cherbourg, the enemy's steamer *Kearsarge* was lying at Flushing. On the 14th of June, or three days after

our arrival, she steamed into the harbor of Cherbourg, sent a boat on shore to communicate with the authorities, and, without anchoring, steamed out again, and took her station off the breakwater. We had heard, a day or two before, of the expected arrival of this ship, and it was generally understood among my crew that I intended to engage her. . . .

I now addressed a note to Mr. Bonfils, our agent, requesting him to inform Captain Winslow, through the United States Consul, that if he would wait until I could receive some coal on board—my supply having been nearly exhausted, by my late cruising—I would come out and give him battle. This message was duly conveyed, and the defiance was understood to have been accepted.

We commenced coaling ship immediately, and making other preparations for battle; as sending down all useless yards and top-hamper, examining the gun equipments, and overhauling the magazine and shell-rooms. My crew seemed not only willing, but anxious for the combat, and I had every confidence in their steadiness and drill; but they labored under one serious disadvantage. They had had but very limited opportunities of actual practice at target-firing, with shot and shell. The reason is obvious. I had no means of replenishing either shot or shell, and was obliged, therefore, to husband the store I had on hand for actual conflict. . . .

As for the two ships, though the enemy was superior to me, both in size, stanchness of construction, and armament, they were of force so nearly equal, that I cannot be charged with rashness in having offered battle. The *Kearsarge* mounted seven guns:—two eleven-inch Dahlgrens, four 32-pounders, and a rifled 28-pounder. Though the *Alabama* carried one gun more than her antagonist, it is seen that the battery of the latter enabled her to throw more metal at a broadside— there being a difference of three inches in the bore of the shell-guns of the two ships.

Still the disparity was not so great, but that I might hope to beat my enemy in a fair fight. But he did not show me a fair fight, for, as it afterward turned out, his ship was iron-clad. It was the same thing, as if two men were to go out to fight a duel, and one of them, unknown to the other, were to put a shirt of mail under his outer garment. The days of chivalry being past, perhaps it would be unfair to charge Captain Winslow with deceit in withholding from me the fact that he meant to wear armor in the fight. He may have reasoned that it was my duty to find it out for myself. Besides, if he had disclosed this fact to me, and so prevented the engagement, the Federal Secretary of the Navy would have cut his head off to a certainty.

An anonymous eyewitness of the fight wrote in the London Daily News: *"The* Kearsarge *is spoken of as being iron-clad; she was no more iron-clad than the* Alabama *might have been, had they taken the precaution. She simply had a double row of chains hanging over her sides to protect her machinery. Two shots from the* Alabama *struck these chains, and fell harmlessly into the water."*

Semmes's excuses on record, he told the story of the fight:

. . . In the way of crew, the *Kearsarge* had 162, all told—the *Alabama*, 149. I had communicated my intention to fight this battle to Flag-Officer Barron, my senior officer in Paris, a few days before, and that officer had generously left the matter to my own discretion. I completed my preparations on Saturday evening, the 18th of June, and notified the Port-Admiral of my intention to go out on the following morning. The next day dawned beautiful and bright. The cloudy, murky weather of some days past had cleared off, and a bright sun, a gentle breeze, and a smooth sea, were to be the concomitants of the battle. Whilst I was still in my cot, the Admiral sent an officer off to say to me that the iron-clad frigate *Couronne* would accompany me a part of the way out, to see that the neutrality of French waters was not violated. My crew had turned in early, and gotten a good night's rest, and I permitted them to get their breakfasts comfortably—not turning them to until nine o'clock—before any movement was made toward getting under way, beyond lighting the fires in the furnaces. . . .

The day being Sunday, and the weather fine, a large concourse of people—many having come all the way from Paris—collected on the heights above the town, in the upper stories of such of the houses as commanded a view of the sea, and on the walls and fortifications of the harbor. Several French luggers employed as pilot-boats went out, and also an English steam-yacht, called the *Deerhound*. Everything being in readiness between nine and ten o'clock, we got under way, and proceeded to sea, through the western entrance of the harbor; the *Couronne* following us. As we emerged from behind the mole, we discovered the *Kearsarge* at a distance of between six and seven miles from the land. She had been apprised of our intention of coming out that morning, and was awaiting us. The *Couronne* anchored a short distance outside of the harbor. We were three quarters of an hour in running out to the *Kearsarge,* during which time we had gotten our people to quarters, cast loose the battery, and made all the other necessary preparations for battle. The yards had been previously slung in chains, stoppers prepared for the rigging, and preventer braces rove. It only remained to open the magazine and shell-rooms, sand down the decks, and fill the requisite number of tubs with water. The crew had been particularly neat in their dress on that morning, and the officers were all in the uniforms appropriate to their rank. As we were approaching the enemy's ship, I caused the crew to be sent aft, within convenient reach of my voice, and mounting a gun-carriage, delivered them the following brief address. I had not spoken to them in this formal way since I had addressed them on the memorable occasion of commissioning the ship.

"OFFICERS AND SEAMEN OF THE ALABAMA!—You have, at length, another opportunity of meeting the enemy—the first that has been presented to you, since you sank the *Hatteras!* * In the meantime, you have been all over the world, and it is not too much to say, that you have destroyed, and driven for protection under neutral flags, one half of the enemy's commerce, which, at the beginning of the war, covered every sea. This is an achievement of which you may well be proud; and a grateful country will not be unmindful of it. The name of your ship has become a household word wherever civilization extends. Shall that name be tarnished by defeat? The thing is impossible! Remember that you are in the English Channel, the theatre of so much of the naval glory of our race, and that the eyes of all Europe are at this moment, upon you. The flag that floats over you is that of a young Republic, who bids defiance to her enemies, whenever, and wherever found. Show the world that you know how to uphold it! Go to your quarters."

The utmost silence prevailed during the delivery of this address, broken only once, in an enthusiastic burst of *Never! never!* when I asked my sailors if they would permit the name of their ship to be tarnished by defeat. My official report of the engagement, addressed to Flag-Officer Barron, in Paris, will describe what now took place. . . .

SOUTHHAMPTON, June 21, 1864.

SIR:—I have the honor to inform you, that, in accordance with my intentions as previously announced to you, I steamed out of the harbor

---

* In January of 1863, the *Alabama,* posing as "Her Majesty's steamer *Vixen,*" tricked the *Hatteras* into approaching. Within a hundred yards of the Federal warship, the *Alabama* revealed her true nature by running up Confederate colors and opening with a broadside.

of Cherbourg between nine and ten o'clock on the morning of the 19th of June, for the purpose of engaging the enemy's steamer *Kearsarge*, which had been lying off, and on the port, for several days previously. After clearing the harbor, we descried the enemy, with his head off shore, at the distance of about seven miles. We were three quarters of an hour in coming up with him. I had previously pivotted my guns to starboard, and made all preparations for engaging the enemy on that side. When within about a mile and a quarter of the enemy, he suddenly wheeled, and, bringing his head in shore, presented his starboard battery to me. By this time, we were distant about one mile from each other, when I opened on him with solid shot, to which he replied in a few minutes, and the action became active on both sides. The enemy now pressed his ship under a full head of steam, and to prevent our passing each other too speedily, and to keep our respective broadsides bearing, it became necessary to fight in a circle; the two ships steaming around a common centre, and preserving a distance from each other of from three quarters to half a mile. When we got within good shell range, we opened upon him with shell. Some ten or fifteen minutes after the commencement of the action, our spanker-gaff was shot away, and our ensign came down by the run. This was immediately replaced by another at the mizzen-masthead. The firing now became very hot, and the enemy's shot and shell soon began to tell upon our hull, knocking down, killing, and disabling a number of men, at the same time, in different parts of the ship. Perceiving that our shell, though apparently exploding against the enemy's sides, were doing him but little damage, I returned to solid-shot firing, and from this time onward alternated with shot and shell.

After the lapse of about one hour and ten minutes, our ship was ascertained to be in a sinking condition, the enemy's shell having exploded in our side, and between decks, opening large apertures through which the water rushed with great rapidity. For some few minutes I had hopes of being able to reach the French coast, for which purpose I gave the ship all steam, and set such of the fore-and-aft sails as were available.* The ship filled so rapidly, however, that before we had made much progress, the fires were extinguished in the furnaces, and we were evidently on the point of sinking. I now hauled down my colors,

---

* Semmes displayed a great want of generosity toward Winslow, whose seamanship had been superb. Semmes appeared to avoid close action, and Winslow forced a battle in a series of circular tracks so that Semmes was prevented from making a dash for shore. When the fight ended, the *Alabama* was nearly five miles off the coast with no chance of escaping within French jurisdiction.

to prevent the further destruction of life, and dispatched a boat to inform the enemy of our condition. Although we were now but 400 yards from each other, the enemy fired upon me five times after my colors had been struck. It is charitable to suppose that a ship of war of a Christian nation could not have done this intentionally.

Captain Semmes's "charitable" supposition was correct. Winslow, in his official report of the action, wrote: "I saw now that she [the Alabama] *was at our mercy, and a few more guns well directed brought down her flag. I was unable to ascertain whether it had been hauled down or shot away; but a white flag having been displayed over the stern, our fire was reserved. Two minutes had not more than elapsed before she again opened on us with the two guns on the port side. This drew our fire again, and the* Kearsarge *was immediately steamed ahead and laid across her bows for raking. The white flag was still flying, and our fire was again reserved. Shortly after this, her boats were seen to be lowering, and an officer in one of them came alongside, and informed us the ship had surrendered and was fast sinking."*

To the end, Semmes remained querulous:

We now directed all our exertions toward saving the wounded, and such of the boys of the ship as were unable to swim. These were dispatched in my quarter-boats, the only boats remaining to me; the waist-boats having been torn to pieces. Some twenty minutes after my furnace-fires had been extinguished, and when the ship was on the point of settling, every man, in obedience to a previous order which had been given the crew, jumped overboard, and endeavored to save himself. There was no appearance of any boat coming to me from the enemy, until after my ship went down. Fortunately, however, the steam-yacht *Deerhound*, owned by a gentleman of Lancashire, England— Mr. John Lancaster—who was himself on board, steamed up in the midst of my drowning men, and rescued a number of both officers and men from the water. I was fortunate enough myself thus to escape to the shelter of the neutral flag, together with about forty others, all told. About this time the *Kearsarge* sent one, and then, tardily, another boat. Accompanying, you will find lists of the killed and wounded, and of those who were picked up by the *Deerhound;* the remainder, there is reason to hope, were picked up by the enemy, and by a couple of French pilot boats, which were also fortunately near the scene of action.

According to the London Daily News *correspondent, "the* Kearsarge *picked up sixty-three men, one dead body, and two who died afterward on board. She also took five officers."*

But Semmes pressed his allegation that he had been unfairly treated:

At the end of the engagement, it was discovered by those of our officers who went alongside of the enemy's ship, with the wounded, that her mid-ship section, on both sides, was thoroughly iron-coated; this having been done with chains, constructed for the purpose, placed perpendicularly, from the rail to the water's edge, the whole covered over by a thin outer planking, which gave no indication of the armor beneath. This planking had been ripped off, in every direction, by our shot and shell, the chain broken, and indented in many places, and forced partly into the ship's side. She was effectually guarded, however, in this section, from penetration. The enemy was much damaged, in other parts, but to what extent it is now impossible to say. It is believed he is badly crippled. My officers and men behaved steadily and gallantly, and though they have lost their ship, they have not lost honor. . . . The enemy was heavier than myself, both in ship, battery, and crew; but I did not know until the action was over, that she was also iron-clad. Our total loss in killed and wounded, is 30, to wit: 9 killed, and 21 wounded.

Yet Semmes, essaying the difficult role of propagandist-historian, would meet his match in Gideon Welles, who wrote Winslow:[2]

NAVY DEPARTMENT, July 6, 1864.

SIR—Your very brief dispatches of the 19th and 20th ultimo, informing the Department that the piratical craft "Alabama," or "290," had been sunk on the 19th of June near meridian, by the "Kearsarge," under your command, were this day received. I congratulate you on your good fortune in meeting this vessel, which had so long avoided the fastest ships and some of the most vigilant and intelligent officers of the service; and for the ability displayed in this combat you have the thanks of the Department.

You will please express to the officers and crew of the "Kearsarge" the satisfaction of the Government at the victory over a vessel superior in tonnage, superior in number of guns, and superior in the number of her crew. The battle was so brief, the victory so decisive, and the comparative results so striking, that the country will be reminded of the brilliant actions of our infant Navy, which have been repeated and illustrated in this engagement.

The "Alabama" represented the best maritime effort of the most skilled English workshops. Her battery was composed of the well-tried 32-pounders of 57-hundred weight, of the famous 68-pounder of the British Navy, and of the only successful rifled 100-pounder yet produced in England. The crew were generally recruited in Great Britain, and many of them received superior training on board Her Majesty's gunnery ship, the "Excellent."

The "Kearsarge" is one of the first gun-boats built at our Navy Yards at the commencement of the rebellion, and lacks the improvements of vessels now under construction. The principal guns composing her battery had never been previously tried in an exclusively naval engagement, yet in one hour you succeeded in sinking your antagonist, thus fully ending her predatory career, and killed many of her crew without injury to the "Kearsarge," or the loss of a single life on your vessel.

Our countrymen have reason to be satisfied that in this, as in every naval action of this unhappy war, neither the ships, the guns nor the crew have been deteriorated, but that they maintain the abilities and continue the renown which ever adorned our naval annals.

The President has signified his intention to recommend that you receive a vote of thanks, in order that you may be advanced to the grade of commodore.

Lieutenant-Commander James S. Thornton, the executive officer of the "Kearsarge," will be recommended to the Senate for advancement ten numbers in his grade, and you will report to the Department the names of any other of the officers or crew whose good conduct on the occasion entitles them to especial mention.

Very respectfully,
GIDEON WELLES,
Secretary of the Navy.

CAPTAIN JOHN A. WINSLOW,
Commanding U. S. Steamer "Kearsarge,"
Cherbourg, France.

II

Far from the coast of France, Robert E. Lee came to a decision. He could not shake off this man Grant, but the Federal authorities might be induced to relieve the pressure. In mid-June Lee ordered Jubal A. Early to take the Second Corps of the Army of Northern Virginia with

*two battalions of artillery, move up the Shenandoah Valley toward
Harpers Ferry and, if practicable, give Washington the scare of its life.*

*In the second week of July Gideon Welles—no friend of Secretary of
War Stanton—awoke to the fact that a powerful Confederate force was
approaching the capital, and that the capital was vulnerable:*[3]

July 9, Saturday. The Rebel invasion of Maryland, if not so large or
formidable as last year and year before, looks to me very annoying, the
more so because I learn nothing satisfactory or reliable from the War
Office, and am persuaded there is both neglect and ignorance there. It
is evident there have not been sufficient preparations, but they are beginning to move. Yet they hardly have any accurate information. . . .

July 10, Sunday. When at the Department, Sunday morning, the
10th, examining my mail, one of the clerks came in and stated that the
Rebel pickets were on the outskirts of Georgetown, within the District
lines. There had been no information to warn us of this near approach
of the enemy, but my informant was so positive—and soon confirmed
by another—that I sent to the War Department to ascertain the facts.
They were ignorant—had heard street rumors, but they were unworthy of notice—and ridiculed my inquiry. . . .

July 11, Monday. The Rebels are upon us. . . .

*Early, on the outskirts of Washington, saw difficulties which the
panicky inhabitants overlooked:*[4]

We moved at daylight on the 11th; McCausland moving on the
Georgetown pike, while the infantry, preceded by Imboden's cavalry
under Colonel Smith, turned to the left at Rockville, so as to reach
the 7th street pike which runs by Silver Spring into Washington. Jackson's cavalry moved on the left flank. The previous day had been very
warm, and the roads were exceedingly dusty, as there had been no rain
for several weeks. The heat during the night had been very oppressive,
and but little rest had been obtained. This day was an exceedingly
hot one, and there was no air stirring. While marching, the men were
enveloped in a suffocating cloud of dust and many of them fell by the
way from exhaustion. Our progress was therefore very much impeded,
but I pushed on as rapidly as possible, hoping to get into the fortifications around Washington before they could be manned. Smith drove
a small body of cavalry before him into the works on the 7th street pike,

and dismounted his men and deployed them as skirmishers. I rode ahead of the infantry, and arrived in sight of Fort Stevens on this road a short time after noon, when I discovered that the works were but feebly manned.*

Rodes, whose division was in front, was immediately ordered to bring it into line as rapidly as possible, throw out skirmishers, and move into the works if he could. My whole column was then moving by flank, which was the only practicable mode of marching on the road we were on, and before Rodes' division could be brought up, we saw a cloud of dust in the rear of the works towards Washington, and soon a column of the enemy filed into them on the right and left, and skir-

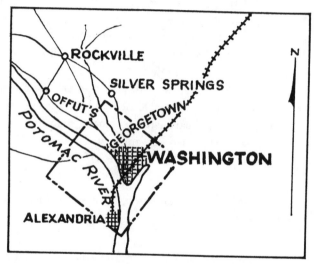

WASHINGTON AND VICINITY, 1864

mishers were thrown out in front, while an artillery fire was opened on us from a number of batteries. This defeated our hopes of getting possession of the works by surprise, and it became necessary to reconnoitre.

Rodes' skirmishers were thrown to the front, driving those of the enemy to the cover of the works, and we proceeded to examine the fortifications in order to ascertain if it was practicable to carry them by

* Welles found Lincoln at Fort Stevens. Tradition insists that Oliver Wendell Holmes, then a captain on the staff of General Horatio G. Wright, had seen the President peering over the parapet. Unaware of the tall man's identity, Holmes shouted, "Get down, you damn fool, before you get shot!"

assault. They were found to be exceedingly strong, and consisted of what appeared to be enclosed forts for heavy artillery, with a tier of lower works in front of each pierced for an immense number of guns, the whole being connected by curtains with ditches in front, and strengthened by palisades and abattis. The timber had been felled within cannon range all around and left on the ground, making a formidable obstacle, and every possible approach was raked by artillery. On the right was Rock Creek, running through a deep ravine which had been rendered impassable by the felling of timber on each side, and beyond were the works on the Georgetown pike which had been reported to be the strongest of all. On the left, as far as the eye could reach, the works appeared to be of the same impregnable character. The position was naturally strong for defence, and the examination showed, what might have been expected, that every appliance of science and unlimited means had been used to render the fortifications around Washington as strong as possible. This reconnoissance consumed the balance of the day.

The rapid marching which had broken down a number of the men who were barefooted or weakened by previous exposure, and had been left in the Valley and directed to be collected at Winchester, and the losses in killed and wounded at Harper's Ferry, Maryland Heights, and Monocacy, had reduced my infantry to about 8,000 muskets. Of those remaining, a very large number were greatly exhausted by the last two days marching, some having fallen by sunstroke, and I was satisfied, when we arrived in front of the fortifications, that not more than one-third of my force could have been carried into action. I had about forty pieces of field artillery, of which the largest were 12 pounder Napoleons, besides a few pieces of horse artillery with the cavalry. McCausland reported the works on the Georgetown pike too strongly manned for him to assault. We could not move to the right or the left without its being discovered from a signal station on the top of the "Soldier's Home," which overlooked the country, and the enemy would have been enabled to move in his works to meet us. Under the circumstances, to have rushed my men blindly against the fortifications, without understanding the state of things, would have been worse than folly. If we had any friends in Washington, none of them came out to give us information, and this satisfied me that the place was not undefended.

Welles visited the fortifications to see the situation for himself. He kept his head—and confided his disgust to his diary:[5]

I rode out this evening [July 11] to Fort Stevens, latterly called Fort Massachusetts. Found General Wright and General McCook with what I am assured is an ample force for its defense. Passed and met as we returned three or four thousand, perhaps more, volunteers under General Meigs, going to the front. Could see the line of pickets of both armies in the valley, extending a mile or more. There was continual firing, without many casualties so far as I could observe, or hear. . . .

I inquired where the Rebel force was, and the officers said over the hills, pointing in the direction of Silver Spring. Are they near Gunpowder or Baltimore? Where are they? Oh! within a short distance, a mile or two only. I asked why their whereabouts was not ascertained, and their strength known. The reply was that we had no fresh cavalry.

The truth is the forts around Washington have been vacated and the troops sent to General Grant, who was promised reinforcements to take Richmond. . . . Citizens are volunteering, and the employees in the navy yard are required to man the fortifications left destitute. Stanton and Halleck . . . are now the most alarmed men in Washington.

I am sorry to see so little reliable intelligence. It strikes me that the whole demonstration is weak in numbers but strong in conception. . . . I am satisfied no attack is now to be apprehended on the city; the Rebels have lost a remarkable opportunity. But on our part there is neglect, ignorance, folly, imbecility, in the last degree. The Rebels are making a show of fight while they are stealing horses, cattle, etc., through Maryland. They might easily have captured Washington. Stanton, Halleck, and Grant are asleep or dumb.

Early, sizing up the odds against him, decided that he had accomplished all that could be expected:[6]

After dark on the 11th, I held a consultation with Major-Generals Breckinridge, Rodes, Gordon and Ramseur, in which I stated to them the danger of remaining where we were, and the necessity of doing something immediately, as the probability was that the passes of the South Mountain and the fords of the upper Potomac would soon be closed against us. After interchanging views with them, being very reluctant to abandon the project of capturing Washington, I determined to make an assault on the enemy's works at daylight next morning, unless some information should be received before that time showing its impracticability, and so informed those officers. During the night a dispatch was received from Gen. Bradley Johnson from near Baltimore, informing me that he had received information, from a reliable source, that two corps had arrived from Gen. Grant's army, and that his whole army was probably in motion. This caused me to delay the attack until I could examine the works again, and, as soon as it was light enough to see, I rode to the front and found the parapets lined with troops. I had, therefore, reluctantly, to give up all hopes of capturing Washington, after I had arrived in sight of the dome of the Capitol, and given the Federal authorities a terrible fright.

Lincoln, like Welles, suspected that the defense of Washington, or at least the pursuit of the Rebels who had had the temerity to threaten the city, could have been better managed.
John Hay sketched the mood of a disgruntled President:[7]

July 13, 1864. The news this morning would seem to indicate that the enemy is retiring from every point.

The President thinks we should push our whole column right up the River Road & cut off as many as possible of the retreating raiders. . . .

July 14, 1864. Nothing of importance yet. This evening as the President started to the Soldiers' Home I asked him *quid nunc* & he said, "Wright telegraphs that he thinks the enemy are all across the Potomac but that he has halted & sent out an infantry reconnoissance, for fear he might come across the rebels & catch some of them." The Chief is evidently disgusted.

III

While Early threw Washington into panic and Grant weakened his own forces by sending a corps and two divisions to the relief of the Capital, Sherman pressed relentlessly toward Atlanta. After his repulse at Kenesaw Mountain he skirted that obstacle, only to encounter Johnston strongly intrenched in front of the Chattahoochee. Sherman's scouts found fords. Johnston, his rear endangered, took up a new line of defense along Peach Tree Creek, ten miles from Atlanta.

Suddenly the campaign took on a new aspect. Confederate Captain Thomas J. Key, who commanded a battery in Cleburne's division, noted news of moment in his diary:[8]

July 18th. This morning the whole army was surprised by the announcement that the Secretary of War had removed General Johnston from command of this army and placed it in the hands of General Hood.

Every man looked sad and disheartened at this information, and felt that evil would result from the removal of Johnston, whom they esteem and love above any previous commander. His address touched every heart, and every man thought that his favorite General had been grievously wronged. The cause for this procedure on the part of the President at this eventful moment when the enemy is pressing us we have been unable to conjecture. General Hood is a gallant man, but Johnston has been tried and won the confidence of the soldiery. . . .

July 19th. The rumor prevailed that General Johnston was still in command of this army. The report cheered the despondent hearts, but I was of the impression that it was done to prevent desertions and to cause the troops to fight with their former bravery in the now approaching conflict. So soon as I dispatched a hasty breakfast, I mounted my horse, which I call General Longstreet, and rode with the other officers of the battalion along the line of battle to select the commanding points for artillery. . . . Most of Sherman's thieves are across the Chattahoochee River and are now skirmishing about two miles from the lines of rifle pits that we are now constructing. They are making some bold maneuvers for Atlanta, but at the same time will not come up fearlessly and fight us on the ground of our choice. . . .

Sherman gauged cautiously both the Confederate defenses and the character of his new chief opponent:[9]

During the night [July 20], I had full reports from all parts of our line, most of which was partially intrenched as against a sally, and finding that McPherson was stretching out too much on his left flank, I wrote him a note early in the morning not to extend so much by his left; for we had not troops enough to completely invest the place, and I intended to destroy utterly all parts of the Augusta Railroad to the east of Atlanta, then to withdraw from the left flank and add to the right. In that letter I ordered McPherson not to extend any farther to the left, but to employ General Dodge's corps (Sixteenth), then forced out of position, to destroy every rail and tie of the railroad, from Decatur up to his skirmish-line, and I wanted him (McPherson) to be ready, as soon as General Garrard returned from Covington (whither I had sent him), to move to the extreme right of Thomas, so as to reach if possible the railroad below Atlanta, viz., the Macon road. In the morning we found the strong line of parapet, "Peach-Tree line," to the front of Schofield and Thomas, abandoned, and our lines were advanced rapidly close up to Atlanta. For some moments I supposed the enemy intended to evacuate, and in person was on horseback at the head of Schofield's troops, who had advanced . . . to some open ground, from which we could plainly see the whole rebel line of parapets, and I saw their men dragging up from the intervening valley, by the distillery, trees and saplings for abatis. Our skirmishers found the enemy down in this valley, and we could see the rebel main line strongly manned, with guns in position at intervals. Schofield was dressing forward his lines, and I could hear Thomas farther to the right engaged, when General Mc-Pherson and his staff rode up. We went back to the Howard House, a double-frame building with a porch, and sat on the steps, discussing the chances of battle, and of Hood's general character. McPherson had also been of the same class at West Point with Hood, Schofield, and Sheridan. We agreed that we ought to be unusually cautious and prepared at all times for sallies and hard fighting, because Hood, though not deemed much of a scholar, or of great mental capacity, was undoubtedly a brave, determined, and rash man; and the change of commanders at that particular crisis argued the displeasure of the Confederate Government with the cautious but prudent conduct of General Jos. Johnston.

If Hood believed himself equal to his new command, he was willing nonetheless by his own testimony to offer an astonishing suggestion:[10]

. . . The order, assigning me to the command of that Army, was received about 11 P.M., on the 17th of July. My predecessor, unwilling to await even the dawn of day, issued his farewell order that memorable night. In despite of my repeated and urgent appeals to him to pocket all dispatches from Richmond, to leave me in command of my own corps, and to fight the battle for Atlanta, he deserted me the ensuing afternoon. He deserted me in violation of his promise to remain and afford me the advantage of his counsel, whilst I shouldered all responsibility of the contest.

I reiterate that it is difficult to imagine a commander placed at the head of an army under more embarrassing circumstances than those against which I was left to contend on the evening of the 18th of July, 1864. I was, comparatively, a stranger to the Army of Tennessee. Moreover General Johnston's mode of warfare formed so strong a contrast to the tactics and strategy which were practiced in Virginia, where far more satisfactory results were obtained than in the West, that I have become a still more ardent advocate of the Lee and Jackson school. The troops of the Army of Tennessee had for such length of time been subjected to the ruinous policy pursued from Dalton to Atlanta that they were unfitted for united action in pitched battle. They had, in other words, been so long habituated to security behind breastworks that they had become wedded to the "timid defensive" policy, and naturally regarded with distrust a commander likely to initiate offensive operations.

The senior Corps Commander [William J. Hardee] considered he had been supplanted through my promotion, and thereupon determined to resign, in consequence, I have no doubt, of my application to President Davis to postpone the order transferring to me the command of the Army; he however, altered his decision, and concluded to remain with his corps.

Five days after Hood assumed command, the battle for Atlanta opened across ground situated approximately halfway between the present heart of the city ("Five Points") and the town square of Decatur, five miles to the east. Captain Thomas J. Key was in the thick of the fighting that twenty-second of July:[11]

. . . About noon the enemy opened his artillery upon our advance, throwing spherical case along the road on which we were advancing. I sought an elevated spot and at once ordered one section of Goldthwaite's battery to return the fire, the Yankees being about six hundred yards distant. Simultaneously, the Captain went into action in the woods with the other section, about 100 yards to my right. Under the fire of artillery and minie balls, General Cleburne's division advanced upon the earth works of the enemy, but the fire was so galling that many faltered in the charge. The enemy's abatis was formed of saplings and bushes cut off and bent over, leaving the butt or stump two feet high.

Notwithstanding these formidable works and tangling obstructions, the brave Confederates charged over all intervening obstacles and took the dirt works together with many prisoners. The most successful movement was performed by two of General Govan's regiments which, finding a ravine across which were no fortifications, moved by the right oblique and after passing the line swung to their left, taking the Yankees in flank and rear. Here some of our men who had gone over the enemy's works were retaken. This caused the Yankees to evacuate all the fortifications protecting their rear and to abandon four pieces of

Napoleon guns. The fire of Captain Goldthwaite's battery, enfilading the enemy, caused them to go over their works to the south. . . . I at once called to the men of the battery for volunteers to go with me across the fortifications and turn the enemy's guns upon them. . . . With a cheer I led them at a double quick through the abatis to the Yankee guns. However, while my men had one gun in the road in full view of a second line of works of the enemy, and were running it up to commence firing, the Yanks from behind the second works poured such a volley of musketry upon those brave cannoneers that they were compelled to abandon the guns and leave the road. The Yanks re-enforced and came back with a charge, and I thought it advisable to retire, which we did in hasty steps and not in good order, knowing that artillerists are defenseless unless they can get their guns in an effective position. Cleburne's men met this charge manfully and in half an hour the Yankees had recrossed their works.

With Cleburne's help, Key's gunners began pounding the Yankees, and at last isolated a pocket of about four hundred that Key wanted very badly to capture:

. . . I tried to get the infantry of General Carter's brigade to charge them while I was firing, but it was impossible to get them forward. . . . I galloped back to Generals Cleburne and Hardee and informed them of . . . how we were driving them, remarking "Generals to the front," which caused a smile to play upon Cleburne's face. They sanctioned my suggestions, and in a few moments Cleburne and I were riding rapidly over the ground that I had gained with Turner's battery. As I rode I told the stragglers to rally—that the Yankees were running—and my remarks seemed to infuse new life into everyone and together we moved forward on the enemy. I also ordered forward the lieutenant commanding the section of Turner's battery and opened a fire upon the retreating foe. In a few moments General Lowrey advanced between my guns and the enemy, and knowing the direction of the Yankee lines I rode to the right and informed Generals Cleburne and Govan of the position. Then, in a few moments, a tremendous and bloody conflict followed. The battery was withdrawn, being no longer serviceable. Our forces carried a portion of the works, but night closed on the bloody tragedy.

The battle on July 22 was not so one-sided as Captain Key suggested.
At noon that day Major W. H. Chamberlin of the Eighty-First Ohio

rode with General Grenville M. Dodge to a luncheon appointment at
General Fuller's headquarters:[12]

Just as General Dodge was about to dismount to accept General
Fuller's hospitality, he heard firing in a south-easterly direction, to the
rear of General Sweeney's division. He took no lunch. He was an intensely active, almost nervously restless, officer. He saw in an instant
that something serious was at hand. He gave General Fuller orders to
form his division immediately, facing south-eastwardly, and galloped
off toward Sweeney's division. He had hardly reached that command
when Hardee's line came tearing wildly through the woods with the
yells of demons. As if by magic, Sweeney's division sprang into line.
The two batteries of artillery (Loomis's and Laird's) had stopped on
commanding ground, and they were promptly in service. General
Dodge's quick eye saw the proper disposition to be made of a portion of
Colonel Mersy's brigade, and, cutting red tape, he delivered his orders
direct to the colonels of the regiments. The orders were executed instantly, and the enemy's advance was checked.* . . . The battle of
General Dodge's corps on this open ground, with no works to protect
the troops of either side, was one of the fiercest of the war. General
Dodge's troops were inspired by his courageous personal presence, for
he rode directly along the lines, and must have been a conspicuous
target for many a Confederate gun. His sturdy saddle-horse was worn
out early in the afternoon, and was replaced by another. There was not
a soldier who did not feel that he ought to equal his general in courage.
. . . We had an advantage in artillery; they in numbers. Their assaults
were repulsed, only to be fearlessly renewed, until the sight of the dead
and wounded lying in their way, as they charged again and again to
break our lines, must have appalled the stoutest hearts. So persistent
were their onslaughts that numbers were made prisoners by rushing
directly into our lines.

Even so, Dodge's left was in danger of crumbling unless he could get
support from McPherson. Lieutenant Colonel W. E. Strong, McPher-
son's chief of staff, saw troops sweep onto that open field:[13]

---

* Sweeney was a West Pointer, Dodge was not. In issuing orders directly to the
colonels, Dodge so hurt Sweeney's military dignity "as to bring on a personal
encounter a few days after the battle, in which he [Dodge] came near losing
his life at the hands of a hot-tempered officer."

The enemy, massed in columns three or four lines deep, moved out of the dense timber several hundred yards from Dodge's position, and, after gaining fairly the open fields, halted and opened fire rapidly on the Sixteenth Corps. They, however, seemed surprised to find our infantry in line of battle prepared for attack, and, after facing for a few minutes the destructive fire from the divisions of Generals Fuller and Sweeney, fell back in disorder to the cover of the woods. Here, however, their lines were quickly re-formed, and they again advanced, evidently determined to carry the position. The scene at this time was grand and impressive. It seemed to us that every mounted officer of the attacking column was riding at the front or at the right or left of the first line of battle. The regimental colors waved and fluttered in advance of the lines, and not a shot was fired by the rebel infantry, although their movement was covered by a heavy and well-directed fire of artillery which was posted in the woods and on higher ground, and which enabled the guns to bear upon our troops with solid shot and shell firing over the attacking column. It seemed impossible, however, for the enemy to face the sweeping, deadly fire from Fuller's and Sweeney's divisions, and the guns of Laird's 14th Ohio and Walker's batteries fairly mowed great swaths in the advancing columns. They showed great steadiness, and closed up the gaps and preserved their alignments; but the iron and leaden hail that was poured upon them was too much for flesh and blood to stand, and before reaching the center of the open field the columns were broken and thrown into great confusion. Taking advantage of this, a portion of Fuller's and Sweeney's divisions, with bayonets fixed, charged the enemy and drove them back to the woods, taking many prisoners. The 81st Ohio charged first, then the 39th and the 27th Ohio. General McPherson's admiration for the steadiness and determined bravery of the Sixteenth Corps was unbounded.

Sherman approached the grimmest moment of the day:[14]

. . . Although the sound of musketry on our left grew in volume, I was not so much disturbed by it as by the sound of artillery back toward Decatur. I ordered Schofield at once to send a brigade back to Decatur (some five miles) and was walking up and down the porch of the Howard House, listening, when one of McPherson's staff, with his horse covered with sweat, dashed up to the porch, and reported that General

McPherson was either "killed or a prisoner." He explained that when they had left me a few minutes before, they had ridden rapidly across the railroad, the sounds of battle increasing as they neared the position occupied by General Giles A. Smith's division, and that McPherson had sent first one, then another of his staff to bring some of the reserve brigades of the Fifteenth Corps over to the exposed left flank; that he had reached the head of Dodge's corps (marching by the flank on the diagonal road as described), and had ordered it to hurry forward to the same point; and then, almost if not entirely alone, he had followed this road leading across the wooded valley behind the Seventeenth Corps, and had disappeared in these woods, doubtless with a sense of absolute security. The sound of musketry was there heard, and McPherson's horse came back, bleeding, wounded, and riderless. . . .

To Sherman the death of James B. McPherson was a severe blow; he ordered the door of the Howard House wrenched from its hinges to provide a sort of table on which Dr. Hewitt examined the stricken general; and Sherman characterized McPherson as a man of "many noble qualities." Grant rated him with Sherman among "the men to whom, above all others, I feel indebted for whatever I have had of success." Major Connolly put the events of the twenty-second in a perspective somewhat different from Sherman's:[15]

. . . The rebels came out and attacked McPherson and Schofield yesterday [July 22], and gained some advantage over them, capturing several pieces of artillery, and many prisoners. McPherson was killed.

That is a severe loss, but his place can be filled; should we lose old father Thomas though, it would hurt us equal to the loss of an entire Division. We have been singularly fortunate during the entire campaign; success has crowned almost every movement, and our losses have been light, but we can't expect to get along always without some pretty tough fighting. The rebels have been more vigorous since we crossed the river than they were before, but it is only the vigor of desperation, and the more frequently they assault us, the sooner their army will be destroyed, for they *can't whip* this army; we are like the big boy, "too big to be whipped." They may gain temporary advantage here and there along our line, they may capture a few guns, but they will capture them at the expense of the blood and muscle of their army, and that they cannot replace; so I don't care how often they assault; we are here to *fight* them and *destroy* them, not to *chase* them, and if they have found their "last ditch" all right, Sherman will soon put them in it, and the oftener they attack the sooner he'll have them in it.

IV

In Virginia, Cold Harbor had convinced Grant that the direct approach to Richmond would cost more men than even the Army of the Potomac could afford to lose. He decided to move around the Confederate capital on the east and strike it through Petersburg, twenty-five miles to the south. On June 15 Grant's leading corps attacked the Petersburg fortifications, manned by sparse troops under Beauregard. The Union forces, anticipating an easy victory, went at their work in sluggish fashion; the Confederates threw everything into the battle. After three days of fighting Lee arrived, stopped the Federal advance, and the two armies settled into a siege.

A few days later Lieutenant Colonel Henry Pleasants of the Forty-eighth Pennsylvania Infantry had an idea:[16]

I was then commanding the first brigade of the second division of the 9th corps. That corps was then under the command of Major General Burnside. While commanding the brigade I frequently had occasion to go to the front line. I noticed a little cup of a ravine near to the enemy's works. I having been a mining and civil engineer many years before the war, it occurred to me that a mine could be excavated there. I examined the ground, and after I had satisfied myself that it could be done, I spoke to the officer next in rank above me, Brigadier General Potter, commanding the division. . . . He received the idea favorably, and wrote a note to General Burnside in relation to it. General Burnside sent for me, and I explained to him carefully the mode of ventilating the mine and everything about it. He seemed very much pleased with the proposition, and told me to go right on with the work.

Pleasants began his tunnel on the twenty-fifth of June. He soon discovered that apathy was a far tougher obstacle than Virginia clay:

My regiment was only about four hundred strong. At first I employed but a few men at a time, but the number was increased as the work progressed, until at last I had to use the whole regiment, non-commissioned officers and all. The great difficulty I had was to dispose of the material got out of the mine. I found it impossible to get any assistance from anybody; I had to do all the work myself. I had to remove all the earth in old cracker boxes. I got pieces of hickory and nailed on the boxes in which we received our crackers, and then iron-clad them with hoops of iron taken from old pork and beef barrels. . . .

Whenever I made application I could not get anything, although General Burnside was very favorable to it. The most important thing was to ascertain how far I had to mine, because if I fell short of or went beyond the proper place the explosion would have no practical effect; therefore I wanted an accurate instrument with which to make the necessary triangulations. I had to make them on the furthest front line, where the enemy's sharpshooters could reach me. I could not get the instrument I wanted, although there was one at army headquarters, and General Burnside had to send to Washington and get an old-fashioned theodolite, which was given to me.

Was there any reason why Headquarters could not have given Pleasants the better instrument?

I do not know. I know this: that General Burnside told me that General Meade and Major Duane, chief engineer of the army of the Potomac, said the thing could not be done; that it was all clap-trap and nonsense; that such a length of mine had never been excavated in military operations, and could not be; that I would either get the men smothered for want of air, or crushed by the falling of the earth; or the enemy would find it out, and it would amount to nothing. I could get no boards and lumber supplied to me for my operations. I had to get a pass and send two companies of my own regiment with wagons outside of our lines to rebel saw-mills and get lumber in that way, after having previously got what lumber I could by tearing down an old bridge. I had no mining picks furnished me, but had to take common army picks and have them straightened for my mining picks.

While Pleasants and his Pennsylvanians labored on their tunnel, Colonel Theodore Lyman wrote home of peaceful, lethargic days when war seemed to have gone off on a summer holiday:[17]

What shall I say of the Fourth? Our celebration could not well amount to much; the men have to stay too close in camp to do such things. The band came in the morning and serenaded, and there was saluting enough in the form of cannon and mortars from our right. This siege—if you choose to call it a siege—is a curious illustration of the customs of old soldiers. On the right—say from the Appomattox to a point opposite the Avery house—the lines are very close and more or less of siege operations are going on; so every finger, or cap, or point of a gun that shows above the works, is instantly shot at, in addition to which batteries and mortars are firing intermittently. Nothing could be more hostile! But pass to the division a little to the left of this, where our lines swing off from the enemy's, and you have a quite reversed state of things. There is not a shot! Behold the picket men, no longer crouching closely in their holes, but standing up and walking about, with the enemy's men, in like fashion, as near to them, in some places, as the length of the Brookline house. At one part, there was a brook between, and our pickets, or theirs, when they want water, hold up a canteen, and then coolly walk down to the neutral stream. All this truce is unofficial, but sacred, and is honorably observed. Also it is a matter of the rank and file. If an officer comes down, they get uneasy and often shout to him to go back, or they will shoot. The other day General Crawford calmly went down, took out an opera-glass and began staring. Very quickly a Reb was seen to write on a scrap of paper, roll it round a pebble and throw it over to our line. Thereon was writ this pithy bit of advice: "Tell the fellow with the spy-glass to clear out, or we shall have to shoot him." Near this same spot occurred a ludicrous thing, which is true, though one would not believe it if seen in a paper. A Reb, either from greenness or by accident, fired his musket, whereupon our people dropped in their holes and were on the point of opening along the whole line, when the Rebs waved their hands and cried: "Don't shoot; you'll see how we'll fix him!" Then they took the musket from the unfortunate grey-back, put a rail on his shoulder, and made him walk up and down for a great while in front of their rifle-pits! If they get orders to open, they call out, "Get into your holes, Yanks, we are ordered to fire"; and their first shots are aimed high, as a sort of warning. Their liberties go too far sometimes, as when two deliberately walked up to our breastwork to exchange papers; whereat General Crawford refused to allow them to return, saying very properly that the truce was not official, and that they had chosen to leave their own works and come over to ours, and that now they could carry back information of our position. They expected an attack on the 4th of July— I suppose as a grand melodramatic stroke on Grant's part; but, instead thereof, the Maryland brigade brought up their band to the trenches and played "Hail Columbia"; upon which, to the surprise of everyone, a North Carolina regiment, lying opposite, rose as a man and gave three cheers!

While the army took a holiday from war, Pleasants completed the tunnel—a main gallery 511 feet long, with left and right lateral galleries of 37 and 38 feet. At the ends of the lateral galleries 8,000 pounds of powder were placed.

The explosion was set for 3:30 A.M., July 30. Burnside's Ninth Corps was to pour into the breach made by the mine and move on to Cemetery Hill, an elevation four hundred yards distant. The Fifth and Eighteenth Corps would follow, fan out, and establish a position which, when exploited, would lead to the fall of Petersburg—and Richmond.

Burnside had planned to have his one division of colored troops lead the charge. The men had not been in battle, but they had been specially trained for weeks and were burning to avenge Fort Pillow. On the night of July 29 Meade ordered a change; white divisions would go in first, the Negroes would follow. The First Division, commanded by a newcomer, General James H. Ledlie, would lead.

Before 3:30 on the morning of July 30 Ledlie's troops were in position. The hour came; nothing happened. Four o'clock; still no explosion. (The fuse had died out at a splice, and two men had gone in to make a new one.) At 4:40 the mine was sprung.

Major William H. Powell of Ledlie's staff witnessed what followed:[18]

It was a magnificent spectacle, and as the mass of earth went up into the air, carrying with it men, guns, carriages, and timbers, and spread out like an immense cloud as it reached its altitude, so close were the Union lines that the mass appeared as if it would descend immediately upon the troops waiting to make the charge. This caused them to break and scatter to the rear, and about ten minutes were consumed in re-forming for the attack. Not much was lost by this delay, however, as it took nearly that time for the cloud of dust to pass off. The order was then given for the advance. As no part of the Union line of breastworks had been removed . . . the troops clambered over them as best they could. This in itself broke the ranks, and they did not stop to re-form, but pushed ahead toward the crater, about 130 yards distant, the debris from the explosion having covered up the abatis and *chevaux-de-frise* in front of the enemy's works.

Little did these men anticipate what they would see upon arriving there: an enormous hole in the ground about 30 feet deep, 60 feet wide, and 170 feet long, filled with dust, great blocks of clay, guns, broken carriages, projecting timbers, and men buried in various ways— some up to their necks, others to their waists, and some with only their feet and legs protruding from the earth. One of these near me was pulled out, and proved to be a second lieutenant of the battery which had been blown up. The fresh air revived him, and he was soon able to walk and talk. . . .

The whole scene of the explosion struck every one dumb with astonishment as we arrived at the crest of the debris. It was impossible for the troops of the Second Brigade to move forward in line, as they had advanced; and, owing to the broken state they were in, every man crowding up to look into the hole, and being pressed by the First Brigade, which was immediately in rear, it was equally impossible to move by the flank, by any command, around the crater. Before the brigade commanders could realize the situation, the two brigades became inextricably mixed, in the desire to look into the hole.

However, Colonel Marshall yelled to the Second Brigade to move forward, and the men did so, jumping, sliding, and tumbling into the hole, over the debris of material, and dead and dying men, and huge blocks of solid clay. . . . A partial formation was made by General Bartlett and Colonel Marshall with some of their troops, but owing to the precipitous walls the men could find no footing except by facing inward, digging their heels into the earth, and throwing their backs against the side of the crater, or squatting in a half-sitting, half-standing posture, and some of the men were shot even there by the fire from the enemy in the traverses. It was at this juncture that Colonel Marshall requested me to go to General Ledlie and explain the condition of affairs. . . .

I found General Ledlie and a part of his staff ensconced in a protected angle of the works. I gave him Colonel Marshall's message, explained to him the situation, and Colonel Marshall's reasons for not being able to move forward. General Ledlie then directed me to return at once and say to Colonel Marshall and General Bartlett that it was General Burnside's order that they should move forward immediately. This message was delivered. But the firing on the crater now was incessant, and it was as heavy a fire of canister as was ever poured continuously upon a single objective point. It was as utterly impracticable to reform a brigade in that crater as it would be to marshal bees into line after upsetting the hive; and equally as impracticable to reform outside of the crater, under the severe fire in front and rear, as it would be to hold a dress parade in front of a charging enemy.

A high command which knew nothing of the real situation continued to send troops forward. Powell again risked death to crawl out of the hellhole and urge Ledlie, for God's sake, to do something:

All the satisfaction I received was an order to go back and tell the brigade commanders to get their men out and press forward to Cemetery Hill. This talk and these orders, coming from a commander sitting in a bomb-proof inside the Union lines, were disgusting. I returned again to the crater and delivered the orders, which I knew beforehand could not possibly be obeyed; and I told General Ledlie so before I left him.*

General John W. Tyler, commanding a division of the Eighteenth Corps, saw Burnside's Negro troops make their belated and hopeless charge. The time was now seven o'clock:[19]

The crater was full of men; they were lying all around, and every point that would give cover to a man was occupied. There was no movement towards Cemetery Hill; the troops were all in confusion and lying down. I asked one or two officers there if an attempt had been made to move on Cemetery Hill. They said the attempt had been made, but it had failed. I then said, "You ought to intrench your position here, and you have too many troops here already to intrench. There are so many troops here that they are in each other's way; they are only exposed to this terrific fire of the enemy," which was then growing warmer and warmer, and was a very severe fire.

While I was talking to an officer—we had sought shelter in the crater —the head of the colored division appeared at the crest of the crater, and the division commenced piling over into the crater and passing across it on the other side as well as they could. I exclaimed, "What are these men sent in here for? It is only adding confusion to the confusion which already exists." The men literally came falling right over

* Six months later the Joint Committee on the Conduct of the War arrived at a conclusion: "Brigadier General J. H. Ledlie, United States volunteers, he having failed to push forward his division promptly according to orders, and thereby blocking up the avenue which was designed for the passage of troops ordered to follow and support his in the assault. It is in evidence that no commander reported to General Burnside that his troops could not be got forward, which the court regard as a neglect of duty on the part of General Ledlie, inasmuch as a timely report of the misbehavior might have enabled General Burnside, commanding the assault, to have made other arrangements for prosecuting it before it became too late. Instead of being with his division during this difficulty in the crater, and by his personal efforts endeavoring to lead his troops forward, he was most of the time in a bomb-proof, ten rods in rear of the mainline of the 9th corps works, where it was impossible for him to see anything of the movements of troops that were going on."—*Report*, Vol. I, 216 (second paging).

into this crater on their hands and knees; they were so thick in there that a man could not walk. Seeing that I was going to be covered up there, and be entirely useless, I thought I would go out. As I had no control over these troops, and supposing there were officers in command, I said, "If you can get these troops beyond this line so that I can get out, I will move my division right out and cover your right flank"; and I went back for the purpose of doing so. I met General Ord on our line at the head of my division. I said, "General, unless a movement is made out of the crater towards Cemetery Hill, it is murder to send more men in there. That colored division should never have been sent in there; but there is a furor there, and perhaps they may move off sufficiently for me to pass my division out." "Well," said he, "do so if they move." A very few moments after, I thought they had started to make a rush towards Cemetery Hill, and I immediately ordered my leading brigade, which was massed by regiments, to charge to the right of the crater. The colored division by that time had nearly, if not quite, all got into the crater; had passed to the right of it by perhaps fifty yards, and were all lying down . . . trying to cover themselves the best way they could.

The gnawing fear, the hatred that caused the war in the first place now broke all bounds. George S. Bernard, Twelfth Virginia Infantry, Mahone's brigade, shuddered at what he saw:[20]

I saw Confederates beating and shooting at the negro soldiers, as the latter, terror-stricken, rushed away from them. I saw one negro running down the trench towards the place where several of us stood, and a Confederate soldier just in his rear drawing a bead on him as he ran. The Confederate fired at the poor creature, seemingly heedless of the fact that his bullet might have pierced his victim and struck some of the many Confederates immediately in its range.

A minute later I witnessed another deed which made my blood run cold: Just about the outer end of the ditch by which I had entered stood a negro soldier . . . begging for his life from two Confederate soldiers, who stood by him, one of them striking the poor wretch with a steel ramrod, the other holding a gun in his hand with which he seemed to be trying to get a shot at the negro. The man with the gun fired it at the negro, but did not seem to seriously injure him, as he only clapped his hand to his hip where he appeared to have been shot, and continued to beg for his life. The man with the ramrod continued to strike the negro therewith, whilst the fellow with the gun deliberately re-loaded it, and, placing its muzzle close against the stomach of the poor negro, fired, at which the latter fell limp and lifeless. . . . It was a brutal, horrible act, and those of us who witnessed it from our position in the trench, a few feet away, could but exclaim: "That is too bad! It is shocking!" Yet this, I have no doubt, from what I saw and afterwards heard, was but a sample of many other bloody tragedies during the first ten minutes after our men got into the trench, many of whom seemed infuriated at the idea of having to fight negroes. Within these ten minutes the whole floor of the trench was strewn with the dead bodies of negroes, in some places in such numbers that it was difficult to make one's way along the trench without stepping on them.

Tyler's men still tried to reach the objective:[21]

My leading brigade charged over our line up to the enemy's works, and took possession of about one hundred yards of it; but there were no movements of the troops in and around the crater to advance on Cemetery Hill. At the time my leading brigade charged I directed the head of my second brigade to move out through a break in our works . . . so as to join hands on the right of the first brigade and charge the enemy's lines beyond. They succeeded in getting only about half way between our lines and the lines of the enemy, when they were stopped by the enemy's fire. The first brigade . . . succeeded in reaching the enemy's works, and took possession of about one hundred yards of it, when they laid down. I immediately sent word to my first brigade commander, who was within hailing distance—within sight, probably seventy-five yards off—to take his leading regiment and charge by the right flank, so as to sweep down the enemy's lines, while I brought up the second brigade. I was in hopes to take possession of a still greater length of the enemy's line. I returned to the brigade commander of my third brigade, and ordered him to mass his troops behind our lines, and hold them in readiness for any exigency. I had but just given him his instructions when my first brigade charged by the right flank, in obedience to my orders. I immediately passed over the line to the second brigade to give the command "Forward!"

I had got, probably, half way between our line and the enemy's lines —which were perhaps only a hundred yards apart at that point, and it was a very broken country, thick underbrush and morass—when, looking to the left, I saw the troops in vast numbers come rushing back, and immediately my whole first brigade came back, and then my second brigade on my right, and everything was swept back in and around the crater, and probably all but about one-third of the original number stampeded back right into our lines.

Men huddled in the crater for hours, groaning from wounds, begging for water. As early as 9:30 A.M. Meade issued a peremptory order for withdrawal. It could not be obeyed—enemy fire was too heavy. In mid-afternoon the Confederates themselves cleared the crater, driving hundreds back to the Union lines, capturing those who remained.

Major William H. Powell summed up the casualties which the Ninth Corps had suffered in two weeks:[22]

In the engagements of the 17th and 18th of June, in order to obtain the position held by the Ninth Corps at the time of the explosion, the three white divisions lost 29 officers and 348 men killed; 106 officers and 1851 men wounded; and 15 officers and 554 men missing—total, 2903. From the 20th of June to the day before the crater fight of July 30th these same divisions lost in the trenches 12 officers and 231 men killed; 44 officers and 851 men wounded; and 12 men missing,—total, 1150. . . . In the engagement of July 30th the four divisions of the Ninth Corps had 52 officers and 376 men killed; 105 officers and 1556 men wounded; and 87 officers and 1652 men captured,—total, 3828.

CHAPTER 33

"WAR IS WAR"

T HE CRATER was more than a ghastly blunder; it was proof that Richmond and Petersburg could be taken only by a long, costly siege. With Sherman apparently stalled before Atlanta, gloom enveloped the North—a gloom so oppressive that even a spectacular naval victory could not dispel it.

I

Protected by powerful forts, Mobile, Alabama remained after three years of war a safe port for blockade-runners. Moreover, during the summer of 1864, a new Confederate ram, the Tennessee, *was being ironclad here. Looking like a great turtle, the* Tennessee, *with six-inch iron plate covering her sloping sides, was considered the strongest, most powerful ironclad ever put afloat.*

One tough old Unionist who was determined that the Tennessee's *career would end where it began—in Mobile Bay—was Admiral David Farragut. A Federal assault force of 5,000 was gathered to capture the garrisons in the forts after a fleet of fourteen wooden ships and four monitors (or ironclads) had cleared the bay of Rebel vessels. On August 12, as "the gray glimmer of dawn was just beginning to struggle through a dense fog," Farragut roused his crews. A hasty repast of sandwiches and coffee was served, for the Admiral insisted that he would have breakfast inside Mobile Bay "at the regular hour." Shortly after five o'clock the Federal fleet steamed up the main channel. There disaster threatened Farragut:*[1]

. . . The vessels outside the bar . . . were all under way by forty minutes past five in the morning . . . two abreast, and lashed to-

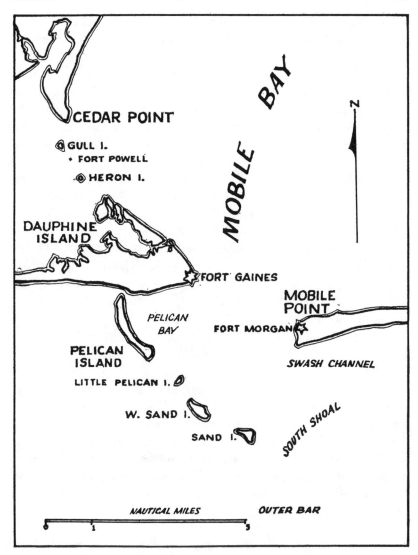

MOBILE BAY

gether. . . . The iron-clads were already inside the bar, and had been ordered to take up their positions on the starboard side of the wooden ships, or between them and Fort Morgan, for the double purpose of keeping down the fire from the water-battery and the parapet guns of the fort, as well as to attack the ram *Tennessee* as soon as the fort was passed.

It was only at the urgent request of the Captains and commanding officers that I yielded to the *Brooklyn* being the leading ship of the line, as she had four chase-guns and an ingenious arrangement for picking up torpedoes [mines], and because, in their judgment, the flagship ought not to be too much exposed. . . .

The attacking fleet steamed steadily up the main ship-channel, the *Tecumseh* firing the first shot at forty-seven minutes past six o'clock. At six minutes past seven the Fort opened upon us, and was replied to by a gun from the *Brooklyn*, and immediately after the action became general.

It was soon apparent that there was some difficulty ahead. The *Brooklyn*, for some cause which I did not then clearly understand, . . . arrested the advance of the whole fleet, while, at the same time, the guns of the Fort were playing with great effect upon that vessel and the *Hartford*. A moment after I saw the *Tecumseh* struck by a torpedo, disappear almost instantly between the waves, carrying with her her gallant commander and nearly all her crew. I determined at once, as I had originally intended, to take the lead, and after ordering the *Metacomet* to send a boat to save, if possible, any of the perishing crew, I dashed ahead with the *Hartford*, and the ships followed on, their officers believing that they were going to a noble death with their commander-in-chief.

I steamed through between the buoys, where the torpedoes were supposed to have been sunk. These buoys had been previously examined by my Flag-Lieutenant, I. Crittenden Watson, in several nightly reconnoissances. Though he had not been able to discover the sunken torpedoes, yet we had been assured by refugees, deserters, and others, of their existence, but, believing that from their having been some time in the water, they were probably innocuous, I determined to take the chance of their explosion.

With Farragut aboard the Hartford *was J. C. Kinney, a signal officer who was to establish communication between the fleet and the army after the forts had been passed. Kinney read the signal from the* Brooklyn, *"Our best monitor is sunk." Farragut answered briefly, "Go on!" Still, "for some mysterious reason," the* Brooklyn *halted, and Kinney felt a trickling of sweat:*[2]

It was the decisive moment of the day. Owing to our position, only our few bowguns could be used, while a deadly rain of shot and shell was falling on us, and our men were being cut down by scores, unable to make reply. The sight on the deck of the *Hartford* was sickening beyond the power of words to portray. Shot after shot came through the side, mowing down the men, deluging the decks with blood, and scattering mangled fragments of humanity so thickly that it was difficult to stand on the deck, so slippery was it. The old expressions of the "scuppers running blood," "the slippery deck," etc., give but the faintest idea of the spectacle on the *Hartford*. The bodies of the dead were placed in a long row on the side, while the wounded were sent below until the surgeons' quarters would hold no more. A solid shot coming through the bow struck a gunner on the neck, completely severing head from body. One poor fellow (afterward an object of interest at the great Sanitary Commission fair in New York) lost both legs by a cannon ball; as he fell he threw up both arms, just in time to have them also carried away by another shot. At one gun, all the crew on one side were swept down by a shot which came crashing through the bulwarks. . . .

Meanwhile, the men were working the guns that could be used, as though the sight and smell of blood had sharpened their appetites. There was no skulking; in fact there was no chance to skulk, if there had been such a disposition. They stood to their work, white and black side by side. There was no thought of social differences then; and whenever a shot was believed to have been well placed, the cheers of the men rang out above the roar of the guns. As our poet laureate, the Admiral's secretary, Harry Howard Brownell, of Hartford, sang of the fight, in the most graphic and truthful description ever written of it:

"Never a nerve that failed,
Never a cheek that paled,
Not a tinge of gloom or pallor.
  There was bold Kentucky grit,
And the old Virginian valor
  And the daring Yankee wit.

"There were blue eyes from the turfy Shannon,
  There were black orbs from the palmy Niger,
But there, alongside the cannon,
  Each man fought like a tiger.

One only doubt was ours,
  Only one fear we knew:
Could the day that dawned so well
Go down for the darker powers?
  Would the fleet get through?"

*The fleet not only went through, but Farragut also fulfilled his boast
and settled down to breakfast inside Mobile Bay at the regular hour.
The meal was suddenly interrupted by a messenger-boy shouting: "The
ram is coming down." J. C. Kinney, rushing onto the quarter-deck,
stood beside the admiral and the fleet-captain:*

The *Tennessee* fired two shots through her bow, and then kept on for
the *Hartford*. The two flag-ships approached each other bow to bow.
The two admirals, Farragut and Buchanan,* had entered our navy together as boys, and up to the outbreak of the war had been warm
friends. But now each was hoping for the overthrow of the other, and
had Buchanan possessed the grit of Farragut, it is probable that moment would have witnessed the destruction of both vessels. For had the
ram struck us square, as it came, bows on, it would have plowed its way
half through the *Hartford*, and, as we sank, we should have carried it
to the bottom, unable to extricate itself. But the rebel admiral was not
desirous of so much glory, and, just as the two vessels were meeting,
the course of the *Tennessee* was slightly changed, enough to strike us
only a glancing blow on the port bow, which left us uninjured, while
the two vessels grated past each other. He tried to sink us with a broadside as he went by, but only one of his guns went off, the primers in all
the others failing. That gun sent a shell through the berth-deck, above
the water-line, killing five men and wounding eight,—the last hostile
shot which has ever touched the *Hartford*. The muzzle of the gun was so
close that the powder blackened the ship's side. The *Hartford* gave the
ram a salute from ten heavy guns, each loaded with thirteen pounds of
powder and a solid shot, but the balls merely dented her side and
bounded into the air. The scene on the *Hartford* during the moment of
contact was of intense excitement. The admiral coolly stood on the port
quarter-rail, holding to the mizzen rigging, from which, at one time, he
almost could have jumped to the deck of the ram. Flag-Lieutenant
Watson, seeing him in this exposed position, secured him to the rigging by a rope's end with his own hands; so that during the day he was
twice "lashed to the rigging." As the ships came together, Captain
Drayton ran to the bow of the *Hartford*, and, as the ram sheered off to
avoid striking a square blow, he shook his lorgnette at it, and exclaimed, "The cowardly rascal; he's afraid of a wooden ship!"

The *Tennessee* now became the target for the whole fleet, all the ves-

* Franklin Buchanan, former Union naval officer, who commanded the Confederate squadron.

sels of which were making toward it, pounding it with shot, and trying to run it down. As the *Hartford* turned to make for it again, we ran in front of the *Lackawanna*, which had already turned and was moving under full headway with the same object. She struck us on our starboard side, amidships, crushing half-way through, knocking two portholes into one, upsetting two Dahlgren guns, and creating general consternation. For a time it was thought that we must sink, and the cry rang out over the deck: "Save the Admiral! save the Admiral!" The port boats were ordered lowered, and in their haste some of the sailors cut the "falls" and two of the cutters dropped into the water wrong side up, and floated astern. But the Admiral, nearly as cool as ever, sprang into the starboard mizzen-rigging, looked over the side of the ship, and, finding there was still a few inches to spare above the water's edge, instantly ordered the ship ahead again at full speed, after the ram. The unfortunate *Lackawanna*, which had struck the ram a second blow, was making for her once more, and, singularly enough, again came up on our starboard side, and another collision seemed imminent. And now the Admiral became a trifle excited. He had no idea of whipping the rebels to be himself sunk by a friend. "Can you say, 'For God's sake' by signal?" he inquired. "Yes, sir," was the reply. "Then say to the *Lackawanna,* 'For God's sake get out of our way and anchor!' " In my haste to send the message, I brought the end of my signal flag-staff down with considerable violence upon the head of the Admiral, who was standing nearer than I thought, causing him to wince perceptibly but I could not apologize until I finished signaling. . . .

The remainder of the story is soon told. The ram was unable to strike a single one of the Union vessels, while the concentration of fire upon it tore away everything except the solid iron. First, the rebel flag-staff fell; then the smoke-stack was shot away, and finally a well-placed shot from the monitor *Chickasaw* broke the rudder-chain, so that the great ram would no longer mind the helm, and she lay like a huge monster at bay. Already a fifteen-inch solid shot from the *Manhattan* had crushed through the iron armor and let the daylight into her, and finally a shell exploded in one of her port-holes, and a fragment seriously wounded the rebel admiral. And then, up through the iron grating of her deck came a staff, bearing a white flag. The firing ceased, and from vessel after vessel of the victorious fleet rang out such cheers as are seldom heard and never forgotten—cheers which meant victory after a hard and very doubtful struggle. And, as the cheering ceased, a dim echo seemed to come from below, where the wounded and dying, knowing the day was at last won, joined in the shouts of triumph, rejoiced that their sacrifice would not be in vain. So ended the fight.

For the wounded, battles never end that neatly, as Farragut knew:[3]

. . . Commander Johnston, formerly of the United States navy, was in command of the *Tennessee,* and came on board the flag-ship, to surrender his sword and that of Admiral Buchanan. The surgeon, Doctor Conrad, came with him, stated the condition of the Admiral, and wished to know what was to be done with him. Fleet Surgeon Palmer, who was on board the *Hartford,* during the action, commiserating the sufferings of the wounded, suggested that those of both sides be sent to Pensacola, where they could be properly cared for. I therefore addressed a note to Brigadier-General R. L. Page, commanding Fort Morgan, informing him that Admiral Buchanan and others of the *Tennessee* had been wounded, and desiring to know whether he would permit one of our vessels, under a flag of truce, to convey them, with or without our wounded, to Pensacola, on the understanding that the vessel should take out none but the wounded, and bring nothing back that she did not take out. This was acceded to by General Page, and the *Metacomet* proceeded on this mission of humanity. . . .

As I had an elevated position in the main rigging near the top, I was able to overlook not only the deck of the *Hartford,* but the other vessels of the fleet. I witnessed the terrible effects of the enemy's shot, and the good conduct of the men at their guns, and although no doubt their hearts sickened, as mine did, when their shipmates were struck down beside them, yet there was not a moment's hesitation to lay their comrades aside, and spring again to their deadly work.

II

The Battle of Mobile Bay and the fall of Fort Gaines and Fort Morgan soon afterward (on August 7 and August 23) gave the Union 104 guns and 1,500 prisoners, and closed one of the last remaining Southern ports; yet many thousands in the North persisted in believing that the South could not be subdued. The men of faint heart made Lincoln their target. On August 22 Thurlow Weed, shrewdest of Republican politicians, wrote to Lincoln's Secretary of State:[4]

When, ten or twelve days since, I told Mr. Lincoln that his re-election was an impossibility, I also told him that the information would soon come to him through other channels. It has doubtless, ere this, reached him. At any rate, nobody here doubts it; nor do I see any body from other States who authorises the slightest hope of success.

Mr. Raymond, who has just left me, says that unless some prompt and bold step be now taken, all is lost.

The People are wild for Peace. They are told that the President will only listen to terms of Peace on condition Slavery be "abandoned."

. . . That *something* should be done and promptly done, to give the Administration a chance for its life, is certain.

Henry J. Raymond, editor of the New York Times *and a Lincoln supporter whose loyalty could not be questioned, warned the President:*[5]

Rooms of the National Union
Executive Committee
Astor House, New York, Aug. 22, 1864

My dear Sir:

I feel compelled to drop you a line concerning the political condition of the country as it strikes me. I am in active correspondence with your staunchest friends in every state and from them all I hear but one report. The tide is setting strongly against us. Hon. E. B. Washburne writes that "were an election to be held now in Illinois we should be beaten." Mr. Cameron writes that Pennsylvania is against us. Gov. Morton writes that nothing but the most strenuous efforts can carry Indiana. This State, according to the best information I can get, would go 50,000 against us tomorrow. And so of the rest.

Nothing but the most resolute and decided action on the part of the Government and its friends, can save the country from falling into hostile hands. . . .

Henry J. Raymond

Raymond urged Lincoln to put Jefferson Davis on the spot by proposing a peace conference. Davis, Raymond was sure, would repel any reasonable offer and thus prove to a faltering North that the end of the war could come only through victory. Lincoln ignored the proposal, but he accepted Raymond's appraisal of public sentiment. Upon the receipt of the editor's letter Lincoln asked the members of his Cabinet to sign their names on the outside of a folded sheet of paper. Inside he had written:[6]

EXECUTIVE MANSION
WASHINGTON, Aug. 23, 1864

This morning, as for some days past, it seems exceedingly probable
that this Administration will not be reelected. Then it will be my duty
to so co-operate with the President elect, as to save the Union between the election and the inauguration; as he will have secured his
election on such ground that he can not possibly save it afterwards.

A. LINCOLN

III

*With victory almost in their possession, the Democrats met in Chicago
on August 29. Noah Brooks, correspondent of the Sacramento* Union,
*reported the temper of the convention and its choice of a candidate to
oppose Lincoln:*[7]

When the convention began to assemble in the great wigwam near
the lake shore, Vallandigham, Alexander Long, and Representative
Harris were the "stars" of the occasion. Calls for them were made at
every possible opportunity, and it was easy to see that these eminent
Peace Democrats were more popular than any other of the delegates
to the convention. It was a noisy assemblage, and it was also a Peace
Democrat convention. While Alexander Long was reading a set of
resolutions, which he proposed to have the convention adopt, asking for
a suspension of the draft until after the election, "Sunset" Cox interfered with a motion to have all resolutions referred, without reading or
debate, to the proper committee; whereupon he was roundly hissed,
and the spectators, who to the number of thousands filled the pit of the
great building, yelled, "Get down, you War Democrat!" much to his
discomfiture. The crowd of on-lookers in the pit was so great that
many of them climbed up and roosted on a fence which separated
them from the delegates, and their weight soon broke down this slender
barrier, creating the greatest confusion. Frantic ushers and policemen
attempted to preserve order; now and then a train crashing by on the
Lake Shore tracks close at hand added to the racket, and filled the
huge building with smoke and cinders.

Horatio Seymour, then governor of New York, was the president of
the Chicago convention; and it must be said that he made a much better
presiding officer than ex-Governor Dennison had proved himself in the
chair of the Republican convention at Baltimore. Seymour was tall,
fine-looking, of an imposing figure, with a good though colorless face,

bright, dark eyes, a high, commanding forehead, dark-reddish hair, and slightly bald. He had a clear, ringing voice, with a slight imperfection in his speech, and he was in the main an attractive and effective speaker, and a capital presiding officer. His opening address, which was very calm and cool, was not well received by the crowd, who evidently wanted something more heart-firing, and who incessantly shouted, "Vallandigham! Vallandigham!" But the distinguished exile, though he was not far away, was discreet enough to remain out of sight until his time came. His name was presented by the State of Ohio for membership of the committee on platform, and it was well known that the most important plank in that structure—that which related to the prosecution of the war—was his. . . . This was the famous clause which explicitly declared that "after four years of failure to restore the Union by the experiment of war, during which, under the pretense of a military necessity, or war power higher than the Constitution, the Constitution itself has been disregarded in every part . . . , the public welfare demands that immediate efforts be made for a cessation of hostilities with a view to an ultimate convention of the States, or other peaceable means to the end that at the earliest practicable moment peace may be restored on the basis of the Federal union of the States." This was the peace platform which Lincoln had expected. The war candidate, of course, was soon to be forthcoming. . . .

Although McClellan was the inevitable nominee of the convention, he did not receive the honor until one formal ballot had been taken. The first ballot gave him 150 votes; Thomas H. Seymour of Connecticut had 43 votes, and Horatio Seymour of New York received 7. There were two scattering votes cast. The roll-call had been finished, but the balloting was practically settled by the action of Missouri, which, having previously voted solidly for Thomas H. Seymour, now divided its strength, and cast 7 votes for McClellan, and 4 for Thomas H. Seymour, amid great cheering. There was then a great landslide of votes for McClellan, until all but the most uncompromising of the Peace Democrats had gone over to the inevitable nominee. Long, Vallandigham, and others held out until the last; and after all changes were made, the final vote was announced thus: McClellan, 202½; Thomas H. Seymour, 23½. Instantly the pent-up feelings of the crowd broke forth in the most rapturous manner: cheers, yells, music, and screams indescribable rent the air, and outside the wigwam a park of cannon volleyed a salute in honor of the nominee. The long agony was over, and men threw up their hats, and behaved as much like bedlamites as men usually do under such circumstances. When order was restored, Vallandigham, who until then had not spoken, mounted the rostrum, and moved that the nomination be made unanimous. It is impossible to describe the tremendous applause which greeted the appearance of the Ohio "martyr," who had only lately returned through Canada from his exile. His appearance on the platform, bland, smiling, and rosy, was the signal for a terrific outburst before he could open his mouth; and when his little speech was done, another whirlwind of applause greeted his magnanimous motion in favor of a war candidate. . . .

George H. Pendleton was nominated for vice-president without much difficulty. . . . The convention broke up in the most admirable disorder, and that night the city of Chicago seemed drunk with political excitement. Although many of the leaders had left by afternoon trains, the marching mobs halted under the windows of all the principal hotels, and demanded speeches until midnight fell, and something like silence reigned in the city.

IV

Before Atlanta, Sherman admitted that he was held in check by a stubborn defense. By late August he was convinced that Hood would hold fast though Federal artillery battered down every house. "It was evident that we must decoy him out to fight us on something like equal terms," Sherman wrote. Within Atlanta, Hood came to sense a change:[8]

The bombardment of the city continued till the 25th of August; it was painful, yet strange, to mark how expert grew the old men, women and children, in building their little underground forts, in which to fly for safety during the storm of shell and shot. Often 'mid the darkness of night were they constrained to seek refuge in these dungeons beneath the earth; albeit, I cannot recall one word from their lips, expressive of dissatisfaction or willingness to surrender.

Sherman had now been over one month continuously moving toward our left and thoroughly fortifying, step by step, as he advanced in the direction of the Macon Railroad. On the night of the 25th, he withdrew from our immediate front; his works, which at an early hour the following morning we discovered to be abandoned, were occupied at a later hour by the corps of Generals Stewart and [Stephen D.] Lee.

This movement of the Federals gave rise to many idle rumors in relation to its object. I felt confident that their plan would soon be developed; accordingly orders were issued to corps commanders to send out scouts in their front, and to keep Army headquarters fully advised of the slightest change in the enemy's position; to issue three days' rations and to be in readiness to move at a moment's warning. Instructions were likewise sent to General Armstrong, commanding the cavalry in vicinity of the West Point Railroad, to be most active in securing all possible information in regard to the operations of the enemy. . . .

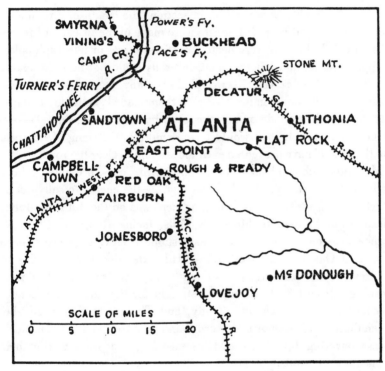

ATLANTA AND VICINITY, 1864

Early [on August 28], the enemy were reported by General Armstrong in large force at Fairburn, on the West Point Road. It became at once evident that General Sherman was moving with his main body to destroy the Macon road, and that the fate of Atlanta depended upon our ability to defeat this movement. . . .

On the 29th, the Federals marched slowly in the direction of Rough and Ready, and Jonesboro. . . . Had Sherman not been doubly protected by the Chattahoochee, deep intervening creeks and ravines extending to the river, beside the wall of parapets behind which he had thus far manoeuvered, I would have moved from East Point with our main body, and have attacked his Army whilst effecting these changes of position. This move not being practicable, I was forced to await further developments.

That Monday, August 29, Sherman was at Fairburn on the West Point Railroad, having a wonderful time:[9]

. . . The track was heaved up in sections the length of a regiment, then separated rail by rail; bonfires were made of the ties and of fence-rails on which the rails were heated, carried to trees or telegraph-poles, wrapped around and left to cool. Such rails could not be used again; and, to be still more certain, we filled up many deep cuts with trees, brush and earth, and commingled with them loaded shells, so arranged that they would explode on an attempt to haul out the bushes. The explosion of one such shell would have demoralized a gang of negroes, and thus would have prevented even the attempt to clear the road.

Meantime Schofield, with the Twenty-third Corps, presented a bold front toward East Point, daring and inviting the enemy to sally out to attack him in position. His first movement was on the 30th, to Mount Gilead Church, then to Morrow's Mills, facing Rough and Ready. Thomas was on his right, within easy support, moving by cross-roads from Red Oak to the Fayetteville Road, extending from Couch's to Renfrew's; and Howard was aiming for Jonesboro. . . . The next morning (August 31st) all moved straight for the railroad. Schofield reached it near Rough and Ready, and Thomas at two points between there and Jonesboro. Howard found an intrenched foe (Hardee's corps) covering Jonesboro, and his men began at once to dig their accustomed rifle-pits.

Hood had been outwitted, for all the brave face he put on the tale in his memoirs. Hardee with one corps was opposed by six corps under the command of Sherman. The climax came on the first of September. Tom Key, that adept Confederate artillerist, remembered:[10]

At 2 o'clock A.M. we were ordered to change base to the position occupied by General Lee, and Lee moved back to Atlanta.*. . . About

* Clearly Hood expected an attack from Sherman in front of the city. Since Lee fought with Hardee, the move gave Sherman his 6 to 1 advantage at the critical point.

3 o'clock the enemy made an attack upon General Govan's line which was facing to the north, and Key's and Swett's batteries opened such a deadly fire upon them that the line was broken. The Yankees then brought up three or four additional lines of batteries and concentrating for a desperate assault they charged up in this massed condition upon Govan's lines and against a portion of General Lewis's force which had just been thrown upon the right of Govan and, of course, had no defenses. General Govan's works were fairly strong though manned very thinly, about a rank and a half. Their fire upon the advancing enemy was steady, and that of Swett's and Key's batteries very destructive, but the immense numbers and overwhelming forces of the Yankees ran upon the works, sweeping over the right of Govan's fortifications, striking the lines at both batteries, and capturing the General and several hundred of his gallant Arkansans. The cannoneers continued to pour canister upon the enemy until they were within ten steps of their guns, and all of Key's battery were captured except twelve men. Swett's had a similar loss. . . .

The defense of the Confederates was noble, but they were too weak to contend against such numbers. . . . Night brought the bloody contest to a close, and in my opinion our opponents lost ten men to our one. . . . About midnight we reached Lovejoy Station where we halted for the night. I lay down but there was no sleep for me. The events of the day had been so unexpected and surprising that slumber could not drive sad thoughts from me.

Major James A. Connolly wrote his wife of those tense moments when "Our Corps had the honor of giving the grand finishing stroke to the campaign":[11]

. . . Oh, it was a glorious battle! But this Division suffered terribly. There was no chance of flinching there. Generals, Colonels, Majors, Captains and privates, all had to go forward together over that open field, facing and drawing nearer to death at every step we took, our horses crazy, frantic with the howling of shells, the rattling of canister and the whistling of bullets, ourselves delirious with the wild excitement of the moment, and thinking only of getting over those breast-works—great volleys of canister shot sweeping through our lines making huge gaps, but the blue coated boys filled the gaps and still rushed forward right into the jaws of death—we left hundreds of bleeding comrades behind us at every step, but not one instant did

that line hesitate—it moved steadily forward to the enemy's works
—over the works with a shout—over the cannon—over the rebels, and
then commenced stern work with the bayonet, but the despairing
cries of surrender soon stopped it, the firing ceased, and 1,000 rebels
were hurried to the rear as prisoners of war.

The General rode forward with the front line despite our protests
and had two horses shot under him during the charge, my tent
mate . . . was shot in the right arm, why the other five of us escaped
is one of the strange things found in a battle, when we were all
similarly exposed to the fire. When the cheer went up I recollect finding
myself in a tangled lot of soldiers, on my horse, just against the enemy's
log breast-works, my hat off, and tears streaming from my eyes, but
as happy as a mortal is ever permitted to be. I could have lain down on
that blood stained grass, amid the dying and the dead and wept with
excess of joy. I have no language to express the rapture one feels in the
moment of victory, but I do know that at such a moment one feels
as if the joy were worth risking a hundred lives to attain it. . . .

That night, as we lay on the ground without blankets or tents, we
were aroused by sound of distant explosions away off to the North, in
the direction of Atlanta, and many were the conjectures as to the cause,
but the afternoon brought us the intelligence that the enemy had
"evacuated Atlanta last night, blowing up 86 car loads of ammunition,
and destroying large amounts of public stores." Then went up more
lusty cheers than were ever heard in that part of Georgia before.

V

*"I was not so much pained by the fall of Atlanta," Hood declared, "as
by the recurrence of retreat, which I full well knew would further de-
moralize the Army and renew desertions." War has a meaning for
generals that civilians may not share—a fact that little Carrie Berry
could have explained:*[12]

Sept. 1. Thurs. . . . Directly after dinner Cousin Emma came down
and told us that Atlanta would be evacuated this evening and we might
look for the federals in the morning. It was not long till the hole town
found it out and such excitement there was. We have ben looking for
them all evening but they have not come yet. . . . I finished my stockings to day.

Sept. 2. Fri. We all woke up this morning without sleeping much last
night. The Confederates had four engenes and a long train of box cars

filled with ammunition and set it on fire last night which caused a grate explosion which kept us all awake. It reminded us of the shells—of all the days of excitement, we have had it to day. Everyone has been trying to get all they could before the Federals come in the morning. They have ben running with saques of meal, salt and tobacco. They did act rediculous breaking open stores and robbing them. About twelve o'clock there were a few federals came in. They were picketed. In about an hour the cavalry came dashing in. We were all frightened. We were afraid they were going to treat us badly. It was not long till the Infantry came in. They were orderely and behaved very well. I think I shall like the Yankees very well.

Sept. 3. Sat. The soldiers have ben coming in all day. I went up to Aunties this morning and she said that she had a yankee officer to spend the night with her. We have not seen much of them. Only two of them have ben here to beg some thing to eat. We have had a rainy day and we all feel gloomy.

Mary Rawson Day, whose husband was a captain in the First Georgia Volunteers, was pleasantly surprised those first days of September:[13]

Time after time had we been told of the severity of Gen. Sherman until we came to dread his approach as we would that of a mighty hurricane which sweeps all before it caring naught for justice or humanity. Our fear of his coming did not however prevent it. The forenoon passed slowly with nothing of importance . . . with dinner time came Father, who said that the Federals had taken possession of the city. OH! What a relief for me. I had expected them to enter in disorder, exulting loudly in the success of their enterprise. The capture of Atlanta seems to have been the acme of the ambition of the Northern government.

Atlanta was taken possession of quietly. About ten o'clock in the morning [September 2] the mayor, two councilmen with the principal citizens went out to invite them in. After some hesitation they marched in under the command of Gen. Slocum. . . . Immediately upon entering the town the stars and stripes were seen floating from the flag pole on the Franklin building. Father's store was used as a signal station. The signals were given with a blue flag having a large white star in the center and in the evening they used beautiful lanterns which were moved in different directions. This day has closed and is numbered with those past and gone and the moon once more shines over sleeping, silent Atlanta.

Sherman, who believed that "the brilliant success at Atlanta" had "made the election of Mr. Lincoln certain," probably expected this congratulatory message from Washington:[14]

EXECUTIVE MANSION,
WASHINGTON, D. C., September 3, 1864

The national thanks are rendered by the President to Major-General W. T. Sherman and the gallant officers and soldiers of his command before Atlanta, for the distinguished ability and perseverance displayed in the campaign in Georgia, which, under Divine favor, has resulted in the capture of Atlanta. The marches, battles, sieges, and other military operations that have signalized the campaign, must render it famous in the annals of war, and have entitled those who participated therein to the applause and thanks of the nation.

ABRAHAM LINCOLN,
President of the United States

Next day Sherman heard from an old friend:

CITY POINT, VIRGINIA, September 4, 1864—9 P.M.
MAJOR-GENERAL SHERMAN:

I have just received your dispatch announcing the capture of Atlanta. In honor of your great victory, I have ordered a salute to be fired with *shotted* guns from every battery bearing upon the enemy. The salute will be fired within an hour, amid great rejoicing.

U. S. GRANT, *Lieutenant-General*

VI

George B. McClellan also sensed that the fall of Atlanta made a difference in the presidential campaign. How could a man be elected on a platform which called the war a failure? In accepting the Democratic nomination McClellan threw away the party creed and wrote his own:[15]

ORANGE, N. J., September 8th
To HON. HORATIO SEYMOUR AND OTHERS, COMMITTEE, &c.:

GENTLEMEN: I have the honor to acknowledge the receipt of your letter informing me of my nomination by the Democratic National Convention recently held at Chicago, as their candidate at the next election for President of the United States.

It is unnecessary for me to say to you that this nomination comes to me unsought. I am happy to know that when the nomination was made, the record of my public life was kept in view. The effect of long and varied service in the army, during war and peace, has been to strengthen and make indelible in my mind and heart the love and reverence for the Union, Constitution, laws, and flag of our country impressed upon me in early youth. These feelings have thus far guided the course of my life, and must continue to do so until its end. The existence of more than one Government over the region which once owned our flag, is incompatible with the peace, the power, and the happiness of the people. The preservation of our Union was the sole avowed object for which the war was commenced. It should have been conducted for that object only, and in accordance with those principles which I took occasion to declare when in active service. Thus conducted the work of reconciliation would have been easy, and we might have reaped the benefits of our many victories on land and sea.

The Union was originally formed by the exercise of a spirit of conciliation and compromise. To restore and preserve it, the same spirit must prevail in our councils and in the hearts of the people. The reestablishment of the Union, in all its integrity, is and must continue to be the indispensable condition in any settlement. So soon as it is clear, or even probable, that our present adversaries are ready for peace upon the basis of the Union, we should exhaust all the resources of statesmanship practised by civilized nations and taught by the traditions of the American people, consistent with the honor and interests of the country, to secure such peace, reëstablish the Union, and guarantee for the future the constitutional rights of every State. The Union is the one condition of peace. We ask no more.*

Let me add what I doubt not was, although unexpressed, the sentiment of the Convention, as it is of the people they represent, that when any one State is willing to return to the Union it should be received at once with a full guarantee of all its constitutional rights. If a frank, earnest, and persistent effort to obtain these objects should fail, the responsibility for ulterior consequences will fall upon those who remain in arms against the Union, but the Union must be preserved at all hazards. I could not look in the face my gallant comrades of the army and navy who have survived so many bloody battles, and tell them that their labors and the sacrifice of so many of our slain and wounded

* In McClellan, who was willing to restore the Union with slavery, Frémont soon saw a greater menace than Lincoln. On September 22, Frémont renounced his own candidacy in an effort to strengthen Lincoln's opposition to McClellan.

brethren had been in vain, that we had abandoned that Union for which we had so often perilled our lives. A vast majority of our people, whether in the army or navy or at home, would, as I would, hail with unbounded joy the permanent restoration of peace on the basis of the Union under the Constitution, without the effusion of another drop of blood, but no peace can be permanent without Union. . . .

VII

In Atlanta, Sherman reached a decision:[16]

. . . I took up my headquarters in the house of Judge Lyons, which stood opposite one corner of the Court-House Square, and at once set about a measure already ordered, of which I had thought much and long, viz., to remove the entire civil population, and to deny to all civilians from the rear the expected profits of civil trade. Hundreds of sutlers and traders were waiting at Nashville and Chattanooga, greedy to reach Atlanta with their wares and goods, with which to drive a profitable trade with the inhabitants. I gave positive orders that none of these traders, except three (one for each separate army), should be permitted to come nearer than Chattanooga; and, moreover, I peremptorily required that all the citizens and families resident in Atlanta should go away, giving to each the option to go south or north, as their interests or feelings dictated. I was resolved to make Atlanta a pure military garrison or depot, with no civil population to influence military measures. I had seen Memphis, Vicksburg, Natchez and New Orleans, all captured from the enemy, and each at once was garrisoned by a full division of troops, if not more; so that success was actually crippling our armies in the field by detachments to guard and protect the interests of a hostile population.

I gave notice of this purpose, as early as the 4th of September, to General Halleck, in a letter concluding with these words:

"If the people raise a howl against my barbarity and cruelty, I will answer that war is war, and not popularity-seeking. If they want peace, they and their relatives must stop the war."

Among those who discovered that Sherman meant exactly what he said were Mary Rawson Day and her family:[17]

Thursday [September 8]. The order compelling all persons to evacuate the city was today plainly written out; we could not misunderstand it. All those whose husbands were in the service were to leave on Monday, while the remainder were given fifteen days to pack and leave. Now comes a deliberation as to which home we should choose. My grandparents, aunt and cousins were to leave on Monday for the South; besides I had relations and friends down in Southwestern Georgia. This would have made it much more pleasant for us and in addition to this, the climate was much more congenial in the South. That would undoubtedly have been our choice had not one great barrier here presented itself. This was that all men of the Confederacy were conscripted and were compelled to serve in the Army. This we knew Father could stand only a short time and he had no inclination to enter the Army. But a difficulty equally as great debarred us from entering life in the "Yankee land of Canaan," the difference in the currency occasioned this embarrassment. Father's property mostly consisted in lands and Confederate money so we had not means enough to venture North unless Pa could get something for his tobacco. So we were in a vacillating condition for several days.

Friday. Father made a visit to Col. Beckworth and Col. Easton to find if no disposition could be made of the tobacco, but ill fated weed though much loved and longed for by Yankee soldiery, you seem as ever to be only a source of trouble to those who possess and use you. No success was experienced and evening found us as undecided as in the morning.

Saturday dawns and another day of continued exertion and restless anxiety slowly passes. All of this time we had been wasting our precious fifteen days. Another appeal was made today to Col. Beckworth and he promised to see Gen. Sherman and obtain a written paper allowing us to dispose of our provisions and tobacco if he could. With this assurance we prepared to spend the approaching Sabbath.*

Hood attacked Sherman's order, clearing Atlanta of its civilian population, as a measure which "in studied and ingenious cruelty" surpassed "all acts ever before brought to my attention in the dark history of war." Sherman was ready to match Hood tongue-lashing for tongue-lashing any day:[18]

In the name of common-sense, I ask you not to appeal to a just God in such a sacrilegious manner. You who, in the midst of peace and

---

* Three days later Sherman gave his consent, and Mary wrote that they had resolved "to brave the severities of the cold North West, so we immediately prepared to emigrate to the prairies of Iowa."

prosperity, have plunged a nation into war—dark and cruel war—who dared and badgered us to battle, insulted our flag, seized our arsenals and forts that were left in the honorable custody of ordnance-sergeants, seized and made "prisoners of war" the very garrisons sent to protect your people against negroes and Indians, long before any overt act was committed by the (to you) hated Lincoln Government; tried to force Kentucky and Missouri into rebellion, spite of themselves; falsified the vote of Louisiana; turned loose your privateers to plunder unarmed ships; expelled Union families by the thousands, burned their houses, and declared, by an act of your Congress, the confiscation of all debts due Northern men for goods had and received! Talk thus to the marines, but not to me, who have seen these things, and who will this day make as much sacrifice for the peace and honor of the South as the best-born Southerner among you! If we must be enemies, let us be men, and fight it out as we propose to do, and not deal in such hypocritical appeals to God and humanity. God will judge us in due time, and he will pronounce whether it be more humane to fight with a town full of women and the families of a brave people at our back, or to remove them in time to places of safety among their own friends and people.

Some residents—among them the family of Maxwell R. Berry—could not find a way of leaving Atlanta (or did not honestly try to do so). As September faded in the occupied city, his ten-year-old daughter, Carrie, preserved the tedium and dreariness of a life disrupted by war:[19]

Sat. Sept. 24. This has ben a bright day and we all have ben ironing and cleaning up. We have had so much rain that a sun shiny day seems quite pleasant.

Sun. Sept. 25. Another long and lonely day without church. So cloudy we all lay about and read until we are all tired.

Mon. Sept. 26. I have not done much to day. I have ben up to Aunties several times to see Cousin Emma and Willie for the last time. They are going off to night for the north. We all feel so sorry to see her leave for we all feel so lonesome.

Tues. Sept. 27. This has been wash day. I went up to Aunties this evening and she gave me some quilt peaces and some doll clothes.

Wed. Sept. 28. This has been another rainy day. I have ben sewing some to day. I went up to Aunties and we brushed her hair for her.

Thurs. Sept. 29. We ironed to day and we got done by two o'clock and I went up to Aunties after I was done here and she gave me some rasenes.

Fri. Sept. 30. I have ben sewing some to day on my apron. There are so many soldiers pacing backward and forward.

From May to September, inclusive, Sherman calculated that the Atlanta campaign had cost him 4,423 killed, 22,822 wounded, and 4,442 missing—an aggregate loss of 31,687. The comparative Confederate casualties, by his reckoning, were 3,044 killed, 18,952 wounded, 12,983 missing—an aggregate loss of 34,979. But even in victory Sherman found reason for concern:[20]

General Thomas occupied a house on Marietta Street, which had a veranda with high pillars. We were sitting there one evening, talking about things generally, when General Thomas asked leave to send his trains back to Chattanooga, for the convenience and economy of forage. I inquired of him if he supposed we would be allowed much rest at Atlanta, and he said he thought we would, or that at all events it would not be prudent for us to go much further into Georgia because of our already long line of communication, viz., three hundred miles from Nashville. This was true; but there we were, and we could not afford to remain on the defensive, simply holding Atlanta and fighting for the safety of its railroad. I insisted on his retaining all trains, and on keeping all his divisions ready to move at a moment's warning. All the army, officers and men, seemed to relax more or less and sink into a condition of idleness. General Schofield was permitted to go to Knoxville, to look after matters in his Department of Ohio; and Generals Blair and Logan went home to look after politics. Many of the regiments were entitled to, and claimed, their discharge, by reason of the expiration of their term of service; so that with victory and success came also many causes of disintegration.

VIII

In Virginia, while an August sun still burned, Colonel Theodore Lyman went on an excursion down the James River to the headquarters of General Benjamin F. Butler, commanding the Army of the James:[21]

This was quite a festal day for us. The General, accompanied by the Frenchies,* Rosencrantz, Bache, Biddle and myself, paid a grand

* Two French officers, Colonel de Chanal and Captain Guzman, sent as a commission to observe the campaign, were the "Frenchies" aboard.

visit to Butler. Butler was in high feather. He is as proud of all his "fixin's" as a farmer over a prime potato patch. We first got on the Greyhound, an elegant steamer (Butler believes in making himself comfortable), and proceeded down the Appomattox, past City Point, and then bore up the James, passing Bermuda Hundred, with its flotilla of schooners and steamers. . . . We had got a good bit above Bermuda Hundred and were paddling along bravely when we came in sight of two gunboats; that is, common steamers with some heavy guns on board. There are many in the river and they go up and down to keep it clear. As we drew near, I saw the men were at quarters and the guns run out. We passed between the first boat and the high wooded bank, when I beheld the gunboat captain dancing up and down on the paddle-box and roaring to us: "The left bank is lined with sh-a-a-rp-shooters!" It would have edified you to have seen the swift dignity with which General Meade and his gallant Staff stepped from the open, upper deck to the shady seclusion of the cabin! Our skipper jingled "Stop her," with his engine-room bell, and stop she did. Here was a chance for war-god Butler. "Hey? What? Sharpshooters? Pshaw! Fiddledeedee! Stop her! Who said stop her? Mr. DeRay, tell the Captain to go on, *instantly!*" And Butler danced out on the open deck and stood, like George II at Dettingen, in "an attitude of fence." I, who looked for a brisk volley of musketry, fully expected to see him get a bullet in his extensive stomach. Meanwhile the Captain went on, and, as soon as we were clear, the naval party in the rear (or "astern," we ought to say) let go one big gun, with a tremendous *whang!* and sent a projectile about the size of a flour barrel on shore, severely wounding a great many bushes and trees. The other gunboat went ahead of us and kept up a little marine combat, all on her own hook. Whether there really were sharpshooters, I know not: I only think, if there *were*, it would be difficult to say which party was the more scared. . . .

During the summer stalemate, Horace Porter greeted important guests:[22]

Mrs. Grant had come East with the children, and Colonel Dent, her brother, was sent to meet them at Philadelphia, and bring them to City Point to pay a visit to the general. The children consisted of Frederick D., then fourteen years old; Ulysses S., Jr., twelve; Nellie R., nine; and Jesse R., six. Nellie was born on the 4th of July, and when a child an innocent deception had been practised upon her by her father in letting her believe that all the boisterous demonstrations and display of fire-works on Independence day were in honor of her birthday. The general was exceedingly fond of his family, and his meeting with them afforded him the happiest day he had seen since they parted. They were com-fortably lodged aboard the headquarters steamboat, but spent most of their time in camp. The morning after their arrival, when I stepped into the general's tent, I found him in his shirt-sleeves engaged in a rough-and-tumble wrestling-match with the two older boys. He had become red in the face, and seemed nearly out of breath from the exertion. The lads had just tripped him up, and he was on his knees on the floor grappling with the youngsters, and joining in their merry laughter, as if he were a boy again himself. I had several despatches in my hand, and when he saw that I had come on business, he disentangled him-self after some difficulty from the young combatants, rose to his feet, brushed the dust off his knees with his hand, and said in a sort of apologetic manner: "Ah, you know my weaknesses—my children and my horses." The children often romped with him, and he joined in their frolics as if they were all playmates together. The younger ones would hang about his neck while he was writing, making a terrible mess of his papers, and turn everything in his tent into a toy: but they were never once reproved for any innocent sport; they were governed solely by an appeal to their affections. They were always respectful, and never failed to render strict obedience to their father when he told them seriously what he wanted them to do.

Inside the Confederate lines Sidney Lanier watched Lee:[23]

The last time I saw him with mortal eyes—for with spiritual eyes many, many times have I contemplated him since—the scene was so beautiful, the surroundings were so rare, nay, time and circumstance did so fitly frame him as it were, that I think the picture should not be lost. There was nothing melodramatic in the circumstances, nothing startling, nothing sensational—which was all the more particularly in accord with his character, for this was one of those grand but modest, sweet souls that love simplicity and shrink from all that is loud and vulgar.

It was at fateful Petersburg on a glorious Sunday morning whilst the armies of Grant and Butler were investing our last stronghold there. It had been announced to those who happened to be stationed in the neighborhood of General Lee's headquarters that religious services would be conducted on that morning by Major General Pendleton of the artillery. At the appointed time I strolled over to Dunn's Hill where General Lee's tent was pitched and found General Pendleton ensconced under a magnificent tree, and a small party of soldiers with a few ladies from the dwellings near by, collected about him. In a few moments General Lee appeared with his camp chair and sat down. The services began. That terrible battery, Number Five, was firing very slowly, each report of the great gun making the otherwise profound silence still more profound. Even Hoke's line was quiet. I sat down on the grass and gazed, with such reverence as I had never given to mortal man before, upon the grand face of General Lee.

He had been greatly fatigued by loss of sleep. As the services progressed and the immortal words of the Christian doctrine came to our hearts and comforted us, sweet influences born of the liberal sunlight that lay warm upon the grass, of the waving leaves and trembling flowers, seemed to steal over the General's soul. Presently his eyelids closed and he fell gently asleep. Not a muscle of him stirred, not a nerve of his grand countenance twitched, there was no drooping of the head nor bowing of the figure. . . . As he slumbered so, sitting erect with his arms folded upon his chest in an attitude of majestic repose such as I never saw assumed by mortal man before; as the lazy cannon of the enemy anon hurled a screaming shell to within a few hundred yards of where we sat; as finally a bird flew into the tree overhead and piped small blissful notes in unearthly contrast with the roar of the war engines; it seemed to me as if the present earth floated off through the sunlight and the antique earth returned out of the past and some majestic god sat on a hill sculptured in stone presiding over a terrible yet sublime contest of human passions.

IX

North and South, newspapers reported what was happening in and around Atlanta and Richmond. Soon a campaign in the Shenandoah Valley dominated the news. Near Winchester, armies commanded by Jubal A. Early and Phil Sheridan, newly detached from the Army of the Potomac, faced each other. Early made the fatal error of underrating an unknown opponent:[24]

The relative positions which we occupied rendered my communications to the rear very much exposed, but I could not avoid it without giving up the lower Valley. The object of my presence there was to keep up a threatening attitude towards Maryland and Pennsylvania, and prevent the use of the Baltimore and Ohio railroad, and the Chesapeake and Ohio canal, as well as to keep as large a force as possible from Grant's army to defend the Federal Capital. Had Sheridan, by a prompt movement, thrown his whole force on the line of my communications, I would have been compelled to attempt to cut my way through, as there was no escape for me to the right or left, and my force was too weak to cross the Potomac while he was in my rear. I knew my danger, but I could occupy no other position that would have enabled me to accomplish the desired object. If I had moved up the valley at all [i.e., to the southwest], I could not have stopped short of New Market, for between that place and the country in which I was there was no forage for my horses; and this would have enabled the enemy to resume the use of the railroad and canal, and return all the troops from Grant's army to him. Being compelled to occupy the position where I was, and being aware of its danger as well as apprized of the fact that very great odds were opposed to me, my only resource was to use my forces so as to display them at different points with great rapidity, and thereby keep up the impression that they were much larger than they really were. The events of the last month had satisfied me that the commander opposed to me was without enterprise, and possessed an excessive caution which amounted to timidity. If it was his policy to produce the impression that his force was too weak to fight me, he did not succeed, but if it was to convince me that he was not an able or energetic commander, his strategy was a complete success, and subsequent events have not changed my opinion.

By September 19 Sheridan was ready. Two days later a future President of the United States—Rutherford B. Hayes—wrote to his wife:[25]

CAMP NEAR STRASBURG, VIRGINIA
September 21, 1864

. . . The fighting began at daylight Monday (19th), with our cavalry. Then the Sixth Corps fighting pretty well, joined in; and about 10:30 A.M. the Nineteenth took part—some portions of it behaving badly, losing ground, two guns, and some prisoners. We in the meantime were guarding the wagons (!). Since the fight they say Crook's command was the *reserve!*

By noon the battle was rather against [us]. The Rebels were jubilant and in Winchester were cheering and rejoicing over the victory.

We were sent for. General Crook in person superintended the whole
thing. At one o'clock, having passed around on the Rebel left, we
passed under a fire of cannon and musketry and pushed direct for a
battery on their extreme flank. This division was our extreme right. My
brigade in front, supported by Colonel White's old brigade. As soon as
we felt their fire we moved swiftly forward going directly at the battery.
The order was to walk fast, keep silent, until within about one hundred
yards of the guns, and then with a yell to charge at full speed. We
passed over a ridge and were just ready to begin the rush when we

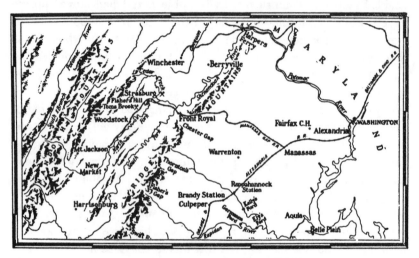

THE SHENANDOAH VALLEY, 1864
From *Atlas of American History*

came upon a deep creek with high banks, boggy, and perhaps twenty-
five yards wide.

The Rebel fire now broke out furiously. Of course the line stopped.
To stop was death. To go on was probably the same; but on we
started again. My horse plunged in and mired down hopelessly, just as
by frantic struggling he reached about the middle of the stream. I
jumped off, and down on all fours, succeeded in reaching the Rebel side
—but alone. Perhaps some distance above or below others were across.
I was about the middle of the brigade and saw nobody else, but hundreds were struggling in the stream. . . .

Soon they came flocking, all regiments mixed up—all order gone.
No chance of ever reforming, but pell-mell, over the obstructions, went
the crowd. Two cannons were captured; the rest run off. The whole of

Crook's command (both divisions) were soon over, with the general swinging his sword, and the Rebel position was successfully flanked, and victory in prospect for the first time that day.

We chased them three to five hundred yards, when we came in sight of a second line, strongly posted. We steadily worked towards them under a destructive fire. Sometimes we would be brought to a standstill by the storm of grape and musketry, but the flags (*yours* as advanced as any) would be pushed on and a straggling crowd would follow. With your flag were Twenty-third, Thirty-fourth, Thirty-sixth, and Seventy-first men, and so of all the others. Officers on horseback were falling faster than others, but all were suffering. . . .

Things began to look dark. The Nineteenth Corps next on our left were in a splendid line, but they didn't push. They stood and fired at long range! Many an anxious glance was cast that way. They were in plain sight, but no, or very little, effective help came from that handsome line. It was too far off. At the most critical moment a large body of that splendid cavalry, with sabres drawn, moved slowly around our right beyond the creek. They at a trot and finally with shouts at a gallop charged right into the Rebel lines. We pushed on and away broke the Rebels. The cavalry came back, and an hour later and nearly a mile back, the same scene again; and a third time; and the victory was ours just at sundown. . . .

We are following the retreating Rebels. They will get into an entrenched position before fighting again, and I suspect we shall not assault them in strong works. So I look for no more fighting with General Early this campaign.

Early continued to belittle his opponent, and his own losses:[26]

This battle, beginning with the skirmishing in Ramseur's front, had lasted from daylight until dark, and, at the close of it, we had been forced back two miles, after having repulsed the enemy's first attack with great slaughter to him, and subsequently contested every inch of ground with unsurpassed obstinacy. We deserved the victory, and would have had it, but for the enemy's immense superiority in cavalry, which alone gave it to him. . . .

A skillful and energetic commander of the enemy's forces would have crushed Ramseur before any assistance could have reached him, and thus ensured the destruction of my whole force; and, later in the day, when the battle had turned against us, with the immense superiority in cavalry which Sheridan had, and the advantage of the open country, would have destroyed my whole force and captured everything I had. As it was, considering the immense disparity in numbers and equipment, the enemy had very little to boast of. I had lost a few pieces of artillery and some very valuable officers and men, but the main part of my force and all my trains had been saved, and the enemy's loss in killed and wounded was far greater than mine. When I look back to this battle, I can but attribute my escape from utter annihilation to the incapacity of my opponent.

John B. Gordon, one of Early's major generals, faced facts:[27]

The pursuit was pressed far into the twilight, and only ended when night came and dropped her protecting curtains around us.

Drearily and silently, with burdened brains and aching hearts, leaving our dead and many of the wounded behind us, we rode hour after hour, with our sore-footed, suffering men doing their best to keep up, anxiously inquiring for their commands and eagerly listening for orders to halt and sleep.

Lucky was the Confederate private who on that mournful retreat knew his own captain, and most lucky was the commander who knew where to find the main body of his own troops. The only lamps to guide us were the benignant stars, dimly lighting the gray surface of the broad limestone turnpike. It was, however, a merciful darkness. It came too slowly for our comfort; but it came at last, and screened our weary and confused infantry from further annoyance by Sheridan's horsemen. Little was said by any officer. Each was left to his own thoughts and the contemplation of the shadows that were thickening around us. What was the morrow to bring, or the next month, or the next year? There was no limit to lofty courage, to loyal devotion, and the spirit of self-sacrifice; but where were the men to come from to take the places of the maimed and the dead? Where were the arsenals from which to replace the diminishing materials of war so essential to our future defence? It was evident that these thoughts were running through the brains of rank and file; for now and then there came a cheering flash of rustic wit or grim humor from the privates: "Cheer up, boys; don't be worried. We'll lick them Yankees the first fair chance, and get more grub and guns and things than our poor old quartermaster mules can pull." Distinct in my memory now (they will be there till I die) are those startling manifestations of a spirit which nothing could break, that strange commingling of deep-drawn sighs and merry songs, the marvellous blending of an hour of despair with an hour of bounding hope, inspired by the most resolute manhood ever exhibited in any age or country. . . .

When the night was far spent and a sufficient distance between the Confederate rear and the Union front had been reached, there came the order to halt—more grateful than sweetest music to the weary soldiers' ears; and down they dropped on their beds of grass or earth, their heads pillowed on dust-covered knapsacks, their rifles at their sides, and their often shoeless feet bruised and aching.

But they slept. Priceless boon—sleep and rest for tired frame and heart and brain!

Gordon saw no reason to minimize the Confederate defeat at Fisher's Hill, with which Sheridan capped his victory at Winchester:

General Sheridan graciously granted us two days and a part of the third to stop and rest and pull ourselves together for the struggle of September 22. The battle, or, to speak more accurately, the bout at Fisher's Hill, was so quickly ended that it may be described in a few words. Indeed, to all experienced soldiers the whole story is told in one word—"flanked."

We had again halted and spread our banners on the ramparts which nature built along the Shenandoah's banks. Our stay was short, however, and our leaving was hurried, without ceremony or concert. It is the old story of failure to protect flanks. Although the Union forces more than doubled Early's army, our position was such that in our stronghold we could have whipped General Sheridan had the weak point on our left been sufficiently protected. Sheridan demonstrated in front while he slipped his infantry around our left and completely enveloped that flank. An effort was made to move Battle and Wharton to the enveloped flank in order to protect it, but the effort was made too late. The Federals saw their advantage, and seized and pressed it. The Confederates saw the hopelessness of their situation, and realized that they had only the option of retreat or capture. They were not long in deciding. The retreat (it is always so) was at first stubborn and slow, then rapid, then—a rout.

CHAPTER 34

THE TEST
OF FREEDOM

O CTOBER BECAME a troublesome month for Sherman. Hood, intent on restoring the "fighting spirit" in his Army of Tennessee, endeavored to turn Sherman's right flank, destroy his communications, and thus force the Federals to loosen their hold on Atlanta. On the fourth of October, Hood struck the railroad at Acworth and Big Shanty, capturing some four hundred prisoners. But Hood was playing for much bigger game—the more than a million Federal rations at Allatoona.

I

Sherman rushed down troops from Rome to save those rations, but floods had spread the railroad tracks and at least a third of a badly outnumbered Federal force never reached the field. For the Union commander, John Corse, the situation looked glum. Yet few generals could excel Corse at fighting like a bobcat:[1]

Under a brisk cannonade, kept up for near two hours, with sharp skirmishing on our south front and our west flank, the enemy pushed a brigade of infantry around north of us, cut the railroad and telegraph, severing our communication with Cartersville and Rome. The cannonading and musketry had not ceased, when, at half-past eight A.M., I received by flag of truce, which came from the north, on the Cartersville road, the following summons to surrender:

AROUND ALLATOONA, October 5, 1864
COMMANDING OFFICER U. S. FORCES, ALLATOONA:

SIR: I have placed the forces under my command in such positions, that you are surrounded, and to avoid a needless effusion of blood, I call on you to surrender your forces at once and unconditionally. Five minutes will be allowed you to decide. Should you accede to this, you will be treated in the most honorable manner as prisoners of war. I have the honor to be, very respectfully yours,

S. G. FRENCH,
Major-General Commanding Forces C. S.

To which I made the following reply:

HEADQUARTERS FOURTH DIVISION, FIFTEENTH ARMY CORPS,
ALLATOONA, GA., 8.30 A.M., October 5, 1864.
MAJOR-GENERAL S. G. FRENCH, C. S. ARMY, ETC.:

Your communication demanding surrender of my command, I acknowledge receipt of, and respectfully reply that we are prepared for the "needless effusion of blood," whenever it is agreeable to you. I am, very respectfully, your obedient servant,

JOHN M. CORSE,
Brigadier-General Commanding Forces U. S.

I then hastened to my different commands, informing them of the object of the flag, etc., my answer, and the importance and necessity of their preparing for hard fighting. I directed Colonel Rowett to hold the spur, on which the Thirty-ninth Iowa and Seventh Illinois were formed; sent Colonel Tourtelotte over to the east hill, with orders to hold it to the last, sending to me for reënforcements, if needed. Taking two companies of the Ninety-third Illinois down a spur parallel with railroad and along the brink of the cut, so disposed them as to hold the north side as long as possible. Three companies of the Ninety-third, which had been driven in from the west end of the ridge, were distributed in the ditch south of the redoubt, with instructions to keep the town well covered by their fire and watch the dépôt, where were stored over a million rations. The remaining battalion, under Major Fisher, lay between the redoubt and Rowett's line, ready to reënforce wherever most needed.

I had hardly issued the incipient orders, when the storm broke in all its fury on the Thirty-ninth Iowa and Seventh Illinois.* Young's brigade of Texans, one thousand nine hundred strong, had gained the west end of the ridge, and moved with great impetuosity along its crest, till they struck Rowett's command, where they received a severe check; but, undaunted, they came again and again. Rowett, reënforced by the Ninety-third Illinois, and aided by the gallant Redfield, encouraged me to hope we were safe here, when I observed a brigade of the enemy, under General Sears, moving from the north, its left extending across the railroad.

I rushed to the two companies of the Ninety-third Illinois, which were on the brink of the cut running north from the redoubt and parallel with the railroad, they having been reënforced by the retreating pickets, and urged them to hold on to the spur; but it was of no avail. The enemy's line of battle swept us like so much chaff, and struck the Thirty-ninth Iowa in flank, threatening to engulf our little band without further ado. Fortunately for us, Colonel Tourtelotte's fire caught Sears in flank, and broke him so badly as to enable me to get a staff-officer over the cut with orders to bring the Fiftieth Illinois over to reënforce Rowett, who had lost very heavily.

However, before the regiment sent for could arrive, Sears and Young both rallied, and made their assaults in front and on the flank with so much vigor and in such force, as to break Rowett's line, and had not the Thirty-ninth Iowa fought with the desperation it did, I never would have been able to get a man back into the redoubt. As it was, their hand-to-hand conflict and stubborn stand broke the enemy to that extent, he must stop and reform, before undertaking the assault on the fort. Under cover of the blow they gave the enemy, the Seventh and Ninety-third Illinois, and what remained of the Thirty-ninth Iowa, fell back into the fort.

The fighting up to this time (about eleven A.M.) was of a most extraordinary character. Attacked from the north, from the west, and from the south, these three regiments, Thirty-ninth Iowa, Seventh and Ninety-third Illinois, held Young's and a portion of Sears's and Cockerel's brigades at bay for nearly two hours and a half. The gallant Colonel Redfield, of the Thirty-ninth Iowa, fell shot in four places, and the extraordinary valor of the men and officers of this regiment, and of the Seventh Illinois, saved to us Allatoona. So completely disorganized

* Illinois had sent six volunteer regiments to the Mexican War. In the history of the state, they were revered. Therefore, the first of the Illinois Civil War regiments was numbered the Seventh.

was the enemy, that no regular assault could be made on the fort, till I had the trenches all filled, and the parapets lined with men.

The Twelfth Illinois and Fiftieth Illinois arriving from the east hill, enabled us to occupy every foot of trench and keep up a line of fire that, as long as our ammunition lasted, would render our little fort impregnable.

The broken pieces of the enemy enabled them to fill every hollow and take every advantage of the rough ground surrounding the fort, filling every hole and trench, seeking shelter behind every stump and log that lay within musket-range of the fort. We received their fire from the north, south, and west face of the redoubt, completely in face of the murderous fire of the enemy now concentrated upon us. The artillery was silent for want of ammunition, and a brave fellow, whose name I regret having forgotten, volunteered to cross the cut, which was under fire of the enemy, and go to the fort on the east hill and procure some ammunition. Having executed his mission successfully, he returned in a short time with an arm-load of canister and case-shot. About half-past two P.M., the enemy were observed massing a force behind a small house and the ridge on which the house was located, distant north-west from the fort about one hundred and fifty yards.

The dead and wounded were moved aside, so as to enable us to move a piece of artillery to an embrasure commanding the house and ridge. A few shots from the gun threw the enemy's column into great confusion, which, being observed by our men, caused them to rush to the parapet and open such a heavy and continuous musketry-fire that it was impossible for the enemy to rally.

From this time until near four P.M., we enfilading our ditches and rendering it almost impracticable for a man to expose his person above the parapet, an effort was made to carry our work by assault, but the battery (Twelfth Wisconsin) was so ably manned and so gallantly fought as to render it impossible for a column to live within one hundred yards of the work. Officers labored constantly to stimulate the men to exertion, and most all that were killed or wounded in the fort met their fate while trying to get the men to expose themselves above the parapet and nobly setting them the example.

The enemy kept up a constant and intense fire, gradually closing around us and rapidly filling our little fort with the dead and dying.

About one P.M., I was wounded by a rifle-ball, which rendered me insensible for some thirty or forty minutes, but managed to rally on hearing some person or persons cry, "Cease firing!" which conveyed to me the impression that they were trying to surrender the fort.

Again I urged my staff, the few officers left unhurt, and the men around me, to renewed exertion, assuring them that Sherman would soon be there with reënforcements.

The gallant fellows struggled to keep their heads above the ditch and parapet, had the advantage of the enemy, and maintained it with such success that they were driven from every position, and finally fled in confusion, leaving the dead and wounded and our little garrison in possession of the field.

Sherman pressed hard after Hood, for, as the Union general subsequently confessed, a "wild" scheme possessed him:[2]

On the sixth and seventh, I pushed my cavalry well toward Burnt Hickory and Dallas, and discovered that the enemy had moved westward, and inferred that he would attempt to break our railroad again in the neighborhood of Kingston. Accordingly, on the morning of the eighth, I put the army in motion through Allatoona Pass to Kingston, reaching that point on the tenth. There I learned that the enemy had feigned on Rome, and was passing the Coosa River on a pontoon-bridge about eleven miles below Rome. I therefore, on the eleventh, moved to Rome, and pushed Garrard's cavalry and the Twenty-third corps, under General Cox, across the Oostenaula, to threaten the flanks of the enemy passing north. Garrard's cavalry drove a cavalry brigade of the enemy to and beyond the Narrows, leading into the valley of the Chattooga, capturing two field-pieces and taking some prisoners.

The enemy had moved with great rapidity, and made his appearance at Resaca; and Hood had in person demanded its surrender. I had from Kingston reënforced Resaca by two regiments of the army of the Tennessee. I at first intended to move the army into the Chattooga valley, to interpose between the enemy and his line of retreat down the Coosa, but feared that General Hood would, in that event, turn eastward by Spring Place, and down the Federal Road, and therefore moved against him at Resaca. Colonel Weaver, at Resaca, afterward reënforced by General Raum's brigade, had repulsed the enemy from Resaca, but he had succeeded in breaking the railroad from Tilton to Dalton, and as far north as the Tunnel.

Arriving at Resaca on the evening of the fourteenth, I determined to strike Hood in flank, or force him to battle, and directed the army of the Tennessee, General Howard, to move to Snake Creek Gap, which was held by the enemy, whilst General Stanley, with the Fourth and Fourteenth corps, moved by Tilton across the mountains to the rear of Snake Creek Gap, in the neighborhood of Villanow.

The army of the Tennessee found the enemy occupying our old lines in the Snake Creek Gap, and on the fifteenth skirmished for the purpose of holding him there until Stanley could get to his rear. But the enemy gave way about noon, and was followed through the Gap, escaping before General Stanley had reached the further end of the Pass. The next day, the sixteenth, the armies moved directly toward La Fayette, with a view to cut off Hood's retreat. We found him intrenched in Ship's Gap, but the leading division (Wood's) of the Fifteenth corps rapidly carried the advanced posts held by two companies of a South-Carolina regiment, making them prisoners. The remaining eight companies escaped to the main body near La Fayette. The next morning we passed over into the valley of the Chattooga, the army of the Tennessee moving in pursuit by La Fayette and Alpine, toward Blue Pond; the army of the Cumberland by Summerville and Melville Post-Office to Gaylesville; and the army of the Ohio and Garrard's cavalry from Villanow, Dirttown Valley, and Goover's Gap to Gaylesville. Hood, however, was little encumbered with trains, and marched with great rapidity, and had succeeded in getting into the narrow gorge formed by the Lookout Range abutting against the Coosa River, in the neighborhood of Gadsden. He evidently wanted to avoid a fight.

On the nineteenth, all the armies were grouped about Gaylesville, in the rich valley of the Chattooga, abounding in corn and meat, and I determined to pause in my pursuit of the enemy, to watch his movements and live on the country. I hoped that Hood would turn toward Guntersville and Bridgeport. The army of the Tennessee was posted near Little River, with instructions to feel forward in support of the cavalry, which was ordered to watch Hood in the neighborhood of Wills's Valley, and to give me the earliest notice possible of his turning northward. The army of the Ohio was posted at Cedar Bluff, with orders to lay a pontoon across the Coosa, and to feel forward to centre, and down in the direction of Blue Mountain. The army of the Cumberland was held in reserve at Gaylesville; and all the troops were instructed to draw heavily for supplies from the surrounding country. In the mean time communications were opened to Rome, and a heavy force set to work in repairing the damages done to our railroads. Atlanta was abundantly supplied with provisions, but forage was scarce; and General Slocum was instructed to send strong foraging parties out in the direction of

South River, and collect all the corn and fodder possible, and to put his own trains in good condition for further service.

Hood's movements and strategy had demonstrated that he had an army capable of endangering at all times my communications, but unable to meet me in open fight. To follow him would simply amount to being decoyed away from Georgia, with little prospect of overtaking and overwhelming him. To remain on the defensive, would have been bad policy for an army of so great value as the one I then commanded; and I was forced to adopt a course more fruitful in results than the naked one of following him to the South-West. I had previously submitted to the Commander-in-Chief a general plan, which amounted substantially to the destruction of Atlanta and the railroad back to Chattanooga, and sallying forth from Atlanta through the heart of Georgia, to capture one or more of the great Atlantic seaports. This I renewed from Gaylesville, modified somewhat by the change of events.

II

In the Shenandoah Valley Sheridan carried out a policy which Grant had decided upon three months earlier. On July 19, a few days after Early had frightened Washington, Grant had written to Halleck: "If the enemy has left Maryland, as I suppose he has, he should have upon his heels veterans, militiamen, men on horseback and everything that can be got to follow, to eat out Virginia clear and clean as far as they go, so that crows flying over it for the balance of this season will have to carry their provender with them."

The Valley had been granted a respite until Winchester and Fisher's Hill. Then its time came. Sheridan reported to Grant:[3]

WOODSTOCK, October 7, 1864—9 P.M.

I have the honor to report my command at this point tonight. I commenced moving back from Port Republic, Mount Crawford, Bridgewater, and Harrisonburg yesterday morning. The grain and forage in advance of these points up to Staunton had previously been destroyed. In moving back to this point the whole country from the Blue Ridge to the North Mountains has been made untenable for a rebel army. I have destroyed over 2,000 barns filled with wheat, hay, and farming implements; over seventy mills filled with flour and wheat; have driven in front of the army over 4,000 head of stock, and have killed and issued to the troops not less than 3,000 sheep. This destruction embraces the Luray Valley and Little Fort Valley, as well as the main valley. A large number of horses have been obtained, a proper estimate of which I cannot now make. Lieut. John R. Meigs, my engineer officer, was murdered beyond Harrisonburg, near Dayton. For this atrocious act all the houses within five miles were burned. Since I came into the Valley, from Harper's Ferry up to Harrisonburg, every train, every small party, and every straggler has been bushwhacked by people, many of whom have protection papers from commanders who have been hitherto in this valley. From the vicinity of Harrisonburg over 400 wagonloads of refugees have been sent back to Martinsburg; most of these people were Dunkers and had been conscripted. The people here are getting sick of the war; heretofore they have had no reason to complain, because they have been living in great abundance. . . .

Tomorrow I will continue the destruction of wheat, forage, etc., down to Fisher's Hill. When this is completed the Valley, from Winchester up to Staunton, ninety-two miles, will have but little in it for man or beast.

Henry Kyd Douglas, Confederate cavalry officer, confirmed Sheridan's report:[4]

Then [October 1], . . . Sheridan set his cavalry to work on their campaign of arson, rapine, and starvation. . . .

I try to restrain my bitterness at the recollection of the dreadful scenes I witnessed. I rode down the Valley with the advance after Sheridan's retreating cavalry beneath great columns of smoke which almost shut out the sun by day, and in the red glare of bonfires, which, all across that Valley, poured out flames and sparks heavenward and crackled mockingly in the night air; and I saw mothers and maidens tearing their hair and shrieking to Heaven in their fright and despair, and little children, voiceless and tearless in their pitiable terror. I saw a beautiful girl, the daughter of a clergyman, standing in the front door of her home while its stable and outbuildings were burning, tearing the yellow tresses from her head, taking up and repeating the oaths of passing skirmishers and shrieking with wild laughter, for the horrors of the night had driven her mad. It is little wonder that General Grant in his *Memoirs* passes over this work as if he could not bear to touch it, and that no reputable historian of the North has ventured to tell the truth about it and defend it, for it is an insult to civilization and to God to pretend that the Laws of War justify such warfare.

III

While Sheridan burned and ravaged in the Valley, Early re-formed his battered troops and started after the Federals. On October 18 Sheridan

*made a quick trip to Washington. The following morning, while he was
still at Winchester on his way back, Early struck. John B. Gordon reported an initial Confederate victory—and an inexplicable lapse on
Early's part:*[5]

The whole situation was unspeakably impressive. Everything conspired to make the conditions both thrilling and weird. The men were
resting, lying in long lines on the thickly matted grass or reclining in
groups, their hearts thumping, their ears eagerly listening for the orders: "Attention, men!" "Fall in!" "Forward!" At brief intervals
members of the staff withdrew to a point where they could safely strike
a match and examine watches in order to keep me advised of the time.
In the still starlit night, the only sounds heard were the gentle rustle of
leaves by the October wind, the low murmur of the Shenandoah flowing swiftly along its rocky bed and dashing against the limestone cliffs
that bordered it, the churning of the water by the feet of horses on
which sat Sheridan's faithful pickets, and the subdued tones or half-
whispers of my men as they thoughtfully communed with each other as
to the fate which might befall each in the next hour. . . .

The minute-hand of the watch admonished us that it was time to
move in order to reach Sheridan's flank at the hour agreed upon. General Payne of Virginia, one of the ablest and most knightly soldiers in
the Confederate army, plunged with his intrepid cavalry into the river,
and firing as they went upon Sheridan's mounted pickets and supporting squadrons, the Virginians dashed in pursuit as if in steeplechase
with the Union riders, the coveted goal for both being the rear of Sheridan's army. The Federals sought it for safety. Payne was seeking it to
spread confusion and panic in the Federal ranks and camps; and magnificently did he accomplish his purpose. . . .

As soon as Payne had cleared the ford for the infantry, Evans, with
his Virginians, North Carolinians, and Georgians, the old Stonewall
Brigade leading, rushed into the cold current of the Shenandoah, chilled
as it was by the October nights and frosts. The brave fellows did not
hesitate for a moment. Reaching the eastern bank drenched and cold,
they were ready for the "double quick," which warmed them up and
brought them speedily to the left flank of Sheridan's sleeping
army. . . .

The surprise was complete. The victory was won in a space of time
inconceivably short, and with a loss to the Confederates incredibly
small. Sheridan's brave men had lain down in their tents on the preced-

ing night feeling absolutely protected by his intrenchments and his faithful riflemen who stood on guard. They were startled in their dreams and aroused from their slumbers by the rolls of musketry in nearly every direction around them, and terrified by the whizzing of Minié balls through their tents and the yelling of exultant foemen in their very midst. They sprang from their beds to find Confederate bayonets at their breasts. Large numbers were captured. Many hundreds were shot down as they attempted to escape. Two entire corps, the Eighth and Nineteenth, constituting more than two thirds of Sheridan's army, broke and fled, leaving the ground covered with arms, accoutrements, knapsacks, and the dead bodies of their comrades. Across the open fields they swarmed in utter disorganization, heedless of their officers' commands—heedless of all things save getting to the rear. There was nothing else for them to do; for Sheridan's magnificent cavalry was in full retreat before Rosser's bold troopers, who were in position to sweep down upon the other Union flank and rear.

A little after sunrise we had captured nearly all of the Union artillery; we had scattered in veriest rout two thirds of the Union army; while less than one third of the Confederate forces had been under fire, and that third intact and jubilant. Only the Sixth Corps of Sheridan's entire force held its ground. It was on the right rear and had been held in reserve. It stood like a granite breakwater, built to beat back the oncoming flood; but it was also doomed unless some marvellous intervention should check the Confederate concentration which was forming against it. . . . It was at that hour largely outnumbered, and I had directed every Confederate command then subject to my orders to assail it in front and upon both flanks simultaneously. At the same time I had directed the brilliant chief of artillery, Colonel Thomas H. Carter of Virginia . . . to gallop along the broad highway with all his batteries and with every piece of captured artillery available, and to pour an incessant stream of shot and shell upon this solitary remaining corps, explaining to him at the same time the movements I had ordered the infantry to make. As Colonel Carter surveyed the position of Sheridan's Sixth Corps (it could not have been better placed for our purposes), he exclaimed: "General, you will need no infantry. With enfilade fire from my batteries I will destroy that corps in twenty minutes."

At this moment General Early came upon the field, and said:

"Well, Gordon, this is glory enough for one day. This is the 19th. Precisely one month ago today we were going in the opposite direction."

His allusion was to our flight from Winchester on the 19th of September. I replied: "It is very well so far, general; but we have one more blow to strike, and then there will not be left an organized company of infantry in Sheridan's army."

I pointed to the Sixth Corps and explained the movements I had ordered, which I felt sure would compass the capture of that corps—certainly its destruction. When I had finished, he said: "No use in that; they will all go directly."

"That is the Sixth Corps, general. It will not go unless we drive it from the field."

"Yes, it will go too, directly."

My heart went into my boots. Visions of the fatal halt on the first day at Gettysburg, and of the whole day's hesitation to permit an assault on Grant's exposed flank on the 6th of May in the Wilderness, rose before me. And so it came to pass that the fatal halting, the hesitation, the spasmodic firing, and the isolated movements in the face of the sullen, slow, and orderly retreat of this superb Federal corps, lost us the great opportunity. . . .

Sheridan heard the distant roar of artillery just in time:[6]

Toward 6 o'clock the morning of the 19th, the officer on picket duty at Winchester came to my room, I being yet in bed, and reported artillery firing from the direction of Cedar Creek. I asked him if the firing was continuous or only desultory, to which he replied that it was not a sustained fire, but rather irregular and fitful. I remarked: "It's all right; Grover has gone out this morning to make a reconnoissance, and he is merely feeling the enemy." I tried to go to sleep again, but grew so restless that I could not, and soon got up and dressed myself. A little later the picket officer came back and reported that the firing, which could be distinctly heard from his line on the heights outside of Winchester, was still going on. I asked him if it sounded like a battle, and as he again said that it did not, I still inferred that the cannonading was caused by Grover's division banging away at the enemy simply to find out what he was up to. However, I went down-stairs and requested that breakfast be hurried up, and at the same time ordered the horses to be saddled and in readiness, for I concluded to go to the front before any further examinations were made in regard to the defensive line.

We mounted our horses between half-past 8 and 9, and as we were proceeding up the street which leads directly through Winchester . . .

to the Valley pike, I noticed that there were many women at the windows and doors of the houses, who kept shaking their skirts at us and who were otherwise markedly insolent in their demeanor, but supposing this conduct to be instigated by their well-known and perhaps natural prejudices, I ascribed to it no unusual significance. On reaching the edge of the town I halted a moment, and there heard quite distinctly the sound of artillery firing in an unceasing roar. Concluding from this that a battle was in progress, I now felt confident that the women along the street had received intelligence from the battle-field by the "grape-vine telegraph," and were in raptures over some good news, while I as yet was utterly ignorant of the actual situation. Moving on, I put my head down toward the pommel of my saddle and listened intently, trying to locate and interpret the sound, continuing in this position till we crossed Mill Creek, about half a mile from Winchester. The result of my efforts in the interval was the conviction that the travel of the sound was increasing too rapidly to be accounted for by my own rate of motion, and that therefore my army must be falling back.

At Mill Creek my escort fell in behind, and we were going ahead at a regular pace, when, just as we made the crest of the rise beyond the stream, there burst upon our view the appalling spectacle of a panic-stricken army—hundreds of slightly wounded men, throngs of others unhurt but utterly demoralized, and baggage-wagons by the score, all pressing to the rear in hopeless confusion, telling only too plainly that a disaster had occurred at the front. On accosting some of the fugitives, they assured me that the army was broken up, in full retreat, and that all was lost; all this with a manner true to that peculiar indifference that takes possession of panic-stricken men. . . .

For a short distance I traveled on the road, but soon found it so blocked with wagons and wounded men that my progress was impeded, and I was forced to take to the adjoining fields to make haste. When most of the wagons and wounded were past I returned to the road, which was thickly lined with unhurt men, who, having got far enough to the rear to be out of danger, had halted, without any organization, and begun cooking coffee, but when they saw me they abandoned their coffee, threw up their hats, shouldered their muskets, and as I passed along turned to follow with enthusiasm and cheers. To acknowledge this exhibition of feeling I took off my hat, and with Forsyth and O'Keefe rode some distance in advance of my escort, while every mounted officer who saw me galloped out on either side of the pike to tell the men at a distance that I had come back. In this way the news was spread to the stragglers off the road, when they, too, turned their faces to the front and marched toward the enemy, changing in a moment from the depths of depression to the extreme of enthusiasm. I already knew that even in the ordinary condition of mind enthusiasm is a potent element with soldiers, but what I saw that day convinced me that if it can be excited from a state of despondency its power is almost irresistible. I said nothing except to remark, as I rode among those on the road: "If I had been with you this morning this disaster would not have happened. We must face the other way; we will go back and recover our camp."

John B. Gordon, bitter at Early's indecision, saw Confederate victory slip away:[7]

When the long hours of dallying with the Sixth Corps had passed, and our afternoon alignment was made, there was a long gap, with scarcely a vedette to guard it between my right and the main Confederate line. . . . Every Confederate commander of our left wing foresaw the crash which speedily came. One after another of my staff was directed to ride with all speed to General Early and apprise him of the hazardous situation. Receiving no satisfactory answer, I myself finally rode to headquarters to urge that he re-enforce the left and fill the gap, which would prove a veritable death-trap if left open many minutes longer; or else that he concentrate his entire force for desperate defence or immediate withdrawal. He instructed me to stretch out the already weak lines and take a battery of guns to the left. I rode back at a furious gallop to execute these most unpromising movements. It was too late. The last chance had passed of saving the army from the doom which had been threatened for hours. Major Kirkpatrick had started with his guns, rushing across the plain to the crumbling Confederate lines like fire-engines tearing through streets in the vain effort to save a building already wrapped in flames and tumbling to the ground. I reached my command only in time to find the unresisted columns of Sheridan rushing through this gap, and, worse still, to find Clement A. Evans, whom I left in command, almost completely surrounded by literally overwhelming numbers; but he was handling the men with great skill, and fighting in almost every direction with characteristic coolness. It required counter-charges of the most daring character to prevent the utter destruction of the command and effect its withdrawal. At the same instant additional Union forces, which had penetrated through the vacant space, were assailing our main line on the flank and rolling it up like a scroll. Regiment after regiment, brigade after brigade, in rapid succession was crushed, and, like hard clods of clay under a pelting rain, the superb commands crumbled to pieces. The sun was sinking, but the spasmodic battle still raged. Wrapped in clouds of smoke and gathering darkness, the overpowered Confederates stubbornly yielded before the advancing Federals.

There was no yelling on the one side, nor huzzahs on the other. The gleaming blazes from hot muzzles made the murky twilight lurid. The line of light from Confederate guns grew shorter and resistance fainter. The steady roll of musketry, punctuated now and then by peals of thunder from retreating or advancing batteries, suddenly ceased; and resistance ended as the last organized regiment of Early's literally overwhelmed army broke and fled in the darkness. As the tumult of battle died away, there came from the north side of the plain a dull, heavy swelling sound like the roaring of a distant cyclone, the omen of additional disaster. It was unmistakable. Sheridan's horsemen were riding furiously across the open fields of grass to intercept the Confederates before they crossed Cedar Creek. Many were cut off and captured. As the sullen roar from horses' hoofs beating the soft turf of the plain told of the near approach of the cavalry, all effort at orderly retreat was abandoned. The only possibility of saving the rear regiments was in unrestrained flight—every man for himself. Mounted officers gathered here and there squads of brave men who poured volleys into the advancing lines of blue; but it was too late to make effective resistance.

In the dim starlight, after crossing the creek, I gathered around me a small force representing nearly every command in Early's army, intending to check, if possible, the further pursuit, or at least to delay it long enough to enable the shattered and rapidly retreating fragments to escape. The brave fellows responded to my call and formed a line across the pike. The effort was utterly fruitless, however, and resulted only in hair-breadth escapes and unexampled experiences. . . .

At the point where I attempted to make a stand at night, the pike ran immediately on the edge of one of those abrupt and rugged limestone cliffs down which it was supposed not even a rabbit could plunge without breaking his neck; and I proved it to be nearly true. One end of my short line of gray-jackets rested on the pike at this forbidding precipice. I had scarcely gotten my men in position when I discovered that Sheridan's dragoons had crossed the creek higher up, and that I was surrounded by them on three sides, while on the other was this breakneck escarpment. These enterprising horsemen in search of their game had located my little band, and at the sound of the bugle they came in head-long charge. Only one volley from my men and the Federal cavalry were upon them. Realizing that our capture was imminent, I shouted to my men to escape, if possible, in the darkness. One minute more and I should have had a Yankee carbine at my head, inviting my surrender. The alternatives were the precipice or Yankee prison. There was no time to debate the question, not a moment. Wheeling my horse to the dismal brink, I drove my spurs into his flanks, and he plunged downward and tumbled headlong in one direction, sending me in another. How I reached the bottom of that abyss I shall never know; for I was rendered temporarily unconscious. Strangely enough, I was only stunned, and in no way seriously hurt. My horse, too, though bruised, was not disabled. For a moment I thought he was dead, for he lay motionless and prone at full length. However, he promptly responded to my call and rose to his feet; and although the bare places on his head and hips showed that he had been hurt, he was ready without a groan to bear me again in any direction I might wish to go. . . .

It was, perhaps, an hour or more after nightfall, and yet the vanguard of Sheridan's army had not halted. Considerable numbers of them were now between me and the retreating Confederates. The greater part of the country on each side of the pike, however, was open, and I was fairly familiar with it all. There was no serious difficulty, therefore, in passing around the Union forces, who soon went into camp for the night. Lonely, thoughtful, and sad—sadder and more thoughtful, if possible, on this nineteenth night of October than on the corresponding night of the previous month at Winchester—I rode through open fields, now and then finding squads of Confederates avoiding the pike to escape capture, and occasionally a solitary soldier as lonely, if not as sad and thoughtful, as I.

IV

With the election of 1864 drawing near, the Confederate government decided on a bold action to bring the war home to the people of the North. To lead a raid without parallel, the Rebels selected Lieutenant Bennett H. Young, twenty-one years of age and a veteran of Morgan's highly individualistic campaigns. Twice during 1864 Young had failed in attempts to release Confederate prisoners in Northern camps. When in October Young left Canada and journeyed through the night "with twenty reliable men" the little town toward which he traveled never ex-

pected to behold a bona fide Confederate. His objective: St. Albans, Vermont, fifteen miles south of the border.

Promptly at three o'clock on the afternoon of October 19, 1864, Young and his raiders took possession of St. Albans in the name of the Confederate States of America. John W. Headley, one of the invaders, told a crisp story:[8]

. . . All the citizens on the street were ordered to go into the square and remain. This was ridiculed by a number of citizens, when the Confederates began to shoot at men who hesitated to go, and one was wounded. The citizens now realized that the exhibition was not a joke.

The Confederates were prepared with fifty four-ounce bottles of Greek Fire * each, and while three men went to each bank and secured their money, the others were firing the hotels and other buildings, and securing horses and equipments.

The citizens had been held at bay during the proceedings, which had consumed perhaps three-quarters of an hour. But the city contained about 5,000 inhabitants, and many men began to come into the public square. A number of Federal soldiers appeared among them, and preparations were being made for an attack upon the Confederates, who were now ready to go when a few more horses were equipped.

Suddenly the people began to fire from windows, and three of the Confederates were seriously wounded. A skirmish now ensued, and one citizen was killed. The Confederates dashed their Greek Fire against the houses all about on the square, and began their march to escape, with the citizens and a few soldiers, some in buggies and some on horseback, in pursuit. Lieutenant Young took the road to Shelburne, some eight miles distant, and was beyond the reach of the pursuers until at Shelburne he reached a bridge over a river, on which a team was found crossing with a load of hay, for which he was obliged to wait. The pursuers approached, when the Confederates halted and opened fire, at the same time halting the team and turning it upon the bridge set fire to the hay, which fired and destroyed the bridge. The pursuers did not again overtake the Confederates. Lieutenant Young and his men, however,

---

* Greek fire, an inflammable chemical mixture, was used by Byzantine Greeks during the Middle Ages to set fire to enemy ships and to defend Constantinople. The Confederate raiders knew very little about it, except that the moment it was exposed to air it would blaze and burn everything it touched. It was a colorless liquid.

pushed forward and reached the border line of Canada about nine
o'clock that night. . . .

Next day Young learned that some of his men had been arrested at
Phillipsburg, Quebec. He had decided to give himself up to the Cana-
dian authorities, but the Vermonters got there first:

Young stopped at a farm-house, and leaving his revolvers in an adjoining room, he sat at the only fire, which was in the kitchen, to get
warm. To his surprise, about twenty-five people from St. Albans, in
pursuit of his party, learning that there was a stranger in the house,
suddenly rushed in and reached Young before he could get to his pistols, which they secured. They promptly seized him and at once proceeded to beat him with the pistols and with swords.

The American party now started with Young to return to St. Albans.
They could have killed him, but doubtless deemed it important to deliver him alive in St. Albans for several reasons. They put Young in an
open wagon with two men on each side and one in his rear, all in the
wagon. The men were excited and carried their pistols cocked, badger-
ing him with threats to shoot, while they denounced him in unmeasured
terms. Young, however, continued to protest against their proceedings,
insisting that they were in violation of British neutrality, but they said
they did not care a d--n for British law or the British nation. The front
gate was some two hundred feet from the house. The road which passed
in front of the house led from the United States to Phillipsburg. When
they reached the gate to pass out, Young suddenly knocked the men
from each side with his arms, seized the reins, and quickly turning the
horses, drove toward Phillipsburg. But his captors, who were apparently paralyzed for a moment, soon recovered, and pounced upon him
with their pistols and swords. In the midst of the melee, and fortunately
for Young, a British officer happened upon the scene. Young told him
of his character—that of a Confederate officer on British soil and entitled to protection, that his captors were Americans who proposed to
take him without any authority to the United States in violation of British neutrality and in defiance of British law.

Assured by the British officer that other Confederate captives would be
sent to St. Albans next day, the Vermonters agreed that Young should
be taken to Phillipsburg—the last they would see of him:

That night Lieutenant Young and his five men were carried to St. Johns, a distance of about twenty miles, and placed in jail. Here a large garrison of British Regulars was stationed, who manifested the warmest friendship for the prisoners. They went so far as to suggest to Lieutenant Young that he and his men might be rescued. They extended every courtesy, and the citizens were likewise friendly and hospitable to the prisoners. Lieutenant Young and his comrades concluded that it would be unwise now to evade the issue and preferred to await their fate in the courts of Canada, since their extradition had been demanded by the Government of the United States.*

V

Mobile Bay had been closed to the Confederacy, Atlanta had fallen, the Shenandoah Valley—granary of Lee's army—could no longer provide food for a regiment. Yet Jefferson Davis, addressing the Confederate Congress on November 7, could see no reason for discouragement in recent events:[9]

. . . At the beginning of the year the State of Texas was partially in possession of the enemy, and large portions of Louisiana and Arkansas lay apparently defenseless. Of the Federal soldiers who invaded Texas, none are known to remain except as prisoners of war. In northwestern Louisiana a large and well-appointed army, aided by a powerful fleet, was repeatedly defeated, and deemed itself fortunate in finally escaping with a loss of one-third of its numbers, a large part of its military trains, and many transports and gunboats. The enemy's occupation of that State is reduced to the narrow district commanded by the guns of his fleet. Arkansas has been recovered with the exception of a few fortified posts, while our forces have penetrated into central Missouri, affording to our oppressed brethren in that State an opportunity, of which many have availed themselves, of striking for liberation from the tyranny to which they have been subjected.

On the east of the Mississippi, in spite of some reverses, we have much cause for gratulation. The enemy hoped to effect during the present year, by concentration of forces, the conquest which he had previously failed to accomplish by more extended operations. Compelled therefore to withdraw or seriously to weaken the strength of the armies

* Canadian sentiment in that locality favored Young and his raiders. They were set free.

of occupation at different points, he has afforded us the opportunity of recovering possession of extensive districts of our territory. Nearly the whole of northern and western Mississippi, of northern Alabama, and of western Tennessee are again in our possession, and all attempts to penetrate from the coast line into the interior of the Atlantic and Gulf States have been baffled. On the entire ocean and gulf coast of the Confederacy the whole success of the enemy, with the enormous naval forces at his command, has been limited to the capture of the outer defenses of Mobile Bay.

If we now turn to the results accomplished by the two great armies, so confidently relied on by the invaders as sufficient to secure the subversion of our Government and the subjugation of our people to foreign domination, we have still greater cause for devout gratitude to Divine Power. In southwestern Virginia successive armies, which threatened the capture of Lynchburg and Saltville, have been routed and driven out of the country, and a portion of eastern Tennessee reconquered by our troops. In northern Virginia extensive districts formerly occupied by the enemy are now free from their presence. In the lower Valley their general, rendered desperate by his inability to maintain a hostile occupation, has resorted to the infamous expedient of converting a fruitful land into a desert by burning its mills, granaries, and homesteads, and destroying the food, standing crops, live stock, and agricultural implements of peaceful noncombatants. The main army, after a series of defeats in which its losses have been enormous, after attempts by raiding parties to break up our railroad communications, which have resulted in the destruction of a large part of the cavalry engaged in the work, after constant repulse of repeated assaults on our defensive lines, is, with the aid of heavy reënforcements, but with, it is hoped, waning prospect of further progress in the design, still engaged in an effort commenced more than four months ago to capture the town of Petersburg.

The army of General Sherman, although succeeding at the end of the summer in obtaining possession of Atlanta, has been unable to secure any ultimate advantage from this success. The same general, who in February last marched a large army from Vicksburg to Meridian with no other result than being forced to march back again, was able, by the aid of greatly increased numbers and after much delay, to force a passage from Chattanooga to Atlanta, only to be for the second time compelled to withdraw on the line of his advance without obtaining control of a single line of territory beyond the narrow track of his march, and without gaining aught beyond the precarious possession of a few fortified points in which he is compelled to maintain heavy garrisons and which are menaced with recapture.

Davis advanced a novel theory of military invincibility:

The lessons afforded by the history of this war are fraught with instruction and encouragement. Repeatedly during the war have formidable expeditions been directed by the enemy against points ignorantly supposed to be of vital importance to the Confederacy. Some of these expeditions have, at immense cost, been successful, but in no instance have the promised fruits been reaped. Again, in the present campaign was the delusion fondly cherished that the capture of Atlanta and Richmond would, if effected, end the war by the overthrow of our Government and the submission of our people. We can now judge by experience how unimportant is the influence of the former event upon our capacity for defense, upon the courage and spirit of our people, and the stability of the Government. We may in like manner judge that if the campaign against Richmond had resulted in success instead of failure; if the valor of the army, under the leadership of its accomplished commander, had resisted in vain the overwhelming masses which were, on the contrary, decisively repulsed; if we had been compelled to evacuate Richmond as well as Atlanta—the Confederacy would have remained as erect and defiant as ever. Nothing could have been changed in the purpose of its Government, in the indomitable valor of its troops, or in the unquenchable spirit of its people. The baffled and disappointed foe would in vain have scanned the reports of your proceedings, at some new legislative seat, for any indication that progress had been made in his gigantic task of conquering a free people. The truth so patent to us must ere long be forced upon the reluctant Northern mind. There are no vital points on the preservation of which the continued existence of the Confederacy depends. There is no military success of the enemy which can accomplish its destruction. Not the fall of Richmond, nor Wilmington, nor Charleston, nor Savannah, nor Mobile, nor all of them combined, can save the enemy from the constant and exhaustive drain of blood and treasure which must continue until he shall discover that no peace is attainable unless based on the recognition of our indefeasible rights.

Davis saw hope for the Confederacy in the Northern peace movement:

The disposition of this Government for a peaceful solution of the issues which the enemy has referred to the arbitrament of arms has been too often manifested and is too well known to need new assurances. But while it is true that individuals and parties in the United States have indicated a desire to substitute reason for force, and by negotiations to stop the further sacrifice of human life, and to arrest the calamities which now afflict both countries, the authorities who control the Government of our enemies have too often and too clearly expressed their resolution to make no peace, except on terms of our unconditional submission and degradation, to leave us any hope of the cessation of hostilities until the delusion of their ability to conquer us is dispelled. Among those who are already disposed for peace many are actuated by principle and by disapproval and abhorrence of the iniquitous warfare that their Government is waging, while others are moved by the conviction that it is no longer to the interest of the United States to continue a struggle in which success is unattainable. Whenever this fast-growing conviction shall have taken firm root in the minds of a majority of the Northern people, there will be produced that willingness to negotiate for peace which is now confined to our side. Peace is manifestly impossible unless desired by both parties to this war, and the disposition for it among our enemies will be best and most certainly evoked by the demonstration on our part of ability and unshaken determination to defend our rights, and to hold no earthly price too dear for their purchase. Whenever there shall be on the part of our enemies a desire for peace, there will be no difficulty in finding means by which negotiation can be opened; but it is obvious that no agency can be called into action until this desire shall be mutual. When that contingency shall happen, the Government, to which is confided the treaty-making power, can be at no loss for means adapted to accomplish so desirable an end. In the hope that the day will soon be reached when under Divine favor these States may be allowed to enter on their former peaceful pursuits and to develop the abundant natural resources with which they are blessed, let us, then, resolutely continue to devote our united and unimpaired energies to the defense of our homes, our lives, and our liberties. This is the true path to peace. Let us tread it with confidence in the assured result.

VI

Davis's reading of the Northern public mind was two months out of date. Soldiers whose states permitted them to vote in the field forecast the verdict of the North. Captain J. N. Jones, of the Sixth New Hamp-

shire, watched a lifelong Democrat succumb to some Republican electioneering:[10]

On the morning of that [election] day, at roll-call, I told the men of my company that there would be no drill, and that at nine o'clock A.M. opportunity to vote would be given all of them who were legal voters in New Hampshire. The law made the three ranking officers in each company judges of election. Having no lieutenant, I invited two sergeants to assist me. My tent was about six feet by seven, and sunk into the ground twelve or fifteen inches for greater security against bullets that might come straying around at any time. It was noticed, however, that on that day the rebels were unusually quiet, firing scarcely a shot. A cigar box answered for a ballot box. The state furnished blanks for recording each voter's name, together with that of the town he claimed to be his residence, and for whom he voted. In case, therefore, a man voted who had no right to do so, his vote could be thrown out. The polls having been declared open, and both Democratic and Republican votes placed upon the table,* the men came up, were registered, voted and retired. There was one man, a good specimen of the New Hampshire voter who goes to town meeting and makes a day of it. He seemed in no hurry to vote, and I invited him to take a seat on a hard-bread box at the mouth of the tent. He had served almost three years; had been with the regiment in its every battle; had been slightly wounded several times—was, indeed, a good soldier. At last he said,—"Say, captain, what do you think of the election?" To my reply, "I guess it is all right," he responded, "Well, what do you think of voting? I have always been a Democrat, and never voted anything but the Democratic ticket in my life." "All right," said I, "there are Democratic ballots—vote just as you please. If you can't do so after having gone through what you have, we had better all go home. I shall vote for Lincoln, but do you vote just as you choose." "Well," said he, "I have been thinking about voting for Lincoln. I believe he is a pretty good man." Then taking a Republican ballot in one hand and a Democratic ballot in the other, he rested his elbows on his knees and scanned the tickets in silence. Seeing his dilemma, I read aloud and as impressively as I could, the following lines of poetry printed on the back of the Republican ticket, while he listened attentively:

* The Australian or secret ballot was still a device of the future. In 1864 a voter registered his choice by taking the printed ballot of his party and depositing it in the ballot box.

"What! hoist the white flag when our triumph is nigh!
What! crouch before treason—make freedom a lie!
What! spike all our guns when the foe is at bay,
With his flags and black banners fast dropping away!"

I added the response, "Not much!" and he, without saying a word, put the Lincoln ballot into the box, had his name recorded, and walked away. Company F voted solid for Lincoln, of free choice and without undue influence. And it is gratifying to record the fact that the soldiers' election was likewise a fair one throughout the army.

In Union lines before Petersburg, cheers resounded. Theodore Gerrish of the Twentieth Maine discovered why:[11]

On Tuesday, November 8th, our regiment voted for the candidates for the Presidency; Abraham Lincoln received one hundred and thirty-seven votes, George B. McClellan, thirteen. When the news of the re-election of President Lincoln by such an overwhelming majority reached the army of the Potomac, the men were wild with excitement. From the Weldon railroad, along our entire line, past Petersburgh, across the James river, in the intrenchments away round to Richmond, our men cheered until they were hoarse. The rebels heard the cheering, and supposing that we had learned of some greater victory to our arms, were anxious to know the news. At a point where the lines came within a few rods of each other, our men heard a voice from behind the rebel breastworks, "Say, Yank." "Hilloa, Johnny." "Don't fire, Yank." "All right, Johnny." "What are you'uns all cheering for?" "Big victory on our side." "What is it, Yank?" came the eager response. "Old Abe has cleaned all your fellers out up North." "You don't say so, Yank?" "Fact; gobbled the whole concern, there is not peace men enough left in the whole North to make a corporal's guard." Then there was an anxious conversation among the rebels, and the voice of the spokesman was again heard. "Well, Yank, we cheered when we heard that your little Mac was nominated, but we don't feel much like cheering now."

In Washington, John Hay sketched a President unperturbed by the uncertainties of election day:[12]

Nov. 8. The house has been still and almost deserted today. Everybody in Washington, not at home voting, seems ashamed of it and stays away from the President.

I was talking with him today. He said, "It seems a little singular that I, who am not a vindictive man, should have always been before the people for election in canvasses marked for their bitterness: always but once; when I came to Congress it was a quiet time. But always besides that the contests in which I have been prominent have been marked with great rancor."

. . . During the afternoon few despatches were received.

At night, at 7 o'clock we started over to the War Department to spend the evening. Just as we started we received the first gun from Indianapolis, showing a majority of 8,000 there, a gain of 1,500 over Morton's vote. The vote itself seemed an enormous one for a town of that size and can only be accounted for by considering the great influx since the war of voting men from the country into the State centres where a great deal of Army business is done. There was less significance in this vote on account of the October victory which had disheartened the enemy and destroyed their incentive to work.*

The night was rainy, steamy and dark. We splashed through the grounds to the side door of the War Department where a soaked and smoking sentinel was standing in his own vapor with his huddled-up frame covered with a rubber cloak. Inside a half-dozen idle orderlies, upstairs the clerks of the telegraph. As the President entered they handed him a despatch from Forney claiming ten thousand Union majority in Philadelphia. "Forney is a little excitable." Another comes from Felton, Baltimore, giving us "15,000 in the city, 5,000 in the state. All Hail, Free Maryland." That is superb. A message from Rice to Fox, followed instantly by one from Sumner to Lincoln, claiming Boston by 5,000, and Rice's and Hooper's elections by majorities of 4,000 apiece. A magnificent advance on the chilly dozens of 1862.

Eckert came in shaking the rain from his cloak, with trousers very disreputably muddy. We sternly demanded an explanation. He had slipped, he said, & tumbled prone, crossing the street. He had done it watching a fellow-being ahead and chuckling at his uncertain footing. Which reminded the Tycoon, of course. The President said, "For such an awkward fellow, I am pretty sure-footed. It used to take a pretty dextrous man to throw me. I remember, the evening of the day in 1858, that decided the contest for the Senate between Mr. Douglas and myself, was something like this, dark, rainy & gloomy. I had been reading the returns, and had ascertained that we had lost the Legis-

* In its election for state officers, October 11, Indiana had gone Republican by a safe margin.

lature and started to go home. The path had been worn hog-back and was slippery. My foot slipped from under me, knocking the other one out of the way, but I recovered myself & lit square, and I said to myself, 'It's a slip and not a fall.' "

The President sent over the first fruits to Mrs. Lincoln. He said, "She is more anxious than I."

. . . Despatches kept coming in all the evening showing a splendid triumph in Indiana, showing steady, small gains all over Pennsylvania, enough to give a fair majority this time on the home vote. Guesses from New York and Albany which boiled down to about the estimated majority against us in the city, 35,000, and left the result in the State still doubtful.

A despatch from Butler was picked up & sent by Sanford, saying that the City had gone 35,000 McC. & the State 40,000. This looked impossible. The State had been carefully canvassed & such a result was impossible except in view of some monstrous and undreamed of frauds. After a while another came from Sanford correcting the former one & giving us the 40,000 in the State. . . .

Towards midnight we had supper, provided by Eckert. The President went awkwardly and hospitably to work shovelling out the fried oysters. He was most agreeable and genial all the evening in fact. Fox was abusing the coffee for being so hot—saying quaintly, it kept hot all the way down to the bottom of the cup as a piece of ice staid cold till you finished eating it.

We got later in the evening a scattering despatch from the West, giving us Michigan, one from Fox promising Missouri certainly, but a loss in the first district from that miserable split of Knox & Johnson, one promising Delaware, and one, too good for ready credence, saying Raymond & Dodge & Darling had been elected in New York City.

Capt. Thomas came up with a band about half-past two, and made some music and a small hifalute.

The President answered from the window with rather unusual dignity and effect & we came home.

Two nights later, in response to a serenade, Lincoln related the meaning of the election to the central issue of the war:[13]

It has long been a grave question whether any government, not *too* strong for the liberties of its people, can be strong *enough* to maintain its own existence, in great emergencies.

On this point the present rebellion brought our republic to a severe test; and a presidential election occurring in regular course during the rebellion added not a little to the strain. If the loyal people, *united*, were put to the utmost of their strength by the rebellion, must they not fail when *divided*, and partially paralized, by a political war among themselves?

But the election was a necessity.

We can not have free government without elections; and if the rebellion could force us to forego, or postpone a national election, it might fairly claim to have already conquered and ruined us. The strife of the election is but human nature practically applied to the facts of the case. What has occurred in this case, must ever recur in similar cases. Human nature will not change. In any future great national trial, compared with the men of this, we shall have as weak, and as strong; as silly and as wise; as bad and good. Let us, therefore, study the incidents of this, as philosophy to learn wisdom from, and none of them as wrongs to be revenged.

But the election, along with its incidental, and undesirable strife, has done good too. It has demonstrated that a people's government can sustain a national election, in the midst of a great civil war. Until now it has not been known to the world that this was a possibility. It shows also how *sound*, and how *strong* we still are. It shows that, even among candidates of the same party, he who is most devoted to the Union, and most opposed to treason, can receive most of the people's votes. It shows also, to the extent yet known, that we have more men now, than we had when the war began. Gold is good in its place; but living, brave, patriotic men, are better than gold.

But the rebellion continues; and now that the election is over, may not all, having a common interest, reunite in a common effort, to save our common country? For my own part I have striven, and shall strive to avoid placing any obstacle in the way. So long as I have been here I have not willingly planted a thorn in any man's bosom.

While I am deeply sensible to the high compliment of a re-election; and duly grateful, as I trust, to Almighty God for having directed my countrymen to a right conclusion, as I think, for their own good, it adds nothing to my satisfaction that any other man may be disappointed or pained by the result.

May I ask those who have not differed with me, to join with me, in this same spirit towards those who have?

And now, let me close by asking three hearty cheers for our brave soldiers and seamen and their gallant and skilful commanders.

CHAPTER 35

WHILE ALL GEORGIA HOWLED

I STOOD BY HIM when he was drunk," Sherman said.

The cause of Sherman's umbrage toward Ulysses S. Grant was a be-lief that the lieutenant general had hedged at Sherman's plan to march from Atlanta to the sea.

No new objection or counterproposal could daunt Sherman. He could make the march, he insisted. He would "make all Georgia howl."

I

Twenty-two years later, in a letter to R. L. Johnson, associate editor of Century Magazine, *Sherman admitted that in 1864 he had blamed the wrong man:*[1]

One single fact about the "March to the Sea" unknown to me was re-vealed by General Grant in his Memoirs. . . . "I was in favor of Sherman's plan from the time it was first submitted to me. My Chief of Staff, however, was very bitterly opposed to it; and as I learned sub-sequently, finding that he could not move me, he appealed to the au-thorities at Washington to stop it."

I had been acquainted with Genl. Jno. A. Rawlins, Gen. Grant's "Chief of Staff," from the beginning of the war. He was always most loyal & devoted to his Chief, an enthusiastic patriot, and of real ability. He was a neighbor of General Grant in Galena at the break-ing out of the war, a lawyer in good practice, an intense thinker and a man of vehement expression: a soldier by force of circumstances rather than of education or practice yet of infinite use to his Chief throughout the war and up to the hour of his death as Secretary of War in 1869. General Rawlins was enthusiastically devoted to his friends in the Western Army, with which he had been associated from Cairo to Vicksburg and Chattanooga, and doubtless like many others at the time, October 1864, feared that I was about to lead his comrades in a "wild goose chase," and not fully comprehending the objects and also that I on the spot had better means of accurate knowledge than he in the distance. He did not possess the magnificent equipoise of General Grant, nor the confidence in my military sagacity which his Chief did, and I am not at all surprised to learn that he went to Washington from City Point to obtain an order from the President or Secretary of War to compel me with an army of sixty-five thousand of the best soldiers which America had ever produced to remain idle when an opportunity was offered such as never occurs twice to any man on Earth. General Rawlins was right according to the lights he possessed, and I remember well my feeling of uneasiness that something of the kind *might* happen, and how free and glorious I felt when the . . . telegraph was cut which prevented the possibility of orders of any kind from the rear coming to delay or hinder us from fulfilling what I knew was comparatively easy of execution and was sure to be a long stride toward the goal we all aimed at, victory and peace from Virginia to Texas. He was one of the many referred to by Mr. Lincoln, who sat in darkness, but after the event saw a great light and never revealed to me his other doubts.

Sherman believed that he had given General George H. Thomas at Nashville sufficient forces to handle Hood. On November 1 Grant wired Sherman, "If you can see a chance of destroying Hood's army, attend to that first, and make your other move secondary." Promptly Sherman replied, "No single army can catch Hood, and I am convinced the best results will follow from our defeating Jeff. Davis's cherished plan of making me leave Georgia by manoeuvring." The wire Sherman wanted came at last:[2]

CITY POINT, VIRGINIA, November 2, 1864—11.30 A.M.
MAJOR-GENERAL SHERMAN:
    Your dispatch of 9 A.M. yesterday is just received. I dispatched you the same date, advising that Hood's army, now that it had worked so far north, ought to be looked upon now as the "object." With the

force, however, that you have left with General Thomas, he must be able to take care of Hood and destroy him.

I do not see that you can withdraw from where you are to follow Hood, without giving up all we have gained in territory. I say, then, go on as you propose.

U. S. GRANT, *Lieutenant-General*

Within a week Sherman issued a special field order:

HEADQUARTERS MILITARY DIVISION OF THE MISSISSIPPI, IN THE FIELD, KINGSTON, GEORGIA, November 9, 1864.

1. For the purpose of military operations, this army is divided into two wings viz.:

The right wing, Major-General O. O. Howard commanding, composed of the Fifteenth and Seventeenth Corps; the left wing, Major-General H. W. Slocum commanding, composed of the Fourteenth and Twentieth Corps.

2. The habitual order of march will be, wherever practicable, by four roads, as nearly parallel as possible, and converging at points hereafter to be indicated in orders. The cavalry, Brigadier-General Kilpatrick commanding, will receive special orders from the commander-in-chief.

3. There will be no general train of supplies, but each corps will have its ammunition-train and provision-train, distributed habitually as follows: Behind each regiment should follow one wagon and one ambulance; behind each brigade should follow a due proportion of ammunition-wagons, provision-wagons, and ambulances. In case of danger, each corps commander should change this order of march, by having his advance and rear brigades unencumbered by wheels. The separate columns will start habitually at 7 A.M., and make about fifteen miles per day, unless otherwise fixed in orders.

4. The army will forage liberally on the country during the march. To this end, each brigade commander will organize a good and sufficient foraging party, under the command of one or more discreet officers, who will gather, near the route traveled, corn or forage of any kind, meat of any kind, vegetables, corn-meal, or whatever is needed by the command, aiming at all times to keep in the wagons at least ten days' provisions for his command, and three days' forage. Soldiers must not enter the dwellings of the inhabitants, or commit any trespass; but, during a halt or camp, they may be permitted to gather turnips,

potatoes, and other vegetables, and to drive in stock in sight of their camp. To regular foraging-parties must be intrusted the gathering of provisions and forage, at any distance from the road traveled.

5. To corps commanders alone is intrusted the power to destroy mills, houses, cotton-gins, etc.; and for them this general principle is laid down: In districts and neighborhoods where the army is un-molested, no destruction of such property should be permitted; but should guerrillas or bushwhackers molest our march, or should the inhabitants burn bridges, obstruct roads, or otherwise manifest local hostility, then army commanders should order and enforce a devasta-tion more or less relentless, according to the measure of such hostil-ity.

6. As for horses, mules, wagons, etc., belonging to the inhabitants, the cavalry and artillery may appropriate freely and without limit; dis-criminating, however, between the rich, who are usually hostile, and the poor and industrious, usually neutral or friendly. Foraging-parties may also take mules or horses, to replace the jaded animals of their trains, or to serve as pack-mules for the regiments or brigades. In all foraging, of whatever kind, the parties engaged will refrain from abusive or threatening language, and may, where the officer in command thinks proper, give written certificates of the facts, but no receipts; and they will endeavor to leave with each family a reasonable portion for their maintenance.

7. Negroes who are able-bodied and can be of service to the several columns may be taken along; but each army commander will bear in mind that the question of supplies is a very important one, and that his first duty is to see to those who bear arms.

8. The organization, at once, of a good pioneer battalion for each army corps, composed if possible of negroes, should be attended to. This battalion should follow the advance-guard, repair roads and double them if possible, so that the columns will not be delayed after reaching bad places. Also, army commanders should practise the habit of giving the artillery and wagons the road, marching their troops on one side, and instruct their troops to assist wagons at steep hills or bad crossings of streams.

9. Captain O. M. Poe, chief-engineer, will assign to each wing of the army a pontoon-train, fully equipped and organized; and the com-manders thereof will see to their being properly protected at all times.

By order of Major-General W. T. Sherman,

L. M. DAYTON, *Aide-de-Camp*

II

Sherman pushed ahead with his preparations. The diary of ten-year-old Carrie M. Berry revealed the harrowing days that followed:[3]

Fri. Nov. 11. This is the last day that cars are going out to Chattanooga. We are erbliged to stay here now. Aunt Marthy went down to the carshed and I expect that she got off as she has not ben back.

Sat. Nov. 12. We were fritened almost to death last night. Some mean soldiers set several houses on fire in different parts of the town. I could not go to sleep for fear that they would set our house on fire. We all dred the next few days to come for they said that they would set the last house on fire if they had to leave this place.

Sun. Nov. 13. The federal soldiers have ben coming to day and burning houses and I have ben looking at them come in nearly all day.

Mon. Nov. 14. They came burning Atlanta to day. We all dread it because they say that they will burn the last house before they stop. We will dread it.

Tues. Nov. 15. This has ben a dreadful day. Things have ben burning all around us. We dread to night because we do not know what moment that they will set our house on fire. We have had a gard a little while after dinner and we feel a little more protected.

Wed. Nov. 16. Oh what a night we had. They came burning the store house and about night it looked like the whole town was on fire. We all set up all night. If we had not sat up our house would have ben burnt up for the fire was very near and the soldiers were going around setting houses on fire where they were not watched. They behaved very badly. They all left the town about one o'clock this evening and we were glad when they left for no body knows what we have suffered since they came in.

Carrie's assertion that the Yankees "behaved very badly" drew no denial from Major James A. Connolly of the 123rd Illinois:[4]

Our Commissaries have been busily engaged all day [November 15] in loading rations, and our Quarter Masters in issuing clothing and shoes to the troops. Up to about 3 P.M. this issuing was carried on with something like a show of regularity, but about that time fires began to break out in various portions of the city, and it soon became evident that these fires were but the beginning of a general conflagration which would sweep over the entire city and blot it out of existence;

so Quartermasters and Commissaries ceased trying to issue clothing or load rations, and told the soldiers to go in and take what they wanted before it burned up. The soldiers found many barrels of whisky and of course they drank it until they were drunk; then new fires began to spring up, all sorts of discordant noises rent the air, drunken soldiers on foot and horseback raced up and down the streets while the buildings on either side were solid sheets of flame, they gathered in crowds before the finest structures and sang "Rally around the Flag" while the flames enwrapped these costly edifices, and shouted and danced and sang again while pillar and roof and dome sank into one common ruin. The night, for miles around was bright as midday; the city of Atlanta was one mass of flame, and the morrow must find it a mass of ruins. Well, the soldiers fought for it, and the soldiers won it, now let the soldiers enjoy it; and so I suppose Gen. Sherman thinks, for he is somewhere near by, now, looking on at all this, and saying not one word to prevent it. All the pictures and verbal descriptions of hell I have ever seen never gave me half so vivid an idea of it, as did this flame wrapped city to-night. Gate City of the South, farewell!

A harrowing picture of desolated Atlanta was drawn by General W. P. Howard of the Georgia militia:[5]

The city hall is damaged but not burned. The Second Baptist, Second Presbyterian, Trinity and Catholic churches, and all the residences between Mitchell and Peters streets, running south of east, and Lloyd and Washington streets, running south of west, are safe, all attributable to Father O'Riley, who refused to give up his parsonage to the yankees, who were looking out for fine houses for quarters, and there being a large number of Catholics in the yankee army, who volunteered to protect their church and parsonage, and would not allow any house adjacent to be fired that would endanger them. As a proof of their attachment to their church, and love for Father O'Riley, a soldier who attempted to fire Colonel Calhoun's house, the burning of which would have endangered the whole block, was shot and killed and his grave is now marked. So to Father O'Riley the country is indebted for the protection of the city hall, churches, etc.

Dr. Quintard's Protestant Episcopal, the Christian and African churches were burned. The medical college was saved by Dr. D'Alvigny, who was left in charge of our wounded. The female college was torn down for the purpose of obtaining brick with which to construct winter quarters. All institutions of learning were destroyed. The African church was used as an academy for educating negroes. . . . Very few negroes remained in the city. . . .

Many of the finest houses mysteriously left unburned were filled with the finest furniture, carpets, pianos, mirrors, etc., and occupied by parties, who six months ago lived in humble style.

About fifty families remained during the occupancy of the city by the enemy, and about the same number have returned since its abandonment.* From two to three thousand dead carcasses of animals remain in the city limits.

Horses were turned loose in the cemetery to graze upon the grass and shrubbery. The ornaments of graves, such as marble lambs, miniature statuary, souvenirs of departed little ones, are broken and scattered abroad.

The crowning act of all their wickedness and villainy was committed by our ungodly foe in removing the dead from the vaults in the cemetery, and robbing the coffins of the silver name plates and tippings, and depositing their own dead in the vaults.

With bands playing, Sherman's army left Atlanta next morning. The general was in exuberant spirits:[6]

About 7 A.M. of November 16th we rode out of Atlanta by the Decatur road, filled by the marching troops and wagons of the Fourteenth Corps; and reaching the hill, just outside of the old rebel works, we naturally paused to look back upon the scenes of our past battles. We stood upon the very ground whereon was fought the bloody battle of July 22d, and could see the copse of wood where McPherson fell. Behind us lay Atlanta, smouldering and in ruins, the black smoke rising high in air, and hanging like a pall over the ruined city. Away off in the distance, on the McDonough road, was the rear of Howard's column, the gun-barrels glistening in the sun, the white-topped wagons stretching away to the south; and right before us the Fourteenth Corps, marching steadily and rapidly, with a cheery look and swinging pace, that made light of the thousand miles that lay between us and Richmond. Some band, by accident, struck up the anthem of "John Brown's soul goes marching on;" the men caught up the strain, and never be-

* General Howard's report to Governor Joseph E. Brown was dated December 7, 1864.

fore or since have I heard the chorus of "Glory, glory, hallelujah!" done with more spirit, or in better harmony of time and place.

Then we turned our horses' heads to the east; Atlanta was soon lost behind the screen of trees, and became a thing of the past. Around it clings many a thought of desperate battle, of hope and fear, that now seem like the memory of a dream; and I have never seen the place since. The day was extremely beautiful, clear sunlight, with bracing air, and an unusual feeling of exhilaration seemed to pervade all minds— a feeling of something to come, vague and undefined, still full of venture and intense interest. Even the common soldiers caught the inspira-

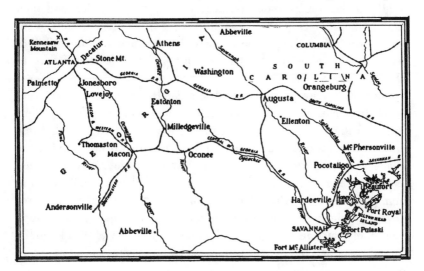

FROM ATLANTA TO SAVANNAH

From *Atlas of American History*

tion, and many a group called out to me as I worked my way past them, "Uncle Billy, I guess Grant is waiting for us at Richmond!" Indeed, the general sentiment was that we were marching for Richmond, and that there we should end the war, but how and when they seemed to care not; nor did they measure the distance, or count the cost in life, or bother their brains about the great rivers to be crossed, and the food required for man and beast, that had to be gathered by the way. There was a "devil-may-care" feeling pervading officers and men, that made me feel the full load of responsibility, for success would be accepted as a matter of course, whereas, should we fail, this "march" would be adjudged the wild adventure of a crazy fool. I had no purpose to march direct for Richmond by way of Augusta and

Charlotte, but always designed to reach the sea-coast first at Savannah or Port Royal, South Carolina, and even kept in mind the alternative of Pensacola.

The first night out we camped by the road-side near Lithonia. Stone Mountain, a mass of granite, was in plain view, cut out in clear outline against the blue sky; the whole horizon was lurid with the bonfires of rail-ties, and groups of men all night were carrying the heated rails to the nearest trees, and bending them around the trunks. Colonel Poe had provided tools for ripping up the rails and twisting them when hot; but the best and easiest way is the one I have described, of heating the middle of the iron-rails on bonfires made of the cross-ties, and then winding them around a telegraph-pole or the trunk of some convenient sapling. I attached much importance to this destruction of the railroad, gave it my own personal attention, and made reiterated orders to others on the subject.

The next day we passed through the handsome town of Covington, the soldiers closing up their ranks, the color-bearers unfurling their flags, and the bands striking up patriotic airs. The white people came out of their houses to behold the sight, spite of their deep hatred of the invaders, and the negroes were simply frantic with joy. Whenever they heard my name, they clustered about my horse, shouted and prayed in their peculiar style, which had a natural eloquence that would have moved a stone. I have witnessed hundreds, if not thousands, of such scenes; and can now see a poor girl, in the very ecstasy of the Methodist "shout," hugging the banner of one of the regiments, and jumping up to the "feet of Jesus."

III

Sherman found many points of interest when he reached the state capital, but his greatest fascination was reading the Southern newspapers that fell into his hands:

. . . By the 23d, I was in Milledgeville with the left wing, and was in full communication with the right wing at Gordon. The people of Milledgeville remained at home, except the Governor (Brown), the State officers, and Legislature, who had ignominiously fled, in the utmost disorder and confusion; standing not on the order of their going, but going at once—some by rail, some by carriages, and many on foot. Some of the citizens who remained behind described this flight of the "brave and patriotic" Governor Brown. He had occupied a public building known as the "Governor's Mansion," and had hastily stripped it of carpets, curtains, and furniture of all sorts, which were removed to a train of freightcars, which carried away these things—even the cabbages and vegetables from his kitchen and cellar—leaving behind muskets, ammunition, and the public archives.

On arrival at Milledgeville I occupied the same public mansion, and was soon overwhelmed with appeals for protection. General Slocum had previously arrived with the Twentieth Corps, had taken up his quarters at the Milledgeville Hotel, established a good provost-guard, and excellent order was maintained. The most frantic appeals had been made by the Governor and Legislature for help from every quarter, and the people of the State had been called out *en masse* to resist and destroy the invaders of their homes and firesides. Even the prisoners and convicts of the penitentiary were released on condition of serving as soldiers, and the cadets were taken from their military college for the same purpose. These constituted a small battalion, under General Harry Wayne, a former officer of the United States Army, and son of the then Justice Wayne of the Supreme Court. But these hastily retreated east across the Oconee River, leaving us a good bridge, which we promptly secured.

At Milledgeville we found newspapers from all the South, and learned the consternation which had filled the Southern mind at our temerity; many charging that we were actually fleeing for our lives and seeking safety at the hands of our fleet on the sea-coast. All demanded that we should be assailed, "front, flank, and rear;" that provisions should be destroyed in advance, so that we would starve; that bridges should be burned, roads obstructed, and no mercy shown us. Judging from the tone of the Southern press of that day, the outside world must have supposed us ruined and lost. I give a few of these appeals as samples, which to-day must sound strange to the parties who made them:

CORINTH, MISSISSIPPI, November 18, 1864.
TO THE PEOPLE OF GEORGIA:

Arise for the defense of your native soil! Rally around your patriotic Governor and gallant soldiers! Obstruct and destroy all the roads in Sherman's front, flank, and rear, and his army will soon starve in your midst. Be confident. Be resolute. Trust in an overruling Providence, and success will soon crown your efforts. I hasten to join you in the defense of your homes and firesides.

P. G. T. BEAUREGARD

RICHMOND, November 18, 1864.

TO THE PEOPLE OF GEORGIA:

You have now the best opportunity ever yet presented to destroy the enemy. Put every thing at the disposal of our generals; remove all provisions from the path of the invader, and put all obstructions in his path.

Every citizen with his gun, and every negro with his spade and axe, can do the work of a soldier. You can destroy the enemy by retarding his march.

Georgians, be firm! Act promptly, and fear not!

B. H. HILL, *Senator*

I most cordially approve the above.

JAMES A. SEDDON, *Secretary of War*

RICHMOND, November 19, 1864

TO THE PEOPLE OF GEORGIA:

We have had a special conference with President Davis and the Secretary of War, and are able to assure you that they have done and are still doing all that can be done to meet the emergency that presses upon you. Let every man fly to arms! Remove your negroes, horses, cattle, and provisions from Sherman's army, and burn what you cannot carry. Burn all bridges, and block up the roads in his route. Assail the invader in front, flank, and rear, by night and by day. Let him have no rest.

JULIAN HARTRIDGE, MARK BLAUFORD,
J. H. REYNOLDS, GENERAL N. LESTER,
JOHN T. SHOEMAKER, JOSEPH M. SMITH,
Members of Congress

Of course, we were rather amused than alarmed at these threats, and made light of the feeble opposition offered to our progress. Some of the officers (in the spirit of mischief) gathered together in the vacant hall of Representatives, elected a Speaker, and constituted themselves the Legislature of the State of Georgia! A proposition was made to repeal the ordinance of secession, which was well debated, and resulted in its repeal by a fair vote! I was not present at these frolics, but heard of them at the time, and enjoyed the joke.

Colonel William Hawley, commanding the Third Wisconsin Volunteers, gave a businesslike report of the manner in which Sherman's boys destroyed the capital of Georgia:[7]

On the twenty-second day of November, 1864, while the Twentieth army corps was approaching the city, I was directed by the Major-General commanding left wing of the army, to occupy the city as commandant of the post, with my own regiment and the One Hundred and Seventh New-York volunteers. My instructions were, to guard all public property, to maintain good order, and to perform all the duties of post commander. I immediately proceeded to establish patrols in the streets, and detailed suitable guards for the public buildings, including the State House, two arsenals, one dépôt, one magazine for powder and ammunition, and other buildings containing cotton, salt, and other contraband property. I also appointed a competent officer to take as correct an inventory of the property, contained in these and other buildings, as possible. The limited time in which I had command of the city, precluded the possibility of my getting a perfectly full and correct inventory of all the property found and destroyed, as this, in my opinion, would have required at least a week to obtain. The following is a list of the most important and valuable articles found, with the disposition made of the same:

One powder magazine, blown up; railroad dépôt and surrounding buildings, burned; two thousand three hundred muskets, smooth bore, calibre sixty-nine, burned; three hundred sets accoutrements, burned; ten thousand rounds ammunition, calibre sixty-nine, burned; five thousand lances, burned; one thousand five hundred cutlasses, burned; fifteen boxes United States standard weights and measures, burned; sixteen hogsheads salt, thrown into the river; one hundred and seventy boxes fixed ammunition, and two hundred kegs powder. Turned over all that was valuable to Major Reynolds, and threw the balance into the river. About one thousand five hundred pounds tobacco were distributed among the troops. A large quantity of cotton—say one thousand eight hundred bales—was disposed of by General Sherman; manner not made known to me. One large three-story building in the square, near the State House, was burned, together with a large number of miscellaneous articles, as parts of harness and saddles, a repair-shop, with all the necessary tools for repairing all kinds of war materials, etc.

Sherman and his marchers began to add their own idioms to the American language. A twisted railroad rail became known as "Sherman's hairpin." And "Sherman's bummers" were those deftly organized foraging parties which, operating on the flanks of his armies, kindled hatred in the hearts of plantation owners like Dolly Summer Lunt:[8]

. . . I hastened back to my frightened servants and told them that they had better hide, and then went back to the gate to claim protection and a guard. But like demons they rush in! My yards are full. To my smokehouse, my dairy, pantry, kitchen and cellar, like famished wolves they came, breaking locks and whatever is in their way. The thousand pounds of meat in my smokehouse is gone in a twinkling, my flour, my meat, my lard, butter, eggs, pickles of various kinds—both in vinegar and brine—wine, jars and jugs are all gone. My eighteen fat turkeys, my hens, chickens, and fowls, my young pigs, are shot down in my yard and hunted as if they were Rebels themselves. . . . There go my mules, my sheep, and worse than all, my boys! . . . They are not friends to the slaves. We have never made the poor cowardly Negro fight, and it is strange, passing strange, that the all-powerful Yankee nation with the whole world to back them, their ports open, their armies filled with soldiers from all nations, should at last take the poor Negro to help them out against this little Confederacy which was to have been brought back into the Union in sixty days' time!

. . . Ovens, skillets, coffee-mills, of which we had three, coffee-pots —not one have I left. . . . As the sad moments rolled on, they swept not only in front of my house, but behind; they tore down my garden palings, made a road through my back yard and lot field, driving their stock and riding through, tearing down my fences and desolating my home—wantonly doing it when there was no necessity for it.

Such a day, if I live to the age of Methuselah, may God spare me from ever seeing again!

Deep in the Georgia pine country, Major Connolly of the 123rd Illinois recounted an unusual evening:[9]

A lot of refugee negroes who are encamped near our headquarters got up a regular "Plantation Dance" to-night, and some of us went over and watched the performance which was highly amusing. The dress, general appearance, action, laughter, music and dancing of the genuine plantation negro is far more grotesque and mirth-provoking than the broadest caricatures of "Christy's Minstrels." They require neither fiddle nor banjo to make music for their ordinary plantation dances, and the dancers need no prompter, but kick, and caper and shuffle in the most complicated and grotesque manner their respective fancies can invent, while all who are not actually engaged as dancers stand in a ring around the dancers, clapping their hands, stamping their feet, swinging their bodies, and singing as loud and as fast and furious as they can, a sort of barbaric chant, unlike anything I ever heard from the lips of white mortals; I observed, however, that there is a tone of melancholy (I know of no other mode of describing it) pervading all their rude music, which was plainly discernible even when the mirth of the dancers and singers had apparently reached its highest pitch. There is more fact than fiction in the saying that a "Soldier's life is always gay," for here we are in the midst of a hostile country, engaged in a campaign which probably the whole world, at this moment, is predicting will end in our complete destruction, and yet I have spent the evening laughing at the oddities of these negroes until my head and sides are aching.

Occasionally Rebel cavalry under Joseph A. Wheeler nipped at the heels of Sherman's army; the effect was that of a military flea-bite— a nuisance. Connolly's interest remained absorbed by the Negroes:

Contrabands are still swarming to us in immense numbers. The General [Absalom Baird] is a nephew of Gerritt Smith's and is quite an abolitionist. He delights in talking with these contrabands when we halt by the roadside and in extracting information concerning their "masters and mistresses" from them. He picked up quite an original character today who calls himself "Jerry." Jerry is a lively, rollicking, fun loving fellow, with a good deal of shrewdness; about 20 years old and rather a good looking boy. Jerry got an old horse, made a rope bridle, mounted horseback and rode alongside the General all the afternoon, talking to him continually. As we rode along Jerry was silent a few minutes, then he suddenly burst into a loud laugh, shook himself all over, and turning to the General remarked: "Golly, I wish ole massa could see me now, ridin' wid de Ginrals."

After getting into camp tonight "Jerry" entertained us for two or three hours with his oddities. He told us about an old preacher in this neighborhood named Kilpatrick (Gen. Kilpatrick's headquarters are at his house tonight) and said he knew Old Kilpatrick's sermon, he had heard him preach it so often, so we got "Jerry" to preach Old Kilpatrick's sermon. I only remember part of it: "O Lord! suffer our ene*mees to Chaste* after us no longer, but turn *dem* gently round, O,

Lord, for we's got *notin* but our rights and our property, *an* if our ene-
mees *chaste* after us any longer we won't have *notin* for our *chillen.*
Bend *dar* hard hearts *an probate* necks, O, Lord, *an* suffer *dem* to
Chaste after us no longer, but turn *dem* gently round." Jerry would
roll up his eyes, and deliver this, and much more, in true ministerial
style, until we almost split our sides with laughter.

We asked "Jerry" how many "Yankees" he thought he had seen today, and he replied about "five hundred thousand." I have noticed that
it is almost universal amongst the negroes in this country, when they
first see our column come along on the road to exclaim: "Good Lord!
looks like de whole world was comin."

*Camp pets—dogs and cats, a small donkey, even a raccoon—amused
Major George Ward Nichols, aide-de-camp to Sherman:*[10]

. . . When the column is moving, haughty gamecocks are seen
mounted upon the breech of a cannon, tied to the pack saddle of a mule,
among pots and pans, or carried lovingly in the arms of a mounted
orderly; crowing with all his might from the interior of a wagon, or
making the woods re-echo with his triumphant notes as he rides perched
upon the knapsack of a soldier. These cocks represent every known
breed, Polish and Spanish, Dorkings, Shanghais, and Bantams—high-
blooded specimens traveling with those of their species who may not
boast of noble lineage. They must all fight, however, or be killed and
eaten. Hardly has the army gone into camp before these feathery combats begin. The cocks use only the spurs with which Nature furnishes
them; for the soldiers have not yet reached the refinement of applying
artificial gaffs, and so but little harm is done. The gamecocks which
have come out of repeated conflicts victorious are honored with such
names as "Bill Sherman," "Johnny Logan," etc.; while the defeated
and bepecked victim is saluted with derisive appellations, such as
"Jeff. Davis," "Beauregard," or "Bob Lee."

*Along the roadside one day Major Nichols encountered a sour-faced
old man, who was in a philosophical mood:*

"They say you are retreating, but it is the strangest sort of retreat I
ever saw. Why dog bite them, the newspapers have been lying in this
way all along. They allers are whipping the Federal armies, and they
allers fall back after the battle is over. It was that ar' idee that first

opened my eyes. Our army was always whipping the Feds, and we allers fell back. I allers told 'em it was a damned humbug, and now by Jesus I know it, for here you are right on [my] place; hogs, potatoes, corn, and fences all gone. I don't find any fault. I expected it all.

"Jeff Davis and the rest talk about splitting the Union. Why if South Carolina had gone out by herself, she would have been split in four pieces by this time. Splitting the Union! Why (with a round oath) the State of Georgia is being split right through from end to end. It is these rich fellows who are making this war, and keeping their precious bodies out of harm's way. There's John Franklin went through here the other day, running away from your army. I could have played dominoes on his coat-tails. There's my poor brother sick with smallpox at Macon, working for eleven dollars a month, and hasn't got a cent of the damned stuff for a year. 'Leven dollars a month and eleven thousand bullets a minute. I don't believe in it, sir!"

Negroes by the hundred trailing after the Federal columns, cavalry skirmishes, tightened mouths at the discovery of a prison pen at Millen —of such images was the march to the sea composed. Major Connolly was far from amused by an incident that occurred on the eighth of December:[11]

When the head of the column reached the "Ebenezer Causeway" I went ahead with one of Genl. [Jefferson C.] Davis' aids who had come back to point out our ground for camping, and as I reached the bridge, I found there Major Lee, Provost Marshal of the Corps, engaged, by Genl. Davis' order, in turning off the road, into the swamp all the fugitive negroes that came along. When we should cross I knew it was the intention that the bridge should be burned, and I inquired if the negroes were not to be permitted to cross; I was told that Genl. Davis had ordered that they should not. This *I* knew, and Genl. Davis knew must result in all these negroes being recaptured or perhaps brutally shot down by the rebel cavalry tomorrow morning. The idea of five or six hundred black women, children and old men being thus returned to slavery by such an infernal copperhead as Jeff. C. Davis was entirely too much for my Democracy; I suppose loss of sleep, and fatigue made me somewhat out of humor too, and I told his staff officers what I thought of such an inhuman, barbarous proceeding in language which may possibly result in reprimand from his serene Highness, for I know his toadies will repeat it to him, but I don't care a fig; I am determined

to expose this act of his publicly, . . . I expect this will cost me
my Brevet as Lieut. Colonel, but let it go, I wouldn't barter my convictions of right, nor seal my mouth for any promotion.*

IV

*In mid-October, Hood had started northward toward Nashville, where
he hoped to defeat Union forces under Schofield and Thomas, gain recruits, and then re-enforce Lee at Richmond.*

*Hood made slow progress. Not until the last day of November did
he have a chance to throw his troops at Schofield, in a strong position
at Franklin, twenty miles south of Nashville.*

*Captain Irving A. Buck, on the staff of Confederate Major General
Patrick R. Cleburne—an abler officer than Hood—saw brave men in
gray and butternut charge in vain against the Federal lines:*[12]

At dawn, November 30, the Confederate army was put in motion towards Franklin, 18 miles distant. . . . The town is located on the south
side and in a bend of the Big Harpeth River, which completely en-
circles it on three sides, crescent in shape. The Federal entrenchments
extended from a point east to one north, in a sharp curve near the
bridge of the Nashville and Decatur Railroad, thence to another curve
west, both flanks resting on the river, their line crossing the neck of a
peninsula. On the high ground north of the river was a strong redoubt,
Fort Granger, for the protection of which and their train was stationed
the Third Division of the Fourth Federal corps. Their entrenchments on
the south side of the river were built in front of the now celebrated
Carter house, a one-story brick building, west of the Columbia pike,
and a large gin house stood on the east side of it. The pike ran through
the entrenchments, while to the east side of it was the railroad. On a
slope half a mile in front of the main works two brigades of Wagner's
Federal division had been halted, and proceeded to throw up breastworks. . . .

General Hood formed his line of battle behind Winstead's Hill
about two and a half miles from Carter's Hill, the Federal position.
. . . Upon arrival General Cheatham had ridden to the top of Winstead's Hill to make observation of the Federal position, which he at
once saw was very strong and well protected, and he knew that to try

* Connolly's report on the incident, addressed to his congressman, appeared in
substance in the New York *Tribune*. A subsequent investigation "exonerated"
Davis.

to dislodge them would be a desperate attempt. Going to General Hood he said, "I do not like the looks of this fight; the enemy has an excellent position and is well fortified." "I prefer to fight them here where they have had only eighteen hours to fortify, than to strike them at Nashville where they have been strengthening themselves for three years," replied Hood. General Forrest was also opposed to a front at-

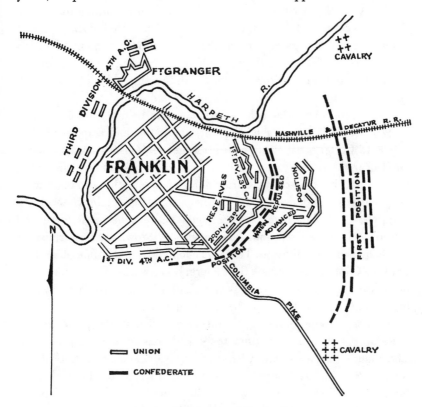

THE BATTLE OF FRANKLIN

From Lossing, *Pictorial History of the Civil War*

tack, advising that the enemy be flanked by moving to the right across the Harpeth River, which was fordable, and offered to attempt it with his cavalry if adequately supported by an infantry column. . . .

The day before the battle of Franklin the road upon which Cleburne was marching ran by Ashwood, 6 miles from Columbia, where is located the church and burial ground of the Polk family.* It was a romantic

* The family of Leonidas Polk, Episcopal bishop turned soldier, who was killed at Pine Mountain, Georgia, June 14, 1864.

place. The beautiful little Episcopal church was in the purest Gothic style, its walls and sharp-pointed roof concealed by ivy, while the flowers and shrubbery looked fresh and green even on this bleak November day. Cleburne reined in his horse and lingered for a moment to admire a place of such singular beauty, and said to one of his staff that it was "almost worth dying for, to be buried in such a beautiful spot."

. . . Upon his arrival at Winstead's Hill, whilst awaiting the formation of his command, he ascended to the summit, rested his field-glasses upon a stump, and gazed long at the enemy's entrenchments. He simply remarked, "They are very formidable." Seating himself upon the stump, he wrote rapidly for a few minutes in a small blank-book, which he returned to his pocket. . . .

The ground over which the advance was to be made from the base of Winstead's Hill was a level plain, about two and a quarter miles across to Carter's Hill, and save for a hedge of osage orange on the knoll near the railroad cut, and a considerable thicket of locust trees, close to and in front of the Carter house, it was entirely unobstructed and fenceless, and every part of the advance in plain view of the Federals. . . . The advance was begun between half-past three and four o'clock in the afternoon. A regiment was thrown out as skirmishers in advance of each division. There was no halt from the time of starting until the Confederates struck the Federal breastworks. The first was that of the two exposed brigades of Wagner's division in the detached works half a mile to the front of the main line. . . .

Wagner's troops broke in confusion and fled to the protection of these works. For a long time there had existed a rivalry between Cheatham's (Brown's) and Cleburne's division, and as the line rushed forward, the former troops shouted to the latter, as the Federals scattered, "We will go into the works with them," and the two divisions were pushed so rapidly that on the right of the Franklin–Columbia pike Cleburne's reached the entrenchments almost as soon as did Wagner's demoralized men. To describe truly that which followed is beyond the power of tongue or pen. In the reckless disregard of life, and in tenacity of purpose displayed, the attack has rarely been equalled, never exceeded. The men fought like demons. Often the combatants were near enough to use clubbed muskets and the bayonet. The first desperate charge by Cheatham was repeated again and again, while Stewart, on his right, threw his force upon the Federals in their entrenchments and fought with the same daring and determination that Cheatham's men had shown. Inside the Federal works a new raw regiment broke and ran to the rear, and into the gap thus created Brown's and Cleburne's men rushed, but from losses they were too weak to hold the ground against the reinforcements of the seasoned and well-disciplined brigade of Gen. Emerson Opdyke. Besides, of their leaders the inspiring voice of Cleburne was already hushed in death, and Brown lay wounded on the field.

Schofield watched the battle with different emotions:[13]

General Stanley and I, who were then together on the north side of the river, rode rapidly to our posts, he to his corps on the south side, and I to the high redoubt on the north bank, overlooking the entire field.

There I witnessed the grandest display possible in war. Every battalion and battery of the Union army in line was distinctly seen. The corps of the Confederate army which were advancing or forming for the attack could also be seen, though less clearly on account of their greater distance, while the Confederate cavalry could be dimly discerned moving to the fords of the river above Franklin. Only a momentary view was permitted of this scene of indescribable grandeur when it was changed to one of the most tragic interest and anxiety. The guns of the redoubt on the parapet on which I stood with two or three staff officers had fired only a few shots over the heads of our troops at the advancing enemy when his heavy line overwhelmed Wagner's two brigades and rapidly followed their fragments in a confused mass over our light intrenchments. The charging ranks of the enemy, the flying remnants of our broken troops, and the double ranks of our first line of defense, coming back from the trenches together, produced the momentary impression of an overwhelming mass of the enemy passing over our parapets.

It is hardly necessary to say that for a moment my "heart sank within me." But instantly Opdycke's brigade and the 12th and 16th Kentucky sprang forward, and steadily advanced to the breach. Up to this moment there had been but little firing at that point, because of our own troops and the enemy coming in pell-mell; hence there was not much smoke, and the whole could be seen. But now all became enveloped in a dense mass of smoke, and not a man was visible except the fragments of the broken brigades and others, afterward known to be prisoners, flocking to the rear. A few seconds of suspense and intense anxiety followed, then the space in the rear of our line became clear of fugitives, and the steady roar of musketry and artillery and the dense volume of smoke rising along the entire line told me that "the breach is restored, the victory won"! That scene, and the emotion of that one moment, were worth all the losses and dangers of a soldier's lifetime.

Buck witnessed a curious phenomenon: a victorious army in retreat. Before the new month of December was out, the reason for this strange strategical move would be revealed:[14]

The deepening shadows of the afternoon betokening the approach of night, brought no relief to the weary but determined combatants. Darkness came, but the struggle continued. Flashes of the guns upon one side would furnish light by which a volley would be directed by the other. The opposing lines at points were within easy reach of each other, and kept up the fusillade until between 9 and 10 o'clock, when it abated, simply because both sides were actually worn out physically, and human endurance could bear no further strain. Between 11 o'clock and midnight the Federals took advantage of this cessation to slip away quietly in retreat towards Nashville.

V

That November, still stalemated in Virginia, Grant decided to enjoy a holiday. Horace Porter described a streetcar conductor who wouldn't be fooled by a cock-and-bull story:[15]

As the apprehension throughout the North had been allayed, and as there were no operations in contemplation in Virginia, General Grant started on the 17th of November, and made a short trip to Burlington, New Jersey, to see his children, who had been placed at school there, and his wife, who was with them. There went with the party an expert telegraph operator, familiar with the cipher used in official despatches, who was used in keeping up telegraphic communication with the front. On November 19 news was received at headquarters, through Confederate sources, that Lee had recalled Early's command from the valley of Virginia. This was instantly communicated to the general-in-chief. He telegraphed at once to Sheridan, mentioning this news, and saying that if he was satisfied that it was so, to send Wright's corps to City Point without delay, and move with his cavalry to cut the Virginia Central Railroad. There was destined to be no respite for the general-in-chief. Even while snatching a couple of days' rest in the quiet of his little family, he was still called on to direct important movements in the field.

Finding that there was no immediate need of his presence at the front, he decided to run over to New York for a couple of days. He had promised Mrs. Grant to go there on a shopping expedition, and he also felt some curiosity to take a look at the city, as he had not seen it since he was graduated from the Military Academy, twenty-one years before. He went with Mrs. Grant to the Astor House, quietly and unannounced, being particularly desirous of avoiding any public demonstrations. He did not realize, however, the sensation which his arrival in the metropolis would create. The news spread rapidly throughout the city, and the greatest eagerness was manifested on the part of the people to get a sight of the famous commander. The foremost citizens presented themselves at the hotel to pay their respects to him, and enthusiastic crowds filled the streets and stood for hours gazing at the windows of his rooms, in the hope of catching a glimpse of him.

Entertainments of every kind were tendered him, and invitations poured in from every quarter. He received many prominent citizens in his rooms, and had a great many interesting talks with them; but the invitations to entertainments were declined, and all public demonstrations avoided as much as possible. The next morning after his arrival the general strolled out into the streets with a former staff-officer then living in New York, and being in plain citizen's clothes, was for some time unobserved; but finally his features, which had been made known by means of the portraits everywhere displayed, were recognized, and finding a crowd surrounding him, he stepped into a street-car. The gentleman with him, finding no vacant seat, asked the conductor to have the people sit closer together and make room for General Grant. The conductor put on a broad grin, and quietly winked one eye, as much as to say, "You can't fool me with such a cock-and-bull story as that"; and the general quietly took hold of a strap, and rode throughout the trip standing with a number of others who had crowded into the car.

VI

By less than a week, Grant missed an effort by eight Confederate conspirators to burn New York City. John W. Headley, the historian of the raid on St. Albans, Vermont, recounts his part in the events of the evening of November 26, 1864:[16]

I reached the Astor House at 7:20 o'clock, got my key, and went to my room in the top story. It was the lower corner front room on Broadway. After lighting the gas jet I hung the bed-clothes loosely on the headboard and piled the chairs, drawers of the bureau, and wash-stand on the bed. Then stuffed some newspapers about among the mass and poured a bottle of turpentine over it all. I concluded to unlock my door and fix the key on the outside, as I might have to get out in a hurry, for I did not know whether the Greek Fire would make a noise or not. I opened a bottle carefully and quickly, and spilled it on the pile of rubbish. It blazed up instantly and the whole bed seemed to be in flames before I could get out. I locked the door and walked down the hall. . . .

Across at the City Hotel I proceeded in the same manner. Then in going down to the Everett House I looked over at my room in the Astor House. A bright light appeared within but there were no indications below of any alarm. After getting through at the Everett House I started to the United States Hotel, when the fire bells began to ring up town. I got through at the United States Hotel without trouble, but in leaving my key the clerk, I thought, looked at me a little curiously. It occurred to me that it had been discovered that my satchel had no baggage in it and that perhaps the clerk had it in mind to mention the fact.

As I came back to Broadway it seemed that a hundred bells were ringing, great crowds were gathering on the street, and there was general consternation. I concluded to go and see how my fires were doing. There was no panic at the Astor House, but to my surprise a great crowd was pouring out of Barnum's Museum nearly opposite the Astor. It was now a quarter after nine o'clock by the City Hall tower clock.

Presently the alarm came from the City Hotel and the Everett. The surging crowds were frantic. But the greatest panic was at Barnum's Museum. People were coming out and down ladders from the second and third floor windows and the manager was crying out for help to get his animals out. It looked like people were getting hurt running over each other in the stampede, and still I could not help some astonishment for I did not suppose there was a fire in the Museum.

In accordance with our plan, I went down Broadway and turned across to the North River Wharf. The vessels and barges of every description were lying along close together and not more than twenty yards from the street. I picked dark spots to stand in, and jerked a bottle in six different places. They were ablaze before I left. One had struck a barge of baled hay and made a big fire. There were wild scenes here the last time I looked back. I started straight for the City Hall.

There was still a crowd around the Astor House and everywhere, but I edged through and crossed over to the City Hall, where I caught a car just starting up town. . . .

Nineteen hotels were fired, yet the plot failed. Through the help of W. L. McDonald, a piano merchant, the eight conspirators escaped. Later, however, luck ran out for Robert Cobb Kennedy, as this confession, which was also his death warrant, attested:[17]

. . . After we had been in New York three weeks, we were told the object of the expedition was to retaliate on the North for the atrocities in the Shenandoah Valley. It was designed to set fire to the city on the night of the Presidential election; but the phosphorus was not ready, and it was put off until the 25th [26th] of November. I was stopping at the Belmont House, but moved into Prince Street. I set fire to four places—in Barnum's Museum, Lovejoy's Hotel, Tammany Hotel, and the New England House. The others only started fires in the house where each was lodging, and then ran off. Had they all done as I did, we would have had thirty-two fires, and played a huge joke on the fire department. I know that I am to be hung for setting fire to Barnum's Museum,* but that was only a joke. I had no idea of doing it. I had been drinking, and went in there with a friend, and, just to scare the people, I emptied a bottle of phosphorus on the floor. We knew it wouldn't set fire to the wood, for we had tried it before, and at one time concluded to give the whole thing up.

There was no fiendishness about it. After setting fire to my four places, I walked the streets all night, and went to the Exchange Hotel early in the morning. We all met there that morning and the next night. My friend and I had rooms there, but we sat in the office nearly all the time, reading the papers, while we were watched by the detectives, of whom the hotel was full.† I expected to die then, and if I had, it would have been all right; but now it seems rather hard. I escaped to Canada, and was glad enough when I crossed the bridge in safety.

I desired, however, to return to my command, and started with my friend for the Confederacy, *via* Detroit. Just before entering the city, he received an intimation that the detectives were on the lookout for us, and, giving me a signal, he jumped from the cars. I didn't notice the signal, but kept on, and was arrested in the depot.

* Kennedy was hanged in New York City a short time after this confession.
† Secretary of State Seward had been warned through the American consul at Halifax to expect plots against Northern cities on the eve of the election, and Richmond papers had openly boasted of these schemes.

I wish to say that killing women and children was the last thing thought of. We wanted to let the people of the North understand that there were two sides to this war, and that they can't be rolling in wealth and comfort, while we at the South are bearing all the hardships and privations.

In retaliation for Sheridan's atrocities in the Shenandoah Valley, we desired to destroy property, not the lives of women and children, although that would, of course, have followed in its train.

Done in the presence of

LIEUT.-COL. MARTIN BURKE,
And J. HOWARD, JR.

March 24 [1865], 10:30 P.M.

CHAPTER 36

A GIFT FOR
MR. LINCOLN

B Y LATE 1864 an overland telegraph between America and Europe by way of Bering Strait and Asiatic Russia was under construction. Since 1860, discoveries of gold, silver and cinnabar deposits in the Sierra Nevadas and the Rockies had drawn thousands of brawling but hard-working miners to those regions. The votes cast in the presidential election of 1864 had demonstrated, Lincoln asserted, that "we have *more* men *now* than we had when the war *began;* that we are not exhausted, nor in process of exhaustion; that we are *gaining* strength, and may, if need be, maintain the contest indefinitely." These three events were among those that the President emphasized on December 6, 1864, when he reported to Congress on the state of the Union.

I

Other paragraphs in the President's message discussed the military situation:[1]

The war continues. Since the last annual message all the important lines and positions then occupied by our forces have been maintained, and our arms have steadily advanced; thus liberating the regions left in rear, so that Missouri, Kentucky, Tennessee and parts of other States have again produced reasonably fair crops.

The most remarkable feature in the military operations of the year is General Sherman's attempted march of three hundred miles directly through the insurgent region. It tends to show a great increase of our

relative strength that our General-in-Chief should feel able to confront
and hold in check every active force of the enemy, and yet to detach a
well-appointed large army to move on such an expedition. The result
not yet being known, conjecture in regard to it is not here indulged.

*Lincoln believed that in the recent election he had heard the voice of the
people:*

Important movements have also occurred during the year to the effect of moulding society for durability in the Union. Although short of
complete success, it is much in the right direction, that twelve thousand
citizens in each of the States of Arkansas and Louisiana have organized
loyal State governments with free constitutions, and are earnestly
struggling to maintain and administer them. The movements in the
same direction, more extensive, though less definite in Missouri, Kentucky and Tennessee, should not be overlooked. But Maryland presents
the example of complete success.* Maryland is secure to Liberty and
Union for all the future. The genius of rebellion will no more claim
Maryland. Like another foul spirit, being driven out, it may seek to tear
her, but it will woo her no more.

At the last session of Congress a proposed amendment of the Constitution abolishing slavery throughout the United States, passed the
Senate, but failed for lack of the requisite two-thirds vote in the
House of Representatives. Although the present is the same Congress,
and nearly the same members, and without questioning the wisdom or
patriotism of those who stood in opposition, I venture to recommend
the reconsideration and passage of the measure at the present session.
Of course the abstract question is not changed; but an intervening
election shows, almost certainly, that the next Congress will pass the
measure if this does not. Hence there is only a question of *time* as to
when the proposed amendment will go to the States for their action.
And as it is to so go, at all events, may we not agree that the sooner the
better? It is not claimed that the election has imposed a duty on members to change their views or their votes, any further than, as an additional element to be considered, their judgment may be affected by it.
It is the voice of the people now, for the first time, heard upon the question. In a great national crisis, like ours, unanimity of action among
those seeking a common end is very desirable—almost indispensable.

* On October 13, 1864, Maryland abolished slavery by popular vote.

And yet no approach to such unanimity is attainable, unless some deference shall be paid to the will of the majority, simply because it is the will of the majority. In this case the common end is the maintenance of the Union; and, among the means to secure that end, such will, through the election, is most clearly declared in favor of such constitutional amendment.

Whither the road to peace? Lincoln thought he knew:

The public purpose to re-establish and maintain the national authority is unchanged, and, as we believe, unchangeable. The manner of continuing the effort remains to choose. On careful consideration of all the evidence accessible it seems to me that no attempt at negotiation with the insurgent leader could result in any good. He would accept nothing short of severance of the Union—precisely what we will not and cannot give. His declarations to this effect are explicit and oft-repeated. He does not attempt to deceive us. He affords us no excuse to deceive ourselves. He cannot voluntarily re-accept the Union; we cannot voluntarily yield it. Between him and us the issue is distinct, simple, and inflexible. It is an issue which can only be tried by war, and decided by victory. If we yield, we are beaten; if the Southern people fail him, he is beaten. Either way, it would be the victory and defeat following war. What is true, however, of him who heads the insurgent cause, is not necessarily true of those who follow. Although he cannot re-accept the Union, they can. Some of them, we know, already desire peace and reunion. The number of such may increase. They can, at any moment, have peace simply by laying down their arms and submitting to the national authority under the Constitution. After so much, the government could not, if it would, maintain war against them. The loyal people would not sustain or allow it. If questions should remain, we would adjust them by the peaceful means of legislation, conference, courts, and votes, operating only in constitutional and lawful channels. . . .

In presenting the abandonment of armed resistance to the national authority on the part of the insurgents, as the only indispensable condition to ending the war on the part of the government, I retract nothing heretofore said as to slavery. I repeat the declaration made a year ago, that "while I remain in my present position I shall not attempt to retract or modify the emancipation proclamation, nor shall I return to slavery any person who is free by the terms of that proclamation, or by any of the Acts of Congress." If the people should, by whatever mode or means, make it an Executive duty to re-enslave such persons, another, and not I, must be their instrument to perform it.

In stating a single condition of peace, I mean simply to say that the war will cease on the part of the government, whenever it shall have ceased on the part of those who began it.

II

The weather held fine in Georgia, and Sherman's troops joked over how by Christmas they would be feasting on oysters. The general was within reach of his goal:[2]

In approaching Savannah, General Slocum struck the Charleston Railroad near the bridge, and occupied the river-bank as his left flank, where he had captured two of the enemy's river-boats and had prevented two others (gunboats) from coming down the river to communicate with the city; while General Howard, by his right flank, had broken the Gulf Railroad. . . , and occupied the railroad itself down to the Little Ogeechee . . . so that no supplies could reach Savannah by any of its accustomed channels.

We, on the contrary, possessed large herds of cattle, which we had brought along or gathered in the country, and our wagons still contained a reasonable amount of breadstuffs and other necessaries, and the fine rice crops of the Savannah and Ogeechee rivers furnished to our men and animals a large amount of rice and rice-straw.

We also held the country to the south and west of the Ogeechee as foraging ground.

Still, communication with the fleet was of vital importance, and I directed General Kilpatrick to cross the Ogeechee by a pontoon-bridge, to reconnoitre Fort McAllister, and to proceed to St. Catherine's Sound, in the direction of Sunbury or Kilkenny Bluff, and open communication with the fleet. General Howard had previously, by my direction, sent one of his best scouts down the Ogeechee in a canoe for a like purpose. But more than this was necessary. We wanted the vessels and their contents, and the Ogeechee River, a navigable stream close to the rear of our camps, was the proper avenue of supply.

The enemy had burned the road-bridge across the Ogeechee, just below the mouth of the Camochee, known as "King's Bridge." This was reconstructed in an incredibly short time in the most substantial manner by the Fifty-eighth Indiana, Colonel Buel, under the direction of Captain Reese, of the Engineer corps, and on the morning of the thirteenth December, the Second division of the Fifteenth corps, under command of Brigadier-General Hazen, crossed the bridge to the west bank of the Ogeechee, and marched down with orders to carry by assault Fort McAllister, a strong inclosed redoubt, manned by two companies of artillery and three of infantry, in all about two hundred men, and mounting twenty-three guns, *en barbette,* and one mortar.

General Hazen reached the vicinity of Fort McAllister about one P.M., deployed his division about the place, with both flanks resting upon the river, posted his skirmishers judiciously behind the trunks of trees whose branches had been used for abattis, and about five P.M. assaulted the place with nine regiments at three points, all of them successfully. I witnessed the assault from a rice-mill on the opposite bank of the river, and can bear testimony to the handsome manner in which it was accomplished.

General William B. Hazen commanded the old division with which Sherman had fought at Shiloh and Vicksburg. These were the hard-bitten veterans who saw, three miles across a salt marsh, Rebel flags flying on Fort McAllister. By eleven o'clock on the morning of December 13, Hazen had almost closed in on the enemy:[3]

. . . About one mile from the Fort a picket was captured, revealing the whereabouts of a line of torpedoes across the road. Some time was lost in safely removing them, when, leaving eight regiments at that point, nine were carried forward to about six hundred yards from the Fort, and deployed, with a line of skirmishers thrown sufficiently near the Fort to keep the gunners from working their guns with any effect; those firing to the rear being in barbette.

The grounds to the right of the Fort being marshy, cut through by deep streams, rendered the deployment of that part of the line slow and difficult, and was not completely effected till forty-five minutes past four P.M., at which time, every officer and man of the nine regiments being instructed what to do, the bugle sounded the forward, and at precisely five o'clock the Fort was carried.

The troops were deployed in our line as thin as possible, the result being that no man in the assault was struck till they came to close quarters. Here the fighting became desperate and deadly. Just outside the works, a line of torpedoes had been placed, many of which were exploded by the tread of the troops, blowing many men to atoms; but the line moved on without checking, over, under, and through abattis, ditches, palisading, and parapet, fighting the garrison through the Fort to their bomb-proofs, from which they still fought, and only succumbed as each man was individually overpowered. Our losses were, twenty-four officers and men killed, and one hundred and ten officers and men wounded.

Meanwhile Union warships had reached the coastal sounds immediately below Savannah—Wassaw, Ossabaw, St. Catherines—and waited for a chance to help Sherman. Rear Admiral John A. Dahlgren reported to Welles how the Navy played its part as Sherman's army finally marched to the sea:[4]

On the eighteenth, General Sherman came on board the flag-ship. Having fully invested Savannah on the land side, whilst the navy held every avenue by water, General Sherman sent a summons to surrender, which was declined by General Hardee on the ground that he held his two lines of defence, and was in communication with his superior authority. General Sherman therefore prepared to attack. His army was gradually drawing closer on Savannah River, and in order to cut off the escape of the rebel forces, he concluded it would be better to send a division to reënforce the troops of General Foster, up Broad River, and make a serious attack there in the direction of the railroad, whilst that on Beaulieu would be limited to the naval cannonade, which I must not omit to mention had been begun and continued with deliberation by Lieutenant Commander Scott, in the *Sonoma*, assisted for a day or so by the mortar of the *Griffiths*, Acting-Master Ogilvie. To insure the exact concurrence of the several ports, the General went with me to Hilton Head in my steamer, and General Foster was made fully acquainted with the design. Late on Monday I put to sea, but to avoid detention from the increasing gale, the pilot preferred to follow the interior passage, and when near Ossabaw my steamer grounded. We started in the barge to pull, and were nearly in the waters of Ossabaw when a tug came along with the following telegram for General Sherman:

FROM STATION NEAR HEADQUARTERS,
December 4, 1864—M.

To GENERAL SHERMAN:

General Howard reports one of General Leggett's brigades near Savannah, and no enemy. Prisoners say the city is abandoned and enemy gone to Hardeeville.

Wood captured six guns. Slocum got eight guns, and is moving on the city.

DAYTON,

Aid-de-Camp.

It was now about three P.M. General Sherman hastened to his head-quarters, and I to the division of vessels lying in front of Beaulieu. The facts of the case were soon apparent. Captain Scott, of the *Sonoma,* was in possession of Fort Beaulieu and Rosedew. I landed at the former, and after giving some brief directions, was on my way from it when I received a note from General Sherman, dated half-past six P.M., with two telegrams from General Howard, one saying, "Tatnall intends to run the blockade tonight;" the other: "Rebel boat *Savannah,* with Tatnall in, is just out of our reach."

I did not apprehend that this intention to escape could be carried into effect.

The two iron-clads which I had at Wassaw blocked the best way out, and I did not believe that the rebel ram could be brought over the shallows of Savannah River, save under the most favorable circumstances of a high tide and an easterly wind. At this time it was blowing a gale from the north-west.

Still it did not seem proper to allow the public interest to incur the least risk in a matter so important. So I ordered the *Pawnee* to tow the *Nantucket* to Savannah River, and her commander being too ill to be on deck, Fleet-Captain Bradford volunteered for the duty.

It was three o'clock on the morning of the twenty-first when I lay down for a few hours' rest; and as my steamer was still aground, got into my barge at seven A.M., pulled to Wassaw, then across the sound into the pass to the Savannah River, and had nearly reached the Savannah River when a tug came along and relieved the faithful seamen of their severe labor in a heavy gale, wet to the skin as they were. I arrived about noon, hoisted my flag in the *Wissahickon,* Captain Johnson, and proceeded up the river with the *Winona,* Captain Dana, and two tugs.

About four P.M., the obstructions across the channel near the head of Elba Island compelled me to anchor a short distance below the city. . . .

The glorious flag of the Union once more waved over the ramparts of the forts, and the city, and the vessels of the navy on the water. Savannah has been taken in the only way probably that it was assailable. In every other the defences were complete and powerful, extending over every approach, and including the rivers that traversed the country to the southward; so that an attack in those quarters could not have succeeded. It is one of the first fruits of the brilliant campaign commencing at Atlanta, and of that fine conception—the march through Georgia.

But it is not the last, and General Sherman has but to follow out his plans in order to reap still greater advantages for the country and renown for himself.

III

In Tennessee, on the first day of December, General John Bell Hood made what seemed to him to be a logical decision:[5]

After the failure of my cherished plan to crush Schofield's Army before it reached its strongly fortified position around Nashville, I remained with an effective force of only twenty-three thousand and fifty-three. I was therefore well aware of our inability to attack the Federals in their new stronghold with any hope of success, although Schofield's troops had abandoned the field at Franklin, leaving their dead and wounded in our possession, and had hastened with considerable alarm into their fortifications. . . . I knew equally well that in the absence of the prestige of complete victory, I could not venture with my small force to cross the Cumberland river into Kentucky, without first receiving reinforcements from the Trans-Mississippi Department. I felt convinced that the Tennesseeans and Kentuckians would not join our forces, since we had failed in the first instance to defeat the Federal Army and capture Nashville. The President [Davis] was still urgent in his instructions relative to the transference of troops to the Army of Tennessee from Texas, and I daily hoped to receive the glad tidings of their safe passage across the Mississippi river.

Thus, unless strengthened by these long-looked for reinforcements, the only remaining chance of success in the campaign, at this juncture, was to take position, entrench around Nashville, and await Thomas's attack which, if handsomely repulsed, might afford us an opportunity to follow up our advantage on the spot, and enter the city on the heels of the enemy.

I could not afford to turn southward, unless for the *special* purpose of forming a junction with the expected reinforcements from Texas, and with the avowed intention to march back again upon Nashville. In truth, our Army was in that condition which rendered it more judicious the men should face a decisive issue rather than retreat—in other words, rather than renounce the honor of their cause, without having made a last and manful effort to lift up the sinking fortunes of the Confederacy.

I therefore determined to move upon Nashville, to entrench, to accept the chances of reinforcements from Texas, and, even at the risk of an attack in the meantime by overwhelming numbers, to adopt the only feasible means of defeating the enemy with my reduced numbers, viz., to await his attack, and, if favored by success, to follow him into his works. . . .

In accordance with these convictions, I ordered the Army to move forward on the 1st of December in the direction of Nashville. . . .

Grant chafed to think that Hood and his army hadn't been finished off by now. Sherman, prodded by Grant to do whatever he could to budge Thomas, admitted that he was "somewhat astonished by the attitude of things in Tennessee." Yet Sherman reminded Grant that while Thomas was "slow in mind and action" he was "judicious and brave," and in time, Sherman believed, Thomas would "outmanoeuvre and destroy Hood." Thomas also chafed under the pressure being exerted on him.

Colonel Henry Stone of Thomas' staff felt a deep sympathy for his chief:[6]

Probably no commander ever underwent two weeks of greater anxiety and distress of mind than General Thomas during the interval between Hood's arrival and his precipitate departure from the vicinity of Nashville. . . . From the 2d of December until the battle was fought on the 15th, the general-in-chief did not cease, day or night, to send him from the headquarters at City Point, Va., most urgent and often most uncalled-for orders in regard to his operations, culminating in an order on the 9th relieving him, and directing him to turn over his command to General Schofield, who was assigned to his place—an order which, had it not been revoked, the great captain would have obeyed with loyal single-heartedness. This order, though made out at the Adjutant-General's office in Washington, was not sent to General Thomas, and he did not know of its existence until told of it some years later. . . . He felt, however, that something of the kind was impending. General Halleck dispatched to him, on the morning of the 9th: "Lieutenant-General Grant expresses much dissatisfaction at your delay in attacking the enemy." His reply shows how entirely he understood the situation: "I feel conscious I have done everything in my power, and that the troops could not have been gotten ready before this. If General Grant should order me to be relieved, I will submit without a murmur." As he was writing this—2 o'clock in the afternoon of December 9th—a terrible storm of freezing rain had been pouring down since daylight, and it kept on pouring and freezing all that day and a part of the next. That night General Grant notified him that the order relieving him—which he had divined—was suspended. But he did not know who had been designated as his successor. With this threat hanging over him; with the utter impossibility, in that weather, of making any movement; with the prospect that the labors of his whole life were about to end in disappointment, if not disaster—he never, for an instant, abated his energy or his work of preparation. Not an hour, day and night, was he idle. Nobody—not even his most trusted staff-officers—knew the contents of the telegrams that came to him. But it was very evident that something greatly troubled him. While the rain was falling and the fields and roads were ice-bound, he would sometimes sit by the window for an hour or more, not speaking a word, gazing steadily out upon the forbidding prospect, as if he were trying to will the storm away. It was curious and interesting to see how, in this gloomy interval, his time was occupied by matters not strictly military. Now, it was a visit from a delegation of the city government, in regard to some municipal regulation; again, somebody whose one horse had been seized and put into the cavalry; then, a committee of citizens, begging that wood might be furnished, to keep some poor families from freezing; and, of evenings, Governor Andrew Johnson—then Vice-President elect—would unfold to him, with much iteration, his fierce views concerning secession, rebels, and reconstruction. To all he gave a patient and kindly hearing, and he often astonished Governor Johnson by his knowledge of constitutional and international law. But, underneath all, it was plain to see that General Grant's dissatisfaction keenly affected him, and that only by the proof which a successful battle would furnish could he hope to regain the confidence of the general-in-chief.

So when, at 8 o'clock on the evening of December 14th, after having laid his plans before his corps commanders, and dismissed them, he dictated to General Halleck the telegram, "The ice having melted away today, the enemy will be attacked tomorrow morning," he drew a deep sigh of relief, and for the first time for a week showed again something of his natural buoyancy and cheerfulness. He moved about more briskly; he put in order all the little last things that remained to be done; he signed his name where it was needed in the letter-book, and then, giving orders to his staff-officers to be ready at 5 o'clock the next morning, went gladly to bed.

The ice had not melted a day too soon; for, while he was writing the telegram to General Halleck, General Logan was speeding his way to Nashville, with orders from General Grant that would have placed him in command of all the Union forces there assembled. General Thomas, fortunately, did not then learn this second proof of General Grant's lack of confidence; and General Logan, on reaching Louisville, found that the work intended for him was already done—and came no farther. At the very time when these orders were made out at Washington, in obedience to General Grant's directions, a large part of the cavalry was unmounted; two divisions were absent securing horses and proper outfit; wagons were unfinished and mules lacking or unbroken; pontoons unmade and pontoniers untrained; the ground was covered with a glare of ice which made all the fields and hillsides impassable for horses and scarcely passable for foot-men. The natives declared that the Yankees brought their weather as well as their army with them. Every corps commander in the army protested that a movement under such conditions would be little short of madness, and certain to result in disaster.

Hood commanded troops that were largely "confused and demoralized." That redoubtable Tennessee historian, Sam Watkins, remembered that on the morning of December 15 he glanced at Hood and recognized "how feeble and decrepit he looked, with an arm in a sling and a crutch in the other hand, trying to guide and control his horse." Colonel Stone watched Thomas that same morning, and saw his blue-clad columns swarm up a hillside:

It was not daylight, on the morning of the 15th of December, when the army began to move. In most of the camps reveille had been sounded at 4 o'clock, and by 6 everything was ready. It turned out a warm, sunny, winter morning. A dense fog at first hung over the valleys and completely hid all movements, but by 9 o'clock this had cleared away. . . .

When . . . the sun began to burn away the fog, the sight from General Thomas's position was inspiring. A little to the left, on Montgomery Hill, the salient of the Confederate lines, and not more than six hundred yards distant from Wood's salient, on Lawrens Hill, could be seen the advance line of works, behind which an unknown force of the enemy lay in wait. Beyond, and along the Hillsboro' Pike, were stretches of stone wall, with here and there a detached earth-work, through whose embrasures peeped the threatening artillery. To the right, along the valley of Richland Creek, the dark line of Wilson's advancing cavalry could be seen slowly making its difficult way across the wet, swampy ground. Close in front, and at the foot of the hill, its right joining Wilson's left, was A. J. Smith's corps, full of cheer and enterprise, and glad to be once more in the open field. Then came the Fourth Corps, whose left, bending back toward the north, was hidden behind Lawrens Hill. Already the skirmishers were engaged, the Confederates slowly falling back before the determined and steady pressure of Smith and Wood.

By the time that Wilson's and Smith's lines were fully extended and brought up to within striking distance of the Confederate works, along the Hillsboro' Pike, it was noon. Post's brigade of Wood's old division . . . which lay at the foot of Montgomery Hill, full of dash and spirit, had since morning been regarding the works at the summit with covetous eyes. At Post's suggestion, it was determined to see which party wanted them most. Accordingly, a charge was ordered—and in a moment the brigade was swarming up the hillside, straight for the enemy's advanced works. For almost the first time since the grand assault on Missionary Ridge, a year before, here was an open field where everything could be seen. From General Thomas's headquarters everybody looked on with breathless suspense, as the blue line, broken and irregular, but with steady persistence, made its way up the steep hillside against a fierce storm of musketry and artillery. Most of the shots, however, passed over the men's heads. It was a struggle to keep up with the colors, and, as they neared the top, only the strongest were at the front. Without a moment's pause, the color-bearers and those who had kept up with them, Post himself at the head, leaped the parapet. As the colors waved from the summit, the whole line swept forward and was over the works in a twinkling, gathering in prisoners and guns. Indeed, so large was the mass of prisoners that a few minutes later was seen heading toward our own lines, that a number of officers at General Thomas's headquarters feared the assault had failed and the prisoners were Confederate reserves who had rallied and retaken the works. But the fear was only momentary; for the wild outburst of cheers that rang across the valley told the story of complete success. . . .

The salient at the center . . . was still firmly held. Post's successful assault had merely driven out or captured the advance forces; the main line was intact. As soon as word came of the successful assault on the

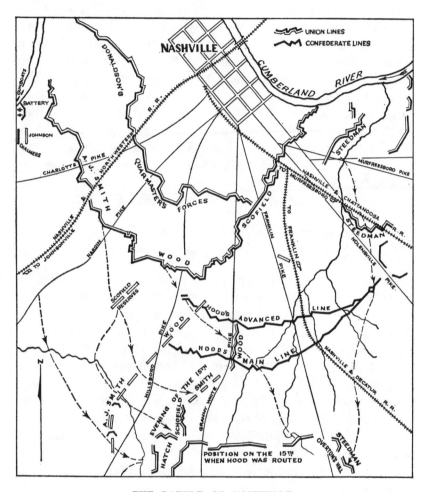

THE BATTLE OF NASHVILLE

From Lossing, *Pictorial History of the Civil War*

right, General Thomas sent orders to General Wood, commanding the Fourth Corps, to prepare to attack the salient. The staff-officer by whom this order was sent did not at first find General Wood; but seeing the two division commanders whose troops would be called upon for the work, gave them the instructions. As he was riding along the line he met one of the brigade commanders—an officer with a reputation for exceptional courage and gallantry—who, in reply to the direction to prepare for the expected assault, said, "You don't mean that we've got to go in here and attack the works on that hill?" "Those are the orders," was the answer. Looking earnestly across the open valley, and at the steep hill beyond, from which the enemy's guns were throwing shot and shell with uncomfortable frequency and nearness, he said, "Why, it would be suicide, sir; perfect suicide." "Nevertheless, those are the orders," said the officer; and he rode on to complete his work. Before he could rejoin General Thomas the assault was made, and the enemy were driven out with a loss of guns, colors, and prisoners, and their whole line was forced to abandon the works along the Hillsboro' Pike and fall back to the Granny White Pike. The retreating line was followed by the entire Fourth Corps (Wood's), as well as by the cavalry and Smith's troops; but night soon fell, and the whole army went into bivouac in the open fields wherever they chanced to be.

The Hood of Nashville was the Hood of Cassville, Kenesaw, Atlanta, Allatoona, Spring Hill, and Franklin. He accepted no blame:[7]

The 10th of December, Generals Stewart and Cheatham were directed to construct detached works in rear of their flanks, which rested near the river, in order to protect these flanks against an effort by the Federals to turn them. Although every possible exertion was made by these officers, the works were not completed when, on the 15th, the Federal Army moved out, and attacked both flanks, whilst the main assault was directed against our left. It was my intention to have made these defences self-sustaining, but time was not allowed, as the enemy attacked on the morning of the 15th. Throughout that day, they were repulsed at all points of the general line with heavy loss, and only succeeded towards evening in capturing the infantry outposts on our left, and with them the small force together with the artillery posted in these unfinished works.

Thomas sent Halleck a factual report and a promise:[8]

NASHVILLE, TENN.,
December 15, 1864—9 P.M.

MAJ. GEN. H. W. HALLECK,
WASHINGTON, D. C.

I attacked the enemy's left this morning and drove it from the river, below the city, very nearly to the Franklin pike, a distance about eight miles. Have captured General Chalmers' headquarters and train, and a second train of about 20 wagons, with between 800 and 1,000 prisoners and 16 pieces of artillery. The troops behaved splendidly, all taking their share in assaulting and carrying the enemy's breast-works. I shall attack the enemy again tomorrow, if he stands to fight, and, if he retreats during the night, will pursue him, throwing a heavy cavalry force in his rear, to destroy his trains, if possible.

Confederate Major General Carter L. Stevenson, commanding the right of Hood's line, saw Thomas' troops accept heavy punishment to fulfill their commander's promise:[9]

The enemy advanced early in heavy force in front of the new line which we had constructed late the previous night, my division extending its entire length, part of it in two and part of it in one thin rank, from a short distance to the left of the Franklin pike. The skirmishers of the right of Lee's corps (Clayton's) and mine maintained their position so well, though in small force, that in their subsequent accounts the enemy have seen fit to magnify their affair with them into a desperate assault by two corps upon our first line, which was finally successful, but attended with heavy loss. Soon afterward their forces advanced to the assault. . . . Their success the previous day had emboldened them, and they rushed forward with great spirit, only to be driven back with dreadful slaughter. Finding at last that they could make no impression upon our lines, they relinquished their attempt and contented themselves with keeping up an incessant fire of small arms at long range and an artillery fire which I have never seen surpassed for heaviness, continuance, and accuracy. This state of things continued until evening, doing, however, but little damage, my men keeping closely in the trenches and perfectly cool and confident.

General James T. Holtzclaw, commanding a Confederate brigade, testified to the bravery—and the shocking losses—of the assaulting force:

About 10 o'clock [the enemy] made a desperate charge, but was driven back, with loss. He then commenced a most furious shelling from three six-gun batteries, concentrating his fire mainly upon my right. One battery of unusually heavy guns was brought down the pike to within 600 yards of my line. The conformation of the ground prevented me sharpshooting it sufficiently to drive it away. At 12 M. the enemy made a most determined charge on my right. Placing a negro brigade in front they gallantly dashed up to the abatis, forty feet in front, and were killed by hundreds. Pressed on by their white brethren in the rear they continued to come up in masses to the abatis, but they came only to die. I have seen most of the battle-fields of the West, but never saw dead men thicker in front of my two right regiments; the great masses and disorder of the enemy enabling the left to rake them in flank, while the right, with a coolness unexampled, scarcely threw away a shot at their front. The enemy at last broke and fled in wild disorder. With great difficulty I prevented my line from pursuing; with a supporting line I should certainly have done so; but covering the pike, which would be our only line of retreat in case of disaster, I did not feel justified in hazarding the position for what might only have been a temporary success. A color-bearer of the negro brigade brought his standard to within a few feet of my line. He was shot down, and Lieutenant Knox, of the Thirty-sixth Alabama Regiment, sprang over the shattered works and brought it in. Another flag was carried off by an officer after five different bearers had fallen in the vain effort to plant it in my works. At 2 P.M. the enemy attempted a second charge, less determined than the first. Their brave officers could neither lead nor drive their men to such certain death; I noticed as many as three mounted who fell far in advance of their commands urging them forward. The shelling of the enemy's batteries between 12 and 3 P.M. was the most furious I ever witnessed, while the range was so precise that scarce a shell failed to explode in the line. The enemy seemed now to be satisfied that he could not carry my position, and contented himself by shelling and sharpshooting everything in sight.

But the weight of Union men and metal was too heavy for Confederate resistance, no matter how valiant. General Stevenson related an unexpected turn of events:

Toward evening General Lee sent me information that things were going badly on the left, and that it might be necessary to retire under cover of the approaching night. I at once hurried off orders for the artillery horses, which had been removed some distance to the rear to protect them from the fire of the enemy's artillery, under which they could not have lived half an hour, to be brought up. (It was proper to observe that about the middle of the day mist and rain arose, which entirely prevented my seeing any thing that was going on beyond my own line.) The messengers had hardly gone for the horses before the break, which, commencing some distance beyond the left of Lee's corps, extended to my line. Seeing it, the men on my left commenced leaving the works, but at the call of their officers returned at once and held the line until the enemy were within fifty steps of them on their flank and pouring a fire into them from the flank and rear. When the true situation of affairs became apparent, and it was evident that the whole army, with the exception of my division and Clayton's, had been broken and scattered, the order for their withdrawal was given, an effort being made to deploy skirmishers from my left brigade at right angles to the works to cover, in some measure, the movement. Amid the indescribable confusion of other troops, and with the enemy pouring in their fire upon their flanks and from the front—having rushed toward the break and then forward when they perceived that the troops on my left had broken—it was impossible to withdraw the command in order, and it became considerably broken and confused. Many of them were unable to get out of the ditches in time and were captured. . . . The artillery horses of Rowan's battery, on the left of my line, could not be brought up in time, and one of the guns of Corput's battery was lost by being driven at full speed against a tree and the carriage broken. The different brigade and regimental commanders had sent off their horses, there being no protection for them near the breast-works, and, being thus unable to move about more rapidly than the men, were prevented from reforming their commands as quickly as could have been desired and extricating them from the throng of panic-stricken stragglers from other commands who crowded the road. This was done at last, and the line of march taken up for Franklin.

On December 16, while the outcome of the battle was still unknown in Washington, Lincoln had wired Thomas: "You made a magnificent beginning. A grand consummation is within your reach. Do not let it slip."

Lincoln need not have worried; Thomas, as his record showed, had let few chances to win "slip." The general responded to Lincoln, Stanton, Grant and Johnson on the events of a day when, by the testimony of Sam Watkins, Hood's Army of Tennessee "degenerated into a mob . . .":[10]

HEADQUARTERS DEPARTMENT OF THE CUMBERLAND,
EIGHT MILES FROM NASHVILLE, December 16, 1864—6 P.M.
THE PRESIDENT OF THE UNITED STATES,
HON. E. M. STANTON,
LIEUT. GEN. U. S. GRANT, AND
GOVERNOR ANDREW JOHNSON, NASHVILLE:

This army thanks you for your approbation of its conduct yesterday, and to assure you that it is not misplaced. I have the honor to report that the enemy has been pressed at all points today on his line of retreat to the Brentwood Hills, and Brigadier-General Hatch, of Wilson's corps of cavalry, on the right, turned the enemy's left, and captured a large number of prisoners, number not yet reported. Major-General Schofield's troops, next on the left of cavalry, carried several heights, captured many prisoners and six pieces of artillery. Brevet Major-General Smith, next on left of Major-General Schofield, carried the salient point of the enemy's line with McMillen's brigade, of McArthur's division, capturing 16 pieces of artillery, 2 brigadier-generals, and about 2,000 prisoners. Brigadier-General Garrard's division, of Smith's command, next on the left of McArthur's division, carried the enemy's intrenchments, capturing all the artillery and troops of the enemy on the line. Brigadier-General Wood's corps, on the Franklin pike, took up the assault, carrying the enemy's intrenchments in his front, captured 8 pieces of artillery, something over 600 prisoners, and drove the enemy within one mile of the Brentwood Pass. Major-General Steedman, commanding detachments of the different armies of the Military Division of the Mississippi, most nobly supported General Wood's left, and bore a most honorable part in the operations of the day. I have ordered the pursuit to be continued in the morning at daylight, although the troops are very much fatigued. The greatest enthusiasm prevails. I must not forget to report the operations of Brigadier-General Johnson, in successfully driving the enemy, with the co-operation of the gun-boats, under Lieutenant-Commander Fitch, from their established batteries on the Cumberland River below the city of Nashville, and of the services of Brigadier-General Croxton's brigade, in covering and relieving our right and rear, in the operations of yesterday and today. Although I have no report of the number of prisoners captured by Johnson's and Croxton's commands, I know they have made a large number. I am glad to be able to state that the number of prisoners captured yesterday greatly exceeds the number reported by me last evening. The woods, fields, and intrenchments are strewn with

the enemy's small-arms, abandoned in their retreat. In conclusion, I am
happy to state that all this has been effected with but a very small loss
to us. Our loss does not probably exceed 3,000; very few killed.

GEO. H. THOMAS,
Major-General, U. S. Volunteers,
Commanding

IV

In less than a week after Thomas triumphed at Nashville, Sherman
entered Savannah:[11]

Generals Slocum and Howard moved their headquarters at once into
the city, leaving the bulk of their troops in camps outside. On the
morning of December 22d I followed with my own headquarters, and
rode down Bull Street to the custom-house, from the roof of which we
had an extensive view over the city, the river, and the vast extent of
marsh and rice-fields on the South Carolina side. The navy-yard, and
the wreck of the iron-clad ram *Savannah*, were still smouldering, but
all else looked quiet enough. Turning back, we rode to the Pulaski
Hotel, which I had known in years long gone, and found it kept by a
Vermont man with a lame leg, who used to be a clerk in the St. Louis
Hotel, New Orleans, and I inquired about the capacity of his
hotel for headquarters. He was very anxious to have us for boarders,
but I soon explained to him that we had a full mess equipment along,
and that we were not in the habit of paying board; that one wing of the
building would suffice for our use, while I would allow him to keep an
hotel for the accommodation of officers and gentlemen in the remainder. I then dispatched an officer to look around for a livery-stable that
could accommodate our horses, and, while waiting there, an English
gentleman, Mr. Charles Green, came and said that he had a fine house
completely furnished, for which he had no use, and offered it as headquarters. . . .

I was disappointed that Hardee had escaped with his army, but
on the whole we had reason to be content with the substantial fruits of
victory. The Savannah River was found to be badly obstructed by torpedoes, and by log piers stretched across the channel below the city,
which piers were filled with the cobble stones that formerly paved the
streets. Admiral Dahlgren was extremely active, visited me repeatedly
in the city, while his fleet still watched Charleston, and all the avenues,
for the blockade-runners that infested the coast, which were no-

toriously owned and managed by Englishmen, who used the island of New Providence (Nassau) as a sort of entrepot. One of these small blockade-runners came into Savannah after we were in full possession, and the master did not discover his mistake till he came ashore to visit the custom-house. Of course his vessel fell a prize to the navy. A heavy force was at once set to work to remove the torpedoes and obstructions in the main channel of the river, and, from that time forth, Savannah became the great depot of supply for the troops operating in that quarter.

A "shrewd" Yankee, who understood Lincoln, offered a suggestion that Sherman accepted:

Within an hour of taking up my quarters in Mr. Green's house, Mr. A. G. Browne, of Salem, Massachusetts, United States Treasury agent for the Department of the South, made his appearance to claim possession, in the name of the Treasury Department, of all captured cotton, rice, buildings, etc. Having use for these articles ourselves, and having fairly earned them, I did not feel inclined to surrender possession, and explained to him that the quartermaster and commissary could manage them more to my liking than he; but I agreed, after the proper inventories had been prepared, if there remained any thing for which we had no special use, I would turn it over to him. It was then known that in the warehouses were stored at least twenty-five thousand bales of cotton, and in the forts one hundred and fifty large, heavy sea-coast guns; although afterward, on a more careful count, there proved to be more than two hundred and fifty sea-coast or siege guns, and thirty-one thousand bales of cotton. At that interview Mr. Browne, who was a shrewd, clever Yankee, told me that a vessel was on the point of starting for Old Point Comfort, and, if she had good weather off Cape Hatteras, would reach Fortress Monroe by Christmas-day, and he suggested that I might make it the occasion of sending a welcome Christmas gift to the President, Mr. Lincoln, who peculiarly enjoyed such pleasantry. I accordingly sat down and wrote on a slip of paper, to be left at the telegraph-office at Fortress Monroe for transmission, the following:

"SAVANNAH, GEORGIA, December 22, 1864.

"To HIS EXCELLENCY PRESIDENT LINCOLN, WASHINGTON, D. C.:

"I beg to present you as a Christmas-gift the city of Savannah, with one hundred and fifty heavy guns and plenty of ammunition, also about twenty-five thousand bales of cotton.

"W. T. SHERMAN, *Major-General.*"

This message actually reached him on Christmas-eve, was extensively published in the newspapers, and made many a household unusually happy on that festive day; and it was in the answer to this dispatch that Mr. Lincoln wrote me the letter of December 26th, already given, beginning with the words, "Many, many thanks," etc., which he sent at the hands of General John A. Logan, who happened to be in Washington, and was coming to Savannah, to rejoin his command.

In 1861 Sherman had been "sadly disappointed" in Lincoln and had damned him along with politicians generally who had "got things in a hell of a fix." Now Sherman placed the President first among the wise men of the country. Years later, he gave his reasons to R. L. Johnson, associate editor of Century Magazine:[12]

. . . Mr. Lincoln was the wisest man of our day, and now truly and kindly gave voice to my secret thoughts and feeling when he wrote me at Savannah from Washington under date of Dec. 26, 1864:

"When you were about leaving Atlanta for the Atlantic coast, I was anxious if not fearful; but feeling that you were the better judge, and remembering 'nothing risked, nothing gained,' I did not interfere. Now the undertaking being a success, the honor is all yours; for I believe none of us went further than to acquiesce; and, taking the work of General Thomas into account, as it should be taken, it is indeed a great success. Not only does it afford the obvious and immediate military advantages, but, in showing to the world that your army could be divided, putting the stronger part to an important new service, and yet leaving enough to vanquish the old opposing force of the whole, Hood's army, it brings those who sat in darkness to see a great light. But what next? I suppose it will be safer if I leave General Grant and yourself to decide."

So highly do I prize this testimonial that I possess Mr. Lincoln's letter, every word in his own hand writing, unto this day; and if I know myself I believe on receiving it I experienced more satisfaction in giving to his overburdened and weary soul one gleam of satisfaction and happiness, than of selfish pride in an achievement which has given me among men a larger measure of fame than any single act of my life. . . .

V

The month that had begun with the President promising Congress that final victory was near now had ended. Thomas held Nashville, and in

Savannah Negroes began dating all events from "de Time Tecumpsey was here." Above the Mason and Dixon line every song-writer seemed busy at a new ballad to commemorate the march to the sea. Among them was D. A. Warden, who produced "Sherman's on the Track":[13]

> Oh look away out yonder,
>   For de dust am rising high,
> Gen'ral Sherman's comin' 'long,
>   And Massa's goin' to die,
> He's got some nigger soldiers
>   Dat make de rebels run,
> Just hold your breff a little while,
>   And see de glorious fun,
> Just hold your breff a little while,
>   And see de glorious fun.
> Chorus.—Shout! darkies shout!
>   Old Sherman's on de track,
>   He's knock'd de breff from poor old Jeff,
>   And laid him on his back, whack!

Two stanzas later Mr. Warden composed an accurate report of the general situation:

> The railroads hab been torn to smash,
>   De lokies cannot run,
> Old Hood has got his boiler bust
>   And dat hab stopt *his* fun,
> Poor Beauregard *lies* berry sick,
>   Wid rupture and wid gout,
> While Bobby Lee begins to see
>   De game am most played out,
> While Bobby Lee begins to see
>   De game am most played out.

1865

CHAPTER 37

A KING'S CURE
FOR ALL EVILS

————

T ED UPSON remembered a day back home in Lima, Indiana, during March 1859—Ted was going on fourteen then—when Cooper Dayton, his mother's brother from Nashville, and the Reverend Cory "got to talking right away and both got pretty mad for Preachers."

"Now, Brother Cory," Cooper Dayton asked, "if you had your own way what would you do with the slaves?"

"Free them, sir! Free them at once! You have no right to hold them a day longer in slavery."

Cooper Dayton looked at Cory. "My!" he said. "How you must love a Nigger!"

I

Almost four years of war had changed people, attitudes, circumstances.

Theodore Upson, of Company C, 100th Indiana Infantry—Ted was going on twenty now—was one of Sherman's boys who were finding the Christmas holidays in Savannah a midwinter picnic:[1]

We have been having a Christmas Jubilee. The boys raised some money and I went down into the City to get some stuff. We have a Darky cook, and he said, "You alls get the greginces and I will get you alls up a fine dinner sure." I got some chickens, canned goods, condensed milk, and a dozen eggs. These cost me pretty dear—$3.00 per doz. I wouldn't have minded so much, but when we came to use them there was only one of the lot that was at all fit to use and that was not any too good. But we had the dinner just the same and it was fine. Some of the officers had a banquet—they called it. I dont know if they had egg nog. If they did their eggs must have been better than ours, but I know they must have had some sort of nog for the Provost Guard had to help some of them to their Quarters.

Major James A. Connolly, older, maturer than Upson, wrote to his wife on January 19, 1865:[2]

Our headquarters are in the city. My office is in a fine brick building on "Oglethorpe Square," and Captain ———, aide de camp, and myself have private rooms in another fine residence on the same square. We have gas light, coal fires, sofas, fine beds, bath room with hot and cold water, and all such luxuries; so it won't do for us to remain here long or we shall be completely spoiled for soldiering. Our beds should be at the roots of the cypress trees of Carolina instead of the luxurious couches of Savannah. Soldiers may *be* gentlemen but they can't *live* like gentlemen and do soldier's duty.

I shall leave Savannah very favorably impressed with it as a city. I have been most courteously treated by all its citizens with whom I have come in contact, and I hope that its beautiful squares, its elegant mansions, and its delightful streets may never hear any but peaceful sounds. Our whole army has fallen in love with this city and we all leave it with regret.

II

Four hundred miles to the northeast there was action. An ominous telegram sped from the fort which commanded the entrance to the Cape Fear River and kept Wilmington, North Carolina, open to blockade runners:[3]

FORT FISHER,
January 12, 1865

MAJOR HILL:

There are a number of signal lights shown northeast and southeast; they are not the blockade signals, but the old fleet signals. Today at noon one of the blockaders ran very close down from battery Gatlin and turned off toward the fleet; when two and a half to three miles from us her decks seemed crowded, but not unusually so. I am just officially informed that a sergeant and three men deserted from Battery Gatlin last night.

LAMB,
Colonel

Another telegram came from a nearby post:

MASONBOROUGH,
January 12, 1865

MAJ. J. H. HILL:

The lights from the fleet have increased. Thirty and more vessels in view moving toward Fisher; 10 o'clock.

T. J. LIPSCOMB,
Colonel, Commanding

General W. H. C. Whiting, commanding the Confederate garrison at Wilmington, hurried to Fort Fisher. From there he sent a series of urgent appeals to Braxton Bragg, who had a small force at Sugar Loaf, between Fort Fisher and Wilmington:[4]

FORT FISHER,
January 13, 1865

GENERAL BRAGG:

The enemy have landed in large force. Garrison too weak to resist assault and prevent their advance. You must attack them at once.

WHITING,
General

FORT FISHER,
January 13, 1865

GENERAL BRAGG:

Enemy have landed a large force. They will assault me tonight, or try to do it. You must attack.

W. H. C. WHITING,
Major-General

FORT FISHER,
January 13, 1865—8 P.M.

GENERAL BRAXTON BRAGG:

Enemy are on the beach, where they have been all day. Why are they not attacked? Our casualties about forty, after a furious bombardment. I have ordered troops from the other posts. Our submarine cable and telegraph cut by shell. Enemy ceased firing at 6 o'clock.

WHITING,
General

Next day Whiting was even more forceful:[5]

FORT FISHER,
January 14, 1865—1:30 P.M.

GENERAL BRAGG:

I send this boat, *Cape Fear*, to town for coal and wood, with the request that she return at once; she is necessary here for our communication. The game of the enemy is very plain to me. They are now furiously bombarding my land front; they will continue to do that, in order, if possible, to silence my guns until they are satisfied that their land force has securely established itself across the neck and rests on the river; then Porter will attempt to force a passage to co-operate with the force that takes the river bank. I have received dispatches from you stating that the enemy had extended to the river-bank. This they should never have been allowed to do; and if they are permitted to remain there the reduction of Fort Fisher is but a question of time. This has been notified heretofore frequently both to yourself and to the Department. I will hold this place till the last extremities; but unless you drive that land force from its position I cannot answer for the security of this harbor. The fire has been and continues to be exceedingly heavy, surpassing not so much in its volume as in its extraordinary condition even the fire of Christmas. The garrison is in good spirits and condition.

I am, general, very respectfully, your obedient servant,

W. H. C. WHITING
Major-General

Bragg, ever the optimist, reported to Lee:[6]

SUGAR LOAF,
January 14, 1865—8 P.M.

GENERAL R. E. LEE,
RICHMOND, VA.:

The enemy succeeded last night in extending his line across the peninsula, and interposed between us and Fort Fisher. His line has been closely examined by myself and General Hoke, and he considers it too hazardous to assault with such an inferior force. Fisher has been re-enforced with sufficient veterans to make it safe. The width of the river is such the enemy cannot control it from his position even with artillery, and he has yet landed none. Weather continues fine and sea smooth. Bombardment today light.

BRAXTON BRAGG

Whiting, desperate, renewed his appeals to Bragg:

FORT FISHER,
January 15, 1865.

GENERAL BRAXTON BRAGG:

Is Fisher to be besieged, or you to attack? Should like to know. The fire on the fort from iron-clads heavy, but casualties so far during the fight 3 killed and 32 wounded.

W. H. C. WHITING,
Major-General

FORT FISHER,
January 15, 1865—6:30 P.M.

GENERAL BRAXTON BRAGG:

The enemy are assaulting us by land and sea. Their infantry out-number us. Can't you help us? I am slightly wounded.

WHITING,
General

Officers at batteries near Fort Fisher reported the collapse of the defense:[7]

BATTERY LAMB,
January 15, 1865

GENERAL BRAGG:

Fort Fisher evacuated; troops rushed in confusion to Battery Buchanan. I landed at Buchanan just as the enemy was going in, and barely escaped. I will report to you tonight. There is no mistake in this information. Lieutenant Bright is here with thirty men, and wishes instruction.

A. H. COLQUITT,
Brigadier-General

BATTERY LAMB,
January 15, 1865—4:20 P.M.
(Received 4:45 P.M.)

GENERAL HÉBERT: *

Enemy still hold east part of land face of Fisher. Mound and Buchanan still firing. Flag still waving over the Mound and Buchanan.

BRIGHT,
Lieutenant

BATTERY LAMB,
January 15, 1865—10:30 P.M.
(Received 12 midnight.)

GENERAL HÉBERT:

All at once firing has ceased; also signals; and the whole fleet are now throwing rockets up—all colors. It is fully believed that the fort has surrendered. . . .

J. J. BRIGHT

Once more Bragg had the duty of announcing a result far different from what he had predicted:[8]

SUGAR LOAF,
January 16, 1865—1 A.M.

GENERAL R. E. LEE,
PETERSBURG:

I am mortified at having to report the unexpected capture of Fort Fisher, with most of its garrison, at about 10 o'clock tonight. Particulars not known.

BRAXTON BRAGG

Alexander H. Stephens, who wore no blinders, assessed the importance to the Confederacy of the loss of Fort Fisher:[9]

The fall of this Fort was one of the greatest disasters which had befallen our cause from the beginning of the war—not excepting the loss of Vicksburg or Atlanta. Forts Fisher and Caswell guarded the entrance to the Cape Fear River, and prevented the complete blockade of the port of Wilmington, through which a limited Foreign Commerce had been carried on during the whole time. It was by means of what

* General Louis Hébert, chief engineer of the Department of North Carolina.

cotton could thus be carried out, that we had been enabled to get along financially, as well as we had; and at this point also, a considerable number of arms and various munitions of war, as well as large supplies of subsistence, had been introduced. All other ports . . . had long since been closed by Naval siege. . . . Fort Sumter at Charleston, it is true, had still held out, and had never been taken, but the harbor there had been virtually closed by a strict blockade; so that the closing of the port of Wilmington was the complete shutting out of the Confederate States from all intercourse by sea with Foreign Countries.

III

Suddenly Washington and the halls of Congress became the greatest battlefield of the war. The objective to be won was the consent of Americans to a constitutional amendment abolishing slavery. When the first phase of the campaign had been fought the previous spring, the President of the United States had led the attack. Charles A. Dana had admired him greatly:[10]

Lincoln was a supreme politician. He understood politics because he understood human nature. I had an illustration of this in the spring of 1864. The administration had decided that the Constitution of the United States should be amended so that slavery should be prohibited. This was not only a change in our national policy, it was also a most important military measure. It was intended not merely as a means of abolishing slavery forever, but as a means of affecting the judgment and the feelings and the anticipations of those in rebellion. It was believed that such an amendment to the Constitution would be equivalent to new armies in the field, that it would be worth at least a million men, that it would be an intellectual army that would tend to paralyze the enemy and break the continuity of his ideas.

In order thus to amend the Constitution, it was necessary first to have the proposed amendment approved by three fourths of the States. When that question came to be considered, the issue was seen to be so close that one State more was necessary. The State of Nevada was organized and admitted into the Union to answer that purpose. I have sometimes heard people complain of Nevada as superfluous and petty, not big enough to be a State; but when I hear that complaint, I always hear Abraham Lincoln saying, "It is easier to admit Nevada than to raise another million of soldiers."

In March, 1864, the question of allowing Nevada to form a State government finally came up in the House of Representatives. There was strong opposition to it. For a long time beforehand the question had been canvassed anxiously. At last, late one afternoon, the President came into my office, in the third story of the War Department. He used to come there sometimes rather than send for me, because he was fond of walking and liked to get away from the crowds in the White House. He came in and shut the door.

"Dana," he said, "I am very anxious about this vote. It has got to be taken next week. The time is very short. It is going to be a great deal closer than I wish it was."

"There are plenty of Democrats who will vote for it," I replied. "There is James E. English, of Connecticut; I think he is sure, isn't he?"

"Oh, yes; he is sure on the merits of the question."

"Then," said I, "there's 'Sunset' Cox, of Ohio. How is he?"

"He is sure and fearless. But there are some others that I am not clear about. There are three that you can deal with better than anybody else, perhaps, as you know them all. I wish you would send for them."

He told me who they were; it isn't necessary to repeat the names here. One man was from New Jersey and two from New York.

"What will they be likely to want?" I asked.

"I don't know," said the President; "I don't know. It makes no difference, though, what they want. Here is the alternative: that we carry this vote, or be compelled to raise another million, and I don't know how many more, men, and fight no one knows how long. It is a question of three votes or new armies."

"Well, sir," said I, "what shall I say to these gentlemen?"

"I don't know," said he; "but whatever promise you make to them I will perform."

I sent for the men and saw them one by one. I found that they were afraid of their party. They said that some fellows in the party would be down on them. Two of them wanted internal revenue collector's appointments. "You shall have it," I said. Another one wanted a very important appointment about the custom house of New York. I knew the man well whom he wanted to have appointed. He was a Republican, though the congressman was a Democrat. I had served with him in the Republican county committee of New York. The office was worth perhaps twenty thousand dollars a year. When the congressman stated the case, I asked him, "Do you want that?"

"Yes," said he.

"Well," I answered, "you shall have it."

"I understand, of course," said he, "that you are not saying this on your own authority?"

"Oh, no," said I; "I am saying it on the authority of the President."

Now, in January 1865, with the Thirteenth Amendment again before Congress, Lincoln eagerly renewed the fight. James A. Rollins, a Representative from Missouri, described an interview with the President:[11]

The President had several times in my presence expressed his deep anxiety in favor of the passage of this great measure. He and others had repeatedly counted votes in order to ascertain, as far as they could, the strength of the measure upon a second trial in the House. He was doubtful about its passage, and some ten days or two weeks before it came up for consideration before the House, I received a note from him, written in pencil on a card, while sitting at my desk in the House, stating that he wished to see me, and asking that I call on him at the White House. I responded that I would be there the next morning at nine o'clock. I was prompt in calling upon him and found him alone in his office. He received me in the most cordial manner, and said in his usual familiar way: "Rollins, I have been wanting to talk to you for some time about the thirteenth amendment proposed to the Constitution of the United States, which will have to be voted on now, before a great while." I said: "Well, I am here, and ready to talk upon that subject." He said: "You and I were old whigs, both of us followers of that great statesman, Henry Clay, and I tell you I never had an opinion upon the subject of slavery in my life that I did not get from him. I am very anxious that the war should be brought to a close at the earliest possible date, and I don't believe this can be accomplished as long as those fellows down South can rely upon the border states to help them; but if the members from the border states would unite, at least enough of them to pass the thirteenth amendment to the Constitution, they would soon see that they could not expect much help from that quarter, and be willing to give up their opposition and quit their war upon the government; this is my chief hope and main reliance to bring the war to a speedy close, and I have sent for you as an old whig friend to come and see me, that I might make an appeal to you to vote for this amendment. It is going to be very close, a few votes one way or the other will decide it."

To this I responded: "Mr. President, so far as I am concerned you

need not have sent for me to ascertain my views on this subject, for although I represent perhaps the strongest slave district in Missouri, and
have the misfortune to be one of the largest slave-owners in the county
where I reside, I had already determined to vote for the thirteenth
amendment." He arose from his chair, and grasping me by the hand,
gave it a hearty shake, and said: "I am most delighted to hear that."

He asked me how many more of the Missouri delegates in the House
would vote for it. I said I could not tell; the Republicans of course
would; General Loan, Mr. Blow, Mr. Boyd, and Colonel McClurg. He
said: "Won't General Price * vote for it? He is a good Union
man." I said I could not answer. "Well, what about Governor King?" I
told him I did not know. He then asked about Judges Hall and Norton.
I said they would both vote against it, I thought.

"Well," he said, "are you on good terms with Price and King?" I
responded in the affirmative, and that I was on easy terms with the
entire delegation. He then asked me if I would not talk with those who
might be persuaded to vote for the amendment, and report to him as
soon as I could find out what the prospect was. I answered that I would
do so with pleasure, and remarked at the same time, that when I was
a young man, in 1848, I was the whig competitor of King for Governor
of Missouri and as he beat me very badly, I thought now he should pay
me back by voting as I desired him on this important question. I promised the President I would talk to this gentleman upon the subject. He
said: "I would like you to talk to all the border state men whom you
can approach properly, and tell them of my anxiety to have the measure
pass; and let me know the prospect of the border state vote," which I
promised to do. He again said: "The passage of this amendment will
clinch the whole subject; it will bring the war, I have no doubt, rapidly
to a close."

*Nicolay and Hay, eyewitnesses, described the critical vote in the House
of Representatives:*[12]

The issue was decided in the afternoon of the 31st of January, 1865.
. . . The galleries were filled to overflowing; the Members watched
the proceedings with unconcealed solicitude. "Up to noon," said a
contemporaneous formal report, "the pro-slavery party are said to
have been confident of defeating the amendment, and, after that time

---

* Thomas Lawson Price, elected as a Democrat in 1862.

had passed, one of the most earnest advocates of the measure said, ' 'Tis the toss of a copper.' " There were the usual pleas for postponement and for permission to offer amendments or substitutes, but at four o'clock the House came to a final vote, and the roll-call showed, yeas, 119; nays, 56; not voting, 8. Scattering murmurs of applause had followed the announcement of affirmative votes from several of the Democratic Members. This was renewed when by direction of the Speaker [Schuyler Colfax, of Indiana] the clerk called his name and he voted aye.

Colfax announced that the amendment had received the requisite two-thirds majority. According to the Washington Globe, *emotions could no longer be contained:*

The announcement was received by the House and by the spectators with an outburst of enthusiasm. The Members on the Republican side of the House instantly sprung to their feet, and, regardless of parliamentary rules, applauded with cheers and clapping of hands. The example was followed by the male spectators in the galleries, which were crowded to excess, who waved their hats and cheered loud and long, while the ladies, hundreds of whom were present, rose in their seats and waved their handkerchiefs, participating in and adding to the general excitement and intense interest of the scene. This lasted for several minutes.

The following night a jubilant procession marched to the White House. The band played until Lincoln appeared at a window:[13]

The President said he supposed the passage through Congress of the Constitutional amendment for the abolishment of Slavery throughout the United States, was the occasion to which he was indebted for the honor of this call. [Applause.] The occasion was one of congratulation to the country and to the whole world. But there is a task yet before us —to go forward and consummate by the votes of the States that which Congress so nobly began yesterday. [Applause and cries—"They will do it," &c.] He had the honor to inform those present that Illinois was a little ahead. He thought this measure was a very fitting if not an indispensable adjunct to the winding up of the great difficulty. He wished the reunion of all the States perfected and so effected as to remove all causes of disturbance in the future; and to attain this end it was necessary that the original disturbing cause should, if possible, be rooted out. He thought all would bear him witness that he had never shrunk from doing all that he could to eradicate Slavery by issuing an emancipation proclamation. [Applause.] But that proclamation falls far short of what the amendment will be when fully consummated. A question might be raised whether the proclamation was legally valid. It might be added that it only aided those who came into our lines and that it was inoperative as to those who did not give themselves up, or that it would have no effect upon the children of the slaves born hereafter. In fact it would be urged that it did not meet the evil. But this amendment is a King's cure for all the evils. [Applause.] It winds the whole thing up. He would repeat that it was the fitting if not indispensable adjunct to the consummation of the great game we are playing. He could not but congratulate all present, himself, the country and the whole world upon this great moral victory.

IV

With the end of slavery in sight, Lincoln made a move, though with little hope, to end the war. Early in January Francis P. Blair, Sr., an old friend of Jefferson Davis, made an unofficial visit to Richmond in a one-man effort to bring the war to a close. To Blair, Davis expressed his willingness that a conference should be held "with a view to secure peace to the two countries." Lincoln wrote of his desire that peace should come "to the people of our one common country"—a phrase that indicated no narrowing of the gap that had separated North and South for almost four years—yet he agreed to meet Confederate commissioners within the Union lines.

On February 3 Alexander H. Stephens, R. M. T. Hunter, former Confederate Secretary of State, and John A. Campbell who, though opposed to secession, had resigned as an associate justice of the United States Supreme Court when secession became a fact, were escorted to the steamer River Queen *in Hampton Roads. Stephens renewed an old friendship:*[14]

The interview took place in the Saloon of the steamer, on board of which were Mr. Lincoln and Mr. Seward, and which lay at anchor near Fortress Monroe. The Commissioners were conducted into the Saloon first. Soon after, Mr. Lincoln and Mr. Seward entered. After usual salutations on the part of those who were previously acquainted, and introductions of the others who had never met before, conversation was immediately opened by the revival of reminiscences and associations of former days.

This was commenced by myself addressing Mr. Lincoln, and alluding to some of the incidents of our Congressional acquaintance—especially, to the part we had acted together in effecting the election of General Taylor in 1848. To my remarks he responded in a cheerful and cordial manner, as if the remembrance of those times, and our connection with the incidents referred to, had awakened in him a train of agreeable reflections, extending to others. . . .

With this introduction I said in substance: Well, Mr. President, is there no way of putting an end to the present trouble, and bringing about a restoration of the general good feeling and harmony *then* existing between the different States and Sections of the country?

. . . Mr. Lincoln in reply said, in substance, that there was but one way that he knew of, and that was, for those who were resisting the laws of the Union to cease that resistance. All the trouble came from an armed resistance against the National Authority.

But, said I, is there no other question that might divert the attention of both Parties, for a time, from the questions involved in their present strife, until the passions on both sides might cool, when they would be in better temper to come to an amicable and proper adjustment of those points of difference out of which the present lamentable collision of arms has arisen? Is there no Continental question, said I, which might thus temporarily engage our attention? We have been induced to believe that there is.

Mr. Lincoln seemed to understand my allusion instantly, and said in substance: I suppose you refer to something that Mr. Blair has said. Now it is proper to state at the beginning, that whatever he said was of his own accord, and without the least authority from me. When he applied for a passport to go to Richmond, with certain ideas which he wished to make known to me, I told him flatly that I did not want to hear them. If he desired to go to Richmond of his own accord, I would give him a passport; but he had no authority to speak for me in any way whatever. When he returned and brought me Mr. Davis's letter, I gave him the one to which you alluded in your application for leave to cross the lines. I was always willing to hear propositions for peace on the conditions of this letter and on no other. The restoration of the Union is a *sine qua non* with me, and hence my instructions that no conference was to be held except upon that basis.

From this I inferred that he simply meant to be understood, in the first place, as disavowing whatever Mr. Blair had said as coming authoritatively from him; and, in the second place, that no arrangement could be made on the line suggested by Mr. Blair, without a previous pledge or assurance being given, that the Union was to be ultimately restored.

After a short silence, I continued: But suppose, Mr. President, a line of policy should be suggested, which, if adopted, would most probably lead to a restoration of the Union without further bloodshed, would it not be highly advisable to act on it, even without the absolute pledge of ultimate restoration being required to be first given? May not such a policy be found to exist in the line indicated by the interrogatory propounded? Is there not now such a Continental question in which all the parties engaged in our present war feel a deep and similar interest? I allude, of course, to Mexico, and what is called the "Monroe Doctrine,"—the principles of which are involved in the contest now waging there. From the tone of leading Northern papers and from public speeches of prominent men, as well as from *other* sources, we are under the impression that the Administration at Washington is decidedly opposed to the establishment of an Empire in Mexico by France, and is desirous to prevent it. In other words, they wish to sustain the principle of the Monroe Doctrine, and that, as I understand it, is, that the United States will maintain the right of Self-government to all People on this Continent, against the domination or control of any European power.

Mr. Lincoln and Mr. Seward both concurred in the expression of opinion that such was the feeling of a majority of the people of the North.

Could not both parties then, said I, in our contest, come to an understanding and agreement to postpone their present strife, by a suspension of hostilities between themselves, until this principle is maintained in behalf of Mexico; and might it not, when successfully sustained there, naturally, and would it not almost inevitably, lead to a peaceful and harmonious solution of their own difficulties? Could any pledge now given, make a permanent restoration or re-organization of the Union more probable, or even so probable, as such a result would?

Mr. Lincoln replied with considerable earnestness, that he could entertain no proposition for ceasing active military operations, which was not based upon a pledge first given, for the ultimate restoration of the Union. He had considered the question of an Armistice fully, and he could not give his consent to any proposition of that sort, on the basis suggested. The settlement of our existing difficulties was a question now of supreme importance, and the only basis on which he would entertain a proposition for a settlement was the recognition and re-establishment of the National Authority throughout the land.

These pointed and emphatic responses seemed to put an end to the Conference on the subject contemplated in our Mission, as we had no authority to give any such pledge. . . .

In spite of the impasse, the discussion continued, with Stephens emphasizing again the desirability of joint action against the French in Mexico. The North and South, he argued, could act together simply by adopting a military convention. Lincoln reiterated that he would take no step unless it was first agreed that resistance to national authority would cease.

The conversation turned to the status of slaves who had not been affected by the Proclamation of Emancipation. Lincoln had some comments on that subject:

He said it was not his intention in the beginning to interfere with Slavery in the States; that he never would have done it, if he had not been compelled by necessity to do it, to maintain the Union; that the subject presented many difficult and perplexing questions to him; that he had hesitated for some time, and had resorted to this measure, only when driven to it by public necessity; that he had been in favor of the General Government prohibiting the extension of Slavery into the Territories, but did not think that that Government possessed power over the subject in the States, except as a war measure; and that he had always himself been in favor of emancipation, but not immediate emancipation, even by the States. Many evils attending this appeared to him.

After pausing for some time, his head rather bent down, as if in deep reflection, while all were silent, he rose up and used these words, almost, if not quite identical:

Stephens, if I were in Georgia, and entertained the sentiments I do—though, I suppose, I should not be permitted to stay there long with them; but if I resided in Georgia, with my present sentiments, I'll tell you what I would do, if I were in your place: I would go home and get the Governor of the State to call the Legislature together, and get them to recall all the State troops from the war; elect Senators and Members to Congress, and ratify this Constitutional Amendment [the thirteenth] *prospectively*, so as to take effect—say in five years. Such a ratification would be valid in my opinion. . . . Whatever may have been the views of your people before the war, they must be convinced now, that Slavery is doomed. It cannot last long in any event, and the best course, it seems to me, for your public men to pursue, would be to adopt such a policy as will avoid, as far as possible, the evils of immediate emancipation. This would be my course, if I were in your place. . . .

Mr. Seward said, that the Northern people were weary of the war. They desired peace and a restoration of harmony, and he believed would be willing to pay as an indemnity for the slaves, what amount would be required to continue the war, but stated no amount.

After thus going through with all these matters, in a conversation of about four hours . . . , there was a pause, as if all felt that the interview should close. I arose and said that it seemed our mission would be entirely fruitless, unless we could do something in the matter of the Exchange of Prisoners. This brought up that subject.

Mr. Lincoln expressed himself in favor of doing something on it, and concluded by saying that he would put the whole matter in the hands of General Grant, then at City Point, with whom we could interchange views upon our return. Some propositions were then made for immediate special exchanges, which were readily agreed to.*

I then said: I wish, Mr. President, you would reconsider the subject of an Armistice on the basis which has been suggested. Great questions, as well as vast interests, are involved in it. If, upon so doing, you shall change your mind, you can make it known through the Military.

Well, said he, as he was taking my hand for a farewell leave, and with a peculiar manner very characteristic of him: Well, Stephens, I will re-consider it, but I do not think my mind will change, but I will re-consider.

The two parties then took formal and friendly leave of each other, Mr. Lincoln and Mr. Seward withdrawing first from the saloon together. Col. Babcock, our escort, soon came in to conduct us back to the steamer on which we came.

* On February 10 Lincoln wrote to Stephens: "According to our agreement, your nephew, Lieut. Stephens, goes to you, bearing this note. Please, in return, to select and send to me, that officer of the same rank, imprisoned at Richmond, whose physical condition most urgently requires his release."

Stephens reported the failure of the conference to Davis. He found the Confederate President obsessed with the conviction that in spite of ever-mounting odds, the South could still win its independence:

On the return of the Commissioners to Richmond, everybody was very much disappointed, and no one seemed to be more so than Mr. Davis. He thought Mr. Lincoln had acted in bad faith in the matter, and attributed this change in his policy to the fall of Fort Fisher. . . .

I thought the publicity of the Mission was enough to account for its failure, without attributing it to any bad faith, either on the part of Mr. Blair or Mr. Lincoln; that I had expressed the opinion to Judge Campbell and Mr. Hunter, when we saw our departure announced in the papers as it was (the whole North being in a stir upon the subject by the time we reached City Point), that this would most probably defeat our accomplishing anything, even if Mr. Lincoln really intended to do anything on that line; and that it was in this view of the subject *solely*, I had made the request of him, at the close of the interview, to *reconsider* the matter of the Armistice.

I called Mr. Davis's attention specially to the fact, that in reply to that request Mr. Lincoln declared he *would reconsider* it; and notwithstanding the qualification with which he made the declaration, yet I thought if there ever had been *really* anything in the *projèt*, Mr. Davis would still hear from it in a quiet way through the Military, after all the then "hubbub" about Peace Negotiations had subsided. In this view of the subject, I gave it to him as my opinion, that there should be no written report by the Commissioners touching the Conference, especially as a full disclosure of its *real objects* could not, with propriety, then be made; and that any report without this, however consistent with the facts, as far as they should be set forth, would fail to give full information upon the *exact* posture of the affairs to which it related, by which the public mind in reference to it would be more or less misled.

He insisted that a written report should be made, and the other Commissioners concurring with him, I again yielded my views on that point . . . , believing, as I did, that if I declined, more harm would certainly result from a misconstruction of my course and reasons in the matter, than would by conforming to his views and those of my Colleagues.

The question then was, what was next to be done?

Mr. Davis's position was, that inasmuch as it was now settled beyond question, by the decided and pointed declarations of Mr. Lincoln, that there could be no Peace short of *Unconditional Submission* on the part of the People of the Confederate States, with an entire change of their Social Fabric throughout the South, the People ought to be, and could be, more thoroughly aroused by Appeals through the Press and by Public Addresses, to the full consciousness of the necessity of renewed and more desperate efforts, for the preservation of themselves and their Institutions. By these means they might yet be saved from the most humiliating threatened degradation. In these lay the only hope left of escaping such a calamity. He himself seemed more interested than ever to fight it out on this line, and to risk all upon the issue.

By the course he proposed, I understood him to hold the opinion, that Richmond could *still* be defended, notwithstanding Sherman had already made considerable progress on his march from Savannah; and that our cause could *still* be successfully maintained, without any change in the internal policy upon the subjects referred to before.

THE HARD HAND
OF WAR

———————

ANOTHER SPRING APPROACHED—the fourth since those early days in 1861 when elderly gentlemen in Charleston enlisted as Home Guardsmen and practiced military evolutions so that they would be ready for the Negro insurrection certain to follow Mr. Lincoln's inauguration. Judge Campbell, who had accompanied Stephens to the Peace Conference at Hampton Roads, had said that spring of 1861: "Who can give self-control to Southern members [of Congress] or prevent them from showing that slavery is ordained by Heaven?" The Union armies had undertaken to give an answer in a war that now squeezed the Confederacy into an ever-diminishing stockade.

I

Ending that war quickly, effectively, had become the burning passion —with Sherman, certainly, who had no intention of lolling at ease in Savannah, or sending his army north in transports as Grant proposed. On December 24, less than two days after entering Savannah, Sherman began sketching for Grant the outline of new bold ventures:[1]

. . . I feel no doubt whatever as to our future plans. I have thought them over so long and well that they appear as clear as daylight. I left Augusta untouched on purpose, because the enemy will be in doubt as to my objective point, after we cross the Savannah River, whether it be Augusta or Charleston, and will naturally divide his forces. I will then move either on Branchville or Columbia, by any curved line that gives us the best supplies, breaking up in our course as much railroad as possible; then, ignoring Charleston and Augusta both, I would occupy Columbia and Camden, pausing there long enough to observe the effect. I would then strike for the Charleston & Wilmington Railroad, somewhere between the Santee and Cape Fear Rivers, and, if possible, communicate with the fleet under Admiral Dahlgren. . . . Then I would favor an attack on Wilmington, in the belief that Porter and Butler will fail in their present undertaking.* Charleston is now a mere desolated wreck, and is hardly worth the time it would take to starve it out. Still, I am aware that, historically and politically, much importance is attached to the place, and it may be that, apart from its military importance, both you and the Administration may prefer I should give it more attention; and it would be well for you to give me some general idea on that subject, for otherwise I would treat it as I have expressed, as a point of little importance, after all its railroads leading into the interior have been destroyed or occupied by us. But, on the hypothesis of ignoring Charleston and taking Wilmington, I would then favor a movement direct on Raleigh. The game is then up with Lee, unless he comes out of Richmond, avoids you and fights me; in which case I should reckon on your being on his heels. Now that Hood is used up by Thomas, I feel disposed to bring the matter to an issue as quick as possible. I feel confident that I can break up the whole railroad system of South Carolina and North Carolina, and be on the Roanoke, either at Raleigh or Weldon, by the time spring fairly opens; and, if you feel confident that you can whip Lee outside of his intrenchments, I feel equally confident that I can handle him in the open country. . . .

In a letter written on the same day to Halleck, Sherman advanced another argument in favor of his plan of campaign:

* A combined assault in the last week of December, 1864, which failed miserably. "Your reputation as a prophet may soon equal that as a general," Halleck wrote from Washington after Porter and Butler, in Sherman's term, "fizzled" in their attack on Wilmington. "Thank God," Halleck added, "that I had nothing to do with it, except to express the opinion that Butler's torpedo ship would have as much effect on the forts as if he should ——— at them." Sherman was no less frank, writing Halleck, "I am rejoiced that the current of events has carried Butler to Lowell where he should have stayed and confined his bellicose operations to the factory girls."

. . . I attach more importance to these deep incisions into the enemy's country, because this war differs from European wars in this particular: We are not only fighting hostile armies, but a hostile people, and must make old and young, rich and poor, feel the hard hand of war, as well as their organized armies. I know that this recent movement of mine through Georgia has had a wonderful effect in this respect. Thousands who had been deceived by their lying newspapers to believe that we were being whipped all the time now realize the truth, and have no appetite for a repetition of the same experience. To be sure, Jeff. Davis has his people under pretty good discipline, but I think faith in him is much shaken in Georgia, and before we have done with her South Carolina will not be quite so tempestuous.

I will bear in mind your hint as to Charleston, and do not think "salt" will be necessary. When I move, the Fifteenth Corps will be on the right of the right wing, and their position will naturally bring them into Charleston first; and, if you have watched the history of that corps, you will have remarked that they generally do their work pretty well. The truth is, the whole army is burning with an insatiable desire to wreak vengeance upon South Carolina. I almost tremble at her fate, but feel that she deserves all that seems in store for her. . . .

II

Grant gave his assent without reservations. Sherman had hoped to start north by mid-January but heavy rains sent the Savannah River out of its banks and made the roads impassable. Once the skies had cleared, Sherman took stock:[2]

On the 1st day of February . . . the army designed for the active campaign from Savannah northward was composed of two wings, commanded respectively by Major-Generals Howard and Slocum, and was substantially the same that had marched from Atlanta to Savannah. The same general orders were in force, and this campaign may properly be classed as a continuance of the former.

The right wing, less Corse's division, Fifteenth Corps, was grouped at or near Pocotaligo, South Carolina, with its wagons filled with food, ammunition, and forage, all ready to start, and only waiting for the left wing, which was detained by the flood in the Savannah River. . . .

The left wing, with Corse's division and Kilpatrick's cavalry, was at and near Sister's Ferry, forty miles above the city of Savannah, engaged in crossing the river, then much swollen. . . .

The actual strength of the army . . . was at the time sixty thousand and seventy-nine men, and sixty-eight guns. The trains were made up of about twenty-five hundred wagons, with six mules to each wagon, and about six hundred ambulances, with two horses each. The contents of the wagons embraced an ample supply of ammunition for a great battle; forage for about seven days, and provisions for twenty days, mostly of bread, sugar, coffee, and salt, depending largely for fresh meat on beeves driven on the hoof and such cattle, hogs, and poultry, as we expected to gather along our line of march. . . .

The enemy occupied the cities of Charleston and Augusta, with garrisons capable of making a respectable if not successful defense, but

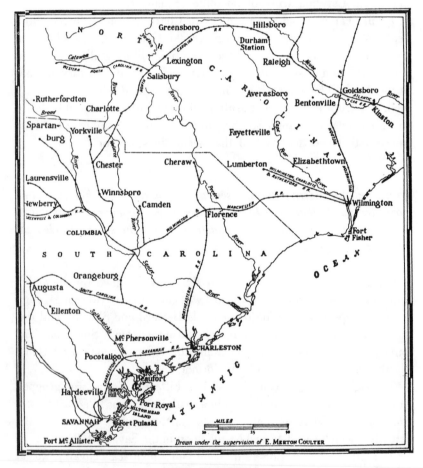

THE CAROLINAS

From *Atlas of American History*

utterly unable to meet our veteran columns in the open field. To resist or delay our progress north, General Wheeler had his division of cavalry (reduced to the size of a brigade by his hard and persistent fighting ever since the beginning of the Atlanta campaign), and General Wade Hampton had been dispatched from the Army of Virginia to his native State of South Carolina, with a great flourish of trumpets, and extraordinary powers to raise men, money, and horses, with which "to stay the progress of the invader," and "to punish us for our insolent attempt to invade the glorious State of South Carolina!" He was supposed at the time to have, at and near Columbia, two small divisions of cavalry commanded by himself and General Butler.*

. . . I knew full well at the time that the broken fragments of Hood's army (which had escaped from Tennessee) were being hurried rapidly across Georgia, by Augusta, to make junction in my front; estimating them at the maximum twenty-five thousand men, and Hardee's, Wheeler's, and Hampton's forces at fifteen thousand, made forty thousand; which, if handled with spirit and energy, would constitute a formidable force, and might make the passage of such rivers as the Santee and Cape Fear a difficult undertaking. Therefore, I took all possible precautions, and arranged with Admiral Dahlgren and General Foster to watch our progress inland by all the means possible, and to provide for us points of security along the coast. . . .

The question of supplies remained still the one of vital importance, and I reasoned that we might safely rely on the country for a considerable quantity of forage and provisions, and that, if the worst came to the worst, we could live several months on the mules and horses of our trains. Nevertheless, time was equally material, and the moment I heard that General Slocum had finished his pontoon-bridge at Sister's Ferry, and that Kilpatrick's cavalry was over the river, I gave the general orders to march, and instructed all the columns to aim for the South Carolina Railroad to the west of Branchville, about Blackville and Midway.

III

One of Sherman's aides, Major George Ward Nichols, described the progress of "the great march":[3]

February 10th.—Another important step is gained. We have crossed the south fork of the Edisto, and hold the main road beyond,

* Matthew Calbraith Butler, recently ordered to South Carolina from Richmond.

while the left wing of the army, which has been delayed so long by the
Freshet that submerged the roads leading from Sister's Ferry, is at
last coming into position with the remainder of the army. . . .

The crossing of the South Edisto was a feat worth mentioning somewhat in detail. It was Mower's fortune to have the lead. Upon the arrival
of his division at the place known as Bennaker's Bridge, which he
found burned, he was met with a sharp cannonading from the Rebels,
who were in position on the other side. This was in the afternoon. He
at once set to work to cross the stream. A little lower down, by dint of
wading and swimming, he managed to get into the water four pontoon
boats. Upon these, about eight o'clock in the evening, just as the moon
was rising, he crossed his division. This night attack was something
the Rebels were not prepared for, accustomed as they are to the strange
doings of the "Yankees." The moon rose above the tree-tops in all her
queenly splendor. Mower thought it was light enough to whip Rebels
by. He was now well out of the swamp, and knew that the sooner he
gained the high road the better. So, as we say in the army, he "went in,"
and the result was that the Rebels went out; that is, all who were not
killed or captured. . . .

ORANGEBURG, February 12th.—Today another difficult task has been
achieved. We have crossed the north fork of the Edisto, and occupy
Orangeburg. . . .

Tonight we are encamped upon the place of one of South Carolina's
most high-blooded chivalry—one of those persons who believed himself to have been brought into the world to rule over his fellow-creatures,
a sort of Grand Pasha, and all that sort of thing. How the negro pioneers
are making away with the evergreens and rose-bushes of his artistically
arranged walks, flower-beds, and drives! These black men in blue
are making brooms of his pet shrubs, with which they clear the ground
in front of the tents.

We find very few wealthy planters; the inhabitants we meet, mostly
women, are of the poorer class; they are frightened fearfully, and
expect all sorts of outrages to be perpetrated, and appear to be correspondingly grateful that their lives and houses are spared. The
stories they are told and credit are so absurd that I will not repeat
them. It is enough that these foolish, ignorant people have believed
them. . . .

Each day, as the army moves forward, large additions are made
to the droves of cattle. Our conscription is remorseless. Every species of
four-footed beast that South Carolina planters cherished among their

live-stock is swept in by our flanking foragers, and the music of the animal creation mingles with the sound of the footfall of the army.

IV

As Sherman's 60,000 veterans swept northward almost unopposed, South Carolina trembled. Even before the army had moved out of Savannah the same Albert G. Magrath who, upon Lincoln's election, had ripped off the robes of a Federal judge in melodramatic rage pleaded, as governor of South Carolina, with Jefferson Davis to defend Charleston at all costs:[4]

CHARLESTON, January 22, 1865

PRESIDENT DAVIS:

I am so impressed with the belief that in the military operations in the next few days in this State the fate of the Confederation is deeply involved, that I am here to urge upon General Hardee the defense of Charleston to the last moment, in the hope that meanwhile re-enforcements will enable us to hold it. I am using all influence with Governor Brown and Governor Vance to keep our States together and each give its help to the other, but confidence is almost lost and hope is to a great extent gone. To restore these and rally the people here and elsewhere there must be a stand-point to which all should look as the place where the purposes and strength of our Government are exhibited. Circumstances have plainly made Charleston and its connections that place. The loss of these, added to our other losses, will spread dismay, and I fear that such a loss will be taken as proof that our cause is without life or hope, and any effectual resistance cannot be prolonged. My intelligence from adjoining States confirms these apprehensions most fully.

Give General Hardee the help with which he can oppose General Sherman and I assure you that the spirit of the people will rise again. Not to sustain him is to confirm the belief that our cause is already lost. . . . It is because I feel the fate of Charleston and of Branchville to a great extent will determine that of other States, and with it the cause of the Confederation, that I urge the necessity for aid upon you in the most impressive manner. Richmond will hereby fall when Charleston is lost. To retain Richmond until Charleston is lost is to sacrifice both. If Charleston can be saved, and in doing that the means of resistance for the whole Confederation can be preserved, then, although to give succor to Charleston might hasten the fall of Richmond, yet to give that succor without delay is, to me, the obvious policy. God forbid that

I should urge you to give up an inch of the soil of Virginia that can be saved; but if it must be inevitably lost, to delay that inevitable necessity at such a cost as to endanger our whole cause, is not to accomplish any good.

In mid-February Pierre Gustave Toutant Beauregard, the hero of Fort Sumter, told Jefferson Davis that Charleston would have to be evacuated. The Confederate President replied on February 16:[5]

Your telegrams of yesterday received. You can better judge of the necessity for evacuating Charleston than I can. Such full preparations had been made that I had hoped for other and better results, and the disappointment is to me extremely bitter. The re-enforcements calculated on from reserves and militia of Georgia and South Carolina, together with the troops ordered from Mississippi, must have fallen much short of estimate. What can be done with the naval squadron, the torpedo boats, and your valuable heavy guns at Charleston? Do not allow cotton stored there to become prize of the enemy, as was the case at Savannah. From reverse, however sad, if you are sustained by unity and determination among the people, we can look hopefully forward. . . .

Three weeks later the colonel of a Negro regiment pleaded for aid to the suffering residents of the cradle of secession:[6]

HEADQUARTERS POST OF CHARLESTON.
CHARLESTON, S. C., March 6, 1865
REV. JOSEPH P. THOMPSON, D.D.,
PRESIDENT OF THE AMERICAN UNION COMMISSION, NEW YORK CITY:
REVEREND AND DEAR SIR: Mr. Mahlon T. Hewitt, of your city, has called upon me in behalf of the American Union Mission to ascertain the true condition of the people of Charleston, and to devise some method by which the suffering and want occasioned by the rebellion may be most surely alleviated. We thank you for this prompt indication that the men of the North sympathize in the afflictions of their fellow countrymen, and desire to meet them when returning to loyalty in the true spirit of a Christian brotherhood. The suffering here is great, nor is it confined to the poorer classes alone. Charleston is today cut off from the back country by the presence of intervening armies. Families who have heretofore derived their income from country

estates are now, of necessity, in want. Others whose property has been gradually absorbed into rebel bonds are penniless. The rebel currency is worthless. Thus many who have been tenderly reared are now suffering. Instances of want come daily and hourly to my notice, which I am powerless to alleviate. Major-General Gilmore, commanding this department, generously turned over most of the rice captured in the city to a committee, who are distributing it for the relief of the most necessitous. But this supply can only last for a few days at the best, and does not begin to answer our wants. We need money, provisions, clothing, and medicines and delicacies for the sick. You cannot do too much for us. Your agent, Mr. Hewitt, has, at my suggestion, invited several prominent residents of Charleston, to organize as an auxiliary association to your commission, and thus insure the safe and equitable distribution of the charity which you so nobly offer. These gentlemen have accepted, and the loyal people of the North may rely upon the faithful performance of the trust. I believe that the nation will respond to the appeal which your commission makes in behalf of this great charity, and look forward hopefully to the day when the olive branch you proffer shall be planted beside hearthstones made desolate by war, and bear the golden fruitage of reconciliation and peace.

Very respectfully, your obedient servant,
STEWART L. WOODFORD,
Colonel 103d U. S. Colored Troops,
Commanding the City

v

On February 17 Sherman's forces occupied Columbia. Many a man in the Union ranks remembered that except for a sudden epidemic of smallpox the Ordinance of Secession would have been adopted here rather than in Charleston. That night fire destroyed nearly fourteen hundred residences and stores. Sherman insisted that he was not responsible for the holocaust. William Gilmore Simms, the South's favorite romantic novelist and a refugee in Columbia at the time, told another story:[7]

Among the first fires of evening was one about dark, which broke out in a filthy purlieu of low houses, of wood, on Gervais Street, occupied mostly as brothels. Almost at the same time a body of soldiers scattered over the Eastern outskirts of the city, fired severally the dwellings of Mr. Secretary Trenholm, General Wade Hampton, Dr.

John Wallace, and many others. There were then some twenty fires in full blast, in as many different quarters, and while the alarm sounded from these quarters, a similar alarm went up almost simultaneously from Cotton Town, the northernmost limit of the city, and from Main Street in its very centre . . . thus enveloping in flames almost every section of the devoted city. At this period, thus early in the evening, there were few shows of that drunkenness which prevailed at a late hour in the night, and only after all the grocery shops on Main Street had been rifled. The men engaged in this were well prepared with all the appliances essential to their work. They did not need the torch. They carried with them, from house to house, pots and vessels containing combustible liquids, composed probably of phosphorous and other similar agents, turpentine, etc., and with balls of cotton saturated in this liquid, with which they also overspread the floors and walls; they conveyed the flames with wonderful rapidity from dwelling to dwelling. Each had his ready box of Lucifer matches, and, with a scrape upon the walls, the flames began to rage. Where houses were closely contiguous, a brand from one was the means of conveying destruction to the other. . . .

Sherman placed the responsibility for the disaster upon a Confederate general:[8]

. . . In anticipation of the occupation of the city, I had made written orders to General Howard touching the conduct of the troops. These were to destroy, absolutely, all arsenals and public property not needed for our own use, as well as all railroads, depots, and machinery useful in war to an enemy, but to spare all dwellings, colleges, schools, asylums, and harmless private property. I was the first to cross the pontoon bridge, and in company with General Howard rode into the city. The day was clear, but a perfect tempest of wind was raging. The brigade of Colonel Stone was already in the city, and was properly posted. Citizens and soldiers were on the streets, and general good order prevailed. General Wade Hampton, who commanded the Confederate rear-guard of cavalry, had, in anticipation of our capture of Columbia, ordered that all cotton, public and private, should be moved into the streets and fired, to prevent our making use of it. Bales were piled everywhere, the rope and bagging cut, and tufts of cotton were blown about in the wind, lodged in the trees and against houses, so as to resemble a snow storm. Some of these piles of cotton were burning, especially one in the very heart of the city, near the Court-house, but the fire was partially subdued by the labor of our soldiers. During the day the Fifteenth corps passed through Columbia and out on the Camden road. The Seventeenth did not enter the town at all; and, as I have before stated, the left wing and cavalry did not come within two miles of the town.

Before one single public building had been fired by order, the smoldering fires, set by Hampton's order, were rekindled by the wind, and communicated to the buildings around. About dark they began to spread, and got beyond the control of the brigade on duty within the city. The whole of Wood's division was brought in, but it was found impossible to check the flames, which, by midnight, had become unmanageable, and raged until about four A.M., when the wind subsiding, they were got under control. I was up nearly all night, and saw Generals Howard, Logan, Woods, and others, laboring to save houses and protect families thus suddenly deprived of shelter, and of bedding and wearing apparel. I disclaim on the part of my army any agency in this fire, but on the contrary, claim that we saved what of Columbia remains unconsumed. And without hesitation, I charge General Wade Hampton with having burned his own city of Columbia, not with a malicious intent, or as the manifestations of a silly "Roman stoicism," but from folly and want of sense, in filling it with lint, cotton, and tinder. Our officers and men on duty worked well to extinguish the flames; but others not on duty, including the officers who had long been imprisoned there, rescued by us, may have assisted in spreading the fire after it had once begun, and may have indulged in unconcealed joy to see the ruin of the capital of South Carolina.

Little affection ever was lost between Sherman and Hampton, who soon were engaged in a brittle exchange of letters:

HEADQUARTERS MILITARY DIVISION OF THE MISSISSIPPI,
IN THE FIELD, February 24, 1865
GENERAL: It is officially reported to me that our foraging parties are murdered after capture, and labelled "Death to all foragers." One instance of a lieutenant and seven men near Chesterville, and another of twenty, "near a ravine eighty rods from the main road," about three miles from Feasterville. I have ordered a similar number of prisoners in our hands to be disposed of in like manner.

I hold about a thousand prisoners, captured in various ways, and can stand it as long as you, but I hardly think these murders are committed with your knowledge, and would suggest that you give notice to the people at large that every life taken by them simply results in the death of one of your confederates.

Of course you cannot question my right to "forage on the country." It is a war-right as old as history. The manner of exercising it varies with circumstances, and if the civil authorities will supply my requisitions I will forbid all foraging. But I find no civil authorities who can respond to calls for forage or provisions, therefore must collect directly of the people. I have no doubt this is the occasion of much misbehavior on the part of our men, but I cannot permit an enemy to judge, or punish with wholesale murder.

Personally I regret the bitter feelings engendered by this war; but they were to be expected; and I simply allege that those who struck the first blow, and made war inevitable, ought not, in fairness, to reproach us for the natural consequences. I merely assert our war-right to forage, and my resolve to protect my foragers to the extent of life for life.

I am, with respect,

Your obedient servant
W. T. SHERMAN,
Major-General United States Army

LIEUTENANT-GENERAL WADE HAMPTON,
Commanding Cavalry Forces, C.S.A.

Hampton retorted venomously:

HEADQUARTERS IN THE FIELD,
February 27, 1865

GENERAL: Your communication of the twenty-fourth inst. reached me to-day. In it you state that it has been officially reported that your foraging parties are "murdered" after capture. You go on to say that you have "ordered a similar number of prisoners in your hands to be disposed of in like manner;" that is to say, you have ordered a number of Confederate soldiers to be "murdered." You characterize your order in proper terms, for the public voice, even in your own country, where it seldom dares to express itself in vindication of truth, honor, or justice, will surely agree with you in pronouncing you guilty of murder, if your order is carried out. Before dismissing this portion of your letter, I beg to assure you, that for every soldier of mine "mur dered" by you, I shall have executed at once *two* of yours, giving, in all cases, preference to any officers who may be in my hands.

In reference to the statement you make regarding the death of your foragers, I have only to say that I know nothing of it; that no orders given by me authorize the killing of prisoners after capture, and I do not believe my men killed any of yours except under circumstances in which it was perfectly legitimate and proper they *should* kill them. It is a part of the system of the thieves whom you designate as your foragers to fire the dwellings of those citizens whom they have robbed. To check this inhuman system, which is justly execrated by every civilized nation, I have directed my men to shoot down all of your men who are caught burning houses. This order shall remain in force so long as you disgrace the profession of arms by allowing your men to destroy private dwellings.

You say that I cannot, of course, question your right to forage on the country. "It is a right as old as history." I do not, sir, question this right. But there is a right older even than this, and one more inalienable—the right that every man has to defend his home, and to protect those who are dependent on him; and from my heart I wish that every old man and boy in my country, who can fire a gun, would shoot down, as he would a wild beast, the men who are desolating their land, burning their homes, and insulting their women.

You are particular in defining and claiming "war-rights." May I ask if you enumerate among these the right to fire upon a defenceless city without notice; to burn that city to the ground after it had been surrendered by the inhabitants, who claimed, though in vain, that protection which is always accorded in civilized warfare to non-combatants; to fire the dwelling-houses of citizens after robbing them, and to perpetrate even darker crimes than these—crimes too black to be mentioned.

You have permitted, if you have not ordered, the commission of these offences against humanity and the rules of war. You fired into the city of Columbia without a word of warning, after its surrender by the mayor, who demanded protection to private property; you laid the whole city in ashes, leaving amidst its ruins thousands of old men and helpless women and children, who are likely to perish of starvation and exposure. Your line of march can be traced by the lurid light of burning houses; and in more than one household there is an agony far more bitter than that of death. The Indian scalped his victim regardless of age or sex, but with all his barbarity he always respected the persons of his female captives. Your soldiers, more savage than the Indian, insult those whose natural protectors are absent.

In conclusion, I have only to request that whenever you have any of my men "murdered" or "disposed of"—for the terms seem synonymous with you—you will let me hear of it, that I may know what action to take in the matter. In the meantime I shall hold fifty-six of your men as hostages for those whom you have ordered to be executed.

I am yours, &c.,
WADE HAMPTON,
Lieutenant-General
MAJOR-GENERAL W. T. SHERMAN, U. S. A.

VI

Sherman reached Cheraw, South Carolina, on March 3 and took the town after a brisk but minor engagement. The next day Major George W. Nichols, Sherman's aide, noted in his diary:[9]

March 4th.—The capture of Cheraw is of more value than we anticipated, although the force opposed to us was not so large as had been reported. The Rebel cavalry was a division of Hampton's men, and the infantry were those who had been brought up from Charleston. Their line was first formed at Thompson's Creek, which they were driven from instantly by the impetuosity of our troops, who did not give them time to reform, but drove the entire force through the town at the double-quick. Our soldiers were at one end of the bridge while the Rebels were leaving the other, but too late to save it from the flames. We captured twenty-five cannon which had been brought to this place from Charleston; they were Blakelys, twenty-pound Parrotts, and two of Rebel manufacture. All but the Blakelys have been destroyed. These guns, used so effectively upon our fleet at Charleston, will be carried to the seacoast as trophies. General Mower fired them today in a salute in honor of the inauguration for his second term. Our honored President would have been as glad and proud as we, could he have heard the roaring of our cannon and our shouts of joy and victory. His first inauguration was not celebrated in South Carolina by loyal hearts and hands; but the glorification over the beginning of his second term goes to make up the deficiency.

Lincoln's second inauguration began less auspiciously than Nichols and the mindful Mower could have imagined. Vice President Andrew John-

son, recovering from the debilitating effect of a recent illness, had forti-
fied himself with a stiff drink of whisky—perhaps several stiff drinks
—and in consequence delivered his inaugural address and took the
oath of office with tipsy loquacity. But a day that began in gloom and
scandal turned into one of promise. Noah Brooks described the
metamorphosis:[10]

The newly chosen senators were sworn in, and the procession for the
inauguration platform, which had been built on the east front of the
Capitol, was formed. There was a sea of heads in the great plaza in
front of the Capitol, as far as the eye could reach, and breaking in
waves along its outer edges among the budding foliage of the grounds
beyond. When the President and the procession of notables appeared,
a tremendous shout, prolonged and loud, arose from the surging ocean
of humanity around the Capitol building. Then the sergeant-at-arms of
the Senate . . . arose and bowed, with his shining black hat in hand,
in dumb-show before the crowd, which thereupon became still, and
Abraham Lincoln, rising tall and gaunt among the groups about him,
stepped forward and read his inaugural address, which was printed in
two broad columns upon a single page of large paper. As he advanced
from his seat, a roar of applause shook the air, and, again and again
repeated, finally died far away on the outer fringe of the throng, like a
sweeping wave upon the shore. Just at that moment the sun, which had
been obscured all day, burst forth in its unclouded meridian splendor,
and flooded the spectacle with glory and with light. Every heart beat
quicker at the unexpected omen, and doubtless not a few mentally
prayed that so might the darkness which had obscured the past four
years be now dissipated by the sun of prosperity,

> Till danger's troubled night depart,
> And the star of peace return.

The inaugural address was received in the most profound silence.
Every word was clear and audible as the ringing and somewhat shrill
tones of Lincoln's voice sounded over the vast concourse.

Lincoln said:

At this second appearing to take the oath of the presidential office,
there is less occasion for an extended address than there was at the
first. Then a statement, somewhat in detail, of a course to be pursued,

seemed fitting and proper. Now, at the expiration of four years, during which public declarations have been constantly called forth on every point and phase of the great contest which still absorbs the attention, and engrosses the energies of the nation, little that is new could be presented. The progress of our arms, upon which all else chiefly depends, is as well known to the public as to myself; and it is, I trust, reasonably satisfactory and encouraging to all. With high hope for the future, no prediction in regard to it is ventured.

On the occasion corresponding to this four years ago, all thoughts were anxiously directed to an impending civil war. All dreaded it—all sought to avert it. While the inaugural address was being delivered from this place, devoted altogether to *saving* the Union without war, insurgent agents were in the city seeking to *destroy* it without war— seeking to dissolve the Union, and divide effects, by negotiation. Both parties deprecated war; but one of them would *make* war rather than let the nation survive; and the other would *accept* war rather than let it perish. And the war came.

One eighth of the whole population were colored slaves, not distributed generally over the Union, but localized in the Southern part of it. These slaves constituted a peculiar and powerful interest. All knew that this interest was, somehow, the cause of the war. To strengthen, perpetuate, and extend this interest was the object for which the insurgents would rend the Union, even by war; while the government claimed no right to do more than to restrict the territorial enlargement of it. Neither party expected for the war, the magnitude, or the duration, which it has already attained. Neither anticipated that the *cause* of the conflict might cease with, or even before, the conflict itself should cease. Each looked for an easier triumph, and a result less fundamental and astounding. Both read the same Bible, and pray to the same God; and each invokes His aid against the other. It may seem strange that any men should dare to ask a just God's assistance in wringing their bread from the sweat of other men's faces; but let us judge not that we be not judged. The prayers of both could not be answered; that of neither has been answered fully. The Almighty has His own purposes. "Woe unto the world because of offences! for it must needs be that offences come; but woe to that man by whom the offence cometh!" If we shall suppose that American Slavery is one of those offences which, in the providence of God, must needs come, but which, having continued through His appointed time, He now wills to remove, and that He gives to both North and South, this terrible war, as the woe due to those by whom the offence came, shall we discern therein any departure from those divine attributes which the believers in a Living God always ascribe to Him? Fondly do we hope—fervently do we pray—that this mighty scourge of war may speedily pass away. Yet, if God wills that it continue, until all the wealth piled by the bond-man's two hundred and fifty years of unrequited toil shall be sunk, and until every drop of blood drawn with the lash, shall be paid by another drawn with the sword, as was said three thousand years ago, so still it must be said, "the judgments of the Lord, are true and righteous altogether."

With malice toward none; with charity for all; with firmness in the right, as God gives us to see the right, let us strive on to finish the work we are in; to bind up the nation's wounds; to care for him who shall have borne the battle, and his widow, and his orphan—to do all which may achieve and cherish a just, and a lasting peace, among ourselves, and with all nations.

At the conclusion of Lincoln's address (Brooks wrote):

There were many cheers and many tears. . . . Silence being restored, the President turned toward Chief Justice Chase, who, with his right hand uplifted, directed the Bible to be brought forward by the clerk of the Supreme Court. Then Lincoln, laying his right hand upon the open page, repeated the oath of office administered to him by the Chief Justice, after which, solemnly saying, "So help me God," he bent forward and reverently kissed the Book, then rose up inaugurated President of the United States for four years from March 4, 1865. A salvo of artillery boomed upon the air, cheer upon cheer rang out, and then, after turning, and bowing to the assembled hosts, the President retired into the Capitol, and, emerging by a basement entrance, took his carriage and was escorted back to the White House by a great procession.

VII

Sherman pressed forward relentlessly, taking Fayetteville, North Carolina, where the Confederates had an important arsenal, on March 12 and Averysboro, on the road to Raleigh, five days later. The next day the wily general switched his objective to Goldsboro, fifty miles southeast of Raleigh.

Major General Henry W. Slocum, out in front with the left wing, described the development of a battle which neither he nor Sherman had expected:[11]

General Sherman rode with me on the 18th [of March] and left me at 6 A.M. on the 19th to join General Howard, who was marching on roads several miles to our right. On leaving me General Sherman expressed the opinion that Hardee had fallen back to Raleigh, and that I could easily reach the Neuse River on the following day. I felt confident I could accomplish the task. We moved forward at 6 A.M., and soon met the skirmishers of the enemy. The resistance to our advance became very stubborn. Carlin's division was deployed and ordered to advance. I believed that the force in my front consisted only of cavalry with a few pieces of artillery. Fearing that the firing would be heard by General Sherman and cause the other wing of the army to delay its march, I sent Major E. W. Guindon of my staff to General Sherman, to tell him that I had met a strong force of cavalry, but that I should not need assistance, and felt confident I should be at the Neuse at the appointed time.

Soon after the bearer of the message to General Sherman had left me, word came from Carlin that he had developed a strong force of the enemy in an intrenched position. About the same time one of my officers brought me an emaciated, sickly appearing young man about twenty-two or twenty-three years of age, dressed in the Confederate gray. He had expressed great anxiety to see the commanding officer at once. I asked him what he had to say. He said he had been in the Union army, had been taken prisoner, and while sick and in prison had been induced to enlist in the Confederate service. He said he had enlisted with the intention of deserting when a good opportunity presented itself, believing he should die if he remained in prison. In reply to my questions he informed me that he had formerly resided at Syracuse, New York, and had entered the service at the commencement of the war, in a company raised by Captain Butler. I had been a resident of Syracuse, and knew the history of his company and regiment. While I was talking with him one of my aides, Major William G. Tracy, rode up and at once recognized the deserter as an old acquaintance whom he had known at Syracuse before the war. I asked how he knew General Johnston was in command and what he knew as to the strength of his force. He said General Johnston rode along the line early that morning, and that the officers had told all the men that "Old Joe" had caught one of Sherman's wings beyond the reach of support, that he intended to *smash* that wing and then go for the other. The man stated that he had had no chance of escaping till that morning, and had come to me to warn me of my danger. He said, "There is a very large force immediately in your front, all under command of General Joe Johnston." While he was making his statement General Carlin's division with four pieces of artillery became engaged with the enemy. A line for defense was at once selected, and as the troops came up they were placed in position and ordered to collect fence-rails and everything else available for barricades. The men used their tin cups and hands as shovels, and needed no urging to induce them to work. I regretted that I had sent the message to Sherman assuring him I needed no help, and saw the necessity of giving him information at once as to the situation. This information was carried to General Sherman by a young man, not then twenty years of age, but who was full of energy and activity and was always reliable.

Slocum's young man was Lieutenant Joseph B. Foraker, who would one day be Governor of Ohio and a United States Senator. Slocum told him: "Ride well to the right so as to keep clear of the enemy's left flank, and don't *spare horse-flesh."*
Foraker never forgot his mission:

I reached General Sherman just about sundown. He was on the left side of the road on a sloping hillside, where, as I understood, he had halted only a few minutes before for the night. His staff were about him. I think General Howard was there, but I do not now remember seeing him—but on the hillside twenty yards farther up Logan was lying on a blanket. Sherman saw me approaching and walked briskly toward me, took the message, tore it open, read it, and called out "John Logan! where is Logan?" Just then Logan jumped up and started toward us. He too walked briskly, but before he had reached us Sherman had informed him of the situation and ordered him to turn Hazen back and report to you [Slocum]. It was not yet dark when I rode away. . . . It was after midnight when I got back, the ride back being so much longer in point of time because the road was full of troops, it was dark, and my "horse-flesh" was used up.

Slocum saw the Confederates drive back Carlin's division:

. . . They were handled with skill and fell back without panic or demoralization, taking places in the line established. The Twentieth Corps held the left of our line, with orders to connect with the Fourteenth. A space between the two corps had been left uncovered, and

Cogswell's brigade of the Twentieth Corps, ordered to report to General Davis, filled the gap just before the enemy reached our line.

The enemy fought bravely, but their line had become somewhat broken in advancing through the woods, and when they came up to our line, posted behind slight intrenchments, they received a fire which compelled them to fall back. The assaults were repeated over and over again until a late hour, each assault finding us better prepared for resistance. During the night Hazen reported to me, and was placed on the right of the Fourteenth Corps. Early on the next morning Generals Baird and Geary, each with two brigades, arrived on the field. Baird was placed in front of our works and moved out beyond the advanced position held by us on the preceding day. The 20th was spent in strengthening our position and developing the line of the enemy. On the morning of the 21st the right wing arrived. This wing had marched twenty miles over bad roads, skirmishing most of the way with the enemy. On the 21st General Johnston found Sherman's army united, and in position on three sides of him. On the other side was Mill Creek. Our troops were pressed closely to the works of the enemy, and the entire day was spent in skirmishing. During the night of the 21st the enemy crossed Mill Creek and retreated toward Raleigh. The plans of the enemy to surprise us and destroy our army in detail were well formed and well executed, and would have been more successful had not the men of the Fourteenth and Twentieth corps been veterans, and the equals in courage and endurance of any soldiers of this or any other country.

Bentonville was the last serious resistance which the Confederate army made to the march through the Carolinas. On March 22 Sherman entered Goldsboro. There he was joined by the armies of Schofield and Terry from New Bern and Wilmington. Thus strengthened, and with Schofield available for temporary command, Sherman set out for City Point and a conference with Grant. Arriving on March 27, he learned that Lincoln had been present for several days. The two generals proceeded to the River Queen, *the steamer on which the President had taken quarters. After extending a warm welcome, Lincoln asked many questions about Sherman's march and about military operations of the near future. More than once, Sherman remembered, the President exclaimed: "Must more blood be shed? Cannot this last bloody battle be avoided?"*

The next day Grant and Sherman, accompanied by Admiral Porter, boarded the River Queen *again. Sherman, writing seven years later, recalled the interview:*[12]

We all took seats in the after cabin, and the conversation became general. I explained to Mr. Lincoln that Admiral Porter had given me the *Bat,* a very fleet vessel to carry me back to Newbern, and that I was ready to start back then. It seemed to relieve him, as he was afraid that something might go wrong at Goldsboro in my absence. I had no such fears, and the most perfect confidence in Gen. Schofield and I doubt not I said as much.

I ought not and must not attempt to recall the words of that conversation. Of course none of us then foresaw the tragic end of the principal figure of that group, so near at hand; and none of us saw the exact manner in which the war would close; but I know that I felt, and believe the others did, that the end of the war was near. The imminent danger was that Lee seeing the meshes closing surely around him, would not remain passive; but would make one more desperate effort; and General Grant was providing for it, by getting General Sheridan's cavalry well to his left flank, so as to watch the first symptoms, and to bring the Rebel army to bay till the infantry could come up.

Meanwhile I only asked two weeks stay—the "status quo"—when we would have our wagons loaded, and would start from Goldsboro for Burkesville via Raleigh. Though I can not attempt to recall the words spoken by any one of the persons present on that occasion, I know we talked generally about what was to be done when Lee's & Johnston's armies were beaten and dispersed. On this point Mr. Lincoln was very full. He said that he had long thought of it, that he hoped the end could be reached without more bloodshed, but in any event, he wanted us to get the deluded men of the Rebel armies disarmed and back to their homes, that he contemplated no revenge—no harsh measures, but quite the contrary, and that their suffering and hardships in the war, would make them the more submissive to Law. I cannot say that Mr. Lincoln or anybody else used this language at the time but I know I left his presence with the conviction that he had in his mind, or that his Cabinet had, some plan of settlement ready for application the moment Lee & Johnston were defeated. . . .

That afternoon I embarked on the *Bat,* and we steamed down the coast to Hatteras Inlet, which we entered, and proceeded to Newbern—and from Newbern to Goldsboro by rail, which I reached the night of March 30.

CHAPTER 39

"AN
AFFECTIONATE
FAREWELL"

GRANT DEPARTED next morning, March 29, by railroad. The President walked down to the station to say goodbye. Horace Porter believed that Lincoln looked "more serious," with "the rings under his eyes . . . of a darker hue." Aboard the train, Grant and his staff raised their hats in a final token of respect for the President. Obviously affected, Lincoln returned the salute and called:

"Goodbye, gentlemen. God bless you all! Remember, your success is my success."

Grant sat by the train window afterward, smoking a cigar and seeming absorbed in the passing scenery. Turning to Horace Porter, the general revealed that his thoughts remained with Lincoln.

"I think we can send him some good news in a day or two," Grant said.

I

Throughout the fall and winter Grant had been hamstrung before Petersburg. With the spring of 1865 he intended to finish the war. Impatiently he waited for the end of abnormally heavy rains, and the return of Sheridan, with his magnificent cavalry, from the Valley. By late March the rains had stopped, the roads were drying, and Sheridan was back.

*On the night of March 29 Grant started columns southwestward to-
ward Dinwiddie Court House, thirty miles from City Point. Lee's
troops, uneasy when they were pressed back to the vital Southside Railroad, fought sharply. Grant pushed out his lines in parallels east and
west of the Southside. Clearly, he intended to sever this line and beyond
it, the Richmond and Danville, on which Lee depended for supplies.
Grant also meant to occupy Five Forks, ten miles north of Dinwiddie
Court House.*

*At Five Forks, on the edge of a dry, well-watered forest, five good
roads came together. To take Five Forks was to unlock all the surrounding country. Grant sent Sheridan to do the job. The talented George
Alfred Townsend, who had returned to reporting battles after three
years of lecturing and traveling in Europe, discovered that the war had
changed during his absence. Cavalry no longer made saber charges.
Even the generals had discovered that horses could take men to a point
where they were needed, faster than they could march; once there, cavalrymen dismounted and fought as foot soldiers.*

*On April 1, at Five Forks, Townsend learned what a mighty punch
Sheridan could deliver in this style of warfare:*[1]

A colonel with a shattered regiment came down upon us in a charge.
The bayonets were fixed; the men came on with a yell; their gray uniforms seemed black amidst the smoke; their preserved colors, torn by
grape and ball, waved yet defiantly; twice they halted, and poured in
volleys, but came on again like the surge from the fog, depleted, but determined; yet, in the hot faces of the carbineers, they read a purpose as
resolute, but more calm, and, while they pressed along, swept all the
while by scathing volleys, a group of horsemen took them in flank. It
was an awful instant; the horses recoiled; the charging column trembled like a single thing, but at once the Rebels, with rare organization,
fell into a hollow square, and with solid sheets of steel defied our cen-
taurs. The horsemen rode around them in vain; no charge could break
the shining squares, until our dismounted carbineers poured in their
volleys afresh, making gaps in the spent ranks, and then in their wavering time the cavalry thundered down. The Rebels could stand no more;
they reeled and swayed, and fell back broken and beaten. And on the
ground their colonel lay, sealing his devotion with his life.

Through wood and brake and swamp, across field and trench, we
pushed the fighting defenders steadily. For a part of the time, Sheridan
himself was there, short and broad, and active, waving his hat, giving

orders, seldom out of fire, but never stationary, and close by fell the long yellow locks of Custer, sabre extended, fighting like a Viking, though he was worn and haggard with much work. At four o'clock the Rebels were behind their wooden walls at Five Forks, and still the cavalry pressed them hard, in feint rather than solemn effort, while a battalion dismounted, charged squarely upon the face of their breastworks which lay in the main on the north side of the White Oak road. Then, while the cavalry worked round toward the rear, the infantry of Warren, though commanded by Sheridan, prepared to take part in the battle.

Townsend believed that the "genius" with which Sheridan now disposed his infantry "should place him as high in infantry tactics as he has heretofore shown himself superior in cavalry." Townsend watched as Sheridan, extending his lines, drove the Rebels into their breastworks. Dismounting his cavalry, he charged on front and flank:

. . . At last, every Rebel was safe behind his intrenchments. Then the signal was given, and the concealed infantry, many thousand strong, sprang up and advanced by echelon to the right. Imagine a great barn door shutting to, and you have the movement, if you can also imagine the door itself, hinge and all, moving forward also. This was the door:

AYRES—CRAWFORD—GRIFFIN

Stick a pin through Ayres and turn Griffin and Crawford forward as you would a spoke in a wheel, but move your pin up also a very little. In this way Ayres will advance, say half a mile, and Griffin, to describe a quarter revolution, will move through a radius of four miles. But to complicate this movement by echelon, we must imagine the right when half way advanced cutting across the centre and reforming, while Crawford became the right and Griffin the middle of the line of battle. Warren was with Crawford on this march. Edgar M. Gregory commanded the skirmishers. Ayres was so close to the Rebel left that he might be said to hinge upon it; and at 6 o'clock the whole corps column came crash upon the full flank of the astonished Rebels. Now came the pitch of the battle.

We were already on the Rebel right in force, and thinly in their rear. Our carbineers were making feint to charge in direct front, and our infantry, four deep, hemmed in their entire left. All this they [the Confederates] did not for an instant note, so thorough was their confusion; but seeing it directly, they, so far from giving up, concentrated all their energy and fought like fiends. They had a battery in position, which belched incessantly, and over the breastworks their musketry made one unbroken roll, while against Sheridan's prowlers on their left, by skirmish and sortie, they stuck to their sinking fortunes, so as to win unwilling applause from mouths of wisest censure.

It was just at the coming up of the infantry that Sheridan's little band was pushed the hardest. At one time, indeed, they seemed about to undergo extermination; not that they wavered, but that they were so vastly overpowered. It will remain to the latest time a matter of marvel that so paltry a cavalry force could press back sixteen thousand infantry; but when the infantry blew like a great barn door—the simile best applicable—upon the enemy's left, the victory that was to come had passed the region of strategy and resolved to an affair of personal courage. We had met the enemy; were they to be ours? To expedite this consummation every officer fought as if he were the forlorn hope. Mounted on his black pony, the same which he rode at Winchester, Sheridan galloped everywhere, his flushed face all the redder, and his plethoric but nervous figure all the more ubiquitous. He galloped once straight down the Rebel front, with but a handful of his staff. A dozen bullets whistled for him together; one grazed his arm, at which a faithful orderly rode; the black pony leaped high, in fright, and Sheridan was untouched, but the orderly lay dead in the field, and the saddle dashed afar, empty. . . .

Townsend wrote with the enthusiasm of a reporter to whom such scenes were new: "Imagine along a line of a full mile, thirty thousand men struggling for life and prestige; the woods gathering about them —but yesterday the home of hermit hawks and chipmunks—now ablaze with bursting shells, and showing in the dusk the curl of flames in the tangled grass, and, rising up the boles of the pine trees, the scaling, scorching tongues."

Yet Townsend missed the real story of Five Forks. Orders from Robert E. Lee to Fitzhugh Lee and Pickett had urged: "Hold Five Forks at all hazards." Then General Tom Rosser had arrived with a mess of fresh shad. Pickett and Fitzhugh Lee were picking the bones clean when Sheridan came storming down, catching the three Confederate commanders flat-footed. In a letter home Pickett accepted his rout philosophically:[2]

Well, I made the best arrangements of which the nature of the ground admitted. . . . About two o'clock in the afternoon, Sheridan made a heavy demonstration with his cavalry, threatening also the right flank. Meantime Warren's corps swept around the left flank and rear of the infantry line . . . and the attack became general. . . .

I succeeded in getting a sergeant and enough men to man one piece, but after firing eight rounds the axle broke. Floweree's regiment fought hand to hand after all their cartridges had been used. The small cavalry force, which had gotten into place gave way, and the enemy poured in. . . . We were completely entrapped. . . .

My darling, overpowered, defeated, cut to pieces, starving, captured, as we were, those that were left of us formed front and north and south and met with sullen desperation their double onset. With the members of my own staff and the general officers and their staff officers we compelled a rally . . . enabling many of us to escape capture. . . .

The birds were hushed in the woods when I started to write, and now one calls to its mate, "Cheer up—cheer up." Let's listen and obey the birds, my darling.

II

Sunday, April 2, 1865—a beautiful day in Richmond. That morning Jefferson Davis attended services in St. Paul's Church. There a messenger brought him the grim news that Lee's lines had broken and his troops were in full retreat toward Danville. President Davis, going to his office, assembled the heads of departments and bureaus "as far as they could be found" to plan an orderly transfer of government from doomed Richmond to Danville. Quickly the streets filled with wagons of every description as the race to quit the city gained momentum. The last uniformed Confederate to leave Richmond was Captain Clement Sulivane, who "saw few sleeping eyes during the pandemonium of that night": [3]

The division of General G. W. C. Lee, of Ewell's corps, at that time rested in the trenches eight miles below Richmond, with its right on the James River, covering Chaffin's Bluff. I was at the time its assistant adjutant general, and was in the city on some detached duty connected with the "Local Brigade" belonging to the division—a force composed of the soldiers of the army detailed on account of their mechanical skill to work in the arsenals, etc., and of clerks and other employes of the War, Treasury, Quartermaster and other departments.

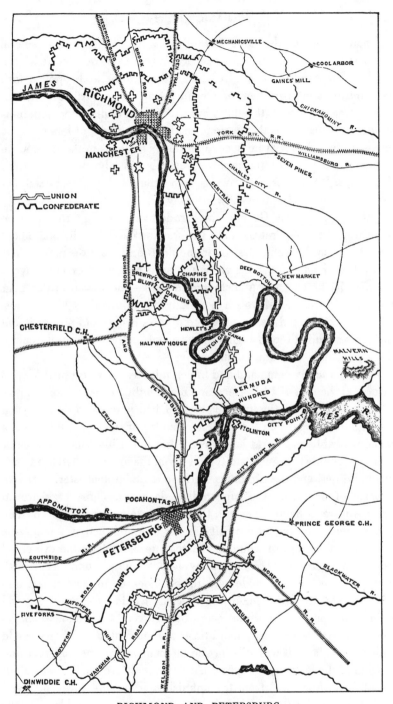

RICHMOND AND PETERSBURG

From Lossing, *Pictorial History of the Civil War*

Upon receipt of the news from Petersburg I reported to General Ewell (then in Richmond) for instructions, and was ordered to assemble and command the Local Brigade, cause it to be well supplied with ammunition and provisions, and await further orders. All that day and night I was engaged in this duty, but with small result, as the battalions melted away as fast as they were formed, mainly under orders from the heads of departments who needed all their employes in the transportation and guarding of the archives, etc., but partly, no doubt, from desertions. When morning dawned, fewer than 200 men remained, under command of Captain Edward Mayo.

Shortly before day General Ewell rode to my headquarters and informed me that General G. W. C. Lee was then crossing the pontoon at Drewry's; that he would destroy it and press on to join the main army; that all the bridges over the river had been destroyed except Mayo's, between Richmond and Manchester; and that the wagon bridge over the canal in front of Mayo's had already been burned by Union emissaries. My command was to hasten to Mayo's bridge and protect it and the one remaining foot-bridge over the canal leading to it, until General Gary of South Carolina should arrive.

I hurried to my command and fifteen minutes later occupied Mayo's bridge, at the foot of 14th street, and made military dispositions to protect it to the last extremity. This done, I had nothing to do but listen for sounds and gaze on the terrible splendor of the scene. And such a scene probably the world has never witnessed. Either incendiaries or (more probably) fragments of bombs from the arsenals, had fired various buildings, and the two cities, Richmond and Manchester, were like a blaze of day amid the surrounding darkness. Three high arched bridges were in flames; beneath them the waters sparkled and dashed and rushed on by the burning city. Every now and then, as a magazine exploded, a column of white smoke rose up as high as the eye could reach, instantaneously followed by a deafening sound. The earth seemed to rock and tremble as with the shock of an earthquake, and immediately afterward hundreds of shells would explode in air and send their iron spray down far below the bridge. As the immense magazines of cartridges ignited, the rattle as of thousands of musketry would follow, and then all was still for the moment except the dull roar and crackle of the fast-spreading fires. At dawn we heard terrific explosions about "The Rockets," from the unfinished iron-clads down the river.

By daylight on the 3rd a mob of men, women and children, to the number of several thousands, had gathered at the corner of 14th and

Cary streets and other outlets in front of the bridge, attracted by the vast commissary depot at that point; for it must be remembered that in 1865 Richmond was a half-starved city, and the Confederate government had that morning removed its guards and abandoned the removal of the provisions, which was impossible for the want of transportation. The depot doors were forced open and a demoniacal struggle for the countless barrels of hams, bacon, whisky, flour, sugar, coffee, etc., raged about the buildings among the hungry mob. The gutters ran whisky, and it was lapped as it flowed down the streets, while all fought for a share of the plunder. The flames came nearer and nearer, and at last caught in the commissariat itself.

At daylight the approach of the Union forces could be plainly discerned. After a little came the clatter of horses' hoofs galloping up Main street. My infantry guard stood to arms, the picket across the canal was withdrawn, and the engineer officer lighted a torch of fat pine. By direction of the Engineer Department barrels of tar, surrounded by pine knots, had been placed at intervals on the bridge, with kerosene at hand, and a lieutenant of engineers had reported for the duty of firing them at my order. The noisy train proved to be Gary's ambulances, sent forward preparatory to his final rush for the bridge. The muleteers galloped their animals about half-way down, when they were stopped by the dense mass of human beings. Rapidly communicating to Captain Mayo my instructions from General Ewell, I ordered that officer to stand firm at his post until Gary got up. I rode forward into the mob and cleared a lane. The ambulances were galloped down to the bridge, I retired to my post, and the mob closed in after me and resumed its wild struggle for plunder.

A few minutes later a long line of cavalry in gray turned into 14th street and, sword in hand, galloped straight down to the river. Gary had come. The mob scattered right and left before the armed horsemen, who reined up at the canal. Presently a single company of cavalry appeared in sight, and rode at headlong speed to the bridge. "My rearguard," explained Gary. Touching his hat to me, he called out, "All over! Good-bye! Blow her to h--l!" and trotted over the bridge. That was the last I ever saw of General Gary of South Carolina.

In less than sixty seconds Captain Mayo was in column of march, and as he reached the little island about half-way across the bridge, the single piece of artillery loaded with grape-shot that had occupied that spot arrived on the Manchester side of the river. The engineer officer, Dr. Lyons, and I walked leisurely to the island, setting fire to the provided combustible material as we passed along, and leaving the north section of Mayo's bridge wrapped in flame and smoke. At the island we stopped to take a view of the situation north of the river, and saw a line of blue-coated horsemen galloping in furious haste up Main street. Across 14th street they stopped, and then dashed down 14th street to the flaming bridge. They fired a few random shots at us three on the island, and we retreated to Manchester. I ordered my command forward, the lieutenant of engineers saluted and went about his business, and myself and my companion sat on our horses for nearly half an hour watching the occupation of Richmond. We saw another string of horsemen in blue pass up Main street, then we saw a dense column of infantry march by, seemingly without end; we heard the very welkin ring with cheers as the United States forces reached Capitol Square, and then we turned and slowly rode on our way.

A fretful Stanton wired Lincoln at City Point not to expose himself. The President replied in a gay mood, "Thanks for your caution; but I have already been to Petersburg." Horace Porter saw him there:[4]

Mr. Lincoln soon after arrived, accompanied by Robert, who had ridden back to the railroad-station to meet him, and by his little son, "Tad," and Admiral Porter. He dismounted in the street, and came in through the front gate with long and rapid strides, his face beaming with delight. He seized General Grant's hand as the general stepped forward to greet him, and stood shaking it for some time, and pouring out his thanks and congratulations with all the fervor of a heart which seemed overflowing with its fullness of joy. I doubt whether Mr. Lincoln ever experienced a happier moment in his life. The scene was singularly affecting, and one never to be forgotten. He said: "Do you know, general, I had a sort of sneaking idea all along that you intended to do something like this; but I thought some time ago that you would so manoeuver as to have Sherman come up and be near enough to co-operate with you." "Yes," replied the general; "I thought at one time that Sherman's army might advance far enough to be in supporting distance of the Eastern armies when the spring campaign against Lee opened; but I had a feeling that it would be better to let Lee's old antagonists give his army the final blow, and finish up the job. If the Western troops were even to put in an appearance against Lee's army, it might give some of our politicians a chance to stir up sectional feeling in claiming everything for the troops from their own section of country. The Western armies have been very successful in their campaigns, and it is due to the Eastern armies to let them vanquish their old enemy single-handed." "I see," said Mr. Lincoln; "but I never thought of it in that light. In fact, my anxiety has been so great that I didn't care where the help came from, so that the work was perfectly done." "Oh," General Grant continued, "I do not suppose it would have given rise to much of the bickering I mentioned, and perhaps the idea would not have occurred to any one else. I feel sure there would have been no such feeling among the soldiers. Of course I would not have risked the result of the campaign on account of any mere sentiment of this kind. I have always felt confident that our troops here were amply able to handle Lee." Mr. Lincoln then began to talk about the civil complications that would follow the destruction of the Confederate armies in the field, and showed plainly the anxiety he felt regarding the great problems in statecraft which would soon be thrust upon him. He intimated very plainly, in a conversation that lasted nearly half an hour, that thoughts of leniency to the conquered were uppermost in his heart.

Meanwhile his son Tad, for whom he always showed a deep affection, was becoming a little uneasy, and gave certain appealing looks, to which General Sharpe, who seemed to understand the mute expressions of small boys, responded by producing some sandwiches, which he offered to him, saying: "Here, young man, I guess you must be hungry." Tad seized them as a drowning man would seize a life-preserver, and cried out: "Yes, I am; that's what's the matter with me." This greatly amused the President and the general-in-chief, who had a hearty laugh at Tad's expense.

Safely back at City Point, the President gave Stanton no peace of mind. Lincoln's wire to the Secretary continued: "It is certain now that Richmond is in our hands, and I think I will go there tomorrow. I can take care of myself."

Thomas Thatcher Graves, on the staff of General Godfrey Weitzel, who commanded the troops occupying Richmond, could hardly believe his eyes on the morning of April 4:[5]

On passing out from Clay street, from Jefferson Davis's house, I saw a crowd coming, headed by President Lincoln, who was walking with his usual long, careless stride, and looking about with an interested air and taking in everything. Upon my saluting he said: "Is it far to Presi-

dent Davis's house?" I accompanied him to the house, which was occupied by General Weitzel as headquarters. . . .

At the Davis house, he was shown into the reception-room, with the
remark that the housekeeper had said that that room was President
Davis's office. As he seated himself he remarked, "This must have
been President Davis's chair," and, crossing his legs, he looked far off
with a serious, dreamy expression. At length he asked me if the housekeeper was in the house. Upon learning that she had left he jumped
up and said, with a boyish manner, "Come, let's look at the house!"
We went pretty much over it; I retailed all that the housekeeper had
told me, and he seemed interested in everything. As we came down
the staircase General Weitzel came in, in breathless haste, and at once
President Lincoln's face lost its boyish expression as he realized that
duty must be resumed. Soon afterward Judge Campbell, General Anderson (Confederates), and others called and asked for an interview
with the President. It was granted, and took place in the parlor with
closed doors.

I accompanied President Lincoln and General Weitzel to Libby
Prison and Castle Thunder, and heard General Weitzel ask President
Lincoln what he (General Weitzel) should do in regard to the conquered people. President Lincoln replied that he did not wish to give
any orders on that subject, but, as he expressed it, "If I were in your
place I'd let 'em up easy, let 'em up easy."

*That afternoon A. W. Bartlett, of the Twelfth New Hampshire, saw
the wild enthusiasm of Richmond's Negroes:*[6]

When it became certain that it was really "Marsa Abraham" that
was in their midst, there was such a rush to see and speak with him
that it was almost impossible, at times, for his carriage to move. A number of bright eyed and woolly headed urchins, taking advantage of
this delay, climbed upon the top of the carriage and took a peep at him
over the rim, greatly to the amusement of the President. His reception
in a city which, only a day or two before, had been the headquarters
and centre of the Rebellion, was most remarkable; and more resembled the triumphant return from, than an entry into the enemy's capital. Instead of the streets being silent and vacated, they were filled with
men, women, and children, shouting and cheering wherever he went.

"I'd rather see him than Jesus," excitedly exclaims one woman, as
she runs ahead of the crowd to get a full view of his benign counte-

nance. "De kingdom's come, and de Lord is wid us," chants another. "Hallelujah!" shouts a third; and so on through a whole volume of prayers, praises, blessings, and benedictions showered down upon him, the great emancipator of a race, and the saviour of his country, thus redeemed, as he walked slowly forward with smiling face and uncovered head. . . .

But it was not the colored population alone which welcomed the Union troops and their great commander-in-chief into the city of Richmond. Thousands of the white citizens were glad to be again under the protection of the flag of their fathers; and some, who had been true to it from the first, keeping it safely hidden away as a sacred emblem of their loyalty, were more happy, if possible, though less demonstrative, than the negro, as they once more were allowed the privilege of spreading its bright folds to the free air of heaven.

Another early visitor to Richmond, George Alfred Townsend, revealed to readers of the New York Herald *that not all Southerners had supported the Confederacy. At Castle Thunder, the state prison, an abandoned record book made him shudder:*[7]

These are some of the entries:

"George Barton,—giving food to Federal prisoners of war; forty lashes upon the bare back. Approved. Sentence carried into effect July 2.

"Peter B. Innis,—passing forged government notes; chain and ball for twelve months; forty lashes a day. Approved.

"Arthur Wright,—attempting to desert to the enemy; sentenced to be shot. Approved. Carried into effect, March 26.

"John Morton,—communicating with the enemy; to be hung. Approved. Carried into effect, March 26."

In an inner room are some fifty pairs of balls and chains, with anklets and handcuffs upon them, which have bent the spirit and body of many a resisting heart. Within are two condemned cells, perfectly dark—a faded flap over the window peep-hole—the smell from which would knock a strong man down.

For in their centre lies the sink, ever open, and the floors are sappy with uncleanliness. To the right of these, a door leads to a walled yard not forty feet long, nor fifteen wide, overlooked by the barred windows of the main prison rooms, and by sentry boxes upon the wall-top. Here the wretched were shot and hung in sight of their trembling comrades.

The brick wall at the foot of the yard is scarred and crushed by balls
and bullets which first passed through some human heart and wrote
here their damning testimony. The gallows had been suspended from
a wing in the ledge, and in mid-air the impotent captive swung, none
daring or willing to say a good word for him; and not for any offence
against God's law, not for wronging his neighbor, or shedding blood,
or making his kind miserable, but for standing in the way of an up-
start organization, which his impulse and his judgment alike impelled
him to oppose. This little yard, bullet-marked, close, and shut from all
sympathy, is to us the ghastliest spot in the world. Can Mr. Davis visit
it, and pray as he does so devoutly afterward? When men plead the
justice of the South, and arguments are prompt to favor them, let this
prison yard rise up and say that no such crimes in liberty's name have
ever been committed, on this continent, at least.

Charles Dana also had reached Richmond:[8]

Immediately upon arriving I began to make inquiries about official
papers. I found that the records and documents of the departments
and of Congress had generally been removed before the evacuation,
and that during the fire the Capitol had been ransacked and the documents there scattered. In the rooms of the Secretary of the Senate and
of the Military Committee of the House of Representatives in the State
House we found some papers of importance. . . .

General Weitzel told me that he had found about twenty thousand
people in Richmond, half of them of African descent. He said that
when President Lincoln entered the town on the 4th [5th] he received
a most enthusiastic reception from the mass of the inhabitants.* All
the members of Congress had escaped, and only the Assistant Secretary
of War, Judge John Archibald Campbell, remained in the fallen capital
of the Confederacy. Most of the newspaper editors had fled, but the
Whig appeared on the 4th as a Union paper, with the name of its
former proprietor at its head. The night after I arrived [that is,
April 6th] the theater opened.

There was much suffering and poverty among the population, the
rich as well as the poor being destitute of food. Weitzel had decided to
issue supplies to all who would take the oath. In my first message to
Mr. Stanton I spoke of this. He immediately answered: "Please ascer-

* Judith Brockenbrough McGuire insisted, however, that those who greeted Mr.
Lincoln so warmly represented the "low, lower, lowest of creation."

tain from General Weitzel under what authority he is distributing rations to the people of Richmond, as I suppose he would not do it without authority; and direct him to report daily the amount of rations distributed by his order to persons not belonging to the military service, and not authorized by law to receive rations, designating the color of the persons, their occupation, and sex." Mr. Stanton seemed to be satisfied when I wired that Weitzel was working under General Ord's orders, approved by General Grant, and that he was paying for the rations by selling captured property.

The important question which the President had on his mind when I reached Richmond was how Virginia could be brought back to the Union. He had already had an interview with Judge Campbell and other prominent representatives of the Confederate Government. All they asked, they said, was an amnesty and a military convention to cover appearances. Slavery they admitted to be defunct. The President did not promise the amnesty, but he told them he had the pardoning power, and would save any repentant sinner from hanging. They assured him that, if amnesty could be offered, the rebel army would be dissolved and all the States return.

III

Lee's one idea, falling back from Petersburg, was to join with Joe Johnston's troops in North Carolina. Foreseeing some such emergency as now happened, Lee, days before, had instructed Richmond to send supplies to Amelia Court House, forty miles southwest of Richmond, on the Richmond and Danville Railroad. On the fourth of April he led his hungry, gaunt-eyed soldiers into this depot on their route to Danville. There were no supplies. Francis Lawley, correspondent for the London Times, *watched the Army of Northern Virginia stumble forward:*[9]

The country through which we were passing was a tract of straggling woods and pine barrens with occasional little patches of clearings. The foraging parties had to go so far afield in quest of food that they were taken prisoners by wholesale. In the face of such suffering as they left behind, it cannot be wondered at if some of the poor fellows courted capture.

Those foragers who returned to Lee brought little or nothing with them. The sufferings of the men from the pangs of hunger have not been approached in the military annals of the last fifty years. But the sufferings of the mules and horses must have been even keener; for the men assuaged their craving by plucking the buds and twigs of trees just shooting in the early spring, whereas the grass had not yet started from its winter sleep and food for the unhappy quadrupeds there was none. As early as the morning of the 4th, Lee sent off half his artillery toward the railroad to relieve the famished horses. This artillery making slow progress, thanks to the exhaustion of the horses, was captured by the Federals on the 8th, but not until General Lindsay Walker had buried many of his guns, which were of course subsequently exhumed (70 of them at one haul) by their captors.

It is easy to see that the locomotion of an army in such a plight must have been slow and slower. The retreat was conducted in the following fashion: About midnight the Confederates slipped out of their hasty works, which they had thrown up and held during the previous day, and fell back until ten or eleven o'clock the next morning. Then they halted, and immediately threw up earthworks for their protection during the day. It was not long before the wolves were again at their heels, and from their earthworks the Confederates exchanged a heavy fire

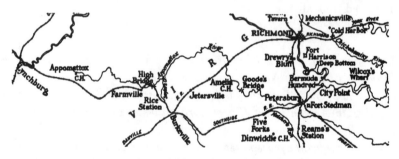

FROM RICHMOND TO APPOMATTOX

From *Atlas of American History*

with their pursuers throughout the day. Delayed by the necessity of guarding a train from thirty-five to forty miles in length, enfeebled by hunger and sleeplessness, the retreating army was able to make only ten miles each night. This delay enabled the active Sheridan to get ahead with his cavalry and destroy the depot of provisions along the railroad between Burkeville and Danville.

Upon the 5th, many of the mules and horses ceased to struggle. It became necessary to burn hundreds of wagons. At intervals the enemy's cavalry dashed in and struck the interminable train here or there, capturing and burning dozens upon dozens of wagons. Toward evening of the 5th, and all day long upon the 6th, hundreds of men dropped from exhaustion and thousands let fall their muskets from inability to carry them further.

The scenes of the 5th, 6th, 7th and 8th were of a nature which can be apprehended in its vivid reality only by men who are thoroughly familiar with the harrowing details of war. Behind and on either flank an ubiquitous and increasingly adventurous enemy—every mud-hole and every rise in the road choked with blazing wagons, the air filled with the deafening reports of ammunition exploding and shells bursting when touched by the flames, dense columns of smoke ascending to heaven from the burning and exploding vehicles—exhausted men, worn-out mules and horses lying down side by side—gaunt famine glaring hopelessly from sunken lack-lustre eyes—dead horses, dead mules, dead men everywhere—death many times welcomed as God's blessing in disguise—who can wonder if many hearts, tried in the fiery furnace of four years' unparalleled suffering and never hitherto found wanting, should have quailed in presence of starvation, fatigue, sleeplessness, misery, unintermitted for five or six days and culminating in hopelessness.

Riding hard on the heels of the retreating Confederates, Colonel Theodore Lyman knew Lee's flight was hopeless:[10]

> HEADQUARTERS ARMY OF POTOMAC
> RICHMOND AND BURKEVILLE R.R.
> 10 MILES NORTH OF BURKEVILLE
> April 6, 1865

We are pelting after Old Lee as hard as the poor doughboys' legs can go. I estimate our prisoners at 16,000, with lots of guns and colors. At six A.M. the three infantry corps advanced in line of battle, on Amelia Court House; 2d on the left; 5th in the centre; and 6th on the right. Sheridan's cavalry, meantime, struck off to the left, to head off their waggon-trains in the direction of the Appomattox River. We did not know just then, you perceive, in what precise direction the enemy was moving. Following the railroad directly towards Amelia C.H., General Meade received distinct intelligence, at nine o'clock, that the enemy was moving on Deatonsville, intending probably to cross the Appomattox at High Bridge. Instantly General Meade gave orders for the 6th Corps to face about and move by the left flank and seek roads in the direction of High Bridge, with the idea of supporting the cavalry in their attempt to head off the enemy; the 2d Corps were turned into the left-hand road nearest Jetersville, and directed to push on and strike the enemy wherever they could. At nine we got to the left-hand road lying some way beyond Jetersville, and here the 5th Corps was turned in, with orders to follow the road through Paineville and attack whatever they found. These prompt dispositions ensured the grand success of the day, which the newspapers have gracefully handed over to General Sheridan!

Here I may as well say that Lee was trying to escape with his large artillery and waggon trains. At first he thought to move directly along the railroad, through Burkeville, to Danville. Cut off by the 5th Corps and the cavalry, he *now* was trying to march "cross lots" and get to the Danville road, somewhere below us. . . . At ten, we got back to Jetersville, a collection of half-a-dozen houses with a country church. From the second story of a house I witnessed a most curious spectacle —a fight, four miles off in a straight line! At that point was a bare ridge, a little above Deatonsville, and there, with my good glass, I could see a single man very well. It was just like a play of marionettes! and the surrounding woods made side scenes to this stage. At first, I saw only the Rebel train, moving along the ridge towards Deatonsville, in all haste: there now goes a pigmy ambulance drawn by mouse-like horses, at a trot. Here come more ambulances and many waggons from the woods, and disappear, in a continuous procession, over the ridge. Suddenly—*boom! boom!* and the distant smoke of Humphreys' batteries curls above the pine trees. At this stimulus the Lilliputian procession redoubles its speed (I am on the point of crying "bravo!" at this brilliant stroke of the gentleman who is pulling the wires). But now enter from the woods, in some confusion, a good number of Rebel cavalry; they form on the crest—but, *boom! boom!* go the cannon, and they disappear. Ah! here come the infantry! Now for a fight! Yes, a line of battle in retreat, and covering the rear. There are mounted officers; they gallop about, waving their tiny swords. Halt! The infantry form a good line on the crest; you can't scare *them*. What are they carrying? Spears? No, *rails;* that's what it is, rails for to revet a breastwork. They scramble about like ants. You had better hurry up, Yanks, if you want to carry that crest! (The stage manager informs me the Yanks *are* hurrying and the next act will be—Enter Duke Humphrey, in haste.) Hullo! There come six fleet mice dragging something, followed by more: yes, a battery. They unlimber: a pause: Flash!—(count twenty-two seconds by Captain Barrows's watch) then, *bang! bang!*

There come in their skirmishers! running for their lives; certainly the Yanks are in those woods. Now they turn their guns more to the left; they are getting flanked. Their officers gallop wildly. You seem to hear them shout, "Change front to the rear!" anyhow they do so, at a double-quick. Then one volley of musketry, and they are gone, guns and all! The next moment our skirmishers go swarming up the hill; up goes a battery, and down goes the curtain.

There is no rest for the wicked. All day long the peppery Humphreys, glaring through those spectacles, presses hotly in their rear; the active Sheridan is felling trees across their front; on their right is the Appomattox, impassable; and now, as the afternoon closes, here comes the inevitable Wright, grimly on their left flank, at Sailor's Creek. The 6th Corps charges; they can't be stopped—result, five Rebel generals; 8600 prisoners, 14 cannon; the Rebel rear-guard annihilated! As we get to our camp, beyond Deatonsville, there comes a Staff officer with a despatch. "*I* attacked with two divisions of the 6th Corps. *I* captured many thousand prisoners, etc., etc. P. H. Sheridan." "Oh," said Meade, "so *General Wright wasn't there.*" "Oh, yes!" cried the Staff officer, as if speaking of some worthy man who had commanded a battalion, "Oh, yes, General Wright *was* there." Meade turned on his heel without a word, and Cavalry Sheridan's despatch proceeded—to the newspapers!

The uneven contest at Sailor's (Saylor's) Creek, that saw a Confederate corps terribly hacked and General Ewell captured, ended on April 7. Horace Porter described another memorable event of that day:[11]

A little before noon on April 7, 1865, General Grant, with his staff, rode into the little village of Farmville, on the south side of the Appomattox River, a town that will be memorable in history as the place where he opened the correspondence with Lee which, two days later, led to the surrender of the Army of Northern Virginia. He drew up in front of the village hotel, a comfortable brick building, dismounted, and established headquarters on its broad piazza. News came in that Crook was fighting large odds with his cavalry on the north side of the river, and I was directed to go to his front and see what was necessary to be done to assist him. I found that he was being driven back, the enemy (Munford's and Rosser's cavalry divisions, under Fitzhugh Lee) having made a bold stand north of the river. Humphreys was also on the north side, isolated from the rest of our infantry, confronted by a large portion of Lee's army, and having some heavy fighting. On my return to general headquarters that evening, Wright's corps was ordered to cross the river and move rapidly to the support of our troops there. Notwithstanding their long march that day, the men sprang to their feet with a spirit that made every one marvel at their pluck, and came swinging through the main street of the village with a step that seemed as elastic as on the first day of their toilsome tramp. It was now dark, but they spied the general-in-chief watching them with evident pride from the piazza of the hotel as they marched past. Then was witnessed one of the most inspiring scenes of the campaign. Bonfires were lighted on the sides of the street; the men seized straw and pine-knots, and improvised torches; cheers arose from their throats, already hoarse with shouts of victory; bands played, banners waved, and muskets were swung in the air. A regiment now broke forth with the song of "John Brown's body," and soon a whole division was shouting the swelling chorus of the popular air, which had risen to the dignity of a national anthem. The night march had become a grand review, with Grant as the reviewing officer.

Ord and Gibbon had visited the general at the hotel, and he had spoken with them, as well as with Wright, about sending some communication to Lee that might pave the way to the stopping of further bloodshed. Dr. Smith, formerly of the regular army, a native of Virginia, and a relative of General Ewell, now one of our prisoners, had told General Grant the night before that Ewell had said in conversation that their cause was lost when they crossed the James River, and he considered that it was the duty of the authorities to negotiate for peace then, while they still had a right to claim concessions, adding that now they were not in condition to claim anything. He said that for every man killed after this somebody would be responsible, and it would be little better than murder. He could not tell what General Lee would do, but he hoped that he would at once surrender his army. This statement, together with the news that had been received from Sheridan, saying that he had heard that General Lee's trains of provisions, which had come by rail, were at Appomattox, and that he expected to capture them before Lee could reach them, induced the general to write. . . .

Grant detailed the historic correspondence that followed:[12]

Feeling now that General Lee's chance of escape was utterly hopeless, I addressed him the following communication from Farmville:

"April 7, 1865

"GENERAL: The result of the last week must convince you of the hopelessness of further resistance on the part of the Army of Northern Virginia in this struggle. I feel that it is so, and regard it as my duty to shift from myself the responsibility of any further effusion of blood, by asking of you the surrender of that portion of the Confederate States army known as the Army of Northern Virginia.

"U. S. GRANT,
"*Lieutenant-General*

"GENERAL R. E. LEE."

Early on the morning of the eighth, before leaving, I received at Farmville the following:

"April 7, 1865

"GENERAL: I have received your note of this date. Though not entertaining the opinion you express on the hopelessness of further resistance on the part of the army of Northern Virginia, I reciprocate your desire to avoid useless effusion of blood, and therefore, before considering your proposition, ask the terms you will offer on condition of its surrender.

"R. E. LEE,
"*General*

"LIEUTENANT-GENERAL U. S. GRANT."

To this I immediately replied:

"April 8, 1865

"GENERAL: Your note of last evening, in reply to mine of same date, asking the condition on which I will accept the surrender of the army of Northern Virginia, is just received. In reply I would say that, *peace* being my great desire, there is but one condition I would insist upon, namely: That the men and officers surrendered shall be disqualified for taking up arms again against the Government of the United States until properly exchanged. I will meet you, or will designate officers to meet any officers you may name for the same purpose, at any point agreeable to you, for the purpose of arranging definitely the terms upon which the surrender of the army of Northern Virginia will be received.

"U. S. GRANT,
"*Lieutenant-General*

"GENERAL R. E. LEE."

Early on the morning of the eighth the pursuit was resumed. General Meade followed north of the Appomattox, and General Sheridan, with all the cavalry, pushed straight for Appomattox Station, followed by General Ord's command and the Fifth corps. During the day General Meade's advance had considerable fighting with the enemy's rear guard, but was unable to bring on a general engagement. Late in the evening General Sheridan struck the railroad at the Appomattox station, drove the enemy from there, and captured twenty-five pieces of artillery, a hospital train, and four trains of cars loaded with supplies for Lee's army. During this day I accompanied General Meade's column, and about midnight received the following communication from General Lee:

"April 8, 1865

"GENERAL: I received at a late hour your note of to-day. In mine of yesterday I did not intend to propose the surrender of the Army of Northern Virginia, but to ask the terms of your proposition. To be frank, I do not think the emergency has arisen to call for the surrender of this army; but as the restoration of peace should be the sole object of all, I desired to know whether your proposals would lead to that end. I cannot, therefore, meet you with a view to surrender the Army of Northern Virginia; but as far as your proposal may affect the Confederate States forces under my command, and tend to the restoration of peace, I should be pleased to meet you at ten A.M. to-morrow on the old stage road to Richmond, between the picket lines of the two armies.

"R. E. LEE,
"General

"LIEUTENANT-GENERAL U. S. GRANT."

Early on the morning of the ninth I returned him an answer as follows, and immediately started to join the column south of the Appomattox:

"April 9, 1865

"GENERAL: Your note of yesterday is received. I have no authority to treat on the subject of peace; the meeting proposed for A.M. to-day could lead to no good. I will state, however, General, that I am equally anxious for peace with yourself, and the whole North entertains the same feeling. The terms upon which peace can be had are well understood. By the South laying down their arms they will hasten that most desirable event, save thousands of human lives, and hundreds of millions of property not yet destroyed. Seriously hoping that all our difficulties may be settled without the loss of another life, I subscribe myself, &c.,

> "U. S. GRANT,
> "*Lieutenant-General*

"GENERAL R. E. LEE."

On the morning of the ninth General Ord's command and the Fifth corps reached Appomattox station just as the enemy was making a desperate effort to break through our cavalry. The infantry was at once thrown in. Soon after a white flag was received, requesting a suspension of hostilities pending negotiations for surrender.

Before reaching General Sheridan's headquarters, I received the following from General Lee:

> "April 9, 1865
> "GENERAL: I received your note of this morning on the picket line, whither I had come to meet you, and ascertain definitely what terms were embraced in your proposal of yesterday with reference to the surrender of this army. I now ask an interview in accordance with the offer contained in your letter of yesterday for that purpose.
> "R. E. LEE,
> "*General*

"LIEUTENANT-GENERAL U. S. GRANT."

IV

Colonel Theodore Lyman described a truce that upset two Union generals:[13]

. . . At 10.30 came, one after the other, two negroes, who said that some of our troops entered Lynchburg yesterday; and that Lee was now cut off near Appomattox Court House. This gave us new wings! An aide-de-camp galloped on, to urge Humphreys to press the pursuit, and all waggons were ordered out of the road, that the 6th Corps might close in immediately on his rear. Away went the General again, full tilt, along the road crowded by the infantry, every man of whom was footing it, as if a lottery prize lay just ahead! A bugler trotted ahead, blowing to call the attention of the troops, while General Webb followed, crying, "Give way to the right! Give way to the right!" Thus we ingeniously worked our way, amid much pleasantry. "Fish for sale!" roared one doughboy. "Yes," joined in a pithy comrade, "and a tarnation big one, too!" The comments on the General were endless. "That's Meade." "Yes, that's him." "Is he sick?" "I expect he is; he looks kinder wild!" "Guess the old man hain't had much sleep lately."

The heavy artillery firing we had earlier heard, now had suddenly ceased, and there was a perfect stillness—a suspicious circumstance that gave us new hope. Somewhat before noon we got to General Humphreys, some five miles east of the Court House and at the very head of his men. He reported that he had just struck the enemy's skirmish line, and was preparing to drive them back. At that moment an officer rode up and said the enemy were out with a white flag. "They shan't stop *me!*" retorted the fiery H.; "receive the message but push on the skirmishers!" Back came the officer speedily, with a note. General Lee stated that General Ord had agreed to a suspension of hostilities, and he should ask for the same on this *end* of the line. "Hey! what!" cried General Meade, in his harsh, suspicious voice, "I have no sort of authority to grant such suspension. General Lee has already refused the terms of General Grant. Advance your skirmishers, Humphreys, and bring up your troops. We will pitch into them at once!" But lo! here comes now General Forsyth, who had ridden through the Rebel army, from General Sheridan (under a flag), and who now urged a brief suspension. "Well," said the General, "in order that you may get back to Sheridan, I will wait till two o'clock, and then, if I get no communication from General Lee, I shall attack!" So back went Forsyth, with a variety of notes and despatches. We waited, not without excitement, for the appointed hour. Meantime, negroes came in and said the Rebel pickets had thrown down their muskets and gone leisurely to their main body; also that the Rebels were "done gone give up." Presently, the General pulled out his watch and said: "Two o'clock—no answer—go forward." But they had not advanced far, before we saw a Rebel and a Union officer coming in. They bore an order from General Grant to halt the troops. Major Wingate, of General Lee's Staff, was a military-looking man, dressed in a handsome grey suit with gold lace, and a gold star upon the collar. He was courageous, but plainly mortified to the heart. "We had done better to have burnt our whole train three days ago," he said bitterly. "In trying to save a train, we have lost an army!" And there he struck the pith of the thing.

The reporter Sylvanus Cadwallader was at Appomattox Court House on that historic ninth of April, 1865:[14]

. . . The news of the pending negotiations for the surrender spread rapidly through both armies. As we came out on the open ground near the village, both armies were in plain view. The soldiers of each were in line of battle, and ready to renew the contest on short notice. Officers were galloping in all directions, colors were flying, and it had more the appearance of a grand review of troops, than of contending hosts. A nearer view, however, disclosed dirty, tattered, ranks of soldiers, none of them well clad, and nearly all officers in fatigue dress.

We struck the upper or south end of the principal street of the village, and turned northward to the Court House. Lee's army still lay north and east of the town. A close lookout was kept for Gen. Lee. When nearly in front of a two-story brick house on the right, or east side of the street, an orderly in rebel uniform was seen holding a couple of horses near the north end of the building. One was a dapple-gray, with a Grimsley saddle and plain single-reined bridle on him, without anything to denote rank.

A staff officer dashed across the open blue grass yard and inquired whose horses they were. The orderly said they belonged to Gen. Lee, who was in the house. The house stood back several rods from the street. The front fence was wholly down, and mostly carried away. So Gen. Grant rode across the yard to the front entrance to a long porch which extended the whole length of the house, dismounted, ascended a half dozen steps onto the porch, and was about to enter the half-open door of a wide hall which separated the ground floor into two suites of rooms, when Gen. Lee met him, exchanged salutations, and conducted him into the front room on the left side of the hall. The staff all remained on their horses. In a few minutes Gen. Grant came to the front, and beckoned to us to come in. . . .

Grant remembered his emotions when he shook the hand of Lee:[15]

What General Lee's feelings were I do not know. As he was a man of much dignity, with an impassible face, it was impossible to say whether he felt inwardly glad that the end had finally come, or felt sad over the result, and was too manly to show it. Whatever his feelings, they were entirely concealed from my observation; but my own feelings, which had been quite jubilant on the receipt of his letter, were sad and depressed. I felt like anything rather than rejoicing at the downfall of a foe, who had fought so long and valiantly, and had suffered so much for a cause, though that cause was, I believe, one of the worst for which a people ever fought, and one for which there was the least excuse.

With Grant in the McLean House that day was Horace Porter:[16]

The contrast between the two commanders was singularly striking, and could not fail to attract marked attention as they sat, six or eight feet apart, facing each other. General Grant, then nearly forty-three years of age, was five feet eight inches in height, with shoulders slightly stooped. His hair and full beard were nut-brown, without a trace of gray in them. He had on his single-breasted blouse of dark-blue flannel, unbuttoned in front and showing a waistcoat underneath. He wore an ordinary pair of top-boots, with his trousers inside, and was without spurs. The boots and portions of his clothes were spattered with mud. . . . His felt "sugar-loaf," stiff-brimmed hat was resting on his lap. He had no sword or sash, and a pair of shoulder-straps was all there was about him to designate his rank. . . .

Lee, on the other hand, was six feet and one inch in height, and erect for one of his age, for he was Grant's senior by sixteen years. His hair and full beard were a silver-gray, and thick, except that the hair had become a little thin in front. He wore a new uniform of Confederate gray, buttoned to the throat, and a handsome sword and sash. . . . His top-boots were comparatively new, and had on them near the top some ornamental stitching of red silk. Like his uniform, they were clean. On the boots were handsome spurs with large rowels. A felt hat which in color matched pretty closely that of his uniform, and a pair of long, gray buckskin gauntlets, lay beside him on the table. . . .

Grant recalled, with a hint of chagrin, "I must have contrasted very strangely with a man so handsomely dressed." The two generals talked for a time of old army days until, Grant admitted, "General Lee called my attention to the object of our meeting":[17]

. . . I called to General Parker, secretary on my staff, for writing materials, and commenced writing out the following terms:

APPOMATTOX C.H., VA.,
Ap'l 9th, 1865

GEN. R. E. LEE,
COMD'G C. S. A.

GEN.: In accordance with the substance of my letter to you of the 8th inst., I propose to receive the surrender of the Army of N. Va. on the following terms, to wit: Rolls of all the officers and men to be made in duplicate. One copy to be given to an officer designated by me, the other to be retained by such officer or officers as you may designate. The officers to give their individual paroles not to take up arms against the Government of the United States until properly exchanged, and each company or regimental commander sign a like parole for the men of their commands. The arms, artillery and public property to be parked and stacked, and turned over to the officer appointed by me to receive them. This will not embrace the side-arms of the officers, nor their private horses or baggage. This done, each officer and man will be allowed to return to their homes, not to be disturbed by United States authority so long as they observe their paroles and the laws in force where they may reside.

Very respectfully,
U. S. GRANT,
Lt.-Gen.

When I put my pen to the paper I did not know the first word that I should make use of in writing the terms. I only knew what was in my mind, and I wished to express it clearly, so that there could be no mistaking it. . . .

Grant's letter was handed to Lee. Horace Porter watched intently:[18]

Lee pushed aside some books and two brass candlesticks which were on the table, then took the book and laid it down before him, while he drew from his pocket a pair of steel-rimmed spectacles, and wiped the glasses carefully with his handkerchief. He crossed his legs, adjusted the spectacles very slowly and deliberately, took up the draft of the terms, and proceeded to read them attentively. When he reached the top line of the second page, he looked up, and said to General Grant: "After the words 'until properly' the word 'exchanged' seems to be omitted. You doubtless intended to use that word."

"Why, yes," said Grant; "I thought I had put in the word 'exchanged.' "

"I presumed it had been omitted inadvertently," continued Lee; "and, with your permission, I will mark where it should be inserted."

"Certainly," Grant replied.

Lee felt in his pocket as if searching for a pencil, but he did not seem to be able to find one. Seeing this, I handed him my lead-pencil. . . .

To Grant, receiving a surrender was part of the business of war. He continued his narrative without embellishment:[19]

No conversation, not one word, passed between General Lee and myself, either about private property, side arms, or kindred subjects. He appeared to have no objections to the terms first proposed; or if he had a point to make against them he wished to wait until they were in writing to make it. When he read over that part of the terms about side arms, horses and private property of the officers, he remarked, with some feeling, I thought, that this would have a happy effect upon his army.

Then, after a little further conversation, General Lee remarked to me again that their army was organized a little differently from the army of the United States (still maintaining by implication that we were two countries); that in their army the cavalrymen and artillerists owned their own horses; and he asked if he was to understand that the men who so owned their horses were to be permitted to retain them. I told him that as the terms were written they would not; that only the officers were permitted to take their private property. He then, after reading over the terms a second time, remarked that that was clear.

I then said to him that I thought this would be about the last battle of the war—I sincerely hoped so; and I said further I took it that most of the men in the ranks were small farmers. The whole country had been so raided by the two armies that it was doubtful whether they would be able to put in a crop to carry themselves and their families through the next winter without the aid of the horses they were then riding. The United States did not want them, and I would, therefore, instruct the officers I left behind to receive the paroles of his troops to let every man of the Confederate army who claimed to own a horse or mule take the animal to his home. Lee remarked again that this would have a happy effect. . . .

The much talked of surrendering of Lee's sword and my handing it back, this and much more that has been said about it is the purest romance.

V

The two generals signed the papers. Then Lee shook hands with Grant, bowed to the other officers, and left the room. Waiting on the porch for his horse, Lee three times struck the palm of his left hand with his right fist. At a slow trot, he rode back to his army. Horace Porter described the jubilant scene inside the McLean House:[20]

Mr. McLean had been charging about in a manner which indicated that the excitement was shaking his nervous system to its center; but his real trials did not begin until the departure of the chief actors in the surrender. Then relic-hunters charged down upon the manor-house, and began to bargain for the numerous pieces of furniture. Sheridan paid the proprietor twenty dollars in gold for the table on which General Grant wrote the terms of surrender, for the purpose of presenting it to Mrs. Custer, and handed it over to her dashing husband, who galloped off to camp bearing it upon his shoulders. Ord paid forty dollars for the table at which Lee sat, and afterward presented it to Mrs. Grant, who modestly declined it, and insisted that Mrs. Ord should become its possessor. General Sharpe paid ten dollars for the pair of brass candlesticks; Colonel Sheridan, the general's brother, secured the stone inkstand; and General Capehart the chair in which Grant sat. . . . A child's doll was found in the room, which the younger officers tossed from one to the other, and called the "silent witness."

Colonel Charles Marshall, who had accompanied Lee on his meeting with Grant, described a different scene and mood:[21]

On the night of April 9th after our return from McLean's house General Lee sat with several of us at a fire in front of his tent, and after some conversation about the army and the events of the day in which his feelings towards his men were strongly expressed, he told me to prepare an order to the troops.

The next day it was raining and many persons were coming and going, so that I was unable to write without interruption until about 10 o'clock, when General Lee finding that the order had not been prepared, directed me to get into his ambulance, which stood near his tent, and placed an orderly to prevent anyone from approaching us. I made a draft in pencil and took it to General Lee who struck out a paragraph, which he said would tend to keep alive the feeling existing between the North and the South, and made one or two other changes. I then returned to the ambulance, recopied the order and gave it to a clerk in the office of the Adjutant General to write in ink.

After the first draft of the order had been made and signed by General Lee, other copies were made for transmission to the corps commanders and the staff of the army. All these copies were signed by the General and a good many persons sent other copies which they had made or procured and obtained his signature. In this way many of the orders had the General's name signed as if they were originals.

The full text of the order follows:

GENERAL ORDER NO. 9

HEADQUARTERS ARMY OF NORTHERN VIRGINIA, 10th April 1865

After four years of arduous service marked by unsurpassed courage and fortitude the Army of Northern Virginia has been compelled to yield to overwhelming numbers and resources.

I need not tell the survivors of so many hard fought battles, who have remained steadfast to the last, that I have consented to this result from no distrust of them. But feeling that valor and devotion could accomplish nothing that could compensate for the loss that would have accompanied the continuance of the contest, I determined to avoid the useless sacrifice of those whose past services have endeared them to their country.

By the terms of the agreement Officers and men can return to their homes and remain there until exchanged. You will take with you the satisfaction that proceeds from the consciousness of duty faithfully performed and I earnestly pray that a merciful God will extend to you his blessing and protection.

With an unceasing admiration of your constancy and devotion to your country and a grateful remembrance of your kind and generous consideration of myself, I bid you all an affectionate farewell.

R. E. LEE
General

Meade, obviously satisfying his curiosity, took Colonel Theodore Ly-
man on a fascinating ride next morning:[22]

. . . Monday April 10 is a day worthy of description, because I
saw the remains of our great opponent, the Army of Northern Virginia.
The General proposed to ride through the Rebel lines to General Grant,
who was at Appomattox Court House; and he took George and myself
as aides; a great chance! for the rest were not allowed to go, no communication being permitted between the armies. At 10.30 we rode off,
and, passing along the state road, soon got to the picket line, where a
row of our men were talking comfortably with an opposite row of
theirs. There the General sent me ahead to see some general of theirs
who might give us a guide through the lines. I rode a little beyond a
wood, and came on several regiments, camped there. The arms were
neatly stacked and the well-known battle-flags were planted by the arms.
The men, looking tired and indifferent, were grouped here and there.
I judged they had nothing to eat, for there was no cooking going on.
A mounted officer was shown me as General Field, and to him I applied. He looked something like Captain Sleeper, but was extremely
moody, though he at once said he would ride back himself to General
Meade, by whom he was courteously received, which caused him to
thaw out considerably. We rode about a mile and then turned off to
General Lee's Headquarters, which consisted in one fly with a campfire in front. I believe he had lost most of his baggage in some of the
trains, though his establishment is at all times modest. He had ridden
out, but, as we turned down the road again, we met him coming up,
with three or four Staff officers. As he rode up General Meade took
off his cap and said: "Good-morning, General." Lee, however, did not
recognize him, and, when he found who it was, said: "But what are
you doing with all that grey in your beard?" To which Meade promptly
replied: "You have to answer for most of it!" Lee is, as all agree, a
stately-looking man; tall, erect and strongly built, with a full chest. His
hair and closely trimmed beard, though thick, are now nearly white.
He has a large and well-shaped head, with a brown, clear eye, of unusual depth. His face is sunburnt and rather florid. In manner he is
exceedingly grave and dignified—this, I believe, he always has; but
there was evidently added an extreme depression, which gave him
the air of a man who kept up his pride to the last, but who was entirely
overwhelmed. From his speech I judge he was inclined to wander in

his thoughts. You would not have recognized a Confederate officer from his dress, which was a blue military overcoat, a high grey hat, and well-brushed riding boots.

As General Meade introduced his two aides, Lee put out his hand and saluted us with all the air of the oldest blood in the world. I did not think, when I left, in '63, for Germantown, that I should ever shake the hand of Robert E. Lee, prisoner of war! He held a long conference with General Meade, while I stood over a fire, with his officers, in the rain. Colonel Marshall, one of his aides, was a very sensible and gentlemanly man, and seemed in good spirits. He told me that, at one time during the retreat, he got no sleep for seventy-two hours, the consequence of which was that his brain did not work at all, or worked all wrong. A quartermaster came up to him and asked by what route he should move his train: to which Marshall replied, in a lucid manner: "Tell the Captain that I *should* have sent that cane as a present to his baby; but I could not, because the baby turned out to be a girl instead of a boy!" We were talking there together, when there appeared a great oddity—an old man, with an angular, much-wrinkled face, and long, thick white hair, brushed *à la* Calhoun; a pair of silver spectacles and a high felt hat further set off the countenance, while the legs kept up their claim of eccentricity by encasing themselves in grey blankets, tied somewhat in a bandit fashion. The whole made up no less a person than Henry A. Wise, once Governor of the loyal state of Virginia, now Brigadier-General and prisoner of war. By his first wife he is Meade's brother-in-law, and had been sent for to see him. I think *he* is punished already enough: old, sick, impoverished, a prisoner, with nothing to live for, not even his son, who was killed at Roanoke Island, he stood there in his old, wet, grey blanket, glad to accept at our hands a pittance of biscuit and coffee, to save him and his Staff from starvation! While they too talked, I asked General Lee after his son "Ronnie," who was about there somewhere. It was the "Last Ditch" indeed! He too is punished enough: living at this moment at Richmond, on the food doled out to him by our government, he gets his ration just like the poorest negro in the place! We left Lee, and kept on through the sad remnants of an army that has its place in history. It would have looked a mighty host, if the ghosts of all its soldiers that now sleep between Gettysburg and Lynchburg could have stood there in the lines, beside the living.

CHAPTER 40

"WHERE I LEFT OFF"

T HE PEOPLE ARE FULL OF REJOICING," the editors of *Harper's Weekly* commented in their lead article for April 22, 1865. "The war for the Union has been *their* war, fought in their interest, sustained by their patriotism—a patriotism that has withheld neither property nor life. Let the people rejoice, then, in the final triumph, with a consciousness of their own strength, but especially with a conviction of the righteousness of their victory and a sense of overwhelming gratitude to the God of Battles. Their *Hail Columbia* is fitly accompanied by their *Te Deums*."

I

On March 27, 1865, Secretary of War Edwin M. Stanton had ordered: "That at the hour of noon on the 14th of April 1865 Brevet Maj. Gen. Anderson will raise and plant upon the ruins of Fort Sumter in Charleston harbor the same United States flag which floated over the Battlements of that fort during the rebel assault and which was lowered and saluted by him and the small force of his command, when the works were evacuated on the 14th day of April 1861." Dr. F. Milton Willis witnessed this restoration of national authority:[1]

Sergeant Hart, who had replaced the flag after it had been shot away in the first assault, stepped forward with the Fort Sumter mail-bag in his hand. As he quietly drew forth from its long seclusion the same old flag of '61, the wildest shouts went up. The old symbol of union was quickly attached to the halyards by three sailors from the fleet who were in the first fight, and crowned with a wreath of evergreen set with clusters of rosebuds and orange blossoms. . . .

General Robert Anderson, the hero of the day, stepped forward and with uncovered head and voice trembling with emotion, said:

"I am here, my friends, my fellow-citizens and fellow-soldiers, to perform an act of duty to my country dear to my heart, and which all of you will appreciate and feel. Had I observed the wishes of my heart it should have been done in silence; but in accordance with the request of the Honorable Secretary of War, I make a few remarks, as by his order, after four long, long years of war, I restore to its proper place this dear flag, which floated here during peace before the first act of this cruel rebellion. (Taking the halyards in his hands, he said:) I thank God that I have lived to see this day, and to be here, to perform this, perhaps the last act of my life, of duty to my country. My heart is filled with gratitude to that God who has so signally blessed us, who has given us blessings beyond measure. May all the nations bless and praise the name of the Lord, and all the world proclaim, 'Glory to God in the highest, and on earth peace, good-will toward men.' "

"Amen! Amen!" the multitude responded. Then the old veteran grasped the halyards with firm and steady hand and drew aloft the starry banner; and as, all tattered by shot and shell, it rose above the battlements into its native air, a loud and prolonged shout, from fort and fleet, greeted it. The whole audience sprang to their feet. Bands began to play their most inspiring music. Men swung their hats and grasped each other by the hand; women and children waved their handkerchiefs, and many wept for joy. As it rested at length in its old place at the top of the staff, and waved its victorious folds toward the recovered city which had first disowned it, the enthusiasm became tumultuous and overpowering, till at last it found relief in the national song:

"The star spangled banner, O long may it wave,
O'er the land of the free, and the home of the brave!"

II

After Appomattox the complete collapse of the Confederacy became inevitable. Official telegrams and newspaper dispatches charted the wave of surrenders. The Secretary of War to Major General John A. Dix, commanding the Department of the East:[2]

War Department, Washington, D. C.
April 28, 1865—3 o'clock p.m.
Major-Gen. Dix: A dispatch from Gen. Grant, dated at Raleigh,
10 p.m., April 26, just received by this Department, states that "Johnston surrendered the forces in his command, embracing all from
here to the Chattahoochie, to Gen. Sherman on the basis agreed upon
between Lee and myself for the Army of Northern Virginia."
                                                    Edwin M. Stanton

General E. R. S. Canby to Military Headquarters at Memphis:

Hdqrs. Military Division of West Mississippi,
Citronelle, May 4
Lieut-Gen. Taylor has this day surrendered to me with the forces
under his command, on substantially the same terms as those accepted
by Gen. Lee.

The New York Tribune, *May 29:*

PEACE!
KIRBY SMITH SURRENDERS
THE OLD FLAG WAVES FROM MAINE TO THE RIO GRANDE!
OFFICIAL ANNOUNCEMENT

War Department,
Washington, Saturday, May 27, 1865
Major-Gen. Dix: A dispatch from General Canby, dated at New
Orleans, yesterday, the 26th inst., states that arrangements for the surrender of the Confederate forces in the Trans-Mississippi Department
have been concluded. They include the men and materiel of the army
and navy.
                                    Edwin M. Stanton, *Secretary of War*

III
*Alexander H. Stephens, Vice President of the Confederate States of
America, had reached a decision as early as the Hampton Roads con-
ference. He would be the first of the captains and the kings to depart:*[3]

I saw nothing to prevent Sherman himself from proceeding right on
to Richmond and attacking Lee in the rear, to say nothing of any move-

ments by Grant, who then had an Army in front of not much, if any, under 200,000 men. Lee's forces were not over one fourth of that number. Sherman's army, when united with Schofield's and Terry's, who were joining him from Wilmington, North Carolina, would be swelled to near 100,000. To meet these, the Confederates had in his front nothing but the fragments of shattered armies, amounting in all to not one half the number of the Federals.

When the programme of action, thus indicated by Mr. Davis [resistance to the end] . . . was clearly resolved upon, I, *then*, for the first time, in view of all the surroundings, considered the Cause as utterly hopeless.

It was then that I withdrew from Richmond. . . . He [Davis] inquired what it was my purpose to do? I told him it was to go home and remain there. I should neither make any speech, nor even make known to the public in any way my views of the general condition of affairs, but quietly abide the issues of fortune, whatever they might be. Differing as we did, at that time, upon these points, as we had upon others, we parted in the same friendship which had on all occasions marked our personal intercourse. . . .

I, therefore, left on the 9th of February, and reached home the 20th, where I remained in perfect retirement, until I was arrested on the 11th of May.*

James Russell Lowell remembered a "startled April morning" when the news flashed across the country:[4]

WASHINGTON, Friday, April 14, 1865

The President was shot in a theater tonight, and perhaps mortally wounded.

(Later)

WASHINGTON, Friday, April 14, 1865

Like a clap of thunder out of clear sky spread the announcement that President Lincoln was shot while sitting in his box at Ford's Theater. The city is wild with excitement. A gentleman who was present thus describes the event: At about 10½ o'clock, in the midst of one of the acts, a pistol shot was heard, and at the same instant a man leaped upon the stage from the same box occupied by the President, brandished a

* Stephens was confined in Fort Warren, Boston harbor, for five months and then released on his own parole.

long knife, and shouted, *"Sic semper tyrannis!"* then rushed to the rear of the scenes and out of the back door of the theater. So sudden was the whole thing that most persons in the theater supposed it a part of the play, and it was some minutes before the fearful tragedy was comprehended. The man was pursued, however, by some one connected with the theater to the outer door and seen to mount a horse and ride rapidly away.

WAR DEPARTMENT,

WASHINGTON, April 15, 1865

MAJOR-GENERAL DIX: Abraham Lincoln died this morning at twenty-two minutes after 7 o'clock.

EDWIN M. STANTON, *Secretary of War*

Walt Whitman wrote: "Mother prepared breakfast—and other meals afterward—as usual; but not a mouthful was eaten all day by either of us. We each drank half a cup of coffee; that was all. Little was said. We got every newspaper morning and evening, and the frequent extras of that period, and passed them silently to each other."

Whitman began at once Lincoln's greatest eulogy:

O Captain! my Captain! our fearful trip is done,
The ship has weathered every rack, the prize we sought is won,
The port is near, the bells I hear, the people all exulting,
While follow eyes the steady keel, the vessel grim and daring;
  But O heart! heart! heart!
   O the bleeding drops of red,
    Where on the deck my Captain lies,
     Fallen cold and dead.

O Captain! my Captain! rise up and hear the bells;
Rise up—for you the flag is flung—for you the bugle trills,
For you bouquets and ribboned wreaths—for you the shores
         a-crowding
For you they call, the swaying mass, their eager faces turning;
  Here Captain! dear father!
   This arm beneath your head!
    It is some dream that on the deck
     You've fallen cold and dead.

My Captain does not answer, his lips are pale and still,
My father does not feel my arm, he has no pulse nor will,

The ship is anchored safe and sound, its voyage closed and done,
From fearful trip the victor ship comes in with object won;
  Exult O shores, and ring O bells!
    But I, with mournful tread,
      Walk the deck my Captain lies,
        Fallen cold and dead.

While Whitman grieved in New York, another great American, un-
aware of the President's death, reached home:[5]

General Robert E. Lee, lately commanding the rebel armies, arrived
in Richmond yesterday afternoon, at half-past three o'clock. The first
intimation of the arrival of the General was the call made upon Lieutenant H. S. Merrell, Post Quartermaster of Richmond, for forage
and stabling for twenty horses in behalf of General Lee. Shortly after
three o'clock General Lee arrived on the pontoon bridge that spans
the James between Richmond and Manchester, an opposite town. Here
an immense crowd had collected to receive him, and he was greeted
with cheers upon cheers, the acclamations of the people, so generously
and heartily bestowed, visibly affecting him. Whenever he passed Union officers they raised their caps. . . . As he proceeded along the
streets to his residence in Franklin Street the crowd increased in
numbers, and the cheers grew louder.

The General was accompanied by five members of his staff, General Lee and all wearing swords. As he dismounted at his residence
the thousands of people who surrounded him again greeted him with
acclaims, and so many as could get near his person shook him heartily
by the hand. . . . The good feeling in relation to General Lee was
common to both Unionists and rebels, and was fully shared in by all.

A month later the war ended for Jefferson Davis. The Secretary of War
wired Major General Dix:[6]

WAR DEPARTMENT, WASHINGTON, May 13
  The following dispatch, just received from Gen. Wilson, announces
the surprise and capture of Jefferson Davis and his staff, by Col. Pritchard and the Michigan Cavalry, on the morning of the 10th inst., at
Irwinsville, in Irwin County, Georgia.

"MACON, GA., May 12, 1865—11 A.M.
"LIEUT. GEN. U. S. GRANT AND HON. SECRETARY OF WAR,
WASHINGTON, D. C.:

"I have the honor to report that at daylight of the 10th inst., Col. Pritchard, commanding 4th Michigan Cavalry, captured Jeff. Davis and family, with Reagan, Postmaster-General; Col. Harrison, Private Secretary; Col. Johnson, A. D. C.; Col. Morris, Col. Lubbeck, Lieut. Hathaway and others. Col. Pritchard surprised their camp at Irwinsville, in Irwin County, Ga., 75 miles southeast of this place. They will be here tomorrow night, and will be forwarded under strong guard without delay.*. . .

"J. H. WILSON, *Brevet Major-General*"

Harper's Weekly *told how, in Virginia, history completed a cycle:*[7]

Edmund Ruffin, the father of secession in Virginia, and who fired the first gun on Fort Sumter, committed suicide June 17, 1865. A memorandum was found among his papers stating that he preferred death to living under the United States Government. He was upward of seventy-four years old when he committed this act of self-murder. At the time of his death he was staying in Amelia County, Virginia. The suicide was a deliberate act, the deluded man taking a musket loaded with buckshot, and placing the muzzle in his mouth, with the aid of a stick touched the trigger. The first cap failed to explode, when he replaced it with a better one, fired the piece, and was instantly killed. The upper portion of his head was entirely blown off.

. . . His death seems a fit close to that stage of his life which he devoted to rebellion against his Government. He that taketh the sword must perish by the sword, even though it be through madness and by his own act.

IV

Since the summer of 1864, in countless homes, North and South, families had gathered around the parlor piano to sing:

"The men will cheer, the boys will shout,
The ladies they will all turn out,

---

* Davis was confined in Fortress Monroe, off Hampton Roads, for two years. On May 13, 1867, on a writ of habeas corpus, he was admitted to bail in the amount of $100,000. The first name on the bail bond was that of Horace Greeley.

And we'll all feel gay,
When Johnny comes marching home."

Yet for Emma Florence LeConte, a seventeen-year-old girl who had lived through the burning of Columbia, South Carolina, the promise of the song was not fulfilled:[8]

The troops are coming home. One meets long-absent, familiar faces on the streets, and congregations once almost strictly feminine are now mingled with returned soldiers. Our boys—Cousin Johnny and Julian —have come home, too. It was pleasant to see them again, but the meeting was more sad than glad. We would have waited many years if only we could have received them back triumphant. For four years we have looked forward to this day—the day when the troops would march home. We expected to meet them exulting and victorious. That was to be a day of wildest joy, when the tidings of peace should reach us, and the thought of that time used to lighten our hearts and nerve us to bear every trial and privation. Then we determined, after our independence was acknowledged and the time came for Gen. Lee to disband his army, to go on to Richmond to see the glorious sight, to see the hero take leave of his brave victorious men. The army is disbanded now—oh! Merciful God!—the hot tears rush into my eyes and I cannot write.

Captain S. H. M. Byers, rescued by Sherman in February 1865 after fifteen months in Confederate prisons, found that he stood alone:[9]

At last my accounts were ready. "But your regiment," said the Assistant War Secretary, "does not exist. What was left of them were all put into a cavalry troop long ago. *You are the last man of the regiment.*" Across the face of my paper he wrote: "Discharged as a supernumerary officer."

Henry Kyd Douglas, whose brigade was the last to lay down its arms at Appomattox, left Fort Delaware where he had been imprisoned for parole violation:

On the 23rd of August, the General issued Special Order No. 328 saying that as my sentence had expired—I think I had only been there about a month or a little over—I would be discharged and furnished transportation to my home at Shepherdstown. On that day, accompanied by his wife and daughter and staff, he took me to Wilmington on his boat and gave an excellent dinner on board. At Wilmington I took my leave of them, with sincere expressions of thanks for their uniform courtesy, one and all, while I was the unwilling guest of the Government at Fort Delaware.

For me, the War was over, at last!

Leander Stillwell, Sixty-first Illinois, received his discharge at Springfield and made his way home:[10]

I arrived at the little village of Otterville about sundown. It was a very small place in 1865. There was just one store, (which also contained the postoffice,) a blacksmith shop, the old stone school-house, a church, and perhaps a dozen or so private dwellings. There were no sidewalks, and I stalked up the middle of the one street the town afforded, with my sword poised on my shoulder, musket fashion, and feeling happy and proud.

I looked eagerly around as I passed along, hoping to see some old friend. As I went by the store, a man who was seated therein on the counter leaned forward and looked at me, but said nothing. A little further up the street a big dog sprang off the porch of a house, ran out to the little gate in front, and standing on his hind legs with his fore-paws on the palings, barked at me loudly and persistently—but I attracted no further attention. . . .

I now had only two miles to go, and was soon at the dear old boyhood home. My folks were expecting me, so they were not taken by surprise. There was no "scene" when we met, nor any effusive display, but we all had a feeling of profound contentment and satisfaction which was too deep to be expressed by mere words.

When I returned home I found that the farm work my father was then engaged in was cutting and shocking corn. So, the morning after my arrival, September 29th, I doffed my uniform of first lieutenant, put on some of my father's old clothes, armed myself with a corn knife, and proceeded to wage war on the standing corn. The feeling I had while engaged in this work was sort of queer. It almost seemed, sometimes, as if I had been away only a day or two, and had just taken up the farm work where I had left off.

CHAPTER 1

1. John G. Nicolay and John Hay, *Abraham Lincoln: A History* (New York, 1890), II, 306–07; hereafter cited as Nicolay and Hay.
2. Nicolay and Hay, II, 307–14.
3. New York *Tribune*, Nov. 12, 1860; in Herbert Mitgang (ed.), *Lincoln as They Saw Him* (New York, 1956), 212–14.
4. Samuel W. Crawford, *The Genesis of the Civil War* (Hartford, Conn., 1887), 12–13.
5. Mary Boykin Chesnut, *A Diary from Dixie* (New York, 1905; reissued, Boston, 1949), 3.
6. *War of the Rebellion . . . Official Records of the Union and Confederate Armies* (Washington, D. C., 1880–1901), Ser. 1, I, 74–76; hereafter cited as *Official Records*.
7. Daniel E. H. Smith, Alice R. H. Smith and Arney R. Childs (eds.), *Mason Smith Family Letters, 1860–1868* (Columbia, S. C., 1950), 3–4.
8. *Official Records*, Ser. 1, I, 90.
9. Crawford, *The Genesis of the Civil War*, 48–55.
10. Abner Doubleday, *Reminiscences of Forts Sumter and Moultrie in 1860–'61* (New York, 1876), 64–67.
11. Frank Moore (ed.), *The Rebellion Record: A Diary of American Events* (New York, 1861–1868), I, 8–9; hereafter cited as *Rebellion Record*.

CHAPTER 2

1. *The Crime Against Kansas, Speech of Hon. Charles Sumner,* *19th and 20th May, 1856* (Washington, D. C., 1856. Pamphlet).
2. Paul M. Angle (ed.), *Created Equal? The Complete Lincoln-Douglas Debates of 1858* (Chicago 1958), 110–11, 112–13.
3. Angle, *Created Equal?*, 267–68.
4. Angle, *Created Equal?*, 332–33.
5. *Report of Select Committee of the Senate on the Harper's Ferry Invasion* (Washington, D. C., 1860), 40.
6. Quoted in "The Hanging of John Brown" by Boyd B. Stutler, *American Heritage*, No. 2, 6–9.
7. Allan Nevins, *The Emergence of Lincoln* (New York, 1950), II, 98–107.

CHAPTER 3

1. Roy P. Basler (ed.), *The Collected Works of Abraham Lincoln* (New Brunswick, N. J., 1953), IV, 195–96; hereafter cited as *Collected Works*.
2. Dunbar Rowland (ed.), *Jefferson Davis Constitutionalist, His Letters, Papers and Speeches* (Jackson, Miss., 1923), V, 47–48; hereafter cited as *Davis Constitutionalist*.
3. Rowland, *Davis Constitutionalist*, V, 49–53.
4. *Collected Works*, IV, 255–61.
5. Nicolay and Hay, III, 378–79.
6. Nicolay and Hay, III, 380–81.
7. Thomas C. DeLeon, *Four Years in Rebel Capitals* (Mobile, Ala., 1890), 24–26.
8. *Official Records*, Ser. 1, I, 13–14.
9. *Official Records*, Ser. 1, I, 29.
10. Robert Underwood Johnson and Clarence Clough Buell (eds.), *Battles and Leaders of the Civil*

War (New York, 1884–1888), "Inside Sumter in '61," I, 66–69; hereafter cited as *B. & L.*

11. *Official Records*, Ser. 1, I, 11.
12. Katherine M. Jones (ed.), *Heroines of Dixie* (Indianapolis, 1955), 17–22.
13. Crawford, *The Genesis of the Civil War*, 435–37.
14. *Official Records*, Ser. 1, I, 12.
15. Jones, *Heroines of Dixie*, 20–22.
16. Quoted in Roy F. Nichols, *The Disruption of American Democracy* (New York, 1948), 395–96.
17. Stephen Vincent Benét, *John Brown's Body* (New York, 1927), 71–72.

CHAPTER 4

1. Nicolay and Hay, IV, 71.
2. Nicolay and Hay, IV, 76–77, 79–80.
3. Associated Press dispatch, April 15, 1861.
4. *Official Records*, Ser. 3, I, 70–87.
5. *Official Records*, Ser. 3, I, 70–83.
6. *Official Records*, Ser. 4, I, 225–35.
7. Chicago *Tribune*, April 17, 1861.
8. *Rebellion Record*, I, 28.
9. Chicago *Tribune*, April 17, 1861.
10. John Beauchamp Jones, *A Rebel War Clerk's Diary* (Philadelphia, 1866), I, 21–23.
11. Henry Kyd Douglas, *I Rode With Stonewall* (Chapel Hill, N. C., 1940), 5.
12. Capt. Robert E. Lee, *Recollections and Letters of General Robert E. Lee* (New York, 1904), 26–27.
13. S. H. M. Byers, *With Fire and Sword* (New York, 1911), 11–13.
14. Jessie Grant Cramer (ed.), *Letters of Ulysses S. Grant* (New York, 1912), 24–26.
15. William G. Stevenson, *Thirteen Months in the Rebel Army* (New York, 1862), 35–39.
16. Mary Anna Jackson, *Memoirs of Stonewall Jackson* (Louisville, Ky., 1895), 145–46.

17. William Tecumseh Sherman, *Memoirs of General W. T. Sherman, written by himself* (New York, 1875; corrected, 1876), I, 167–68.
18. Samuel L. Clemens, *Works* (Hartford, Conn., 1899), XXI, 236–39.
19. John W. Hanson, *Historical Sketch of the Old Sixth Regiment of Massachusetts Volunteers* (Boston, 1866), 23–29, 31–32.
20. Helen Nicolay, *Lincoln's Secretary, A Biography of John G. Nicolay* (New York, 1949), 95–96.
21. Nicolay and Hay, IV, 156–57.
22. Tyler Dennett (ed.), *Lincoln and the Civil War, In the Diaries and Letters of John Hay* (New York, 1939), 20–21.
23. Jefferson Davis, *The Rise and fall of the Confederate Government* (New York, 1881), I, 328–30.

CHAPTER 5

1. Judith Brockenbrough McGuire, *Diary of a Southern Refugee During the War* (New York, 1867), 17–18.
2. *Collected Works*, IV, 385–86.
3. Benjamin F. Butler, *Butler's Book* (Boston, 1892), 256–60.
4. *Official Records*, Ser. 1, II, 719–21.
5. Joseph E. Johnston, *Narrative of Military Operations, Directed, during the Late War Between the States* (New York, 1874), 33–34.
6. *Report of Committee on the Conduct of the War*, Senate Document, 37th Congress, 3rd Session, 1862–1863, Pt. II, 56–57; hereafter cited as *C.C.W.*
7. Johnston, *Narrative of Military Operations*, 36–38.
8. Sherman, *Memoirs*, I, 180–81.

9. George W. Bicknell, *History of the Fifth Regiment Maine Volunteers* (Portland, 1871), 28–30.
10. *B. & L.*, I, 209–10.
11. Davis, *The Rise and Fall of the Confederate Government*, I, 349–50.
12. *B. & L.*, I, 212–13.
13. Josiah M. Favill, *The Diary of a Young Officer* (Chicago, 1909), 34–36.
14. *Official Records*, Ser. 1, II, 320–21.
15. Lyman Trumbull to Mrs. Lyman Trumbull, Washington, D. C., July 22, 1861, in Horace White, *The Life of Lyman Trumbull* (Boston, 1913), 166–67.
16. *C.C.W.*, Pt. II, 76.

CHAPTER 6

1. Quoted in G. F. R. Henderson, *The Civil War, A Soldier's View* (Chicago, 1958), 121–22.
2. Ulysses S. Grant, *Personal Memoirs* (New York, 1885), I, 243, 246–50.
3. Clemens, *Works*, XXI, 256–57.
4. Grant, *Memoirs*, I, 138–39.
5. George Brinton McClellan, *McClellan's Own Story* (New York, 1887), 57–62.
6. Sherman, *Memoirs*, I, 194–97.
7. McClellan, *Own Story*, 84–92.
8. Walter H. Taylor, *Four Years with General Lee* (New York, 1878), 24.
9. Capt. Robert E. Lee, *Recollections and Letters*, 39–41.
10. John Beatty, *Memoirs of a Volunteer* (New York, 1946), 60.
11. *The Annals of the War* (Philadelphia, 1879), 89–90.
12. Capt. Robert E. Lee, *Recollections and Letters*, 44–46.
13. J. F. C. Fuller, *Grant and Lee* (reissued, Bloomington, Ind., 1957), 117–29.
14. Sherman, *Memoirs*, II, 406–08.
15. Capt. Robert E. Lee, *Recollections and Letters*, 105–06.

CHAPTER 7

1. *B. & L.*, I, 264–66.
2. *B. & L.*, I, 267–68.
3. *B. & L.*, I, 269–71.
4. *B. & L.*, I, 282.
5. *Rebellion Record*, II, 516–17.
6. *Rebellion Record*, II, 497–98.
7. *Rebellion Record*, II, 517–18.
8. *Collected Works*, IV, 506.
9. *Collected Works*, IV, 531–32.
10. Cramer, *Letters of Ulysses S. Grant*, 64–67.
11. Grant, *Memoirs*, I, 274–77.
12. *Rebellion Record*, III, 299.
13. *Rebellion Record*, III, 232–33.

CHAPTER 8

1. *Collected Works*, V, 544–45.
2. *B. & L.*, I, 675–76.
3. *B. & L.*, I, 684–86.
4. McClellan, *Own Story*, 173–74.
5. Quoted in Lloyd Lewis, *Sherman, Fighting Prophet* (New York, 1932), 201.
6. Henry Adams, *The Education of Henry Adams* (Privately printed, 1906; Boston, 1918), 122–23.
7. Sarah Agnes Wallace and Frances Elma Gillespie (eds.), *The Journal of Benjamin Moran 1857–1865* (Chicago, 1949), II, 912–17; hereafter cited as *Moran Journal*.
8. Donaldson Jordan and Edwin J. Pratt, *Europe and the American Civil War* (Boston, 1931), 29–31.
9. *Moran Journal*, II, 925.
10. *Proceedings of the Massachusetts Historical Society*, Nov., 1911, 128–29.
11. *Collected Works*, V, 29–30.
12. *Rebellion Record*, Supplements: II, 31, 47, 71, 87, 99; III, 9, 24, 36, 37, 48.

CHAPTER 9

1. *Annals of the War*, 76–79.
2. *Collected Works*, V, 96–97.
3. *Rebellion Record*, IV, 30.
4. *Rebellion Record*, IV, 41–42.

5. *Rebellion Record*, IV, 43, 47.
6. *Rebellion Record*, IV, 73–74.
7. *Rebellion Record*, IV, 75.
8. *Rebellion Record*, IV, 75–76.
9. Grant, *Memoirs*, I, 294–99.
10. *Rebellion Record*, IV, 173, 174.
11. *Rebellion Record*, IV, 185–86.
12. *Rebellion Record*, IV, 207–09.
13. *Rebellion Record*, IV, 210.
14. McClellan, *Own Story*, 215–17.
15. McClellan, *Own Story*, 195–96.
16. Edward Younger (ed.), *Inside the Confederate Government, The Diary of Robert Garlick Hill Kean* (New York, 1957), 23–24.
17. Julia Ward Howe, *Reminiscences of Julia Ward Howe, 1819–1899* (Boston, 1899), 274–75.
18. *The Atlantic Monthly,* Feb., 1862, 145.

CHAPTER 10

1. *Annals of the War*, 20.
2. *Rebellion Record*, IV, 273–74.
3. *Rebellion Record*, IV, 467.
4. *Rebellion Record*, IV, 275–76.
5. *Annals of the War*, 24–25.
6. *Rebellion Record*, IV, 267–68.
7. *Rebellion Record*, IV, 270–71.
8. *Moran Journal*, II, 971–72.
9. *Annals of the War*, 679–80.
10. *Annals of the War*, 682–83.
11. *Rebellion Record*, IV, 381–82.
12. *Rebellion Record*, IV, 388.
13. *Rebellion Record*, IV, 388; Stevenson, *Thirteen Months in the Rebel Army*, 115–16; *Iowa Journal of History*, July, 1954, 242, 251, 254, 265.
14. *Rebellion Record*, IV, 393–94.
15. *Rebellion Record*, IV, 382–83.
16. J. F. C. Fuller, *The Generalship of Ulysses S. Grant* (New York, 1929), 108–11.
17. Sherman, *Memoirs*, I, 254–55.
18. Grant, *Memoirs*, I, 368–69.

CHAPTER 11

1. *B. & L.*, II, 710–11.
2. *Rebellion Record*, Supplement I, 286–87.

3. *B. & L.*, II, 713–14.
4. *Rebellion Record*, Supplement I, 287–88.
5. *Rebellion Record*, Supplement I, 280–82.
6. *B. & L.*, II, 14–15.
7. *B. & L.*, II, 16–17.
8. *B. & L.*, II, 18.
9. *B. & L.*, II, 19–21.
10. Edward A. Pollard, *The Second Year of the War* (New York, 1865), 19–21.
11. Quoted in Richard B. Harwell (ed.), *The Confederate Reader* (New York, 1957), 105.
12. Pollard, *Second Year of the War*, 21.
13. Benjamin F. Butler, *Private and Official Correspondence of Gen. Benjamin F. Butler during the Period of the Civil War* (Privately issued [Norwood, Mass.] 1917), II, 35–36.
14. Butler, *Private Correspondence*, II, 36–37.
15. Butler, *Private Correspondence*, II, 70–71.
16. *Rebellion Record*, VI, 270–71.

CHAPTER 12

1. *Collected Works*, V, 157–58.
2. George Alfred Townsend, *Rustics in Rebellion* (Chapel Hill, 1950), 36–38 [original title: *Campaigns of a Non-Combatant* (New York, 1866)].
3. McClellan, *Own Story*, 306–17.
4. *Collected Works*, V, 185.
5. Townsend, *Rustics*, 93–95.
6. McClellan, *Own Story*, 306–17.
7. Chesnut, *Diary from Dixie*, 216–17.
8. *Rebellion Record*, V, 6.
9. Pollard, *Second Year of the War*, 29–31.
10. Pollard, *Second Year of the War*, 31 n–32 n.
11. Thomas W. Hyde, *Following the Greek Cross or, Memories of the Sixth Army Corps* (Boston, 1894), 50–53.

12. McClellan, *Own Story*, 352–57.
13. George C. Gorham, *Life and Public Services of Edwin M. Stanton* (Boston, 1899), I, 400.
14. David Donald (ed.), *Inside Lincoln's Cabinet, The Civil War Diaries of Salmon P. Chase* (New York, 1954), 84–86.
15. McClellan, *Own Story*, 352–57.
16. Jones, *Rebel War Clerk's Diary*, I, 123–25.
17. Townsend, *Rustics*, 58–60.
18. Townsend, *Rustics*, 67.
19. *Collected Works*, V, 216; McClellan, *Own Story*, 394–402.
20. Townsend, *Rustics*, 86–89.
21. William Child, *A History of the Fifth Regiment New Hampshire Volunteers* (Bristol, N. H., 1893), 82–84.
22. *Rebellion Record*, V, 88.
23. Rebellion Record, V, 97.
24. McClellan, *Own Story*, 394–402.

CHAPTER 13

1. Earl Schenck Miers, *Robert E. Lee, A Great-Life-in-Brief* (New York, 1956), 73–75.
2. *B. & L.*, II, 442–45.
3. *Rebellion Record*, V, 192–93.
4. *Rebellion Record*, V, 196–97.
5. *B. & L.*, II, 347.
6. Pollard, *Second Year of the War*, 311.
7. McClellan, *Own Story*, 441.
8. *Rebellion Record*, V, 238.
9. Pollard, *Second Year of the War*, 315–16.
10. *Southern Bivouac*, II, 655.
11. Stanley F. Horn, *The Robert E. Lee Reader* (Indianapolis, 1949), 190–91.
12. McClellan, *Own Story*, 424–25.
13. *Rebellion Record*, V, 242–43.
14. *Rebellion Record*, V, 244.
15. *Rebellion Record*, V, 244–45.
16. Robert Stiles, *Four Years under Marse Robert* (New York, 1903), 97.
17. Pollard, *Second Year of the War*, 321–24.

18. Comte de Paris, *History of the Civil War in America* (Philadelphia, 1876), II, 144–46.
19. Jones, *Rebel War Clerk's Diary*, I, 142.

CHAPTER 14

1. *Rebellion Record*, V, 179–80.
2. James D. McCabe, *Life and Campaigns of General Robert E. Lee* (Philadelphia, 1870), 644.
3. Townsend, *Rustics*, 206, 220, 224–26.
4. Roebling Papers, Ms., Rutgers University Library.
5. *Rebellion Record*, V, 402–03.
6. Roebling Papers.
7. W. W. Blackford, *War Years With Jeb Stuart* (New York, 1946), 132–34.
8. Blackford, *War Years*, 123.
9. Blackford, *War Years*, 120–22.
10. Joseph T. Durkin (ed.), *John Dooley, Confederate Soldier* (Washington, D. C., 1945), 20–22, 23–24.
11. Roebling Papers.
12. William Butler Papers, MS., Chicago Historical Society.
13. *Rebellion Record*, V, 615–16.
14. *Collected Works*, VI, 6–7.

CHAPTER 15

1. *Official Records*, Ser. 1, XIX, Pt. 2, 600, 601–02.
2. *B. & L.*, II, 604.
3. *Rebellion Record*, V, 606–07.
4. *War Talks in Kansas* (Kansas City, 1906), 250.
5. G. Moxley Sorrel, *Recollections of a Confederate Staff Officer* (Jackson, Tenn., 1958), 101.
6. *Rebellion Record*, V, 432–33.
7. Blackford, *War Years*, 144–45.
8. *Rebellion Record*, V, 447.
9. *Rebellion Record*, V, 467–69.
10. *Rebellion Record*, V, 467–69.
11. Blackford, *War Years*, 150–51.
12. Durkin, *John Dooley*, 45–48.
13. Rufus R. Dawes, *Service with the Sixth Wisconsin Volunteers* (Marietta, Ohio, 1890), 90–92.

14. Charles Francis Adams, Jr., "Historians and Historical Societies," *Proceedings of the Massachusetts Historical Society,* Second Series, XIII, 105–06.
15. *B. & L.,* II, 690–93.
16. *B. & L.,* II, 681.

CHAPTER 16

1. *Rebellion Record,* Supplement I, 305–306.
2. *Rebellion Record,* Supplement I, 308.
3. *Rebellion Record,* Supplement I, 317.
4. *Rebellion Record,* Supplement I, 321–22.
5. *Collected Works,* V, 144–46.
6. Davis, *Rise and Fall of the Confederate Government,* II, 180.
7. *Collected Works,* V, 169, 222–23.
8. *Collected Works,* V, 278–79.
9. David Homer Bates, *Lincoln in the Telegraph Office* (New York, 1907), 138–41.
10. Francis B. Carpenter, *Six Months in the White House with Abraham Lincoln* (New York, 1866), 20–22.
11. *Collected Works,* V, 317–19.
12. Davis, *Rise and Fall of the Confederate Government,* II, 184–86.
13. *Collected Works,* V, 388–89.
14. *Collected Works,* V, 419–21.
15. *Collected Works,* V, 423–24.
16. *Collected Works,* V, 425; Chase Diary, *Annual Report, American Historical Association, 1902,* Vol. II. (Washington, D. C., 1903), 87–89.
17. Davis, *Rise and Fall of the Confederate Government,* II, 190–91.
18. *Collected Works,* V, 438–39.
19. *Harper's Weekly,* Oct. 4, 1862.

CHAPTER 17

1. Grant, *Memoirs,* I, 408–12.
2. Grant, *Memoirs,* I, 412–13.
3. Grant, *Memoirs,* I, 416–17.
4. Grant, *Memoirs,* I, 417–19.

5. Philip Henry Sheridan, *Personal Memoirs* (New York, 1904), I, 190–92.
6. Sheridan, *Memoirs,* I, 193–95.
7. Sheridan, *Memoirs,* I, 195–98.
8. *Rebellion Record,* VI, 23–24.
9. *Moran Journal,* II, 1063–64.
10. Adams, *Education,* 154–56.
11. Grant, *Memoirs,* I, 426–27.
12. Ulysses S. Grant, *Headquarters Records,* Ms., Library of Congress.
13. Cadwallader Ms., Illinois State Historical Library, Springfield.
14. Grant, *Memoirs,* I, 429.
15. Lewis, *Sherman, Fighting Prophet,* 257–59.

CHAPTER 18

1. *Collected Works,* V, 505–06.
2. *Collected Works,* V, 514–15.
3. *Collected Works,* V, 531–32, 537.
4. *Rebellion Record,* VI, 94–95.
5. *Rebellion Record,* VI, 95–96.
6. *Rebellion Record,* VI, 103.
7. *Rebellion Record,* VI, 97.
8. *Rebellion Record,* VI, 97–98.
9. *Rebellion Record,* VI, 105.
10. *Rebellion Record,* VI, 98–99.
11. *Rebellion Record,* VI, 103–04.
12. *Rebellion Record,* VI, 110–11.
13. *Rebellion Record,* VI, 111.
14. Eugene A. Cory, *A Private's Recollections of Fredericksburg* (Providence, 1884), 24–25.
15. *B. & L.,* III, 78.
16. Capt. D. P. Conyngham, *The Irish Brigade* (Boston, 1869), 346.
17. *Rebellion Record,* VI, 79.
18. *Collected Works,* VI, 13.
19. Sherman, *Memoirs,* I, 291–92.
20. John Beatty, *Memoirs of a Volunteer* (New York, 1946), 152.
21. *Rebellion Record,* VI, 118–19.
22. *Rebellion Record,* VI, 158–59.
23. *Rebellion Record,* VI, 165.
24. Beatty, *Memoirs,* 155–56.
25. *Rebellion Record,* VI, 166; Beatty, *Memoirs,* 156–57.
26. *Rebellion Record,* VI, 166.

27. *Rebellion Record,* VI, 161.
28. Pollard, *Second Year of the War,* 183–86.

CHAPTER 19

1. Nicolay and Hay, IV, 421, 429–30.
2. *Collected Works,* VI, 29–30.
3. Thomas Wentworth Higginson, *Army Life in a Black Regiment* (Boston, 1870), 39–42.
4. Rowland, *Davis Constitutionalist,* V, 409–11.
5. *Rebellion Record,* VI, 343–44.
6. *Rebellion Record,* VI, 357–58, 360–61.
7. Emma Martin Maffitt, *The Life and Public Services of John Newland Maffitt* (New York, 1906), 267–69.
8. *Rebellion Record,* VI, 430–31.
9. James Russell Soley, *The Blockade and the Cruisers* (New York, 1885), 156–60.
10. Thomas Taylor, *Running the Blockade* (New York, 1896), 44–54.
11. *Harper's New Monthly Magazine,* Sept., 1866, 498–99; *Official Records,* Navies, Ser. 1, VIII, 417; Soley, *The Blockade,* 165–66.
12. *Official Records,* Navies, Ser. 1, VIII, 417, 459, 471.
13. Soley, *The Blockade,* 165–66.

CHAPTER 20

1. *Official Records,* Ser. 1, XXI, 916–18.
2. *Official Records,* Ser. 1, XXI, 944–45.
3. *Official Records,* Ser. 1, XXI, 953–54.
4. *Rebellion Record,* VI, 398–400.
5. *Collected Works,* VI, 78–79.
6. Regis de Trobriand, *Four Years with the Army of the Potomac* (Boston, 1889), 413–14.
7. Charles Francis Adams, Jr., *An Autobiography* (Boston, 1916), 161.
8. *C.C.W.,* I, Pt. 2, 112–13.

9. *B. & L.,* IV, 35–41.
10. *B. & L.,* III, 155–56.
11. *B. & L.,* III, 203.
12. *B. & L.,* III, 205.
13. John O. Casler, *Four Years in the Stonewall Brigade* (Guthrie, Okla., 1893), 216–22.
14. *B. & L.,* III, 211–14.
15. *B. & L.,* III, 165–71.
16. *Official Records,* Ser. 1, XXV, 805.
17. *B. & L.,* III, 214.
18. G. F. R. Henderson, *Stonewall Jackson and the American Civil War* (London, 1898), II, 579.

CHAPTER 21

1. Quoted in Henry Adams, *The Great Secession Winter of 1860–61 and Other Essays* (New York, 1958), 146–47, 152.
2. *Harper's Weekly,* Feb. 3, 1863.
3. Charles W. Ramsdell, *Behind the Lines in the Southern Confederacy* (Baton Rouge, 1944), 12–13.
4. *Rebellion Record,* VIII, 272, 273.
5. Quoted in Jones, *Rebel War Clerk's Diary,* I, 250, 252–53.
6. Quoted in Ramsdell, *Behind the Lines,* 47–48.
7. *Harper's Weekly,* Feb. 21, 1863.
8. Jones, *Rebel War Clerk's Diary,* I, 284–86.
9. Bell Irvin Wiley, *The Plain People of the Confederacy* (Baton Rouge, 1944), 54–55, 56–57, 60–62, 65–66.
10. Charles A. Dana, *Recollections of the Civil War* (New York, 1898), 18–19.
11. *Annals of the War,* 706–07, 709, 713, 719–21.
12. Charles S. Winslow, "Historical Events of Chicago," Ms., Chicago Historical Society.
13. New York *Times,* June 17, 1863.
14. *Rebellion Record,* XI, 23–24.
15. Edward Dicey, *Six Months in the Federal States* (London, 1863), II, 220–23.

16. Francis Trevelyan Miller (ed.), *The Photographic History of the American Civil War* (New York, 1912), IX, 132, 176, 351.

CHAPTER 22

1. *Harper's Weekly*, Mar. 14, 1863.
2. *The American Annual Cyclopaedia and Register of Important Events*, 1863, 271, 273–74.
3. James L. Vallandigham, *A Life of Clement L. Vallandigham* (Baltimore, 1872), 224–26.
4. Vallandigham, *Life*, 458–59, 464.
5. Vallandigham, *Life*, 250–52.
6. Vallandigham, *Life*, 255–59.
7. *The Trial of Clement L. Vallandigham by a Military Commission* (Cincinnati, 1863), 13–16.
8. *Collected Works*, VI, 266–69.
9. James Ford Rhodes, *History of the United States from the Compromise of 1850 to the Final Restoration of Home Rule at the South in 1877* (New York, 1892–1906), IV, 251–52.
10. Chicago *Times*, June 5, 1863.
11. New York *Tribune*, June 4, 1863.

CHAPTER 23

1. *Official Records*, Ser. 1, XVII, 710.
2. *Official Records*, Ser. 1, XVII, 780–81.
3. *Collected Works*, VI, 48–49.
4. Grant, *Memoirs*, I, 442–44.
5. Benjamin P. Thomas (ed.), *Three Years with Grant as Recalled by War Correspondent Sylvanus Cadwallader* (New York, 1955), 54–55 [Ms. in Illinois State Historical Library, Springfield].
6. John Q. Anderson (ed.), *Brokenburn: The Journal of Kate Stone 1861–1868* (Baton Rouge, 1955), 168–73.
7. David D. Porter, *Naval History of the Civil War* (Hartford, Conn., 1886), 303–04.
8. Porter, *Naval History*, 305–06.

9. Thomas, *Three Years with Grant*, 61–62.
10. Dana, *Recollections*, 30–32.
11. James Harrison Wilson, *Under the Old Flag* (New York, 1912), I, 163–64.
12. Dana, *Recollections*, 37–38.
13. Porter, *Naval History*, 311.
14. *Transactions of the Illinois State Historical Society*, 1907, 127–29.
15. *Trans., Ill. St. Hist. Soc.*, 1907, 129–30.
16. Porter, *Naval History*, 313–15.
17. Grant, *Memoirs*, I, 477–81.
18. Grant, *Memoirs*, I, 490–93.
19. Dana, *Recollections*, 48–50.
20. *B. & L.*, III, 486–87.
21. Thomas, *Three Years with Grant*, 69–70.
22. Thomas, *Three Years with Grant*, 70–72.
23. *B. & L.*, III, 478–79.
24. Thomas, *Three Years with Grant*, 73–75.

CHAPTER 24

1. *Official Records*, Ser. 1, XXVII, Pt. 3, 882.
2. Jones, *Rebel War Clerk's Diary*, I, 327–28.
3. *War Sketches and Incidents, as Related by Companions in the Iowa Commandery, Military Order of the Loyal Legion* (Des Moines, 1893), 208–14.
4. Grant, *Memoirs*, I, 515–17.
5. *Annals of the War*, 343–46.
6. Grant, *Memoirs*, I, 519–20.
7. *Rebellion Record*, X, 572.
8. Grant, *Memoirs*, I, 529–31.
9. McClernand Papers, Illinois State Historical Library, Springfield.
10. Thomas, *Three Years with Grant*, 90–92.
11. Dickey Papers, Illinois State Historical Library, Springfield.
12. Tupper Papers, Illinois State Historical Library, Springfield.
13. *Rebellion Record*, X, 576.
14. *Century Magazine*, Sept., 1885, 771–73.

15. Lord Journal, Manuscript Division, Library of Congress.
16. Vicksburg *Daily Citizen*, July 2–4, 1863.
17. Clemens, *Works*, IV, 280–82.
18. William Ward Orme, *Civil War Letters of Brigadier General William Ward Orme—1862-1866* (Springfield, Ill. 1930. Pamphlet); reprinted from *Journal of the Illinois State Historical Society* (Vol. XXIII), 280–81.
19. *B. & L.*, III, 540–42.
20. Wilbur F. Crummer, *With Grant at Fort Donelson, Shiloh and Vicksburg* (Oak Park, Ill., 1915), 137–42.
21. Michael Jacobs, *Notes on the Rebel Invasion of Maryland and Pennsylvania and the Battle of Gettysburg* (Philadelphia, 1864), 15–18.

CHAPTER 25

1. Broadhead Ms., Library, National Parks Service, Gettysburg, Pa.
2. Mrs. Tillie (Pierce) Alleman, *At Gettysburg, or What a Girl Saw and Heard of the Battle* (New York, 1889), 19–20.
3. Bayly Ms., Library, National Park Service, Gettysburg, Pa.
4. *Annals of the War*, 208.
5. Blackford, *War Years*, 224–25.
6. Durkin, *John Dooley*, 98–99.
7. Alleman, *At Gettysburg*, 21–22.
8. Broadhead Ms.
9. Bayly Ms.
10. Oliver Otis Howard, *Autobiography* (New York, 1908), I, 412, 413–14.
11. Miller, *Photographic History*, II, 211.
12. Bret Harte, *The Lost Galleon* (San Francisco, 1867), 27–28.
13. Charles Carleton Coffin, *The Boys of '61, or Four Years of Fighting* (Boston, 1896), 293–95.
14. Alleman, *At Gettysburg*, 43–45.
15. Frank Aretas Haskell, *The Battle of Gettysburg* (Wisconsin

History Commission, 1910), 18–30. [Earlier editions, privately issued, were dated "about 1880," 1898 and 1908.]
16. *Annals of the War*, 420–22.
17. Alleman, *At Gettysburg*, 49–50.
18. Arthur James Lyon Freemantle, *Three Months in the Southern States* (London, 1863), 257–60.
19. Haskell, *Gettysburg*, 41–43.
20. Haskell, *Gettysburg*, 42, 43–4.
21. *Rebellion Record*, X, 179.
22. William C. Oates, *The War Between the Union and the Confederacy and Its Lost Opportunities* (New York, 1905), 216, 221–22, 228–29.
23. Ziba B. Graham, *On to Gettysburg, Two Days from My Diary of 1863* (Detroit, 1889), 12.
24. Haskell, *Gettysburg*, 54–57.
25. *B. & L.*, III, 313–14.
26. George Edward Pickett, *The Heart of a Soldier* (New York, 1913), 94–95, 98–99.
27. Durkin, *John Dooley*, 101–02.
28. Haskell, *Gettysburg*, 97–103.
29. Philadelphia *Weekly Times*, Aug. 11, 1877.
30. Haskell, *Gettysburg*, 113–14.
31. Durkin, *John Dooley*, 105–07.
32. Haskell, *Gettysburg*, 119–26.
33. Broadhead Ms.
34. Alleman, *At Gettysburg*, 71–74.
35. Pickett, *The Heart of a Soldier*, 99–100.
36. Bayly Ms.; Harte, *The Lost Galleon*, 28.
37. Grant, *Memoirs*, I, 557–59, 563–64.

CHAPTER 26

1. *Harper's Weekly*, Jan. 17, 1863.
2. James A. Connolley, *Three Years in the Army of the Cumberland* (Bloomington, Ind., 1959), 89–90, 90–94.
3. Basil W. Duke, *History of Morgan's Cavalry* (Cincinnati, 1867), 434–35; F. Senour, *Morgan and His Captors* (Cincinnati, 1865), 124–25, 155–59.

4. Duke, *Morgan's Cavalry*, 458–61.
5. Stanley F. Horn, *The Army of Tennessee* (Norman, Okla., 1953), 233.
6. *Frank Leslie's Illustrated Newspaper*, July 25, 1863.
7. *Harper's Weekly*, Aug. 1, 1863.
8. Rhodes, *History of the U. S.*, IV, 330.
9. [J. S. Boughton], *The Lawrence Massacre by a Band of Missouri Ruffians under Quantrell* (Lawrence, Kans., n.d. Pamphlet).
10. Dana, *Recollections*, 110–11, 111–14.
11. *B. & L.*, III, 666–67.
12. Beatty, *Memoirs of a Volunteer*, 250–51.
13. James Longstreet, *From Manassas to Appomattox* (Philadelphia, 1896), 455–56.
14. Thomas B. Van Horne, *The Life of Major-General George H. Thomas* (New York, 1882), 148–49.
15. *B. & L.*, III, 662.
16. James D. Bulloch, *The Secret Service of the Confederate States in Europe* (London, 1883), I, 385–86, 409–12.
17. George E. Baker (ed.), *The Works of William H. Seward* (Boston, 1884), V, 387–88.
18. *Diplomatic Correspondence of the United States*, 1863, Pt. I, 367.
19. Worthington Chauncey Ford (ed.), *A Cycle of Adams Letters, 1861–1865* (Boston, 1920), II, 82–83.
20. Bulloch, *Secret Service*, I, 420–22.

CHAPTER 27

1. Grant, *Memoirs*, II, 24–25.
2. Grant, *Memoirs*, II, 38–39.
3. Grant, *Memoirs*, II, 40–41.
4. Dennett, *Lincoln and the Civil War*, 121; *Collected Works*, VII, 21.
5. Connolly, *Three Years*, 151–52.
6. Connolly, *Three Years*, 152–55.

7. Connolly, *Three Years*, 155–59.
8. Sam R. Watkins, *"Co. Aytch," Maury Grays, First Tennessee Regiment* (Nashville, 1882), 104–05.
9. *B. & L.*, III, 727.
10. Watkins, *"Co. Aytch,"* 105.
11. Rowland, *Davis Constitutionalist*, VI, 95–96.
12. Rowland, *Davis Constitutionalist*, VI, 94–95.
13. Rowland, *Davis Constitutionalist*, VI, 96, 104–05.
14. Rowland, *Davis Constitutionalist*, VI, 127–28.
15. *Collected Works*, VII, 48–53.
16. *Atlantic Monthly*, Jan., 1864, 122.

CHAPTER 28

1. Bell Irvin Wiley (ed.), *This Infernal War, The Confederate Letters of Sgt. Edwin H. Fay* (Austin, Tex., 1958), 346–47.
2. Merrilies Diary, Ms., Chicago Historical Society.
3. Child, *The Fifth Regiment New Hampshire Volunteers*, 193.
4. Dickinson Diary, Ms., Chicago Historical Society.
5. Pitts Diary, Ms., Chicago Historical Society.
6. Wiley, *This Infernal War*, 329; Johnston Ms., Chicago Historical Society.
7. *Rebellion Record*, VII, 411.
8. Carl Schurz, *The Reminiscences of Carl Schurz* (New York, 1908), III, 339–40.
9. Henrietta Stratton Jaquette (ed.), *South After Gettysburg, Letters of Cornelia Hancock from the Army of the Potomac 1863–1865* (Philadelphia, 1937), 17, 19, 23, 24.
10. Phoebe Yates Pember, *A Southern Woman's Story* (New York, 1879), 133–36.
11. H. H. Cunningham, *Doctors in Gray: The Confederate Medical Service* (Baton Rouge, 1958), 264–66.

12. "Civil War Diary of William Micajah Barrow," *Louisiana Historical Quarterly*, Oct., 1934, 722–23; *Ibid.*, 723–29.
13. F. F. Cavada, *Libby Life: Experiences of a Prisoner of War* (Philadelphia, 1864), 19–27.
14. Henry H. Eby, *Observations of an Illinois Boy in Battle, Camp and Prisons, 1861–1865* (Mendota, Ill., 1910), 137–44.
15. S. S. Boggs, *Eighteen Months a Prisoner under the Rebel Flag* (Lovington, Ill., 1887), 17, 22–24, 26–27.
16. Virginia Confederate, *In Vinculis, or The Prisoner of War* (Petersburg, Va., 1866), 58–63, 138–47.
17. Rowland, *Davis Constitutionalist*, VI, 122–23.
18. Clement Eaton, *A History of the Southern Confederacy* (New York, 1954), 106.
19. Rhodes, *History of the U. S.*, V, 508.

CHAPTER 29

1. *Rebellion Record*, VIII, 278–79.
2. *Rebellion Record*, VIII, 304–05.
3. *Official Records*, Ser. 1, XXXII, Pt. 1, 561–62.
4. *Official Records*, Ser. 1, XXXII, Pt. 1, 528–29.
5. *Official Records*, Ser. 1, XXXII, Pt. 1, 525–26.
6. *Official Records*, Ser. 1, XXXII, Pt. 1, 610.
7. *Collected Works*, VII, 302–03.
8. John A. Wyeth, *Life of General Nathan Bedford Forrest* (New York, 1899), 367–68.
9. *Official Records*, Ser. 1, XXXIV, Pt. 1, 510, 514–15.
10. *Rebellion Record*, VIII, 546–47.
11. *C.C.W.*, *II*, 217–18.
12. *Rebellion Record*, VIII, 549–50.
13. *Rebellion Record*, VIII, 521.
14. *Rebellion Record*, VIII, 529–31.
15. Lawrence Van Alstyne, *Diary of an Enlisted Man* (New Haven, Conn., 1910), 320–21.

16. *Official Records*, Ser. 1, XXXIV, Pt. 1, 546–48.

CHAPTER 30

1. Horace Porter, *Campaigning with Grant* (New York, 1897) 18–21.
2. Grant, *Memoirs*, II, 116–23.
3. Sheridan, *Memoirs*, I, 355–56.
4. Grant, *Memoirs*, II, 141–42.
5. Letter owned by Stanley F. Horn, Nashville; quoted in Stanley F. Horn, *The Robert E. Lee Reader* (Indianapolis, 1949), 362–63.
6. Sorrel, *Recollections*, 226–27.
7. *Rebellion Record*, XI, 440–41.
8. George R. Agassiz (ed.), *Meade's Headquarters 1863–1865, Letters of Colonel Theodore Lyman from the Wilderness to Appomattox* (Boston, 1922), 91–92.
9. Porter, *Campaigning with Grant*, 68–70.
10. Agassiz, *Meade's Headquarters*, 93–94.
11. Sorrel, *Recollections*, 230–31.
12. Agassiz, *Meade's Headquarters*, 95–97.
13. *Rebellion Record*, XI, 442–43.
14. Sorrel, *Recollections*, 231–35.
15. Agassiz, *Meade's Headquarters*, 98–99.
16. Porter, *Campaigning with Grant*, 78–79.
17. Agassiz, *Meade's Headquarters*, 100, 102.
18. Sheridan, *Memoirs*, I, 377–78.
19. H. B. McClellan, *Southern Historical Society Papers*, VII, 142–43.
20. McClellan, *Southern Hist. Soc. Papers*, VII, 107–09.
21. Porter, *Campaigning with Grant*, 110–11.
22. Agassiz, *Meade's Headquarters*, 132–33.
23. Agassiz, *Meade's Headquarters*, 106.

24. Porter, *Campaigning with Grant*, 174–75.
25. William Swinton, *Army of the Potomac* (New York, 1866), 495.
26. Oates, *The War Between the Union and the Confederacy*, 366–67.
27. Grant, *Memoirs*, II, 276–77.
28. Agassiz, *Meade's Headquarters*, 147–48.

CHAPTER 31

1. *B. & L.*, IV, 250.
2. John Bell Hood, *Advance and Retreat* (New Orleans, 1880), 89, 91–92, 95.
3. Connolly, *Three Years*, 208–09.
4. Johnston, *Narrative of Military Operations*, 321–22.
5. Hood, *Advance and Retreat*, 99.
6. Sherman, *Memoirs*, II, 39, 42, 44–45.
7. Johnston, *Narrative of Military Operations*, 330–31.
8. Connolly, *Three Years*, 213–14.
9. *Annual American Cyclopaedia*, 1864, 785.
10. Washburne Ms., Library of Congress.
11. *Proceedings of the Massachusetts Historical Society*, Vol. 58, 135.
12. D. F. Murphy, *Proceedings of the National Union Convention* (New York, 1864), 63–66.
13. "Diary of Edward Bates," *Annual Report, American Historical Association*, 1930, Vol. 14, 374.
14. Edward McPherson, *The Political History of the United States . . . during the Great Rebellion* (Washington, D. C., 1865), 412.
15. Nicolay and Hay, IX, 40–41.
16. Merrilies Diary, Ms., Chicago Historical Society.
17. Samuel G. French, "Kennesaw Mountain," *The Kennesaw Gazette* (n.d.).

CHAPTER 32

1. Raphael Semmes, *Memoirs of Service Afloat* (Baltimore, 1869), 752–59.
2. Porter, *Naval History*, 655.
3. Gideon Welles, *Diary of Gideon Welles* (Boston, 1911), II, 70–71.
4. Jubal A. Early, *A Memoir of the Last Year of the War for Independence* (Lynchburg, Va., 1867), 56–58.
5. Welles, *Diary*, II, 72–73.
6. Early, *Memoir*, 58–59.
7. Dennett, *Letters and Diary of John Hay*, 209–10.
8. Wirt Armistead Cate (ed.), *Two Soldiers: The Campaign Diaries of Thomas J. Key, C.S.A. and Robert J. Campbell, U.S.A.* (Chapel Hill, 1938), 89–90.
9. Sherman, *Memoirs*, II, 74–75.
10. Hood, *Advance and Retreat*, 161–62.
11. Cate, *Two Soldiers*, 94–97.
12. *B. & L.*, IV, 326.
13. *B. & L.*, IV, 327–28.
14. Sherman, *Memoirs*, II, 76–77.
15. Connolly, *Three Years*, 240.
16. *C.C.W.*, I, 112–13 [second paging].
17. Agassiz, *Meade's Headquarters*, 181–82.
18. *B. & L.*, IV, 551–54.
19. *C.C.W.*, I, 120–21 [second paging].
20. George S. Bernard, *The Battle of the Crater* (Petersburg, Va., 1892), 159–60.
21. *C.C.W.*, I, 120–21 [second paging].
22. *B. & L.*, IV, 559.

CHAPTER 33

1. *Rebellion Record*, VIII, 101–02.
2. *Scribner's Monthly*, May, 1881, 204–05, 207–08 [ownership actually had passed to *Century Magazine*].
3. *Rebellion Record*, VIII, 102.

4. Robert Todd Lincoln Papers, Library of Congress.
5. Robert Todd Lincoln Papers.
6. *Collected Works*, VII, 514.
7. Noah Brooks, *Washington in Lincoln's Time* (New York, 1896), 182–88.
8. Hood, *Advance and Retreat*, 202–04.
9. Sherman, *Memoirs*, II, 105–06, 107.
10. Cate, *Two Soldiers*, 126–28.
11. Connolly, *Three Years*, 257–59.
12. Carrie Berry Diary, Ms., Atlanta Historical Society.
13. Rawson Diary, Ms., Atlanta Historical Society.
14. Sherman, *Memoirs*, II, 110.
15. *Annual American Cyclopaedia*, 1864, 794.
16. Sherman, *Memoirs*, II, 110–11.
17. Rawson Diary.
18. Sherman, *Memoirs*, II, 120–21.
19. Berry Diary.
20. Sherman, *Memoirs*, II, 130.
21. Agassiz, *Meade's Headquarters*, 204–05.
22. Porter, *Campaigning with Grant*, 283–84.
23. Ethel Armes, *Stratford on the Potomac* (Greenwich, Conn., 1928), 5.
24. Early, *Memoir*, 79–80.
25. Charles Richard Williams (ed.), *Diary and Letters of Rutherford B. Hayes* (Columbus, O., 1922), II, 508–11.
26. Early, *Memoir*, 90–91.
27. John B. Gordon, *Reminiscences of the Civil War* (New York, 1904), 323–26.

CHAPTER 34

1. *Rebellion Record*, IX, 179–80.
2. *Rebellion Record*, IX, 2–3.
3. *Official Records*, Ser. 1, XLIII, 30–31.
4. Douglas, *I Rode With Stonewall*, 314–16.
5. Gordon, *Reminiscences*, 337–42.
6. Sheridan, *Personal Memoirs*, II, 68–80.

7. Gordon, *Reminiscences*, 347–51.
8. John W. Headley, *Confederate Operations in Canada and New York* (New York, 1906), 259–61.
9. Rowland, *Davis Constitutionalist*, VI, 384–98.
10. Lyman Jackman, *History of the Sixth New Hampshire Regiment* (Concord, N. H., 1891), 344–46.
11. Theodore Gerrish, *Army Life: A Private's Reminiscences of the Civil War* (Portland, Me., 1882), 219–20.
12. Dennett, *Diaries and Letters of John Hay*, 232–36.
13. *Collected Works*, VIII, 100–01.

CHAPTER 35

1. Ms., Collection of Alfred M. Stearn, Chicago.
2. Sherman, *Memoirs*, II, 166, 174–76.
3. Berry Diary.
4. Connolly, *Three Years*, 301–02.
5. W. P. Howard, Official Report, *Macon (Ga.) Telegraph*, Dec. 10, 1864.
6. Sherman, *Memoirs*, II, 178–80, 188–90.
7. *Rebellion Record*, IX, 147.
8. Lunt, Dolly Sumner, *A Woman's Wartime Journal* (New York, 1918), 25, 29–42.
9. Connolly, *Three Years*, 332–33, 339–40.
10. George Ward Nichols, *The Story of the Great March, from the Diary of a Staff Officer* (New York, 1865), 74–77.
11. Connolly, *Three Years*, 354–55.
12. Irving A. Buck, *Cleburne and His Command* (New York, 1908), 326–33.
13. John A. Schofield, *Forty-Six Years in the Army* (New York, 1897), 177–79.
14. Buck, *Cleburne and His Command*, 333.
15. Porter, *Campaigning with Grant*, 325–26.

16. Headley, *Confederate Operations*, 274–76.
17. Benn Pitman, *The Assassination of President Lincoln and the Trial of the Conspirators* (New York, 1865), 54.

CHAPTER 36

1. *Collected Works*, VIII, 148–49, 151–52.
2. *Rebellion Record*, IX, 5.
3. *Rebellion Record*, IX, 175.
4. *Rebellion Record*, IX, 202–03.
5. Hood, *Advance and Retreat*, 299–300.
6. *B. & L.*, IV, 454–60.
7. Hood, *Advance and Retreat*, 302.
8. *Official Records*, Ser. 1, XLV, Pt. 2, 194.
9. *Official Records*, Ser. 1, XLV, Pt. 1, 694–95, 705–06.
10. *Official Records*, Ser. 1, XLV, Pt. 2, 210–11.
11. Sherman, *Memoirs*, II, 217–19, 231–32.
12. Ms., Collection of Alfred Stearn, Chicago.
13. Broadside, Emory University Library, Emory University, Ga.

CHAPTER 37

1. Theodore F. Upson, *With Sherman to the Sea* (Bloomington, Ind., 1958), 145.
2. Connolly, *Three Years*, 374–75.
3. *Official Records*, Ser. 1, XLVI, Pt. 2, 1043.
4. *Official Records*, Ser. 1, XLVI, Pt. 2, 1048.
5. *Official Records*, Ser. 1, XLVI, Pt. 2, 1056.
6. *Official Records*, Ser. 1, XLVI, Pt. 2, 1053, 1064–65.
7. *Official Records*, Ser. 1, XLVI, Pt. 2, 1071.
8. *Official Records*, Ser. 1, XLVI, Pt. 2, 1078.
9. Alexander H. Stephens, *Constitutional View of the Late War between the States* (Philadelphia, 1868–70), II, 619–20.
10. Dana, *Recollections*, 174–77.

11. I. N. Arnold, *The Life of Abraham Lincoln* (Chicago, 1885), 358–59.
12. Nicolay and Hay, X, 85–86.
13. *Collected Works*, VIII, 254–55; Stephens, *Constitutional View*, II, 599–602, 613–14, 618–23.

CHAPTER 38

1. Sherman, *Memoirs*, II, 225, 227–28.
2. Sherman, *Memoirs*, II, 268–72.
3. Nicholas, *Story of the Great March*, 145–51.
4. *Official Records*, Ser. 1, XLVII, Pt. 2, 1035–36.
5. *Official Records*, Ser. 1, XLVII, Pt. 2, 1201.
6. *Official Records*, Ser. 1, XLVII, Pt. 2, 711.
7. *Who Burnt Columbia?* (Charleston, S. C., 1875. Pamphlet).
8. *Rebellion Record*, XI, 377, 387–88.
9. Nichols, *Story of the Great March*, 198–99.
10. Brooks, *Washington in Lincoln's Time*, 238–40.
11. *B. & L.*, IV, 692–93, 695.
12. Letter to Isaac N. Arnold, Nov. 28, 1872, Ms., Chicago Historical Society.

CHAPTER 39

1. Townsend, *Rustics*, 252–55.
2. Pickett, *The Heart of a Soldier*, 172–75.
3. *B. & L.*, IV, 725.
4. Porter, *Campaigning with Grant*, 450–52.
5. *B. & L.*, IV, 727–28.
6. A. W. Bartlett, *History of the Twelfth Regiment New Hampshire Volunteers* (Concord, N. H., 1897), 271–73.
7. Townsend, *Rustics*, 270–71.
8. Dana, *Recollections*, 265–67.
9. *Confederate Veteran* (Atlanta, Ga.), Vol. I, 211.
10. Agassiz, *Meade's Headquarters*, 348–51.

11. Porter, *Campaigning with Grant*, 458–59.
12. *Rebellion Record*, XI, 356–57.
13. Agassiz, *Meade's Headquarters*, 356–58.
14. Thomas, *Three Years with Grant*, 325–26.
15. Grant, *Memoirs*, II, 489.
16. Porter, *Campaigning with Grant*, 473–74.
17. Grant, *Memoirs*, II, 491–92.
18. Porter, *Campaigning with Grant*, 477–78.
19. Grant, *Memoirs*, II, 492–94.
20. Porter, *Campaigning with Grant*, 486–87.
21. Maj.-Gen. Sir Frederick Maurice (ed.), *An Aide-de-Camp of Lee* (Boston, 1927), 275.
22. Agassiz, *Meade's Headquarters*, 359–62.

CHAPTER 40

1. Dr. F. Milton Willis, "Replacing the Flag upon Sumter," *Fort Sumter Memorial* (New York, 1915), 37–39.
2. New York *Tribune*, April 29, May 12 and May 29, 1865.
3. Stephens, *Constitutional View*, II, 624–26.
4. New York *Tribune*, April 15 and April 17, 1865.
5. New York *Weekly Herald*, April 22, 1865.
6. New York *Tribune*, May 15, 1865.
7. *Harper's Weekly*, July 29, 1865.
8. Earl Schenck Miers (ed.), *When the World Ended: The Diary of Emma LeConte* (New York, 1957), 98–99.
9. Byers, *With Fire and Sword*, 202; Douglas, *I Rode with Stonewall*, 349.
10. Leander Stillwell, *The Story of a Common Soldier, or Army Life in the Civil War* (Erie, Kans., 1917), 154.

PAUL M. ANGLE *is the country's foremost living scholar on Abraham Lincoln. He has been more influential than any other man in throwing new light on Lincoln's thought and activity and in documenting the importance of the Middle West in the Civil War. He was for many years executive secretary of the Abraham Lincoln Association; since 1945 he has been director of the Chicago Historical Society, which has been called "the Athenaeum of mid-America." A graduate of Miami University in Oxford, Ohio, he has been awarded four honorary degrees. He is the author of a long list of important monographs on the Civil War, including* The Lincoln Reader, Created Equal *and* Mary Lincoln, Wife and Widow, *which he wrote with Carl Sandburg. In 1959, the sesquicentennial year of Lincoln's birth, he was sent by the State Department to lecture on Lincoln in Japan.*

EARL SCHENCK MIERS, *who lives in Edison, New Jersey, left a career in publishing to become an independent scholar and writer, also specializing in the Civil War period. He has only one honorary degree, from Rutgers, where he also did his undergraduate studying. He has also written many specialized books on the Civil War, including* The Great Rebellion, The General March to Hell, The Web of Victory: Grant at Vicksburg *and* Robert E. Lee. *Most recently he has served as editor-in-chief of* Lincoln Day by Day, *the three-volume product of the Lincoln Sesquicentennial Commission. In reviewing this work, Carl Sandburg called Mr. Miers "one of the more free-going and vivid writers on Lincoln and the Civil War."*

Other DACAPO titles of interest